CASES AND MATERIALS

# LEGISLATION AND REGULATION

*by*

JOHN F. MANNING
Bruce Bromley Professor of Law
Harvard School of Law

MATTHEW C. STEPHENSON
Professor of Law
Harvard School of Law

FOUNDATION PRESS
2010

THOMSON REUTERS

© 2010 By THOMSON REUTERS/FOUNDATION PRESS

      1 New York Plaza, 34th Floor

      New York, NY 10004

      Phone Toll Free 1–877–888–1330

      Fax (646) 424–5201

      foundation–press.com

Printed in the United States of America

**ISBN** 978–1–59941–726–4

Mat #40877640

*The editors dedicate this book
to their families*

# PREFACE

This casebook is designed for a first-year course on Legislation and Regulation. Harvard Law School introduced such a course as part of a more general package of reforms to the first-year curriculum in September 2006. The purpose of this new required Legislation and Regulation course was to bring the first-year law school curriculum more into line with the realities of modern legal practice and the structure of our legal system—in particular, the centrality of statutes and regulations. The objective of this course is to teach students both how federal statutory and regulatory law is made, and how judges and administrative interpreters construe these legal materials. The course also serves as a foundation for courses in the upper-level curriculum, including Environmental Law, Labor Law, Securities Law, Employment Law, Bankruptcy, Taxation, and numerous other courses in which statutes and regulations are central.

The casebook consists of five chapters. Chapters One and Two focus on the "legislation" element of the course, introducing students to the theory and practice of statutory interpretation. Chapter One introduces classic themes and controversies in statutory interpretation, such as the conflict between a statute's text and apparent purpose, different approaches to construing statutory language, and the appropriate role of extrinsic materials (particularly legislative history) in statutory interpretation. Chapter Two continues the exploration of the theory and practice of statutory interpretation by examining the role of "canons of construction" (both semantic and substantive) in statutory interpretation.

Chapters Three and Four focus on the "regulation" element of the course, introducing students to the legal architecture that both enables and constrains regulatory policymaking by administrative agencies. Chapter Three explores the constitutional framework of the modern administrative state and presents the core doctrines and practices that structure the relationship between the agencies and the President and Congress. Chapter Four deals with the administrative rulemaking process and related topics, focusing in particular on the legal apparatus established by the Administrative Procedure Act (APA) and the judicial decisions construing that statute.

Chapter Five integrates the "legislation" and "regulation" aspects of the course by focusing on judicial review of agencies' interpretations of the statutes that they administer. Chapter Five thus revisits many of the issues covered in Chapters One and Two, but in the context of statutes interpreted in the first instance by administrative agencies. This gives students an opportunity to consider the appropriate allocation of interpretative authority between courts and agencies, as well as a chance to consolidate their understanding of some of the core concepts of interpretation found in Chapters One and Two. It also lends itself to review and further consideration of issues pertaining to the appropriate role and function of agencies in our system of government (the central theme of Chapters Three and Four).

A few words on our general approach to constructing this casebook: First, the two of us sought to meld somewhat different perspectives. One of the editors (Manning) takes a more doctrinal, structural, and historical approach to the material. The other (Stephenson) approaches many of the same questions from a more pragmatic, instrumentalist, and social scientific perspective. Each editor is friendly to the other's approach, and we tried to craft a book that blended a broad range of doctrinal, political science, historical, economic, and philosophical perspectives on the cases and materials we selected. Second, we erred on the side of including somewhat more of the principal cases, making the excerpted cases somewhat longer than in other casebooks. Our experience in teaching these materials has been that cutting the cases too much can make the cases harder to understand by disrupting the flow or omitting key elements of the argument. (One style point: In our editing of the principal cases, we indicate with ellipses where we were omitting substantive material, but we generally do not indicate where we omit citations.) Third, we have tried, in the notes following the cases, to give the students context for understanding how the case fits in with the fabric of the law more generally and with related material in the casebook. In so doing, we have tried to make the notes as modular as possible, permitting instructors to assign the ones that most interest them. Finally, we have tried to lay out basic concepts in a way that makes the book accessible for first-years, but we have sought to make the treatment in-depth enough to engage of interest to upper level students as well.

This casebook has been the product of tremendous effort by a large number of people. Neither the book nor the Harvard Legislation and Regulation course would exist without the vision and leadership of Elena Kagan and Martha Minow, who spearheaded the curricular reform and oversaw the development of the course, or without the invaluable contributions of our colleagues David Barron, Jody Freeman, Todd Rakoff, Mark Tushnet, and Adrian Vermeule. We also benefitted tremendously from our colleagues who either spoke to us in during the early development of these materials, or used them in draft form, or both: Rachel Barkow, Einer Elhauge, Jody Freeman, Roderick Hills, David Lewis, David Marcus, Anne Joseph O'Connell Todd Rakoff, Samuel Rascoff, Christina Rodriguez, Peter Strauss, Adrian Vermeule, and Alexander Volokh. We thank our outstanding research assistants–Janet Kim, Leif Overvold, Ryan Park, Paul Ray, Colleen Roh, and Benjamin Snyder–who performed heroic feats of substantive analysis, proofreading, and cite-checking. Their excellent work saved us from error and vastly improved the quality of the book. We are grateful to John Bloomquist, Jim Coates, JoAnn Grinstead, and Robb Westawker of Foundation Press for their good advice, excellent editing, and strong support. We are also grateful to Margaret Flynn and Sarah Davitt for their vigilant and unflagging faculty assistance in the preparation of these materials. Last but not least, we thank the hundreds of students in our Legislation and Regulation classes who road tested these materials and whose comments made them better.

JFM

MCS

June 2010

# SUMMARY OF CONTENTS

# TABLE OF CONTENTS

# TABLE OF CASES

Principal cases are in bold type. Non-principal cases are in roman type. References are to Pages.

# TABLE OF AUTHORITIES

References are to Pages.

CASES AND MATERIALS

# LEGISLATION AND REGULATION

# CHAPTER ONE

# THE LEGISLATIVE PROCESS AND STATUTORY INTERPRETATION

### CONTENTS

## I. INTRODUCTION TO THE SUBJECT MATTER

The classic vision of lawmaking made popular by high school civics teachers entails the passage of a bill by both Houses of Congress, its submission to the President for signature or veto, and, if vetoed, its return to Congress to see if legislators can muster a two-thirds vote of each House to override that veto. In reality, only a small proportion of binding legal rules in the federal system are made that way. Put to one side the fact that the Constitution expressly contemplates two other forms of federal law-making—the adoption of the Constitution and amendments thereto (*see* U.S. CONST. arts. V, VII) and the adoption of treaties proposed by the President and ratified by two thirds of the Senate (*see* U.S. CONST. art. II, § 2, cl. 2). The reality today is that most of the nitty-gritty detail of federal law emerges from implementation or interpretation of the statutes that Congress enacts. This implementation and interpretation is principally the work of courts and regulatory agencies.

The main reason for this is the inevitable incompleteness of legislative commands. No legislature has the foresight, skill, time, patience, and resources to anticipate and provide for all of the contingencies that may arise. Even a simple command like "no vehicles in the park" leaves many ambiguities to be worked out by the executive officials who enforce it and the judges who adjudicate cases arising under it. Certainly, the "no vehicles in the park" statute has areas of clarity. It plainly applies to cars, trucks, and probably motorcycles. By the same token, it seems equally plain that the statute would not interfere with your ability to go to the park with your dog or in your sneakers or with a picnic basket. But does it apply to bicycles? Tricycles? A remote-control toy car? How about an inoperative M–1 Abrams tank placed in the park as a monument to veterans? Once we get past the easy cases, how do we decide the ones on the margin? *See* Lon L. Fuller, *Positivism and Fidelity to Law—A Reply to Professor Hart*, 71 HARV. L. REV. 630, 662–664 (1958); H.L.A. Hart, *Positivism and the Separation of Law and Morals*, 71 HARV. L. REV. 593, 607 (1958). Much of a lawyer's career is spent grappling with, and arguing about, how to fill in or flesh out the details of vague, ambiguous, or incomplete legal commands in concrete cases.

This course will consider different theories and techniques of lawmaking, legal interpretation, and implementation. We will examine whether and how the characteristics of particular lawmaking processes affect the responsibilities of courts and executive officers charged with interpreting the law. We will begin by focusing on legislation, considering the methods that federal courts use to read statutes, and how competing techniques of interpretation do or do not fit with basic values and assumptions about our system of government. Some of the questions we will consider include:

- Is the courts' job to figure out precisely what Congress would have wanted in the circumstances of a given case, or should courts apply statutes according to the plain import of their terms because the words are what Congress enacted into law?

- Should courts consult the purposes of the statute—the reasons that Congress likely passed it in the first place—when interpreting the statute's specific provisions? How can courts figure out what those purposes are?

- Should courts pay attention to what legislators said about the statute during the process leading up to its enactment? Should they pay special attention to what a bill's sponsors said they thought it meant? What about the views expressed by the specialized legislative committees that initially considered and proposed the legislation?

- Should courts use specialized rules of thumb (in trade lingo, "canons of construction") to help resolve statutory ambiguities?

- Do we get help with any of these questions by considering the way different techniques fit in with our governmental traditions?

## A. THE SNAIL DARTER CASE: *TVA v. HILL*

To begin to think about these questions, it helps to focus on a real statute and a leading case interpreting it. Consider the following statute—the Endangered Species Act of 1973. This statute had to wend its way through a complicated process to secure enactment. Many actors had to bargain over how far it would extend, how strict it would be, how stringently it was to be enforced, and countless other questions. Look at the following language, which comes from the preamble to the statute (its declaration of purpose and policy) and from the operative part of the statute instructing government agencies not to jeopardize endangered or threatened species. What types of policy choices do you see in the operative provisions of Section 7? How strict is the protection provided? Is the language of Section 7 absolute? In interpreting Section 7, how much influence should interpreters give to the statement of policy and purpose found in Section 2? Is there room for common sense exceptions to its seemingly broad command? These questions are taken up in Tennessee Valley Authority v. Hill, 437 U.S. 153 (1978), which is excerpted after the statute.

---

## The Endangered Species Act of 1973
### Section 2 (16 U.S.C. § 1531)

. . .

(b) Purposes

The purposes of this chapter are to provide a means whereby the ecosystems upon which endangered species and threatened species depend may be conserved, [and] to provide a program for the conservation of such endangered species and threatened species. . . .

(c) Policy

(1) It is further declared to be the policy of Congress that all Federal departments and agencies shall seek to conserve endangered species and threatened species and shall utilize their authorities in furtherance of the purposes of this chapter.

(2) It is further declared to be the policy of Congress that Federal agencies shall cooperate with State and local agencies to resolve water resource issues in concert with conservation of endangered species.

### Section 7 (16 U.S.C. § 1536)

(a) Federal agency actions and consultations

. . .

(2) Each Federal agency shall . . . insure that any action authorized, funded, or carried out by such agency . . . is not likely to jeopardize the continued existence of any endangered species or threatened species or result in the destruction or adverse modification of habitat of such species which is determined by the Secretary [of the Interior], after consultation as appropriate with affected States, to be critical. . . .

---

## Tennessee Valley Authority v. Hill

Supreme Court of the United States
437 U.S. 153 (1978)

■ MR. CHIEF JUSTICE BURGER delivered the opinion of the Court.

The question[] presented in this case [is] whether the Endangered Species Act of 1973 requires a court to enjoin the operation of a virtually completed federal dam—which had been authorized prior to 1973—when, pursuant to authority vested in him by Congress, the Secretary of the Interior has determined that operation of the dam would eradicate an endangered species. . . .

I

. . .

In th[e] area of the Little Tennessee River[,] the Tennessee Valley Authority, a wholly owned public corporation of the United States, began constructing the Tellico Dam and Reservoir Project in 1967, shortly after Congress appropriated initial funds for its development. . . . Of particular relevance to this case is one aspect of the project, a dam which TVA determined to place on the Little Tennessee, a short distance from where the river's waters meet with the Big Tennessee. . . .

The Tellico Dam has never opened, however, despite the fact that construction has been virtually completed and the dam is essentially ready for operation. Although Congress has appropriated monies for Tellico every year since 1967, progress was delayed, and ultimately stopped, by a tangle of lawsuits and administrative proceedings. . . .

[In 1973,] a University of Tennessee ichthyologist, Dr. David A. Etnier, found a previously unknown species of perch, the snail darter, or Percina (Imostoma) tanasi. This three-inch, tannish-colored fish, whose numbers are estimated to be in the range of 10,000 to 15,000, would soon engage the attention of environmentalists, the TVA, the Department of the Interior, the Congress of the United States, and ultimately the federal courts....

Until recently the finding of a new species of animal life would hardly generate a cause célèbre. This is particularly so in the case of darters, of which there are approximately 130 known species, 8 to 10 of these having been identified only in the last five years. The moving force behind the snail darter's sudden fame came some four months after its discovery, when the Congress passed the Endangered Species Act of 1973. This legislation, among other things, authorizes the Secretary of the Interior to declare species of animal life "endangered" and to identify the "critical habitat" of these creatures. When a species or its habitat is so listed, the following portion of the Act—relevant here—becomes effective:

> "The Secretary [of the Interior] shall review other programs adminis-tered by him and utilize such programs in furtherance of the purposes of this chapter. All other Federal departments and agencies shall, in consultation with and with the assistance of the Secretary, utilize their authorities in furtherance of the purposes of this chapter by carrying out programs for the conservation of endangered species and threat-ened species listed pursuant to section 1533 of this title and *by taking such action necessary to insure that actions authorized, funded, or carried out by them do not jeopardize the continued existence of such endangered species and threatened species or result in the destruction or modification of habitat of such species* which is determined by the Secretary, after consultation as appropriate with the affected States, to be critical." 16 U.S.C. § 1536 (1976 ed.) (emphasis added).

... [T]he Secretary formally listed the snail darter as an endangered species on October 8, 1975.... [T]he Secretary determined that the snail darter apparently lives only in that portion of the Little Tennessee River which would be completely inundated by the reservoir created as a conse-quence of the Tellico Dam's completion. The Secretary went on to explain the significance of the dam to the habitat of the snail darter:

> "[T]he snail darter occurs only in the swifter portions of shoals over clean gravel substrate in cool, low-turbidity water. Food of the snail darter is almost exclusively snails which require a clean gravel sub-strate for their survival. *The proposed impoundment of water behind the proposed Tellico Dam would result in total destruction of the snail darter's habitat.*" (emphasis added).

... Using these determinations as a predicate, and notwithstanding the near completion of the dam, the Secretary declared that pursuant to § 7 of the Act, "all Federal agencies must take such action as is necessary to insure that actions authorized, funded, or carried out by them do not result in the destruction or modification of this critical habitat area." This notice, of course, was pointedly directed at TVA and clearly aimed at halting completion or operation of the dam. . . .

Meanwhile, Congress had also become involved in the fate of the snail darter. Appearing before a Subcommittee of the House Committee on Appropriations in April 1975—some seven months before the snail darter was listed as endangered—TVA representatives described the discovery of the fish and the relevance of the Endangered Species Act to the Tellico Project. . . . TVA presented a position which it would advance in successive forums thereafter, namely, that the Act did not prohibit the completion of a project authorized, funded, and substantially constructed before the Act was passed. . . . Thereafter, the House Committee on Appropriations, in its June 20, 1975, Report, stated the following in the course of recommending that an additional $29 million be appropriated for Tellico:

> "The *Committee* directs that the project, for which an environmental impact statement has been completed and provided the Committee, should be completed as promptly as possible. . . ." (Emphasis added.)

Congress then approved the TVA general budget, which contained funds for continued construction of the Tellico Project. In December 1975, one month after the snail darter was declared an endangered species, the President signed the bill into law.

In February 1976, . . . respondents filed the case now under review, seeking to enjoin completion of the dam and impoundment of the reservoir on the ground that those actions would violate the Act by directly causing the extinction of the species *Percina (Imostoma) tanasi* . . . . Shortly thereafter the House and Senate held appropriations hearings which would include discussions of the Tellico budget.

At these hearings, TVA Chairman Wagner reiterated the agency's position that the Act did not apply to a project which was over 50% finished by the time the Act became effective and some 70% to 80% complete when the snail darter was officially listed as endangered. . . .

[After trial, the] District Court found that closure of the dam and the consequent impoundment of the reservoir would "result in the adverse modification, if not complete destruction, of the snail darter's critical habitat," making it "highly probable" that "the continued existence of the snail darter" would be "jeopardize[d]." Despite these findings, the District Court declined to embrace the plaintiffs' position . . . that once a federal project was shown to jeopardize an endangered species, a court . . . is compelled to issue an injunction restraining violation of the Endangered Species Act.

In reaching this result, the District Court stressed that the entire project was then about 80% complete and, based on available evidence, "there [were] no alternatives to impoundment of the reservoir, short of scrapping the entire project." The District Court also found that if the Tellico Project was permanently enjoined, "some $53 million would be lost in nonrecoverable obligations," meaning that a large portion of the $78 million already expended would be wasted. The court also noted that the

Endangered Species Act of 1973 was passed some seven years after construction on the dam commenced and that Congress had continued appropriations for Tellico, with full awareness of the snail darter problem. Assessing these various factors, the District Court concluded:

> "At some point in time a federal project becomes so near completion and so incapable of modification that a court of equity should not apply a statute enacted long after inception of the project to produce an unreasonable result.... Where there has been an irreversible and irretrievable commitment of resources by Congress to a project over a span of almost a decade, the Court should proceed with a great deal of circumspection."

To accept the plaintiffs' position, the District Court argued, would inexorably lead to what it characterized as the absurd result of requiring "a court to halt impoundment of water behind a fully completed dam if an endangered species were discovered in the river on the day before such impoundment was scheduled to take place. We cannot conceive that Congress intended such a result."

Less than a month after the District Court decision, the Senate and House Appropriations Committees recommended the full budget request of $9 million for continued work on Tellico...

On June 29, 1976, both Houses of Congress passed TVA's general budget, which included funds for Tellico; the President signed the bill on July 12, 1976....

Thereafter, in the Court of Appeals, respondents argued that the District Court had abused its discretion by not issuing an injunction in the face of "a blatant statutory violation." The Court of Appeals agreed....

The Court of Appeals ... rejected TVA's contention that the word "actions" in § 7 of the Act was not intended by Congress to encompass the terminal phases of ongoing projects. Not only could the court find no "positive reinforcement" for TVA's argument in the Act's legislative history, but also such an interpretation was seen as being "inimical to ... its objectives." ...

We granted certiorari to review the judgment of the Court of Appeals.

## II

We begin with the premise that operation of the Tellico Dam will either eradicate the known population of snail darters or destroy their critical habitat....

### (A)

It may seem curious to some that the survival of a relatively small number of three-inch fish among all the countless millions of species extant would require the permanent halting of a virtually completed dam for which Congress has expended more than $100 million. The paradox is not minimized by the fact that Congress continued to appropriate large sums of public money for the project, even after congressional Appropriations

Committees were apprised of its apparent impact upon the survival of the snail darter. We conclude, however, that the explicit provisions of the Endangered Species Act require precisely that result.

One would be hard pressed to find a statutory provision whose terms were any plainer than those in § 7 of the Endangered Species Act. Its very words affirmatively command all federal agencies *"to insure* that actions *authorized, funded, or carried out* by them do not jeopardize the continued existence"* of an endangered species or *"result* in the destruction or modification of habitat of such species...."* (Emphasis added.) This language admits of no exception. Nonetheless, petitioner urges, as do the dissenters, that the Act cannot reasonably be interpreted as applying to a federal project which was well under way when Congress passed the Endangered Species Act of 1973. To sustain that position, however, we would be forced to ignore the ordinary meaning of plain language. It has not been shown, for example, how TVA can close the gates of the Tellico Dam without "carrying out" an action that has been "authorized" and "funded" by a federal agency. Nor can we understand how such action will *"insure"* that the snail darter's habitat is not disrupted.[18] Accepting the Secretary's determinations, as we must, it is clear that TVA's proposed operation of the dam will have precisely the opposite effect, namely the eradication of an endangered species.

Concededly, this view of the Act will produce results requiring the sacrifice of the anticipated benefits of the project and of many millions of dollars in public funds. But examination of the language, history, and structure of the legislation under review here indicates beyond doubt that Congress intended endangered species to be afforded the highest of priorities....

[The Court undertook a long discussion of the legislative background to the 1973 Act, demonstrating that the Act was designed to strengthen prior legislative efforts to protect endangered species.]

As it was finally passed, the Endangered Species Act of 1973 represented the most comprehensive legislation for the preservation of endangered species ever enacted by any nation. Its stated purposes were "to provide a

---

**18.** In dissent, Mr. Justice Powell argues that the meaning of "actions" in § 7 is "far from 'plain,'" and that "it seems evident that the 'actions' referred to are not all actions that an agency can ever take, but rather actions that the agency is deciding whether to authorize, to fund, or to carry out." Aside from this bare assertion, however, no explanation is given to support the proffered interpretation. This recalls Lewis Carroll's class advice on the construction of language:

"'When I use a word,' Humpty Dumpty said, in rather a scornful tone, 'it means just what I choose it to mean-neither more nor less.'" Through the Looking Glass, in The Complete Works of Lewis Carroll 196 (1939).

Aside from being unexplicated, the dissent's reading of § 7 is flawed on several counts. First, under its view, the words "or carry out" in § 7 would be superfluous since all prospective actions of an agency remain to be "authorized" or "funded." Second, the dissent's position logically means that an agency would be obligated to comply with § 7 only when a project is in the planning stage. But if Congress had meant to so limit the Act, it surely would have used words to that effect....

means whereby the ecosystems upon which endangered species and threatened species depend may be conserved," and "to provide a program for the conservation of such ... species." 16 U.S.C. § 1531(b). In furtherance of these goals, Congress expressly stated in § 2(c) that "all Federal departments and agencies *shall* seek to *conserve endangered species* and threatened species." 16 U.S.C. § 1531(c). Lest there be any ambiguity as to the meaning of this statutory directive, the Act specifically defined "conserve" as meaning "to use and the use of *all methods and procedures which are necessary* to bring *any endangered species* or threatened species to the point at which the measures provided pursuant to this chapter are no longer necessary." § 1532(2) (Emphasis added.). Aside from § 7, other provisions indicated the seriousness with which Congress viewed this issue: Virtually all dealings with endangered species, including taking, possession, transportation, and sale, were prohibited, 16 U.S.C. § 1538, except in extremely narrow circumstances, see § 1539(b). The Secretary [of the Interior] was also given extensive power to develop regulations and programs for the preservation of endangered and threatened species. § 1533(d). Citizen involvement was encouraged by the Act, with provisions allowing interested persons to petition the Secretary to list a species as endangered or threatened, § 1533(c)(2), and bring civil suits in United States district courts to force compliance with any provision of the Act, §§ 1540(c) and (g).

Section 7 of the Act, which of course is relied upon by respondents in this case, provides a particularly good gauge of congressional intent.... [T]his provision had its genesis in the Endangered Species Act of 1966, but that legislation qualified the obligation of federal agencies by stating that they should seek to preserve endangered species only *"insofar as is practicable and consistent with the[ir] primary purposes...."* Likewise, every bill introduced in 1973 contained a qualification similar to that found in the earlier statutes. Exemplary of these was the administration bill, H.R. 4758, which in § 2(b) would direct federal agencies to use their authorities to further the ends of the Act *"insofar as is practicable and consistent with the[ir] primary purposes."* ... This type of language did not go unnoticed by those advocating strong endangered species legislation. A representative of the Sierra Club, for example, attacked the use of the phrase "consistent with the primary purpose" in proposed H.R. 4758, cautioning that the qualification "could be construed to be a declaration of congressional policy that other agency purposes are necessarily more important than protection of endangered species and would always prevail if conflict were to occur." ...

What is very significant in this sequence is that the final version of the 1973 Act carefully omitted all of the reservations described above. In the bill which the Senate initially approved (S. 1983), however, the version of the current § 7 merely required federal agencies to "carry out such programs *as are practicable* for the protection of species listed...." S. 1983, § 7(a). (Emphasis added.). By way of contrast, the bill that originally passed the House, H.R. 37, contained a provision which was essentially a mirror image of the subsequently passed § 7–indeed all phrases which might have qualified an agency's responsibilities had been omitted from the bill. . . .

Resolution of this difference in statutory language, as well as other variations between the House and Senate bills, was the task of a Conference Committee. See 119 Cong.Rec. 30174–30175, 31183 (1973). [T]he Conference Report, H.R. Conf.Rep. No. 93–740 (1973), U.S.Code Cong. & Admin.News 1973, p. 2989, basically adopted the Senate bill, S. 1983; but the conferees rejected the Senate version of § 7 and adopted the stringent, mandatory language in H.R. 37. . . . Representative Dingell, provided an interpretation of what the Conference bill would require, making it clear that the mandatory provisions of § 7 were not casually or inadvertently included:

> "[Section 7] substantially amplifie[s] the obligation of [federal agencies] to take steps within their power to carry out the purposes of this act. A recent article . . . illustrates the problem which might occur absent this new language in the bill. It appears that the whooping cranes of this country, perhaps the best known of our endangered species, are being threatened by Air Force bombing activities along the gulf coast of Texas. Under existing law, the Secretary of Defense has some discretion as to whether or not he will take the necessary action to see that this threat disappears. . . . [O]nce the bill is enacted, [the Secretary of Defense] *would be required to take the proper steps. . . .*" 119 Cong.Rec. 42913 (1973). (Emphasis added.) . . .

It is against this legislative background that we must measure TVA's claim that the Act was not intended to stop operation of a project which, like Tellico Dam, was near completion when an endangered species was discovered in its path. While there is no discussion in the legislative history of precisely this problem,[29] the totality of congressional action makes it abundantly clear that the result we reach today is wholly in accord with both the words of the statute and the intent of Congress. The plain intent of Congress in enacting this statute was to halt and reverse the trend toward species extinction, whatever the cost. . . .

It is not for us to speculate, much less act, on whether Congress would have altered its stance had the specific events of this case been anticipated. In any event, we discern no hint in the deliberations of Congress relating to the 1973 Act that would compel a different result than we reach here. Indeed, the repeated expressions of congressional concern over what it saw as the potentially enormous danger presented by the eradication of any endangered species suggest how the balance would have been struck had the issue been presented to Congress in 1973.

---

**29.** When confronted with a statute which is plain and unambiguous on its face, we ordinarily do not look to legislative history as a guide to its meaning. Ex parte Collett, 337 U.S. 55, 61 (1949), and cases cited therein. Here it is not necessary to look beyond the words of the statute. We have undertaken such an analysis only to meet Mr. Justice Powell's suggestion that the "absurd" result reached in this case . . . is not in accord with congressional intent.

Furthermore, it is clear Congress foresaw that § 7 would, on occasion, require agencies to alter ongoing projects in order to fulfill the goals of the Act. [For example,] Congressman Dingell's discussion of Air Force practice bombing, for instance, obviously pinpoints a particular activity—intimately related to the national defense—which a major federal department would be obliged to alter in deference to the strictures of § 7....

One might dispute the applicability of these examples to the Tellico Dam by saying that in this case the burden on the public through the loss of millions of unrecoverable dollars would greatly outweigh the loss of the snail darter.[33] But neither the Endangered Species Act nor Art. III of the Constitution provides federal courts with authority to make such fine utilitarian calculations. On the contrary, the plain language of the Act, buttressed by its legislative history, shows clearly that Congress viewed the value of endangered species as "incalculable." Quite obviously, it would be difficult for a court to balance the loss of a sum certain—even $100 million—against a congressionally declared "incalculable" value, even assuming we had the power to engage in such a weighing process, which we emphatically do not....

Notwithstanding Congress' expression of intent in 1973, we are urged to find that the continuing appropriations for Tellico Dam constitute an implied repeal of the 1973 Act, at least insofar as it applies to the Tellico Project. In support of this view, TVA points to the statements found in various House and Senate Appropriations Committees' Reports; ... those Reports generally reflected the attitude of the Committees either that the Act did not apply to Tellico or that the dam should be completed regardless of the provisions of the Act. Since we are unwilling to assume that these latter Committee statements constituted advice to ignore the provisions of a duly enacted law, we assume that these Committees believed that the Act simply was not applicable in this situation. But even under this interpretation of the Committees' actions, ... [t]here is nothing in the appropriations measures, as passed, which states that the Tellico Project was to be completed irrespective of the requirements of the Endangered Species Act. These appropriations, in fact, represented relatively minor components of the lump-sum amounts for the entire TVA budget.[35] To find a repeal of the Endangered Species Act under these circumstances would surely do vio-

---

**33.** Mr. Justice POWELL's dissent places great reliance on Church of the Holy Trinity v. United States, 143 U.S. 457, 459 (1892), to support his view of the 1973 Act's legislative history. This Court, however, later explained *Holy Trinity* as applying only in "rare and exceptional circumstances.... And there must be something to make plain the intent of Congress that the letter of the statute is not to prevail." Crooks v. Harrelson, 282 U.S. 55, 60 (1930). As we have seen from our explication of the structure and history of the 1973 Act, there is nothing to support the assertion that the literal meaning of § 7 should not apply in this case.

**35.** The Appropriations Acts did not themselves identify the projects for which the sums had been appropriated; identification of these projects requires reference to the legislative history. Thus, unless a Member scrutinized in detail the Committee proceedings concerning the appropriations, he would have no knowledge of the possible conflict between the continued funding and the Endangered Species Act.

lence to the "'cardinal rule . . . that repeals by implication are not favored.'" . . .

. . . We recognize that both substantive enactments and appropriations measures are "Acts of Congress," but the latter have the limited and specific purpose of providing funds for authorized programs. When voting on appropriations measures, legislators are entitled to operate under the assumption that the funds will be devoted to purposes which are lawful and not for any purpose forbidden. Without such an assurance, every appropriations measure would be pregnant with prospects of altering substantive legislation, repealing by implication any prior statute which might prohibit the expenditure. Not only would this lead to the absurd result of requiring Members to review exhaustively the background of every authorization before voting on an appropriation, but it would flout the very rules the Congress carefully adopted to avoid this need. House Rule XXI(2), for instance, specifically provides:

> "No appropriation shall be reported in any general appropriation bill, or be in order as an amendment thereto, for any expenditure not previously authorized by law, unless in continuation of appropriations for such public works as are already in progress. *Nor shall any provision in any such bill or amendment thereto changing existing law be in order*." (Emphasis added.)

. . .

Perhaps mindful of the fact that it is "swimming upstream" against a strong current of well-established precedent, TVA argues for an exception to the rule against implied repealers in a circumstance where, as here, Appropriations Committees have expressly stated their "understanding" that the earlier legislation would not prohibit the proposed expenditure. We cannot accept such a proposition. Expressions of committees dealing with requests for appropriations cannot be equated with statutes enacted by Congress, particularly not in the circumstances presented by this case. First, the Appropriations Committees had no jurisdiction over the subject of endangered species, much less did they conduct the type of extensive hearings which preceded passage of the earlier Endangered Species Acts, especially the 1973 Act. . . .

Second, there is no indication that Congress as a whole was aware of TVA's position, although the Appropriations Committees apparently agreed with [TVA's] views. . . .

(B)

. . . Our system of government is . . . a tripartite one, with each branch having certain defined functions delegated to it by the Constitution. While "[i]t is emphatically the province and duty of the judicial department to say what the law is," Marbury v. Madison, 1 Cranch 137 (1803), it is equally— and emphatically—the exclusive province of the Congress not only to formulate legislative policies and mandate programs and projects, but also to establish their relative priority for the Nation. Once Congress, exercising its delegated powers, has decided the order of priorities in a given area, it is for the Executive to administer the laws and for the courts to enforce them when enforcement is sought.

Here we are urged to view the Endangered Species Act "reasonably," and hence shape a remedy "that accords with some modicum of common sense and the public weal." But is that our function? We have no expert knowledge on the subject of endangered species, much less do we have a mandate from the people to strike a balance of equities on the side of the Tellico Dam. Congress has spoken in the plainest of words, making it abundantly clear that the balance has been struck in favor of affording endangered species the highest of priorities, thereby adopting a policy which it described as "institutionalized caution."

Our individual appraisal of the wisdom or unwisdom of a particular course consciously selected by the Congress is to be put aside in the process of interpreting a statute. Once the meaning of an enactment is discerned and its constitutionality determined, the judicial process comes to an end. We do not sit as a committee of review, nor are we vested with the power of veto. The lines ascribed to Sir Thomas More by Robert Bolt are not without relevance here:

> "The law, Roper, the law. I know what's legal, not what's right. And I'll stick to what's legal. . . . I'm not [G-d]. The currents and eddies of right and wrong, which you find such plain-sailing, I can't navigate, I'm no voyager. But in the thickets of the law, oh there I'm a forester. . . . What would you do? Cut a great road through the law to get after the Devil? . . . And when the last law was down, and the Devil turned round on you-where would you hide, Roper, the laws all being flat? . . . This country's planted thick with laws from coast to coast— Man's laws, not [G-d's]—and if you cut them down . . . d'you really think you could stand upright in the winds that would blow then? . . . Yes, I'd give the Devil benefit of law, for my own safety's sake." R. Bolt, A Man for All Seasons, Act I, p. 147 (Three Plays, Heinemann ed. 1967).

We agree with the Court of Appeals that in our constitutional system the commitment to the separation of powers is too fundamental for us to pre-empt congressional action by judicially decreeing what accords with "common sense and the public weal." Our Constitution vests such responsibilities in the political branches. . . .

■ Mr. Justice Powell, with whom Mr. Justice Blackmun joins, dissenting.

The Court today holds that § 7 of the Endangered Species Act requires a federal court, for the purpose of protecting an endangered species or its habitat, to enjoin permanently the operation of any federal project, whether completed or substantially completed. This decision casts a long shadow over the operation of even the most important projects, serving vital needs of society and national defense, whenever it is determined that continued operation would threaten extinction of an endangered species or its habitat.

This result is said to be required by the "plain intent of Congress" as well as by the language of the statute.

In my view § 7 cannot reasonably be interpreted as applying to a project that is completed or substantially completed when its threat to an endangered species is discovered. Nor can I believe that Congress could have intended this Act to produce the "absurd result"—in the words of the District Court—of this case. If it were clear from the language of the Act and its legislative history that Congress intended to authorize this result, this Court would be compelled to enforce it. It is not our province to rectify policy or political judgments by the Legislative Branch, however egregiously they may disserve the public interest. But where the statutory language and legislative history, as in this case, need not be construed to reach such a result, I view it as the duty of this Court to adopt a permissible construction that accords with some modicum of common sense and the public weal.

## I

... In a decision of May 25, 1976, the District Court for the Eastern District of Tennessee held that "the Act should not be construed as preventing completion of the project." An opposite construction, said the District Court would be unreasonable. . . .

Observing that respondents' argument, carried to its logical extreme, would require a court to enjoin the impoundment of water behind a fully completed dam if an endangered species were discovered in the river on the day before the scheduled impoundment, the District Court concluded that Congress could not have intended such a result. . . .

The Court of Appeals for the Sixth Circuit nevertheless ... held that the Act was intended to create precisely the sort of dramatic conflict presented in this case. . . . Judicial resolution of that conflict, the Court of Appeals reasoned, would represent usurpation of legislative power. It quoted the District Court's statement that respondents' reading of the Act, taken to its logical extreme, would compel a court to halt impoundment of water behind a dam if an endangered species were discovered in the river on the day before the scheduled impoundment. The Court of Appeals, however, rejected the District Court's conclusion that such a reading was unreasonable and contrary to congressional intent, holding instead that "[c]onscientious enforcement of the Act requires that it be taken to its logical extreme." . . .

## II

Today the Court, like the Court of Appeals below, adopts a reading of § 7 of the Act that gives it a retroactive effect and disregards 12 years of consistently expressed congressional intent to complete the Tellico Project. With all due respect, I view this result as an extreme example of a literalist construction, not required by the language of the Act and adopted without regard to its manifest purpose. Moreover, it ignores established canons of statutory construction.

A

The starting point in statutory construction is, of course, the language of § 7 itself. [That provision] can be viewed as a textbook example of fuzzy language, which can be read according to the "eye of the beholder." The critical words direct all federal agencies to take "such action [as may be] necessary to insure that actions authorized, funded, or carried out by them do not jeopardize the continued existence of ... endangered species ... or result in the destruction or modification of [a critical] habitat of such species...." Respondents ... read these words as sweepingly as possible to include all "actions" that any federal agency ever may take with respect to any federal project, whether completed or not.

The Court today embraces this sweeping construction. Under the Court's reasoning, the Act covers every existing federal installation, including great hydroelectric projects and reservoirs, every river and harbor project, and every national defense installation—however essential to the Nation's economic health and safety. The "actions" that an agency would be prohibited from "carrying out" would include the continued operation of such projects or any change necessary to preserve their continued usefulness. The only precondition, according to respondents, to thus destroying the usefulness of even the most important federal project in our country would be a finding by the Secretary of the Interior that a continuation of the project would threaten the survival or critical habitat of a newly discovered species of water spider or amoeba.

"[F]requently words of general meaning are used in a statute, words broad enough to include an act in question, and yet a consideration of the whole legislation, or of the circumstances surrounding its enactment, or of the absurd results which follow from giving such broad meaning to the words, makes it unreasonable to believe that the legislator intended to include the particular act." Church of the Holy Trinity v. United States, 143 U.S. 457, 459 (1892).[14] The result that will follow in this case by virtue of the Court's reading of § 7 makes it unreasonable to believe that Congress intended that reading. Moreover, § 7 may be construed in a way that avoids an "absurd result" without doing violence to its language.

The critical word in § 7 is "actions" and its meaning is far from "plain." It is part of the phrase: "actions authorized, funded or carried out." In terms of planning and executing various activities, it seems evident

---

**14.**   ... The Court suggests that the precept stated in *Church of the Holy Trinity* was somehow undermined in Crooks v. Harrelson, 282 U.S. 55, 60 (1930). Only a year after the decision in Crooks, however, the Court declared that a "literal application of a statute which would lead to absurd consequences is to be avoided whenever a reasonable application can be given which is consistent with the legislative purpose." [United States v. Ryan, 284 U.S 167, 175 (1931)]. In the following year, the Court expressly relied upon *Church of the Holy Trinity* on this very point. [Sorrells v. United States, 287 U.S. 435, 448 (1932)]. The real difference between the Court and myself on this issue arises from our perceptions of the character of today's result. The Court professes to find nothing particularly remarkable about the result produced by its decision in this case. Because I view it as remarkable indeed, and because I can find no hint that Congress actually intended it, I am led to conclude that the congressional words cannot be given the meaning ascribed to them by the Court.

that the "actions" referred to are not all actions that an agency can ever take, but rather actions that the agency is deciding whether to authorize, to fund, or to carry out. In short, these words reasonably may be read as applying only to prospective actions, i.e., actions with respect to which the agency has reasonable decisionmaking alternatives still available, actions not yet carried out. . . .

This is a reasonable construction of the language and also is supported by the presumption against construing statutes to give them a retroactive effect. As this Court stated in United States Fidelity & Guaranty Co. v. United States ex rel. Struthers Wells Co., 209 U.S. 306, 314 (1908), the "presumption is very strong that a statute was not meant to act retrospectively, and it ought never to receive such a construction if it is susceptible of any other." This is particularly true where a statute enacts a new regime of regulation. . . .

### B

The Court recognizes that the first purpose of statutory construction is to ascertain the intent of the legislature. The Court's opinion reviews at length the legislative history, with quotations from Committee Reports and statements by Members of Congress. The Court then ends this discussion with curiously conflicting conclusions.

It finds that the "totality of congressional action makes it abundantly clear that the result we reach today [justifying the termination or abandonment of any federal project] is wholly in accord with both the words of the statute and the intent of Congress." Yet, in the same paragraph, the Court acknowledges that "there is no discussion in the legislative history of precisely this problem." The opinion nowhere makes clear how the result it reaches can be "abundantly" self-evident from the legislative history when the result was never discussed. While the Court's review of the legislative history establishes that Congress intended to require governmental agencies to take endangered species into account in the planning and execution of their programs, there is not even a hint in the legislative history that Congress intended to compel the undoing or abandonment of any project or program later found to threaten a newly discovered species.

If the relevant Committees that considered the Act, and the Members of Congress who voted on it, had been aware that the Act could be used to terminate major federal projects authorized years earlier and nearly completed, or to require the abandonment of essential and long-completed federal installations and edifices, we can be certain that there would have been hearings, testimony, and debate concerning consequences so wasteful, so inimical to purposes previously deemed important, and so likely to arouse public outrage. The absence of any such consideration by the Committees or in the floor debates indicates quite clearly that no one participating in the legislative process considered these consequences as within the intendment of the Act.

As indicated above, this view of legislative intent at the time of enactment is abundantly confirmed by the subsequent congressional actions and expressions. We have held, properly, that post-enactment statements by individual Members of Congress as to the meaning of a statute are entitled to little or no weight. *See, e.g.*, Regional Rail Reorganization Act Cases, 419 U.S. 102, 132 (1974). The Court also has recognized that subsequent Appropriations Acts themselves are not necessarily entitled to significant weight in determining whether a prior statute has been superseded. See United States v. Langston, 118 U.S. 389, 393 (1886). But these precedents are inapposite. There was no effort here to "bootstrap" a post-enactment view of prior legislation by isolated statements of individual Congressmen. Nor is this a case where Congress, without explanation or comment upon the statute in question, merely has voted apparently inconsistent financial support in subsequent Appropriations Acts. Testimony on this precise issue was presented before congressional committees, and the Committee Reports for three consecutive years addressed the problem and affirmed their understanding of the original congressional intent. We cannot assume—as the Court suggests—that Congress, when it continued each year to approve the recommended appropriations, was unaware of the contents of the supporting Committee Reports. All this amounts to strong corroborative evidence that the interpretation of § 7 as not applying to completed or substantially completed projects reflects the initial legislative intent. * * *

■ [Justice Rehnquist's separate dissent is omitted.]

### The Court's Tools of Construction

Consider the range of resources that the majority and dissent analyzed in articulating their competing views of whether the Endangered Species Act (ESA) required the Tennessee Valley Authority to abandon the expensive, almost-finished Tellico Dam project in order to save the snail darter from certain destruction. Think about the different ways in which the majority and the dissent handled various clues about statutory meaning. The sections and chapters that follow will consider, in some detail, the issues raised below. For now, think a bit about the questions posed by the common threads and differences between the majority's and dissent's approaches to the various tools of construction.

*a.* ***The text***—Both the majority and dissent agreed on one point: the starting point for analysis is the text of the statute. But they disagreed sharply about the ordinary meaning of the operative terms and about the importance of the text relative to other tools of construction. The Court wrote that "[o]ne would be hard pressed to find a statutory provision whose terms were any plainer" and that "the ordinary meaning of the plain language" applies to "a federal project which was well under way when Congress passed the [Act.]" In contrast, the dissent characterized the operative provision as "a textbook example of fuzzy language, which can be read according to 'the eye of the beholder'" and accused the majority of adopting a "literalist construction." As we go through sections that follow, consider the following questions: Why did both the majority and dissent think it appropriate to start with the text? What criteria, if any, should a judge use to determine the "ordinary meaning" of the statutory text? And how does one settle disagreements about the meaning of statutory language?

*b.   The legislative history*—The majority noted that some earlier versions of the bill had contained a qualifier that might have addressed the problem of a project already in progress (such as the Tellico Dam), but that the conference committee appointed to reconcile the House and Senate versions of the bill deleted the qualifier and, according to a member of the committee, made compliance with the Act's provisions nondiscretionary. The dissent countered that the legislative history did not squarely address the problem presented in the case and that, if the relevant committees had believed that the language required the result announced by the Court, "there would have been hearings, testimony, and debate concerning consequences so wasteful, so inimical to purposes previously deemed important, and so likely to arouse public outrage." The Court has long used legislative history as a tool of construction, though the practice has been contested in recent years (*see* Part IV, *infra*). Think about the reason that both the Court and the dissent invoked legislative history (or the lack thereof): to ferret out the likely intent of the law's primary drafters. Why is that intent relevant to the law's meaning? Does the disagreement between the majority and dissent about the import of the legislative history reflect merely a different view of the same evidence or a difference in interpretive philosophy?

*c.   The purpose of the statute as a whole*—Notice that the Court examined a number of provisions of the ESA, concluding that Congress's purpose in passing the Act was to adopt "the most comprehensive legislation for the preservation of endangered species ever enacted by any nation." This perception of the statute's broad goals appears to have reinforced the Court's determination that the statute precluded completion of the Tellico Dam. If the statute's *overall purpose* had cut against the majority's view, would that have justified the majority in adopting a different interpretation of the statute, notwithstanding its view of the ordinary meaning of the text?

*d.   Avoiding absurdity*—The dissent believed that the majority's reading of the statute would produce "absurd results," because the majority's interpretation would require the government to shut down any *existing* federally funded project that threatened an endangered species, no matter how many resources Congress had already committed to a project or how "essential to the Nation's economic health and safety" it was. The dissent appeared to assume that Congress, which legislates with limited foresight and necessarily expresses complex policies in general terms, would not have intended the Act to give rise to such results if they had come to Congress's attention. The majority argued that because "Congress has spoken in the plainest of words," the Court had no "mandate" to consider the "balance of equities." Under what circumstances, if any, is the Court justified in deviating from a statute's ordinary meaning in order to avoid absurd results?

*e.  **Subsequent legislation***—The dissent found it significant that even after passing the ESA, Congress continued to appropriate money to the Tennessee Valley Authority, making clear in committee reports that a significant sum each year was to go to completing the Tellico Dam. Why should an interpreter trying to make sense of a statute enacted in 1973 care about whether its interpretation of that statute fits with legislation that Congress passed in subsequent years? Does it help to determine legislative intent? Is it the Court's job to make the law more coherent, if possible, independent of Congress's specific intent?

*f.  **Canons of construction***—In rejecting the relevance of the subsequent appropriations bills, the majority relied on two established *canons of construction*—that is, rules of thumb that courts apply to decode language in the specialized context of legislation. First, given the tension between the Court's assumption that the ESA required the closing of the dam and the seemingly contrary intent of the subsequent bills authorizing further funding for the dam, the Court applied the well-settled canon that subsequent bills (*i.e.*, the appropriations acts) do not impliedly repeal earlier legislation unless the intent to do so is unmistakably clear. Second, and relatedly, the Court applied the presumption that Congress does not alter substantive law through appropriations measures. The dissent invoked a different presumption—namely, that Congress does not impose new regulatory burdens retroactively without clearly saying so. Where do these canons come from and what justifies them? If multiple canons cut in opposite directions in a given case, how does the Court decide which canon takes priority?

## B.  Foundational Theories of Statutory Interpretation

The American legal tradition encompasses a range of views about the proper role of the judge in statutory interpretation cases. Although many theories occupy the academic landscape, the Court has tended to alternate among three foundational approaches: *intentionalism*, *purposivism*, and *textualism*. This tripartite categorization is an oversimplification: There is a great deal of diversity within each of these interpretive traditions, as well as a great deal of common ground among them. Yet this way of framing different approaches to the problem of interpretation is useful, as these labels have become convenient shorthand for related clusters of ideas.

***Intentionalism***—Intentionalism is perhaps the most traditional approach to statutory interpretation, though it has fallen out of favor in recent years. Intentionalism holds that when a judge confronts a difficult issue of statutory interpretation—when the statute is unclear, or seems to dictate a troublesome result—the judge should try to reconstruct, as best he or she can, the *likely intent* of the legislature respecting the problem at hand. That is, the intentionalist judge tries to figure out what the legislature would have *specifically intended* if it had confronted the particular interpretive question before the Court.

***Purposivism***—Purposivism is similar to intentionalism, but purposivists view specific legislative intent—what the legislators would have done if they had confronted the precise question at issue—as illusory or too difficult to reconstruct. Purposivists nonetheless maintain that Congress adopts legislation for a reason and that courts should read specific statutory provisions to advance the purpose or *general aims* of the legislation, as derived from a variety of sources.

***Textualism***—A third interpretive school, textualism, holds that interpreters should strive to discern how reasonable people would understand the *semantic import* or *usage* of the precise statutory language that Congress adopted. Textualists argue that going beyond the text to further some elusive notion of congressional intent or purpose is both illegitimate in principle and unworkable in practice.

To illustrate the differences among these three approaches, consider the hypothetical "no vehicles in the park" statute. *See supra* p. 2. If one were to ask if the statute precludes a bicycle rider from pedaling into the park, intentionalists, purposivists, and textualists would emphasize different factors in answering this question. An intentionalist might find it highly significant if, preceding the statute's enactment, one of the statute's sponsors had assured a worried colleague that the bill was "not intended to reach standard recreational activities such as bicycling." A purposivist might be more interested in what inspired the enactment. If the legislature appeared to have been principally concerned with noise and pollution, a purposivist interpreter would be inclined to decide that bicycling in the park does not violate the statute. On the other hand, if the legislation seemed to have been a response to concerns about dangerous collisions between pedestrians and vehicles of various kinds, a purposivist would be more likely to read the statute as covering bicycles. A textualist would take more interest in how people ordinarily use the word "vehicle." Is it strained to refer to a bicycle as a "vehicle"? How does the dictionary define that term? Has "vehicle" in legal parlance come to be equated with "motor vehicles" such as cars, trucks, and motorcycles?

Although they vary in important respects, these three approaches also have significant common points of reference. First, all three approaches rely on many of the same tools of construction, even if they *emphasize* different ones. For example, purposivists pay close attention to the semantic meaning of the text, following it as long as it does not contradict the statute's apparent overall purpose, while textualists will credit certain kinds of evidence of purpose if the statutory text is ambiguous. *Compare, e.g.*, United States v. American Trucking Ass'ns, 310 U.S. 534, 543 (1940) (endorsing purposivism but observing that "[t]here is . . . no more persuasive evidence of the purpose of a statute than the words by which the legislature undertook to give expression to its wishes"), *with* National Tax Credit Partners, L.P. v. Havlik, 20 F.3d 705, 707 (7th Cir. 1994) (endorsing textualism and remarking that "[k]nowing the purpose behind a rule may help a court decode an ambiguous text"). Textualists, it turns out, care about intended meaning (though they do not regard all of the traditional tools for ascertaining "intent" to be reliable). *See, e.g.*, Antonin Scalia, *Common–Law Courts in a Civil Law System: The Role of United States Federal Courts in Interpreting the Constitution and Laws*, *in* A MATTER OF INTERPRETATION: FEDERAL COURTS AND THE LAW 3, 16–17 (Amy Gutmann ed., 1997) (noting that textualists look for " 'objectified' intent—the intent that a reasonable person would gather from the text of the law"); *see also* Caleb Nelson, *What Is Textualism?*, 91 VA. L. REV. 347 (2005). Similarly, almost all interpreters seem to shrink from interpretations that would produce absurd results, though perhaps for different reasons and in different degrees. And virtually all sides now agree that statutory interpretation entails some reliance on canons of construction, though they vary in which canons they prefer and how they use them. *See* John F. Manning, *Legal Realism and the Canons' Revival*, 5 GREEN BAG 2D 283 (2002).

Second, each of these approaches is grounded in the principle of *legislative supremacy*, which encapsulates the related ideas that in the United States's constitutional system, acts of Congress enjoy primacy as long as they remain within constitutional bounds, and that judges must act as Congress's *faithful agents*. Although there have been some important challenges to that conception of the role of judges (*see* pp. 214–217, *infra*), the standard account of federal judicial power builds directly on the faithful agent assumption. *See* Cass R. Sunstein, *Interpreting Statutes in the Regulatory State*, 103 HARV. L. REV. 405, 415 (1989). Indeed, the mainstream versions of all three foundational approaches seek their justification in the premise of legislative supremacy. *See, e.g.*, United States v. Klinger, 199 F.2d 645, 648 (2d Cir. 1952) (Hand, J.) (intentionalism) ("Flinch as we may, what we do, and must do, is to project ourselves, as best we can, into the position of those who uttered the words, and to impute to them how they would have dealt with the concrete occasion."), aff'd by an equally divided court, 345 U.S. 979 (1953) (per curiam); West Va. Univ. Hosps., Inc. v. Casey, 499 U.S. 83, 115 (1991) (Stevens, J., dissenting) (purposivism) ("In the domain of statutory interpretation, Congress is the master.... [W]e do the country a disservice when we needlessly ignore persuasive evidence of Congress' actual purpose and require it to take the time to revisit the matter and to restate its purpose in more precise English whenever its work product suffers from an omission or inadvertent error.") (citation omitted) (internal quotation marks omitted); Frank H. Easterbrook, *Text, History, and Structure in Statutory Interpretation*, 17 HARV. J.L. & PUB. POL'Y 61, 63 (1994) (textualism) ("We are supposed to be faithful agents, not independent principals. Having a wide field to play—not only the statute but also the debates, not only the rules but also the values they advance, and so on—liberates judges. This is objectionable on grounds of democratic theory as well as on grounds of predictability.").

This common starting point of legislative supremacy means that all three of these foundational approaches are concerned with "legislative intent," though they understand this phrase somewhat differently. At its most basic level, the emphasis on "legislative intent" derives from the idea that the object of interpretation is to enforce a decision that is attributable to the legislature—to ascertain the *legislature's* directions or instructions or will or meaning or preferences or desires. At that level of generality, the concept of legislative intent is a cornerstone of any system of interpretation predicated on the idea of legislative supremacy. As the legal philosopher Joseph Raz put it, "[i]t makes no sense to give any person or body law-making power unless it is assumed that the law they make is the law they intended to make." Joseph Raz, *Intention in Interpretation, in* THE AUTONOMY OF LAW: ESSAYS ON LEGAL POSITIVISM 249, 258 (Robert P. George ed., 1996). Professor Raz elaborates by asking, if one were to assume that "the law made by legislation is not the one intended by the legislator ... why does it matter who the members of the legislature are, whether they are democratically elected or not, whether they represent different regions in the country, or classes in the population, whether they are adults or children, sane or insane? Since the law they will end by making does not represent their intentions, the fact that their intentions are foolish or wise, partial or impartial, self-serving or public spirited, makes no difference." *Id.* at 258–59.

When you consider the contrasting approaches of intentionalists, purposivists, and textualists in the materials that follow, ask yourself: (a) how these approaches differ in their understanding of "legislative intent" and the principle of "legislative supremacy"; (b) how these differences, or other differences in perspective among the approaches, affect the tools that proponents of each approach use to ascertain statutory meaning; and (c) what practical consequences each interpretive strategy holds for the operation of our federal lawmaking system.

## C.  A BRIEF OVERVIEW OF THE LEGISLATIVE PROCESS

In evaluating the comparative virtues of various approaches to statutory construction, it is helpful to have a sense of how the legislative process works and thus how legislators in our system formulate the policy instructions that the judiciary must interpret. Some of the procedures for enacting federal legislation are constitutional, derived principally from Article I, Section 7. Other procedural rules are created by Congress, pursuant to the authority granted by Article I, Section 5 to each house of Congress to establish its own rules of procedure. We will consider each in turn. As you read the following material, consider whether the nature of the legislative process should affect the way we think about the interpretation of statutes, and if so, what effect it should have.

### 1.  Article I, Section 7: Bicameralism and Presentment

The constitutional process for enacting federal statutes is, by design, quite cumbersome. Most significantly, Article I, Section 7 of the Constitution requires *bicameralism and presentment*:

> Every Bill which shall have passed the House of Representatives and the Senate, shall, before it become a Law, be presented to the

President of the United States; If he approve he shall sign it, but if not he shall return it, with his Objections to that House in which it shall have originated, who shall enter the Objections at large on their Journal, and proceed to reconsider it. If after such Reconsideration two thirds of that House shall agree to pass the Bill, it shall be sent, together with the Objections, to the other House, by which it shall likewise be reconsidered, and if approved by two thirds of that House, it shall become a Law. But in all such Cases the Votes of both Houses shall be determined by Yeas and Nays, and the Names of the Persons voting for and against the Bill shall be entered on the Journal of each House respectively. If any Bill shall not be returned by the President within ten Days (Sundays excepted) after it shall have been presented to him, the Same shall be a Law, in like Manner as if he had signed it, unless the Congress by their Adjournment prevent its Return, in which Case it shall not be a Law.

Every Order, Resolution, or Vote to which the Concurrence of the Senate and House of Representatives may be necessary (except on a question of Adjournment) shall be presented to the President of the United States; and before the Same shall take Effect, shall be approved by him, or being disapproved by him, shall be repassed by two thirds of the Senate and House of Representatives, according to the Rules and Limitations prescribed in the Case of a Bill.

U.S. CONST. art. I, § 7, cls. 2–3. To put this in plain English, before a bill can become law, it must pass both the House and the Senate (bicameralism), and if it does, Congress must then send the bill to the President to sign or veto (presentment). If the President signs the bill, it becomes law. If the President vetoes the bill, it can still become law if each House of Congress can muster a two-thirds supermajority to override the veto.

Consider some additional facts. Presidents, Senators, and Representatives are elected at different times, and for different terms. *See* U.S. CONST. art. I, § 2, cl. 1 (House of Representatives to be selected "every second Year"); *id.* art. II, § 3, cls. 1–2 (Senators to be selected "for six Years" and to be divided into three classes to be elected to staggered terms); *id.* art. II, § 1 (President "shall have a Term of four Years"). This means that at any given moment, two thirds of the Senators were elected at a different time from members of the House, and two thirds of the Senators were elected at a different time from the President. Half the time, the entire House has been elected in a different cycle from the President. Furthermore, each of the three actors answers to a different constituency. Representatives are elected from single-member districts allocated to the states in proportion to their population. *See id.* art. I, § 2, cl. 3. In perhaps the crucial compromise underlying the Constitution, each state has two Senators regardless of population. *See id.* § 3, cl. 1; *see also id.* art. V. This means that Wyoming has as many Senators as California, even though California has fifty-three times more Representatives in the House after the 2000 census. The President, in turn, is selected by electors chosen by each state in the manner prescribed by the state legislature. *See id.* art. II, § 1, cl. 2. Each state has a number of electors equal to the combined number of its Representatives and its Senators. *See id.* So even though California has approximately fifty-three times the population of Wyoming, it has only about eighteen times as much influence in selecting the President. The methods for selecting the Senate and the President quite obviously provide smaller states with disproportionate influence.

What goals might be served by the division of power along those particular dimensions? What purposes might such an elaborate lawmaking process serve? If one were a rational constitution designer, why would one make it so hard to adopt a statute? What reason might one have for staggering the historical moments when different elements of the three lawmaking actors are elected? Why provide for such different types of constituencies for each of the institutions? Consider some classic justifications for the Article I lawmaking process:

*a.* ***Checks and balances***—The Article I bicameralism and presentment provisions mean that a great deal of consensus is required before policy proposals may be enacted into law. The division of power between two houses that have been elected by different voters is functionally similar to a supermajority requirement. *See* James M. Buchanan & Gordon Tullock, The Calculus of Consent 233–48 (1962); William H. Riker, Commentary, *The Merits of Bicameralism*, 12 Int'l Rev. L. & Econ. 166, 167–68 (1992). The fragmented structure of the federal government, and the resulting need for broad-based consensus as a precondition for enacting legislation, means that each of the three actors involved in the legislative process (the House, the Senate, and the President) may act as a check against the ill-motivated decisions of the other two. James Madison thus said of bicameralism:

> [A] senate, as a second branch of the legislative assembly distinct from and dividing power with the first, must be in all cases a salutary check on the government. It doubles the security to the people by requiring the concurrence of two distinct bodies in schemes of usurpation or perfidy, where the ambition or corruption of one would otherwise be sufficient.

The Federalist No. 62, at 378–79 (James Madison) (Clinton Rossiter ed., 1961). James Wilson, one of the most influential of the Constitution's framers, similarly wrote:

> When a single legislature is determined to depart from the principles of the constitution—and its incontrollable power may prompt the determination—there is no constitutional authority to arrest its progress.... Far different will the case be, when the legislature consists of two branches. If one of them should depart, or attempt to depart from the principles of the constitution; it will be drawn back by the other.

James Wilson, *Lectures on Law, in* 1 The Works of James Wilson 69, 291–92 (Robert Green McCloskey ed., 1967).

Is that persuasive? What about the rejoinder that, although this constitutional structure might be effective in preventing one faction or branch of government from abusing its power through ill-advised or unjustified *action*, this structure makes it easier for one branch or faction to abuse its power to *block* legislative initiatives, at the expense of the general welfare? Madison fully recognized that concern, acknowledging that "this complicated check on legislation may in some instances be injurious as well as beneficial." The Federalist No. 62, *supra*, at 378. Alexander Hamilton likewise observed that "the power of preventing bad laws includes that of preventing good laws." *Id*. No. 73, at 443. Madison, Wilson, Hamilton, and others, however, saw the risks of legislative overreaching as more salient than the risks of legislative inaction. Madison thus contended that "the facility and excess of law-making," and not the converse, "seem to be the diseases to which our governments are most liable." *Id*. No. 62, at 378. And for Hamilton, "[t]he injury which may possibly be done by defeating a few good laws will be amply compensated by preventing a number of bad ones." *Id*. No. 73, at 444. Do you agree that government action is a greater danger to welfare and liberty than government passivity or inertia? Why or why not? Is it possible that even if this premise was true at the time of the founding, it is no longer true? *See* Cass R. Sunstein, After the Rights Revolution: Reconceiving the Regulatory State (1990).

**b. Deliberation and cooling off**—Not only might the cumbersome procedures for enacting federal statutes enable different branches to check each others' excesses, but this process might also foster a more careful and deliberative lawmaking process. Requiring lawmakers to clear multiple hurdles, on this view, permits a period of "cooling off," tamping down the tendency of legislatures to adopt ill-considered legislation in hasty response to the passions of the moment. Consider the following exchange attributed to George Washington and Thomas Jefferson:

> There is a tradition that, on his return from France, Jefferson called Washington to account at the breakfast-table for having agreed to a second chamber. 'Why,' asked Washington, 'did you pour that coffee into your saucer?' 'To cool it,' quoth Jefferson. 'Even so,' said Washington, 'we pour legislation into the senatorial saucer to cool it.'

3 The Records of the Federal Convention of 1787, at 359 (Max Farrand ed., rev. ed. 1966). This "cooling off" effect may also facilitate rational deliberation and public participation. That is, bicameralism and presentment may make it more likely that the legislative process will produce a public airing of disagreements and of arguments for and against different courses of action. The Supreme Court thus observed that "[t]he division of the Congress into two distinctive bodies assures that the legislative power would be exercised only after opportunity for full study and debate in separate settings." INS v. Chadha, 462 U.S. 919, 951 (1983). But might this "cooling off" effect also have a downside? If the design of the legislative process facilitates gridlock, does it make it harder for more loosely-organized constituencies to sustain political momentum? Do you find this critique persuasive? Why or why not?

## 2.   Congressional Rules of Procedure

The Constitution provides that "[e]ach House may determine the Rules of its Proceedings." U.S. CONST. art. I, § 5, cl. 2. And each House of Congress does, in fact, have an elaborate set of written rules as well as a large set of unwritten traditions or procedural norms. These congressionally created procedures determine how agendas are set in Congress, how bills make it to the floor, how they are amended, how (and if) they receive a final vote in each House, and how the two Houses of Congress reconcile their differences when they pass different bills on the same subject. Although it is impossible to provide a summary of these procedures that is both concise and comprehensive, this short overview will lend some perspective on their complexities.[1]

*a. Introduction of bills and referral to committees*—Many bills that result in major legislation are proposed by the executive branch or significant interest groups. Typically, either the chair of a standing committee or some other influential member of Congress formally introduces such bills. Once introduced, bills are typically referred to one or more appropriate standing committees.[2] Although the vast majority of such referrals are routine, "[p]recedent, public laws, turf battles, and the jurisdictional mandates of the committees as set forth in the rules of the House and Senate determine which committees receive what kinds of bills." (Oleszek 82). Even a casual perusal of the committee lists from either House reveals that any piece of major legislation could fall within the jurisdiction of multiple committees. Often, lawmakers try to draft bills so that the subject matter appears to fall within the jurisdiction of a committee apt to be favorably disposed to the legislation. The Speaker of the House or Senate Majority Leader (or, more accurately, a parliamentarian acting on his or her behalf) ultimately makes the assignment. This authority is an important one for the elected leadership in each chamber. (Oleszek 82–85).

*b. Committee consideration*—Many things can happen to a bill after it is referred to the appropriate committee. A committee may report the bill to the appropriate House as submitted; it may amend the bill and submit it; it may rewrite the bill from scratch; or it may refuse to act on the bill. If the committee refuses to act, a bill typically dies. (Although

---

**1.**   Citations in the text are to WALTER J. OLESZEK, CONGRESSIONAL PROCEDURES AND THE POLICY PROCESS (7th ed. 2007). For reasons of space and presentation, we have simplified the complex process that Mr. Oleszek's excellent book so thoughtfully and thoroughly describes.

**2.**   The Senate's standing committees are: Agriculture, Nutrition, and Forestry; Appropriations; Armed Services; Banking, Housing, and Urban Affairs; Budget; Commerce, Science, and Transportation; Energy and Natural Resources; Environment and Public Works; Finance; Foreign Relations; Health, Education, Labor, and Pensions; Homeland Security and Government Affairs; Judiciary; Rules and Administration; Small Business and Entrepreneurship; and Veterans' Affairs. In the House, the following committees divide up substantive jurisdiction: Agriculture; Appropriations; Armed Services; Budget; Education and Labor; Energy and Commerce; Financial Services; Foreign Affairs; Homeland Security; House Administration; Judiciary; Natural Resources; Oversight and Government Reform; Rules; Science and Technology; Small Business; Standards of Official Conduct; Transportation and Infrastructure; Veterans' Affairs; and Ways and Means.

there are procedures available to circumvent a recalcitrant committee in each chamber, those procedures are cumbersome and rarely used.) In determining how to shape a bill, committees often conduct hearings. "Hearings are perhaps the most orchestrated phase of policymaking and usually are part of any overall strategy to get bills enacted into law. Committee members and staff typically plan with care who should testify, when, and on what issues." (Oleszek 96). After hearings, the committee meets to "mark up"—that is, determine whether and how to amend—the proposed bill and to put it in final form for report to the chamber. (Oleszek 98). When a marked-up bill is reported to the chamber, it is typically accompanied by an explanatory report—the House Report or Senate Report—which is prepared in the respective chambers by the committee staff at the behest of the committee chair. (Oleszek 106).

    *c.  **Floor debate and amendment**—*After a bill clears committee, it must get to the floor. Scheduling business for the floor is one of the most important forms of authority enjoyed by the majority leadership in each chamber. In the House of Representatives, the path to the floor for most legislation runs through the Rules Committee. The Rules Committee is appointed by the Speaker and the Minority Leader, and is heavily weighted to the majority party. The Rules Committee decides on the "rule" that determines the order in which a bill will be taken up, sets the amount of time for general debate, decides whether to permit amendments to be entertained on the House floor, prescribes the number of amendments, and specifies what parts of the bill are and are not open to amendment. (Oleszek 125–42).

    The Senate works much differently. The process for scheduling a bill that has been reported favorably out of committee is much more informal, typically involving an effort to secure unanimous consent to bring the bill to the floor. Under Senate rules, unlimited debate on legislation is available unless three fifths (sixty) of the Senators vote for "cloture." In addition, the Senate has a tradition allowing individual Senators to place a three-day anonymous hold on consideration of legislation simply by making a request to the leadership. Although the tradition permits anonymous holds to last only for a few days, it is possible for Senators to use what are known as "rolling holds," through which a succession of Senators agree to renew the hold over a period of time. These practices mean that almost nothing could get done in the Senate without "unanimous consent agreements," which can predetermine the amount of time for debate and may impose restrictions on the amendments that can be proposed to a committee bill. For major legislation, such agreements "are often the product of intensive and extensive negotiations, with drafts of agreements . . . exchanged on and off the floor among concerned senators," and "once an accord is reached among the key actors, each side will try to sell the [unanimous consent agreement] to their other colleagues." (Oleszek 203–208).

    *d.  **Reconciliation**—*When a bill passes both chambers in different forms, the two forms must be reconciled before they are presented to the President. Sometimes one chamber will recede to the other's bill in order to facilitate passage, particularly if the two chambers vote the bill out shortly before Congress adjourns. (Oleszek 256–57). The other common procedure is for the House and Senate to agree to appoint a "conference committee." The Speaker of the House and the Majority Leader of the Senate select the conferees, in consultation with the chairs and ranking minority members of the committee that reported the bill. Conference committees sometimes divide into subconferences to focus on particular issues. (Oleszek 263, 266). As with other parts of the legislative process, the conference process "is subject to outside pressure" from "special-interest groups, executive agency officials, and sometimes even the president." (Oleszek 269). When a majority of conferees from each chamber have agreed on a revised bill, they instruct the conference committee staff to write a report that explains the compromise reached. (Oleszek 275). Then, if each chamber agrees to the conference version of the bill, the final legislation or "enrolled bill" is presented to the President for his or her signature or veto. If the President signs the legislation, or if two thirds of each chamber votes to override a presidential veto, the bill becomes law.

\* \* \* \*

What impression do the foregoing descriptions give you of the legislative process? How much do legislative procedures allow the elected majority leadership in each chamber to control or influence the shape of legislation? How easy is it to translate basic policy impulses into detailed legislation? How much authority does the process confer upon subsets of the legislature to block or shape legislation, even if it has fairly broad political support? And what implications, if any, does this all have for how courts should interpret unclear or incomplete statutory language?

## II. THE LETTER OF THE LAW VERSUS THE SPIRIT OF THE LAW

As we observed in Part I, statutes inevitably pose problems of generality and incompleteness. Human language is imprecise, and legislators must act with limited foresight about the particular situations that interpreters will encounter when a statute is applied in real-world cases. Accordingly, in some of its applications a statute's text will appear over-or under-inclusive in relation to the apparent general aims or purposes for which the legislature enacted it. This potential mismatch between the rules embedded in a statutory text (the "letter of the law") and the general background purpose of the statute (the "spirit of the law") has troubled statutory interpreters and legal theorists for millennia. *See, e.g.*, WILLIAM D. POPKIN, STATUTES IN COURT: THE HISTORY AND THEORY OF STATUTORY INTERPRETATION (1999); John F. Manning, *Textualism and the Equity of the Statute*, 101 COLUM. L. REV. 1 (2001). On this topic, Aristotle famously wrote:

> When the law speaks universally, ... and a case arises on which it is not covered by the universal statement, then it is right, where the legislator fails us and has erred by over-simplicity, to correct the

omission—to say what the legislator himself would have said had he been present, and would have put into his law if he had known. The Nichomachean Ethics of Aristotle 133 (Sir David Ross trans., 1925).

As this notion of interpretation later developed, it came to stand for the idea that the judge should assume that when the letter of the law fails to capture its reason or spirit, enforcing the spirit of the law better approximates what the legislator would have done had he or she expressly dealt with the case at hand. On this view the spirit of the law, rather than the letter, is the essence of the law. Sir Edmund Plowden, a famous sixteenth-century lawyer who compiled English law reports, thus wrote:

> [I]t is not the words of the law, but the internal sense of it that makes the law, and our law (like all others) consists of two parts, *viz.* of body and soul, the letter of the law is the body of the law, and the sense and reason of the law is the soul of the law, *quia ratio legis est anima legis*.... And it often happens that when you know the letter, you know not the sense, for sometimes the sense is more confined and contracted than the letter, and sometimes it is more large and extensive. And equity, which in Latin is called *equitas*, enlarges or diminishes the letter....
>
> So that a man ought not to rest upon the letter only, ... but he ought to rely upon the sense, which is temperated and guided by equity, and therein he reaps the fruit of the law.... And in order to form a right judgment when the letter of a statute is restrained, and when enlarged, by equity, it is a good way, when you peruse a statute, to suppose that the law-maker is present, and that you have asked him the question you want to know touching the equity, then you must give yourself such an answer as you imagine he would have done, if he had been present.

Eyston v. Studd, (1574) 75 Eng. Rep. 688, 696, 700 (K.B.) (Plowden's note) (emphasis omitted).

Or, finally, consider the following excerpt from Sir William Blackstone's *Commentaries on the Laws of England*, which purported to give an account of the principles of English law in the late eighteenth century. Many believe that Blackstone's *Commentaries* was the most influential law treatise in the formative years of the United States. His account of statutory interpretation sets forth with clarity the tension that runs through many of the cases:

> The fairest and most rational method to interpret the will of the legislator, is by exploring his intentions at the time when the law was made, by *signs* the most natural and probable. And these signs are either the words, the context, the subject matter, the effects and consequence, or the spirit and reason of the law. Let us take a short view of them all.
>
> 1. Words are generally to be understood in their usual and most known signification; not so much regarding the propriety of grammar, as their general and popular use.... [T]erms of art, or technical terms,

must be taken according to the acceptation of the learned in each art, trade, and science. . . .

2.   If words happen to be still dubious, we may establish their meaning from the context; with which it may be of singular use to compare a word, or a sentence, whenever they are ambiguous, equivocal, or intricate. Thus the proeme, or preamble, is often called in to help the construction of an act of parliament. Of the same nature and use is the comparison of a law with other laws, that are made by the same legislator, that have some affinity with the subject, or that expressly relate to the same point. . . .

3.   As to the subject matter, words are always to be understood as having a regard thereto; for that is always supposed to be in the eye of the legislator, and all his expressions directed to that end. . . .

4.   As to the effects and consequence, the rule is, where words bear either none, or a very absurd signification, if literally understood, we must a little deviate from the received sense of them. Therefore the Bolognian law, mentioned by Puffendorf, which enacted "that whoever drew blood in the streets should be punished with the utmost severity," was held after long debate not to extend to the surgeon, who opened the vein of a person that fell down in the street with a fit.

5.   But, lastly, the most universal and effectual way of discovering the true meaning of a law, when the words are dubious, is by considering the reason and spirit of it; or the cause which moved the legislator to enact it. For when this reason ceases, the law itself ought likewise to cease with it. . . . . From this method of interpreting laws, by the reason of them, arises what we call *equity*; which is thus defined by Grotius, "the correction of that, wherein the law (by reason of its universality) is deficient." For since in laws all cases cannot be foreseen or expressed, it is necessary, that when the general decrees of the law come to be applied to particular cases, there should be somewhere a power vested of excepting those circumstances, which (had they been foreseen) the legislator . . . would have excepted.

Equity thus depending, essentially, upon the particular circumstances of each individual case, there can be no established rules and fixed precepts of equity laid down, without destroying it's [sic] very essence, and reducing it to a positive law. And, on the other hand, the liberty of considering all cases in an equitable light must not be indulged too far, lest thereby we destroy all law, and leave the decision of every question entirely in the breast of the judge. And law, without equity, tho' hard and disagreeable, is much more desirable for the public good, than equity without law; which would make every judge a legislator, and introduce most infinite confusion; as there would be then almost as many different rules of action laid down in our courts, as there are differences of capacity and sentiment in the human mind.

1 WILLIAM BLACKSTONE, COMMENTARIES *59–62. Although some aspects of Blackstone's framework have fallen out of favor in contemporary federal

practice (*see* Section III.B, *infra*), Blackstone's approach had substantial influence on U.S. courts for many years. How well do his five rules match up with your intuitions about the way to interpret written laws? How large of an exception is "reason and spirit" (rule 5) to the earlier admonition to give words in a statute "their usual and most known signification" (rule 1)?

## A. THE CLASSIC APPROACH

The following cases are famous examples of the tension between the letter of the law and the spirit of the law, and how courts may use the latter to trump the former. As you read these cases, consider whether the courts do a good job ascertaining the statutes' purposes. And, assuming that the court is correct in its understanding of statutory purpose, you might ask further whether these cases are good candidates for departing from the ordinary meaning of the enacted words in order to effectuate the spirit of the law.

---

## Riggs v. Palmer

Court of Appeals of New York
115 N.Y. 506, 22 N.E. 188 (1889)

■ EARL, J.

On the 13th day of August, 1880, Francis B. Palmer made his last will and testament, in which he gave small legacies to his two daughters, Mrs. Riggs and Mrs. Preston, the plaintiffs in this action, and the remainder of his estate to his grandson, the defendant Elmer E. Palmer. . . . At the date of the will, and subsequently to the death of the testator, Elmer lived with him as a member of his family, and at his death was 16 years old. He knew of the provisions made in his favor in the will, and, that he might prevent his grandfather from revoking such provisions, . . . he willfully murdered him by poisoning him. He now claims the property, and the sole question for our determination is, can he have it?

The defendants say that the testator is dead; that his will was made in due form . . .; and that therefore it must have effect according to the letter of the law. It is quite true that statutes regulating the making, proof, and effect of wills and the devolution of property, if literally construed, and if their force and effect can in no way and under no circumstances be controlled or modified, give this property to the murderer. The purpose of those statutes was to enable testators to dispose of their estates to the objects of their bounty at death, and to carry into effect their final wishes legally expressed; and in considering and giving effect to them this purpose must be kept in view. It was the intention of the law-makers that the donees in a will should have the property given to them. But it never could have been their intention that a donee who murdered the testator to make the will operative should have any benefit under it. If such a case had been present to their minds, and it had been supposed necessary to make some provision of law to meet it, it cannot be doubted that they would have provided for it. It is a familiar canon of construction that a thing which is within the intention of the makers of a statute is as much within the statute as if it were within the letter; and a thing which is within the letter of the statute is not within the statute unless it be within the intention of the makers. The writers of laws do not always express their intention perfectly, but either exceed it or fall short of it, so that judges are to collect it from probable or rational conjectures only, and this is called "rational interpretation;" and Rutherford, in his *Institutes* . . . says: "Where we make use of rational interpretation, sometimes we restrain the meaning of the writer so as to take in less, and sometimes we extend or enlarge his meaning so as to take in more, than his words express." Such a construction ought to be put upon a statute as will best answer the intention which the makers had in view . . . and in Smith's *Commentaries* . . . many cases are mentioned where it was held that matters embraced in the general words of statutes nevertheless were not within the statutes, because it could not have been the intention of the law-makers that they should be included. They were taken out of the statutes by an equitable construction; and it is said in Bacon: "By an equitable construction a case not within the letter of a statute is sometimes holden to be within the meaning, because it is within the mischief for which a remedy is provided. The reason for such construction is that the law-makers could not set down every case in express terms. In order to form a right judgment whether a case be within the equity of a statute, it is a good way to suppose the law-maker present, and that you have asked him this question: Did you intend to comprehend this case? Then you must give yourself such answer as you imagine he, being an upright and reasonable man, would have given. If this be that he did mean to comprehend it, you may safely hold the case to be within the equity of the statute; for while you do no more than he would have done, you do not act contrary to the statute, but in conformity thereto." In some cases the letter of a legislative act is restrained by an equitable construction; in others, it is enlarged; in others, the construction is contrary to the letter. . . . If the law-makers could, as to this case, be consulted, would they say that they intended by their general language that the property of a testator or of an ancestor should pass to one who had taken his life for the express purpose of getting his property? In [Blackstone's *Commentaries*], the learned author, speaking of the construction of statutes, says: "If there arise out of them collaterally any absurd consequences manifestly contradictory to common reason, they are with regard to those collateral consequences void. . . . Where some collateral matter arises out of the general words, and happens to be unreasonable, there the judges are in decency to conclude that this consequence was not foreseen by the parliament, and therefore they are at liberty to expound the statute by equity, and only *quoad hoc* disregard it;" and he gives as an illustration, if an act of parliament gives a man power to try all causes that arise within his manor of Dale, yet, if a cause should arise in which he himself is party, the act is construed not to extend to that, because it is unreasonable that any man should determine his own quarrel. There was a statute in Bologna that whoever drew blood in the streets should be severely punished, and yet it was held not to apply to the case of a barber who opened a vein in the street. It is commanded in the decalogue that no work shall be done upon the Sabbath, and yet giving the command a rational interpretation founded upon its design the Infallible Judge held that it did not prohibit works of necessity, charity, or benevolence on that day.

What could be more unreasonable than to suppose that it was the legislative intention in the general laws passed for the orderly, peaceable, and just devolution of property that they should have operation in favor of one who murdered his ancestor that he might speedily come into the possession of his estate? Such an intention is inconceivable. We need not, therefore, be much troubled by the general language contained in the laws. Besides, all laws ... may be controlled in their operation and effect by general, fundamental maxims of the common law. No one shall be permitted to profit by his own fraud, or to take advantage of his own wrong, or to found any claim upon his own iniquity, or to acquire property by his own crime. These maxims are dictated by public policy, have their foundation in universal law administered in all civilized countries, and have nowhere been superseded by statute....

Here there was no certainty that this murderer would survive the testator, or that the testator would not change his will, and there was no certainty that he would get this property if nature was allowed to take its course. He therefore murdered the testator expressly to vest himself with an estate. Under such circumstances, what law, human or divine, will allow him to take the estate and enjoy the fruits of his crime? ... My view of this case does not inflict upon Elmer any greater or other punishment for his crime than the law specifies. It takes from him no property, but simply holds that he shall not acquire property by his crime, and thus be rewarded for its commission....

■ GRAY, J., (*dissenting.*)

This appeal presents an extraordinary state of facts, and the case, in respect of them, I believe, is without precedent in this state. The respondent, a lad of 16 years of age, being aware of the provisions in his grandfather's will, which constituted him the residuary legatee of the testator's estate, caused his death by poison, in 1882. For this crime he was tried, and was convicted of murder in the second degree, and at the time of the commencement of this action he was serving out his sentence in the state reformatory. This action was brought by two of the children of the testator for the purpose of having those provisions of the will in the respondent's favor canceled and annulled. The appellants' argument for a reversal of the judgment, which dismissed their complaint, is that the respondent unlawfully prevented a revocation of the existing will, or a new will from being made, by his crime; and that he terminated the enjoyment by the testator of his property, and effected his own succession to it, by the same crime. They say that to permit the respondent to take the property willed to him would be to permit him to take advantage of his own wrong.

To sustain their position the appellants' counsel has submitted an able and elaborate brief, and, if I believed that the decision of the question could be effected by considerations of an equitable nature, I should not hesitate to assent to views which commend themselves to the conscience. But the matter does not lie within the domain of conscience. We are bound by the rigid rules of law, which have been established by the legislature, and within the limits of which the determination of this question is confined. The question we are dealing with is whether a testamentary disposition can be altered, or a will revoked, after the testator's death, through an appeal to the courts, when the legislature has by its enactments prescribed exactly when and how wills may be made, altered, and revoked, and apparently, as it seems to me, when they have been fully complied with, has left no room for the exercise of an equitable jurisdiction by courts over such matters. Modern jurisprudence, in recognizing the right of the individual, under more or less restrictions, to dispose of his property after his death, subjects it to legislative control, both as to extent and as to mode of exercise. . . . To the statutory restraints which are imposed upon the disposition of one's property by will are added strict and systematic statutory rules for the execution, alteration, and revocation of the will, which must be, at least substantially, if not exactly, followed to insure validity and performance. The reason for the establishment of such rules, we may naturally assume, consists in the purpose to create those safeguards about these grave and important acts which experience has demonstrated to be the wisest and surest. That freedom which is permitted to be exercised in the testamentary disposition of one's estate by the laws of the state is subject to its being exercised in conformity with the regulations of the statutes. The capacity and the power of the individual to dispose of his property after death, and the mode by which that power can be exercised, are matters of which the legislature was assumed the entire control, and has undertaken to regulate with comprehensive particularity.

The appellants' argument is not helped by reference to those rules of the civil law, or to those laws of other governments, by which the heir, or legatee, is excluded from benefit under the testament if he has been convicted of killing, or attempting to kill, the testator. In the absence of such legislation here, the courts are not empowered to institute such a system of remedial justice. The deprivation of the heir of his testamentary succession by the Roman law, when guilty of such a crime, plainly was intended to be in the nature of a punishment imposed upon him. The succession, in such a case of guilt, escheated to the exchequer. See Dom. Civil Law, pt. 2, bk. 1, tit. 1, § 3. I concede that rules of law which annul testamentary provisions made for the benefit of those who have become unworthy of them may be based on principles of equity and of natural justice. It is quite reasonable to suppose that a testator would revoke or alter his will, where his mind has been so angered and changed as to make him unwilling to have his will executed as it stood. But these principles only suggest sufficient reasons for the enactment of laws to meet such cases.

The statutes of this state have prescribed various ways in which a will may be altered or revoked; but the very provision defining the modes of alteration and revocation implies a prohibition of alteration or revocation in any other way. The words of the section of the statute are: "No will in writing, except in the cases hereinafter mentioned, nor any part thereof, shall be revoked or altered otherwise," etc. Where, therefore, none of the cases mentioned are met by the facts, and the revocation is not in the way described in the section, the will of the testator is unalterable. I think that a valid will must continue as a will always, unless revoked in the manner provided by the statutes. Mere intention to revoke a will does not have the effect of revocation. The intention to revoke is necessary to constitute the effective revocation of a will, but it must be demonstrated by one of the acts contemplated by the statute.... The finding of fact of the referee that presumably the testator would have altered his will had he known of his grantor's murderous intent cannot affect the question. We may concede it to the fullest extent; but still the cardinal objection is undisposed of,—that the making and the revocation of a will are purely matters of statutory regulation, by which the court is bound in the determination of questions relating to these acts.

    ... I cannot find any support for the argument that the respondent's succession to the property should be avoided because of his criminal act, when the laws are silent. Public policy does not demand it; for the demands of public policy are satisfied by the proper execution of the laws and the punishment of the crime. There has been no convention between the testator and his legatee nor is there any such contractual element, in such a disposition of property by a testator, as to impose or imply conditions in the legatee. The appellants' argument practically amounts to this: that, as the legatee has been guilty of a crime, by the commission of which he is placed in a position to sooner receive the benefits of the testamentary provision, his rights to the property should be forfeited, and he should be divested of his estate. To allow their argument to prevail, would involve the diversion by the court of the testator's estate into the hands of persons whom, possibly enough, for all we know, the testator might not have chosen or desired as its recipients. Practically the court is asked to make another will for the testator. The laws do not warrant this judicial action, and mere presumption would not be strong enough to sustain it. But, more than this, to concede the appellants' views would involve the imposition of an additional punishment or penalty upon the respondent. What power or warrant have the courts to add to the respondent's penalties by depriving him of property? The law has punished him for his crime, and we may not say that it was an insufficient punishment. In the trial and punishment of the respondent the law has vindicated itself for the outrage which he committed, and further judicial utterance upon the subject of punishment or deprivation of rights is barred...

---

*1.  Language, Purpose, and Legislative Supremacy*—Both the majority and the dissent in *Riggs* agreed that New York's Statute of Wills clearly stated that anyone named in a will would inherit except in cases of fraud, duress, or incapacity at the time the will was made. Thus, as the majority put it, the relevant "statutes regulating the making, proof, and effect of wills and the devolution of property, if literally construed, and if their force and effect can in no way and under no circumstances be controlled or modified, give this property to [Elmer]." How important a role should this consideration have played in the Court's analysis?

The starting presumption in American law is that legislators choose their words to express their intended meaning. *See, e.g.,* Connecticut Nat'l Bank v. Germain, 503 U.S. 249, 253–54 (1992) ("[C]ourts must presume that a legislature says in a statute what it means and means in a statute what it says there."); Park 'N Fly, Inc. v. Dollar Park and Fly, Inc., 469 U.S. 189, 194 (1985) ("Statutory construction must begin with the language employed by Congress and the assumption that the ordinary meaning of that language accurately expresses the legislative purpose."). Although not universally accepted, this presumption finds support in common sense intuitions about communication. "The words [a legislator] uses are the instruments by means of which he expects or hopes to effect ... changes [in society]. What gives him this expectation or this hope is his belief that he can anticipate how others (*e.g.,* judges and administrators) will understand these words." Gerald C. MacCallum, Jr., *Legislative Intent*, 75 YALE L.J. 754, 758 (1966). If that is the starting point, under what circumstances should judges feel justified in departing from the ordinary or conventional meaning of the text?

The majority in *Riggs* concluded that despite the clarity of the statutory text, the legislature's intention plainly ran counter to the expressed meaning of its chosen words *in this situation*. "If such a case had been present [in the minds of the legislators]," the majority asserted, "it cannot be doubted that they would have provided [that a donee who murdered the testator to make the will operative could not have any benefit under it]." But how do we know that it could not have been the legislators' intention that Elmer Palmer inherit according to the terms of the will? If the Statute of Wills provided that the expressed wishes of the testator govern except in the case of fraud, duress, or incapacity when the will was made, isn't it possible that the intention of the legislature was simply to provide a clear road map for a testator to articulate, in a binding way, his or her intentions? Could the legislative intention to provide for certainty in estate planning trump the fact that the mechanisms designed to ensure this certainty might occasionally produce results that the testator would not want?

Given that the court recognized that "[t]he purpose of those statutes was to enable testators to dispose of their estates to the objects of their bounty at death, and to carry into effect their final wishes legally expressed," his decision might be thought to rest, in part, on the idea that Francis Palmer, the testator, would surely have revised his will had he known that his nephew Elmer would murder him to collect his inheritance. But how easily is such a rule of decision limited? Suppose that Elmer had done no harm to Francis, but between the latter's death and the probate of the estate, Elmer had murdered someone else, perhaps a dear relative of Francis's. Or consider the possibility that Elmer joined a political movement that almost anyone, including Francis, would have found abhorrent. One could frame the intention of the legislature as being (a) to ensure that murderers do not inherit by virtue of their criminal act or (b) to ensure that heirs do not inherit when it is unmistakably obvious that the testator would have revised the will if subsequent facts had been known to him or her. Once one opens the door for exceptions not specified in the statute, how easy is it to articulate what the legislature must have intended in a given case?

**2.  *Background Principles and Legislative Intent*—**The majority in *Riggs* tried to articulate the legislature's purpose by invoking the common law maxim that a person shall not profit from his or her own wrongdoing. Like almost every state (all except Louisiana), New York is a common law jurisdiction. In the absence of controlling statutes, state courts in common law jurisdictions have presumptive authority to prescribe rules of decision for cases sounding in tort, contract, property, and the like. *See* Thomas W. Merrill, *Judicial Prerogative*, 12 PACE L. REV. 327, 345–46 (1992). In common law jurisdictions, should background common law principles also influence the interpretation of legislation? If so, what is the basis for that conclusion?

Perhaps the idea that courts should interpret statutes in light of common law principles derives from a venerable—but deeply controversial—maxim of interpretation according to which statutes in derogation of the common law should be narrowly construed. *See, e.g.*, Norfolk Redevelopment & Hous. Auth. v. Chesapeake & Potomac Tel. Co., 464 U.S. 30, 35–36 (1983). One might extend this principle to presume that legislators enact statutes against the common law background and do not usually intend to deviate from fundamental common law principles, even when the literal text of the statute might be susceptible to such a reading. In his influential commentary on *Riggs*, Professor Ronald Dworkin suggests that Justice Earl thought it "sensible to assume that legislators have a general and diffuse intention to respect traditional principles of justice unless they clearly indicate to the contrary." RONALD DWORKIN, LAW'S EMPIRE 19 (1986). Along similar lines, the Supreme Court has suggested that "where a common-law principle is well established, . . . the courts may take it as given that Congress has legislated with an expectation that the principle will apply except 'when a statutory purpose to the contrary is evident.'" Astoria Fed. Sav. & Loan Ass'n v. Solimino, 501 U.S. 104, 108 (1991) (quoting Isbrandtsen Co. v. Johnson, 343 U.S. 779, 783 (1952)).

Does it seem realistic to assume that members of the New York legislature had the maxim that "no one should profit by his or her own wrong" in mind when they enacted the Statute of Wills? If not, does the foregoing interpretive presumption really serve the interest in legislative supremacy? Furthermore, as Professor Reed Dickerson argues: "Except with respect to pure statutory codifications of existing common law, the rule [against construing statutes to derogate from common law principles] makes little sense, because most statutes that affect the common law are enacted for the very purpose of changing it. How, then, can we plausibly assume in areas of doubt that the legislature did not intend to change the common law or that it intended to change the common law to the lesser, rather than the greater, degree?" REED DICKERSON, THE INTERPRETATION AND APPLICATION OF STATUTES 206–07 (1975). Indeed, if common law is judge-made law and statutory law reflects the work product of the legislature, the judicial impulse to give narrow scope to statutes in derogation of the common law may in fact protect judicial power against perceived legislative encroachment. *See, e.g.,* Roscoe Pound, *Common Law and Legislation,* 21 HARV. L. REV. 383 (1908). At the same time, at least in jurisdictions that assign common law powers to their courts, might the common law supply a ready and predictable means of filling in gaps and omissions in complex statutory schemes, even if one believes that courts should not rely on the common law to restrict otherwise clear statutory language? *See, e.g.,* William N. Eskridge, Jr., *Public Values in Statutory Interpretation,* 137 U. PA. L. REV. 1007, 1051–55 (1989).

Or perhaps thinking about the case in terms of what the legislature wanted or was trying to achieve is the wrong way to frame the problem. Professor Dworkin said of *Riggs* that "it seems likely that the New York legislators did not have the case of murderers in mind at all. They did not intend that murderers inherit, but neither did they intend that they should not. They had no active intention either way." DWORKIN, *supra,* at 19. Does that seem correct? If so, then maybe the principle of "legislative suprema-cy" is of little help in resolving the case, and interpreters must look elsewhere for guiding principles. Professor Dworkin emphasizes the importance of *coherence,* explaining that, "since a statute forms a part of a larger intellectual system, the law as a whole, it should be constructed so as to make that larger system coherent in principle." *Id.* at 19–20. How satisfying is that approach? Does it seem more honest than the majority's efforts to tie its outcome to the imputed intention of the legislature? If the question does not boil down to imputing a plausible legislative intention, should coherence necessarily be the touchstone, or can judges defend their interpretive rules of thumb based on other values dear to them? *See, e.g.,* Jonathan R. Macey, *Promoting Public–Regarding Legislation Through Statutory Interpretation: An Interest–Group Model,* 86 COLUM. L. REV. 223, 264–65 (1986) (arguing that the canon protecting against derogation of the common law promotes efficiency); David L. Shapiro, *Continuity and Change in Statutory Interpretation,* 67 N.Y.U. L. REV. 921 (1992) (arguing that it promotes continuity). How does one choose among competing values when designing a rule of interpretation whose justification does not rest upon the pursuit of some plausible account of legislative instructions?

---

## Church of the Holy Trinity v. United States

Supreme Court of the United States
143 U.S. 457 (1892)

■ MR. JUSTICE BREWER delivered the opinion of the court.

Plaintiff in error is a corporation duly organized and incorporated as a religious society under the laws of the state of New York. E. Walpole

Warren was, prior to September, 1887, an alien residing in England. In that month the plaintiff in error made a contract with him, by which he was to remove to the city of New York, and enter into its service as rector and pastor; and, in pursuance of such contract, Warren did so remove and enter upon such service. It is claimed by the United States that this contract on the part of the plaintiff in error was forbidden by chapter 164, 23 St. p. 332; and an action was commenced to recover the penalty prescribed by that act. . . .

The first section describes the act forbidden, and is in these words:

> "Be it enacted by the senate and house of representatives of the United States of America, in congress assembled, that from and after the passage of this act it shall be unlawful for any person, company, partnership, or corporation, in any manner whatsoever, to prepay the transportation, or in any way assist or encourage the importation or migration, of any alien or aliens, any foreigner or foreigners, into the United States, its territories, or the District of Columbia, under contract or agreement, parol or special, express or implied, made previous to the importation or migration of such alien or aliens, foreigner or foreigners, to perform labor or service of any kind in the United States, its territories, or the District of Columbia."

It must be conceded that the act of the corporation is within the letter of this section, for the relation of rector to his church is one of service, and implies labor on the one side with compensation on the other. Not only are the general words labor and service both used, but also, as it were to guard against any narrow interpretation and emphasize a breadth of meaning, to them is added "of any kind;" and, further ... the fifth section, which makes specific exceptions, among them professional actors, artists, lecturers, singers, and domestic servants, strengthens the idea that every other kind of labor and service was intended to be reached by the first section. While there is great force to this reasoning, we cannot think congress intended to denounce with penalties a transaction like that in the present case. It is a familiar rule that a thing may be within the letter of the statute and yet not within the statute, because not within its spirit nor within the intention of its makers. This has been often asserted, and the Reports are full of cases illustrating its application. This is not the substitution of the will of the judge for that of the legislator; for frequently words of general meaning are used in a statute, words broad enough to include an act in question, and yet a consideration of the whole legislation, or of the circumstances surrounding its enactment, or of the absurd results which follow from giving such broad meaning to the words, makes it unreasonable to believe that the legislator intended to include the particular act. As said in Stradling v. Morgan, Plow. 205: "From which cases it appears that the sages of the law heretofore have construed statutes quite contrary to the letter in some appearance, and those statutes which comprehend all things in the letter they have expounded to extend to but some things, and those which generally prohibit all people from doing such an act they have interpreted to permit some people to do it, and those which include every person in the letter they have adjudged to reach to some persons only, which expositions have always been founded upon the intent of the legislature, which they have collected sometimes by considering the cause and necessity of making the act, sometimes by comparing one part of the act with another, and sometimes by foreign circumstances."

In Margate Pier Co. v. Hannam, 3 Barn. & Ald. 266, ABBOTT, C. J., quotes from Lord Coke as follows: "Acts of parliament are to be so construed as no man that is innocent or free from injury or wrong be, by a literal construction, punished or endangered." In the case of State v. Clark, 29 N. J. Law, 96, 99, it appeared that an act had been passed, making it a misdemeanor to willfully break down a fence in the possession of another person. Clark was indicted under that statute. The defense was that the act of breaking down the fence, though willful, was in the exercise of a legal right to go upon his own lands. The trial court rejected the testimony offered to sustain the defense, and the supreme court held that this ruling was error. In its opinion the court used this language: "The act of 1855, in terms, makes the willful opening, breaking down, or injuring of any fences belonging to or in the possession of any other person a misdemeanor. In what sense is the term willful used? In common parlance, willful is used in the sense of intentional, as distinguished from accidental or involuntary. Whatever one does intentionally, he does willfully. Is it used in that sense in this act? Did the legislature intend to make the intentional opening of a fence for the purpose of going upon the land of another indictable, if done by permission or for a lawful purpose? ... We cannot suppose such to have been the actual intent. To adopt such a construction would put a stop to the ordinary business of life. The language of the act, if construed literally, evidently leads to an absurd result. If a literal construction of the words of a statute be absurd, the act must be so construed as to avoid the absurdity. The court must restrain the words. The object designed to be reached by the act must limit and control the literal import of the terms and phrases employed." ... It will always, therefore, be presumed that the legislature intended exceptions to its language which would avoid results of this character. The reason of the law in such cases should prevail over its letter. The common sense of man approves the judgment mentioned by Puffendorf, that the Bolognian law which enacted "that whoever drew blood in the streets should be punished with the utmost severity," did not extend to the surgeon who opened the vein of a person that fell down in the street in a fit. The same common sense accepts the ruling, cited by Plowden, that the statute of 1 Edw. II., which enacts that a prisoner who breaks prison shall be guilty of felony, does not extend to a prisoner who breaks out when the prison is on fire, "for he is not to be hanged because he would not stay to be burnt." And we think that a like common sense will sanction the ruling we make, that the act of congress which punishes the obstruction or retarding of the passage of the mail, or of its carrier, does not apply to a case of temporary detention of the mail caused by the arrest of the carrier upon an indictment for murder." ...

Among other things which may be considered in determining the intent of the legislature is the title of the act. We do not mean that it may be used to add to or take from the body of the statute, but it may help to interpret its meaning. In ... U.S. v. Fisher, 2 Cranch, 358, 386, Chief Justice Marshall said: "On the influence which the title ought to have in construing the enacting clauses, much has been said, and yet it is not easy to discern the point of difference between the opposing counsel in this respect. Neither party contends that the title of an act can control plain words in the body of the statute; and neither denies that, taken with other parts, it may assist in removing ambiguities. Where the intent is plain, nothing is left to construction. Where the mind labors to discover the design of the legislature, it seizes everything from which aid can be derived; and in such case the title claims a degree of notice, and will have its due share of consideration." And in the case of U.S. v. Palmer, 3 Wheat. 610, 631, the same judge applied the doctrine in this way: "The words of the section are in terms of unlimited extent. The words 'any person or persons' are broad enough to comprehend every human being. But general words must not only be limited to cases within the jurisdiction of the state, but also to those objects to which the legislature intended to apply them. Did the legislature intend to apply these words to the subjects of a foreign power, who in a foreign ship may commit murder or robbery on the high seas? The title of an act cannot control its words, but may furnish some aid in showing what was in the mind of the legislature. The title of this act is, 'An act for the punishment of certain crimes against the United States.' It would seem that offenses against the United States, not offenses against the human race, were the crimes which the legislature intended by this law to punish."

It will be seen that words as general as those used in the first section of this act were by that decision limited, and the intent of congress with respect to the act was gathered partially, at least, from its title. Now, the title of this act is, "An act to prohibit the importation and migration of foreigners and aliens under contract or agreement to perform labor in the United States, its territories, and the District of Columbia." Obviously the thought expressed in this reaches only to the work of the manual laborer, as distinguished from that of the professional man. No one reading such a title would suppose that congress had in its mind any purpose of staying the coming into this country of ministers of the gospel, or, indeed, of any class whose toil is that of the brain. The common understanding of the terms labor and laborers does not include preaching and preachers, and it is to be assumed that words and phrases are used in their ordinary meaning. So whatever of light is thrown upon the statute by the language of the title indicates an exclusion from its penal provisions of all contracts for the employment of ministers, rectors, and pastors.

Again, another guide to the meaning of a statute is found in the evil which it is designed to remedy; and for this the court properly looks at contemporaneous events, the situation as it existed, and as it was pressed upon the attention of the legislative body. U.S. v. Railroad Co., 91 U.S. 72, 79. The situation which called for this statute was briefly but fully stated by Mr. Justice BROWN when, as district judge, he decided the case of U.S. v. Craig, 28 Fed. Rep. 795, 798: "The motives and history of the act are matters of common knowledge. It had become the practice for large capitalists in this country to contract with their agents abroad for the shipment of great numbers of an ignorant and servile class of foreign laborers, under contracts by which the employer agreed, upon the one hand, to prepay their passage, while, upon the other hand, the laborers agreed to work after their arrival for a certain time at a low rate of wages. The effect of this was to break down the labor market, and to reduce other laborers engaged in like occupations to the level of the assisted immigrant. The evil finally became so flagrant that an appeal was made to congress for relief by the passage of the act in question, the design of which was to raise the standard of foreign immigrants, and to discountenance the migration of those who had not sufficient means in their own hands, or those of their friends, to pay their passage."

It appears, also, from the petitions, and in the testimony presented before the committees of congress, that it was this cheap, unskilled labor which was making the trouble, and the influx of which congress sought to prevent. It was never suggested that we had in this country a surplus of brain toilers, and, least of all, that the market for the services of Christian ministers was depressed by foreign competition. Those were matters to which the attention of congress, or of the people, was not directed. So far, then, as the evil which was sought to be remedied interprets the statute, it also guides to an exclusion of this contract from the penalties of the act.

A singular circumstance, throwing light upon the intent of congress, is found in this extract from the report of the senate committee on education and labor, recommending the passage of the bill: "The general facts and considerations which induce the committee to recommend the passage of this bill are set forth in the report of the committee of the house. The committee report the bill back without amendment, although there are certain features thereof which might well be changed or modified, in the hope that the bill may not fail of passage during the present session. Especially would the committee have otherwise recommended amendments, substituting for the expression, 'labor and service,' whenever it occurs in the body of the bill, the words 'manual labor' or 'manual service,' as sufficiently broad to accomplish the purposes of the bill, and that such amendments would remove objections which a sharp and perhaps unfriendly criticism may urge to the proposed legislation. The committee, however, believing that the bill in its present form will be construed as including only those whose labor or service is manual in character, and being very desirous that the bill become a law before the adjournment, have reported the bill without change." Page 6059, Congressional Record, 48th Cong. And, referring back to the report of the committee of the house, there appears this language: "It seeks to restrain and prohibit the immigration or importation of laborers who would have never seen our shores but for the inducements and allurements of men whose only object is to obtain labor at the lowest possible rate, regardless of the social and material well-being of our own citizens, and regardless of the evil consequences which result to American laborers from such immigration. This class of immigrants care nothing about our institutions, and in many instances never even heard of them. They are men whose passage is paid by the importers. They come here under contract to labor for a certain number of years. They are ignorant of our social condition, and, that they may remain so, they are isolated and prevented from coming into contact with Americans. They are generally from the lowest social stratum, and live upon the coarsest food, and in hovels of a character before unknown to American workmen. They, as a rule, do not become citizens, and are certainly not a desirable acquisition to the body politic. The inevitable tendency of their presence among us is to degrade American labor, and to reduce it to the level of the imported pauper labor." Page 5359, Congressional Record, 48th Cong.

We find, therefore, that the title of the act, the evil which was intended to be remedied, the circumstances surrounding the appeal to congress, the reports of the committee of each house, all concur in affirming that the intent of congress was simply to stay the influx of this cheap, unskilled labor.

But, beyond all these matters, no purpose of action against religion can be imputed to any legislation, state or national, because this is a religious people.... [The court then canvassed a variety of pre- and post-constitutional expressions concerning the importance of religion to American society.] There is no dissonance in these declarations.... These, and many other matters which might be noticed, add a volume of unofficial declarations to the mass of organic utterances that this is a Christian nation. In the face of all these, shall it be believed that a Congress of the United States intended to make it a misdemeanor for a church of this country to contract for the services of a Christian minister residing in another nation?

Suppose, in the congress that passed this act, some member had offered a bill which in terms declared that, if any Roman Catholic church in this country should contract with Cardinal Manning to come to this country, and enter into its service as pastor and priest; or any Episcopal church should enter into a like contract with Canon Farrar; or any Baptist church should make similar arrangements with Rev. Mr. Spurgeon; or any Jewish synagogue with some eminent rabbi, such contract should be adjudged unlawful and void, and the church making it be subject to prosecution and punishment. Can it be believed that it would have received a minute of approving thought or a single vote? Yet it is contended that such was, in effect, the meaning of this statute. The construction invoked cannot be accepted as correct. It is a case where there was presented a definite evil, in view of which the legislature used general terms with the purpose of reaching all phases of that evil; and thereafter, unexpectedly, it is developed that the general language thus employed is broad enough to reach cases and acts which the whole history and life of the country affirm could not have been intentionally legislated against. It is the duty of the courts, under those circumstances, to say that, however broad the language of the statute may be, the act, although within the letter, is not within the intention of the legislature, and therefore cannot be within the statute.

***1.*** **Holy Trinity *and the Tradition of Strong Purposivism*—***Holy Trinity*** has become the most important marker for the idea that when the letter of the law and spirit of the law conflict, the former must yield to the latter. *See, e.g.*, Michael C. Dorf, *The Supreme Court, 1997 Term—Foreword: The Limits of Socratic Deliberation*, 112 HARV. L. REV. 4, 15 (1998). The case has perhaps earned that status because it so crisply explains the reasons for preferring spirit to letter. The Court started by stating, in no uncertain terms, that the hiring of Reverend Warren fell within the prohibition of the Alien Contract Labor Act. Indeed, Justice Brewer's opinion seems not merely to concede the point, but to take pains to establish it. Nonetheless, once the Court concluded from various sources that Congress had enacted the statute with the general purpose of halting "the influx of . . . cheap unskilled labor," the Court had little difficulty deciding that its job, as Congress's faithful agent, was to cut back the statute to give effect to its background purpose or general aim. The Court thought it "unreasonable to believe that the legislat[ure] intended to include the particular act" of hiring a pastor from abroad. Accordingly, the Court concluded that reshaping the text to fit its apparent purpose was not "the substitution of the will of the judge for that of the legislator," but rather a superior way of giving effect to the true legislative will or intent.

*Holy Trinity*'s reasoning defined the Court's tradition of strong purposivism. That approach competed throughout the late nineteenth and early twentieth century with the "plain meaning" rule, which stated that "[w]here the language is plain and admits of no more than one meaning, the duty of interpretation does not arise." Caminetti v. United States, 242 U.S. 470, 485 (1917). By the close of the New Deal, however, the Court had made clear that it subscribed fully to *Holy Trinity*'s strong purposivism. In a landmark case decided in 1940, the Court reiterated that "the function of the courts" in cases of statutory interpretation "is to construe the language so as to give effect to the intent of Congress." United States v. American Trucking Ass'ns, 310 U.S. 534, 542 (1940). In keeping with *Holy Trinity*, the *American Trucking* Court instructed judges about the Supreme Court's practices for ascertaining such intent:

> When [plain] meaning has led to absurd or futile results, . . . this Court has looked beyond the words to the purpose of the act. Frequently, however, even when the plain meaning did not produce absurd results but merely an unreasonable one "plainly at variance with the policy of the legislation as a whole" this Court has followed that purpose, rather than the literal words. When aid to construction of the meaning of words, as used in the statute, is available, there certainly can be no "rule of law" which forbids its use, however clear the words may appear on "superficial examination."

*Id*. at 543–44 (citations omitted).

In the aftermath of *American Trucking*, law professors and judges developed a more elaborate intellectual foundation for strong purposivism that grounded this approach in the principle of legislative supremacy but that did not turn on the idea that courts could or should discern the legislature's specific intent regarding any particular fact situation. The basic idea was that Congress enacts laws to achieve a purpose, and that interpreters should read those laws accordingly. *See* Archibald Cox, *Judge Learned Hand and the Interpretation of Statutes*, 60 HARV. L. REV. 370, 374 (1947); Felix Frankfurter, *Some Reflections on the Reading of Statutes*, 47 COLUM. L. REV. 527, 538–39 (1947). No one stated the point more clearly than Max Radin, who explained that "[t]he legislature that put [a] statute on the books had the constitutional right and power to set [the statute's] purpose as a desirable one for the community, and the court or administrator has the undoubted duty to obey it." Max Radin, *A Short Way with Statutes*, 56 HARV. L. REV. 388, 398 (1942). Because the drafter chose the words "primarily to let us know the statutory purpose," interpreters should undertake their responsibility with that function in mind. *Id.* at 400. From that starting point, Radin concluded:

> To say that the legislature is "presumed" to have selected its phraseology with meticulous care as to every word is in direct contradiction to known facts and injects an improper element into the relation of courts to the statutes. The legislature has no constitutional warrant to demand reverence for the words in which it frames its directives.

*Id.* at 406. Accordingly, "if the purpose is clear, . . . the implemental part of the statute should be subordinated to it." *Id.* at 407.

After World War II, this basic idea took on a canonical form in the highly influential Legal Process teaching materials prepared by Henry M. Hart, Jr., and Albert M. Sacks of the Harvard Law School. *See* HENRY M. HART, JR. & ALBERT M. SACKS, THE LEGAL PROCESS 1374 (William N. Eskridge, Jr. & Philip P. Frickey eds., 1994) (tent. ed. 1958); *see also, e.g.*, William N. Eskridge, Jr. & Philip P. Frickey, *The Making of The Legal Process*, 107 HARV. L. REV. 2031, 2046–47 (1994) (discussing the influence of the Legal Process teaching materials). Their basic theme was much like Radin's. They believed that "[t]he idea of a statute without an intelligible purpose is foreign to the idea of law and inadmissible." HART & SACKS, *supra*, at 1124. Hence, the interpreter must "[d]ecide what purpose ought to be attributed to the statute and to any subordinate provision of it which may be involved; and then . . . [i]nterpret the words of the statute immediately in question so as to carry out the purpose as best it can." *Id.* at 1374. In so doing, moreover, the judge should assume "that the legislature was made up of reasonable persons pursuing reasonable purposes reasonably." *Id.* at 1378.

How well do those premises square with the realities of the legislative process? Even if they do not describe how statutes are made, do purposivist theories represent a defensible normative account of how judges should act?

**2.  Holy Trinity *and the Identification of Legislative Purpose*—** In addition to articulating the essence of the purposivist approach, *Holy Trinity* is also notable for the ways in which the Court went about discerning the legislature's purpose. Consider the sources on which the Court relied:

*a.  The statute's title*—The Court noted that the Alien Contract Labor Act's formal title is: "An act to prohibit the importation and migration of foreigners and aliens under contract or agreement to perform labor in the United States, its territories, and the District of Columbia." It is black letter law that interpreters may consult the title of a statute in order to help resolve *ambiguity* in its operational provisions. *See, e.g.,* Pennsylvania Dep't of Corr. v. Yeskey, 524 U.S. 206, 212 (1998); Brotherhood of R.R. Trainmen v. Baltimore & O.R. Co., 331 U.S. 519, 528–29 (1947). Presumably, the title tells interpreters something useful about how Congress conceived of its reasons for acting, thereby shedding light on the statute's purpose. But should the general terms of a statutory title take precedence over the more specific operative provisions when the text of the latter is clear? If the title merely refers to "labor," but the Act's operative prohibition bars the importation of persons "to perform labor or service of any kind," why should the more directly relevant terms of the operative provision yield? Similarly, sometimes statutes contain preambles or findings that explicitly articulate the legislative purpose (though this was not true in *Holy Trinity*). *See, e.g.,* General Dynamics Land Sys., Inc. v. Cline, 540 U.S. 581, 589–93 (2004) (deriving the statutory purpose, in part, from enacted findings of purpose) (*see* pp. 68–78, *infra*). In such cases, should the findings of purpose stated in the preamble ever trump the specific semantic meaning of a particular operative provision when the two conflict?

*b.  The "mischief"*—The mischief rule is one of the oldest, most venerable rules of statutory construction. Its most famous statement is found in *Heydon's Case*, 76 Eng. Rep. 637, 638 (K.B. 1584), which instructed that "the office of all the Judges is always to make such . . . construction as shall suppress the mischief, and advance the remedy, and to suppress subtle inventions and evasions for continuance of the mischief, and . . . to add force and life to the cure and remedy, according to the true intent of the makers of the Act." The idea is simple: If the interpreter can identify the mischief the statute was trying to remedy, that fact will say a great deal about the purpose of the legislation. In *Holy Trinity*, the Court "look[ed] at contemporaneous events, the situation as it existed, and as it was pressed upon the attention of the legislative body." How should a judge determine such facts? Newspaper articles? Petitions to the legislature for action? Blue Ribbon Commission reports? Justice Brewer merely observed in *Holy Trinity* that "[t]he motives and history of the act are matters of common knowledge." Assuming that he is correct, does it necessarily follow that a piece of legislation is designed to address fully the mischief that inspired its enactment in the first place, or that the legislation is limited only to addressing that particular mischief?

*c.  Legislative history*—*Holy Trinity* is an early example of the how the Court sometimes relies on legislative history—statements by legislators, witnesses, or originating committees, as well as the evolution of a bill as it moves through the legislative process—to determine the statute's purpose. Most notably, the Court observed that the Senate Report both acknowledged the potential overbreadth of the phrase "labor or service of any kind" and noted that the Committee would have substituted the more appropriate terms "manual labor" or "manual service," if the Committee had not thought it more important to ensure the bill's passage "during the present session." In other words, the committee responsible for drafting the Senate bill not only directly expressed its understanding of the bill's narrower purpose, but also explained why the legislation was not being amended to express its more restricted scope.

Part IV of this chapter (pp. 140–201, *infra*) considers questions concerning the reliability and legitimacy of legislative history as evidence of legislative intent, purpose, or semantic meaning. For present purposes, it suffices to note that Professor Adrian Vermeule has unearthed some rather interesting evidence about the Senate Report on which the *Holy Trinity* Court relied. *See* Adrian Vermeule, *Legislative History and the Limits of Judicial Competence: The Untold Story of* Holy Trinity Church, 50 Stan. L. Rev. 1833 (1998). Although the Senate Committee Report stated that the Committee did not wish to propose the clarifying amendment because the committee wanted to assure the bill's swift passage during the first session of the 47th Congress, the bill did not in fact pass until the second session. *See id.* at 1848–51. Senators offered numerous amendments during the bill's ultimate consideration, but the bill's managers never offered the simple clarifying amendment to which they adverted in the Senate Committee Report—a fact that leads Professor Vermeule to conclude that they did not believe that they could secure the legislation's enactment on those terms. *See id.* at 1851–52.

Assuming Professor Vermeule is correct, why do you think the Senate committee might have stated an understanding of the bill's purpose that was at odds with the bill managers' apparent sense of what the Senate as a whole would accept? Perhaps it suggests that, although the committee is supposed to be an agent of the chamber, there may be some "slack" in this agency relationship: Maybe the committee was trying to manipulate the legislative history in order to secure a result that it would not have been able to achieve if it had proposed an amendment to the statutory text. Or perhaps the bill's managers chose not to back such an amendment, even though it probably would have attracted widespread support, because the complexity of the legislative process means that opening the door even to a generally popular amendment might have complicated the bill's chances for passage. Indeed, there is evidence that this is why the bill's managers were reluctant to open up discussion of more amendments to the scope of the bill's coverage during floor consideration. *See* John F. Manning, *The Absurdity Doctrine*, 116 Harv. L. Rev. 2387, 2427–28 & n.157 (2003). More generally, despite the suspicious procedural circumstances identified by Professor Vermeule, Professor Carol Chomsky suggests that it was nonetheless appropriate for the Court to narrow the statute in light of the tenor of the legislative history as a whole, which strongly suggested that the legislation was, in fact, directed at preventing the influx of low-cost, unskilled labor. *See* Carol Chomsky, *Unlocking the Mysteries of* Holy Trinity: *Spirit, Letter, and History in Statutory Interpretation*, 100 Colum. L. Rev. 901, 923–35 (2000). What probative value, if any, would you ascribe to the legislative history under the circumstances?

*d.   Societal values*—Perhaps the best known aspect of *Holy Trinity* is its suggestion that "no purpose of action against religion can be imputed to any legislation, state or national, because this is a religious people." This reasoning presupposes (a) that judges can infer the broadly and deeply held values of American society and (b) that legislators choose not to act in the teeth of such values either because, as Americans, they share those values or because, as legislators, they would not wish to inflame their constituents by flouting their values. *See* John F. Manning, *The Absurdity Doctrine*, 116 HARV. L. REV. 2387, 2405–08 (2003). The *Holy Trinity* Court went so far as to characterize as "absurd" a reading of the statute that would cover pastors. (We discuss this "absurdity canon" in more detail at pp. 85–101, *infra*.) But *Holy Trinity* might also be read as endorsing the broader principle that statutory purposes, and hence statutory meaning, should be inferred in light of deeply held background values. Is that right? Is this similar to the interpretive move made by Justice Earl in *Riggs v. Palmer* (pp. 33 & 37–38, *supra*)?

*e.   Other evidence of statutory purpose*—In addition to the sources employed in *Holy Trinity*, courts adopting a purposivist approach to interpretation have looked to other sorts of evidence as well. For example, courts sometimes look to the overall structure created by a statutory scheme to infer the statute's purpose, which the court then uses to interpret specific provisions. If a statute creates a complex and reticulated remedial scheme, for example, the Court might infer that the statutory remedies were meant to be exclusive. *See* United States v. Fausto, 484 U.S. 439, 448 (1988). The classic discussion of the art of structural inference is found in CHARLES L. BLACK, JR., STRUCTURE AND RELATIONSHIP IN CONSTITUTIONAL LAW (1969). More generally, courts may try to infer the meaning of a particular provision by the apparent purpose of the statute as a whole. *See, e.g.*, Commissioner v. Estate of Sternberger, 348 U.S. 187, 206 (1955). (If you read *TVA v. Hill* (pp. 4–17, *supra*) you may recall that the Court noted that the highly protective character of the various provisions of the Endangered Species Act made it easily conceivable that Congress would have meant to save the snail darter, even at the expense of the almost-completed Tellico Dam.) A statute's relationship to other statutes concerning the same general subject matter may also help to reveal its purpose. *See, e.g.*, Keifer & Keifer v. Reconstruction Fin. Corp., 306 U.S. 381, 389 (1939) ("The Congressional will must be divined, and by a process of interpretation which, in effect, is the ascertainment of policy immanent not merely in the single statute . . . but in a series of statutes. . . ."). Viewed from a Legal Process perspective (*see* p. 45, *supra*), to impute to Congress inexplicable differences in approach across statutes would be to assume that Congress acted arbitrarily, rather than reasonably.

Do these assumptions reflect Congress's real-world practice? Might a given institutional structure be consistent with multiple purposes? If so, is the presumption of a single purpose defensible as a normative assumption that improves the law without intruding upon congressional prerogatives, at least in the case of ambiguity?

\* \* \* \*

Ultimately, the Court may infer the "purpose" of a statute from some or all of the foregoing sources. Given the inevitable uncertainties associated with each, perhaps the most important factor is the Court's ability to find confirmation of its sense of the legislative purpose, where possible, in multiple sources.

## B.  THE NEW TEXTUALISM

Near the close of the twentieth century, a group of self-described "textualist" judges—most prominently, Justice Antonin Scalia and Judge Frank Easterbrook—challenged many of the key assumptions defining traditional purposivism. Many associate this "new textualism" principally with the rejection of legislative history as a tool of statutory interpretation (*see infra* Section IV.B, pp. 163–181, *infra*), but the new textualist position is much broader than a critique of one particular interpretive source. Rather, textualists build on the premise of legislative supremacy to argue that judges must hew closely to the meaning of a clear statutory text even when the result contradicts the statute's apparent purpose, however derived. Consider, for example, the question whether a statute that states "no dogs are allowed in the park" would prohibit a person (an eccentric person, perhaps) from bringing a pet wolf into the park. Even if in ordinary usage a wolf would not be considered a "dog," a purposivist judge might reason that the statute nevertheless applies, on the logic that any conceivable reason for adopting this statutory prohibition (*e.g.*, public safety or sanitary concerns) would apply to wolves. A textualist, however, would most likely read the word "dogs" in its usual sense, because respect for legislative supremacy requires enforcing the statute as written when its semantic meaning is clear in context. Modern textualists emphasize that judges must respect the *legislative compromise* embedded in the statutory text. This idea has had a significant influence on the Court's approach to the conflict of text and purpose. The following case was one of the first Supreme Court opinions that embraced this modern textualist approach.

---

## West Virginia University Hospitals, Inc. v. Casey

Supreme Court of the United States
499 U.S. 83 (1991)

■ JUSTICE SCALIA delivered the opinion of the Court.

This case presents the question whether fees for services rendered by experts in civil rights litigation may be shifted to the losing party pursuant to 42 U.S.C. § 1988, which permits the award of "a reasonable attorney's fee."

### I

Petitioner West Virginia University Hospitals, Inc. (WVUH), operates a hospital in Morgantown, W.Va., near the Pennsylvania border. The hospital is often used by Medicaid recipients living in southwestern Pennsylvania.

In January 1986, Pennsylvania's Department of Public Welfare notified WVUH of new Medicaid reimbursement schedules for services provided to Pennsylvania residents by the Morgantown hospital. In administrative proceedings, WVUH unsuccessfully objected to the new reimbursement rates on both federal statutory and federal constitutional grounds. After exhausting administrative remedies, WVUH filed suit in Federal District Court under 42 U.S.C. § 1983. . . .

Counsel for WVUH employed Coopers & Lybrand, a national accounting firm, and three doctors specializing in hospital finance to assist in the preparation of the lawsuit and to testify at trial. WVUH prevailed at trial in May 1988. The District Court subsequently awarded fees pursuant to 42 U.S.C. § 1988,[1] including over $100,000 in fees attributable to expert services. The District Court found these services to have been "essential" to presentation of the case—a finding not disputed by respondents.

Respondents appealed both the judgment on the merits and the fee award. The Court of Appeals for the Third Circuit affirmed as to the former, but reversed as to the expert fees, disallowing them except to the extent that they fell within the $30–per–day fees for witnesses prescribed by 28 U.S.C. § 1821(b). WVUH petitioned this Court for review of that disallowance; we granted certiorari.

## II

Title 28 U.S.C. § 1920 provides:

"A judge or clerk of any court of the United States may tax as costs the following:

"(1) Fees of the clerk and marshal;

"(2) Fees of the court reporter for all or any part of the stenographic transcript necessarily obtained for use in the case;

"(3) Fees and disbursements for printing and witnesses;

"(4) Fees for exemplification and copies of papers necessarily obtained for use in the case;

"(5) Docket fees under section 1923 of this title;

"(6) Compensation of court appointed experts, compensation of interpreters, and salaries, fees, expenses, and costs of special interpretation services under section 1828 of this title."

Title 28 U.S.C. § 1821(b) limits the witness fees authorized by § 1920(3) as follows: "A witness shall be paid an attendance fee of $30 per day for each day's attendance. A witness shall also be paid the attendance fee for the time necessarily occupied in going to and returning from the place of attendance. . . ." In Crawford Fitting Co. v. J.T. Gibbons, Inc., 482 U.S. 437

---

**1.** Title 42 U.S.C. § 1988 provides in relevant part: "In any action or proceeding to enforce a provision of sections 1981, 1982, 1983, 1985, and 1986 of this title, title IX of Public Law 92–318 . . ., or title VI of the Civil Rights Act of 1964 . . ., the court, in its discretion, may allow the prevailing party, other than the United States, a reasonable attorney's fee as part of the costs."

(1987), we held that these provisions define the full extent of a federal court's power to shift litigation costs absent express statutory authority to go further. . . .

As to the testimonial services of the hospital's experts, therefore, *Crawford Fitting* plainly requires, as a prerequisite to reimbursement, the identification of "explicit statutory authority." . . . The question before us, then, is—with regard to both testimonial and nontestimonial expert fees— whether the term "attorney's fee" in § 1988 provides the "explicit statutory authority" required by *Crawford Fitting*.

### III

The record of statutory usage demonstrates convincingly that attorney's fees and expert fees are regarded as separate elements of litigation cost. While some fee-shifting provisions, like § 1988, refer only to "attorney's fees," many others explicitly shift expert witness fees as well as attorney's fees. In 1976, just over a week prior to the enactment of § 1988, Congress passed those provisions of the Toxic Substances Control Act which provide that a prevailing party may recover "the costs of suit and reasonable fees for attorneys and *expert witnesses*." Also in 1976, Congress amended the Consumer Product Safety Act, which as originally enacted in 1972 shifted to the losing party "cost[s] of suit, including a reasonable attorney's fee[.]" In the 1976 amendment, Congress altered the fee-shifting provisions to their present form by adding a phrase shifting expert witness fees in addition to attorney's fees. Two other significant Acts passed in 1976 contain similar phrasing: the Resource Conservation and Recovery Act of 1976 ("costs of litigation (including reasonable attorney and expert witness fees)"), and the Natural Gas Pipeline Safety Act Amendments of 1976 ("costs of suit, including reasonable attorney's fees and reasonable expert witnesses fees").

Congress enacted similarly phrased fee-shifting provisions in numerous statutes both before 1976, see, *e.g.*, Endangered Species Act of 1973 ("costs of litigation (including reasonable attorney and expert witness fees)"), and afterwards, see, *e.g.*, Public Utility Regulatory Policies Act of 1978 ("reasonable attorneys' fees, expert witness fees, and other reasonable costs incurred in preparation and advocacy of [the litigant's] position" ). These statutes encompass diverse categories of legislation, including tax, administrative procedure, environmental protection, consumer protection, admiralty and navigation, utilities regulation, and, significantly, civil rights: The Equal Access to Justice Act (EAJA), the counterpart to § 1988 for violation of federal rights by federal employees, states that " 'fees and other expenses' . . . includes the reasonable expenses of expert witnesses . . . and reasonable attorney fees." At least 34 statutes in 10 different titles of the United States Code explicitly shift attorney's fees and expert witness fees.

The laws that refer to fees for nontestimonial expert services are less common, but they establish a similar usage both before and after 1976: Such fees are referred to *in addition to* attorney's fees when a shift is intended. A provision of the Criminal Justice Act of 1964 directs the court to reimburse appointed counsel for expert fees necessary to the defense of indigent criminal defendants—even though the immediately preceding provision already directs that appointed defense counsel be paid a designated hourly rate plus "expenses reasonably incurred." . . .

To the same effect is the 1980 EAJA, which provides: " 'fees and other expenses' . . . includes the reasonable expenses of expert witnesses, *the reasonable cost of any study, analysis, engineering report, test, or project* which is found by the court to be necessary for the preparation of the party's case, and reasonable attorney fees." (emphasis added). If the reasonable cost of a "study" or "analysis"—which is but another way of describing nontestimonial expert services—is by common usage already included in the "attorney fees," again a significant and highly detailed part of the statute becomes redundant. The Administrative Procedure Act and the Tax Equity and Fiscal Responsibility Act of 1982 contain similar language. Also reflecting the same usage are two railroad regulation statutes, the Regional Rail Reorganization Act of 1973 ("costs and expenses (including reasonable fees of accountants, experts, and attorneys) actually incurred"), and the Railroad Revitalization and Regulatory Reform Act of 1976 ("costs and expenses (including fees of accountants, experts, and attorneys) actually and reasonably incurred").[5]

We think this statutory usage shows beyond question that attorney's fees and expert fees are distinct items of expense. If, as WVUH argues, the one includes the other, dozens of statutes referring to the two separately become an inexplicable exercise in redundancy.

### IV

WVUH argues that at least in pre–1976 *judicial* usage the phrase "attorney's fees" included the fees of experts. To support this proposition, it relies upon two historical assertions: first, that pre–1976 courts, when exercising traditional equitable discretion in shifting attorney's fees, taxed as an element of such fees the expenses related to expert services; and second, that pre–1976 courts shifting attorney's fees pursuant to statutes identical in phrasing to § 1988 allowed the recovery of expert fees. We disagree with these assertions. The judicial background against which Congress enacted § 1988 mirrored the statutory background: expert fees were regarded not as a subset of attorney's fees, but as a distinct category of litigation expense.

Certainly it is true that prior to 1976 some federal courts shifted expert fees to losing parties pursuant to various equitable doctrines—

---

**5.** WVUH cites a House Conference Committee Report from a statute passed in 1986, stating: "The conferees intend that the term 'attorneys' fees as part of the costs' include reasonable expenses and fees of expert witnesses and the reasonable costs of any test or evaluation which is found to be necessary for the preparation of the . . . case." (discussing the Handicapped Children's Protection Act of 1986). In our view this undercuts rather than supports WVUH's position: The specification would have been quite unnecessary if the ordinary meaning of the term included those elements. The statement is an apparent effort to depart from ordinary meaning and to define a term of art.

sometimes in conjunction with attorney's fees. But they did not shift them as an element of attorney's fees. . . .

Even where the courts' holdings treated attorney's fees and expert fees the same (i.e., granted both or denied both), their analysis discussed them as separate categories of expense. We have found no support for the proposition that, at common law, courts shifted expert fees *as an element of* attorney's fees.

Of arguably greater significance than the courts' treatment of attorney's fees *versus* expert fees at common law is their treatment of those expenses under statutes containing fee-shifting provisions similar to § 1988. WVUH contends that in some cases courts shifted expert fees as well as the statutorily authorized attorney's fees—and thus must have thought that the latter included the former. We find, however, that the practice, at least in the overwhelming majority of cases, was otherwise.

Prior to 1976, the leading fee-shifting statute was the Clayton Act (shifting "the cost of suit, including a reasonable attorney's fee"). As of 1976, four Circuits (six Circuits, if one includes summary affirmances of district court judgments) had held that this provision did not permit a shift of expert witness fees. No court had held otherwise. Also instructive is pre–1976 practice under the federal patent laws, which provided that "[t]he court in exceptional cases may award reasonable attorney fees to the prevailing party." Again, every court to consider the matter as of 1976 thought that this provision conveyed no authority to shift expert fees. . . .

In sum, we conclude that at the time this provision was enacted neither statutory nor judicial usage regarded the phrase "attorney's fees" as embracing fees for experts' services.

V

WVUH suggests that a distinctive meaning of "attorney's fees" should be adopted with respect to § 1988 because this statute was meant to overrule our decision in Alyeska Pipeline Service Co. v. Wilderness Society, 421 U.S. 240 (1975). As mentioned above, prior to 1975 many courts awarded expert fees and attorney's fees in certain circumstances pursuant to their equitable discretion. In *Alyeska*, we held that this discretion did not extend beyond a few exceptional circumstances long recognized by common law. Specifically, we rejected the so-called "private attorney general" doctrine recently created by some lower federal courts, which allowed equitable fee shifting to plaintiffs in certain types of civil rights litigation. WVUH argues that § 1988 was intended to restore the pre–*Alyeska* regime—and that, since expert fees were shifted then, they should be shifted now.

Both chronology and the remarks of sponsors of the bill that became § 1988 suggest that at least some members of Congress viewed it as a response to *Alyeska*. It is a considerable step, however, from this proposition to the conclusion the hospital would have us draw, namely, that § 1988 should be read as a reversal of *Alyeska* in all respects.

By its plain language and as unanimously construed in the courts, § 1988 is both broader and narrower than the pre–*Alyeska* regime. Before *Alyeska*, civil rights plaintiffs could recover fees pursuant to the private attorney general doctrine only if private enforcement was necessary to defend important rights benefiting large numbers of people, and cost barriers might otherwise preclude private suits. Section 1988 contains no similar limitation—so that in the present suit there is no question as to the propriety of shifting WVUH's attorney's fees, even though it is highly doubtful they could have been awarded under pre–*Alyeska* equitable theories. In other respects, however, § 1988 is not as broad as the former regime. It is limited, for example, to violations of specified civil rights statutes—which means that it would not have reversed the outcome of *Alyeska* itself, which involved not a civil rights statute but the National Environmental Policy Act of 1969. Since it is clear that, in many respects, § 1988 was not meant to return us precisely to the pre–*Alyeska* regime, the objective of achieving such a return is no reason to depart from the normal import of the text.

WVUH further argues that the congressional purpose in enacting § 1988 must prevail over the ordinary meaning of the statutory terms. It quotes, for example, the House Committee Report to the effect that "the judicial remedy [must be] full and complete," and the Senate Committee Report to the effect that "[c]itizens must have the opportunity to recover what it costs them to vindicate [civil] rights in court[.]" As we have observed before, however, the purpose of a statute includes not only what it sets out to change, but also what it resolves to leave alone. The best evidence of that purpose is the statutory text adopted by both Houses of Congress and submitted to the President. Where that contains a phrase that is unambiguous—that has a clearly accepted meaning in both legislative and judicial practice—we do not permit it to be expanded or contracted by the statements of individual legislators or committees during the course of the enactment process. Congress could easily have shifted "attorney's fees and expert witness fees," or "reasonable litigation expenses," as it did in contemporaneous statutes; it chose instead to enact more restrictive language, and we are bound by that restriction.

WVUH asserts that we have previously been guided by the "broad remedial purposes" of § 1988, rather than its text, in a context resolving an "analogous issue": In Missouri v. Jenkins, 491 U.S. 274, 285 (1989), we concluded that § 1988 permitted separately billed paralegal and law clerk time to be charged to the losing party. The trouble with this argument is that *Jenkins* did not involve an "analogous issue," insofar as the relevant considerations are concerned. The issue there was not, as WVUH contends, whether we would permit our perception of the "policy" of the statute to overcome its "plain language." It was not remotely plain in *Jenkins* that the phrase "attorney's fee" did not include charges for law clerk and paralegal services. Such services, like the services of "secretaries, messengers, librarians, janitors, and others whose labor contributes to the work product," had traditionally been included in calculation of the lawyers' hourly rates. Only recently had there arisen "the 'increasingly widespread custom of separately billing for [such] services[.]' " By contrast, there has never been, to our knowledge, a practice of including the cost of expert services within attorneys' hourly rates. There was also no record in *Jenkins*—as there is a lengthy record here—of statutory usage that recognizes a distinction between the charges at issue and attorney's fees. We do not know of a single statute that shifts clerk or paralegal fees separately; and even those, such as the EAJA, which comprehensively define the assessable "litigation costs" make no separate mention of clerks or paralegals. In other words, *Jenkins* involved a respect in which the term "attorney's fees" (giving the losing argument the benefit of the doubt) was genuinely ambiguous; and we resolved that ambiguity not by invoking some policy that supersedes the text of the statute, but by concluding that charges of this sort had traditionally been included in attorney's fees and that separate billing should make no difference. The term's application to expert fees is not ambiguous; and if it were the means of analysis employed in *Jenkins* would lead to the conclusion that since such fees have not traditionally been included within the attorney's hourly rate they are not attorney's fees.

WVUH's last contention is that, even if Congress plainly did not include expert fees in the fee-shifting provisions of § 1988, it would have done so had it thought about it. Most of the pre–§ 1988 statutes that explicitly shifted expert fees dealt with environmental litigation, where the necessity of expert advice was readily apparent; and when Congress later enacted the EAJA, the federal counterpart of § 1988, it explicitly included expert fees. Thus, the argument runs, the 94th Congress simply forgot; it is our duty to ask how they would have decided had they actually considered the question.

This argument profoundly mistakes our role. Where a statutory term presented to us for the first time is ambiguous, we construe it to contain that permissible meaning which fits most logically and comfortably into the body of both previously and subsequently enacted law. We do so not because that precise accommodative meaning is what the lawmakers must have had in mind (how could an earlier Congress know what a later Congress would enact?), but because it is our role to make sense rather than nonsense out of the *corpus juris*. But where, as here, the meaning of the term prevents such accommodation, it is not our function to eliminate clearly expressed inconsistency of policy and to treat alike subjects that different Congresses have chosen to treat differently. The facile attribution of congressional "forgetfulness" cannot justify such a usurpation. Where what is at issue is not a contradictory disposition within the same enactment, but merely a difference between the more parsimonious policy of an earlier enactment and the more generous policy of a later one, there is no more basis for saying that the earlier Congress forgot than for saying that the earlier Congress felt differently. In such circumstances, the attribution of forgetfulness rests in reality upon the judge's assessment that the later statute contains the *better* disposition. But that is not for judges to prescribe. We thus reject this last argument for the same reason that

Justice Brandeis, writing for the Court, once rejected a similar (though less explicit) argument by the United States:

> "[The statute's] language is plain and unambiguous. What the Government asks is not a construction of a statute, but, in effect, an enlargement of it by the court, so that what was omitted, presumably by inadvertence, may be included within its scope. To supply omissions transcends the judicial function." Iselin v. United States, 270 U.S. 245, 250–251 (1926).[7]

For the foregoing reasons, we conclude that § 1988 conveys no authority to shift expert fees....

■ [JUSTICE MARSHALL's separate dissent is omitted.]

■ JUSTICE STEVENS, with whom JUSTICE MARSHALL and JUSTICE BLACKMUN join, dissenting.

... In the early 1970's, Congress began to focus on the importance of public interest litigation, and since that time, it has enacted numerous fee-shifting statutes. In many of these statutes, which the majority cites at length, Congress has expressly authorized the recovery of expert witness fees as part of the costs of litigation. The question in this case is whether, notwithstanding the omission of such an express authorization in 42 U.S.C. § 1988, Congress intended to authorize such recovery when it provided for "a reasonable attorney's fee as part of the costs." In my view, ... the omission of express authorization for expert witness fees in a fee-shifting provision should not preclude the award of expert witness fees. We should look at the way in which the Court has interpreted the text of this statute in the past, as well as this statute's legislative history, to resolve the question before us, rather than looking at the text of the many other statutes that the majority cites in which Congress expressly recognized the need for compensating expert witnesses....

## II

The Senate Report on the Civil Rights Attorney's Fees Awards Act of 1976 explained that the purpose of the proposed amendment to 42 U.S.C. § 1988 was "to remedy anomalous gaps in our civil rights laws created by the United States Supreme Court's recent decision in *Alyeska Pipeline Service Co. v. Wilderness Society* and to achieve consistency in our civil rights laws."[7] The Senate Committee on the Judiciary wanted to level the

---

**7.** WVUH at least asks us to guess the preferences of the *enacting* Congress. Justice STEVENS apparently believes our role is to guess the desires of the *present* Congress, or of Congresses yet to be. "Only time will tell," he says, "whether the Court, with its literal reading of § 1988, has correctly interpreted the will of Congress[.]" The implication is that today's holding will be proved wrong if Congress amends the law to conform with his dissent. We think not. The "will of Congress" we look to is not a will evolving from Session to Session, but a will expressed and fixed in a particular enactment. Otherwise, we would speak not of "interpreting" the law but of "intuiting" or "predicting" it. Our role is to say what the law, as hitherto enacted, *is*; not to forecast what the law, as amended, *will be*.

**7.** In *Alyeska Pipeline Service Co. v. Wilderness Society*, the Court held that courts were not free to fashion new exceptions to the American Rule, according to which each side assumed the cost of its own attorney's fees....

playing field so that private citizens, who might have little or no money, could still serve as "private attorneys general" and afford to bring actions, even against state or local bodies, to enforce the civil rights laws. The Committee acknowledged that "[i]f private citizens are to be able to assert their civil rights, and if those who violate the Nation's fundamental laws are not to proceed with impunity, then citizens must have the opportunity to recover *what it costs them* to vindicate these rights in court." According to the Committee, the bill would create "no startling new remedy," but would simply provide "the technical requirements" requested by the Supreme Court in *Alyeska*, so that courts could "continue the practice of awarding attorneys' fees which had been going on for years prior to the Court's May decision."

To underscore its intention to return the courts to their pre–*Alyeska* practice of shifting fees in civil rights cases, the Senate Committee's Report cited with approval not only several cases in which fees had been shifted, but also all of the cases contained in Legal Fees, Hearings before the Subcommittee on Representation of Citizen Interests of the Senate Committee on the Judiciary, 93d Cong., 1st Sess., pt. 3 (1973). The cases collected in the 1973 Senate Hearings included many in which courts had permitted the shifting of costs, including expert witness fees. At the time when the Committee referred to these cases, though several were later reversed, it used them to make the point that prior to *Alyeska*, courts awarded attorney's fees and costs, including expert witness fees, in civil rights cases, and that they did so in order to encourage private citizens to bring such suits. It was to this pre–*Alyeska* regime, in which courts could award expert witness fees along with attorney's fees, that the Senate Committee intended to return through the passage of the fee-shifting amendment to § 1988.

The House Report expressed concerns similar to those raised by the Senate Report. It noted that "[t]he effective enforcement of Federal civil rights statutes depends largely on the efforts of private citizens" and that the House bill was "designed to give such persons effective access to the judicial process...." The House Committee on the Judiciary concluded that "civil rights litigants were suffering very severe hardships because of the *Alyeska* decision," and that the case had had a "devastating impact" and had created a "compelling need" for a fee-shifting provision in the civil rights context.

According to both Reports, the record of House and Senate subcommittee hearings, consisting of the testimony and written submissions of public officials, scholars, practicing attorneys, and private citizens, and the questions of the legislators, makes clear that both committees were concerned with preserving access to the courts and encouraging public interest litigation.[9]

---

**9.** A frequently expressed concern was the need to undo the damage to public interest litigation caused by *Alyeska*. See, *e.g.*, Awarding of Attorneys' Fees, Hearings before the Subcommittee on Courts, Civil Liberties, and the Administration of Justice of the House Committee on the Judiciary, 94th Cong., 1st Sess. (1975). Many who testified expressed the view that attorneys needed fee-shifting provisions so that they could afford to work on public

It is fair to say that throughout the course of the hearings, a recurring theme was the desire to return to the pre–*Alyeska* practice in which courts could shift fees, including expert witness fees, and make those who acted as private attorneys general whole again, thus encouraging the enforcement of the civil rights laws.

The case before us today is precisely the type of public interest litigation that Congress intended to encourage by amending § 1988 to provide for fee shifting of a "reasonable attorney's fee as part of the costs." . . .

### III

In recent years the Court has vacillated between a purely literal approach to the task of statutory interpretation and an approach that seeks guidance from historical context, legislative history, and prior cases identifying the purpose that motivated the legislation. Thus, for example, in Christiansburg Garment Co. v. EEOC, 434 U.S. 412 (1978), we rejected a "mechanical construction" of the fee-shifting provision in § 706(k) of Title VII of the Civil Rights Act of 1964 that the prevailing defendant had urged upon us. Although the text of the statute drew no distinction between different kinds of "prevailing parties," we held that awards to prevailing plaintiffs are governed by a more liberal standard than awards to prevailing defendants. That holding rested entirely on our evaluation of the relevant congressional policy and found no support within the four corners of the statutory text. Nevertheless, the holding was unanimous and, to the best of my knowledge, evoked no adverse criticism or response in Congress.[11]

---

interest litigation, and private citizens needed fee-shifting provisions so that they could be made whole again. For example, the private citizen who was brought into court by the Government and who later prevailed would still not be made whole, because he had to bear the costs of his own attorney's fees. The Senate Hearings also examined the average citizen's lack of access to the legal system.

**11.** Other examples of cases in which the Court eschewed the literal approach include Steelworkers v. Weber, 443 U.S. 193 (1979), and Johnson v. Transportation Agency, Santa Clara County, 480 U.S. 616 (1987). Although the dissenters had the better textual argument in both cases, and urged the Court to read the words of the statute literally, the Court, in both cases, opted for a reading that took into account congressional purpose and historical context. Neither decision prompted an adverse congressional response.

Although there have been those who have argued that congressional inaction cannot be seen as an endorsement of this Court's interpretations, see, *e.g.*, Johnson v. Transportation Agency, 480 U.S., at 671–672 (SCALIA, J., dissenting); Patterson v. McLean Credit Union, 491 U.S. 164, 175, n.1 (1989), that charge has been answered by the observation that "when Congress has been displeased with [the Court's] interpretation . . ., it has not hesitated to amend the statute to tell us so. . . . Surely, it is appropriate to find some probative value in such radically different congressional reactions to this Court's interpretations. . . ." Johnson v. Transportation Agency, 480 U.S., at 629–630, n. 7; see Patterson v. McLean Credit Union, 491 U.S., at 200 (BRENNAN, J., concurring in judgment in part and dissenting in part) ("Where our prior interpretation of congressional intent was plausible, . . . we have often taken Congress' subsequent inaction as probative to varying degrees, depending upon the circumstances, of its acquiescence"). Since Congress has had an opportunity, albeit brief, to correct our broad reading of attorney's fees in *Jenkins* if it thought that we had misapprehended its purpose, the

On those occasions, however, when the Court has put on its thick grammarian's spectacles and ignored the available evidence of congressional purpose and the teaching of prior cases construing a statute, the congressional response has been dramatically different. It is no coincidence that the Court's literal reading of Title VII, which led to the conclusion that disparate treatment of pregnant and nonpregnant persons was not discrimination on the basis of sex was repudiated by the 95th Congress; that its literal reading of the "continuous physical presence" requirement in § 244(a)(1) of the Immigration and Nationality Act, which led to the view that the statute did not permit even temporary or inadvertent absences from this country was rebuffed by the 99th Congress; that its literal reading of the word "program" in Title IX of the Education Amendments of 1972, which led to the Court's gratuitous limit on the scope of the antidiscrimination provisions of Title IX was rejected by the 100th Congress; or that its refusal to accept the teaching of earlier decisions in Wards Cove Packing Co. v. Atonio, 490 U.S. 642 (1989) (reformulating order of proof and weight of parties' burdens in disparate-impact cases), and Patterson v. McLean Credit Union, 491 U.S. 164 (1989) (limiting scope of 42 U.S.C. § 1981 to the making and enforcement of contracts), was overwhelmingly rejected by the 101st Congress, and its refusal to accept the widely held view of lower courts about the scope of fraud was quickly corrected by the 100th Congress.

In the domain of statutory interpretation, Congress is the master. It obviously has the power to correct our mistakes, but we do the country a disservice when we needlessly ignore persuasive evidence of Congress' actual purpose and require it "to take the time to revisit the matter" and to restate its purpose in more precise English whenever its work product suffers from an omission or inadvertent error. As Judge Learned Hand explained, statutes are likely to be imprecise.

> "All [legislators] have done is to write down certain words which they mean to apply generally to situations of that kind. To apply these literally may either pervert what was plainly their general meaning, or leave undisposed of what there is every reason to suppose they meant to provide for. Thus it is not enough for the judge just to use a dictionary. If he should do no more, he might come out with a result which every sensible man would recognize to be quite the opposite of what was really intended; which would contradict or leave unfulfilled its plain purpose." L. Hand, How Far Is a Judge Free in Rendering a Decision?, in *The Spirit of Liberty* 103, 106 (I. Dilliard ed.1952).

The Court concludes its opinion with the suggestion that disagreement with its textual analysis could only be based on the dissenters' preference for a "better" statute. It overlooks the possibility that a different view may be more faithful to Congress' command. The fact that Congress has consistently provided for the inclusion of expert witness fees in fee-shifting statutes when it considered the matter is a weak reed on which to rest the

---

Court has no reason to change its approach to the fee-shifting provision of § 1988, as the majority does today.

conclusion that the omission of such a provision represents a deliberate decision to forbid such awards. Only time will tell whether the Court, with its literal reading[19] of § 1988, has correctly interpreted the will of Congress with respect to the issue it has resolved today. . . .

---

*1. **Textualism, Purposivism, and Assumptions about the Legislative Process**—*Justice Stevens' dissent plainly falls within the purposivist tradition of Hart and Sacks and the Legal Process school. Justice Stevens started from the proposition that courts should presume that Congress rationally fulfills its apparent goals and that its work product is relatively coherent. Given the timing and public context of the legislation in question, one can scarcely doubt that the *general aim* or *background purpose* of § 1988 was to overrule the *Alyeska Pipeline* case. Bracketing for the moment the question whether legislative history is a reliable and legitimate source for discerning legislative purpose, it is clear from the hearings and the accompanying committee reports that the bill's drafters sought to ensure that civil rights plaintiffs and defendants played on a level playing field in which plaintiffs had meaningful access to the judicial process, and that the drafters concluded that, to advance this goal, prevailing civil rights plaintiffs should be able to recover the costs they incurred in pursuing litigation. As Justice Stevens argued, those background purposes point strongly in the direction of permitting the recovery of both attorney's fees and expert fees. Justice Stevens then made the classic purposivist move: he argued that the principle of legislative supremacy not only permits, but actually requires the Court to deviate from the conventional meaning of the text: "[W]e do the country a disservice when we needlessly ignore persuasive evidence of Congress' actual purpose and require it 'to take the time to revisit the matter' and to restate its purpose in more precise English whenever its work product suffers from an omission or inadvertent error." Justice Stevens' view of the legislative process thus appears to be that Congress usually acts from coherent background purposes, but inevitably adopts language that fails to capture those purposes fully. As Judge Posner, who wrote a lower court opinion taking the same position with regard to the fee-shifting provisions of § 1988, explained:

> [J]udges realize in their heart of hearts that the superficial clarity to which they are referring when they call the meaning of a statute

---

**19.** Seventy years ago, Justice Cardozo warned of the dangers of literal reading, whether of precedents or statutes:

> "[Some judges'] notion of their duty is to match the colors of the case at hand against the colors of many sample cases spread out upon their desk. The sample nearest in shade supplies the applicable rule. But, of course, no system of living law can be evolved by such a process, and no judge of a high court, worthy of his office, views the function of his place so narrowly. If that were all there was to our calling, there would be little of intellectual interest about it. The man who had the best card index of the cases would also be the wisest judge. It is when the colors do not match, when the references in the index fail, when there is no decisive precedent, that the serious business of the judge begins." *The Nature of the Judicial Process*, at 20–21.

"plain" is treacherous footing for interpretation. They know that statutes are purposive utterances and that language is a slippery medium in which to encode a purpose. They know that legislatures, including the Congress of the United States, often legislate in haste, without considering fully the potential application of their words to novel settings.

Friedrich v. City of Chicago, 888 F.2d 511, 514 (7th Cir. 1989), vacated mem., 499 U.S. 933 (1991). Accordingly, if the judge can discern "what Congress probably was driving at," he or she should read the statute "to bring about the end that the legislators would have specified had they thought about it more clearly or used a more perspicuous form of words." *Id.* Noting the fallacy of "legislative omniscience," Judge Posner thought it important that an interpretation that awarded expert fees "would be obvious to one familiar with the circumstances of enactment." *Id.* at 517.

Given the factual background of the legislation and the statements found in the hearings and committee reports, doesn't it seem plausible that Justice Stevens and Judge Posner are right in thinking that the bill's sponsors and perhaps even the average voter in each House would have understood the bill to give the broader coverage urged by the plaintiffs? If so, should that be the end of the matter from the standpoint of legislative supremacy?

Justice Scalia's majority opinion provides a nice illustration not only of the basic textualist position, but also of how that position derives from a conception of the legislative process that diverges substantially from the purposivist vision. Justice Scalia's principal argument was that the *semantic meaning* of "reasonable attorney's fee" cannot include expert fees. His opinion for the Court did not draw this from the "plain meaning" of the statute; indeed, the opinion recognized that in the specialized parlance of the legal profession an "attorney's fee" might easily refer to something more than a lawyer's billable hours. What convinced the Court that "expert fees" did not count as attorney's fees under § 1988 was the *usage* of the term in legal parlance. In countless other fee-shifting statutes, including some passed by the same Congress that enacted § 1988, "attorney's fees" and "expert fees" appeared as separate items of expense, making it clear that Congress did not use the former expression to include the latter item of expense. Assuming that the Court correctly determined the statute's semantic meaning, why should that be decisive if all other evidence of legislative purpose points in a different direction?

The answer lies in a view of the legislative process that is different—and grittier—than the one that underlies strong purposivism. Rather than seeing the legislative process as coherent and reasonable, the new textualists emphasize the rough-and-tumble of political compromise. While purposivists tend to see mismatch between a statute's text and apparent purpose as reflecting some sort of inadvertent legislative omission or failure of foresight, textualists are more likely to see such apparent misalignment as the consequence of the inevitable conflict, bargaining, and compromise among hundreds of elected federal officials and countless constituents and interest groups. The Court first articulated this view in 1986 in an opinion by Chief Justice Burger:

> The "plain purpose" of legislation . . . is determined in the first instance with reference to the plain language of the statute itself. Application of "broad purposes" of legislation at the expense of specific provisions ignores the complexity of the problems Congress is called upon to address and the dynamics of legislative action. Congress may be unanimous in its intent to stamp out some vague social or economic evil; however, because its Members may differ sharply on the means for effectuating that intent, the final language of the legislation may reflect hard-fought compromises. Invocation of the "plain purpose" of legislation at the expense of the terms of the statute itself takes no account of the processes of compromise and, in the end, prevents the effectuation of congressional intent.

Board of Governors of Fed. Res. Sys. v. Dimension Fin. Corp, 474 U.S. 361, 373–74 (1986) (internal citation omitted). Judge Easterbrook has developed that same theme: "If [a given statutory outcome] is unprincipled, it is the way of compromise. Law is a vector rather than an arrow. Especially when you see the hand of interest groups." Frank H. Easterbrook, *Text, History, and Structure in Statutory Interpretation*, 17 HARV. J.L. & PUB. POL'Y 61, 68 (1994). In other words, laws will be messy, uneven, and ill-fitting with their apparent purposes not because Congress is short-sighted or imprecise, but rather because legislation entails compromise, and compromise is untidy by nature. This phenomenon is further amplified by the cumbersome and fragmented federal legislative process (pp. 22–28, *supra*), which gives political minorities extraordinary power to block or slow down legislation. This means that political minorities—sometimes multiple competing political minorities—have considerable power to extract concessions as a condition of their assent. This feature of the legislative process may have considerable benefits, but it also means that legislative compromises will often be even more awkward and unprincipled.

From this observation, textualists conclude that respect for legislative supremacy requires judicial respect for these often arbitrary legislative compromises, rather than a judicial attempt to derive (and impose) a coherent statutory "purpose." According to textualists, if the judiciary regards itself as having authority to smooth over every oddly shaped statute in order to make it more congruent with its overall purpose, that practice risks disrupting the lines of compromise that emerged from the complex and arduous legislative process and made their way into the final statutory text. *See* John F. Manning, *Textualism and the Equity of the Statute*, 101 COLUM. L. REV. 1, 70–78 (2001). How convincing is that account of textualism? Why should judges assume that an awkward statute reflects the fruits of legislative compromise, rather than legislative omission or lack of foresight?

It is important to emphasize that, while textualists and purposivists emphasize different features of the legislative process, neither purposivists nor textualists are naïve. Purposivists understand that the legislative process sometimes involves unprincipled compromises and horse trading, while textualists agree that language is inevitably imprecise and that legislators lack perfect foresight. So, when a court confronts a case in which the most plausible semantic meaning of a statute's text conflicts with the most plausible reconstruction of the statute's purpose, the court has to balance these different sorts of threats to legislative supremacy. If courts presume that tension between text and purpose usually reflects a failure of legislative expression, and therefore strive to read statutes consistently with some kind of coherent purpose, then the statutory law of the United States will be, on balance, more coherent and probably more just. On the other hand, if courts presume that statutory awkwardness reflects legislative compromise, the rights of minority stakeholders in the legislative process will receive greater protection against inadvertent dilution. What presumption should courts adopt? The answer to this question may depend not only on empirical questions about the actual reasons for misalignment between text and purpose, but also the competing values at stake. How should courts go about deciding which values merit greater protection in the design of rules of interpretation?

**2. Textualists' Disaggregation of "Purpose"**—The textualist critique of purposivism also asserts that, even putting aside the messy realities of the legislative process and the need to respect legislative compromise, the traditional notion that judges can discern a single statutory "purpose" is flawed. First of all, the "purpose" of a statute can be framed at different levels of generality. How, for example, would one define the "purpose" of the attorney fee recovery provision in § 1988? Is the purpose of this provision to reimburse civil rights plaintiffs for their attorney costs? If so, then the "purpose" and "text" become equivalent. So purposivists must have a higher level of generality in mind. But how high a level? Is the purpose of the attorney fee provision in § 1988 to reimburse plaintiffs for all reasonable litigation costs? To level the playing field between civil rights plaintiffs and defendants? To promote civil rights litigation? To promote a just society? At what point does the purpose become too remote to overcome the semantic meaning of the rules embedded in the text? Max Radin explained this level of generality problem as follows:

> There are purposes and purposes. It is not so much that the same statute may be an obvious instrument to several ends simultaneously, which is, after all, unlikely, but that nearly every end is a means to another end. We distinguish in our conduct and our thinking between immediate and ulterior purposes.... If we [take a statute that makes gambling contracts void], can we say simply that its purpose is to discourage gambling? That is obviously a remoter purpose, but the immediate purpose is something less. It is to make it impossible to sue on gambling contracts, or at any rate to make their gambling character a defense.... [T]o interpret a law by its purposes requires the court to select one of a concatenated sequence of purposes, and this choice is to be determined by motives which are usually suppressed.

Max Radin, *Statutory Interpretation*, 43 HARV. L. REV. 863, 876, 878 (1930). At the highest level of generality, Radin observed, "the avowed and ultimate purposes of all statutes, because of all law, are justice and security." *Id.* at 876.

Radin's observation leads into a second textualist objection to the conventional conception of legislative "purpose": While traditional purposivists think of purpose in terms of a statute's *ends*, textualists emphasize that statutes embody choices about both *ends and means*. The means adopted give interpreters important information about the price the legislature was willing to pay to achieve its ends. For example, one of the legislature's central choices concerning means is whether to rely on *rules* or *standards* to implement their policies. Thus, Judge Easterbrook has written:

> A legislature that seeks to achieve Goal $X$ can do so in one of two ways. First, it can identify the goal and instruct courts or agencies to design rules to achieve the goal. In that event, the subsequent selection of rules implements the actual legislative decision, even if the rules are not what the legislature would have selected itself. The second approach is for the legislature to pick the rules. It pursues Goal $X$ by Rule $Y$. The selection of $Y$ is a measure of what Goal $X$ was worth to the legislature, of how best to achieve $X$, and of where to stop in pursuit of $X$. Like any other rule, $Y$ is bound to be imprecise, to be over- and under-inclusive. This is not a good reason for a court, observing the inevitable imprecision, to add to or subtract from Rule $Y$ on the argument that, by doing so, it can get more of Goal $X$. The judicial selection of means to pursue $X$ displaces and directly overrides the legislative selection of ways to obtain $X$. It denies to legislatures the choice of creating or withholding gapfilling authority.

Frank H. Easterbrook, *Statutes' Domains*, 50 U. CHI. L. REV. 533, 546–47 (1983) (citations omitted). Accordingly, when purposivists rely on "an imputed 'spirit' to convert one approach into another," they "dishonor[] the legislative choice as effectively as expressly refusing to follow the law." Frank H. Easterbrook, *Text, History, and Structure in Statutory Interpretation*, 17 HARV. J.L. & PUB. POL'Y 61, 68 (1994). This is likely what Justice Scalia meant when he wrote for the Court in *Casey* that "the purpose of a statute includes not only what it sets out to change, but also what it resolves to leave alone" and that "[t]he best evidence of that purpose is the statutory text adopted by both Houses of Congress and submitted to the President."

How persuasive do you find this critique of the concept of legislative purpose? In recent years, the Justices who subscribe to (or are sympathetic to) textualism have been able to attract majorities for the proposition that legislation entails compromise and that interpreters should therefore pay close attention to not only the ends pursued by a statute, but also the means chosen for effecting those ends. *See, e.g.*, Ragsdale v. Wolverine World Wide, Inc., 535 U.S. 81, 93–94 (2002) (Kennedy, J.) (noting that "any key term in an important piece of legislation" typically reflects "the result of compromise between groups with marked but divergent interests in the contested provision" and that "[c]ourts and agencies must respect and give effect to these sorts of compromises"); MCI Telecomms. Corp. v. AT & T Co., 512 U.S. 218, 231 n.4 (1994) (Scalia, J.) (holding that judges "are bound, not only by the ultimate purposes Congress has selected, but by the means it has deemed appropriate, and prescribed, for the pursuit of those purposes"). Perhaps more strikingly, even non-textualist judges sometimes sound similar themes. *See, e.g.*, Landgraf v. USI Film Prods., 511 U.S. 244, 286 (1994) (Stevens, J.) ("Statutes are seldom crafted to pursue a single goal, and compromises necessary to their enactment may require adopting means other than those that would most effectively pursue the main goal."); Pension Benefit Guar. Corp. v. LTV Corp., 496 U.S. 633, 646–47 (1990) (Blackmun, J.) ("[N]o legislation pursues its purposes at all costs. Deciding what competing values will or will not be sacrificed to the achievement of a particular objective is the very essence of legislative choice—and it frustrates rather than effectuates legislative intent simplistically to assume that *whatever* furthers the statute's primary objective must be the law.") (alteration in original) (quoting Rodriguez v. United States, 480 U.S. 522, 525–26 (1987) (per curiam)) (internal quotation marks omitted). Do such opinions suggest that at least some modern purposivists have implicitly endorsed elements of the textualist critique? Or do they show that purposivism can be sensitive to such process concerns without sacrificing the fundamental commitment to give priority to the reason and spirit of the law, rather than its narrow literal meaning?

*3. Congressional Override of Judicial Statutory Interpretation Decisions*—In arguing that purposivism is more consistent than textualism with the principle of legislative supremacy, Justice Stevens pointed out that Congress had recently overridden a number of decisions resting on strict textual analysis, but had left in place other decisions that employed a purposive approach. Justice Stevens' anecdotal claim that Congress is more likely to override textualist interpretations has been substantiated by more systematic empirical research. *See* Daniel J. Bussel, *Textualism's Failures: A Study of Overruled Bankruptcy Decisions*, 53 Vand. L. Rev. 887 (2000); William N. Eskridge, Jr., *Overriding Supreme Court Statutory Interpretation Decisions*, 101 Yale L.J. 331 (1991); Michael E. Solimine & James L. Walker, *The Next Word: Congressional Response to Supreme Court Statutory Decisions*, 65 Temp. L. Rev. 425, 446 (1992). Furthermore, Justice Stevens' prediction that Congress would amend § 1988 to overturn the Supreme Court's decision in *Casey* was fulfilled when Congress enacted, as part of the Civil Rights Act of 1991, an amendment to § 1988 that provided for recovery of expert fees. *See* Pub. L. No. 102–166, Title I, §§ 103, 113(a)(2), Nov. 21, 1991, 105 Stat. 1074, 1079. Perhaps this evidence collectively demonstrates that purposivism is more likely to answer the interpretive question correctly than is textualism, and that Justice Stevens had the better of the argument in *Casey*.

Then again, perhaps it doesn't. A textualist might plausibly respond, first, that what Congress wants, or is able to enact, at the present moment tells us little about the legislative compromise that facilitated the enactment of the statute in the first place. On one plausible (but sometimes contested) view, the point of interpretation is to respect the supremacy of the *enacting* legislature, not the current legislature. Indeed, perhaps the greater override rate for textualist decisions is really evidence that textualists are typically more faithful to the intent of the enacting legislature, while purposivists (perhaps subconsciously) tailor their decisions to the preferences of the sitting legislature.

Second, isn't there a sense in which the frequent congressional "correction" of textualist decisions actually supports the textualist position rather than the purposivist position? After all, textualists often respond to accusations that their interpretations lead to unwise or unjust results by insisting that "if Congress doesn't like it, Congress can fix it." A subtler version of this argument maintains that textualism operates as a kind of "penalty default rule" that improves the legislative process: The idea here is that the Court's reliance on text is more likely to provoke Congress to clarify an ambiguous or imprecise statute, and this effect may enhance, rather than detract from, the legitimacy of the interpretive practice. *Cf.* EINER ELHAUGE, STATUTORY DEFAULT RULES 149–223 (2008). Purposivists usually counter that these arguments fail to account for the complexities and difficulties of the legislative process.

Third, a closer inquiry into these congressional overrides of textualist decisions reveals that the story is sometimes more complicated than it first appears. Consider the 1991 Civil Rights Act amendment to § 1988 that overturned *Casey*. It turns out that this amendment only overturned *Casey* with respect to a subset of cases covered by § 1988, not to all the cases that would have been covered had *Casey* come out the other way. Doesn't Congress's refusal to extend expert fees to all categories of litigation under § 1988 at least indicate that the question whether to provide for both attorney's fees *and* expert fees was not perfectly obvious and might have been a topic on which to strike a compromise—perhaps even an awkward one?

> **4.   *The Problem of Inconsistency in Interpretive Method*—**What are the implications of the fact that the Court is often inconsistent in the application of interpretive methods? Consider Justice Stevens' observation in *Casey* that "[i]n recent years the Court has vacillated between a purely literal approach to the task of statutory interpretation and an approach that seeks guidance from historical context, legislative history, and prior cases identifying the purpose that motivated the legislation." Justice Stevens' main point was to argue for the latter approach as superior to the former, but might the vacillation itself be a problem? Wouldn't it be better if there were a consistent set of background interpretive norms against which Congress could legislate? A number of commentators have urged the Court to develop clear, consistent interpretive practices. *See, e.g.,* Sydney Foster, *Should Courts Give Stare Decisis Effect to Statutory Interpretation Methodology*, 96 GEO. L.J. 1863 (2008); Cass R. Sunstein, *Interpreting Statutes in the Regulatory State*, 103 HARV. L. REV. 405, 505 (1989). Why do you think the Court has been unable to do so thus far? Is the main problem

that the heterogeneous collection of federal judges and justices will simply never be able to establish a coherent approach to interpretation? *See* Frank H. Easterbrook, *Ways of Criticizing the Court*, 95 Harv. L. Rev. 802 (1982); Adrian Vermeule, *The Judiciary Is a They, Not an It: Interpretive Theory and the Fallacy of Division*, 14 J. Contemp. Legal Issues 549 (2005); Alexander Volokh, *Choosing Interpretive Methods: A Positive Theory of Judges and Everyone Else*, 83 N.Y.U. L. Rev. 769 (2008). Or is it simply that many individual judges and justices are unwilling to commit themselves to a particular set of interpretive rules? *See* Jonathan R. Siegel, *The Polymorphic Principle and the Judicial Role in Statutory Interpretation*, 84 Tex. L. Rev. 339, 385–90 (2005). Or is there some other explanation?

## C.  Textually-Constrained Purposivism

Over the last quarter-century, textualism has had an extraordinary influence on how federal courts approach questions of statutory interpretation. When the Court finds the text to be clear in context, it now routinely enforces the statute as written. *See, e.g.,* Carcieri v. Salazar, 129 S.Ct. 1058, 1066–67 (2009) ("[C]ourts must presume that a legislature says in a statute what it means and means in a statute what it says there." (citation omitted) (internal quotation mark omitted)); Jimenez v. Quarterman, 129 S.Ct. 681, 685 (2009) ("It is well established that, when the statutory language is plain, we must enforce it according to its terms."); Ali v. Federal Bureau of Prisons, 552 U.S. 214, 128 S.Ct. 831, 841 (2008) ("We are not at liberty to rewrite the statute to reflect a meaning we deem more desirable. I[nstead, we must g]ive effect to the text [C]ongress enacted...." (footnote omitted)). One measure of the success of the textualist critique of purposivism is that the Supreme Court has not cited *Holy Trinity* favorably in a majority opinion in over two decades. (The most recent favorable citation in a majority opinion was in Public Citizen v. United States Department of Justice, 491 U.S. 440, 454 (1989) (*see* pp. 89–96, *infra*)). The Court's apparent unease with *Holy Trinity*-style strong purposivism, however, does not mean that the Court has abandoned the use of purpose in statutory analysis. There may be fissures on the Court concerning whether and in what circumstances one should use particular sources, such as legislative history, as evidence of statutory purpose (*see* Part IV). But no one—not even the staunchest textualist—denies that statutory purpose is sometimes relevant to the resolution of statutory ambiguity. *See, e.g.,* National Tax Credit Partners, L.P. v. Havlik, 20 F.3d 705, 707 (7th Cir. 1994) (Easterbrook, J.) ("Knowing the purpose behind a rule may help a court decode an ambiguous text, but first there must be some ambiguity." (citations omitted)); Antonin Scalia, *Judicial Deference to Administrative Interpretations of Law*, 1989 Duke L.J. 511, 515 ("Surely one of the most frequent justifications courts give for choosing a particular construction is that the alternative interpretation would produce ... results less compatible with the reason or purpose of the statute.").

Consider the following case, in which the Court relied heavily on the purpose of the Age Discrimination in Employment Act, but first took pains to establish that the statutory language was elastic enough to accommodate the interpretation favored by the Court. Does this analysis represent a new strain of textually-constrained purposivism?

---

# General Dynamics Land Systems, Inc. v. Cline

Supreme Court of the United States
540 U.S. 581 (2004)

■ Justice Souter delivered the opinion of the Court.

The Age Discrimination in Employment Act of 1967 (ADEA or Act), 81 Stat. 602, 29 U.S.C. § 621 et seq., forbids discriminatory preference for the young over the old. The question in this case is whether it also prohibits favoring the old over the young. We hold it does not.

## I

In 1997, a collective-bargaining agreement between petitioner General Dynamics and the United Auto Workers eliminated the company's obligation to provide health benefits to subsequently retired employees, except as to then-current workers at least 50 years old. Respondents (collectively, Cline) were then at least 40 and thus protected by the Act, see 29 U.S.C. § 631(a), but under 50 and so without promise of the benefits. All of them objected to the new terms, although some had retired before the change in order to get the prior advantage, some retired afterwards with no benefit, and some worked on, knowing the new contract would give them no health coverage when they were through.

Before the Equal Employment Opportunity Commission (EEOC or Commission) they claimed that the agreement violated the ADEA, because it "discriminate[d against them] ... with respect to ... compensation, terms, conditions, or privileges of employment, because of [their] age," § 623(a)(1)....

A divided panel of the Sixth Circuit [held] ... that the prohibition of § 623(a)(1), covering discrimination against "any individual ... because of such individual's age," is so clear on its face that if Congress had meant to limit its coverage to protect only the older worker against the younger, it would have said so.... Judge Cole, concurring, saw the issue as one of plain meaning that produced no absurd result.... Judge Williams dissented [based on contrary precedent in another circuit], thinking it "obvious that the older a person is, the greater his or her needs become."

We granted certiorari to resolve [a] conflict among the Circuits, and now reverse.

## II

The common ground in this case is the generalization that the ADEA's prohibition covers "discriminat[ion] ... because of [an] individual's age," 29 U.S.C. § 623(a)(1), that helps the younger by hurting the older. In the abstract, the phrase is open to an argument for a broader construction, since reference to "age" carries no express modifier and the word could be read to look two ways. This more expansive possible understanding does not, however, square with the natural reading of the whole provision prohibiting discrimination, and in fact Congress's interpretive clues speak almost unanimously to an understanding of discrimination as directed against workers who are older than the ones getting treated better.

Congress chose not to include age within discrimination forbidden by Title VII of the Civil Rights Act of 1964, § 715, 78 Stat. 265, being aware that there were legitimate reasons as well as invidious ones for making employment decisions on age. Instead it called for a study of the issue by the Secretary of Labor, ibid., who concluded that age discrimination was a serious problem, but one different in kind from discrimination on account of race. The Secretary spoke of disadvantage to older individuals from arbitrary and stereotypical employment distinctions (including then-common policies of age ceilings on hiring), but he examined the problem in light of rational considerations of increased pension cost and, in some cases, legitimate concerns about an older person's ability to do the job. Wirtz Report 2. When the Secretary ultimately took the position that arbitrary discrimination against older workers was widespread and persistent enough to call for a federal legislative remedy, id., at 21–22, he placed his recommendation against the background of common experience that the potential cost of employing someone rises with age, so that the older an employee is, the greater the inducement to prefer a younger substitute. The report contains no suggestion that reactions to age level off at some point, and it was devoid of any indication that the Secretary had noticed unfair advantages accruing to older employees at the expense of their juniors.

Congress then asked for a specific proposal, Fair Labor Standards Amendments of 1966, § 606, 80 Stat. 845, which the Secretary provided in January 1967. 113 Cong. Rec. 1377 (1967); see also Public Papers of the Presidents, Lyndon B. Johnson, Vol. 1, Jan. 23, 1967, p. 37 (1968) (message to Congress urging that "[o]pportunity . . . be opened to the many Americans over 45 who are qualified and willing to work"). Extensive House and Senate hearings ensued. See Age Discrimination in Employment: Hearings on H.R. 3651 et al. before the General Subcommittee on Labor of the House Committee on Education and Labor, 90th Cong., 1st Sess. (1967) (hereinafter House Hearings); Age Discrimination in Employment: Hearings on S. 830 and S. 788 before the Subcommittee on Labor of the Senate Committee on Labor and Public Welfare, 90th Cong., 1st Sess. (1967) (hereinafter Senate Hearings). See generally EEOC v. Wyoming, 460 U.S. 226, 229–233 (1983).

The testimony at both hearings dwelled on unjustified assumptions about the effect of age on ability to work. See, *e.g.*, House Hearings 151 (statement of Rep. Joshua Eilberg) ("At age 40, a worker may find that age restrictions become common. . . . By age 45, his employment opportunities are likely to contract sharply; they shrink more severely at age 55 and virtually vanish by age 65"); *id.*, at 422 (statement of Rep. Claude Pepper) ("We must provide meaningful opportunities for employment to the thousands of workers 45 and over who are well qualified but nevertheless denied jobs which they may desperately need because someone has arbitrarily decided that they are too old"); Senate Hearings 34 (statement of Sen. George Murphy) ("[A]n older worker often faces an attitude on the part of some employers that prevents him from receiving serious consideration or even an interview in his search for employment"). The hearings specifically addressed higher pension and benefit costs as heavier drags on hiring workers the older they got. See, *e.g.*, House Hearings 45 (statement of Norman Sprague) (Apart from stereotypes, "labor market conditions, seniority and promotion-from-within policies, job training costs, pension and insurance costs, and mandatory retirement policies often make employers reluctant to hire older workers"). The record thus reflects the common facts that an individual's chances to find and keep a job get worse over time; as between any two people, the younger is in the stronger position, the older more apt to be tagged with demeaning stereotype. Not surprisingly, from the voluminous records of the hearings, we have found (and Cline has cited) nothing suggesting that any workers were registering complaints about discrimination in favor of their seniors.

Nor is there any such suggestion in the introductory provisions of the ADEA, 81 Stat. 602, which begins with statements of purpose and findings that mirror the Wirtz Report and the committee transcripts. *Id.*, § 2. The findings stress the impediments suffered by "older workers . . . in their efforts to retain . . . and especially to regain employment," *id.*, § 2(a)(1); "the [burdens] of arbitrary age limits regardless of potential for job performance," id., § 2(a)(2); the costs of "otherwise desirable practices [that] may work to the disadvantage of older persons," *ibid.*; and "the incidence of unemployment, especially long-term unemployment[, which] is, relative to the younger ages, high among older workers," *id.*, § 2(a)(3). The statutory objects were "to promote employment of older persons based on their ability rather than age; to prohibit arbitrary age discrimination in employment; [and] to help employers and workers find ways of meeting problems arising from the impact of age on employment." *Id.*, § 2(b).

In sum, except on one point, all the findings and statements of objectives are either cast in terms of the effects of age as intensifying over time, or are couched in terms that refer to "older" workers, explicitly or implicitly relative to "younger" ones. The single subject on which the statute speaks less specifically is that of "arbitrary limits" or "arbitrary age discrimination." But these are unmistakable references to the Wirtz Report's finding that "[a]lmost three out of every five employers covered by [a] 1965 survey have in effect age limitations (most frequently between 45 and 55) on new hires which they apply without consideration of an applicant's other qualifications." Wirtz Report 6. The ADEA's ban on "arbitrary limits" thus applies to age caps that exclude older applicants, necessarily to the advantage of younger ones.

Such is the setting of the ADEA's core substantive provision, § 4 (as amended, 29 U.S.C. § 623), prohibiting employers and certain others from "discriminat[ion] . . . because of [an] individual's age," whenever (as originally enacted) the individual is "at least forty years of age but less than sixty-five years of age," § 12, 81 Stat. 607. The prefatory provisions and their legislative history make a case that we think is beyond reasonable doubt, that the ADEA was concerned to protect a relatively old worker from discrimination that works to the advantage of the relatively young.

Nor is it remarkable that the record is devoid of any evidence that younger workers were suffering at the expense of their elders, let alone that a social problem required a federal statute to place a younger worker in parity with an older one. Common experience is to the contrary, and the testimony, reports, and congressional findings simply confirm that Congress used the phrase "discriminat[ion] ... because of [an] individual's age" the same way that ordinary people in common usage might speak of age discrimination any day of the week. One commonplace conception of American society in recent decades is its character as a "youth culture," and in a world where younger is better, talk about discrimination because of age is naturally understood to refer to discrimination against the older.

This same, idiomatic sense of the statutory phrase is confirmed by the statute's restriction of the protected class to those 40 and above. If Congress had been worrying about protecting the younger against the older, it would not likely have ignored everyone under 40. The youthful deficiencies of inexperience and unsteadiness invite stereotypical and discriminatory thinking about those a lot younger than 40, and prejudice suffered by a 40–year–old is not typically owing to youth, as 40–year–olds sadly tend to find out. The enemy of 40 is 30, not 50. See H.R.Rep. No. 805, 90th Cong., 1st Sess., 6 (1967), U.S.Code Cong. & Admin.News 1967, pp. 2213, 2219 ("[T]estimony indicated [40] to be the age at which age discrimination in employment becomes evident"). Even so, the 40–year threshold was adopted over the objection that some discrimination against older people begins at an even younger age; female flight attendants were not fired at 32 because they were too young, ibid. See also Senate Hearings 47 (statement of Sec'y Wirtz) (lowering the minimum age limit "would change the nature of the proposal from an over-age employment discrimination measure"). Thus, the 40–year threshold makes sense as identifying a class requiring protection against preference for their juniors, not as defining a class that might be threatened by favoritism toward seniors. ...

### III

Cline and amicus EEOC proffer [the following] rejoinders in favor of their competing view that the prohibition works both ways. First, they say (as does Justice Thomas) that the statute's meaning is plain when the word "age" receives its natural and ordinary meaning and the statute is read as a whole giving "age" the same meaning throughout. And even if the text does not plainly mean what they say it means, they argue that the soundness of their version is shown by a colloquy on the floor of the Senate involving Senator Yarborough, a sponsor of the bill that became the ADEA.... On each point, however, we think the argument falls short of unsettling our view of the natural meaning of the phrase speaking of discrimination, read in light of the statute's manifest purpose.

## A

The first response to our reading is the dictionary argument that "age" means the length of a person's life, with the phrase "because of such individual's age" stating a simple test of causation: "discriminat[ion] . . . because of [an] individual's age" is treatment that would not have occurred if the individual's span of years had been longer or shorter. The case for this reading calls attention to the other instances of "age" in the ADEA that are not limited to old age, such as 29 U.S.C. § 623(f), which gives an employer a defense to charges of age discrimination when "age is a bona fide occupational qualification." Cline and the EEOC argue that if "age" meant old age, § 623(f) would then provide a defense (old age is a bona fide qualification) only for an employer's action that on our reading would never clash with the statute (because preferring the older is not forbidden).

The argument rests on two mistakes. First, it assumes that the word "age" has the same meaning wherever the ADEA uses it. But this is not so, and Cline simply misemploys the "presumption that identical words used in different parts of the same act are intended to have the same meaning." Atlantic Cleaners & Dyers, Inc. v. United States, 286 U.S. 427, 433(1932). Cline forgets that "the presumption is not rigid and readily yields whenever there is such variation in the connection in which the words are used as reasonably to warrant the conclusion that they were employed in different parts of the act with different intent." *Ibid.*; see also United States v. Cleveland Indians Baseball Co., 532 U.S. 200, 213 (2001) (phrase "wages paid" has different meanings in different parts of Title 26 U.S.C.); Robinson v. Shell Oil Co., 519 U.S. 337, 343–344 (1997) (term "employee" has different meanings in different parts of Title VII). The presumption of uniform usage thus relents when a word used has several commonly understood meanings among which a speaker can alternate in the course of an ordinary conversation, without being confused or getting confusing.

"Age" is that kind of word. As JUSTICE THOMAS agrees, the word "age" standing alone can be readily understood either as pointing to any number of years lived, or as common shorthand for the longer span and concurrent aches that make youth look good. Which alternative was probably intended is a matter of context; we understand the different choices of meaning that lie behind a sentence like "Age can be shown by a driver's license," and the statement, "Age has left him a shut-in." So it is easy to understand that Congress chose different meanings at different places in the ADEA, as the different settings readily show. Hence the second flaw in Cline's argument for uniform usage: it ignores the cardinal rule that "[s]tatutory language must be read in context [since] a phrase 'gathers meaning from the words around it.'" Jones v. United States, 527 U.S. 373, 389 (1999) (quoting Jarecki v. G.D. Searle & Co., 367 U.S. 303, 307 (1961)). The point here is that we are not asking an abstract question about the meaning of "age"; we are seeking the meaning of the whole phrase "discriminate . . . because of such individual's age," where it occurs in the ADEA, 29 U.S.C. § 623(a)(1). As we have said, social history emphatically reveals an understanding of age discrimination as aimed against the old, and the statutory reference to age discrimination in this idiomatic sense is confirmed by legislative history. For the very reason that reference to context shows that "age" means "old age" when teamed with "discrimination," the provision of an affirmative defense when age is a bona fide occupational qualification readily shows that "age" as a qualification means comparative youth. As context tells us that "age" means one thing in § 623(a)(1) and another in § 623(f), so it also tells us that the presumption of uniformity cannot sensibly operate here.

The comparisons JUSTICE THOMAS urges, to McDonald v. Santa Fe Trail Transp. Co., 427 U.S. 273 (1976), and Oncale v. Sundowner Offshore Services, Inc., 523 U.S. 75 (1998), serve to clarify our position. Both cases involved Title VII of the Civil Rights Act of 1964, 42 U.S.C. § 2000e et seq., and its prohibition on employment discrimination "because of [an] individual's *race* . . . [or] *sex*," § 2000e–2(a)(1) (emphasis added). The term "age" employed by the ADEA is not, however, comparable to the terms "race" or "sex" employed by Title VII. "Race" and "sex" are general terms that in every day usage require modifiers to indicate any relatively narrow application. We do not commonly understand "race" to refer only to the black race, or "sex" to refer only to the female. But the prohibition of age discrimination is readily read more narrowly than analogous provisions dealing with race and sex. That narrower reading is the more natural one in the textual setting, and it makes perfect sense because of Congress's demonstrated concern with distinctions that hurt older people.

### B

The second objection has more substance than the first, but still not enough. The record of congressional action reports a colloquy on the Senate floor between two of the legislators most active in pushing for the ADEA, Senators Javits and Yarborough. Senator Javits began the exchange by raising a concern mentioned by Senator Dominick, that "the bill might not forbid discrimination between two persons each of whom would be between the ages of 40 and 65." 113 Cong. Rec. 31255 (1967). Senator Javits then gave his own view that, "if two individuals ages 52 and 42 apply for the same job, and the employer selected the man aged 42 solely . . . because he is younger than the man 52, then he will have violated the act," and asked Senator Yarborough for his opinion. *Ibid.* Senator Yarborough answered that "[t]he law prohibits age being a factor in the decision to hire, as to one age over the other, whichever way [the] decision went." *Ibid.*

Although in the past we have given weight to Senator Yarborough's views on the construction of the ADEA because he was a sponsor, see, *e.g.*, Public Employees Retirement System of Ohio v. Betts, 492 U.S. 158, 179 (1989), his side of this exchange is not enough to unsettle our reading of the statute. . . . What matters is that the Senator's remark, "whichever way [the] decision went," is the only item in all the 1967 hearings, reports, and debates going against the grain of the common understanding of age discrimination. Even from a sponsor, a single outlying statement cannot stand against a tide of context and history, not to mention 30 years of judicial interpretation producing no apparent legislative qualms. See Consumer Product Safety Comm'n v. GTE Sylvania, Inc., 447 U.S. 102 (1980) ("'[O]rdinarily even the contemporaneous remarks of a single legislator who sponsors a bill are not controlling in analyzing legislative history"). . . .

### IV

We see the text, structure, purpose, and history of the ADEA, along with its relationship to other federal statutes, as showing that the statute does not mean to stop an employer from favoring an older employee over a younger one. The judgment of the Court of Appeals is

*Reversed.*

■ [JUSTICE SCALIA dissented on the ground that the Court should have deferred to the contrary opinion of the Equal Employment Opportunity Commission, the agency responsible for enforcing the ADEA.]

■ JUSTICE THOMAS, with whom JUSTICE KENNEDY joins, dissenting.

This should have been an easy case. The plain language of 29 U.S.C. § 623(a)(1) mandates a particular outcome: that the respondents are able to sue for discrimination against them in favor of older workers. The agency charged with enforcing the statute has adopted a regulation and issued an opinion as an adjudicator, both of which adopt this natural interpretation of the provision. And the only portion of legislative history relevant to the question before us is consistent with this outcome. Despite the fact that these traditional tools of statutory interpretation lead inexorably to the conclusion that respondents can state a claim for discrimination against the relatively young, the Court, apparently disappointed by this result, today adopts a different interpretation. In doing so, the Court, of necessity, creates a new tool of statutory interpretation, and then proceeds to give this newly created "social history" analysis dispositive weight. Because I cannot agree with the Court's new approach to interpreting antidiscrimination statutes, I respectfully dissent.

### I

"The starting point for [the] interpretation of a statute is always its language," Community for Creative Non–Violence v. Reid, 490 U.S. 730 (1989), and "courts must presume that a legislature says in a statute what it means and means in a statute what it says there," Connecticut Nat. Bank v. Germain, 503 U.S. 249, 253–254 (1992). Thus, rather than looking through the historical background of the Age Discrimination in Employment Act of 1967 (ADEA), I would instead start with the text of § 623(a)(1) itself, and if "the words of [the] statute are unambiguous," my "judicial inquiry [would be] complete." Id., at 254 (internal quotation marks omitted).

The plain language of the ADEA clearly allows for suits brought by the relatively young when discriminated against in favor of the relatively old. The phrase "discriminate ... because of such individual's age," 29 U.S.C. § 623(a)(1), is not restricted to discrimination because of relatively older age. If an employer fired a worker for the sole reason that the worker was under 45, it would be entirely natural to say that the worker had been discriminated against because of his age. I struggle to think of what other phrase I would use to describe such behavior. I wonder how the Court would describe such incidents, because the Court apparently considers such usage to be unusual, atypical, or aberrant. See ante, at 1243 (concluding that the "common usage" of language would exclude discrimination against the relatively young from the phrase "discriminat[ion] ... because of [an] individual's age").

The parties do identify a possible ambiguity, centering on the multiple meanings of the word "age." As the parties note, "age" does have an alternative meaning, namely, "[t]he state of being old; old age." American Heritage Dictionary 33 (3d ed.1992); see also Oxford American Dictionary 18 (1999); Webster's Third New International Dictionary 40 (1993). First, this secondary meaning is, of course, less commonly used than the primary meaning, and appears restricted to those few instances where it is clear in the immediate context of the phrase that it could have no other meaning. The phrases "hair white with age," American Heritage Dictionary, supra, at 33, or "*eyes ... dim with age*," Random House Dictionary of the English Language 37 (2d ed.1987), cannot possibly be using "age" to include "young age," unlike a phrase such as "he fired her because of her age." Second, the use of the word "age" in other portions of the statute effectively destroys any doubt. The ADEA's advertising prohibition, 29 U.S.C. § 623(e), and the bona fide occupational qualification defense, § 623(f)(1), would both be rendered incoherent if the term "age" in those provisions were read to mean only "older age." Although it is true that the " 'presumption that identical words used in different parts of the same act are intended to have the same meaning' " is not "rigid" and can be overcome when the context is clear, *ante*, at 1245 (quoting Atlantic Cleaners & Dyers, Inc. v. United States, 286 U.S. 427, 433 (1932)), the presumption is not rebutted here. As noted, the plain and common reading of the phrase "such individual's age" refers to the individual's chronological age. At the very least, it is manifestly unclear that it bars *only* discrimination against the relatively older. Only by incorrectly concluding that § 623(a)(1) clearly and unequivocally bars only discrimination as "against the older," can the Court then conclude that the "context" of §§ 623(f)(1) and 623(e) allows for an alternative meaning of the term "age," ante, at 1246.

The one structural argument raised by the Court in defense of its interpretation of "discriminates ... because of such individual's age" is the provision limiting the ADEA's protections to those over 40 years of age. See 29 U.S.C. § 631(a). At first glance, this might look odd when paired with the conclusion that § 623(a)(1) bars discrimination against the relatively young as well as the relatively old, but there is a perfectly rational explanation. Congress could easily conclude that age discrimination directed against those under 40 is not as damaging, since a young worker unjustly fired is likely to find a new job or otherwise recover from the discrimination. A person over 40 fired due to irrational age discrimination (whether because the worker is too young or too old) might have a more difficult time recovering from the discharge and finding new employment. Such an interpretation also comports with the many findings of the Wirtz report, United States Dept. of Labor, The Older American Worker: Age Discrimination in Employment (June 1965), and the parallel findings in the ADEA itself. See, *e.g.*, 29 U.S.C. § 621(a)(1) (finding that "older workers find themselves disadvantaged in their efforts to retain employment, and especially to regain employment when displaced from jobs"); § 621(a)(3) (finding that "the incidence of unemployment, especially long-term unemployment with resultant deterioration of skill, morale, and employer acceptability is, relative to the younger ages, high among older workers").

This plain reading of the ADEA is bolstered by the interpretation of the agency charged with administering the statute. . . .

Finally, the only relevant piece of legislative history addressing the question before the Court—whether it would be possible for a younger individual to sue based on discrimination against him in favor of an older individual—comports with the plain reading of the text. Senator Yarborough, in the only exchange that the parties identified from the legislative history discussing this particular question, confirmed that the text really meant what it said. See 113 Cong. Rec. 31255 (1967). Although the statute is clear, and hence there is no need to delve into the legislative history, this history merely confirms that the plain reading of the text is correct.

## II

Strangely, the Court does not explain why it departs from accepted methods of interpreting statutes. It does, however, clearly set forth its principal reason for adopting its particular reading of the phrase "discriminate ... based on [an] individual's age" in Part III–A of its opinion. "The point here," the Court states, "is that we are not asking an abstract question about the meaning of 'age'; we are seeking the meaning of the whole phrase 'discriminate ... because of such individual's age.' ... As we have said, *social history* emphatically reveals an understanding of age discrimination as aimed against the old, and the statutory reference to age discrimination in this idiomatic sense is confirmed by legislative history" (emphasis added). The Court does not define "social history," although it is apparently something different from legislative history, because the Court refers to legislative history as a separate interpretive tool in the very same sentence. Indeed, the Court has never defined "social history" in any previous opinion, probably because it has never sanctioned looking to "social history" as a method of statutory interpretation. Today, the Court takes this unprecedented step, and then places dispositive weight on the new concept.

It appears that the Court considers the "social history" of the phrase "discriminate ... because of [an] individual's age" to be the principal evil that Congress targeted when it passed the ADEA. In each section of its analysis, the Court pointedly notes that there was no evidence of widespread problems of antiyouth discrimination, and that the primary concerns of Executive Branch officials and Members of Congress pertained to problems that workers generally faced as they increased in age. The Court reaches its final, legal conclusion as to the meaning of the phrase (that "ordinary people" employing the common usage of language would "talk about discrimination because of age [as] naturally [referring to] discrimination against the older") only after concluding both that "the ADEA was concerned to protect a relatively old worker from discrimination that works to the advantage of the relatively young" and that "the record is devoid of any evidence that younger workers were suffering at the expense of their elders, let alone that a social problem required a federal statute to place a younger worker in parity with an older one." Hence, the Court apparently concludes that if Congress has in mind a particular, principal, or primary form of discrimination when it passes an antidiscrimination provision prohibiting persons from "discriminating because of [some personal quality]," then the phrase "discriminate because of [some personal quality]" only covers the principal or most common form of discrimination relating to this personal quality.

The Court, however, has not typically interpreted nondiscrimination statutes in this odd manner. "[S]tatutory prohibitions often go beyond the principal evil to cover reasonably comparable evils, and it is ultimately the provisions of our laws rather than the principal concerns of our legislators by which we are governed." Oncale v. Sundowner Offshore Services, Inc., 523 U.S. 75, 79 (1998). The oddity of the Court's new technique of statutory interpretation is highlighted by this Court's contrary approach to the racial-discrimination prohibition of Title VII of the Civil Rights Act of 1964, 78 Stat. 253, as amended, 42 U.S.C. § 2000e et seq.

There is little doubt that the motivation behind the enactment of the Civil Rights Act of 1964 was to prevent invidious discrimination against racial minorities, especially blacks. . . . The congressional debates and hearings, although filled with statements decrying discrimination against racial minorities and setting forth the disadvantages those minorities suffered, contain no references that I could find to any problem of discrimination against whites. . . . I find no evidence that even a single legislator appeared concerned about whether there were incidents of discrimination against whites, and I find no citation to any such incidents. . . . In light of the Court's opinion today, it appears that this Court has been treading down the wrong path with respect to Title VII since at least 1976. See McDonald v. Santa Fe Trail Transp. Co., 427 U.S. 273 (1976) (holding that Title VII protected whites discriminated against in favor of racial minorities). . . .

It is abundantly clear, then, that the Court's new approach to antidiscrimination statutes would lead us far astray from well-settled principles of statutory interpretation. The Court's examination of "social history" is in serious tension (if not outright conflict) with our prior cases in such matters. Under the Court's current approach, for instance, *McDonald* and

*Oncale* are wrongly decided. One can only hope that this new technique of statutory interpretation does not catch on, and that its errors are limited to only this case. . . .

\* \* \*

As the ADEA clearly prohibits discrimination because of an individual's age, whether the individual is too old or too young, I would affirm the Court of Appeals. Because the Court resorts to interpretive sleight of hand to avoid addressing the plain language of the ADEA, I respectfully dissent.

---

***1. The Transformation of Purposivism***—Whatever one thinks about the particular disagreement between the majority and the dissent in *Cline*, isn't the style of the majority's opinion, in some sense, the most important aspect of the case? Before the developments of the past quarter-century, it seems likely that the Court would simply have explained that although age, read literally, would refer to the years of someone's life, the spirit of the ADEA trumps the letter. That is, the Court likely would not have felt any compulsion to demonstrate that its purposive interpretation fit within the semantic boundaries of the text.

*Cline* is not the only recent example of this new, textually constrained approach to purposivism. In Zuni Pub. Sch. Dist. No. 89 v. Department of Educ., 550 U.S. 81 (2007), the Court considered the administration of federal education grants to the states under the Impact Aid Act, 108 Stat. 3749, which requires the Secretary of Education to determine in certain circumstances whether the state receiving the aid has a program to "equalize expenditures" on school funding throughout the state. 20 U.S.C. § 7709(b)(1) (2006). In making that calculation, the Act directs the Secretary to "disregard [school districts] with per-pupil expenditures ... above the ninety-fifth percentile or below the fifth percentile of such expenditures." 20 U.S.C. § 7709(b)(2)(B)(i). The question presented in *Zuni* was whether the statute required the Secretary to calculate the fifth and ninety-fifth percentiles based on the simple number of school districts (*e.g.*, pick the top and bottom five out of one hundred districts) or to do so based on their enrollment (*e.g.*, pick those districts that in aggregate contain the top and bottom 5000 students out of 100,000). The Secretary chose the latter method.

Justice Breyer's opinion for the Court began by stating that "[c]onsiderations other than [statutory] language provide us with unusually strong indications that Congress intended to leave the Secretary free to use the calculation method before us and that the Secretary's chosen method is a reasonable one." 550 U.S. at 90. The Court then proceeded to consider the "legislative history" and various other indicia of the "purpose" of the statutory provision at issue. *Id.* at 90–93. Despite leading with that analysis, however, Justice Breyer's opinion took pains to examine the "literal language" of the governing statute, "for normally neither the legislative history nor the reasonableness of the Secretary's method would be determinative if the plain language of the statute unambiguously indicated that

Congress sought to foreclose the Secretary's interpretation." *Id.* at 94. Justice Breyer's opinion spent pages examining "mainstream and technical" dictionary definitions of the term "percentile," as well as its usage in other statutes, in order to show that the Secretary's approach fit within the provision's understood semantic meaning. *See id.* at 94–99.

This decision drew a sharp protest from Justice Scalia, whose dissent (joined by Chief Justice Roberts and Justice Thomas) argued that the statutory language plainly referred to the top and bottom five percent of districts, not pupils. From that starting point, he accused the Court of reviving *Holy Trinity. Id.* at 108 (Scalia, J., dissenting). Interestingly, the majority did not concede Justice Scalia's argument that it was elevating the statutory purpose over the statutory text; instead, the majority defended its interpretation as consistent with the text, and disputed Justice Scalia's contrary assertions. *See id.* at 97–98. Only Justice Stevens offered an unapologetic defense of traditional purposivism, arguing that:

> [JUSTICE SCALIA] correctly observes that a judicial decision that departs from statutory text may represent "policy-driven interpretation." As long as that driving policy is faithful to the intent of Congress . . .—which it must be if it is to override a strict interpretation of the text—the decision is also a correct performance of the judicial function. Justice SCALIA's argument today rests on the incorrect premise that every policy-driven interpretation implements a judge's personal view of sound policy, rather than a faithful attempt to carry out the will of the legislature. Quite the contrary is true of the work of the judges with whom I have worked for many years. If we presume that our judges are intellectually honest—as I do—there is no reason to fear "policy-driven interpretation[s]" of Acts of Congress.

*Id.* at 105 (Stevens, J., concurring) (alteration in original) (citation omitted).

What are the advantages and disadvantages of the "new" purposivism represented by cases like *Cline* and *Zuni*? Is the approach in these cases significantly different from the more traditional version of purposivism associated with cases like *Holy Trinity*? Or, as Justice Stevens' *Zuni* concurrence suggests—and Justice Scalia's *Zuni* dissent insists—is the "new" purposivism really nothing more than a change in rhetoric?

**2. *Derivation of Statutory Purpose, Redux*—**Even if the new purposivism differs from traditional purposivism in its acceptance of more textual constraints, many of the same difficulties related to discerning and defining legislative purpose persist. Did you find the *Cline* majority's derivation of purpose convincing? The hearing testimony, as well as statements by Johnson Administration officials supporting the legislation, does suggest that the impetus for enacting the ADEA was a concern for the disadvantages faced by older workers. But the fact that Congress was concerned about discrimination against older workers, and expressed that view explicitly, does not necessarily mean that Congress was not *also* concerned with discrimination against younger workers. Perhaps the references to discrimination against older workers were merely examples, or the most salient form, of the general problem that Congress was trying to address. Moreover, as the Court has said in other contexts, "the reach of a statute often exceeds the precise evil to be eliminated" and that "it is not, and cannot be, our practice to restrict the unqualified language of a statute to the particular evil that Congress was trying to remedy." Brogan v. United States, 522 U.S. 398, 403 (1998). Consider also the fact that the sponsors of the legislation believed that it would have a broader reach, protecting younger workers as well as older workers. Does that suggest that ADEA's purpose itself was ambiguous?

And what about the majority's reliance on the "social history" of age discrimination as evidence of legislative purpose? Justice Thomas's dissent suggested that this reference to social history was novel and dangerous. Does the reference to social history merely describe the mischief that provoked the legislation, much in the same way that the Court in *Holy Trinity* relied on the labor conditions that gave rise to calls for immigration legislation? Is an informed understanding of the social conditions that gave rise to legislation a more or less reliable tool of statutory construction than legislative history generated in the legislative process?

## D.   LEGISLATIVE PURPOSE AND DYNAMIC STATUTORY INTERPRETATION

How much authority should judges have to adapt statutes to unforeseen or unforeseeable circumstances, even if the adaptation contradicts the specific intent or clear text underlying the original enactment? Consider the infamous decision in Commonwealth v. Welosky, 276 Mass. 398 (1931), in which the Supreme Judicial Court (SJC) of Massachusetts restrictively interpreted a jury service statute to exclude women. The statute read as follows: "A person qualified to vote for representatives to the [state legislature] shall be liable to serve as a juror." When the statute was adopted in the nineteenth century, women did not have the right to vote, and they did not secure it in Massachusetts until the adoption of the Nineteenth Amendment to the U.S. Constitution and the enactment of conforming Massachusetts laws. Yet despite the fact that women were "person[s] qualified to vote" for the state legislature when *Welosky* was decided in 1931, the SJC concluded that the statute did not authorize their jury service. Although acknowledging that women fell within the literal terms of the statute, the SJC reasoned:

> [Words] are to be construed according to their natural import in common and approved usage. The imperfections of language to express intent often render necessary further inquiry. Statutes are to be interpreted, not alone according to their simple, literal or strict verbal meaning, but in connection with their development, their progression through the legislative body, the history of the times, prior legislation, contemporary customs and conditions and the system of positive law of which they are part, and in the light of the constitution and of the common law, to the end that they be held to cover the subjects presumably within the vision of the Legislature and, on the one hand,

be not unduly constricted so as to exclude matters fairly within their scope, and, on the other hand, be not stretched by enlargement of signification to comprehend matters not within the principle and purview on which they were founded when originally framed and their words chosen. General expressions may be restrained by relevant circumstances showing a legislative intent that they be narrowed and used in a particular sense.

*Id.* at 401–02.

Finding that the word "person" had been used in many senses in the law (including to refer to corporations and to males), the SJC concluded that because the voting rules prescribed by the Massachusetts Constitution had, until after the Nineteenth Amendment, confined the franchise to men, "the intent of the Legislature must have been, in using the word 'person' in statutes concerning jurors and jury lists, to confine its meaning to men." Although acknowledging that the Nineteenth Amendment and the conforming laws in Massachusetts had changed an important predicate, the court nevertheless concluded:

> Statutes framed in general terms commonly look to the future and may include conditions as they arise from time to time not even known at the time of enactment, provided they are fairly within the sweep and the meaning of the words and falling within their obvious scope and purpose. But statutes do not govern situations not within the reason of their enactment and *giving rise to radically diverse circumstances presumably not within the dominating purpose of those who framed and enacted them.*

*Id.* at 403 (emphasis added). The statute was framed flexibly, the court suggested, with the intent of permitting new classes of male inhabitants to sit on juries as property qualifications in the Commonwealth were gradually relaxed. As for the changes brought about after the Nineteenth Amendment, the court wrote:

> The Nineteenth Amendment to the federal Constitution.... did not extend the right to vote to members of an existing classification theretofore disqualified, but created a new class. It added to qualified voters those who did not fall within the meaning of the word 'person' in the jury statutes. No member of the class thus added to the body of voters had ever theretofore in this commonwealth had the right to vote for candidates for offices created by the Constitution. The change in the legal status of women wrought by the Nineteenth Amendment was radical, drastic and unprecedented. While it is to be given full effect in its field, it is not to be extended by implication. It is unthinkable that those who first framed and selected the words for the [Massachusetts jury service statute] had any design that it should ever include women within its scope.... When they used the word 'person' in connection with those qualified to vote for members of the more numerous branch of the [state legislature], to describe those liable to jury service, no one contemplated the possibility of women becoming so qualified.

*Id.* at 407–08. The SJC thus engaged in what we would now call "imaginative reconstruction"—the process whereby a judge tries "to think his [or her] way as best he [or she] can into the minds of the enacting legislators and imagine how they would have wanted the statute applied to the case at bar." Richard A. Posner, *Statutory Interpretation—in the Classroom and in the Courtroom*, 50 U. CHI. L. REV. 800, 817 (1983).

Even assuming that the SJC correctly thought its way into the minds of the legislature that adopted the jury statute, should courts feel bound by such an intention when faced with circumstances that legislators could not have been foreseen? Many believe that for important functional reasons, the answer should be no. *See, e.g.*, T. Alexander Aleinikoff, *Updating Statutory Interpretation*, 87 MICH. L. REV. 20 (1988); Peter L. Strauss, *The Common Law and Statutes*, 70 U. COLO. L. REV. 225 (1999). The most prominent proponent of this sort of "dynamic statutory interpretation" is Professor William Eskridge, who has argued that, even if one embraces a robust conception of legislative supremacy, this need not imply that judges must enforce only the specific intentions behind, or ordinary semantic meaning of, a statutory text. WILLIAM N. ESKRIDGE, JR., DYNAMIC STATUTORY INTERPRETATION 120–30 (1994). Rather, because statutes remain on the books for many years through many changes in legal and factual contexts, Professor Eskridge argues that the right analogy for the judicial role in statutory interpretation is the *relational agent*—an agent in an ongoing contractual relationship whose "primary obligation is to use her best efforts to carry out the general goals and specific orders [of her principal] over time." *Id.* at 125. Professor Eskridge explains:

> Like the relational agent, the judge is the subordinate in an ongoing enterprise and follows directives issued by the legislature. Like the relational contract, statutes are often phrased in general terms, written long before an interpretive issue arises. . . . Like the relational principal, the legislature will often speak on a specific question just once, leaving it to the judge (agent) to fill in details and implement the statute in unforeseen situations over a long period of time. Hence, like the relational agent, the judge must often exercise creativity in applying prior legislative directives to specific situations.

*Id.* In implementing a statute over time, the relational agent will encounter changed circumstances of various sorts that he or she will appropriately take into account in implementing the statute, sometimes leading to decisions contrary to the plain import or specific intention of the original directive. Even if the principal has a *specific intent* with respect to a particular issue, the relational agent may also have a relevant *general intent* about the aims of the enterprise and a rationally inferable *meta-intent* about how to reconcile conflicts between the specific and the general intent.

To flesh this out, Eskridge builds on an example first developed by Professor Francis Lieber. FRANCIS LIEBER, LEGAL AND POLITICAL HERMENEUTICS, OR PRINCIPLES OF INTERPRETATION AND CONSTRUCTION IN LAW AND POLITICS, WITH REMARKS ON PRECEDENTS AND AUTHORITIES (The Lawbook Exchange, Ltd.

2002) (1839). Imagine a situation involving the head of a household (Williams) and a domestic employee (Diamond), who is minding the house and children while Williams is out of the country. Suppose Williams has given Diamond the following explicit directive: "[F]etch five pounds of soup meat every Monday ... so that [you] can prepare enough for the entire week." ESKRIDGE, *supra*, at 125. While this directive is quite specific, it will quickly require adjustment in the face of changed circumstances. If there are *changes in social context*—for example, if one of the children is discovered to be allergic to soup meat—then Williams' *specific* intent appropriately yields to "her general intent that [Diamond] act to protect the children's health and [to] her meta-intent that Diamond adapt specific directives to that end." *Id.* at 126. Similarly, *new directives* from the principal may make it appropriate to revise the original directive, even if the new directives do not expressly withdraw or alter the original directive. For example, if Williams sends Diamond a follow-up note instructing him to feed the children cholesterol-lowering muffins, Diamond may be justified in substituting low-cholesterol chicken for high-cholesterol soup meat. *Id.* at 126–27. Finally, new *meta-policies* that potentially constrain the principal's discretion—such as the town's decision to ration soup meat—may require the relational agent to alter the program. *See id.* at 127. In short, Professor Eskridge concludes that, however specific the original directive may be, a faithful relational agent (and hence a good interpreter) "must first understand the assumptions underlying the original directive, including its purpose," and then "must figure out how the statute can best meet its goal(s) in a world that is not the world of its framers." *Id.* at 128. What is true of the hypothetical relationship between Williams and Diamond, Professor Eskridge concludes, is equally true of the real-world relationship between the legislature and the judiciary.

Professor Eskridge's advocacy of dynamic statutory interpretation, and his relational agent theory of judging more generally, has much to recommend it. Its greatest virtue is that it seems to solve inevitable problems of statutory obsolescence. But in emphasizing the desirability of dynamic adaptation of statutory meaning to new circumstances, does Eskridge's position perhaps understate some of the dangers associated with allowing judges to engage in this sort of statutory updating? *See, e.g.,* Philip P. Frickey, *Faithful Interpretation*, 73 WASH. U. L.Q. 1085, 1089 (1995); John Copeland Nagle, *Newt Gingrich, Dynamic Statutory Interpreter*, 143 U. PA. L. REV. 2209 (1995) (book review). Consider three dangers in particular:

First, judges may not be all that good at figuring out when new developments justify deviation from a clear, specific statutory directive. Not all deviations, after all, would really serve the principal's interest. Imagine that when Diamond goes to the market, he notices that the price of soup meat has risen, but there's a sale on potatoes. He might reason, "Williams wanted me to manage the household's affairs efficiently, and even though he told me to buy soup meat, I would serve Williams' general intent more faithfully if I made potato soup this week instead. So, as a good relational agent, that's what I'll do." This would be a serious mistake if Williams had specified soup meat because he wanted to ensure the children got enough protein. A perfect relational agent would not make these mistakes, but if real-world agents—including judges—are prone to such errors, it might be better for agents to follow the dictates of the original command until it is explicitly changed or there is some sort of emergency. This may be the best approach even if the agent always tries to act in the principal's best interest; once we consider the possibility of agents with their own agendas, the argument for constraining the agent's discretion, even at the cost of sacrificing some desirable adaptation, is stronger.

Second, we might worry that the dynamic approach to statutory interpretation does not adequately respect the constitutional and other safeguards built into the lawmaking process. This process has been deliberately designed to be slow, cumbersome, and fragmented. That sort of process has obvious costs, among them the difficulty of updating outdated laws. But the system has been designed that way in part because of the presumption in favor of the status quo, and in part because of a desire to empower minorities and to ensure sufficient deliberation and political consensus as a precondition for legal change. A dynamic approach to judicial construction of statutes facilitates more rapid and flexible legal change in response to changed circumstances, but precisely for that reason it may undermine the interest in ensuring that changes in the law are carefully considered and backed by substantial majorities.

Third, dynamic statutory interpretation may undermine the interest in legal stability and predictability as such. Sometimes, legislatures may adopt rigid, inflexible statutory directives deliberately, because even though they will not always be appropriate in all contingencies, it is important for potentially affected parties to be able to plan their affairs around legal rules that are easily ascertainable and predictable. Furthermore, legislatures may sometimes want to commit themselves in advance to certain policies, because the fact that the policy is unlikely to change in response to changed circumstances affects behavior in desirable ways.

Maybe it is a mistake to try to decide, as a general matter, whether courts should adopt the dynamic approach to statutory interpretation advocated by Professor Eskridge. Perhaps instead courts should consider statutes on a case-by-case basis, asking whether in the particular case at hand Congress would have preferred the court to act as a relational agent or rather to adhere to the specific statutory command. Some statutes do not seem to leave much room for dynamic updating. Imagine that Congress passes a statute stating as follows: "In order to fund the refurbishment of the nation's bridges and tunnels, the Secretary of Transportation shall hereby collect a 2% surcharge on the retail sale of any gallon of gasoline." If it turned out that the nation's infrastructure was decaying more quickly than expected or that gas prices fell during an unexpectedly lengthy economic downturn, surely the Secretary would not have the authority to charge 3%, even if it would serve the goals of the original directive in circumstances very different from those anticipated by the framers. That conclusion perhaps reflects the judgment that Congress sends a particular kind of signal by choosing a bright-line numerical rule. *Cf.* Richard A.

Posner, *Legal Formalism, Legal Realism, and the Interpretation of Statutes and the Constitution*, 37 Case W. Res. L. Rev. 176, 191 (1986). But in other statutes Congress leaves more room for dynamic interpretation by framing the statute in more open-ended, goal-oriented terms. Should courts try to distinguish those statutes for which dynamic interpretation is appropriate from those for which it is not, depending on other indicia of Congress's intent on this meta-question? If so, how should they go about it?

Professor Eskridge frames his theory of dynamic statutory interpretation principally as an alternative to textualism, and in many respects his position seems to adopt a more purposivist approach. And indeed, the conventional wisdom is that purposivism offers the greatest flexibility in updating statutes, since the premise of the purposivist approach is that courts properly rectify inevitable legislative failures of foresight or expression. But, as *Commonwealth v. Welosky* shows, there is not necessarily a one-to-one correlation between purposivism and flexibility: Sometimes the purpose of a statute will be broader than the norms embedded in the text and sometimes it will be narrower. In *Welosky*, after all, the *text* of the statute is apparently more susceptible to dynamic change over time (as the background legal rules change): The statute provides that "[a] person qualified to vote for representatives to the [state legislature] shall be liable to serve as a juror." Even assuming that the SJC correctly identified the statute's purpose as being to provide a metric that would permit the rolls of male jurors to grow as property qualifications for voting receded, a textualist would surely conclude that "in the context of an unambiguous statutory text that [narrower purpose] is irrelevant." Pennsylvania Dep't of Corr. v. Yeskey, 524 U.S. 206, 212 (1998) (Scalia, J). Whether the statutory text or external indicia of statutory purpose are more likely to constrain interpretive flexibility is an empirical question, the answer to which is not obvious. The important point here is that the aims of dynamic statutory interpretation are not *necessarily* better served by relying on a purposivist rather than a textualist approach in all cases.

## E. Judicial Correction of Legislative Mistakes

### a. The Absurdity Doctrine

Both *Riggs* and *Holy Trinity* insisted not only that a literal reading of the statutory text would be contrary to legislative purpose or intent, but also that adhering to a literal reading would produce *absurd results*. This characterization of outcomes as "absurd" is important, because one of the oldest and most well-established principles of statutory interpretation holds that statutes should not be construed to create absurd results. This was one of Blackstone's fundamental principles of statutory interpretation (*see* p. 30, *supra*), and it has been a staple of American legal culture since the founding. In Sturges v. Crowninshield, 17 U.S. (4 Wheat.) 122, 203 (1819), Chief Justice Marshall wrote for the Court that the judicial obligation to enforce the statutory text abated when "the absurdity and injustice of applying the provision to the case, would be so monstrous, that all mankind would, without hesitation, unite in rejecting the application," and this premise has guided the Court ever since. Indeed, even the Court's decisions that have aggressively defended the "plain meaning" rule have commonly also acknowledged an exception for absurd results. *See, e.g.*, United States v. Missouri Pac. R.R. Co., 278 U.S. 269, 278 (1929). Indeed, most proponents of both textualism and purposivism find common ground when the application of a statute's plain meaning produces a result that can only be described as "absurd." In this subsection, we examine what qualifies as an absurd result, and what, if anything, justifies excluding absurd results that otherwise fall within the scope of a clearly worded statutory text.

The following case, *United States v. Kirby*, is a particularly famous example of the absurdity doctrine. *Kirby* is notable for its succinct statement of the doctrine, and also because it involves perhaps one of the least controversial applications of the absurdity doctrine in a real case.

## United States v. Kirby

Supreme Court of the United States
74 U.S. 482 (1868)

The defendants were indicted for knowingly and wilfully obstructing and retarding the passage of the mail and of a mail carrier, in the District Court for the District of Kentucky. The case was certified to the Circuit Court for that district.

The indictment was founded upon the ninth section of the act of Congress, of March 3, 1825, ... which provides "that, if any person shall knowingly and wilfully obstruct or retard the passage of the mail, or of any driver or carrier, or of any horse or carriage carrying the same, he shall, upon conviction, for every such offence, pay a fine not exceeding one hundred dollars...."

The indictment contained four counts, and charged the defendants with knowingly and wilfully obstructing the passage of the mail of the United States, in the district of Kentucky, on the first of February, 1867, contrary to the act of Congress; and with knowingly and wilfully obstructing and retarding at the same time in that district, the passage of one Farris, a carrier of the mail, while engaged in the performance of this duty; and with knowingly and wilfully retarding at the same time in that district, the passage of the steamboat General Buell, which was then carrying the mail of the United States from the city of Louisville, in Kentucky, to the city of Cincinnati, in Ohio.

To this indictment the defendants, among other things, pleaded ... that at the September Term, 1866, of the Circuit Court of Gallation County, in the State of Kentucky, ... two indictments were found by the grand jury of the county against the said Farris for murder; that by order of the court bench warrants were issued upon these indictments, and placed in the hands of Kirby, one of the defendants, who was then sheriff of the county, commanding him to arrest the said Farris and bring him before the court to answer the indictments; that in obedience to these warrants he arrested Farris, and was accompanied by the other defendants as a posse, who were lawfully summoned to assist him in effecting the arrest; that they entered the steamboat Buell to make the arrest, and only used such force as was necessary to accomplish this end; and that they acted without any intent or purpose to obstruct or retard the mail, or the passage of the steamer. To this plea the district attorney of the United States demurred, and upon the argument of the demurrer two questions arose:

First. Whether the arrest of the mail-carrier upon the bench warrants from the Circuit Court of Kentucky was, under the circumstances, an obstruction of the mail within the meaning of the act of Congress.

Second. Whether the arrest was obstructing or retarding the passage of a carrier of the mail within the meaning of that act. . . .

■ Mr. Justice Field, after stating the case, delivered the opinion of the court, as follows:

There can be but one answer, in our judgment, to the questions certified to us. The statute of Congress by its terms applies only to persons who "knowing and wilfully" obstruct or retard the passage of the mail, or of its carrier; that is, to those who know that the acts performed will have that effect, and perform them with the intention that such shall be their operation. When the acts which create the obstruction are in themselves unlawful, the intention to obstruct will be imputed to their author, although the attainment of other ends may have been his primary object. The statute has no reference to acts lawful in themselves, from the execution of which a temporary delay to the mails unavoidably follows. All persons in the public service are exempt, as a matter of public policy, from arrest upon civil process while thus engaged. Process of that kind can, therefore, furnish no justification for the arrest of a carrier of the mail. . . . The rule is different when the process is issued upon a charge of felony. No officer or employee of the United States is placed by his position, or the services he is called to perform, above responsibility to the legal tribunals of the country, and to the ordinary processes for his arrest and detention, when accused of felony, in the forms prescribed by the Constitution and laws. The public inconvenience which may occasionally follow from the temporary delay in the transmission of the mail caused by the arrest of its carriers upon such charges, is far less than that which would arise from extending to them the immunity for which the counsel of the government contends. Indeed, it may be doubted whether it is competent for Congress to exempt the employees of the United States from arrest on criminal process from the State courts, when the crimes charged against them are not merely *mala prohibita*, but are *mala in se*. But whether legislation of that character be constitutional or not, no intention to extend such exemption should be attributed to Congress unless clearly manifested by its language. All laws should receive a sensible construction. General terms should be so limited in their application as not to lead to injustice, oppression, or an absurd consequence. It will always, therefore, be presumed that the legislature intended exceptions to its language, which would avoid results of this character. The reason of the law in such cases should prevail over its letter.

The common sense of man approves the judgment mentioned by Puffendorf, that the Bolognian law which enacted, "that whoever drew blood in the streets should be punished with the utmost severity," did not extend to the surgeon who opened the vein of a person that fell down in the street in a fit. The same common sense accepts the ruling, cited by Plowden, that the statute of 1st Edward II, which enacts that a prisoner who breaks prison shall be guilty of felony, does not extend to a prisoner who breaks out when the prison is on fire—"for he is not to be hanged because he would not stay to be burnt." And we think that a like common sense will sanction the ruling we make, that the act of Congress which punishes the obstruction or retarding of the passage of the mail, or of its carrier, does not apply to a case of temporary detention of the mail caused by the arrest of the carrier upon an indictment for murder.

The questions certified to us must be answered IN THE NEGATIVE; and it is SO ORDERED.

---

***The Rationale for the Absurdity Doctrine***—The Court has traditionally defended the absurdity doctrine as a method of discerning legislative intent. The connection between absurdity and intent is straightforward. As *Kirby* states, an absurdity is something that contradicts "common sense," understood as society's widely and deeply held values. On the assumption that legislators represent a cross-section of society (or that they must answer to constituents who do), the Court presumes that a statutory application which offends widely and deeply held social values must represent a failure of expression or foresight, which the legislators would surely have corrected had it come to their attention. Understood that way, the absurdity doctrine fits comfortably with intentionalist or purposivist modes of statutory interpretation. Indeed, the absurdity doctrine may be thought of simply as a special (and extreme) case of the general proposition that courts should deviate from the plain language of a statute when doing so is necessary to give effect to the will of the legislators or the purpose of the legislation. But what about textualist approaches? Even the staunchest textualists have, at times, endorsed the absurdity doctrine. *See, e.g.*, INS v. Cardoza–Fonseca, 480 U.S. 421, 452 (1987) (Scalia, J., concurring in the judgment); Kerr v. Puckett, 138 F.3d 321, 323 (7th Cir. 1998) (Easterbrook, J.). Is this embrace of the absurdity doctrine consistent with the textualist approach to statutory interpretation? If, as textualists typically argue, the principle of legislative supremacy requires courts to enforce the clear import of the enacted text, rather than some vague notion of legislative intent or purpose, what difference should it make if the outcome is, by some measure, "absurd"?

Consider the following possible distinction: One important textualist critique of purposivism (discussed in more detail at pp. 49–67, *supra*) is that statutes embody legislative compromises, and so a statute may not have a single, coherent "purpose." On this view, courts must respect legislative supremacy by respecting these compromises, even when they seem arbitrary. But in a case of true absurdity, courts might conclude that the absurd result could not possibly have been the product of a deliberate compromise. Consider this argument in the context of *Kirby*. Is it conceivable that the result dictated by the evident semantic meaning of the statute in *Kirby*—convicting a local law enforcement officer for arresting a mail carrier charged with murder—could possibly have been the product of a legislative compromise? In contrast, in a case like *Holy Trinity*, there may be plausible arguments as to why the back and forth of the legislative process would have produced a statute that made no exception for clergy, even if we stipulate that most legislators probably wouldn't have wanted that result. It is perhaps for this reason that most modern textualists would accept the result in *Kirby* as legitimate, but reject the result in *Holy Trinity* as judicial usurpation.

Is that analysis convincing? Can you think of process reasons for resisting the absurdity doctrine, even in cases in which it would be unthinkable that Members of Congress affirmatively bargained to get the particular absurd result? What about the argument that the absurdity doctrine is too elastic and easily abused? How should courts go about distinguishing outcomes that are truly "absurd" from outcomes that are merely unlikely, or in tension with the larger purposes or spirit of the law? Let us consider those questions in the context of a more recent case, *Public Citizen v. U.S. Department of Justice*, in which the Justices divided sharply over the meaning and application of the absurdity doctrine:

---

# Public Citizen v. United States Department of Justice

Supreme Court of the United States
491 U.S. 440 (1989)

■ JUSTICE BRENNAN delivered the opinion of the Court.

The Department of Justice regularly seeks advice from the American Bar Association's Standing Committee on Federal Judiciary regarding potential nominees for federal judgeships. The question before us is whether the Federal Advisory Committee Act (FACA) applies to these consultations.... We hold that FACA does not apply to this special advisory relationship....

I

A

... Since 1952 the President, through the Department of Justice, has requested advice from the American Bar Association's Standing Committee on Federal Judiciary (ABA Committee) in making [judicial] nominations.

The American Bar Association is a private voluntary professional association of approximately 343,000 attorneys. It has several working committees, among them the advisory body whose work is at issue here....

B

FACA was born of a desire to assess the need for the "numerous committees, boards, commissions, councils, and similar groups which have been established to advise officers and agencies in the executive branch of the Federal Government." Its purpose was to ensure that new advisory committees be established only when essential and that their number be minimized; that they be terminated when they have outlived their usefulness; that their creation, operation, and duration be subject to uniform standards and procedures; that Congress and the public remain apprised of their existence, activities, and cost; and that their work be exclusively advisory in nature.

To attain these objectives, FACA directs the Director of the Office of Management and Budget and agency heads to establish various administrative guidelines and management controls for advisory committees. It also imposes a number of requirements on advisory groups. For example, FACA requires that each advisory committee file a charter and keep detailed minutes of its meetings. Those meetings must be chaired or attended by an officer or employee of the Federal Government who is authorized to adjourn any meeting when he or she deems its adjournment in the public interest. FACA also requires advisory committees to provide advance notice of their meetings and to open them to the public, unless the President or the agency head to which an advisory committee reports determines that it may be closed to the public in accordance with the Government in the Sunshine Act. In addition, FACA stipulates that advisory committee minutes, records, and reports be made available to the public, provided they do not fall within one of the Freedom of Information Act's exemptions, and the Government does not choose to withhold them. Advisory committees established by legislation or created by the President or other federal officials must also be "fairly balanced in terms of the points of view represented and the functions" they perform. Their existence is limited to two years, unless specifically exempted by the entity establishing them.

C

In October 1986, appellant Washington Legal Foundation (WLF) brought suit against the Department of Justice after the ABA Committee refused WLF's request for the names of potential judicial nominees it was considering and for the ABA Committee's reports and minutes of its meetings. WLF asked the District Court for the District of Columbia to declare the ABA Committee an "advisory committee" as FACA defines that term. WLF further sought an injunction ordering the Justice Department to cease utilizing the ABA Committee as an advisory committee until it complied with FACA. . . .

III

Section 3(2) of FACA, as set forth in 5 U.S.C.App. § 3(2), defines "advisory committee" as follows:

"For the purpose of this Act—

. . .

"(2) The term 'advisory committee' means any committee, board, commission, council, conference, panel, task force, or other similar group, or any subcommittee or other subgroup thereof (hereafter in this paragraph referred to as 'committee'), which is—

"(A) established by statute or reorganization plan, or

"(B) established or utilized by the President, or

"(C) established or utilized by one or more agencies, in the interest of obtaining advice or recommendations for the President or one or more agencies or officers of the Federal Government, except that such term excludes (i) the Advisory Commission on Intergovernmental Relations, (ii) the Commission on Government Procurement, and (iii) any committee which is composed wholly of full-time officers or employees of the Federal Government."

. . . Whether the ABA Committee constitutes an "advisory committee" for purposes of FACA therefore depends upon whether it is "utilized" by the President or the Justice Department as Congress intended that term to be understood.

### A

There is no doubt that the Executive makes use of the ABA Committee, and thus "utilizes" it in one common sense of the term. As the District Court recognized, however, "reliance on the plain language of FACA alone is not entirely satisfactory." "Utilize" is a woolly verb, its contours left undefined by the statute itself. Read unqualifiedly, it would extend FACA's requirements to any group of two or more persons, or at least any formal organization, from which the President or an Executive agency seeks advice. We are convinced that Congress did not intend that result. A nodding acquaintance with FACA's purposes, as manifested by its legislative history and as recited in § 2 of the Act, reveals that it cannot have been Congress' intention, for example, to require the filing of a charter, the presence of a controlling federal official, and detailed minutes any time the President seeks the views of the National Association for the Advancement of Colored People (NAACP) before nominating Commissioners to the Equal Employment Opportunity Commission, or asks the leaders of an American Legion Post he is visiting for the organization's opinion on some aspect of military policy.

Nor can Congress have meant—as a straightforward reading of "utilize" would appear to require—that all of FACA's restrictions apply if a President consults with his own political party before picking his Cabinet. It was unmistakably not Congress' intention to intrude on a political party's freedom to conduct its affairs as it chooses, or its ability to advise elected officials who belong to that party, by placing a federal employee in charge of each advisory group meeting and making its minutes public property. FACA was enacted to cure specific ills, above all the wasteful expenditure of public funds for worthless committee meetings and biased proposals; although its reach is extensive, we cannot believe that it was intended to cover every formal and informal consultation between the President or an Executive agency and a group rendering advice.[9] As we said in Church of the Holy Trinity v. United States, 143 U.S. 457, 459 (1892): "[F]requently words of general meaning are used in a statute, words broad enough to include an act in question, and yet a consideration of the whole legislation, or of the circumstances surrounding its enactment, or of the absurd results which follow from giving such broad meaning to the words, makes it unreasonable to believe that the legislator intended to include the particular act."

Where the literal reading of a statutory term would "compel an odd result," Green v. Bock Laundry Machine Co., 490 U.S. 504, 509 (1989), we must search for other evidence of congressional intent to lend the term its proper scope.... "The circumstances of the enactment of particular legislation," for example, "may persuade a court that Congress did not intend words of common meaning to have their literal effect." Watt v. Alaska, 451 U.S. 259, 266 (1981). Even though, as Judge Learned Hand said, "the words used, even in their literal sense, are the primary, and ordinarily the most reliable, source of interpreting the meaning of any writing," nevertheless "it is one of the surest indexes of a mature and developed jurisprudence not to make a fortress out of the dictionary; but to remember that statutes always have some purpose or object to accomplish, whose sympathetic and imaginative discovery is the surest guide to their meaning." Cabell v. Markham, 148 F.2d 737, 739 (CA2), aff'd, 326 U.S. 404 (1945). Looking beyond the naked text for guidance is perfectly proper when the result it apparently decrees is difficult to fathom or where it seems inconsistent with Congress' intention, since the plain-meaning rule is "rather an axiom of experience than a rule of law, and does not preclude consideration of persuasive evidence if it exists." Boston Sand & Gravel Co. v. United States, 278 U.S. 41, 48 (1928) (Holmes, J.)....

---

**9.** JUSTICE KENNEDY agrees with our conclusion that an unreflective reading of the term "utilize" would include the President's occasional consultations with groups such as the NAACP and committees of the President's own political party. Having concluded that groups such as these are covered by the statute when they render advice, however, JUSTICE KENNEDY refuses to consult FACA's legislative history ... because this result would not, in his estimation, be "absurd." Although this Court has never adopted so strict a standard for reviewing [the legislative history], ... even if "absurdity" were the test, one would think it was met here. The idea that Members of Congress would vote for a bill subjecting their own political parties to bureaucratic intrusion and public oversight when a President or Cabinet officer consults with party committees concerning political appointments is outlandish. Nor does it strike us as in any way "unhealthy," or undemocratic, to use all available materials in ascertaining the intent of our elected representatives, rather than read their enactments as requiring what may seem a disturbingly unlikely result, provided only that the result is not "absurd." Indeed, the sounder and more democratic course, the course that strives for allegiance to Congress' desires in all cases, not just those where Congress' statutory directive is plainly sensible or borders on the lunatic, is the traditional approach we reaffirm today.

## B

... [A] literalistic reading of § 3(2) would bring the Justice Department's advisory relationship with the ABA Committee within FACA's terms, particularly given FACA's objective of opening many advisory relationships to public scrutiny except in certain narrowly defined situations. A literalistic reading, however, would catch far more groups and consulting arrangements than Congress could conceivably have intended. And the careful review which this interpretive difficulty warrants of earlier efforts to regulate federal advisory committees and the circumstances surrounding FACA's adoption strongly suggests that FACA's definition of "advisory committee" was not meant to encompass the ABA Committee's relationship with the Justice Department.... Weighing the deliberately inclusive statutory language against other evidence of congressional intent, it seems to us a close question whether FACA should be construed to apply to the ABA Committee, although on the whole we are fairly confident it should not....

■ Justice Scalia took no part in the consideration or decision of these cases.

■ Justice Kennedy, with whom The Chief Justice and Justice O'Connor join, concurring in the judgment.

... [T]his suit presents two distinct issues of the separation of powers. The first concerns the rules this Court must follow in interpreting a statute passed by Congress and signed by the President. On this subject, I cannot join the Court's conclusion that the Federal Advisory Committee Act (FACA) does not cover the activities of the American Bar Association's Standing Committee on Federal Judiciary in advising the Department of Justice regarding potential nominees for federal judgeships. The result seems sensible in the abstract; but I cannot accept the method by which the Court arrives at its interpretation of FACA, which does not accord proper respect to the finality and binding effect of legislative enactments. The second question in the case is the extent to which Congress may interfere with the President's constitutional prerogative to nominate federal judges. On this issue, which the Court does not reach because of its conclusion on the statutory question, I think it quite plain that the application of FACA to the Government's use of the ABA Committee is unconstitutional.

## I

The statutory question in this suit is simple enough to formulate. FACA applies to "any committee" that is "established or utilized" by the President or one or more agencies, and which furnishes "advice or recommendations" to the President or one or more agencies... The only question we face ... is whether the ABA Committee is "utilized" by the Department of Justice or the President.

There is a ready starting point, which ought to serve also as a sufficient stopping point, for this kind of analysis: the plain language of the statute. Yet the Court is unwilling to rest on this foundation, for several reasons. One is an evident unwillingness to define the application of the statute in terms of the ordinary meaning of its language. We are told that "utilize" is "a woolly verb," and therefore we cannot be content to rely on what is described, with varying levels of animus, as a "literal reading," a "literalistic reading," and "a dictionary reading" of this word. We also are told in no uncertain terms that we cannot rely on (what I happen to regard as a more accurate description) "a straightforward reading of 'utilize.'" Reluctance to working with the basic meaning of words in a normal manner undermines the legal process. These cases demonstrate that reluctance of this sort leads instead to woolly judicial construction that mars the plain face of legislative enactments.

The Court concedes that the Executive Branch "utilizes" the ABA Committee in the common sense of that word. Indeed, this point cannot be contested.... This should end the matter. The Court nevertheless goes through several more steps to conclude that, although "it seems to us a close question," Congress did not intend that FACA would apply to the ABA Committee.

Although I believe the Court's result is quite sensible, I cannot go along with the unhealthy process of amending the statute by judicial interpretation. Where the language of a statute is clear in its application, the normal rule is that we are bound by it. There is, of course, a legitimate exception to this rule, which the Court invokes, and with which I have no quarrel. Where the plain language of the statute would lead to "patently absurd consequences," United States v. Brown, 333 U.S. 18, 27 (1948), that "Congress could not *possibly* have intended," FBI v. Abramson, 456 U.S. 615, 640 (1982) (O'CONNOR, J., dissenting) (emphasis added), we need not apply the language in such a fashion. When used in a proper manner, this narrow exception to our normal rule of statutory construction does not intrude upon the lawmaking powers of Congress, but rather demonstrates a respect for the coequal Legislative Branch, which we assume would not act in an absurd way.

This exception remains a legitimate tool of the Judiciary, however, only as long as the Court acts with self-discipline by limiting the exception to situations where the result of applying the plain language would be, in a genuine sense, absurd, i.e., where it is quite impossible that Congress could have intended the result, and where the alleged absurdity is so clear as to be obvious to most anyone. A few examples of true absurdity are given in the *Holy Trinity* decision cited by the Court, such as where a sheriff was prosecuted for obstructing the mails even though he was executing a warrant to arrest the mail carrier for murder, or where a medieval law against drawing blood in the streets was to be applied against a physician who came to the aid of a man who had fallen down in a fit. In today's opinion, however, the Court disregards the plain language of the statute not because its application would be patently absurd, but rather because, on the basis of its view of the legislative history, the Court is "fairly confident" that "FACA should [not] be construed to apply to the ABA Committee." I believe the Court's loose invocation of the "absurd result" canon of statutory construction creates too great a risk that the Court is exercising its own "WILL instead of JUDGMENT," with the consequence of "substituti[ng] [its own] pleasure to that of the legislative body." The Federalist No. 78, p. 469 (C. Rossiter ed. 1961) (A. Hamilton).

The Court makes only a passing effort to show that it would be absurd to apply the term "utilize" to the ABA Committee according to its commonsense meaning. It offers three examples that we can assume are meant to demonstrate this point: the application of FACA to an American Legion Post should the President visit that organization and happen to ask its opinion on some aspect of military policy; the application of FACA to the meetings of the National Association for the Advancement of Colored People (NAACP) should the President seek its views in nominating Commissioners to the Equal Employment Opportunity Commission; and the application of FACA to the national committee of the President's political party should he consult it for advice and recommendations before picking his Cabinet.

None of these examples demonstrate the kind of absurd consequences that would justify departure from the plain language of the statute. A commonsense interpretation of the term "utilize" would not necessarily reach the kind of ad hoc contact with a private group that is contemplated by the Court's American Legion hypothetical.... As for the more regular use contemplated by the Court's examples concerning the NAACP and the national committee of the President's political party, it would not be at all absurd to say that, under the Court's hypothetical, these groups would be "utilized" by the President to obtain "advice or recommendations" on appointments, and therefore would fall within the coverage of the statute. Rather, what is troublesome about these examples is that they raise the very same serious constitutional questions [about the president's appointment power upon which we rely below].... The Court confuses the two points. The fact that a particular application of the clear terms of a statute might be unconstitutional does not, in and of itself, render a straightforward application of the language absurd, so as to allow us to conclude that the statute does not apply.

Unable to show that an application of FACA according the plain meaning of its terms would be absurd, the Court turns instead to the task of demonstrating that a straightforward reading of the statute would be inconsistent with the congressional purposes that lay behind its passage. To the student of statutory construction, this move is a familiar one. It is, as the Court identifies it, the classic *Holy Trinity* argument. "[A] thing may be within the letter of the statute and yet not within the statute, because not within its spirit, nor within the intention of its makers." I cannot embrace this principle. Where it is clear that the unambiguous language of a statute embraces certain conduct, and it would not be patently absurd to apply the statute to such conduct, it does not foster a democratic exegesis for this Court to rummage through unauthoritative materials to consult the spirit of the legislation in order to discover an alternative interpretation of the statute with which the Court is more comfortable. It comes as a surprise to no one that the result of the Court's lengthy journey through the legislative history is the discovery of a congressional intent not to include the activities of the ABA Committee within the coverage of FACA. The problem with spirits is that they tend to reflect less the views of the world whence they come than the views of those who seek their advice.

Lest anyone think that my objection to the use of the *Holy Trinity* doctrine is a mere point of interpretive purity divorced from more practical considerations, I should pause for a moment to recall the unhappy genesis of that doctrine and its unwelcome potential. . . .

The central support for the [*Holy Trinity*] Court's ultimate conclusion that Congress did not intend the [immigration] law to cover Christian ministers is its lengthy review of the "mass of organic utterances" establishing that "this is a Christian nation," and which were taken to prove that it could not "be believed that a Congress of the United States intended to make it a misdemeanor for a church of this country to contract for the services of a Christian minister residing in another nation." I should think the potential of this doctrine to allow judges to substitute their personal predelictions for the will of the Congress is so self-evident from the case which spawned it as to require no further discussion of its susceptibility to abuse. . . .

## II

Although I disagree with the Court's conclusion that FACA does not cover the Justice Department's use of the ABA Committee, I concur in the judgment of the Court because, in my view, the application of FACA in this context would be a plain violation of the Appointments Clause of the Constitution. . . .

---

**1. *Is Absurdity in the Eye of the Beholder?***—Does Justice Brennan's opinion for the Court in *Public Citizen* hold that it would be absurd to impose FACA's reporting and disclosure requirements on the ABA's Standing Committee on the Judiciary? If so, is that result correct? Is it fair to say that this application of FACA would be "absurd" in the relevant sense? It would certainly be odd, and there's a good argument that such a result would not have been anticipated or intended by the legislators who enacted the statute. At the same time, applying FACA to the ABA Standing Committee doesn't seem to present the sort of irrationality that one sees in a case like *Kirby*, or in the litany of classic examples the *Kirby* opinion cites. Is there a qualitative difference between the type of absurdity identified in those classic examples and the type identified in *Public Citizen*? In his concurring opinion, Justice Kennedy argued that the Court should "limit[] the exception to situations where the result of applying the plain language would be, in a genuine sense, absurd, i.e., where it is quite impossible that Congress could have intended the result, and where the alleged absurdity is so clear as to be obvious to most anyone." Is that standard firm enough to provide a workable line of demarcation?

Consider the following applications of the absurdity doctrine by the Supreme Court. Which, if any, of the following conclusions about absurdity seem justified?

(a.) It would be absurd to permit individuals, but not corporations, to seek expedited Supreme Court review of the constitutionality of the Line Item Veto Act. *See* Clinton v. New York, 524 U.S. 417, 429 (1998).

(b.) It would be absurd for a Federal Rule of Evidence to make it more burdensome for civil plaintiffs than for civil defendants to introduce an opposing witness's past criminal conviction in order to impeach that witness's credibility. *See* Green v. Bock Laundry Mach. Co., 490 U.S. 504, 509–11 (1989).

(c.) It would be absurd to think that Congress, in passing an otherwise unqualified criminal statute, would not wish to provide for a defense for "entrapment"—the practice whereby undercover government agents induce criminal behavior from a person who does not have an extant propensity to commit such a crime. *See* Sorrells v. United States, 287 U.S. 435, 448–49 (1932).

Which of these applications of the absurdity doctrine seem persuasive to you? Which do not? How can you distinguish them?

**2. *Absurdity and the Level of Generality Problem*—**If the Court indeed understood *Public Citizen* as an application of the absurdity doctrine, a striking feature of Justice Brennan's analysis is that it did not focus on the alleged absurdity of the particular application of FACA at issue. Rather, it relied on the fact that, if one were to give the word "utilize" its conventional meaning, this would necessarily imply *other* results that would (in the majority's view) be clearly absurd: If one were to accept the petitioners' "plain meaning" argument, Justice Brennan explained, FACA would be triggered "any time the President seeks the views of the National Association for the Advancement of Colored People (NAACP) before nominating Commissioners to the Equal Employment Opportunity Commission, or asks the leaders of an American Legion Post he is visiting for the organization's opinion on some aspect of military policy."

It is debatable whether such results would actually follow from a broad reading of "utilize," or whether those results would necessarily be absurd. But suppose we stipulate for the moment both that those results would indeed be absurd and that the application of FACA to the ABA Standing Committee would *not* be absurd. This raises a question about the level of generality at which the absurdity doctrine works. Does the identification of absurd applications that are not before the Court empower the Court to conclude, more generally, that the language of the statute cannot be read in its ordinary sense, thereby opening the door for consideration of extra-textual indicia of intent or purpose? That is certainly the suggestion of Justice Brennan's opinion for the Court. Does that approach unwisely extend the reach of the absurdity doctrine? Couldn't the Court instead have read the statute according to the ordinary meaning of its terms, except in those *specific instances* where a literal reading would produce absurd results? If the Court had adopted that approach, then presumably the NAACP and American Legion examples would be irrelevant—the only question ought to have been whether the particular application of FACA before the Court was itself absurd. Then again, perhaps the Court was getting at the following argument: If a straightforward reading of a statutory term would lead to a *range* of absurd results, this may be *prima facie* evidence that the *term itself* must have a narrower meaning (in all cases) than it would appear at first. On that account, the *Public Citizen* Court was not truly invoking the absurdity canon in the same way that *Kirby* was; instead, the *Public Citizen* Court was using possible absurd results as a way to make a more general argument about statutory meaning.

Might the Court's approach also be understood as extending the absurdity doctrine in another respect? In particular, the Court did not seem to apply classic absurdity analysis to support its concerns about applying FACA to executive branch consultations with the NAACP, the American Legion, or the President's political party. That is, the Court did not treat the possibility of FACA's applying to such consultations as absurd on the ground that it would violate some deeply and widely held social value. Rather, the Court appeared to be making an assessment of what Congress would have intended, given the purposes of the bill and the dynamics of Washington politics. If the Court was indeed extending the absurdity doctrine in that direction, is such an extension justified? If the Court is prepared to determine that Congress could not have intended a particular result because it offended widely held social values and was thus absurd, why shouldn't it, in principle, be able to make the same determination if it is perfectly clear that a particular result would have been utterly unacceptable politically to the Congress that adopted the statute being interpreted? Does Justice Kennedy's concurring opinion present a convincing—and judicially administrable—distinction between the two situations?

**3. *Policy Versus Process Rationality*—**Assume for the moment that Justice Brennan was correct that the typical Member of Congress would not have intended the "odd result" of applying FACA to outside consultative groups like the ABA's Standing Committee. Might there still be a process explanation that accounts for the breadth of the statute as written? Both the Senate and House bills originally provided for narrow coverage, applying FACA only to advisory committees "established" (House) or "established or organized" (Senate) by a federal agency. *See* H.R. Rep. No. 92–1017, at 3 (1972); S. Rep. No. 92–1098, at 6 (1972). The broad phraseology ultimately adopted—"established or *utilized* by one or more agencies, in the interest of obtaining advice or recommendations"— was substituted, without explanation, by the conference committee that reconciled the conflicting House and Senate versions of the bill. *See* H.R. Rep. No. 92–1403, at 9 (1972) (Conf. Rep.). Even if rank-and-file Members of Congress would have opted for a narrower conception of "advisory committee," isn't it conceivable that a sufficient number of the conferees preferred the broader result? And since Congress votes up or down on the language reported by the commerce committee, isn't it also conceivable that the conferees expected the rank-and-file legislators to prefer to vote for an undesirably broad statute than to see the bill fail entirely?

Put more generally, in a complex legislative process, even widely held preferences or values do not pass unfiltered into law (*see* pp. 22–28, *supra*). "[A] large majority of the legislature may want to alter the text of a bill to include or exclude a particular statutory application; but because the legislative bargaining necessary to achieve that alteration is apt to go beyond the application itself, the drafting question is always more complicated than the underlying policy question." John F. Manning, *The Absurdity Doctrine*, 116 Harv. L. Rev. 2387, 2409 (2003). Furthermore, legislative drafters may have to cast their positions in very general or very narrow terms in order to mask disagreements over specifics that might upset the chances of enacting the legislation if dealt with explicitly. Does the absurdity doctrine take for granted the idea that Congress would have been able to frame its legislation precisely enough to avoid the absurd application even if the problem had come into view?

This view of the legislative process, which is typical of the "new textualist" school of interpretation more generally (*see* Section II.B, *supra*) may be having an impact on how the Supreme Court applies the absurdity doctrine. Most notably, in Barnhart v. Sigmon Coal Co., 534 U.S. 438 (2002), the Court rejected a substantial absurdity claim on the basis of legislative process considerations. In 1992, Congress enacted the Coal Industry Retiree Health Benefit Act, 26 U.S.C. §§ 9701–9722, as a way to address looming insolvency in coal-industry retirement plans created pursuant to a number of collective bargaining agreements. To fund the obligations under those plans, the Act required contributions from (1) coal companies ("signatory operators") that had signed any of the collective bargaining agreements in question and (2) other firms ("related persons") that had enjoyed specified forms of business affiliation with signatory operators. The Act contained an undoubted anomaly. The Act explicitly required contributions from any company that was a *successor-in-interest* to a *related person* (by virtue of having purchased its assets), but imposed no such requirements on the *successor-in-interest* to a *signatory operator*. No one denied that this interpretation produced a glaring incongruity in the Act's coverage. As the dissent in *Barnhart* emphasized, a conventional reading of the statute would produce the following absurd result: If a signatory coal operator had been affiliated with a dairy farm (in a way that made the farm a "related person"), and if the coal company and dairy farm each sold its assets to different buyers, the Act would impose financial responsibility for the signatory's retirees upon the dairy's successor but not the signatory's successor. *Id.* at 465 (Stevens, J., dissenting).

Yet the *Barnhart* majority refused to apply the absurdity doctrine. Without denying the oddity of the result, Justice Thomas's opinion for the Court emphasized that the outcome may have been perfectly rational from a process standpoint, even if incongruous from a substantive perspective:

> [N]egotiations surrounding enactment of this bill tell a typical story of legislative battle among interest groups, Congress, and the President. Indeed, this legislation failed to ease tensions among many of the interested parties. Its delicate crafting reflected a compromise amidst highly interested parties attempting to pull the provisions in different directions. As such, a change in any individual provision could have unravelled the whole. It is quite possible that a bill that assigned liability to successors of signatory operators would not have survived the legislative process. The deals brokered during a Committee mark-up, on the floor of the two Houses, during a joint House and Senate Conference, or in negotiations with the President are not for us to judge or second-guess.

*Id.* at 461. How would *Public Citizen* have been decided under the *Barnhart* framework? What about *Kirby*? If the process-oriented approach in *Barn-hart* leaves more absurdities in place, what benefit does it produce? Modern textualists have emphasized the fact that introducing clarifying amend-ments to address absurdities may open a Pandora's Box that ultimately scuttles proposed legislation—but does that alter the reality that inherent imperfections in the legislative process sometimes lead to absurd results that no rational legislature would have endorsed? If that's so, why shouldn't courts refuse to impose those results?

**4. *Congressional Response to the Absurdity Doctrine*—**One ar-gument against the absurdity doctrine is that the risks of "false positives" in applying the doctrine (finding absurdity when there is none) are signifi-cantly greater than the risks of "false negatives" (failing to prohibit an absurd application). The reasoning is that if an application of the statute as written is truly absurd—something that virtually every participant in the legislative process would oppose—then one would expect that Congress would quickly amend the statute to fix the problem. It should be relatively easy, then, to correct false negatives. On the other hand, false positives—overly expansive applications of the absurdity doctrine—might go uncor-rected, because legislators and interest groups who favor the court's inter-pretation may be able to block corrective legislation. Do you find that persuasive? Is it true that "absurd" outcomes are likely to be quickly corrected? Or are the obstacles to legislative action great enough that they may not be corrected quickly, or even at all? And what about the interim costs of having to live with absurd results in the period before the legislature gets around to fixing the statute?

Another argument sometimes advanced against the absurdity doctrine is that if courts give effect to the language Congress enacts, and refuse to "rescue" Congress from careless or overly broad statutory language, then Congress will legislate more carefully, and will pay more attention to potentially problematic applications of statutory language. But perhaps, as Professor Einer Elhauge argues, eliminating or cutting back on the absurd-ity doctrine would require Congress to specify an unrealistically large amount of statutory detail. *See* EINER ELHAUGE, STATUTORY DEFAULT RULES 144–46 (2008). Which position do you find more convincing? What sorts of empirical evidence would be required to arbitrate between these competing claims?

**5.  *Other Techniques for Avoiding Absurdity*—**Could some of the problems addressed by the absurdity doctrine be handled through judicial conventions that are more precise and regularized than an unchannelled grant of authority to avoid absurdity? Consider some examples:

(a.) In *Kirby*, the Court held it absurd to apply a criminal prohibition against willful obstruction of the mails to convict a law enforcement officer for arresting a postal carrier charged with murder. Could the Court have achieved the same result by applying the venerable maxim that "[c]riminal prohibitions do not generally apply to reasonable enforcement actions by officers of the law"? Brogan v. United States, 522 U.S. 398, 406 (1998). *See* pp. 86–88, *supra*.

(b.) In defending the absurdity doctrine, the Court has often invoked Plowden's discussion of the ruling that a statute that punishes escape from prison does not apply to a prisoner who breaks out when the prison is on fire. *See, e.g.*, Baender v. Barnett, 255 U.S. 224, 272 (1921); Holy Trinity Church v. United States, 143 U.S. 457, 461 (1892); United States v. Kirby, 74 U.S. 482, 487 (1868). If one construed all criminal statutes against the background of the commonly-accepted defenses (such as self-defense, duress, and necessity), might the same result be obtained by applying the accepted defense of necessity? *See, e.g.*, United States v. Bailey, 444 U.S. 394, 410 (1980).

(c.) In Puffendorf's example, is there a way apart from the absurdity doctrine to avoid convicting a surgeon for "draw[ing] blood in the streets" when he or she has merely performed emergency surgery to save someone who has fallen ill on the roadside? If one reads language *in context*, the concept of "drawing blood" may have different meanings. It means one thing to say "the dog drew blood" (a violent puncture) and "the nurse drew blood" (a medical procedure). Is it possible that the meaning of "draws blood" means one thing in the context of the criminal code and another in the context of the public health code? Might this sort of contextual interpretation avoid absurdity not by asserting a judicial authority to *depart* from the statutory text, but rather by adopting a reasonable method to *determine* the meaning of the statutory text? *See* pp. 126–140, *infra*.

Even if the foregoing examples permit the avoidance of absurd results through more regularized legal conventions, does the law still require the flexibility afforded by the absurdity doctrine to handle the countless unforeseeable applications of any complex statute? Why is it legitimate for courts to rely on maxims of interpretation such as the reasonable-law-enforcement maxim and the doctrine of necessity? Where did they come from in the first place?

## b.  The Scrivener's Error Doctrine

On rare occasions, the federal judiciary will correct what is known as a "scrivener's error"—an obvious mistake in the *transcription* of the legislature's policies into words. *See, e.g.*, United States Nat'l Bank of Ore. v. Independent Ins. Agents of America, Inc., 508 U.S. 439, 462 (1993) (unanimous decision concluding that "the placement of the quotation marks in the 1916 Act was a simple scrivener's error, a mistake made by someone unfamiliar with the law's object and design"). Although these cases also involve departures from the text of the statute in order to avoid obviously unintended results, some prominent textualists—perhaps less than fully at ease with the absurdity doctrine—have sought to distinguish that doctrine from the scrivener's error doctrine. Justice Scalia explains this distinction as being one between cases in which "the legislature obviously misspoke" and cases in which it "obviously overlegislated." Antonin Scalia, *Common–Law Courts in a Civil–Law System: The Role of United States Federal Courts in Interpreting the Constitution and Laws*, in A MATTER OF INTERPRETATION: FEDERAL COURTS AND THE LAW 3, 21 (Amy Gutmann ed., 1997). In other words, scrivener's errors are instances "where on the very face of the statute it is clear to the reader that a mistake of expression (rather than of legislative wisdom) has been made." *Id.* at 20.

Is there really a qualitative difference between absurdity and scrivener's error? How does one detect a scrivener's error? Consider the disagreement between Justice Marshall's opinion for the Court and Justice Stevens' dissent in the following case:

---

## United States v. Locke

Supreme Court of the United States
471 U.S. 84 (1985)

■ JUSTICE MARSHALL delivered the opinion of the Court.

.   .   .

### I

From the enactment of the general mining laws in the 19th century until 1976, those who sought to make their living by locating and developing minerals on federal lands were virtually unconstrained by the fetters of federal control. . . . Congress in 1976 enacted the [Federal Land Policy and Management Act (FLPMA)], Pub.L. 94–579, 90 Stat. 2743 (codified at 43 U.S.C. § 1701 *et seq.*). Section 314 of the Act establishes a federal recording system that is designed both to rid federal lands of stale mining claims and to provide federal land managers with up-to-date information that allows them to make informed land management decisions. For claims located before FLPMA's enactment, the federal recording system [requires that] in the year of the initial recording, and "prior to December 31" of every year after that, the claimant must file with state officials and with BLM a notice of intention to hold the claim, an affidavit of assessment work performed on the claim, or a detailed reporting form. Section 314(c) of the Act provides that failure to comply with [this requirement] "shall be deemed conclusively to constitute an abandonment of the mining claim ... by the owner."

... [T]he annual filing obligation ... has created the dispute underlying this appeal. Appellees, four individuals engaged "in the business of operating mining properties in Nevada," purchased in 1960 and 1966 10 unpatented mining claims on public lands near Ely, Nevada. These claims were major sources of gravel and building material: the claims are valued at several million dollars, and, in the 1979–1980 assessment year alone, appellees' gross income totaled more than $1 million. Throughout the period during which they owned the claims, appellees complied with annual state-law filing and assessment work requirements. In addition, appellees satisfied FLPMA's initial recording requirement by properly filing with BLM a notice of location, thereby putting their claims on record for purposes of FLPMA.

At the end of 1980, however, appellees failed to meet on time their first annual obligation to file with the Federal Government. After allegedly receiving misleading information from a BLM employee,[7] appellees waited until December 31 to submit to BLM the annual notice of intent to hold or proof of assessment work performed required under § 314(a) of FLPMA. As noted above, that section requires these documents to be filed annually "prior to December 31." Had appellees checked, they further would have discovered that BLM regulations made quite clear that claimants were required to make the annual filings in the proper BLM office "on or before December 30 of each calendar year." 43 CFR § 3833.2–1(a) (1980) (current version at 43 CFR § 3833.2–1(b)(1) (1984)). Thus, appellees' filing was one day too late.

This fact was brought painfully home to appellees when they received a letter from the BLM Nevada State Office informing them that their claims had been declared abandoned and void due to their tardy filing. In many cases, loss of a claim in this way would have minimal practical effect; the claimant could simply locate the same claim again and then rerecord it with

---

**7.** An affidavit submitted to the District Court by one of appellees' employees stated that BLM officials in Ely had told the employee that the filing could be made at the BLM Reno office "on or before December 31, 1980." Affidavit of Laura C. Locke 3. The 1978 version of a BLM question and answer pamphlet erroneously stated that the annual filings had to be made "on or before December 31" of each year. Staking a Mining Claim on Federal Lands 9–10 (1978). Later versions have corrected this error to bring the pamphlet into accord with the BLM regulations that require the filings to be made "on or before December 30."

Justice Stevens and Justice Powell seek to make much of this pamphlet and of the uncontroverted evidence that appellees were told a December 31 filing would comply with the statute. However, at the time appellees filed in 1980, BLM regulations and the then-current pamphlets made clear that the filing was required "on or before December 30." Thus, the dissenters' reliance on this pamphlet would seem better directed to the claim that the United States was equitably estopped from forfeiting appellees' claims, given the advice of the BLM agent and the objective basis the 1978 pamphlet provides for crediting the claim that such advice was given. The District Court did not consider this estoppel claim. Without expressing any view as to whether, as a matter of law, appellees could prevail on such a theory, we leave any further treatment of this issue, including fuller development of the record, to the District Court on remand.

BLM. In this case, however, relocation of appellees' claims, which were initially located by appellees' predecessors in 1952 and 1954, was prohibited by the Common Varieties Act of 1955; that Act prospectively barred location of the sort of minerals yielded by appellees' claims. Appellees' mineral deposits thus escheated to the Government. . . .

## III

### A

Before the District Court, appellees asserted that the § 314(a) requirement of a filing "prior to December 31 of each year" should be construed to require a filing "on or before December 31." Thus, appellees argued, their December 31 filing had in fact complied with the statute, and the BLM had acted ultra vires in voiding their claims. . . . It is clear to us that the plain language of the statute simply cannot sustain the gloss appellees would put on it. As even counsel for appellees conceded at oral argument, § 314(a) "is a statement that Congress wanted it filed by December 30th. I think that is a clear statement. . . ." . . . While we will not allow a literal reading of a statute to produce a result "demonstrably at odds with the intentions of its drafters," Griffin v. Oceanic Contractors, Inc., 458 U.S. 564, 571 (1982), with respect to filing deadlines a literal reading of Congress' words is generally the only proper reading of those words. To attempt to decide whether some date other than the one set out in the statute is the date actually "intended" by Congress is to set sail on an aimless journey, for the purpose of a filing deadline would be just as well served by nearly any date a court might choose as by the date Congress has in fact set out in the statute. "Actual purpose is sometimes unknown," United States Railroad Retirement Board v. Fritz, 449 U.S. 166, 180 (1980) (STEVENS, J., concurring), and such is the case with filing deadlines; as might be expected, nothing in the legislative history suggests why Congress chose December 30 over December 31, or over September 1 (the end of the assessment year for mining claims, 30 U.S.C. § 28), as the last day on which the required filings could be made. But "[d]eadlines are inherently arbitrary," while fixed dates "are often essential to accomplish necessary results." United States v. Boyle, 469 U.S. 241, 249 (1985). Faced with the inherent arbitrariness of filing deadlines, we must, at least in a civil case, apply by its terms the date fixed by the statute. Cf. *United States Railroad Retirement Board v. Fritz, supra,* 449 U.S., at 179.[10]

Moreover, BLM regulations have made absolutely clear since the enactment of FLPMA that "prior to December 31" means what it says. As the current version of the filing regulations states:

---

**10.** Statutory filing deadlines are generally subject to the defenses of waiver, estoppel, and equitable tolling. See Zipes v. Trans World Airlines, Inc., 455 U.S. 385, 392–398 (1982). Whether this general principle applies to deadlines that run in favor of the Government is a question on which we express no opinion today. In addition, no showing has been made that appellees were in any way "unable to exercise the usual care and diligence" that would have allowed them to meet the filing deadline or to learn of its existence. See United States v. Boyle, 469 U.S. 241, 253 (1985) (BRENNAN, J., concurring). Of course, at issue in *Boyle* was an explicit provision in the Internal Revenue Code that provided a reasonable-cause exception to the Code's filing deadlines, while FLPMA contains no analogous provision.

"The owner of an unpatented mining claim located on Federal lands ... shall have filed or caused to have been filed on or before December 30 of each calendar year ... evidence of annual assessment work performed during the previous assessment year or a notice of intention to hold the mining claim." 43 CFR § 3833.2–1(b)(1) (1984).

... If appellees, who were businessmen involved in the running of a major mining operation for more than 20 years, had any questions about whether a December 31 filing complied with the statute, it was incumbent upon them, as it is upon other businessmen, *see United States v. Boyle, supra,* to have checked the regulations or to have consulted an attorney for legal advice. Pursuit of either of these courses, rather than the submission of a last-minute filing, would surely have led appellees to the conclusion that December 30 was the last day on which they could file safely.

In so saying, we are not insensitive to the problems posed by congressional reliance on the words "prior to December 31." But the fact that Congress might have acted with greater clarity or foresight does not give courts a carte blanche to redraft statutes in an effort to achieve that which Congress is perceived to have failed to do. "There is a basic difference between filling a gap left by Congress' silence and rewriting rules that Congress has affirmatively and specifically enacted." Mobil Oil Corp. v. Higginbotham, 436 U.S. 618, 625 (1978). Nor is the Judiciary licensed to attempt to soften the clear import of Congress' chosen words whenever a court believes those words lead to a harsh result. On the contrary, deference to the supremacy of the Legislature, as well as recognition that Congressmen typically vote on the language of a bill, generally requires us to assume that "the legislative purpose is expressed by the ordinary meaning of the words used." Richards v. United States, 369 U.S. 1, 9 (1962). "Going behind the plain language of a statute in search of a possibly contrary congressional intent is 'a step to be taken cautiously' even under the best of circumstances." American Tobacco Co. v. Patterson, 456 U.S. 63, 75 (1982). When even after taking this step nothing in the legislative history remotely suggests a congressional intent contrary to Congress' chosen words, and neither appellees nor the dissenters have pointed to anything that so suggests, any further steps take the courts out of the realm of interpretation and place them in the domain of legislation. The phrase "prior to" may be clumsy, but its meaning is clear.[11] Under these circumstances, we are obligated to apply the "prior to December 31" language by its terms.

The agency's regulations clarify and confirm the import of the statutory language by making clear that the annual filings must be made on or before December 30. These regulations provide a conclusive answer to appellees' claim, for where the language of a filing deadline is plain and the agency's construction completely consistent with that language, the agen-

---

**11.** Legislative drafting books are filled with suggestions that the phrase "prior to" be replaced with the word "before," see, e.g., R. Dickerson, Materials on Legal Drafting 293 (1981), but we have seen no suggestion that "prior to" be replaced with "on or before"—a phrase with obviously different substantive content.

cy's construction simply cannot be found "sufficiently unreasonable" as to be unacceptable.

We cannot press statutory construction "to the point of disingenuous evasion".... Moore Ice Cream Co. v. Rose, 289 U.S. 373, 379 (1933) (Cardozo, J.).[12] We therefore hold that BLM did not act ultra vires in concluding that appellees' filing was untimely....

■ [JUSTICE O'CONNOR'S concurring opinion is omitted.]

■ [JUSTICE POWELL'S dissent is omitted].

■ JUSTICE STEVENS, with whom JUSTICE BRENNAN joins, dissenting.

The Court's opinion is contrary to the intent of Congress ... and unjustly creates a trap for unwary property owners.... [T]he choice of the language "prior to December 31" when read in context ... is, at least, ambiguous, and, at best, "the consequence of a legislative *accident*, perhaps caused by nothing more than the unfortunate fact that Congress is too busy to do all of its work as carefully as it should." [citation omitted]. In my view, Congress actually intended to authorize an annual filing at any time prior to the close of business on December 31st, that is, prior to the end of the calendar year to which the filing pertains....

Congress enacted § 314 of the Federal Land Policy and Management Act to establish for federal land planners and managers a federal recording system designed to cope with the problem of stale claims, and to provide "an easy way of discovering which Federal lands are subject to either valid or invalid mining claim locations." I submit that the appellees' actions in this case did not diminish the importance of these congressional purposes; to the contrary, their actions were entirely consistent with the statutory purposes, despite the confusion created by the "inartful draftsmanship" of the statutory language.

A careful reading of § 314 discloses at least three respects in which its text cannot possibly reflect the actual intent of Congress. First, the description of what must be filed in the initial filing and subsequent annual filings is quite obviously garbled. Read literally, § 314(a)(2) seems to require that

---

**12.** We note that the United States Code is sprinkled with provisions that require action "prior to" some date, including at least 14 provisions that contemplate action "prior to December 31." See 7 U.S.C. § 609(b)(5); 12 U.S.C. § 1709(*o*)(1)(E); 12 U.S.C. § 1823(g); 12 U.S.C. § 1841(a)(5)(A); 22 U.S.C. § 3784(c); 26 U.S.C. § 503(d)(1); 33 U.S.C. § 1319(a)(5)(B); 42 U.S.C. § 415(a)(7)(E)(ii) (1982 ed., Supp. III); 42 U.S.C. § 1962(d)–17(b); 42 U.S.C. § 5614(b)(5); 42 U.S.C. § 7502(a)(2); 42 U.S.C. § 7521(b)(2); 43 U.S.C. § 1744(a); 50 U.S.C.App. § 1741(b)(1). Dozens of state statutes and local ordinances undoubtedly incorporate similar "prior to December 31" deadlines. In addition, legislatures know how to make explicit an intent to allow action on December 31 when they employ a December 31 date in a statute. See, *e.g.*, 7 U.S.C. § 609(b)(2); 22 U.S.C. §§ 3303(b)(3)(B) and (c); 43 U.S.C. § 256a.

It is unclear whether the arguments advanced by the dissenters are meant to apply to all of these provisions, or only to some of them; if the latter, we are given little guidance as to how a court is to go about the rather eclectic task of choosing which "prior to December 31" deadlines it can interpret "flexibly." Understandably enough, the dissenters seek to disavow any intent to call all these "prior to December 31" deadlines into question.... The only thing we can find unique about this particular December 31 deadline is that the dissenters are willing to go through such tortured reasoning to evade it.

a notice of intent to hold the claim and an affidavit of assessment work performed on the claim must be filed "on a detailed report provided by § 28–1 of Title 30." One must substitute the word "or" for the word "on" to make any sense at all out of this provision. This error should cause us to pause before concluding that Congress commanded blind allegiance to the remainder of the literal text of § 314.

Second, the express language of the statute is unambiguous in describing the place where the second annual filing shall be made. If the statute is read inflexibly, the owner must "file in the office of the Bureau" the required documents. Yet the regulations that the Bureau itself has drafted, quite reasonably, construe the statute to allow filing in a mailbox, provided that the document is actually received by the Bureau prior to the close of business on January 19 of the year following the year in which the statute requires the filing to be made. A notice mailed on December 30, 1982, and received by the Bureau on January 19, 1983, was filed "in the office of the Bureau" during 1982 within the meaning of the statute, but one that is hand-delivered to the office on December 31, 1982, cannot be accepted as a 1982 "filing."

The Court finds comfort in the fact that the implementing regulations have eliminated the risk of injustice. But if one must rely on those regulations, it should be apparent that the meaning of the statute itself is not all that obvious. To begin with, the regulations do not use the language "prior to December 31;" instead, they use "on or before December 30 of each year."[10] The Bureau's drafting of the regulations using this latter phrase indicates that the meaning of the statute itself is not quite as "plain" as the Court assumes; if the language were plain, it is doubtful that the Bureau would have found it necessary to change the language at all. Moreover, the Bureau, under the aegis of the Department of the Interior, once issued a pamphlet entitled "Staking a Mining Claim on Federal Lands" that contained the following information:

> "Owners of claims or sites located on or before Oct. 21, 1976, have until Oct. 22, 1979, to file evidence of assessment work performed the preceding year or to file a notice of intent to hold the claim or site. Once the claim or site is recorded with BLM, *these documents must be filed on or before December 31 of each subsequent year.*" Id., at 9–10 (1978) (emphasis added).

"Plain language" indeed. . . .

---

**10.** 43 CFR § 3833.2–1(b)(1) (1984). It is undisputed that the regulations did not come to the attention of the appellees. To justify the forfeiture in this case on the ground that appellees are chargeable with constructive notice of the contents of the Federal Register is no more acceptable to me today than it would have been to Justice Jackson in 1947. "To my mind, it is an absurdity to hold that every farmer who insures his crops knows what the Federal Register contains or even knows that there is such a publication. If he were to peruse this voluminous and dull publication as it is issued from time to time in order to make sure whether anything has been promulgated that affects his rights, he would never need crop insurance, for he would never get time to plant any crops." Federal Crop Insurance Corporation v. Merrill, 332 U.S. 380, 387 (1947) (Jackson, J., dissenting).

In light of the foregoing, I cannot believe that Congress intended the words "prior to December 31 of each year" to be given the literal reading the Court adopts today. The statutory scheme requires periodic filings on a calendar-year basis. The end of the calendar year is, of course, correctly described either as "prior to the close of business on December 31," or "on or before December 31," but it is surely understandable that the author of § 314 might inadvertently use the words "prior to December 31" when he meant to refer to the end of the calendar year. As the facts of this case demonstrate, the scrivener's error is one that can be made in good faith. The risk of such an error is, of course, the greatest when the reference is to the end of the calendar year. That it was in fact an error seems rather clear to me because no one has suggested any rational basis for omitting just one day from the period in which an annual filing may be made, and I would not presume that Congress deliberately created a trap for the unwary by such an omission.

It would be fully consistent with the intent of Congress to treat any filing received during the 1980 calendar year as a timely filing for that year. Such an interpretation certainly does not interfere with Congress' intent to establish a federal recording system designed to cope with the problem of stale mining claims on federal lands. The system is established, and apparently, functioning. Moreover, the claims here were *active*; the Bureau was well aware that the appellees intended to hold and to operate their claims.

Additionally, a sensible construction of the statute does not interfere with Congress' intention to provide "an easy way of discovering which Federal lands are subject to either valid or invalid mining claim locations." The Bureau in this case was well aware of the existence and production of appellees' mining claims; only by blinking reality could the Bureau reach the decision that it did. It is undisputed that the appellees made the first 1980 filing on August 29, 1980, and made the second required filing on December 31, 1980; the Bureau did not declare the mining claims "abandoned and void" until April 4, 1981. Thus, appellees lost their entire livelihood for no practical reason, contrary to the intent of Congress, and because of the hypertechnical construction of a poorly drafted statute, which an agency interprets to allow "filings" far beyond December 30 in some circumstances, but then interprets inflexibly in others. Appellants acknowledge that "[i]t may well be that Congress wished to require filing by the end of the calendar year and that the earlier deadline resulted from careless draftmanship." I have no doubt that Congress would have chosen to adopt a construction of the statute that filing take place by the end of the calendar year if its attention had been focused on this precise issue. . . . [15]

I respectfully dissent.

---

**15.** The Court lists [in footnote 12 of its opinion] several provisions in the United States Code as supportive of its position that "prior to December 31" is somehow less ambiguous because of its occasional use in various statutory provisions. It then states that it "is unclear whether the arguments advanced by the dissenters are meant to apply to all of the provisions, or only to some of them." However, the provisions cited for support illustrate the lack of justification for the Court's approach, and highlight the uniqueness of the provision in this case. Eleven of the provisions refer to a one-time specific date; the provision at issue here

*1. Scrivener's Errors and Absurdity*—How would one be able to tell that there was a "scrivener's error" in *Locke*? Does the determination depend largely on the conclusion that the statute, as written, doesn't make sense given the policy underlying this provision? Consider Justice Stevens' reasoning in his dissent. Given the nature of the statutory scheme, Justice Stevens concluded that it obviously sought to require "periodic filings on a calendar-year basis." While acknowledging that the statutory text did not "correctly describe[]" the end of the year, he thought it "understandable that the author [of the statute] might inadvertently use the words 'prior to December 31' when he meant to refer to the end of the calendar year." This conclusion was buttressed by the fact that other provisions of the statute contained incongruities that were unquestionably scrivener's errors. Among them was the anomaly, noted by Judge Posner, that "the same section of the statute distinguishes between claims 'located prior to October 21, 1976' and claims 'located after October 21, 1976,' thus leaving a void for claims located on October 21, 1976—if 'prior to' is read literally." Richard A. Posner, *Legal Formalism, Legal Realism, and the Interpretation of Statutes and the Constitution*, 37 CASE W. RES. L. REV. 179, 204 (1986). Perhaps more importantly, beyond relying on other examples of errors in the text, Justice Stevens found it obvious that the statute's phraseology was a scrivener's error "because no one has suggested any rational basis for omitting just one day from the period in which an annual filing may be made."

If Justice Stevens' reasoning typifies the search for a scrivener's error, does the doctrine differ meaningfully from the absurdity doctrine? How much does the finding of a scrivener's error rest on the proposition that enforcing the statute as written would depart obviously from the statute's purpose? Would the scrivener's error doctrine avoid some of the concerns associated with the absurdity doctrine if it required that a statute be interpreted as written unless the judge was unable to conceive of any rational basis for the statutory provision sought to be avoided?

More generally, would it be possible—or desirable—to craft a doctrine that permitted deviation from the clear terms of an enacted text only when it was possible to point to obvious clerical or typographical errors? There are indeed cases in which the text of the statute, read literally, simply makes no linguistic or semantic sense—in which it is apparent that the legislature used the wrong word or simply made a common grammatical or punctuation mistake that makes linguistic nonsense of an otherwise comprehensible sentence. *See, e.g.,* United States v. Scheer, 729 F.2d 164, 169 (2d Cir. 1984); Commonwealth *ex rel.* Smathers v. Taylor, 28 A. 348, 352 (Pa. 1894). There are also cases in which the statute uses a cross-reference

---

requires specific action on a continual annual basis, thus involving a much greater risk of creating a trap for the unwary. Further, each of the specific dates mentioned in the 11 provisions is long past; thus, contrary to the Court's premise, this decision would have no effect on them because they require no future action . . . .

that, in context, could refer only to a nearby section other than the one actually named. *See, e.g.*, United States v. Coatoam, 245 F.3d 553, 557 (6th Cir. 2001); King v. Housing Auth., 670 F.2d 952, 954 n.4 (11th Cir. 1982). In situations like these, is there any reasonable probability that the apparent clerical error was the product of legislative compromise? If not, would a narrowly drawn scrivener's error doctrine be available to someone who rejects the absurdity doctrine? Would such a narrower doctrine be satisfactory? Consider Cernauskas v. Fletcher, 211 Ark. 678 (1947), which involved an Arkansas state statute that gave municipalities the power to "vacate public streets and alleys" if certain conditions are met. The statute also included a clause that said: "All laws and parts of laws . . . are hereby repealed." The Arkansas Supreme Court concluded that this was clearly a scrivener's error: "No doubt," the Court reasoned, "the legislature meant to repeal all laws in conflict with that act, and, by error of the author or the typist, left out the usual words 'in conflict herewith', which we will imply by necessary construction." *Id.* at 680. That conclusion seems entirely sensible. Yet could a court reach it if the scrivener's error doctrine is limited to situations involving an obvious grammatical error, mislabeled cross-reference, or linguistically nonsensical result? It is not incoherent to pass a statute repealing all statutory law and reverting to common law— but it is extremely unlikely that this is what the Arkansas legislature meant to do. Can the result in *Cernauskas* be defended as an application of a narrow version of the scrivener's error doctrine, or does the eminently reasonable result in the case demonstrate that courts must look beyond the text to the likely intentions and expectations of the legislators? *See* EINER ELHAUGE, STATUTORY DEFAULT RULES 147–48 (2008); Jonathan R. Siegel, *What Statutory Drafting Errors Teach Us About Statutory Interpretation*, 69 GEO. WASH. L. REV. 309 (2001).

**2. *The Importance of Punctuation***—The preceding discussion of the scrivener's error doctrine—and in particular the courts' willingness to overlook or read around obvious grammatical or punctuation mistakes— should not be misinterpreted as an indication that courts are lax or forgiving about matters of grammar or punctuation. Especially in recent years, as the textualist influence on the federal judiciary has grown, courts have not hesitated to emphasize rules of grammar and proper punctuation in determining the meaning of legislation, treating these rules as elements of a statute's "plain meaning." A number of Supreme Court statutory interpretation cases have turned at least in part, for example, on the placement or omission of commas. *See, e.g.*, International Primate Prot. League v. Administrators of Tulane Educ. Fund, 500 U.S. 72, 80 (1991); United States v. Ron Pair Enters., Inc., 489 U.S. 235, 241–42 (1989).

Does that make sense? Do you think that Members of Congress pay close attention to commas? Must legislators consciously consider the way a statute uses grammar and punctuation in order to internalize the implications of those practices? *See* Jonathan R. Macey & Geoffrey P. Miller, *The Canons of Statutory Construction and Judicial Preferences*, 45 VAND. L. REV. 647, 651 (1992) (noting "that people who do not know the rules of grammar can employ grammatically correct language when speaking English"). When should a court disregard the strict rules of grammar and punctuation because of an inferred scrivener's error, and when is that illegitimate? Should interpreters more readily assume that legislative drafters have made a punctuation mistake than that the legislators mistakenly chose a word that failed to capture their true intent? *See, e.g.*, Costanzo v. Tillinghast, 287 U.S. 341, 344 (1932) ("[P]unctuation is not decisive of the construction of a statute. Upon like principle we should not apply the rules of syntax to defeat the evident legislative intent.") (citations omitted); Barrett v. Van Pelt, 268 U.S. 85, 91 (1925) (" 'Punctuation is a minor, and not a controlling, element in interpretation, and courts will disregard the punctuation of a statute, or re-punctuate it, if need be, to give effect to what otherwise appears to be its purpose and true meaning.' ") (internal quotation marks omitted). Do those decisions reflect the teachings of an era in which the Court paid less attention to the semantic import of the statutory text itself, or should the Court remain willing to disregard punctuation that seems at odds with other indicia of meaning?

## III. What Is the Text?

The Supreme Court has repeatedly held "that the starting point for interpreting a statute is the language of the statute itself." CPSC v. GTE Sylvania, Inc., 447 U.S. 102, 108 (1980). Indeed, all three of the foundational approaches to statutory interpretation—intentionalism, purposivism, and of course textualism—rely in varying degrees on the text. Even those who believe that the judge's primary task is implementing the general aims or purpose of a statute accept that "[t]here is . . . no more persuasive evidence of the purpose of a statute than the words by which the legislature undertook to give expression to its wishes," and that deciphering the semantic meaning of statutory language is frequently "sufficient . . . to determine the purpose of the legislation." United States v. American Trucking Ass'ns, 310 U.S. 534, 543 (1940).

But often figuring out the meaning of the text is not nearly as straightforward as we might think. At one time, the Court's view of how to determine textual meaning reflected a now-discredited theory of language that presupposed that the statutory text could have an intrinsic meaning that Congress simply enacted into law. So from time to time, the Court would say that it was deriving an interpretation from "within the four corners" of a statute, White v. United States, 191 U.S. 545, 551 (1903), or declare that "[w]here the language is plain and admits of no more than one meaning, the duty of interpretation does not arise." Caminetti v. United States, 242 U.S. 470, 485 (1917). Modern understandings are more complex. No one—not even the most text-focused judge—today believes that language has intrinsic meaning. Instead, judges have accepted the insight that language has meaning only because it reflects practices and conventions shared by a community of speakers and listeners. *See* Ludwig Wittgenstein, Philosophical Investigations §§ 134–142 (G.E.M. Anscombe trans., 2d ed. 1958).

This does not mean that words have no meaning; rather, the meaning of words is determined by the shared understandings and expectations of the relevant linguistic community. There is nothing magical about the word "vehicle," but we have a rough idea of what a "no vehicle in the park" statute might mean because our society has come to agreement about what we mean when we say "vehicle." And, of course, that term, like many others, has different meanings in different contexts. A "vehicle" may mean "[t]hat in or on which a person or thing is or may be carried," but also "[a]n art form or device used to convey an effect." WEBSTER'S NEW COLLEGI-ATE DICTIONARY 943 (1953). But we immediately see that the "no vehicles in the park" statute uses the word in the first sense rather than the second, without consciously thinking about it. So, words have meaning to us because we have the linguistic and cultural competence to recognize the way they are used in their surrounding contexts, and this is true of statutes no less than it is true of everyday conversation. Consider what the philosopher Jeremy Waldron has to say about why legislatures can communicate instructions to judges, administrators, and the public:

> A legislator who votes for (or against) a provision like 'No vehicle shall be permitted to enter any state or municipal park' does so on the assumption that—to put it crudely—what the words mean to him is identical to what they will mean to those to whom they are addressed (in the event that the provision is passed). . . . That such assumptions pervade the legislative process shows how much law depends on language, on the shared conventions that constitute a language, and on the reciprocity of intentions that conventions comprise.

Jeremy Waldron, *Legislators' Intentions and Unintentional Legislation, in* LAW AND INTERPRETATION: ESSAYS, IN LEGAL PHILOSOPHY 329, 339 (Andrei Marmor ed., 1995).

But there is a twist. We can discern what words mean in context because we are part of a community that has implicitly agreed upon practices and conventions for communicating with one another. There are, however, many such communities. Doctors, chemists, building contractors, artists, and lawyers all communicate with one another using jargon or shorthand that may deviate from the ordinary way that people use words in everyday speech or writing. *See, e.g.*, Felix Frankfurter, *Some Reflections on the Reading of Statutes*, 47 COLUM. L. REV. 527, 537 (1947). Accordingly, what is plain to those within a specialized linguistic community may be obscure to the man or woman on the street, and the same word or phrase may mean different things to different linguistic communities. It is therefore vitally important to pay attention to specialized meanings and conventions within the community in which the communication is taking place. Furthermore, when the same word or phrase may have different meanings, judges need some way of determining which meaning was intended or understood by the legislators who enacted that word or phrase into law. The following cases provide examples of the sorts of issues and questions that can arise when courts try to ascertain the meaning of "the text."

## A. SCIENTIFIC OR ORDINARY MEANING?

## Nix v. Hedden

Supreme Court of the United States
149 U.S. 304 (1893)

This was an action brought February 4, 1887, against the collector of the port of New York to recover back duties paid under protest on tomatoes imported by the plaintiff from the West Indies in the spring of 1886, which the collector assessed under ... the Tariff Act of March 3, 1883, ... imposing a duty on "vegetables in their natural state, or in salt or brine, not specially enumerated or provided for in this act, ten per centum ad valorem;" and which the plaintiffs contended came within the clause in the free list of the same act, "Fruits, green, ripe, or dried, not specially enumerated or provided for in this act." ...

■ MR. JUSTICE GRAY:

The single question in this case is whether tomatoes, considered as provisions, are to be classed as "vegetables" or as "fruit," within the meaning of the Tariff Act of 1883....

... The passages cited from the dictionaries define the word "fruit" as the seed of plants, or that part of plants which contains the seed, and especially the juicy, pulpy products of certain plants, covering and containing the seed. These definitions have no tendency to show that tomatoes are "fruit," as distinguished from "vegetables," in common speech, or within the meaning of the Tariff Act.

There being no evidence that the words "fruit" and "vegetables" have acquired any special meaning in trade or commerce, they must receive their ordinary meaning. Of that meaning the court is bound to take judicial notice, as it does in regard to all words in our own tongue; and upon such a question dictionaries are admitted, not as evidence, but only as aids to the memory and understanding of the court.

Botanically speaking, tomatoes are the fruit of a vine, just as are cucumbers, squashes, beans, and peas. But in the common language of the people, whether sellers or consumers of provisions, all these are vegetables which are grown in kitchen gardens, and which, whether eaten cooked or raw, are, like potatoes, carrots, parsnips, turnips, beets, cauliflower, cabbage, celery, and lettuce, usually served at dinner in, with, or after the soup, fish, or meats which constitute the principal part of the repast, and not, like fruits generally, as dessert.

The attempt to class tomatoes as fruit is not unlike a recent attempt to class beans as seeds, of which Mr. Justice Bradley, speaking for this court, said: "We do not see why they should be classified as seeds, any more than walnuts should be so classified. Both are seeds, in the language of botany or natural history, but not in commerce nor in common parlance. On the other hand in speaking generally of provisions, beans may well be included under the term 'vegetables.' As an article of food on our tables, whether baked or boiled, or forming the basis of soup, they are used as a vegetable, as well when ripe as when green. This is the principal use to which they are put. Beyond the common knowledge which we have on this subject, very little evidence is necessary, or can be produced." Robertson v. Salomon, 130 U. S. 412, 414.

---

**1.  *Ordinary or Specialized Meaning?*—***Nix* illustrates the difficulties that may arise when words and phrases have both ordinary and specialized meanings. The problem is not so much that there's no correct answer to the question whether a tomato is a fruit or a vegetable, but rather that the correct answer depends on the context and the community. A botanist might (correctly) assert that a tomato is a fruit, while a chef might (correctly) assert that it's a vegetable. (Actually, a botanist might say that a tomato is a fruit *and* a vegetable, because botanists define a vegetable as any edible part of a plant other than the flower. The important point is that a botanist might classify a tomato as a fruit, whereas a chef presumably would not.) In cases like *Nix*, how do we know when to treat words in a statute as having a specialized meaning as opposed to an ordinary meaning?

One way to approach this question is to consider whom the legislature was addressing. As Justice Frankfurter explained, "If a statute is written for ordinary folk, it would be arbitrary not to assume that Congress intended its words to be read with the minds of ordinary [people]. If they are addressed to specialists, they must be read by judges with the minds of specialists." Felix Frankfurter, *Some Reflections on the Reading of Statutes,* 47 COLUM. L.REV. 527, 536 (1947). But even if that is a reasonable starting point, it is incomplete because the statute's target audience will not always be obvious. The Court has dealt with this problem in part by adopting a starting presumption that "the ordinary meaning of [the statutory] language expresses the legislative purpose." Park 'N Fly, Inc. v. Dollar Park and Fly, Inc., 469 U.S. 189, 194 (1985). *See also* Perrin v. United States, 444 U.S. 37, 42 (1979) ("A fundamental canon of statutory construction is that, unless otherwise defined, words will be interpreted as taking their ordinary, contemporary, common meaning."). Justice Gray seemed to make use of something like this presumption in *Nix* when he declared, "There being no evidence that the words 'fruit' and 'vegetables' have acquired any special meaning in trade or commerce, they must receive their ordinary meaning."

Is that a convincing analysis? Certainly, tariff laws are directed primarily to the world of trade and commerce. But in reaching his conclusion, Justice Gray did not cite any specific evidence for the proposition that merchants would understand terms like "fruit" and "vegetable" in their ordinary rather than technical sense. How should the Court have determined trade practice or understanding? Should the answer depend entirely on the likely understanding of the audience or should the Court have looked, perhaps in the legislative history, at whether Members of Congress understood themselves to be using terms such as "fruit" in their ordinary or technical sense? (*See* Section IV.D, *infra*.) If the statute at issue regulated the practice of farmers instead of merchants, should the outcome have been different? Or might one have reasoned from the structure of the statute that Congress could not have had the botanical definitions in mind, because botanically the category "fruit" is a subset of the category "vegetable," such that the use of the botanical definitions would be inconsistent with the tariff statute's use of "fruits" and "vegetables" as separate, presumably exclusive categories?

**2.  *Other Ways of Resolving the Ambiguity***—Imagine that the Court in *Nix* had no good basis for determining, one way or the other, whether to treat the word "fruit" in its ordinary or technical sense. As noted above, one way to resolve a case like that would be to apply the presumption that Congress uses words in their ordinary sense. But there are other presumptions or rules of thumb that a court might use. For example, the Court has long applied a presumption that "[i]n case of doubt [tax statutes] are construed most strongly against the government, and in favor of the citizen." Gould v. Gould, 245 U.S. 151, 153 (1917). This rule, moreover, applies to customs duties—a form of taxation upon imports. *See, e.g.*, American Net & Twine Co. v. Worthington, 141 U.S. 468, 474 (1891). If this legal convention was firmly established prior to the enactment of the tariff at issue in *Nix*, should the Court have resolved any doubt about the ordinary versus technical meaning in the light of that convention? Note that in *Nix* the presumption that Congress uses words in their ordinary sense and the convention that tariff statutes are to be construed in favor of the citizen point in opposite directions, as the ordinary classification of a tomato as a vegetable would mean the importer has to pay the tax. Which interpretive presumption ought to take precedence, and why?

## B.  Legal Terms of Art

One important subcommunity that has developed its own specialized jargon is the legal profession. Statutes, of course, are legal documents. But statutes are also (usually) addressed to the wider world. This raises the question of whether, or to what extent, courts should consider themselves as bound by "legalese," as opposed to ordinary meaning, when they interpret a statute. The case that follows, *Moskal v. United States*, illustrates this problem. In *Moskal*, the majority read the operative term in a criminal statute ("falsely made") according to its ordinary meaning, giving rise to criminal liability for the implementation of an odometer tampering scheme. The dissent treated the operative term as a narrower, technical legal term of art—a reading which would have relieved the defendant of liability. In reading the case, consider the criteria that courts should use to determine when to read words with distinctly legal meanings in their ordinary sense. Should the Court adopt a blanket presumption that *legal* terms of art should be construed in their technical rather than ordinary sense, reversing the usual presumption?

## Moskal v. United States

Supreme Court of the United States
498 U.S. 103 (1990)

■ JUSTICE MARSHALL delivered the opinion of the Court.

The issue in this case is whether a person who knowingly procures genuine vehicle titles that incorporate fraudulently tendered odometer readings receives those titles "knowing [them] to have been *falsely made*." 18 U.S.C. § 2314 (emphasis added). We conclude that he does.

### I

Petitioner Raymond Moskal participated in a "title-washing" scheme. Moskal's confederates purchased used cars in Pennsylvania, rolled back the cars' odometers, and altered their titles to reflect those lower mileage figures. The altered titles were then sent to an accomplice in Virginia, who submitted them to Virginia authorities. Those officials, unaware of the alterations, issued Virginia titles incorporating the false mileage figures. The "washed" titles were then sent back to Pennsylvania, where they were used in connection with car sales to unsuspecting buyers. Moskal played two roles in this scheme: He sent altered titles from Pennsylvania to Virginia; he received "washed" titles when they were returned.

The Government indicted and convicted Moskal under 18 U.S.C. § 2314 for receiving two washed titles, each recording a mileage figure that was 30,000 miles lower than the true number. Section 2314 imposes fines or imprisonment on anyone who, "with unlawful or fraudulent intent, transports in interstate . . . commerce any falsely made, forged, altered, or counterfeited securities . . . , knowing the same to have been falsely made, forged, altered or counterfeited." On appeal, Moskal maintained that the washed titles were nonetheless genuine and thus not "falsely made." The Court of Appeals disagreed, finding that "the purpose of the term 'falsely made' was to . . . prohibit the fraudulent introduction into commerce of falsely made documents regardless of the precise method by which the introducer or his confederates effected their lack of authenticity." United States v. Davis, 888 F.2d 283, 285 (CA3 1989) [citations and internal quotation marks omitted].

. . . [W]e granted certiorari to resolve a divergence of opinion among the Courts of Appeals. We now affirm petitioner's conviction.

### II

As indicated, § 2314 prohibits the knowing transportation of "falsely made, forged, altered, or counterfeited securities" in interstate commerce. Moskal acknowledges that he could have been charged with violating this provision when he sent the Pennsylvania titles to Virginia, since those titles were "altered" within the meaning of § 2314. But he insists that he did not violate the provision in subsequently receiving the washed titles from Virginia because, although he was participating in a fraud (and thus no doubt had the requisite intent under § 2314), the washed titles themselves were not "falsely made." He asserts that when a title is issued by appropriate state authorities who do not know of its falsity, the title is "genuine" or valid as the state document it purports to be and therefore not "falsely made."

Whether a valid title that contains fraudulently tendered odometer readings may be a "falsely made" security for purposes of § 2314 presents a conventional issue of statutory construction, and we must therefore determine what scope Congress intended § 2314 to have. . . .

## A

"In determining the scope of a statute, we look first to its language," United States v. Turkette, 452 U.S. 576, 580 (1981), giving the "words used" their "ordinary meaning," Richards v. United States, 369 U.S. 1, 9 (1962). We think that the words of § 2314 are broad enough, on their face, to encompass washed titles containing fraudulently tendered odometer readings. Such titles are "falsely made" in the sense that they are made to contain false, or incorrect, information.

Moskal resists this construction of the language on the ground that the state officials responsible for issuing the washed titles did not know that they were incorporating false odometer readings. We see little merit in this argument. As used in § 2314, "falsely made" refers to the character of the securities being transported. In our view, it is perfectly consistent with ordinary usage to speak of the security as *being* "falsely made" regardless of whether the party responsible for the physical production of the document knew that he was making a security in a manner that incorporates false information. . . .

Short of construing "falsely made" in this way, we are at a loss to give *any* meaning to this phrase independent of the other terms in § 2314, such as "forged" or "counterfeited." By seeking to exclude from § 2314's scope any security that is "genuine" or valid, Moskal essentially equates "falsely made" with "forged" or "counterfeited." His construction therefore violates the established principle that a court should " 'give effect, if possible, to every clause and word of a statute.' " United States v. Menasche, 348 U.S. 528, 538–539 (1955).

Our conclusion that "falsely made" encompasses genuine documents containing false information is supported by Congress' purpose in enacting § 2314. Inspired by the proliferation of interstate schemes for passing counterfeit securities, see 84 Cong.Rec. 9412 (statement of Sen. O'Mahoney), Congress in 1939 added the clause pertaining to "falsely made, forged, altered or counterfeited securities" as an amendment to the National Stolen Property Act. 53 Stat. 1178. Our prior decisions have recognized Congress' "general intent" and "broad purpose" to curb the type of trafficking in fraudulent securities that often depends for its success on the exploitation of interstate commerce. In United States v. Sheridan, 329 U.S.

379 (1946), we explained that Congress enacted the relevant clause of § 2314 in order to "com[e] to the aid of the states in detecting and punishing criminals whose offenses are complete under state law, but who utilize the channels of interstate commerce to make a successful getaway and thus make the state's detecting and punitive processes impotent." Id., at 384. This, we concluded, "was indeed one of the most effective ways of preventing further frauds." *Ibid.*; see also McElroy v. United States, 455 U.S. 642, 655 (1982)....

We think that "title-washing" operations are a perfect example of the "further frauds" that Congress sought to halt in enacting § 2314. As Moskal concedes, his title-washing scheme is a clear instance of fraud involving securities. And as the facts of this case demonstrate, title washes involve precisely the sort of fraudulent activities that are dispersed among several States in order to elude state detection....

To summarize our conclusions as to the meaning of "falsely made" in § 2314, we find both in the plain meaning of those words and in the legislative purpose underlying them ample reason to apply the law to a fraudulent scheme for washing vehicle titles.

B

Petitioner contends that such a reading of § 2314 is nonetheless precluded by a further principle of statutory construction. "[W]here a federal criminal statute uses a common-law term of established meaning without otherwise defining it, the general practice is to give that term its common-law meaning." United States v. Turley, 352 U.S. 407, 411 (1957). Petitioner argues that, at the time Congress enacted the relevant clause of § 2314, the term "falsely made" had an established common-law meaning equivalent to forgery. As so defined, "falsely made" excluded authentic or genuine documents that were merely false in content. Petitioner maintains that Congress should be presumed to have adopted this common-law definition when it amended the National Stolen Property Act in 1939 and that § 2314 therefore should be deemed not to cover washed vehicle titles that merely contain false odometer readings. We disagree for two reasons.

First, Moskal has failed to demonstrate that there was, in fact, an "established" meaning of "falsely made" at common law. Rather, it appears that there were divergent views on this issue in American courts. Petitioner and respondent agree that many courts interpreted "falsely made" to exclude documents that were false only in content.... But the [asserted] view—that "falsely made" excluded documents "genuinely" issued by the person purporting to make them and false only in content— was not universal. For example, in United States v. Hartman, 65 F. 490 (ED Mo.1894), the defendant procured a "notary certificate" containing falsehoods. Finding that this conduct fell within the conduct proscribed by a statute barring certain falsely made, forged, altered, or counterfeited writings, the judge stated:

"I cannot conceive how any significance can be given to the words 'falsely make' unless they shall be construed to mean the statements in a certificate which in fact are untrue. 'Falsely' means in opposition to the truth. 'Falsely makes' means to state in a certificate that which is not true. . . ." *Id.*, at 491.

[Moreover,] [o]ther common-law courts, accepting the equation of "falsely making" with "forgery," treated as "forged" otherwise genuine documents fraudulently procured from innocent makers. In State v. Shurtliff, 18 Me. 368 (1841), a landowner signed a deed conveying his farm under the misapprehension that the deed pertained to a different land parcel. Although this deed was "genuine" in the sense that the owner had signed it, the court held it was "falsely made" by the grantee, who had tendered this deed for the owner's signature instead of one previously agreed upon by the parties. Id., at 371. In concluding that the deed was falsely made, the court explained: "[I]t is not necessary, that the act [of falsely making] should be done, in whole or in part, by the hand of the party charged. It is sufficient if he cause or procure it to be done." *Ibid.* . . . . See also Annot., Genuine Making of Instrument for Purpose of Defrauding as Constituting Forgery, 41 A.L.R. 229, 247 (1926).

This plurality of definitions of "falsely made" substantially undermines Moskal's reliance on the "common-law meaning" principle. That rule of construction, after all, presumes simply that Congress accepted the *one* meaning for an undefined statutory term that prevailed at common law. Where, however, no fixed usage existed at common law, we think it more appropriate to inquire which of the common-law readings of the term best accords with the overall purposes of the statute rather than to simply assume, for example, that Congress adopted the reading that was followed by the largest number of common-law courts. " 'Sound rules of statutory interpretation exist to discover and not to direct the Congressional will.' " Huddleston v. United States, 415 U.S. 814, 831 (1974), quoting United States ex rel. Marcus v. Hess, 317 U.S. 537, 542 (1943).

Our second reason for rejecting Moskal's reliance on the "common-law meaning" rule is that, as this Court has previously recognized, Congress' general purpose in enacting a law may prevail over this rule of statutory construction. . . . The position of those common-law courts that defined "falsely made" to exclude documents that are false only in content does not accord with Congress' broad purpose in enacting § 2314—namely, to criminalize trafficking in fraudulent securities that exploits interstate commerce. We conclude, then, that it is far more likely that Congress adopted the common-law view of "falsely made" that encompasses "genuine" documents that are false in content. . . .

For all of the foregoing reasons, the decision of the Court of Appeals is [a]ffirmed.

■ Justice Souter took no part in the consideration or decision of this case.

■ Justice Scalia, with whom Justice O'Connor and Justice Kennedy join, dissenting.

. . .

## I

The Court's decision rests ultimately upon the proposition that, pursuant to "ordinary meaning," a "falsely made" document includes a document which is genuinely what it purports to be, but which contains information that the maker knows to be false, or even information that the maker does not know to be false but that someone who causes him to insert it knows to be false. It seems to me that such a meaning is quite *extraordinary*. Surely the adverb preceding the word "made" naturally refers to the manner of making, rather than to the nature of the product made. An inexpensively made painting is not the same as an inexpensive painting. A forged memorandum is "falsely made"; a memorandum that contains erroneous information is simply "false."

One would not expect general-usage dictionaries to have a separate entry for "falsely made," but some of them do use precisely the phrase "to make falsely" to define "forged." See, *e.g.*, Webster's New International Dictionary 990 (2d ed. 1945); Webster's Third New International Dictionary 891 (1961). The Court seeks to make its interpretation plausible by the following locution: "Such titles are 'falsely made' in the sense that they are made to contain false, or incorrect, information." This sort of word-play can transform virtually anything into "falsely made." Thus: "The building was falsely made in the sense that it was made to contain a false entrance." This is a far cry from "ordinary meaning." . . .

The Court maintains, however, that giving "falsely made" what I consider to be its ordinary meaning would render the term superfluous, offending the principle of construction that if possible each word should be given some effect. United States v. Menasche, 348 U.S. 528, 538–539 (1955). The principle is sound, but its limitation ("if possible") must be observed. It should not be used to distort ordinary meaning. Nor should it be applied to the obvious instances of iteration to which lawyers, alas, are particularly addicted-such as "give, grant, bargain, sell, and convey," "aver and affirm," "rest, residue, and remainder," or "right, title, and interest." See generally B. Garner, A Dictionary of Modern Legal Usage 197–200 (1987). The phrase at issue here, "falsely made, forged, altered, or counterfeited," is, in one respect at least, uncontestedly of that sort. As the United States conceded at oral argument, and as any Webster's 2d dictionary will confirm, "forged" and "counterfeited" mean the same thing. . . . The entire phrase "falsely made, forged, altered, or counterfeited" is self-evidently not a listing of differing and precisely calibrated terms, but a collection of near synonyms which describes the product of the general crime of forgery.

## II

Even on the basis of a layman's understanding, therefore, I think today's opinion in error. But in declaring that understanding to be the governing criterion, rather than the specialized legal meaning that the term "falsely made" has long possessed, the Court makes a mistake of greater consequence. The rigid and unrealistic standard it prescribes for establishing a specialized legal meaning, and the justification it announces for ignoring such a meaning, will adversely affect many future cases.

The Court acknowledges, as it must, the doctrine that when a statute employs a term with a specialized legal meaning relevant to the matter at hand, that meaning governs. As Justice Jackson explained for the Court in Morissette v. United States, 342 U.S. 246, 263 (1952):

> "[W]here Congress borrows terms of art in which are accumulated the legal tradition and meaning of centuries of practice, it presumably knows and adopts the cluster of ideas that were attached to each borrowed word in the body of learning from which it was taken and the meaning its use will convey to the judicial mind unless otherwise instructed. In such a case, absence of contrary direction may be taken as satisfaction with widely accepted definitions, not as departure from them."

Or as Justice Frankfurter more poetically put it: "[I]f a word is obviously transplanted from another legal source, whether the common law or other legislation, it brings its soil with it." *Some Reflections on the Reading of Statutes*, 47 Colum.L.Rev. 527, 537 (1947).

We have such an obvious transplant before us here. Both Black's Law Dictionary and Ballentine's Law Dictionary contain a definition of the term "false making." The former reads as follows:

> "*False making*. An essential element of forgery, where material alteration is not involved. Term has reference to manner in which writing is made or executed rather than to its substance or effect. A falsely made instrument is one that is fictitious, not genuine, or in some material particular something other than it purports to be and without regard to truth or falsity of facts stated therein." Black's Law Dictionary 602 (6th ed. 1990).

... Blackstone defined forgery as "the *fraudulent making* or alteration of a writing to the prejudice of another man's right." 4 W. Blackstone, Commentaries 245 (1769) (emphasis added). The most prominent 19th-century American authority on criminal law wrote that "[f]orgery, at the common law, is the *false making* or materially altering, with intent to defraud, of any writing which, if genuine, might apparently be of legal efficacy or the foundation of a legal liability." 2 J. Bishop, Criminal Law § 523, p. 288 (5th ed. 1872) (emphasis added)....

In 1939, when the relevant portion of § 2314 was enacted, the States and the Federal Government had been using the "falsely made" terminology for more than a century in their forgery statutes. *E.g.*, Ky.Penal Laws § 22 (1802) ("falsely make, forge or counterfeit"); Ind.Rev.Stat., ch. 53, § 26 (1843) ( "falsely make, deface, destroy, alter, forge, or counterfeit"); Del.Rev.Code, ch. 151 (passed 1852) ("falsely make, forge, or counterfeit"). More significantly still, the most common statutory definition of forgery had been a formulation employing precisely the four terms that appear in § 2314: falsely make, alter, forge, and counterfeit. [Citation omitted of one federal and eighteen state statutes containing that precise formulation]. By

1939, several federal courts and eight States had held that the formula "falsely make, alter, forge or counterfeit" did not encompass the inclusion of false information in a genuine document. United States v. Davis, 231 U.S. 183, 187–188 (1913) (dictum); United States v. Staats, 8 How. 41, 46 (1850) (dictum); United States ex rel. Starr v. Mulligan, 59 F.2d 200 (CA2 1932); United States v. Smith, 262 F. 191 (Ind.1920); United States v. Glasener, 81 F. 566 (SD Cal.1897); United States v. Moore, 60 F. 738 (NDNY 1894); United States v. Cameron, 3 Dak. 132 (1882); United States v. Wentworth, 11 F. 52 (CCNH 1882); People v. Kramer, 352 Ill. 304 (1933); Goucher v. State, 113 Neb. 352 (1925); De Rose v. People, 64 Colo. 332 (1918); State v. Ford, 89 Ore. 121 (1918); Territory v. Gutierrez, 13 N.M. 312 (1906); People v. Bendit, 111 Cal. 274 (1896); State v. Corfield, 46 Kan. 207 (1890); State v. Willson, 28 Minn. 52 (1881). Only one federal court had disagreed. United States v. Hartman, 65 F. 490 (ED Mo.1894). ([But] this case was not followed and has been implicitly overruled.) Even statutes that used "falsely made" without accompaniment of the other three terms used in § 2314 were interpreted not to include falsity of content. People v. Mann, 75 N.Y. 484 (1878); State v. Young, [46 N.H. 266 (1865)]. Indeed, as far as I am aware, the only state courts that held a genuine document containing false information to be "forged" did so under governing texts that did not include the term "falsely made." See Moore v. Commonwealth, 92 Ky. 630 (1892); Luttrell v. State, 85 Tenn. 232 (1886). Even they were in the minority, however. See Bank of Detroit v. Standard Accident Insurance Co., 245 Mich. 14 (1928) ("forged"); Dexter Horton National Bank of Seattle v. United States Fidelity & Guaranty Co., 149 Wash. 343 (1928) ("forged"); Barron v. State, 12 Ga.App. 342 (1913) ("fraudulently make").

Commentators in 1939 were apparently unanimous in their understanding that "false making" was an element of the crime of forgery, and that the term did not embrace false contents. May's Law of Crimes § 292 (K. Sears & H. Weihofen eds., 4th ed. 1938); W. Clark & W. Marshall, Law of Crimes § 394 (3d ed. 1927); 2 J. Bishop, Criminal Law §§ 523, 582, 582a (9th ed. 1923); 1 H. Brill, Cyclopedia of Criminal Law § 557 (1922). (Contemporary commentators remain unanimous that falsity of content does not establish forgery. See, e.g., R. Perkins & R. Boyce, Criminal Law 418–420 (3d ed. 1982); 4 C. Torcia, Wharton's Criminal Law 130–132 (14th ed. 1981); W. Lafave & A. Scott, Criminal Law 671 (1972).) . . .

I think it plain that "falsely made" had a well-established common-law meaning at the time the relevant language of § 2314 was enacted—indeed, that the entire formulary phrase "falsely made, forged, altered, or counterfeited" had a well-established common-law meaning; and that that meaning does not support the present conviction. . . .

## IV

The Court acknowledges the principle that common-law terms ought to be given their established common-law meanings, but asserts that the principle is inapplicable here because the meaning of "falsely made" I have described above "was not universal." For support it cites three cases and an A.L.R. annotation. The annotation itself says that one of the three cases, United States v. Hartman, 65 F. 490 (ED Mo.1894), "has generally been disapproved, and has not been followed." Annot., 41 A.L.R. 229, 249 (1926). The other two cases ... discuss not falsity of content but genuineness of the instrument. As for the annotation itself, that concludes that "the better view, and that supported by the majority opinion, is that ... the genuine making of an instrument for the purpose of defrauding does not constitute the crime of forgery." 41 A.L.R., at 231. "Majority opinion" is an understatement. The annotation lists 16 States and the United States as supporting the view, and only 2 States (Kentucky and Tennessee) as opposing it. If such minimal "divergence"—by States with statutes that did not include the term "falsely made"—is sufficient to eliminate a common-law meaning long accepted by virtually all the courts and by apparently all the commentators, the principle of common-law meaning might as well be frankly abandoned....

The Court's second reason for refusing to give "falsely made" its common-law meaning is that "Congress' general purpose in enacting a law may prevail over this rule of statutory construction." That is undoubtedly true in the sense that an explicitly stated statutory purpose that contradicts a common-law meaning (and that accords with another, "ordinary" meaning of the contested term) will prevail. The Court, however, means something quite different. What displaces normal principles of construction here, according to the Court, is "Congress' broad purpose in enacting § 2314—namely, to criminalize trafficking in fraudulent securities that exploits interstate commerce." But that analysis does not rely upon any explicit language, and is simply question-begging. The whole issue before us here is how "broad" Congress' purpose in enacting § 2314 was. Was it, as the Court simply announces, "to criminalize trafficking in *fraudulent* securities"? Or was it to exclude trafficking in *forged* securities? The answer to that question is best sought by examining the language that Congress used—here, language that Congress has used since 1790 to describe not fraud but forgery .... It is perverse to find the answer by assuming it, and then to impose that answer upon the text....

For the foregoing reasons, I respectfully dissent.

---

**1. Ordinary Meaning, Legal Meaning, and Legislative Intent**— Taking the phrase "falsely made" in its ordinary sense, it seems clear that Justice Marshall had a strong argument that the inclusion of a false odometer reading would render an automobile title "falsely made." It also seems clear from the evidence collected by Justice Scalia that the term "falsely made" has a technical legal meaning that is considerably narrower—much closer to "forged"—that applies to an inauthentic document rather than an authentic document that contains false information. Which reading should an interpreter attribute to Congress?

Justice Scalia quoted Justice Jackson's famous opinion in *Morissette v. United States*, which states that when Congress uses a legal term of art, "it presumably knows and adopts the cluster of ideas that were attached to each borrowed word in the body of learning from which it was taken and the meaning its use will convey to the judicial mind unless otherwise instructed." Is that a reasonable presumption? If Congress passed a statute that authorizes suit against HMOs for "negligent refusal to authorize medical treatment," it would be odd for legislators to choose a term such as "negligent," which is so obviously fraught with technical legal meaning, unless they meant to use that word in its technical sense. But what of a term such as "falsely made"? Is it so obvious that Members of Congress would have understood the term in its technical sense? The evidence Justice Scalia amasses regarding the phrase's use as a technical term of art is certainly impressive, and it is likely that some participants in the legislative process must have been familiar with the technical meaning of "falsely made." After all, it would be quite a coincidence if the drafters had randomly selected a term that just happened to have a well-established common law meaning. But isn't the most realistic scenario that someone in the process—a sponsor who was particularly interested in the bill or, perhaps more likely, a staff member—picked up the technical phrase from some other legal source and inserted it into the statute? And doesn't it seem likely that most of the rank-and-file legislators who voted in favor of 18 U.S.C. § 2314 had no view one way or the other on either the question whether the phrase "falsely made" should be taken in its ordinary or technical sense, or the question whether the type of scheme concocted and executed by Moskal should fall within the statute's proscriptions? If Congress likely had no specific intention one way or the other, what is the justification for reading a phrase like "falsely made" in its technical rather than its ordinary sense?

One of the most compelling answers to that question comes from a theory of objective intent associated with legal philosopher Joseph Raz. He believes that the object of interpretation must be to ascertain *some version* of legislative intent, or else it would be hard to justify the interpretive outcomes as the product of a system of legislative supremacy. (*See* pp. 21–22, *supra*.) Acknowledging that Congress may not have an *actual* or *genuine* (*i.e.*, *subjective*) intention concerning most difficult interpretive questions, Raz argues that the theoretical requirement of legislative intent is satisfied by the plausible assumption that legislators intend to enact a law that will be decoded according to the interpretive conventions prevailing in the relevant legal culture:

> Th[at] minimal intention is sufficient to preserve the essential idea that legislators have control over the law. Legislators who have the minimal intention know that they are, if they carry the majority, making law, and they know how to find out what law they are making. All they have to do is establish the meaning of the text in front of them, when understood as it will be according to their legal culture assuming that it will be promulgated on that occasion.

Joseph Raz, *Intention in Interpretation, in* THE AUTONOMY OF LAW: ESSAYS ON LEGAL POSITIVISM 249, 267 (Robert P. George ed., 1996). Under that assumption, even if a legislator has formed no intent concerning a given statutory detail (such as the meaning of "falsely made"), the legal system charges that legislator with the intention "to say what one would be normally understood as saying, given the circumstances in which one said it." *Id.* at 268.

Consistent with Professor Raz's position, textualists look for "a sort of 'objectified' intent—the intent that a reasonable person would gather from the text of the law, placed alongside the remainder of the *corpus juris.*" Antonin Scalia, *Common–Law Courts in a Civil–Law System: The Role of the United States Federal Courts in Interpreting the Constitution and Laws,* in A Matter of Interpretation 3, 17 (Amy Gutmann ed., 1997). *See also* Frank H. Easterbrook, *The Role of Original Intent in Statutory Construction,* 11 Harv. J.L. & Pub. Pol'y 59, 65 (1988) (arguing that courts "should look at the statutory structure and hear the words as they would sound in the mind of *a skilled, objectively reasonable user of words*") (emphasis added). The textualists' reasonable user of language recognizes that because it is impossible to ascertain subjective legislative intent on almost any hard interpretive question, the best one can do is to attribute to Congress the meaning that a reasonable legislator conversant with applicable social and linguistic conventions would have understood the text to mean. On that theory, even if no one in Congress *actually* knew the technical meaning of "falsely made," one would impute to Congress the understandings of a reasonable person conversant with applicable legal conventions.

Does that theory weld statutory interpretation to legislative supremacy in a convincing way? If not, what are the alternatives? One alternative, of course is the more purposivist approach adopted by Justice Marshall's majority opinion in *Moskal.* Of course, Justice Marshall's opinion rejected the dissent's assertion that "falsely made" has a clear technical meaning at common law. But Justice Marshall also argued that "Congress' general purpose in enacting a law may prevail over th[e] rule of statutory construction [directing courts to give technical legal terms their common law meaning]." Because "Congress' broad purpose in enacting § 2314 . . . [was] to criminalize trafficking in fraudulent securities that exploits interstate commerce," it is more than plausible that Congress meant to adopt the majority's broader understanding of "falsely made." If we assume that the weight of the evidence supports Justice Scalia's claims about the common law understanding of "falsely made," but that Justice Marshall was right about the general purpose of the statute, what should the result be? Should the broad *general purpose* of the statute trump the *specific meaning* of that common law term? Does this conflict present the same questions of letter versus spirit as in cases like *Riggs* (pp. 31–35, *supra*) and *Holy Trinity* (pp. 38–43, *supra*), or does the conflict over the ordinary versus technical meaning of "falsely made" make this case more like *Cline* (pp. 68–78, *supra*), in which purpose was invoked to resolve a textual ambiguity? Does the answer depend on one's sense of how well-established the common law meaning is?

**2.   *The Relevant Audience and the Rule of Lenity*—**Recall Justice Frankfurter's statement (*supra* p. 114) that the choice between ordinary and technical meaning depends upon the identity of the audience to whom the statutory provision is directed. This approach seemingly offers one way to resolve the choice of meaning, but as we have seen, statutes may have more than one audience. This fact may significantly complicate the application of Justice Frankfurter's proposed rule to resolve the interpretive problem. Most statutes, after all, are directed at least in part at lawyers—indeed, for many statutory provisions, it is unlikely that anyone *other* than lawyers ever parses the statutory text closely. On the other hand, most statutes are ultimately designed to influence the conduct of non-lawyers. Does this mean that courts should adopt a very strong presumption that statutes should be given their ordinary meaning, even when a technical legal meaning is quite clear, on the logic that potentially affected parties are unlikely to be familiar with legal terms of art?

This latter idea is related to an important (and ancient) interpretive principle in criminal law known as the "rule of lenity," discussed in greater detail in Chapter Two (pp. 327–337, *infra*). In brief, the rule of lenity instructs courts to construe ambiguous criminal laws in favor of defendants. *See, e.g.,* United States v. Wiltberger, 18 U.S. (5 Wheat.) 76, 95 (1820) (Marshall, C.J.). Courts and commentators have offered a variety of justifications for the rule of lenity; for present purposes, the most relevant justification is that the rule of lenity ensures "that laws give the person of ordinary intelligence a reasonable opportunity to know what is prohibited, so that he [or she] may act accordingly." Grayned v. City of Rockford, 408 U.S. 104, 108 (1972). Does that principle mean that courts should eschew reliance on the technical common law meaning of terms in criminal statutes, at least when such reliance would expand rather than contract the scope of criminal liability?

## C.   COLLOQUIAL MEANING OR DICTIONARY MEANING?

If textual interpretation requires courts to determine how a reasonable person conversant with relevant social and linguistic conventions would have used or understood the statutory terms at issue, what evidence should courts use to make that determination? As we have seen, sometimes the question is whether to follow the "ordinary meaning" of statutory terms or to give them a more specialized or technical meaning. But what about the basic question of how to determine what the "ordinary meaning" of statutory terms actually is? Sometimes we feel instinctively that we simply know what a word or phrase would mean to an ordinary speaker of English—a category that, after all, includes us. But what should we do when we are less sure?

One thing we might do, if we want to know what a word means (or can mean), is to look the word up in the dictionary. In recent years, the Supreme Court has dramatically increased its reliance on dictionaries, both in absolute terms and relative to other interpretive resources. *See, e.g.,* Samuel A. Thumma & Jeffrey L. Kirchmeier, *The Lexicon Has Become a Fortress: The United States Supreme Court's Use of Dictionaries*, 47 BUFF. L. REV. 227, 252–60 (1999). Do such resources capture the range of contextual nuance in a rich human language? What if the dictionary includes definitions that are broader or narrower than our instinctive sense of how we would ordinarily use the word or phrase in question? More generally, if the same word or phrase can have more than one "ordinary meaning"—if the same general linguistic community sometimes uses a term in one sense, and sometimes uses the same term in a quite different sense, how can courts decide which of several possible "ordinary meanings" is the correct one? Let us consider these questions in the context of the following case:

## Smith v. United States

Supreme Court of the United States
508 U.S. 223 (1993)

■ JUSTICE O'CONNOR delivered the opinion of the Court.

We decide today whether the exchange of a gun for narcotics constitutes "use" of a firearm "during and in relation to . . . [a] drug trafficking crime" within the meaning of 18 U.S.C. § 924(c)(1). We hold that it does.

I

Petitioner John Angus Smith and his companion went from Tennessee to Florida to buy cocaine; they hoped to resell it at a profit. While in Florida, they met petitioner's acquaintance, Deborah Hoag. Hoag agreed to, and in fact did, purchase cocaine for petitioner. She then accompanied petitioner and his friend to her motel room, where they were joined by a drug dealer. While Hoag listened, petitioner and the dealer discussed petitioner's MAC–10 firearm, which had been modified to operate as an automatic. The MAC–10 apparently is a favorite among criminals. It is small and compact, lightweight, and can be equipped with a silencer. Most important of all, it can be devastating: A fully automatic MAC–10 can fire more than 1,000 rounds per minute. The dealer expressed his interest in becoming the owner of a MAC–10, and petitioner promised that he would discuss selling the gun if his arrangement with another potential buyer fell through.

Unfortunately for petitioner, Hoag had contacts not only with narcotics traffickers but also with law enforcement officials. In fact, she was a confidential informant. Consistent with her post, she informed the Broward County Sheriff's Office of petitioner's activities. The Sheriff's Office responded quickly, sending an undercover officer to Hoag's motel room. . . . Upon arriving at Hoag's motel room, the undercover officer presented himself to petitioner as a pawnshop dealer. Petitioner, in turn, presented the officer with a proposition: He had an automatic MAC–10 and silencer with which he might be willing to part. Petitioner then pulled the MAC–10 out of a black canvas bag and showed it to the officer. The officer examined the gun and asked petitioner what he wanted for it. Rather than asking for money, however, petitioner asked for drugs. He was willing to trade his MAC–10, he said, for two ounces of cocaine. . . .

A grand jury sitting in the District Court for the Southern District of Florida returned an indictment charging petitioner with, among other offenses, two drug trafficking crimes. . . . Most important here, the indictment alleged that petitioner knowingly used the MAC–10 and its silencer during and in relation to a drug trafficking crime. Under 18 U.S.C. § 924(c)(1), a defendant who so uses a firearm must be sentenced to five years' incarceration. And where, as here, the firearm is a "machinegun" or is fitted with a silencer, the sentence is 30 years. The jury convicted petitioner on all counts.

On appeal, petitioner argued that § 924(c)(1)'s penalty for using a firearm during and in relation to a drug trafficking offense covers only situations in which the firearm is used as a weapon. According to petitioner, the provision does not extend to defendants who use a firearm solely as a medium of exchange or for barter. . . .

## II

Section 924(c)(1) requires the imposition of specified penalties if the defendant, "during and in relation to any crime of violence or drug trafficking crime[,] uses or carries a firearm." By its terms, the statute requires the prosecution to make two showings. First, the prosecution must demonstrate that the defendant "use[d] or carrie[d] a firearm." Second, it must prove that the use or carrying was "during and in relation to" a "crime of violence or drug trafficking crime."

## A

Petitioner argues that exchanging a firearm for drugs does not constitute "use" of the firearm within the meaning of the statute. He points out that nothing in the record indicates that he fired the MAC–10, threatened anyone with it, or employed it for self-protection. In essence, petitioner argues that he cannot be said to have "use[d]" a firearm unless he used it as a weapon, since that is how firearms most often are used. Of course, § 924(c)(1) is not limited to those cases in which a gun is used; it applies with equal force whenever a gun is "carrie[d]." In this case, however, the indictment alleged only that petitioner "use[d]" the MAC–10. Accordingly, we do not consider whether the evidence might support the conclusion that petitioner carried the MAC–10 within the meaning of § 924(c)(1). Instead we confine our discussion to what the parties view as the dispositive issue in this case: whether trading a firearm for drugs can constitute "use" of the firearm within the meaning of § 924(c)(1).

When a word is not defined by statute, we normally construe it in accord with its ordinary or natural meaning. Surely petitioner's treatment of his MAC–10 can be described as "use" within the everyday meaning of that term. Petitioner "used" his MAC–10 in an attempt to obtain drugs by offering to trade it for cocaine. Webster's defines "to use" as "[t]o convert to one's service" or "to employ." Webster's New International Dictionary

2806 (2d ed. 1939). Black's Law Dictionary contains a similar definition: "[t]o make use of; to convert to one's service; to employ; to avail oneself of; to utilize; to carry out a purpose or action by means of." Black's Law Dictionary 1541 (6th ed. 1990). Indeed, over 100 years ago we gave the word "use" the same gloss, indicating that it means " 'to employ' " or " 'to derive service from.' " Astor v. Merritt, 111 U.S. 202, 213 (1884). Petitioner's handling of the MAC–10 in this case falls squarely within those definitions. By attempting to trade his MAC–10 for the drugs, he "used" or "employed" it as an item of barter to obtain cocaine; he "derived service" from it because it was going to bring him the very drugs he sought.

In petitioner's view, § 924(c)(1) should require proof not only that the defendant used the firearm, but also that he used it as a weapon. But the words "as a weapon" appear nowhere in the statute. Rather, § 924(c)(1)'s language sweeps broadly, punishing any "us[e]" of a firearm, so long as the use is "during and in relation to" a drug trafficking offense. Had Congress intended the narrow construction petitioner urges, it could have so indicated. It did not, and we decline to introduce that additional requirement on our own.

Language, of course, cannot be interpreted apart from context. The meaning of a word that appears ambiguous if viewed in isolation may become clear when the word is analyzed in light of the terms that surround it. Recognizing this, petitioner and the dissent argue that the word "uses" has a somewhat reduced scope in § 924(c)(1) because it appears alongside the word "firearm." Specifically, they contend that the average person on the street would not think immediately of a guns-for-drugs trade as an example of "us[ing] a firearm." Rather, that phrase normally evokes an image of the most familiar use to which a firearm is put—use as a weapon. Petitioner and the dissent therefore argue that the statute excludes uses where the weapon is not fired or otherwise employed for its destructive capacity. Indeed, relying on that argument—and without citation to authority—the dissent announces its own, restrictive definition of "use." "To use an instrumentality," the dissent argues, "ordinarily means to use it for its intended purpose."

There is a significant flaw to this argument. It is one thing to say that the ordinary meaning of "uses a firearm" *includes* using a firearm as a weapon, since that is the intended purpose of a firearm and the example of "use" that most immediately comes to mind. But it is quite another to conclude that, as a result, the phrase also *excludes* any other use. Certainly that conclusion does not follow from the phrase "uses ... a firearm" itself. As the dictionary definitions and experience make clear, one can use a firearm in a number of ways. That one example of "use" is the first to come to mind when the phrase "uses ... a firearm" is uttered does not preclude us from recognizing that there are other "uses" that qualify as well. In this case, it is both reasonable and normal to say that petitioner "used" his MAC–10 in his drug trafficking offense by trading it for cocaine; the dissent does not contend otherwise.

The dissent's example of how one might "use" a cane suffers from a similar flaw. To be sure, "use" as an adornment in a hallway is not the first "use" of a cane that comes to mind. But certainly it does not follow that the *only* "use" to which a cane might be put is assisting one's grandfather in walking. Quite the opposite: The most infamous use of a cane in American history had nothing to do with walking at all, see J. McPherson, Battle Cry of Freedom 150 (1988) (describing the caning of Senator Sumner in the United States Senate in 1856); and the use of a cane as an instrument of punishment was once so common that "to cane" has become a verb meaning "[t]o beat with a cane." Webster's New International Dictionary. In any event, the only question in this case is whether the phrase "uses . . . a firearm" in § 924(c)(1) is most reasonably read as *excluding* the use of a firearm in a gun-for-drugs trade. The fact that the phrase clearly *includes* using a firearm to shoot someone, as the dissent contends, does not answer it. . . .

We are not persuaded that our construction of the phrase "uses . . . a firearm" will produce anomalous applications. . . . [Section] 924(c)(1) requires not only that the defendant "use" the firearm, but also that he use it "during and in relation to" the drug trafficking crime. As a result, the defendant who "uses" a firearm to scratch his head, or for some other innocuous purpose, would avoid punishment for that conduct altogether: Although scratching one's head with a gun might constitute "use," that action cannot support punishment under § 924(c)(1) unless it facilitates or furthers the drug crime; that the firearm served to relieve an itch is not enough. . . .

In any event, the "intended purpose" of a firearm is not that it be used in any offensive manner whatever, but rather that it be used in a particular fashion—by firing it. The dissent's contention therefore cannot be that the defendant must use the firearm "as a weapon," but rather that he must fire it or threaten to fire it, "as a gun." Under the dissent's approach, then, even the criminal who pistol-whips his victim has not used a firearm within the meaning of § 924(c)(1), for firearms are intended to be fired or brandished, not used as bludgeons. . . . The universal view of the courts of appeals, however, is directly to the contrary. . . .

To the extent there is uncertainty about the scope of the phrase "uses . . . a firearm" in § 924(c)(1), we believe the remainder of § 924 appropriately sets it to rest. Just as a single word cannot be read in isolation, nor can a single provision of a statute. As we have recognized:

> "Statutory construction . . . is a holistic endeavor. A provision that may seem ambiguous in isolation is often clarified by the remainder of the statutory scheme—because the same terminology is used elsewhere in a context that makes its meaning clear, or because only one of the permissible meanings produces a substantive effect that is compatible with the rest of the law." United Savings Assn. of Texas v. Timbers of Inwood Forest Associates, Ltd., 484 U.S. 365, 371 (1988) (citations omitted).

Here, Congress employed the words "use" and "firearm" together not only in § 924(c)(1), but also in § 924(d)(1), which deals with forfeiture of firearms. Under § 924(d)(1), any "firearm or ammunition intended to be used" in the various offenses listed in § 924(d)(3) is subject to seizure and forfeiture. Consistent with petitioner's interpretation, § 924(d)(3) lists offenses in which guns might be used as offensive weapons. But it also lists offenses in which the firearm is not used as a weapon but instead as an item of barter or commerce. For example, any gun intended to be "used" in an interstate "transfer, s[ale], trade, gi[ft], transport, or deliver[y]" of a firearm prohibited under § 922(a)(5) where there is a pattern of such activity, or in a federal offense involving "the exportation of firearms," is subject to forfeiture. In fact, none of the offenses listed in four of the six subsections of § 924(d)(3) involves the bellicose use of a firearm; each offense involves use as an item in commerce. Thus, it is clear from § 924(d)(3) that one who transports, exports, sells, or trades a firearm "uses" it within the meaning of § 924(d)(1)—even though those actions do not involve using the firearm as a weapon. Unless we are to hold that using a firearm has a different meaning in § 924(c)(1) than it does in § 924(d)— and clearly we should not—we must reject petitioner's narrow interpretation.

The evident care with which Congress chose the language of § 924(d)(1) reinforces our conclusion in this regard. Although § 924(d)(1) lists numerous firearm-related offenses that render guns subject to forfeiture, Congress did not lump all of those offenses together and require forfeiture solely of guns "used" in a prohibited activity. Instead, it carefully varied the statutory language in accordance with the guns' relation to the offense. For example, with respect to some crimes, the firearm is subject to forfeiture not only if it is "used," but also if it is "involved in" the offense. Examination of the offenses to which the "involved in" language applies reveals why Congress believed it necessary to include such an expansive term. One of the listed offenses, violation of § 922(a)(6), is the making of a false statement material to the lawfulness of a gun's transfer. Because making a material misstatement in order to acquire or sell a gun is not "use" of the gun even under the broadest definition of the word "use," Congress carefully expanded the statutory language. As a result, a gun with respect to which a material misstatement is made is subject to forfeiture because, even though the gun is not "used" in the offense, it is "involved in" it. Congress, however, did not so expand the language for offenses in which firearms were "intended to be used," even though the firearms in many of those offenses function as items of commerce rather than as weapons. Instead, Congress apparently was of the view that one could use a gun by trading it. In light of the common meaning of the word "use" and the structure and language of the statute, we are not in any position to disagree.

The dissent suggests that our interpretation produces a "strange dichotomy" between "using" a firearm and "carrying" one. We do not see why that is so. Just as a defendant may "use" a firearm within the meaning of § 924(c)(1) by trading it for drugs *or* using it to shoot someone, so too would a defendant "carry" the firearm by keeping it on his person whether he intends to exchange it for cocaine or fire it in self-defense. The dichotomy arises, if at all, only when one tries to extend the phrase " 'uses ... a firearm' " to any use " 'for any purpose whatever.' " For our purposes, it is sufficient to recognize that, because § 924(d)(1) includes both using a firearm for *trade* and using a firearm as a *weapon* as "us[ing] a firearm," it is most reasonable to construe § 924(c)(1) as encompassing both of those "uses" as well.

Finally, it is argued that § 924(c)(1) originally dealt with use of a firearm during crimes of violence; the provision concerning use of a firearm during and in relation to drug trafficking offenses was added later. From this, the dissent infers that "use" *originally* was limited to use of a gun "as a weapon." That the statute in its current form employs the term "use" more broadly is unimportant, the dissent contends, because the addition of the words " 'drug trafficking crime' would have been a peculiar way to *expand* its meaning." Even if we assume that Congress had intended the term "use" to have a more limited scope when it passed the original version of § 924(c) in 1968, we believe it clear from the face of the statute that the Congress that amended § 924(c) in 1986 did not. Rather, the 1986 Congress employed the term "use" expansively, covering both use as a weapon, as the dissent admits, and use as an item of trade or barter, as an examination of § 924(d) demonstrates. Because the phrase "uses ... a firearm" is broad enough in ordinary usage to cover use of a firearm as an item of barter or commerce, Congress was free in 1986 so to employ it. The language and structure of § 924 indicates that Congress did just that. Accordingly, we conclude that using a firearm in a guns-for-drugs trade may constitute "us[ing] a firearm" within the meaning of § 924(c)(1).

B

Using a firearm, however, is not enough to subject the defendant to the punishment required by § 924(c)(1). Instead, the firearm must be used "during and in relation to" a "crime of violence or drug trafficking crime." 18 U.S.C. § 924(c)(1). Petitioner does not deny that the alleged use occurred "during" a drug trafficking crime. Nor could he. The indictment charged that petitioner and his companion conspired to possess cocaine with intent to distribute. There can be no doubt that the gun-for-drugs trade was proposed during and in furtherance of that interstate drug conspiracy. Nor can it be contended that the alleged use did not occur during the "attempt" to possess cocaine with which petitioner also was charged; the MAC–10 served as an inducement to convince the undercover officer to provide petitioner with the drugs that petitioner sought.

Petitioner, however, does dispute whether his use of the firearm was "in relation to" the drug trafficking offense. The phrase "in relation to" is expansive.... Nonetheless, the phrase does illuminate § 924(c)(1)'s boundaries. According to Webster's, "in relation to" means "with reference to" or "as regards." Webster's New International Dictionary. The phrase "in relation to" thus, at a minimum, clarifies that the firearm must have some purpose or effect with respect to the drug trafficking crime; its presence or involvement cannot be the result of accident or coincidence. . . .

We need not determine the precise contours of the "in relation to" requirement here, however, as petitioner's use of his MAC–10 meets any reasonable construction of it. The MAC–10's presence in this case was not the product of happenstance. . . . Without it, the deal would not have been possible. . . .

C

Finally, the dissent and petitioner invoke the rule of lenity. The mere possibility of articulating a narrower construction, however, does not by itself make the rule of lenity applicable. Instead, that venerable rule is reserved for cases where, "[a]fter 'seiz[ing] every thing from which aid can be derived,' " the Court is "left with an ambiguous statute." United States v. Bass, 404 U.S. 336, 347 (1971) (quoting United States v. Fisher, 2 Cranch 358, 386 (1805)). This is not such a case. Not only does petitioner's use of his MAC–10 fall squarely within the common usage and dictionary definitions of the terms "uses . . . a firearm," but Congress affirmatively demonstrated that it meant to include transactions like petitioner's as "us[ing] a firearm" by so employing those terms in § 924(d).

Imposing a more restrictive reading of the phrase "uses . . . a firearm" does violence not only to the structure and language of the statute, but to its purpose as well. When Congress enacted the current version of § 924(c)(1), it was no doubt aware that drugs and guns are a dangerous combination. . . . The fact that a gun is treated momentarily as an item of commerce does not render it inert or deprive it of destructive capacity. Rather, as experience demonstrates, it can be converted instantaneously from currency to cannon. We therefore see no reason why Congress would have intended courts and juries applying § 924(c)(1) to draw a fine metaphysical distinction between a gun's role in a drug offense as a weapon and its role as an item of barter; it creates a grave possibility of violence and death in either capacity.

We have observed that the rule of lenity "cannot dictate an implausible interpretation of a statute, nor one at odds with the generally accepted contemporary meaning of a term." Taylor v. United States, 495 U.S. 575, 596 (1990). That observation controls this case. Both a firearm's use as a weapon and its use as an item of barter fall within the plain language of § 924(c)(1), so long as the use occurs during and in relation to a drug trafficking offense; both must constitute "uses" of a firearm for § 924(d)(1) to make any sense at all; and both create the very dangers and risks that Congress meant § 924(c)(1) to address. We therefore hold that a criminal who trades his firearm for drugs "uses" it during and in relation to a drug trafficking offense within the meaning of § 924(c)(1). . . .

■ [JUSTICE BLACKMUN'S separate concurrence is omitted.]

■ JUSTICE SCALIA, with whom JUSTICE STEVENS and JUSTICE SOUTER join, dissenting.

Section 924(c)(1) mandates a sentence enhancement for any defendant who "during and in relation to any crime of violence or drug trafficking crime . . . uses . . . a firearm." 18 U.S.C. § 924(c)(1). The Court begins its analysis by focusing upon the word "use" in this passage, and explaining that the dictionary definitions of that word are very broad. It is, however, a "fundamental principle of statutory construction (and, indeed, of language itself) that the meaning of a word cannot be determined in isolation, but must be drawn from the context in which it is used." Deal v. United States, 508 U.S. 129, 132 (1993). That is particularly true of a word as elastic as "use," whose meanings range all the way from "to partake of" (as in "he uses tobacco") to "to be wont or accustomed" (as in "he used to smoke tobacco"). See Webster's New International Dictionary 2806 (2d ed. 1939).

In the search for statutory meaning, we give nontechnical words and phrases their ordinary meaning. To use an instrumentality ordinarily means to use it for its intended purpose. When someone asks, "Do you use a cane?," he is not inquiring whether you have your grandfather's silver-handled walking stick on display in the hall; he wants to know whether you walk with a cane. Similarly, to speak of "using a firearm" is to speak of using it for its distinctive purpose, *i.e.*, as a weapon. To be sure, "one can use a firearm in a number of ways," including as an article of exchange, just as one can "use" a cane as a hall decoration—but that is not the ordinary meaning of "using" the one or the other.[1] The Court does not appear to grasp the distinction between how a word can be used and how it *ordinarily* is used. It would, indeed, be "both reasonable and normal to say that petitioner 'used' his MAC–10 in his drug trafficking offense by trading it for cocaine." It would also be reasonable and normal to say that he "used" it to scratch his head. When one wishes to describe the action of employing the instrument of a firearm for such unusual purposes, "use" is assuredly a verb one could select. But that says nothing about whether the *ordinary* meaning of the phrase "uses a firearm" embraces such extraordinary employments. It is unquestionably not reasonable and normal, I think, to say simply "do not use firearms" when one means to prohibit selling or scratching with them. . . .

Given our rule that ordinary meaning governs, and given the ordinary meaning of "uses a firearm," it seems to me inconsequential that "the words 'as a weapon' appear nowhere in the statute"; they are reasonably implicit. Petitioner is not, I think, seeking to introduce an "additional requirement" into the text, but is simply construing the text according to its normal import.

---

**1.** The Court asserts that the "significant flaw" in this argument is that "to say that the ordinary meaning of 'uses a firearm' *includes* using a firearm as a weapon" is quite different from saying that the ordinary meaning "also *excludes* any other use." The two are indeed different—but it is precisely the latter that I assert to be true: The ordinary meaning of "uses a firearm" does *not* include using it as an article of commerce. I think it perfectly obvious, for example, that the objective falsity requirement for a perjury conviction would not be satisfied if a witness answered "no" to a prosecutor's inquiry whether he had ever "used a firearm," even though he had once sold his grandfather's Enfield rifle to a collector.

The Court seeks to avoid this conclusion by referring to the next subsection of the statute, § 924(d), which does not employ the phrase "uses a firearm," but provides for the confiscation of firearms that are "used in" referenced offenses which include the crimes of transferring, selling, or transporting firearms in interstate commerce. The Court concludes from this that *whenever* the term appears in this statute, "use" of a firearm must include nonweapon use. I do not agree. We are dealing here not with a technical word or an "artfully defined" legal term, but with common words that are, as I have suggested, inordinately sensitive to context. Just as adding the direct object "a firearm" to the verb "use" narrows the meaning of that verb (it can no longer mean "partake of"), so also adding the modifier "in the offense of transferring, selling, or transporting firearms" to the phrase "use a firearm" *expands* the meaning of that phrase (it then includes, as it previously would not, nonweapon use). But neither the narrowing nor the expansion should logically be thought to apply to all appearances of the affected word or phrase. Just as every appearance of the word "use" in the statute need not be given the narrow meaning that word acquires in the phrase "use a firearm," so also every appearance of the phrase "use a firearm" need not be given the expansive connotation that phrase acquires in the broader context "use a firearm in crimes such as unlawful sale of firearms." When, for example, the statute provides that its prohibition on certain transactions in firearms "shall not apply to the loan or rental of a firearm to any person for temporary use for lawful sporting purposes," I have no doubt that the "use" referred to is *only* use as a sporting *weapon*, and not the use of pawning the firearm to pay for a ski trip. Likewise when, in § 924(c)(1), the phrase "uses ... a firearm" is not employed in a context that necessarily envisions the unusual "use" of a firearm as a commodity, the normally understood meaning of the phrase should prevail.

Another consideration leads to the same conclusion: § 924(c)(1) provides increased penalties not only for one who "uses" a firearm during and in relation to any crime of violence or drug trafficking crime, but also for one who "carries" a firearm in those circumstances. The interpretation I would give the language produces an eminently reasonable dichotomy between "using a firearm" (as a weapon) and "carrying a firearm" (which in the context "uses or carries a firearm" means carrying it in such manner as to be ready for use as a weapon). The Court's interpretation, by contrast, produces a strange dichotomy between "using a firearm for any purpose whatever, including barter," and "carrying a firearm."[3]

Finally, although the present prosecution was brought under the portion of § 924(c)(1) pertaining to use of a firearm "during and in relation

---

**3.** The Court responds to this argument by abandoning all pretense of giving the phrase "uses a firearm" even a *permissible* meaning, much less its ordinary one. There is no problem, the Court says, because it is not contending that "uses a firearm" means "uses for any purpose," only that it means "uses as a weapon or for trade." Unfortunately, that is not one of the options that our mother tongue makes available. "Uses a firearm" can be given a broad meaning ("uses for any purpose") or its more ordinary narrow meaning ("uses as a weapon"); but it can not possibly mean "uses as a weapon or for trade."

to any . . . drug trafficking crime," I think it significant that that portion is affiliated with the pre-existing provision pertaining to use of a firearm "during and in relation to any crime of violence," rather than with the firearm trafficking offenses defined in § 922 and referenced in § 924(d). The word "use" in the "crime of violence" context has the unmistakable import of use as a weapon, and that import carries over, in my view, to the subsequently added phrase "or drug trafficking crime." Surely the word "use" means the same thing as to both, and surely the 1986 addition of "drug trafficking crime" would have been a peculiar way to *expand* its meaning (beyond "use as a weapon") for crimes of violence.

Even if the reader does not consider the issue to be as clear as I do, he must at least acknowledge, I think, that it is eminently debatable—and that is enough, under the rule of lenity, to require finding for the petitioner here. "At the very least, it may be said that the issue is subject to some doubt. Under these circumstances, we adhere to the familiar rule that, 'where there is ambiguity in a criminal statute, doubts are resolved in favor of the defendant.'" Adamo Wrecking Co. v. United States, 434 U.S. 275, 284–285 (1978), quoting United States v. Bass, 404 U.S. 336, 348.[4]

For the foregoing reasons, I respectfully dissent.

---

***1. The Use and Abuse of Dictionaries***—The majority opinion in *Smith* relied heavily on the dictionary definition of "use," citing both WEBSTER'S NEW INTERNATIONAL DICTIONARY 2806 (2d ed. 1939) and BLACK'S LAW DICTIONARY 1541 (6th ed. 1990) for broad definitions that include "to employ" or "to utilize." The Court's practice of using dictionaries to determine meaning, although increasingly common, is controversial. The main objection—that focusing on dictionary definitions will miss or undervalue the policy impulses that inspired the legislation—is well captured by Judge Learned Hand's famous admonition "not to make a fortress out of the dictionary; but to remember that statutes always have some purpose or object to accomplish, whose sympathetic and imaginative discovery is the surest guide to their meaning." Cabell v. Markham, 148 F.2d 737, 739 (2d Cir. 1945), *aff'd*, 326 U.S. 404 (1945). Even Judge Easterbrook has observed that the dictionary is merely "a museum of words, an historical catalog rather than a means to decode the work of legislatures." Frank H. Easterbrook, *Text, History, and Structure in Statutory Interpretation*, 17 HARV. J.L. & PUB. POL'Y 61, 67 (1994).

At the same time, doesn't it make sense to conclude that dictionaries can often shed light on statutory meaning? Dictionaries provide a historical record of how people use language in context, and that can provide at least

---

**4.** The Court contends that giving the language its ordinary meaning would frustrate the purpose of the statute, since a gun "can be converted instantaneously from currency to cannon." Stretching language in order to write a more effective statute than Congress devised is not an exercise we should indulge in. But in any case, the ready ability to use a gun that is at hand as a weapon is perhaps one of the reasons the statute sanctions not only *using* a firearm, but *carrying* one. Here, however, the Government chose not to indict under that provision.

a starting point for considering how a reasonable person would have used or understood a given word or phrase. Perhaps the most important purposivists of the twentieth century—Professors Hart and Sacks—thus wrote: "Judges answer many questions of the linguistically correct meaning of particular words out of their own experience and judgment.... It is nice, however, when such questions can be answered by reference to impersonal authority. Such an authority is provided by reputable dictionaries." Henry M. Hart, Jr. & Albert M. Sacks, The Legal Process: Basic Problems in the Making and Application of Law 1190 (William N. Eskridge, Jr. & Philip P. Frickey eds., 1994) (tent. ed. 1958). The Supreme Court's most dedicated purposivists, moreover, have no difficulty consulting dictionaries as a useful starting point for identifying the purposes Congress sought to achieve through its chosen words. *See, e.g.*, Muscarello v. United States, 524 U.S. 125, 127–31 (1998) (Breyer, J.) (using dictionaries to identify the "primary meaning" of the word "carry"); Dunn v. Commodity Futures Trading Comm'n, 519 U.S. 465, 470 (1997) (Stevens, J.) (citing Black's Law Dictionary to help determine "the ordinary meaning of the key word 'in' ").

Likewise, even the strictest textualist would agree that dictionaries, though helpful, cannot conclusively answer questions of statutory construction. Words may have technical connotations that a conventional dictionary has not recorded. And, because dictionaries do not have an infinite capacity to record nuance, interpreters must be sensitive to the possibility of colloquial meanings that the dictionary has not picked up. Justice Scalia argued that the latter circumstance obtained in *Smith*. What did you make of Justice Scalia's argument that the word "use" in the context of § 924(c)(1) did not have the sweeping meaning one might infer from the dictionary, but rather had the narrower colloquial meaning of "using [a firearm] for its distinctive purpose, i.e., as a weapon"? As a staunch textualist, Justice Scalia's argument was not that the ordinary meaning of "use" should be narrowed in light of the statute's purpose. Rather, Justice Scalia insisted that a reasonable person would have understood the *semantic* meaning of the term "use a firearm" in that narrow sense.

How did he know? He invoked other, similar instances of the word's usage. Justice Scalia thus wrote: "When someone asks, 'Do you use a cane?,' he is not inquiring whether you have your grandfather's silver-handled walking stick on display in the hall; he wants to know whether you walk with a cane." By the same token, he thought "it perfectly obvious ... that the objective falsity requirement for a perjury conviction would not be satisfied if a witness answered 'no' to a prosecutor's inquiry whether he had ever 'used a firearm,' even though he had once sold his grandfather's Enfield rifle to a collector." Is that type of argument persuasive? Is the particular argument about the contextual meaning of the word "use" a convincing one? Imagine that instead of joining Justice Scalia's dissent, Justice Stevens had dissented on the ground that Congress had an obvious purpose to limit the phrase "use[] ... a firearm" to instances in which a perpetrator actively used a gun to assist in the commission of the crime. Would that reason for narrowing the word "use" have been any less legitimate than Justice Scalia's narrowing the dictionary definition of "use" in light of his perception of the colloquial meaning of the phrase "use a firearm"?

**2. *Disagreement and Clear Meaning*—**Textualism presupposes that interpreters can discern and agree upon the clear import of a statutory text. In *Smith*, does the disagreement over the relevance of dictionary meaning (preferred by the majority) versus colloquial meaning (pressed by the dissent) cast doubt on judges' capacity to draw clear meaning from statutory text? How does one resolve the conflict among specialized, dictionary, and colloquial meanings when judges have such difficulty agreeing on which type of meaning is relevant in a given case? Judge Posner has written that a statute is clear when "all or most persons, having the linguistic and cultural competence assumed by the authors of the text, would agree on its meaning." Richard A. Posner, *Legal Formalism, Legal Realism, and the Interpretation of Statutes and the Constitution*, 37 CASE W. RES. L. REV. 179, 187 (1986). If judges, as in *Smith*, disagree about the meaning of a word or phrase, does that negate any contention that the meaning is clear? Perhaps when courts and commentators assert that a statute is "clear," they do not mean that the meaning of the statute is so certain that no disagreement is possible. After all, some degree of uncertainty is present in all legal analysis, including statutory interpretation. Therefore, as Professor Gary Lawson has argued, interpreters routinely make judgments about the relative *probabilities* that competing interpretations of a given text are correct. *See* Gary Lawson, *Proving the Law*, 86 NW. U. L. REV. 859, 890–94 (1992). In most cases in which judges describe the outcome of an interpretive question as clear, they are merely describing their conclusion that there is a high probability that most reasonable people would understand the statute in the way that the judge describes. Is that satisfactory?

**3. *Earlier Examples Revisited*—**The dispute in *Smith* demonstrates that reasonable people (and reasonable Justices) can disagree about the ordinary meaning of language, and that assertions about statutory clarity are often more problematic than they appear. In that light, let us revisit two problems arising out of statutory language discussed earlier in this Chapter—one imaginary ("no dogs in the park") and one real (*Holy Trinity*). Recall that we had earlier treated the semantic meaning of both statutes as clear in context. To what extent is that treatment warranted? To what extent can the questions of statutory meaning in these cases be resolved by reference to semantic evidence?

**a. *"No dogs in the park"*—**May one take a pet wolf into a park with a "no dogs allowed" rule? A standard dictionary defines "dog" as follows:

>     **1.** A domesticated carnivorous animal (*Canis familiaris*) related to the foxes and wolves and raised in a wide variety of breeds. **2.** Any of various carnivorous mammals of the family Canidae, such as the dingo. **3.** A male animal of the family Canidae, especially of the fox or a domesticated breed. **4.** Any of various other animals, such as the prairie dog.

THE AMERICAN HERITAGE DICTIONARY OF THE ENGLISH LANGUAGE 531 (4th. ed. 2000). If one then goes to the closest reference for the family Canidae—"Canid"—the definition is "[a]ny of various widely distributed carnivorous mammals of the family Canidae, which includes the foxes, wolves, dogs, jackals, and coyotes." *Id*. at 271–72. Looking from the other direction, "wolf" is relevantly defined as "[e]ither of two carnivorous mammals of the family Canidae, especially the gray wolf of northern regions, that typically live and hunt in hierarchical packs and prey on livestock and game animals." *Id*. at 1977. Those definitions, considered cumulatively, suggest that the term "dog" presumptively means something distinct from "wolf," but could potentially be used to encompass wolves. Here, the dictionary definitions seem to pick up some ambivalence among English speakers. One could imagine a passer-by noticing a pet wolf and saying "Beautiful dog!" Conversely, one could imagine someone yelling with alarm, "That's not a dog in the pasture; that's a wolf!" When the dictionary is unclear, what besides intuition could help resolve the issue? Do you lean one way on the question yourself?

**b. "Labor or service of any kind"**—In *Holy Trinity* (pp. 38–43, *supra*), the Court assumed that the ordinary meaning of "labor or service of any kind" in the Alien Contract Labor Act would cover the English pastor; this is why the Court had to invoke considerations of legislative intent and purpose to avoid this reading of the statute. But Professor William Eskridge has contested this view, as follows:

> [T]here is reason to think that some ordinary speakers of the English language would have limited the statutory language to manual workers and would not have extended it to brain toilers such as the Holy Trinity Church pastor. The first definition of the term "labor" listed in the 1879 and 1886 editions of Webster's Dictionary was "Physical toil or bodily exertion . . . hard muscular effort directed to some useful end, as agriculture, manufactures, and the like. . . ." The first, and pre-ferred, definition supports Brewer's intuition that brain toilers were not targeted by the statute. . . . The second listed definition, "intellec-tual exertion, mental effort," was broad enough to include brain as well as manual toilers, but judges of the period were more likely to follow the primary definition. . . .
>
> The contemporary definition of "service" was also narrow. Web-ster's first, and only relevant, definition of the term was: "The act of serving; the occupation of a servant; the performance of labor for the benefit of another, or at another's command; attendance of an inferior, or hired helper, or slave, & c., on a superior, employer, master, or the like. . . ." Legal dictionaries of the period defined "service" more broadly, as "being employed to serve another; duty or labor to be rendered by one person to another." When lawyers spoke of profession-al work, they appear to have used the term "services" rather than "service."

William N. Eskridge, Jr., *Textualism: The Unknown Ideal?*, 96 MICH. L. REV. 1509, 1518 (1998) (book review) (citations omitted). How persuasive is

Professor Eskridge's account? Even if the primary definition of "service" in Webster's Dictionary referred to work done by physical toilers, doesn't the availability of a broader definition of "service" in legal dictionaries of the era support giving the statute a wide scope, given that the term "labor or service" is modified by the qualifier "of any kind"?

## IV.  LEGISLATIVE HISTORY

Of the tools that courts might use to discern statutory meaning, perhaps none has attracted as much modern comment and controversy as legislative history (though the interpretive canons, discussed in Chapter Two, may be a close second). Many of the cases earlier in this chapter have contained some discussion of legislative history, and some of them have adverted to the controversy about its use. We now focus directly on this issue.

There are many forms of legislative history that courts might look to when interpreting statutory language. The history of changes and amendments to a bill may reveal what legislators considered—and what they rejected—in settling upon the language ultimately enacted. Furthermore, the originating committee in each chamber typically produces a report that explains why the committee members framed the bill the way they did, what they sought to achieve, and sometimes even what they specifically understood certain words and phrases to mean. Additional explanations will frequently emerge in the debates on the floor of the House and the Senate. Often, remarks in the debates will come from rank-and-file Members sending a message to their constituents. Sometimes, they will involve pre-planned colloquies between a rank-and-file Member and the bill's sponsor or floor manager, in which the latter will offer his or her understanding of the intentions or goals that underlay the bill. Some or all of these materials have for many years been understood to offer useful insights into statutory meaning. Yet critics have attacked judicial use of legislative history as unsound in theory and unwise in practice.

To understand the terms of the current debate, it is helpful to begin with a brief historical overview. In the first several decades of the Republic, use of legislative history was disfavored. Consider the statement made by a unanimous Supreme Court in 1845:

> In expounding this law, the judgment of the court cannot, in any degree, be influenced by the construction placed upon it by individual members of Congress in the debate which took place on its passage, nor by the motives or reasons assigned by them for supporting or opposing amendments that were offered. The law as it passed is the will of the majority of both houses, and the only mode in which that will is spoken is in the act itself; and we must gather their intention from the language there used, comparing it, when any ambiguity exists, with the laws upon the same subject,

> and looking, if necessary, to the public history of the times in
> which it was passed.

Aldridge v. Williams, 44 U.S. (3 How.) 9, 24 (1845). Beginning in 1860,
however, the Court began to invoke legislative history from time to time in
order to clarify the meaning of language in a piece of legislation, *see, e.g.,*
Dubuque & Pac. R.R. v. Litchfield, 64 U.S. (23 How.) 66, 87 (1860), or even
to assist in ascertaining that the surface meaning of the statutory text did
not capture legislative intent, *see, e.g., Church of the Holy Trinity v. United
States,* 143 U.S. 457 (1892) (pp. 38–43, *supra*). Nonetheless, use of legislative history in statutory interpretation, while increasing, was still relatively
sporadic between 1860 and 1940. *See* Note, *Why Learned Hand Would
Never Consult Legislative History Today*, 105 HARV. L. REV. 1005, 1008–11
(1992).

Beginning around 1940, however, things began to change. In the
landmark case of United States v. American Trucking Ass'ns, 310 U.S. 534,
542–44 (1940), the Court made clear that it would not exclude any ''aid to
construction of the meaning of words, as used in the statute.'' This seminal
opinion ushered in a long era of increasing reliance on legislative history.
*See* HENRY M. HART, JR. & ALBERT M. SACKS, THE LEGAL PROCESS: BASIC
PROBLEMS IN THE MAKING AND APPLICATION OF LAW 1237 (William N. Eskridge,
Jr. & Philip P. Frickey eds., 1994) (tent. ed. 1958). While the figures vary
somewhat year to year, one indication of the increase in the use of
legislative history over this period is the fact that the Supreme Court cited
legislative history only 19 times in 1938, but cited it 336 times in 1978.
Jorge L. Carro & Andrew R. Brann, *The U.S. Supreme Court and the Use of
Legislative Histories: A Statistical Analysis*, 22 JURIMETRICS J. 294, 303
(1982). This reliance became so pronounced that by the early 1970s, the
Court was able to state, without any sense of irony: ''The legislative history
. . . is ambiguous. . . . Because of this ambiguity it is clear that we must
look primarily to the statutes themselves to find the legislative intent.''
Citizens to Preserve Overton Park v. Volpe, 401 U.S. 402, 412 n.29 (1971).

The post–*American Trucking* trend toward reliance on legislative history may have been a pragmatic response to the fact that New Deal statutes
passed between 1933 and 1940 tended to be more open-ended than statutes
traditionally had been, thereby requiring greater reliance on extrinsic
materials in order to ascertain meaning. Or perhaps because legislative
history is easier to produce than enacted statutory text (because the whole
chamber need not assent to legislative history), increased judicial reliance
on legislative history may have reflected a broader New Deal impulse to
facilitate the lawmaking thought to be necessary to cope with the increased
demands of a complex industrial society and the Great Depression. *See, e.g.,*
JAMES M. LANDIS, THE ADMINISTRATIVE PROCESS (1938).

Beginning in the 1980s, some new textualists—most notably Justice
Scalia and Judge Easterbrook—began to challenge the legitimacy and
reliability of legislative history as an indicator of statutory meaning. The
textualist critique of legislative history has had a major impact on the
Court's decisionmaking, leading to a noticeable reduction in the use of
legislative history. It has also stimulated a vigorous debate about the

nature of the interpretive enterprise. Before turning to the critique and response, however, it is helpful first to get some sense of how the Court used legislative history during the period between *American Trucking* and the rise of the new textualism in the 1980s.

## A.  The Post-New Deal Approach to Legislative History

Consider the following decision, which in many respects typifies the post–New Deal consensus on the use of legislative history. Notice that while both the majority and the dissent seek to justify their positions in terms of the language of the statute, by far the larger part of both opinions goes to dissecting the legislative history of the enactment. As you read the opinions, think about the resources that the Court and dissent draw upon to ascertain intent. What assumptions do their analyses convey about the nature of the legislative process?

---

## North Haven Board of Education v. Bell

Supreme Court of the United States
456 U.S. 512 (1982)

■ Justice Blackmun delivered the opinion of the Court.

At issue here is the validity of regulations promulgated by the Department of Education pursuant to Title IX of the Education Amendments of 1972, Pub.L.92–318, 86 Stat. 373, as amended, 20 U.S.C. § 1681 *et seq.* These regulations prohibit federally funded education programs from discriminating on the basis of gender with respect to employment.

### I

Title IX proscribes gender discrimination in education programs or activities receiving federal financial assistance. Patterned after Title VI of the Civil Rights Act of 1964, Title IX, as amended, contains two core provisions. The first is a "program-specific" prohibition of gender discrimination:

> "No person in the United States shall, on the basis of sex, be excluded from participation in, be denied the benefits of, or be subjected to discrimination under any education program or activity receiving Federal financial assistance...." § 901(a), 20 U.S.C. § 1681(a).

Nine statutory exceptions to § 901(a)'s coverage follow. See §§ 901(a)(1)–(9).[1]

---

**1.** Section 901(a)(1) provides that, with respect to admissions, § 901(a) applies only to institutions of vocational education, professional education, and graduate higher education, and to public institutions of undergraduate higher education. Specific exceptions are made for the admissions policies of schools that begin admitting students of both sexes for the first time, § 901(a)(2); religious schools, § 901(a)(3); military schools, § 901(a)(4); the admissions policies of public institutions of undergraduate higher education that traditionally and

The second core provision relates to enforcement. Section 902, 20 U.S.C. § 1682, authorizes each agency awarding federal financial assistance to any education program to promulgate regulations ensuring that aid recipients adhere to § 901(a)'s mandate. The ultimate sanction for noncompliance is termination of federal funds or denial of future grants. . . .

In 1975, the Department of Health, Education, and Welfare (HEW) invoked its § 902 authority to issue regulations governing the operation of federally funded education programs.[4] These regulations extend, for example, to policies involving admissions, textbooks, and athletics. See 34 CFR pt. 106 (1980). Interpreting the term "person" in § 901(a) to encompass employees as well as students, HEW included among the regulations a series entitled "Subpart E," which deals with employment practices, ranging from job classifications to pregnancy leave. See 34 CFR §§ 106.51– 106.61 (1980). Subpart E's general introductory section provides:

"No person shall, on the basis of sex, be excluded from participation in, be denied the benefits of, or be subjected to discrimination in employment, or recruitment, consideration, or selection therefor, whether full-time or part-time, under any education program or activity operated by a recipient which receives or benefits from Federal financial assistance." § 106.51(a)(1).

## II

Petitioners are two Connecticut public school boards that brought separate suits challenging HEW's authority to issue the Subpart E regulations. Petitioners contend that Title IX was not meant to reach the employment practices of educational institutions[, but rather only discrimination in regard to availability or implementation of educational programs]. . . .

## III

### A

Our starting point in determining the scope of Title IX is, of course, the statutory language. Section 901(a)'s broad directive that "no person" may be discriminated against on the basis of gender appears, on its face, to include employees as well as students. Under that provision, employees, like other "persons," may not be "excluded from participation in," "denied

---

continually have admitted students of only one gender, § 901(a)(5); social fraternities and sororities, and voluntary youth service organizations, § 901(a)(6); Boys/Girls State/Nation conferences, § 901(a)(7); father-son and mother-daughter activities at educational institutions, § 901(a)(8); and scholarships awarded in "beauty" pageants by institutions of higher education, § 901(a)(9).

**4.** HEW's functions under Title IX were transferred in 1979 to the Department of Education by § 301(a)(3) of the Department of Education Organization Act, Pub.L. 96–88, 93 Stat. 678, 20 U.S.C. § 3441(a)(3) (1976 ed., Supp. IV). Because many of the relevant actions in this case were taken by HEW prior to reorganization, both agencies are referred to herein as HEW.

the benefits of," or "subjected to discrimination under" education programs receiving federal financial support.

Employees who directly participate in federal programs or who directly
benefit from federal grants, loans, or contracts clearly fall within the first
two protective categories described in § 901(a). In addition, a female
employee who works in a federally funded education program is "subjected
to discrimination under" that program if she is paid a lower salary for like
work, given less opportunity for promotion, or forced to work under more
adverse conditions than are her male colleagues.

There is no doubt that "if we are to give [Title IX] the scope that its
origins dictate, we must accord it a sweep as broad as its language." United
States v. Price, 383 U.S. 787, 801 (1966). Because § 901(a) neither expressly nor impliedly excludes employees from its reach, we should interpret the
provision as covering and protecting these "persons" unless other considerations counsel to the contrary. After all, Congress easily could have
substituted "student" or "beneficiary" for the word "person" if it had
wished to restrict the scope of § 901(a).

Petitioners, however, point to the nine exceptions to § 901(a)'s coverage set forth in §§ 901(a)(1)–(9). See n. 1, supra. The exceptions, the school
boards argue, are directed only at students, and thus indicate that § 901(a)
similarly applies only to students. But the exceptions are not concerned
solely with students and student activities: two of them exempt an entire
class of institutions—religious and military schools—and are not limited to
student-related activities at such schools. See §§ 901(a)(3), (4). Moreover,
petitioners' argument rests on an inference that is by no means compelled;
in fact, the absence of a specific exclusion for employment among the list of
exceptions tends to support the Court of Appeals' conclusion that Title IX's
broad protection of "person[s]" does extend to employees of educational
institutions. See Andrus v. Glover Construction Co., 446 U.S. 608, 616–617
(1980).

Although the statutory language thus seems to favor inclusion of
employees, nevertheless, because Title IX does not expressly include or
exclude employees from its scope, we turn to the Act's legislative history for
evidence as to whether Congress meant somehow to limit the expansive
language of § 901.

### B

In the early 1970's, several attempts were made to enact legislation
banning discrimination against women in the field of education. Although
unsuccessful, these efforts included prohibitions against discriminatory
employment practices.

In 1972, the provisions ultimately enacted as Title IX were introduced
in the Senate by Senator Bayh during debate on the Education Amendments of 1972. In addition to prohibiting gender discrimination in federally
funded education programs and threatening termination of federal assistance for noncompliance, the amendment included provisions extending the

coverage of Title VII and the Equal Pay Act to educational institutions. Summarizing his proposal, Senator Bayh divided it into two parts—first, the forerunner of § 901(a), and then the extensions of Title VII and the Equal Pay Act:

"Amendment No. 874 is broad, but basically it closes loopholes in existing legislation relating to general education programs and employment resulting from those programs. . . . *[T]he heart of this amendment* is a provision banning sex discrimination in educational programs receiving Federal funds. The amendment would cover such crucial aspects as admissions procedures, scholarships, and *faculty employment*, with limited exceptions. Enforcement powers include fund termination provisions—and appropriate safeguards—parallel to those found in title VI of the 1964 Civil Rights Act. *Other important provisions* in the amendment would extend the equal employment opportunities provisions of title VII of the 1964 Civil Rights Act to educational institutions, and extend the Equal Pay for Equal Work Act to include executive, administrative and professional women." 118 Cong.Rec. 5803 (1972) (emphasis added).

The Senator's description of § 901(a), the "heart" of his amendment, indicates that it, as well as the Title VII and Equal Pay Act provisions, was aimed at discrimination in employment.

Similarly, in a prepared statement summarizing the amendment, Senator Bayh discussed the general prohibition against gender discrimination:

"Central to my amendment are sections 1001–1005, which would prohibit discrimination on the basis of sex in federally funded education programs. . . .

. . .

"This portion of the amendment covers discrimination in all areas where abuse has been mentioned—*employment practices for faculty and administrators*, scholarship aid, admissions, access to programs within the institution such as vocational education classes, and so forth." 118 Cong.Rec. 5807 (1972) (emphasis added).

Petitioners observe that the discussion of this portion of the amendment appears under the heading "A. Prohibition of Sex Discrimination in Federally Funded Education Programs," while the provisions involving Title VII and the Equal Pay Act are summarized under the heading "B. Prohibition of Education–Related Employment Discrimination." But we are not willing to ascribe any particular significance to these headings. The Title VII and Equal Pay Act portions of the Bayh amendment are more narrowly focused on employment discrimination than is the general ban on gender discrimination, and the headings reflect that difference. Especially in light of the explicit reference to employment practices in the description of the amendment's general provision, however, the headings do not negate

Senator Bayh's intent that employees as well as students be protected by the first portion of his amendment.[15]

The final piece of evidence from the Senate debate on the Bayh amendment appears during a colloquy between Senator Bayh and Senator Pell, chairman of the Senate Subcommittee on Education and floor manager of the education bill. In response to Senator Pell's inquiry about the scope of the sections that in large part became §§ 901(a) and (b), Senator Bayh stated:

> "As the Senator knows, we are dealing with three basically different types of discrimination here. We are dealing with discrimination in admission to an institution, discrimination of available services or studies within an institution once students are admitted, and *discrimination in employment within an institution*, as a member of a faculty or whatever.
>
> "*In the area of employment, we permit no exceptions.*" (emphasis added.)[16]

Although the statements of one legislator made during debate may not be controlling, see, *e.g.*, Chrysler Corp. v. Brown, 441 U.S. 281, 311 (1979), Senator Bayh's remarks, as those of the sponsor of the language ultimately enacted, are an authoritative guide to the statute's construction. See, e.g., FEA v. Algonquin SNG, Inc., 426 U.S. 548, 564 (1976) (such statements "deserv[e] to be accorded substantial weight ..."). And, because §§ 901 and 902 originated as a floor amendment, no committee report discusses the provisions; Senator Bayh's statements—which were made on the same day the amendment was passed, and some of which were prepared rather than spontaneous remarks—are the only authoritative indications of congressional intent regarding the scope of §§ 901 and 902.

The legislative history in the House is even more sparse. H.R. 7248, 92d Cong., 1st Sess. (1971), the Higher Education Act of 1971, contained, as part of its Title X, a general prohibition against gender discrimination in federally funded education programs that was identical to the corresponding section of the Bayh amendment and to § 901(a) as ultimately enacted. But § 1004 of Title X, like § 604 of Title VI, see 42 U.S.C. § 2000d–3, provided that nothing in Title X authorized action "by any department or agency with respect to any employment practice ... except where a

---

**15.** The headings and corresponding divisions of Senator Bayh's summary of his amendment do suggest, however, that the Senator's reference to "sections 1001–1005" in describing the prohibition of discrimination in federally funded education programs is of little significance. Although, as the dissent points out, § 1005 of the amendment comprised the Title VII provisions, the detailed discussion of the Title VII amendments in part B of the summary, the absence of any further mention of those provisions in part A's description of Title IX, and the fact that the Title VII provisions were not limited to "federally funded education programs" indicate that the Senator's reference to § 1005 in part A was inadvertent.

**16.** Moreover, in reply to Senator Pell's questions regarding Title IX's application to the faculty of religious and military schools, Senator Bayh made clear that such institutions were explicitly excepted from the reach of § 901(a). See 118 Cong.Rec. 5813 (1972). His response makes no sense if Senator Bayh thought that the provision was not aimed at protecting any employees; in that event, he could have answered Senator Pell's questions simply by stating that employment discrimination was dealt with in the Title VII and Equal Pay Act portions of the amendment, rather than in § 901.

primary objective of the Federal financial assistance is to provide employment." The debate on Title X included no discussion of this limitation. See 117 Cong.Rec. 39248–39263 (1971).

When the House and Senate versions of Title IX were submitted to the Conference Committee, § 1004 was deleted. The Conference Reports simply explained:

"[T]he House amendment, but not the Senate amendment, provided that nothing in the title authorizes action by any department or agency with respect to any employment practice of any employer, employment agency, or labor organization except where a primary objective of the Federal financial assistance is to provide employment. The House recedes." S.Conf.Rep.No.92–798, p. 221 (1972); H.R.Conf.Rep.No.92–1085, p. 221 (1972).

Expressly a conscious choice, therefore, the omission of § 1004 suggests that Congress intended that § 901 prohibit gender discrimination in employment.

Petitioners and the dissent contend, however, that § 1004 was deleted in order to avoid an inconsistency: Title IX included provisions relating to the Equal Pay Act, which obviously concerned employment, and § 1004 conflicted with those portions of the Act. See Sex Discrimination Regulations: Hearings before the Subcommittee on Postsecondary Education of the House Committee on Education and Labor, 94th Cong., 1st Sess., 409 (1975) (1975 Hearings) (remarks of Rep. O'Hara) (arguing that Title IX was a "cut and paste job," using "a Xerox" of Title VI, and that § 1004 "got in through a drafting error"). As the Court of Appeals observed, however, the Conference Committee could easily have altered the wording of § 1004 to make clear that its limitation applied only to § 901 or could have noted in the Conference Reports that the omission was necessitated by the apparent inconsistency. Instead, by stating that "[t]he House recedes," the Reports suggest that the Senate version of Title IX, which was intended to ban discriminatory employment practices, prevailed for substantive reasons. See Gulf Oil Corp. v. Copp Paving Co., 419 U.S. 186, 199–200 (1974) (deletion of a provision by a Conference Committee "militates against a judgment that Congress intended a result that it expressly declined to enact"). . . .

In our view, the legislative history thus corroborates our reading of the statutory language and verifies the Court of Appeals' conclusion that employment discrimination comes within the prohibition of Title IX.[21] . . .

### IV

[Discussion of the program-specific nature of Title IX's prohibition is omitted].

It is so ordered.

---

**21.** Thus, we do not, as the dissent charges, "rel[y] on legislative history to add omitted words. . . ." Rather, we use the legislative history as a guide to interpreting the "critical words" that Congress did include in Title IX. It is the dissent that uses the legislative history—of a different statute—to rewrite Title IX so as to restrict its reach.

■ JUSTICE POWELL, with whom THE CHIEF JUSTICE and JUSTICE REHNQUIST join, dissenting.

Title IX of the Education Amendments of 1972, 86 Stat. 373, as amended, 20 U.S.C. § 1681 et seq., prohibits discrimination on the basis of sex in education programs and activities receiving federal funds. In 1975, the Department of Health, Education, and Welfare (HEW) promulgated regulations prohibiting discrimination on the basis of gender in employment by fund recipients. 34 CFR § 106.51(a)(1). Today, the Court upholds the validity of these regulations. . . . Because I believe the Court's interpretation is neither consistent with the statutory language nor supported by its legislative history, I dissent.

### I

Although the Court begins with the language of the statute, it quotes the relevant language in its entirety only in the opening paragraphs of the opinion. In the section considering the statute's meaning, the Court quotes two words of the statute and paraphrases the rest, thereby suggesting an interpretation actually at odds with the language used in the statute. Thus, according to the Court, "[s]ection 901(a)'s broad directive that 'no person' may be discriminated against on the basis of gender appears, on its face, to include employees as well as students." This is not what the statutory language provides.

In relevant part, the statute states:

"No person in the United States shall, on the basis of sex, be excluded from participation in, be denied the benefits of, or be subjected to discrimination under any education program or activity receiving Federal financial assistance. . . ." Education Amendments of 1972, § 901(a), 20 U.S.C. § 1681(a).

A natural reading of these words would limit the statute's scope to discrimination against those who are enrolled in, or who are denied the benefits of, programs or activities receiving federal funding. It tortures the language chosen by Congress to conclude that not only teachers and administrators, but also secretaries and janitors, who are discriminated against on the basis of sex in employment, are thereby (i) denied participation in a program or activity; (ii) denied the *benefits* of a program or activity; or (iii) subject to discrimination *under* an education program or activity. Moreover, Congress made no reference whatever to employers or employees in Title IX, in sharp contrast to quite explicit language in other statutes regulating employment practices.[4] . . .

### II

### A

The Court acknowledges, as it must, that § 901 of Title IX "does not expressly include . . . employees." But it finds a strong negative inference

---

**4.** See, *e.g.*, 42 U.S.C. § 2000e–2(a) (Title VII: "[i]t shall be an unlawful employment practice for an employer–"); 29 U.S.C. § 206(d)(1) (Equal Pay Act: "[n]o employer having employees . . .").

in the fact that § 901 does not "exclude employees from its scope." The Court then turns to the legislative history for evidence as to whether or not § 901 was meant to prohibit employment discrimination. I agree with the several Courts of Appeals that have concluded unequivocally that the statutory language cannot fairly be read to proscribe employee discrimination. Only rarely may legislative history be relied upon to read into a statute operative language that Congress itself did not include. To justify such a reading of a statute, the legislative history must show clearly and unambiguously that Congress did intend what it failed to state. The Court's elaborate exposition of the history of Title IX falls far short of this standard.

Title IX originated in a floor amendment sponsored by Senator Bayh to Senate bill S. 659, 92d Cong., 2d Sess. (1972). The amendment was intended to close loopholes in earlier civil rights legislation; three problem areas had been identified in hearings by a special House Committee in 1970. Title VII of the Civil Rights Act of 1964, though generally barring employment discrimination on the basis of sex, race, religion, or national origin, did not apply to discrimination "with respect to the employment of individuals to perform work connected with the educational activities of [educational] institutions." And the Equal Pay Act of 1963 banned discrimination in wages on the basis of sex, 29 U.S.C. § 206(d)(1), but it did not apply to administrative, executive, or professional workers, including teachers. See 29 U.S.C. § 213(a)(1) (1970 ed.) (no longer in force). Finally, Title VI of the Civil Rights Act of 1964, 42 U.S.C. § 2000d, barred discrimination on the basis of "race, color, or national origin," but not sex, in any federally funded programs and activities.

The Bayh floor amendment, No. 874, introduced in 1972, closed these loopholes. Section 1005 amended Title VII to cover employment discrimination in educational institutions. Sections 1009–1010 amended the Equal Pay Act so that discrimination in pay on the basis of sex was barred, even for teachers and other professionals. And §§ 1001–1003 created a new Title IX banning discrimination on the basis of sex in federally funded *educational* programs and activities, thus effectively extending Title VI's prohibition to sex discrimination in such programs.

Since the amendments to Title VII and the Equal Pay Act explicitly covered discrimination in employment in educational institutions, there was no need to include §§ 1001–1003 of the Bayh amendment to proscribe such discrimination. Instead, Title IX presumably was enacted, as its language clearly indicates, to bar discrimination against beneficiaries of federally funded educational programs and activities. . . .

B

[A discussion of the relationship between Title VI, which does not proscribe discrimination in employment, and Title IX, is omitted.]

C

In concluding that the legislative history indicates Title IX was intended to extend to employment discrimination, the Court is forced to rely primarily on the statements of a single Senator.[11] The first statement is ambiguous. Senator Bayh did state that faculty employment would be covered by his amendment after mentioning the sections enacting Title IX but prior to any mention of those amending Title VII and the Equal Pay Act. Immediately thereafter, however, he stated that Title IX's enforcement powers paralleled those in Title VI. Yet Title VI has never provided for fund termination to redress discrimination in employment.

Next, the Court quotes Bayh's statements that (i) he regarded "sections 1001–1005" as "[c]entral to [his] amendment" and (ii) "[t]his portion of the amendment covers discrimination in all areas," including employment. But § 1005 of the Bayh Amendment is the section amending Title VII and thus §§ 1001–1005 cover employment discrimination regardless of whether Title IX does. Moreover, the Court uses an ellipsis rather than include the following words from the second Bayh statement:

> "Discrimination against the beneficiaries of federally assisted programs and activities is already prohibited by title VI of the 1964 Civil Rights Act, but unfortunately the prohibition does not apply to discrimination on the basis of sex. In order to close this loophole, my amendment sets forth prohibition and enforcement provisions which generally parallel the provisions of title VI." 118 Cong.Rec. 5807 (1972) (in ellipsis, *ante,* at 1920).

Thus, for a second time, Bayh indicated to the Senate that he regarded Title IX of his amendment as parallel to Title VI rather than as a substantial departure from Title VI.

In the third Bayh statement, the Senator was responding to a question from Senator Pell regarding Title IX, and the Court assumes that each sentence in that response refers to Title IX. But, [some of that response may have been directed to the amendment concerning Title VII and the Equal pay Act.]

Rather than supporting the Court's view, the legislative history accords with the natural reading of the statute. Title IX prohibits discrimination only against beneficiaries of federally funded programs and activities, not all employment discrimination by recipients of federal funds. Title IX is modeled after Title VI, which is explicitly so limited—and to the extent statements of Senator Bayh can be read to the contrary, they are ambiguous. . . .

### III

As the sole issue before us is the meaning of § 901(a) of Title IX, I repeat the relevant language:

> "No person in the United States shall, on the basis of sex, be excluded from participation in, be denied the benefits of, or be subjected to

---

**11.**  The most dependable sources of legislative intent are the reports of the responsible committees. Because Title IX is the result of a floor amendment, there is no explanation of its meaning in reports from the relevant House and Senate Committees.

discrimination under any education program or activity receiving Federal financial assistance...."

The Court acknowledges that, in view of the lack of support for its position in this language, it must look to the legislative history for evidence as to whether or not § 901 was meant to prohibit employment discrimination. Although the Court examines at length the truncated legislative history, it ignores other factors highly relevant to congressional intent: (i) whether the ambiguity easily could have been avoided by the legislative draftsman; (ii) whether Congress had prior experience and a certain amount of expertise in legislating with respect to this particular subject; and (iii) whether existing legislation clearly and adequately proscribed, and provided remedies for, the conduct in question. When these factors are considered, there is no justification for reading sex employment discrimination language into § 901.

If there had been such an intent, no competent legislative draftsman would have written § 901 as above set forth. The draftsman would have been guided, of course, by the employment-discrimination language in Title VII and the Equal Pay Act, language specifically addressing this problem. Moreover, although these other statutes had been enacted by an earlier Congress, at the time Title IX was being drafted and considered Title VII and the Equal Pay Act also were amended to proscribe explicitly employment discrimination in educational institutions on the basis of sex. Congress hardly would have enacted a third statute addressing this problem, but, in contrast to the other two, use language ambiguous at best.

In addition, a comparison of the provisions of Title VII and Title IX suggests that Congress would not have enacted the inconsistent provisions of the latter with respect to remedies and procedures. Title VII is a comprehensive antidiscrimination statute with carefully prescribed procedures for conciliation by the EEOC, federal-court remedies available within certain time limits, and certain specified forms of relief, designed to make whole the victims of illegal discrimination and available unless discriminatory conduct falls within one of several exceptions. See 42 U.S.C. § 2000e et seq. (1976 ed. and Supp.IV). This thoughtfully structured approach is in sharp contrast to Title IX, which contains only one extreme remedy, fund termination, apparently now available at the request of any female employee who can prove discrimination in employment in a federally funded program or activity. This cutoff of funds, at the expense of innocent beneficiaries of the funded program, will not remedy the injustice to the employee. Indeed, Title IX does not authorize a single action, such as employment, reemployment, or promotion, to rectify *employment* discrimination. And Title IX, unlike Title VII, has no time limits for action, no conciliation provisions, and no guidance as to procedure. Compare 20 U.S.C. § 1681 et seq. (Title IX) with 42 U.S.C. § 2000e *et seq.* (1976 ed. and Supp.IV) (Title VII). The Solicitor General conceded at oral argument that appropriate relief for the two employees who initiated this suit was available under Title VII....

In sum, the Court's decision today, finding an unarticulated intent on the part of Congress, is predicated on five perceptions of congressional action that I am unable to share: (i) that Congress neglectfully or forgetfully failed to include language in § 901 with respect to discrimination that would have made clear its intent; (ii) that Congress enacted a third statute proscribing sex discrimination in employment in educational institutions in the absence of any showing of a need for such duplicative legislation; (iii) that Congress failed to include in the third statute appropriate procedural and remedial provisions relevant to employment discrimination; (iv) that it vested the authority to enforce the third statute in HEW, a department that even the Solicitor General concedes lacks the experience and the qualifications to oversee and enforce employment legislation; and, (v) finally that in Title IX, it gave a new "remedy" for sex discrimination in employment, but did not make that remedy available to those discriminated against on the basis of race. . . .

---

The Court's decision in *Bell* relied on a variety of different forms of legislative history. In determining whether and to what extent to rely on legislative history as authoritative evidence of legislative intent or purpose, what criteria should courts use? Consider the traditional view of perhaps the most common forms of legislative history:

***1. Committee Reports***—The conventional wisdom has been that the most reliable form of legislative history consists of the reports prepared by the House and Senate committees, which accompany bills favorably reported to the chamber, and the conference committee reports which accompany the reconciled version of the House and Senate bills. Between the 1940s and the 1980s, it became commonplace for the Court to equate the views expressed in a committee report with the intent of Congress. *See, e.g.,* Thornburg v. Gingles, 478 U.S. 30, 43 n.7 (1986) (Brennan, J.) (plurality opinion) ("We have repeatedly recognized that the authoritative source for legislative intent lies in the Committee Reports on the bill.") (citing Garcia v. United States, 469 U.S. 70, 76 & n.3 (1984), and Zuber v. Allen, 396 U.S. 168, 186 (1969)); J.W. Bateson Co. v. United States *ex rel.* Bd. of Trs. of the Nat'l Automatic Sprinkler Indus. Pension Fund, 434 U.S. 586, 591 (1978) (observing that "the authoritative Committee Reports . . . squarely focus on the question at issue here" and "leave[] no room for doubt about Congress' intent"). Indeed, by 1953, Justice Frankfurter could remark: "Whatever we may think about the loose use of legislative history, it has never been questioned that reports of committees and utterances of those in charge of legislation constitute authoritative exposition of the meaning of legislation." Orloff v. Willoughby, 345 U.S. 83, 98 (1953) (Frankfurter, J., dissenting).

A nice illustration of this reliance on committee reports is the Court's decision in Steadman v. Securities and Exchange Commission, 450 U.S. 91 (1981). The substantive question in *Steadman* involved the standard of proof applied by an administrative agency, the Securities and Exchange Commission (SEC), in determining whether to penalize an investment adviser or securities broker alleged to have violated certain securities laws. The question was whether the standard of proof that the SEC had been applying was consistent with a statute called the Administrative Procedure Act (APA). Justice Brennan's majority opinion began with the assertion that "the task of determining the appropriate standard of proof in the instant case is one of discerning congressional intent." Although the Court explained that "[t]he search for congressional intent begins with the language of the statute," it found the "language of the statute [] somewhat opaque concerning the precise standard of proof to be used." The majority did not find this much of a problem, however, in light of its conclusion that "[t]he legislative history ... clearly reveals the Congress' intent," and in particular that "[a]ny doubt as to the intent of Congress is removed by the House [Committee] Report, which expressly adopted a preponderance-of-the-evidence standard."

The reliance on committee reports as evidence of congressional intent was not, however, completely uncontroversial. Well before the new textualist critique of legislative history, prominent scholars had questioned not only the reliance on committee reports, but the underlying intentionalist methodology on which that reliance was based. Consider Professor Max Radin's analysis of both the concept of "legislative intention" and the use of committee reports to discern it:

> That the intention of the legislature is undiscoverable in any real sense is almost an immediate inference from a statement of the proposition. The chances that of several hundred [legislators] each will have exactly the same determinate situations in mind as possible reductions of [an ambiguous statutory phrase], are infinitesimally small. The chance is still smaller that ... the litigated issue, will not only be within the minds of all these [legislators] but will be certain to be selected by all of them as the present limit to which the [ambiguous phrase] should be narrowed. In an extreme case, it might be that we could learn all that was in the mind of the draftsman, or of a committee of half a dozen men who completely approved of every word. But when this draft is submitted to the legislature and at once accepted without a dissentient voice and without debate, what have we then learned of the intentions of the four or five hundred approvers? Even if the contents of the minds of the legislature were uniform, we have no means of knowing that content except by the external utterances or behavior of these hundreds of [legislators], and in almost every case the only external act is the extremely ambiguous one of acquiescence, which may be motivated in literally hundreds of ways, and which by itself indicates little or nothing of the pictures which the statutory descriptions imply. It is not impossible that this knowledge could be obtained. But how probable it is, even venturesome mathematicians will scarcely undertake to compute.

Max Radin, *Statutory Interpretation*, 43 HARV. L. REV. 863, 870–71 (1930).

Radin's critique drew an immediate response from a variety of quarters. Perhaps the most prominent response, from Professor James Landis, asserted that rank-and-file legislators looked to the committees for their understanding of legislation:

> The assumption that the meaning of a representative assembly attached to the words used in a particular statute is rarely discoverable, has little foundation in fact. The records of legislative assemblies once opened and read with a knowledge of legislative procedure often reveal the richest kind of evidence. To insist that each individual legislator besides his aye vote must also have expressed the meaning he attaches to the bill as a condition precedent to predicating an intent on the part of the legislature, is to disregard the realities of legislative procedure. Through the committee report, the explanation of the committee chairman and otherwise, a mere expression of assent becomes in reality a concurrence in the expressed views of another.

James M. Landis, *A Note on "Statutory Interpretation,"* 43 Harv. L. Rev. 886, 888–89 (1930) (citations omitted); *see also* J.P. Chamberlain, *The Courts and Committee Reports*, 1 U. Chi. L. Rev. 81, 82 (1933) (contending that because Congress has assigned committees "the actual work" of establishing a factual basis for legislation and devising an appropriate remedy, "it is fair to assume that Congress has adopted as its intent the intent of the committee"). This theory was soon taken up in a famous opinion by Judge Learned Hand, one of the most respected jurists of the twentieth century, who wrote:

> It is of course true that members who vote upon a bill do not all know, probably very few of them know, what has taken place in committee. On the most rigid theory possibly we ought to assume that they accept the words just as the words read, without any background of amendment or other evidence as to their meaning. But courts have come to treat the facts more really; they recognize that while members deliberately express their personal position upon the general purposes of the legislation, as to the details of its articulation they accept the work of the committees; so much they delegate because legislation could not go on in any other way.

SEC v. Robert Collier & Co., 76 F.2d 939, 941 (2d Cir. 1935), *rev'd sub nom.* SEC v. Stock Mkt. Fin., 79 F.2d 1010 (2d Cir. 1935).

How warranted are the assumptions about committees expressed by Professor Landis and Judge Hand? At a minimum, wouldn't one want to know why rank-and-file members would wish to delegate to committees the authority to supply the details of legislative policy? Given that the responsible committees and their staffs take the lead in drafting legislation, wouldn't the implicit arrangement that Professor Landis discusses give committees something of a perverse incentive to leave ambiguity in the statutory text, which is voted on by the whole body and is often subject to amendment on the floor, while placing in the committee reports an increasing amount of statutory detail? *See* Daniel R. Ortiz, *The Self–Limitation of Legislative History: An Intrainstitutional Perspective*, 12 Int'l Rev. L. & Econ. 232, 233–34 (1992).

An alternative theory for judicial reliance on congressional committee reports was advanced by Professor Harry Wilmer Jones, who defended reliance on legislative history as the lesser of two evils in cases of statutory ambiguity: "[T]he choice before the judges is that they must either derive the meaning of a statute solely from its language and from conjecture as to its purposes, or must accept as the 'legislative intention' the understanding of the committee experts and other interested legislators really responsible for its formulation." Harry Wilmer Jones, *Extrinsic Aids in the Federal Courts*, 25 Iowa L. Rev. 737, 743 (1940). Accordingly, even if committees do not perfectly reflect the median legislator's preferences, as a matter of probability committee reports (and sponsors' statements) seemed to offer "the best available evidence" of the common legislative understanding of the way statutory words had been used in context. Harry Wilmer Jones, *Statutory Doubts and Legislative Intention*, 40 Colum. L. Rev. 957, 969 (1940). For a candid articulation of such a view by the Court, see United States v. O'Brien, 391 U.S. 367, 383–84 (1968) ("When the issue is simply the interpretation of legislation, the Court will look to statements by legislators for guidance as to the purpose of the legislature, because the benefit to sound decision-making in this circumstance is thought sufficient to risk the possibility of misreading Congress' purpose."). Notice that the foregoing articles, which established the intellectual basis for the growth of judicial reliance on legislative history, depend explicitly upon assumptions concerning legislative behavior. So too did the Court's practice. If the legitimacy of relying on committee reports depends on such essentially empirical assumptions, is it subject to disproof? For further discussion, *see* pp. 176–178, *infra*.

**2. Statements of Individual Legislators**—While committee reports are the most widely used and influential form of legislative history, courts sometimes draw inferences from the statements of individual legislators—particularly statements by a bill's sponsors, but also statements by rank-and-file members during floor debates, and colloquies between legislators and witnesses at committee hearings. The Court has drawn some clear distinctions concerning the weight it will attach to the statements of individual legislators made outside the context of an official committee report. The Court's practice concerning the use of individual legislator statements has, however, varied dramatically, even within a short time frame. Still, it is possible to make certain generalizations.

**a. Floor statements in general**—Although the Court's reliance on floor debates was not unheard of in the nineteenth century, its official position more often was that floor statements were not to be used. *See, e.g.*, United States v. Union Pac. R.R. Co., 91 U.S. 72, 79 (1875) ("In construing an act of Congress, we are not at liberty to recur to the views of individual members in debate, nor to consider the motives which influenced them to vote for or against its passage. The act itself speaks the will of Congress, and this is to be ascertained from the language used."); Aldridge v. Williams, 44 U.S. (3 How.) 9, 24 (1845). Indeed, on the eve of the twentieth century, the Court reiterated this position in strong terms:

All that can be determined from the debates and reports is that various members had various views, and we are left to determine the meaning of this act, as we determine the meaning of other acts, from the language used therein.

There is, too, a general acquiescence in the doctrine that debates in congress are not appropriate sources of information from which to discover the meaning of the language of a statute passed by that body.

The reason is that it is impossible to determine with certainty what construction was put upon an act by the members of a legislative body that passed it by resorting to the speeches of individual members thereof. Those who did not speak may not have agreed with those who did, and those who spoke might differ from each other; the result being that the only proper way to construe a legislative act is from the language used in the act, and, upon occasion, by a resort to the history of the times when it was passed.

United States v. Trans–Missouri Freight Ass'n, 166 U.S. 290, 318–19 (1897) (citations omitted).

Even at the height of its post–New Deal enthusiasm for legislative history, the Court placed relatively little weight on floor statements. In an influential concurring opinion, Justice Jackson thus wrote:

I think we should not go beyond Committee reports, which presumably are well considered and carefully prepared.... [T]o select casual statements from floor debates, not always distinguished for candor or accuracy, as a basis for making up our minds what law Congress intended to enact is to substitute ourselves for the Congress in one of its important functions.

Schwegmann Bros. v. Calvert Distillers Corp., 341 U.S. 384, 395–396 (1951) (Jackson, J., concurring). The idea that committee reports are more reliable than floor debates has been echoed in numerous other opinions as well. *See, e.g.,* Zuber v. Allen, 396 U.S. 168, 186 (1969) (stating that committee reports reflect "the considered and collective understanding of those Congressmen involved in drafting and studying proposed legislation," while "[f]loor debates reflect at best the understanding of individual Congressmen").

Notwithstanding those concerns, the Court has occasionally treated floor debates as useful evidence of legislative intent. The Court sometimes finds, for example, that the floor debates as a whole corroborate other evidence of meaning or demonstrate a widespread sense of the legislation's objectives. *See, e.g.,* Patsy v. Board of Regents, 457 U.S. 496, 503–04 (1982); Alyeska Pipeline Serv. Co. v. Wilderness Soc'y, 421 U.S. 240, 262 n.36 (1975). Consider the following statement about floor debates by Professor Harry Wilmer Jones:

A judge is certainly not bound to accept the construction put upon a statute by a legislator who may have been speaking only for himself, but as a judge he will surely have had sufficient experience in weighing evidence to enable him to make an accurate estimate of the degree to which a statement made during debate reflects the general understanding of the legislative body as a whole.

The discovered circumstance that no objection was taken to the construction placed upon a bill by a speaker in debate would be at least some evidence that the speaker's understanding of its meaning was shared by other members. If, moreover, a comparison of the several speeches made in debate on a measure indicates that each speaker was of the same belief as to the meaning or legal effect of the statute, that concordance would be highly persuasive evidence of a prevailing legislative judgment. The flat exclusionary rule, barring any introduction of the records of debate, would withhold from the consideration of the judges evidence of "intention" which might be of great assistance in difficult cases, especially when the other legislative sources are silent or conflicting.

Harry Wilmer Jones, *Extrinsic Aids in the Federal Courts*, 25 IOWA L. REV. 737, 751–52 (1940). Do Jones's remarks seem sound? Should judges determine the weight they will attach to floor debates based on the content of the particular statement, the identity of the speaker, and the context in which the statement is made? Do judges have the requisite knowledge of the subtleties of the legislative process to sort the wheat from the chaff?

And what of the fact that many "floor statements" found in the legislative history were never actually spoken during floor debates, or even uttered before the legislation passed? It turns out that for most of the post–*American Trucking* period of extensive judicial reliance on legislative history, members of Congress could freely insert floor statements into the record after the fact. *See* Note, *Why Learned Hand Would Never Consult Legislative History Today*, 105 HARV. L. REV. 1005, 1014 (1992). In 1978, Congress adopted a reform measure requiring that a "bullet" accompany a statement in the Congressional Record if the legislator had not read at least part of it from the floor, but members of Congress discovered various ingenious methods of circumventing the "bulleting" rule. Among other things, legislators could "avoid a bullet by delivering as little as one sentence of a speech on the floor and extending their remarks afterwards," and "clerks on the floor often ignore[d] the bulleting rule when specifically asked to by a member of Congress." OFFICE OF LEGAL POLICY, U.S. DEP'T OF JUSTICE, USING AND MISUSING LEGISLATIVE HISTORY: A RE-EVALUATION OF THE STATUS OF LEGISLATIVE HISTORY IN STATUTORY INTERPRETATION 54 (1989). Subsequent reforms sought to address those second-generation abuses:

In 1985, the House replaced the "bullet" system with a system in which legislators, while on the floor, asked for permission to revise and extend their remarks for the record. Material inserted under such permission was to be printed in different typeface from the substantially verbatim presentation of the representatives' remarks made on the floor of the House. In 1995, the Republican majority in the House of Representatives again changed the rules for compiling the Congressional Record to reduce further representatives' power to edit their remarks.

Bernard W. Bell, *R–E–S–P–E–C–T: Respecting Legislative Judgments in Interpretive Theory*, 78 N.C. L. Rev. 1253, 1319 (2000) (citation omitted). How much does the trend toward more accurate documentation of what was actually said during floor debates help judges seeking to use legislative history as an interpretive resource? Even if a judge can tell which statements were actually spoken on the floor, how can a judge ascertain after the fact who agreed with the statements made?

***b. Statements made during hearings***—A similar set of questions arise with respect to statements made by legislators and witnesses during a committee's hearings on a bill. The Court has frequently expressed deep suspicion about the probative value of statements made during hearings that did not make it into the official committee reports. *See, e.g.,* Kelly v. Robinson, 479 U.S. 36, 51 n.13 (1986); S & E Contractors, Inc. v. United States, 406 U.S. 1, 13 n.9 (1972). Despite these expressions of skepticism, the post–New Deal Supreme Court consulted hearings for various purposes, often to reinforce inferences drawn from other legislative history or to show what problems or circumstances had been brought to Congress's attention when it was considering a bill. *See, e.g.,* Gwaltney of Smithfield, Ltd. v. Chesapeake Bay Found., Inc., 484 U.S. 49, 61 (1987); Japan Whaling Ass'n v. American Cetacean Soc'y, 478 U.S. 221, 226 (1986).

Consider the following reasons why testimony at hearings may shed light on statutory meaning: (1) Hearing transcripts may disclose the problems, factual circumstances, and legal assumptions that witnesses brought to the attention of the drafters; (2) Hearings may reveal the political dynamics leading up to the proposal and adoption of a bill, including the role of the executive branch in bringing about the legislation; (3) Hearing transcripts may contain the expressed views of key legislators (including the committee chair) who took the lead in framing the legislation. Does the relevance of such considerations depend on whether rank-and-file members of Congress were aware of the content of the hearing testimony when they voted? Does it matter whether the hearing testimony is, in some sense, "cooked"—that is, worked out in advance between the witnesses and key members of the committee and their staff? Consider Professor Reed Dickerson's comments on this score:

> What is said at [committee] hearings is so unreliable, even when it appears to make good sense, that courts should pay little heed to it, except possibly for confirmatory purposes. It tends to be highly adversarial, but without even the elementary safeguards for balance that our judicial system provides. As for witnesses, the cards are likely to be heavily stacked in favor of the proponents of the bill. There are few guarantees of thoroughness. Nor is such material reasonably available to the legislative audience.

Reed Dickerson, *Dipping into Legislative History*, 11 Hofstra L. Rev. 1125, 1131 (1983) (citations omitted). Given that the responsible committees typically prepare committee reports that set forth the factual, legal, and policy grounds for the committee's decision, why would the Court ever choose to rely on hearings as a proxy for the committee's understanding?

*c. Sponsors' statements*—Sponsors' statements have a unique status among statements by individual Members. The Court has described the views of sponsors or floor managers as weighty, or even authoritative. *See, e.g.,* Schwegmann Bros. v. Calvert Distillers Corp., 341 U.S. 384, 394–95 (1951) ("It is the sponsors that we look to when the meaning of the statutory words is in doubt."). The Court's rationales for giving special weight to sponsors' statements are straightforward and bear strong resemblance to the rationales for crediting committee reports. First, if the sponsor or floor manager has taken the lead in framing legislation, his or her statements may offer an especially well-informed view of the factual, legal, or policy context in which it was drafted. *See, e.g.,* Jacobus tenBroek, *Admissibility of Congressional Debates in Statutory Construction by the United States Supreme Court*, 25 CAL. L. REV. 326, 329 n.20 (1937). Second, such statements may be entitled to special weight "because the sponsors are the Members of Congress most likely to know what the proposed legislation is all about, and other Members can be expected to pay heed to their characterizations of the legislation." William N. Eskridge, Jr., *The New Textualism*, 37 UCLA L. REV. 621, 638 (1990). In other words, rank-and-file members may develop a practice of deferring to sponsors, thereby effectively delegating to them the authority to explain the bill authoritatively.

On the other hand, might sponsors' statements be even more susceptible to opportunistic manipulation than are committee reports, which at least require negotiation among the diverse interests represented on the committees? The Court has never given sponsors' statements quite the authoritative status that it has conferred on committee reports. *See, e.g.,* CPSC v. GTE Sylvania, Inc., 447 U.S. 102, 118 (1980) ("[O]rdinarily even the contemporaneous remarks of a single legislator who sponsors a bill are not controlling in analyzing legislative history."). Why should the views of a bill's sponsor merit *any* special weight, absent some implicit agreement among rank-and-file legislators to accord them such weight?

*3. Successive Versions of a Statute*—In *Bell*, the Court gave interpretive significance to the deletion of a provision during the House–Senate conference. When, if ever, should a Court take into account the changes made during the drafting process when trying to figure out the meaning of the enacted text? Many influential commentators have argued that changes to draft bills during the legislative process, as well as rejections of proposed changes, should carry essentially no weight. Professor Max Radin thus wrote:

> Successive drafts of a statute are not stages in its development. They are separate things of which we can only say that they followed each other in a definite sequence, and that one was not the other. But that fact gives us little information about the final form, since we never really know why one gave way to any other. There were doubtless many reasons, some of them likely enough to be personal, arbitrary, and capricious—the fondness of the draftsman for a special locution, his repugnance to another, a misconception of the associations of some

word, a chance combination, and often enough a mere inadvertence. That is not to say that some conclusions, principally negative ones, can not be drawn from the legislative history of a statute. But in the end, all that we know is that the final form displaced the others, and that fact is not disputed.

Max Radin, *Statutory Interpretation*, 43 Harv. L. Rev. 863, 873 (1930); *see also* Reed Dickerson, The Interpretation and Application of Statutes 160 (1975) (footnotes omitted) ("Although often relied on by courts for help in interpreting or applying statutes, the nonadoption or rejection of a proposed amendment to a pending bill is a circumstance that, standing alone, is normally inadequate as a basis for inferring legislative intent.... [B]eing consistent with many possible explanations, it has little probative value for interpretation."). This skeptical view of statutory drafting history may have had some impact even during the post–New Deal period. *See, e.g.,* Gemsco, Inc. v. Walling, 324 U.S. 244, 261–63 (1945).

But perhaps the claim that one can learn *nothing* from successive drafts of a bill, or from rejected amendments or alternatives, is overly broad. As Judge Hand once argued, if a bill is "changed in a most significant way," and a court can discern a reason for the change that makes sense of the enacted text, then to disregard such evidence would be "the last measure of arid formalism." SEC v. Robert Collier & Co., 76 F.2d 939, 941 (2d Cir. 1935). The Court has generally found it uncontroversial to consider changes in wording in successive versions of a bill, whether those changes were effected through floor amendments or through reconciliation by a conference committee. *See, e.g.,* Pacific Gas & Elec. Co. v. State Energy Res. Conservation & Dev. Comm'n, 461 U.S. 190, 220 (1983); Busic v. United States, 446 U.S. 398, 406 n.11 (1980); United States v. Great N. Ry. Co., 287 U.S. 144, 155 (1932). Still, even if one accepts that changes can sometimes be probative, there is reason for caution. As one commentator put it: "[A] bill as originally introduced may have been amended with the mere intention of making the same statutory direction more clear and understandable.... Similarly, an amendment may have been rejected as unnecessary rather than as an unwise alteration of the legislative policy." Harry Wilmer Jones, *Extrinsic Aids in the Federal Courts*, 25 Iowa L. Rev. 737, 756 (1940). If that assessment is correct, does the probative value of successive drafts depend on the reasons that legislators offer in support of their amendments? If so, does the legitimacy of reliance on successive drafts mirror the debate over the legitimacy of relying on explanations of individual legislators?

***4. Subsequent Legislative Action (or Inaction)***—Sometimes courts have considered legislative activity (or inactivity) *after* the enactment of a contested statutory provision to determine what that provision means. It is not clear whether this potential interpretive resource is properly categorized as "legislative history," but we include it here because, like more conventional forms of legislative history, when courts look to so-called "post-enactment legislative history," they are drawing inferences about the meaning of enacted text from legislative choices other than the choice to enact that text.

The most common form of post-enactment legislative history involves alleged legislative *acquiescence* in a judicial or administrative construction of a statutory provision. Suppose that a statute is ambiguous—it could mean $X$ or $Y$. Shortly after its enactment, a court or an administrative agency charged with implementing the statute declares that the better reading of the statute is $X$. Several years pass, and eventually a case comes before a court in which a litigant argues that the best reading of the statute is $Y$, not $X$. Suppose that the court is inclined to agree with that claim, as $Y$ is the most natural reading of the text, given the context and other indicia of semantic meaning. Nonetheless, the court might conclude that $X$ is the proper interpretation. Why? If the earlier interpretation was issued by a court, one reason for adhering to interpretation $X$ is the ordinary principle of *stare decisis*—the idea the courts should be reluctant to overturn precedents, in order to preserve legal stability and predictability. But in the context of statutory interpretation, there may be an additional reason to adhere to the prior decision: If Congress has persistently refused to overturn the prior judicial or administrative decision, this may amount to an implicit legislative judgment that the prior interpretation was correct, at least if there is reason for Congress to be aware of the precedent in question. *See, e.g.*, Flood v. Kuhn, 407 U.S. 258, 283–84 (1972) (refusing "to overturn [certain] cases judicially when Congress, by its positive inaction, has allowed those decisions to stand for so long and, far beyond mere inference and implication, has clearly evinced a desire not to disapprove them legislatively"); *see also* Johnson v. Transportation Agency, Santa Clara County, Cal., 480 U.S. 616, 629 n.7 (1987). Courts are also apt to find such legislative acquiescence if Congress has "considered, but not enacted, legislation" that would have overturned that precedent in whole or part. United States v. Johnson, 481 U.S. 681, 686 n.6 (1987).

In recent cases, the Court has shown growing skepticism of acquiescence arguments. In Central Bank of Denver v. First Interstate Bank of Denver, 511 U.S. 164 (1994), for example, the Court exemplified its new attitude by stating:

> [O]ur observations on the acquiescence doctrine indicate its limitations as an expression of congressional intent. "It does not follow ... that Congress' failure to overturn a statutory precedent is reason for this Court to adhere to it. It is 'impossible to assert with any degree of assurance that congressional failure to act represents' affirmative congressional approval of the [courts'] statutory interpretation.... Congress may legislate, moreover, only through the passage of a bill which is approved by both Houses and signed by the President. See U.S. CONST., art. I, § 7, cl. 2. Congressional inaction cannot amend a duly enacted statute." Patterson v. McLean Credit Union, 491 U.S. 164, 175, n.1 (1989) (quoting Johnson v. Transportation Agency, Santa Clara Cty., 480 U.S. 616, 672 (1987) (SCALIA, J., dissenting)); see Helvering v. Hallock, 309 U.S. 106, 121 (1940) (Frankfurter, J.) ("[W]e

walk on quicksand when we try to find in the absence of corrective legislation a controlling legal principle").

*Id.* at 186 (alterations in original) (citations omitted). Which approach reflects a more plausible understanding of the legislative process? How important is the fact that it is very difficult to enact new legislation? Couldn't there be countless reasons that prevent Congress from overturning an interpretation that it disfavors? Other matters might sit higher on the legislative agenda; a gatekeeping committee might bottle up override legislation that had majority support in both Houses; or an override bill might become a pawn in legislative negotiations over unrelated legislation. The legislative acquiescence argument might be particularly problematic when the relevant judicial precedents were issued by the courts of appeals rather than the Supreme Court, as Congress might be less aware of, or less concerned about, a lower court's construction of a statute. *See* Amy Coney Barrett, *Statutory Stare Decisis in the Courts of Appeals*, 73 GEO. WASH. L. REV. 317 (2005).

While these objections have force, might there nonetheless be sound reasons for courts to draw at least modest inferences from Congress's failure to disapprove or modify interpretive decisions? If one thinks of the life of a statute as an ongoing process in which the courts, Congress, and federal administrative agencies act collaboratively in the implementation of legislation for which they share responsibility, why shouldn't congressional failure to react count as a positive signal concerning the interpretations advanced by those who administer the law? *See* Peter L. Strauss, *On Resegregating the Worlds of Statute and Common Law*, 1994 SUP. CT. REV. 429, 512–13. Would the objection to relying on inaction in that situation be purely formal? If so, would it be persuasive?

A variant on the "legislative acquiescence" situation may arise when Congress reenacts a piece of legislation that has been authoritatively interpreted by a court or agency, or extensively amends such legislation without overturning the prior interpretation, or enacts substantially identical language in a new statute. When this occurs, it is sometimes taken to be a *ratification* of the prior interpretation. *See* Bragdon v. Abbott, 524 U.S. 624, 644–45 (1998); Herman & McClean v. Huddleston, 459 U.S. 375, 385–86 (1983); Lorillard v. Pons, 434 U.S. 575, 580–81 (1978). Ratification is thought to be less controversial than acquiescence because it is the product of an affirmative act of legislation. But is the empirical basis for ratification much sounder than the one underlying acquiescence? When Congress enacts a large and complex piece of regulatory legislation that happens to contain a previously interpreted word or phrase, is there reason to believe that a constitutionally sufficient majority is aware of the judicial or administrative opinions interpreting such a phrase? What do you think is more likely—that key Members of Congress know the contents of legislative history, or that they know how a court or agency has previously interpreted a particular word or phrase in a regulatory statute?

## B.  THE TEXTUALIST CRITIQUE OF LEGISLATIVE HISTORY

By the 1970s, legislative history had become perhaps *the* central focus of the Court's statutory interpretation jurisprudence. Beginning in the mid–1980s, the new textualists—most prominently, Justice Scalia and Judge Easterbrook—questioned the utility of legislative history as a window into collective legislative intent and raised constitutional concerns rooted in Article I, Section 7's bicameralism and presentment requirements, as well as a somewhat vaguer conception that judges impermissibly acquire added policymaking discretion by relying on legislative history. *See generally* Philip P. Frickey, *From the Big Sleep to the Big Heat: The Revival of Theory in Statutory Interpretation*, 77 MINN. L. REV. 241 (1992). The following cases illustrate the new textualist critique of the traditional use of legislative history:

---

## Blanchard v. Bergeron

Supreme Court of the United States
489 U.S. 87 (1989)

■ JUSTICE WHITE delivered the opinion of the Court.

[A jury awarded Blanchard $10,000 in damages on his claim that a sheriff's deputy had deprived him of his civil rights under 42 U.S.C. § 1983. The district court awarded Blanchard $7,500 in attorney's fees under 42 U.S.C. § 1988, which provides that a court, "in its discretion, may allow . . . a reasonable attorney's fee" to a prevailing party in federal civil rights actions under § 1983. The court of appeals reduced the fee award to $4,000, ruling that petitioner's 40% contingent-fee arrangement with his lawyer served as a cap on fees.]

### II

Section 1988 provides that the court, "in its discretion, may allow . . . a reasonable attorney's fee." The section does not provide a specific definition of "reasonable" fee, and the question is whether the award must be limited to the amount provided in a contingent-fee agreement. The legislative history of the Act is instructive insofar as it tells us: "In computing the fee, counsel for prevailing parties should be paid, as is traditional with attorneys compensated by a fee-paying client, 'for all time reasonably expended on a matter.'" S.Rep. No. 94–1011, p. 6 (1976).

In many past cases considering the award of attorney's fees under § 1988, we have turned our attention to Johnson v. Georgia Highway Express, Inc., [488 F.2d 714, 718 (5th Cir. 1974),] a case decided before the enactment of [Section 1988]. . . . *Johnson* provides guidance to Congress' intent because both the House and Senate Reports refer to the 12 factors set forth in *Johnson* for assessing the reasonableness of an attorney's fee award.[5] The Senate Report, in particular, refers to three District Court decisions that "correctly applied" the 12 factors laid out in *Johnson.*

In the course of its discussion of the factors to be considered by a court in awarding attorney's fees, the *Johnson* court dealt with fee arrangements:

> " 'Whether or not [a litigant] agreed to pay a fee and in what amount is not decisive. Conceivably, a litigant might agree to pay his counsel a fixed dollar fee. This might be even more than the fee eventually allowed by the court. Or he might agree to pay his lawyer a percentage contingent fee that would be greater than the fee the court might ultimately set. Such arrangements should not determine the court's decision. The criterion for the court is not what the parties agree but what is reasonable.' " 488 F.2d, at 718 (quoting Clark v. American Marine Corp., 320 F.Supp. 709, 711 (ED La.1970), aff'd 437 F.2d 959 (CA5 1971)).

Yet in the next sentence, *Johnson* says, "In no event, however, should the litigant be awarded a fee greater than he is contractually bound to pay, if indeed the attorneys have contracted as to amount." This latter statement, never disowned in the Circuit, was the basis for the decision below. But we doubt that Congress embraced this aspect of *Johnson*, for it pointed to the three District Court cases in which the factors are "correctly applied." Those cases clarify that the fee arrangement is but a single factor and not determinative. In Stanford Daily v. Zurcher, 64 F.R.D. 680 (ND Cal. 1974), aff'd 550 F.2d 464 (CA9 1977), rev'd on other grounds, 436 U.S. 547 (1978), for example, the District Court considered a contingent-fee arrangement to be a factor, but not dispositive, in the calculation of a fee award. In Davis v. County of Los Angeles, [8 EPD ¶ 9444 (CD Cal. 1974)], the court permitted a fee award to counsel in a public interest firm which otherwise would have been entitled to no fee. Finally, in Swann v. Charlotte–Mecklenburg Board of Education, 66 F.R.D. 483 (WDNC 1975), the court stated that reasonable fees should be granted regardless of the individual plaintiff's fee obligations. *Johnson*'s "list of 12" thus provides a useful catalog of the many factors to be considered in assessing the reasonableness of an award of attorney's fees; but the one factor at issue here, the attorney's private fee arrangement, standing alone, is not dispositive.

The *Johnson* contingency-fee factor is simply that, a factor. The presence of a pre-existing fee agreement may aid in determining reasonableness.... But as we see it, a contingent-fee contract does not impose an

---

**5.** The 12 factors set forth by the *Johnson* court for determining fee awards under § 706(k) of Title VII of the Civil Rights Act of 1964 are: (1) the time and labor required; (2) the novelty and difficulty of the questions; (3) the skill requisite to perform the legal service properly; (4) the preclusion of other employment by the attorney due to acceptance of the case; (5) the customary fee; (6) whether the fee is fixed or contingent; (7) time limitations imposed by the client or the circumstances; (8) the amount involved and the results obtained; (9) the experience, reputation, and ability of the attorneys; (10) the "undesirability" of the case; (11) the nature and length of the professional relationship with the client; and (12) awards in similar cases.

automatic ceiling on an award of attorney's fees, and to hold otherwise would be inconsistent with the statute and its policy and purpose.... 

■ Justice Scalia, concurring in part and concurring in the judgment.

I concur in the judgment and join the opinion of the Court except that portion which rests upon detailed analysis of the Fifth Circuit's opinion in Johnson v. Georgia Highway Express, Inc., 488 F.2d 714 (1974), and the District Court decisions in Swann v. Charlotte–Mecklenburg Board of Education, 66 F.R.D. 483 (WDNC 1975); Stanford Daily v. Zurcher, 64 F.R.D. 680 (ND Cal. 1974); and Davis v. County of Los Angeles, 8 EPD ¶ 9444 (CD Cal. 1974). The Court carefully examines those opinions, separating holding from dictum, much as a lower court would study our opinions in order to be faithful to our guidance. The justification for this role reversal is that the Senate and House Committee Reports on the Civil Rights Attorney's Fees Awards Act of 1976 referred approvingly to Johnson, and the Senate Report alone referred to the three District Court opinions as having "correctly applied" Johnson. The Court resolves the difficulty that Johnson contradicts the three District Court opinions on the precise point at issue here by concluding in effect that the analysis in Johnson was dictum, whereas in the three District Court opinions it was a holding. Despite the fact that the House Report referred only to Johnson, and made no mention of the District Court cases, the Court "doubt[s] that Congress embraced this aspect of Johnson, for it pointed to the three District Court cases in which the factors are 'correctly applied.' "

In my view Congress did no such thing. Congress is elected to enact statutes rather than point to cases, and its Members have better uses for their time than poring over District Court opinions. That the Court should refer to the citation of three District Court cases in a document issued by a single committee of a single house as the action of Congress displays the level of unreality that our unrestrained use of legislative history has attained. I am confident that only a small proportion of the Members of Congress read either one of the Committee Reports in question, even if (as is not always the case) the Reports happened to have been published before the vote; that very few of those who did read them set off for the nearest law library to check out what was actually said in the four cases at issue (or in the more than 50 other cases cited by the House and Senate Reports); and that no Member of Congress came to the judgment that the District Court cases would trump Johnson on the point at issue here because the latter was dictum. As anyone familiar with modern-day drafting of congressional committee reports is well aware, the references to the cases were inserted, at best by a committee staff member on his or her own initiative, and at worst by a committee staff member at the suggestion of a lawyer-lobbyist; and the purpose of those references was not primarily to inform the Members of Congress what the bill meant (for that end Johnson would not merely have been cited, but its 12 factors would have been described, which they were not), but rather to influence judicial construction. What a heady feeling it must be for a young staffer, to know that his or her citation of obscure district court cases can transform them into the law of the land, thereafter dutifully to be observed by the Supreme Court itself.

I decline to participate in this process. It is neither compatible with our judicial responsibility of assuring reasoned, consistent, and effective application of the statutes of the United States, nor conducive to a genuine effectuation of congressional intent, to give legislative force to each snippet of analysis, and even every case citation, in committee reports that are increasingly unreliable evidence of what the voting Members of Congress actually had in mind. By treating *Johnson* and the District Court trilogy as fully authoritative, the Court today expands what I regard as our cases' excessive preoccupation with them—and with the 12–factor *Johnson* analysis in particular.... Except for the few passages to which I object, today's opinion admirably follows our more recent approach of seeking to develop an interpretation of the statute that is reasonable, consistent, and faithful to its apparent purpose, rather than to achieve obedient adherence to cases cited in the committee reports. I therefore join the balance of the opinion.

---

## Continental Can Company, Inc. v. Chicago Truck Drivers, Helpers and Warehouse Workers Union

U.S. Court of Appeals for the Seventh Circuit
916 F.2d 1154 (7th Cir. 1990)

■ Easterbrook, Circuit Judge.

Would a company whose customer paid 50.1% of the bill think it had received "substantially all" of the price? Not likely. Nonetheless, Continental Can Company insists that when a majority of a pension fund's assets come from firms engaged in the trucking business, contributing employers qualify for a treatment that is available only if "substantially all of the contributions required under the plan are made by employers primarily engaged in the long and short haul trucking industry", 29 U.S.C. § 1383(d)(2).

"Substantially all" sounds like "less than all, but not much less". Arbitrators and courts must convert this phrase to a percentage in order to make it work, which raises the question why Congress did not enact a percentage in the first place. It is easy to write "a majority" or "two thirds" or "three quarters" or 85% or $e^{-0.162}$ as it is to write "substantially all"—and any of the former choices would have prevented disputes of this kind. Perhaps, however, "substantially all" is an attractive standard because it enables Members of Congress to say different things to different interest groups. The genesis of § 1383(d)(2) ... suggests something of this kind—although it is also consistent with the possibility that the sponsor pulled the wrong language out of his pocket.

On May 22, 1980, the House unanimously passed H.R. 3904, its bill to establish a system of withdrawal liability for under-funded pension plans. This bill lacked an exclusion for the trucking industry. Many of that industry's plans are chronically under-funded. . . . When the Senate's Labor and Human Resources and Finance Committees reported the Senate equivalent of H.R. 3904 to the floor on July 24, 1980, the bill had a special rule for the trucking business, in exactly the language that became § 4203(d)(2). The report accompanying the bill did not discuss the meaning of "substantially all".

The House accepted most of the Senate's amendments to H.R. 3904. Representative Thompson, the floor manager, commented on this particular change:

> The [Senate] bill also contains a special withdrawal liability rule for certain trucking industry plans where substantially all of the contributions are made by employers primarily engaged in the long and short haul trucking industry, the household goods moving industry or the public warehousing industry. The phrase "substantially all" appears in several provisions of the tax laws—including the industrial development bond and the private foundation rules—where the Internal Revenue Service has interpreted the phrase to mean at least 85 percent. It is our intent that, as used in this special trucking industry withdrawal liability rule, the substantially all requirement would only be satisfied where at least 85 percent of the contributions to the plan are made by employers who are primarily engaged in the specified industries.

The House passed the legislation unanimously the same day.

One day later the Senate also passed H.R. 3904. . . . In a text sandwiched between two "speeches" marked by a ● (indicating that the remarks were inserted after the debate rather than delivered on the floor) Sen. Durenberger explained why special treatment for the trucking industry is appropriate and added:

> [I]t should be observed that if the majority of the contributions to any pension plan are made by employers engaged in over the road (long) and short haul trucking . . . this withdrawal liability procedure will apply to all employers who contribute to such a plan.

This remark, coming after both House and Senate had agreed to the language of § 4203(d)(2), is the first time anyone implied that "substantially all" means "majority".

Because the House was unwilling to accept all of the Senate's further amendments, the chambers held a conference. Section 4203(d)(2), language common to the two versions, was not mentioned in the Conference Committee's report. On September 26, 1980, President Carter signed the bill into law. That was not, however, the end of Senator Durenberger's efforts to explain his amendment. On November 19, 1980, the Senator inserted into the Congressional Record still another bulleted statement:

> Recently . . . I found out that on the very day that I clarified the intent of this special withdrawal liability procedure for the trucking industry, Mr. Thompson told the House of Representatives that this special rule would only apply if at least 85 percent of the contributions

to the plan were made by employers previously engaged in the specified industries. Mr. Thompson based his statement upon unrelated interpretations of the phrase "substantially all."

Since this amendment originated in the Senate without Mr. Thompson's participation, I am amazed that he would undertake an interpretation of the intent of the language.

My interpretation was based on information supplied to me as to the diversity of Teamster representation, and I am convinced that an 85–percent contribution requirement would emasculate the special withdrawal procedure.

Therefore, as a final clarification, I will reiterate that the withdrawal liability procedure will apply to any multiemployer pension plan in the trucking industry if the majority (50.1 percent) of contributions to the plan are made by employers who are primarily engaged in the long-and short-haul trucking industry, the household goods moving industry, or the public warehousing industry.

Representative Thompson did not file a surrebuttal, perhaps thinking that the race is to the swift—for he had gotten his thoughts into the record before the House voted, while Senator Durenberger's two statements came after the Senate first adopted § 4203(d)(2), and the Senator's second statement came nearly two months after the bill became law.

Although Senator Durenberger was "amazed" that anyone would dare to interpret language he had not written, we do not view Representative Thompson's speech as an exercise in temerity. The Senate amended H.R. 3904 and wanted the House to accept its revisions. Members of the House were entitled to form their own understanding of the language before deciding whether to enact it. Words do not have meanings given by natural law. You don't have to be Ludwig Wittgenstein or Hans–Georg Gadamer to know that successful communication depends on meanings shared by interpretive communities. Texts are addressed to readers, in this case initially to the Representatives. Authors' private meanings—meanings subjectively held but not communicated—do not influence the readers' beliefs. The Senate, and then the House, and the Senate once again, passed § 4203(d)(2) without knowing Senator Durenberger's belief that "substantially all" means 50.1%. At the time the President signed the bill, Rep. Thompson's specific statement of August 25 and Sen. Durenberger's vague one of August 26 were the only ones on paper. Representative Thompson's was in line with a frequent meaning of the phrase and must have supplied the meaning for the bulk of Members and the President, if the phrase was ever present to their minds. That is why statements after enactment do not count; the legislative history of a bill is valuable only to the extent it shows genesis and evolution, making "subsequent legislative history" an oxymoron.

Continental Can presses on us an extreme version of the belief that the "real" law lies in the "intent" of Congress, of which the words of the statute are just evidence. It is an extreme version because here the only intent is the author's; Continental Can wants us to disregard the intent of all the other Members of Congress and the President, even though their assent was necessary to put Sen. Durenberger's text into force. But we need not worry about whether the argument is modest or extreme, because its premise is wrong. The text of the statute, and not the private intent of the legislators, is the law. Only the text survived the complex process for proposing, amending, adopting, and obtaining the President's signature (or two-thirds of each house). It is easy to announce intents and hard to enact laws; the Constitution gives force only to what is enacted. So the text is law and legislative intent a clue to the meaning of the text, rather than the text being a clue to legislative intent.

"Substantially all" may have a special meaning. Statutes contain words of art, whose meaning may appear strange to a lay reader. "Substantially all" is one of those phrases with a special legal meaning. Congress uses it all the time in tax statutes, and the Internal Revenue Service decodes it as meaning 85%.... *All* of the regulations we could find, not just substantially all, quantify this phrase as 85% or more....

Because language is an exercise in shared understanding, one Senator's idiosyncratic meaning does not count. This was the point of the exchange between Alice and Humpty Dumpty. If everyone accepts a new meaning for a word, then the language has changed; if one speaker chooses a private meaning, we have babble rather than communication.

The question, then, is whether anyone other than Senator Durenberger used "substantially all" to signify 50.1% rather than 85%. Nothing in the debates suggests that they did. Representative Thompson's statement, the only one delivered on the floor in advance of passage, shows that he at least (and likely the House) used the phrase in the customary way. Senator Durenberger's two comments, inserted in the Congressional Record after the fact, could not have influenced anyone in the House and probably did not come to the attention of anyone in the Senate; anyway it was too late. Efforts of this kind to change the meaning of a text without bothering to change the text itself demonstrate why the use of legislative history has come under such vigorous attack.... If Senator Durenberger wanted to see whether his colleagues would agree to an amendment exempting funds the majority of which came from the trucking industry, he had only to propose words such as "majority" or "50.1%" or "more than half" or "most". Instead he chose a formula with a known meaning and tipped into the Congressional Record a novel interpretation. Perhaps he believed that language expressly using a preponderance-of-the-assets standard would not have been enacted but he expected the federal courts to accept the legislative "history". Perhaps instead he meant to propose an amendment saying "majority" but slipped, and did the best he could later on to convey what he had meant to propose. Either way, what Congress enacted, as opposed to what Sen. Durenberger wishes it had enacted, means 85%....

---

**1. The Formalist Argument: Legislative History Is Not Law—** Justice Scalia's partial concurrence in *Blanchard* and Judge Easterbrook's

*Continental Can* opinion are illustrative of the new textualists' critique of the use of legislative history. The textualists' rejection of legislative history as a means of discerning legislative intent stems in large measure from their rejection of the idea that there is any meaningful or legitimate notion of "legislative intent" beyond the "objectified intent" manifest in the semantic meaning of the words of the statute that Congress enacted. Textualists argue that only the text of the statute, not the subjective intentions of individual legislators, is the law. As Justice Scalia succinctly declared in a 1993 concurring opinion:

> The greatest defect of legislative history is its illegitimacy. We are governed by laws, not by the intentions of legislators. As the Court said in 1844: "The law as it passed is the will of the majority of both houses, *and the only mode in which that will is spoken is in the act itself....*".

Conroy v. Aniskoff, 507 U.S. 511, 519 (1993) (Scalia, J., concurring in the judgment) (quoting Aldridge v. Williams, 44 U.S. (3 How). 9, 24 (1845) (emphasis added by Justice Scalia)). Legislative history thus lacks legitimacy because it has not gone through the constitutionally mandatory processes of bicameral passage by the House and Senate and presentment to the President for approval or veto, as required by Article I, § 7 (*see* pp. 22–25, *supra*).

In a series of opinions and articles, Judge Easterbrook gave a common-sensical twist to this theme. Consider the following explanation of the legitimacy deficit associated with reliance on legislative history as authoritative evidence of legislative intent:

> [T]he technique [of using legislative history to discern legislative intent] assumes that intentions are "the law." Why are they? If we took an opinion poll of Congress today on a raft of issues and found out its views, would those views become the law? Certainly not. They must run the gamut of the process—and process is the essence of legislation. That means committees, fighting for time on the floor, compromise because other members want some unrelated objective, passage, exposure to veto, and so on....
>
> Yet the whole process of interpretation from intent is an end run around [this] process. It is a translation from intent to law that we would find repulsive if proposed explicitly. Imagine how we would react to a bill that said, "From today forward, the result of any opinion poll among members of Congress shall have the effect of law." We would think the law a joke at best, unconstitutional at worst. This silly "law" comes uncomfortably close, however, to the method by which courts deduce the content of legislation when they look to subjective intent.

Frank H. Easterbrook, *The Role of Original Intent in Statutory Construction*, 11 HARV. J. L. & PUB. POL'Y 59, 64–65 (1988) (citations omitted). *See also In re* Sinclair, 870 F.2d 1340, 1342–44 (7th Cir. 1989); Frank H. Easterbrook, *What Does Legislative History Tell Us?*, 66 CHI.-KENT L. REV. 441, 445 (1990).

Is this objection persuasive? Critics of modern textualism contend that the textualists' bicameralism-and-presentment argument misunderstands why and how judges consult legislative history. Typical of this line of argument is then-Judge Breyer's famous critique of the textualists' objection to legislative history's legitimacy:

> The "statute-is-the-only-law" argument misses the point. No one claims that legislative history is a statute, or even that, in any strong sense, it is "law." Rather, legislative history is helpful in trying to understand the meaning of the words that do make up the statute or the "law." A judge cannot interpret the words of an ambiguous statute without looking beyond its words for the words have simply ceased to provide univocal guidance to decide the case at hand. Can the judge, for example, ignore a dictionary or the historical interpretive practice of the agency that customarily applies some words? Is a dictionary or an historic agency interpretive practice "law?"

Stephen Breyer, *On the Uses of Legislative History in Interpreting Statutes*, 65 S. CAL. L. REV. 845, 863 (1992). Does Judge Breyer have a point? Certainly, textualists rely on all sorts of extrinsic, unenacted materials to interpret statutes. They rely on unenacted dictionaries to establish ordinary meaning, unenacted case law to establish the technical meaning of common law terms of art, unenacted background interpretive conventions and presumptions, and other unenacted extrinsic sources. If those extrinsic sources do not offend Article I, § 7, why would legislative history create difficulties?

Then again, given the way that judges use legislative history, is it fully satisfying to say that the courts don't treat legislative history as enacted text? Consider *Blanchard*, in which the question was what constitutes a "reasonable attorney's fee" for purposes of 42 U.S.C. § 1988. The Court equated that open-ended "reasonableness" standard with the Fifth Circuit's highly detailed twelve-factor *Highway Express* test for calculating attorney's fees owed to a prevailing plaintiff. Since the twelve-factor test did not represent the well-settled technical meaning of a term of art, the Court's sole basis for ascribing that meaning to § 1988 was because the Senate and House committees declared that they intended the statute to have that meaning. In effect, the Court treated the text of the committee reports as the authoritative source of the statute's policy details. How does that differ from treating legislative history as equivalent to statutory text? Of course, even if legislative history was misused in *Blanchard*, does that necessarily mean that the use of legislative history is *always* illegitimate?

**2.  *Does Judicial Use of Legislative History Facilitate Circumvention of Article I?***—Textualists have responded to the argument that they rely on unenacted dictionaries or other extrinsic sources of meaning by asserting that legislative history is qualitatively different from other extrinsic aids because *legislative actors* are responsible for generating legislative history, and may often do so with the primary or sole intent of influencing judicial interpretation. Perhaps, then, the principal concern with legislative history is not so much that it is unenacted, but that legislators and interest groups may deliberately use legislative history as a way to *circumvent* the Article I, § 7 process.

This concern is a favorite theme of many textualists, who argue that parochial interest groups often induce legislators to create favorable legislative history to achieve private-interest goals that the groups would not be able to persuade the entire Congress to endorse. As Judge Buckley put it, "to the degree that judges are perceived as grasping at any fragment of legislative history for insights into congressional intent, to that degree will legislators be encouraged to salt the legislative record with unilateral interpretations of statutory provisions they were unable to persuade their colleagues to accept." International Bhd. of Elec. Workers, Local Union No. 474 v. NLRB, 814 F.2d 697, 717 (D.C. Cir. 1987) (IBEW) (Buckley, J., concurring). *See also* Frank H. Easterbrook, *Text, History, and Structure in Statutory Interpretation*, 17 HARV. J.L. & PUB. POL'Y 61, 61 (1994) ("These clues [in the legislative history] are slanted, drafted by the staff and perhaps by private interest groups."); Kenneth W. Starr, *Observations about the Use of Legislative History*, 1987 DUKE L.J. 371, 376 ("Lobbyists maneuver to get their clients' opinions into the mass of legislative materials . . . .").

How do we know if the textualists' empirical assertions about legislative history are accurate? Certainly they are true some of the time. But if the textualists are correct that committee reports are rife with surreptitious attempts to circumvent the views of the chamber as a whole, why does the chamber tolerate this behavior by deferring so extensively to the committees? Does it make sense to presume instead that, as long as the committee reports were published and available to Congress prior to the final vote on a piece of legislation, the rank-and-file members implicitly endorsed those reports? *See* Jonathan R. Siegel, *The Use of Legislative History in a System of Separated Powers*, 53 VAND. L. REV. 1457 (2000). After all, because Congress lacks the capacity to identify and agree as a body on all the details of complex legislation, rank-and-file legislators may tacitly agree to leave the details of the meaning of legislation to be determined by committees and sponsors. *See, e.g.*, SEC v. Robert Collier & Co., 76 F.2d 939, 941 (2d Cir. 1935) (Hand, J.) (recognizing that "while members [of Congress] deliberately express their personal position upon the general purposes of the legislation, as to the details of its articulation they accept the work of the committees; so much they delegate because legislation could not go in any other way"); HENRY J. FRIENDLY, *Mr. Justice Frankfurter and the Reading of Statutes*, in BENCHMARKS 196, 216 (1967) (deeming it "very likely most [legislators] knew only of the general purpose [of a piece of legislation], relied for the details on members who sat on the committees particularly concerned, and were quite willing to adopt these committees' will on subordinate points as their own").

Can judicial use of legislative history—particularly committee reports—be justified on this "delegation" theory? Consider the following exchange between Justice Stevens and Justice Scalia in Bank One Chicago v. Midwest Bank & Trust Co., 516 U.S. 264 (1996). In a concurrence,

Justice Stevens responded to the new textualists' empirical claims about the reliability of committee reports as indicia of legislative intent as follows:

> Legislators, like other busy people, often depend on the judgment of trusted colleagues when discharging their official responsibilities. If a statute . . . has bipartisan support and has been carefully considered by committees familiar with the subject matter, Representatives and Senators may appropriately rely on the views of the committee members in casting their votes. In such circumstances, since most Members are content to endorse the views of the responsible committees, the intent of those involved in the drafting process is properly regarded as the intent of the entire Congress.

*Id.* at 276–77. Justice Scalia's partial concurrence took issue with this argument:

> [A]ssuming Justice STEVENS is right about this desire to leave details to the committees, the very first provision of the Constitution forbids it. Article I, § 1, provides that "[a]ll legislative Powers herein granted shall be vested in a Congress of the United States, which shall consist of a Senate and a House of Representatives." It has always been assumed that these powers are nondelegable—or, as John Locke put it, that legislative power consists of the power "to make laws, . . . not to make legislators." No one would think that the House of Representatives could operate in such fashion that only the broad outlines of bills would be adopted by vote of the full House, leaving minor details to be written, adopted, and voted upon only by the cognizant committees. Thus, if legislation consists of forming an "intent" rather than adopting a text (a proposition with which I do not agree), Congress cannot leave the formation of that intent to a small band of its number, but must, as the Constitution says, form an intent of the *Congress*. There is no escaping the point: Legislative history that does not represent the intent of the whole Congress is nonprobative; and legislative history that does represent the intent of the whole Congress is fanciful.

*Id.* at 280 (Scalia, J., concurring in part and concurring in the judgment) (alteration in original) (citations omitted). Justice Scalia's position, in other words, is that even if Congress wished to make a tacit assignment of law-elaboration authority to committees, the Constitution prohibits such arrangements. Where does Justice Scalia's position come from? Is he saying that it is unconstitutional for courts to rely on legislative history or for legislators to produce it with the expectation that courts will use it for purposes of interpretation? Is it purely a formalistic argument, or is Justice Scalia correct that legislative self-delegation (to committees or sponsors) presents particular cause for concern about the circumvention of Article I, Section 7? *See* John F. Manning, *Textualism as a Nondelegation Doctrine*, 97 COLUM. L. REV. 673 (1997).

**3. *Is Collective Legislative Intent a Coherent Concept?*—**In addition to arguing that judicial consideration of subjective legislative intent is illegitimate, the new textualists have made much of the claim that subjective legislative intent is simply an incoherent concept because legislatures, as collective bodies, do not have an "intent." Even if every individual participant in the legislative process has some intent in enacting a particular statute, their intents still may be quite different even if they vote for the same statutory text. This means that trying to figure out what "the legislature wanted" (or would have wanted) by looking to indicia of *individual* legislative preferences is hopeless and misleading.

The basic insight has its roots in the Marquis de Condorcet's famous demonstration, in his 1785 *Essay on the Application of Analysis to the Probability of Majority Decisions*, that it may not be possible to use majority rule to aggregate individual preferences into a consistent collective choice. A version of Condorcet's Paradox is as follows: Suppose three legislators have to choose among three options (*A*, *B*, and *C*), and suppose the legislators have the following preferences:

Legislator 1: *A* is better than *B*, which is better than *C*;

Legislator 2: *B* is better than *C*, which is better than *A*;

Legislator 3: *C* is better than *A*, which is better than *B*.

Which outcome, *A*, *B*, or *C*, is preferred by the "majority"? It's impossible to say. A majority prefers *A* to *B*, and *B* to *C*, but a majority also prefers *C* to *A*. This does not necessarily mean that these three legislators could not make a decision. There may be some procedure that determines which alternatives can be proposed, and in which order. But if an ambiguous statute emerges from this process—say, a statute that could mean *A*, *B*, or *C*—we cannot try to resolve the ambiguity by asking which outcome the legislature "intended" or "preferred." Likewise, suppose the text of the statute seems to imply meaning *C*, but a litigant cites legislative history indicating that Legislators 1 and 2 preferred *B* to *C*. Is that a reason to reject interpretation *C* in favor of interpretation *B*? Clearly not: Even though a majority of legislators preferred *B* to *C*, a majority also preferred *A* to *B*, and *C* to *A* (and so on).

This insight was subsequently developed and generalized by a branch of economics called "social choice theory," which studies how individual preferences are aggregated into collective decisions. Particularly important were the seminal contributions of Professor Kenneth Arrow, who demonstrated that there is no non-dictatorial collective choice mechanism that always satisfies certain minimal criteria for rationality. *See* KENNETH J. ARROW, SOCIAL CHOICE AND INDIVIDUAL VALUES (Yale Univ. Press 1963) (1951). The idea that legislatures, as collective entities, do not have a single "intent" was hardly new. *See, e.g.*, Max Radin, *Statutory Interpretation*, 43 HARV. L. REV. 863, 870 (1930). But textualists picked up on the social choice theorists' more rigorous analysis of the problem to develop a thoroughgoing critique of the notion of congressional intent. In Judge Easterbrook's words:

> Although legislators have individual lists of desires, priorities, and preferences, it turns out to be difficult, sometimes impossible, to aggregate these lists into a coherent collective choice. Every system of voting has flaws. The one used by legislatures is particularly dependent

on the order in which decisions are made. Legislatures customarily consider proposals one at a time and then vote them up or down. This method disregards third or fourth options and the intensity with which legislators prefer one option over another. Additional options can be considered only in sequence, and this makes the order of decision vital. It is fairly easy to show that someone with control of the agenda can manipulate the choice so that the legislature adopts proposals that only a minority support. The existence of agenda control makes it impossible for a court—even one that knows each legislator's complete table of preferences—to say what the whole body would have done with a proposal it did not consider in fact.

Frank H. Easterbrook, *Statutes' Domains*, 50 U. CHI. L. REV. 533, 547–48 (1983) (citations omitted). It follows that even if a committee or sponsor indicates a given preference on an issue left opaque by the statute as adopted, one cannot reason straightforwardly from that evidence to the outcome that the legislature would have reached collectively.

How powerful is this critique? Are you persuaded that it makes no sense to try to discern the intent or purpose of the legislature, with legislative history or any other source, because there is no such thing as collective intent—that is, because Congress is a "they," not an "it"? *See* Kenneth A. Shepsle, *Congress Is a "They," Not an "It": Legislative Intent as Oxymoron*, 12 INT'L REV. L. & ECON. 239 (1992). One response to this critique is that even though it may *sometimes* be impossible to aggregate individual preferences into a coherent majority decision in a non-arbitrary way, this is not invariably true. Imagine, for example, that in the example given above, Legislators 1 and 2 had the same preferences, preferring $A$ to $B$ to $C$. Couldn't we then say that the legislature preferred $A$ to $B$ to $C$? Does the coherence of the concept of collective legislative intent depend on whether the problematic situations identified by Condorcet, Arrow, and other theorists are frequently present in real legislatures?

Furthermore, Professors Farber and Frickey have suggested that the impossibility of coherent collective choice under "pure" majority rule strengthens rather than undermines the case for looking to at least certain forms of legislative history. If "pure majority rule is incoherent," they argue, then the outputs of our legislative process must be understood in light of the filtering procedures that Congress has put in place to aggregate its preferences into a meaningful collective decision. DANIEL A. FARBER & PHILIP P. FRICKEY, LAW AND PUBLIC CHOICE: A CRITICAL INTRODUCTION 61 (1991). In other words, if committees make legislation possible, then a reasonable interpretive theory may permit, perhaps even require, courts to heed committees' expressed understanding of the legislation they have put forward pursuant to their agenda-setting authority.

Professors Matthew McCubbins, Roger Noll, and Barry Weingast (who write collectively under the name of McNollgast) have offered another route to the same conclusion. They suggest that legislative committees, sponsors, and floor managers speak as agents of the congressional majority and have an incentive to represent the majority's intentions regarding the legislation that these key actors are managing. If they use legislative history to adopt an outlying position not subscribed to by the majority, these actors—who, like other legislators, are repeat players—will be penalized and mistrusted by the leadership in future legislative projects:

> In practice, political actors have two routes to enforce truthfulness. First, members who prevaricate can be and occasionally are removed from gatekeeping positions, such as party leadership or committee chairs. Second, because Congress passes a very large number of legislative provisions each year, the same member is likely to be in a position of delegated authority on many occasions. To succeed in accomplishing numerous legislative objectives over a lifetime in politics, a legislator will find it valuable to develop a reputation for not taking strategic advantage when acting as an agent for other members.

McNollgast, *Legislative Intent: The Use of Positive Political Theory in Statutory Interpretation*, LAW & CONTEMP. PROBS., Winter 1994, at 3, 26.

Are you persuaded? If we accept the claim that there is no such thing as the "majority" preference, but instead only individual preferences that must be aggregated according to some arbitrary set of agenda-setting and decisionmaking rules, does this weaken the case for judicial use of legislative history, or strengthen it? Or does it make no difference whatsoever?

### 4. *The Probative Value of Legislative History*—Textualists' main arguments against legislative history emphasize the illegitimacy and incoherence (in their view) of any concept of a "legislative intent" other than the objectified intent manifest in the statutory text, read in context. In addition to these in-principle objections, textualists also argue that even if there were such a thing as the collective intent of the legislature, and even if such collective intent were legally relevant, courts still should not look to legislative history because legislative history is unreliable and possibly misleading. Indeed, as Justice Scalia's *Blanchard* concurrence and Judge Easterbrook's panel opinion in *Continental Can* make clear, textualists believe that even the forms of legislative history traditionally thought to be most authoritative—committee reports and sponsors' statements—do not supply reliable information, and may supply misinformation. As Justice Scalia has written:

> [The view expressed in the committee reports] does not necessarily say anything about what Congress as a whole thought. Assuming that all the members of the ... Committees in question ... actually adverted to the interpretive point at issue here—which is probably an unrealistic assumption—and assuming further that they were in *unanimous* agreement on the point, they would still represent less than two-fifths of the Senate, and less than one-tenth of the House. It is most unlikely that many Members of either Chamber read the pertinent portions of the Committee Reports before voting on the bill—assuming (we cannot be sure) that the Reports were available before the vote....
>
> All we know for sure is that the full Senate adopted the text that we have before us here, as did the full House, pursuant to the

procedures prescribed by the Constitution; and that that text, having been transmitted to the President and approved by him, again pursuant to the procedures prescribed by the Constitution, became law.

Wisconsin Pub. Intervenor v. Mortier, 501 U.S. 597, 620–21 (1991) (Scalia, J., concurring in the judgment). Justice Scalia argues that committee reports are an unreliable guide to congressional intent for two closely related reasons. First, the views of committee members are not representative of the chamber as a whole; and, second, rank-and-file Members of Congress do not constructively embrace the committee's views as their own when they vote for legislation—indeed, the committee's views are unlikely to inform how rank-and-file members interpret the legislation before they vote on it.

Note that both of these arguments rest in part on empirical claims about how Congress operates. Take the first claim—that the views of the members of the committees with jurisdiction over a given bill are unlikely to be representative of the views of the chamber. Part of the idea here is simply the observation that the committees consist of fewer members than the chamber as a whole. But the claim of non-representativeness goes farther than that: Textualists suggest that committee members are likely to be "preference outliers," with views that diverge quite substantially from the chamber. Why might this be? First, as some political scientists suggest, Members of Congress self-select onto committees where they (or their constituents) have particularly intense policy interests. Thus a disproportionate number of representatives from farm states serve on the Agriculture Committee, representatives with military bases in their districts are more likely to sit on the Armed Services Committee, and so forth. *See, e.g.,* Kenneth A. Shepsle & Barry R. Weingast, *The Institutional Foundations of Committee Power*, 81 AM. POL. SCI. REV. 85 (1987); Barry R. Weingast & William J. Marshall, *The Industrial Organization of Congress; or, Why Legislatures, Like Firms, Are Not Organized as Markets*, 96 J. POL. ECON. 132 (1988). Second, interest groups with a particular stake in certain issue areas may form relationships with the relevant committees that are close—perhaps too close—and can exert sway over those committees that exceeds their sway over the chamber as a whole.

There is, however, an alternative image of congressional committees. This image—associated with the more traditional judicial approach to legislative history—views committees more favorably, as subgroups of the chamber that have developed specialized expertise in certain subject areas. On this view, committees are likely to be reasonably representative of the chamber, and even if there is some divergence between committee preferences and chamber preferences, the chamber benefits sufficiently from the committee's specialization that this "non-representativeness" is not much of a problem. *See* David P. Baron, *Legislative Organization with Informational Committees*, 44 AM. J. POL. SCI. 485 (2000); Thomas W. Gilligan & Keith Krehbiel, *Organization of Informative Committees by a Rational Legislature*, 34 AM. J. POL. SCI. 531 (1990). A number of political scientists have investigated the question whether committees tend to be preference outliers or tend to be reasonably representative of the parent chamber. This has proven to be a very challenging question to answer empirically, and the results are mixed. *See, e.g.,* Richard L. Hall & Bernard Grofman, *The Committee Assignment Process and the Conditional Nature of Committee Bias*, 84 AM. POL. SCI. REV. 1149 (1990); John Londregan & James M. Snyder, Jr., *Comparing Committee and Floor Preferences*, 19 LEGISLATIVE STUD. Q. 233 (1994). How much does or should the question of whether judges should look to committee reports turn on this unsettled empirical question?

The second element of the textualists' critique of the reliability of committee reports as evidence of statutory meaning is the claim that rank-and-file legislators are unlikely ever to read the committee report. Justice Scalia emphasized this claim in the excerpt from *Wisconsin Public Intervenor* quoted above, and other textualist judges have echoed the argument. *See, e.g.,* Wallace v. Christensen, 802 F.2d 1539, 1560 (9th Cir. 1986) (en banc) (Kozinksi, J., concurring in the judgment) ("Reports are usually written by staff or lobbyists, not legislators; few if any legislators read the reports; they are not voted on by the committee whose views they supposedly represent, much less by the full Senate or House of Representatives . . . ."). How accurate is this characterization of legislative behavior? Judge Posner has argued, to the contrary, that, at least when a bill is complex and technical, legislators are more likely to base their votes on the legislative history than on the language of the bill itself:

> Legislative history is in bad odor in some influential judicial quarters, but . . . in the case of statutory language as technical and arcane as that of [an international corporate tax statute's] provisions, the slogan that Congress votes on the bill and not on the report strikes us as pretty empty. Even advised by his personal staff a member of Congress would have great difficulty figuring out the purport of [the statutory provision at issue] without the aid of the committee reports. If he (or his staff) cannot rely on them as a guide to the meaning of the statute, we are not sure what he is supposed to do.

Archer–Daniels–Midland Co. v. United States, 37 F.3d 321, 323–24 (7th Cir. 1994) (Posner, C.J.) (citation omitted). Other observers of the legislative process have echoed Judge Posner's observation, arguing that if rank-and-file members (or their staffs) read anything before deciding how to vote on a piece of legislation, they are at least as likely to read the committee report as the bill itself. If true, what implications follow? Does this observation undercut the textualist claim that committee reports are an unreliable guide to the views of the chamber? Does it make any difference that, whether they have read the bill, the legislative history, or neither, the legislators ultimately vote for the bill but do not vote for the legislative history?

**5.  *Does Legislative History Expand Judicial Discretion?*—**Part of the new textualists' objection to legislative history was connected to a more general anxiety about "judicial activism"—a concern about judges' going beyond the legitimate exercise of judicial discretion, using an overly loose and undisciplined form of "interpretation" to implement their own views of sound public policy at the expense of the legislative and executive branches. Many textualists view the practice of referring to legislative history as facilitating this sort of activism. Justice Scalia in particular has emphasized that, with complex modern statutes, legislative history will be so vast and varied that it will give judges considerable discretion to select the outcome they prefer as a policy matter:

> On balance, [legislative history] has facilitated rather than deterred decisions that are based upon the courts' policy preferences, rather than neutral principles of law. Since there are no rules as to how much weight an element of legislative history is entitled to, it can usually be either relied upon or dismissed with equal plausibility. If the willful judge does not like the committee report, he will not follow it; he will call the statute not ambiguous enough, the committee report too ambiguous, or the legislative history (this is a favorite phrase) "as a whole, inconclusive." It is ordinarily very hard to demonstrate that this is false so convincingly as to produce embarrassment.... In any piece of major legislation, the legislative history is extensive, and there is something for everybody. As Judge Harold Leventhal used to say, the trick is to look over the heads of the crowd and pick out your friends.

Antonin Scalia, *Common–Law Courts in a Civil–Law System: The Role of the United States Federal Courts in Interpreting the Constitution and Laws, in* A MATTER OF INTERPRETATION 3, 35–36 (Amy Gutmann ed., 1997); *see also* Frederick Schauer, *Statutory Interpretation and the Coordinating Function of Plain Meaning*, 1990 SUP. CT. REV. 231 (discussing the use of plain meaning as a common point of reference that limits interpretive discretion).

Critics of textualism, however, have resisted the claim that judges are more constrained when they eschew use of legislative history. First, critics insist that the relative elasticity of language gives willful judges just as much leeway to reach results they desire, rather than results intended by Congress, when the judges purport to rely only on the semantic meaning of the text. *See, e.g.*, William N. Eskridge, Jr., *Textualism: The Unknown Ideal?*, 96 MICH. L. REV. 1509, 1533–35 (1998) (book review); Philip P. Frickey, *Wisdom on* Weber, 74 TUL. L. REV. 1169, 1180–81 (2000); A. Raymond Randolph, *Dictionaries, Plain Meaning, and Context in Statutory Interpretation*, 17 HARV. J.L. & PUB. POL'Y 71 (1994). Second, they argue that legislative history may, on balance, constrain rather than liberate judges: If a statute is genuinely ambiguous, doesn't a court's ability to consult an authoritative committee report or sponsor's statement ensure that some form of *legislative* signal will resolve the ambiguity, rather than the judge's own conception of which interpretation better completes the statutory scheme? *See* James J. Brudney & Corey Ditslear, *Liberal Justices' Reliance on Legislative History: Principle, Strategy, and the Scalia Effect*, 29 BERKELEY J. EMP. & LAB. L. 117, 158–60 (2008). A related point is that if courts look to legislative history, it is easier for Congress to specify in greater detail the policies it wishes to adopt at lower bargaining costs than it would take to embed them in the text. *See, e.g.,* Jerry L. Mashaw, *Textualism, Constitutionalism, and the Interpretation of Federal Statutes*, 32 Wm. & Mary L. Rev. 827, 836–37 (1991). Do the legislative history-rich decisions excerpted above, and elsewhere in this chapter, make this tool of construction appear more constraining or more liberating for the judges? If legislative history is, in fact, used to specify a degree of statutory detail that the legislature would not otherwise be able to achieve through the cumbersome process of bicameralism and presentment, does that lend credence to textualist concerns about the circumvention of that process? *See* John F. Manning, *Lawmaking Made Easy*, 10 Green Bag 2d 191 (2007).

**6. *Legislative History and Congressional Expectations*—**Textualists have never suggested that their proposed revision of how courts use legislative history be applied only prospectively—that is, only to cases involving statutes enacted after the sought-after abandonment of the use of legislative history as a tool of construction. Does this create a bait-and-switch problem? Consider what Professors Eskridge and Ferejohn have said about the necessarily complementary relationship between legislators and courts:

> When legislators vote on statutes or logroll to cement statutory deals and compromises, they are assuming consequences they expect statutes to have in the world.... Because these consequences depend on how statutes are interpreted by courts and agencies, legislator assumptions involve their understanding of how courts and agencies will go about interpreting statutes.

William N. Eskridge, Jr. & John Ferejohn, *Politics, Interpretation, and the Rule of Law, in* Nomos XXXVI: The Rule of Law 265, 273 (Ian Shapiro ed., 1994). This premise, moreover, is reflected in the Court's well-established presumption "that Congress legislates with knowledge of our basic rules of statutory construction." McNary v. Haitian Refugee Ctr., Inc., 498 U.S. 479, 496 (1991). In light of those principles, consider the following point:

> From the 1940's until at least the late 1980's, Congress could rely on the federal courts' receptivity to legislative intent expressed in what the courts had viewed as the more authoritative and reliable sources of legislative history—primarily, committee reports and statements of officials actively involved in the legislative effort [such as sponsor's statements]. Ignoring the legislative history of [a statute enacted during that period] ... violate[s] the interpretive regime that had been in place ... when Congress adopted the ... statute.

Philip P. Frickey, *Interpretive–Regime Change*, 38 Loy. L.A. L. Rev. 1971, 1982 (2005). Does this observation counsel in favor of a strong principle of *stare decisis* with respect to principles of statutory interpretation? *See* Sydney Foster, *Should Courts Give Stare Decisis Effect to Statutory Interpretation Methodology*, 96 Geo. L.J. 1863 (2008). Does it suggest that, for textualism to be persuasive, it must ultimately rest upon constitutional arguments that are capable of overcoming entrenched legislative expectations?

*7. Legislative History and Judicial Decision Costs*—Recently, Professor Adrian Vermeule has provided a fundamentally different theoretical foundation for textualism generally, and for the rejection of legislative history more specifically. Rather than engage in formalistic or empirical debates about the legitimacy or probative value of legislative history, Professor Vermeule attempts to break conceptual and empirical stalemates over high-level theories of statutory interpretation by introducing into the equation what he describes as "lower-level institutional analysis," much of it rooted in modern decision theory. With respect to competing claims about the reliability of legislative history as evidence of intended statutory meaning, Professor Vermeule concludes that attempts to test the relative merits of different approaches empirically would be "daunting," perhaps intractable. It is simply impossible to tell whether judicial reliance on legislative history averts more error than it causes, or vice versa. Professor Vermeule then argues that in the face of such "severe uncertainty," judges should eschew legislative history for the simple reason that "the costs of legislative-history research and litigation to courts and parties ... are high." If we don't know whether legislative history will help or hurt on the merits, we might as well not waste time considering it. ADRIAN VERMEULE, JUDGING UNDER UNCERTAINTY: AN INSTITUTIONAL THEORY OF LEGAL INTERPRETATION 192–195 (2006).

Is that persuasive? Professor Vermeule is surely right that claims about the impact of reliance on legislative history on the accuracy of judicial decisionmaking are speculative at best. Does it follow that courts should dispense with the practice? Should one apply that principle more generally, using the lowest-cost method of decisionmaking whenever the efficacy of more costly methods is extremely uncertain? Is Professor Vermeule's claim that the empirical arguments about the effects of legislative history are hopelessly stalemated itself an empirical claim? For in-depth assessments of Professor Vermeule's intriguing approach, see, e.g., William N. Eskridge, Jr., *No Frills Textualism*, 119 HARV. L. REV. 2041 (2006) (book review); Caleb Nelson, *Statutory Interpretation and Decision Theory*, 74 U. CHI. L. REV. 329 (2007) (book review).

## C. THE NEW SYNTHESIS

Both proponents and opponents of the use of legislative history have made substantial cases for their positions, and reasonable people can surely differ about how much, and in what manner, judges should rely upon legislative history to interpret statutes. At a minimum, it is fair to say that in contrast with the state of the legal culture a quarter-century ago, the utility of legislative history as a source of statutory meaning is no longer taken for granted. To put the point more strongly, while lawyers still cite legislative history and most judges still use it, the Supreme Court today would generally try to ascertain first whether the statutory text speaks clearly to an issue and would not typically or uncritically treat legislative history as the primary indicium of legislative intent or statutory meaning. As Professor Philip Frickey has written:

Justice Scalia's arguments have had some effect upon the Supreme Court. The Court is less likely to cite legislative history today, and when it does, the citations seem less important to the outcome. The Court pays careful attention to statutory text and is much more likely than in earlier eras to use dictionaries to assist in constructing textual meaning.

Philip P. Frickey, *Revisiting the Revival of Theory in Statutory Interpretation: A Lecture in Honor of Irving Younger*, 84 MINN. L. REV. 199, 205 (1999). This observation has been substantiated by a number of empirical studies of judicial decisionmaking. Although the techniques for measuring the relevant phenomena are inevitably rough, most studies suggest that the new textualism has had a pronounced—but incomplete—influence on how federal courts decide statutory interpretation cases. Most notably, over the last quarter-century the Supreme Court and the federal courts of appeals have reduced their reliance on legislative history, which is cited much less often than it was in the early 1980s, and have placed greater emphasis on the text and on sources of semantic meaning, like dictionaries. *See, e.g.,* James J. Brudney & Corey Ditslear, *The Decline and Fall of Legislative History?*, 89 JUDICATURE 220 (2006); Michael H. Koby, *The Supreme Court's Declining Reliance on Legislative History: The Impact of Justice Scalia's Critique*, 36 HARV. J. ON LEGIS. 369, 386–87 (1999); Thomas W. Merrill, Essay, *Textualism and the Future of the* Chevron *Doctrine*, 72 WASH. U. L.Q. 351, 356 (1994); Samuel A. Thumma & Jeffrey L. Kirchmeier, *The Lexicon Has Become a Fortress: The United States Supreme Court's Use of Dictionaries*, 47 BUFF. L. REV. 227, 252–60 (1999). *But see* Frank B. Cross, Essay, *The Significance of Statutory Interpretive Methodologies*, 82 NOTRE DAME L. REV. 1971, 1979–88 (2007); Jane S. Schacter, *The Confounding Common Law Originalism in Recent Supreme Court Statutory Interpretation: Implications for the Legislative History Debate and Beyond*, 51 STAN. L. REV. 1 (1998); Charles Tiefer, *The Reconceptualization of Legislative History in the Supreme Court*, 2000 WIS. L. REV. 205.

What accounts for the new textualism's influence on statutory interpretation practice, and in particular its impact on the use of legislative history? Part of the effect might be due simply to the fact that a number of the Justices appointed in the 1980s and early 1990s (particularly Justices Scalia, Kennedy, and Thomas) use legislative history parsimoniously or not at all. *See* Brudney & Ditslear, *supra*, at 222–23. Furthermore, these Justices—especially Justice Scalia—have been steadfast in their refusal to join any opinion, or any part of an opinion, that relies on legislative history. On a closely divided Court, this can have a powerful effect on citation practices. As Professor Thomas Merrill has observed:

> Justice Scalia's practice of refusing to join any part of another Justice's opinion that relies on legislative history. . . . means that in any case in which another Justice needs the vote of Justice Scalia to form a majority or controlling opinion, the writing Justice knows that if legislative history is employed he or she will lose majority status with respect to at least a portion of the opinion. The arrival of Justice

Thomas, who has taken up a similar stance, effectively doubles Justice Scalia's voting clout in this regard.

On the other side of the ledger.... neither Justice Stevens nor any other Justice has adopted a policy of declining to join any opinion that *fails* to ground statutory interpretation in a conception of legislative purpose derived from legislative history. The simple logic of coalition building thus points powerfully toward suppression of legislative history: two sure votes lost if you use it, no votes necessarily lost if you ignore it.

In short, the internal dynamic on the Court is such that each Justice now has an incentive to abandon all references to legislative history in his or her opinions, at least if the Justice has any hope of attracting the votes of Justices Scalia and Thomas....

Merrill, *supra*, at 365–66. *See also* James J. Brudney & Corey Ditslear, *Liberal Justices' Reliance on Legislative History: Principle, Strategy, and the Scalia Effect*, 29 BERKELEY J. EMP. & LAB. L. 117, 160–71 (2008).

But the influence of the textualist critique of legislative history cannot be attributed solely to the idiosyncratic internal dynamics of the Court. Even opponents of the new textualism have acknowledged the validity of some of the textualist criticisms about potential overreliance on, or abuse of, legislative history. Thus, Professor William Eskridge, one of the leading critics of the new textualism, has argued that even if the new textualists do not (and should not) succeed in what he described as a "radical" program to eliminate judicial reliance on legislative history, at least three positive developments might emerge from their efforts. First, the new textualism underscores that "the Court should devote more of its energy to analyzing statutory *texts*," while "reminding courts and attorneys that legislative history is, at best, secondary and supporting evidence of statutory meaning." Second, the new textualism might inspire the Court to eschew reliance on legislative history altogether "where [the] statutory text is clear, and where that clarity is consistent with the statutory structure and the apparent statutory policy." Third, the new approach might induce the Court to be "more critical of the legislative history it uses," making sure that the legislative history in question has sufficient indicia of reliability and relevance. William N. Eskridge, Jr., *The New Textualism*, 37 UCLA L. REV. 621, 625 (1990). *See also* Jerry L. Mashaw, *Textualism, Constitutionalism, and the Interpretation of Federal Statutes*, 32 WM. & MARY L. REV. 827, 833–34 (1991). Professor Eskridge's argument suggests that the textualist challenge might improve the practice of using legislative history. Indeed, most judges and Justices seems to have responded to the textualist critique of legislative history with something of a mend-it-don't-end-it attitude, taking a more critical view of legislative history than prevailed in the practice's post–New Deal heyday, but rejecting the outright exclusionary position that new textualists like Justice Scalia might prefer.

Do these observations suggest the possibility of some convergence to a more moderate position, even if this convergence stops short of full agreement? *See* Jonathan T. Molot, *The Rise and Fall of Textualism*, 106 COLUM.

L. Rev. 1, 36 (2006) (ARGUING THAT, AS THE COMPETING POSITIONS HAVE DEVEL-
OPED, "THAT WHICH UNITES TEXTUALISTS AND PURPOSIVISTS SEEMS TO OUTWEIGH
THAT WHICH DIVIDES THEM"). OR ARE THE DISAGREEMENTS ABOUT THE LEGITIMACY
AND UTILITY OF THE USE OF LEGISLATIVE HISTORY TOO FUNDAMENTAL TO PERMIT EVEN A
PARTIAL RECONCILIATION OF THE COMPETING POSITION? *SEE* JONATHAN R. SIEGEL,
*THE INEXORABLE RADICALIZATION OF TEXTUALISM,* 158 U. Pa. L. Rev. 117 (2009).

The following case, *Exxon Mobil Corp. v. Allapattah Services, Inc.,*
provides a particularly interesting context in which to consider the different positions on the use of legislative history. The underlying question of
statutory interpretation at issue in *Exxon Mobil* is fairly complex, but a
brief summary should provide the necessary context for understanding the
methodological dispute in the case over the proper role of legislative
history.

*Exxon Mobil* involved a class action (a civil suit in which a large
number of similarly-situated plaintiffs sue the same defendant for a shared
or similar injury) brought in federal court. Although the legal claims in
*Exxon Mobil* were grounded in state law rather than federal law, a federal
statute, 28 U.S.C. § 1332(a), gives the federal district courts original
jurisdiction over "diversity" actions—civil cases in which the plaintiff and
the defendant are citizens of different states. The statute, however, only
confers federal jurisdiction over diversity actions if the "amount in controversy" exceeds a particular threshold, currently $75,000. 28 U.S.C.
§ 1332(a). Some of the plaintiffs in *Exxon Mobil* had claims exceeding
$75,000, but others did not. The question, then, was whether the federal
court could hear the case (exercising so-called "supplemental jurisdiction"
over the claims with a value below $75,000). Prior to 1990, the answer to
that question would clearly have been no, in light of a 1973 Supreme Court
case called Zahn v. International Paper Co., 414 U.S. 291 (1973). But in
1990, Congress enacted a new provision, 28 U.S.C. § 1367, as part of a
package of amendments known as the Judicial Improvements Act, Pub. L.
101–650. Section 1367 provided, in relevant part:

> (a) Except as provided in subsections (b) and (c) or as expressly
> provided otherwise by Federal statute, in any civil action of which the
> district courts have original jurisdiction, the district courts shall have
> supplemental jurisdiction over all other claims that are so related to
> claims in the action within such original jurisdiction that they form
> part of the same case or controversy under Article III of the United
> States Constitution. Such supplemental jurisdiction shall include
> claims that involve the joinder or intervention of additional parties.

> (b) In any civil action of which the district courts have original
> jurisdiction founded solely on section 1332 of this title, the district
> courts shall not have supplemental jurisdiction under subsection (a)
> over claims by plaintiffs against persons made parties under Rule 14,
> 19, 20, or 24 of the Federal Rules of Civil Procedure, or over claims by
> persons proposed to be joined as plaintiffs under Rule 19 of such rules,
> or seeking to intervene as plaintiffs under Rule 24 of such rules, when

exercising supplemental jurisdiction over such claims would be inconsistent with the jurisdictional requirements of section 1332.

The origins of § 1367 are helpful to understanding the subsequent debate over its meaning. In 1989, the Supreme Court decided a case called Finley v. United States, 490 U.S. 545 (1989), which raised a question concerning a supplemental jurisdiction issue that was similar to, but distinct from, the issue the Court had resolved in *Zahn*. While *Zahn* had involved a diversity action, *Finley* was a so-called "federal question" case, in which the plaintiff asserted claims "arising under the Constitution, laws, or treaties of the United States," 28 U.S.C. § 1331. In addition to these federal law claims, the plaintiff in *Finley* had also tried to add related state law claims against other defendants. Even though all the claims arose out of the same underlying dispute, the Supreme Court held that a federal court could not exercise supplemental jurisdiction over these other claims. The result in *Finley* was widely criticized. Most notably, a subcommittee of the Federal Court Study Committee (a blue-ribbon commission created pursuant to an Act of Congress to study the federal courts and to recommend legislative reforms) addressed *Finley*, as well as more general questions regarding the exercise of supplemental jurisdiction by the federal district courts. This subcommittee, chaired by Judge Richard Posner, proposed statutory language that Congress used as the basis for § 1367.

Everyone agreed that § 1367 overruled *Finley*. The more difficult question, which the Court addressed in *Exxon Mobil*, was whether § 1367 also overruled *Zahn*. In other words, did § 1367 permit a federal district court to assume jurisdiction in a diversity class action when some but not all of the plaintiffs satisfied the amount-in-controversy requirement? Justice Kennedy's opinion for the Court concluded, after a lengthy and intricate analysis of the interrelated statutory provisions, that the answer was yes: Section 1367 did indeed overrule *Zahn*. Justice Ginsburg, in a dissent joined by Justices Stevens, O'Connor, and Breyer, argued that although the majority's reading of § 1367 was plausible, an alternative reading was also plausible, and that this alternative reading would be less disruptive of pre-existing jurisprudence, easier to square with other statutory provisions, and more consistent with Congress's apparent intent. The dispute between Justice Kennedy and Justice Ginsburg over the best way to read the text of § 1367 is extremely complicated and not immediately relevant for our purposes here. The most pertinent feature of the case, for present purposes, is the dispute between Justice Kennedy (for the majority) and Justice Stevens (in a separate dissent joined by Justice Breyer) over the meaning and relevance of the legislative history of § 1367.

---

# Exxon Mobil Corp. v. Allapattah Services, Inc.
Supreme Court of the United States
545 U.S. 546 (2005)

■ JUSTICE KENNEDY delivered the opinion of the Court.

. . . .

[The defendants and the dissenters] insist that . . . we should look to other interpretive tools [besides the text and structure of the statute], including the legislative history of § 1367, which supposedly demonstrate Congress did not intend § 1367 to overrule *Zahn*. We can reject this argument at the very outset simply because § 1367 is not ambiguous. . . . Even if we were to stipulate, however, that the reading [the dissenters] urge upon us is textually plausible, the legislative history cited to support it would not alter our view as to the best interpretation of § 1367.

Those who urge that the legislative history refutes our interpretation rely primarily on the House Judiciary Committee Report on the Judicial Improvements Act. This Report explained that § 1367 would "authorize jurisdiction in a case like *Finley*, as well as essentially restore the pre–*Finley* understandings of the authorization for and limits on other forms of supplemental jurisdiction." . . . The Report then remarked that § 1367(b) "is not intended to affect the jurisdictional requirements of [§ 1332] in diversity-only class actions, as those requirements were interpreted prior to *Finley*," citing, without further elaboration, *Zahn* and Supreme Tribe of Ben–Hur v. Cauble, 255 U.S. 356 (1921). . . .

As we have repeatedly held, the authoritative statement is the statutory text, not the legislative history or any other extrinsic material. Extrinsic materials have a role in statutory interpretation only to the extent they shed a reliable light on the enacting Legislature's understanding of otherwise ambiguous terms. Not all extrinsic materials are reliable sources of insight into legislative understandings, however, and legislative history in particular is vulnerable to two serious criticisms. First, legislative history is itself often murky, ambiguous, and contradictory. Judicial investigation of legislative history has a tendency to become, to borrow Judge Leventhal's memorable phrase, an exercise in " 'looking over a crowd and picking out your friends.' " Second, judicial reliance on legislative materials like committee reports, which are not themselves subject to the requirements of Article I, may give unrepresentative committee members—or, worse yet, unelected staffers and lobbyists—both the power and the incentive to attempt strategic manipulations of legislative history to secure results they were unable to achieve through the statutory text. We need not comment here on whether these problems are sufficiently prevalent to render legislative history inherently unreliable in all circumstances, a point on which Members of this Court have disagreed. It is clear, however, that in this instance both criticisms are right on the mark.

First of all, the legislative history of § 1367 is far murkier than selective quotation from the House Report would suggest. The text of § 1367 is based substantially on a draft proposal contained in a Federal Court Study Committee working paper, which was drafted by a Subcommittee chaired by Judge Posner. While the Subcommittee explained, in language echoed by the House Report, that its proposal "basically restores the law as it existed prior to *Finley*," it observed in a footnote that its proposal would overrule *Zahn* and that this would be a good idea. Although the Federal Courts Study Committee did not expressly adopt the Subcommittee's specific reference to *Zahn*, it neither explicitly disagreed with the Subcommittee's conclusion that this was the best reading of the proposed text nor substantially modified the proposal to avoid this result. Therefore, even if the House Report could fairly be read to reflect an understanding that the text of § 1367 did not overrule *Zahn*, the Subcommittee Working Paper on which § 1367 was based reflected the opposite understanding. The House Report is no more authoritative than the Subcommittee Working Paper. The utility of either can extend no further than the light it sheds on how the enacting Legislature understood the statutory text. Trying to figure out how to square the Subcommittee Working Paper's understanding with the House Report's understanding, or which is more reflective of the understanding of the enacting legislators, is a hopeless task.

Second, the worst fears of critics who argue legislative history will be used to circumvent the Article I process were realized in this case. The telltale evidence is the statement, by three law professors who participated in drafting § 1367, that § 1367 "on its face" permits "supplemental jurisdiction over claims of class members that do not satisfy section 1332's jurisdictional amount requirement, which would overrule [*Zahn*]. [There is] a disclaimer of intent to accomplish this result in the legislative history. . . . It would have been better had the statute dealt explicitly with this problem, and the legislative history was an attempt to correct the oversight." Rowe, Burbank, & Mengler, Compounding or Creating Confusion About Supplemental Jurisdiction? A Reply to Professor Freer, 40 Emory L.J. 943, 960, n. 90 (1991). The professors were frank to concede that if one refuses to consider the legislative history, one has no choice but to "conclude that section 1367 has wiped *Zahn* off the books." So there exists an acknowledgment, by parties who have detailed, specific knowledge of the statute and the drafting process, both that the plain text of § 1367 overruled *Zahn* and that language to the contrary in the House Report was a post hoc attempt to alter that result. One need not subscribe to the wholesale condemnation of legislative history to refuse to give any effect to such a deliberate effort to amend a statute through a committee report.

In sum, even if we believed resort to legislative history were appropriate in these cases—a point we do not concede—we would not give significant weight to the House Report. The distinguished jurists who drafted the Subcommittee Working Paper, along with three of the participants in the drafting of § 1367, agree that this provision, on its face, overrules *Zahn*. This accords with the best reading of the statute's text, and nothing in the legislative history indicates directly and explicitly that Congress understood the phrase "civil action of which the district courts have original jurisdiction" to exclude cases in which some but not all of the diversity plaintiffs meet the amount in controversy requirement.

No credence, moreover, can be given to the claim that, if Congress understood § 1367 to overrule *Zahn*, the proposal would have been more controversial. We have little sense whether any Member of Congress would have been particularly upset by this result. This is not a case where one can plausibly say that concerned legislators might not have realized the possible effect of the text they were adopting. Certainly, any competent legislative aide who studied the matter would have flagged this issue if it were a matter of importance to his or her boss, especially in light of the Subcommittee Working Paper. There are any number of reasons why legislators did not spend more time arguing over § 1367, none of which are relevant to our interpretation of what the words of the statute mean. . . .

■ JUSTICE STEVENS, with whom JUSTICE BREYER joins, dissenting.

JUSTICE GINSBURG's carefully reasoned opinion demonstrates the error in the Court's rather ambitious reading of this opaque jurisdictional statute. She also has demonstrated that "ambiguity" is a term that may have different meanings for different judges, for the Court has made the remarkable declaration that its reading of the statute is so obviously correct—and JUSTICE GINSBURG's so obviously wrong—that the text does not even qualify as "ambiguous." Because ambiguity is apparently in the eye of the beholder, I remain convinced that it is unwise to treat the ambiguity *vel non* of a statute as determinative of whether legislative history is consulted. Indeed, I believe that we as judges are more, rather than less, constrained when we make ourselves accountable to all reliable evidence of legislative intent.

The legislative history of 28 U.S.C. § 1367 provides powerful confirmation of JUSTICE GINSBURG's interpretation of that statute. It is helpful to consider in full the relevant portion of the House Report, which was also adopted by the Senate:

> "This section would authorize jurisdiction in a case like *Finley*, as well as essentially restore the pre–*Finley* understandings of the authorization for and limits on other forms of supplemental jurisdiction. In federal question cases, it broadly authorizes the district courts to exercise supplemental jurisdiction over additional claims, including claims involving the joinder of additional parties. In diversity cases, the district courts may exercise supplemental jurisdiction, except when doing so would be inconsistent with the jurisdictional requirements of the diversity statute.

> \* \* \* \* \*

> "[§ 1367(b)] prohibits a district court in a case over which it has jurisdiction founded solely on the general diversity provision, 28 U.S.C. § 1332, from exercising supplemental jurisdiction in specified circumstances. [Footnote 16: 'The net effect of subsection (b) is to implement the principal rationale of Owen Equipment & Erection Co. v. Kroger, 437 U.S. 365 (1978)'.] In diversity-only actions the district courts may not hear plaintiffs' supplemental claims when exercising supplemental jurisdiction would encourage plaintiffs to evade the jurisdictional requirement of 28 U.S.C. § 1332 by the simple expedient of naming initially only those defendants whose joinder satisfies section 1332's requirements and later adding claims not within original federal jurisdiction against other defendants who have intervened or been joined on a supplemental basis. In accord with case law, the subsection also

prohibits the joinder or intervention of persons as plaintiffs if adding them is inconsistent with section 1332's requirements. The section is not intended to affect the jurisdictional requirements of 28 U.S.C. § 1332 in diversity-only class actions, as those requirements were interpreted prior to *Finley*. [Footnote 17: 'See Supreme Tribe of Ben–Hur v. Cauble, 255 U.S. 356 (1921); Zahn v. International Paper Co., 414 U.S. 291 (1973)'.] ['']...

Not only does the House Report specifically say that § 1367 was not intended to upset [*Zahn*], but its entire explanation of the statute demonstrates that Congress had in mind a very specific and relatively modest task—undoing this Court's 5-to-4 decision in [*Finley*]. In addition to overturning that unfortunate and much-criticized decision, the statute, according to the Report, codifies and preserves the "the pre–*Finley* understandings of the authorization for and limits on other forms of supplemental jurisdiction[]" ....

The Court's reasons for ignoring this virtual billboard of congressional intent are unpersuasive. That a subcommittee of the Federal Courts Study Committee believed that an earlier, substantially similar version of the statute overruled *Zahn* only highlights the fact that the statute is ambiguous. What is determinative is that the House Report explicitly rejected that broad reading of the statutory text. Such a report has special significance as an indicator of legislative intent. In Congress, committee reports are normally considered the authoritative explication of a statute's text and purposes, and busy legislators and their assistants rely on that explication in casting their votes.

The Court's second reason—its comment on the three law professors who participated in drafting § 1367—is similarly off the mark. In the law review article that the Court refers to, the professors were merely saying that the text of the statute was susceptible to an overly broad (and simplistic) reading, and that clarification in the House Report was therefore appropriate. Significantly, the reference to *Zahn* in the House Report does not at all appear to be tacked-on or out of place; indeed, it is wholly consistent with the Report's broader explanation of Congress' goal of overruling *Finley* and preserving pre–*Finley* law. To suggest that these professors participated in a "deliberate effort to amend a statute through a committee report," reveals an unrealistic view of the legislative process, not to mention disrespect for three law professors who acted in the role of public servants. To be sure, legislative history can be manipulated. But, in the situation before us, there is little reason to fear that an unholy conspiracy of "unrepresentative committee members," law professors, and "unelected staffers and lobbyists," endeavored to torpedo Congress' attempt to overrule (without discussion) ... longstanding features of this Court's diversity jurisprudence....

■ [JUSTICE GINSBURG's dissent joined by JUSTICE STEVENS, JUSTICE O'CONNOR, and JUSTICE BREYER, is omitted.]

*1. **Legislative History and Statutory Ambiguity***—Justice Kennedy's majority opinion in *Exxon Mobil* takes what has become the standard modern doctrinal line on the use of legislative history: It is permissible for a court to consult the statute's legislative history if, but only if, the court first determines that the statute is ambiguous. On this view, although legislative history may be used to *resolve* statutory ambiguity, it may not be used to create statutory ambiguity or to overcome the clear semantic meaning of the text. It is for this reason that Justice Kennedy insisted that his discussion of legislative history in *Exxon Mobil* was not actually necessary for the holding. If one takes Justice Kennedy at his word, then even if he were to concede that Justice Stevens was absolutely right that the legislative history incontrovertibly demonstrated that Congress did not intend for § 1367 to overrule *Zahn*, this would not matter because the semantic reading of the statute, when read in context and in light of the overall statutory structure, was clear.

That approach to legislative history attempts to strike a balance between the more traditional view of legislative history associated with the *American Trucking* era—and still embraced by Justice Stevens—and the more skeptical view advanced by the new textualists. Legislative history, on this compromise view, is a deeply flawed instrument that should be used sparingly, and only when necessary to resolve questions of interpretation that cannot be resolved on the basis of the statutory text. Does that seem like a reasonable middle ground? Or is it just a way for courts to dance around the issue, dodging the fundamental questions about whether legislative history is a legitimate and reliable interpretive tool? If legislative history is as bad as the textualists say it is—if it facilitates circumvention of Article I, has no connection to any legitimate notion of objectified legislative intent, and has virtually no probative value with respect to how most rank-and-file legislators understood the statutory terms—then why should courts use it even when the statute's semantic meaning is unclear? There are, after all, plenty of other ways to resolve semantic ambiguities. On the flip side, if courts embrace the position that legislative history can be legitimately used to resolve statutory ambiguities, why can't especially clear and powerful legislative history influence a court's interpretation of statutory text even if the semantic meaning would otherwise seem clear?

Another concern here is just how one defines or determines "ambiguity" in the statute's semantic meaning. Was it problematic for Justice Kennedy to insist that the meaning of § 1367 is unambiguous when four of his colleagues concluded, even without reference to the legislative history, that the statute meant something else? More generally, the doctrine as Justice Kennedy stated it seems to characterize statutory ambiguity as a binary variable—either a statute is clear or it is ambiguous. But wouldn't it be fairer to say that statutory clarity is more of a continuum, ranging from extremely clear to totally opaque? If that's so, isn't there something odd about treating certain types of extrinsic evidence as potentially decisive if a statute is "ambiguous," but treating the same evidence as totally irrelevant if the statute is "clear"?

Then again, maybe that's not the right way to think about the function of the rule that says to look first to the text, and only turn to the legislative history when the text is ambiguous. Maybe in practice this is just a way to remind courts of the primacy of the text, lest judges otherwise leap too quickly to consideration of other extrinsic evidence of statutory meaning. Does that seem plausible?

**2.  *Close Scrutiny of the Particular Legislative History*—**One notable feature of the *Exxon Mobil* majority's discussion of legislative history is that it eschewed broad statements about the reliability or legitimacy of legislative history as such, and instead focused on the reliability or legitimacy of the *particular* pieces of legislative history at issue in the case. One important reason for this may simply be the composition of the majority coalition, which included not only Justices Scalia and Thomas— who take a hard line against use of legislative history—but also Justice Souter, who often defends the utility of legislative history as an interpretive tool, as well as Chief Justice Rehnquist and Justice Kennedy, who are somewhere in between. In a 5–4 decision, Justice Kennedy had a strong interest in keeping his coalition together, and this may have required him to finesse the language of the opinion in such a way that he could respond to the dissent's legislative history argument while holding his majority.

But perhaps *Exxon Mobil* suggests a more refined, case-by-case approach to the evaluation of legislative history. If so, is this a good development? Do you think courts are capable of parsing the legislative history closely enough to make these sorts of determinations? Does the *Exxon Mobil* opinion increase or decrease your confidence that courts are capable of making meaningful case-specific assessments?

**3.  *Distinguishing* Types *of Legislative History*—**As discussed earlier (*see* pp. 152–162, *supra*), there has traditionally been a rough hierarchy of legislative history sources, with committee reports at the top, sponsor statements somewhere in the middle, and other statements in floor debates and hearings closer to the bottom. One of the striking features of the *Exxon Mobil* opinion is its explicit rejection of the idea that the committee reports are entitled to any special status. Rather, the *Exxon Mobil* majority treated the House Committee Report on § 1367 as on a par, in terms of probative value, with the report of the Federal Courts Study Committee, a committee appointed by the Chief Justice pursuant to an Act of Congress that established the committee to study and recommend reforms to various aspects of judicial administration. *See* Pub. L. 100–702, Title I, Nov. 19, 1988, 102 Stat. 4644. Although the Federal Courts Study Committee in fact proposed the statutory language that eventually became § 1367, it was otherwise not part of the legislative process and was not composed of members of Congress. Why did the *Exxon Mobil* Court equate these two types of legislative history? Was it right to do so?

This raises the more general question: In light of what we know (or think we know) about how the legislative process operates, *should* courts draw distinctions among various types of legislative history? Some recent scholars who have defended the use of legislative history in statutory interpretation have argued that the best account of the utility of legislative history may require distinctions of this sort. Professor Einer Elhauge, for example, maintains that courts should consult legislative history to resolve statutory ambiguity, but not because he believes that legislative history can shed meaningful light on actual statutory meaning or legislative intent. Rather, Professor Elhauge contends that most legislators would prefer a rule of consulting legislative history in cases of ambiguity—that is, the judicial practice of consulting legislative history is consistent with a plausible notion of legislative supremacy, because legislators (if they put the matter to a vote) would prefer that courts employ this interpretive tool. EINER ELHAUGE, STATUTORY DEFAULT RULES: HOW TO INTERPRET UNCLEAR LEGISLATION 116 (2008). But, although Professor Elhauge's theory leads him to conclude that courts should be open to a wide range of legislative history materials, it also leads him to distinguish among different types of legislative history: On his view, the views of opponents or statements that come late in the process should count for little, whereas those of a committee or sponsor should count for a lot if other legislators do not expressly dissent. *See id*. at 124–26. Professor Elhauge argues, moreover, that such an interpretive rule would improve the overall accuracy of legislative history by giving legislators an incentive to speak out in opposition to committee reports or sponsors' statements with which they disagree. *See id*. at 125–26.

In a somewhat similar vein, Professors Daniel Rodriguez and Barry Weingast have suggested that statutory interpretation needs to take explicit account of the structure of legislative decisionmaking. Daniel B. Rodriguez & Barry R. Weingast, *The Positive Political Theory of Legislative History: New Perspectives on the 1964 Civil Rights Act and Its Interpretation*, 151 U. PA. L. REV. 1417, 1438–39 (2003). In particular, they believe interpretive questions can be valuably illuminated by identifying the pivotal group—the marginal legislators whose support for the legislation was most uncertain, and whose views were therefore most critical to the bill's ultimate fate—and studying the patterns of votes over time as a bill makes its way through Congress. Professors Rodriguez and Weingast argue that the ultimate enactment of the legislation "depends on whether the ardent supporters [of the legislation] and the pivotal legislators negotiate an effective compromise." *Id*. at 1442. This dynamic, they suggest, can help courts to distinguish those statements in the legislative history that are "cheap talk"—empty rhetoric that does not affect the bill's chances for passage—from those statements that are "costly signals" of the bill's intended meaning. *Id*. at 1445–46. Identifying the pivotal legislators and carefully distinguishing the cheap talk from the costly signaling enables interpreters, on Rodriguez and Weingast's view, to sort probative from unreliable legislative history:

> Because ardent supporters have an incentive to bias the interpretation of an act in their favor and away from the final compromise needed to ensure passage, we must give greater weight to their costly signals than to their cheap talk. Pivotal legislators, in contrast, have strong incentives to provide a clear understanding of the compromise, and

thus their statements and understandings tend to be the least problematic. In parallel with traditional theories, our approach gives the least weight to statements by the act's opponents. We focus on the statements by pivots in part because they have the strongest incentives to communicate reliably the act's meaning, whereas ardent supporters have countervening incentives and opportunities for cheap talk, causing many of their statements to be misleading.

*Id.* at 1448 (citations omitted).

Do you find Elhauge's or Rodriguez and Weingast's arguments for distinguishing among different forms of legislative history convincing? Do their premises about legislative preferences and the nature of the legislative process seem plausible? With respect to Rodriguez and Weingast's approach in particular, does this seem like something that federal judges could effectively implement? More generally, the theories of Elhauge, Rodriquez and Weingast, and others writing in this vein reflect advances (or at least changes) in political scientists' understandings of the legislative process. To what degree should interpretive theories change as underlying theories of legislative decisionmaking change? On the one hand, given the degree to which various interpretive theories are grounded in assertions about legislative process, it would seem natural that those theories should reflect the most current thinking on how that process operates. On the other hand, judges need workable rules, and the legal system as a whole needs a degree of stability and predictability. Might those considerations militate in favor of somewhat cruder principles that are slower to change, even if they do not perfectly capture the legislative process?

## D. OTHER POTENTIAL USES OF LEGISLATIVE HISTORY

This section thus far has dealt with the legitimacy and utility of legislative history as authoritative evidence of legislative intent. Would the concerns about legitimacy pressed by the new textualists abate in situations in which courts relied on legislative history not as a statement of intent, but rather as a source of information about specialized meaning, industry practice, the problems being addressed by the legislation, and other externally verifiable facts about the world? Consider the following case.

## Corning Glass Works v. Brennan

Supreme Court of the United States
417 U.S. 188 (1974)

■ MR. JUSTICE MARSHALL delivered the opinion of the Court.

These cases arise under the Equal Pay Act of 1963, 29 U.S.C. § 206(d)(1), which added to § 6 of the Fair Labor Standards Act of 1938 the principle of equal pay for equal work regardless of sex. The principal question posed is whether Corning Glass Works violated the Act by paying a higher base wage to male night shift inspectors than it paid to female inspectors performing the same tasks on the day shift, where the higher wage was paid in addition to a separate night shift differential paid to all employees for night work. . . .

## I

Prior to 1925, Corning operated its plants in Wellsboro and Corning only during the day, and all inspection work was performed by women. Between 1925 and 1930, the company began to introduce automatic production equipment which made it desirable to institute a night shift. During this period, however, both New York and Pennsylvania law prohibited women from working at night. As a result, in order to fill inspector positions on the new night shift, the company had to recruit male employees from among its male dayworkers. The male employees so transferred demanded and received wages substantially higher than those paid to women inspectors engaged on the two day shifts. . . . Thus a situation developed where the night inspectors were all male, the day inspectors all female, and the male inspectors received significantly higher wages.

In 1944, Corning plants at both locations were organized by a labor union and a collective-bargaining agreement was negotiated for all production and maintenance employees. This agreement for the first time established a plantwide shift differential, but this change did not eliminate the higher base wage paid to male night inspectors. Rather, the shift differential was superimposed on the existing difference in base wages between male night inspectors and female day inspectors.

Prior to June 11, 1964, the effective date of the Equal Pay Act, the law in both Pennsylvania and New York was amended to permit women to work at night. It was not until some time after the effective date of the Act, however, that Corning initiated efforts to eliminate the differential rates for male and female inspectors. Beginning in June 1966, Corning started to open up jobs on the night shift to women. . . .

On January 20, 1969, a new collective-bargaining agreement went into effect. . . . The new agreement abolished for the future the separate base wages for day and night shift inspectors and imposed a uniform base wage for inspectors exceeding the wage rate for the night shift previously in effect. All inspectors hired after January 20, 1969, were to receive the same base wage, whatever their sex or shift. The collective-bargaining agreement further provided, however, for a [provision that] served essentially to perpetuate the differential in base wages between day and night inspectors.

The Secretary of Labor brought these cases to enjoin Corning from violating the Equal Pay Act. . . .

## II

Congress' purpose in enacting the Equal Pay Act was to remedy what was perceived to be a serious and endemic problem of employment discrimination in private industry—the fact that the wage structure of "many segments of American industry has been based on an ancient but outmoded belief that a man, because of his role in society, should be paid more than a woman even though his duties are the same." S.Rep. No. 176, 88th Cong., 1st Sess., 1 (1963). The solution adopted was quite simple in principle: to require that "equal work will be rewarded by equal wages."

The Act's basic structure and operation are similarly straightforward. In order to make out a case under the Act, the Secretary must show that an employer pays different wages to employees of opposite sexes "for equal work on jobs the performance of which requires equal skill, effort, and responsibility, and which are performed under similar working conditions." . . .

. . . Corning argues that the Secretary has failed to prove that Corning ever violated the Act because day shift work is not "performed under similar working conditions" as night shift work. The Secretary maintains that day shift and night shift work are performed under "similar working conditions" within the meaning of the Act. . . .

The most notable feature of the history of the Equal Pay Act is that Congress recognized early in the legislative process that the concept of equal pay for equal work was more readily stated in principle than reduced to statutory language which would be meaningful to employers and workable across the broad range of industries covered by the Act. As originally introduced, the Equal Pay bill required equal pay for "equal work on jobs the performance of which requires equal skills." There were only two exceptions—for differentials "made pursuant to a seniority or merit increase system which does not discriminate on the basis of sex. . . ."

In both the House and Senate committee hearings, witnesses were highly critical of the Act's definition of equal work and of its exemptions. Many noted that most of American industry used formal, systematic job evaluation plans to establish equitable wage structures in their plants. Such systems, as explained coincidentally by a representative of Corning Glass Works who testified at both hearings, took into consideration four separate factors in determining job value—skill, effort, responsibility and working conditions—and each of these four components was further systematically divided into various subcomponents. Under a job evaluation plan, point values are assigned to each of the subcomponents of a given job, resulting in a total point figure representing a relatively objective measure of the job's value.

In comparison to the rather complex job evaluation plans used by industry, the definition of equal work used in the first drafts of the Equal Pay bill was criticized as unduly vague and incomplete. Industry representatives feared that as a result of the bill's definition of equal work, the Secretary of Labor would be cast in the position of second-guessing the validity of a company's job evaluation system. They repeatedly urged that the bill be amended to include an exception for job classification systems, or otherwise to incorporate the language of job evaluation into the bill. Thus Corning's own representative testified:

"Job evaluation is an accepted and tested method of attaining equity in wage relationship.

"A great part of industry is committed to job evaluation by past practice and by contractual agreement as the basis for wage administration.

" 'Skill' alone, as a criterion, fails to recognize other aspects of the job situation that affect job worth.

"We sincerely hope that this committee in passing legislation to eliminate wage differences based on sex alone, will recognize in its language the general role of job evaluation in establishing equitable rate relationship."

We think it plain that in amending the bill's definition of equal work to its present form, the Congress acted in direct response to these pleas. Spokesmen for the amended bill stated, for example, during the House debates:

"The concept of equal pay for jobs demanding equal skill has been expanded to require also equal effort, responsibility, and similar working conditions. These factors are the core of all job classification systems. They form a legitimate basis for differentials in pay."

Indeed, the most telling evidence of congressional intent is the fact that the Act's amended definition of equal work incorporated the specific language of the job evaluation plan described at the hearings by Corning's own representative—that is, the concepts of "skill," "effort," "responsibility," and "working conditions."

Congress' intent, as manifested in this history, was to use these terms to incorporate into the new federal Act the well-defined and well-accepted principles of job evaluation so as to ensure that wage differentials based upon bona fide job evaluation plans would be outside the purview of the Act. The House Report emphasized:

"This language recognizes that there are many factors which may be used to measure the relationships between jobs and which establish a valid basis for a difference in pay. These factors will be found in a majority of the job classification systems. Thus, it is anticipated that a bona fide job classification program that does not discriminate on the basis of sex will serve as a valid defense to a charge of discrimination." H.R.Rep.No.309, at 3, U.S.Code Cong. & Admin.News, 1963, pp. 688, 689.

It is in this light that the phrase "working conditions" must be understood, for where Congress has used technical words or terms of art, "it (is) proper to explain them by reference to the art or science to which they (are) appropriate." Greenleaf v. Goodrich, 101 U.S. 278, 284 (1880). This principle is particularly salutary where, as here, the legislative history reveals that Congress incorporated words having a special meaning within the field regulated by the statute so as to overcome objections by industry representatives that statutory definitions were vague and incomplete.

While a layman might well assume that time of day worked reflects one aspect of a job's "working conditions," the term has a different and much more specific meaning in the language of industrial relations. As Corning's own representative testified at the hearings, the element of working conditions encompasses two subfactors: "surroundings" and "hazards." "Surroundings" measures the elements, such as toxic chemicals or fumes, regularly encountered by a worker, their intensity, and their frequency. "Hazards" takes into account the physical hazards regularly encountered, their frequency, and the severity of injury they can cause. This definition of "working conditions" is not only manifested in Corning's own job evaluation plans but is also well accepted across a wide range of American industry.

Nowhere in any of these definitions is time of day worked mentioned as a relevant criterion. The fact of the matter is that the concept of "working conditions," as used in the specialized language of job evaluation systems, simply does not encompass shift differentials. Indeed, while Corning now argues that night inspection work is not equal to day inspection work, all of its own job evaluation plans, including the one now in effect, have consistently treated them as equal in all respects, including working conditions.... [T]he inspection work at issue in this case, whether performed during the day or night, is "equal work" as that term is defined in the Act....

■ MR. JUSTICE STEWART took no part in the consideration or decision of these cases.

■ [CHIEF JUSTICE BURGER, JUSTICE BLACKMUN, and JUSTICE REHNQUIST dissented, without a separate opinion. Their brief statement indicated that they agreed with the analysis of the court of appeals opinion below, which had had also relied principally on legislative history, albeit a different piece of legislative history. In particular, the court of appeals opinion gave great weight to the statement of one of the sponsors of the legislation, Representative Goodell, who stated that "hours of work [and] difference in shift ... would logically fall within the working condition factor." 109 Cong.Rec. 9209 (1963) (quoted in Brennan v. Corning Glass Works, 480 F.2d 1254, 1259–60 (1973)).]

---

*1. Distinguishing Uses of Legislative History*—Is there a difference between relying on legislative history as an authoritative source of legislative intent and relying on it as a source of evidence for facts about the world? Consider, in this regard, Judge Easterbrook's account of different uses of legislative history, and their respective value and dangers:

> [Courts must] distinguish[] among uses of legislative history.... Language is a process of communication that works only when authors and readers share a set of rules and meanings. What "clearly" means one thing to a reader unacquainted with the circumstances of the

utterance—including social conventions prevailing at the time of drafting—may mean something else to a reader with a different background. Legislation speaks across the decades, during which legal institutions and linguistic conventions change. To decode words one must frequently reconstruct the legal and political culture of the drafters. Legislative history may be invaluable in revealing the setting of the enactment and the assumptions its authors entertained about how their words would be understood. It may show, too, that words with a denotation "clear" to an outsider are terms of art, with an equally "clear" but different meaning to an insider. It may show too that the words leave gaps, for short phrases cannot address all human experience; understood in context, the words may leave to the executive and judicial branches the task of adding flesh to bones. These we take to be the points of cases . . . holding that judges may learn from the legislative history even when the text is "clear". Clarity depends on context, which legislative history may illuminate. The process is objective; the search is not for the contents of the authors' heads but for the rules of language they used.

Quite different is the claim that legislative intent is *the* basis of interpretation, that the text of the law is simply evidence of the real rule. In such a regime legislative history is not a way to understand the text but is a more authentic, because more proximate, expression of legislators' will. One may say in reply that legislative history is a poor guide to legislators' intent because it is written by the staff rather than by members of Congress, because it is often losers' history ("If you can't get your proposal into the bill, at least write the legislative history to make it look as if you'd prevailed"), because it becomes a crutch ("There's no need for us to vote on the amendment if we can write a little legislative history"), because it complicates the task of execution and obedience (neither judges nor those whose conduct is supposed to be influenced by the law can know what to do without delving into legislative recesses, a costly and uncertain process). Often there is so much legislative history that a court can manipulate the meaning of a law by choosing which snippets to emphasize and by putting hypothetical questions—questions to be answered by inferences from speeches rather than by reference to the text, so that great discretion devolves on the (judicial) questioner. Sponsors of opinion polls know that a small change in the text of a question can lead to large differences in the answer. Legislative history offers wilful judges an opportunity to pose questions and devise answers, with predictable divergence in results. These and related concerns have lead to skepticism about using legislative history to find legislative intent.

In re Sinclair, 870 F.2d 1340, 1342–43 (7th Cir. 1989) (citations omitted). If certain uses of legislative history would pass muster even for a strict textualist such as Judge Easterbrook, what criteria should courts apply to ensure that it is being properly used, rather than misused?

Based on the distinctions drawn above, should textualists find the use of legislative history in *Corning Glass Works* legitimate? In the passage from *Sinclair*, Judge Easterbrook says that legislative history "may show . . . that words with a denotation 'clear' to an outsider are terms of art, with an equally 'clear' but different meaning to an insider." Is that how the *Corning Glass Works* Court is using legislative history? Should textualists view such uses of legislative history as legitimate—as no different in kind from looking at other extrinsic sources, like human resource manuals or trade journal articles, to determine when words are being used in a technical rather than ordinary sense? Then again, textualists often emphasize the possibility that committee members might manipulate legislative history to achieve results they could not get enacted into law. Wouldn't that concern apply to the Court's use of legislative history in *Corning Glass Works*? If the Court began to rely principally on legislative history as evidence of contextual meaning, savvy legislators bent on creating records favorable to their constituents' interests might learn how to frame the legislative history to their advantage, perhaps describing terms as technical terms of art in favorable ways so as to produce desirable interpretive results. Given this possibility, when a court relies on legislative history for contextual information, at the very least it must take care to verify independently the persuasiveness of the representations made in the materials, rather than taking them at face value or giving them additional weight because of their congressional source. *See* John F. Manning, *Textualism as a Nondelegation Doctrine*, 97 COLUM. L. REV. 673, 731–37 (1997).

There are a few other narrow contexts in which strong textualists have sometimes relied in part on legislative history. Consider the following two opinions by Justice Scalia.

First, in United States v. Fausto, 484 U.S. 439 (1988), the Court determined that by prescribing an elaborate remedial scheme for personnel actions involving a given class of federal employees, the Civil Service Reform Act of 1978 (CSRA) displaced other, more general statutory remedies that such employees could have invoked prior to the Act. To this end, Justice Scalia's opinion for the Court cited a Senate Committee Report for the proposition that "[a] leading purpose of the CSRA was to replace the haphazard arrangements for administrative and judicial review of personnel action, part of the 'outdated patchwork of statutes and rules built up over almost a century.'" *Id*. at 444 (quoting S. Rep. No. 95–969, at 3 (1978)). Although the Court initially relied on the Senate Report to identify the mischief, however, its analysis did not stop with the report. Rather, the Court went on to examine a host of pre–Act regulations and judicial decisions, which verified that the committee's account of the difficulties in the pre–Act system corresponded to the reality of the situation. *See id*. at 444–45. Does this use of legislative history satisfy concerns about its legitimacy and reliability? Is it analogous to the Court's reliance on legislative history in *Corning Glass Works*? If not, does Justice Scalia's use of legislative history seem more or less probative and reliable?

Second, in *Green v. Bock Laundry Machine Co.*, 490 U.S. 504 (1989), Justice Scalia wrote an opinion concurring in the judgment in a case that, in his view and the Court's, identified an absurd result that would arise if the Federal Rules of Evidence were given their most natural semantic meaning. The facts of *Bock Laundry* are too complicated to warrant recitation. For present purposes, the important point is this: In discussing the absurdity doctrine, Justice Scalia noted that he would use legislative history to help determine the existence of an absurdity:

> I think it entirely appropriate to consult all public materials, including the background of [the relevant Federal Rule of Evidence] and the legislative history of its adoption, to verify that what seems to us an unthinkable disposition . . . was indeed unthought of, and thus to justify a departure from the ordinary meaning of . . . the Rule.

*Id.* at 527 (Scalia, J., concurring in the judgment). Does this seem consistent with textualism? Presumably, the justification for looking to legislative history in this case is that the absurdity doctrine presupposes that Congress somehow overlooked an application so troubling that it never would have intended to cover it had the matter come to light during the legislative process; if someone in the legislative process in fact mentioned the application, then the Court might find it more difficult to conclude that the absurd result had simply been overlooked. But if Justice Scalia doubts that most legislators read or agree with any particular item of legislative history—including committee reports—how can he equate the mention of an absurd application in the legislative history with *Congress's* having thought of the problem?

**2. *Specialized Meanings and the Problem of Multiple Audiences, Redux*—**The Court in *Corning Glass Works* decided that the Equal Pay Act used the term "working conditions" in the technical sense it had acquired in industrial job evaluation systems—a sense that took into account hazards and surroundings, but not time of day. Assume that the Court properly relied on the hearing testimony to establish that most employers—including Corning Glass—would have understood the phrase "working conditions" in that technical sense. What is the significance, if any, of the fact that the statute is addressed not only to those employers, but also to other audiences? Three other audiences in particular might be relevant: *First*, not all employers subject to the Equal Pay Act use these elaborate point systems for classifying jobs; these other employers might not have been aware of the details of such systems, or even that they exist. *Second*, not all employees or potential employees might be familiar with the technical definition of "working conditions." *Third*, a statute like the Equal Pay Act arguably has a broader expressive significance to the general public, in that it endorses certain norms and a certain balance between competing values. What, if anything, is the significance of the fact that these other audiences might not have understood the provisions of the Equal Pay Act in the specialized technical sense the Court ascribes to them?

**3. *Changes in Specialized Meaning over Time*—**Suppose that the *Corning Glass Works* Court was correct in its conclusion that when Congress used the term "similar working conditions," it meant to use that phrase with the specialized meaning it had acquired in the context of industrial job classification systems. Now suppose that some years after the statute was enacted, industry employers changed their job classification practices, expressly expanding the definition of "working conditions" to include surroundings, hazards, and *time of day*. As a result of this change, day shift jobs and night shift jobs are assigned different point values under the now-standard job evaluation system—they are treated as *dissimilar*. What are the implications, if any, for the correct interpretation of the term "similar working conditions" in the Equal Pay Act?

One possibility—the one most courts would probably endorse—is that the change in industry usage does not matter for purposes of the Equal Pay Act, because the relevant interpretive question is what the statute was intended or understood to mean *at the time of enactment*. But wouldn't it be plausible to argue that by using the specialized term "working conditions," Congress meant to *incorporate by reference* whatever meaning that term had in the relevant community *at the time of enforcement*? This latter interpretation is arguably more consistent with Congress's purpose in adopting this specialized language in the first place, as the idea seems to have been to preserve companies' autonomy to rely on industry best practices for classifying jobs as similar or dissimilar for purposes of determining salary. Then again, maybe this approach is troublesome not only because the meaning of statutory terms can change over time, but also because the meaning of statutory terms can be changed by private actors, without any direct legislative action. Is that a problem? Why or why not?

## V. The Judicial Power and Equitable Interpretation

The three dominant foundational theories of statutory interpretation—intentionalism, purposivism, and textualism—all proceed on the assumption that judges must act as Congress's faithful agent. But although the "faithful agent" model is the standard account of the role of the judge in the federal system, it is not the only model. Some have argued that the judge interpreting a statute acts not so much as Congress's faithful agent, but rather as Congress's junior partner. On this view, judges have more freedom to shape legislation through a process of "interpretation" that, while proceeding from the statute and from the instructions of Congress, is not strictly bound by those things. Thus, Justice Stone urged his fellow judges to reject the "illusion that in interpreting [statutes] our only task is to discover the legislative will," and instead to "treat a statute much more as we treat a judicial precedent, as both a declaration and a source of law, and as a premise for legal reasoning." Harlan F. Stone, *The Common Law in the United States*, 50 Harv. L. Rev. 4, 13, 15 (1936). Although this view of the judicial role is not the prevalent view today, the idea has prominent modern proponents such as Judge Guido Calabresi of the U.S. Court of

Appeals for the Second Circuit and the legal philosopher Ronald Dworkin. *See* Guido Calabresi, A Common Law for the Age of Statutes 7 (1982) (proposing "a new relationship between courts and statutes, a relationship that would enable us to retain the legislative initiative in lawmaking ... while restoring to courts their common law function of seeing to it that the law is kept up to date"); Ronald Dworkin, Law's Empire 313 (1986) (arguing that a judge should ideally "see his own role as fundamentally the creative one of a partner continuing to develop, in what he believes is the best way, the statutory scheme Congress began").

The following case, *United States v. Marshall*, provides an opportunity to think about questions regarding the appropriate role of judges, and how different conceptions of the judicial role affect approaches to statutory interpretation. The case involves a statute, originally enacted in 1970, called the Comprehensive Drug Abuse Prevention and Control Act. According to the report of the House committee with principal jurisdiction over the bill, the purpose of this Act was "to deal in a comprehensive fashion with the growing menace of drug abuse in the United States" through a variety of means, including an "overall balanced scheme of criminal penalties for offenses involving drugs" (H.R. Rep. No. 91–1444, at 1 (1970)). Title II of the Act, also known as the Controlled Substances Act (CSA), specified criminal penalties for various drug offenses. Congress has amended the CSA's penalty provisions several times, most importantly in 1984 and 1986. As amended, the CSA establishes the following penalties for drug offenses:

## Controlled Substances Act Part D: Offenses and Penalties

### 21 U.S.C. § 841

(a) Unlawful acts

Except as authorized by this subchapter, it shall be unlawful for any person knowingly or intentionally—

(1) to manufacture, distribute, or dispense, or possess with intent to manufacture, distribute, or dispense, a controlled substance; ...

(b) Penalties

Except as otherwise provided in [other sections of the statute], any person who violates subsection (a) of this section shall be sentenced as follows:

(1)(A) In the case of a violation of subsection (a) of this section involving—

> (i) 1 kilogram or more of a mixture or substance containing a detectable amount of heroin;

> (ii) 5 kilograms or more of a mixture or substance containing a detectable amount of [cocaine];

> (iii) 50 grams or more of a mixture or substance ... which contains cocaine base;

(iv) 100 grams or more of phencyclidine (PCP) or 1 kilogram or more of a mixture or substance containing a detectable amount of phencyclidine (PCP);

(v) 10 grams or more of a mixture or substance containing a detectable amount of lysergic acid diethylamide (LSD);

(vi) 400 grams or more of a mixture or substance containing a detectable amount of N–phenyl–N–[1–(2–phenylethyl)–4–piperidinyl] propanamide or 100 grams or more of a mixture or substance containing a detectable amount of any analogue of N–phenyl–N–[1–(2–phenylethyl)–4–piperidinyl] propanamide;

(vii) 1000 kilograms or more of a mixture or substance containing a detectable amount of marijuana, or 1,000 or more marijuana plants regardless of weight; or

(viii) 50 grams or more of methamphetamine . . . or 500 grams or more of a mixture or substance containing a detectable amount of methamphetamine . . . ;

such person shall be sentenced to a term of imprisonment which may not be less than 10 years or more than life and if death or serious bodily injury results from the use of such substance shall be not less than 20 years or more than life. . . .

(B) In the case of a violation of subsection (a) of this section involving—

(i) 100 grams or more of a mixture or substance containing a detectable amount of heroin;

(ii) 500 grams or more of a mixture or substance containing a detectable amount of [cocaine];

(iii) 5 grams or more of a mixture or substance . . . which contains cocaine base;

(iv) 10 grams or more of phencyclidine (PCP) or 100 grams or more of a mixture or substance containing a detectable amount of phencyclidine (PCP);

(v) 1 gram or more of a mixture or substance containing a detectable amount of lysergic acid diethylamide (LSD);

(vi) 40 grams or more of a mixture or substance containing a detectable amount of N–phenyl–N–[1–(2–phenylethyl)–4–piperidinyl] propanamide or 10 grams or more of a mixture or substance containing a detectable amount of any analogue of N–phenyl–N–[1–(2–phenylethyl)–4–piperidinyl] propanamide;

(vii) 100 kilograms or more of a mixture or substance containing a detectable amount of marijuana, or 100 or more marijuana plants regardless of weight; or

(viii) 5 grams or more of methamphetamine . . . or 50 grams or more of a mixture or substance containing a detectable amount of methamphetamine . . . ;

such person shall be sentenced to a term of imprisonment which may not be less than 5 years and not more than 40 years and if death or serious bodily injury results from the use of such substance shall be not less than 20 years or more than life. . . .

---

The CSA, as you can see, establishes very strict "mandatory minimum" penalties for drug manufacturing and distribution offenses, and the applicability of these penalties in most cases depends on weight. Applying these statutory penalties in particular cases may seem to involve little more than some fairly mechanical fact-finding. But, as the *Marshall* case excerpted below illustrates, the mandatory minimum provisions for LSD raised a difficult question of legal interpretation.

---

## United States v. Marshall

U.S. Court of Appeals for the Seventh Circuit
908 F.2d 1312 (7th Cir. 1990) (en banc), *aff'd*, 500 U.S. 453 (1991)

■ Easterbrook, Circuit Judge.

. . . Stanley J. Marshall was convicted after a bench trial and sentenced to 20 years' imprisonment for conspiring to distribute, and distributing, more than ten grams of LSD, enough for 11,751 doses. Patrick Brumm, Richard L. Chapman, and John M. Schoenecker were convicted by a jury of selling ten sheets (1,000 doses) of paper containing LSD. Because the total weight of the paper and LSD was 5.7 grams, a five-year mandatory minimum applied. The district court sentenced Brumm to 60 months (the minimum), Schoenecker to 63 months, and Chapman to 96 months' imprisonment. All four defendants confine their arguments on appeal to questions concerning their sentences.

The [primary question is this]: Whether 21 U.S.C. § 841(b)(1)(A)(v) and (B)(v), which set mandatory minimum terms of imprisonment—five years for selling more than one gram of a "mixture or substance containing a detectable amount" of LSD, ten years for more than ten grams—exclude the weight of a carrier medium. . . .

I

According to the Sentencing Commission, the LSD in an average dose weighs 0.05 milligrams. Twenty thousand pure doses are a gram. But 0.05 mg is almost invisible, so LSD is distributed to retail customers in a carrier. Pure LSD is dissolved in a solvent such as alcohol and sprayed on paper or gelatin; alternatively the paper may be dipped in the solution. After the solvent evaporates, the paper or gel is cut into one-dose squares and sold by the square. Users swallow the squares or may drop them into a beverage, releasing the drug. Although the gelatin and paper are light, they weigh much more than the drug. Marshall's 11,751 doses weighed 113.32 grams; the LSD accounted for only 670.72 mg of this, not enough to activate the five-year mandatory minimum sentence, let alone the ten-year minimum. The ten sheets of blotter paper carrying the 1,000 doses Chapman and confederates sold weighed 5.7 grams; the LSD in the paper did not approach the one-gram threshold for a mandatory minimum sentence. This disparity between the weight of the pure LSD and the weight of LSD-plus-carrier underlies the defendants' arguments.

### A

If the carrier counts in the weight of the "mixture or substance containing a detectable amount" of LSD, some odd things may happen. Weight in the hands of distributors may exceed that of manufacturers and wholesalers. Big fish then could receive paltry sentences or small fish draconian ones. Someone who sold 19,999 doses of pure LSD (at 0.05 mg per dose) would escape the five-year mandatory minimum of § 841(b)(1)(B)(v) and be covered by § 841(b)(1)(C), which lacks a minimum term and has a maximum of "only" 20 years. Someone who sold a single hit of LSD dissolved in a tumbler of orange juice could be exposed to a ten-year mandatory minimum. Retailers could fall in or out of the mandatory terms depending not on the number of doses but on the medium: sugar cubes weigh more than paper, which weighs more than gelatin. One way to eliminate the possibility of such consequences is to say that the carrier is not a "mixture or substance containing a detectable amount" of the drug. Defendants ask us to do this.

Defendants' submission starts from the premise that the interaction of the statutory phrase "mixture or substance" with the distribution of LSD by the dose in a carrier creates a unique probability of surprise results. The premise may be unwarranted. The paper used to distribute LSD is light stuff, not the kind used to absorb ink. Chapman's 1,000 doses weighed about 0.16 ounces. More than 6,000 doses, even in blotter paper, weigh less than an ounce. Because the LSD in one dose weighs about 0.05 milligrams, the combination of LSD-plus-paper is about 110 times the weight of the LSD. The impregnated paper could be described as "0.9% LSD"....

This is by no means an unusual dilution rate for illegal drugs. Heroin sold on the street is 2% to 3% opiate and the rest filler. Jerome J. Platt, *Heroin Addiction: Theory, Research, and Treatment* 48–50 (1986). Sometimes the mixture is even more dilute, approaching the dilution rate for LSD in blotter paper. E.g., United States v. Buggs, 904 F.2d 1070, 1072 (7th Cir.1990) (conviction for sale of 9.95 grams of 1.2% heroin). Heroin and crack cocaine, like LSD, are sold on the streets by the dose, although they are sold by weight higher in the distributional chain. All of the "designer drugs" and many of the opiates are sold by the dose, often conveniently packaged in pills. The Sentencing Commission lists MDA, PCP, psilocin, psilocybin, methaqualone, phenmetrazine, and amphetamines (regular and meth-) along with LSD as drugs sold by the dose in very dilute form. Other drugs, such as dilaudid and dolaphine, are sold by the pill rather than weight, and it is safe to assume that all have far less than 100% active ingredients....

B

It is not possible to construe the words of § 841 to make the penalty turn on the net weight of the drug rather than the gross weight of carrier and drug. The statute speaks of "mixture or substance containing a detectable amount" of a drug. "Detectable amount" is the opposite of "pure"; the point of the statute is that the "mixture" is not to be converted to an equivalent amount of pure drug.

The structure of the statute reinforces this conclusion. The 10–year minimum applies to any person who possesses, with intent to distribute, "100 grams or more of phencyclidine (PCP) or 1 kilogram or more of a mixture or substance containing a detectable amount of phencyclidine (PCP)." Congress distinguished the pure drug from a "mixture or substance containing a detectable amount of" it. All drugs other than PCP are governed exclusively by the "mixture or substance" language. Even brute force cannot turn that language into a reference to pure LSD. Congress used the same "mixture or substance" language to describe heroin, cocaine, amphetamines, and many other drugs that are sold after being cut— sometimes as much as LSD. There is no sound basis on which to treat the words "substance or mixture containing a detectable amount of", repeated verbatim for every drug mentioned in § 841 except PCP, as *different* things for LSD and cocaine although the language is identical, while treating the "mixture or substance" language as meaning the *same* as the reference to pure PCP in 21 U.S.C. § 841(b)(1)(A)(iv) and (B)(iv).

Although the "mixture or substance" language shows that the statute cannot be limited to pure LSD, it does not necessarily follow that blotter paper is a "mixture or substance containing" LSD. That phrase cannot include all "carriers". One gram of crystalline LSD in a heavy glass bottle is still only one gram of "statutory LSD". So is a gram of LSD being "carried" in a Boeing 747. How much mingling of the drug with something else is essential to form a "mixture or substance"? The legislative history is silent, but ordinary usage is indicative.

"Substance" may well refer to a chemical compound, or perhaps to a drug in a solvent. LSD does not react chemically with sugar, blotter paper, or gelatin, and none of these is a solvent. "Mixture" is more inclusive. Cocaine often is mixed with mannitol, quinine, or lactose. These white powders do not react, but it is common ground that a cocaine-mannitol mixture is a statutory "mixture".

LSD and blotter paper are not commingled in the same way as cocaine and lactose. What is the nature of their association? The possibility most favorable to defendants is that LSD sits on blotter paper as oil floats on water. Immiscible substances may fall outside the statutory definition of "mixture". The possibility does not assist defendants—not on this record, anyway. LSD is applied to paper in a solvent; after the solvent evaporates, a tiny quantity of LSD remains. Because the fibers absorb the alcohol, the LSD solidifies inside the paper rather than on it. You cannot pick a grain of LSD off the surface of the paper. Ordinary parlance calls the paper containing tiny crystals of LSD a mixture.

United States v. Rose, 881 F.2d 386 (7th Cir.1989), like every other appellate decision that has addressed the question, concludes that the carrier medium for LSD, like the "cut" for heroin and cocaine, is a "mixture or substance containing a detectable amount" of the drug. Although a chemist might be able to offer evidence bearing on the question whether LSD and blotter paper "mix" any more fully than do oil and water, the record contains no such evidence. Without knowing more of the chemistry than this record reveals, we adhere to the unanimous conclusion of the other courts of appeals that blotter paper treated with LSD is a "mixture or substance containing a detectable quantity of" LSD. . . .

### III

. . .

[In response to the dissent's contention that the scheme as written is irrational, the majority responded, in part:] Both the statute and the guidelines make the sentence increase with quantity. The greater the quantity, the greater the sentence. This is a rational way to proceed. Whether the potential created by failure to adjust for purity will be realized depends not only on the range of purity that actually occurs but also on what can be done about the extreme cases. Do we see major suppliers of LSD skipping out the courthouse door because their pure drug falls outside the mandatory minima . . .? Do we see people going to jail for ten years because they sold one dose of LSD in a soft drink? . . .

We do not see an inverted system of penalties. Counsel have not called to our attention, and we could not find, even one prosecution for selling a single dose of LSD, let alone a single-dose prosecution that ended in a preposterously high sentence. In the broad middle ground of retail and wholesale sales, in which (to judge from recent decisions) LSD almost always is sold in blotter paper, § 841 and the guidelines work as they should: the more doses, the greater the weight; the greater the weight, the longer the sentence. Marshall, wholesaler of 11,751 doses, gets 20 years; the other three defendants, retailers of 1,000, get five to eight years. As for the high end: any manufacturer or wholesaler who is in the business in a big way will trigger either § 841(b)(1)(A)(v) {10 years to life for 10 grams or more of LSD} or § 841(b)(1)(B)(v) {5 to 40 years for 1 gram or more of LSD}. A person who cannot be linked to even one gram is not such a big fish after all.

Even a "minor manufacturer" is covered by § 841(b)(1)(C), which authorizes a maximum sentence of 20 years without parole. . . . [In addition,] [t]he *real* punishment for a manufacturer or a major wholesaler of any drug is not set by § 841. It is set by the Continuing Criminal Enterprise statute, 21 U.S.C. § 848. This law, "a carefully crafted prohibition . . . designed to reach the 'top brass' in the drug rings", Garrett v. United States, 471 U.S. 773, 781 (1985), comes into play whenever a person organizes or supervises a criminal enterprise, involving at least five others, from which he earns substantial income. Major distributors fall within the statute, as do those who aid and abet the drug chieftains. . . . The CCE offense carries a minimum term of 20 years' imprisonment. If the defendant is "the principal administrator" and the enterprise has gross receipts of $10 million per year, the mandatory penalty is life without parole, 21 U.S.C. § 848(b). There is in theory little risk, and in practice none, that the major players in the manufacture and distribution of LSD or any other illegal drug will be treated lightly compared with the four middlemen now before us. Defendants might have established that, despite all appearances, sentences are unrelated (or inversely related) to the amount of pure LSD involved. Yet they introduced no evidence to this effect, and none has been published in the social science literature....

Although the parties say that Congress legislated in ignorance, we lack support for that belief. Congress itself says the opposite, that it selected the weights in the table "after consulting with a number of DEA agents and prosecutors about the distribution patterns for these various drugs". H.R.Rep. No. 99–845, 99th Cong., 2d Sess. 11 (1986). Agents and prosecutors are well-acquainted with the effects of different drugs and the details of their distribution. The numbers in § 841 are not hat sizes. Yet even if we attribute unfamiliarity to Congress, we must recognize our own innocence of data. We do not know whether LSD leaves the factory (a) pure and dry, (b) on blotter paper, or (c) dissolved in alcohol (and, if in solution, at what rate of dilution). The range of weights per dose spans at least three orders of magnitude. If LSD is shipped in solution, then the higher-ups draw longer sentences per dose than do retailers; if shipped in blotter paper the sentences are the same per dose. We do not know the extent to which blotter paper dominates retail sales; if it holds the lion's share, then the risk of erratic sentences at the retail tier is small. We do not know the actual distribution of sentences. For all we can tell, sentences in LSD cases come *closer* to a smooth upward graduation per dose than do sentences for cocaine and heroin. Lacking these facts, we are in no position to condemn this act of Congress as arbitrary in operation....

Although sentences under §§ 841, 846, and 848 together may be proportional to the number of doses sold, it would not matter if they were not. All Congress needs is a rational basis for making the penalties depend on gross rather than net weight. There are at least three.

First, LSD is sold at retail for a low price (a few dollars per dose). Blotter paper apparently has contributed to the renewed success of the drug, making it easy to transport, store, conceal, and sell. Because the carrier medium is an ingredient in the drug distribution business, it is rational to design a schedule of penalties based on that tool of the trade.... Second, extracting the "pure" drug and debating whether that task has been done properly is unnecessary if, in 99% of all cases, LSD is sold in blotter paper. Why reduce the amount to a pure measure if that almost never spells a difference? No one has been prosecuted for distributing LSD in sugar cubes in the last 20 years. Similarly, no one has been prosecuted for possessing significant quantities of pure LSD in the last decade. Why worry about how to treat manufacturers caught red-handed with pure dry LSD if they are never nabbed? Statutes rationally may be addressed to the main cases rather than the exceptions. Congress may count on prosecutorial discretion to take care of the absurd cases (one dose in a quart of lemonade) .... Third, extracting LSD from blotter paper and weighing the drug *accurately* may be difficult.... Congress rationally may decide to avoid a costly and imprecise process. ...

Affirmed.

■ [Judge Cummings' dissent is omitted].

■ Posner, Circuit Judge, joined by Bauer, Chief Judge, and Cummings, Wood, Jr., and Cudahy, Circuit Judges, dissenting.

... Based as it is on weight, the system [for sentencing defendants under § 841] works well for drugs that are sold by weight; and ordinarily the weight quoted to the buyer is the weight of the dilute form, although of course price will vary with purity. The dilute form is the product, and it is as natural to punish its purveyors according to the weight of the product as it is to punish moonshiners by the weight or volume of the moonshine they sell rather than by the weight of the alcohol contained in it. So, for example, under Florida law it is a felony to possess one or more gallons of moonshine, and a misdemeanor to possess less than one gallon, regardless of the alcoholic content.

LSD, however, is sold to the consumer by the dose; it is not cut, diluted, or mixed with something else. Moreover, it is incredibly light. An average dose of LSD weighs .05 milligrams, which is less than two millionths of an ounce. To ingest something that small requires swallowing something much larger. Pure LSD in granular form is first diluted by being dissolved, usually in alcohol, and then a quantity of the solution containing one dose of LSD is sprayed or eyedropped on a sugar cube, or on a cube of gelatin, or, as in the cases before us, on an inch-square section of "blotter" paper.... After the solution is applied to the carrier medium, the alcohol or other solvent evaporates, leaving an invisible (and undiluted) spot of pure LSD on the cube or blotter paper. The consumer drops the cube or the piece of paper into a glass of water, or orange juice, or some other beverage, causing the LSD to dissolve in the beverage, which is then drunk.... [A] quart of orange juice containing one dose of LSD is not more, in any relevant sense, than a pint of juice containing the same one dose, and it would be loony to punish the purveyor of the quart more heavily than the purveyor of the pint. It would be like basing the punishment for selling cocaine on the combined weight of the cocaine and of the vehicle (plane, boat, automobile, or whatever) used to transport it or the syringe used to inject it or the pipe used to smoke it. The blotter paper, sugar cubes, etc. are the vehicles for conveying LSD to the consumer.

The weight of the carrier is vastly greater than that of the LSD, as well as irrelevant to its potency. There is no comparable disparity between the pure and the mixed form (if that is how we should regard LSD on blotter paper or other carrier medium) with respect to the other drugs in section 841, with the illuminating exception of PCP. There Congress specified alternative weights, for the drug itself and for the substance or mixture containing the drug. For example, the five-year minimum sentence for a seller of PCP requires the sale of either ten grams of the drug itself or one hundred grams of a substance or mixture containing the drug.

Ten sheets of blotter paper, containing a thousand doses of LSD, weigh almost six grams. The LSD itself weighs less than a hundredth as much. If the thousand doses are on gelatin cubes instead of sheets of blotter paper, the total weight is less, but it is still more than two grams, which is forty times the weight of the LSD. In both cases, if the carrier plus the LSD constitutes the relevant "substance or mixture" (the crucial "if" in this case), the dealer is subject to the minimum mandatory sentence of five years. One of the defendants before us (Marshall) sold almost 12,000 doses of LSD on blotter paper. This subjected him to the ten-year minimum.... Since it takes 20,000 doses of LSD to equal a gram, Marshall would not have been subject to even the five-year mandatory minimum had he sold the LSD in its pure form. And a dealer who sold fifteen times the number of doses as Marshall—180,000—would not be subject to the ten-year mandatory minimum sentence if he sold the drug in its pure form, because 180,000 doses is only nine grams.

At the other extreme, if Marshall were not a dealer at all but dropped a square of blotter paper containing a single dose of LSD into a glass of orange juice and sold it to a friend at cost (perhaps 35 cents), he would be subject to the ten-year minimum. The juice with LSD dissolved in it would be the statutory mixture or substance containing a detectable amount of the illegal drug and it would weigh more than ten grams.... So a person who sold one dose of LSD might be subject to the ten-year mandatory minimum sentence while a dealer who sold 199,999 doses in pure form would be subject only to the five-year minimum....

All this seems crazy but we must consider whether Congress might have had a reason for wanting to key the severity of punishment for selling LSD to the weight of the carrier rather than to the number of doses or to some reasonable proxy for dosage (as weight is, for many drugs). The only one suggested is that it might be costly to determine the weight of the LSD in the blotter paper, sugar cube, etc., because it is so light! That merely underscores the irrationality of basing the punishment for selling this drug on weight rather than on dosage. But in fact the weight is reported in every case I have seen, so apparently it can be determined readily enough.... If the weight of the LSD is difficult to determine, the difficulty is easily overcome by basing punishment on the number of doses, which makes much more sense in any event. To base punishment on the weight of the carrier medium makes about as much sense as basing punishment on the weight of the defendant.

A person who sells LSD on blotter paper is not a worse criminal than one who sells the same number of doses on gelatin cubes, but he is subject to a heavier punishment. A person who sells five doses of LSD on sugar cubes is not a worse person than a manufacturer of LSD who is caught with 19,999 doses in pure form, but the former is subject to a ten-year mandatory minimum no-parole sentence while the latter is not even subject to the five-year minimum. . . . This is a quilt the pattern whereof no one has been able to discern. The legislative history is silent, and since even the Justice Department cannot explain the why of the punishment scheme that it is defending, the most plausible inference is that Congress simply did not realize how LSD is sold. The inference is reinforced by the statutory treatment of PCP. . . .

Th[e] irrationality is magnified when we compare the sentences for people who sell other drugs prohibited by 21 U.S.C. § 841. Marshall, remember, sold fewer than 12,000 doses and was sentenced to twenty years. Twelve thousand doses sounds like a lot, but to receive a comparable sentence for selling heroin Marshall would have had to sell ten kilograms, which would yield between one and two million doses. To receive a comparable sentence for selling cocaine he would have had to sell fifty kilograms, which would yield anywhere from 325,000 to five million doses. While the corresponding weight is lower for crack—half a kilogram—this still translates into 50,000 doses. . . .

Well, what if anything can we judges do about this mess? The answer lies in the shadow of a jurisprudential disagreement that is not less important by virtue of being unavowed by most judges. It is the disagreement between the severely positivistic view that the content of law is exhausted in clear, explicit, and definite enactments by or under express delegation from legislatures, and the natural lawyer's or legal pragmatist's view that the practice of interpretation . . . authorize[s] judges to enrich positive law with the moral values and practical concerns of civilized society. Judges who in other respects have seemed quite similar, such as Holmes and Cardozo, have taken opposite sides of this issue. Neither approach is entirely satisfactory. The first buys political neutrality and a type of objectivity at the price of substantive injustice, while the second buys justice in the individual case at the price of considerable uncertainty and, not infrequently, judicial willfulness. It is no wonder that our legal system oscillates between the approaches. The positivist view, applied unflinchingly to this case, commands the affirmance of prison sentences that are exceptionally harsh by the standards of the modern Western world, dictated by an accidental, unintended scheme of punishment nevertheless implied by the words (taken one by one) of the relevant enactments. The natural law or pragmatist view leads to a freer interpretation, one influenced by norms of equal treatment; and let us explore the interpretive possibilities here. One is to interpret "mixture or substance containing a detectable amount of [LSD]" to exclude the carrier medium—the blotter paper, sugar or gelatin cubes, and orange juice or other beverage. . . .

Interpreted to exclude the carrier, the punishment schedule for LSD would make perfectly good sense; it would not warp the statutory design. The comparison with heroin and cocaine is again illuminating. The statute imposes the five-year mandatory minimum sentence on anyone who sells a substance or mixture containing a hundred grams of heroin, equal to 10,000 to 20,000 doses. One gram of pure LSD, which also would trigger the five-year minimum, yields 20,000 doses. The comparable figures for cocaine are 3,250 to 50,000 doses, placing LSD in about the middle. So Congress may have wanted to base punishment for the sale of LSD on the weight of the pure drug after all, using one and ten grams of the pure drug to trigger the five-year and ten-year minima (and corresponding maxima— twenty years and forty years). This interpretation leaves "substance or mixture containing" without a referent, so far as LSD is concerned. But we must remember that Congress used the identical term in each subsection that specifies the quantity of a drug that subjects the seller to the designated minimum and maximum punishments. In thus automatically including the same term in each subsection, Congress did not necessarily affirm that, for each and every drug covered by the statute, a substance or mixture containing the drug *must* be found. . . .

The literal interpretation adopted by the majority is not inevitable. All interpretation is contextual. The words of the statute—interpreted against a background that includes a . . . constitutional commitment to rationality, an evident failure by . . . Congress . . . to consider how LSD is actually produced, distributed, and sold, and an equally evident failure . . . to consider the interaction between heavy mandatory minimum sentences and the Sentencing Guidelines—will bear an interpretation that distinguishes between the carrier vehicle of the illegal drug and the substance or mixture containing a detectable amount of the drug. The punishment of the crack dealer is not determined by the weight of the glass tube in which he sells the crack; we should not lightly attribute to Congress a purpose of punishing the dealer in LSD according to the weight of the LSD carrier. We should not make Congress's handiwork an embarrassment to the members of Congress and to us.

---

**1.  *The Semantic Meaning of the Statutory Text*—**Judge Posner's dissent framed the challenge of this case as resolving a tension between the best semantic reading of the statutory text (the majority's interpretation) and the reading that seems more sensible, just, and consistent with the overall goals of the legislative scheme (the dissent's interpretation). Though the case is interesting principally as an opportunity to think about different ways of resolving that sort of tension, it is worth considering at the outset that the semantic and pragmatic arguments might not necessarily point so strongly in the directions that Judges Easterbrook and Posner suggested.

Consider first the semantic arguments about the ordinary meaning of the statutory text. Judge Easterbrook's starting premise was that LSD on blotter paper is clearly a "mixture or substance containing a detectable amount of [LSD]." He found it important that the grains of LSD were interspersed with the fibers of the blotter paper and could not be "pick[ed] . . . off the surface of the paper." On that basis, he concluded that "[o]rdinary parlance calls the paper containing tiny crystals of LSD a mixture." According to Judge Easterbrook, even though the result of including the weight of the blotter paper in calculating the penalty might produce odd results, such a regime was compelled by the language and structure of the statute.

Could Judge Posner have challenged Judge Easterbrook's conclusion about the ordinary meaning of the statutory text head-on? Is it true that in "ordinary parlance" we would call LSD crystals interspersed with paper fibers a "mixture"? If you spilled coffee on a work paper, would you call the coffee-stained end product a "mixture" of coffee and paper? Judge Easterbrook was correct that the technical definition of "mixture," as used in chemistry, is a "composition of two or more substances that are not chemically combined with each other and are capable of being separated." American Heritage Dictionary of the English Language 1128 (4th ed. 2000). But if the person on the street would not use the term "mixture" to describe LSD sprayed on paper, should the court credit the commonplace meaning or the technical meaning? (*See* pp. 113–115, *supra*.) On the one hand, because the statute unquestionably regulates chemical compounds, perhaps it is appropriate to use the chemists' definition. On the other hand, the statute imposes criminal penalties, which may counsel in favor of adopting the everyday understanding of the term, at least when it supplies the narrower definition (*see* pp. 327–337, *infra*). Why didn't Judge Posner engage Judge Easterbrook in these terms? Do you think that he was consciously trying to shift the terms of the debate?

**2.   *The Rationality of the Statutory Scheme***—Assume for present purposes that Judge Easterbrook correctly understood the statute's semantic meaning. Did Judge Posner make a convincing case that the statutory penalties for LSD, on a textualist reading of the statute, are arbitrary and irrational? Judge Posner cited two dimensions along which the statute seems arbitrary. First, under Judge Easterbrook's interpretation, the penalties for distributing LSD seem radically disproportionate to the penalties for distributing other serious narcotics under the statute. To get a comparable sentence for selling approximately 12,000 doses of LSD, one would have had to sell a quantity of heroine that would generate "between one and two million doses" or an amount of cocaine that "would yield anywhere from 325,000 to five million doses." Second, Judge Posner noted that the penalties for LSD will vary wildly depending on the medium in which it is sold: "A person who sells five doses of LSD on sugar cubes is not a worse person than a manufacturer of LSD who is caught with 19,999 doses in pure form, but the former is subject to a ten-year mandatory minimum no-parole sentence while the latter is not even subject to the five-year minimum."

Judge Easterbrook's principal response was that even if the statute appears to compel odd results, that is Congress's prerogative. Congress can constitutionally adopt what Judge Posner referred to as a "quilt"—a statute that draws odd, hard-to-explain lines—as long as it satisfies a minimum standard of rationality; the result in this case, though harsh, is not so absurd that it is inconceivable that Congress could have intended it. Beyond this, though, Judge Easterbrook also took issue with Judge Posner's assertion that a plain reading of the statute is irrational, especially when considered alongside the penalties for manufacturers or wholesalers prescribed by other statutes, the history of prosecutions for LSD, and the real-world practice concerning LSD's retail distribution. Furthermore,

Judge Easterbrook emphasized that the criteria established by the text of the statute might not be irrational because, even though they might sometimes compel strange disproportionalities in sentences, tying sentences to an easily-measurable variable like weight might serve administrative interests relating to the ease of measuring quantity. Is that persuasive?

**3. *Inferences from Statutory Structure***—In addition to his close semantic reading of the text of the LSD sentencing provision, Judge Easterbrook also emphasized that a nearby statutory provision—one that prescribed different penalties for a "mixture or substance containing a detectable amount of [PCP]" and for pure PCP—precluded the court from adopting the defendants' position that the court should base sentences on the weight of pure LSD apart from the blotter paper. The essence of Judge Easterbrook's argument is that the differentiation between the pure substance and a mixture in the PCP provision demonstrates that Congress was aware of the fact that some drugs were sold by the dose on carrier media with variable weight, and that Congress was capable of writing statutory language to reflect this distinction when it chose to. From this, according to Judge Easterbrook, it follows that Congress (for whatever reason) implicitly considered and rejected making an analogous distinction in the context of LSD. Furthermore, adopting the reading of "mixture or substance" favored by Judge Posner for the LSD provision, if applied to the identical language in the PCP provision, would render the careful distinction drawn in the latter provision nonsensical.

How convincing is Judge Easterbrook's structural argument? Might Judge Posner plausibly respond that the PCP provision demonstrates not that Congress made a deliberate decision not to draw an analogous distinction for LSD, but rather that Congress recognized that it would be irrational to base penalties solely on the weight of the mixture for narcotics that are sold by the dose rather than by weight? On this view, Congress's failure to draw a similar distinction in the LSD provision was more likely an oversight than a deliberate (and otherwise inexplicable) decision. Is Judge Posner's explanation more plausible as an empirical claim about why these provisions are structured as they are? Or do you find Judge Easterbrook's account more convincing? And if Judge Posner is right, what follows? Suppose we knew with certainty that Congress's failure to draw a distinction in the LSD provision that parallels the distinction drawn in the PCP provision was an oversight rather than a deliberate decision. Suppose, in other words, that we could be sure that Congress would have drawn a similar distinction for LSD had it considered the issue explicitly. Putting aside the question of whether we could ever have evidence that established that fact convincingly in a real case, should it matter? Presumably a textualist would say no, an intentionalist would say yes, and a purposivist would probably also say yes if the conventional meaning of the text would conflict with the broader purposes of the statute. What do you think?

**4. *What Is the Judge's Role?***—Assume for the sake of argument that Judge Easterbrook had the better of the argument with respect to the statute's semantic meaning, while Judge Posner was correct that Judge

Easterbrook's text-bound interpretation would lead to arbitrary and unjust results that Judge Posner's more freewheeling interpretation would avoid. If that's what the case is about—as Judge Posner insisted—then the case is really a referendum on the proper conception of the role of federal judges in statutory interpretation cases. Judge Posner was admirably evenhanded in discussing the pros and cons of Judge Easterbrook's "positivist" approach and what Judge Posner described as a "natural law" or "pragmatic" approach, in which judges have more freedom to depart from the text in order to "enrich positive law with the moral values and practical concerns of civilized society." As Judge Posner put it, the positivist approach "buys political neutrality and a type of objectivity at the price of substantive injustice," while the pragmatic approach that he favors "buys justice in the individual case at the price of considerable uncertainty and, not infrequently, judicial willfulness." Judge Easterbrook might quibble a bit with Judge Posner's phraseology, but it is likely that he would agree with Judge Posner's framing of the problem, even though he came out the other way. Which conception of the judge's role do you find more attractive? Given these costs and benefits, how should judges decide which approach to adopt? What is the basis for your conclusion?

Is the dispute between Judge Easterbrook and Judge Posner in *Marshall* a conflict between textualism and purposivism, or is the disagreement even deeper and more fundamental? One could characterize the dispute as a conflict between textualism and purposivism if one concludes that Judge Posner's position was ultimately grounded on the view that a conventional reading of the LSD sentencing provisions in the Controlled Substances Act would be contrary to the ends *Congress* was trying to achieve in enacting the statute (for example, a more rational scheme of narcotics regulation that ties the severity of punishment to the severity of the offense). But Judge Posner's language hinted that he was going farther than that, suggesting that judges may legitimately interpret statutes to advance pragmatic and moral ends, even when those ends are not expressly tied to some notion of what Congress intended. What do you think Judge Posner meant to suggest here? Do you think there's a significant difference between these views in practice, or is the nature of purposivist interpretation such that the purposes the judge ascribes to the legislature generally reflect the sort of moral and pragmatic concerns that Judge Posner had in mind? *Cf.* Elizabeth Garrett & Adrian Vermeule, *Institutional Design of a Thayerian Congress*, 50 DUKE L.J. 1277, 1293 (2001) ("[I]maginative reconstruction [of legislative intent or purpose] collapses into substantive decisionmaking, because the best way to figure out what the . . . legislators . . . would do is to figure out what the best answer is.").

**5. Equitable Interpretation and the "Judicial Power"**—If Judge Posner was indeed advocating a conception of the judicial role that is more akin to a junior partner than a faithful agent, then this may not sit well with those who believe our federal system is grounded in the principle of legislative supremacy. Indeed, it may seem flatly inconsistent with conventional notions of the judicial function even to suggest that judges could deviate from the text or the intent of the enacting legislature to further the judges' conceptions of justice or wise policy. Yet advocates of this alternative "junior partner" conception of judging have pointed out that it is not in fact a radical reconceptualization of the judicial role, but is instead grounded in the ancient English practice of "equitable interpretation," pursuant to which "exceptions dictated by sound policy were written by judges into loose statutory generalizations, and, on the other hand, situations were brought within the reach of the statute that admittedly lay without its express terms." James McCauley Landis, *Statutes and the Sources of Law, in* Harvard Legal Essays 213, 215 (Roscoe Pound ed., 1934).

Building on this observation, Professor William Eskridge has argued that the "judicial power" vested in the federal courts by Article III of the Constitution was understood at the time of the founding to include this power of equitable interpretation. *See, e.g.,* William N. Eskridge, Jr., Dynamic Statutory Interpretation 116–18 (1994); William N. Eskridge, Jr., *All About Words: Early Understandings of the "Judicial Power" in Statutory Interpretation, 1776–1806*, 101 Colum. L. Rev. 990 (2001). Those who framed and ratified the Constitution were schooled in English law and legal tradition, so it is likely, Professor Eskridge contends, that they would have understood equitable interpretation to be part of "the judicial Power." Furthermore, in founding-era debates over ratification of the Constitution, Anti–Federalists asserted that the meaning of the Constitution's text would expand over time by virtue of the federal judges' inherent power of equitable interpretation—an assumption that Federalists never expressly disputed, even when defending the Constitution's allocation of judicial power on other grounds. Finally, state courts in the founding era often employed the technique of equitable interpretation, as did some of the early opinions of the Supreme Court under Chief Justices Jay and Ellsworth. Professor Eskridge and others believe that this evidence establishes not only that equitable interpretation is normatively attractive, but also that this approach was implicitly endorsed by the Constitution's assignment of "the judicial power" to the federal courts. This argument is important for modern debates about statutory interpretation because much of the textualist critique of non-textualist approaches is grounded in the notion that legislative supremacy requires textualist interpretation. Even if this were true—a point that most non-textualists would not concede—it would matter much less if the Article III judicial power imbued the federal courts with the traditional English judicial power of equitable interpretation.

But is it really so clear that the "judicial power" assigned by Article III of the Constitution was based on the prevailing English understanding of judicial power? After all, English government at the time of the founding involved a considerable commingling of judicial and legislative powers (*e.g.,* judges frequently wrote statutes, and the Upper House of Parliament served as the court of last resort). Given that the U.S. Constitution rejected that model in favor of a strict separation of legislative and judicial powers, isn't it plausible that the American conception of the appropriate scope of "judicial power" differed sharply from the English conception? By the same token, state judicial practice in the founding era may have only limited probative value as to the prevailing understanding of *federal* judicial power, as many state governments were structured differently from the federal government. Another difficulty for the hypothesis that the Article III judicial power was understood in the founding era to encompass equitable interpretation is the fact that the Marshall Court—composed of members of the founding generation, and extremely influential in shaping American constitutional understandings—generally focused on the text and articulated a strong conception of the faithful agent theory of the judicial role. Professor Eskridge maintains that Chief Justice Marshall's ostensible textualism was strategic, but it is not clear that that was in fact the case, and even if it were, isn't the Marshall Court's practice at least indicative that the constitutional culture surrounding the Article III power had settled around the faithful agent theory once the implications of the new Constitution had been worked out? *See* John F. Manning, *Textualism and the Equity of the Statute*, 101 Colum. L. Rev. 1 (2001); John F. Manning, *Deriving Rules of Statutory Interpretation from the Constitution*, 101 Colum. L. Rev. 1648 (2001).

If one cannot conclusively resolve the conflict between the "faithful agent" and "junior partner" understandings of the Article III power by reference to history or to the text of the Constitution, how should this conflict be resolved? How much authority should federal judges possess to smooth out the rough edges of legislation and to act in common law fashion to ensure the statutory law's consistency and rationality? And, if one relaxes the faithful agency assumption, then interpretation requires not only a theory of legislation, but also a theory of adjudication that does not depend solely on the judge's ability to trace his or her decision back to a choice made by Congress. What would such a theory look like, and what would it be based on? Some conception of "natural law"? Pragmatic considerations of wise policy, viewed in light of the relative institutional competencies of legislatures and judges?

It is important to emphasize that the faithful agent conception of the judicial role remains the dominant one in our legal and political culture. Although the alternative junior partner conception has been endorsed in one form or another by distinguished jurists and scholars, it remains a minority position. As a lawyer, you would be unwise to argue explicitly to a judge that she has the power to modify Congress's statutory command in order to further an interest in substantive justice or sound policy. Yet this alternative understanding of the judicial role is important to understand, not least because it may exert a powerful yet subtle influence over interpretive theories and practices that are conducted, on the surface, in terms of legislative supremacy.

CHAPTER TWO

# CANONS OF CONSTRUCTION

### CONTENTS

# I. Introduction to Canons of Construction

The topic of this chapter is a set of interpretive tools known as "canons of construction." These canons are interpretive principles or presumptions that judges use to discern—or, at times, to construct—statutory meaning. Some of these canons are "semantic" (or "linguistic" or "syntactic"): They are generalizations about how the English language is conventionally used and understood, which judges may use to "decode" statutory terms. The use of semantic canons can therefore be understood simply as a form of textual analysis.

Other canons are substantive, rather than merely semantic. A substantive canon is a judicial presumption—maybe weak, maybe strong, maybe super-strong—in favor of or against a particular substantive outcome. It is possible to conceive of such canons as representing generic approximations of congressional intent: Because the judge thinks it extremely unlikely that Congress would want result $X$, the judge will categorically refuse to read the statute to mandate result $X$ unless the statute clearly requires it. Such canons may also be understood as "conditions on the effectual exercise of legislative power" that "promote objectives of the legal system which transcend the wishes of any particular session of the legislature." HENRY M. HART, JR. & ALBERT M. SACKS, THE LEGAL PROCESS: BASIC PROBLEMS IN THE MAKING AND APPLICATION OF LAW 1376 (William N. Eskridge, Jr. & Philip P. Frickey eds., 1994). On that understanding, the substantive canons are judge-made principles, grounded in commitment to certain systemic (perhaps constitutional) values rather than any empirical beliefs about actual congressional intent.

The following case, *McBoyle v. United States*, packs several interpretive techniques—including both semantic and substantive canons of construction—into a very short opinion. The case is useful both as a recap of the material covered in Chapter One—including textual analysis and consideration of legislative context and history—and as an introduction to the material to be covered in this chapter. Read the case carefully and try to identify all of Justice Holmes's reasons for his conclusion—which may seem counter-intuitive to a modern reader—that an airplane is not a "vehicle."

## McBoyle v. United States

Supreme Court of the United States
283 U.S. 25 (1931)

■ MR. JUSTICE HOLMES delivered the opinion of the Court.

The petitioner was convicted of transporting from Ottawa, Illinois, to Guymon, Oklahoma, an airplane that he knew to have been stolen, and was sentenced to serve three years' imprisonment and to pay a fine of $2,000.... A writ of certiorari was granted by this Court on the question whether the National Motor Vehicle Theft Act applies to aircraft.... That Act provides: "Sec. 2. That when used in this Act: (a) The term 'motor vehicle' shall include an automobile, automobile truck, automobile wagon, motor cycle, or any other self-propelled vehicle not designed for running on rails; ... Sec. 3. That whoever shall transport or cause to be transported in interstate or foreign commerce a motor vehicle, knowing the same to have been stolen, shall be punished by a fine of not more than $5,000, or by imprisonment of not more than five years, or both."

Section 2 defines the motor vehicles of which the transportation in interstate commerce is punished in Section 3. The question is the meaning of the word "vehicle" in the phrase "any other self-propelled vehicle not designed for running on rails." No doubt etymologically it is possible to use the word to signify a conveyance working on land, water or air, and sometimes legislation extends the use in that direction.... But in everyday speech "vehicle" calls up the picture of a thing moving on land.... So here, the phrase under discussion calls up the popular picture. For after including automobile truck, automobile wagon and motor cycle, the words 'any other self-propelled vehicle not designed for running on rails' still indicate that a vehicle in the popular sense, that is a vehicle running on land is the theme. It is a vehicle that runs, not something, not commonly called a vehicle, that flies. Airplanes were well known in 1919 when this statute was passed, but it is admitted that they were not mentioned in the reports or in the debates in Congress. It is impossible to read words that so carefully enumerate the different forms of motor vehicles and have no reference of any kind to aircraft, as including airplanes under a term that usage more and more precisely confines to a different class. The counsel for the petitioner have shown that the phraseology of the statute as to motor vehicles follows that of earlier statutes of Connecticut, Delaware, Ohio, Michigan and Missouri, not to mention the late Regulations of Traffic for the District of Columbia, none of which can be supposed to leave the earth.

Although it is not likely that a criminal will carefully consider the text of the law before he murders or steals, it is reasonable that a fair warning should be given to the world in language that the common world will understand, of what the law intends to do if a certain line is passed. To make the warning fair, so far as possible the line should be clear. When a rule of conduct is laid down in words that evoke in the common mind only the picture of vehicles moving on land, the statute should not be extended to aircraft simply because it may seem to us that a similar policy applies, or upon the speculation that if the legislature had thought of it, very likely broader words would have been used....

---

**1. A Recap: Ordinary Meaning and Statutory Background—** Two of the interpretive moves that Justice Holmes made in *McBoyle* may be familiar if you have covered the material in Chapter One. First, Justice Holmes noted that although it is "etymologically ... possible" to construe the category "vehicle" as including airplanes, the term "vehicle," as used in "everyday speech," calls to mind only vehicles that move on land. So, we can think of the interpretive issue in *McBoyle* as involving a tension between a broad construction of a term that is consistent with that term's dictionary definition, and a narrower construction that is more consistent with how the term is ordinarily used. This is similar to the dispute in *Smith v. United States* about whether the phrase "use a firearm" includes exchanging a firearm for narcotics—on the logic that this is consistent with the dictionary definition of "use"—or whether that phrase, in context, covers only use of a firearm as a weapon, as that is what we ordinarily think of when we hear or read the phrase "use a firearm." *See* pp. 127–136, *supra*. If we stipulate that Justice Holmes was correct that the "popular picture" called to mind by the word "vehicle" in 1919 would have been limited to land vehicles, do you agree with his resolution of the case? Or would you have held that, notwithstanding the "everyday" or "popular" image of a "vehicle," an airplane is unambiguously a vehicle according to the accepted dictionary definition of that word?

Justice Holmes also invoked the legislative history of the statute, pointing out that Congress was well aware of the existence of airplanes when the National Motor Vehicle Theft Act was enacted in 1919, yet airplanes "were not mentioned in the reports or in the debates in Congress." Furthermore, *McBoyle* noted that the text of the federal Act was based on the text in previously enacted state statutes, as well as traffic regulations for the District of Columbia, which were passed before airplanes were in widespread use, and so could not possibly have been meant to cover airplanes. Did you find these arguments from legislative history convincing? Why or why not?

**2. *A Preview of the Canons of Construction*—**In addition to the sorts of arguments just discussed, Justice Holmes made two other interpretive moves that implicitly invoked the sorts of general rules—or canons—of statutory construction that are the focus of this chapter.

First, Justice Holmes emphasized that the term "vehicle" appears at the end of a list of more specific terms ("automobile," "truck," "wagon," and "motor cycle"). These more specific terms, Justice Holmes explained, provide guidance regarding the proper construction of the more general word "vehicle." Without saying so, Justice Holmes here was employing a semantic canon of construction sometimes known by the Latin phrase *ejusdem generis* ("of the same type"). The idea is that human beings—including, or perhaps especially, legislators—tend to group together words that have a common characteristic. *See* pp. 249–266, *infra*.

Second, in the final paragraph of the opinion Justice Holmes emphasized that criminal statutes ought to be clear, and that courts should not construe a statute to impose criminal penalties on a defendant if the statute could plausibly be read as not covering the defendant's conduct. Here Justice Holmes appeared to be alluding to a classic substantive canon of construction, the "rule of lenity." *See* pp. 327–337, *infra*.

Do these arguments strike you as compelling?

## II. SEMANTIC CANONS OF CONSTRUCTION

The enactment of a law is a form of communication through language—from the law-giver to those affected by the law, as well as to those who must enforce, apply, or interpret the law. This sort of communication is only possible if the participants have a set of shared practices and conventions that permit them to convey meaning to each other. At the most basic level, intelligible communication requires that both parties attach the same meaning to the same sounds or signs. Furthermore, we often need to be able to tell which of several possible meanings is intended by considering the context in which a word is used. Our shared practices and conventions also go beyond word meanings. The rules of grammar and syntax, for example, represent shared conventions that assist us in decoding the communications of others.

In the law of statutory interpretation, courts have developed or recognized a number of rules of thumb for decoding legal language. These rules of thumb—often described as semantic (or linguistic or syntactic) canons of construction—have sometimes been given Latin names that make them seem more alien and technical than they really are. Many of these canons in fact resemble the practices and conventions that we would use in ordinary conversation. For example, in *McBoyle*, one of the reasons that Justice Holmes gives for the conclusion that an airplane is not a "vehicle" within the meaning of the National Motor Vehicle Theft Act is that the relevant statutory term "vehicle" appears as a catch-all term at the end of a list that includes only vehicles that run on land, like cars, trucks, and motorcycles. As Justice Holmes explains, "a vehicle running on land is the theme," and it "is impossible to read words that so carefully enumerate the different forms of motor vehicles and have no reference to any kind of aircraft, as including airplanes...." That kind of contextual inference is sometimes described as the application of a canon called *ejusdem generis* ("of the same type"), but really all Justice Holmes is doing is relying on a generalization about what people, including legislators, usually have in mind when they include a general catch-all term at the end of a list of more specific items.

There are many such semantic canons of construction. One of the most famous (and infamous) is the *expressio unius* canon (short for *expressio unius est exclusio alterius*: the expression of one thing implies the exclusion of others). The *expressio unius* canon (sometimes alternatively known as the *inclusio unius* canon) is a shorthand way of expressing a commonsense idea: When a parent tells a child that she "may have a glass of orange juice," that permission impliedly precludes her from reaching for the Diet Dr. Pepper next to it on the refrigerator shelf. Or consider the canon *noscitur a sociis*, which means that a word is known by its associates. If a statute authorizes regulation of "banks," we will not be sure what "bank" means until we know if the surrounding language deals with financial institutions or navigable riverways. *See* Lawrence Lessig, *Understanding*

*Changed Readings: Fidelity and Theory*, 47 Stan. L. Rev. 395, 407–08 (1995). Justice Scalia has described these sorts of semantic canons as "so commonsensical that, were the canons not couched in Latin, you would find it hard to believe anyone could criticize them." Antonin Scalia, *Common-Law Courts in a Civil–Law System: The Role of United States Federal Courts in Interpreting the Constitution and Laws, in* A Matter of Interpretation 3, 26 (Amy Gutmann ed., 1997). Less colorfully, Justice Holmes described the semantic canons as "axiom[s] of experience" about the way we use language. Boston Sand & Gravel Co. v. United States, 278 U.S. 41, 48 (1928).

Nonetheless, the semantic canons have proven to be controversial. Indeed, until recently, few scholars had anything nice to say about them. This disfavor may be almost entirely attributable to a 1950 article published by Professor Karl Llewellyn. Llewellyn argued that every canon has an equal and opposite counter-canon, and that judges deciding statutory interpretation cases simply invoke the canon that favors the result they wish to reach. He famously wrote:

> When it comes to presenting a proposed construction in court, there is an accepted conventional vocabulary. As in argument over points of case-law, the accepted convention still, unhappily requires discussion as if only one single correct meaning could exist. Hence there are two opposing canons on almost every point. . . . Plainly, [therefore,] to make any canon take hold in a particular instance, the construction contended for must be sold, essentially, by means other than use of the canon. . . .

Karl N. Llewellyn, *Remarks on the Theory of Appellate Decision and the Rules or Canons About How Statutes Are to Be Construed*, 3 Vand. L. Rev. 395, 401 (1950). Llewellyn appended to his article a chart listing twenty-eight pairs of canons drawn from various cases and treatises, where each canon appeared to contradict the one with which it was paired. To give a flavor, consider the first two pairs. First, Llewellyn juxtaposed the canon that "[a] statute cannot go beyond its text" with the counter-canon that "[t]o effect its purpose a statute may be implemented beyond its text." The second pairing combined the canon that "[s]tatutes in derogation of the common law will not be extended by construction" with the counter-canon that "[s]uch acts will be liberally construed if their nature is remedial."

Richard Posner subsequently built on Llewellyn's critique by noting that many of the canons rest on unrealistic assumptions about the legislative process. Richard A. Posner, *Statutory Interpretation—in the Classroom and in the Courtroom*, 50 U. Chi. L. Rev. 800, 805–18 (1983). For example, he wrote that "the canon that every word of a statute must be given significance [and that] nothing in the statute can be treated as surplusage" rests on a false "assumption of legislative omniscience." *Id*. at 812. As Judge Posner observed: "No one would suggest that judicial opinions or academic articles contain no surplusage; are these documents less carefully prepared than statutes?" *Id*.

Despite these criticisms, courts and judges have continued to invoke semantic canons when resolving questions of statutory interpretation. Recently, there has been something of a revival of scholarly interest in the canons, with some suggesting that critiques of the sort advanced by Llewellyn and Posner may be overstated. Justice Scalia, for example, has observed that Llewellyn's pairings of canons and counter-canons do not show that the use of canons in statutory interpretation is "a fraud," but rather shows only that any particular canon "is not absolute." *Scalia, supra*, at 27. For example, the twelfth pairing on Llewellyn's chart matches the canon "[i]f language is plain and unambiguous it must be given effect" with the counter-canon "[n]ot when literal interpretation would lead to absurd or mischievous consequences or thwart manifest purpose." *Llewellyn, supra*, at 403. The latter "canon" seems to be an exception to the former that applies *if and only if* specified conditions are satisfied. This suggests that, contrary to Llewellyn's criticisms, the canons may provide useful interpretive guidance if judges develop conventions for determining which canon applies *in context*. Consider the observations of Professors Jonathan Macey and Geoffrey Miller on this score:

> The canons present no greater opportunity for judicial willfulness than do other techniques of statutory interpretation.... Rather, in a wide array of situations, common sense or practical wisdom will inform judges' decisions about which canon to employ in a given context. For example, one may tell a person standing on the edge of a deep gorge "he who hesitates is lost." One also might say "look before you leap." But, of course, common sense dictates that the latter maxim is more appropriate than the former in this context. Common sense similarly will inform the decision in other situations. Thus, while it is true that no meta-rule or formal model is available to instruct judges in picking and choosing among canons, in the same way that people who do not know the rules of grammar can employ grammatically correct language when speaking English, it seems plausible that judges can select among canons in a sensible and coherent fashion even in the absence of known rules to guide them.

Jonathan R. Macey & Geoffrey P. Miller, *The Canons of Statutory Construction and Judicial Preferences*, 45 VAND. L. REV. 647, 650–51 (1992).

The cases in this section will give you an opportunity to consider the scope, nature, and appropriateness of a variety of semantic canons of construction. As you read the cases, think about how the criticisms of the canons—and the efforts to rehabilitate them—square with your impressions of the cases. Consider also how the canons square with the rules of thumb you bring to understanding conversations with others.

## A.  THE *EXPRESSIO UNIUS* CANON

One of the most frequently invoked, and frequently criticized, semantic canons of construction is the *expressio unius* (or *inclusio unius*) canon—the principle that when a statutory provision explicitly expresses or includes particular things, other things are implicitly excluded. Like most semantic canons, *expressio unius*—despite its fancy-sounding Latin name—is really just a shorthand way of expressing an intuitive idea about how language is used and understood. Yet as the following case illustrates, it is often unclear when the expression of one thing really does imply the exclusion of others, and when it implies no such thing. How does one know when to apply the *expressio unius* canon? Is it, as Professor Llewellyn suggested, an arbitrary *post hoc* justification for decisions reached on other grounds? Or is it simply a matter of sensitivity to context, no different in kind from other forms of semantic interpretation? If the latter, then does characterizing this particular aspect of contextual interpretation as a "canon"—a general rule or principle with a special name—make any practical difference? Does this characterization helpfully clarify the reasons for particular textual inferences, or does it unhelpfully make this sort of interpretation seem more rule-bound then it really is?

---

# Silvers v. Sony Pictures Entertainment, Inc.

U.S. Court of Appeals for the Ninth Circuit
402 F.3d 881 (9th Cir. 2005) (en banc)

■ Graber, Circuit Judge.

May an assignee who holds an accrued claim for copyright infringement, but who has no legal or beneficial interest in the copyright itself, institute an action for infringement? After analyzing the 1976 Copyright Act and its history . . ., we answer that question "no." . . .

### FACTUAL AND PROCEDURAL BACKGROUND

Nancey Silvers wrote the script of a made-for-television movie called "The Other Woman." Although Silvers wrote "The Other Woman" script, she did not hold the copyright, because "The Other Woman" was a work-for-hire that Silvers completed for Frank & Bob Films. . . . Frank & Bob Films was the original owner of the copyright to "The Other Woman," and remains so today.

About three years after "The Other Woman" aired on a broadcast network, Sony Pictures Entertainment, Inc., released the motion picture "Stepmom." After the release of "Stepmom," Frank & Bob Films executed an "Assignment of Claims and Causes of Action" in favor of Silvers. Frank & Bob Films retained ownership of the underlying copyright to "The Other Woman" script, but assigned to Silvers "all right, title and interest in and to any claims and causes of action against Sony Pictures Entertainment, Inc., Columbia TriStar, and any other appropriate persons or entities, with respect to the screenplay 'The Other Woman' . . . and the motion picture 'Stepmom.' "

Silvers then filed a complaint against Sony for copyright infringement, alleging that the movie "Stepmom" was substantially similar to the script for "The Other Woman." Sony moved to dismiss on the ground that Silvers lacked standing to bring an action for copyright infringement in the absence of some legal or beneficial ownership in the underlying copyright. . . .

## DISCUSSION

### A. The Statute

. . . Section 501(b) of the 1976 Copyright Act establishes who is legally authorized to sue for infringement of a copyright:

> The *legal or beneficial owner of an exclusive right under a copyright* is entitled, subject to the requirements of section 411, to institute an action for any infringement of that particular right committed while he or she is the owner of it.

17 U.S.C. § 501(b) (emphasis added). The meaning of that provision appears clear. To be entitled to sue for copyright infringement, the plaintiff must be the "legal or beneficial owner of an exclusive right under a copyright." . . .

Section 106 of the 1976 Copyright Act, in turn, defines "exclusive rights":

> (1) to reproduce the copyrighted work in copies or phonorecords;

> (2) to prepare derivative works based upon the copyrighted work;

> (3) to distribute copies or phonorecords of the copyrighted work to the public by sale or other transfer of ownership, or by rental, lease, or lending;

> (4) in the case of literary, musical, dramatic, and choreographic works, pantomimes, and motion pictures and other audiovisual works, to perform the copyrighted work publicly;

> (5) in the case of literary, musical, dramatic, and choreographic works, pantomimes, and pictorial, graphic, or sculptural works, including the individual images of a motion picture or other audiovisual work, to display the copyrighted work publicly; and

> (6) in the case of sound recordings, to perform the copyrighted work publicly by means of a digital audio transmission.

17 U.S.C. § 106. The right to sue for an accrued claim for infringement is not an exclusive right under § 106. Section 201(d) refers to exclusive rights and provides:

> (1) The ownership of a copyright may be transferred in whole or in part by any means of conveyance or by operation of law, and may be bequeathed by will or pass as personal property by the applicable laws of intestate succession.

> (2) Any of the exclusive rights comprised in a copyright, including any subdivision of any of the rights specified by section 106, may be transferred as provided by clause (1) and owned separately. The owner of any particular exclusive right is entitled, to the extent of that right,

to all of the protection and remedies accorded to the copyright owner
by this title.

17 U.S.C. § 201(d). Exclusive rights in a copyright may be transferred and
owned separately, but § 201(d) creates no exclusive rights other than those
listed in § 106, nor does it create an exception to § 501(b).

... Returning to the operative section, under § 501(b) the plaintiff
must have a legal or beneficial interest in at least one of the exclusive
rights described in § 106. Additionally, in order for a plaintiff to be
"entitled ... to institute an action" for infringement, the infringement
must be "committed while he or she is the owner of" the particular
exclusive right allegedly infringed.

The statute does not say expressly that *only* a legal or beneficial owner
of an exclusive right is entitled to sue. But, under traditional principles of
statutory interpretation, Congress' explicit listing of who *may* sue for
copyright infringement should be understood as an *exclusion of others* from
suing for infringement. The doctrine of *expressio unius est exclusio alterius*
"as applied to statutory interpretation creates a presumption that when a
statute designates certain persons, things, or manners of operation, all
omissions should be understood as exclusions." Boudette v. Barnette, 923
F.2d 754, 756–57 (9th Cir.1991).

There are two particularly important reasons to apply such a presumption here. First, we are mindful of the principle with which we began our
discussion: Copyright is a creature of statute, so we will not lightly insert
common law principles that Congress has left out. Second, the durational
limitation in § 501(b) shows that Congress restricted even the legal or
beneficial owner of a copyright; the owner is not entitled to sue unless the
alleged infringement occurred "while he or she [was] the owner of it." In
other words, Congress' grant of the right to sue was carefully circumscribed....

■ [Judge Berzon's dissent, which Judge Reinhardt joined, is omitted.]

■ Bea, Circuit Judge, with whom Kleinfeld, Circuit Judge, joins, dissenting:

The question presented in this case is whether an assignee of an
accrued cause of action for copyright infringement, who has no legal or
beneficial interest in the copyright itself, has standing to sue for copyright
infringement....

## I.

... Section 501(b) of the 1976 Act provides, in pertinent part:

The legal or beneficial owner of an exclusive right under a copyright is
entitled, subject to the requirements of section 411, to institute an
action for any infringement of that particular right committed while he
or she is the owner of it.

Turning to first principles, then, it is well-established that courts
should interpret a statute according to its plain meaning.... However,
where a statute is ambiguous, courts should consult a statute's legislative

history to discern Congressional intent. Here, as the Majority acknowledges, the statute does not address the present question and is therefore ambiguous. . . .

The key to understanding the legislative history of the 1976 Act, then, is an understanding of the history of standing to sue under copyright law as it existed prior to the 1976 Act. When read in context with copyright law that existed before the 1976 Act, and the portions of the law that were not changed by such Act, a conclusion different from the Majority's reading emerges.

### A.   History of the 1909 Copyright Act

Under the Copyright Act of 1909 ("1909 Act") (codifying copyright law before the enactment of the 1976 Act), the "proprietor" of a copyright was afforded the right to sue for copyright infringement. 17 U.S.C. § 101(b) (1909). While the 1909 Act did not define the term "proprietor," courts interpreted that term to mean the "sole owner" of the copyright. *See, e.g.,* Gardner v. Nike, Inc., 279 F.3d 774, 777–778 (9th Cir.2002). . . .

The 1909 Act was predicated on the "doctrine of indivisibility." *Id.* at 778. That is, under the Act, a copyright owner possessed an indivisible "bundle of rights" which were "incapable of assignment in part." *Id.* Accordingly, assignment under the 1909 Act included "the totality of rights commanded by copyright." *Id.* Transfer of "[a]nything less than an assignment was considered a license." *Id.* Regardless [of] the particular use of the copyright, "only the copyright *proprietor* (which would include an *assignee* but *not* a *licensee*) had standing to bring an infringement action." *Id.* (emphasis added).

Even though the statute granted standing solely to the "proprietor" of the entire copyright, courts nevertheless allowed *assignees* of an accrued cause of action for copyright infringement to sue for infringement of their property rights. . . . The infringement claim, like any other contingent asset, could be sold, much like the copyright holder's claim against a trade debtor or a coupon clipped from the copyright holder's bond portfolio.

Moreover, all defenses against the assignor were valid against the assignee, who "stood in the shoes" of the assignor. See T.B. Harms & Francis, Day & Hunter v. Stern, 231 F. 645, 647 (2d Cir.1916). . . .

### B.   History of the 1976 Copyright Act

The 1976 Act was the result of 15 years of debate on proposed legislation and was precipitated by Congress's recognition that the nature of copyrighted works had changed. Congress noted that, during the half-century since the passage of the 1909 Act, "a wide range of new techniques for capturing and communicating printed matter, visual images, and recorded sounds have come into use." H.R.Rep. No. 94–1476 at 159. For example, no longer was an opera performed only in a theater, but such a work could be performed in movies, television, videos, records, and other forms. Such technical advances "generated new industries and new methods for the production and dissemination of copyrighted works, and the

business relations between authors and users have evolved new patterns."
*Id.*

Toward that end, Congress recognized the commercial need to divide and "infinitely subdivide" copyright uses in recognition of increasing technologically driven varieties of means of reproduction and distribution. Thus, one main purpose of the 1976 Act was, for the first time, to recognize the principle of "divisibility" of uses of a copyright, and the ability to convey the rights to uses separately to various reproducers, which divisible rights did not exist under the 1909 Act. See H.R.Rep. No. 94–1476 at 159.

Congress further recognized that allowing for "divisibility" of the copyright required a mechanism whereby heretofore barred owners of exclusive licenses could now sue for copyright infringement. Accordingly, Congress enacted Section 501 of the 1976 Act to provide access to the courts for the owner of one or more rights to exclusive use, but did not mention the right of the owner of the overall copyright to sue. See 17 U.S.C. § 501(b).

Indeed, in providing for the right *of exclusive licensees* to sue, the drafters of the 1976 Act stated:

> *The principle of the divisibility of copyright ownership, established by section 201(d), carries with it the need in infringement actions to safeguard the rights of all copyright owners and to avoid a multiplicity of suits.* Subsection (b) of section 501 enables the owner of a particular right to bring an infringement action in that owner's name alone, while at the same time insuring to the extent possible that the other owners whose rights may be affected are notified and given a chance to join the action.

H.R.Rep. No. 94–1476 at 159 (emphasis added).

... [T]he statement above in italics ... demonstrates that Congress intended to *enlarge* the ability to bring suit to the owners of exclusive rights.

Read in context with provisions of the 1909 Act (to the extent the acts are not inconsistent), and contrary to the Majority's conclusion, the 1976 Act's Section 501(b) was an *enlargement* of infringement action rights. Henceforth, standing was not limited only to the "proprietor" of the original copyright; a legal or beneficial owner of exclusive rights severed by assignment from the original copyright also had standing to sue for infringement. However, nothing in the 1976 Act eliminated the rights of copyright owners under ... the 1909 Act to their remedies, nor the right of property owners to enjoy the property rights granted by the statute, including the assignment and enforcement of accrued causes of action....

## II.

The Majority concludes that because the statute does not *expressly* grant standing to assignees of an accrued cause of action, such persons do not have standing. Rather, the Majority reasons that, applying the maxim of statutory construction *expressio unius exclusio alterius est*, "Congress' explicit listing of who *may* sue for copyright infringement should be understood as an *exclusion of others* from suing for infringement." (emphasis in original). In my view, the Majority misapplies this maxim of statutory construction.

*First*, such maxims of statutory construction are to be used only when Congressional intent cannot be discerned. Indeed, we have noted:

> Most strongly put, the *expressio unius*, or *inclusio unius*, principle is that '[w]hen a statute limits a thing to be done in a particular mode, it includes a negative of any other mode.' This is a rule of interpretation, not a rule of law. The maxim is 'a product of logic and common sense,' properly applied only when it makes sense as a matter of legislative purpose.... [T]he *expressio unius* principle describes what we usually mean by a particular manner of expression, but does not prescribe how we must interpret a phrase once written. Understood as a descriptive generalization about language rather than a prescriptive rule of construction, the maxim usefully describes a common syntactical implication. 'My children are Jonathan, Rebecca and Seth' means 'none of my children are Samuel.' Sometimes there is no negative pregnant: 'get milk, bread, peanut butter and eggs at the grocery' probably does not mean 'do not get ice cream.' "

Longview Fibre Co. v. Rasmussen, 980 F.2d 1307, 1313 (9th Cir.1992) (internal citations omitted). See also Nat'l R.R. Passenger Corp. v. Nat'l Ass'n of R.R. Passengers, 414 U.S. 453, 458 (1974) ("This principle of statutory construction reflects an ancient maxim—*expressio unius est exclusio alterius*.... But even the most basic general principles of statutory construction must yield to clear contrary evidence of legislative intent."). Here, Congressional intent is readily discernible, and, as demonstrated above, contrary to the Majority's application of the maxim.

*Second*, commentators have noted that the use of maxims of statutory construction such as "*expressio unius*" are problematic insofar as there is no hierarchy of maxims of statutory interpretation. Why choose *expressio unius* rather than another maxim, indeed, the exact opposite: that listing some cases may include others? In his recent book, *A Matter of Interpretation*, Justice Scalia wrote, "[t]he hard truth of the matter is that American courts have no intelligible, generally accepted, and consistently applied theory of statutory interpretation."[9] Antonin Scalia, *A Matter of Interpretation*, 14 (1997) (quoting Henry M. Hart, Jr. & Albert M. Sacks, *The Legal Process* 1169 (William N. Eskridge, Jr. & Philip P. Frickey eds., 1994)).

---

**9.** See Stephen J. Safranek, Scalia's Lament, 8 Tex. Rev. L. & Pol. 315, 316 (Spring 2004) (noting the lack of hierarchy among maxims of statutory interpretation; "in the cases where judges apply interpretive aids, the aids are often used in isolation and are not necessarily the controlling method by which the statute is interpreted."); see also Karl N. Llewellyn, Remarks on the Theory of Appellate Decision and The Rules or Canons About How Statutes Are to Be Construed, 3 Vand. L. Rev. 395, 405 (1949–1950) (noting that "there are two opposing canons on almost every point"; and noting that the opposing canon for the *expressio unius exclusio alterius est* is "[t]he language may fairly comprehend many different cases where some only are expressly mentioned by way of example").

*Third*, while maxims of statutory construction may, indeed, be *helpful* in interpreting statutes, they are not *binding*. The Founders, including Alexander Hamilton, recognized as much. See Alexander Hamilton, *The Federalist Papers*, No. 83 at 464 (Clinton Rossiter ed., 1961) ("The rules of legal interpretation are rules of common sense, adopted by the courts in the construction of laws. The true test of a just application of them is its conformity with the source from which they are derived.").

Hence, rather than be guided by a Latin maxim nowhere mentioned by the 1976 Act or our jurisprudence as hierarchically preferable to other means of statutory interpretation, we should be guided by plain legislative intent, which, as our Supreme Court reminds us, trumps the ancient Latin maxim underpinning the Majority Opinion's conclusion. See *Nat'l R.R. Passenger Corp.*, 414 U.S. at 459.

Indeed, it should be noted that where Congress chooses to expressly prohibit assignment, it knows how to do so explicitly.... Here, that Congress did not prohibit assignment of infringement claims may well carry a negative pregnant that it intended not to prohibit assignment....

---

**1. *When Does the Canon Apply?***—The introduction to this section discussed Karl Llewellyn's famous critique of the canons of construction: that for every canon, there is a contradictory counter-canon (or, at least, a qualification or exception that renders the principal canon indeterminate in practice). Judge Bea's dissent made specific reference to Llewellyn's critique of the *expressio unius* canon: while many cases cite the principle that the expression of specific items implicitly excludes others not mentioned, other cases state that sometimes specific items are mentioned expressly only by way of example, and thus do not impliedly exclude other items that the statute might otherwise be read to cover. There is a sense in which Professor Llewellyn (and Judge Bea) must be correct: There are countless examples of statements where the express inclusion of some things in no way implies the exclusion of others. Professor Max Radin, a contemporary of Llewellyn, famously wrote that the *expressio unius* canon stands "in direct contradiction to the habits of speech of most persons," adding by way of example that "[t]o say that all men are mortal does not mean that all women are not." Max Radin, *Statutory Interpretation*, 43 HARV. L. REV. 863, 873 (1930). Judge Bea's dissent quoted a more prosaic example from an earlier Ninth Circuit decision, pointing out that an instruction to "get milk, bread, peanut butter and eggs at the grocery" usually does not imply that the shopper should not also get ice cream.

Yet at the same time, isn't it true that *sometimes* the expression or enumeration of certain things really does imply the exclusion of others, in a way that any reasonable person would recognize? Consider Professor Geoffrey Miller's example that "if a statute says, 'All cats born on or after January 1, 1989, shall be vaccinated for feline leukemia,' this is not inconsistent logically with the proposition that cats born *before* January 1, 1989, shall be vaccinated; yet any reader would understand intuitively that construing the statute to cover this second class of cats would flout a standard convention of interpretation." Geoffrey P. Miller, *Pragmatics and the Maxims of Interpretation*, 1990 WIS. L. REV. 1179, 1196.

If one concludes that the *expressio unius* canon is sometimes, but not always, a sensible way to interpret statutory language, what follows? Is the canon's application simply dependent on context, as is every linguistic convention? *See* Jonathan R. Macey & Geoffrey P. Miller, *The Canons of Statutory Construction and Judicial Preferences*, 45 VAND. L. REV. 647, 650–51 (1992). If so, should we trust judges to understand when a statutory list or specification justifies a negative implication in context, just as we trust ourselves to do so in ordinary conversation? Or should courts specify with greater precision the circumstances in which particular canons, including *expressio unius*, do or do not apply? In recent years, the Supreme Court has made some efforts along these lines. *See, e.g.,* Barnhart v. Peabody Coal Co., 537 U.S. 149, 168 (2003) ("[T]he canon *expressio unius est exclusio alterius* does not apply to every statutory listing or grouping; it has force only when the items expressed are members of an 'associated group or series,' justifying the inference that items not mentioned were excluded by deliberate choice, not inadvertence.") (*quoting* United States v. Vonn, 535 U.S. 55, 65 (2002)). Moreover, some commentators have suggested that the Supreme Court has systematic incentives to engage in precisely that kind of clarification, given the Justices' awareness of the problem and of Llewellyn's criticism. *See* William N. Eskridge, Jr. & Philip P. Frickey, *The Supreme Court, 1993 Term—Foreword: Law As Equilibrium*, 108 HARV. L. REV. 26, 66 (1994). Do you think such efforts are likely to be effective? If we need a second tier of rules of thumb to understand how to apply the first tier of rules of thumb (the canons), then will we eventually need a third tier to understand how to apply the second tier, and so on?

**2. The Expressio Unius *Canon and Congressional Intent*—** Although parts of Judge Bea's dissent seemed to embrace Llwellyn's position that the *expressio unius* canon is generally useless, it is possible to read the dissent as taking the more moderate position that although *expressio unius* is *sometimes* helpful in resolving statutory ambiguities, judges should invoke this canon (and others like it) only when "Congressional intent cannot be discerned." In the *Silvers* case, Judge Bea believed that the intent of Congress could be inferred from the legislative history and overall structure of the statute. But isn't it problematic to assert that judges should invoke semantic canons only when the intent of Congress is unclear? After all, haven't we said that the semantic canons, including *expressio unius*, are merely shorthand ways of expressing commonsense principles of linguistic interpretation, comparable to the rules of grammar or syntax? If that's so, then what can it possibly mean to say that one should "use" or "apply" the *expressio unius* canon only if the statute is ambiguous? If the *expressio unius* canon is just a way of describing a standard form of textual interpretation, then presumably application of the canon is part of the process of determining whether the statute is textually ambiguous in the first place. Or is the idea that the textual inferences one would draw from something like the *expressio unius* canon are sufficiently weak that other indicia of congressional intent (including, perhaps, extrinsic sources like legislative history) take precedence?

This question about the order of priority of different tools of statutory interpretation keeps coming up, because although courts often declare that certain interpretive tools should be used only when a statute is ambiguous, the courts are typically less clear on which of these ambiguity-resolving tools ought to be used *first*. To illustrate the problem, suppose we have a statute that is ambiguous—it could mean $X$ or $Y$. The case law says that if a statute is ambiguous, a court may use a semantic canon (say, *expressio unius*) to resolve that ambiguity. Suppose that an application of the *expressio unius* principle would support interpretation $X$. But the case law might also establish that if a statute is ambiguous, a court may legitimately look to extrinsic sources (such as legislative history). Suppose that the legislative history implies that interpretation $Y$ is more consistent with congressional intent. So, what is a court to do? In the post-New Deal period, when the Supreme Court was most enthusiastic about using legislative history, the Court frequently emphasized that semantic canons, such as *expressio unius*, necessarily yielded to persuasive evidence of legislative intent or purpose. *See, e.g.*, Andrus v. Glover Constr. Co., 446 U.S. 608, 616–617 (1980); National R.R. Passenger Corp. v. National Ass'n of R.R. Passengers, 414 U.S. 453, 458 (1974). In recent years, in keeping with the greater focus on the semantic meaning of statutory texts and increased skepticism of legislative history, the Court has been more inclined to use semantic canons like *expressio unius* to ascertain a sufficiently clear textual meaning to preclude consultation of legislative history. *See, e.g.*, Barnhart v. Sigmon Coal Co., 534 U.S. 438, 457 & n.15 (2002); United States v. Gonzales, 520 U.S. 1, 5–6 (1997); *see also* James J. Brudney & Corey Ditslear, *Canons of Construction and the Elusive Quest for Neutral Reasoning*, 58 Vand. L. Rev. 1, 45–49 (2005). Does that seem like a sound approach? Should courts invoke the *expressio unius* canon before turning to legislative history, on the logic that statutory text should take priority over extrinsic evidence of statutory meaning, and that the *expressio unius* canon is a way of interpreting the text itself? Or should courts look to the legislative history before invoking *expressio unius*, on the logic that the canons like *expressio unius* are weak linguistic generalizations that courts can use to make educated guesses about congressional intent when no better evidence is available, but that sufficiently clear legislative history provides much surer guidance?

## B.  The *Noscitur A Sociis* Canon, the Presumption Favoring Consistent Meaning, and the Presumption Against Surplus Language

In statutory interpretation cases, judges often try to discern the meaning of ambiguous terms by looking to other terms in the statute and making assumptions about how these other terms relate to the ambiguous language at issue. That is, judges apply semantic canons that pertain to the relationship between different statutory terms. The following case, *Gustafson v. Alloyd Co.*, illustrates three such canons: *first*, the presumption that the same word or phrase has the same meaning in different sections of the same statute; *second*, the presumption that a word's meaning can be clarified—and often narrowed—by the words around it (the *noscitur a sociis* canon); and *third*, the presumption that each word in a statute has meaning, such that interpretations which would render certain statutory language redundant or otherwise superfluous are disfavored. As you read the majority and dissenting opinions in *Gustafson*, consider the role that these interpretive canons do or should play in resolving a case like this. Consider also whether the case supports Professor Llewellyn's claim that the canons are manipulable *post hoc* rationalizations for decisions reached on other grounds, or whether the case illustrates instead Justice Scalia's argument that these so-called canons simply describe intuitive and familiar techniques that we all use, sometimes unconsciously, in understanding language in context.

## Gustafson v. Alloyd Company, Inc.

Supreme Court of the United States
513 U.S. 561 (1995)

■ JUSTICE KENNEDY delivered the opinion of the Court.

Under § 12(2) of the Securities Act of 1933 buyers have an express cause of action for rescission [that is, the undoing of a contract] against sellers who make material misstatements or omissions "by means of a prospectus." The question presented is whether this right of rescission extends to a private, secondary transaction, on the theory that recitations in the purchase agreement are part of a "prospectus."

I

Petitioners Gustafson, McLean, and Butler (collectively Gustafson) were in 1989 the sole shareholders of Alloyd, Inc.... . In 1989, Gustafson decided to sell Alloyd.... Wind Point Partners II, L.P., agreed to buy substantially all of the issued and outstanding stock.... 

On December 20, 1989, Gustafson and [Wind Point] executed a contract of sale. [Wind Point] agreed to pay Gustafson and his coshareholders $18,709,000 for the sale of the stock plus a payment of $2,122,219, which reflected the estimated increase in Alloyd's net worth from the end of the previous year.... 

The year-end audit of Alloyd revealed that Alloyd's actual earnings for 1989 were lower than the estimates relied upon by the parties in negotiating the adjustment amount of $2,122,219.... [T]he newly formed company (now called Alloyd Co., the same as the original company) and Wind Point brought suit in the United States District Court for the Northern District of Illinois, seeking outright rescission of the contract under § 12(2) of the

Securities Act of 1933 (1933 Act or Act). Alloyd (the new company) claimed that statements made by Gustafson and his coshareholders regarding the financial data of their company were inaccurate, rendering untrue the representations and warranties contained in the contract. The buyers further alleged that the contract of sale was a "prospectus," so that any misstatements contained in the agreement gave rise to liability under § 12(2) of the 1933 Act. . . .

## II

The rescission claim against Gustafson is based upon § 12(2) of the 1933 Act, 48 Stat. 84, as amended, 15 U.S.C. § 77l(2)[, which provides in relevant part] that any person who

> "offers or sells a security . . . by the use of any means or instruments of transportation or communication in interstate commerce or of the mails, by means of a prospectus or oral communication, which includes an untrue statement of a material fact or omits to state a material fact necessary in order to make the statements, in the light of the circumstances under which they were made, not misleading . . . , and who shall not sustain the burden of proof that he did not know, and in the exercise of reasonable care could not have known, of such untruth or omission, . . . shall be liable to the person purchasing such security from him, who may sue [for rescission of the transaction] . . . ."

As this case reaches us, we must assume that the stock purchase agreement contained material misstatements of fact made by the sellers and that Gustafson would not sustain its burden of proving due care. On these assumptions, Alloyd would have a right to obtain rescission [of the contract pursuant to § 12(2)] if those misstatements were made "by means of a prospectus or oral communication." . . . The determinative question, then, is whether the contract between Alloyd and Gustafson is a "prospectus" as the term is used in the 1933 Act.

Alloyd argues that "prospectus" is defined in a broad manner, broad enough to encompass the contract between the parties. This argument is echoed by the dissents. . . . Gustafson, by contrast, maintains that prospectus in the 1933 Act means a communication soliciting the [general] public to purchase securities from the [original issuer of the securities]. . . .

Three sections of the 1933 Act are critical in resolving the definitional question on which the case turns: § 2(10), which defines a prospectus; § 10, which sets forth the information that must be contained in a prospectus; and § 12, which imposes liability based on misstatements in a prospectus. In seeking to interpret the term "prospectus," we adopt the premise that the term should be construed, if possible, to give it a consistent meaning throughout the Act. That principle follows from our duty to construe statutes, not isolated provisions. . . .

## A

We begin with § 10. It provides, in relevant part:

"Except to the extent otherwise permitted or required pursuant to this subsection or subsections (c), (d), or (e) of this section—

"(1) a prospectus relating to a security other than a security issued by a foreign government or political subdivision thereof, shall contain the information contained in the registration statement [filed with the SEC prior to an initial public offering] . . . ;

"(2) a prospectus relating to a security issued by a foreign government or political subdivision thereof shall contain the information contained in the registration statement . . ."

Section 10 does not provide that some prospectuses must contain the information contained in the registration statement. Save for the explicit and well-defined exemptions for securities listed under § 3, . . . its mandate is unqualified: "[A] prospectus . . . shall contain the information contained in the registration statement."

Although § 10 does not define what a prospectus is, it does instruct us what a prospectus cannot be if the Act is to be interpreted as a symmetrical and coherent regulatory scheme, one in which the operative words have a consistent meaning throughout. There is no dispute that the contract in this case was not required to contain the information contained in a registration statement and that no statutory exemption was required to take the document out of § 10's coverage. It follows that the contract is not a prospectus under § 10. That does not mean that a document ceases to be a prospectus whenever it omits a required piece of information. It does mean that a document is not a prospectus within the meaning of that section if, absent an exemption, it need not comply with § 10's requirements in the first place.

An examination of § 10 reveals that, whatever else "prospectus" may mean, the term is confined to a document that, absent an overriding exemption, must include the "information contained in the registration statement." By and large, only public offerings by an issuer of a security, or by controlling shareholders of an issuer, require the preparation and filing of registration statements. . . . It follows, we conclude, that a prospectus under § 10 is confined to documents related to public offerings by an issuer or its controlling shareholders.

This much (the meaning of prospectus in § 10) seems not to be in dispute. Where the courts are in disagreement is with the implications of this proposition for the entirety of the Act, and for § 12 in particular. . . . We conclude that the term "prospectus" must have the same meaning under §§ 10 and 12. In so holding, we do not, as the dissent by JUSTICE GINSBURG suggests, make the mistake of treating § 10 as a definitional section. . . . Instead, we find in § 10 guidance and instruction for giving the term a consistent meaning throughout the Act.

The 1933 Act, like every Act of Congress, should not be read as a series of unrelated and isolated provisions. Only last Term we adhered to the "normal rule of statutory construction" that "identical words used in different parts of the same act are intended to have the same meaning."

Department of Revenue of Ore. v. ACF Industries, Inc., 510 U.S. 332, 342 (1994) (internal quotation marks and citations omitted).... That principle applies here. If the contract before us is not a prospectus for purposes of § 10—as all must and do concede—it is not a prospectus for purposes of § 12 either....

... [A]ccepting Alloyd's argument that any written offer is a prospectus under § 12 would require us to hold that the word "prospectus" in § 12 refers to a broader set of communications than the same term in § 10.... In the name of a plain meaning approach to statutory interpretation, the dissents discover in the Act two different species of prospectuses: formal (also called § 10) prospectuses, subject to both §§ 10 and 12, and informal prospectuses, subject only to § 12 but not to § 10. Nowhere in the statute, however, do the terms "formal prospectus" or "informal prospectus" appear. Instead, the Act uses one term—"prospectus"—throughout.... [W]e cannot accept the conclusion that this single operative word means one thing in one section of the Act and something quite different in another....

## B

Alloyd's contrary argument rests to a significant extent on § 2(10), or, to be more precise, on one word of that section. Section 2(10) provides that "[t]he term 'prospectus' means any prospectus, notice, circular, advertisement, letter, or communication, written or by radio or television, which offers any security for sale or confirms the sale of any security." Concentrating on the word "communication," Alloyd argues that any written communication that offers a security for sale is a "prospectus." Inserting its definition into § 12(2), Alloyd insists that a material misstatement in any communication offering a security for sale gives rise to an action for rescission, without proof of fraud by seller or reliance by the purchaser. In Alloyd's view, § 2(10) gives the term "prospectus" a capacious definition that, although incompatible with § 10, nevertheless governs in § 12.

The flaw in Alloyd's argument, echoed in the dissenting opinions, is its reliance on one word of the definitional section in isolation. To be sure, § 2(10) defines a prospectus as, *inter alia*, a "communication, written or by radio or television, which offers any security for sale or confirms the sale of any security." The word "communication," however, on which Alloyd's entire argument rests, is but one word in a list, a word Alloyd reads altogether out of context.

The relevant phrase in the definitional part of the statute must be read in its entirety, a reading which yields the interpretation that the term "prospectus" refers to a document soliciting the public to acquire securities. We find that definition controlling. Alloyd's argument that the phrase "communication, written or by radio or television," transforms any written communication offering a security for sale into a prospectus cannot consist with at least two rather sensible rules of statutory construction. First, the Court will avoid a reading which renders some words altogether redundant. If "communication" included every written communication, it would render "notice, circular, advertisement, [and] letter" redundant, since each of these are forms of written communication as well. Congress with ease could have drafted § 2(10) to read: "The term 'prospectus' means any communication, written or by radio or television, that offers a security for sale or confirms the sale of a security." Congress did not write the statute that way, however, and we decline to say it included the words "notice, circular, advertisement, [and] letter" for no purpose.

The constructional problem is resolved by the second principle Alloyd overlooks, which is that a word is known by the company it keeps (the doctrine of *noscitur a sociis*). This rule we rely upon to avoid ascribing to one word a meaning so broad that it is inconsistent with its accompanying words, thus giving "unintended breadth to the Acts of Congress." Jarecki v. G.D. Searle & Co., 367 U.S. 303, 307 (1961). The rule guided our earlier interpretation of the word "security" under the 1934 Act. The 1934 Act defines the term "security" to mean, inter alia, "any note." We concluded, nevertheless that, in context "the phrase 'any note' should not be interpreted to mean literally 'any note,' but must be understood against the background of what Congress was attempting to accomplish in enacting the Securities Acts." Reves v. Ernst & Young, 494 U.S. 56, 63 (1990). These considerations convince us that Alloyd's suggested interpretation is not the correct one.

There is a better reading. From the terms "prospectus, notice, circular, advertisement, [or] letter," it is apparent that the list refers to documents of wide dissemination. In a similar manner, the list includes communications "by radio or television," but not face-to-face or telephonic conversations. Inclusion of the term "communication" in that list suggests that it too refers to a public communication.

When the 1933 Act was drawn and adopted, the term "prospectus" was well understood to refer to a document soliciting the public to acquire securities from the issuer.... In this respect, the word "prospectus" is a term of art, which accounts for congressional confidence in employing what might otherwise be regarded as a partial circularity in the formal, statutory definition.... The use of the term "prospectus" to refer to public solicitations explains as well Congress' decision in § 12(2) to grant buyers a right to rescind without proof of reliance....

The list of terms in § 2(10) prevents a seller of stock from avoiding liability by calling a soliciting document something other than a prospectus, but it does not compel the conclusion that Alloyd urges us to reach and that the dissenting opinions adopt. Instead, the term "written communication" must be read in context to refer to writings that, from a functional standpoint, are similar to the terms "notice, circular, [and] advertisement." The term includes communications held out to the public at large but that might have been thought to be outside the other words in the definitional section....

■ Justice Thomas, with whom Justice Scalia, Justice Ginsburg, and Justice Breyer join, dissenting.

From the majority's opinion, one would not realize that § 12(2) of the Securities Act of 1933 (1933 Act or Act) was involved in this case until one had read more than halfway through. In contrast to the majority's approach of interpreting the statute, I believe the proper method is to begin with the provision actually involved in this case, § 12(2), and then turn to the 1933 Act's definitional section, § 2(10), before consulting the structure of the Act as a whole. Because the result of this textual analysis shows that § 12(2) applies to secondary or private sales of a security as well as to initial public offerings, I dissent.

## I

## A

As we have emphasized in our recent decisions, " '[t]he starting point in every case involving construction of a statute is the language itself.' " Landreth Timber Co. v. Landreth, 471 U.S. 681, 685 (1985) (quoting Blue Chip Stamps v. Manor Drug Stores, 421 U.S. 723, 756 (1975) (Powell, J., concurring)). Unfortunately, the majority has decided to interpret the word "prospectus" in § 12(2) by turning to sources outside the four corners of the statute, rather than by adopting the definition provided by Congress.

Section 12(2) creates a cause of action when the seller of a security makes a material omission or misstatement to the buyer by means of a prospectus or oral communication. If the seller acted negligently in making the misstatements, the buyer may sue to rescind the sale. I agree with the majority that the only way to interpret § 12(2) as limited to initial offerings is to read "by means of a prospectus or oral communication" narrowly. I also agree that in the absence of any other statutory command, one could understand "prospectus" as "a term of art which describes the transmittal of information concerning the sale of a security in an initial distribution." But the canon that "we construe a statutory term in accordance with its ordinary or natural meaning" applies only "[i]n the absence of [a statutory] definition." FDIC v. Meyer, 510 U.S. 471, 476 (1994).

There is no reason to seek the meaning of "prospectus" outside of the 1933 Act, because Congress has supplied just such a definition in § 2(10). That definition is extraordinarily broad:

"When used in this subchapter, unless the context otherwise requires—

. . . . .

"(10) The term 'prospectus' means any prospectus, notice, circular, advertisement, letter, or communication, written or by radio or television, which offers any security for sale or confirms the sale of any security." 15 U.S.C. § 77b(10).

For me, the breadth of these terms forecloses the majority's position that "prospectus" applies only in the context of initial distributions of securities. Indeed, § 2(10)'s inclusion of a prospectus as only one of the many different documents that qualify as a "prospectus" for statutory purposes indicates that Congress intended "prospectus" to be more than a mere "term of art." Likewise, Congress' extension of prospectus to include documents that merely *confirm* the sale of a security underscores Congress' intent to depart from the term's ordinary meaning. . . .

The majority seeks to avoid this reading by attempting to create ambiguities in § 2(10). According to the majority, the maxim *noscitur a sociis* (a word is known by the company it keeps) indicates that the circulars, advertisements, letters, or other communications referred to by § 2(10) are limited by the first word in the list: "prospectus." Thus, we are told that these words define the forms a prospectus may take, but the covered communications still must be "prospectus-like" in the sense that they must relate to an initial public offering. *Noscitur a sociis*, however, does not require us to construe *every* term in a series narrowly because of the meaning given to just one of the terms. See Russell Motor Car Co. v. United States, 261 U.S. 514, 519 (1923).

The majority uses the canon in an effort to *create* doubt, not to *reduce* it. The canon applies only in cases of ambiguity, which I do not find in § 2(10). "*Noscitur a sociis* is a well established and useful rule of construction where words are of obscure or doubtful meaning; and then, but only then, its aid may be sought to remove the obscurity or doubt by reference to the associated words." *Russell*, 261 U.S. at 520. There is obvious breadth in "notice, circular, advertisement, letter, or communication, written or by radio or television." To read one word in a long list as controlling the meaning of all the other words would defy common sense; doing so would prevent Congress from giving effect to expansive words in a list whenever they are combined with one word with a more restricted meaning. Section 2(10)'s very exhaustiveness suggests that "prospectus" is merely the first item in a long list of covered documents, rather than a brooding omnipresence whose meaning cabins that of all the following words. The majority also argues that a broad definition of prospectus makes much of § 2(10) redundant. But the majority fails to see that "communication, written or by radio or television," is a catchall. It operates as a safety net that Congress used to sweep up anything it had forgotten to include in its definition. This is a technique Congress employed in several other provisions of the 1933 Act and the Securities Exchange Act of 1934 (1934 Act). See, *e.g.*, 15 U.S.C. § 77b(1) ("term 'security' means any note, stock, treasury stock, bond, debenture . . . or, in general, any interest or instrument commonly known as a 'security' "); § 77b(9) ("term 'write' or 'written' shall include printed, lithographed, or any means of graphic communication"); § 78c(a)(6) ("term 'bank' means (A) a banking institution organized under the laws of the United States, (B) a member bank of the Federal Reserve System, (C) any other banking institution"). In fact, it is the majority's approach that creates redundancies. The majority cannot account for Congress' decision to begin its definition of "prospectus" with the term "prospectus," which is then followed by the rest of § 2(10)'s list. As a result, the majority must conclude that the use of the term is a "partial circularity," a reading that deprives the word of its meaning.

B

The majority correctly argues that other sections of the 1933 Act employ a narrower understanding of "prospectus" as a document related to an initial public offering.... In fact, the majority builds its entire argument on the proposition that it must give "prospectus" the same meaning in both §§ 10 and 12. Since § 10 assumes a narrower definition of prospectus, the majority believes that its definition must control that of § 12. Although the majority denies that it reads § 10 as a definitional section, it admits that § 10 "does instruct us what a prospectus cannot be if the Act is to be interpreted as a symmetrical and coherent regulatory scheme."

I agree with the majority that [§ 10] cannot embrace fully the broad definition of prospectus supplied by § 2(10) and used by § 12(2). I also recognize the general presumption that a given term bears the same meaning throughout a statute. But this presumption is overcome when Congress indicates otherwise. Here, there are several indications that Congress did not use the word "prospectus" in the same sense throughout the statute. First, § 2(10) defines "prospectus" to include not only a document that "offers any security for sale" (which is consistent with the majority's reading), but also one that "confirms the sale of any security." But the majority does not claim that § 10 uses the term "prospectus" to include confirmation slips. It would be radical to say that every confirmation slip must contain all the information that § 10 requires; only the documents accompanying an initial public offering must contain that information. Despite the majority's protestations, it is absolutely clear that the 1933 Act uses "prospectus" in two different ways. As a result, any justification for the majority's twisted reading of § 2(10) disappears.

Second, this understanding is reinforced by § 2's preface that its definitions apply "unless the context otherwise requires." This phrase indicates that Congress intended simply to provide a "default" meaning for "prospectus." Further, nothing in § 12(2) indicates that the "context otherwise requires" the use of a definition of "prospectus" other than the one provided by § 2(10). If anything, it is § 10's "context" that seems to require the use of a definition that is different from that of § 2(10).

Third, the dual use of "prospectus" in § 2(10), which both defines "prospectus" broadly and uses it as a term of art, makes clear that the statute is using the word in at least two different senses, and paves the way for such variations in the ensuing provisions. To adopt the majority's argument would force us to eliminate § 2(10) in favor of some narrower, common law definition of "prospectus." Our mandate to interpret statutes does not allow us to recast Congress' handiwork so completely.

The majority transforms § 10 into the tail that wags the 1933 Act dog. An analogy will illustrate the point. Suppose that the Act regulates cars, and that § 2(10) of the Act defines a "car" as any car, motorcycle, truck, or trailer. Section 10 of this hypothetical statute then declares that a car shall have seatbelts, and § 5 states that it is unlawful to sell cars without seatbelts. Section 12(2) of this Act then creates a cause of action for misrepresentations that occur during the sale of a car. It is reasonable to conclude that §§ 5 and 10 apply only to what we ordinarily refer to as "cars," because it would be absurd to require motorcycles and trailers to have seatbelts. But the majority's reasoning would lead to the further conclusion that § 12(2) does not cover sales of motorcycles, when it is clear that the Act includes such sales....

### III

... Unfortunately, the majority's decision ... turns on its head the commonsense approach to interpreting legal documents. The majority begins by importing a definition of "prospectus" from beyond the four corners of the 1933 Act that fits the precise use of the term in § 10. Initially ignoring the definition of "prospectus" provided at the beginning of the statute by Congress, the majority finally discusses § 2(10) to show that it does not utterly preclude its preferred meaning. Only then does the majority decide to parse the language of the provision at issue. However, when one interprets a contract provision, one usually begins by reading the provision, and then ascertaining the meaning of any important or ambiguous phrases by consulting any definitional clauses in the contract. Only if those inquiries prove unhelpful does a court turn to extrinsic definitions or to structure. I doubt that the majority would read in so narrow and peculiar a fashion most other statutes, particularly one intended to restrict causes of action in securities cases....

■ JUSTICE GINSBURG, with whom JUSTICE BREYER joins, dissenting.

... As JUSTICE THOMAS persuasively demonstrates, the statute's language does not support the Court's reading. Section 12(2) contains no terms expressly confining the provision to public offerings, and the statutory definition of "prospectus"—"any prospectus, notice, circular, advertisement, letter, or communication, written or by radio or television, which offers any security for sale or confirms the sale of any security," § 2(10)—is capacious....

### I

To construe a legislatively defined term, courts usually start with the defining section. Section 2(10) defines prospectus capaciously as "any prospectus, notice, circular, advertisement, letter, or communication, written or by radio or television, which offers any security for sale or confirms the sale of any security[.]" The items listed in the defining provision, notably "letters" and "communications," are common in private and secondary sales, as well as in public offerings. The § 2(10) definition thus does not confine the § 12(2) term "prospectus" to public offerings.

The Court bypasses § 2(10).... Instead of beginning at the beginning, by first attending to the definition section, the Court starts with § 10, a substantive provision. The Court correctly observes that the term "prospectus" has a circumscribed meaning in that context. A prospectus within the contemplation of § 10 is a formal document, typically a document composing part of a registration statement; a § 10 prospectus, all agree, appears only in public offerings. The Court then proceeds backward; it reads into the literally and logically prior definition section, § 2(10), the meaning "prospectus" has in § 10.

To justify its backward reading—proceeding from § 10 to § 2(10) and not the other way round—the Court states that it "cannot accept the conclusion that [the operative word 'prospectus'] means one thing in one section of the Act and something quite different in another." Our decisions, however, constantly recognize that "a characterization fitting in certain contexts may be unsuitable in others." NationsBank of N.C., N.A. v. Variable Annuity Life Ins. Co., [513 U.S. 251, 262 (1995)]. . . .

See also Cook, "Substance" and "Procedure" in the Conflict of Laws, 42 Yale L.J. 333, 337 (1933) ("The tendency to assume that a word which appears in two or more legal rules, and so in connection with more than one purpose, has and should have precisely the same scope in all of them, runs all through legal discussions. It has all the tenacity of original sin and must constantly be guarded against."). . . .

---

***1. The Presumption of Consistent Usage***—Justice Kennedy's opinion for the Court made much of the fact that the interpretation of "prospectus" favored by the plaintiffs and the dissenters would be nonsensical if applied to § 10 of the Securities Act, which requires that a "prospectus" contain the information found in the registration statement that securities issuers are required to file with the SEC. Of course, the plaintiff in *Gustafson* did not allege a violation of § 10. The only reason § 10 is relevant at all is because of a presumption—which the Court described as a "normal rule of statutory construction"—that "identical words used in different parts of the same act are intended to have the same meaning."

Just how strong is this presumption—and how strong should it be? The *Gustafson* case revealed substantial disagreement among the Justices about these questions. Justice Kennedy's majority opinion seemed to endorse a strong version of the presumption of consistent usage, suggesting that this presumption is necessary "if the Act is to be interpreted as a symmetrical and coherent regulatory scheme." Justice Thomas's dissent acknowledged "the general presumption that a given term bears the same meaning throughout a statute," but Justice Thomas emphasized that this is just a presumption, one that "is overcome when Congress indicates otherwise," as it had in the definitions section of the Securities Act. Indeed, as Justice Thomas pointed out, § 2 says explicitly that its definition of "prospectus" applies "unless the context otherwise requires." Justice Ginsburg's dissent took an even more critical line, warning against a reflexive impulse to give the same term a consistent meaning in different sections of the statute, without regard to context or purpose. Justice Ginsburg quoted Professor Walter Wheeler Cook's admonition that the presumption that "a word which appears in two or more legal rules . . . should have precisely the same scope . . . has all the tenacity of original sin and must constantly be guarded against." Which of these positions strikes you as the more persuasive? When, if ever, does it make sense to presume that statutory words and phrases have the same meaning in different sections of the same statute? If we do have such a presumption, when or under what conditions should it be overcome?

Should the same presumption apply when Congress uses similar language to address similar subject matter in *different* statutes? The Court has suggested that when two statutes use similar language, it is generally appropriate to read that as "a strong indication that [they] should be interpreted *pari passu* [side by side]." Northcross v. Board of Ed. of Memphis City Schools, 412 U.S. 427, 428 (1973) (per curiam). The Court has sometimes endorsed this rule in strong terms:

> The correct rule of interpretation is, that if divers statutes relate to the same thing, they ought all to be taken into consideration in construing any one of them.... If a thing contained in a subsequent statute, be within the reason of a former statute, it shall be taken to be within the meaning of that statute; and if it can be gathered from a subsequent statute *in pari materia*, what meaning the legislature attached to the words of a former statute, they will amount to a legislative declaration of its meaning, and will govern the construction of the first statute.

United States v. Freeman, 44 U.S. (3 How.) 556, 564–565 (1845) (citations omitted).

Does the so-called *in pari materia* ("on the same subject") canon make sense? As a matter of legislative intent, is it empirically plausible that Congress is typically aware of earlier statutes and desires uniform construction on similar subject matters? *See* William W. Buzbee, *The One–Congress Fiction in Statutory Interpretation*, 149 U. PA. L. REV. 171 (2000). If the *in pari materia* rule is implausible as an empirical presumption about the legislative process, might the rule nonetheless be defended as a desirable principle of *judicial* behavior, in that it instructs judges to strive to make the law coherent over time? *See, e.g.,* West Va. Univ. Hosps., Inc. v. Casey, 499 U.S. 83, 100–01 (1991) (pp. 49–60, *supra*) (arguing for reading statutes together "not because that precise accommodative meaning is what the lawmakers must have had in mind ..., but because it is [the judiciary's] role to make sense rather than nonsense out of the *corpus juris*"); *see also* Buzbee, *supra*, at 221–25 (discussing debates over this justification for the *in pari materia* canon). If that is the most plausible basis for the canon, what are its limits? The Court has made clear that this norm of interpretation must yield to contrary indicia of legislative intent or meaning. *See, e.g.,* General Dynamics Land Systems, Inc. v. Cline, 540 U.S. 581, 595 (2004) (pp. 68–78, *supra*); *cf.* Atlantic Cleaners & Dyers, Inc. v. United States, 286 U.S. 427, 433 (1932) (discussing factors that indicate that the same word is used in different ways in different parts of the statute). How strong must those contrary indicia of legislative intent be in order to justify departing from the presumption? Should the *in pari materia* canon yield to persuasive evidence from the legislative history? Or should the principle be considered a technique for ascertaining the clear meaning of the text? *See*

W. Va. Hosps., *supra* (treating the usage of the term "attorney's fees" as consistent across various statutes, despite legislative history suggesting a different meaning in the particular statute at issue in the case).

*2. The* **Noscitur a Sociis** *Canon*—The definitions section of the Securities Act, § 2, defines a "prospectus" as "any prospectus, notice, circular, advertisement, letter, or communication, written or by radio or television, which offers any security for sale or confirms the sale of any security." Although the contract at issue in *Gustafson* offered securities for sale, it was not a traditional prospectus, nor would it likely count as a notice, circular, advertisement, or letter. The question, then, is whether this contract was a "communication" within the meaning of the Securities Act. One might conclude, as did the *Gustafson* dissenters, that the answer is clearly yes, given the ordinary meaning (and dictionary definition) of "communication." Yet Justice Kennedy's majority opinion read "communication" more narrowly as including only "documents of wide dissemination" or other forms of communication to the general public, rather than to a particular party. Justice Kennedy reached this conclusion in part by emphasizing a traditional semantic canon known as *noscitur a sociis*—"[a word is] known by its associates"—and pointing out that the other words in the definition of "prospectus" all entail a more general communication with the public at large.

Application of the *noscitur* canon is a form of contextual interpretation, designed to avoid giving a word a broad meaning unintended by Congress. It is easiest to illustrate the logic of the canon with an example involving synonyms that have totally unrelated meanings. Suppose, for instance, that a local zoning ordinance forbids excessive noise within fifty yards of "an office, bank, or school." We wouldn't interpret such an ordinance to apply to someone making lots of noise within fifty yards of the edge of a river, even though that is also a "bank." Even if there were no other indication of legislative intent or purpose, we could tell from the other words around "bank" which meaning was intended. Likewise, if an ordinance imposed special penalties for excessive noise within fifty yards of a "shore, beach, bank, or levy," it would be equally obvious that "bank," in context, means the edge of a river, not a financial institution.

But that sort of situation is not the typical context in which judges invoke the *noscitur* canon. Rather, the typical *noscitur* case involves a statutory term that can have a broad meaning or a narrow meaning, and the surrounding terms may offer some clue as to which meaning was intended. In *Gustafson*, for example, "communication" could mean literally anything that conveys information from one person or entity to another (a broad reading), but could also, at least according to the majority, refer only to a message that is widely disseminated (a narrower reading). The majority believed that the other words in the § 2 definition of "prospectus" indicated that the latter meaning was the one Congress intended.

But is that correct? Why should an apparently broad term in a statutory list be construed narrowly, just because other terms in the same list have a narrower meaning? Justice Thomas insisted that the *noscitur* canon, as the majority applied it, would mean that every time a broad statutory term appeared in a list with more restrictive terms, the meaning of the broad term would be artificially narrowed, and that this would disable Congress ever from combining broad terms with narrow terms. Is that critique persuasive? How might Justice Kennedy respond? And if Justice Thomas's critique seems like a powerful one to you, can you identify realistic situations in which use of the *noscitur* canon would nevertheless be appropriate? After all, Justice Thomas acknowledged that the *noscitur* canon is *sometimes* useful in interpreting statutes. But almost all real cases where the canon might apply involve reading a term more narrowly than one might otherwise, given the words around it. Does Justice Thomas's critique therefore prove too much?

Perhaps the basic conundrum here is that judges can err both by construing a statutory term too broadly and by construing it too narrowly: The *noscitur* canon is useful in preventing judges from giving an overly sweeping meaning to terms that Congress intended more narrowly (Justice Kennedy's concern), but an overly zealous application of the canon may lead to unduly narrow readings of terms that Congress meant to sweep broadly (Justice Thomas's concern). How should judges strike the right balance? Does the canon's utility require that judges can sort out appropriate linguistic cues in context?

Another, closely related point of disagreement between Justice Kennedy's majority opinion and Justice Thomas's dissent had to do with when it becomes appropriate for judges to invoke semantic canons like *noscitur a sociis*. Justice Thomas viewed the *noscitur* canon as useful and appropriate only when the relevant statutory terms are ambiguous. If those terms are clear, it would be inappropriate to use the *noscitur* canon to create doubt or ambiguity that would not have been present otherwise. Justice Kennedy, on the other hand, deployed the *noscitur* canon as an element of his textual analysis of § 2(10) of the Securities Act, rather than as a separate interpretive tool. (The *Silvers v. Sony Pictures* case, pp. 225–231 *supra*, also raised this issue in the context of the *expressio unius* canon.) If semantic canons (including *expressio unius* and *noscitur a sociis*) are merely commonsense principles of linguistic interpretation—comparable to rules of grammar and syntax—then perhaps Justice Kennedy had the better of the argument on this point. We would not, after all, say that a judge can invoke the rules of grammar if the statute is "ambiguous" but cannot do so if the text of the statute is "clear"—the very statement is nonsensical, because grammatical rules are an integral part of understanding the meaning of the text. On the other hand, perhaps Justice Thomas had a point, insofar as semantic canons, unlike the rules of grammar, are relatively weak rules of thumb that are sometimes helpful but often inappropriate when a different meaning is clear in context. Perhaps Justice Thomas's point was simply that *other* tools of textual interpretation are more powerful and reliable than the idea that a word's meaning is informed by surrounding words, and that the majority erred in prioritizing this weak linguistic presumption over the more significant indicia of textual meaning available in the *Gustafson* case.

Consider another example of the *noscitur a sociis* canon in action. In Jarecki v. G.D. Searle & Co., 367 U.S. 303 (1961), the Supreme Court considered a statutory provision that exempted "abnormal income" from a special "excess profits" tax imposed during the Korean War. The statute defined "abnormal income" as including income "resulting from exploration, discovery, or prospecting, or any combination of the foregoing, extending over a period of more than 12 months." A pharmaceutical company that had developed two new drugs and a camera company that had invented a new type of camera argued that these inventions were "discoveries" within the meaning of the abnormal income exemption. The Supreme Court disagreed, relying in part on the *noscitur* canon:

> "Discovery" is a word usable in many contexts and with various shades of meaning. Here, however, it does not stand alone, but gathers meaning from the words around it. . . . The three words in conjunction, "exploration," "discovery" and "prospecting," all describe income-producing activity in the oil and gas and mining industries, but it is difficult to conceive of any other industry to which they all apply. . . . The maxim *noscitur a sociis* . . . while not an inescapable rule, is often wisely applied where a word is capable of many meanings in order to avoid the giving of unintended breadth to the Acts of Congress. . . . The application of the maxim here leads to the conclusion that 'discovery' in [this Act] means only the discovery of mineral resources."

*Id.* at 307 (citations omitted). Does this holding seem convincing to you? Do you find this application of the *noscitur* canon more or less convincing than the application of that canon in *Gustafson*?

**3. The Presumption Against Superfluous Statutory Language**—The *Gustafson* majority invoked yet a third semantic canon of statutory construction to support its reading of "prospectus": the canon that judges should construe statutes so that every term and provision is meaningful, if it is possible to do so. In other words, interpretations that render certain statutory language superfluous are disfavored. According to Justice Kennedy's majority opinion, this principle militated against the broad reading of "communication" favored by the dissenting Justices. Justice Kennedy reasoned that if the statutory term "communication" included everything that would count as a communication under the broad reading of that term, then the more specific statutory terms "notice," "circular," "advertisement," and "letter" would be redundant, as all of these things would qualify as "communications" under the broad definition. So, Justice Kennedy concluded, Congress could not have intended such a broad interpretation, or else it would simply have defined "prospectus" in the statute as including "any communication, written or by radio or television, that offers a security for sale or confirms the sale of a security."

What is the basis for the presumption against surplus statutory language? Is this presumption, like other semantic canons of construction, premised on the way ordinary speakers use and understand language? If so, does the claim strike you as plausible? Is it true that we usually express ourselves in ways that minimize redundancy or other forms of superfluity?

There are reasons to be skeptical of this claim: While it is probably true that most speakers and writers are usually not deliberately redundant, it is probably *not* true that redundancy is exceedingly rare in everyday communication. Indeed, it seems quite common. *See* Richard A. Posner, *Statutory Interpretation—in the Classroom and in the Courtroom*, 50 U. CHI. L. REV. 800, 812 (1983) ("There is no evidence for this improbable proposition; what evidence we have, much of it from the statutes themselves, is to the contrary.")

Of course, legislation is different from everyday communication, because the enactment of a law is a special kind of communicative act. But it is not clear which way that cuts. Perhaps the deliberation associated with the statutory drafting process, coupled with legislators' awareness of the significance of every statutory phrase, implies that we can be much more confident that each statutory term was carefully chosen, and therefore likely to have independent significance. On the other hand, the fact that legislative drafting and enactment is a collective process that takes place over a long period of time, with many opportunities for addition, subtraction, and modification of language, may mean that redundant or otherwise superfluous language is *more* likely to appear in statutes than in other forms of communication. If that latter view is correct, then doesn't it seem like a mistake to draw any particularly strong inference from the fact that certain interpretations create more superfluity than do others? Or perhaps one should adopt a more nuanced view: Maybe the fact that an interpretation that renders certain *terms* duplicative may not be much of a problem, but an interpretation that renders a *substantive provision* of a statute entirely superfluous is something courts should strain to avoid. Does that distinction make sense?

Returning to *Gustafson*, one might question whether Justice Kennedy has really avoided the redundancy problem he identified, because even on his narrower interpretation of "communication" as including only "documents of wide dissemination," presumably a "notice," "circular," "advertisement," or "letter" would all still count as types of "communication." But there is a ready answer to this objection: the more specific terms are important—and not at all superfluous—because their presence is essential to indicate that Congress intended a narrower meaning for "communication." Without these more specific terms, after all, the *noscitur* canon on which the majority relied would have been inapplicable. So, although under the majority's interpretation the terms "notice," "circular," "advertisement," and "letter" are still in a sense redundant (because they are all subsumed by "communication"), they are not superfluous, because they collectively indicate the sort of communication that Congress had in mind when it defined "prospectus" for purposes of the Securities Act.

That interpretive dispute relates to a more general question about the relationship between the *noscitur a sociis* canon and the presumption against superfluous statutory language. There is arguably a tension between these principles, in that the *noscitur* canon counsels judges to give potentially ambiguous terms a meaning that is similar to nearby terms, while the presumption against surplus statutory language emphasizes that where possible each statutory term should be construed to have independent meaning (and therefore should mean something *different* than nearby terms). An aggressive application of the *noscitur* canon might render a statutory term superfluous in light of the surrounding terms from which the ambiguous term "draws meaning." Perhaps this tension is an illustration of Professor Llewellyn's critique of the canons: In a case like *Gustafson*, if a court wants to read a term like "communication" narrowly, it can invoke *noscitur a sociis*; if the court wants to read the term broadly, it can emphasize that a narrow reading would deprive the term of independent significance. But that critique may be overdrawn: Perhaps the best interpretation is one that gives each term independent significance, but appropriately limits the sweep of potentially broad terms in light of the contextual evidence, including related (but distinct) terms nearby. Does that seem like a reasonable accommodation of these canons? Or do you think the tension will be impossible to avoid in most cases?

## C. The *Ejusdem Generis* Canon

Many statutes contain lists of specific terms followed by a more open-ended residual term at the end. Often, the residual term can have a very broad meaning—so broad that it would go well beyond the sorts of things specifically enumerated. In these cases, courts sometimes invoke another semantic canon known as *ejusdem generis* ("of the same kind") in order to read the general residual term more narrowly, so that it encompasses only things that are similar to the items that are specifically mentioned.

*McBoyle v. United States* (pp. 219–220, *supra*) is a case of this type: The National Motor Vehicle Theft Act covered theft of an "automobile, automobile truck, automobile wagon, motor cycle, or any other self-propelled vehicle not designed for running on rails." Justice Holmes interpreted the residual "any other vehicle" category as including only vehicles that run on the ground—a characteristic shared by automobiles, trucks, wagons, and motorcycles—not vehicles that fly. Justice Holmes did not invoke the *ejusdem generis* canon by its Latin name, but *McBoyle* is a classic example of an application of this canon. If that particular application of the canon seems unpersuasive to you, then consider another example: The Illinois Supreme Court construed a statute that allowed a state government agency to sell "gravel, sand, earth or other material" from state-owned park land not to allow sales of timber harvested from that land, even though timber is clearly a kind of "material." To reach this conclusion, the Illinois Supreme Court applied the *ejusdem generis* canon, reasoning that "other material" in that context refers only to other material that is similar to sand, gravel, and earth. Sierra Club v. Kenney, 429 N.E.2d 1214, 1222 (Ill. 1981). Do you find that convincing?

Like other semantic canons, *ejusdem generis* can plausibly be described and defended as a commonsense form of contextual interpretation. But like other semantic canons, there are serious questions concerning its scope and determinacy. Perhaps chief among these is the problem of extracting from the enumerated statutory terms the particular characteristic or quality that limits the general residual term. The following case provides a nice illustration of that difficulty.

---

## People v. Smith

Supreme Court of Michigan
393 Mich. 432 (1975)

■ T.G. KAVANAGH, CHIEF JUSTICE.

. . . Defendant and three others were charged with carrying a concealed weapon in a motor vehicle [in violation of Michigan state law], M.C.L.A. § 750.227. . . .

Detroit Police Officer Ward testified at the preliminary examination that he and his partner observed a Ford Econoline van, in which defendant Smith was a passenger, make several erratic U-turns. The van was stopped and Officer Ward while approaching the vehicle observed through the right window what he believed to be the stock of a rifle. He opened the door and grabbed an M–1 rifle from underneath the second seat. Defendant Smith was sitting on the third seat with his feet up. A cartridge belt and clips containing ammunition were found in the front seat between co-defendants Gaut and Turner.

Defendants filed motions to quash, defendant Smith contending that an M–1 rifle was not a dangerous weapon within the meaning of the [concealed weapon] statute. . . .

The defendant urges [the following] question[]: . . .

"Is a rifle over 30 inches in length a dangerous weapon within the meaning of MCLA 750.227 if said section is interpreted consistently with the constitution of the State of Michigan and with the intent of the Michigan Legislature?"

. . . The statute provides:

"Sec. 227. *Carrying concealed weapons*—Any person who shall carry a dagger, dirk, stiletto, or *other dangerous weapon except hunting knives adapted and carried as such*, concealed on or about his person, or whether concealed or otherwise in any vehicle operated or occupied by him, except in his dwelling house or place of business or on other land possessed by him; and any person who shall carry a pistol concealed on or about his person, or, whether concealed or otherwise, in any vehicle operated or occupied by him, except in his dwelling house or place of business or on other land possessed by him, without a license to so carry said pistol as provided by law, shall be guilty of a felony, punishable by imprisonment in the state prison for not more than 5 years, or by fine of not more than 2,500 dollars." . . .

The trial court concluded that because an M–1 is a military rifle it comes within the classification of a dangerous weapon. The Court of

Appeals majority, observing that the 43 inch rifle is heavy and could also be used as a club, eschewed analysis of the statute because they had "no doubt that the legislature, when they said 'dangerous weapon', they in fact meant dangerous weapon...."

This misses the real question.

No one suggests that an M–1 rifle is not a dangerous weapon. The question is whether this statute proscribes the carrying of *all* dangerous weapons or only those of the types specified.

In construing statutes in an effort to ascertain and give effect to the legislative interest, courts are guided by a rule of construction known as "ejusdem generis."

This is a rule whereby in a statute in which general words follow a designation of particular subjects, the meaning of the general words will ordinarily be presumed to be and construed as restricted by the particular designation and as including only things of the same kind, class, character or nature as those specifically enumerated....

Thus here the phrase "or other dangerous weapon except hunting knives adapted and carried as such" following those specified types of stabbing weapons, under the rule would be limited to stabbing weapons. As to that part of the statute we see no intent to include firearms of any sort in the phrase "other dangerous weapon."

Nor can we read the word "pistol" in M.C.L.A. § 750.227; M.S.A. § 28.424 as applying to an M–1 rifle. "Pistol" is defined in M.C.L.A. § 28.421; M.S.A. § 28.91 to mean any firearm, loaded or unloaded 30 inches or less in length, or any firearm, loaded or unloaded, which by its construction and appearance conceals it as a firearm.

In sum, M.C.L.A. § 750.227; M.S.A. § 28.424 applies only to those dangerous weapons enumerated therein. M–1 rifles are not so included. In reaching this conclusion it is important to stress, however, that the Legislature did not, through inadvertence or intent, neglect to consider the problems and dangers posed by the carrying about of long barreled firearms. The Legislature made specific provision on point in an earlier section of the same act, which reads as follows:

> "*Carrying firearm or dangerous weapon with unlawful intent*—Any person who, with intent to use the same unlawfully against the person of another, goes armed with a pistol or other *firearm* or dagger, dirk, razor, stiletto, or knife having a blade over 3 inches in length, or any other dangerous or deadly weapon or instrument, shall be guilty of a felony, punishable by imprisonment in the state prison for not more than 5 years or by a fine of not more than 2,500 dollars." M.C.L.A. § 750.226; M.S.A. § 28.423.

Without any question whatever, an M–1 rifle is a "firearm" within the scope of M.C.L.A. § 750.226. Concluding that M–1s are covered by M.C.L.A. § 750.226 and not by M.C.L.A. § 750.227 not only accords with a strict reading of both statutes involved, it reflects as well an ordered regulatory scheme enacted by the Legislature. The prohibition against carrying long barreled firearms does not reasonably belong in a "concealed" weapons class of crimes.

The greater difficulty in prosecuting crimes proscribed under M.C.L.A. § 750.226 which does require proof of "intent to use the [weapon] unlawfully" in order to support a conviction does not, of course, escape us. It appears, however, that the Legislature was cognizant of the fact that to hold that rifles are included within the proscription of M.C.L.A. § 750.227 would be to subject most weekend hunters, for example, to potential *felony* prosecution under M.C.L.A. § 750.227 notwithstanding their lack of intent to unlawfully use their hunting rifles.[2] Whether the crime situation presently requires consideration of more stringent regulation of the carrying of long guns, under different conditions or with different intent from that set out in M.C.L.A. § 750.226, would require legislative resolution and is beyond the proper authority of the judiciary.

In short, what we hold herein, should not be taken in any way, shape or form to legalize the carrying about of M–1 rifles or any other sort of weapon hitherto considered "dangerous" with unlawful intent. In light of the extant statutory scheme, we merely hold that the prosecution erred in charging and trying defendant under the inapposite auspices of M.C.L.A. § 750.227. . . .

Reversed.

■ T.M. KAVANAGH, COLEMAN, WILLIAMS and SWAINSON, JJ., concur.

---

**1. *What Sorts of Things Count as "of the Same Kind"?***—The *ejusdem generis* canon has some intuitive appeal: It is often clear in context that when someone uses a broad term they actually have a narrower meaning in mind, given the more specific items proffered as examples of the more general category. A lease contract that allows a tenant to withhold rent if she discovers that her apartment building is inhabited by "rats, mice, termites, or other pests" would presumably not allow nonpayment if the tenant discovers she has a particularly annoying next-door neighbor. Similarly, a statute that forbids people from bringing "cats, dogs, and other animals" into a public park presumably does not bar mounted police from riding their horses in the park, as one can infer that the statute meant to bar domestic animals kept as pets. *See* David L. Shapiro, *Continuity and Change in Statutory Interpretation*, 67 N.Y.U. L. REV. 921, 930 (1992). But it is often difficult to determine what the shared characteristic of the listed items actually is—or, perhaps more precisely, *which* shared characteristic of the specific terms limits the more general term. After all, the enumerated items will share many common features, not all of which

---

**2.** . . . There are also other specific statutes which apply to dangerous weapons other than those specified in the statute under which the defendant was charged. See, for example, M.C.L.A. § 750.224; M.S.A. § 28.421 which applies to the manufacture, sale or possession of a machine gun, silencer, bomb, blackjack, slung shot, billy, metallic knuckels [sic], sand club, bludgeon, or gas container.

should limit the more general residual term. An absurd example may help illustrate the point. In *McBoyle*, the enumerated vehicles—automobile, truck, wagon, and motorcycle—all have an even number of wheels (typically two or four). Does that mean that, in light of the *ejusdem generis* canon, the statute would not cover someone who steals a three-wheeled off-road vehicle and transports it across state lines, simply because that vehicle had an odd number of wheels? Presumably the answer would be no. Indeed, the suggestion seems silly. The point of the example, though, is to illustrate that judges applying the *ejusdem generis* canon must make implicit judgments about which common characteristics of the enumerated terms are *relevant*, though the criteria for relevance are rarely spelled out.

Consider, in this regard, a few hypothetical examples that are somewhat less absurd. The statute at issue in *Smith* made it unlawful for a person to carry a "dagger, dirk, stiletto, or other dangerous weapon except hunting knives . . . concealed on or about his person, or whether concealed or otherwise in any vehicle operated or occupied by him." Would this prohibition cover someone who carried a sword-cane (a cane that contains a long concealed blade)? The *Smith* opinion implied that the answer would be yes, since *Smith* used the *ejusdem generis* canon to limit the scope of the statute to "stabbing weapons." But couldn't the defendant in this hypothetical case argue that the specifically enumerated weapons—daggers, dirks, and stilettos (as well as the exempted hunting knives)—are all knife-like weapons with *short* blades, used for stabbing at close range, while a sword is a fundamentally different kind of stabbing weapon? If your instinct is to reject that argument, what explanation can you give? Why should the enumeration of daggers, dirks, stilettos, and knives limit the "dangerous weapon" category only to "stabbing weapons," rather than to "short-bladed stabbing weapons"? Is there a principled basis for drawing the line in this way?

Here's another example that illustrates the difficulty of specifying the relevant shared characteristics of the listed items: Suppose that instead of an M–1 rifle, the defendant in *Smith* was found with nunchaku sticks concealed on his person. (Nunchaku sticks, also known as nunchucks, are a traditional Japanese weapon consisting of two heavy sticks joined by a short rope or chain.) Would this defendant be guilty of violating the Michigan concealed weapons statute? Presumably the answer would be no, since *Smith* limited the scope of the "other dangerous weapon" category to "stabbing weapons." But couldn't the *Smith* court just as easily have defined the *ejusdem generis* category as "weapons designed for use in hand-to-hand combat"—a category that would exclude the M–1 rifle but include the nunchaku sticks? (For cases reaching different conclusions on whether concealed weapon statutes similar to the Michigan statute cover nunchakus, compare State v. Muliufi, 643 P.2d 546 (Haw. 1982), with State v. Tucker, 558 P.2d 1244 (Or. App. 1977).)

The preceding examples suggest four different ways that the court could plausibly have defined the relevant common characteristic of the specifically mentioned statutory items (dirks, daggers, stilettos, and knives): (1) Perhaps the relevant common characteristic of these items is simply that they are capable of inflicting serious bodily injury (in which case the rifle, sword-cane, and nunchakus would all fall within the ambit of the statute); (2) Perhaps the relevant common characteristic, as *Smith* concluded, is that the enumerated weapons are all stabbing weapons (in which case the statute covers the sword-cane, but not the rifle or nunchakus); (3) Alternatively, we might conclude that the listed weapons are all *short-bladed* stabbing weapons (meaning that the statute would not cover the rifle, sword-cane, or nunchakus); (4) Maybe instead the common characteristic of these items is that they are designed for use in close-range combat (in which case the sword-cane and nunchakus are covered, but the rifle isn't). Other specifications of common characteristics are also possible. How, then, should a court define the relevant category?

**2.   *The Relationship Between* Ejusdem Generis *and* Noscitur a Sociis**—As may be immediately apparent, the *ejusdem generis* canon and the *noscitur a sociis* canon are closely related—so closely, in fact, that they are often conflated. Both of these canons typically involve narrowing the range of meaning of a particular term by reading it in the context of related terms. The main difference is that courts typically invoke *ejusdem generis* when the ambiguous term in question is a residual catch-all category at the end (or occasionally the beginning) of a list of more specific enumerated items. In contrast, *noscitur a sociis* stands for the general proposition that "a word is given meaning by those around it." Antonin Scalia, *Common-Law Courts in a Civil–Law System: The Role of United States Federal Courts in Interpreting the Constitution and Laws, in* A Matter of Interpretation 3, 26 (Amy Gutmann ed., 1997). Hence, "[i]f you tell me, 'I took the boat out on the 'bay,' I understand 'bay' to mean one thing; if you tell me, 'I put the saddle on the bay,' I understand it to mean something else." *Id.* That said, certain applications of the *noscitur* canon—like that in *Gustafson* (pp. 234–243, *supra*)—are quite similar to applications of the *ejusdem generis* canon, in that such *noscitur* cases involve using the meanings of certain terms in a list to narrow the meaning of another one of the terms in that list (a term that might conceivably have a much broader meaning). So, if a statute says, "This rule applies to A, B, C, or any other X," and we use the meanings of specific items A, B, and C to narrow the meaning of general catch-all category X, then we have an *ejusdem generis* case. But if the statute says, "This rule applies to A, B, C, or D," and we use the meanings of items A, B, and C to narrow the meaning of item D, then we have a *noscitur a sociis* case. Still, the principle underlying both canons is essentially the same—as are the problems and difficulties—and you should not get too hung up on carefully distinguishing *noscitur a sociis* cases from *ejusdem generis* cases.

**3.   *The Issue of When To Apply the Canons, Redux*—**An issue that came up with respect to the *expressio unius* canon and the *noscitur a sociis* canon concerned the appropriate point in the interpretive process at which to apply these canons. (*See* p. 246, *supra*.) More specifically, we considered whether it is appropriate to use these semantic canons to *determine* the "clear meaning" of a statutory text, or whether courts could properly resort to these semantic canons only when the text was ambiguous (and perhaps also when the legislative history failed to clarify this ambiguity). This issue arises in *ejusdem generis* cases as well.

In *Smith*, would it be fair to say that the court took a clear position on this question? After all, the court acknowledged that "[n]o one suggests that an M–1 rifle is not a dangerous weapon." Since the statute on its face applied to anyone who carries "any dangerous weapon" (other than a hunting knife) concealed on his person, one might think that the statute is not ambiguous. So, if it were appropriate to apply the *ejusdem generis* canon only if the statute is ambiguous prior to the canon's application, then presumably *Smith* would have come out the other way. But the *Smith* court used the *ejusdem generis* canon to determine that the phrase "any dangerous weapon" in the statute did *not* actually include all dangerous weapons, but only certain *types* of dangerous weapons. Doesn't that amount to a rejection of the proposition that resort to *ejusdem generis* is appropriate only if the statute is ambiguous? Or does the *ejusdem generis* canon also capture something about ordinary habits of speech? Is that the right approach?

Consider also whether the rule on this question of priority should be different for different semantic canons. Could you make a plausible argument, for example, that resort to the *expressio unius* canon is appropriate only if the statute is otherwise ambiguous, while use of the *ejusdem generis* canon is appropriate at the initial stage to determine whether the statute has a clear meaning? What would such an argument look like?

\* \* \* \*

The next principal case, *Circuit City Stores, Inc. v. Adams*, raises some additional questions about the role of the *ejusdem generis* canon in statutory construction. As you read the case, consider whether you find the majority's application of the *ejusdem generis* canon in *Circuit City* more or less persuasive than the application we saw in *People v. Smith*.

# Circuit City Stores, Inc. v. Adams

Supreme Court of the United States
532 U.S. 105 (2001)

■ Justice Kennedy delivered the opinion of the Court.

Section 1 of the Federal Arbitration Act (FAA or Act) excludes from the Act's coverage "contracts of employment of seamen, railroad employees, or any other class of workers engaged in foreign or interstate commerce." 9 U.S.C. § 1. All but one of the Courts of Appeals which have addressed the issue interpret this provision as exempting contracts of employment of transportation workers, but not other employment contracts, from the FAA's coverage. A different interpretation has been adopted by the Court of Appeals for the Ninth Circuit, which construes the exemption so that all contracts of employment are beyond the FAA's reach, whether or not the worker is engaged in transportation.... We now decide that the better interpretation is to construe the statute, as most of the Courts of Appeals have done, to confine the exemption to transportation workers.

## I

In October 1995, respondent Saint Clair Adams applied for a job at petitioner Circuit City Stores, Inc., a national retailer of consumer electronics. Adams signed an employment application which included [a provision calling for binding arbitration of any employment disputes].... Adams was hired as a sales counselor in Circuit City's store in Santa Rosa, California.

Two years later, Adams filed an employment discrimination lawsuit against Circuit City in state court, asserting claims under California's Fair Employment and Housing Act and other claims based on general tort theories under California law. Circuit City filed suit in the United States District Court for the Northern District of California, seeking to enjoin the state-court action and to compel arbitration of respondent's claims pursuant to the FAA. The District Court entered the requested order. Respondent, the court concluded, was obligated by the arbitration agreement to submit his claims against the employer to binding arbitration. An appeal followed.

... [T]he Court of Appeals held the arbitration agreement between Adams and Circuit City was contained in a "contract of employment," and so was not subject to the FAA....

## II

### A

Congress enacted the FAA in 1925. As the Court has explained, the FAA was a response to hostility of American courts to the enforcement of arbitration agreements.... The FAA's coverage provision, § 2, provides that

> "[a] written provision in any maritime transaction or a contract evidencing a transaction involving commerce to settle by arbitration a controversy thereafter arising out of such contract or transaction, or the refusal to perform the whole or any part thereof, or an agreement in writing to submit to arbitration an existing controversy arising out of such a contract, transaction, or refusal, shall be valid, irrevocable, and enforceable, save upon such grounds as exist at law or in equity for the revocation of any contract."

We had occasion in Allied–Bruce [Terminix Companies, Inc. v. Dobson, 513 U.S. 265 (1995)], to consider the significance of Congress' use of the words "involving commerce" in § 2.... [T]he Court interpreted § 2 as implementing Congress' intent "to exercise [its] commerce power to the full."

The instant case, of course, involves not the basic coverage authorization under § 2 of the Act, but the exemption from coverage under § 1. The exemption clause provides the Act shall not apply "to contracts of employment of seamen, railroad employees, or any other class of workers engaged in foreign or interstate commerce." 9 U.S.C. § 1. . . .

### B

Respondent, at the outset, contends that we need not address the meaning of the § 1 exclusion provision to decide the case in his favor. In his view, an employment contract is not a "contract evidencing a transaction involving interstate commerce" at all, since the word "transaction" in § 2 extends only to commercial contracts. . . . This line of reasoning proves too much, for it would make the § 1 exclusion provision superfluous. If all contracts of employment are beyond the scope of the Act under the § 2 coverage provision, the separate exemption for "contracts of employment of seamen, railroad employees, or any other class of workers engaged in . . . interstate commerce" would be pointless. . . . If, then, there is an argument to be made that arbitration agreements in employment contracts are not covered by the Act, it must be premised on the language of the § 1 exclusion provision itself.

Respondent . . . relies on the asserted breadth of the words "contracts of employment of . . . any other class of workers engaged in . . . commerce." Referring to our construction of § 2's coverage provision in *Allied–Bruce*—concluding that the words "involving commerce" evidence the congressional intent to regulate to the full extent of its commerce power—respondent contends § 1's interpretation should have a like reach, thus exempting all employment contracts. The two provisions, it is argued, are coterminous; under this view the "involving commerce" provision brings within the FAA's scope all contracts within the Congress' commerce power, and the "engaged in . . . commerce" language in § 1 in turn exempts from the FAA all employment contracts falling within that authority.

This reading of § 1, however, runs into an immediate and, in our view, insurmountable textual obstacle. Unlike the "involving commerce" language in § 2, the words "any other class of workers engaged in . . . commerce" constitute a residual phrase, following, in the same sentence, explicit reference to "seamen" and "railroad employees." Construing the residual phrase to exclude all employment contracts fails to give independent effect to the statute's enumeration of the specific categories of workers which precedes it; there would be no need for Congress to use the phrases "seamen" and "railroad employees" if those same classes of workers were subsumed within the meaning of the "engaged in . . . commerce" residual clause. The wording of § 1 calls for the application of the maxim *ejusdem generis*, the statutory canon that "[w]here general words follow specific words in a statutory enumeration, the general words are construed to embrace only objects similar in nature to those objects enumerated by the preceding specific words." 2A N. Singer, Sutherland on Statutes and Statutory Construction § 47.17 (1991). . . . Under this rule of construction the residual clause should be read to give effect to the terms "seamen" and "railroad employees," and should itself be controlled and defined by reference to the enumerated categories of workers which are recited just before it; the interpretation of the clause pressed by respondent fails to produce these results.

Canons of construction need not be conclusive and are often countered, of course, by some maxim pointing in a different direction. The application of the rule *ejusdem generis* in this case, however, is in full accord with other sound considerations bearing upon the proper interpretation of the clause. For even if the term "engaged in commerce" stood alone in § 1, we would not construe the provision to exclude all contracts of employment from the FAA. Congress uses different modifiers to the word "commerce" in the design and enactment of its statutes. The phrase "affecting commerce" indicates Congress' intent to regulate to the outer limits of its authority under the Commerce Clause. . . . The "involving commerce" phrase, the operative words for the reach of the basic coverage provision in § 2, was at issue in *Allied–Bruce*. . . . Considering the usual meaning of the word "involving," and the pro-arbitration purposes of the FAA, *Allied-Bruce* held the "word 'involving,' like 'affecting,' signals an intent to exercise Congress' commerce power to the full." Unlike those phrases, however, the general words "in commerce" and the specific phrase "engaged in commerce" are understood to have a more limited reach. In *Allied–Bruce* itself the Court said the words "in commerce" are "often-found words of art" that we have not read as expressing congressional intent to regulate to the outer limits of authority under the Commerce Clause. . . .

It is argued that we should assess the meaning of the phrase "engaged in commerce" in a different manner here, because the FAA was enacted when congressional authority to regulate under the commerce power was to a large extent confined by our decisions. . . . When the FAA was enacted in 1925, respondent reasons, the phrase "engaged in commerce" was not a term of art indicating a limited assertion of congressional jurisdiction; to the contrary, it is said, the formulation came close to expressing the outer limits of Congress' power as then understood. . . . Were this mode of interpretation to prevail, we would take into account the scope of the Commerce Clause, as then elaborated by the Court, at the date of the FAA's enactment in order to interpret what the statute means now.

A variable standard for interpreting common, jurisdictional phrases would contradict our earlier cases and bring instability to statutory interpretation. The Court has declined in past cases to afford significance, in construing the meaning of the statutory jurisdictional provisions "in commerce" and "engaged in commerce," to the circumstance that the statute predated shifts in the Court's Commerce Clause cases. . . .

The Court's reluctance to accept contentions that Congress used the words "in commerce" or "engaged in commerce" to regulate to the full extent of its commerce power rests on sound foundation, as it affords objective and consistent significance to the meaning of the words Congress uses when it defines the reach of a statute. To say that the statutory words "engaged in commerce" are subject to variable interpretations depending upon the date of adoption, even a date before the phrase became a term of art, ignores the reason why the formulation became a term of art in the first place: The plain meaning of the words "engaged in commerce" is narrower than the more open-ended formulations "affecting commerce" and "involving commerce." . . . It would be unwieldy for Congress, for the Court, and for litigants to be required to deconstruct statutory Commerce Clause phrases depending upon the year of a particular statutory enactment.

In rejecting the contention that the meaning of the phrase "engaged in commerce" in § 1 of the FAA should be given a broader construction than justified by its evident language simply because it was enacted in 1925 rather than 1938, we do not mean to suggest that statutory jurisdictional formulations "necessarily have a uniform meaning whenever used by Congress." . . . We must, of course, construe the "engaged in commerce" language in the FAA with reference to the statutory context in which it is found and in a manner consistent with the FAA's purpose. These considerations, however, further compel that the § 1 exclusion provision be afforded a narrow construction. As discussed above, the location of the phrase "any other class of workers engaged in . . . commerce" in a residual provision, after specific categories of workers have been enumerated, undermines any attempt to give the provision a sweeping, open-ended construction. And the fact that the provision is contained in a statute that "seeks broadly to overcome judicial hostility to arbitration agreements," . . . gives no reason to abandon the precise reading of a provision that exempts contracts from the FAA's coverage.

In sum, the text of the FAA forecloses . . . a construction which would exclude all employment contracts from the FAA. . . . While it is of course possible to speculate that Congress might have chosen a different jurisdictional formulation had it known that the Court would soon embrace a less restrictive reading of the Commerce Clause, the text of § 1 precludes interpreting the exclusion provision to defeat the language of § 2 as to all employment contracts. Section 1 exempts from the FAA only contracts of employment of transportation workers.

## C

As the conclusion we reach today is directed by the text of § 1, we need not assess the legislative history of the exclusion provision. . . . We do note, however, that the legislative record on the § 1 exemption is quite sparse. Respondent points to no language in either Committee Report addressing the meaning of the provision, nor to any mention of the § 1 exclusion during debate on the FAA on the floor of the House or Senate. Instead, respondent places greatest reliance upon testimony before a Senate subcommittee hearing suggesting that the exception may have been added in response to the objections of the president of the International Seamen's Union of America. . . . Legislative history is problematic even when the attempt is to draw inferences from the intent of duly appointed committees of the Congress. It becomes far more so when we consult sources still more steps removed from the full Congress and speculate upon the significance of the fact that a certain interest group sponsored or opposed particular legislation.... We ought not attribute to Congress an official purpose based on the motives of a particular group that lobbied for or against a certain proposal—even assuming the precise intent of the group can be determined, a point doubtful both as a general rule and in the instant case. It is for the Congress, not the courts, to consult political forces and then decide how best to resolve conflicts in the course of writing the objective embodiments of law we know as statutes....

■ [JUSTICE STEVENS' dissent, which was joined by JUSTICE GINSBURG and JUSTICE BREYER, and joined in part by JUSTICE SOUTER, is omitted.]

■ JUSTICE SOUTER, with whom JUSTICE STEVENS, JUSTICE GINSBURG, and JUSTICE BREYER join, dissenting.

Section 2 of the Federal Arbitration Act (FAA or Act) provides for the enforceability of a written arbitration clause in "any maritime transaction or a contract evidencing a transaction involving commerce," 9 U.S.C. § 2, while § 1 exempts from the Act's coverage "contracts of employment of seamen, railroad employees, or any other class of workers engaged in foreign or interstate commerce." Whatever the understanding of Congress's implied admiralty power may have been when the Act was passed in 1925, the commerce power was then thought to be far narrower than we have subsequently come to see it. As a consequence, there are two quite different ways of reading the scope of the Act's provisions. One way would be to say, for example, that the coverage provision extends only to those contracts "involving commerce" that were understood to be covered in 1925; the other would be to read it as exercising Congress's commerce jurisdiction in its modern conception in the same way it was thought to implement the more limited view of the Commerce Clause in 1925. The first possibility would result in a statutory ambit frozen in time, behooving Congress to amend the statute whenever it desired to expand arbitration clause enforcement beyond its scope in 1925; the second would produce an elastic reach, based on an understanding that Congress used language intended to go as far as Congress could go, whatever that might be over time.

In *Allied–Bruce*, we decided that the elastic understanding of § 2 was the more sensible way to give effect to what Congress intended when it legislated to cover contracts "involving commerce," a phrase that we found an apt way of providing that coverage would extend to the outer constitutional limits under the Commerce Clause. The question here is whether a similarly general phrase in the § 1 exemption, referring to contracts of "any ... class of workers engaged in foreign or interstate commerce," should receive a correspondingly evolutionary reading, so as to expand the exemption for employment contracts to keep pace with the enhanced reach of the general enforceability provision. If it is tempting to answer yes, on the principle that what is sauce for the goose is sauce for the gander, it is sobering to realize that the Courts of Appeals have ... overwhelmingly rejected the evolutionary reading of § 1 accepted by the Court of Appeals in this case. A majority of this Court now puts its *imprimatur* on the majority view among the Courts of Appeals.

The number of courts arrayed against reading the § 1 exemption in a way that would allow it to grow parallel to the expanding § 2 coverage reflects the fact that this minority view faces two hurdles, each textually based and apparent from the face of the Act. First, the language of coverage (a contract evidencing a transaction "involving commerce") is different from the language of the exemption (a contract of a worker "engaged in ... commerce"). Second, the "engaged in ... commerce" catchall phrase in the exemption is placed in the text following more specific exemptions for employment contracts of "seamen" and "railroad employees." The placement possibly indicates that workers who are excused from arbitrating by virtue of the catchall exclusion must resemble seamen and railroad workers, perhaps by being employees who actually handle and move goods as they are shipped interstate or internationally.

Neither hurdle turns out to be a bar, however. The first objection is at best inconclusive and weaker than the grounds to reject it; the second is even more certainly inapposite, for reasons the Court itself has stated but misunderstood.

## I

Is Congress further from a plenary exercise of the commerce power when it deals with contracts of workers "engaged in ... commerce" than with contracts detailing transactions "involving commerce?" The answer is an easy yes, insofar as the former are only the class of labor contracts, while the latter are not so limited. But that is not the point. The question is whether Congress used language indicating that it meant to cover as many contracts as the Commerce Clause allows it to reach within each class of contracts addressed. In *Allied-Bruce* we examined the 1925 context and held that "involving commerce" showed just such a plenary intention, even though at the time we decided that case we had long understood "affecting commerce" to be the quintessential expression of an intended plenary exercise of commerce power.

Again looking to the context of the time, I reach the same conclusion about the phrase "engaged in commerce" as a description of employment contracts exempted from the Act. When the Act was passed (and the commerce power was closely confined) our case law indicated that the only employment relationships subject to the commerce power were those in which workers were actually engaged in interstate commerce.... Thus, by using "engaged in" for the exclusion, Congress showed an intent to exclude to the limit of its power to cover employment contracts in the first place, and it did so just as clearly as its use of "involving commerce" showed its intent to legislate to the hilt over commercial contracts at a more general level. That conclusion is in fact borne out by the statement of the then-Secretary of Commerce, Herbert Hoover, who suggested to Congress that the § 1 exclusion language should be adopted "[i]f objection appears to the inclusion of workers' contracts in the law's scheme."

The Court cites [several cases] for the proposition that "engaged in" has acquired a more restricted meaning as a term of art, immune to tampering now. But none of the cited cases dealt with the question here, whether exemption language is to be read as petrified when coverage language is read to grow. Nor do the cases support the Court's unwillingness to look beyond the four corners of the statute to determine whether the words in question necessarily " 'have a uniform meaning whenever used by Congress' " . . . .

The Court has no good reason, therefore, to reject a reading of "engaged in" as an expression of intent to legislate to the full extent of the commerce power over employment contracts. The statute is accordingly entitled to a coherent reading as a whole . . . by treating the exemption for employment contracts as keeping pace with the expanded understanding of the commerce power generally.

## II

The second hurdle is cleared more easily still, and the Court has shown how. . . . [T]he majority today finds great significance in the fact that the generally phrased exemption for the employment contracts of workers "engaged in commerce" does not stand alone, but occurs at the end of a sequence of more specific exemptions: for "contracts of employment of seamen, railroad employees, or any other class of workers engaged in foreign or interstate commerce." . . . [T]his Court sees the sequence as an occasion to apply the interpretive maxim of *ejusdem generis*, that is, when specific terms are followed by a general one, the latter is meant to cover only examples of the same sort as the preceding specifics. Here, the same sort is thought to be contracts of transportation workers, or employees of transporters, the very carriers of commerce. And that, of course, excludes respondent Adams from benefit of the exemption, for he is employed by a retail seller.

Like many interpretive canons, however, *ejusdem generis* is a fallback, and if there are good reasons not to apply it, it is put aside.[2] There are good reasons here. As Adams argued, it is imputing something very odd to the working of the congressional brain to say that Congress took care to bar application of the Act to the class of employment contracts it most obviously had authority to legislate about in 1925, contracts of workers employed by carriers and handlers of commerce, while covering only employees "engaged" in less obvious ways, over whose coverage litigation might be anticipated with uncertain results. It would seem to have made more sense either to cover all coverable employment contracts or to exclude them all. In fact, exclusion might well have been in order based on concern that

---

**2.** What is more, the Court has repeatedly explained that the canon is triggered only by uncertain statutory text, . . . and that it can be overcome by, *inter alia*, contrary legislative history. . . . The Court today turns this practice upside down, using *ejusdem generis* to establish that the text is so clear that legislative history is irrelevant.

arbitration could prove expensive or unfavorable to employees, many of whom lack the bargaining power to resist an arbitration clause if their prospective employers insist on one. And excluding all employment contracts from the Act's enforcement of mandatory arbitration clauses is consistent with Secretary Hoover's suggestion that the exemption language would respond to any "objection ... to the inclusion of workers' contracts."

[Finally,] ... Congress already had spoken on the [employment relations] of sailors and rail workers and had tailored the legislation to the particular circumstances of the sea and rail carriers.... [M]aking the specific references [in § 1] was ... [thus] an act of special care to make sure that the FAA not be construed to modify the existing legislation so exactly aimed; that was no reason at all to limit the general FAA exclusion from applying to employment contracts that had not been targeted with special legislation.... The Court has understood this point before, holding that the existence of a special reason for emphasizing specific examples of a statutory class can negate any inference that an otherwise unqualified general phrase was meant to apply only to matters *ejusdem generis*. On the Court's own reading of the history, then, the explanation for the catchall is not *ejusdem generis*; instead, the explanation for the specifics is *ex abundanti cautela*, abundance of caution....

---

### 1.  Is the Term "Involving Commerce" Elastic?—To understand the central issue in *Circuit City*, it is helpful to begin with a brief summary of the 1995 case *Allied–Bruce Terminix Companies v. Dobson*. The issue in *Allied–Bruce* concerned the proper interpretation of the phrase "involving commerce" in § 2 of the Federal Arbitration Act (FAA), and in particular whether the meaning of this phrase changes over time, as the judicial doctrine on what counts as "commerce" changes.

Section 2 of the FAA imposes certain federal law requirements on contracts "involving commerce." Congress's authority to impose such federal law requirements derives from Article I, Section 8, Clause 3 of the Constitution (the Commerce Clause), which grants Congress the power to "regulate commerce ... among the several states...." The precise scope and extent of Congress's Commerce Clause power is the subject of considerable debate. For present purposes, the most important thing to know is that the Supreme Court's doctrine on what counts as interstate commerce broadened considerably between 1925, when the FAA was enacted, and 1995, when the Supreme Court decided *Allied–Bruce*. *Allied–Bruce* involved a homeowner who sued a termite control company for breach of contract. The contract contained an arbitration clause, and the question before the Court was whether the FAA applied. This sort of contract would probably not have qualified as a contract involving interstate commerce in 1925; it would follow that the federal government lacked the constitutional authority under the Commerce Clause to regulate such contracts. *See, e.g.*, A.L.A. Schechter Poultry Corp. v. United States, 295 U.S. 495, 546 (1935) (holding that Congress may regulate intrastate transactions only when they have a "direct" effect on interstate commerce). Yet by 1995, the prevailing legal doctrine would likely treat such a contract as sufficiently connected to interstate commerce so as to permit federal regulation under the Commerce Clause. *See, e.g.,* Wickard v. Filburn, 317 U.S. 111, 128–29 (1942) (holding that Congress can regulate individual intrastate transactions pursuant to the Commerce Clause if the cumulative effect of all such transactions would have a "substantial effect" on interstate commerce). The question before the Supreme Court in *Allied–Bruce* was whether § 2's reference to contracts "involving commerce" included only those contracts that Congress would have been able to regulate under its Commerce Clause power as that power was understood in 1925 (when the FAA was enacted), or whether it included contracts that Congress could regulate under the Commerce Clause given prevailing doctrine in 1995 (when the Supreme Court decided the case). The Supreme Court held in *Allied–Bruce* that the latter conclusion was correct.

This holding is notable because in most cases courts strive to interpret statutory language in a way that is consistent with the meaning that language would have had when the statute was enacted. That approach seems logical; usually we cannot sensibly interpret the meaning of a text—especially one from some time in the past—without attention to what the words meant at the time the text was written. If Congress in 1925 would have understood the phrase "involving commerce" as extending only to the set of interstate commercial activities that it had the power to regulate under Commerce Clause doctrine as it stood in 1925, how can the Court interpret that language seventy years later to have a much broader reach? The answer, according to *Allied-Bruce*, is that the phrase "involving commerce" (like the functionally equivalent phrase "affecting . . . commerce," interpreted in Russell v. United States, 471 U.S. 858, 859 (1985)) is a kind of term of art that Congress uses to signify its intention to exercise its powers to the limit of federal authority under the Commerce Clause. (*Cf.* pp. 115–126, *supra.*) On this view, although the scope of the statutory term "involving commerce" will change over time, this is not because the *courts* are giving the term a different meaning. Rather, it is because the phrase *itself* has an elastic meaning: It is as if the FAA covered "contracts that the federal government has the constitutional authority to regulate under the Commerce Clause," or, perhaps more simply, as if the FAA covered "all contracts," with the implicit expectation that courts would refuse to enforce those applications of the FAA that exceeded Congress's constitutional authority. Do you find this approach persuasive? Or do you think that § 2 should have been read more narrowly, applying only to those contracts that Congress could plausibly have believed it could regulate given prevailing Supreme Court doctrine in 1925?

Turning now to *Circuit City*, if the term "involving commerce" in § 2 is a term of art that indicates that Congress is legislating to the limits of its powers under the Commerce Clause, then does the phrase "engaged in . . . interstate commerce" in § 1 have a similarly elastic quality? Justice Souter's dissent asserted that the answer is yes, but Justice Kennedy's majority opinion disagreed. One of the majority's main reasons for this conclusion, to which we will turn in a moment, involved the application of the *ejusdem generis* canon. But Justice Kennedy's majority opinion also argued that even if the *ejusdem generis* canon had no applicability in this case, the Court would *still* have found that the phrase "engaged in commerce" had a different and narrower meaning than the phrase "involving commerce." According to the majority, while "involving commerce" and "affecting commerce" are terms of art that expand as the scope of Congress's Commerce Clause authority expands, the phrase "engaged in commerce," as well as the phrase "in commerce," are terms of art with a more circumscribed meaning. Do you find that persuasive? If we put the *ejusdem generis* issue to one side, would you have held that the phrase "engaged in . . . interstate commerce" has an elastic meaning that can expand as Commerce Clause doctrine changes, or a narrower meaning that reflects Congress's understanding of what counted as commerce subject to federal regulation in 1925?

Finally, though the Court did not mention it, does it matter that § 1 refers to workers "engaged in . . . *interstate* commerce" (emphasis added), while § 2 refers only to transactions "involving commerce," with no specific reference to *interstate* commerce? Why or why not?

**2. *The Relationship Between* Ejusdem Generis *and the Presumption Against Superfluous Statutory Language*—**The *Circuit City* majority drew an explicit connection between the *ejusdem generis* canon and the canon of construction (discussed at pp. 247–249, *supra*) that disfavors constructions that render statutory language redundant or otherwise superfluous. As Justice Kennedy's majority opinion pointed out, if the term "workers engaged in foreign or interstate commerce" includes any workers whose contracts Congress has the constitutional authority to regulate, then the specific terms "seamen" and "railroad employees" would be redundant: The statute could simply have carved out an exemption for "contracts of employment of workers engaged in foreign or interstate commerce," or even more simply, for "contracts of employment."

Of course, even on the majority's reading, the terms "seamen" and "railroad employees" are redundant with the more general "workers engaged in foreign or interstate commerce," since seamen and railroad employers would fall into that category even on the narrower reading preferred by the *Circuit City* majority. But on the majority's reading, those terms are not superfluous, since their inclusion helps delimit the scope of the more general category. In this sense, the analysis here is similar to the majority opinion in *Gustafson v. Alloyd Co.*, also written by Justice Kennedy. *See* pp. 234–238, *supra*.

But if *ejusdem generis* is essentially an application of the principle that interpretations that create surplus statutory language are disfavored, then the *ejusdem generis* canon may be vulnerable to the many criticisms of that principle—chief among them that a strong presumption against superfluous language is inconsistent both with ordinary communication and with what we know about how the legislative process actually works. *See, e.g.,* Richard A. Posner, *Statutory Interpretation—in the Classroom and in the*

*Courtroom*, 50 U. CHI. L. REV. 800, 812 (1983). For instance, as Justice Souter's *Circuit City* dissent pointed out, Congress might have specifically mentioned seamen and railroad employees in § 1 not because Congress meant to limit the scope of the exemption to employees who were in some sense "similar to" sailors and railway workers, but rather because Congress had already enacted statutes addressing the employment relations of those particular types of workers, and Congress wanted to ensure that the FAA was not construed to disrupt those more specific statutory regimes. This would still create a "redundancy," but one that is entirely understandable in light of the fact that people often list specific examples of a more general category out of a desire to specially emphasize certain applications, rather than out of a desire to place implicit limits on the more general category. Perhaps channeling the spirit of Karl Llewellyn, Justice Souter suggested that the best explanation for the apparent redundancy is not the maxim *ejusdem generis*, but the counter-maxim *ex abundanti cautela* ("abundance of caution").

Is this response limited to the circumstances of this particular case? Or can specific examples *always* be explained by Congress's desire to emphasize that those examples are included within the statutory provision, rather than a congressional intent to limit the scope of the more general term? Is this alternative explanation plausible in other cases that apply the *ejusdem generis* maxim, like *McBoyle v. United States* (pp. 219–220, *supra*) and *People v. Smith* (pp. 127–136, *supra*)?

## III.   SUBSTANTIVE CANONS OF CONSTRUCTION

Semantic canons of construction like *expressio unius*, *noscitur a sociis*, and *ejusdem generis* purport to be neutral with respect to substantive outcomes; these canons are, at least in principle, about deciphering language, not about favoring or disfavoring particular results. There is another important set of canons, however, that is more substantive. Unlike semantic canons, these substantive canons do not purport to be neutral formalizations of background understandings about the way people use and understand the English language. Instead, these substantive canons ask interpreters to put a thumb on the scale in favor of some value or policy that courts have identified as worthy of special protection (or, equivalently, a thumb on the scale against a result that courts have identified as undesirable).

Many of these substantive canons take the form of "clear statement rules" that instruct courts to construe statutes to promote a favored value or avoid a disfavored one unless the statute demands the contrary with greater clarity than would ordinarily be required. One well-known clear statement rule is the rule of lenity, which instructs courts to resolve ambiguities in criminal statutes in favor of the accused. Justice Holmes's opinion in *McBoyle v. United States* at the beginning of this chapter (pp. 219–220, *supra*) alluded to the rule of lenity in holding that an airplane is not a "vehicle" within the meaning of the National Motor Vehicle Theft

Act. "Although it is not likely that a criminal will carefully consider the text of the law before he murders or steals," Justice Holmes explained in *McBoyle*, "it is reasonable that a fair warning should be given to the world in language that the common world will understand, of what the law intends to do if a certain line is passed. To make the warning fair, so far as possible the line should be clear." Justice Holmes implied, consistent with the rule of lenity, that doubts about the meaning of a criminal statute—in that case, doubts about whether an airplane counts as a "vehicle"—should be construed in favor of the defendant. (*See* pp. 327–337, *infra.*)

Notice that in order for a clear statement rule like the rule of lenity to do any work, it must be the case that in the absence of the rule the court would have reached a different conclusion. Suppose, for example, that a court finds a criminal statute ambiguous, but thinks that on the better reading of the statute, the defendant's conduct is lawful. In that case, although the court might invoke the rule of lenity to buttress its conclusion, in fact the rule of lenity is unnecessary to the outcome. The rule of lenity would have bite only if the court thought that the better reading of the criminal statute would cover the defendant's conduct, but that the statute is sufficiently ambiguous that a contrary reading is at least plausible. In such a case, the rule of lenity might alter the outcome, because the court could find that although the statute probably covered the defendant's conduct, it failed to do so with sufficient clarity.

The rule of lenity is but one example of a large set of substantive canons of statutory interpretation. Another especially significant substantive canon instructs courts to construe statutes so as to avoid serious constitutional problems, if it is possible to do so. Other substantive canons are designed to protect values that purport to originate in the Constitution itself, such as federalism and due process, even in the absence of a serious concern about avoiding actual violations of the constitutional text. Still other canons are designed to avoid conflicts with foreign governments or international law. The various substantive canons are nicely catalogued and discussed in William N. Eskridge, Jr. & Philip P. Frickey, *Quasi–Constitutional Law: Clear Statement Rules as Constitutional Lawmaking*, 45 Vand. L. Rev. 593 (1992).

As you work through the material in this section, think about whether, or under what conditions, it is legitimate for courts to develop and apply substantive canons. When, if ever, can one plausibly justify such canons on grounds of presumed congressional intent? If courts believe that Congress is unlikely to have desired a particular kind of outcome, is it legitimate for them to adopt a categorical rule to construe statutes to avoid that sort of outcome unless the statute is very clear? *Cf.* Church of the Holy Trinity v. United States, 143 U.S. 457 (1892) (construing an otherwise clear statute to avoid contradicting a deeply held social value in favor of religion) (*see* pp. 38–43, *supra*). Substantive canons might alternatively be understood as techniques that courts employ in order to advance particular values that the *courts* have determined are important, regardless of the likely preferences of Congress. On this view, the substantive canons "constitute conditions on the effectual exercise of legislative power" that "promote objectives of the legal system which transcend the wishes of any particular session of the legislature." HENRY M. HART, JR. & ALBERT M. SACKS, THE LEGAL PROCESS: BASIC PROBLEMS IN THE MAKING AND APPLICATION OF LAW 1376 (William N. Eskridge, Jr. & Philip N. Frickey eds., 1994). If that is right, how do courts derive the values that they wish to protect? Is the process of derivation a principled one? Is it legitimate, in our system, for courts to do this at all? We will consider these and other questions as we work through a handful of prominent substantive canons of construction.

## A.  AVOIDING SERIOUS CONSTITUTIONAL QUESTIONS

One of the most important and controversial substantive canons is the doctrine that courts should construe statutes to avoid serious constitutional problems. To give some necessary background, in Marbury v. Madison, 5 U.S. (1 Cranch) 137, 177 (1803), the Supreme Court recognized that "the judicial Power" includes the power to pass on the constitutionality of legislation, and that "an act of the legislature, repugnant to the constitution, is void." *Id*. Although this premise is now deeply embedded in American jurisprudence, the resultant power has proven a consistent source of anxiety. As Justice Holmes once wrote, passing on the constitutionality of an Act of Congress "is the gravest and most delicate duty that th[e] Court is called upon to perform." Blodgett v. Holden, 275 U.S. 142, 148 (1927) (Holmes, J., concurring). This sense perhaps reflects the so-called "countermajoritarian difficulty"—the felt "reality that when the Supreme Court declares unconstitutional a legislative act or the action of an elected executive, it thwarts the will of representatives of the actual people of the here and now." ALEXANDER M. BICKEL, THE LEAST DANGEROUS BRANCH: THE SUPREME COURT AT THE BAR OF POLITICS 16–17 (2d ed., 1962). In light of this concern, the Supreme Court has expressed a strong presumption in favor of upholding statutes as constitutional. *See, e.g.*, United States Dep't of Labor v. Triplett, 494 U.S. 715, 721 (1990) (emphasizing "the heavy presumption of constitutionality to which a 'carefully considered decision of a coequal and representative branch of our Government' is entitled") (quoting Walters v. National Ass'n of Radiation Survivors, 473 U.S. 305, 319 (1985)); Brown v. Maryland, 25 U.S. (12 Wheat.) 419, 436 (1827) (Marshall, C.J.) ("It has been truly said, that the presumption is in favour of every legislative act, and that the whole burthen of proof lies on him who denies its constitutionality."). The Court has also devised a number of techniques to avoid having to address constitutional objections to congressional statutes in the first place. *See* RICHARD H. FALLON, JR., JOHN F. MANNING, DANIEL J. MELTZER, AND DAVID L. SHAPIRO, HART & WECHSLER'S THE FEDERAL COURTS AND THE FEDERAL SYSTEM 76–80 (6th ed., 2009) (cataloguing such techniques).

The canon of constitutional avoidance is one of the most important of such techniques. This canon—often known as the "avoidance canon"—has appeared in one form or another in Supreme Court jurisprudence since at least the early nineteenth century, although as we discuss below (p. 270, *infra*) the meaning and scope of the canon has changed over time. Perhaps the best-known and most influential articulation of the constitutional avoidance doctrine is Justice Brandeis's concurrence in Ashwander v. Tennessee Valley Authority, 297 U.S. 288, 341 (1936). The underlying dispute and the majority opinion in *Ashwander* are not particularly interesting. Rather, the case is remembered largely for Justice Brandeis's concurrence, in which he went well beyond the issues directly presented in the case in order to lay out a set of seven rules which, he said, the Supreme Court had developed in order to "avoid passing upon a large part of all the constitutional questions pressed upon it for decision." *Id.* at 346. Of these seven rules, two (number 4 and number 7) are especially salient to the discussion of the constitutional avoidance doctrine in statutory interpretation:

> 4. The Court will not pass upon a constitutional question although properly presented by the record, if there is also present some other ground upon which the case may be disposed of. . . . Thus, if a case can be decided on either of two grounds, one involving a constitutional question, the other a question of statutory construction or general law, the Court will decide only the latter. . . .

> 7. When the validity of an act of the Congress is drawn in question, and even if a serious doubt of constitutionality is raised, it is a cardinal principle that this Court will first ascertain whether a construction of the statute is fairly possible by which the question may be avoided. . . .

297 U.S. at 347–48 (Brandeis, J., concurring) (internal citations and quotation marks omitted).

The first of these two principles (Justice Brandeis's fourth *Ashwander* rule) is not really about *how* courts should interpret statutes, but rather about *when* they should do so. This rule states that courts should always try to resolve a case on statutory (or other) grounds *before* addressing constitutional objections. Suppose, for example, that a website operator is convicted of violating a federal anti-pornography statute, and on appeal the operator argues, first, that the material on his website was not pornographic within the meaning of the statute, and, second, that the statute is an unconstitutional interference with the First Amendment's guarantee of freedom of speech. A court applying Justice Brandeis's fourth *Ashwander* rule would address the statutory issue first, because if the court finds in favor of the website operator on statutory grounds, the court does not need to reach the constitutional question at all. But Justice Brandeis's fourth *Ashwander* rule does not say anything about *how* the court should conduct the statutory analysis; it just says that the court should address the statutory issue before the constitutional issue, in the hope of avoiding the latter.

By contrast, the second of the two rules stated above (Justice Brandeis's seventh *Ashwander* rule) has to do with *how*, not simply when, the court should interpret the statute. In particular, Justice Brandeis's seventh *Ashwander* rule says that if there is a "serious doubt" about the constitutionality of a federal statute, the court should see whether "a construction of the statute is fairly possible by which the question may be avoided." It is this principle that is generally known as the "constitutional avoidance" or "constitutional doubt" canon. In the hypothetical example involving the website operator convicted of violating an anti-pornography statute, a court applying Justice Brandeis's seventh *Ashwander* rule would try to avoid having to reach the constitutional issue by seeing if it is possible to interpret the anti-pornography statute so that the website operator is not in violation. If there are two plausible constructions of the statute, one of which would prohibit the operator's conduct (and therefore raise a serious First Amendment problem) and one of which would not, the constitutional avoidance canon (Brandeis's seventh *Ashwander* rule) would instruct the court to adopt the latter interpretation, thereby obviating the need to address the First Amendment issue.

An important feature of Justice Brandeis's formulation of the avoidance canon is that the canon applies as long as an otherwise plausible interpretation would raise a "serious doubt" about the statute's constitutionality. This position contrasts, subtly but importantly, with an earlier version of the avoidance canon—the "classical avoidance canon"—according to which courts are supposed to interpret statutes in order to avoid constructions that would be *actually* unconstitutional. The "modern avoidance canon" articulated by Justice Brandeis in *Ashwander* (and generally traced to the earlier decision in United States ex rel. Attorney General v. Delaware & Hudson Co., 213 U.S. 366 (1909)) differs from the "classical avoidance canon" in that under "modern avoidance," the presence of a serious constitutional *doubt* or *question* about one possible construction of a statute is a sufficient reason to adopt a different construction, so long as that alternative construction is "fairly possible." *See* John Copeland Nagle, Delaware & Hudson *Revisited*, 72 NOTRE DAME L. REV. 1495 (1997); Adrian Vermeule, *Saving Constructions*, 85 GEO. L.J. 1945 (1997). *But see* William N. Eskridge, Jr., *All About Words: Early Understandings of the "Judicial Power" in Statutory Interpretation, 1776–1806*, 101 COLUM. L. REV. 990, 1105 (2001) (suggesting that there is precedential support in early federal judicial practice for both versions of the avoidance canon). While classical avoidance is designed to avoid judicial invalidation of statutes on constitutional grounds, classical avoidance does not allow the court to avoid deciding the constitutional issue, because the court cannot apply the classical version of the avoidance canon until the court first determines that a given interpretation of the statute would render the statute actually unconstitutional. Modern avoidance, by contrast, allows courts to avoid ever even deciding the constitutional issue—indeed, that sort of avoidance is the express purpose of the modern version of the canon.

What is the justification for the avoidance canon, particularly in its modern form? How should the canon be applied, and what is its proper scope? The opinions in the following Supreme Court case, *National Labor Relations Board v. Catholic Bishop of Chicago*, illustrate that even Justices who agree in general terms that the avoidance canon is a legitimate tool of statutory construction have quite different views on when, or how, judges ought to apply that canon. Before proceeding to the case, a bit of background on the statutory and constitutional provisions may be helpful.

The dispute in *Catholic Bishop* concerned the applicability of the prohibition on "unfair labor practices" in § 8 of the National Labor Relations Act (NLRA) to religiously affiliated schools that employ lay teachers to teach secular subjects. Section 8 of the NLRA makes it an unfair labor practice for an employer "to refuse to bargain collectively with the representatives of [its] employees," if those representatives are authorized to bargain on the employees' behalf. 29 U.S.C. § 158(a)(5). It is also an unfair labor practice for an employer "to interfere with, restrain, or coerce employees" in the exercise of their right to organize a union and bargain collectively. 29 U.S.C. § 158(a)(1). The statutory question in *Catholic Bishop* concerned the definition of "employer" for purposes of these provisions. Section 2 of the NLRA defines "employer" as follows: "The term 'employer' includes any person acting as an agent of an employer . . ., but shall not include the United States or any wholly owned Government corporation, or any Federal Reserve Bank, or any State or political subdivision thereof, or any person subject to the Railway Labor Act . . ., or any labor organization (other than when acting as an employer), or anyone acting in the capacity of officer or agent of such labor organization." 29 U.S.C. § 152(2).

The constitutional question at issue in *Catholic Bishop* involved the Religion Clauses of the First Amendment. While you do not need to know the details of First Amendment doctrine to understand the central questions of statutory construction in *Catholic Bishop*, the following background might nevertheless be useful in understanding the case. The First Amendment contains two separate clauses pertaining to religion—the prohibition on government *establishment* of religion, and the bar on government interference with the *free exercise* of religion. ("Congress shall make no law respecting an establishment of religion, or prohibiting the free exercise thereof. . . ." U.S. Const. amend. 1.) The First Amendment questions that came up in *Catholic Bishop* had to do with the Free Exercise Clause, not the Establishment Clause. That said, in the 1971 Establishment Clause decision *Lemon v. Kurtzman*, 403 U.S. 602, the Supreme Court had held that state aid to religious schools involved excessive government "entanglement" with religion, in violation of the Establishment Clause. At the time *Catholic Bishop* was decided there was some question as to whether, or under what conditions, government regulation of religious organizations could lead to a similar sort of "entanglement" that would give rise to a constitutional violation under the Free Exercise Clause.

---

# NLRB v. Catholic Bishop of Chicago

Supreme Court of the United States
440 U.S. 490 (1979)

■ Mr. Chief Justice Burger delivered the opinion of the Court.

This case arises out of the National Labor Relations Board's exercise of jurisdiction over lay faculty members at two groups of Catholic high schools. We granted certiorari to consider two questions: (a) Whether teachers in schools operated by a church to teach both religious and secular subjects are within the jurisdiction granted by the National Labor Relations Act; and (b) if the Act authorizes such jurisdiction, does its exercise violate the guarantees of the Religion Clauses of the First Amendment?

## I

One group of schools is operated by the Catholic Bishop of Chicago...; the other group is operated by the Diocese of Fort Wayne–South Bend, Inc. The [schools] operated by the Catholic Bishop of Chicago ... provide special religious instruction not offered in other Catholic secondary schools. [They] also offer essentially the same college-preparatory curriculum as public secondary schools....

The Diocese of Fort Wayne–South Bend, Inc., has five high schools.... [T]hese high schools seek to provide a traditional secular education but oriented to the tenets of the Roman Catholic faith; religious training is also mandatory....

In 1974 and 1975, separate representation petitions were filed with the Board by interested union organizations...; representation was sought only for lay teachers. The schools challenged the assertion of jurisdiction on two grounds: (a) that they do not fall within the Board's discretionary jurisdictional criteria; and (b) that the Religion Clauses of the First Amendment preclude the Board's jurisdiction....

## IV

That there are constitutional limitations on the Board's actions has been repeatedly recognized by this Court even while acknowledging the broad scope of the grant of jurisdiction. The First Amendment, of course, is a limitation on the power of Congress. Thus, if we were to conclude that the Act granted the challenged jurisdiction over these teachers we would be required to decide whether that was constitutionally permissible under the Religion Clauses of the First Amendment.

Although the respondents press their claims under the Religion Clauses, the question we consider first is whether Congress intended the Board to have jurisdiction over teachers in church-operated schools. In a number of cases the Court has heeded the essence of Mr. Chief Justice Marshall's admonition in Murray v. The Charming Betsy, 2 Cranch 64 (1804), by holding that an Act of Congress ought not be construed to violate the Constitution if any other possible construction remains available....

... In keeping with the Court's prudential policy it is incumbent on us to determine whether the Board's exercise of its jurisdiction here would give rise to serious constitutional questions. If so, we must first identify "the affirmative intention of the Congress clearly expressed" before concluding that the Act grants jurisdiction.

V

[W]e have recognized the critical and unique role of the teacher in fulfilling the mission of a church-operated school. What was said of the schools in Lemon v. Kurtzman, 403 U.S. 602, 617 (1971), is true of the schools in this case: "Religious authority necessarily pervades the school system." The key role played by teachers in such a school system has been the predicate for our conclusions that governmental aid channeled through teachers creates an impermissible risk of excessive governmental entanglement in the affairs of the church-operated schools....

Only recently we again noted the importance of the teacher's function in a church school: "Whether the subject is 'remedial reading,' 'advanced writing,' or simply 'reading,' a teacher remains a teacher, and the danger that religious doctrine will become intertwined with secular instruction persists." Meek v. Pittenger, 421 U.S. 349, 370 (1975). Cf. Wolman v. Walter, 433 U.S. 229, 244 (1977). Good intentions by government—or third parties—can surely no more avoid entanglement with the religious mission of the school in the setting of mandatory collective bargaining than in the well-motivated legislative efforts consented to by the church-operated schools which we found unacceptable in *Lemon*, *Meek*, and *Wolman*.

The Board argues that it can avoid excessive entanglement since it will resolve only factual issues such as whether an anti-union animus motivated an employer's action. But at this stage of our consideration we are not compelled to determine whether the entanglement is excessive as we would were we considering the constitutional issue. Rather, we make a narrow inquiry whether the exercise of the Board's jurisdiction presents a significant risk that the First Amendment will be infringed.

Moreover, it is already clear that the Board's actions will go beyond resolving factual issues. The Court of Appeals' opinion refers to charges of unfair labor practices filed against religious schools. The court observed that in those cases the schools had responded that their challenged actions were mandated by their religious creeds. The resolution of such charges by the Board, in many instances, will necessarily involve inquiry into the good faith of the position asserted by the clergy-administrators and its relationship to the school's religious mission....

The Board's exercise of jurisdiction will have at least one other impact on church-operated schools. The Board will be called upon to decide what are "terms and conditions of employment" and therefore mandatory subjects of bargaining....

The church-teacher relationship in a church-operated school differs from the employment relationship in a public or other nonreligious school. We see no escape from conflicts flowing from the Board's exercise of jurisdiction over teachers in church-operated schools and the consequent serious First Amendment questions that would follow. We therefore turn to an examination of the National Labor Relations Act to decide whether it must be read to confer jurisdiction that would in turn require a decision on the constitutional claims raised by respondents.

## VI

There is no clear expression of an affirmative intention of Congress that teachers in church-operated schools should be covered by the Act. Admittedly, Congress defined the Board's jurisdiction in very broad terms; we must therefore examine the legislative history of the Act to determine whether Congress contemplated that the grant of jurisdiction would include teachers in such schools.

In enacting the National Labor Relations Act in 1935, Congress sought to protect the right of American workers to bargain collectively. The concern that was repeated throughout the debates was the need to assure workers the right to organize to counterbalance the collective activities of employers which had been authorized by the National Industrial Recovery Act. But congressional attention focused on employment in private industry and on industrial recovery.

Our examination of the statute and its legislative history indicates that Congress simply gave no consideration to church-operated schools. It is not without significance, however, that the Senate Committee on Education and Labor chose a college professor's dispute with the college as an example of employer-employee relations *not* covered by the Act.

Congress' next major consideration of the jurisdiction of the Board came during the passage of the Labor Management Relations Act of 1947—the Taft–Hartley Act. In that Act Congress amended the definition of "employer" in § 2 of the original Act to exclude nonprofit hospitals. There was [in the legislative deliberations] some discussion of the scope of the Board's jurisdiction but the consensus was that nonprofit institutions in general did not fall within the Board's jurisdiction because they did not affect commerce. . . .

The most recent significant amendment to the Act was passed in 1974, removing the exemption of nonprofit hospitals. The Board relies upon that amendment as showing that Congress approved the Board's exercise of jurisdiction over church-operated schools. A close examination of that legislative history, however, reveals nothing to indicate an affirmative intention that such schools be within the Board's jurisdiction. Since the Board did not assert jurisdiction over teachers in a church-operated school until after the 1974 amendment, nothing in the history of the amendment can be read as reflecting Congress' tacit approval of the Board's action.

During the debate there were expressions of concern about the effect of the bill on employees of religious hospitals whose religious beliefs would not permit them to join a union. The result of those concerns was an amendment which reflects congressional sensitivity to First Amendment guarantees:

> "Any employee of a health care institution who is a member of and adheres to established and traditional tenets or teachings of a bona fide religion, body, or sect which has historically held conscientious objections to joining or financially supporting labor organizations shall not be required to join or financially support any labor organization as a

condition of employment; except that such employee may be required, in lieu of periodic dues and initiation fees, to pay sums equal to such dues and initiation fees to a nonreligious charitable fund exempt from taxation under section 501(c)(3) of title 26, chosen by such employee from a list of at least three such funds, designated in a contract between such institution and a labor organization, or if the contract fails to designate such funds, then to any such fund chosen by the employee." 29 U.S.C. § 169.

The absence of an "affirmative intention of the Congress clearly expressed" fortifies our conclusion that Congress did not contemplate that the Board would require church-operated schools to grant recognition to unions as bargaining agents for their teachers.

... Accordingly, in the absence of a clear expression of Congress' intent to bring teachers in church-operated schools within the jurisdiction of the Board, we decline to construe the Act in a manner that could in turn call upon the Court to resolve difficult and sensitive questions arising out of the guarantees of the First Amendment Religion Clauses.

■ MR. JUSTICE BRENNAN, with whom MR. JUSTICE WHITE, MR. JUSTICE MARSHALL, and MR. JUSTICE BLACKMUN join, dissenting.

The Court today holds that coverage of the National Labor Relations Act does not extend to lay teachers employed by church-operated schools. That construction is plainly wrong in light of the Act's language, its legislative history, and this Court's precedents. It is justified solely on the basis of a canon of statutory construction seemingly invented by the Court for the purpose of deciding this case. I dissent.

## I

The general principle of construing statutes to avoid unnecessary constitutional decisions is a well-settled and salutary one. The governing canon, however, is *not* that expressed by the Court today. The Court requires that there be a "clear expression of an affirmative intention of Congress" before it will bring within the coverage of a broadly worded regulatory statute certain persons whose coverage might raise constitutional questions. But those familiar with the legislative process know that explicit expressions of congressional intent in such broadly inclusive statutes are not commonplace. Thus, by strictly or loosely applying its requirement, the Court can virtually remake congressional enactments. This flouts Mr. Chief Justice Taft's admonition "that amendment may not be substituted for construction, and that a court may not exercise legislative functions to save [a] law from conflict with constitutional limitation." Yu Cong Eng v. Trinidad, 271 U.S. 500, 518 (1926)....

The settled canon for construing statutes wherein constitutional questions may lurk was stated in Machinists v. Street, 367 U.S. 740 (1961) ...:

" 'When the validity of an act of the Congress is drawn in question, and even if a serious doubt of constitutionality is raised, it is a cardinal principle that this Court will first ascertain whether a construction of the statute is *fairly possible* by which the question may be avoided.' Crowell v. Benson, 285 U.S. 22, 62." Id., at 749–750 (emphasis added).

... This limitation to constructions that are "fairly possible," and "reasonable," ... acts as a brake against wholesale judicial dismemberment of congressional enactments. It confines the judiciary to its proper role in construing statutes, which is to interpret them so as to give effect to congressional intention. The Court's new "affirmative expression" rule releases that brake.

II

The interpretation of the National Labor Relations Act announced by the Court today is not "fairly possible." The Act's wording, its legislative history, and the Court's own precedents leave "the intention of the Congress ... revealed too distinctly to permit us to ignore it because of mere misgivings as to power." Moore Ice Cream Co. v. Rose, 289 U.S., at 379. Section 2(2) of the Act, 29 U.S.C. § 152(2), defines "employer" as

> "... any person acting as an agent of an employer, directly or indirectly, *but shall not include* the United States or any wholly owned Government corporation, or any Federal Reserve Bank, or any State or political subdivision thereof, or any person subject to the Railway Labor Act, as amended from time to time, or any labor organization (other than when acting as an employer), or anyone acting in the capacity of officer or agent of such labor organization." (Emphasis added.)

Thus, the Act covers all employers not within the eight express exceptions. The Court today substitutes amendment for construction to insert one more exception—for church-operated schools. This is a particularly transparent violation of the judicial role: The legislative history reveals that Congress itself considered and rejected a very similar amendment.

The pertinent legislative history of the NLRA begins with the Wagner Act of 1935. Section 2(2) of that Act, identical in all relevant respects to the current section, excluded from its coverage neither church-operated schools nor any other private nonprofit organization. Accordingly, in applying that Act, the National Labor Relations Board did not recognize an exception for nonprofit employers, even when religiously associated. An argument for an implied nonprofit exemption was rejected because the design of the Act was as clear then as it is now: "[N]either charitable institutions nor their employees are exempted from operation of the Act by its terms, although certain other employers and employees are exempted." Central Dispensary & Emergency Hospital, 44 N.L.R.B. 533, 540 (1942) (footnotes omitted), enf'd, 79 U.S.App.D.C. 274, 145 F.2d 852 (1944). Both the lower courts and this Court concurred in the Board's construction....

The Hartley bill, which passed the House of Representatives in 1947, would have provided the exception the Court today writes into the statute:

"The term 'employer' ... shall not include ... any corporation, community chest, fund, or foundation organized and operated exclusively for *religious*, charitable, scientific, literary, or *educational* purposes, ... no part of the net earnings of which inures to the benefit of any private shareholder or individual...." (Emphasis added.).

But the proposed exception was not enacted.[5] The bill reported by the Senate Committee on Labor and Public Welfare did not contain the Hartley exception. Instead, the Senate proposed an exception limited to nonprofit hospitals, and passed the bill in that form. The Senate version was accepted by the House in conference, thus limiting the exception for nonprofit employers to nonprofit hospitals.

Even that limited exemption was ultimately repealed in 1974. In doing so, Congress confirmed the view of the Act expressed here: that it was intended to cover all employers—including nonprofit employers—unless expressly excluded, and that the 1947 amendment excluded only nonprofit hospitals. Moreover, it is significant that in considering the 1974 amendments, the Senate expressly rejected an amendment proposed by Senator Ervin that was analogous to the one the Court today creates—an amendment to exempt nonprofit hospitals operated by religious groups. Senator Cranston, floor manager of the Senate Committee bill and primary opponent of the proposed religious exception, explained:

"[S]uch an exception for religiously affiliated hospitals would seriously erode *the existing national policy which holds religiously affiliated institutions generally such as* proprietary nursing homes, residential communities, and *educational facilities to the same standards as their nonsectarian counterparts.*" 120 Cong.Rec. 12957 (1974), 1974 Leg.Hist. 137 (emphasis added)....

In construing the Board's jurisdiction to exclude church-operated schools, therefore, the Court today is faithful to neither the statute's language nor its history. Moreover, it is also untrue to its own precedents.... As long as an employer is within the reach of Congress' power under the Commerce Clause—and no one doubts that respondents are—the Court has held him to be covered by the Act regardless of the nature of his activity....

Thus, the available authority indicates that Congress intended to include—not exclude—lay teachers of church-operated schools. The Court does not counter this with evidence that Congress *did* intend an exception it never stated. Instead, despite the legislative history to the contrary, it construes the Act as excluding lay teachers only because Congress did not state explicitly that they were covered. In Mr. Justice Cardozo's words, this

---

**5.** A number of reasons were offered for the rejection of the Hartley bill's exception. Some Congressmen strongly opposed the exception; some were opposed to additional exceptions to the Board's jurisdiction; and some thought it unnecessary.... But whatever the reasons, it is clear that an amendment similar to that made by the Court today was proposed and rejected in 1947.

presses "avoidance of a difficulty . . . to the point of disingenuous evasion." Moore Ice Cream Co. v. Rose, 289 U.S., at 379.

### III

Under my view that the NLRA includes within its coverage lay teachers employed by church-operated schools, the constitutional questions presented would have to be reached. I do not now do so only because the Court does not. I repeat for emphasis, however, that while the resolution of the constitutional question is not without difficulty, it is irresponsible to avoid it by a cavalier exercise in statutory interpretation which succeeds only in defying congressional intent. A statute is not "a nose of wax to be changed from that which the plain language imports. . . ." Yu Cong Eng v. Trinidad, 271 U.S., at 518.

---

***1.  When Can a Constitutional Problem Be Avoided?***—Chief Justice Burger's majority opinion and Justice Brennan's dissent both accepted the legitimacy of the avoidance canon, but they characterized the canon in very different ways. Justice Brennan emphasized that the Court may only adopt an interpretation that avoids a constitutional problem if that interpretation is "reasonable" or "fairly possible." If the text of the statute is not ambiguous—if the only way to avoid the constitutional question is to stretch or twist the statute in ways that amount to "disingenuous evasion"—then the avoidance canon has no place. Justice Brennan reasoned that the Catholic Church was clearly the lay teachers' "employer" in the ordinary meaning of that term, and that the statute does not include an exemption for religious organizations despite the inclusion of a number of other specific exemptions. (Note that the latter argument was an implicit application of the *expressio unius* canon. *See* pp. 224–233, *supra.*) In the absence of the avoidance canon, one would be hard-pressed to find any plausible justification for reading the NLRA's definition of "employer" as excluding religious organizations, especially religious organizations that employ lay teachers to teach secular subjects. So, Justice Brennan reasoned, the statute is not ambiguous, and the avoidance canon therefore did not apply.

Chief Justice Burger's majority opinion had a much different understanding of how the avoidance canon works and when it comes into play. On Justice Brennan's understanding, the avoidance canon can be used only to resolve a statutory ambiguity that would exist independently of the canon. For Chief Justice Burger, the avoidance canon functions more like a clear statement rule, according to which general terms should not be applied in ways that create serious constitutional problems. On this view, if Congress wants a general statute to reach constitutionally problematic cases, Congress must provide a "clear expression" of its "affirmative intent" to do so: The fact that a religious organization would be an "employer" within the ordinary meaning of the statutory definition is not enough to justify the conclusion that such an organization is an "employer" for NLRA purposes; rather, because applying NLRA rules to religious organizations would raise a serious constitutional question, Congress would have had to say something like "employer, including a religious organization" if it wanted the NLRA to reach such employers.

So, we seem to have two competing versions of the avoidance canon: the majority's strong "clear statement" version, and the dissent's weaker "ambiguity-resolving" version. Which is correct? Perhaps a more general way to frame the question would be: How much should a court be willing to deviate from the apparent meaning of the statute in order to avoid a constitutional question? It is important to emphasize that although the clear statement version of the avoidance canon prevailed in *Catholic Bishop*, the case did *not* decisively resolve that question as a matter of formal doctrine. The Supreme Court and the lower federal courts have not been particularly consistent in how they apply the canon.

A closely related issue concerns the relative priority of the avoidance canon vis-à-vis other tools of construction, like semantic canons and legislative history. Consider Justice Brennan's implicit application of the *expressio unius* canon in *Catholic Bishop*: the fact that the definition of "employer" lists eight specific exemptions, but does not include an exemption for religious organizations, implies that no such exemption was intended or contemplated. Suppose, for the sake of argument, that in the absence of this consideration, the term "employer" would be sufficiently ambiguous that it would be appropriate to apply the avoidance canon in order to read "employer" as not extending to religious organizations. Does Justice Brennan's *expressio unius* argument render the statute sufficiently clear that the avoidance canon would no longer be relevant? Or is an *expressio unius* inference sufficiently weak (either as a general matter or in this particular case) that the avoidance canon should take precedence?

Likewise, suppose that the text of the statute were sufficiently ambiguous that it would ordinarily be proper to apply the avoidance canon so as to avoid reading "employer" as including religious organizations, but suppose further that some compelling legislative history points in the other direction. For instance, suppose the original House bill contained an explicit exemption for religious schools, but an amendment to strike that provision passed after extensive debate. Or imagine that the House and Senate committee reports on the NLRA included religious schools as examples of "employers" that would be covered by the Act's prohibition on unfair labor practices. What should a judge do? Even if a judge would otherwise be inclined to use legislative history to resolve statutory ambiguity, can legislative history provide a sufficiently clear indication that Congress intended the constitutionally problematic application to meet the higher burden imposed by the avoidance canon?

**2. *How Serious Must the Constitutional Problem Be?*—**One of the most difficult questions that comes up with respect to the avoidance canon concerns just how serious the constitutional problem must be to trigger application of the canon. As noted earlier, the classical version of the avoidance canon required the court to find that its otherwise-preferred interpretation of the statute would be *actually unconstitutional* before the court could legitimately adopt an alternative reading of the statute. The modern version of the avoidance canon differs in that it requires only the presence of a "serious constitutional problem" (or, in a common alternative formulation, a "grave constitutional doubt"), rather than a finding of actual unconstitutionality. But how "serious" or "grave" must the constitutional problem be? Is the presence of a non-frivolous constitutional objection sufficient to trigger the canon? Or is something more required, such as the conclusion that a given interpretation would *likely* be unconstitutional, or that resolution of the constitutional issue would require resolution of particularly complex and uncertain questions of constitutional law?

*Catholic Bishop* did not address this issue directly. Chief Justice Burger's majority opinion concluded, without much analysis, that the constitutional problem was sufficiently serious to trigger the avoidance canon, while the dissent did not address the issue at all in light of Justice Brennan's conclusion that the statutory language simply did not permit the majority's reading no how matter how grave the constitutional problem might be. But it is easy to imagine how this issue could arise in a case like *Catholic Bishop*. Suppose, for example, that under prevailing First Amendment doctrine, application of the NLRA to lay teachers at religiously affiliated schools would seem constitutionally unproblematic, but the church advances a novel—though by no means unreasonable—constitutional theory that might lead to a different conclusion. What should the Court do? Should it refuse to apply the avoidance doctrine, on the grounds that Congress would not have perceived any constitutional difficulty at the time it enacted the statute, and then proceed to address the church's novel constitutional theory on the merits? Or should the presence of a serious, perhaps complicated, First Amendment question impel the court to construe the statute so as to avoid that issue entirely? Does this question depend on the proper rationale for applying the canon in the first place?

**3. What Is the Justification (If Any) for the Avoidance Canon?**—The preceding questions about how courts should apply the avoidance canon are probably impossible to answer without thinking more carefully about exactly why we have this canon—or whether we should have it at all. Courts and commentators have suggested a number of reasons why the avoidance canon might be desirable, though all of these justifications have been attacked by the canon's critics. Let us consider three of the most prominent arguments in favor of the canon, as well as critiques of those arguments.

**a. An empirical claim about likely congressional intent**—One possible justification for the constitutional avoidance canon is that it reflects a reasonable presumption about what Congress actually intended. This argument proceeds from the empirical claim that Congress tries to respect the constitutional limits on its legislative authority and generally steers clear of legislating in ways that would raise serious constitutional issues. This assumption about congressional preferences implies that when a court encounters a statute that seems, on an initial reading, to raise a serious constitutional question, the court can reasonably conclude that this reading was probably not the one that Congress intended. If another reading is possible, the court should adopt that reading out of respect for Congress's likely intent. As the Supreme Court explained in *Clark v. Martinez*, the avoidance canon rests "on the reasonable presumption that Congress did not intend the [interpretation] which raises serious constitutional doubts." 543 U.S. 371, 381 (2005). *See also* Rust v. Sullivan, 500 U.S. 173, 191 (1991) (the avoidance canon "is followed out of respect for Congress, which we assume legislates in the light of constitutional limitations"); Yates v. United States, 354 U.S. 298, 319 (1957) ("In [construing a statute] we should not assume that Congress chose to disregard a constitutional danger zone so clearly marked. . . .").

Perhaps the greatest virtue of this rationale for the avoidance canon is that it grounds the canon in the policy preferences of Congress, rather than in those of the judiciary. Perhaps the greatest weakness of this rationale, however, is that its empirical predicate is doubtful at best. Although there is reason to suppose that Congress typically prefers to have its statutes upheld rather than struck down, there is not much evidence that Congress is otherwise averse to enacting legislation that raises difficult constitutional issues. As Judge Henry Friendly once wrote:

> It does not seem in any way obvious, as a matter of interpretation, that the legislature would prefer a narrow construction which does not raise constitutional doubts to a broader one which does raise them. For there is always the chance, usually a good one, that the doubts will be settled favorably, and if they are not, the conceded rule of construing to avoid unconstitutionality will come into operation and save the day. People in such a heads-I-win, tails-you-lose position do not readily sacrifice it; the idea that Congress must use strong language to show it wanted the Supreme Court even to consider the constitutional question . . . seems rather fanciful.

HENRY J. FRIENDLY, BENCHMARKS 210 (1967). *See also* William K. Kelley, *Avoiding Constitutional Questions as a Three–Branch Problem*, 86 CORNELL L. REV. 831, 846–55 (2001); Lawrence C. Marshall, *Divesting the Courts: Breaking the Judicial Monopoly on Constitutional Interpretation*, 66 CHI.–KENT L. REV. 481, 489–90 (1990); Frederick Schauer, Ashwander *Revisited*, 1995 SUP. CT. REV. 71, 92–93;.

If the assertion that Congress is reluctant to enact legislation that raises serious constitutional questions is empirically problematic, perhaps the judicial presumption that Congress intends to steer clear of such questions can be better understood as a legal fiction designed to show judicial *respect* for Congress. Even if we do not really believe that Congress actually tries to steer clear of the constitutional "danger zone" when it legislates, perhaps courts should proceed *as if* Congress behaved in this way. But although judicial opinions sometimes use language suggesting this rationale, it is not clear why it makes sense. Why wouldn't the court show more "respect" to Congress by presuming that Congress had carefully considered the constitutional question and decided that the statute was likely constitutional?

Then again, perhaps we should not dismiss too quickly Congress's interest in avoiding judicial invalidation of its statutes on constitutional grounds. Perhaps, as Justice Breyer has suggested, the constitutional avoidance doctrine is premised on the assumption "that Congress would prefer a less-than-optimal interpretation of its statute to the grave risk of a constitutional holding that would set the statute entirely aside." F.C.C. v. Fox Television Stations, Inc., 129 S.Ct. 1800, 1840 (2009) (Breyer, J., dissenting). But even if that were correct, would it justify the modern avoidance doctrine, in which a serious doubt suffices to trigger the canon, or only the classical version, which required a finding that the otherwise optimal interpretation is actually unconstitutional? Also, wouldn't Justice Breyer's argument make sense only in those (unusual) cases where the alternative to the strained interpretation of the statute is wholesale invalidation of the *entire statute*, rather than constitutional invalidation of particular *applications*? After all, in a case like *Catholic Bishop*, even if the Court had reached the constitutional issue and decided that applying the NLRA to religious organizations violated the First Amendment, the result would not have been the invalidation of the entire NLRA, but rather the NLRA's inapplicability to religious organizations—exactly the same substantive result as that induced by the holding in the real case. Does this suggest that the relevance of the avoidance canon should depend in part on the consequences, for the rest of the statutory scheme, of an adverse decision on the constitutional issue?

***b. A prudential tool of judicial restraint***—An alternative (though not mutually exclusive) justification for the avoidance canon is that, whether or not it accurately captures Congress's likely intent, the canon is a valuable prudential tool of judicial restraint. Indeed, the interest in avoiding unnecessary adjudication of constitutional issues seems to have been Justice Brandeis's principal concern in his *Ashwander* concurrence. The Supreme Court has emphasized this rationale in subsequent opinions as well, characterizing the avoidance canon as "a fundamental rule of judicial restraint." Three Affiliated Tribes v. Wold Engineering, P.C., 467 U.S. 138, 157 (1984).

The judicial restraint justification for the avoidance canon proceeds from the assumption that constitutional decisions are a much more significant judicial constraint on the other branches of government than are statutory decisions. This is in part because constitutional decisions are significantly harder to undo or alter than are decisions that rest on statutory grounds: If Congress is unhappy with how the Supreme Court interpreted a federal statute, it can amend the statute, but a constitutional ruling can be altered only by a subsequent judicial decision to overturn the earlier constitutional holding (unlikely) or by a constitutional amendment (even more unlikely). Moreover, constitutional rulings are generally more likely than statutory rulings to affect other areas of the law. In *Catholic Bishop*, for example, if the Court reached the constitutional issue, it may have had to say something general about when government regulation of ostensibly secular activities at religious institutions violates the First Amendment. Whatever the Court said on this point could have had implications extending well beyond the NLRA. In contrast, a statutory ruling makes no new constitutional law, so its impact is more confined.

The Supreme Court elaborated this basic prudential argument in *Rescue Army v. Municipal Court of Los Angeles*, explaining that the constitutional avoidance canon's

> ultimate foundations ... lie in all that goes to make up the unique place and character, in our scheme, of judicial review of governmental action for constitutionality. They are found in[, among other things,] the delicacy of that function, particularly in view of possible consequences for others stemming also from constitutional roots [and] the comparative finality of those consequences; the consideration due to the judgment of other repositories of constitutional power... [and] in the paramount importance of constitutional adjudication in our system.

331 U.S. 549, 571 (1947). For these and other reasons, the avoidance canon may also be a way for the court to avoid the friction or conflict with Congress that would be inherent in a ruling that a statute actually violates the Constitution. *See* Almendarez–Torres v. United States, 523 U.S. 224, 238 (1998) (claiming that the avoidance canon "seeks ... to minimize disagreement between the branches by preserving congressional enactments that might otherwise founder on constitutional objections").

Although judicial opinions often laud the avoidance canon as a tool of judicial restraint, many scholars—and some judges—have argued that the modern avoidance canon in fact has precisely the opposite effect. As Professor Frederick Schauer has argued, "avoidance is only important in those cases in which the result is different from what the result would have been by application of a judge's or court's preconstitutional views about how a statute should be interpreted," and therefore a court applying the canon will "frequently interpret[ ] a statute in ways that its drafters did not anticipate ... [and] may not have preferred." Frederick Schauer, Ashwander *Revisited*, 1995 SUP. CT. REV. 71, 74, 89. Because the modern avoidance canon invites judges to deviate from the most natural reading of the statutory text in the presence of a constitutional *doubt*, rather than an actual constitutional *violation*, the canon enlarges rather than restricts the ability of judges to rely on constitutional considerations to nullify congressional enactments. *Id.* at 89. Moreover, since the modern avoidance canon (in contrast to the classical avoidance canon) relieves courts of the need actually to adjudicate the constitutional question, a court invoking the modern avoidance canon need not analyze the constitutional issues in as much detail, or apply the extant constitutional doctrine with as much rigor, as would be expected in a case where the court was actually ruling on the constitutional issue. *Id.* at 89–90. In *Catholic Bishop*, for example, it is not at all clear that requiring religious organizations to bargain collectively with their lay employees would violate the First Amendment, and it is entirely possible that the Court could not (or would not) write an opinion reaching such a result as a matter of constitutional law. Certainly there is nothing in the *Catholic Bishop* majority opinion that analyzed the First Amendment issue in the depth that would be expected in a decision that rested on constitutional grounds. Yet the Court was able to issue a quasi-constitutional holding—the NLRA does not apply to religious organizations, in light of First Amendment concerns—without the burden of explaining and justifying this holding as a matter of constitutional law. For those who believe that the judicial obligation to give reasons is one of the most important constraints on judicial willfulness (*see, e.g.,* Frederick Schauer, *Giving Reasons*, 47 Stan. L. Rev. 633 (1995)); David L. Shapiro, *In Defense of Judicial Candor*, 100 Harv. L. Rev. 731, 737 (1987), it is troubling that the avoidance canon apparently allows courts to make quasi-constitutional decisions on the cheap.

Of course, if a court resolves a case on avoidance grounds, Congress could in theory amend the statute to force the constitutional issue, whereas Congress could not overcome a constitutional ruling by passing a new statute. That, again, is one of the principal arguments as to why the avoidance canon is a tool of judicial restraint. But the critics insist that this distinction is more often than not an illusory one. As Judge Posner has written:

> Congress's practical ability to overrule a judicial decision miscon-struing one of its statutes, given all the other matters pressing for its attention, is less today than ever before, and probably was never very great. The practical effect of interpreting statutes to avoid raising constitutional questions is therefore to enlarge the already vast reach of constitutional prohibition beyond even the most extravagant modern interpretation of the Constitution—to create a judge-made constitutional "penumbra" that has the same prohibitory effect as the judge-made (or at least judge-amplified) Constitution itself.

Richard A. Posner, *Statutory Interpretation—in the Classroom and in the Courtroom*, 50 U. Chi. L. Rev. 800, 816 (1983). Perhaps Judge Posner's concerns are overstated: Congress has, after all, shown considerable ability to overturn statutory interpretation decisions with which it disagrees. *See, e.g.,* William N. Eskridge, Jr., *Overriding Supreme Court Statutory Inter-pretation Decisions*, 101 Yale L.J. 331 (1991). But if a court—especially the Supreme Court—has resolved a statutory interpretation case on constitu-tional avoidance grounds, hasn't the court sent a strong signal of its inclinations regarding the merits of the constitutional objections? Despite the possibility that the Court would later uphold the statute after more direct engagement with the constitutional question that it sidestepped through avoidance, might Congress be disinclined to press the issue in light of the signals from the Court that the effort may ultimately prove unavail-ing?

Another line of criticism is that the whole notion that courts should assiduously avoid making constitutional decisions, in the name of judicial "restraint," is misguided. It may well be that courts should presume that congressional statutes are constitutional, and should exercise the power of constitutional judicial review sparingly and carefully. But the presumption that courts should err on the side of avoiding constitutional *invalidation* of statutes is distinct from the presumption that courts should avoid *reaching and deciding* questions of constitutional law. After all, clarifying difficult questions of constitutional law is widely regarded as one of the most important functions of the federal courts, particularly the Supreme Court. Even if the Court should limit itself to deciding only those constitutional issues that arise in a concrete case, why does it follow that the Court should adopt a strained interpretation of a statute simply to avoid making a constitutional decision that would elaborate constitutional doctrine and provide better guidance for future cases? *See* Lisa A. Kloppenberg, Playing It Safe: How the Supreme Court Sidesteps Hard Cases and Stunts the Development of the Law (2001); *cf.* Adrian Vermeule, *Holmes on Emergencies*, 61 Stan. L. Rev. 163, 177–78 (2008).

Do you find these criticisms persuasive, or do you agree with Justice Brandeis and others who defend the avoidance canon as a mechanism of judicial restraint? Does your answer depend on how the canon is applied?

  *c. Protecting constitutional values*—One of the standard critiques of the avoidance canon, as we have just seen, is that it does not actually foster judicial restraint, but instead expands the degree to which courts may draw on constitutional considerations to limit the scope or application of congressional statutes. Some defenders of the constitutional avoidance canon, however, consider this a virtue rather than a vice. To them, the avoidance canon may be desirable precisely because it enables courts to take constitutional considerations into account in ways that would not be possible if the court were limited to a simple yes-or-no decision on whether the statute at issue is constitutional. There are two variants on this argument, one of which is more process-oriented, the other of which is more unapologetically substantive.

  The process-oriented argument emphasizes that when Congress considers legislation in a "constitutional danger zone"—that is, when the proposed statute at least arguably infringes on constitutional rights—it is important that Congress deliberate more carefully than it ordinarily would about the constitutional issue before acting. If one accepts that premise, then the avoidance canon provides courts with a means to avoid giving effect to constitutionally problematic statutory mandates when Congress has not engaged in the requisite degree of careful deliberation. *See* Cass R. Sunstein, *Nondelegation Canons*, 67 U. Chi. L. Rev. 315, 331 (2000). To illustrate, in *Catholic Bishop*, there is no evidence that Congress ever explicitly considered whether or how the NLRA should apply to religious organizations in light of the serious First Amendment concerns involved. Accordingly, by insisting that Congress address constitutionally problematic issues explicitly, the avoidance canon may improve the legislative process by encouraging more candid and searching analysis of constitutional questions regarding a statute's reach. *See, e.g.*, Cass R. Sunstein, After the Rights Revolution: Reconceiving the Regulatory State 154–55 (1990); Dan T. Coenen, *A Constitution of Collaboration: Protecting Fundamental Values with Second–Look Rules of Interbranch Dialogue*, 42 Wm. & Mary L. Rev. 1575, 1609 (2001).

While the preceding argument emphasizes the avoidance canon's desirable effects on the legislative *process*—fostering careful deliberation on constitutional issues—some defenders of the avoidance canon make a related argument that is more overtly substantive. According to this view, the Constitution enshrines certain public values, and courts can properly enforce and promote those values not only by striking down legislative enactments that clearly contravene the Constitution's text, but also by reading statutes narrowly to avoid trenching on constitutional values unless Congress has clearly forced the issue. This is a kind of "soft" enforcement of a broader set of constitutional values that lie behind the more hard-edged constitutional prohibitions embodied in the text and doctrine. As Professor Ernest Young elaborates this point:

> [N]ot all constitutional principles have a 'line in the sand' quality, such that all government acts short of that line are valid and all government acts falling over that line are invalid. Rather, some constitutional principles take the form of 'resistance norms'—norms that may be more or less yielding to governmental action, depending on the strength of the government's interest, the degree of institutional support for the challenged action, or the clarity of purpose that the legislature has expressed.

Ernest A. Young, *Constitutional Avoidance, Resistance Norms, and the Preservation of Judicial Review*, 78 Tex. L. Rev. 1549, 1552 (2000). *See also* Dan T. Coenen, *The Rehnquist Court, Structural Due Process, and Semi-substantive Constitutional Review*, 75 S. Cal. L. Rev. 1281, 1294–95 (2002) (asserting that by using the avoidance canon, "the Court can and does protect fundamental values by eschewing interpretations otherwise ascribable to statutes that would push those statutes into constitutional danger zones"); Matthew C. Stephenson, *The Price of Public Action: Constitutional Doctrine and the Judicial Manipulation of Legislative Enactment Costs*, 118 Yale L.J. 2, 40–42 (2008) (arguing that the avoidance canon raises the costs to legislators of implementing constitutionally problematic results, and therefore "is a method for gauging indirectly the strength of the [threatened] constitutional value relative to the other public interests at stake," *id.* at 40).

Proponents of this argument might defend the decision in *Catholic Bishop* in the following terms: The Free Exercise Clause of the First Amendment is meant to advance a particular set of public values having to do with limiting state interference with religious practice. Courts enforce this guarantee in part by holding that certain government actions with respect to religion are absolutely impermissible. But that form of enforcement by itself is inadequate, because there's a big grey area consisting of cases in which some government action would trench on the values the Free Exercise Clause is meant to protect, but it's not clear the action goes so far that a court would or should be willing to prohibit it absolutely. Application of the NLRA to religious organizations is one of the cases in this grey area. For these cases, it is arguably legitimate for courts to require a more overt and unambiguous indication of congressional intent before confronting the constitutional issue, as doing so reduces constitutionally problematic state interference with religion without expanding the scope of the constitutional prohibition so broadly that Congress is disabled from legislating in the grey area altogether. *See* Philip P. Frickey, *Getting from Joe to Gene (McCarthy): The Avoidance Canon, Legal Process Theory, and Narrowing Statutory Interpretation in the Early Warren Court*, 93 CAL. L. REV. 397 (2005); Young, *supra*, at 1589.

These defenses of the avoidance canon concede that the canon empowers rather than restrains judges. For exactly that reason, such defenses run into powerful objections. *First*, with respect to the more process-oriented version of the argument, one might ask where a court gets the authority to deviate from the most natural reading of the statute Congress actually passed in order to "improve" the legislative process. If one believes—as most do—that courts are supposed to be faithful agents of the legislature when interpreting statutes (*see* pp. 21–22, *supra*), isn't it problematic for a court to refuse to enforce a statute as written because it concludes Congress should have been more careful in its deliberations?

*Second*, with respect to the more substantive version of the argument, why is it legitimate for a court to adopt strained readings of statutes in order to protect constitutional values if the court has not identified any actual violation of the Constitution? Critics of the "constitutional values" defense of the avoidance canon argue that the invocation of constitutional values, or the suggestion that a given interpretation of a statute falls into a constitutional "danger zone" or "grey area," is simply a way for courts to dodge what ought to be the real issue, which is whether the statute violates the Constitution or not. These critics argue that the Constitution does not adopt freestanding values, but rather prescribes particular means to implement those values, and to balance them against other considerations. *See* John F. Manning, *Clear Statement Rules and the Constitution*, 110 COLUM. L. REV. 399 (2010). In a case like *Catholic Bishop*, proponents of this view would argue that the First Amendment (as clarified by its implementing doctrine) does not simply protect the "value" of limiting state interference with religion, but rather establishes a complex scheme and carefully designed criteria for determining the scope of legitimate government regulation of religious practice. By asking simply whether the NLRA's application would offend the value of nonentanglement between government and religion, the critics would argue, the *Catholic Bishop* majority bypassed the complex balance of considerations that the Court's own First Amendment decisions have made relevant. Furthermore, the concern about judicial willfulness may be especially acute when judges claim the authority not only to enforce constitutional prohibitions, but also to enforce more loosely defined constitutional values, or to improve the legislative process, through canons of statutory interpretation. *See, e.g.*, William N. Eskridge, Jr., *Textualism, the Unknown Ideal?*, 96 MICH. L. REV. 1509, 1545–46 (1998) (book review) (arguing that clear statement rules and other substantive canons are selectively applied); Bradford C. Mank, *Textualism's Selective Canons of Statutory Construction: Reinvigorating Individual Liberties, Leg-*

*islative Authority, and Deference to Executive Agencies*, 86 Ky. L.J. 527, 527 (1998) (same).

What do you think? Can the constitutional avoidance canon be defended not as a doctrine of judicial restraint, but as a legitimate tool of judicial empowerment? Or does this defense of the avoidance canon endorse an illegitimate and unwise role for judges in our system? Does your answer depend on empirical claims or assumptions regarding the practical effects of judicial use of the avoidance canon? To what extent do you think these issues can be resolved as a matter of principle, without reference to empirical arguments?

## B.   Protecting State Sovereignty and Autonomy

The constitutional avoidance canon instructs courts to construe statutes so as to avoid serious constitutional problems. Although the avoidance canon is sometimes defended as a means for protecting more general constitutional "values," it still requires some substantial probability that the otherwise-preferable construction of the statute would actually violate the Constitution. (Just how substantial the likelihood of actual unconstitutionality must be to trigger the canon is not entirely clear, as we have seen. *See* pp. 279–280, *supra.*) There are other substantive canons, however, that do not require a substantial likelihood that an otherwise-preferable interpretation be unconstitutional, or otherwise unlawful, in order to avoid it. These canons are intended to further particular substantive values, and while these substantive values are often connected to or derived from the Constitution in some way, these canons are distinct from the avoidance canon in that they may apply even in the absence of any plausible concern that the statute might actually be unconstitutional.

Among the most important and controversial of these substantive canons are those designed to protect the sovereignty and autonomy of state governments in our federal system. Questions about the appropriate balance between state and federal power—and the appropriate role for the federal courts in maintaining that balance—have been among the most significant and difficult issues throughout U.S. constitutional and political history. In the process of struggling with these issues, the Supreme Court has developed a number of substantive canons of construction aimed at protecting state autonomy and sovereignty by construing federal statutes narrowly to avoid excessive encroachment on state prerogatives.

This section first considers a family of canons that are meant to protect state governments from liability under federal law, focusing in particular on a canon that requires an especially clear and explicit statement before a federal statute will be read to interfere with certain core aspects of state government operations. We then turn to a substantive canon that is designed to limit the degree to which federal law displaces (or "preempts") state law. As we will see, in all these cases there are significant disagreements about the scope and legitimacy of these "pro-federalism" canons.

## a.  Federal Regulation of State Governmental Functions

In the following case, *Gregory v. Ashcroft*, the Supreme Court applied a clear statement rule designed to protect states from undue federal interference with core state activities or functions. To understand the case, it is useful first to have some background on the evolution of the Supreme Court's doctrine on the meaning of the Tenth Amendment of the Constitution, which provides that "[t]he powers not delegated to the United States by the Constitution, nor prohibited by it to the States, are reserved to the States respectively, or to the people." U.S. Const. amend. X.

There is a longstanding jurisprudential and scholarly debate over whether the Tenth Amendment imposes substantive limits on the requirements that the federal government may impose upon the states, or whether the Amendment merely declares that the federal government does not have any power that is not elsewhere granted to it by the Constitution. In National League of Cities v. Usery, 426 U.S. 833 (1976), the Supreme Court appeared to adopt the former view, holding that the Tenth Amendment barred application of the federal Fair Labor Standards Act (FLSA) to state governments. Although the Court had previously held, in United States v. Darby, 312 U.S. 100 (1941), that the FLSA was a legitimate exercise of Congress's constitutional power to regulate interstate commerce, then-Justice Rehnquist's majority opinion in *National League of Cities* reasoned that in light of the Tenth Amendment, "Congress may not exercise [its commerce power] so as to force directly upon the States its choices as to how essential decisions regarding the conduct of integral governmental functions are to be made." 426 U.S. at 855. Applying the FLSA's wages-and-hours rules to state government employees, the Court reasoned, would interfere with these sorts of essential decisions, and so was unconstitutional. The more expansive view of the Tenth Amendment adopted in *National League of Cities*, however, proved short-lived. In Garcia v. San Antonio Metropolitan Transit Authority, 469 U.S. 528 (1985), the Supreme Court overruled *National League of Cities* and held that the FLSA did indeed apply to state governments. Justice Blackmun, who wrote the *Garcia* opinion, had concurred in *National League of Cities*, but he had gradually come to the conclusion that the sort of balancing test he originally favored was unworkable. He thus wrote for the *Garcia* majority that as long as Congress has the constitutional authority under the Commerce Clause (or some other source) to enact federal statutory requirements, the Tenth Amendment did not impose any substantive limit on Congress's ability to apply those requirements to state governments.

Perhaps the most interesting aspect of *Garcia* is the majority opinion's endorsement of the so-called "political safeguards of federalism" as an adequate means to protect state sovereignty and to preserve an appropriate balance between state and federal power. The "political safeguards" argument, developed initially in a famous article by Professor Herbert Wechsler and subsequently refined and elaborated by other scholars, maintains that aggressive judicial protection of state sovereignty (for example, by reading the Tenth Amendment as imposing substantive limits on federal power) is unwise and unnecessary, because the structural provisions of the Constitution (or other political and institutional considerations) are sufficient to prevent excessive federal encroachment on state sovereignty. *See* Herbert Wechsler, *The Political Safeguards of Federalism: The Role of States in the Composition and Selection of the National Government*, 54 Colum. L. Rev. 543 (1954); *see also* Jesse H. Choper, Judicial Review and the National Political Process 175–84 (1980); Larry D. Kramer, *Putting the Politics Back into the Political Safeguards of Federalism*, 100 Colum. L. Rev. 215 (2000); D. Bruce La Pierre, *The Political Safeguards of Federalism Redux: Intergovernmental Immunity and the States as Agents of the Nation*, 60 Wash. U. L.Q. 779 (1982). As *Garcia* explained, "Apart from the limitation on federal authority inherent in the delegated nature of Congress' Article I powers, the principal means chosen by the Framers to ensure the role of the States in the federal system lies in the structure of the Federal Government itself. It is no novelty to observe that the composition of the Federal Government was designed in large part to protect the States from overreaching by Congress." 469 U.S. at 550–51 (citing Wechsler, Choper, and La Pierre, *supra*). *See also* South Carolina v. Baker, 485 U.S. 505, 512 (1988) ("The Tenth Amendment limits on Congress' authority to regulate state activities . . . are structural, not substantive. . . . States must find their protection from congressional regulation through the national political process, not through judicially defined spheres of unregulable state activity.").

This "political safeguards of federalism" argument has attracted considerable scholarly criticism. Critics emphasize the inadequacy of such political safeguards and the concomitant need for meaningful judicial enforcement of substantive limits on congressional interference with state prerogatives. *See, e.g.,* John O. McGinnis & Ilya Somin, *Federalism vs. States' Rights: A Defense of Judicial Review in a Federal System*, 99 Nw. U. L. Rev. 89, 103–05 (2004); Saikrishna B. Prakash & John C. Yoo, *The Puzzling Persistence of Process–Based Federalism Theories*, 79 Tex. L. Rev. 1459 (2001); Ernest A. Young, *Making Federalism Doctrine: Fidelity, Institutional Competence, and Compensating Adjustments*, 46 Wm. & Mary L. Rev. 1733, 1815–44 (2005). Such criticisms are manifest in the opinions of the four dissenters in *Garcia* (Chief Justice Burger and Justices Rehnquist, Powell, and O'Connor). *See Garcia*, 469 U.S. at 564–67 (Powell, J., dissenting); *id.* at 580–89 (O'Connor, J., dissenting).

In *Garcia* the political safeguards view, coupled with skepticism about the workability of judicial enforcement of the Tenth Amendment, carried the day, and *Garcia* has not been overruled. That said, the concerns that animated *National League of Cities* persisted, and many Justices—particularly the *Garcia* dissenters—remained interested in limiting the degree to which federal statutory requirements interfered with core state functions. One possible way to do so is through substantive canons of statutory interpretation, as the *Gregory* decision illustrates.

# Gregory v. Ashcroft

Supreme Court of the United States
501 U.S. 452 (1991)

■ Justice O'Connor delivered the opinion of the Court.

Article V, § 26, of the Missouri Constitution provides that "[a]ll judges other than municipal judges shall retire at the age of seventy years." We consider whether this mandatory retirement provision violates the federal Age Discrimination in Employment Act of 1967 (ADEA or Act). . . .

I

Petitioners are Missouri state judges. . . .

[They] filed suit against John D. Ashcroft, the Governor of Missouri, . . . challenging the validity of the mandatory retirement provision. . . .

II

The ADEA makes it unlawful for an "employer" "to discharge any individual" who is at least 40 years old "because of such individual's age." 29 U.S.C. §§ 623(a), 631(a). The term "employer" is defined to include "a State or political subdivision of a State." § 630(b)(2). Petitioners . . . contend that the Missouri mandatory retirement requirement for judges violates the ADEA.

A

As every schoolchild learns, our Constitution establishes a system of dual sovereignty between the States and the Federal Government. This Court also has recognized this fundamental principle. . . .

The Constitution created a Federal Government of limited powers. "The powers not delegated to the United States by the Constitution, nor prohibited by it to the States, are reserved to the States respectively, or to the people." U.S. Const., Amdt. 10. The States thus retain substantial sovereign authority under our constitutional system. . . .

This federalist structure of joint sovereigns preserves to the people numerous advantages. It assures a decentralized government that will be more sensitive to the diverse needs of a heterogeneous society; it increases opportunity for citizen involvement in democratic processes; it allows for more innovation and experimentation in government; and it makes government more responsive by putting the States in competition for a mobile citizenry. . . .

Perhaps the principal benefit of the federalist system is a check on abuses of government power. . . . Just as the separation and independence of the coordinate branches of the Federal Government serve to prevent the accumulation of excessive power in any one branch, a healthy balance of power between the States and the Federal Government will reduce the risk of tyranny and abuse from either front. Alexander Hamilton explained to the people of New York, perhaps optimistically, that the new federalist system would suppress completely "the attempts of the government to establish a tyranny":

> "[I]n a confederacy the people, without exaggeration, may be said to be entirely the masters of their own fate. Power being almost always the rival of power, the general government will at all times stand ready to check the usurpations of the state governments, and these will have the same disposition towards the general government. The people, by throwing themselves into either scale, will infallibly make it preponderate. If their rights are invaded by either, they can make use of the other as the instrument of redress." The Federalist No. 28, pp. 180–181 (C. Rossiter ed. 1961).

... One fairly can dispute whether our federalist system has been quite as successful in checking government abuse as Hamilton promised, but there is no doubt about the design. If this "double security" is to be effective, there must be a proper balance between the States and the Federal Government. These twin powers will act as mutual restraints only if both are credible. In the tension between federal and state power lies the promise of liberty.

The Federal Government holds a decided advantage in this delicate balance: the Supremacy Clause. U.S. Const., Art. VI, cl. 2. As long as it is acting within the powers granted it under the Constitution, Congress may impose its will on the States. Congress may legislate in areas traditionally regulated by the States. This is an extraordinary power in a federalist system. It is a power that we must assume Congress does not exercise lightly.

The present case concerns a state constitutional provision through which the people of Missouri establish a qualification for those who sit as their judges. This provision goes beyond an area traditionally regulated by the States; it is a decision of the most fundamental sort for a sovereign entity. . . .

Congressional interference with this decision of the people of Missouri, defining their constitutional officers, would upset the usual constitutional balance of federal and state powers. For this reason, "it is incumbent upon the federal courts to be certain of Congress' intent before finding that federal law overrides" this balance. [Atascadero State Hospital v. Scanlon, 473 U.S. 234, 243 (1985)]. We explained recently:

> "[I]f Congress intends to alter the 'usual constitutional balance between the States and the Federal Government,' it must make its intention to do so 'unmistakably clear in the language of the statute.' Atascadero State Hospital v. Scanlon, 473 U.S. 234, 242 (1985); see also Pennhurst State School and Hospital v. Halderman, 465 U.S. 89, 99 (1984)[. . . .] 'In traditionally sensitive areas, such as legislation affecting the federal balance, the requirement of clear statement assures that the legislature has in fact faced, and intended to bring into issue, the critical matters involved in the judicial decision.' United States v. Bass, 404 U.S. 336, 349 (1971)." Will v. Michigan Dept. of State Police, 491 U.S. 58, 65 (1989).

This plain statement rule is nothing more than an acknowledgment that the States retain substantial sovereign powers under our constitutional scheme, powers with which Congress does not readily interfere....

We are constrained in our ability to consider the limits that the state-federal balance places on Congress' powers under the Commerce Clause [to interfere with how States determine the qualifications of their government officials]. See Garcia v. San Antonio Metropolitan Transit Authority, 469 U.S. 528 (1985) (declining to review limitations placed on Congress' Commerce Clause powers by our federal system). But there is no need to do so if we hold that the ADEA does not apply to state judges. Application of the plain statement rule thus may avoid a potential constitutional problem. Indeed, inasmuch as this Court in *Garcia* has left primarily to the political process the protection of the States against intrusive exercises of Congress' Commerce Clause powers, we must be absolutely certain that Congress intended such an exercise. "[T]o give the state-displacing weight of federal law to mere congressional *ambiguity* would evade the very procedure for lawmaking on which *Garcia* relied to protect states' interests." L. Tribe, American Constitutional Law § 6–25, p. 480 (2d ed. 1988).

## B

In 1974, Congress extended the substantive provisions of the ADEA to include the States as employers. At the same time, Congress amended the definition of "employee" to exclude all elected and most high-ranking government officials. Under the Act, as amended:

> "The term 'employee' means an individual employed by any employer except that the term 'employee' shall not include any person elected to public office in any State or political subdivision of any State by the qualified voters thereof, or any person chosen by such officer to be on such officer's personal staff, or an appointee on the policymaking level or an immediate adviser with respect to the exercise of the constitutional or legal powers of the office." 29 U.S.C. § 630(f).

Governor Ashcroft contends that the § 630(f) exclusion of certain public officials also excludes judges, like petitioners, who are appointed to office by the Governor and are then subject to retention election. The Governor points to two passages in § 630(f). First, he argues, these judges are selected by an elected official and, because they make policy, are "appointee[s] on the policymaking level."

Petitioners counter that judges merely resolve factual disputes and decide questions of law; they do not make policy. Moreover, petitioners point out that the policymaking-level exception is part of a trilogy, tied closely to the elected-official exception. Thus, the Act excepts elected officials and: (1) "any person chosen by such officer to be on such officer's personal staff"; (2) "an appointee on the policymaking level"; and (3) "an immediate advisor with respect to the exercise of the constitutional or legal powers of the office." Applying the maxim of statutory construction *noscitur a sociis*—that a word is known by the company it keeps—petitioners argue that since (1) and (3) refer only to those in close working relationships with elected officials, so too must (2). Even if it can be said that judges may make policy, petitioners contend, they do not do so at the behest of an elected official.

Governor Ashcroft relies on the plain language of the statute: It exempts persons appointed "at the policymaking level." The Governor argues that state judges, in fashioning and applying the common law, make policy.... The common law, unlike a constitution or statute, provides no definitive text; it is to be derived from the interstices of prior opinions and a well-considered judgment of what is best for the community....

Governor Ashcroft contends that Missouri judges make policy in other ways as well. The Missouri Supreme Court and Courts of Appeals have supervisory authority over inferior courts. The Missouri Supreme Court has the constitutional duty to establish rules of practice and procedure for the Missouri court system, and inferior courts exercise policy judgment in establishing local rules of practice. The state courts have supervisory powers over the state bar, with the Missouri Supreme Court given the authority to develop disciplinary rules.

The Governor stresses judges' policymaking responsibilities, but it is far from plain that the statutory exception requires that judges actually make policy. The statute refers to appointees "on the policymaking level," not to appointees "who make policy." It may be sufficient that the appointee is in a position requiring the exercise of discretion concerning issues of public importance....

Nonetheless, "appointee at the policymaking level," particularly in the context of the other exceptions that surround it, is an odd way for Congress to exclude judges; a plain statement that judges are not "employees" would seem the most efficient phrasing. But in this case we are not looking for a plain statement that judges are excluded. We will not read the ADEA to cover state judges unless Congress has made it clear that judges are *included*. This does not mean that the Act must mention judges explicitly, though it does not. Rather, it must be plain to anyone reading the Act that it covers judges. In the context of a statute that plainly excludes most important state public officials, "appointee on the policymaking level" is sufficiently broad that we cannot conclude that the statute plainly covers appointed state judges. Therefore, it does not....

■ JUSTICE WHITE, with whom JUSTICE STEVENS joins, concurring in part, dissenting in part, and concurring in the judgment.

I agree with the majority that neither the Age Discrimination in Employment Act of 1967 (ADEA) nor the Equal Protection Clause prohibits Missouri's mandatory retirement provision as applied to petitioners.... I cannot agree, however, with the majority's reasoning in Part II of its opinion, which ignores several areas of well-established precedent and announces a rule that is likely to prove both unwise and infeasible. That the majority's analysis in Part II is completely unnecessary to the proper resolution of this case makes it all the more remarkable.

## I

... The majority ... holds that whether or not the ADEA can fairly be read to exclude state judges from its scope, "[w]e will not read the ADEA to cover state judges unless Congress has made it clear that judges are *included*." (emphasis in original). I cannot agree with this "plain statement" rule because it is unsupported by the decisions upon which the majority relies, contrary to our Tenth Amendment jurisprudence, and fundamentally unsound.

... The dispute in this case ... is not whether Congress has outlawed age discrimination by the States. It clearly has. The only question is whether petitioners fall within the definition of "employee" in the Act, § 630(f), which contains exceptions for elected officials and certain appointed officials. If petitioners *are* "employee[s]," Missouri's mandatory retirement provision clearly conflicts with the antidiscrimination provisions of the ADEA.... Pre-emption therefore is automatic, since "state law is preempted to the extent that it actually conflicts with federal law." Pacific Gas & Elec. Co. v. State Energy Resources Conservation and Development Comm'n, 461 U.S. 190, 204 (1983). The majority's federalism concerns are irrelevant to such "actual conflict" pre-emption....

While acknowledging this principle of federal legislative supremacy, the majority nevertheless imposes upon Congress a "plain statement" requirement. The majority claims to derive this requirement from the plain statement approach developed in ... Atascadero State Hospital v. Scanlon, 473 U.S. 234, 243 (1985), and applied two Terms ago in Will v. Michigan Dept. of State Police, 491 U.S. 58, 65 (1989). The issue in those cases, however, was whether Congress intended a particular statute to extend to the States at all.... In the present case, by contrast, Congress has expressly extended the coverage of the ADEA to the States and their employees. Its intention to regulate age discrimination by States is thus "unmistakably clear in the language of the statute." *Atascadero*, 473 U.S., at 242.... The only dispute is over the precise details of the statute's application. We have never extended the plain statement approach that far, and the majority offers no compelling reason for doing so.

... The majority's plain statement rule is not only unprecedented, it directly contravenes our decisions in Garcia v. San Antonio Metropolitan Transit Authority, 469 U.S. 528 (1985), and South Carolina v. Baker, 485 U.S. 505 (1988). In those cases we made it clear "that States must find their protection from congressional regulation through the national political process, not through judicially defined spheres of unregulable state activity." *Id.*, at 512. We also rejected as "unsound in principle and unworkable in practice" any test for state immunity that requires a judicial determination of which state activities are " 'traditional,' " " 'integral,' " or " 'necessary.' " *Garcia*, 469 U.S., at 546. The majority disregards those decisions in its attempt to carve out areas of state activity that will receive special protection from federal legislation.

The majority's approach is also unsound because it will serve only to confuse the law. First, the majority fails to explain the scope of its rule. Is the rule limited to federal regulation of the qualifications of state officials? Or does it apply more broadly to the regulation of any "state governmental functions"? Second, the majority does not explain its requirement that Congress' intent to regulate a particular state activity be "plain to anyone reading [the federal statute]." Does that mean that it is now improper to look to the purpose or history of a federal statute in determining the scope of the statute's limitations on state activities? If so, the majority's rule is completely inconsistent with our pre-emption jurisprudence. The vagueness of the majority's rule undoubtedly will lead States to assert that various federal statutes no longer apply to a wide variety of state activities if Congress has not expressly referred to those activities in the statute. Congress, in turn, will be forced to draft long and detailed lists of which particular state functions it meant to regulate.

. . . The majority asserts that its plain statement rule is helpful in avoiding a "potential constitutional problem." It is far from clear, however, why there would be a constitutional problem if the ADEA applied to state judges, in light of our decisions in *Garcia* and *Baker*, discussed above. As long as "the national political process did not operate in a defective manner, the Tenth Amendment is not implicated." *Baker, supra,* at 513. There is no claim in this case that the political process by which the ADEA was extended to state employees was inadequate to protect the States from being "unduly burden[ed]" by the Federal Government. See *Garcia, supra,* 469 U.S., at 556. In any event, as discussed below, a straightforward analysis of the ADEA's definition of "employee" reveals that the ADEA does not apply here. Thus, even if there were potential constitutional problems in extending the ADEA to state judges, the majority's proposed plain statement rule would not be necessary to avoid them in this case. Indeed, because this case can be decided purely on the basis of statutory interpretation, the majority's announcement of its plain statement rule, which purportedly is derived from constitutional principles, violates our general practice of avoiding the unnecessary resolution of constitutional issues. . . .

II

■ [JUSTICE WHITE concluded that, as a matter of straightforward statutory interpretation, the ADEA does not cover state judges because they fall into the exception for appointees "on the policymaking level."]

■ [JUSTICE BLACKMUN'S dissent, jointed by JUSTICE MARSHALL, is omitted.]

---

**1. *What Is the* Gregory *Clear Statement Rule?*—**The scope and source of the interpretive canon the majority deployed in *Gregory* were not entirely clear. At one point the Court stated that application of the clear statement rule "avoid[s] a potential constitutional problem," which suggests that the Court was applying the constitutional avoidance canon. But, as the dissent pointed out, cases like *Garcia* and *Baker* (pp. 289–290, *supra*) would seem to establish that there would not be any constitutional problem with applying an otherwise valid federal statute to state government employees. Justice O'Connor's majority opinion seemed to admit as much when it recognized that, "[a]s long as it is acting within the powers granted it under the Constitution, Congress may impose its will on the States." (It is perhaps not coincidental that Justice O'Connor dissented in both *Garcia* and *Baker*. Indeed, no Justice voted with the majority in both *Garcia* and *Gregory*, just as no Justice dissented in both cases.) So, while it may be that at least some members of the *Gregory* majority perceived a constitutional problem, the prevailing constitutional doctrine—which the *Gregory* majority chose not to disturb—makes it difficult to defend the result in *Gregory* as a straightforward application of the constitutional avoidance canon.

Probably for that reason, *Gregory* is usually read not as an application of the constitutional avoidance canon, but rather as standing for a *different* substantive canon, according to which a clear statement is required before a court will construe a federal statute as interfering with fundamental aspects of state sovereignty. Indeed, *Gregory v. Ashcroft*—together with other cases cited by the *Gregory* majority, including United States v. Bass, 404 U.S. 336 (1971), Pennhurst State School and Hospital v. Halderman, 465 U.S. 89 (1984), Atascadero State Hospital v. Scanlon, 473 U.S. 234 (1985), and Will v. Michigan Dept. of State Police, 491 U.S. 58 (1989)—are usually viewed as establishing a clear statement rule (or cluster of closely related clear statement rules) that are designed to protect state governments from federal interference. If *Gregory* did indeed rely on this sort of clear statement rule, is the decision sound? And what, exactly, can we conclude about the scope and strength of the clear statement rule that *Gregory* embraced?

With respect to the *scope* of the rule, what sorts of state activities would (or should) fall within the scope of the *Gregory* presumption? Justice White's dissent accused the majority of creating confusion by failing to explain whether its clear statement rule was limited to federal regulation of the qualifications of state officials, or whether would apply more broadly to federal regulation of any state government function. Is that a fair criticism? How do you think Justice O'Connor would respond? How would you address that issue, if you were called on to explain or refine the scope of the *Gregory* presumption?

With respect to the *strength* of the *Gregory* presumption, how much of a burden does or should this presumption place on those who would read a statute to disturb the state-federal balance? Perhaps because *Gregory* demanded "absolute[] certain[ty]" that Congress intended such an exercise" of "federal power," some commentators view *Gregory* as adopting a "superstrong" clear statement rule. William N. Eskridge, Jr., & Philip P. Frickey, *Quasi–Constitutional Law: Clear Statement Rules as Constitutional Lawmaking*, 45 Vand. L. Rev. 593, 623–24 (1992). Does that assessment, however, necessarily follow from the facts of the case? After all, the ADEA contains an express exemption for appointees "on the policymaking level," which could plausibly be read as including judges. (Notwithstanding familiar political rhetoric about how judges merely apply the law, everyone with even a passing familiarity with how the legal system actually operates understands that judges, especially appellate judges, have a great deal of discretion not only to decide individual cases, but to formulate doctrines and to issue interpretations that could plausibly be characterized as "policy.") For this reason, Justice White concurred in the judgment, even though he rejected the majority's clear statement rule. The majority was less sure that the most natural reading of this exemption would include judges, but reasoned that because the exemption *can* be read as excluding appointed state judges, the clear statement rule implies that is how the exemption *should* be read. In that light, can the *Gregory* canon be understood as endorsing a somewhat weaker presumption that merely instructs courts how to choose among textually plausible readings of an ambiguous statutory term? How would (or should) the Court's analysis in *Gregory* have been different if the statute itself were not otherwise ambiguous? Suppose, for example, that the ADEA did not contain the exemption for "appointee[s] on the policymaking level"? How should that hypothetical case come out? How do you think Justice O'Connor would have ruled in such a case?

In this regard, it is perhaps worth noting that other cases that invoke pro-federalism clear statement rules involve statutes that do not explicitly impose federal law on state governments, but rather impose federal law on some broad category that would seem clearly to include state governments. For example, some federal statutes impose requirements on "any recipient" of federal funds. *See Atascadero, supra*. In contrast, the ADEA provision at issue in *Gregory* was explicit about its applicability to state government employees, but it failed to contain a clear statement that it applied to state *judges*. Justice White's partial dissent in *Gregory* treated this distinction as highly significant: He argued that the Court should insist on a clear statement only when there was some question "whether Congress intended a particular statute to extend to the States at all" (as in cases like *Atascadero*), but not when "[t]he only dispute is over the precise details of the statute's application." Do you agree?

Another question pertaining to the strength of the *Gregory* presumption concerns the sort of evidence sufficient to overcome it. Suppose that the legislative history of the ADEA had contained statements indicating that many members of Congress, including sponsors of the House and Senate bills, specifically intended the ADEA to apply to state judges, and understood the statute's general language as having that effect. Would this influence your assessment of the case? This question is a variant of the more general issue of when, or under what conditions, a substantive presumption can be overcome by evidence in the legislative history. Does it matter, in answering this question, whether the substantive canon at issue is based on an assertion about likely congressional intent, or whether it is more overtly based on an independent judicial value judgment?

**2. *The* Gregory *Rule and the Protection of Federalism*—**Let us assume, as is widely believed, that *Gregory* recognized and applied a clear statement rule meant to protect state sovereignty and autonomy, even when there is no serious constitutional question—much less any actual constitutional violation—lurking in the background. On that account, the *Gregory* clear statement rule derives from the impulse to safeguard an important constitutional *value* (the commitment to federalism) through tools of statutory construction that require Congress to pay an extra price—the incremental bargaining costs for extra statutory clarity—when legislation presses against constitutionally derived values such as federalism. *See, e.g.,* Matthew C. Stephenson, *The Price of Public Action: Constitutional Doctrine and the Judicial Manipulation of Legislative Enactment Costs,* 118 YALE L.J. 2, 11–16 (2008); Ernest A. Young, *Constitutional Avoidance, Resistance Norms, and the Preservation of Judicial Review,* 78 TEX. L. REV. 1549, 1585–93 (2000). Thus, as was true in the closely analogous context of the constitutional avoidance canon (*see* pp. 285–287, *supra*), *Gregory* might be defended as providing an additional remedial device that supplements *Marbury*-style judicial review. Indeed, some have argued that enforcing the Constitution's federalism values through *Gregory*-style clear statement rules is preferable to a more aggressive approach (for example, overruling *Garcia*), because the former approach preserves federalism values while avoiding instability and maintaining a respectful posture toward Congress. *See* Thomas W. Merrill, *Rescuing Federalism after* Raich*: The Case for Clear Statement Rules,* 9 LEWIS & CLARK L. REV. 823, 825–28 (2005).

A defense of *Gregory* that emphasizes the protection of "constitutional values," however, invites many of the same critiques leveled at the analogous defense of the modern constitutional avoidance canon. *See* pp. 287–288, *supra.* As we have seen, there are serious questions about whether this is a legitimate approach for courts to adopt, as well as questions about how courts can or should define the substantive value that deserves special protection. One might reasonably ask why, if a straightforward reading of a statute does not offend any express constitutional provision, Congress should have to go back and re-enact it with additional clarity. *See* John F. Manning, *Clear Statement Rules and the Constitution,* 110 COLUM. L. REV. 399 (2010).

Moreover, one might also question the premise that the Constitution embodies a freestanding commitment to "federalism." After all, the Constitution unquestionably represents "a bundle of compromises." MAX FARRAND, THE FRAMING OF THE CONSTITUTION OF THE UNITED STATES 201 (1913). Unsurprisingly, therefore, the document safeguards federalism in a number of rather specific ways. First, it creates a government of limited and carefully enumerated powers. *See* U.S. CONST. art. I, § 8. Second, it imposes concrete limitations on congressional power to intrude upon the states. *See* U.S. CONST. art. I, § 9 (providing, among other things, that "[n]o Tax or Duty shall be laid on Articles exported from any State"). Third, the constitutional structure expressly assigns states significant responsibility over the selection of key federal officials. *See, e.g.,* U.S. CONST. art. II, § 1, cl. 2

(providing that "[e]ach State shall appoint" presidential electors "in such Manner as the Legislature thereof may direct"). Fourth, the Supremacy Clause, U.S. CONST. art. VI, cl. 2, carefully delineates the types of federal law that may preempt state law—namely, "[t]his Constitution, and the Laws . . . which shall be made in pursuance thereof; and all treaties made, or which shall be made, under the Authority of the United States"—an enumeration that some regard as codifying the political safeguards of federalism. *See, e.g.*, Bradford R. Clark, *Separation of Powers as a Safeguard of Federalism*, 79 TEX. L. REV. 1321 (2001). In addition, many aspects of the Constitution—including the broad grant of congressional authority conferred by the Necessary and Proper Clause, U.S. CONST. art. I, § 8, cl. 18, and the express limitations on state financial, diplomatic, and military authority prescribed by Article I, § 10—unquestionably promote the competing value of a strong central government. *See, e.g.*, Roderick M. Hills, Jr., *Against Preemption: How Federalism Can Improve the National Legislative Process*, 82 N.Y.U. L. REV. 1, 5 (2007); Carlos Manuel Vázquez, *The Separation of Powers as a Safeguard of Nationalism*, 83 NOTRE DAME L. REV. 1601, 1604 (2008). Because the Constitution divides power between the federal and state governments in such particular ways, does it make sense to imagine that the document *also* adopts a freestanding federalism norm? Or should one assume that "federalism"—which was an innovation of the U.S. Constitution—is defined by the balance struck between state and national power in those particular provisions? *See* John F. Manning, *Federalism and the Generality Problem in Constitutional Interpretation*, 122 HARV. L. REV. 2003 (2009).

    **3. *Federalism as a Constitutional Value***—Given that so much of the *Gregory* decision turned on the impulse to safeguard "federalism"—the sovereignty and autonomy of the state governments in our federal system— it is worth pausing to consider what functional considerations, if any, might explain and justify substantive canons designed to protect state prerogatives. Justice O'Connor's opinion in *Gregory* offered the following arguments:

    *Responsiveness*—A decentralized system, according to Justice O'Connor, is "more sensitive to the diverse needs of a heterogeneous society." The idea here seems to be that, because the values and interests of the citizenry vary by region, states can adopt policies that are tailored to their populations, and mobile citizens can "sort" into different states. (This argument is often associated with a famous article by the economist Charles Tiebout, *A Pure Theory of Local Expenditures*, 64 J. POL. ECON. 416 (1956).)

    *Participation*—State governments are smaller and closer to the people than is the federal government, and therefore, explained Justice O'Connor, a system in which state governments have more power "increases opportunity for citizen involvement in democratic processes[.]"

    *Innovation*—Following Justice Brandeis's famous assertion that state legislatures are "laborator[ies]" of democracy, New State Ice Co. v. Liebmann, 285 U.S. 262, 311 (1932) (Brandeis, J., dissenting), the *Gregory* majority suggested that, compared to a centralized system, a federal system "allows for more innovation and experimentation in government[.]"

*Competition*—Federalism "makes government more responsive by putting the States in competition for a mobile citizenry"—a benefit sometimes referred to as a "race to the top." *See* Michael W. McConnell, *Federalism: Evaluating the Founders' Design*, 54 U. Chi. L. Rev. 1484, 1498–1500 (1987) (book review).

*Vertical Division of Power*—Justice O'Connor's *Gregory* opinion declared that the "principal benefit of the federalist system" is the capacity of such a system to check abuses of power, a benefit comparable to that associated with the horizontal separation of powers within the federal government. The idea, most famously articulated by Alexander Hamilton in Federalist 28, is that the state governments can restrain federal power grabs and abuses—but only if the states are themselves sufficiently powerful and autonomous.

Do you find any or all of these arguments sufficiently compelling to justify the clear statement rule adopted in *Gregory*? Critics might respond in three ways. First, many of the virtues allegedly associated with federalism may be grossly overstated, and really more applicable to *local* rather than state governments. Is a state government—particularly of a large state like California, New York or Texas—really that much "closer to the people" than the federal government? If what we really want is a greater degree of local self-government, it is not obvious whether we would see more of *that* kind of decentralization in a system with strong states or in a system with a strong federal government. *See* Edward L. Rubin & Malcolm Feeley, *Federalism: Some Notes on a National Neurosis*, 41 UCLA L. Rev. 903 (1994).

Second, even if a federalist system with strong states has some of the virtues ascribed to it, those virtues must be compared to its vices—and those vices may be substantial. States can innovate in desirable ways, to be sure, but they can also "innovate" in ways that are normatively troubling. Recall James Madison's concerns about political behavior in a small, as opposed to an extended, political unit:

> The smaller the society, the fewer probably will be the distinct parties and interests composing it; the fewer the distinct parties and interests, the more frequently will a majority be found of the same party; and the smaller the number of individuals composing a majority, and the smaller the compass within which they are placed, the more easily will they concert and execute their plans of oppression. Extend the sphere and you take in a greater variety of parties and interests; you make it less probable that a majority of the whole will have a common motive to invade the rights of other citizens; or if such a common motive exists, it will be more difficult for all who feel it to discover their own strength and to act in unison with each other.

THE FEDERALIST NO. 10, pp. 82–84 (Clinton Rossiter ed., 1961). Perhaps unsurprisingly, therefore, important aspects of the history of the struggle for civil rights in the United States have involved efforts by the federal government to remedy discriminatory behavior by individual states. *See, e.g.*, Pasadena City Bd. of Educ. v. Spangler, 427 U.S. 424 (1976) (Attorney General suing to desegregate schools); Cooper v. Aaron, 358 U.S. 1 (1958) (enforcing federal court's desegregation decree against recalcitrant state and local officials). And while proponents of state authority celebrate the desirable effects of interstate competition (the "race to the top"), skeptics point out the problem of a "race to the bottom," in which the mobility of human and financial capital causes state governments to compete in ways that result in suboptimal levels of regulation and fewer public goods. *See, e.g.*, PAUL E. PETERSON, THE PRICE OF FEDERALISM 121–24 (1995); Richard B. Stewart, *Pyramids of Sacrifice? Problems of Federalism in Mandating State Implementation of National Environmental Policy*, 86 YALE L.J. 1196, 1212 (1977). *But see, e.g.*, Richard L. Revesz, *Rehabilitating Interstate Competition: Rethinking the "Race-to-the-Bottom" Rationale for Federal Environmental Regulation*, 67 N.Y.U. L. REV. 1210 (1992); Peter H. Schuck, *Some Federal–State Developments in Immigration Law*, 58 N.Y.U. ANN. SURV. AM. L. 387, 389 (2002).

Third, a more moderate criticism of the argument advanced in cases like *Gregory* is that it will not do for the Court to extol the virtues of federalism in the abstract. Rather, it is incumbent upon the Court to show how the *particular* federal regulation of states at issue threatens to undermine one or more of the benefits associated with a decentralized federal system. How, specifically, would an application of the federal ADEA to state court judges interfere with desirable interstate competition to provide optimal levels of public goods, or to adopt innovative public policy? Is it really plausible that this relatively modest federal antidiscrimination law will undermine the vertical division of powers between the states and the federal government, especially if the Court remains willing to enforce firm, constitutionally grounded limits on federal power? If the Court had not really established that the most natural reading of the federal ADEA would actually pose a threat to the federalism values the Court discussed, then perhaps it was improper for the Court to invoke those values to justify the *Gregory* clear statement rule. But in response to that, supporters of *Gregory* might reply in the words of the constitutional law scholar Laurence Tribe (who is generally unsympathetic to much of modern federalism doctrine):

> [N]o one expects Congress to obliterate the states, at least in one fell swoop. If there is any danger, it lies in the tyranny of small decisions— in the prospect that Congress will nibble away at state sovereignty, bit by bit, until someday essentially nothing is left but a gutted shell.

LAURENCE H. TRIBE, AMERICAN CONSTITUTIONAL LAW 302 (1978). Do you find Professor Tribe's argument compelling?

***4. Improving the Legislative Process***—Another prominent defense of clear statement rules of the sort applied in *Gregory* is that such rules improve the legislative drafting process by encouraging the explicit consideration and clear resolution of particularly problematic issues, such as the impact of the federal statute on traditional state prerogatives. *See, e.g.,* Cass R. Sunstein, *Nondelegation Canons*, 67 U. Chi. L. Rev. 315, 331 (2000). (You may recall that a similar argument is often made on behalf of the avoidance canon. *See* p. 285, *supra.*) On this view, clear statement rules do not entail undue judicial interference with legislative prerogatives, because if Congress really does (for example) want to impose federal requirements on areas of traditional state authority, it can (so long as Congress has the constitutional authority to do so). At the same time, if Congress fails to consider the issue or cannot reach consensus, or if the statute's drafters are deliberately vague in the hopes of avoiding controversy, Congress is aware that the statute will be construed in a particular way—in this case, as *not* upsetting the traditional state prerogative to determine qualifications for state officials. So, not only does the canon put a thumb on the scale in favor of a preferred result, but it improves the legislative process by eliciting a more accurate and transparent indication of congressional intent in those cases where Congress really does mean to take some extraordinary action that upsets the usual federal-state balance.

There are several serious objections to this rationale for judicially-imposed substantive canons of construction, however. *First*, even if proponents of the argument are correct about the effects of these rules, why is it legitimate for a court to "improve" the legislative drafting process in this way, rather than simply giving effect to whatever the enacting Congress intended or understood the statute to mean? (*See* p. 287, *supra.*) *Second*, judicial insistence upon additional clarity may have adverse effects on the legislative process, "increas[ing] the risk of misspecification and sharpen[ing] the focus of value conflicts." Colin S. Diver, *The Optimal Precision of Administrative Rules*, 93 Yale L.J. 65, 73 (1983). *Third*, even if the Court acts legitimately when it creates clear statement rules, it is far from certain, as an empirical matter, that Members of Congress are even aware of, let alone responsive to, canons of construction or other interpretive principles when they draft and vote on statutory language.

On that third point, the evidence on whether or how Congress reacts to judicial canons is surprisingly sparse. As Judge Posner observed over twenty-five years ago:

> There is no evidence that members of Congress, or their assistants who do the actual drafting, know the [judicially-created set of interpretive rules] or if they know, they pay attention to it. Nor, in truth, is there any evidence that they do not; it is remarkable how little research has been done on a question that one might have thought lawyers would regard as fundamental to their enterprise.

Richard A. Posner, *Statutory Interpretation—in the Classroom and in the Courtroom*, 50 U. Chi. L. Rev. 800, 806 (1983). While acknowledging the absence of strong evidence either way, Judge Posner expressed skepticism that Congress paid attention to judicial canons in the drafting process. Abner Mikva, who served as a member of the House of Representatives and later as a federal judge on the Court of Appeals for the D.C. Circuit, shared this skepticism: "When I was in Congress," Judge Mikva once quipped, "the only 'canons' we talked about were the ones the Pentagon bought that could not shoot straight." Abner J. Mikva, *Reading and Writing Statutes*, 48 U. PITT. L. REV. 627, 629 (1987). There is some limited, though certainly not decisive, evidence that corroborates the skepticism shared by Judges Posner and Mikva. Professors Victoria Nourse and Jane Schacter, for instance, interviewed staffers who worked for the Senate Judiciary Committee and found that although these staffers (many of whom were lawyers) were "certainly [] aware of canons," most of them "did not view canons as a central factor in drafting legislation." Victoria Nourse & Jane Schacter, *The Politics of Legislative Drafting: A Congressional Case Study*, 77 N.Y.U. L. REV. 575, 600 (2002). *See also* James J. Brudney, *Recalibrating Federal Judicial Independence*, 64 OHIO STATE L.J. 149, 180 n.113 (2003) ("Reliance on the judicially constructed canons is especially problematic because it is not clear that Congress, with its steadily declining proportion of lawyer-members, has any serious awareness of their existence, much less their specific applicability.").

Yet isn't there something irrational about legislators (or the interest groups who lobby them) systematically ignoring substantive canons, if those canons have a substantial impact on the actual effect of the legislation? Perhaps the explanation is that the practical effects of canons are less important than lawyers and judges think they are. Or perhaps the failure of Congress to consider seriously canons of construction derives from the fact that the application of the canons across different courts and over time is so unpredictable that legislators rationally discount or ignore them. There is some evidence that this inter-judge and inter-temporal variation in application of substantive canons is indeed significant. *See* James J. Brudney & Corey Ditslear, *Canons of Construction and the Elusive Quest for Neutral Reasoning*, 58 VAND. L. REV. 1 (2005). Does that observation militate in favor of the position that the courts should pick canons, articulate them clearly, and stick to them consistently? *See* Sydney Foster, *Should Courts Give Stare Decisis Effect to Statutory Interpretation Methodology?*, 96 GEO. L.J. 1863, 1889 & n.144 (2008); Adrian Vermeule, *Interpretive Choice*, 75 N.Y.U. L. REV. 74, 140 (2000). Or does it mean that courts should simply abandon the hope (and the claim) that substantive canons of construction can influence the legislative drafting process in desirable ways?

Another difficulty with the argument that substantive canons merely establish clear default rules for Congress is the fact that in many cases— including *Gregory*—Congress enacted the statutory language at issue before the Court ever articulated the canon. It is all well and good to say that a clear statement rule, once announced, will have desirable effects on legislative deliberation and drafting. But how can that argument justify using a newly-minted canon to reject the otherwise clear meaning of a statute enacted at a time when Congress had no reason to anticipate the canon's creation? *See* William N. Eskridge, Jr. & Philip P. Frickey, *Quasi–Constitutional Law: Clear Statement Rules as Constitutional Lawmaking*, 45 VAND.

L. REV. 593, 638–40 (1992); Amanda L. Tyler, *Continuity, Coherence, and the Canons*, 99 Nw. U. L. REV. 1389, 1419–20 & n.143 (2005). Even if the *Gregory* rule is desirable going forward, should the Court have announced the rule (in dicta) and applied it only to statutes passed *after* the announcement of the rule?

Although this "prospective-only" approach to announcing new substantive canons may seem attractive in the abstract, courts hardly ever proceed in this fashion. One reason might be that there are doubts about whether doing so would be legitimate: There is a longstanding tradition that the federal courts may not issue so-called "advisory opinions" (opinions that discuss how the court would resolve possible future cases not currently before it), which might raise doubts about whether it would be permissible for the Court to announce a canon in a case in which it did not actually apply that canon. *See* RICHARD H. FALLON, JR., JOHN F. MANNING, DANIEL J. MELTZER, & DAVID L. SHAPIRO, HART AND WECHSLER'S THE FEDERAL COURTS AND THE FEDERAL SYSTEM 54–55 (6th ed., 2009). Even if one puts that concern to one side, judges and Justices might be reluctant to make a new canon purely prospective because they are reluctant to admit that they are in fact announcing a new canon. Of course, there may be other reasons for applying a new substantive canon even to statutes enacted prior to judicial articulation of the canon, such as the belief that the clear statement rule really does capture likely congressional intent at the time of the enactment, or the argument that the substantive values safeguarded by the application of the canon derive from constitutional commitments. But is it possible to salvage the "clear-rules-for-Congress" justification for decisions like *Gregory* if one admits the court is announcing a new substantive canon?

**5.  *Congressional Intent and Political Safeguards Theory*—**The introductory note on *Gregory* (pp. 289–290, *supra*) observed that one of the Court's prominent justifications for abandoning the attempt to enforce a substantive version of the Tenth Amendment was the idea that the "political safeguards of federalism"—including, for example, equal representation of states in the Senate, and close ties between the state and national arms of the major political parties—would ensure that the federal government takes sufficient account of state interests when enacting federal legislation. If we assume for the moment that this thesis is broadly accurate, what implications, if any, does it have for the *Gregory* clear statement rule?

One possibility is that accepting the political safeguards thesis implies that the *Gregory* rule is unnecessary, and for that reason undesirable. After all, if we can rely on the federal lawmaking process to protect state sovereignty, why do we need a special substantive canon to protect that same value? If we can rely on Congress to strike the balance correctly, then isn't the application of something like the *Gregory* rule an unjustified judicial interference with Congress's reasoned judgment? On the other hand, some form of *Gregory*'s clear statement requirement is arguably necessary to ensure the operation of the political safeguards of federalism built into the lawmaking process. *See, e.g.,* Bradford R. Clark, *Process–*

*Based Preemption, in* Preemption Choice: The Theory, Law, and Reality of Federalism's Core Question 192, 204–05 (William W. Buzbee ed., 2009). Finally, if the *Gregory* rule is defended as reflecting not an independent judicial value judgment, but rather the likely intent of Congress, then mightn't the "political safeguards" thesis actually bolster the case for some version of the *Gregory* canon? If the structure and process of federal lawmaking is likely to make Congress sensitive to concerns about state sovereignty, then isn't it sensible to presume that Congress would usually not want to do something as dramatic and aggressive as imposing federal qualification rules on state court judges? Of course, if one believes that Congress usually cares too little (or not at all) about state sovereignty, then one might reach the opposite conclusions: It may be harder to defend the *Gregory* canon as reflecting likely congressional intent, but the case for protecting state sovereignty through some other means may become stronger.

### b.  Federal Preemption of State Law

In the system of "dual sovereignty" established by the U.S. Constitution, the state governments have the general authority to legislate on affairs within their respective jurisdictions, while the federal government has only those powers enumerated in the Constitution—such as the power to collect taxes, to regulate interstate and foreign commerce, and to enforce the equal protection and due process provisions in the Fourteenth Amendment. What happens when the federal government enacts a law that conflicts with a state law on the same subject? The constitutional provision known as the Supremacy Clause makes clear that when there is a conflict between federal law and state law, federal law takes precedence: "This Constitution, and the Laws of the United States which shall be made in Pursuance thereof; and all Treaties made, or which shall be made, under the authority of the United States, shall be the supreme Law of the land; and the Judges in every State shall be bound thereby, any Thing in the Constitution or Laws of any State to the Contrary notwithstanding." U.S. Const. art. VI, cl. 2. Thus, as long as the federal government is acting pursuant to a legitimate source of constitutional authority, federal law may "preempt" state law. Yet although it is well-settled that Congress has the power to preempt state law, courts must still figure out when, and to what extent, Congress has in fact exercised that power. To do so, courts must examine the allegedly preemptive federal statute at issue, and perhaps the allegedly preempted state law as well. The question of federal preemption, then, is typically a question of statutory interpretation.

There are two broad types of federal preemption cases. The first type involves *express preemption.* In an express preemption case, the federal statute contains some explicit provision that declares that the federal statute preempts certain categories of state law. Resolution of express preemption claims typically involves interpreting the meaning and scope of the preemption clause in the federal statute, and considering whether the challenged state law is covered by that clause. The second type of federal preemption case involves claims of *implied preemption.* In an implied preemption case, there is no express language in the federal statute declaring that certain categories of state law are preempted, but the court can nonetheless conclude that the federal statute implicitly preempts certain state laws.

The case law and commentary further divides implied preemption cases into three sub-categories. The first involves *conflict preemption* (sometimes referred to as *impossibility preemption*): situations where, although the federal statute does not say anything explicit about preemption, there is an irreconcilable conflict between state and federal law, such that it is impossible to comply with both of them. *See, e.g.,* Southland Corp. v. Keating, 465 U.S. 1 (1984). Second, courts will sometimes find that although compliance with both the state and federal law is technically possible, enforcement of the state law would obstruct or frustrate the purposes of the federal statute. In other words, a court might conclude that the state law is such an obstacle to the achievement of the federal law's objectives that the federal law impliedly preempts the state law. This sort of implied preemption is usually known as *obstacle preemption. See, e.g.,* Hines v. Davidowitz, 312 U.S. 52, 67 (1941). Third, courts sometimes conclude that federal regulation in some substantive area is so pervasive and comprehensive that the federal government has implicitly expressed its desire to "occupy the field," impliedly preempting any state or local regulation in that area. This type of implied preemption is known as *field preemption. See, e.g.,* California v. ARC America Corp., 490 U.S. 93, 100 (1989). (Field preemption might be characterized as a type of obstacle preemption, in that one of the implicit goals of the federal law is to establish an exclusive scheme of federal regulation.)

Although federal preemption of state law is constitutionally legitimate—and often desirable—it raises concerns about the balance between federal and state power. These concerns are related to the sorts of concerns expressed in cases like *Gregory v. Ashcroft.* (*See* pp. 291–296, *supra.*) But they are distinct in that they do not involve the imposition of federal rules on the state governments themselves, but rather the displacement of state law by federal law, often in areas that have historically been the subject of state rather than federal control. How, if at all, should these sorts of federalism concerns influence how courts interpret statutes in preemption cases? Should there be a thumb on the scale—a substantive canon—against finding federal preemption of state law? The following case, *Rice v. Santa Fe Elevator Corp.*, suggests that there should, though as we shall see, subsequent courts and commentators have interpreted *Rice* in quite different ways. As you read the case, see if you can identify the substantive canon that the Court announces, and consider whether you think it is appropriate.

---

# Rice v. Santa Fe Elevator Corporation

Supreme Court of the United States
331 U.S. 218 (1947)

■ Mr. Justice Douglas delivered the opinion of the Court.

Respondents in these two cases are warehousemen engaged in the business of operating public warehouses for the storage of grain in Illinois.

Their warehouses are operated under licenses issued by the Secretary of Agriculture pursuant to the United States Warehouse Act. The Rice partnership, one of the petitioners, is an owner, shipper, and dealer in grain and is a customer of respondents. . . .

In 1944 Rice filed a complaint with the [Illinois Commerce] Commission, charging respondents with [various violations of Illinois state laws administered by the Commission]. . . .

Respondents moved to dismiss on the ground that the United States Warehouse Act superseded the authority of the Commission to regulate in the manner sought by the complaint. . . .

The United States Warehouse Act, as originally enacted in 1916, made federal regulation in this field subservient to state regulation. It provided in § 29 that "nothing in this act shall be construed to conflict with, or to authorize any conflict with, or in any way to impair or limit the effect or operation of the laws of any State relating to warehouses [or] warehousemen. . . ." And § 6 required an applicant for a federal warehouse license to provide a bond 'to secure the faithful performance of his obligations as a warehouseman' under state as well as under federal law.

In 1931 Congress amended the Act. Section 29 was amended to provide that although the Secretary of Agriculture "is authorized to cooperate with State officials charged with the enforcement of State laws relating to warehouses, warehousemen", and their personnel, "the power, jurisdiction, and authority conferred upon the Secretary of Agriculture under this act shall be exclusive with respect to all persons securing a license hereunder so long as said license remains in effect." Section 6 was amended to omit the requirement that the bond be conditioned on compliance with requirements of state law.

. . . Congress in 1931 made the "power, jurisdiction, and authority" of the Secretary of Agriculture conferred by the Act "exclusive with respect to all persons securing a license" under the Act, so long as the license remains in effect. It is argued by respondents that § 29 should be construed to mean that the subjects which the Secretary's authority touches may not be regulated in any way by any state agency, though the scope of federal regulation is not as broad as the regulatory scheme of the State and even though there is or may be no necessary conflict between what the state agency and the federal agency do. On the other hand, petitioners argue that since the area taken over by the Federal Government is limited, the rest may be occupied by the States; that state regulation should not give way unless there is a precise coincidence of regulation or an irreconcilable conflict between the two.

It is clear that since warehouses engaged in the storage of grain for interstate or foreign commerce are in the federal domain, Congress may, if it chooses, take unto itself all regulatory authority over them, share the task with the States, or adopt as federal policy the state scheme of regulation. The question in each case is what the purpose of Congress was.

Congress legislated here in a field which the States have traditionally occupied. So we start with the assumption that the historic police powers of the States were not to be superseded by the Federal Act unless that was the clear and manifest purpose of Congress. Such a purpose may be evidenced in several ways. The scheme of federal regulation may be so pervasive as to make reasonable the inference that Congress left no room for the States to supplement it. Or the Act of Congress may touch a field in which the federal interest is so dominant that the federal system will be assumed to preclude enforcement of state laws on the same subject. Likewise, the object sought to be obtained by the federal law and the character of obligations imposed by it may reveal the same purpose. Or the state policy may produce a result inconsistent with the objective of the federal statute. It is often a perplexing question whether Congress has precluded state action or by the choice of selective regulatory measures has left the police power of the States undisturbed except as the state and federal regulations collide.

A forceful argument is made here for the view that the Illinois regulatory scheme should be allowed to supplement the Federal Act and that the Illinois Commission should not be prevented from acting on any of the matters covered by Rice's complaint, unless what the Commission does runs counter in fact to the federal policy. That is to say, the actual operation of the state system may be harmonious with the "measure of control" over warehousemen which the Federal Act imposes. That, it is said, can only be determined after the Illinois Commission has acted....

At first blush that construction of the Federal Act has great plausibility. It preserves intact the federal system of warehouse regulation, leaves the State free to protect local interests, and strikes down state power only in case what the State does in fact dilutes or diminishes the federal program.

But the special and peculiar history of the Warehouse Act indicates to us that such a construction would thwart the federal policy which Congress adopted when it amended the Act in 1931....

■ MR. JUSTICE FRANKFURTER, with whom MR. JUSTICE RUTLEDGE concurs, dissenting.

... The Court now holds that by the 1931 Amendment to [the Warehouse] Act, Congress not only made the federal legislation independent of State law to the full scope of federal regulation, but also nullified the extensive network of State laws regulating warehouses, even though such laws in their actual operation, in nowise conflict with the operation of the federal law. The Court thereby uproots a vast body of State enactments which in themselves do not collide with the licensing powers of the Secretary of Agriculture. It does so on the ground that Congress, by the 1931 Amendment, provided that "the power, jurisdiction, and authority conferred upon the Secretary of Agriculture under this act shall be exclusive with respect to all persons securing a license hereunder so long as said license remains in effect."...

[O]ur problem is to determine what freedom to regulate its grain warehouses has been left to Illinois, after Congress exercised its constitutional power over such warehouses by adopting a licensing system to be administered by the Secretary of Agriculture under closely defined authority. Underlying the problem is the important fact that we are concerned with an economic enterprise which, while it has important radiations beyond State bounds, does not thereby lose special relations to the State in which it is conducted. And so we have once more the duty of judicially adjusting the interests of both the Nation and the State, where Congress has not clearly asserted its power of preemption so as to leave no doubt that the separate interests of the States are left wholly to national protection.

The general considerations to be taken into account in striking a balance, and not to be acknowledged merely platonically, have been indicated in my opinion in Bethlehem Steel Co. v. New York State Labor Relations Board, 330 U.S. 767. Suffice it to say that due regard for our federalism, in its practical operation, favors survival of the reserved authority of a State over matters that are the intimate concern of the State unless Congress has clearly swept the boards of all State authority, or the State's claim is in unmistakable conflict with what Congress has ordered....

... Evidence is lacking that Congress felt that the correction of the inadequacy which had revealed itself regarding the 1916 Act required withdrawal of federal license holders from the requirements of non-conflicting State regulation. So long as full scope can be given to the amendatory legislation without undermining non-conflicting State laws, nothing but the clearest expression should persuade us that the federal Act wiped out State fixation of rates and other State requirements deeply rooted in their laws. When neither the mischief at which the 1931 Amendment was directed, nor the policy, terms and structure of warehousing legislation by Congress in its entirety necessitate it, disregard of the delicate balance of Federal-State relations ought not to be attributed to Congress....

---

Although the *Rice* majority ultimately found that the federal statute preempted the state laws at issue in the case, *Rice* is best known for its assertion that when Congress legislates in a field which the states have traditionally occupied, the courts will presume "that the historic police powers of the States were not to be superseded by the Federal Act unless that was the clear and manifest purpose of Congress." Although this "presumption against preemption" is well-established, its precise strength and scope is less settled. Indeed, in *Rice* itself Justice Frankfurter's dissent alleged that the majority had failed to apply the presumption correctly, in that the majority was willing to find preemption based on legislative history that did not, in Justice Frankfurter's view, amount to the kind of super-clear indication of congressional intent necessary to displace state law.

The following case, *Cipollone v. Liggett Group*, raises a number of difficult questions about the meaning and scope of the presumption against preemption—in particular, how (or whether) this presumption applies to the interpretation of an express preemption clause.

---

# Cipollone v. Liggett Group, Inc.

Supreme Court of the United States
505 U.S. 504 (1992)

■ Justice Stevens delivered the opinion of the Court, except as to Parts V and VI.

"Warning: The Surgeon General Has Determined That Cigarette Smoking Is Dangerous to Your Health." A federal statute enacted in 1969 requires that warning (or a variation thereof) to appear in a conspicuous place on every package of cigarettes sold in the United States. The questions presented to us by this case are whether that statute ... preempted petitioner's common-law claims against respondent cigarette manufacturers. . . .

## I

. . . [Petitioner's] complaint alleged that Rose Cipollone developed lung cancer because she smoked cigarettes manufactured and sold by the three respondents. . . .

Petitioner's ... complaint alleges several different bases of recovery [under state common law, including failure to warn, breach of warranties, and fraud] . . . .

As one of their defenses, respondents contended that the Federal Cigarette Labeling and Advertising Act, enacted in 1965, and its successor, the Public Health Cigarette Smoking Act of 1969, protected them from any liability based on their conduct after 1965. . . .

## II

. . . In July 1965, Congress enacted the Federal Cigarette Labeling and Advertising Act (1965 Act or Act). The 1965 Act ... mandated warnings on cigarette packages (§ 5(a)), but barred the requirement of such warnings in cigarette advertising (§ 5(b)).

Section 2 of the Act declares the statute's two purposes: (1) adequately informing the public that cigarette smoking may be hazardous to health, and (2) protecting the national economy from the burden imposed by diverse, nonuniform, and confusing cigarette labeling and advertising regulations. In furtherance of the first purpose, § 4 of the Act made it unlawful to sell or distribute any cigarettes in the United States unless the package bore a conspicuous label stating: "Caution: Cigarette Smoking May Be Hazardous to Your Health." In furtherance of the second purpose, § 5, captioned "Preemption," provided in part:

"(a) No statement relating to smoking and health, other than the statement required by section 4 of this Act, shall be required on any cigarette package.

"(b) No statement relating to smoking and health shall be required in the advertising of any cigarettes the packages of which are labeled in conformity with the provisions of this Act."

Although the Act took effect January 1, 1966, § 10 of the Act provided that its provisions affecting the regulation of advertising would terminate on July 1, 1969.

. . . . [T]he Public Health Cigarette Smoking Act of 1969 (1969 Act or Act) . . . amended the 1965 Act in several ways. First, the 1969 Act strengthened the warning label, in part by requiring a statement that cigarette smoking "is dangerous" rather than that it "may be hazardous." Second, the 1969 Act banned cigarette advertising in "any medium of electronic communication subject to [FCC] jurisdiction." Third, and related, the 1969 Act modified the pre-emption provision by replacing the original § 5(b) with a provision that reads:

"(b) No requirement or prohibition based on smoking and health shall be imposed under State law with respect to the advertising or promotion of any cigarettes the packages of which are labeled in conformity with the provisions of this Act."

. . .

### III

Article VI of the Constitution provides that the laws of the United States "shall be the supreme Law of the Land; . . . any Thing in the Constitution or Laws of any state to the Contrary notwithstanding." Art. VI, cl. 2. . . . Consideration of issues arising under the Supremacy Clause "start[s] with the assumption that the historic police powers of the States [are] not to be superseded by . . . Federal Act unless that [is] the clear and manifest purpose of Congress." Rice v. Santa Fe Elevator Corp., 331 U.S. 218, 230 (1947). . . .

Congress' intent may be "explicitly stated in the statute's language or implicitly contained in its structure and purpose." Jones v. Rath Packing Co., 430 U.S. 519, 525 (1977). In the absence of an express congressional command, state law is pre-empted if that law actually conflicts with federal law, or if federal law so thoroughly occupies a legislative field " 'as to make reasonable the inference that Congress left no room for the States to supplement it.' " Fidelity Fed. Sav. & Loan Assn. v. De la Cuesta, 458 U.S. 141, 153 (1982) (quoting Rice v. Santa Fe Elevator Corp., 331 U.S., at 230).

. . . In our opinion, the pre-emptive scope of the 1965 Act and the 1969 Act is governed entirely by the express language in § 5 of each Act. When Congress has considered the issue of pre-emption and has included in the enacted legislation a provision explicitly addressing that issue, and when that provision provides a "reliable indicium of congressional intent with respect to state authority," Malone v. White Motor Corp., 435 U.S. [497,

505 (1978)], "there is no need to infer congressional intent to pre-empt state laws from the substantive provisions" of the legislation. *California Federal Savings & Loan Assn. v. Guerra*, 479 U.S. 272, 282 (1987) (opinion of Marshall, J.). Such reasoning is a variant of the familiar principle of *expressio unius est exclusio alterius*: Congress' enactment of a provision defining the pre-emptive reach of a statute implies that matters beyond that reach are not pre-empted. In this case, the other provisions of the 1965 and 1969 Acts offer no cause to look beyond § 5 of each Act. Therefore, we need only identify the domain expressly pre-empted by each of those sections. As the 1965 and 1969 provisions differ substantially, we consider each in turn.

## IV

In the 1965 pre-emption provision regarding advertising (§ 5(b)), Congress spoke precisely and narrowly: "No *statement* relating to smoking and health shall be required *in the advertising* of [properly labeled] cigarettes." Section 5(a) used the same phrase ("No *statement* relating to smoking and health") with regard to cigarette labeling. As § 5(a) made clear, that phrase referred to the sort of warning provided for in § 4, which set forth verbatim the warning Congress determined to be appropriate. Thus, on their face, these provisions merely prohibited state and federal rulemaking bodies from mandating particular cautionary statements on cigarette labels (§ 5(a)) or in cigarette advertisements (§ 5(b)).

Beyond the precise words of these provisions, this reading is appropriate for several reasons. First, as discussed above, we must construe these provisions in light of the presumption against the pre-emption of state police power regulations. This presumption reinforces the appropriateness of a narrow reading of § 5. Second, the warning required in § 4 does not by its own effect foreclose additional obligations imposed under state law. That Congress requires a particular warning label does not automatically pre-empt a regulatory field. Third, there is no general, inherent conflict between federal pre-emption of state warning requirements and the continued vitality of state common-law damages actions.... All of these considerations indicate that § 5 is best read as having superseded only positive enactments by legislatures or administrative agencies that mandate particular warning labels....

## V

Compared to its predecessor in the 1965 Act, the plain language of the pre-emption provision in the 1969 Act is much broader. First, the later Act bars not simply "statement[s]" but rather "requirement[s] or prohibition[s] ... imposed under State law." Second, the later Act reaches beyond statements "in the advertising" to obligations "with respect to the advertising or promotion" of cigarettes.

Notwithstanding these substantial differences in language, both petitioner and respondents contend that the 1969 Act did not materially alter the pre-emptive scope of federal law. Their primary support for this contention is a sentence in a Committee Report which states that the 1969 amendment "clarified" the 1965 version of § 5(b). We reject the parties' reading as incompatible with the language and origins of the amendments. As we noted in another context, "[i]nferences from legislative history cannot rest on so slender a reed. Moreover, the views of a subsequent Congress form a hazardous basis for inferring the intent of an earlier one." United States v. Price, 361 U.S. 304, 313 (1960). The 1969 Act worked substantial changes in the law.... In the context of such revisions and in light of the substantial changes in wording, we cannot accept the parties' claim that the 1969 Act did not alter the reach of § 5(b).

Petitioner next contends that § 5(b), however broadened by the 1969 Act, does not pre-empt *common-law* actions. He offers two theories for limiting the reach of the amended § 5(b). First, he argues that common-law damages actions do not impose "requirement[s] or prohibition[s]" and that Congress intended only to trump "state statute[s], injunction[s], or executive pronouncement[s]." We disagree; such an analysis is at odds both with the plain words of the 1969 Act and with the general understanding of common-law damages actions. The phrase "[n]o requirement or prohibition" sweeps broadly and suggests no distinction between positive enactments and common law; to the contrary, those words easily encompass obligations that take the form of common-law rules....

... Petitioner's second argument for excluding common-law rules from the reach of § 5(b) hinges on the phrase "imposed under State law." This argument fails as well. At least since Erie R. Co. v. Tompkins, 304 U.S. 64 (1938), we have recognized the phrase "state law" to include common law as well as statutes and regulations. Indeed just last Term, the Court stated that the phrase " 'all other law, including State and municipal law' " "does not admit of [a] distinction ... between positive enactments and common-law rules of liability." Norfolk & Western R. Co. v. Train Dispatchers, 499 U.S. 117, 128 (1991). Although the presumption against pre-emption might give good reason to construe the phrase "state law" in a pre-emption provision more narrowly than an identical phrase in another context, in this case such a construction is not appropriate. As explained above, the 1965 version of § 5 was precise and narrow on its face; the obviously broader language of the 1969 version extended that section's pre-emptive reach. Moreover, while the version of the 1969 Act passed by the Senate pre-empted "any State *statute or regulation* with respect to ... advertising or promotion," the Conference Committee replaced this language with "State *law* with respect to advertising or promotion." In such a situation, § 5(b)'s pre-emption of "state law" cannot fairly be limited to positive enactments.

That the pre-emptive scope of § 5(b) cannot be limited to positive enactments does not mean that that section pre-empts all common-law claims.... For purposes of § 5(b), the common law is not of a piece.

... [W]e must fairly but—in light of the strong presumption against pre-emption—narrowly construe the precise language of § 5(b) and we must look to each of petitioner's common-law claims to determine whether it is in fact pre-empted. The central inquiry in each case is straightforward: we ask whether the legal duty that is the predicate of the common-law damages action constitutes a "requirement or prohibition based on smoking and health ... imposed under State law with respect to ... advertising or promotion," giving that clause a fair but narrow reading. As discussed below, each phrase within that clause limits the universe of common-law claims pre-empted by the statute.

[JUSTICE STEVENS' plurality opinion then considered in turn each of the petitioner's state common law claims, concluding that many were pre-empted by the 1969 Act but that some were not.]

■ JUSTICE BLACKMUN, with whom JUSTICE KENNEDY and JUSTICE SOUTER join, concurring in part, concurring in the judgment in part, and dissenting in part.

## I

The Court today would craft a compromise position concerning the extent to which federal law pre-empts persons injured by cigarette manufacturers' unlawful conduct from bringing state common-law damages claims against those manufacturers. I, however, find the Court's divided holding with respect to the original and amended versions of the federal statute entirely unsatisfactory. Our precedents do not allow us to infer a scope of pre-emption beyond that which clearly is mandated by Congress' language. In my view, *neither* version of the federal legislation at issue here provides the kind of unambiguous evidence of congressional intent necessary to displace state common-law damages claims....

## A

... I ... agree with the Court that we cannot find the state common-law damages claims at issue in this case pre-empted by federal law in the absence of clear and unambiguous evidence that Congress intended that result. The Court describes this reluctance to infer pre-emption in ambiguous cases as a "presumption against the pre-emption of state police power regulations." Although many of the cases in which the Court has invoked such a presumption against displacement of state law have involved implied pre-emption, ... this Court often speaks in general terms without reference to the nature of the pre-emption at issue in the given statutory scheme....

The principles of federalism and respect for state sovereignty that underlie the Court's reluctance to find pre-emption where Congress has not spoken directly to the issue apply with equal force where Congress has spoken, though ambiguously. In such cases, the question is not *whether* Congress intended to pre-empt state regulation, but to what *extent*. We do not, absent unambiguous evidence, infer a scope of pre-emption beyond that which clearly is mandated by Congress' language. I therefore agree with the Court's unwillingness to conclude that the state common-law damages claims at issue in this case are pre-empted unless such result is " 'the clear and manifest purpose of Congress.' "

## B

I also agree with the Court's application of the foregoing principles in Part IV of its opinion, where it concludes that none of petitioner's common-law damages claims are pre-empted by the 1965 Act. . . .

## II

My agreement with the Court ceases at this point. Given the Court's proper analytical focus on the scope of the express pre-emption provisions at issue here and its acknowledgment that the 1965 Act does not pre-empt state common-law damages claims, I find the plurality's conclusion that the 1969 Act pre-empts at least some common-law damages claims little short of baffling. In my view, the modified language of § 5(b) ("No requirement or prohibition based on smoking and health shall be imposed under State law with respect to the advertising or promotion of any cigarettes the packages of which are labeled in conformity with the provisions of this Act"), no more "clearly" or "manifestly" exhibits an intent to pre-empt state common-law damages actions than did the language of its predecessor in the 1965 Act. Nonetheless, the plurality reaches a different conclusion, and its reasoning warrants scrutiny.

## A

The plurality premises its pre-emption ruling on what it terms the "substantial changes" wrought by Congress in § 5(b), notably, the rewording of the provision to pre-empt any "requirement or prohibition" (as opposed merely to any "statement") "imposed under State law." As an initial matter, I do not disagree with the plurality that the phrase "State law," in an appropriate case, can encompass the common law as well as positive enactments such as statutes and regulations. I do disagree, however, with the plurality's conclusion that "State law" as used in § 5(b) represents such an all-inclusive reference. Congress' intention in selecting that phrase cannot be understood without considering the narrow range of actions—any "requirement or prohibition"—that Congress specifically described in § 5(b) as "imposed under" state law. . . .

Although the plurality flatly states that the phrase "no requirement or prohibition" "sweeps broadly" and "easily encompass[es] obligations that take the form of common-law rules," those words are in reality far from unambiguous and cannot be said clearly to evidence a congressional mandate to pre-empt state common-law damages actions. The dictionary definitions of these terms suggest, if anything, specific actions mandated or disallowed by a formal governing authority. . . .

More important, the question whether common-law damages actions exert a regulatory effect on manufacturers analogous to that of positive enactments—an assumption crucial to the plurality's conclusion that the phrase "requirement or prohibition" encompasses common-law actions—is significantly more complicated than the plurality[ ] . . . suggest[s].

The effect of tort law on a manufacturer's behavior is necessarily indirect. Although an award of damages by its very nature attaches additional consequences to the manufacturer's continued unlawful conduct, no particular course of action (*e.g.*, the adoption of a new warning label) is required.... The level of choice that a defendant retains in shaping its own behavior distinguishes the indirect regulatory effect of the common law from positive enactments such as statutes and administrative regulations.... Moreover, tort law has an entirely separate function—compensating victims—that sets it apart from direct forms of regulation....

... In light of the recognized distinction in this Court's jurisprudence between direct state regulation and the indirect regulatory effects of common-law damages actions, it cannot be said that damages claims are clearly or unambiguously "requirements" or "prohibitions" imposed under state law. The plain language of the 1969 Act's modified pre-emption provision simply cannot bear the broad interpretation the plurality would impart to it.

### B

Not only does the text of the revised § 5(b) fail clearly or manifestly to require pre-emption of state common-law damages actions, but there is no suggestion in the legislative history that Congress intended to expand the scope of the pre-emption provision when it amended the statute in 1969. The plurality acknowledges the evidence that Congress itself perceived the changes in § 5(b) to be a mere " 'clarifi[cation]' " of the existing narrow pre-emption provision, ... but it dismisses these statements of legislative intent as the " 'views of a subsequent Congress.' " ... The plurality is wrong not only as a factual matter—for the statements of the Congress that amended § 5(b) are contemporaneous, not "subsequent," to enactment of the revised pre-emption provision—but as a legal matter, as well. This Court accords "great weight" to an amending Congress' interpretation of the underlying statute....

Viewing the revisions to § 5(b) as generally nonsubstantive in nature makes sense. By replacing the word "statement" with the slightly broader term, "requirement," and adding the word "prohibition" to ensure that a State could not do through negative mandate (e.g., banning all cigarette advertising) that which it already was forbidden to do through positive mandate (*e.g.*, mandating particular cautionary statements), Congress sought to "clarif[y]" the existing precautions against confusing and non-uniform state laws and regulations.

Just as it acknowledges the evidence that Congress' changes in the pre-emption provision were nonsubstantive, the plurality admits that "portions of the legislative history of the 1969 Act suggest that Congress was primarily concerned with positive enactments by States and localities." Indeed, the relevant Senate Report explains that the revised pre-emption provision is "intended to include not only action by State statute but by all other administrative actions or local ordinances or regulations by any political subdivisions of any State," a list remarkable for the absence of any reference to common-law damages actions.... [T]he words of § 5(b) ("requirement or prohibition") do not ... "plainly" extend to common-law damages actions, and the plurality errs in placing so much weight on this fragile textual hook.

. . . Finally, there is absolutely no suggestion in the legislative history that Congress intended to leave plaintiffs who were injured as a result of cigarette manufacturers' unlawful conduct without any alternative remedies; yet that is the regrettable effect of the ruling today that many state common-law damages claims are pre-empted. The Court in the past has hesitated to find pre-emption where federal law provides no comparable remedy. . . .

Unlike other federal statutes where Congress has eased the bite of pre-emption by establishing "comprehensive" civil enforcement schemes, the Cigarette Labeling and Advertising Act is barren of alternative remedies. . . . Unlike the plurality, I am unwilling to believe that Congress, without any mention of state common-law damages actions or of its intention dramatically to expand the scope of federal pre-emption, would have eliminated the only means of judicial recourse for those injured by cigarette manufacturers' unlawful conduct.

Thus, not only does the plain language of the 1969 Act fail clearly to require pre-emption of petitioner's state common-law damages claims, but there is no suggestion in the legislative history that Congress intended to expand the scope of the pre-emption provision in the drastic manner that the plurality attributes to it. Our obligation to infer pre-emption only where Congress' intent is clear and manifest mandates the conclusion that state common-law damages actions are not pre-empted by the 1969 Act. . . .

■ JUSTICE SCALIA, with whom JUSTICE THOMAS joins, concurring in the judgment in part and dissenting in part.

Today's decision announces what, on its face, is an extraordinary and unprecedented principle of federal statutory construction: that express pre-emption provisions must be construed narrowly, "in light of the presumption against the pre-emption of state police power regulations." The life-span of this new rule may have been blessedly brief, inasmuch as the opinion that gives it birth in Part I proceeds to ignore it in Part V, by adjudging at least some of the common-law tort claims at issue here pre-empted. In my view, there is no merit to this newly crafted doctrine of narrow construction. Under the Supremacy Clause, our job is to interpret Congress's decrees of pre-emption neither narrowly nor broadly, but in accordance with their apparent meaning. If we did that job in the present case, we would find, under the 1965 Act, pre-emption of petitioner's failure-to-warn claims; and under the 1969 Act, we would find pre-emption of petitioner's claims complete.

I

The Court's threshold description of the law of pre-emption is accurate enough: Though we generally " 'assum[e] that the historic police powers of the States [are] not to be superseded by . . . Federal Act unless that [is] the clear and manifest purpose of Congress,' " we have traditionally not thought that to require express statutory text. Where state law is in actual conflict with federal law, or where it "stands as an obstacle to the accomplishment and execution of the full purposes and objectives of Congress," Hines v. Davidowitz, 312 U.S. 52, 67 (1941), or even where the nature of Congress's regulation, or its scope, convinces us that "Congress left no room for the States to supplement it," *Rice*, 331 U.S., at 230, we have had no difficulty declaring that state law must yield. The ultimate question in each case, as we have framed the inquiry, is one of Congress's intent, as revealed by the text, structure, purposes, and subject matter of the statutes involved.

The Court goes beyond these traditional principles, however, to announce two new ones. First, it says that express pre-emption provisions must be given the narrowest possible construction. This is in its view the consequence of our oft-repeated assumption that, absent convincing evidence of statutory intent to pre-empt, " 'the historic police powers of the States [are] not to be superseded[.]' " But it seems to me that assumption dissolves once there is conclusive evidence of intent to pre-empt in the express words of the statute itself, and the only remaining question is what the *scope* of that pre-emption is meant to be. Thereupon, I think, our responsibility is to apply to the text ordinary principles of statutory construction. . . .

In light of our willingness to find pre-emption in the absence of *any* explicit statement of pre-emptive intent, the notion that such explicit statements, where they exist, are subject to a "plain-statement" rule is more than somewhat odd. To be sure, our jurisprudence abounds with rules of "plain statement," "clear statement," and "narrow construction" designed variously to ensure that, absent unambiguous evidence of Congress's intent, extraordinary constitutional powers are not invoked, or important constitutional protections eliminated, or seemingly inequitable doctrines applied. . . . But *none* of those rules exists alongside a doctrine whereby the same result so prophylactically protected from careless explicit provision can be achieved *by sheer implication*, with no express statement of intent at all. That is the novel regime the Court constructs today.

The results seem odder still when one takes into account the second new rule that the Court announces: "When Congress has considered the issue of pre-emption and has included in the enacted legislation a provision explicitly addressing that issue, . . . we need only identify the domain expressly pre-empted by [that provision]." Once there is an express pre-emption provision, in other words, all doctrines of implied pre-emption are eliminated. This proposition may be correct insofar as implied "field" pre-emption is concerned: The existence of an express pre-emption provision tends to contradict any inference that Congress intended to occupy a field broader than the statute's express language defines. However, with regard to implied "conflict" pre-emption—*i.e.*, where state regulation actually conflicts with federal law, or where state regulation "stands as an obstacle to the accomplishment and execution" of Congress's purposes, *Hines*, 312 U.S., at 67—the Court's second new rule works mischief. If taken seriously, it would mean, for example, that if a federal consumer protection law provided that no state agency or court shall assert jurisdiction under state law over any workplace safety issue with respect to which a federal standard is in effect, then a state agency operating under a law dealing with a subject other than workplace safety (*e.g.*, consumer protection) could impose requirements entirely contrary to federal law—forbidding, for example, the use of certain safety equipment that federal law requires. To my knowledge, we have never expressed such a rule before.... When this second novelty is combined with the first, the result is extraordinary: The statute that says *anything* about pre-emption must say *everything*; and it must do so with great exactitude, as any ambiguity concerning its scope will be read in favor of preserving state power. If this is to be the law, surely only the most sporting of Congresses will dare to say anything about pre-emption.

The proper rule of construction for express pre-emption provisions is, it seems to me, the one that is customary for statutory provisions in general: Their language should be given its ordinary meaning.... When this suggests that the pre-emption provision was intended to sweep broadly, our construction must sweep broadly as well. And when it bespeaks a narrow scope of pre-emption, so must our judgment. Applying its niggardly rule of construction, the Court finds (not surprisingly) that none of petitioner's claims—common-law failure to warn, breach of express warranty, and intentional fraud and misrepresentation—is pre-empted under § 5(b) of the 1965 Act. And save for the failure-to-warn claims, the Court reaches the same result under § 5(b) of the 1969 Act. I think most of that is error. Applying ordinary principles of statutory construction, I believe petitioner's failure-to-warn claims are pre-empted by the 1965 Act, and all his common-law claims by the 1969 Act.

II

■ [JUSTICE SCALIA's dissent then considered each of the petitioner's state common law claims, and concluded that all these claims are preempted.]

---

*1. **Is a State Common Law Duty a "Requirement Under State Law"?**—*The central interpretive issue in *Cipollone* was whether a federal statute that preempts any "requirement or prohibition ... imposed under State law" related to cigarette advertising or promotion preempts state common law tort and contract suits that allege, for example, breach of common law duties to warn, breach of express or implied contractual warranties, fraud, misrepresentation, and so forth. The answer to this question turned on whether a state common law duty is a "requirement or prohibition ... imposed under State law," or whether only a "positive enactment" (that is, a state statute or administrative regulation that specifically mandates or forbids certain behavior) counts as a "requirement or prohibition" within the meaning of the federal statute.

Putting aside for the moment issues related to the presumption against preemption, how would you answer that question, and why? On the one hand, common law duties are similar to direct statutory or administrative regulations, in that both attach adverse legal consequences to certain conduct. A regulation might prohibit selling cigarettes without a warning about the health risks of smoking, and impose a $50,000 fine on any company that violates this regulation. Or, a cigarette company might be found liable for negligent failure to warn if it sells cigarettes without such a warning label, and might expect to pay $50,000 in damages for this breach of its common law duty. From the company's perspective, there would seem to be no difference: if it engages in disfavored conduct $X$ (here, selling cigarettes without an adequate warning), then as a consequence of state law, the company is liable to incur a monetary penalty.

On the other hand, don't common law duties seem different, in some important respects, from positive regulatory or legislative enactments? As Justice Blackmun's partial dissent in *Cipollone* pointed out, the effect of common law liability on a firm's behavior is "necessarily indirect," as common law duties typically do not require any particular course of action. While a state regulation related to cigarette advertising is likely to specify (often in great detail) a *particular* warning statement, a common law judge (or properly instructed jury) will typically ask only whether the defendant's conduct amounts to a breach of duty that caused harm to the plaintiff. That inquiry usually does not turn on whether the defendant provided a specific type of warning, but only whether the defendant's warning was adequate. Also, as Justice Blackmun pointed out, common law actions have a compensatory purpose that distinguishes them from typical regulatory or statutory enactments. Which position do you find more persuasive in this context? Does the phrase "requirement or prohibition . . . imposed under state law" in § 5(b) of the 1969 Public Health Cigarette Smoking Act cover state common law damages actions or not? Do you think the answer is clear, or would you find the statute ambiguous on that point?

*Cipollone* was neither the first nor the last word on the question whether the term "requirement or prohibition," or similar phrasing, covers state common law duties. Four years later, in Medtronic, Inc. v. Lohr, 518 U.S. 470 (1996), the Supreme Court considered the meaning of the preemption clause in the Medical Device Act, which preempted any state law "requirement . . . which is different from, or in addition to," any federal law requirement related to the safety or effectiveness of a medical device. 21 U.S.C. § 360k. Like *Cipollone*, *Medtronic* fractured the Court, producing three separate opinions. Most relevant to the discussion here, Justice Stevens' opinion (joined on this point by Justices Kennedy, Souter, and Ginsburg), concluded that the "any requirement" language in § 360k did *not* include state common law damages actions. A contrary conclusion, Justice Stevens reasoned, would be "implausible," as it would deprive those injured by defective medical devices of any compensatory remedy—a result the plurality thought Congress could not have intended. 518 U.S. at 487. Furthermore, Justice Stevens explained, the term " '[r]equirement' appears to presume that the State is imposing a specific duty on the manufacturer. . . ." *Id.* Justice O'Connor (in a partial dissent joined by Chief Justice Rehnquist and Justices Scalia and Thomas) and Justice Breyer (in a partial concurrence) disagreed, arguing—in keeping with the position of the *Cipollone* majority—that the term "requirements" encompasses common law damages actions.

Most of the Justices who participated in both *Cipollone* and *Medtronic* seem to have staked out consistent positions. But it is striking that Justice Stevens both wrote the opinion in *Cipollone*—which held that the term "requirement" in the preemption clause of the Public Health Cigarette Smoking Act *did* include common law duties—and also concluded in *Medtronic*—that the term "requirement" in the preemption clause of the Medical Device Act *did not* include common law duties. Justice Stevens' *Medtronic* opinion acknowledged the apparent tension with *Cipollone*, but argued that the cases were distinguishable in two respects. First, because the statute at issue in *Cipollone* targeted only a narrow class of requirements—those related to advertising or promotion of cigarettes—reading "requirements" broadly as including common law duties would not have as sweeping an effect as it would in *Medtronic*, and for that reason would not produce as "serious [an] intrusion into state sovereignty. . . ." 518 U.S. at 488. Second, Justice Stevens' *Medtronic* opinion noted that while the statute at issue in *Cipollone* used the term "requirement" only in the preemption clause, the Medical Device Act used the term "requirements" many times throughout the statute's text, and in every other instance that term was used to mean "device-specific enactments of positive law by legislative or administrative bodies, not the application of general rules of common law by judges and juries." *Id.* at 489. So, Justice Stevens reasoned that one can infer, from the usage of the term in other contexts, that when Congress enacted the Medical Device Act it understood the term "requirement" in that Act as including only positive enactments, not common law duties. Do you find these distinctions persuasive? Or is Justice Stevens being inconsistent? If the latter, what do you think explains the inconsistency?

Since the decision in *Medtronic*, the Supreme Court has moved decisively toward the position that common law duties *are* "requirements." *See* Riegel v. Medtronic, Inc., 552 U.S. 312, 324 (2008) ("Congress is entitled to know what meaning this Court will assign to terms regularly used in its enactments. Absent other indication, reference to a State's 'requirements' includes its common-law duties."); *see also* Bates v. Dow Agrosciences LLC, 544 U.S. 431, 443 (2005). So, the *Cipollone* position seems to have prevailed. Nonetheless, the sorts of common law duties or remedies covered by these sorts of preemption clauses continue to generate uncertainty and litigation. *See Bates, supra; Riegel, supra*; Altria Group, Inc. v. Good, 129 S.Ct. 538 (2008).

**2. *The Presumption Against Preemption and Express Preemption Clauses*—**Both Justice Stevens' *Cipollone* plurality opinion and Justice Blackmun's partial dissent invoked the "presumption against preemption" derived from *Rice v. Santa Fe Elevator* (pp. 307–310, *supra*) to read the express preemption clause in the 1969 Public Health Cigarette Smoking Act narrowly. The difference between Justices Stevens and Blackmun seems to turn on just how much ambiguity they found in the Act: Justice Stevens thought that any "requirement or prohibition . . . imposed under State law" clearly includes common law duties, but the presumption against preemption called for the Court to resolve against preemption any ambiguity regarding whether a particular common law duty operates "with respect to the advertisement or promotion of cigarettes." Justice Blackmun viewed the phrase "requirement or prohibition" as itself ambiguous with respect to whether common law duties are covered, such that the presumption against preemption required the Court to read that phrase as including only positive enactments.

Justice Scalia had a very different understanding of the principle that *Rice* and other "presumption against preemption" cases actually stand for. In his view, the so-called presumption against preemption is nothing more than a specific expression of the commonplace admonition that judges should be reluctant to read things into a statute that aren't explicit in the text. In the preemption context, that reluctance to depart from the text implies that judges should eschew a finding of implied preemption unless such preemption is extraordinarily clear. But, Justice Scalia reasoned, when a statute contains an express preemption clause, there is no need for courts to place any thumb on the scale against a finding of preemption. Rather, he insisted, when interpreting express preemption clauses, courts should take the approach that is "customary for statutory provisions in general: Their language should be given its ordinary meaning."

Is that correct? As a matter of existing doctrine and precedent, is Justice Scalia's position consistent with language in prior cases, like *Rice*? It is true that those cases involve implied rather than express preemption. But don't those cases also suggest that special concerns are at stake when the question is whether a federal statute supersedes state legislation "in a field which the States have traditionally occupied"? Why all the special language about a "presumption against preemption" if this "presumption" is nothing more that a particular instantiation of the more general principle that courts should be reluctant to read implied terms into statutes? Moreover, as Justice Blackmun pointed out, the Court has invoked clear statement rules in other contexts to interpret express statutory provisions narrowly when issues of state sovereignty and autonomy were at stake. Why wouldn't the logic of those opinions support a broader construction of the presumption against preemption?

Justice Scalia had a ready answer: While the Court has developed "clear statement rules" to protect federalism (and other values) in other contexts, the preemption context is different because the Court has recognized the legitimacy of finding implied preemption, at least in some cases. Does it make sense to apply a presumption against preemption to an express preemption clause if it is sometimes legitimate to find preemption even in the absence of express statutory text? According to Justice Scalia, the answer must be no. To see his point, consider the question whether it is legitimate for a court to find implied preemption if the statute contains an express preemption clause. If it is, then we have the anomalous result that a court may refuse to give the express preemption clause its most natural reading in order to avoid preempting more state law, but can nonetheless find implied preemption without any express textual indication from Congress that such preemption was intended. This seems bizarre, as "the same result so prophylactically protected from careless explicit provision can be achieved by sheer implication, with no express statement of intent at all." On the other hand, if the inclusion of an express preemption clause precludes (by *expressio unius* logic) any inquiry into implied preemption, then, as Justice Scalia explained, a "statute that says anything about preemption must say everything; and it must do so with great exactitude," which creates a significant disincentive for Congress ever to say anything about preemption. That result is undesirable if we would generally prefer Congress, rather than the courts, to decide the appropriate degree of federal preemption of state law. Do your find this critique of the *Cipollone* plurality's version of the presumption against preemption compelling, or is the dilemma posed by Justice Scalia illusory? Could a court reasonably adopt a presumption against preemption when interpreting an express preemption clause, while still holding open the possibility that the court might find implied preemption of certain state laws that don't fall within the scope of that clause?

The current state of the doctrine on this point is not altogether clear. Seven of the nine Justices in *Cipollone* agreed that the presumption against preemption applies to the interpretation of express preemption clauses, and this finding has been reaffirmed in other cases, despite the continued objections of Justices Scalia and Thomas. *See* Altria Group, Inc. v. Good, 129 S.Ct. 538, 543 (2008); Bates v. Dow Agrosciences, LLC, 544 U.S. 431, 449 (2005); *see also id.* at 458–59 (Thomas, J., concurring in the judgment in part and dissenting in part). These opinions, however, exist alongside others in which the Court has interpreted express preemption clauses broadly, without noting, or apparently applying, a presumption against preemption. *See* Riegel v. Medtronic, Inc., 552 U.S. 312 (2008); *id.* at 333 (Ginsburg, J., dissenting); *Altria*, 129 S.Ct. at 556–58 (2008) (Thomas, J., dissenting) (claiming that "[s]ince *Cipollone*, the Court's reliance on the presumption against pre-emption has waned in the express pre-emption context," citing post-*Cipollone* cases in which the Court had allegedly construed express preemption clauses without applying a presumption against preemption). Notwithstanding Justice Thomas's assertion, however, the *Altria* majority expressly reaffirmed the view that "[w]hen addressing questions of *express or implied* pre-emption, [courts should begin] 'with the assumption that the historic police powers of the States [are] not to be superseded by the Federal Act unless that was the clear and manifest purpose of Congress.' " 129 S.Ct. at 543 (quoting *Rice v. Santa Fe Elevator*) (emphasis added). It appears, then, that the doctrine on this point is still contested.

**3.   *The Presumption Against Preemption and Implied Preemption***—How do doctrines of implied preemption—conflict, obstacle, and field preemption—square with the presumption against preemption? If *Rice* requires evidence of a "clear and manifest purpose" to preempt, can that standard *ever* be satisfied by implication? In a recent concurring opinion, Justice Thomas suggested that it could not, and he announced that he would no longer apply what he called the "purposes and objectives" version of implied preemption. *See* Wyeth v. Levine, 129 S.Ct. 1187, 1205 (2009) (Thomas, J., concurring in the judgment). He began by noting that the Supremacy Clause permits state law to be displaced only by "[t]his Constitution, and the Laws ... made in Pursuance thereof; and all Treaties made, or which shall be made, under the Authority of the United States," U.S. Const. art. VI, cl. 2. *See* 129 S.Ct. at 1206. Starting from the premise that "Laws ... made in pursuance thereof" refers to duly enacted statutes, Justice Thomas reasoned that "purposes and objectives" preemption displaces state law based on the "interpretation of broad federal policy objectives, legislative history, or generalized notions of congressional purposes that are not contained within the text of federal law." *Id.* at 1207. "Congressional and agency musings," he added, "do not satisfy the Art. I, § 7 requirements for enactment of federal law and, therefore, do not preempt state law under the Supremacy Clause." *Id.* Such preemption, moreover, ignores the fact that federal regulatory statutes frequently represent compromises that do not pursue their purposes "at all costs." *Id.* at 1215.

Does Justice Thomas overread the Supremacy Clause? *Compare* Bradford R. Clark, *Separation of Powers as a Safeguard of Federalism*, 79 Tex. L. Rev. 1321 (2001) (arguing that the Supremacy Clause implements the political safeguards of federalism, in part, by permitting statutory preemption only when "the laws of the United States ... made in pursuance [of the Constitution]" affirmatively so require), *with* Peter L. Strauss, *The Perils of Theory*, 83 Notre Dame L. Rev. 1567, 1568–73 (2008) (arguing that the text and history of the clause do not support such an expansive reading). Might Justice Thomas's argument be understood as suggesting that even if one doesn't subscribe to textualism generally, the political safeguards of federalism—as reflected in Article I, § 7 and reinforced by the Supremacy Clause—counsel against judicial reliance on purposive interpretation to find preemption? Even if Justice Thomas's reasoning would rule out *obstacle preemption* and perhaps even *field preemption* (*see* p. 307, *supra*), would his approach eliminate *conflict preemption*, which applies in cases in which the application of a state law would squarely conflict with the requirements of a federal statute? *See* Caleb Nelson, *Preemption*, 86 Va. L. Rev. 225, 231 (2000) (arguing that the original understanding of the Supremacy Clause supports conflict preemption).

### *4. The Presumption Against Preemption and Federalism Values*

—The "state sovereignty" clear statement rules in cases like *Gregory v. Ashcroft* were justified in part as safeguarding values associated with federalism. The presumption against preemption is typically defended in similar terms. Yet many of the Justices who are enthusiastic proponents of the clear statement rules applied in *Gregory* and similar cases take a narrower view of the presumption against preemption, while many of the Justices who embrace the presumption against preemption are critical of the clear statement rules announced in cases like *Gregory*. Why is this?

One possibility is that despite the rhetoric of federalism and state sovereignty, decisions in these cases are driven more by Justices' views of the desirability of civil litigation as a remedy for social harms. In cases like *Gregory*, the "pro-federalism" canon of construction is also pro-defendant, in that it operates to protect a certain class of defendants (state governments) from private antidiscrimination suits brought under federal law. By contrast, the "pro-federalism" presumption against preemption usually favors civil plaintiffs, because in the majority of these cases the issue is whether a federal regulatory scheme preempts private remedies that would otherwise be available under state law. Perhaps for many Justices, federalism concerns take a back seat to views about the virtues and vices of civil litigation. There is some empirical evidence consistent with this view. *See* Frank B. Cross & Emerson H. Tiller, *The Three Faces of Federalism: An Empirical Assessment of Supreme Court Federalism Jurisprudence*, 73 S. Cal. L. Rev. 741, 757–62 (2000); Michael S. Greve & Jonathan Klick, *Preemption in the Rehnquist Court: A Preliminary Empirical Assessment*, 14 Sup. Ct. Econ. Rev. 43, 79–85 (2006); David B. Spence & Paula Murray, *The Law, Economics, and Politics of Federal Preemption Jurisprudence: A Quantitative Analysis*, 87 Cal. L. Rev. 1125, 1129–30, 1184 (1999).

Another possibility might be that although these substantive canons all protect "federalism," the presumption against preemption and the federalism clear statement rules in cases like *Gregory* actually promote quite different federalism values. One set of arguments in favor of a federal system focuses on how such a system can foster a kind of efficient decentralization that produces better public policy. On this view, state autonomy is important primarily because it facilitates responsiveness to local concerns, sensitivity to heterogeneous policy preferences, policy innovation (states as "laboratories of democracy"), or a healthy competition to produce desirable policies (a "race to the top"). (*See* pp. 300–301, *supra.*) If that's why federalism is desirable, then the case for reading federal statutes narrowly to avoid preemption of state law is attractive because the imposition of uniform national rules would undermine these benefits of decentralized policymaking. But on that account of federalism's virtues, it is not clear why the Court should adopt clear statement rules that shield state governments from liability under otherwise applicable federal statutes that do not displace the state's regulatory initiatives. There is, however, another kind of argument in favor of federalism. Perhaps the maintenance of states as strong, independent sovereigns is important because, as Justice O'Connor puts it in *Gregory*, "[i]n the tension between federal and state power lies the promise of liberty." If one is chiefly concerned with maintaining sovereign states as a counterbalance to federal power, the imposition of federal law *on* states—the sort of thing disfavored by clear statement rules of the type applied in *Gregory*—may be of greater concern than the expansion of federal law into areas traditionally regulated *by* states. After all, when a federal statute preempts state law in some area, the federal government has not interfered with the internal operation of state governments, or done anything that directly undermines the ability of the states' citizens to organize their state governments as they please. Are these distinctions convincing? Do you think they explain the Justices' voting patterns in these cases?

## C. The Rule of Lenity

Some substantive canons put a thumb on the scale in favor of certain classes of individuals—often those thought to be particularly vulnerable, or otherwise worthy of special protection. Perhaps the oldest and most well-established canon of this sort is the "rule of lenity," according to which ambiguities in criminal statutes are to be construed in favor of defendants. In *McBoyle*, Justice Holmes implicitly invoked the rule of lenity when he emphasized that, in the context of criminal prohibitions, "it is reasonable that a fair warning should be given to the world in language that the common world will understand, of what the law intends to do if a certain line is passed," and that "[t]o make the warning fair, so far as possible the line should be clear." (*See* p. 220, *supra*.) If you have covered *Smith v. United States* in Chapter One (pp. 127–136, *supra*), you may recall that Justice Scalia's dissent invoked the rule of lenity to argue that the majority erred by reading a criminal prohibition on "us[ing] a firearm" broadly when there was an alternative plausible interpretation of that phrase. The next case, *United States v. Bass*, provides another example of the rule of lenity in action.

---

## United States v. Bass

Supreme Court of the United States
404 U.S. 336 (1971)

■ Mr. Justice Marshall delivered the opinion of the Court.

Respondent was convicted in the Southern District of New York of possessing firearms in violation of Title VII of the Omnibus Crime Control and Safe Streets Act of 1968, 18 U.S.C.App. § 1202(a). In pertinent part, that statute reads:

"Any person who—

(1) has been convicted by a court of the United States or of a State or any political subdivision thereof of a felony . . . and who receives, possesses, or transports in commerce or affecting commerce . . . any firearm shall be fined not more than $10,000 or imprisoned for not more than two years, or both."[12]

---

12. Section 1202(a) reads in full:

"Any person who—

"(1) has been convicted by a court of the United States or of a State or any political subdivision thereof of a felony, or

"(2) has been discharged from the Armed Forces under dishonorable conditions, or

"(3) has been adjudged by a court of the United States or of a State or any political subdivision thereof of being mentally incompetent, or

The evidence showed that respondent, who had previously been convicted of a felony in New York State, possessed on separate occasions a pistol and then a shotgun. There was no allegation in the indictment and no attempt by the prosecution to show that either firearm had been possessed "in commerce or affecting commerce." The Government proceeded on the assumption that § 1202(a)(1) banned all possessions and receipts of firearms by convicted felons, and that no connection with interstate commerce had to be demonstrated in individual cases.

. . . We conclude that § 1202 is ambiguous in the critical respect. Because its sanctions are criminal and because, under the Government's broader reading, the statute would mark a major inroad into a domain traditionally left to the States, we refuse to adopt the broad reading in the absence of a clearer direction from Congress.

## I

Not wishing "to give point to the quip that only when legislative history is doubtful do you go to the statute,"[5] we begin by looking to the text itself. The critical textual question is whether the statutory phrase "in commerce or affecting commerce" applies to "possesses" and "receives" as well as to "transports." If it does, then the Government must prove as an essential element of the offense that a possession, receipt, or transportation was "in commerce or affecting commerce"—a burden not undertaken in this prosecution for possession.

While the statute does not read well under either view, "the natural construction of the language" suggests that the clause "in commerce or affecting commerce" qualifies all three antecedents in the list. Porto Rico Railway Light & Power Co. v. Mor, 253 U.S. 345, 348 (1920). Since "in commerce or affecting commerce" undeniably applies to at least one antecedent, and since it makes sense with all three, the more plausible construction here is that it in fact applies to all three. But although this is a beginning, the argument is certainly neither overwhelming nor decisive.[6]

---

"(4) having been a citizen of the United States has renounced his citizenship, or

"(5) being an alien is illegally or unlawfully in the United States, and who receives, possesses, or transports in commerce or affecting commerce, after the date of enactment of this Act, any firearm shall be fined not more than $10,000 or imprisoned for not more than two years, or both."

**5.**  Frankfurter, Some Reflections on the Reading of Statutes, 47 Col. L. Rev. 527, 543 (1947).

**6.**  The Government, noting that there is no comma after "transports," argues that the punctuation indicates a congressional intent to limit the qualifying phrase to the last antecedent. But many leading grammarians, while sometimes noting that commas at the end of series can avoid ambiguity, concede that use of such commas is discretionary. See, *e.g.,* B. Evans & C. Evans, A Dictionary of Contemporary American Usage 103 (1957); M. Nicholson, A Dictionary of American–English Usage 94 (1957); R. Copperud, A Dictionary of Usage and Style 94–95 (1964); cf. W. Strunk & E. White, The Elements of Style 1–2 (1959). When grammarians are divided, and surely where they are cheerfully tolerant, we will not attach significance to an omitted comma. It is enough to say that the statute's punctuation is fully consistent with the respondent's interpretation, and that in this case grammatical expertise will not help to clarify the statute's meaning.

In a more significant respect, however, the language of the statute does provide support for respondent's reading. Undeniably, the phrase "in commerce or affecting commerce" is part of the "transports" offense. But if that phrase applies *only* to "transports," the statute would have a curious reach. While permitting transportation of a firearm unless it is transported "in commerce or affecting commerce," the statute would prohibit all possessions of firearms, and both interstate and intrastate receipts. Since virtually all transportations, whether interstate or intrastate, involve an accompanying possession or receipt, it is odd indeed to argue that on the one hand the statute reaches all possessions and receipts, and on the other hand outlaws only interstate transportations. Even assuming that a person can "transport" a firearm under the statute without possessing or receiving it, there is no reason consistent with any discernible purpose of the statute to apply an interstate commerce requirement to the "transports" offense alone. . . .

Nevertheless, the Government argues that its reading is to be preferred because the defendant's narrower interpretation would make Title VII redundant with Title IV of the same Act. Title IV, *inter alia*, makes it a crime for four categories of people—including those convicted of a crime punishable for a term exceeding one year—"to ship or transport any firearm or ammunition in interstate or foreign commerce . . . (or) to receive any firearm or ammunition which has been shipped or transported in interstate or foreign commerce." 18 U.S.C. §§ 922(g) and (h). . . . [But] Title VII indeed does complement Title IV. . . . First, although subsections of the two Titles do address their prohibitions to some of the same people, each statute also reaches substantial groups of people not reached by the other.[7] Secondly, Title VII complements Title IV by punishing a broader

---

[Editor's Note: The Court's discussion is in tension with the grammatical "rule of the last antecedent," which has become an accepted canon of statutory construction. *See* 2A N. Singer, Sutherland on Statutory Construction § 47.33, p. 369 (6th rev. ed. 2000) ("Referential and qualifying words and phrases, where no contrary intention appears, refer solely to the last antecedent").]

**7.** Title VII limits the firearm-related activity of convicted felons, dishonorable discharges from the Armed Services, persons adjudged "mentally incompetent," aliens illegally in the country, and former citizens who have renounced their citizenship. See n. 1, *supra*. A felony is defined as "any offense punishable by imprisonment for a term exceeding one year, but does not include any offense (other than one involving a firearm or explosive) classified as a misdemeanor under the laws of a State and punishable by a term of imprisonment of two years or less. . . ." 18 U.S.C.App. § 1202(c)(2).

Title IV reaches persons "under indictment for, or . . . convicted in any court of, a crime punishable by imprisonment for a term exceeding one year"; fugitives from justice; users or addicts of various drugs; persons adjudicated as "mental defective[s] or . . . committed" to a mental institution. 18 U.S.C. §§ 922(g) and (h).

class of behavior. Even under respondent's view, a Title VII offense is made out if the firearm was possessed or received "in commerce or affecting commerce"; however, Title IV apparently does not reach possessions or intrastate transactions at all, even those with an interstate commerce nexus, but is limited to the sending or receiving of firearms as part of an interstate transportation.

In addition, whatever reading is adopted, Title VII and Title IV are, in part, redundant. The interstate commerce requirement in Title VII minimally applies to transportation. Since Title IV also prohibits convicted criminals from transporting firearms in interstate commerce, the two Titles overlap under both readings. The Government's broader reading of Title VII does not eliminate the redundancy, but simply creates a larger area in which there is no overlap. While the Government would be on stronger ground if its reading were necessary to give Title VII some unique and independent thrust, this is not the case here. . . .

. . . [A]spects of the meager legislative history, however, do provide some significant support for the Government's interpretation. On the Senate floor, Senator Long, who introduced § 1202, described various evils that prompted his statute. These evils included assassinations of public figures and threats to the operation of businesses significant enough in the aggregate to affect commerce. Such evils, we note, would be most thoroughly mitigated by forbidding every possession of any firearm by specified classes of especially risky people, regardless of whether the gun was possessed, received, or transported "in commerce or affecting commerce." In addition, specific remarks of the Senator can be read to state that the amendment reaches the mere possession of guns without any showing of an interstate commerce nexus. But Senator Long never specifically says that no connection with commerce need be shown in the individual case. And nothing in his statements explains why, if an interstate commerce nexus is irrelevant in individual cases, the phrase "in commerce or affecting commerce" is in the statute at all. But even if Senator Long's remarks were crystal clear to us, they were apparently not crystal clear to his congressional colleagues. Meager as the discussion of Title VII was, one of the few Congressmen who discussed the amendment summarized Title VII as "mak(ing) it a Federal crime to take, possess, or receive a firearm across State lines. . . ." 114 Cong.Rec. 16298 (statement of Rep. Pollock).

In short, "the legislative history of [the] Act hardly speaks with that clarity of purpose which Congress supposedly furnishes courts in order to enable them to enforce its true will." Universal Camera Corp. v. NLRB, 340 U.S. 474, 483 (1951). . . . While standing alone, the legislative history might tip in the Government's favor, the respondent explains far better the presence of critical language in the statute. The Government concedes that "the statute is not a model of logic or clarity." After "seiz[ing] every thing from which aid can be derived," United States v. Fisher, 2 Cranch 358, 386 (1805) (Marshall, C.J.), we are left with an ambiguous statute.

II

Given this ambiguity, we adopt the narrower reading: the phrase "in commerce or affecting commerce" is part of all three offenses, and the present conviction must be set aside because the Government has failed to show the requisite nexus with interstate commerce. This result is dictated by two wise principles this Court has long followed.

First, as we have recently reaffirmed, "ambiguity concerning the ambit of criminal statutes should be resolved in favor of lenity." Rewis v. United States, 401 U.S. 808, 812 (1971).... In various ways over the years, we have stated that "when choice has to be made between two readings of what conduct Congress has made a crime, it is appropriate, before we choose the harsher alternative, to require that Congress should have spoken in language that is clear and definite." United States v. Universal C.I.T. Credit Corp., 344 U.S. 218, 221–222 (1952). This principle is founded on two policies that have long been part of our tradition. First, "a fair warning should be given to the world in language that the common world will understand, of what the law intends to do if a certain line is passed. To make the warning fair, so fair as possible the line should be clear." McBoyle v. United States, 283 U.S. 25, 27 (1931) (Holmes, J.).[15] ... Second, because of the seriousness of criminal penalties, and because criminal punishment usually represents the moral condemnation of the community, legislatures and not courts should define criminal activity. This policy embodies "the instinctive distaste against men languishing in prison unless the lawmaker has clearly said they should." H. Friendly, Mr. Justice Frankfurter and the Reading of Statutes, in Benchmarks 196, 209 (1967). Thus, where there is ambiguity in a criminal statute, doubts are resolved in favor of the defendant. Here, we conclude that Congress has not "plainly and unmistakably," United States v. Gradwell, 243 U.S. 476, 485 (1917), made it a federal crime for a convicted felon simply to possess a gun absent some demonstrated nexus with interstate commerce.

There is a second principle supporting today's result: unless Congress conveys its purpose clearly, it will not be deemed to have significantly changed the federal-state balance. Congress has traditionally been reluctant to define as a federal crime conduct readily denounced as criminal by the States.... [W]e will not be quick to assume that Congress has meant to effect a significant change in the sensitive relation between federal and state criminal jurisdiction. In traditionally sensitive areas, such as legislation affecting the federal balance, the requirement of clear statement assures that the legislature has in fact faced, and intended to bring into issue, the critical matters involved in the judicial decision.... In the instant case, the broad construction urged by the Government renders

---

**15.** Holmes prefaced his much-quoted statement with the observation that "it is not likely that a criminal will carefully consider the text of the law before he murders or steals...." But in the case of gun acquisition and possession it is not unreasonable to imagine a citizen attempting to "(steer) a careful course between violation of the statute (and lawful conduct)," United States v. Hood, 343 U.S. 148, 151 (1952)....

traditionally local criminal conduct a matter for federal enforcement and would also involve a substantial extension of federal police resources. . . .

■ [Justice Brennan's opinion concurring in part is omitted].

■ Mr. Justice Blackmun, with whom The Chief Justice, joins, dissenting.

I cannot join the Court's opinion and judgment. . . .

1.   The statute, 18 U.S.C.App. § 1202(a), when it speaks of one "who receives, possesses, or transports in commerce or affecting commerce," although arguably ambiguous and, as the Government concedes, "not a model of logic or clarity," is clear enough. The structure of the vital language and its punctuation make it refer to one who receives, to one who possesses, and to one who transports in commerce. If one wished to say that he would welcome a cat, would welcome a dog, or would welcome a cow that jumps over the moon, he would likely say "I would like to have a cat, a dog, or a cow that jumps over the moon." So it is here.

2.   The meaning the Court implants on the statute is justified only by the addition and interposition of a comma after the word "transports." I perceive no warrant for this judicial transfiguration.

3.   In the very same statute the phrase "after the date of enactment of this Act" is separated by commas and undeniably modifies each of the preceding words, "receives," "possesses," and "transports." [That is, the statute imposes penalties on anyone who "receives, possesses, or transports in commerce or affecting commerce, after the date of enactment, a firearm."] Obviously, then, the draftsman—and the Congress—knew the use of commas for phrase modification. We should give effect to the only meaning attendant upon that use.

4.   The specific finding in 18 U.S.C.App. § 1201[3] clearly demonstrates that Congress was attempting to reach and prohibit every possession of a firearm by a felon; that Congress found that such possession, whether interstate or intrastate, affected interstate commerce; and that Congress did not conclude that intrastate possession was a matter of less concern to it than interstate possession. That finding was unnecessary if Congress also required proof that each receipt or possession of a firearm was in or affected interstate or foreign commerce.

5.   Senator Long's explanatory comments reveal clearly the purpose, the intent, and the extent of the legislation:

"I have prepared an amendment which I will offer at an appropriate time, simply setting forth the fact that anybody who has been convicted of a felony . . . is not permitted to *possess* a firearm. . . .

"It might be well to analyze, for a moment, the logic involved. When a man has been convicted of a felony, unless—as this bill sets

---

**3.**   § 1201. Congressional findings and declaration.

"The Congress hereby finds and declares that the receipt, possession, or transportation of a firearm by felons . . . constitutes—

"(1) a burden on commerce or threat affecting the free flow of commerce. . . ."

forth—he has been expressly pardoned by the President and the pardon states that the person is to be permitted to *possess* firearms in the future, that man would have no right to *possess* firearms. He would be punished criminally if he is found in *possession* of them." 114 Cong.Rec. 13868 (emphasis supplied).

"So Congress simply finds that the *possession* of these weapons by the wrong kind of people is either a burden on commerce or a threat that affects the free flow of commerce."

"You cannot do business in an area, and you certainly cannot do as much of it and do it as well as you would like, if in order to do business you have to go through a street where there are burglars, murderers, and arsonists armed to the teeth against innocent citizens. So the threat certainly affects the free flow of commerce." 114 Cong. Rec. 13869 (emphasis supplied).

[JUSTICE BLACKMUN then canvassed other legislative history, to similar effect.]

... One cannot detect in these remarks any purpose to restrict or limit the type of possession that was being considered for proscription.

6. The Court's construction of § 1202(a), limiting its application to interstate possession and receipt, shrinks the statute into something little more than a duplication of 18 U.S.C. § 922(g) and (h). I cannot ascribe to Congress such a gesture of nonaccomplishment.

I thus conclude that § 1202(a) was intended to and does reach all possessions and receipts of firearms by convicted felons....

---

*1. Rationales for the Rule of Lenity*—As the Court's opinion in *Bass* suggested, one important rationale for the rule of lenity is the idea of fair notice—the notion that an individual should not suffer punishment unless he or she has a fair opportunity to know, and bring his or her behavior into conformity with, the requirements of the law. Recall what Justice Holmes said on this score in *McBoyle* (pp. 219–220, *supra*):

> Although it is not likely that a criminal will carefully consider the text of the law before he murders or steals, it is reasonable that a fair warning should be given to the world in language that the common world will understand, of what the law intends to do if a certain line is passed. To make the warning fair, so far as possible the line should be clear.

But while this fair notice argument has a strong intuitive appeal, isn't it significant that, as Justice Holmes conceded, most potential criminals are unlikely to "carefully consider the text of the law" before engaging in wrongdoing? Isn't this especially unlikely when the interpretation of the text of the statute turns on fine points of grammar, punctuation, or syntax? Moreover, courts applying the rule of lenity typically only conclude that a criminal statute is sufficiently ambiguous after consulting other extrinsic interpretive aids as well, such as dictionaries, legislative history, and prior judicial precedent—materials that potential criminal defendants are even less likely to consult. *See* EINER ELHAUGE, STATUTORY DEFAULT RULES 175–76 (2008). In *Bass*, for example, the disagreement between the majority and dissent involved, among other things, the floor debates surrounding the legislation. If fair notice is the underlying rationale for lenity, should the Court ever impose a criminal punishment whose applicability is not evident from the plain language of the statute itself? *See* United States v. R.L.C., 503 U.S. 291, 307 (1992) (Scalia, J., concurring in the judgment) ("In my view it is not consistent with the rule of lenity to construe a textually ambiguous penal statute against a criminal defendant on the basis of legislative history."). If it is unlikely that "a criminal will carefully consider the text of the law," let alone extrinsic interpretive sources, what purpose does the notice serve? Is it a moral obligation to ensure that the law is readily accessible and comprehensible whether or not it is actually consulted?

The Court in *Bass* suggested a second rationale supporting the rule of lenity: The idea that legislatures should define criminal policy. In that sense, the rule of lenity may operate as something of a nondelegation canon, requiring Congress to decide for itself the elements of an offense and the circumstances surrounding its punishment, rather than leaving it to the courts to determine the contours of criminal law through the elaboration of ambiguous terms. *See, e.g.,* Cass R. Sunstein, *Nondelegation Canons*, 67 U. CHI. L. REV. 315, 332 (2000). Why should there be a greater imperative for Congress to specify all the statutory details for criminal matters than for civil matters? Does the impulse come from the Due Process Clause? Isn't that precise line of demarcation difficult to ascribe to the vague language of that clause? Furthermore, at least one scholar has argued that Congress has delegated to courts the authority to elaborate criminal law since the beginning of the Republic. *See* Dan M. Kahan, *Lenity and Federal Common Law Crimes*, 1994 SUP. CT. REV. 345, 347–48. Professor Kahan argues, moreover, that given the difficulties of foreseeing all of the contingencies that may arise in the life of a statute, such "a regime of delegated criminal lawmaking is ... more effective than one in which Congress is obliged to make criminal law without judicial assistance." *Id.* at 348. If Professor Kahan is correct about the history, does this cast doubt on whether the rule of lenity in fact represents a deeply embedded *constitutional* tradition?

Could there be simpler justification for lenity? From the earliest days of the Republic, the Court has instructed that "penal laws are to be construed strictly." United States v. Wiltberger, 18 U.S. (5 Wheat.) 76, 95 (1820) (Marshall, C.J.). Even at that early date, Chief Justice Marshall was able to describe the rule of lenity as "an ancient maxim," one that "is perhaps not much less old than construction itself." *Id.* Accordingly, in contrast with clear statement rules of more recent invention (such as the federalism canons), the rule of lenity has been part of the background against which Congress has enacted penal statutes throughout our history. *See* Antonin Scalia, *Assorted Canards of Contemporary Legal Analysis*, 40 CASE W. RES. L. REV. 581, 583 (1990) (concluding that the rule of lenity has, through long usage, acquired "a sort of prescriptive validity, since the legislature presumably has [it] in mind when it chooses its language"); *see also, e.g.,* McNary v. Haitian Refugee Ctr., Inc., 498 U.S. 479, 496 (1991) (presuming "that Congress legislates with knowledge of our basic rules of statutory construction"). Does that rationale suffice to justify the rule of lenity, whether or not it serves any antecedent constitutional purpose?

2. ***How Much Work Does the Rule of Lenity Do?***—In cases like *Moskal v. United States* (pp. 116–123, *supra*) and *Smith v. United States* (pp. 127–136, *supra*), the Supreme Court did not apply the rule of lenity, despite significant disagreement among the Justices about the meaning of the statutory text. In *Moskal*, Justice Marshall's opinion for the Court found the relevant statutory term ("falsely made") to be clear in light of the statute's broad purpose to halt trafficking in fraudulent securities— notwithstanding that there was substantial disagreement about the technical meaning of the common law term "falsely made." In *Smith*, the Court chose the broad dictionary definition of the operative phrase ("uses ... a firearm"), even though there was a plausible colloquial understanding of that phrase that would have placed the defendant's conduct outside the reach of the statute. If the Court uses the full panoply of tools at its disposal to resolve ambiguity, does the rule of lenity achieve much? Or is the real problem with the rule of lenity the fact that, in the absence of any agreed-upon metric for clarity, the canon is hopelessly manipulable? Consider then-Judge Scalia's assertion that the rule of lenity "provides little more than atmospherics, since it leaves open the crucial question—almost invariably present—of how much ambiguousness constitutes an ambiguity." United States v. Hansen, 772 F.2d 940, 948 (D.C. Cir. 1985). Is that right? How does this skeptical view square with Justice Scalia's subsequent claim, quoted above, that the rule of lenity has "a sort of prescriptive validity" and that Congress legislates with the rule in mind?

3. ***Other Canons That Protect Particular Classes***—In addition to the rule of lenity, there are other substantive canons that appear designed to favor particular classes of individuals in cases of a dispute with the government. For example, while the rule of lenity says that courts should construe statutory ambiguities narrowly to avoid imposing *criminal* liability, a similar substantive canon instructs courts to construe statutory ambiguities narrowly to avoid imposing *tax* liability. "In case of doubt," the Supreme Court explained in Gould v. Gould, 245 U.S. 151, 153 (1917), tax statutes "are construed most strongly against the Government, and in favor of the citizen." *See also* Hassett v. Welch, 303 U.S. 303, 314 (1938) ("[I]f doubt exists as to the construction of a taxing statute, the doubt should be resolved in favor of the taxpayer..."). But the strength of this canon has been called into doubt by cases asserting that "the words of statutes—including revenue acts—should be interpreted where possible in their ordinary, everyday senses"—apparently without a strong thumb on the scale in favor of the taxpayer. Crane v. Commissioner of Internal Revenue, 331 U.S. 1, 6 (1947).

While the rule of lenity and the *Gould* canon instruct courts to construe statutory ambiguities to avoid imposition of liability, there are also analogous canons that instruct courts to construe statutory ambiguities to favor provision of certain kinds of government *benefits*. For example, the Supreme Court declared in King v. St. Vincent's Hospital, 502 U.S. 215, 220 n.9 (1991), that "provisions for benefits to members of the Armed Services are to be construed in the beneficiaries' favor." *See also* Fishgold v. Sullivan Drydock & Repair Corp., 328 U.S. 275, 285 (1946) (veterans' rights statutes are "to be liberally construed for the benefit of those who left private life to serve their country").

Are those canons on less solid grounding than constitutionally derived maxims such as the federalism canons? Is there any limit to the Court's capacity to create presumptions and clear statement rules? Could it legitimately adopt a canon according to which, absent a clear statement to the contrary, all statutes should be construed in ways that enhance rather than diminish environmental protection? Worker safety? Private ordering? Economic growth? Economic equality? *Compare, e.g.*, Cass R. Sunstein, *Interpreting Statutes in the Regulatory State*, 103 HARV. L. REV. 405, 478 (1989) (arguing that judges can legitimately devise and apply new substantive canons designed to address the pathologies in the legislative process), *with* Eben Moglen & Richard J. Pierce, Jr., *Sunstein's New Canons: Choosing the Fictions of Statutory Interpretation*, 57 U. CHI. L. REV. 1203 (1990) (arguing that such an open-ended mandate would give the judiciary excessive authority and would not be judicially administrable).

**4. The Presumption Against Retroactivity**—The Constitution places few significant restrictions on the enactment of legislation that imposes retroactive civil liability. The Court has, however, adopted the presumption that Congress intends to impose new liability only prospectively, unless the statute clearly indicates the contrary. *See, e.g.*, Johnson v. United States, 529 U.S. 694, 701 (2000) ("Absent a clear statement of that intent, we do not give retroactive effect to statutes burdening private interests."). Recently, the Court has defended the canon as reflecting a constitutional value:

> [T]he antiretroactivity principle finds expression in several provisions of our Constitution. The *Ex Post Facto* Clause flatly prohibits retroactive application of penal legislation. Article I, § 10, cl. 1, prohibits States from passing another type of retroactive legislation, laws "impairing the Obligation of Contracts." The Fifth Amendment's Takings Clause prevents the Legislature (and other government actors) from depriving private persons of vested property rights except for a "public use" and upon payment of "just compensation." The prohibitions on "Bills of Attainder" in Art. I, §§ 9–10, prohibit legislatures from singling out disfavored persons and meting out summary punishment for past conduct. The Due Process Clause also protects the interests in fair notice and repose that may be compromised by retroactive legislation; a justification sufficient to validate a statute's prospective application under the Clause may not suffice to warrant its retroactive application.

Landgraf v. USI Film Prods., 511 U.S. 244, 266 (1994) (internal citations and quotation marks omitted).

Understood in those terms, is the anti-retroactivity canon legitimate? What about the objection, similar to the objection made against the claim that the Constitution endorses "federalism," that the Constitution does not adopt a norm against retroactivity in the abstract, but does so in concrete contexts through specific means? (*Cf.* pp. 299–300, *supra*.) For example, although the Court in *Landgraf* cited the Ex Post Facto Clause as one of the sources of the norm against retroactivity, it is well established that the Ex Post Facto Clause prohibits only the imposition of retroactive *criminal* liability. *See, e.g.*, Carpenter v. Pennsylvania, 58 U.S. (17 How.) 456, 463 (1854). To tease from that clause a freestanding anti-retroactivity norm is to ignore the fact that the adopters chose to embrace that norm only as applied to criminal law. See John F. Manning, *Clear Statement Rules and the Constitution*, 110 Colum. L. Rev. 399 (2010).

Whatever one's view of the Court's abstraction of constitutional values, the anti-retroactivity canon may find justification on grounds similar to those on which some defend the rule of lenity. The Court has from the earliest days of the Republic assumed that legislation is by nature prospective, unless it specifies otherwise. *See, e.g.*, Reynolds v. McArthur, 27 U.S. (2 Pet.) 417, 434 (1829) (Marshall, C.J.) ("It is a principle which has always been held sacred in the United States, that laws by which human action is to be regulated, look forwards, not backwards; and are never to be construed retrospectively unless the language of the act shall render such construction indispensable."); United States v. Heth, 7 U.S. (3 Cranch) 399, 413 (1806) (seriatim opinion of Paterson, J.) ("Words in a statute ought not to have a retrospective operation, unless they are so clear, strong, and imperative, that no other meaning can be annexed to them, or unless the intention of the legislature cannot be otherwise satisfied."). If, in fact, Congress enacts statutes against the backdrop of the Court's well-settled canons of construction, does the norm against retroactivity necessarily depend upon its defensibility as a constitutional norm?

## D. Problems of Scope and Application of Substantive Canons

Throughout this section, we have confronted questions concerning the proper scope and application of various substantive canons. The next principal case, *Spector v. Norwegian Cruise Line*, raises a particularly challenging set of such questions.

Before turning to *Spector*, it is useful to provide a preliminary discussion about a pair of cases that the *Spector* opinions discuss at some length: Zadvydas v. Davis, 533 U.S. 678 (2001), and Clark v. Martinez, 543 U.S. 371 (2005). Both *Zadvydas* and *Clark* involved the interpretation of a provision of the immigration laws, 8 U.S.C. § 1231, which authorizes the detention of aliens who have been ordered removed from the United States. Ordinarily, the government may detain an alien for up to 90 days prior to deportation. If the government is not able to remove an alien within the

90–day period (for example, if the alien's life would be at risk if he were sent back to his or her home country, or if there is no country willing to receive the alien), the government may continue to detain the alien if, but only if, the Attorney General determines that the alien is "a risk to the community or unlikely to comply with the order of removal," 8 U.S.C. § 1231(a)(6).

But just how long can the government detain a removable alien pursuant to § 1231(a)(6)? Does the statute authorize *indefinite* detention of such an alien? In *Zadvydas*, the Court considered that question in the context of a *resident alien* who had been ordered deported for serious criminal offenses, but who had not been deported because there was no country willing to receive him. The government argued that because § 1231(a)(6) did not contain any time limit on detention, it could hold the alien indefinitely. In a 5–4 decision, the Supreme Court rejected that claim. Justice Breyer's majority opinion relied principally on the constitutional avoidance canon, explaining that "[a] statute permitting indefinite detention of an alien would raise a serious constitutional problem" under the Due Process Clause. "In our view," the Court reasoned, "the statute, read in light of the Constitution's demands, limits an alien's post-removal-period detention to a period reasonably necessary to bring about that alien's removal from the United States. It does not permit indefinite detention." 533 U.S. at 689. The Court later noted that a "reasonably necessary" detention period should presumptively be six months. *Id.* at 701.

In reaching this holding, however, the Court had to deal with a prior case, Shaughnessy v. United States ex rel. Mezei, 345 U.S. 206 (1953), which had upheld as constitutional the indefinite detention of an alien who was denied entry into the United States and was being held on Ellis Island because the government could not find another country to accept him. The *Zadvydas* Court explained that *Mezei* was not controlling because of the distinction, which "runs throughout immigration law," between "an alien who has effected an entry into the United States and one who has never entered...." 533 U.S. at 693. Importantly, an alien can be physically (and lawfully) present in the United States without legally "entering": Under certain circumstances, the government will "parole" an alien into the country (that is, permit physical entry) but for legal purposes such aliens, as well as aliens stopped at the border, are treated as if they are outside the geographic borders of the United States. So, while the *Zadvydas* Court conceded that there would be no constitutional problem with indefinitely detaining an alien who had been paroled into the country or stopped at the border, "once an alien enters the country, the legal circumstance changes, for the Due Process Clause applies to all 'persons' within the United States, including aliens, whither their presence here is lawful, unlawful, temporary, or permanent."

Justice Scalia (joined by Justice Thomas) and Justice Kennedy (joined by Chief Justice Rehnquist, and joined in part by Justices Scalia and Thomas) dissented. The dissenters argued that the majority's application of the avoidance canon was deeply flawed in two respects: First, the statutory text imposed no time limit on the detention period. Thus, the dissenters concluded that the majority's reading of the statute was simply implausible. Second, cases like *Mezei*—which, according to the dissenters, the majority failed to plausibly distinguish—made clear that there is no constitutional problem with the indefinite detention of aliens prior to their removal.

*Clark v. Martinez* involved an application of § 1231(a)(6) to an alien whose circumstances were analogous to those involved in *Mezei*. In particular, *Clark* involved the detention of two Cubans who had arrived in the United States during the 1980 Mariel boatlift (in which approximately 125,000 Cubans, with the permission of President Fidel Castro, departed Cuba in small boats and arrived in Florida without visas). These two men, like many other Mariel refugees, had been paroled into the United States, but had never lawfully entered. They were subsequently convicted of a number of serious criminal offenses and ordered removed from the United States. Cuba, however, would not receive them, and the aliens were then detained pursuant to § 1231(a)(6). The detainees argued that, under *Zadvydas*, their detention was subject to a presumptive six-month limitation period. In a 7–2 decision, the Supreme Court agreed.

Perhaps surprisingly, the Court's opinion was written by Justice Scalia, who had dissented in *Zadvydas*. Despite the fact that Justice Scalia thought *Zadvydas* was wrongly decided, he concluded that it was nonetheless controlling precedent. Justice Scalia's majority opinion in *Clark* reasoned that once the Court had interpreted § 1231(a)(6) as containing an implicit time limit on detention prior to removal, that interpretation must govern *all* cases covered by the statute. The fact that the indefinite detention of non-admitted aliens would not raise a serious constitutional concern, Justice Scalia explained,

> cannot justify giving the *same* detention provision a different meaning when such aliens are involved. It is not at all unusual to give a statute's ambiguous language a limiting construction called for by one of the statute's applications, even though other of the statute's applications, standing alone, would not support the same limitation. The lowest common denominator, as it were, must govern.

*Clark*, 543 U.S. at 380. *Clark* further elaborated that, "when deciding which of two plausible statutory constructions to adopt, a court must consider the necessary consequences of its choice. If one of them would raise a multitude of constitutional problems, the other should prevail—whether or not those constitutional problems pertain to the particular litigant before the Court." *Id.* at 380–81.

Justice Thomas, joined in part by Chief Justice Rehnquist, dissented. Justice Thomas (on this point writing only for himself) attacked the majority's "lowest common denominator" principle as inconsistent with the Court's prior case law, with the history of the constitutional avoidance canon, and with common sense. In Justice Thomas's view, the correct approach is "simply [to] read ambiguous statutes to avoid as-applied constitutional doubts only if those doubts are present in the case before the Court." *Id.* at 399 (Thomas, J., dissenting). Justice Thomas would allow courts to interpret ambiguous statutes as becoming inoperative when they approach constitutional limits, and he insisted that this is perfectly consistent with the avoidance canon. He argued that "[e]very application of that canon, by rejecting a plausible interpretation of a statute, reads the statute to be inoperative to the extent it raises a constitutional doubt or 'limit.'" *Id.* at 400. Furthermore, Justice Thomas warned, the Court's "lowest common denominator" approach is an invitation to unwarranted judicial activism, in which courts "limit the application of statutes wholesale by searching for hypothetical unconstitutional applications of them—or, worse yet, hypothetical constitutional *doubts*—despite the absence of any facial constitutional problem...." *Id.*

Although Justice Thomas was alone in attacking the majority's approach in *Clark*, barely six months after the *Clark* decision came down the Supreme Court revisited the issue—and seemed to take a somewhat different position—in *Spector v. Norwegian Cruise Line*. In addition to this issue, *Spector* raised important questions about how courts define the scope of the substantive canons they apply—an issue that has come up in our discussion of other substantive canons of construction, such as the presumption against preemption (*see* pp. 322–325, *supra*). *Spector* can be a confusing case not only because of the complexity of these interpretive issues, but also because of the number of opinions: just figuring out which legal propositions command a majority of the Court can be something of a challenge. As you read the case, try to disentangle the various related but distinct questions the Court has to address, and note the different coalitions of Justices on these different issues.

---

## Spector v. Norwegian Cruise Line, Ltd.

Supreme Court of the United States
545 U.S. 119 (2005)

■ JUSTICE KENNEDY announced the judgment of the Court and delivered the opinion of the Court with respect to Parts I, II–A–1, and II–B–2, an opinion with respect to Parts II–A–2, II–B–1, II–B–3, and III–B, in which JUSTICE STEVENS and JUSTICE SOUTER join, and an opinion with respect to Part III–A, in which JUSTICE STEVENS, JUSTICE SOUTER, and JUSTICE THOMAS join.

This case presents the question whether Title III of the Americans with Disabilities Act of 1990 (ADA) applies to foreign-flag cruise ships in United States waters. The Court of Appeals for the Fifth Circuit held Title III did not apply because of a presumption, which it sought to derive from this Court's case law, that, absent a clear indication of congressional intent, general statutes do not apply to foreign-flag ships....

I

The respondent Norwegian Cruise Line Ltd. (NCL), a Bermuda Corporation with a principal place of business in Miami, Florida, operates cruise ships that depart from, and return to, ports in the United States. The ships are essentially floating resorts. They provide passengers with staterooms or cabins, food, and entertainment. The cruise ships stop at different ports of call where passengers may disembark. Most of the passengers on these cruises are United States residents; under the terms and conditions of the tickets, disputes between passengers and NCL are to be governed by United States law; and NCL relies upon extensive advertising in the United States to promote its cruises and increase its revenues.

Despite the fact that the cruises are operated by a company based in the United States, serve predominantly United States residents, and are in most other respects United States-centered ventures, almost all of NCL's cruise ships are registered in other countries, flying so-called flags of convenience. The two NCL cruise ships that are the subject of the present litigation, the Norwegian Sea and the Norwegian Star, are both registered in the Bahamas.

The petitioners are disabled individuals and their companions who purchased tickets in 1998 or 1999 for round-trip cruises on the Norwegian Sea or the Norwegian Star, with departures from Houston, Texas. Naming NCL as the defendant, the petitioners filed a class action in the United States District Court for the Southern District of Texas on behalf of all persons similarly situated. They sought declaratory and injunctive relief under Title III of the ADA, which prohibits discrimination on the basis of disability. The petitioners asserted that cruise ships are covered both by Title III's prohibition on discrimination in places of "public accommodation," and by its prohibition on discrimination in "specified public transportation services." Both provisions require covered entities to make "reasonable modifications in policies, practices, or procedures" to accommodate disabled individuals and require removal of "architectural barriers, and communication barriers that are structural in nature" where such removal is "readily achievable."

... The Court of Appeals for the Fifth Circuit ... reasoned that our cases, particularly Benz v. Compania Naviera Hidalgo, S. A., 353 U.S. 138 (1957), and McCulloch v. Sociedad Nacional de Marineros de Honduras, 372 U.S. 10 (1963), stand for the proposition that general statutes do not apply to foreign-flag vessels in United States territory absent a clear indication of congressional intent.... Title III does not contain a specific provision mandating its application to foreign-flag vessels....

## II

### A

#### 1

Title III of the ADA prohibits discrimination against the disabled in the full and equal enjoyment of public accommodations and public transportation services....

Although the statutory definitions of "public accommodation" and "specified public transportation" do not expressly mention cruise ships, there can be no serious doubt that the NCL cruise ships in question fall within both definitions under conventional principles of interpretation. The Court of Appeals for the Fifth Circuit, nevertheless, held that Title III does not apply to foreign-flag cruise ships in United States waters because the statute has no clear statement or explicit text mandating coverage for these ships. This Court's cases, particularly *Benz* and *McCulloch,* do hold, in some circumstances, that a general statute will not apply to certain aspects of the internal operations of foreign vessels temporarily in United States waters, absent a clear statement. The broad clear statement rule adopted by the Court of Appeals, however, would apply to every facet of the business and operations of foreign-flag ships. That formulation is inconsistent with the Court's case law and with sound principles of statutory interpretation.

2

This Court has long held that general statutes are presumed to apply to conduct that takes place aboard a foreign-flag vessel in United States territory if the interests of the United States or its citizens, rather than interests internal to the ship, are at stake.... The general rule that United States statutes apply to foreign-flag ships in United States territory is subject only to a narrow exception. Absent a clear statement of congressional intent, general statutes may not apply to foreign-flag vessels insofar as they regulate matters that involve only the internal order and discipline of the vessel, rather than the peace of the port. This qualification derives from the understanding that, as a matter of international comity, "all matters of discipline and all things done on board which affec[t] only the vessel or those belonging to her, and [do] not involve the peace or dignity of the country, or the tranquility of the port, should be left by the local government to be dealt with by the authorities of the nation to which the vessel belonged." Wildenhus's Case, 120 U.S. 1, 12 (1887). This exception to the usual presumption, however, does not extend beyond matters of internal order and discipline. "[I]f crimes are committed on board [a foreign-flag vessel] of a character to disturb the peace and tranquility of the country to which the vessel has been brought, the offenders have never by comity or usage been entitled to any exemption from the operation of the local laws." *Ibid.*

The two cases in recent times in which the presumption against applying general statutes to foreign vessels' internal affairs has been invoked, *Benz* and *McCulloch*, concern labor relations. The Court held that the general terms of the National Labor Relations Act (NLRA) did not govern the respective rights and duties of a foreign ship and its crew because the NLRA standards would interfere with the foreign vessel's internal affairs in those circumstances. These cases recognized a narrow rule, applicable only to statutory duties that implicate the internal order of the foreign vessel rather than the welfare of American citizens.... The Court held the NLRA inapplicable to labor relations between a foreign vessel and its foreign crew not because foreign ships are generally exempt from the NLRA, but because the particular application of the NLRA would interfere with matters that concern only the internal operations of the ship.

In contrast, the Court held that the NLRA is fully applicable to labor relations between a foreign vessel and American longshoremen because this relationship, unlike the one between a vessel and its own crew, does not implicate a foreign ship's internal order and discipline. Longshoremen v. Ariadne Shipping Co., 397 U.S. 195, 198–201 (1970).

This narrow clear statement rule is supported by sound principles of statutory construction. It is reasonable to presume Congress intends no interference with matters that are primarily of concern only to the ship and the foreign state in which it is registered. It is also reasonable, however, to presume Congress does intend its statutes to apply to entities in United States territory that serve, employ, or otherwise affect American citizens, or that affect the peace and tranquility of the United States, even if those entities happen to be foreign-flag ships.

Cruise ships flying foreign flags of convenience offer public accommodations and transportation services to over 7 million United States residents annually, departing from and returning to ports located in the United States. Large numbers of disabled individuals, many of whom have mobility impairments that make other kinds of vacation travel difficult, take advantage of these cruises or would like to do so. To hold there is no Title III protection for disabled persons who seek to use the amenities of foreign cruise ships would be a harsh and unexpected interpretation of a statute designed to provide broad protection for the disabled. The clear statement rule adopted by the Court of Appeals for the Fifth Circuit, moreover, would imply that other general federal statutes—including, for example, Title II of the Civil Rights Act of 1964—would not apply aboard foreign cruise ships in United States waters. A clear statement rule with this sweeping application is unlikely to reflect congressional intent.

The relevant category for which the Court demands a clear congressional statement, then, consists not of all applications of a statute to foreign-flag vessels but only those applications that would interfere with the foreign vessel's internal affairs. This proposition does not mean the clear statement rule is irrelevant to the ADA, however. If Title III by its terms does impose duties that interfere with a foreign-flag cruise ship's internal affairs, the lack of a clear congressional statement can mean that those specific applications of Title III are precluded....

## B

### 1

The precise content of the category "internal affairs" (or, as it is variously denoted in the case law, "internal order" or "internal operations") is difficult to define with precision. There is, moreover, some ambiguity in our cases as to whether the relevant category of activities is restricted to matters that affect only the internal order of the ship when there is no effect on United States interests, or whether the clear statement rule further comes into play if the predominant effect of a statutory requirement is on a foreign ship's internal affairs but the requirement also promotes the welfare of United States residents or territory. We need not attempt to define the relevant protected category with precision. It suffices to observe that the guiding principles in determining whether the clear statement rule is triggered are the desire for international comity and the presumed lack of interest by the territorial sovereign in matters that bear no substantial relation to the peace and tranquility of the port.

It is plain that Title III might impose any number of duties on cruise ships that have nothing to do with a ship's internal affairs. . . . The petitioners allege the respondent charged disabled passengers higher fares and required disabled passengers to pay special surcharges; maintained evacuation programs and equipment in locations not accessible to disabled individuals; required disabled individuals, but not other passengers, to waive any potential medical liability and to travel with a companion; and reserved the right to remove from the ship any disabled individual whose presence endangers the "comfort" of other passengers. The petitioners also allege more generally that [the respondent] "failed to make reasonable modifications in policies, practices, and procedures" necessary to ensure the petitioners' full enjoyment of the services the respondent offered. These are bare allegations, and their truth is not conceded. We express no opinion on the factual support for those claims. We can say, however, that none of these alleged Title III violations implicate any requirement that would interfere with the internal affairs and management of a vessel as our cases have employed that term.

At least one subset of the petitioners' allegations, however, would appear to involve requirements that might be construed as relating to the internal affairs of foreign-flag cruise ships. These allegations concern physical barriers to access on board. For example, according to the petitioners, most of the cabins on [the respondent's] cruise ships, including the most attractive cabins in the most desirable locations, are not accessible to disabled passengers. The petitioners also allege that the ships' coamings—the raised edges around their doors—make many areas of the ships inaccessible to mobility-impaired passengers who use wheelchairs or scooters. Removal of these and other access barriers, the petitioners suggest, may be required by Title III's structural barrier removal requirement.

Although these physical barriers affect the passengers as well as the ship and its crew, the statutory requirement could mandate a permanent and significant alteration of a physical feature of the ship—that is, an element of basic ship design and construction. If so, these applications of the barrier removal requirement likely would interfere with the internal affairs of foreign ships. A permanent and significant modification to a ship's physical structure goes to fundamental issues of ship design and construction, and it might be impossible for a ship to comply with all the requirements different jurisdictions might impose. The clear statement rule would most likely come into play if Title III were read to require permanent and significant structural modifications to foreign vessels. It is quite a different question, however, whether Title III would require this. The Title III requirements that might impose permanent and substantial changes to a ship's architecture and design, are, like all of Title III's requirements, subject to the statute's own specific limitations and qualifications. These limitations may make resort to the clear statement rule unnecessary. . . .

III

A

. . . If Title III did impose a duty that required cruise ships to make permanent and significant structural modifications . . . , or if the statute otherwise interfered with a foreign ship's internal affairs, the clear statement rule recognized in *Benz* and *McCulloch* would come into play. . . . The Title III requirement in question, however, would still apply to domestic cruise ships, and Title III requirements having nothing to do with internal affairs would continue to apply to domestic and foreign ships alike.

This application-by-application use of the internal affairs clear statement rule is consistent with how the rule has traditionally operated. In *Benz* and *McCulloch*, the Court concluded that the NLRA did not apply to labor relations between a foreign-flag ship and its foreign crew because of interference with the foreign ships' internal affairs. In *Ariadne Shipping*, however, the Court held that the NLRA does apply to labor relations between a foreign-flag ship and American longshoremen. *Ariadne Shipping* acknowledged the clear statement rule invoked in *Benz* and *McCulloch* but held that the "considerations that informed the Court's construction of the statute in [those cases] are clearly inapplicable" to the question whether the statute applies to foreign ships' labor relations with American longshoremen. *Ariadne Shipping* held that the longshoremen's "short-term, irregular and casual connection with the [foreign] vessels plainly belied any involvement on their part with the ships' 'internal discipline and order.' " Therefore, application of the NLRA to foreign ships' relations with American longshoremen "would have threatened no interference in the internal affairs of foreign-flag ships." If the clear statement rule restricts some applications of the NLRA to foreign ships (*e.g.*, labor relations with the foreign crew), but not others (*e.g.*, labor relations with American longshoremen), it follows that the case-by-case application is also required under Title III of the ADA. The rule, where it is even necessary to invoke it, would restrict some applications of Title III to foreign ships (*e.g.*, certain structural barrier modification requirements), but not others (*e.g.*, the prohibition on discriminatory ticket pricing).

The internal affairs clear statement rule is an implied limitation on otherwise unambiguous general terms of the statute. It operates much like the principle that general statutes are construed not to apply extraterritorially, EEOC v. Arabian American Oil Co., 499 U.S. 244, 260 (1991), or the rule that general statutes are presumed not to impose monetary liability on nonconsenting States, Atascadero State Hospital v. Scanlon, 473 U.S. 234 (1985). Implied limitation rules avoid applications of otherwise unambiguous statutes that would intrude on sensitive domains in a way that Congress is unlikely to have intended had it considered the matter. In these instances, the absence of a clear congressional statement is, in effect, equivalent to a statutory qualification saying, for example, "Notwithstanding any general language of this statute, this statute shall not apply extraterritorially"; or ". . . this statute shall not abrogate the sovereign immunity of nonconsenting States"; or ". . . this statute does not regulate the internal affairs of foreign-flag vessels." These clear statement rules ensure Congress does not, by broad or general language, legislate on a sensitive topic inadvertently or without due deliberation. An all-or-nothing approach, under which a statute is altogether inapplicable if but one of its specific applications trenches on the domain protected by a clear statement rule, would convert the clear statement rule from a principle of interpretive caution into a trap for an unwary Congress. If Congress passes broad legislation that has some applications that implicate a clear statement rule—say, some extraterritorial applications, or some applications that would regulate foreign ships' internal affairs—an all-or-nothing approach would require that the entire statute, or some arbitrary set of applications larger than the domain protected by the clear statement rule, would be nullified. We decline to adopt that posture.

### B

Our holding that the clear statement rule operates only when a ship's internal affairs are affected does not implicate our holding in Clark v. Martinez, 543 U.S. 371 (2005). *Martinez* held that statutory language given a limiting construction in one context must be interpreted consistently in other contexts, "even though other of the statute's applications, standing alone, would not support the same limitation." This was simply a rule of consistent interpretation of the statutory words, with no bearing on the implementation of a clear statement rule addressed to particular statutory applications.

The statute in *Martinez*, 8 U.S.C. § 1231(a)(6), authorized detention of aliens pending their removal. In Zadvydas v. Davis, 533 U.S. 678, 696–699 (2001), the Court had interpreted this statute to impose time limits on detention of aliens held for certain reasons stated in the statute. The Court held that an alternative interpretation, one allowing indefinite detention of lawfully admitted aliens, would raise grave constitutional doubts. Having determined the meaning of § 1231(a)(6)'s text in *Zadvydas*, we were obliged in *Martinez* to follow the same interpretation even in a context where the constitutional concerns were not present. As already made clear, the question was one of textual interpretation, not the scope of some implied exception. The constitutional avoidance canon simply informed the choice among plausible readings of § 1231(a)(6)'s text: "The canon of constitutional avoidance," *Martinez* explained, "comes into play only when, after the application of ordinary textual analysis, the statute is found to be susceptible of more than one construction; and the canon functions as a means of choosing between them." (emphasis deleted).

. . . The internal affairs clear statement rule is an implied limitation rule, not a principle for resolving textual ambiguity. Our cases, then, do not compel or permit the conclusion that if any one application of Title III might interfere with a foreign-flag ship's internal affairs, Title III is inapplicable to foreign ships in every other instance. . . .

■ Justice Ginsburg, with whom Justice Breyer joins, concurring in part and concurring in the judgment.

. . . [T]he "internal affairs" clear statement rule . . ., as I understand it, derives from, and is moored to, the broader guide that statutes "should not be interpreted to regulate foreign persons or conduct if that regulation would conflict with principles of international law." Hartford Fire Ins. Co. v. California, 509 U.S. 764, 815 (1993) (Scalia, J., dissenting). . . . Title III is properly read to avoid such conflict, but should not be hemmed in where there is no potential for international discord.[1]

The first of the modern cases to address the application of a domestic statute to a foreign-flag ship in U.S. waters, Benz v. Compania Naviera Hidalgo, S. A., 353 U.S. 138 (1957), did not resort to the tag, "internal affairs" rule, to explain the Court's decision. Benz held that the Labor Management Relations Act did not reach relations between "a foreign employer and a foreign crew operating under an agreement made abroad under the laws of another nation." As we concluded in Benz, before reading our law to "run interference in such a delicate field of international relations," "where the possibilities of international discord are so evident and retaliative action so certain," the Court should await Congress' clearly expressed instruction.

Six years later, in McCulloch v. Sociedad Nacional de Marineros de Honduras, 372 U.S. 10 (1963), the Court relied on Benz to hold that the National Labor Relations Act does not regulate the representation of alien seamen recruited in Honduras to serve aboard vessels under Honduran flags. Applying our law "to the internal management and affairs" of the vessels in question, we observed, would produce a "head-on collision" with the regulatory regime installed under the Honduran labor code. "[S]uch highly charged international circumstances," we said, called for adherence to the venerable interpretive guide that " 'an act of Congress ought never to be construed to violate the law of nations if any other possible construction remains.' " Ibid. (quoting Schooner Charming Betsy, 2 Cranch, at 118). . . .

The plurality, however, suggests that the clear statement rule has a further office: It may block structural modifications prompted by Title III that . . . do not conflict with international legal obligations . . . but nonetheless "interfer[e] with a foreign ship's internal affairs." I disagree with this conception of the rule. In positing an extended application of the internal affairs rule, the plurality cuts the rule loose from its foundation. As Benz and McCulloch demonstrate, the clear statement rule is an interpretive principle counseling against construction of a statute in a manner productive of international discord. When international relations are not at risk, and there is good reason to apply our own law, asserted

---

1.  Were a clear statement rule in order, I would agree with the plurality's application-by-application approach.

internal affairs of a ship should hold no greater sway than asserted management prerogatives of a landlocked enterprise.

As the plurality rightly notes, Title III is a broad remedial statute designed to protect persons with disabilities in a variety of activities and settings. The United States has a strong interest in ensuring that U.S. resident cruise passengers enjoy Title III's protections on both domestic and foreign ships. Once conflicts with international legal obligations are avoided, I see no reason to demand a clearer congressional statement that Title III reaches the vessels in question, ships that regularly sail to and from U.S. ports and derive most of their income from U.S. passengers. . . .

■ JUSTICE THOMAS, concurring in part, dissenting in part, and concurring in the judgment in part.

When a law regulates the internal order of ships, Congress must clearly express its intent to apply the law to foreign-flag ships. I agree with JUSTICE SCALIA that this rule applies to any structural changes to a ship that Title III . . . might require, for such changes to a ship's physical structure pertain to its internal affairs. I further agree with Justice SCALIA that this clear statement rule applies once the possibility, rather than the certainty, of international discord arises. . . . While I conclude that the rule applies to certain aspects of Title III, I agree with the plurality that it does not require an "all-or-nothing approach." Consequently, those applications of Title III that do not pertain to internal affairs apply to foreign-flag vessels. For that reason, I join part III–A of the plurality opinion. . . .

I reach this result, however, only because I continue to reject the "lowest common denominator" principle the Court articulated for the first time in Clark v. Martinez, 543 U.S. 371, 395–397 (2005). The plurality by contrast, accepts *Clark*. Moreover, it claims that applying Title III of the ADA to matters that are not within the realm of a ship's internal order is consistent with *Clark*. The plurality's efforts to distinguish *Clark* are implausible.

The plurality says that today's case differs from *Clark* because it invokes a clear statement rule to interpret unambiguous text. According to the plurality, *Clark* concerned the application of a previously adopted limiting construction of ambiguous text, which this Court imposed to ameliorate unrelated constitutional doubts. As an initial matter, however, the statute at issue in Zadvydas v. Davis, 533 U.S. 678 (2001), and *Clark* was not ambiguous. Even assuming for the sake of argument that it was ambiguous, the distinction the plurality draws has no basis in *Clark*. In *Clark*, this Court addressed the period of detention 8 U.S.C. § 1231(a)(6) authorized for inadmissible aliens. This was a question left open by *Zadvydas*, which had addressed the period of detention under the same statute but with respect to a different class of aliens—those who had been admitted into the country. In *Zadvydas*, this Court had concluded that the possibility of indefinite detention of admitted aliens raised significant constitutional doubts and, in light of those doubts, it limited the Attorney General's power to detain admitted aliens. Section 1231(a)(6) does not distinguish between the two classes of aliens. Thus, this Court in *Clark* concluded it was compelled to apply that same construction, which was warranted only by the specific constitutional concerns arising for admitted aliens, to the unadmitted aliens before it. *Clark*'s conclusion stemmed from the narrowing construction adopted in *Zadvydas*, not the type of rule or canon that gave rise to that construction.

The plurality's reasoning cannot be squared with *Clark*'s "lowest common denominator" principle.... Just as in *Zadvydas* and *Clark*, this Court is called upon to interpret the same statutory text with respect to two different classes of cases—those that implicate the internal affairs of a vessel and those that do not. And just like the statute at issue in *Zadvydas* and *Clark*, Title III "applies without differentiation" to the internal and external affairs of foreign-flag vessels, as well as the internal and external affairs of domestic-flag ships. Thus, the limiting construction of Title III's definitions excluding foreign cruise ships from those definitions must govern *all* applications of the statute, not just those applications that pertain to internal affairs. According to *Clark*, the Court may not narrow Title III on a case-by-case basis, depending on whether a particular application of Title III interferes with a ship's internal order. In fact, it may not apply Title III to any ship or, for that matter, any entity at all, because Title III does not distinguish between any of the covered entities. This demonstrates why the principle *Clark* established is flawed....

■ JUSTICE SCALIA, with whom THE CHIEF JUSTICE and JUSTICE O'CONNOR join, and with whom JUSTICE THOMAS joins as to Part I–A, dissenting.

I respectfully dissent. The plurality correctly recognizes that Congress must clearly express its intent to apply its laws to foreign-flag ships when those laws interfere with the ship's internal order. Its attempt to place Title III ... outside this rule through ... piecemeal application of its provisions is unsupported by our case law. Title III plainly affects the internal order of foreign-flag cruise ships, subjecting them to the possibility of conflicting international obligations. I would hold that, since there is no clear statement of coverage, Title III does not apply to foreign-flag cruise ships.

## I

### A

As the plurality explains, where a law would interfere with the regulation of a ship's internal order, we require a clear statement that Congress intended such a result. This rule is predicated on the "rule of international law that the law of the flag state ordinarily governs the internal affairs of a ship," McCulloch v. Sociedad Nacional de Marineros de Honduras, 372 U.S. 10, 21 (1963), and is designed to avoid "the possibilit[y] of international discord," Benz v. Compania Naviera Hidalgo, S. A., 353 U.S. 138, 147 (1957)....

... As the plurality concedes, the structural modifications that Title III of the ADA requires under its barrier-removal provisions would plainly affect the ship's "internal order." ... A ship's design and construction ...

are at least as integral to the ship's operation and functioning as the bargaining relationship between shipowner and crew at issue in *Benz* and *McCulloch*.

. . . The purpose of the "internal order" clear-statement requirement is to avoid casually subjecting oceangoing vessels to laws that pose obvious risks of conflict with the laws of the ship's flag state, the laws of other nations, and international obligations to which the vessels are subject. . . .

. . . It has never been a condition for application of the foreign-flag clear-statement rule that an actual conflict with foreign or international law be established. . . . The reason to apply the rule here is that the structure of a ship pertains to the ship's internal order, which is a matter presumably left to the flag state unless Congress indicates otherwise. The basis for that presumption of congressional intent is principally (though perhaps not exclusively) that subjecting such matters to the commands of various jurisdictions raises the *possibility* (not necessarily the certainty) of conflict among jurisdictions and with international treaties. Even if the Court could . . . demonstrate that in this particular instance there would be no conflict with the laws of other nations or with international treaties, it would remain true that a ship's structure is preeminently part of its internal order; and it would remain true that subjecting ship structure to multiple national requirements invites conflict. *That* is what triggers application of the clear-statement rule. . . .

I would therefore hold that, because Title III's barrier-removal provisions clearly have the possibility of subjecting foreign-flag ships to conflicting international obligations, . . . Title III does not apply to foreign-flag ships without a clear statement from Congress.

### B

The plurality holds that, even "[i]f Title III did impose a duty that required [foreign-flag] cruise ships to make permanent and significant structural modifications[,] or . . . otherwise interfered with a foreign ship's internal affairs, . . . Title III requirements having nothing to do with internal affairs would continue to apply to domestic and foreign ships alike." I disagree. Whether or not Title III's prescriptions regarding such matters implicate the "internal order" of the ship, they still relate to the ships' maritime operations and are part of the same Title III. The requirements of that enactment either apply to foreign-flag ships or they do not. It is not within our power to design a statute some of whose provisions apply to foreign-flag ships and other of whose provisions do not—any more than it is within our power to prescribe that the statute applies to foreign-flag cruise ships 60% of whose passengers are United States citizens and does not apply to other foreign-flag cruise ships.

The plurality's assertion that those portions of Title III that do *not* implicate a ship's internal order apply to foreign-flag ships displays a confusion between a principle of interpretation based upon a true-to-fact presumption of congressional intent, and a court-made rule. The plurality seems to forget that it is a matter of determining whether Congress *in fact intended* that its enactment cover foreign-flag ships. To believe that there was any such intent section-by-section and paragraph-by-paragraph is delusional. Either Congress enacted Title III only with domestic entities (and not foreign-flag ships) in mind, or it intended Title III to apply across-the-board. It could not possibly be the real congressional intent that foreign-flag cruise ships be considered "place[s] of public accommodation" or "specified public transportation" for purposes of certain provisions but not for others. That Congress had separate foreign-flag intent with respect to each requirement—and would presumably adopt a clear statement provision-by-provision—is utterly implausible. And far from its being the case that this creates "a trap for an unwary Congress," it is the plurality's disposition that, in piecemeal fashion, applies to foreign-flag ships provisions never enacted with foreign-flag vessels in mind.[7] We recently addressed a similar question in Clark v. Martinez, 543 U.S. 371 (2005), where we explained that a statutory provision must be interpreted consistently from case to case. "It is not at all unusual to give a statut[e] . . . a limiting construction called for by one of the statute's applications, even though other of the statute's applications, standing alone, would not support the same limitation." That principle should apply here. Since some applications of Title III plainly affect the internal order of foreign-flag ships, the absence of a clear statement renders the statute inapplicable—even though some applications of the statute, if severed from the rest, would not require clear statement.

. . . The fine-tuning of legislation that the plurality requires would be better left to Congress. To attempt it through the process of case-by-case adjudication is a recipe for endless litigation and confusion. . . . If Congress desires to impose this time-consuming and intricate process, it is certainly able to do so—though I think it would likely prefer some more manageable solution. But for the plurality to impose it as a novel consequence of the venerable clear-statement rule seems to me unreasonable. I would therefore decline to apply all of Title III to foreign-flag ships without a clear statement from Congress. . . .

---

**1.  A Note on Substantive Canons Concerning Foreign Relations**—Some of the canons discussed in this chapter—like the constitutional avoidance canon, or the various federalism canons—come up quite a bit in litigation. The canon applied in *Spector*, which deals with whether or how courts should apply general federal statutes to foreign-flag vessels in United States territorial waters, is considerably more obscure. That said,

---

**7.** The plurality's discussion of Longshoremen v. Ariadne Shipping Co., 397 U.S. 195 (1970), is misleading. Although *Ariadne* clearly recognized the existence of an internal-order rule in our case law, *Ariadne* did not hold, similarly to what the plurality holds here, that application of the foreign-flag clear-statement rule prevented some provisions of the National Labor Relations Act (NLRA) from being applied to foreign-flag ships but allowed others to be applied. Rather, it held that the clear-statement rule *did not apply at all* to activities that were not "within the 'maritime operations of foreign-flag ships.'" The case is relevant only to questions the Court does not decide here—namely, application of Title III to onshore operations of the foreign-flag ships. . . .

this canon is related to a larger family of important substantive canons that concern foreign affairs. For example, in the influential case of *Murray v. The Schooner Charming Betsy*, 6 U.S. (2 Cranch) 64, 118 (1804), Chief Justice Marshall's opinion for the Court declared that "an act of Congress ought never to be construed to violate the law of nations if any other possible construction remains[.]" Courts frequently invoke this canon to interpret federal statutes so as to avoid abrogation or violation of international treaties (*see, e.g.,* Trans World Airlines, Inc. v. Franklin Mint Corp., 466 U.S. 243, 252 (1984); Cook v. United States, 288 U.S. 102, 120 (1933)), violation of international executive agreements (*see, e.g.,* Weinberger v. Rossi, 456 U.S. 25, 32 (1982)), or inconsistency with so-called "customary" international law (*see, e.g.,* F. Hoffmann–La Roche Ltd. v. Empagran S.A., 542 U.S. 155, 164 (2004)). For general discussions of the *Charming Betsy* canon, see Curtis A. Bradley, *The* Charming Betsy *Canon and Separation of Powers: Rethinking the Interpretive Role of International Law*, 86 Geo. L.J. 479 (1998), and Ralph G. Steinhardt, *The Role of International Law as a Canon of Domestic Statutory Construction*, 43 Vand. L. Rev. 1103 (1990).

A closely related substantive canon disfavors the extraterritorial application of United States law: "[L]egislation of Congress, unless a contrary intent appears, is meant to apply only within the territorial jurisdiction of the United States...." Foley Bros., Inc. v. Filardo, 336 U.S. 281, 285 (1949). *See also* E.E.O.C. v. Arabian American Oil Co., 499 U.S. 244, 248 (1991). This anti-extraterritoriality canon has sometimes been described as an application of the *Charming Betsy* canon; this characterization is premised on the view that there is a customary international law norm against states seeking to apply their law in territory under the jurisdiction of another state. *See* Bradley, *supra,* at 489–90; Harold Hongju Koh, *Is International Law Really State Law?*, 111 Harv. L. Rev. 1824, 1837 n.65 (1998); Ernest A. Young, *Sorting Out the Debate Over Customary International Law*, 42 Va. J. Int'l L. 365, 384 (2002). Sometimes, however, the canon disfavoring extraterritorial application of U.S. law is treated as a related but distinct canon grounded in an interest in preserving international comity or, more generally, in keeping the federal courts out of the sensitive domain of foreign relations. *See* Hartford Fire Ins. Co. v. California, 509 U.S. 764, 814–18 (1993) (Scalia, J., dissenting); Roger P. Alford, *Foreign Relations as a Matter of Interpretation: The Use and Abuse of* Charming Betsy, 67 Ohio St. L.J. 1339, 1359–62 (2006).

The early cases that are the focus of much of the doctrinal debate in *Spector*—particularly Benz v. Compania Naviera Hidalgo, S. A., 353 U.S. 138 (1957) and McCulloch v. Sociedad Nacional de Marineros de Honduras, 372 U.S. 10 (1963)—explicitly drew on the *Charming Betsy* canon and the presumption against extraterritorial application of U.S. law, even though the ships in those cases were in United States territory. And, as you saw, the *Spector* opinions placed considerable emphasis on issues related to international comity and compliance with international law when interpreting the canon articulated in *Benz* and *McCulloch*. So, while the particular substantive canon at issue in *Spector* may seem narrow and obscure, disputes about the correct interpretation and application of this canon are connected to larger debates about a more general set of substantive foreign relations canons.

**2.  *What Is the Scope of the* Benz/McCulloch *Canon?*—**There were two major disputes about the substantive canon in *Spector*. The first concerned the proper definition of that canon: What, exactly, falls within the scope of the *Benz/McCulloch* clear statement rule? In the *Spector* litigation, we see three distinct positions on this question.

First, Justice Ginsburg (joined by Justice Breyer) argued that the *Benz/McCulloch* clear statement rule comes into play only when an otherwise plausible construction of an ambiguous statutory term is likely to produce *actual* international discord. On this view, unless the most natural construction of the statute would produce such discord, the *Benz/McCulloch* clear statement rule has no place.

Second, the Court of Appeals for the Fifth Circuit had held that *Benz* and *McCulloch* established a broad clear statement rule, according to which general federal statutes presumptively do not apply to foreign-flag vessels in United States territory. The Fifth Circuit recognized that this canon is grounded in an interest in international comity, but concluded that the canon applied even without a specific showing that the particular application of general U.S. law to a foreign vessel would actually conflict with foreign law or otherwise trigger international discord. The Fifth Circuit instead construed the *Benz/McCulloch* clear statement rule as a broad, prophylactic presumption—an easily administrable rule designed to avoid even the *potential* for international conflict.

Third, Justice Kennedy's plurality opinion (joined by Justices Stevens and Souter) charted a kind of middle way between the Fifth Circuit's broad conception of the *Benz/McCulloch* clear statement rule and Justice Ginsburg's narrower conception. (Despite their other disagreements with the plurality, both Justice Scalia's dissent and Justice Thomas's partial dissent seemed to agree with the plurality on this understanding of *Benz* and *McCulloch*.) The plurality's approach emphasized a distinction between matters that affect the interests of the United States or its citizens, and matters that concern the internal affairs of the foreign vessel. General statutes presumptively apply to activity aboard foreign-flag ships in U.S. territory if that activity affects the welfare of U.S. citizens or the interests of the United States. For matters that pertain principally to the internal affairs of the foreign vessel, however, general statutes are presumed *not* to apply unless the statute contains a clear statement to the contrary.

Do you find Justice Kennedy's intermediate position attractive? Does it achieve the best of both worlds—avoiding the broad sweep associated with the Fifth Circuit's interpretation of the *Benz/McCulloch* canon, while maintaining a reasonably predictable and administrable prophylactic rule that does not require case-by-case inquiry into the potential for international conflict? Or is Justice Kennedy's middle way actually the worst of both worlds, introducing substantial uncertainty and confusion into the scope of the rule, while at the same time allowing the rule to be applied even in situations where it cannot plausibly be defended as avoiding an actual conflict with a foreign state?

Which of the three approaches seems best to you? Do any of the three seem better grounded in the prior case law, as described in the *Spector* opinions? Or are the earlier cases indeterminate with respect to this issue? How would you have characterized the *Benz/McCulloch* canon?

***3. Does the Clear Statement Rule Apply to the Whole Statutory Provision, or Only Particular Applications of That Provision?***—In addition to the debate over the proper characterization of the *Benz/McCulloch* canon, *Spector* also involved a dispute over the proper application of that canon. In particular, the plurality's distinction between external and internal affairs raised the following question: If *some* applications of the ADA to foreign-flag cruise ships would trigger the *Benz/McCulloch* canon (by interfering with a foreign vessel's internal operations), but *other* applications of the ADA to foreign cruise ships would not do so, is Title III of the ADA *generally* inapplicable to foreign vessels in U.S. waters, or are only those *particular applications* of Title III that would implicate foreign vessels' internal affairs precluded by the *Benz/McCulloch* clear statement rule? This question is very similar to the question presented in *Clark v. Martinez* about whether the constitutional avoidance canon required reading the detention provision in the alien removal statute as implicitly limiting the detention period for *all* aliens covered by that provision, or only for those *particular* aliens whose indefinite detention would raise serious constitutional problems. *See* pp. 339–340, *supra.*

For Justice Scalia (joined in dissent by Chief Justice Rehnquist and Justice O'Connor), the answer to this question was obvious, at least after the decision in *Clark*: If the Court must read Title III of the ADA narrowly to avoid interfering with the internal affairs of a foreign-flag vessel, then that narrow interpretation must apply across the board, even with respect to applications of Title III that do not in and of themselves interfere with a foreign vessel's internal operations. As Justice Scalia put it, "The requirements of [Title III] either apply to foreign-flag ships or they do not." Justice Scalia grounded this position in the assertion that the *Benz/McCulloch* canon is "a principle of interpretation based upon a true-to-fact presumption of congressional intent," not a "court-made rule." The Court must decide simply whether Congress enacted Title III "with domestic entities (and not foreign-flag ships) in mind, or [whether] it intended Title III to apply across-the-board." The *Benz/McCulloch* clear statement rule means that the Court must assume that the former answer is the correct one. This, Justice Scalia insisted, is no different that what the Court held only six months earlier in *Clark*.

Justice Thomas agreed with Justice Scalia that the issue in *Spector* was identical to the issue in *Clark*. But the agreement ended there, because Justice Thomas continued to insist that *Clark* was wrongly decided and ought to be overruled. Indeed, Justice Thomas thought Justice Scalia's application of the *Clark* rule in *Spector* vividly illustrated why the *Clark* holding was so badly flawed. In particular, Justice Thomas emphasized the lack of a principled basis for deciding where to draw the line between those applications of a statute that are barred by the clear statement rule and those that are not. Justice Scalia, as we have seen, would draw that line between domestic vessels and foreign vessels. But, Justice Thomas asked, why is that necessarily the right place to draw the line? Why wouldn't it be just as consistent with Justice Scalia's logic to say that Title III does not cover ships at all, because application of the ADA to *some* ships would contravene the *Benz/McCulloch* clear statement rule? Why is that different from refusing to apply Title III to all activities on foreign-flag ships, if *some* of those activities would trigger the *Benz/McCulloch* rule? Do you find this critique compelling? How might Justice Scalia respond?

Justice Kennedy's plurality opinion also took the view that the *Benz/McCulloch* clear statement rule operated on an application-by-application basis, and had no effect on those Title III requirements that did not implicate a foreign ship's internal operations. But Justice Kennedy (as well as Justices Stevens and Souter) had joined the majority opinion in *Clark*. To square the results in *Spector* and *Clark*, Justice Kennedy drew a distinction between those substantive canons of construction that operate as "principle[s] for resolving textual ambiguity" and those that operate as "implied limitation[s] on otherwise unambiguous [statutory] terms." Canons in the first category are about deciding what a particular statutory term means; once that decision is made, the term must have the same meaning in all cases. The *Clark* "lowest common denominator" principle applies when canons of this sort are used to resolve textual ambiguities, as the same text can't have different meanings in different contexts. In contrast, canons in the second category, though ostensibly principles of statutory "interpretation," are not really about resolving ambiguities in the statutory text; rather, these canons instruct courts to adopt contra-textual interpretations—in the form of implied limitations or qualifications of otherwise clear text—absent an unusually specific instruction from Congress. Such implied limitations on the applicability of general statutory terms, the plurality insisted, should be drawn as narrowly as possible. Justice Kennedy then explained that the constitutional avoidance canon employed by the *Zadvydas* majority is a canon of the first type (a means for resolving textual ambiguity), while the *Benz/McCulloch* clear statement rule is a canon of the second type (an implied limitation on otherwise clear text), and this explains why *Clark* was correct to stick to the *Zadvydas* construction of the detention provision even for aliens whose detention raised no constitutional concern, while *Spector* was correct to apply the *Benz/McCulloch* rule only to those specific ADA applications that actually interfere with foreign ships' internal affairs.

Do you find Justice Kennedy's distinction between different types of substantive canons persuasive? If you think through the canons you have studied, can you confidently sort them into "principles for resolving textual ambiguities" and "implied limitations on otherwise unambiguous statutory terms"? Does the constitutional avoidance canon belong in the former category? Doesn't that seem problematic in light of *Catholic Bishop* (pp. 271–278, *supra*), in which the Court read the general term "employer" as not including religious organizations? For that matter, isn't it something of a stretch for the plurality to assert that in *Zadvydas* "[t]he constitutional avoidance canon simply informed the choice among plausible readings of [the statute's text]," given that the provision at issue in *Zadvydas* said nothing whatsoever about a time limit on the detention period? In the absence of the constitutional concern, doesn't it seem implausible that anyone could have interpreted the statute as imposing such a limit? Or perhaps Justice Kennedy was subtly criticizing the use (or abuse) of the avoidance canon in cases like *Zadvydas* (and perhaps *Catholic Bishop*): Maybe Justice Kennedy believes that the avoidance canon *should* be used only to choose among textually plausible interpretations, rather than to limit otherwise unambiguous text, and he used *Spector* as an occasion to advance that view.

In sum, we appear to have three positions on the underlying question: Justice Scalia would apply the *Clark* "lowest common denominator" principle in all cases; Justice Thomas would take an application-by-application approach in all cases; and Justice Kennedy would look to whether the clear statement rule in question resolves a statutory ambiguity by favoring one textually plausible reading of the statute over another textually plausible reading (in which case the favored reading applies in all cases), or whether the clear statement rule in question reads an implied limitation into otherwise broad but clear text (in which case the clear statement rule is relevant only to the problematic applications of the text). Which approach would you favor? Why?

CHAPTER THREE

# THE CONSTITUTIONAL POSITION OF ADMINISTRATIVE AGENCIES

## CONTENTS

## I.   AN INTRODUCTION TO THE ADMINISTRATIVE STATE
## A.   THE ROLE AND FUNCTION OF ADMINISTRATIVE AGENCIES

In Chapters One and Two, we considered the various tools and techniques that federal courts use to interpret and apply statutes enacted by Congress. We saw how judicial interpretation often entails the exercise of policymaking discretion, and for that reason raises difficult and contested questions about the separation of powers, the appropriate role of the courts, and the nature and ends of the federal lawmaking process. But judicial interpretation of congressional statutes is only part of the picture of how our federal system fashions and implements legal rules, rights, and obligations. A great deal of both the initial lawmaking and the subsequent law-implementing work is done by administrative agencies located (at least nominally) in the Executive Branch of government. These agencies' responsibilities include the promulgation and application of regulations that translate general statutory directives into concrete requirements or prohibitions with which the public must comply.

To illustrate the role of administrative agencies in shaping federal law, consider the familiar prohibition on "insider trading" (the use, by a fiduciary of a publicly traded company, of undisclosed material facts about the company's prospects in order to make profitable securities trades). Insider trading is unlawful under federal law. Where does this prohibition come from? The ultimate source is, of course, the Constitution. In this case, Article I, § 8, clause 3 of the Constitution (the "Commerce Clause") grants Congress the power "[t]o regulate Commerce ... among the several States." Pursuant to that authority, Congress in 1934 enacted the Securities Exchange Act, § 10(b) of which states:

> It shall be unlawful for any person, directly or indirectly, by the use of any means or instrumentality of interstate commerce or of the mails, or of any facility of any national securities exchange—... [t]o use or employ, in connection with the purchase or sale of any security ... any manipulative or deceptive device or contrivance in contravention of such rules and regulations as the [Securities and Exchange Commission (SEC)] may prescribe as necessary or appropriate in the public interest or for the protection of investors.

15 U.S.C. § 78j(b).

Notice that § 10(b) does not, by itself, prohibit insider trading (or anything else). Rather, § 10(b) prohibits only those "manipulative or deceptive" practices that contravene "such rules and regulations as the [SEC] may prescribe as necessary or appropriate in the public interest or for the protection of investors." In other words, instead of Congress's exercising its authority under the Commerce Clause to prohibit a specific set of disfavored practices in securities markets (including insider trading), Congress delegated the authority to develop more specific rules to the SEC, an administrative agency created by Congress in Section 4 of the Securities

Exchange Act. In 1942, the SEC exercised its authority under § 10(b) to promulgate a regulation, known as Rule 10b–5, which contains the following substantive prohibitions:

It shall be unlawful for any person, directly or indirectly, by the use of any means or instrumentality of interstate commerce, or of the mails or of any facility of any national securities exchange,

(a) To employ any device, scheme, or artifice to defraud,

(b) To make any untrue statement of a material fact or to omit to state a material fact necessary in order to make the statements made, in the light of the circumstances under which they were made, not misleading, or

(c) To engage in any act, practice, or course of business which operates or would operate as a fraud or deceit upon any person, in connection with the purchase or sale of any security.

17 C.F.R. 240.10b–5.

Even Rule 10b–5 does not contain an explicit prohibition against insider trading. The SEC, however, interpreted the Rule 10b–5 prohibitions against making "misleading" statements and against engaging in "any act" that would operate as a "deceit upon any person" to include insider trading, and it has made a practice of bringing enforcement actions against securities traders whose conduct, in the SEC's view, violates this interpretation of Rule 10b–5. The SEC announced this position in 1961, explaining:

An affirmative duty to disclose material information has been traditionally imposed on corporate "insiders," particularly officers, directors, or controlling stockholders. We, and the courts have consistently held that insiders must disclose material facts which are known to them by virtue of their position but which are not known to persons with whom they deal and which, if known, would affect their investment judgment.

In the Matter of Cady, Roberts & Co., 40 S.E.C. 907, 911 (1961).

Thus, although the ultimate source of authority for the insider trading prohibition is the Constitution's Commerce Clause and a federal statute enacted pursuant to that Clause, the prohibition itself is contained neither in the Constitution nor the statute, but rather in the SEC *regulation* (as subsequently interpreted by the SEC in a specific case applying that regulation). Notwithstanding the fact that the regulation was not adopted by Congress pursuant to the bicameralism and presentment requirements of Article I, § 7, Rule 10b–5 feels very much like an act of legislation, especially since a separate provision of the Securities Exchange Act provides for stringent civil and criminal penalties (including imprisonment) for willful violations of SEC regulations. *See* 15 U.S.C. § 78ff(a). Indeed, when an administrative agency like the SEC promulgates a valid regulation like Rule 10b–5, the agency "speaks as the legislature, and its pronouncement has the force of a statute." Arizona Grocery Co. v. Atchison, T. & S.F. Ry., 284 U.S. 370, 386 (1932).

Administrative agencies, and the regulations they promulgate, play an extraordinarily important role not only in securities regulation, but also in environmental protection, banking, telecommunications, energy, labor, employment, immigration, transportation, and numerous other fields. Although administrative agencies have been an important part of the federal government since the founding, the number of agencies and the scope of agency regulatory activity expanded dramatically over the course of the twentieth century. Today, the extent of agency lawmaking activity rivals that of Congress: In 2001, for example, Congress enacted 24 major statutes and 112 other laws, while federal administrative agencies cumulatively promulgated 70 regulations that were deemed "significant" (according to the Office of Management and Budget's criteria), along with 3,383 other regulations. *See* Anne Joseph O'Connell, *Political Cycles of Rulemaking: An Empirical Portrait of the Modern Administrative State*, 94 VA. L. REV. 889, 892 (2008); *see also* STEVEN P. CROLEY, REGULATION AND PUBLIC INTERESTS: THE POSSIBILITY OF GOOD REGULATORY GOVERNMENT 108 (2008) (estimating that, over the last several decades, federal administrative agencies have issued an average of approximately 4,500 rules per year, of which 1,100–1,500 are "truly substantive" as opposed to ministerial). The quantity and scope of this administrative activity means that lawyers in most practice areas must deal with regulations, and regulatory agencies, on a regular basis.

This chapter focuses on the awkward position that administrative agencies occupy in our three-branch federal government. Although agencies are nominally part of the executive branch, much of their regulatory activity is difficult to distinguish from exercises of legislative power—a power that Article I of the Constitution apparently vests in Congress. Is it permissible for Congress to delegate to agencies the authority to make legal rules, rather than making the rules itself? The chapter begins by exploring this fundamental concern about the legitimacy of delegation. We then turn to the agencies' relationship with the other branches of government. Given that agencies exercise so much power, it is natural that the elected branches—Congress and the President—may have an interest in influencing how agencies exercise this power, or sometimes in insulating agencies from influence by other actors. The political struggle for control of the administrative state has provoked a great deal of legal controversy about the proper relationship among the President, Congress, the agencies, and the courts. Chapter Four then turns to the regulatory process—the procedural and judicial safeguards that are meant to constrain and channel administrative exercises of delegated lawmaking power—while Chapter Five addresses issues concerning agencies' construction of the statutes they administer—in particular, how courts can ensure that agencies adhere to the terms of congressional statutes without usurping the agencies' appropriate role as principal implementers of these statutes.

## B.   THE CONSTITUTIONAL BACKDROP

Much of the analysis of the delegation problem, and of many other constitutional questions related to the operation of the administrative state, entails arguments about the degree and nature of the U.S. Constitution's commitment to the principle of the *separation of powers*. But what, exactly, does this concept mean? And how much does a general understanding of the separation of powers, as a concept or ideal to which our Constitution aspires, help us to resolve concrete disputes about the proper allocation of power in our federal system—including the legitimate scope (if any) for congressional delegation of lawmaking authority to executive Branch agencies? The following discussion considers that issue, and also provides a brief overview of various techniques that we might use to draw inferences about constitutional meaning.

Under a strict conception of the separation of powers, each of the three branches has authority over the function that the Constitution assigns to it—Congress makes the laws, the President enforces them, and the federal judiciary adjudicates disputes arising under them—and no branch may interfere with the work of the other branches lawfully operating within their respective spheres. On this view, delegating authority to administrative agencies is problematic because it reassigns Congress's exclusive legislative power to another branch of government. In addition, the typical administrative agency not only promulgates statute-like regulations, but also enforces those regulations by deciding which enforcement actions to bring and, at least in the first instance, adjudicates the cases it has brought, often under the regulations it has promulgated. *See, e.g.*, James M. Landis, The Administrative Process 2 (1938); Cass R. Sunstein, After the Rights Revolution 22–23 (1991). As one commentator who is very much in sympathy with modern administrative government has thus written: "Virtually every part of the government Congress has created—the Department of Agriculture as well as the Securities and Exchange Commission—exercises *all three* of the governmental functions the Constitution so carefully allocates among Congress, President, and Court." Peter L. Strauss, *Formal and Functional Approaches to Separation-of-Powers Questions—A Foolish Inconsistency?*, 72 Cornell L. Rev. 488, 492–93 (1987). This confluence of rulemaking, enforcement, and adjudication under the roof of a given agency would appear problematic under the strict view.

But does the strict conception understate the complexity of the Constitution's structural provisions and the degree of historical disagreement about what the principle of "separation of powers" actually entails? Or does it accurately characterize a basic feature of our system of government? Let us consider, then, the text of the Constitution itself, and in particular Articles I, II, and III, which define the role and responsibilities of Congress, the President, and the federal judiciary, respectively.

---

# Constitution of the United States

## Article I.

### Section 1

All legislative Powers herein granted shall be vested in a Congress of the United States, which shall consist of a Senate and House of Representatives.

## Section 2

[1]   The House of Representatives shall be composed of Members chosen every second Year by the People of the several States, and the Electors in each State shall have the Qualifications requisite for Electors of the most numerous Branch of the State Legislature.

[2]   No person shall be a Representative who shall not have attained to the Age of twenty five Years, and been seven Years a Citizen of the United States, and who shall not, when elected, be an Inhabitant of that State in which he shall be chosen.

[3]   Representatives and direct Taxes shall be apportioned among the several States which may be included within this Union, according to their respective Numbers, which shall be determined by adding to the whole Number of free Persons, including those bound to Service for a Term of Years, and excluding Indians not taxed, three fifths of all other Persons. The actual Enumeration shall be made within three Years after the first Meeting of the Congress of the United States, and within every subsequent Term of ten Years, in such Manner as they shall by Law direct. The Number of Representatives shall not exceed one for every thirty Thousand, but each State shall have at Least one Representative. . . .

[4]   When vacancies happen in the Representation from any State, the Executive Authority thereof shall issue Writs of Election to fill such Vacancies.

[5]   The House of Representatives shall chuse their Speaker and other Officers; and shall have the sole Power of Impeachment.

## Section 3

[1]   The Senate of the United States shall be composed of two Senators from each State, chosen by the Legislature thereof, for six Years; and each Senator shall have one Vote.

[2]   Immediately after they shall be assembled in Consequence of the first Election, they shall be divided as equally as may be into three Classes. The Seats of the Senators of the first Class shall be vacated at the Expiration of the second Year, of the second Class at the Expiration of the fourth Year, and of the third Class at the Expiration of the sixth Year, so that one third may be chosen every second Year; and if Vacancies happen by Resignation, or otherwise, during the Recess of the Legislature of any State, the Executive thereof may make temporary Appointments until the next Meeting of the Legislature, which shall then fill such Vacancies.

[3]   No Person shall be a Senator who shall not have attained to the Age of thirty Years, and been nine Years a Citizen of the United States, and who shall not, when elected, be an Inhabitant of that State for which he shall be chosen.

[4]   The Vice President of the United States shall be President of the Senate, but shall have no Vote, unless they be equally divided.

[5]   The Senate shall chuse their other Officers, and also a President pro tempore, in the Absence of the Vice President, or when he shall exercise the Office of President of the United States.

[6]   The Senate shall have the sole Power to try all Impeachments. When sitting for that Purpose, they shall be on Oath or Affirmation. When the President of the United States is tried, the Chief Justice shall preside: and no Person shall be convicted without the Concurrence of two thirds of the Members present.

[7]   Judgment in Cases of Impeachment shall not extend further than to removal from Office, and disqualification to hold and enjoy any Office of honor, Trust or Profit under the United States: but the Party convicted shall nevertheless be liable and subject to Indictment, Trial, Judgment and Punishment, according to Law.

### SECTION 4

[1]   The Times, Places and Manner of holding Elections for Senators and Representatives, shall be prescribed in each State by the Legislature thereof; but the Congress may at any time by Law make or alter such Regulations, except as to the Places of chusing Senators.

[2]   The Congress shall assemble at least once in every Year, and such Meeting shall be on the first Monday in December, unless they shall by Law appoint a different Day.

### SECTION 5

[1]   Each House shall be the Judge of the Elections, Returns and Qualifications of its own Members, and a Majority of each shall constitute a Quorum to do Business; but a smaller Number may adjourn from day to day, and may be authorized to compel the Attendance of absent Members, in such Manner, and under such Penalties as each House may provide.

[2]   Each House may determine the Rules of its Proceedings, punish its Members for disorderly Behaviour, and, with the Concurrence of two thirds, expel a Member

[3]   Each House shall keep a Journal of its Proceedings, and from time to time publish the same, excepting such Parts as may in their Judgment require Secrecy; and the Yeas and Nays of the Members of either House on any question shall, at the Desire of one fifth of those Present, be entered on the Journal.

[4]   Neither House, during the Session of Congress, shall, without the consent of the other, adjourn for more than three days, nor to any other Place than that in which the two Houses shall be sitting.

### SECTION 6

[1]   The Senators and Representatives shall receive a Compensation for their Services, to be ascertained by Law, and paid out of the Treasury of the United States. They shall in all Cases, except Treason, Felony and Breach of the Peace, be privileged from Arrest during their Attendance at

the Session of their respective Houses, and in going to and returning from the same; and for any Speech or Debate in either House, they shall not be questioned in any other Place.

[2] No Senator or Representative shall, during the Time for which he was elected, be appointed to any civil Office under the Authority of the United States, which shall have been created, or the Emoluments whereof shall have been encreased during such time; and no Person holding any Office under the United States, shall be a Member of either House during his Continuance in Office.

## SECTION 7

[1] All Bills for raising Revenue shall originate in the House of Representatives; but the Senate may propose or concur with Amendments as on other Bills.

[2] Every Bill which shall have passed the House of Representatives and the Senate, shall, before it become a Law, be presented to the President of the United States; If he approve he shall sign it, but if not he shall return it, with his Objections to that House in which it shall have originated, who shall enter the Objections at large on their Journal, and proceed to reconsider it. If after such Reconsideration two thirds of that House shall agree to pass the Bill, it shall be sent, together with the Objections, to the other House, by which it shall likewise be reconsidered, and if approved by two thirds of that House, it shall become a Law. But in all such Cases the Votes of both Houses shall be determined by yeas and Nays, and the Names of the Persons voting for and against the Bill shall be entered on the Journal of each House respectively. If any Bill shall not be returned by the President within ten days (Sundays excepted) after it shall have been presented to him, the Same shall be a Law, in like Manner as if he had signed it, unless the Congress by their Adjournment prevent its Return in which Case it shall not be a Law.

[3] Every Order, Resolution, or Vote to which the Concurrence of the Senate and House of Representatives may be necessary (except on a question of Adjournment) shall be presented to the President of the United States; and before the Same shall take Effect, shall be approved by him, or being disapproved by him, shall be repassed by two thirds of the Senate and House of Representatives, according to the Rules and Limitations prescribed in the Case of a Bill.

## SECTION 8

[1] The Congress shall have Power To lay and collect Taxes, Duties, Imposts and Excises, to pay the Debts and provide for the common Defence and general Welfare of the United States; but all Duties, Imposts and Excises shall be uniform throughout the United States;

[2] To borrow Money on the credit of the United States;

[3] To regulate Commerce with foreign Nations, and among the several States, and with the Indian Tribes;

[4]   To establish an uniform Rule of Naturalization, and uniform Laws on the subject of Bankruptcies throughout the United States;

[5]   To coin Money, regulate the Value thereof, and of foreign Coin, and fix the Standard of Weights and Measures;

[6]   To provide for the Punishment of counterfeiting the Securities and current Coin of the United States;

[7]   To establish Post Offices and post Roads;

[8]   To promote the Progress of Science and useful Arts, by securing for limited Times to Authors and Inventors the exclusive Right to their respective Writings and Discoveries;

[9]   To constitute Tribunals inferior to the supreme Court;

[10]   To define and punish Piracies and Felonies committed on the high Seas, and Offences against the Law of Nations;

[11]   To declare War, grant Letters of Marque and Reprisal, and make Rules concerning Captures on Land and Water;

[12]   To raise and support Armies, but no Appropriation of Money to that Use shall be for a longer Term than two Years;

[13]   To provide and maintain a Navy;

[14]   To make Rules for the Government and Regulation of the land and naval Forces;

[15]   To provide for calling forth the Militia to execute the Laws of the Union, suppress Insurrections and repel Invasions;

[16]   To provide for organizing, arming, and disciplining, the Militia, and for governing such Part of them as may be employed in the Service of the United States, reserving to the States respectively, the Appointment of the Officers, and the Authority of training the Militia according to the discipline prescribed by Congress;

[17]   To exercise exclusive Legislation in all Cases whatsoever, over such District (not exceeding ten Miles square) as may, by Cession of particular States, and the Acceptance of Congress, become the Seat of the Government of the United States, and to exercise like Authority over all Places purchased by the Consent of the Legislature of the State in which the Same shall be, for the Erection of Forts, Magazines, Arsenals, dock-Yards, and other needful Buildings;—And

[18]   To make all Laws which shall be necessary and proper for carrying into Execution the foregoing Powers, and all other Powers vested by this Constitution in the Government of the United States, or in any Department or Officer thereof.

## Section 9

[1]   The Migration or Importation of such Persons as any of the States now existing shall think proper to admit, shall not be prohibited by the Congress prior to the Year one thousand eight hundred and eight, but a

Tax or duty may be imposed on such Importation, not exceeding ten dollars for each Person.

[2]   The Privilege of the Writ of Habeas Corpus shall not be suspended, unless when in Cases of Rebellion or Invasion the public Safety may require it.

[3]   No Bill of Attainder or ex post facto Law shall be passed.

[4]   No Capitation, or other direct, Tax shall be laid, unless in Proportion to the Census or Enumeration herein before directed to be taken.

[5]   No Tax or Duty shall be laid on Articles exported from any State.

[6]   No Preference shall be given by any Regulation of Commerce or Revenue to the Ports of one State over those of another: nor shall Vessels bound to, or from, one State, be obliged to enter, clear, or pay Duties in another.

[7]   No Money shall be drawn from the Treasury, but in Consequence of Appropriations made by Law; and a regular Statement and Account of the Receipts and Expenditures of all public Money shall be published from time to time.

[8]   No Title of Nobility shall be granted by the United States: And no Person holding any Office of Profit or Trust under them, shall, without the Consent of the Congress, accept of any present, Emolument, Office, or Title, of any kind whatever, from any King, Prince, or foreign State.

### SECTION 10

[1]   No State shall enter into any Treaty, Alliance, or Confederation; grant Letters of Marque and Reprisal; coin Money; emit Bills of Credit; make any Thing but gold and silver Coin a Tender in Payment of Debts; pass any Bill of Attainder, ex post facto Law, or Law impairing the Obligation of Contracts, or grant any Title of Nobility.

[2]   No State shall, without the Consent of the Congress, lay any Imposts or Duties on Imports or Exports, except what may be absolutely necessary for executing it's [sic] inspection Laws: and the net Produce of all Duties and Imposts, laid by any State on Imports or Exports, shall be for the Use of the Treasury of the United States; and all such Laws shall be subject to the Revision and Controul of the Congress.

[3]   No State shall, without the Consent of Congress, lay any Duty of Tonnage, keep Troops, or Ships of War in time of Peace, enter into any Agreement or Compact with another State, or with a foreign Power, or engage in War, unless actually invaded, or in such imminent Danger as will not admit of delay.

### ARTICLE II

### SECTION 1

[1]   The executive Power shall be vested in a President of the United States of America. He shall hold his Office during the Term of four Years,

and, together with the Vice President, chosen for the same Term, be elected as follows:

[2]  Each State shall appoint, in such Manner as the Legislature thereof may direct, a Number of Electors, equal to the whole Number of Senators and Representatives to which the State may be entitled in the Congress: but no Senator or Representative, or Person holding an Office of Trust or Profit under the United States, shall be appointed an Elector.

[3]  The Electors shall meet in their respective States, and vote by Ballot for two Persons, of whom one at least shall not be an Inhabitant of the same State with themselves.[1] And they shall make a List of all the Persons voted for, and of the Number of Votes for each; which List they shall sign and certify, and transmit sealed to the Seat of the Government of the United States, directed to the President of the Senate. The President of the Senate shall, in the Presence of the Senate and House of Representatives, open all the Certificates, and the Votes shall then be counted. The Person having the greatest Number of Votes shall be the President, if such Number be a Majority of the whole Number of Electors appointed; and if there be more than one who have such Majority, and have an equal Number of Votes, then the House of Representatives shall immediately chuse by Ballot one of them for President; and if no Person have a Majority, then from the five highest on the List the said House shall in like Manner chuse the President. But in chusing the President, the Votes shall be taken by States, the Representation from each State having one Vote; A quorum for this Purpose shall consist of a Member or Members from two thirds of the States, and a Majority of all the States shall be necessary to a Choice. In every Case, after the Choice of the President, the Person having the greatest Number of Votes of the Electors shall be the Vice President. But if there should remain two or more who have equal Votes, the Senate shall chuse from them by Ballot the Vice President.

[4]  The Congress may determine the Time of chusing the Electors, and the Day on which they shall give their Votes; which Day shall be the same throughout the United States.

[5]  No Person except a natural born Citizen, or a Citizen of the United States, at the time of the Adoption of this Constitution, shall be eligible to the Office of President; neither shall any Person be eligible to that Office who shall not have attained to the Age of thirty five Years, and been fourteen Years a Resident within the United States.

---

**1.** [Editors' Note:] The manner of electing the President was altered by the Twelfth Amendment, which, in relevant part, separates the vote for President and Vice President. In particular, the Amendment provides:

> The Electors shall meet in their respective states and vote by ballot for President and Vice–President, one of whom, at least, shall not be an inhabitant of the same state with themselves; they shall name in their ballots the person voted for as President, and in distinct ballots the person voted for as Vice–President, and they shall make distinct lists of all persons voted for as President, and of all persons voted for as Vice–President. . . .

U.S. CONST. amend. XII.

[6]  In Case of the Removal of the President from Office, or of his Death, Resignation, or Inability to discharge the Powers and Duties of the said Office, the Same shall devolve on the Vice president, and the Congress may by Law provide for the Case of Removal, Death, Resignation or Inability, both of the President and Vice President, declaring what Officer shall then act as President, and such Officer shall act accordingly, until the Disability be removed, or a President shall be elected.

[7]  The President shall, at stated Times, receive for his Services, a Compensation, which shall neither be encreased nor diminished during the Period for which he shall have been elected, and he shall not receive within that Period any other Emolument from the United States, or any of them.

[8]  Before he enter on the Execution of his Office, he shall take the following Oath or Affirmation:—"I do solemnly swear (or affirm) that I will faithfully execute the Office of President of the United States, and will to the best of my Ability, preserve, protect and defend the Constitution of the United States."

### SECTION 2

[1]  The president shall be Commander in Chief of the Army and Navy of the United States, and of the Militia of the several States, when called into the actual service of the United States; he may require the Opinion, in writing, of the principal Officer in each of the executive Departments, upon any Subject relating to the Duties of their respective Offices, and he shall have Power to grant Reprieves and Pardons for Offences against the United States, except in Cases of Impeachment.

[2]  He shall have Power, by and with the Advice and Consent of the Senate, to make Treaties, provided two thirds of the Senators present concur; and he shall nominate, and by and with the Advice and Consent of the Senate, shall appoint Ambassadors, other public Ministers and Consuls, Judges of the supreme Court, and all other Officers of the United States, whose Appointments are not herein otherwise provided for, and which shall be established by Law: but the Congress may by Law vest the Appointment of such inferior Officers, as they think proper, in the President alone, in the Courts of Law, or in the Heads of Departments.

[3]  The President shall have Power to fill up all Vacancies that may happen during the Recess of the Senate, by granting Commissions which shall expire at the End of their next Session.

### SECTION 3

He shall from time to time give to the Congress Information of the State of the Union, and recommend to their Consideration such Measures as he shall judge necessary and expedient; he may, on extraordinary Occasions, convene both Houses, or either of them, and in Case of Disagreement between them, with Respect to the Time of Adjournment, he may adjourn them to such Time as he shall think proper; he shall receive Ambassadors and other public Ministers; he shall take Care that the Laws be faithfully executed, and shall Commission all the Officers of the United States.

## Section 4

The President, Vice President and all civil Officers of the United States, shall be removed from Office on Impeachment for, and Conviction of, Treason, Bribery, or other high Crimes and Misdemeanors.

## Article III

### Section 1

The judicial Power of the United States, shall be vested in one supreme Court, and in such inferior Courts as the Congress may from time to time ordain and establish. The Judges, both of the supreme and inferior Courts, shall hold their Offices during good Behaviour, and shall, at stated Times, receive for their Services, a Compensation, which shall not be diminished during their Continuance in Office.

### Section 2

[1] The judicial Power shall extend to all Cases, in Law and Equity, arising under this Constitution, the Laws of the United States, and Treaties made, or which shall be made, under their Authority;—to all Cases affecting Ambassadors, other public Ministers and Consuls;—to all Cases of admiralty and maritime Jurisdiction;—to Controversies to which the United States shall be a Party;—to Controversies between two or more States;—between a State and Citizens of another State;—between Citizens of different States,—between Citizens of the same State claiming Lands under Grants of different States, and between a State, or the Citizens thereof, and foreign States, Citizens or Subjects.

[2] In all cases affecting Ambassadors, other public Ministers and Consuls, and those in which a State shall be Party, the supreme Court shall have original Jurisdiction. In all the other Cases before mentioned, the supreme Court shall have appellate Jurisdiction, both as to Law and Fact, with such Exceptions, and under such Regulations as the Congress shall make.

[3] The Trial of all Crimes, except in Cases of Impeachment, shall be by Jury; and such Trial shall be held in the State where the said Crimes shall have been committed; but when not committed within any State, the Trial shall be at such Place or Places as the Congress may by Law have directed.

### Section 3

[1] Treason against the United States, shall consist only in levying War against them, or in adhering to their Enemies, giving them Aid and Comfort. No Person shall be convicted of Treason unless on the Testimony of two Witnesses to the same overt Act, or on Confession in open Court.

[2]   The Congress shall have Power to declare the Punishment of Treason, but no Attainder of Treason shall work Corruption of Blood, or Forfeiture except during the Life of the Person attainted.

---

*1.  Does the Constitutional Text Mandate a "Separation of Powers"?*—Does an examination of the constitutional text support the view that the U.S. Constitution adopts a strict separation of powers? If the premise of this conception of the separation of powers is that Congress *alone* may exercise legislative powers, that the President *alone* may exercise executive power, and that the Judiciary *alone* may exercise judicial power, nothing in the Constitution explicitly tells us that this is required. A standard account traces the doctrine of the separation of powers to the so-called Vesting Clauses: Article I, § 1 ("[a]ll legislative Powers herein granted shall be vested in a Congress of the United States"); Article II, § 1 ("[t]he executive Power shall be vested in a President of the United States"), and Article III, § 1 ("[t]he judicial Power shall be vested in a supreme Court and in such inferior Courts as the Congress may from time to time ordain and establish"). *See, e.g.*, Akhil Reed Amar, *The Supreme Court 1999 Term–Foreword: The Document and the Doctrine*, 114 Harv. L. Rev. 26, 30 (2000); Gary Lawson, *The Rise and Rise of the Administrative State*, 107 Harv. L. Rev. 1231, 1237–38 (1994). This standard account argues that the assignment of carefully specified powers to a particular branch impliedly precludes the exercise of that power by the other branches. Otherwise, why would the Constitution take the trouble to assign those powers to the respective branches? *See, e.g.*, Marbury v. Madison, 5 U.S. (1 Cranch) 137, 174 (1803) ("Affirmative words are often, in their operation, negative of other objects than those affirmed. . . ."); 1 Joseph Story, Commentaries on the Constitution of the United States § 207, at 155 (Boston: Hilliard, Gray & Co. 1833) ("There can be no doubt, that an affirmative grant of powers in many cases will imply an exclusion of all others.").

How far should that argument carry proponents of the strict view of separation of powers? Many find it unwarranted to read a negative implication into the specification of some but not other items in a list because the failure to specify may reflect inadvertence, an inability to agree, or other factors other than an intention to make the enumeration exclusive. *See, e.g.*, Cass R. Sunstein, *Interpreting Statutes in the Regulatory State*, 103 Harv. L. Rev. 405, 455 (1989); *see also* pp. 231–232, *supra*. In a Constitution that explicitly grants Congress the power "[t]o make all Laws which shall be necessary and proper for carrying into Execution the foregoing Powers, and all other Powers vested by this Constitution in the Government of the United States, or in any Department or Officer thereof," U.S. Const. art. I, § 8, cl. 18, might the Vesting Clauses be understood as placeholders, specifying an initial allocation of power that is subject to legislative mixing and matching?

Along these lines, consider the further fact that the Massachusetts Constitution of 1780 famously incorporated the following provision:

> In the government of this Commonwealth, the legislative department shall never exercise the executive and judicial powers, or either of them: The executive shall never exercise the legislative and judicial powers, or either of them: The judicial shall never exercise the legislative and executive powers, or either of them: to the end it may be a government of laws and not of men.

Ma. Const. art. XXX (1780). Several other early constitutions included similar provisions. *See, e.g.*, N.C. Decl. Rts. art. IV (1776); Ga. Const. art. I (1777); N.H. Const. art. XXXVII (1784); Vt. Const. chap. II, § VI (1786). Does the failure of the U.S. Constitution to include a provision along these lines suggest an intention *not* to adopt a system of separated powers? What other explanations might account for the failure to include an express separation-of-powers clause? Might the structural inferences from the Vesting Clauses alone be sufficiently compelling to suggest such a system?

**2.  *Inferences from the Constitutional Structure*—**In determining how to read a document that creates a governmental structure, it is helpful to consider the document holistically—to try to determine how the various parts work as an integrated whole and to consider the way the component parts sensibly relate to one another. *See* Charles L. Black Jr., Structure and Relationship in Constitutional Law (1969). Does that approach help us to figure out whether the Constitution creates a separation of powers, and if so, exactly what sort of separation it is? Consider the following structural arguments for and against the position that the Constitution's initial assignment of powers to the respective branches was meant to be, in some sense, exclusive:

**a.  *Structural evidence of separated powers.*** Several structural features suggest that the Constitution was designed to separate the three powers. First, the Constitution seeks to minimize each branch's role in the selection of the others. In contrast with a parliamentary system, for example, the legislature does not select the executive. *See* U.S. Const. art. II, § 1, cl. 2. (Congress participates in the selection of the President only in the unusual case in which no candidate secures a majority of electors. *See id.* art. II, § 1, cl. 3 (superseded in other respects by the 12th Amendment in 1804)). Nor does the President have any say in the selection of Members of Congress. *Cf. id.* art. I, § 5, cl. 1. Only with respect to the judiciary do the coordinate branches have a constitutionally mandated role in the selection process, as judges are appointed by the President with the advice and consent of the Senate. *See id.* art. II, § 2, cl. 2. But once selected, federal judges enjoy life tenure and salary protection. *See id.* art. III, § 1.

Second, the ability of the branches to remove an official of *another* branch is limited and cumbersome. Neither the President nor the Judiciary has any role to play in removing Members of Congress. *See* U.S. Const. art. I, § 5, cl. 2. In addition, while Congress has the authority to remove "[t]he President, the Vice President, and all civil Officers of the United States [a category that includes federal judges]," it may do so only "on Impeachment for, and Conviction of, Treason, Bribery, or other high Crimes and Misdemeanors," *id.* art. II, § 4, an enormously difficult proposition that ultimately requires a majority vote of the House for impeachment and a two-thirds vote of the Senate for conviction, *see id.* art. I, § 2, cl. 5; *id.* art. I, § 3, cl. 6. Finally, Article III provides that federal judges hold their office "during good Behavior," *id.* art. III, § 1, which reinforces the judiciary's independence from the other branches.

Third, the Constitution provides a number of limitations on congressional control over the salaries of the other branches. *See* U.S. Const. art. II, § 1, cl. 7; *id.* art. III, § 1. As Alexander Hamilton explained, limiting Congress's control over the President's salary means that Congress can "neither weaken [the President's] fortitude by operating upon his necessities; nor corrupt his integrity, by appealing to his avarice." The Federalist No. 73, at 442 (Alexander Hamilton) (Clinton Rossiter ed., 1961). To similar effect, Hamilton explained that Article III's protection of judicial salaries was a prerequisite for judicial independence from the legislature. *See* The Federalist No. 79, *supra*, at 472.

Fourth, the Constitution's Incompatibility Clause, U.S. Const. art. I, § 6, cl. 2, which prevents any member of the legislative branch from serving simultaneously as a judge or executive officer, precludes both a parliamentary-style system in which legislators hold the senior executive positions and any arrangement in which members of the legislature play a judicial role, as was true of the British House of Lords until 2009. *See* Harold H. Bruff, *The Incompatibility Principle*, 59 Admin. L. Rev. 225 (2007); Ronald J. Krotoszynski, Jr., *The Shot (Not) Heard 'Round the World: Reconsidering the Perplexing U.S. Preoccupation with the Separation of Legislative and Executive Powers*, 51 B.C. L. Rev. 1, 25 & n.126 (2010). Notice, however, that the Incompatibility Clause does not prohibit joint service by the same individual in the executive and judicial branches. To name two prominent examples in the early Republic, John Jay served simultaneously as Chief Justice and as an envoy to England, and John Marshall spent a month serving as both Chief Justice and Secretary of State. *See* Stewart Jay, Most Humble Servants: The Advisory Role of Early Judges (1997). Does that negate any inference that the Incompatibility Clause supports the idea of the separation of powers? *See* Steven G. Calabresi & Joan L. Larsen, *One Person, One Office: Separation of Powers or Separation of Personnel?*, 79 Cornell L. Rev. 1045 (1994) (arguing that the Incompatibility Clause was not originally intended to further the separation of powers, but rather to prevent the President from corrupting Congress).

Finally, the Bill of Attainder Clause, U.S. Const. art. I, § 9, which prohibits the legislative imposition of penalties, serves as "a general safeguard against legislative exercise of the judicial function, or more simply—trial by legislature." United States v. Brown, 381 U.S. 437, 442 (1965).

Would the drafters of the Constitution have taken such pains to provide for the independence of the respective branches from one another if Congress could simply reassign one branch's functions to another branch?

***b. Structural evidence of blending.*** In contrast with the foregoing provisions, much of the Constitution reads as if there is no obvious design to separate the powers exercised by the respective branches, or at least no design to do so strictly or without qualification. Consider the many respects in which the Constitution blends legislative, executive, and judicial power. First, through the exercise of the veto power, the President participates in the legislative process. *See* U.S. Const. art. I, § 7, cl. 2. Second, the Senate has responsibility for trying impeachments, and the Chief Justice presides when the Senate is trying the President of the United States. *See id.* art. I, § 3, cl. 6. Third, although the appointment of executive and judicial officers was traditionally an executive prerogative, the Appointments Clause provides that the President must secure the "Advice and Consent of the Senate" before appointing "Officers of the United States." *See id.* art. II, § 2, cl. 2. Fourth, although power to make treaties was likewise a traditional matter of executive prerogative, the Constitution conditions presidential authority to make treaties on his or her ability to secure the advice and consent of "two thirds of the Senators present." *Id.*

Does this blending negate the premise that the Constitution adopts a separation of powers? If the document itself mixes the powers among the branches, why should one read the document as implying that Congress may not also do so, in some measure, pursuant to its power under the Necessary and Proper Clause? Or does the fact that the document makes targeted exceptions to the initial allocation and separation of powers suggest that separation is the norm, barring the presence of an express exception? How should an interpreter sort out these conflicting structural cues?

**3. *Inferences from Historical Understandings and Practice*—**In addition to whatever inferences we may derive from the text and structure of the Constitution, we might also look to historical understandings of the nature and purposes of the Constitution's allocation of powers as a source of insight. The natural place to begin is with the understandings of the founding generation itself, particularly those principally responsible for drafting and ratifying the Constitution.

The usual account of the purpose of the constitutional separation of powers starts with Montesquieu's view (influential with the founders) that separation of powers preserves liberty by requiring the concurrence of independent legislative, executive, and judicial branches before the power of the state can be brought to bear against an individual. *See* Montesquieu, The Spirit of Laws 202, 210–11 (David W. Carrithers ed., 1977); *see also, e.g.,* William Seal Carpenter, *The Separation of Powers in the Eighteenth Century,* 22 Am. Pol. Sci. Rev. 32, 37 (1928) (explaining Montesquieu's influence on the founders). Montesquieu thus wrote that by checking one another, "[t]hese three powers should naturally form a state of repose or inaction," and the state can act against the individual only when the three "move in concert." Montesquieu, *supra,* at 211.

Yet even if Montesquieu had been the sole expositor of American separation-of-powers doctrine, to say that the branches are to serve as checks on each other cannot tell us what degree or type of check adequately serves the contemplated purpose. Indeed, the concept of the "separation of powers" can be applied to quite a number of different institutional arrangements, and "by the last quarter of the eighteenth century, no single doctrine using the label of separation of powers had emerged that could command general assent." Gerhard Casper, *An Essay in Separation of Powers: Some Early Versions and Practices*, 30 WM. & MARY L. REV. 211, 213 (1989).

The specific historical context of the adoption of the Constitution may shed additional light on the sort of separation-of-powers scheme the Constitution was designed to implement. In particular, its design seems to have been in part a response to the perceived failures of state government systems in which the legislature dominated the other branches. *See, e.g.*, M.J.C. VILE, CONSTITUTIONALISM AND THE SEPARATION OF POWERS 166–168 (2d ed., 1976); GORDON WOOD, THE CREATION OF THE AMERICAN REPUBLIC, 1776–1787, at 132–50, 160–61, 404–07 (1969); *Carpenter, supra*, at 32–33. By 1787, there was a widespread consensus that a system of separated powers—even one that was predicated on representative democracy—required effective checks on the accumulation and concentration of power in any one branch. *See, e.g.*, WOOD, *supra*, at 404–13. Perhaps the most famous articulation of this premise is found in James Madison's defense of the proposed Constitution in The Federalist No. 51:

> In order to lay a due foundation for that separate and distinct exercise of the different powers of government, which to a certain extent is admitted on all hands to be essential to the preservation of liberty, it is evident that each department should have a will of its own; and consequently should be so constituted that the members of each should have as little agency as possible in the appointment of the members of the others. . . .

> It is equally evident, that the members of each department should be as little dependent as possible on those of the others, for the emoluments annexed to their offices. Were the executive magistrate, or the judges, not independent of the legislature in this particular, their independence in every other would be merely nominal.

> But the great security against a gradual concentration of the several powers in the same department, consists in giving to those who administer each department the necessary constitutional means and personal motives to resist encroachments of the others. The provision for defense must in this, as in all other cases, be made commensurate to the danger of attack. Ambition must be made to counteract ambition. . . . If men were angels, no government would be necessary. If angels were to govern men, neither external nor internal controls on government would be necessary. In framing a government which is to be administered by men over men, the great difficulty lies in this: you must first enable the government to control the governed; and in the next place oblige it to control itself. A dependence on the people is, no

doubt, the primary control on the government; but experience has taught mankind the necessity of auxiliary precautions.

The Federalist No. 51, at 321–22 (James Madison) (Clinton Rossiter ed., 1961). Madison further suggested that the blending of authority helped to sustain the underlying separation of powers by permitting each branch to guard against creeping encroachment by others. *See* The Federalist No. 48, *supra,* at 308.

This understanding of the purposes of a separation of powers does not, however, necessarily tell us how to decide concrete cases. Moreover, the separation-of-powers tradition by the late eighteenth century reflected the work of numerous theorists who had attributed to it an array of purposes, including:

(1) to create greater governmental efficiency; (2) to assure that statutory law is made in the common interest; (3) to assure that law is impartially administered and that all administrators are under the law; (4) to allow the people's representatives to call executive officials to account for the abuse of their power; and (5) to establish a balance of governmental powers.

W. B. Gwyn, The Meaning of the Separation of Powers 127–128 (1965). Indeed, in the specific context of the U.S. Constitution, there is substantial evidence that one of the purposes of the separation of powers was to achieve an effective and efficient division of labor—that is, to make government more energetic and effective. *See* Cass R. Sunstein, *Constitutionalism After the New Deal*, 101 Harv. L. Rev. 421, 432–33 (1987). If the separation of powers is associated with a diverse set of purposes—some of which may be in tension with one another—how much can the concept of the separation of powers in the abstract help us to interpret ambiguities in the constitutional structure?

If looking to the general purposes of the "separation of powers" does not shed much light on how to resolve particular disputes about the allocation of governmental power, should the Court focus instead on the text, history, traditions, and functional attributes associated with *the particular clauses* that are said to address a contested constitutional practice? The Court famously observed that "[t]he principle of the separation of powers was not simply an abstract generalization in the minds of the Framers: it was woven into the document that they drafted in Philadelphia in the summer of 1787." Buckley v. Valeo, 424 U.S. 1, 124 (1976). In the cases that follow, does that admonition help to address some of the abstraction of thinking about a freestanding separation-of-powers doctrine divorced from the particular clauses that set up the constitutional structure?

Think also about the degree to which indeterminacies in the constitutional structure might have been resolved over time through the development of settled understandings by the government institutions responsible for implementing the Constitution. Indeed, the framers and ratifiers of the Constitution anticipated that much of it would be ambiguous and that its meaning would be settled over time through its practical construction by the responsible government officials. *See* The Federalist No. 37, at 225 (James Madison) (Clinton Rossiter ed., 1961) ("All new laws, though penned with the greatest technical skill . . ., are considered as more or less obscure and equivocal, until their meaning be liquidated and ascertained by a series of particular discussions and adjudications."); *see also* Caleb R. Nelson, *Originalism and Interpretive Conventions*, 70 U. Chi. L. Rev. 519 (2003); H. Jefferson Powell, *The Original Understanding of Original Intent*, 98 Harv. L. Rev. 885, 911 (1985). And the Court has frequently observed that a "[legislative] construction of the Constitution which has been followed since the founding of our government . . . is entitled to the greatest respect" in interpreting the document. Ex Parte Quirin, 317 U.S. 1, 41–42 (1942); *see also, e.g.,* The Laura, 114 U.S. 411, 416 (1885); Stuart v. Laird, 5 U.S. (1 Cranch) 299, 309 (1803). How justified is such an approach? Certainly, early legislators (and presumably other government officials) "must have had a keen appreciation of the influences which had shaped the Constitution and the restrictions which it embodied, since all questions which related to the Constitution and its adoption must have been, at that early date, vividly impressed on their minds." Knowlton v. Moore, 178 U.S. 41, 56 (1900). But how reliably can one glean a reasoned judgment about constitutional meaning from the deliberations of a multimember political body such as Congress? *See, e.g.,* Note, *Should the Supreme Court Presume that Congress Acts Constitutionally? The Role of the Canon of Avoidance and Reliance on Early Legislative Practice in Constitutional Interpretation*, 116 Harv. L. Rev. 1798 (2003).

Finally, in cases in which a thorough examination of the available materials does not speak with decisive clarity to the Constitution's meaning, think about what rule of thumb the Court should use to evaluate the validity of the Acts of Congress that create the institutions of the federal government. *Compare, e.g.,* James Bradley Thayer, *The Origin and Scope of the American Doctrine of Constitutional Law*, 7 Harv. L. Rev. 129, 144 (1893) (arguing that courts should disturb a legislative judgment only if there has been a "very clear" mistake concerning the measure's constitutionality), *with* Morrison v. Olson, 487 U.S. 654, 704–05 (1988) (Scalia, J., dissenting) (arguing that "where the issue pertains to separation of powers, and the political branches are . . . in disagreement, neither can be presumed correct").

***4. Formalism Versus Functionalism***—Two main schools of thought have developed around the question of how to interpret the constitutional structure, which usually go by the names "formalism" and "functionalism." *See, e.g.,* Peter L. Strauss, *Formal and Functional Approaches to Separation-of-Powers Questions—A Foolish Inconsistency?*, 72 Cornell L. Rev. 488 (1987) [hereinafter Strauss, *Formal and Functional Approaches*] (laying out the distinction); *see also, e.g.,* Rebecca L. Brown, *Separated Powers and Ordered Liberty*, 139 U. Pa. L. Rev. 1513, 1522–29 (1991); M. Elizabeth Magill, *The Real Separation in Separation of Powers Law*, 86 Va. L. Rev. 1127, 1136–47 (2000). Although there is no one authoritative definition of either approach, it is possible to make some generalizations about the distinctive assumptions that formalists and functionalists bring to the task of understanding the evidence of constitutional meaning.

Formalists tend to view the Constitution as drawing relatively sharp lines of demarcation between the powers and responsibilities assigned to the respective branches. As Professor Stephen Carter has written: "The 1787 Constitution reflects the enormous energy that the Founders expended on designing the structure of the federal government. . . . The [constitutional structure] consists of relatively determinate clauses phrased by their authors with highly specific referents in mind." Stephen L. Carter, *Constitutional Improprieties: Reflections on* Mistretta, Morrison, *and Administrative Government*, 57 U. Chi. L. Rev. 357, 367 (1990). From that starting point, formalists argue that it is unconstitutional for Congress to reassign a power from the branch to which it is assigned by the relevant constitutional vesting clause. *See, e.g.*, Martin H. Redish, The Constitution as Political Structure 6–10 (1995); Steven G. Calabresi, *The Vesting Clauses as Power Grants*, 88 Nw. U. L. Rev. 1377, 1390 (1994); Gary Lawson, *Territorial Governments and the Limits of Formalism*, 78 Cal. L. Rev. 853, 859–60 (1990). Formalists are also more likely to find that the Constitution's meaning is fixed by some historical understanding that prevailed at the time of its adoption in 1789, and to conclude that interpreters must abide by that clearly established meaning, even if the result denies Congress the authority to adapt governmental structure and practice to address modern social problems more effectively. *See, e.g.*, Steven G. Calabresi & Kevin Rhodes, *The Structural Constitution: Unitary Executive, Plural Judiciary*, 105 Harv. L. Rev. 1153 (1992); Gary Lawson, *The Rise and Rise of the Administrative State*, 107 Harv. L. Rev. 1231 (1994). In short, like textualists in statutory interpretation, formalists believe that when the Constitution adopts rule-like allocations of power, judges must enforce those rules rather than abstracting to the purposes behind them. *See, e.g., Carter, supra*, at 357. The essence of the formalist position is perhaps best captured by Justice Brandeis's famous observation:

> The doctrine of the separation of powers was adopted by the convention of 1787 not to promote efficiency but to preclude the exercise of arbitrary power. The purpose was not to avoid friction, but, by means of the inevitable friction incident to the distribution of the governmental powers among three departments, to save the people from autocracy.

Myers v. United States, 272 U.S. 52, 293 (1926) (Brandeis, J., dissenting).

Functionalists, in contrast, think of the Constitution as leaving a great deal undecided. As a leading functionalist scholar has written, "[o]ne scanning the Constitution for a sense of the overall structure of the federal government is immediately struck by its silences." Peter L. Strauss, *The Place of Agencies in Government: Separation of Powers and the Fourth Branch*, 84 Colum. L. Rev. 573, 597 (1984) [hereinafter Strauss, *Fourth Branch*]; *see also, e.g.*, Martin S. Flaherty, *The Most Dangerous Branch*, 105 Yale L.J. 1725, 1813 (1996) (arguing that the founders defined the constitutional structure at "a high level of generality"). In particular, Professor Strauss argues that the Constitution tells us a great deal about the heads of the respective branches—Congress, the President, and the federal courts—but very little about administrative agencies *per se*; hence, he and other functionalists stress Congress's broad authority to determine the shape of government pursuant to the Necessary and Proper Clause. *See generally* Strauss, *Fourth Branch, supra.* In general, functionalists favor a more purposive approach to interpreting the Constitution; rather than treating the structural provisions as a series of rules that crisply allocate power, they tend to think it sufficient if a challenged administrative scheme leaves intact the "core" functions of each branch and preserves an appropriate balance of power and creative tension among the branches. *See, e.g.,* Cynthia R. Farina, *Statutory Interpretation and the Balance of Power in the Administrative State,* 89 COLUM. L. REV. 452, 478–99 (1989); Strauss, *Fourth Branch, supra,* at 579; Strauss, *Formal and Functional Approaches, supra,* at 489. To insist instead on a strict and unyielding separation of powers, they say, risks compromising the workability and adaptability of modern government without necessarily furthering the underlying aims of the separation of powers. *See, e.g.,* Dean Alfange, *The Supreme Court and the Separation of Powers: A Welcome Return to Normalcy?,* 58 GEO. WASH. L. REV. 668, 669–70 (1990). Finally, functionalists assert that an embrace of formalism would entail a disruptive and undesirable unraveling of much of the post-New Deal administrative state. The functionalist approach is perhaps best captured by Justice Robert Jackson's celebrated statement:

> The actual art of governing under our Constitution does not and cannot conform to judicial definitions of the power of any of its branches based on isolated clauses or even single Articles torn from context. While the Constitution diffuses power the better to secure liberty, it also contemplates that practice will integrate the dispersed powers into a workable government. It enjoins upon its branches separateness but interdependence, autonomy but reciprocity.

Youngstown Sheet & Tube Co. v. Sawyer, 343 U.S. 579, 635 (1952) (Jackson, J., concurring in the judgment).

Which approach seems to comport better with the constitutional structure? Are the Constitution's provisions on separation of powers detailed and precise, vague and open-ended, or some combination? Does formalism rest on an unrealistically optimistic view of an interpreter's being able to define legislative, executive, and judicial powers? *See infra* Paragraph 5. Does it overestimate the possibility of meaningfully applying eighteenth century understandings to a twenty-first century society and government that involves radically different circumstances and challenges? Does functionalism run into the problems that some have attributed to purposivism? If functionalism seeks to implement "the purposes" behind the separation of powers, how determinate are those purposes? Does functionalism sometimes give too little weight to seemingly specific agreements on structural questions that are evident from the text and historical record?

*5.  **Defining the Three Powers**—*In analyzing questions involving the separation of powers, the Court must frequently grapple with the question of what constitutes legislative, executive, or judicial power. The determination is not a straightforward one. *See, e.g.,* M. Elizabeth Magill, *Beyond Powers and Branches in Separation of Powers Law*, 150 U. PA. L. REV. 603, 612–26 (2001); Thomas O. Sargentich, *The Contemporary Debate About Legislative–Executive Separation of Powers*, 72 CORNELL L. REV. 430, 437–38 (1987). The conventional understanding is that legislative power entails "mak[ing] and alter[ing] the general rules of society," the executive power involves "the execution of these general rules," and the judicial power concerns "the interpretation and application of the laws to controverted cases, in standing tribunals, circumscribed by solemn and settled rules of proceeding." M.J.C. VILE, CONSTITUTIONALISM AND THE SEPARATION OF POWERS 168–176 (2d ed., 1998) (quoting the *Pennsylvania Gazette*, Apr. 28, 1784). But that formulation may be too simple, and may not always help us resolve difficult cases. If Congress hears evidence concerning a claim of debt against the United States and appropriates money based on that evidence, has it exercised legislative or judicial power? If the Federal Communications Commission awards a radio license after hearing evidence about which competing license applicant better fulfills the statutory criteria set forth in the Communications Act of 1934, is the Commission exercising executive or judicial power? If the Supreme Court adopts the Rules of Civil Procedure pursuant to authority delegated to it under the Rules Enabling Act, is the Court exercising legislative or judicial power? Does the enforcement of any meaningful doctrine of separation of powers depend on the Court's capacity to answer those questions in a convincingly principled way?

## II.  THE DELEGATION OF LEGISLATIVE POWER
## A.  THE VIRTUES AND VICES OF DELEGATION

As the introductory note to this chapter observed, Congress frequently enacts statutes that delegate to administrative agencies the power to enact regulations to achieve the goals Congress lays out (often in relatively broad and open-ended terms). The United States Environmental Protection Agency (EPA) provides a nice, succinct explanation of the practice:

> . . . While Congress passes the laws that govern the United States, Congress has also authorized EPA and other government agencies to create and enforce regulations in order to put those laws into effect. EPA regulations cover a range of environmental and public health protection issues, from setting standards for clean water to specifying cleanup levels for toxic waste sites to controlling air pollution from industry and other sources. . . .

> Typically, Congress writes legislation about an environmental or public health protection issue before EPA writes any regulations to address it. Public interest groups, citizens, businesses, or other govern-

ment agencies contact Congress with an issue of concern. Congress may then decide to hold hearings and prepare a bill. If the bill gains approval in Congress, it then goes to the President for signature. If signed, the bill becomes a law. . . .

Through the years, Congress has passed and Presidents have signed numerous laws to protect human health and the environment. These laws give EPA most of its authority to write regulations, and serve as the foundation for achieving the nation's environmental and public health protection goals. However, most laws do not have enough detail to be put into practice right away. EPA is called a regulatory agency because Congress authorizes us to write regulations that explain the critical technical, operational, and legal details necessary to implement laws.

For example, the Resource Conservation and Recovery Act (RCRA) requires us to write standards for managing hazardous waste. RCRA's central mandate requires EPA to develop standards to protect human health and the environment, but does not say precisely what those standards should be. As in many other laws, Congress entrusts EPA to develop most of the details for regulations based on our technical and policy expertise.

U.S. Environmental Protection Agency, *How We Write Regulations: An Online Brochure*, http://www.epa.gov/lawsregs/brochure/index.html (last visited July 30, 2009).

The EPA presents this all very matter-of-factly, but it is worth pausing to ask *why* Congress might prefer to delegate substantial lawmaking authority to executive branch agencies, and whether (or when) such delegation is in the public interest. One obvious argument in favor of delegation is that administrative agencies may have specialized expertise that makes them more effective policymakers, especially in complex technical fields like environmental protection and securities regulation. There was a time—particularly during and immediately after President Roosevelt's New Deal—when many leading scholars and government officials thought that the dispassionate application of technocratic expertise by appropriately trained specialists was the best way to address a variety of social problems. A consequence of this perspective was the view that the best way for *Congress* to address such social problems was to delegate much of the decisionmaking authority to the experts in the agency bureaucracy, so that they could apply their problem-solving skills free from the distorting influence of politics. Few people today subscribe to a vision of the administrative state as involving politically neutral, technocratic problem-solving; indeed, it is not clear how many people ever wholly subscribed to that simplistic characterization of the virtues of agency policymaking. Most people would now agree that regulatory policy decisions involve political value choices, and many observers have also developed a healthy skepticism of bureaucratic agencies' claims to superior wisdom. Yet to conclude that technocratic expertise isn't everything is not necessarily to conclude that it is irrelevant, and the idea that agencies have substantial expertise advantages over legislatures remains pervasive.

But why, exactly, must this specialized competence be located in the *executive* branch of government? After all, most agency heads are political appointees with limited expertise in much of what their agencies do; they rely on large, permanent, professional staffs, as well as consultations with outside advisers, to make critical policy choices. Why couldn't legislators acquire their own expertise, for example by dramatically expanding the staffs of the various legislative committees? If you are skeptical that such measures would really enable the legislative branch to replicate the sort of expertise that executive branch agencies are thought to possess, why is that? Does the fact that executive branch agencies are responsible for applying legal rules in specific cases give them an inherent advantage in developing specialized knowledge about the regulatory field? Is the structure of executive agencies, and the process of promulgating administrative regulations, somehow more conducive to the participation of technical experts in the formulation of policy?

Or perhaps the difference between congressional lawmaking and agency regulation is not so much that agencies have a superior capacity *to generate or acquire* policy-relevant technical information, but rather that agencies have a greater capacity *to utilize effectively* such information in the formulation of policy. Consider three arguments as to why the administrative process may be more conducive to complex, technical policymaking than is the legislative process. *First*, the crowded legislative agenda means that Congress simply does not have time to study, let alone address, the myriad issues and questions that would arise with respect to even a moderately complex statute. If Congress tried to specify all impermissible practices in securities markets, or all the details of how hazardous waste should be handled and treated (down to the thickness of the barrels and the wording of the warning labels), Congress would never get anything done. *Second*, the legislative process is (by design) slow and cumbersome, and this makes it very difficult for Congress to react quickly to new information or changed circumstances. But in complex and rapidly evolving policy areas, effective governance requires dispatch and flexibility. *Third*, the pressures of day-to-day partisan and distributive politics may inhibit sensible, pragmatic application of the best available information to the problems at hand: Legislative decisions regarding military bases and weapons programs may be made not so much to advance the nation's security interests, but to enable powerful legislators to deliver "pork" to their districts; environmental regulations may be distorted by politicians who "grandstand," using simple slogans to obscure the complex trade-offs involved in managing environmental risks; legislators may be unduly responsive to the well-heeled interest groups that finance their campaigns; etc. For these reasons, many observers conclude that delegation to agencies, while certainly no panacea, is often desirable. Indeed, members of Congress may reach this conclusion as well, and may favor delegation as a solution to legislative inefficiencies and pathologies, of which members of Congress are perhaps especially aware.

But these arguments are troubling, in that they seem to reject—or at least to question—our system's fundamental commitments to democratic accountability and the separation of powers. It may be true that the legislative process laid out by Article I, § 7 is slow and cumbersome, and that this limits the amount of federal legislative activity and inhibits rapid policy change. But isn't that precisely the point of this institutional structure? It is *supposed* to be difficult for the federal government to make law; the founders thought this cumbersome lawmaking process would protect individual liberty from government overreaching, and would also preserve the position of the state governments as the principal lawmakers in our federal system. *See, e.g.*, Bradford R. Clark, *Separation of Powers as a Safeguard of Federalism*, 79 Tex. L. Rev. 1321, 1344 (2001). If Congress's inability to delegate would lead Congress to legislate less often, and on fewer subjects (because the costs of acquiring all the relevant information and writing sufficiently detailed legislation are prohibitively high), then perhaps that is all to the good. *See* John F. Manning, *Lawmaking Made Easy*, 10 Greenbag 2d 191 (2007).

And isn't there something deeply anti-democratic about the claim that regulatory policy decisions need to be insulated from politics? The pressures induced by regular democratic elections of course can have adverse effects on legislative decisionmaking; few would assert that representative democracy is a perfect system. But democratic accountability also serves extraordinarily valuable functions, chief among them allowing the people to select the leaders they want and to check legislative abuses through the threat of electoral retaliation. Agencies' insulation from electoral pressure may entail a greater propensity for arbitrary, incompetent, or even abusive decisionmaking, against which voters have little effective recourse. Furthermore, the possibility of delegating to agencies may enable *legislators* to evade accountability for public policy decisions. Imagine a situation in which the public demands that the legislature "do something" about some perceived public problem, but the legislators realize that each of the available policy options might antagonize some powerful constituency, or might simply not work. Legislators caught in this bind might view delegation to agencies an attractive option: They can claim to have "done something," and if the agency's resolution of the problem is popular, they can take credit; if the agency takes unpopular action or fails to solve the problem, they can blame the agency for malfeasance or incompetence. *See, e.g.*, Morris P. Fiorina, Congress: Keystone of the Washington Establishment (1977); Peter H. Aranson, Ernest Gellhorn, & Glen O. Robinson, *A Theory of Legislative Delegation*, 68 Cornell L. Rev. 1, 57–59 (1982); Morris P. Fiorina, *Legislative Choice of Regulatory Forms: Legal Process or Administrative Process?*, 39 Pub. Choice 33, 46–52 (1982). This use of delegation is problematic, in that the principle of democratic accountability may require elected representatives to make the hard policy choices and to take the consequences, not to avoid them by passing them off to someone else.

But perhaps these critiques of delegation are overstated. The fact that agency officials are not directly accountable to the electorate, and are insulated to some degree from day-to-day legislative politics, does not mean that they are entirely immune to democratic constraints. After all, agencies only have the authority that Congress grants to them, and Congress can expand, contract, or eliminate that authority by statute. Congress may also influence agency decisionmaking through other forms of oversight, which (sophisticated) voters can also monitor. On top of that, both the President and the Senate play a role in selecting agency personnel, and agencies are part of an executive branch headed by the President, who is accountable to a national electorate. Voters, moreover, can presumably hold their elected legislators accountable for these decisions regarding the scope and extent of delegation.

As for the claim that federal lawmaking is supposed to be slow, cumbersome, and infrequent, that argument may understate the importance of enabling desirable government action, especially under modern conditions. *See, e.g.,* Thomas W. Merrill, *Rethinking Article I, Section 1: From Nondelegation to Exclusive Delegation*, 104 Colum. L. Rev. 2097, 2145–47 (2004). Perhaps the congressional lawmaking structure was appropriate for achieving that balance in the late eighteenth century, when the federal government's functions "were limited essentially to the prevention of disorder, protection from foreign invasion, the enlargement of national boundaries, the stimulation of international trade, and the creation of a scheme of officials to settle civil disputes." James M. Landis, The Administrative Process 6 (1938). As the country grew, its population expanded, and the social externalities associated with industrialization became a more significant threat to the public welfare, the balance arguably shifted. On this view, delegation to agencies entails not a repudiation of the basic values of our system, but rather a wise and necessary adaptation to changed circumstances. This theme runs deep in the Supreme Court's cases. *See, e.g.,* American Power & Light Co. v. SEC, 329 U.S. 90, 105 (1946) ("The judicial approval accorded these 'broad' standards for administrative action is a reflection of the necessities of modern legislation dealing with complex economic and social problems."). Furthermore, the alternatives to agency delegation, in a modern society that demands federal government action, might not necessarily be fewer, but more detailed, congressional statutes. Prohibiting delegation might lead instead either to crude, ill-thought-out statutory responses to pressing problems, or to vague, open-ended statutes. As a practical matter, the latter possibility would entail a delegation of implementation authority to the judiciary, which might be even less well-suited than executive branch agencies to making quasi-legislative regulatory policy decisions. *See* Peter H. Schuck, *Delegation and Democracy: Comments on David Schoenbrod*, 20 Cardozo L. Rev. 775, 790–91 (1999); David B. Spence & Frank Cross, *A Public Choice Case for the Administrative State*, 89 Geo. L.J. 97, 135–141 (2000).

The preceding discussion only scratches the surface of a rich, complex, and longstanding debate about when, or under what conditions, it is appropriate for Congress to delegate what looks like legislative power to administrative agencies. These normative questions are important, because while the question whether delegation to agencies is *legal* is conceptually distinct from the question whether such delegation is *desirable*, one's views on the risks and benefits of delegation often influence one's assessment of the legal issues. Furthermore, as we will see, our legal and political culture's ambivalent embrace of the administrative state—the felt need for delegation to agencies as a prerequisite for effective governance, combined with a deep anxiety about undemocratic and arbitrary bureaucracy—has influenced the development of many aspects of our administrative law. The remainder of this section will focus specifically on the question whether (or under what conditions, and on what theory) the Constitution permits Congress to delegate lawmaking authority to agencies.

## B.   THE CONSTITUTIONAL STATUS OF THE NONDELEGATION DOCTRINE

As we have just seen, there are powerful normative arguments both for and against broad delegations of lawmaking power from Congress to administrative agencies. In the materials that follow, we will see that there are also conflicting signals about the degree to which such delegations are consistent with the text, structure, and history of the U.S. Constitution. In the cases in this part, you will see the Supreme Court struggle to develop a coherent and meaningful "nondelegation doctrine" that imposes some limits on Congress's authority to delegate legislative power to administrative agencies while acknowledging the reality that all administrative statutes inevitably transfer some policymaking discretion to agencies that implement them. As you read these materials, consider these questions: Has the Court convincingly identified a constitutional source for the nondelegation doctrine? Has the Court developed workable criteria for sorting permissible from impermissible delegations of policymaking discretion? What kind of power do agencies exercise when they promulgate rules pursuant to an open-ended delegation? Legislative? Executive? Something in between?

### a.   The Canonical Formulation of the Nondelegation Doctrine

The following case, *J.W. Hampton, Jr. & Co. v. United States*, contains a canonical and oft-cited formulation of the nondelegation doctrine. *Hampton* both summarizes the basic principles and values at stake, and articulates the test for distinguishing legitimate from illegitimate delegations of discretionary authority to the executive branch. As you read the case, ask yourself whether the *Hampton* standard strikes the right balance. Is it faithful to constitutional principles? Does *Hampton*'s approach to drawing the constitutional line seem sensible and workable? If not, how would you approach the issue?

---

## J. W. Hampton, Jr. & Co. v. United States

Supreme Court of the United States
276 U.S. 394 (1928)

■ MR. CHIEF JUSTICE TAFT delivered the opinion of the Court.

J. W. Hampton, Jr., & Co. [imported] barium dioxide, which the collector of customs assessed at the dutiable rate of six cents per pound. This was two cents per pound more than that fixed by statute.... The rate was raised by the collector by virtue of the proclamation of the President ... issued under, and by authority of, § 315 of Title III of the Tariff Act ..., which is the so-called flexible tariff provision. Protest was made and an appeal was taken.... The pertinent parts of § 315 of Title III of the Tariff Act ... are as follows:

[The Court quoted § 315 of the Tariff Act, which authorized the President to adjust the duties fixed by the statute "whenever the President, upon investigation of the differences in costs of production of articles ... of the United States and of like or similar articles ... of competing foreign countries, shall find ... that the duties fixed in this act do not equalize the said differences in costs of production in the United States and the principal competing country." Upon such a finding, the President was empowered to make such "changes in classifications or increases or decreases in any rate of duty" as were necessary "to equalize" those "costs of production." Section 315 further provided that in making this determination, the President was to take into account:

(1) the differences in conditions in production, including wages, costs of material, and other items in costs of production of such or similar articles in the United States and in competing foreign countries; (2) the differences in the wholesale selling prices of domestic and foreign articles in the principal markets of the United States; (3) advantages granted to a foreign producer by a foreign government, or by a person, partnership, corporation, or association in a foreign country; and (4) any other advantages or disadvantages in competition.

The Act also stated that all investigations into differences in production costs were to be made by the United States Tariff Commission, which was required to "give reasonable public notice of its hearings and ... reasonable opportunity to parties interested to be present, to produce evidence, and to be heard." Pursuant to this authority, President Coolidge had issued a declaration increasing the tariff on barium dioxide from 4 to 6 cents per pound.]

The issue here is as to the constitutionality of § 315, upon which depends the authority for the proclamation of the President and for two of the six cents per pound duty collected from the petitioner. The contention of the taxpayers is ... that the section is invalid in that it is a delegation to the President of the legislative power, which by Article I, § 1 of the Constitution, is vested in Congress....

... It seems clear what Congress intended by § 315. Its plan was to secure by law the imposition of customs duties on articles of imported merchandise which should equal the difference between the cost of producing in a foreign country the articles in question and laying them down for sale in the United States, and the cost of producing and selling like or similar articles in the United States, so that the duties ... enable domestic producers to compete on terms of equality with foreign producers in the markets of the United States. It may be that it is difficult to fix with exactness this difference, but the difference which is sought in the statute is perfectly clear and perfectly intelligible. Because of the difficulty in practically determining what that difference is, Congress seems to have doubted that the information in its possession was such as to enable it to make the adjustment accurately, and also to have apprehended that with changing conditions the difference might vary in such a way that some readjustments would be necessary to give effect to the principle on which the statute proceeds. To avoid such difficulties, Congress adopted in § 315 the method of describing with clearness what its policy and plan was and then authorizing a member of the Executive Branch to carry out this policy and plan and to find the changing difference from time to time and to make the adjustments necessary to conform the duties to the standard underlying that policy and plan. . . .

. . . The Federal Constitution and state Constitutions of this country divide the governmental power into three branches. The first is the legislative, the second is the executive, and the third is the judicial, and the rule is that in the actual administration of the government Congress or the Legislature should exercise the legislative power, the President or the state executive, the Governor, the executive power, and the courts or the judiciary the judicial power, and in carrying out that constitutional division into three branches it is a breach of the national fundamental law if Congress gives up its legislative power and transfers it to the President, or to the judicial branch, or if by law it attempts to invest itself or its members with either executive power or judicial power. This is not to say that the three branches are not co-ordinate parts of one government and that each in the field of its duties may not invoke the action of the two other branches in so far as the action invoked shall not be an assumption of the constitutional field of action of another branch. In determining what it may do in seeking assistance from another branch, the extent and character of that assistance must be fixed according to common sense and the inherent necessities of the governmental co-ordination.

The field of Congress involves all and many varieties of legislative action, and Congress has found it frequently necessary to use officers of the executive branch, within defined limits, to secure the exact effect intended by its acts of legislation, by vesting discretion in such officers to make public regulations interpreting a statute and directing the details of its execution. . . .

Congress may feel itself unable conveniently to determine exactly when its exercise of the legislative power should become effective, because dependent on future conditions, and it may leave the determination of such time to the decision of an executive. . . .

. . . [O]ne of the great functions conferred on Congress by the Federal Constitution is the regulation of interstate commerce and rates to be exacted by interstate carriers for the passenger and merchandise traffic. The rates to be fixed are myriad. If Congress were to be required to fix every rate, it would be impossible to exercise the power at all. Therefore, common sense requires that in the fixing of such rates Congress, may provide a Commission, as it does, called the Interstate Commerce Commission, to fix those rates, after hearing evidence and argument concerning them from interested parties, all in accord with a general rule that Congress first lays down, that rates shall be just and reasonable considering the service given, and not discriminatory. As said by this Court in Interstate Commerce Commission v. Goodrich Transit Co., 224 U.S. 194, 214[:]

> "The Congress may not delegate its purely legislative power to a commission, but, having laid down the general rules of action under which a commission shall proceed, it may require of that commission the application of such rules to particular situations and the investigation of facts, with a view to making orders in a particular matter within the rules laid down by the Congress."

... The same principle that permits Congress to exercise its rate-making power in interstate commerce by declaring the rule which shall prevail in the legislative fixing of rates, and enables it to remit to a rate-making body created in accordance with its provisions the fixing of such rates, justifies a similar provision for the fixing of customs duties on imported merchandise. If Congress shall lay down by legislative act an intelligible principle to which the person or body authorized to fix such rates is directed to conform, such legislative action is not a forbidden delegation of legislative power. If it is thought wise to vary the customs duties according to changing conditions of production at home and abroad, it may authorize the Chief Executive to carry out this purpose, with the advisory assistance of a Tariff Commission appointed under congressional authority....

---

**1. The Rationales for a Constitutionally Grounded Nondelegation Doctrine**—*Hampton* endorses the basic principle that Congress may not delegate its legislative power to the executive—a position that has been repeatedly reaffirmed. *See, e.g.,* Mistretta v. United States, 488 U.S. 361, 371–72 (1989) ("[W]e long have insisted that 'the integrity and maintenance of the system of government ordained by the Constitution' mandate that Congress generally cannot delegate its legislative power to another Branch.") (quoting Marshall Field & Co. v. Clark, 143 U.S. 649, 692 (1892)). But where does this nondelegation doctrine come from? From which constitutional provision or provisions does the Court infer such a doctrine? Consider the following possibilities:

**a. Separation of powers.** The Supreme Court has sometimes asserted that the nondelegation doctrine is an inherent consequence of the Constitution's general commitment to a separation of legislative and executive powers. *See Mistretta,* 488 U.S. at 371. Proponents of this rationale typically cite the work of John Locke, a seventeenth-century English political theorist whose writing greatly influenced the founders. *See, e.g.,* Larry Alexander & Saikrishna Prakash, *Reports of the Nondelegation Doctrine's Death Are Greatly Exaggerated,* 70 U. CHI. L. REV. 1297, 1297

(2003); Ernest Gellhorn, *Returning to First Principles*, 36 Am. U. L. Rev. 345, 347–48 (1987). Locke famously wrote that "[t]he power of the legislative, being derived from the people by a positive voluntary grant and institution, can be no other than what that positive grant conveyed, which being only to make laws, and not to make legislators, the legislative can have no power to transfer their authority of making laws and place it in other hands." John Locke, Second Treatise of Government 75 (C.B. McPherson ed., 1980) (1690).

Yet Locke's observation—although frequently cited—is hardly conclusive. As Professor Thomas Merrill points out, Locke's own work recognizes that the executive must enjoy some lawmaking authority, given the fact that the legislature is often out of session, and that contingencies the legislature could not have foreseen will inevitably arise during its absence. *See* Thomas W. Merrill, *Rethinking Article I, Section 1: From Nondelegation to Exclusive Delegation*, 104 Colum. L. Rev. 2097, 2133 (2004). Locke thus wrote that the prerogatives of the crown necessarily included the

> power to act according to discretion, for the public good, without the prescription of the Law, and sometimes even against it . . .: for since in some governments the lawmaking power is not always in being, and is usually too numerous, and so too slow for the dispatch requisite to execution; and because also it is impossible to foresee, and so by laws to provide for, all accidents and necessities that may concern the public, or to make such laws as will do no harm, if they are executed with an inflexible rigour, on all occasions, and upon all persons that may come in their way; therefore there is a latitude left to the executive power, to do many things of choice which the laws do not prescribe.

Locke, *supra*, at 84. Whether or not the founders would have embraced Locke's broad view of executive prerogative, his description is telling insofar as it undermines the proposition that the separation-of-powers theory read by the founders necessarily supports an absolute legislative monopoly on lawmaking authority. *See also* Blackstone, 1 Commentaries *260–*261 (noting that the crown could issue "binding" proclamations that are grounded in the idea that while "the making of laws is entirely the work of . . . the legislative branch, of the sovereign power, yet the manner, time, and circumstances of putting those laws into execution must frequently be left to the discretion of the executive magistrate"). Furthermore, to the extent that Lockean nondelegation theory rests on the premise that power delegated from the people to the legislature could not be *sub*delegated to another entity, that premise contradicts well-settled eighteenth-century agency theory, which held that the recipient of delegated authority could properly subdelegate that authority when necessary to effectuate the aims of the original delegation. *See* Patrick W. Duff & Horace E. Whiteside, *Delegata Potestas Non Potest Delegari: A Maxim of American Constitutional Law*, 14 Cornell L. Q. 168 (1929).

In light of the foregoing evidence, can the nondelegation doctrine properly be attributed to the separation of powers? If not, does that necessarily rule out the legitimacy of such a doctrine, or does it merely suggest that its grounding must lie in inferences from more specific elements of the constitutional structure?

**b.** **The Article I Vesting Clause.** The Supreme Court has frequently grounded the nondelegation doctrine in the Vesting Clause of Article I, § 1, which provides that "[a]ll legislative Powers herein granted shall be vested in a Congress of the United States." *See, e.g.*, Loving v. United States, 517 U.S. 748, 758 (1996); Touby v. United States, 500 U.S. 160, 164–65 (1991). It is perhaps notable, in this respect, that this clause vests "*[a]ll* legislative powers" in Congress. In contrast, the other two Vesting Clauses vest "[t]he executive Power" and "[t]he judicial Power" in the President and the federal courts, respectively, without stating that *all* such power shall be vested in the branches to which those clauses refer.

Some scholars, however, have questioned the Court's conclusion that the Article I Vesting Clause implies some form of nondelegation principle. *First*, the Necessary and Proper Clause of Article I—which authorizes Congress "[t]o make all Laws which shall be necessary and proper for carrying into Execution the foregoing [legislative] Powers," U.S. Const. art. I, § 8, cl. 18—might be read to give Congress the authority to delegate lawmaking authority when necessary to implement its other Article I powers (such as the power to regulate interstate commerce). *See* Peter M. Shane, *Conventionalism in Constitutional Interpretation and the Place of Administrative Agencies*, 36 Am. U. L. Rev. 573, 597–98 (1987); Harold J. Krent, *Delegation and Its Discontents*, 94 Colum. L. Rev. 710, 736 (1994) (reviewing David Schoenbrod, Power without Responsibility (1993)). *But see* Gary Lawson, *Delegation and Original Meaning*, 88 Va. L. Rev. 327, 347–48 (2002) (arguing that "proper" was a term of art limiting Congress to implemental actions that were otherwise properly within the grant of Article I power, and that a delegation of legislative powers that otherwise contradicts Article I could never be "proper" within the meaning of that clause). *Second*, even if Article I *vests* the legislative power exclusively in Congress, that does not necessarily imply that Congress cannot *transfer* that power. *See, e.g.*, Merrill, *supra*; Eric A. Posner & Adrian Vermeule, *Interring the Nondelegation Doctrine*, 69 U. Chi. L. Rev. 1721, 1729 (2003). *Third*, even if we assume both that Article I vests the "legislative power" exclusively in Congress and that this power is nondelegable, it is not clear that agencies technically exercise "legislative power" when they implement a statute by promulgating rules and regulations. *See, e.g.*, Posner & Vermeule, *supra*, at 1725–26 ("Creating rules pursuant to valid statutory authority isn't lawmaking, but law execution."). Do you find any of these responses sufficiently persuasive to overcome the textual inference that the Article I Vesting Clause assigns legislative power exclusively to Congress and thereby prohibits congressional delegation of lawmaking power to executive branch agencies?

**c.** **Bicameralism and presentment.** The Court's third rationale for the nondelegation doctrine turns on the singular attributes of the congressional lawmaking process, including most importantly bicameral passage and presentment to the President. *See, e.g.*, Loving v. United States, 517 U.S. 748, 757–58 (1996). As discussed in Chapter One (see pp. 22–25, *supra*), that cumbersome process arguably serves several crucial constitutional interests such as making it more difficult for parochial factions to procure legislation that serves their private advantage at the public expense; promoting caution and deliberation; giving special protection to the residents of small states (and other political minorities); and filtering out bad laws by raising the decision costs of passing *any* law. The nondelegation doctrine protects those interests by preventing Congress from circumventing the Article I, § 7 process through the faster and easier alternative of agency lawmaking. This rationale for the nondelegation doctrine also builds upon a well-established canon of structural interpretation that:

> when a [law] gives a new right or a new power, and provides a specific, full, and adequate mode of executing the power or enforcing the right given, the fact that a special mode is prescribed will be regarded as excluding, by implication, the right to resort to any other mode of executing the power or of enforcing the right.

Henry Campbell Black, Handbook on the Construction and Interpretation of the Laws § 72. at 221 (2d ed., 1911); *see also, e.g.*, National R.R. Passenger Corp. v. National Ass'n of R.R. Passengers, 414 U.S. 453, 458 (1974); Botany Worsted Mills v. United States, 278 U.S. 282, 289 (1929). The commonsense theory underlying that canon is that the framers of the Constitution presumably would not have taken the trouble to spell out elaborate procedures for the exercise of a newly granted power if those procedures were not integral to the governmental scheme.

Professors Posner and Vermeule argue, however, that the interests served by bicameralism and presentment do not cut against delegation for a simple reason: If the process of bicameralism and presentment does in fact promote a variety of important public ends, then presumably that process will also filter out delegations that fail to serve those ends. *See* Posner & Vermeule, *supra*, at 1750–51. How persuasive is that claim? Are Posner and Vermeule suggesting that the only constitutional protection for bicameralism and presentment is bicameralism and presentment itself? Could one imagine a situation in which it would be impossible under the cumbersome Article I, § 7 process to muster the political will to create a detailed solution to a social problem (such as insider trading or nonreciprocal tariffs), but quite possible to agree to pass the question off to another institution that was not operating under similar constraints? Does the fact that a delegation itself goes through bicameralism and presentment ensure that the resulting administrative scheme will preserve the values that would have been safeguarded if the regulatory details themselves had had to pass through the Article I, § 7 procedures?

**2. *Historical Practice***—What significance, if any, should we ascribe to the fact that Congress has delegated broad rulemaking power to agencies since the very beginning of the Republic? *See, e.g.*, Kenneth Culp Davis, Discretionary Justice: A Preliminary Inquiry 47–48 (1969); Eric Posner & Adrian Vermeule, *Interring the Nondelegation Doctrine*, 69 U. Chi. L. Rev.

1721, 1735–36 (2003). For example, the First Congress enacted a statute authorizing the payment of military pensions "under such regulations as the President of the United States may direct," Act of Sept. 29, 1789, 1 Stat. 95, and a statute authorizing the executive to issue licenses to trade with Native American tribes "under such rules and regulations as the President may prescribe," Act of July 22, 1790, 1 Stat. 137. In Wayman v. Southard, 23 U.S. (10 Wheat.) 1 (1825), the Supreme Court sustained a statute authorizing the Court to prescribe rules governing the execution of judgments in the federal courts; while Congress could have prescribed those rules itself, Chief Justice Marshall's opinion for the Court concluded that "Congress may certainly delegate to others, powers which the legislature may rightfully exercise itself." *Id*. at 43.

At the same time, the Supreme Court has consistently articulated a constitutional concern about delegation, and has asserted that the Constitution imposes limits on congressional power to delegate lawmaking authority to the other branches. *See, e.g.*, Marshall Field & Co. v. Clark, 143 U.S. 649, 692 (1892) ("That congress cannot delegate legislative power to the president is a principle universally recognized as vital to the integrity and maintenance of the system of government ordained by the constitution."); Wayman v. Southard, 23 U.S. (10 Wheat.) 1, 43 (1825) (stating that Congress may not delegate authority over "important subjects" but can do so with respect to "those of less interest"). Given Congress's self-interest concerning this question, should the *judiciary's* longstanding assertions about the meaning of the Constitution count for more than competing constructions implicit in *legislative* practice? If the Court has perennially articulated a strong nondelegation principle but almost never applied to strike down an Act of Congress, should a modern interpreter go by what the Court has *said* (delegation is impermissible) or what it has *done* (consistently upholding delegations)?

**3. The Intelligible Principle Test**—*Hampton*'s so-called "intelligible principle" test remains the governing doctrinal formulation for distinguishing legitimate from illegitimate delegations. *See, e.g.*, Whitman v. American Trucking Associations, 531 U.S. 457, 472 (2001) (pp. 410–415, *infra*); Loving v. United States, 517 U.S. 748, 771 (1996). As Chief Justice Taft's *Hampton* opinion explains, "If Congress shall lay down by legislative act an intelligible principle to which the person or body authorized to fix such rates is directed to conform, such legislative action is not a forbidden delegation of legislative power." This test purports to reconcile the formal nondelegation requirement with the reality that Congress frequently grants agencies broad authority to flesh out the binding policy details of an open-ended regulatory statute.

The animating principle underlying the intelligible principle test appears to be the idea that courts can draw a meaningful line between an agency's *implementation* of a policy decision made by Congress (which may involve some policy discretion, but is not a "legislative" activity) and an agency's exercise of (delegated) legislative power. *See* Cynthia R. Farina, *Statutory Interpretation and the Balance of Power in the Administrative*

*State*, 89 Colum. L. Rev. 452, 481 (1989). For example, in United States v. Grimaud, 220 U.S. 506 (1911), the Court held that no delegation has occurred "when Congress had legislated and indicated its will, . . . giv[ing] those who were to act under such general provisions 'power to fill up the details' by the establishment of administrative rules and regulations." *Id.* at 517 (quoting Wayman v. Southard, 23 U.S. (10 Wheat.) 1, 43 (1825)). As the Court recently put it, "[t]he intelligible-principle rule seeks to enforce the understanding that Congress may not delegate the power to make laws and so may delegate no more than the authority to make policies and rules that implement its statutes." Loving v. United States, 517 U.S. 748, 771 (1996). How convincing is that rationale for the intelligible principle test? Does it rely too confidently on courts' ability to distinguish between "legislative" lawmaking and "executive" lawmaking? Might one alternatively justify the intelligible principle test as a means for distinguishing *legitimate* delegations of legislative power from *illegitimate* delegations of legislative power? If so, why should the presence of an "intelligible principle" be the measure of a legitimate delegation?

### b.   The (Brief) Rise and (Long) Fall of the Nondelegation Doctrine

In 2000, Professor Cass Sunstein wrote that the nondelegation doctrine "has had one good year, and 211 bad ones (and counting)." Cass R. Sunstein, *Nondelegation Canons*, 67 U. Chi. L. Rev. 315, 322 (2000). By that he meant that although the Court has embraced the nondelegation principle throughout much of the nation's history, the Court has only twice relied on the nondelegation doctrine to invalidate an administrative statute as unconstitutional—both times in 1935, at the height of the Roosevelt Administration's efforts, through the collection of legislative and executive initiatives known as the New Deal, to address the unprecedented economic dislocations of the Great Depression. These two cases, Panama Refining Co. v. Ryan, 293 U.S. 388 (1935), and A.L.A. Schechter Poultry Corp. v. United States, 295 U.S. 495 (1935), invoked the nondelegation doctrine to strike down provisions of the National Industrial Recovery Act (NIRA), a centerpiece of the New Deal. *Panama Refining* struck down a relatively peripheral NIRA provision that allowed the President to make it a violation of federal law to sell oil produced in excess of production quotas imposed by state law. *Schechter Poultry*, on the other hand, invalidated the central provision of the NIRA, § 3, which had authorized the President to approve "codes of fair competition"—essentially production and price controls— that were to be submitted by trade or industrial groups throughout the nation. Under § 3 of the NIRA, once the President approved a code of fair competition, it became binding federal law, and any firm in the relevant industry that did not comply with the code could be prosecuted and sanctioned. *See* National Industrial Recovery Act, § 3(a), 48 Stat. 195, 196.

According to one standard account, *Panama Refining* and *Schechter Poultry* represented part of the broader resistance of a largely conservative Supreme Court to the perceived transformation in size and scope of the federal government during the Roosevelt Administration. *See, e.g.*, Peter H.

Irons, The New Deal Lawyers 13–14, 101–02 (1982); Drew Pearson & Robert S. Allen, The Nine Old Men 2 (1974); Fred Rodell, Nine Men: A Political History of the Supreme Court from 1790 to 1955, at 217 (1955); *but see* Barry Cushman, Rethinking the New Deal Court (1998) (arguing that the story of the Justices' behavior is far more complex). To be sure, the modern administrative state originated well before the New Deal. In 1887, Congress created the Interstate Commerce Commission to ensure that railroads charged reasonable and nondiscriminatory rates, and the early decades of the twentieth century witnessed the creation of numerous important regulatory agencies, including the Federal Reserve Board, the Federal Trade Commission, the Federal Radio Commission, and the Federal Power Commission. *See* Cass R. Sunstein, After the Rights Revolution 19 (1990). But the New Deal appeared to reflect a whole new attitude toward the role of the federal government in our society. As Professor Robert Rabin has written, "what distinguished [Franklin Roosevelt] sharply from all of his predecessors in office was his conviction that government had an affirmative obligation to do whatever was necessary to restore a healthy economy, and as a corollary, his belief that the economy would almost certainly remain debilitated without substantial governmental intervention superseding the normal workings of the market." Robert L. Rabin, *Federal Regulation in Historical Perspective*, 38 Stan. L. Rev. 1189, 1246 (1986). On that view, "[a]ny sector of the economy that was malfunctioning needed government-endorsed controls on trade practices necessary to 'make things right.'" *Id.* Partly for this reason, New Deal reformers regarded the separation of powers as an impediment to needed social and economic reform. *See* Sunstein, *supra*, at 22–23. This New Deal attitude toward the separation of powers is well captured by an influential 1938 book, The Administrative Process, by James Landis, one of the major architects of the New Deal's financial legislation and, as a Commissioner and then Chair of the SEC, an influential executor of the resulting regulatory scheme:

> In terms of political theory, the administrative process springs from the inadequacy of a simple tripartite form of government to deal with modern problems. It represents a striving to adapt governmental technique, that still divides under three rubrics, to modern needs and, at the same time, to preserve those elements of responsibility and those conditions of balance that have distinguished Anglo–American government....

> If in private life we were to organize a unit for the operation of an industry, it would scarcely follow Montesquieu's lines. As yet no organization in private industry either has been conceived along those triadic contours, nor would its normal development, if so conceived, have tended to conform to them. Yet the problems of operating an industry resemble to a great degree those entailed by its regulation.

> .  .  .

> ... The administrative process is, in essence, our generation's answer to the inadequacy of the judicial and the legislative processes....

JAMES M. LANDIS, THE ADMINISTRATIVE PROCESS 1, 10, 46 (1938). In other words, if the federal government was to assume responsibility for the regulation of industry in the name of ensuring social and economic security for the populace, the notion of the separation of powers had to yield to modern conceptions of government rooted in administrative specialization and expertise. *See id.* at 25–34.

*Schechter Poultry* is excerpted below. As you read the case, consider whether the decision embodies principles that can help make sense of the nondelegation doctrine. *See* JOHN HART ELY, DEMOCRACY AND DISTRUST 132–34 (1980). Does the Court's intelligible principle analysis in *Schechter Poultry* successfully distinguish between (impermissible) grants of legislative power and (permissible) grants of executive power to fill in the details of a statutory scheme as Congress's agent?

---

## A.L.A. Schechter Poultry Corp. v. United States

Supreme Court of the United States
295 U.S. 495 (1935)

■ MR. CHIEF JUSTICE HUGHES delivered the opinion of the Court.

Petitioners ... were convicted in the District Court of the United States for the Eastern District of New York on eighteen counts of an indictment charging violations of what is known as the "Live Poultry Code," and on an additional count for conspiracy to commit such violations. By demurrer to the indictment and appropriate motions on the trial, the defendants contended ... that the code had been adopted pursuant to an unconstitutional delegation by Congress of legislative power....

The "Live Poultry Code" was promulgated under § 3 of the National Industrial Recovery Act. [Act of June 16, 1933, c. 90, 48 Stat. 195, 196; 15 U.S.C. § 703 (15 USCA § 703)]. That section, the pertinent provisions of which are set forth in the margin,[4] authorizes the President to approve "codes of fair competition." Such a code may be approved for a trade or

---

4. [The relevant provisions of the National Industrial Recovery Act are as follows:]

"Codes of fair competition.

"Sec. 3.   (a) Upon the application to the President by one or more trade or industrial associations or groups, the President may approve a code or codes of fair competition for the trade or industry or subdivision thereof, represented by the applicant or applicants, if the President finds (1) that such associations or groups impose no inequitable restrictions on admission to membership therein and are truly representative of such trades or industries or subdivisions thereof, and (2) that such code or codes are not designed to promote monopolies or to eliminate or oppress small enterprises and will not operate to discriminate against them, and will tend to effectuate the policy of this title: *Provided,* That such code or codes shall not permit monopolies or monopolistic practices: *Provided further,* That where such code or codes affect the services and welfare of persons engaged in other steps of the economic process, nothing in this section shall deprive such persons of the right to be heard prior to approval by the President of such code or codes. The President may, as a condition of his approval of any such code, impose such conditions (including requirements for the making of reports and the keeping of accounts) for the protection of consumers, competitors, employees, and others, and in furtherance of the

industry, upon application by one or more trade or industrial associations or groups, if the President finds (1) that such associations or groups "impose no inequitable restrictions on admission to membership therein and are truly representative," and (2) that such codes are not designed "to promote monopolies or to eliminate or oppress small enterprises and will not operate to discriminate against them, and will tend to effectuate the policy" of Title I of the act (15 USCA § 701 et seq.). Such codes "shall not permit monopolies or monopolistic practices." As a condition of his approval, the President may "impose such conditions (including requirements for the making of reports and the keeping of accounts) for the protection of consumers, competitors, employees, and others, and in furtherance of the public interest, and may provide such exceptions to and exemptions from the provisions of such code as the President in his discretion deems necessary to effectuate the policy herein declared." Where such a code has not been approved, the President may prescribe one, either on his own motion or on complaint. Violation of any provision of a code (so approved or prescribed) "in any transaction in or affecting interstate or foreign commerce" is made a misdemeanor punishable by a fine of not more than $500 for each offense, and each day the violation continues is to be deemed a separate offense.

The "Live Poultry Code" was approved by the President on April 13, 1934.... The declared purpose is "To effect the policies of title I of the

---

public interest, and may provide such exceptions to and exemptions from the provisions of such code, as the President in his discretion deems necessary to effectuate the policy herein declared.

"(b) After the President shall have approved any such code, the provisions of such code shall be the standards of fair competition for such trade or industry or subdivision thereof. Any violation of such standards in any transaction in or affecting interstate or foreign commerce shall be deemed an unfair method of competition in commerce within the meaning of the Federal Trade Commission Act, as amended (Chapter 2 of this title); but nothing in this title (Chapter) shall be construed to impair the powers of the Federal Trade Commission under such Act, as amended (Chapter 2).

"(c) The several district courts of the United States are hereby invested with jurisdiction to prevent and restrain violations of any code of fair competition approved under this title (Chapter); and it shall be the duty of the several district attorneys of the United States, in their respective districts, under the direction of the Attorney General, to institute proceedings in equity to prevent and restrain such violations.

"(d) Upon his own motion, or if complaint is made to the President that abuses inimical to the public interest and contrary to the policy herein declared are prevalent in any trade or industry or subdivision thereof, and if no code of fair competition therefor has theretofore been approved by the President, the President, after such public notice and hearing as he shall specify, may prescribe and approve a code of fair competition for such trade or industry or subdivision thereof, which shall have the same effect as a code of fair competition approved by the President under subsection (a) of this section.

\* \* \* \* \*

"(f) When a code of fair competition has been approved or prescribed by the President under this title (Chapter), any violation of any provision thereof in any transaction in or affecting interstate or foreign commerce shall be a misdemeanor and upon conviction thereof an offender shall be fined not more than $500 for each offense, and each day such violation continues shall be deemed a separate offense."

National Industrial Recovery Act." The code is established as "a code for fair competition for the live poultry industry of the metropolitan area in and about the City of New York." . . . .

The code fixes the number of hours for workdays. It provides that no employee, with certain exceptions, shall be permitted to work in excess of forty (40) hours in any one week, and that no employee, save as stated, "shall be paid in any pay period less than at the rate of fifty (50) cents per hour." The article containing "general labor provisions" prohibits the employment of any person under sixteen years of age, and declares that employees shall have the right of "collective bargaining" and freedom of choice with respect to labor organizations, in the terms of section 7(a) of the act (15 USCA § 707(a)). The minimum number of employees, who shall be employed by slaughterhouse operators, is fixed; the number being graduated according to the average volume of weekly sales. . . .

The seventh article, containing "trade practice provisions," prohibits various practices which are said to constitute "unfair methods of competition." The final article provides for verified reports, such as the Secretary or Administrator may require, "(1) for the protection of consumers, competitors, employees, and others, and in furtherance of the public interest, and (2) for the determination by the Secretary or Administrator of the extent to which the declared policy of the act is being effectuated by this code." The members of the industry are also required to keep books and records which "will clearly reflect all financial transactions of their respective businesses and the financial condition thereof," and to submit weekly reports showing the range of daily prices and volume of sales' for each kind of produce.

The President approved the code by an executive order (No. 6675–A) in which he found that the application for his approval had been duly made in accordance with the provisions of Title I of the National Industrial Recovery Act; that there had been due notice and hearings; that the code constituted "a code of fair competition" as contemplated by the act and complied with its pertinent provisions, including clauses (1) and (2) of subsection (a) of § 3 of Title I (15 USCA § 703(a)(1, 2)); and that the code would tend "to effectuate the policy of Congress as declared in section 1 of Title I." . . .

Of the eighteen counts of the indictment upon which the defendants were convicted, aside from the count for conspiracy, two counts charged violation of the minimum wage and maximum hour provisions of the code, and ten counts were for violation of the . . . "trade practice provisions". . . . [The other six counts related primarily to violations of local ordinances respecting licensing, reporting, and inspection.] . . .

. . . We recently had occasion to review the pertinent decisions and the general principles which govern the determination of this question. Panama Refining Company v. Ryan, 293 U.S. 388. The Constitution provides that "All legislative powers herein granted shall be vested in a Congress of the United States, which shall consist of a Senate and House of Representatives." Article 1, § 1. And the Congress is authorized "To make all Laws which shall be necessary and proper for carrying into Execution" its general powers. Article 1, § 8, par. 18. The Congress is not permitted to abdicate or to transfer to others the essential legislative functions with which it is thus vested. We have repeatedly recognized the necessity of adapting legislation to complex conditions involving a host of details with which the national Legislature cannot deal directly. We pointed out in the Panama Refining Company Case that the Constitution has never been regarded as denying to Congress the necessary resources of flexibility and practicality, which will enable it to perform its function in laying down policies and establishing standards, while leaving to selected instrumentalities the making of subordinate rules within prescribed limits and the determination of facts to which the policy as declared by the Legislature is to apply. But we said that the constant recognition of the necessity and validity of such provisions, and the wide range of administrative authority which has been developed by means of them, cannot be allowed to obscure the limitations of the authority to delegate, if our constitutional system is to be maintained.

Accordingly, we look to the statute to see whether Congress has overstepped these limitations—whether Congress in authorizing "codes of fair competition" has itself established the standards of legal obligation, thus performing its essential legislative function, or, by the failure to enact such standards, has attempted to transfer that function to others.

The aspect in which the question is now presented is distinct from that which was before us in the case of the Panama Refining Company. There the subject of the statutory prohibition was defined. National Industrial Recovery Act, § 9(c), 15 USCA § 709(c). That subject was the transportation in interstate and foreign commerce of petroleum and petroleum products which are produced or withdrawn from storage in excess of the amount permitted by state authority. The question was with respect to the range of discretion given to the President in prohibiting that transportation. As to the "codes of fair competition," under § 3 of the act, the question is more fundamental. It is whether there is any adequate definition of the subject to which the codes are to be addressed.

What is meant by "fair competition" as the term is used in the act? Does it refer to a category established in the law, and is the authority to make codes limited accordingly? Or is it used as a convenient designation for whatever set of laws the formulators of a code for a particular trade or industry may propose and the President may approve (subject to certain restrictions), or the President may himself prescribe, as being wise and beneficent provisions for the government of the trade or industry in order to accomplish the broad purposes of rehabilitation, correction, and expansion which are stated in the first section of Title I?[9]

---

**9.** That section [15 USCA § 701], under the heading "Declaration of Policy," is as follows: "Section 1. A national emergency productive of widespread unemployment and disorganization of industry, which burdens interstate and foreign commerce, affects the public welfare, and undermines the standards of living of the American people, is hereby declared to exist. It is hereby declared to be the policy of Congress to remove obstructions to the free flow of interstate and foreign commerce which tend to diminish the amount thereof; and to provide

The act does not define "fair competition." "Unfair competition," as known to the common law, is a limited concept. Primarily, and strictly, it relates to the palming off of one's goods as those of a rival trader. Good-year's Rubber Manufacturing Co. v. Good-year Rubber Co., 128 U.S. 598, 604; Howe Scale Co. v. Wyckoff, Seamans & Benedict, 198 U.S. 118, 140; Hanover Star Milling Co. v. Metcalf, 240 U.S. 403, 413. In recent years, its scope has been extended. It has been held to apply to misappropriation as well as misrepresentation, to the selling of another's goods as one's own— to misappropriation of what equitably belongs to a competitor. International News Service v. Associated Press, 248 U.S. 215, 241, 242. Unfairness in competition has been predicated of acts which lie outside the ordinary course of business and are tainted by fraud or coercion or conduct otherwise prohibited by law. *Id.*, 248 U.S. 315, page 258. But it is evident that in its widest range, "unfair competition," as it has been understood in the law, does not reach the objectives of the codes which are authorized by the National Industrial Recovery Act. The codes may, indeed, cover conduct which existing law condemns, but they are not limited to conduct of that sort. The government does not contend that the act contemplates such a limitation. It would be opposed both to the declared purposes of the act and to its administrative construction.

The Federal Trade Commission Act [Section 5 (15 USCA § 45)] introduced the expression "unfair methods of competition," which were declared to be unlawful. That was an expression new in the law. Debate apparently convinced the sponsors of the legislation that the words "unfair competition," in the light of their meaning at common law, were too narrow. We have said that the substituted phrase has a broader meaning, that it does not admit of precise definition, its scope being left to judicial determination as controversies arise. Federal Trade Commission v. Raladam Co., 283 U.S. 643, 648, 649; Federal Trade Commission v. R. F. Keppel, 291 U.S. 304, 310–312. What are "Unfair Methods of Competition" are thus to be determined in particular instances, upon evidence, in the light of particular competitive conditions and of what is found to be a specific and substantial public interest. Federal Trade Commission v. Beech–Nut Packing Co., 257 U.S. 441, 453; Federal Trade Commission v. Klesner, 280 U.S. 19, 27, 28; *Federal Trade Commission v. Raladam Co., supra; Federal Trade Commission v. R. F. Keppel, supra;* Federal Trade Commission v. Algoma Lumber Co., 291 U.S. 67, 73. To make this possible, Congress set up a special procedure. A commission, a quasi-judicial body, was created. Provision was made for formal complaint, for notice and hearing, for appropriate findings of fact supported by adequate evidence, and for judicial review to give

---

for the general welfare by promoting the organization of industry for the purpose of co-operative action among trade groups, to induce and maintain united action of labor and management under adequate governmental sanctions and supervision, to eliminate unfair competitive practices, to promote the fullest possible utilization of the present productive capacity of industries, to avoid undue restriction of production (except as may be temporarily required), to increase the consumption of industrial and agricultural products by increasing purchasing power, to reduce and relieve unemployment, to improve standards of labor, and otherwise to rehabilitate industry and to conserve natural resources."

assurance that the action of the commission is taken within its statutory authority. *Federal Trade Commission v. Raladam Co., supra*; *Federal Trade Commission v. Klesner, supra*.

In providing for codes, the National Industrial Recovery Act dispenses with this administrative procedure and with any administrative procedure of an analogous character. But the difference between the code plan of the Recovery Act and the scheme of the Federal Trade Commission Act lies not only in procedure but in subject-matter. We cannot regard the "fair competition" of the codes as antithetical to the "unfair methods of competition" of the Federal Trade Commission Act. The "fair competition" of the codes has a much broader range and a new significance. The Recovery Act provides that it shall not be construed to impair the powers of the Federal Trade Commission, but, when a code is approved, its provisions are to be the "standards of fair competition" for the trade or industry concerned, and any violation of such standards in any transaction in or affecting interstate or foreign commerce is to be deemed "an unfair method of competition" within the meaning of the Federal Trade Commission Act.

For a statement of the authorized objectives and content of the "codes of fair competition," we are referred repeatedly to the "Declaration of Policy" in section 1 of Title I of the Recovery Act (15 USCA § 701). Thus the approval of a code by the President is conditioned on his finding that it "will tend to effectuate the policy of this title." § 3(a). The President is authorized to impose such conditions "for the protection of consumers, competitors, employees, and others, and in furtherance of the public interest, and may provide such exceptions to and exemptions from the provisions of such code, as the President in his discretion deems necessary to effectuate the policy herein declared." *Id*. The "policy herein declared" is manifestly that set forth in section one. That declaration embraces a broad range of objectives. Among them we find the elimination of "unfair competitive practices." But, even if this clause were to be taken to relate to practices which fall under the ban of existing law, either common law or statute, it is still only one of the authorized aims described in section one. It is there declared to be "the policy of Congress"—"to remove obstructions to the free flow of interstate and foreign commerce which tend to diminish the amount thereof; and to provide for the general welfare by promoting the organization of industry for the purpose of cooperative action among trade groups, to induce and maintain united action of labor and management under adequate governmental sanctions and supervision, to eliminate unfair competitive practices, to promote the fullest possible utilization of the present productive capacity of industries, to avoid undue restriction of production (except as may be temporarily required), to increase the consumption of industrial and agricultural products by increasing purchasing power, to reduce and relieve unemployment, to improve standards of labor, and otherwise to rehabilitate industry and to conserve natural resources."

Under § 3, whatever "may tend to effectuate" these general purposes may be included in the "codes of fair competition." We think the conclusion is inescapable that the authority sought to be conferred by § 3 was not merely to deal with "unfair competitive practices" which offend against existing law, and could be the subject of judicial condemnation without further legislation, or to create administrative machinery for the application of established principles of law to particular instances of violation. Rather, the purpose is clearly disclosed to authorize new and controlling prohibitions through codes of laws which would embrace what the formulators would propose, and what the President would approve or prescribe, as wise and beneficent measures for the government of trades and industries in order to bring about their rehabilitation, correction, and development, according to the general declaration of policy in section one. Codes of laws of this sort are styled "codes of fair competition."

We find no real controversy upon this point and we must determine the validity of the code in question in this aspect. As the government candidly says in its brief: "The words 'policy of this title' clearly refer to the 'policy' which Congress declared in the section entitled 'Declaration of Policy'—§ 1. All of the policies there set forth point toward a single goal— the rehabilitation of industry and the industrial recovery which unquestionably was the major policy of Congress in adopting the National Industrial Recovery Act." . . .

The government urges that the codes will "consist of rules of competition deemed fair for each industry by representative members of that industry—by the persons most vitally concerned and most familiar with its problems." Instances are cited in which Congress has availed itself of such assistance; as, *e.g.*, in the exercise of its authority over the public domain, with respect to the recognition of local customs or rules of miners as to mining claims, or, in matters of a more or less technical nature, as in designating the standard height of drawbars. But would it be seriously contended that Congress could delegate its legislative authority to trade or industrial associations or groups so as to empower them to enact the laws they deem to be wise and beneficent for the rehabilitation and expansion of their trade or industries? Could trade or industrial associations or groups be constituted legislative bodies for that purpose because such associations or groups are familiar with the problems of their enterprises? And could an effort of that sort be made valid by such a preface of generalities as to permissible aims as we find in section 1 of title 1? The answer is obvious. Such a delegation of legislative power is unknown to our law, and is utterly inconsistent with the constitutional prerogatives and duties of Congress.

The question, then, turns upon the authority which § 3 of the Recovery Act vests in the President to approve or prescribe. If the codes have standing as penal statutes, this must be due to the effect of the executive action. But Congress cannot delegate legislative power to the President to exercise an unfettered discretion to make whatever laws he thinks may be needed or advisable for the rehabilitation and expansion of trade or industry. *See Panama Refining Company v. Ryan*, *supra*, and cases there reviewed.

Accordingly we turn to the Recovery Act to ascertain what limits have been set to the exercise of the President's discretion: *First*, the President, as a condition of approval, is required to find that the trade or industrial associations or groups which propose a code, "impose no inequitable restrictions on admission to membership" and are "truly representative." That condition, however, relates only to the status of the initiators of the new laws and not to the permissible scope of such laws. *Second*, the President is required to find that the code is not "designed to promote monopolies or to eliminate or oppress small enterprises and will not operate to discriminate against them." And to this is added a proviso that the code "shall not permit monopolies or monopolistic practices." But these restrictions leave virtually untouched the field of policy envisaged by section one, and, in that wide field of legislative possibilities, the proponents of a code, refraining from monopolistic designs, may roam at will, and the President may approve or disapprove their proposals as he may see fit. That is the precise effect of the further finding that the President is to make—that the code "will tend to effectuate the policy of this title." While this is called a finding, it is really but a statement of an opinion as to the general effect upon the promotion of trade or industry of a scheme of laws. These are the only findings which Congress has made essential in order to put into operation a legislative code having the aims described in the "Declaration of Policy."

Nor is the breadth of the President's discretion left to the necessary implications of this limited requirement as to his findings. As already noted, the President in approving a code may impose his own conditions, adding to or taking from what is proposed, as "in his discretion" he thinks necessary "to effectuate the policy" declared by the act. Of course, he has no less liberty when he prescribes a code on his own motion or on complaint, and he is free to prescribe one if a code has not been approved. The act provides for the creation by the President of administrative agencies to assist him, but the action or reports of such agencies, or of his other assistants—their recommendations and findings in relation to the making of codes—have no sanction beyond the will of the President, who may accept, modify, or reject them as he pleases. Such recommendations or findings in no way limit the authority which § 3 undertakes to vest in the President with no other conditions than those there specified. And this authority relates to a host of different trades and industries, thus extending the President's discretion to all the varieties of laws which he may deem to be beneficial in dealing with the vast array of commercial and industrial activities throughout the country.

Such a sweeping delegation of legislative power finds no support in the decisions upon which the government especially relies. By the Interstate Commerce Act (49 USCA § 1 et seq.), Congress has itself provided a code of laws regulating the activities of the common carriers subject to the act, in order to assure the performance of their services upon just and reasonable terms, with adequate facilities and without unjust discrimination. Congress from time to time has elaborated its requirements, as needs have been disclosed. To facilitate the application of the standards prescribed by the act, Congress has provided an expert body. That administrative agency, in dealing with particular cases, is required to act upon notice and hearing, and its orders must be supported by findings of fact which in turn are sustained by evidence. Interstate Commerce Commission v. Louisville & Nashville Railroad Company, 227 U.S. 88; State of Florida v. United States, 282 U.S. 194; United States v. Baltimore & Ohio Railroad Company, 293 U.S. 454. When the Commission is authorized to issue, for the construction, extension, or abandonment of lines, a certificate of "public convenience and necessity," or to permit the acquisition by one carrier of the control of another, if that is found to be "in the public interest," we have pointed out that these provisions are not left without standards to guide determination. The authority conferred has direct relation to the standards prescribed for the service of common carriers, and can be exercised only upon findings, based upon evidence, with respect to particular conditions of transportation. New York Central Securities Corporation v. United States, 287 U.S. 12, 24, 25; Texas & Pacific Railway Co. v. Gulf, Colorado & Santa Fe Railway Co., 270 U.S. 266, 273; Chesapeake & Ohio Railway Co. v. United States, 283 U.S. 35, 42.

Similarly, we have held that the Radio Act of 1927 established standards to govern radio communications, and, in view of the limited number of available broadcasting frequencies, Congress authorized allocation and licenses. The Federal Radio Commission was created as the licensing authority, in order to secure a reasonable equality of opportunity in radio transmission and reception. The authority of the Commission to grant licenses "as public convenience, interest or necessity requires" was limited by the nature of radio communications, and by the scope, character, and quality of the services to be rendered and the relative advantages to be derived through distribution of facilities. These standards established by Congress were to be enforced upon hearing and evidence by an administrative body acting under statutory restrictions adapted to the particular activity. Federal Radio Commission v. Nelson Brothers Bond & Mtg. Co., 289 U.S. 266.

In Hampton, Jr. & Company v. United States, 276 U.S. 394, the question related to the "flexible tariff provision" of the Tariff Act of 1922. We held that Congress had described its plan "to secure by law the imposition of customs duties on articles of imported merchandise which should equal the difference between the cost of producing in a foreign country the articles in question and laying them down for sale in the United States, and the cost of producing and selling like or similar articles in the United States." As the differences in cost might vary from time to time, provision was made for the investigation and determination of these differences by the Executive Branch so as to make "the adjustments necessary to conform the duties to the standard underlying that policy and plan." *Id.* 276 U.S. 394, pages 404, 405. The Court found the same principle to be applicable in fixing customs duties as that which permitted

Congress to exercise its rate-making power in interstate commerce, "by declaring the rule which shall prevail in the legislative fixing of rates," and then remitting "the fixing of such rates" in accordance with its provisions "to a rate-making body." *Id.* 276 U.S. 394, page 409. The Court fully recognized the limitations upon the delegation of legislative power.

To summarize and conclude upon this point: Section 3 of the Recovery Act is without precedent. It supplies no standards for any trade, industry, or activity. It does not undertake to prescribe rules of conduct to be applied to particular states of fact determined by appropriate administrative procedure. Instead of prescribing rules of conduct, it authorizes the making of codes to prescribe them. For that legislative undertaking, § 3 sets up no standards, aside from the statement of the general aims of rehabilitation, correction, and expansion described in section one. In view of the scope of that broad declaration and of the nature of the few restrictions that are imposed, the discretion of the President in approving or prescribing codes, and thus enacting laws for the government of trade and industry throughout the country, is virtually unfettered. We think that the code-making authority thus conferred is an unconstitutional delegation of legislative power....

■ Mr. Justice Cardozo [with whom Justice Stone joins] concurring.

The delegated power of legislation which has found expression in this code is not canalized within banks that keep it from overflowing. It is unconfined and vagrant, if I may borrow my own words in an earlier opinion. Panama Refining Co. v. Ryan, 293 U.S. 388, 440.

This court has held that delegation may be unlawful, though the act to be performed is definite and single, if the necessity, time, and occasion of performance have been left in the end to the discretion of the delegate. *Panama Refining Co. v. Ryan, supra.* I thought that ruling went too far. I pointed out in an opinion that there had been "no grant to the Executive of any roving commission to inquire into evils and then, upon discovering them, do anything he pleases." Choice, though within limits, had been given him "as to the occasion, but none whatever as to the means." Here, in the case before us, is an attempted delegation not confined to any single act nor to any class or group of acts identified or described by reference to a standard. Here in effect is a roving commission to inquire into evils and upon discovery correct them.

I have said that there is no standard, definite or even approximate, to which legislation must conform. Let me make my meaning more precise. If codes of fair competition are codes eliminating "unfair" methods of competition ascertained upon inquiry to prevail in one industry or another, there is no unlawful delegation of legislative functions when the President is directed to inquire into such practices and denounce them when discovered. For many years a like power has been committed to the Federal Trade Commission with the approval of this court in a long series of decisions.... Delegation in such circumstances is born of the necessities of the occasion. The industries of the country are too many and diverse to make it possible for Congress, in respect of matters such as these, to legislate directly with adequate appreciation of varying conditions. Nor is the substance of the power changed because the President may act at the instance of trade or industrial associations having special knowledge of the facts. Their function is strictly advisory; it is the imprimatur of the President that begets the quality of law. Doty v. Love, 295 U.S. 64. When the task that is set before one is that of cleaning house, it is prudent as well as usual to take counsel of the dwellers.

But there is another conception of codes of fair competition, their significance and function, which leads to very different consequences, though it is one that is struggling now for recognition and acceptance. By this other conception a code is not to be restricted to the elimination of business practices that would be characterized by general acceptation as oppressive or unfair. It is to include whatever ordinances may be desirable or helpful for the well-being or prosperity of the industry affected. In that view, the function of its adoption is not merely negative, but positive; the planning of improvements as well as the extirpation of abuses. What is fair, as thus conceived, is not something to be contrasted with what is unfair or fraudulent or tricky. The extension becomes as wide as the field of industrial regulation. If that conception shall prevail, anything that Congress may do within the limits of the commerce clause for the betterment of business may be done by the President upon the recommendation of a trade association by calling it a code. This is delegation running riot. No such plenitude of power is susceptible of transfer. The statute, however, aims at nothing less, as one can learn both from its terms and from the administrative practice under it. Nothing less is aimed at by the code now submitted to our scrutiny.

The code does not confine itself to the suppression of methods of competition that would be classified as unfair according to accepted business standards or accepted norms of ethics. It sets up a comprehensive body of rules to promote the welfare of the industry, if not the welfare of the nation, without reference to standards, ethical or commercial, that could be known or predicted in advance of its adoption. . . .

---

*1. The NIRA's Criteria*—Although the Court did not invoke the intelligible principle test by name, its analysis rests on the proposition that the NIRA supplies no meaningful statutory criteria to channel the President's discretion to approve or disapprove a code of fair competition. Is that a fair reading of the statute? After all, § 3 permits the President to approve "codes of fair competition"—a phrase that includes a criterion for determining whether a code meets the Act's requirements. To be sure, the phrase "fair competition" has no common law antecedents (in contrast with the phrase "unfair methods of competition" used in the Federal Trade Commission Act (FTCA)), and perhaps, as the *Schechter* Court suggests, this makes it an essentially empty phrase. But what of the fact that § 3 explicitly instructs the President to approve codes that "will tend to effectuate the policy of this title"—an obvious reference to the "Declaration of Policy" in § 1 of the NIRA? That section states that the statute's purpose is

> to remove obstructions to the free flow of interstate and foreign commerce which tend to diminish the amount thereof; and to provide for the general welfare by promoting the organization of industry for the purpose of cooperative action among trade groups, to induce and maintain united action of labor and management under adequate governmental sanctions and supervision, to eliminate unfair competitive practices, to promote the fullest possible utilization of the present productive capacity of industries, to avoid undue restriction of production (except as may be temporarily required), to increase the consumption of industrial and agricultural products by increasing purchasing power, to reduce and relieve unemployment, to improve standards of labor, and otherwise to rehabilitate industry and to conserve natural resources.

15 U.S.C. § 701 (repealed).

Why doesn't the statement of purposes in § 1 provide constitutionally adequate (and "intelligible") legislative guidance, channeling the President's discretion by indicating that the President should interpret the phrase "fair competition" in light of the policies articulated in § 1, and should approve only those codes that will promote economic recovery by one or more of the stated means? Perhaps the problem is that § 1 seems to offer a long list of unranked goals, some of which may even be mutually contradictory—classic signs of a "meaningless [regulatory] standard." *See* Richard J. Pierce, Jr., *The Role of Constitutional and Political Theory in Administrative Law*, 64 TEX. L. REV. 469, 474–78 (1985). Is that what the Court meant when it referred to § 1 as a "preface of generalities"? Or the problem might lie instead in the fact that while § 1 did contain something of an "intelligible principle" (promoting economic recovery), the idea of giving the President such broad authority over all of American industry was simply too large a transfer of policymaking discretion to tolerate. *See* Whitman v. American Trucking Ass'ns, 531 U.S. 457, 474 (2001) (describing the problem in *Schechter* as being that the NIRA gave the President "authority to regulate the entire economy on the basis of no more precise a standard than stimulating the economy by assuring 'fair competition' ").

If stimulating economic recovery is not an "intelligible principle," why isn't it? Is that principle less definite than the goal of equalizing production costs between U.S. and foreign manufacturers—the "intelligible principle" that authorized the President to reset tariffs in *Hampton*? How can one tell at what point a criterion ceases to count as an intelligible principle? Along those lines, if the scruple enforced by the Court in *Schechter* was that Congress cannot hand over to the President control over all American industry, at what point does the legislative authorization of broad discretion cross the line? If Congress passed a statute authorizing the President "to take such measures as are necessary and appropriate in the public interest to preserve and promote the solvency of the automobile industry," would that run afoul of *Schecter*? What if it were "the banking system"? If the *Schechter* Court was concerned about the extent of delegated presidential authority over the economy as a whole, how does that concern translate into a principled distinction between legislative and executive power? Professor Gary Lawson suggests that unless Congress can legitimately establish a "Goodness and Niceness Commission" with authority "to promulgate rules for the promotion of goodness and niceness in all areas within the power of Congress under the Constitution," the Court must draw lines between permissible and impermissible transfers of policymaking discretion to the executive. *See* Gary Lawson, *The Rise and Rise of the Administrative State*, 107 HARV. L. REV. 1231, 1239 (1994). But because all administrative statutes confer *some* discretion, the Court must decide when Congress has "crossed the line" into an "improper delegation of distinctively legislative power"—an exercise that, he acknowledges, boils down to the proposition that "Congress must make whatever policy decisions are sufficiently important to the statutory scheme at issue so that Congress must make them." *Id*. Is that essentially what went on in *Schechter*? What does it tell us about the prospects for the judiciary's development of a meaningful nondelegation doctrine?

**2.    *The Absence of Administrative Procedures*—**In contrasting the NIRA's (impermissible) "codes of fair competition" with the FTCA's (permissible) prohibition against "unfair methods of competition," *Schechter* emphasized, among other things, that the FTCA provided extensive procedures for the Federal Trade Commission to use when ascertaining whether the FTCA had been violated. In particular, *Schechter* found that the existence of unfair competition under the FTCA was "to be determined in particular instances, upon evidence, in the light of particular competitive conditions and of what is found to be a specific and substantial public interest," and that the statute made provision "for formal complaint, for notice and hearing, for appropriate findings of fact supported by adequate evidence, and for judicial review to give assurance that the action of the commission is taken within its statutory authority." *Schechter* stressed that the NIRA "dispenses with this administrative procedure and with any administrative procedure of an analogous character." Indeed, the Court noted, "[t]he act provides for the creation by the President of administrative agencies to assist him, but the action or reports of such agencies, or of his other assistants—their recommendations and findings in relation to the making of codes—have no sanction beyond the will of the President, who may accept, modify, or reject them as he pleases."

Why did the Court care about the absence of procedures? Perhaps the idea is that an agency that must investigate the facts, hold hearings of some sort, and make findings under an articulated standard might seem to fit more accurately the model of law implementer. In contrast, if the President can adopt or reject a code of fair competition without undertaking any factual investigation or making any findings, the result may have the feel of an exercise of raw legislative discretion. How convincing are the Court's efforts to draw such a line? Even if an agency is following settled procedures, the decisions it makes in implementing a vague or open-ended organic act presumably entail some form of lawmaking. *See, e.g.*, Richard J.

Pierce, Jr., Chevron *and Its Aftermath: Judicial Review of Agency Interpretations of Statutory Provisions*, 41 VAND. L. REV. 301, 307–08 (1988); Laurence H. Silberman, Chevron—*The Intersection of Law & Policy*, 58 GEO. WASH. L. REV. 821, 822 (1990). Isn't the challenge in all nondelegation cases to determine when Congress has granted *too much* authority to the agency?

Might the *Schechter* Court's concerns about administrative procedure have reflected the pragmatic impulse to condition delegation on indicia of accountability? As one commentator has written, "since *Schechter*, the Supreme Court's tolerance of broad congressional delegations may be attributable, at least in part, to the greater procedural constraints imposed on statutory delegatees. Procedure provides a check on the potential abuses of statutory delegations, and its absence, particularly when the president is involved, may raise a concern about the arbitrary exercise of power." Kevin M. Stack, *The Statutory President*, 90 IOWA L. REV. 539, 591 (2005); *see also* Robert L. Rabin, *Legitimacy, Discretion, and the Concept of Rights*, 92 YALE L.J. 1174, 1179 (1983) (arguing that "control of agency discretion is the guiding force behind [*Schechter*'s] demand for adequate procedural safeguards"); Cass R. Sunstein, *Is the Clean Air Act Unconstitutional?*, 98 MICH. L. REV. 303, 349 (1999) (noting that under *Schechter* "the procedures serve as surrogate safeguards" for legislative accountability). If the need for public accountability is the touchstone, why is the Court permitted to accept even quite robust forms of agency procedure as substitutes for the precise forms of accountability prescribed by the bicameralism and presentment requirements of Article I, § 7?

Finally, much of the Court's discomfort with the procedures outlined in the Act might be attributable to the fact that the NIRA authorized trade associations to propose codes of fair competition in the first instance: The Court emphasized that any such "delegation of legislative power [to private groups] is unknown to our law, and is utterly inconsistent with the constitutional prerogatives and duties of Congress." Does the role of private initiative exacerbate concerns that delegation will undermine political accountability? Given the premise that bicameralism and presentment were designed, in part, to control the influence of special interest groups, does the transfer of substantial policymaking power to trade associations raise special concerns?

**3. Schechter's Aftermath**—Professor Robert Rabin has written that "*Schechter* arguably retains its authority as a statement of the outer limits of federal regulatory power. Even today, a congressional act which set up a business regulatory commission with plenary power to establish 'fair competitive practices' enumerated by industry trade groups would be of doubtful validity." Robert L. Rabin, *Federal Regulation in Historical Perspective*, 38 STAN. L. REV. 1189, 1257 (1986). Yet while the Court has never overruled either *Schechter* or *Panama Refining*, neither case has shown itself to have much generative capacity. Since *Schechter*, the Court has not invalidated a single Act of Congress as unconstitutional on nondelegation grounds, despite the subsequent enactment of numerous administrative statutes that are breathtaking in both the expanse of their coverage and the vagueness of their standards. Although *Schechter* itself was unanimous—attracting the concurrence of progressive Justices such as Brandeis, Stone, and Cardozo—the Court essentially abandoned its resistance to the structural innovations of the New Deal following President Roosevelt's reelection in 1936 and the appointment of new Justices in the late 1930s and early 1940s. *See, e.g.,* David P. Currie, The Constitution in the Supreme Court: The Second Century, 1888–1986, at 236–38 (1990). The story behind the Court's change in attitude is both complex and historically contested. *See, e.g.,* Barry Cushman, Rethinking the New Deal Court: The Structure of a Constitutional Revolution (1998). For present purposes, what is important is that the Court in the late 1930s essentially got out of the business of enforcing the nondelegation doctrine. While the post-New Deal Court continued to endorse the intelligible principle requirement announced in *Hampton*, in practice the Court routinely blessed the broadest of delegations. *See, e.g.,* National Broadcasting Co. v. United States, 319 U.S. 190, 225–26 (1943) (holding that Congress may grant the Federal Communications Commission the power to allocate broadcasting licenses in "the public interest, convenience, and necessity"); American Power & Light Co. v. SEC, 329 U.S. 90, 105 (1946) (holding that Congress may delegate to the SEC the power to reject corporate reorganizations that are not "fair and equitable"); Lichter v. United States, 334 U.S. 742, 785–86 (1948) (sustaining as constitutional an agency's delegated authority to recoup "excessive profits" on war contracts).

Yakus v. United States, 321 U.S. 414 (1944), provides a particularly good illustration of the Court's approach to nondelegation challenges in the immediate post-New Deal period. In *Yakus*, the Court considered a nondelegation challenge to the Emergency Price Control Act of 1942 (EPCA), a wartime measure that gave an executive branch officer, the Price Administrator, the authority to set maximum commodity prices that "in [the Administrator's] judgment will be generally fair and equitable and will effectuate the purposes of this Act [which included stabilizing prices, eliminating hoarding and profiteering, and ensuring that defense appropriations were not adversely impacted by excessive prices]." *See* 50 U.S.C. App. § 902; *see also id.* § 901(a) (articulating the Act's purposes). The Supreme Court upheld the EPCA as constitutional under the *Hampton* test: "The Act is . . . an exercise by Congress of its legislative power. In it Congress has stated the legislative objective, has prescribed the method of achieving that objective—maximum price fixing—and has laid down standards to guide the administrative determination of both the occasions for the exercise of the price-fixing power, and the particular prices to be established." 321 U.S. at 423. In dissent, Justice Roberts insisted that the EPCA unconstitutionally delegated legislative power in light of the fact that "the Act sets no limits upon the discretion or judgment of the Administrator," who had the power to "take any action with respect to prices which he believes will preserve what he deems a sound economy. . . . His judgment . . . is the final touchstone of the validity of his action." *Id.* at 451–52 (Roberts, J., dissenting). But Chief Justice Stone, writing for the majority, explained that the degree of discretion conferred on the Administrator did not amount to a constitutional violation. In making this argument, Chief Justice Stone articulated a broad, functionalist understanding of how courts should approach nondelegation challenges:

> The Constitution as a continuously operative charter of government does not demand the impossible or the impracticable. It does not require that Congress find for itself every fact upon which it desires to base legislative action or that it make for itself detailed determinations which it has declared to be prerequisite to the application of the legislative policy to particular facts and circumstances impossible for Congress itself properly to investigate. The essentials of the legislative function are the determination of the legislative policy and its formulation and promulgation as a defined and binding rule of conduct—here the rule, with penal sanctions, that prices shall not be greater than those fixed by maximum price regulations which conform to standards and will tend to further the policy which Congress has established. These essentials are preserved when Congress has specified the basic conditions of fact upon whose existence or occurrence, ascertained from relevant data by a designated administrative agency, it directs that its statutory command shall be effective. It is no objection that the determination of facts and the inferences to be drawn from them in the light of the statutory standards and declaration of policy call for the exercise of judgment, and for the formulation of subsidiary administrative policy within the prescribed statutory framework....
>
> Nor does the doctrine of separation of powers deny to Congress power to direct that an administrative officer properly designated for that purpose have ample latitude within which he is to ascertain the conditions which Congress has made prerequisite to the operation of its legislative command. Acting within its constitutional power to fix prices it is for Congress to say whether the data on the basis of which prices are to be fixed are to be confined within a narrow or a broad range. In either case the only concern of courts is to ascertain whether the will of Congress has been obeyed. This depends not upon the breadth of the definition of the facts or conditions which the administrative officer is to find but upon the determination whether the definition sufficiently marks the field within which the Administrator is to act so that it may be known whether he has kept within it in compliance with the legislative will.
>
> As we have said: "The Constitution has never been regarded as denying to the Congress the necessary resources of flexibility and practicality ... to perform its function." Currin v. Wallace, [306 U.S. 1, 15 (1939)]. Hence it is irrelevant that Congress might itself have prescribed the maximum prices or have provided a more rigid standard by which they are to be fixed.... Congress is not confined to that method of executing its policy which involves the least possible delegation of discretion to administrative officers.... It is free to avoid the rigidity of such a system, which might well result in serious hardship,

and to choose instead the flexibility attainable by the use of less restrictive standards. Cf. Hampton v. United States, [276 U.S. 408, 409 (1928)]. Only if we could say that there is an absence of standards for the guidance of the Administrator's action, so that it would be impossible in a proper proceeding to ascertain whether the will of Congress has been obeyed, would we be justified in overriding its choice of means for effecting its declared purpose of preventing inflation.

321 U.S. at 424–26 (majority opinion).

Are the standards in the foregoing cases more "intelligible" than the criterion of "fair competition" that the Court invalidated as an impermissible delegation in *Schechter*? If the Court regularly declines to enforce the nondelegation doctrine—even when confronted with vague, open-ended standards—would it reflect greater judicial candor to abandon the doctrine altogether?

### c.   The Demise of the Nondelegation Doctrine?

## Whitman v. American Trucking Associations, Inc.

Supreme Court of the United States
531 U.S. 457 (2001)

■ JUSTICE SCALIA delivered the opinion of the Court.

. . .

### I

Section 109(a) of the [Clean Air Act (CAA)] . . . requires the Administrator of the [Environmental Protection Agency (EPA)] to promulgate [National Ambient Air Quality Standards (NAAQS)] for [certain air pollutants]. Once a NAAQS has been promulgated, the Administrator must review the standard (and the criteria on which it is based) "at five-year intervals" and make "such revisions . . . as may be appropriate." CAA § 109(d)(1), 42 U.S.C. § 7409(d)(1). These cases arose when, on July 18, 1997, the Administrator revised the NAAQS for particulate matter and ozone. . . . American Trucking Associations, Inc., and its co-respondents . . . challenged the new standards in the Court of Appeals for the District of Columbia Circuit . . . . [Among other things, the respondents argued that § 109, as construed by the EPA, violated the nondelegation doctrine.]

The District of Columbia Circuit . . . agreed that [§ 109] delegated legislative power to the Administrator in contravention of the United States Constitution, Art. I, § 1, because it found that the EPA had interpreted the statute to provide no "intelligible principle" to guide the agency's exercise of authority. American Trucking Assns., Inc. v. EPA, 175 F.3d 1027, 1034 ([C.A.D.C.] 1999). The court thought, however, that the EPA could perhaps avoid the unconstitutional delegation by adopting a restrictive construction of [§ 109], so instead of declaring the section unconstitutional the court remanded the NAAQS to the agency....

### III

Section 109(b)(1) of the CAA instructs the EPA to set "ambient air quality standards the attainment and maintenance of which in the judgment of the Administrator, based on [the] criteria [documents provided for in § 108] and allowing an adequate margin of safety, are requisite to protect the public health." 42 U.S.C. § 7409(b)(1). The Court of Appeals held that this section as interpreted by the Administrator did not provide an "intelligible principle" to guide the EPA's exercise of authority in setting NAAQS. "[The] EPA," it said, "lack[ed] any determinate criteria for drawing lines. It has failed to state intelligibly how much is too much." 175 F.3d, at 1034. The court hence found that the EPA's interpretation (but not the statute itself) violated the nondelegation doctrine. *Id.*, at 1038. We disagree.

In a delegation challenge, the constitutional question is whether the statute has delegated legislative power to the agency. Article I, § 1, of the Constitution vests "[a]ll legislative Powers herein granted ... in a Congress of the United States." This text permits no delegation of those powers, Loving v. United States, 517 U.S. 748, 771 (1996); see *id.*, at 776–777 (SCALIA, J., concurring in part and concurring in judgment), and so we repeatedly have said that when Congress confers decisionmaking authority upon agencies *Congress* must "lay down by legislative act an intelligible principle to which the person or body authorized to [act] is directed to conform." J.W. Hampton, Jr., & Co. v. United States, 276 U.S. 394, 409 (1928). We have never suggested that an agency can cure an unlawful delegation of legislative power by adopting in its discretion a limiting construction of the statute.... Whether the statute delegates legislative power is a question for the courts, and an agency's voluntary self-denial has no bearing upon the answer.

We agree with the Solicitor General that the text of § 109(b)(1) of the CAA at a minimum requires that "[f]or a discrete set of pollutants and based on published air quality criteria that reflect the latest scientific knowledge, [the] EPA must establish uniform national standards at a level that is requisite to protect public health from the adverse effects of the pollutant in the ambient air." Tr. of Oral Arg. in No. 99–1257, p. 5. Requisite, in turn, "mean[s] sufficient, but not more than necessary." *Id.*, at 7. These limits on the EPA's discretion are strikingly similar to the ones we approved in Touby v. United States, 500 U.S. 160 (1991), which permitted the Attorney General to designate a drug as a controlled substance for purposes of criminal drug enforcement if doing so was " 'necessary to avoid an imminent hazard to the public safety.' " *Id.*, at 163. They also resemble the Occupational Safety and Health Act of 1970 provision requiring the agency to " 'set the standard which most adequately assures, to the extent feasible, on the basis of the best available evidence, that no employee will suffer any impairment of health' "—which the Court upheld in Industrial Union Dept., AFL–CIO v. American Petroleum Institute, 448 U.S. 607, 646 (1980), and which even then-JUSTICE REHNQUIST, who alone in that case thought the statute violated the nondelegation doctrine, see *id.*, at 671 (opinion concurring in judgment), would have upheld if, like the statute here, it did not permit economic costs to be considered. See American Textile Mfrs. Institute, Inc. v. Donovan, 452 U.S. 490, 545(1981) (REHNQUIST, J., dissenting).

The scope of discretion § 109(b)(1) allows is in fact well within the outer limits of our nondelegation precedents. In the history of the Court we have found the requisite "intelligible principle" lacking in only two statutes, one of which provided literally no guidance for the exercise of discretion, and the other of which conferred authority to regulate the entire economy on the basis of no more precise a standard than stimulating the economy by assuring "fair competition." See Panama Refining Co. v. Ryan, 293 U.S. 388 (1935); A.L.A. Schechter Poultry Corp. v. United States, 295 U.S. 495 (1935). We have, on the other hand, upheld the validity of § 11(b)(2) of the Public Utility Holding Company Act of 1935, 49 Stat. 821, which gave the Securities and Exchange Commission authority to modify the structure of holding company systems so as to ensure that they are not "unduly or unnecessarily complicate[d]" and do not "unfairly or inequitably distribute voting power among security holders." American Power & Light Co. v. SEC, 329 U.S. 90, 104 (1946). We have approved the wartime conferral of agency power to fix the prices of commodities at a level that " 'will be generally fair and equitable and will effectuate the [in some respects conflicting] purposes of th[e] Act.' " Yakus v. United States, 321 U.S. 414, 420, 423–426 (1944). And we have found an "intelligible principle" in various statutes authorizing regulation in the "public interest." See, e.g., National Broadcasting Co. v. United States, 319 U.S. 190, 225–226 (1943) (Federal Communications Commission's power to regulate airwaves); N.Y. Central Sec. Corp. v. United States, 287 U.S. 12, 24–25 (1932) (Interstate Commerce Commission's power to approve railroad consolidations). In short, we have "almost never felt qualified to second-guess Congress regarding the permissible degree of policy judgment that can be left to those executing or applying the law." Mistretta v. United States, 488 U.S. 361, 416 (1989) (SCALIA, J., dissenting); see *id.*, at 373 (majority opinion).

It is true enough that the degree of agency discretion that is acceptable varies according to the scope of the power congressionally conferred. See *Loving v. United States*, 517 U.S., at 772–773; United States v. Mazurie, 419 U.S. 544, 556–557 (1975). While Congress need not provide any direction to the EPA regarding the manner in which it is to define "country elevators," which are to be exempt from new-stationary-source regulations governing grain elevators, see 42 U.S.C. § 7411(i), it must provide substantial guidance on setting air standards that affect the entire national economy. But even in sweeping regulatory schemes we have never demanded, as the Court of Appeals did here, that statutes provide a "determinate criterion" for saying "how much [of the regulated harm] is too much." 175 F.3d, at 1034. In *Touby,* for example, we did not require the statute to decree how "imminent" was too imminent, or how "necessary" was necessary enough, or even—most relevant here—how "hazardous" was too hazardous. 500 U.S., at 165–167. Similarly, the statute at issue in *Lichter* authorized agencies to recoup "excess profits" paid under wartime Government contracts, yet we did not insist that Congress specify how much profit was too much. 334 U.S., at 783–786. It is therefore not conclusive for delegation purposes that, as respondents argue, ozone and particulate matter are "nonthreshold" pollutants that inflict a continuum of adverse health effects at any airborne concentration greater than zero, and hence require the EPA to make judgments of degree. "[A] certain degree of discretion, and thus of lawmaking, inheres in most executive or judicial action." *Mistretta v. United States, supra*, at 417 (Scalia, J., dissenting) (emphasis deleted); see 488 U.S., at 378–379 (majority opinion). Section 109(b)(1) of the CAA, which ... we interpret as requiring the EPA to set air quality standards at the level that is "requisite"—that is, not lower or higher than is necessary—to protect the public health with an adequate margin of safety, fits comfortably within the scope of discretion permitted by our precedent.

We therefore reverse the judgment of the Court of Appeals remanding for reinterpretation that would avoid a supposed delegation of legislative power. It will remain for the Court of Appeals—on the remand that we direct for other reasons—to dispose of any other preserved challenge to the NAAQS under the judicial-review provisions contained in 42 U.S.C. § 7607(d)(9)....

■ Justice Thomas, concurring.

I agree with the majority that § 109's directive to the agency is no less an "intelligible principle" than a host of other directives that we have approved. I also agree that the Court of Appeals' remand to the agency to make its own corrective interpretation does not accord with our understanding of the delegation issue. I write separately, however, to express my concern that there may nevertheless be a genuine constitutional problem with § 109, a problem which the parties did not address.

The parties to these cases who briefed the constitutional issue wrangled over constitutional doctrine with barely a nod to the text of the Constitution. Although this Court since 1928 has treated the "intelligible principle" requirement as the only constitutional limit on congressional grants of power to administrative agencies, see J.W. Hampton, Jr., & Co. v. United States, 276 U.S. 394, 409 (1928), the Constitution does not speak of "intelligible principles." Rather, it speaks in much simpler terms: "*All* legislative Powers herein granted shall be vested in a Congress." U.S. Const., Art. 1, § 1 (emphasis added). I am not convinced that the intelligible principle doctrine serves to prevent all cessions of legislative power. I believe that there are cases in which the principle is intelligible and yet the significance of the delegated decision is simply too great for the decision to be called anything other than "legislative."

As it is, none of the parties to this case has examined the text of the Constitution or asked us to reconsider our precedents on cessions of legislative power. On a future day, however, I would be willing to address the question whether our delegation jurisprudence has strayed too far from our Founders' understanding of separation of powers.

■ JUSTICE STEVENS, with whom JUSTICE SOUTER joins, concurring in part and concurring in the judgment.

Section 109(b)(1) delegates to the Administrator of the Environmental Protection Agency (EPA) the authority to promulgate national ambient air quality standards (NAAQS). In Part III of its opinion, the Court convincingly explains why the Court of Appeals erred when it concluded that § 109 effected "an unconstitutional delegation of legislative power." American Trucking Assns., Inc. v. EPA, 175 F.3d 1027, 1033 (C.A.D.C.1999) (*per curiam*). I wholeheartedly endorse the Court's result and endorse its explanation of its reasons, albeit with the following caveat.

The Court has two choices. We could choose to articulate our ultimate disposition of this issue by frankly acknowledging that the power delegated to the EPA is "legislative" but nevertheless conclude that the delegation is constitutional because adequately limited by the terms of the authorizing statute. Alternatively, we could pretend, as the Court does, that the authority delegated to the EPA is somehow not "legislative power." Despite the fact that there is language in our opinions that supports the Court's articulation of our holding, I am persuaded that it would be both wiser and more faithful to what we have actually done in delegation cases to admit that agency rulemaking authority is "legislative power."

The proper characterization of governmental power should generally depend on the nature of the power, not on the identity of the person exercising it. See Black's Law Dictionary 899 (6th ed. 1990) (defining "legislation" as, *inter alia,* "[f]ormulation of rule[s] for the future"); 1 K. Davis & R. Pierce, Administrative Law Treatise § 2.3, p. 37 (3d ed. 1994) ("If legislative power means the power to make rules of conduct that bind everyone based on resolution of major policy issues, scores of agencies exercise legislative power routinely by promulgating what are candidly called 'legislative rules' "). If the NAAQS that the EPA promulgated had been prescribed by Congress, everyone would agree that those rules would be the product of an exercise of "legislative power." The same characterization is appropriate when an agency exercises rulemaking authority pursuant to a permissible delegation from Congress.

My view is not only more faithful to normal English usage, but is also fully consistent with the text of the Constitution. In Article I, the Framers vested "All legislative Powers" in the Congress, Art. I, § 1, just as in Article II they vested the "executive Power" in the President, Art. II, § 1. Those provisions do not purport to limit the authority of either recipient of power to delegate authority to others. . . .

It seems clear that an executive agency's exercise of rulemaking authority pursuant to a valid delegation from Congress is "legislative." As long as the delegation provides a sufficiently intelligible principle, there is nothing inherently unconstitutional about it. Accordingly, while I . . . agree with almost everything said in Part III [of the Court's opinion], I would hold that when Congress enacted § 109, it effected a constitutional delegation of legislative power to the EPA.

■ [The opinion of JUSTICE BREYER, concurring in part and concurring in the judgment, is omitted.]

---

*1.* ***Whitman's Hands-Off Approach***—In upholding § 109, the Court implicitly reaffirmed that it would not enforce a meaningful nondelegation principle—at least not in the context of striking down Acts of Congress as unconstitutional on nondelegation grounds. Starting from the premise that some degree of discretion is inherent in most executive or judicial decisionmaking, the Court in *Whitman* emphasized that "we have 'almost never felt qualified to second-guess Congress regarding the permissible degree of policy judgment that can be left to those executing or applying the law.' " (quoting Mistretta v. United States, 488 U.S. 361, 416 (1989) (Scalia, J., dissenting)); *see also Mistretta*, 488 U.S. at 373 (majority opinion); Printz v. United States, 521 U.S. 898, 927 (1997). What does this statement mean? Is the idea that although the Constitution embraces a nondelegation doctrine, the Court does not feel competent to enforce that doctrine through judicial review (except perhaps in extreme cases such as *Schechter* and *Panama Refining*)? In other words, maybe the problem is that because all law implementation entails some exercise of policymaking discretion, it is too hard for courts to draw the line between statutorily conferred discretion that is consistent with an agency's legitimate implementation of the law and that which crosses over into an illegitimate exercise of genuinely legislative power. In the very early days of the Republic, Chief Justice John Marshall recognized this line-drawing problem:

> The difference between the departments undoubtedly is, that the legislature makes, the executive executes, and the judiciary construes the law; but the maker of the law may commit something to the discretion of the other departments, and the precise boundary of this power is a subject of delicate and difficult inquiry, into which a Court will not enter unnecessarily.

Wayman v. Southard, 23 U.S. (10 Wheat.) 1, 46 (1825).

If the Court cannot articulate any test for excessive delegation other than "I know it when I see it," then judicial enforcement of a constitutionally grounded nondelegation doctrine might raise serious concerns about the legitimate exercise of judicial power in our system. As Cass Sunstein has written:

> Because the underlying issue is one of degree, decisions invalidating statutes as unduly open-ended are likely to suffer from the appearance, and perhaps the reality, of judicial hostility to the particular program at issue. For this reason, those concerned about rule-free law are especially likely to be uncomfortable with any large-scale revival of the conventional doctrine. Without much exaggeration, and with tongue

only slightly in cheek, we might even say that judicial enforcement of the conventional doctrine would violate the conventional doctrine—since it could not be enforced without delegating, without clear standards, a high degree of discretionary lawmaking authority to the judiciary.

*See* Cass R. Sunstein, *Nondelegation Canons*, 67 U. Chi. L. Rev. 315, 327 (2000).

How persuasive is that rationale for soft-pedaling or abandoning judicial enforcement of the nondelegation doctrine? Should the Court refrain from enforcing a constitutional requirement simply because it is hard to define? Professor Louis Jaffe once wrote: "[N]early every doctrine of constitutional limitation has been attacked as vague. Essentially the charges go to the institution of judicial review as we have it rather than specifically to the delegation doctrine." Louis L. Jaffe, *An Essay on Delegation of Legislative Power II*, 47 Colum. L. Rev. 561, 577 (1947). Professor David Schoenbrod, a leading proponent of a robust nondelegation doctrine, has suggested, moreover, that the Court can meaningfully tell the difference between "interpretation" and "lawmaking." *See* David M. Schoenbrod, Power Without Responsibility: How Congress Abuses the People Through Delegation 180–91 (1993). He suggests that a statute that speaks clearly to a question invites interpretation, not lawmaking; that a statute that "leaves the agency to strike its own balance between conflicting goals" permits lawmaking; that some statutes purport to define rights and responsibilities directly while others leave such matters for agencies to decide (recall § 10(b) of the Securities Exchange Act); and that interpretations, once made, cannot be changed by the interpreter because they represent the meaning of the statute. *See id.* at 183. Do those criteria sort between interpretations and lawmaking more effectively than the intelligible principle test? If so, do they do so effectively enough to constrain judicial discretion?

**2.   *Delegation as a Matter of Practical Necessity*—**Another argument for a soft-to-nonexistent nondelegation doctrine—one that does not appear in *Whitman*—relates to the belief that Congress must have the capacity to delegate lawmaking authority to agencies if the federal government is to be able to function in a complex modern society. *See supra* p. 383. No one has made this point more clearly than did Chief Justice Taft. Recall his observations about the Commerce Power in *Hampton*:

> [O]ne of the great functions conferred on Congress by the Federal Constitution is the regulation of interstate commerce and rates to be exacted by interstate carriers for the passenger and merchandise traffic. The rates to be fixed are myriad. If Congress were to be required to fix every rate, it would be impossible to exercise the power at all. Therefore, common sense requires that in the fixing of such rates Congress may provide a Commission, as it does, called the Interstate Commerce Commission, to fix those rates, after hearing evidence and argument concerning them from interested parties, all in accord with a general rule that Congress first lays down that rates

shall be just and reasonable considering the service given and not discriminatory.

J.W. Hampton, Jr., & Co. v. United States, 276 U.S. 394, 406 (1928). In other words, if Congress cannot delegate broad authority to administrative agencies, it cannot exercise its Commerce Power to the full extent contemplated by the Constitution.

How persuasive is this pragmatic, functional rationale for the Court's hands-off approach to the nondelegation doctrine? If bicameralism and presentment make lawmaking more cumbersome in order to constrain factions, promote caution, and ensure that legislation is supported by a broad social consensus, does Taft's rationale ultimately work at cross-purposes with the purposes of the bicameralism and presentment requirements? To take Chief Justice Taft's example of railroad regulation, some have argued that the Interstate Commerce Commission's decisionmaking apparatus was captured by the railroads that it was supposed to be regulating. *See, e.g.*, George J. Stigler, *The Theory of Economic Regulation*, 2 BELL J. OF ECON. & MAN. SCI. 3 (1971). If that capture of the policymaking process was made easier because of Congress's delegation of ratemaking authority to an agency, doesn't the Court's hands-off approach to the nondelegation doctrine promote some of the very mischiefs that Article I, § 7 was meant to prevent? On the other hand, if the Court is correct that Congress could not meaningfully exercise its legislative power in the absence of delegation, doesn't such a conclusion inevitably press the Court toward a hands-off approach?

**3.  Competing Conceptions of the Power that the Agency Is Exercising**—While the Court was unanimous in concluding that the CAA delegation at issue in *Whitman* was constitutional, Justice Stevens' opinion concurring in part and concurring in the judgment (which Justice Souter joined), as well as Justice Thomas's separate concurring opinion, expressed perspectives on the nondelegation doctrine than differed somewhat from that presented in Justice Scalia's majority opinion.

While Justice Stevens endorsed the *Hampton* intelligible principle test and agreed that the CAA's delegation to the EPA was permissible under that test, his theoretical justification for this conclusion differed from the Court's. Justice Scalia's majority opinion intimated that the power that the EPA exercises pursuant to its authority under the CAA is not really *legislative* power, but rather a form of policymaking discretion that is inherent in the *executive* power. Justice Stevens insisted that this makes no sense; he argued instead that the Court should "frankly acknowledge[ ] that the power delegated to the EPA is 'legislative' but nevertheless conclude that the delegation is constitutional because adequately limited by the terms of the authorizing statute." In Justice Stevens' view, the Vesting Clauses of Articles I and II "do not purport to limit the authority of either recipient of power to delegate authority to others." Which conception of the EPA's exercise of discretion in setting air quality standards fits more comfortably with the constitutional structure? To be sure, agency rules do function in much the same way as legislation. But if Justice Stevens is correct that none of the Vesting Clauses constrain the respective branches' right to delegate the powers thus vested, why does the organic act have to supply adequate limits on the power conferred? If the agency is exercising legislative power, where does the intelligible principle test come from?

Justice Thomas, meanwhile, wrote separately to express his concern—which the parties had not briefed or argued, and so was not properly presented for decision—that the CAA's delegation to EPA might be unconstitutional not because it lacked an intelligible principle, but simply because the power delegated to EPA was too broad. If the Court were to eschew or supplement the intelligible principle test, by what criterion would it determine, under Justice Thomas's framework, whether the power granted is so broad as to be necessarily "legislative"?

## C.   ALTERNATIVE APPROACHES TO NONDELEGATION

As we saw in the preceding section, since 1935 the Supreme Court has eschewed enforcement of the nondelegation doctrine as a matter of constitutional law. At the same time, courts display a persistent anxiety about the degree to which broad delegations to agencies may subvert fundamental constitutional commitments to democratic accountability and checks and balances. Perhaps for this reason, although the Court has consistently refused to give the intelligible principle standard real teeth, the Court has explored, and in some cases endorsed, softer and more indirect doctrinal strategies for promoting some of the values associated with the nondelegation principle. We consider below some of those doctrinal strategies, starting with the most important one: construing statutory delegations narrowly in order to avoid a serious nondelegation problem.

---

## Industrial Union Department, AFL–CIO v. American Petroleum Institute

Supreme Court of the United States
448 U.S. 607 (1980)

■ MR. JUSTICE STEVENS announced the judgment of the Court and delivered an opinion, in which THE CHIEF JUSTICE and MR. JUSTICE STEWART joined and in Parts I, II, III–A, III–B, III–C and III–E of which MR. JUSTICE POWELL joined.

The Occupational Safety and Health Act of 1970 (Act), 29 U.S.C. § 651 *et seq.*, was enacted for the purpose of ensuring safe and healthful working conditions for every working man and woman in the Nation. This litigation concerns a standard promulgated by the Secretary of Labor to regulate occupational exposure to benzene, a substance which has been shown to cause cancer at high exposure levels. The principal question is whether such a showing is a sufficient basis for a standard that places the most stringent limitation on exposure to benzene that is technologically and economically possible.

The Act delegates broad authority to the Secretary to promulgate different kinds of standards. The basic definition of an "occupational safety and health standard" is found in § 3(8), which provides:

"The term 'occupational safety and health standard' means a standard which requires conditions, or the adoption or use of one or more practices, means, methods, operations, or processes, reasonably necessary or appropriate to provide safe or healthful employment and places of employment." 29 U.S.C. § 652(8).

Where toxic materials or harmful physical agents are concerned, a standard must also comply with § 6(b)(5), which provides:

"The Secretary, in promulgating standards dealing with toxic materials or harmful physical agents under this subsection, shall set the standard which most adequately assures, to the extent feasible, on the basis of the best available evidence, that no employee will suffer material impairment of health or functional capacity even if such employee has regular exposure to the hazard dealt with by such standard for the period of his working life. Development of standards under this subsection shall be based upon research, demonstrations, experiments, and such other information as may be appropriate. In addition to the attainment of the highest degree of health and safety protection for the employee, other considerations shall be the latest available scientific data in the field, the feasibility of the standards, and experience gained under this and other health and safety laws." 29 U.S.C. § 655(b)(5).

Wherever the toxic material to be regulated is a carcinogen, the Secretary has taken the position that no safe exposure level can be determined and that § 6(b)(5) requires him to set an exposure limit at the lowest technologically feasible level that will not impair the viability of the industries regulated. In this case, after having determined that there is a causal connection between benzene and leukemia (a cancer of the white blood cells), the Secretary set an exposure limit on airborne concentrations of benzene of one part benzene per million parts of air (1 ppm)....

I

Benzene is a familiar and important commodity. It is a colorless, aromatic liquid that evaporates rapidly under ordinary atmospheric conditions. Approximately 11 billion pounds of benzene were produced in the United States in 1976....

The entire population of the United States is exposed to small quantities of benzene, ranging from a few parts per billion to 0.5 ppm, in the ambient air. Over one million workers are subject to additional low-level exposures as a consequence of their employment. The majority of these employees work in gasoline service stations, benzene production (petroleum refineries and coking operations), chemical processing, benzene transportation, rubber manufacturing, and laboratory operations.

Benzene is a toxic substance. Although it could conceivably cause harm to a person who swallowed or touched it, the principal risk of harm comes from inhalation of benzene vapors. . . .

Industrial health experts have long been aware that exposure to benzene may lead to various types of nonmalignant diseases. . . . In 1969 the American National Standards Institute (ANSI) adopted a national consensus standard of 10 ppm averaged over an 8–hour period with a ceiling concentration of 25 ppm for 10–minute periods or a maximum peak concentration of 50 ppm. In 1971, after the Occupational Safety and Health Act was passed, the Secretary adopted this consensus standard as the federal standard . . . .

. . . In the late 1960's and early 1970's a number of epidemiological studies were published indicating that workers exposed to high concentrations of benzene were subject to significantly increased risk of leukemia. In a 1974 report recommending a permanent standard for benzene, the National Institute for Occupational Safety and Health (NIOSH), OSHA's research arm,[10] noted that these studies raised the "distinct possibility" that benzene caused leukemia. . . .

In October 1976, NIOSH . . . recommended that a 1 ppm exposure limit be imposed for benzene. . . .

In its published statement giving notice of the proposed permanent standard, OSHA did not ask for comments as to whether or not benzene presented a significant health risk at exposures of 10 ppm or less. Rather, it asked for comments as to whether 1 ppm was the minimum feasible exposure limit. . . . Whenever a carcinogen is involved, OSHA will presume that no safe level of exposure exists in the absence of clear proof establishing such a level and will accordingly set the exposure limit at the lowest level feasible. The proposed 1 ppm exposure limit in this case thus was established not on the basis of a proven hazard at 10 ppm, but rather on the basis of "OSHA's best judgment at the time of the proposal of the feasibility of compliance with the proposed standard by the [a]ffected industries." . . .

. . . The final standard was issued on February 10, 1978[, and required] employers . . . to institute whatever engineering or other controls are necessary to keep exposures at or below 1 ppm.

. . . As presently formulated, the benzene standard is an expensive way of providing some additional protection for a relatively small number of employees. According to OSHA's figures, the standard will require capital investments in engineering controls of approximately $266 million, first-year operating costs (for monitoring, medical testing, employee training, and respirators) of $187 million to $205 million and recurring annual costs

---

**10.** Title 29 U.S.C. § 669(a)(3) requires the Department of Health, Education, and Welfare (HEW) (now in part the Department of Health and Human Services) to develop "criteria" dealing with toxic materials and harmful physical agents that describe "exposure levels that are safe for various periods of employment." HEW's obligations under this section have been delegated to NIOSH.

of approximately $34 million. The figures outlined in OSHA's explanation of the costs of compliance to various industries indicate that only 35,000 employees would gain any benefit from the regulation in terms of a reduction in their exposure to benzene. . . .

Although OSHA did not quantify the benefits to each category of worker in terms of decreased exposure to benzene, it appears from the economic impact study done at OSHA's direction that those benefits may be relatively small. . . .

## II

. . . Any discussion of the 1 ppm exposure limit must, of course, begin with the Agency's rationale for imposing that limit. The written explanation of the standard fills 184 pages of the printed appendix. . . . This discussion demonstrates that there is ample justification for regulating occupational exposure to benzene and that the prior limit of 10 ppm . . . was reasonable. It does not, however, provide direct support for the Agency's conclusion that the limit should be reduced from 10 ppm to 1 ppm. . . .

In the end OSHA's rationale for lowering the permissible exposure limit to 1 ppm was based, not on any finding that leukemia has ever been caused by exposure to 10 ppm of benzene and that it will *not* be caused by exposure to 1 ppm, but rather on a series of assumptions indicating that some leukemias might result from exposure to 10 ppm and that the number of cases might be reduced by reducing the exposure level to 1 ppm. In reaching that result, the Agency first unequivocally concluded that benzene is a human carcinogen. Second, it concluded that industry had failed to prove that there is a safe threshold level of exposure to benzene below which no excess leukemia cases would occur. . . .

Third, the Agency applied its standard policy with respect to carcinogens, concluding that, in the absence of definitive proof of a safe level, it must be assumed that *any* level above zero presents *some* increased risk of cancer. . . .

Fourth, the Agency reiterated its view of the Act, stating that it was required by § 6(b)(5) to set the standard either at the level that has been demonstrated to be safe or at the lowest level feasible, whichever is higher. . . . Because of benzene's importance to the economy, no one has ever suggested that it would be feasible to eliminate its use entirely. . . . Rather, the Agency selected 1 ppm as a workable exposure level, and then determined that compliance with that level was technologically feasible and that "the economic impact of . . . [compliance] will not be such as to threaten the financial welfare of the affected firms or the general economy." It therefore held that 1 ppm was the minimum feasible exposure level within the meaning of § 6(b)(5) of the Act. . . .

## III

Our resolution of the issues in these cases turns, to a large extent, on the meaning of and the relationship between § 3(8), which defines a health and safety standard as a standard that is "reasonably necessary and appropriate to provide safe or healthful employment," and § 6(b)(5), which directs the Secretary in promulgating a health and safety standard for toxic materials to "set the standard which most adequately assures, to the extent feasible, on the basis of the best available evidence, that no employee will suffer material impairment of health or functional capacity. . . ."

In the Government's view, § 3(8)'s definition of the term "standard" has no legal significance or at best merely requires that a standard not be totally irrational. It takes the position that § 6(b)(5) is controlling and that it requires OSHA to promulgate a standard that either gives an absolute assurance of safety for each and every worker or reduces exposures to the lowest level feasible. The Government interprets "feasible" as meaning technologically achievable at a cost that would not impair the viability of the industries subject to the regulation. The respondent industry representatives, on the other hand, argue that the . . . "reasonably necessary and appropriate" language of § 3(8), along with the feasibility requirement of § 6(b)(5), requires the Agency to quantify both the costs and the benefits of a proposed rule and to conclude that they are roughly commensurate.

In our view, it is not necessary to decide whether either the Government or industry is entirely correct. For we think it is clear that § 3(8) does apply to all permanent standards promulgated under the Act and that it requires the Secretary, before issuing any standard, to determine that it is reasonably necessary and appropriate to remedy a significant risk of material health impairment. Only after the Secretary has made the threshold determination that such a risk exists with respect to a toxic substance, would it be necessary to decide whether § 6(b)(5) requires him to select the most protective standard he can consistent with economic and technological feasibility, or whether . . . the benefits of the regulation must be commensurate with the costs of its implementation. Because the Secretary did not make the required threshold finding in these cases, we have no occasion to determine whether costs must be weighed against benefits in an appropriate case.

## A

Under the Government's view, § 3(8), if it has any substantive content at all, merely requires OSHA to issue standards that are reasonably calculated to produce a safer or more healthy work environment. Apart from this minimal requirement of rationality, the Government argues that § 3(8) imposes no limits on the Agency's power, and thus would not prevent it from requiring employers to do whatever would be "reasonably necessary" to eliminate all risks of any harm from their workplaces. With respect to toxic substances and harmful physical agents, the Government takes an even more extreme position. Relying on § 6(b)(5)'s direction to set a standard "which most adequately assures . . . that no employee will suffer material impairment of health or functional capacity," the Government contends that the Secretary is required to impose standards that either guarantee workplaces that are free from any risk of material health impairment, however small, or that come as close as possible to doing so without ruining entire industries.

If the purpose of the statute were to eliminate completely and with absolute certainty any risk of serious harm, we would agree that it would be proper for the Secretary to interpret §§ 3(8) and 6(b)(5) in this fashion. But we think it is clear that the statute was not designed to require employers to provide absolutely risk-free workplaces whenever it is technologically feasible to do so, so long as the cost is not great enough to destroy an entire industry. Rather, both the language and structure of the Act, as well as its legislative history, indicate that it was intended to require the elimination, as far as feasible, of significant risks of harm.

## B

By empowering the Secretary to promulgate standards that are "reasonably necessary or appropriate to provide safe or healthful employment and places of employment," the Act implies that, before promulgating any standard, the Secretary must make a finding that the workplaces in question are not safe. But "safe" is not the equivalent of "risk-free." There are many activities that we engage in every day—such as driving a car or even breathing city air—that entail some risk of accident or material health impairment; nevertheless, few people would consider these activities "unsafe." Similarly, a workplace can hardly be considered "unsafe" unless it threatens the workers with a significant risk of harm.

Therefore, before he can promulgate *any* permanent health or safety standard, the Secretary is required to make a threshold finding that a place of employment is unsafe—in the sense that significant risks are present and can be eliminated or lessened by a change in practices. This requirement applies to permanent standards promulgated pursuant to § 6(b)(5).... [T]here is no reason why § 3(8)'s definition of a standard should not be deemed incorporated by reference into § 6(b)(5). The standards promulgated pursuant to § 6(b)(5) are just one species of the genus of standards governed by the basic requirement. That section repeatedly uses the term "standard" without suggesting any exception from, or qualification of, the general definition; on the contrary, it directs the Secretary to select *"the* standard"—that is to say, one of various possible alternatives that satisfy the basic definition in § 3(8)—that is most protective....[48]

... In the absence of a clear mandate in the Act, it is unreasonable to assume that Congress intended to give the Secretary the unprecedented power over American industry that would result from the Government's view of §§ 3(8) and 6(b)(5), coupled with OSHA's cancer policy. Expert

---

**48.** ... MR. JUSTICE MARSHALL states that our view of § 3(8) would make the first sentence in § 6(b)(5) superfluous. We disagree. The first sentence of § 6(b)(5) requires the Secretary to select a highly protective standard once he has determined that a standard should be promulgated.... Once the Secretary has made the requisite threshold finding, § 6(b)(5) directs him to choose the most protective standard that still meets the definition of a standard under § 3(8), consistent with feasibility.

testimony that a substance is probably a human carcinogen—either because it has caused cancer in animals or because individuals have contracted cancer following extremely high exposures—would justify the conclusion that the substance poses some risk of serious harm no matter how minute the exposure and no matter how many experts testified that they regarded the risk as insignificant. That conclusion would in turn justify pervasive regulation limited only by the constraint of feasibility. In light of the fact that there are literally thousands of substances used in the workplace that have been identified as carcinogens or suspect carcinogens, the Government's theory would give OSHA power to impose enormous costs that might produce little, if any, discernible benefit.

If the Government were correct in arguing that neither § 3(8) nor § 6(b)(5) requires that the risk from a toxic substance be quantified sufficiently to enable the Secretary to characterize it as significant in an understandable way, the statute would make such a "sweeping delegation of legislative power" that it might be unconstitutional under the Court's reasoning in A.L.A. Schechter Poultry Corp. v. United States, 295 U.S. 495, 539, and Panama Refining Co. v. Ryan, 293 U.S. 388. A construction of the statute that avoids this kind of open-ended grant should certainly be favored. . . .

## D

Given the conclusion that the Act empowers the Secretary to promulgate health and safety standards only where a significant risk of harm exists, the critical issue becomes how to define and allocate the burden of proving the significance of the risk in a case such as this, where scientific knowledge is imperfect and the precise quantification of risks is therefore impossible. . . .

. . . As we read the statute, the burden was on the Agency to show, on the basis of substantial evidence, that it is at least more likely than not that long-term exposure to 10 ppm of benzene presents a significant risk of material health impairment. . . .

In this case OSHA did not even attempt to carry its burden of proof. The closest it came to making a finding that benzene presented a significant risk of harm in the workplace was its statement that the benefits to be derived from lowering the permissible exposure level from 10 to 1 ppm were "likely" to be "appreciable." . . . [E]ven if it were supported by substantial evidence, such a finding would not be sufficient to satisfy the Agency's obligations under the Act. . . .

■ [CHIEF JUSTICE BURGER'S concurring opinion is omitted.]

■ MR. JUSTICE POWELL, concurring in part and concurring in the judgment.

. . . I agree that §§ 6(b)(5) and 3(8) of the Occupational Safety and Health Act of 1970 must be read together. They require OSHA to make a threshold finding that proposed occupational health standards are reasonably necessary to provide safe workplaces. . . .

... I do not disagree with the plurality's view that OSHA has failed, on this record, to carry its burden of proof on [this threshold issue].... But even if one assumes that OSHA properly met this burden, I conclude that the statute also requires the agency to determine that the economic effects of its standard bear a reasonable relationship to the expected benefits. An occupational health standard is neither "reasonably necessary" nor "feasible," as required by statute, if it calls for expenditures wholly disproportionate to the expected health and safety benefits.

OSHA contends that § 6(b)(5) not only permits but actually requires it to promulgate standards that reduce health risks without regard to economic effects, unless those effects would cause widespread dislocation throughout an entire industry. Under the threshold test adopted by the plurality today, this authority will exist only with respect to "significant" risks. But the plurality does not reject OSHA's claim that it must reduce such risks without considering economic consequences less serious than massive dislocation. In my view, that claim is untenable.

Although one might wish that Congress had spoken with greater clarity, the legislative history and purposes of the statute do not support OSHA's interpretation of the Act. It is simply unreasonable to believe that Congress intended OSHA to pursue the desirable goal of risk-free workplaces to the extent that the economic viability of particular industries—or significant segments thereof—is threatened. As the plurality observes, OSHA itself has not chosen to carry out such a self-defeating policy in all instances. If it did, OSHA regulations would impair the ability of American industries to compete effectively with foreign businesses and to provide employment for American workers.

I therefore would not lightly assume that Congress intended OSHA to require reduction of health risks found to be significant *whenever* it also finds that the affected industry can bear the costs.... [A] standard-setting process that ignored economic considerations would result in a serious misallocation of resources and a lower effective level of safety than could be achieved under standards set with reference to the comparative benefits available at a lower cost. I would not attribute such an irrational intention to Congress....

■ MR. JUSTICE REHNQUIST, concurring in the judgment.

... [T]his litigation presents the Court with what has to be one of the most difficult issues that could confront a decisionmaker: whether the statistical possibility of future deaths should ever be disregarded in light of the economic costs of preventing those deaths.... [T]he widely varying positions advanced in the briefs of the parties and in the opinions of MR. JUSTICE STEVENS, THE CHIEF JUSTICE, MR. JUSTICE POWELL, and MR. JUSTICE MARSHALL demonstrate, perhaps better than any other fact, that Congress, the governmental body best suited and most obligated to make the choice confronting us in this litigation, has improperly delegated that choice to the Secretary of Labor and, derivatively, to this Court.

I

In his Second Treatise of Civil Government, published in 1690, John Locke wrote that "[t]he power of the legislative, being derived from the people by a positive voluntary grant and institution, can be no other than what that positive grant conveyed, which being only to make laws, and not to make legislators, the legislative can have no power to transfer their authority of making laws and place it in other hands." Two hundred years later, this Court expressly recognized the existence of and the necessity for limits on Congress' ability to delegate its authority to representatives of the Executive Branch: "That Congress cannot delegate legislative power to the president is a principle universally recognized as vital to the integrity and maintenance of the system of government ordained by the Constitution." Field v. Clark, 143 U.S. 649, 692 (1892).

The rule against delegation of legislative power is not, however, so cardinal of principle as to allow for no exception. The Framers of the Constitution were practical statesmen, who saw that the doctrine of separation of powers was a two-sided coin. James Madison, in Federalist Paper No. 48, for example, recognized that while the division of authority among the various branches of government was a useful principle, "the degree of separation which the maxim requires, as essential to a free government, can never in practice be duly maintained." The Federalist No. 48, p. 308 (H. Lodge ed. 1888).

This Court also has recognized that a hermetic sealing-off of the three branches of government from one another could easily frustrate the establishment of a National Government capable of effectively exercising the substantive powers granted to the various branches by the Constitution. . . .

During the third and fourth decades of this century, this Court within a relatively short period of time struck down several Acts of Congress on the grounds that they exceeded the authority of Congress under the Commerce Clause or under the nondelegation principle of separation of powers, and at the same time struck down state statutes because they violated "substantive" due process or interfered with interstate commerce. . . . When many of these decisions were later overruled, the principle that Congress could not simply transfer its legislative authority to the Executive fell under a cloud. Yet in my opinion decisions such as Panama Refining Co. v. Ryan, 293 U.S. 388 (1935), suffer from none of the excesses of judicial policymaking that plagued some of the other decisions of that era. The many later decisions that have upheld congressional delegations of authority to the Executive Branch have done so largely on the theory that Congress may wish to exercise its authority in a particular field, but because the field is sufficiently technical, the ground to be covered sufficiently large, and the Members of Congress themselves not necessarily expert in the area in which they choose to legislate, the most that may be asked under the separation-of-powers doctrine is that Congress lay down the general policy and standards that animate the law, leaving the agency to refine those standards, "fill in the blanks," or apply the standards to particular cases. These decisions, to my mind, simply illustrate the ... principle stated more than 50 years ago by Mr. Chief Justice Taft [in *J.W. Hampton, Jr. & Co v. United States*] that delegations of legislative authority must be judged "according to common sense and the inherent necessities of the governmental co-ordination."

Viewing the legislation at issue here in light of these principles, I believe that it fails to pass muster. Read literally, the relevant portion of § 6(b)(5) is completely precatory, admonishing the Secretary to adopt the most protective standard if he can, but excusing him from that duty if he cannot. In the case of a hazardous substance for which a "safe" level is either unknown or impractical, the language of § 6(b)(5) gives the Secretary absolutely no indication where on the continuum of relative safety he should draw his line. Especially in light of the importance of the interests at stake, I have no doubt that the provision at issue, standing alone, would violate the doctrine against uncanalized delegations of legislative power. For me the remaining question, then, is whether additional standards are ascertainable from the legislative history or statutory context of § 6(b)(5) or, if not, whether such a standardless delegation was justifiable in light of the "inherent necessities" of the situation.

## II

One of the primary sources looked to by this Court in adding gloss to an otherwise broad grant of legislative authority is the legislative history of the statute in question. ...

... [But] the legislative history [here] contains nothing to indicate that the language "to the extent feasible" does anything other than render what had been a clear, if somewhat unrealistic, standard largely, if not entirely, precatory. There is certainly nothing to indicate that these words, as used in § 6(b)(5), are limited to technological and economic feasibility. When Congress has wanted to limit the concept of feasibility in this fashion, it has said so. ... I also question whether the Secretary wants to assume the duties such an interpretation would impose upon him. In these cases, for example, the Secretary actually declined to adopt a standard lower than 1 ppm for some industries, not because it was economically or technologically infeasible, but rather because "different levels for different industries would result in serious administrative difficulties." If § 6(b)(5) authorizes the Secretary to reject a more protective standard in the interest of administrative feasibility, I have little doubt that he could reject such standards for any reason whatsoever, including even political feasibility. ...

## IV

As formulated and enforced by this Court, the nondelegation doctrine serves three important functions. First, and most abstractly, it ensures to the extent consistent with orderly governmental administration that important choices of social policy are made by Congress, the branch of our Government most responsive to the popular will. ... Second, the doctrine guarantees that, to the extent Congress finds it necessary to delegate authority, it provides the recipient of that authority with an "intelligible principle" to guide the exercise of the delegated discretion.... Third, and derivative of the second, the doctrine ensures that courts charged with reviewing the exercise of delegated legislative discretion will be able to test that exercise against ascertainable standards....

I believe the legislation at issue here fails on all three counts. The decision whether the law of diminishing returns should have any place in the regulation of toxic substances is quintessentially one of legislative policy. For Congress to pass that decision on to the Secretary in the manner it did violates, in my mind, John Locke's caveat ... that legislatures are to make laws, not legislators. Nor, as I think the prior discussion amply demonstrates, do the provisions at issue or their legislative history provide the Secretary with any guidance that might lead him to his somewhat tentative conclusion that he must eliminate exposure to benzene as far as technologically and economically possible. Finally, I would suggest that the standard of "feasibility" renders meaningful judicial review impossible.

We ought not to shy away from our judicial duty to invalidate unconstitutional delegations of legislative authority solely out of concern that we should thereby reinvigorate discredited constitutional doctrines of the pre-New Deal era. If the nondelegation doctrine has fallen into the same desuetude as have substantive due process and restrictive interpretations of the Commerce Clause, it is, as one writer has phrased it, "a case of death by association." J. Ely, Democracy and Distrust, A Theory of Judicial Review 133 (1980)....

If we are ever to reshoulder the burden of ensuring that Congress itself make the critical policy decisions, these are surely the cases in which to do it. It is difficult to imagine a more obvious example of Congress simply avoiding a choice which was both fundamental for purposes of the statute and yet politically so divisive that the necessary decision or compromise was difficult, if not impossible, to hammer out in the legislative forge. Far from detracting from the substantive authority of Congress, a declaration that the first sentence of § 6(b)(5) of the Occupational Safety and Health Act constitutes an invalid delegation to the Secretary of Labor would preserve the authority of Congress. If Congress wishes to legislate in an area which it has not previously sought to enter, it will in today's political world undoubtedly run into opposition no matter how the legislation is formulated. But that is the very essence of legislative authority under our system. It is the hard choices, and not the filling in of the blanks, which must be made by the elected representatives of the people. When fundamental policy decisions underlying important legislation about to be enacted are to be made, the buck stops with Congress and the President insofar as he exercises his constitutional role in the legislative process....

■ Mr. Justice Marshall, with whom Mr. Justice Brennan, Mr. Justice White, and Mr. Justice Blackmun join, dissenting.

In cases of statutory construction, this Court's authority is limited. If the statutory language and legislative intent are plain, the judicial inquiry is at an end. Under our jurisprudence, it is presumed that ill-considered or unwise legislation will be corrected through the democratic process; a court is not permitted to distort a statute's meaning in order to make it conform with the Justices' own views of sound social policy.

Today's decision flagrantly disregards these restrictions on judicial authority. The plurality ignores the plain meaning of the Occupational Safety and Health Act of 1970 in order to bring the authority of the Secretary of Labor in line with the plurality's own views of proper regulatory policy. The unfortunate consequence is that the Federal Government's efforts to protect American workers from cancer and other crippling diseases may be substantially impaired. . . .

The first sentence of § 6(b)(5) of the Act provides:

"The Secretary, in promulgating standards dealing with toxic materials or harmful physical agents under this subsection, shall set the standard which most adequately assures, to the extent feasible, on the basis of the best available evidence, that no employee will suffer material impairment of health or functional capacity even if such employee has regular exposure to the hazard dealt with by such standard for the period of his working life." 29 U.S.C. § 655(b)(5).

In this case the Secretary of Labor found, on the basis of substantial evidence, that (1) exposure to benzene creates a risk of cancer, chromosomal damage, and a variety of nonmalignant but potentially fatal blood disorders, even at the level of 1 ppm; (2) no safe level of exposure has been shown; (3) benefits in the form of saved lives would be derived from the permanent standard; (4) the number of lives that would be saved could turn out to be either substantial or relatively small; (5) under the present state of scientific knowledge, it is impossible to calculate even in a rough way the number of lives that would be saved, at least without making assumptions that would appear absurd to much of the medical community; and (6) the standard would not materially harm the financial condition of the covered industries. The Court does not set aside any of these findings. Thus, it could not be plainer that the Secretary's decision was fully in accord with his statutory mandate "most adequately [to] assur[e] . . . that no employee will suffer material impairment of health or functional capacity. . . ."

The plurality's conclusion to the contrary is based on its interpretation of 29 U.S.C. § 652(8), which defines an occupational safety and health standard as one "which requires conditions . . . reasonably necessary or appropriate to provide safe or healthful employment. . . ." According to the plurality, a standard is not "reasonably necessary or appropriate" unless the Secretary is able to show that it is "at least more likely than not" that the risk he seeks to regulate is a "significant" one. Nothing in the statute's language or legislative history, however, indicates that the "reasonably necessary or appropriate" language should be given this meaning. Indeed, both demonstrate that the plurality's standard bears no connection with the acts or intentions of Congress and is based only on the plurality's solicitude for the welfare of regulated industries. . . .

Unlike the plurality, I do not purport to know whether the actions taken by Congress and its delegates to ensure occupational safety represent sound or unsound regulatory policy. The critical problem in cases like the ones at bar is scientific uncertainty. While science has determined that exposure to benzene at levels above 1 ppm creates a definite risk of health impairment, the magnitude of the risk cannot be quantified at the present time. The risk at issue has hardly been shown to be insignificant; indeed, future research may reveal that the risk is in fact considerable. But the existing evidence may frequently be inadequate to enable the Secretary to make the threshold finding of "significance" that the Court requires today. If so, the consequence of the plurality's approach would be to subject American workers to a continuing risk of cancer and other fatal diseases, and to render the Federal Government powerless to take protective action on their behalf. Such an approach would place the burden of medical uncertainty squarely on the shoulders of the American worker, the intended beneficiary of the Occupational Safety and Health Act. . . .

## III

### A

. . . [T]he Secretary's decision was reasonable and in full conformance with the statutory language. . . . On this record, the Secretary could conclude that regular exposure above the 1 ppm level would pose a definite risk resulting in material impairment to some indeterminate but possibly substantial number of employees. . . . Nothing in the Act purports to prevent the Secretary from acting when definitive information as to the quantity of a standard's benefits is unavailable. Where, as here, the deficiency in knowledge relates to the extent of the benefits rather than their existence, I see no reason to hold that the Secretary has exceeded his statutory authority.

### B

The plurality avoids this conclusion through reasoning that may charitably be described as obscure. According to the plurality, the definition of occupational safety and health standards as those "reasonably necessary or appropriate to provide safe or healthful . . . working conditions" requires the Secretary to show that it is "more likely than not" that the risk he seeks to regulate is a "significant" one. The plurality does not show how this requirement can be plausibly derived from the "reasonably necessary or appropriate" clause. Indeed, the plurality's reasoning is refuted by the Act's language, structure, and legislative history, and it is foreclosed by every applicable guide to statutory construction. In short, the plurality's standard is a fabrication bearing no connection with the acts or intentions of Congress.

At the outset, it is important to observe that "reasonably necessary or appropriate" clauses are routinely inserted in regulatory legislation, and in the past such clauses have uniformly been interpreted as general provisos that regulatory actions must bear a reasonable relation to those statutory purposes set forth in the statute's substantive provisions. . . .

The plurality suggests that under the "reasonably necessary" clause, a workplace is not "unsafe" unless the Secretary is able to convince a reviewing court that a "significant" risk is at issue. That approach is particularly embarrassing in this case, for it is contradicted by the plain language of the Act. The plurality's interpretation renders utterly superfluous the first sentence of § 655(b)(5), which, as noted above, requires the Secretary to set the standard "which most adequately assures . . . that no employee will suffer material impairment of health." Indeed, the plurality's interpretation reads that sentence out of the Act. . . . [I]t is an odd canon of construction that would insert in a vague and general definitional clause a threshold requirement that overcomes the specific language placed in a standard-setting provision. The most elementary principles of statutory construction demonstrate that precisely the opposite interpretation is appropriate. . . .

The plurality's interpretation of the "reasonably necessary or appropriate" clause is also conclusively refuted by the legislative history. While the standard-setting provision that the plurality ignores received extensive legislative attention, the definitional clause received *none at all*. . . .

. . . The threshold finding that the plurality requires is the plurality's own invention. It bears no relationship to the acts or intentions of Congress, and it can be understood only as reflecting the personal views of the plurality as to the proper allocation of resources for safety in the American workplace.

### C

. . . I do not pretend to know whether the test the plurality erects today is, as a matter of policy, preferable to that created by Congress and its delegates: the area is too fraught with scientific uncertainty, and too dependent on considerations of policy, for a court to be able to determine whether it is desirable to require identification of a "significant" risk before allowing an administrative agency to take regulatory action. But in light of the tenor of the plurality opinion, it is necessary to point out that the question is not one-sided, and that Congress' decision to authorize the Secretary to promulgate the regulation at issue here was a reasonable one.

In this case the Secretary found that exposure to benzene at levels above 1 ppm posed a definite albeit unquantifiable risk of chromosomal damage, nonmalignant blood disorders, and leukemia. The existing evidence was sufficient to justify the conclusion that such a risk was presented, but it did not permit even rough quantification of that risk. . . .

In these circumstances it seems clear that the Secretary found a risk that is "significant" in the sense that the word is normally used. . . . If the Secretary decided to wait until definitive information was available, American workers would be subjected for the indefinite future to a possibly substantial risk of benzene-induced leukemia and other illnesses. It is unsurprising, at least to me, that he concluded that the statute authorized him to take regulatory action now.

. . . To require a quantitative showing of a "significant" risk . . . would either paralyze the Secretary into inaction or force him to deceive the public by acting on the basis of assumptions that must be considered too speculative to support any realistic assessment of the relevant risk. . . .

. . . Today's decision is objectionable not because it is final, but because it places the burden of legislative inertia on the beneficiaries of the safety and health legislation in question in these cases. By allocating the burden in this fashion, the Court requires the American worker to return to the political arena and to win a victory that he won once before in 1970. I am unable to discern any justification for that result.

## D.

. . . [R]espondents characterize the Act as a pragmatic statute designed to balance the benefits of a safety and health regulation against its costs. Respondents observe that the statute speaks in terms of relative protection by providing that safety must be assured "so far as possible," 29 U.S.C. § 651(b), and by stating that the "no material impairment" requirement is to be imposed only "to the extent feasible."[30] Respondents contend that the term feasible should be read to require consideration of the economic burden of a standard, not merely its technological achievability. . . . But respondents present no argument that the expenditure required by the benzene standard is not feasible in that respect. . . .

Respondents suggest that the feasibility requirement should be understood not merely to refer to a standard's expense, but also to mandate a finding that the benefits of an occupational safety and health standard bear

---

**30.** Finding obscurity in the word "feasible," my Brother REHNQUIST invokes the nondelegation doctrine, which was last used to invalidate an Act of Congress in 1935. A.L.A. Schechter Poultry Corp. v. United States, 295 U.S. 495 (1935). While my Brother REHNQUIST eloquently argues that there remains a place for such a doctrine in our jurisprudence, I am frankly puzzled as to why the issue is thought to be of any relevance here. The nondelegation doctrine is designed to assure that the most fundamental decisions will be made by Congress, the elected representatives of the people, rather than by administrators. Some minimal definiteness is therefore required in order for Congress to delegate its authority to administrative agencies.

Congress has been sufficiently definite here. The word "feasible" has a reasonably plain meaning, and its interpretation can be informed by other contexts in which Congress has used it. Since the term is placed in the same sentence with the "no employee will suffer" language, it is clear that "feasible" means technologically and economically achievable. Under the Act, the Secretary is afforded considerably more guidance than are other administrators acting under different regulatory statutes. In short, Congress has made "the critical policy decisions" in these cases. . . .

The plurality's apparent suggestion that the nondelegation doctrine might be violated if the Secretary were permitted to regulate definite but nonquantifiable risks is plainly wrong. Such a statute would be quite definite and would thus raise no constitutional question under *Schechter Poultry*. Moreover, Congress could rationally decide that it would be better to require industry to bear "feasible" costs than to subject American workers to an indeterminate risk of cancer and other fatal diseases.

a reasonable relation to its costs. I believe that the statute's language, structure, and legislative history foreclose respondents' position. In its ordinary meaning an activity is "feasible" if it is capable of achievement, not if its benefits outweigh its costs. See Webster's Third New International Dictionary 831 (1976). Moreover, respondents' interpretation would render § 655(b)(5) internally inconsistent by reading into the term "feasible" a requirement irreconcilable with the express language authorizing the Secretary to set standards assuring that "no employee will suffer material impairment...." Respondents' position would render that language merely hortatory....

---

*1. A Nondelegation Canon?*—The *Benzene* case presented a serious nondelegation question because § 6(b)(5) of the Occupational Safety and Health Act (the OSH Act) arguably prescribed a meaningless criterion for the Occupational Safety and Health Administration (OSHA) to apply in regulating workplace hazards. In particular, the statute instructed the agency to prescribe a standard that "most adequately assures, to the extent feasible, on the basis of the best available evidence, that no employee will suffer material impairment of health or functional capacity even if such employee has regular exposure to the hazard dealt with by such standard for the period of his working life." As Justice Rehnquist argued in his concurring opinion, § 6(b)(5)'s qualifier—"to the extent feasible"—threatened to transform an otherwise intelligible statutory standard into something "completely precatory, admonishing the Secretary to adopt the most protective standard if he can, but excusing him from that duty if he cannot."

For our purposes, the most interesting and important aspect of the case is the plurality's decision to sidestep the problem. Reasoning that the OSH Act would "give the Secretary unprecedented power over American industry" if "limited only by the constraint of feasibility," the plurality read into the statute a threshold requirement that the agency find a "significant risk" to employee health before adopting a safety standard—a requirement that OSHA had not followed in promulgating its benzene regulation. Although no provision of the OSH Act explicitly required such a finding, the plurality creatively treated it as a reasonable implication of one of the Act's definitional provisions, § 3(8), which defined "occupational safety and health standard" to mean measures "reasonably necessary or appropriate to provide safe or healthful employment and places of employment." 29 U.S.C. § 652(8). The plurality reasoned that "a workplace can hardly be considered 'unsafe' unless it threatens the workers with a significant risk of harm." From that starting point, the plurality reasoned that the only "occupational safety and health standard[s]" that OSHA is authorized to adopt under § 6(b)(5) are those that deal with a workplace that is unsafe within the meaning of § 3(8). The plurality's reading is not the most natural way to read the statutory language; indeed, most commentators agree that the plurality's strained interpretation essentially rewrote the statute. *See, e.g.* Jerry Mashaw, *As If Republican Interpreta-*

*tion*, 97 YALE L.J. 1685, 1691 (1988); Martin Shapiro, *Administrative Discretion: The Next Stage*, 92 YALE L.J. 1487, 1507 (1983); Richard B. Stewart, *Regulatory Jurisprudence: Canons Redux*, 79 CAL. L. REV. 807, 817–18 (1991). The plurality, however, justified its reading in part by emphasizing the judiciary's obligation to read statutes, where possible, to avoid a sweeping and potentially unconstitutional delegation of power.

The plurality's approach in *Benzene* is perhaps the most well-known example of how courts may invoke (explicitly or implicitly) nondelegation principles to interpret statutory delegations narrowly. *See* Mistretta v. United States, 488 U.S. 361, 373 n.7 (1989) ("In recent years, our application of the nondelegation doctrine principally has been limited to the interpretation of statutory texts, and, more particularly, to giving narrow constructions to statutory delegations that might otherwise be thought to be unconstitutional."); *see also, e.g.*, FDA v. Brown & Williamson Tobacco Corp., 529 U.S. 120, 160 (2000) (concluding that the general terms of the Food, Drug, and Cosmetic Act do not authorize the FDA to regulate tobacco and suggesting "that Congress could not have intended to delegate a decision of such economic and political significance to an agency in so cryptic a fashion"); MCI Telecommunications Corp. v. American Telephone & Telegraph Co., 512 U.S. 218, 231 (1994) (deeming it "highly unlikely that Congress would leave the determination of whether an industry will be entirely, or even substantially, rate-regulated to agency discretion"); National Cable Television Ass'n v. FCC, 415 U.S. 336, 341–42 (1974) (reading the Independent Offices Appropriations Act "narrowly to avoid constitutional problems" raised by agency's open-ended authority to impose "fees" on regulated parties); Kent v. Dulles, 357 U.S. 116 (1958) (narrowly construing a statutory grant of the authority to the President to establish regulations for issuance of passports, on the logic that Congress would not have delegated the authority to issue regulations that raise serious constitutional issues).

Is the reconceptualization of the nondelegation doctrine as a substantive canon of statutory construction, rather than as an enforceable principle of constitutional law, a sensible approach? Some have argued that this approach provides judges with "a finer weapon" than does judicial review for constitutionality. *See* Paul Gewirtz, *The Courts, Congress, and Executive Policy–Making: Notes on Three Doctrines*, 40 L. & CONTEMP. PROBS., Summer 1976, at 46, 72. Judges may not be able to draw principled lines between permissible and excessive delegations, but they *can* interpret statutes. *See id.* Accordingly, using the canon of construction to enforce the nondelegation doctrine has been attractive to many who doubt the doctrine's efficacy as a basis for judicial review. *See, e.g.*, Richard B. Stewart, *The Reformation of American Administrative Law*, 88 HARV. L. REV. 1669, 1697 (1975); Cass R. Sunstein, *Interpreting Statutes in the Regulatory State*, 103 HARV. L. REV. 405, 470 (1989). But does recasting the nondelegation doctrine as a canon of statutory interpretation really avoid the line-drawing problems that have hampered the enforcement of a meaningful constitutional version of the doctrine? If courts have trouble identifying the point at which Congress has conferred too much discretion for purposes of judicial review, will it be any easier to identify the point at which an administrative statute confers so much discretion that it presents a serious constitutional question under the nondelegation doctrine? *Compare, e.g.,* John F. Manning, *Lessons from a Nondelegation Canon*, 83 Notre Dame L. Rev. 1541 (2008) (arguing that the administrability problems are no different when the nondelegation doctrine is enforced through the canon of avoidance), *with* Cass R. Sunstein, *Nondelegation Canons*, 67 U. Chi. L. Rev. 315, 338 (2000) (suggesting that the avoidance strategy sidesteps "the hard-to-manage question whether the legislature has exceeded the permissible level of discretion"). Furthermore, the nondelegation version of the avoidance canon may raise many of the same concerns that apply to the constitutional avoidance canon more generally—in particular, the worry that courts will fail to respect congressional decisions on the basis of vaguely specified constitutional concerns. As discussed in Chapter Two, *supra* pp. 268–288, the constitutional avoidance canon is the subject of a vigorous scholarly and jurisprudential debate. Whatever the merits of the canon of avoidance in general, however, is there special reason to be concerned about its use to enforce the nondelegation doctrine? If the avoidance canon authorizes or even requires judges to displace the most natural or probable reading of a statute, does it really serve the crucial interest of the nondelegation doctrine—ensuring *legislative* responsibility for policy outcomes—if the *judiciary* rewrites the statute to narrow its scope to an acceptable range and to supply an intelligible principle? *Compare, e.g.*, John F. Manning, *The Nondelegation Doctrine as a Canon of Avoidance*, 2000 Sup. Ct. Rev. 223, 256–57 (arguing that rewriting a statute to protect Congress's Article I authority "is at best self-defeating"), *with* Eric A. Posner & Adrian Vermeule, *Interring the Nondelegation Doctrine*, 69 U. Chi. L. Rev. 1721, 1759–60 (2002) (arguing that judicial "narrowing" or "rewriting" of a statute is not "legislative behavior" and does not contradict any scruple against delegation).

**2. *The Canon of Avoidance as a Nondelegation Canon***—The previous note suggested that the Court in *Benzene* (and some other cases) may invoke something akin to the constitutional avoidance canon in order to construe statutory delegations narrowly, in order to avoid the arguably serious constitutional concern about an impermissibly broad delegation of legislative power. That is, courts may sometimes recognize a specific "nondelegation canon." Some have also argued that even more conventional applications of the constitutional avoidance canon, or other substantive clear statement rules, might have the valuable collateral effect of promoting the goals of the nondelegation doctrine. *See, e.g.*, Cass R. Sunstein, *Nondelegation Canons*, 67 U. Chi. L. Rev. 315 (2000). On this account, because such canons insist that Congress speak with unusual clarity before the Court will read a statute to invade a particular constitutional value, the net effect is to require Congress to take direct responsibility for any constitutionally suspect or disfavored outcome. Put another way, the application of these substantive canons may prevent Congress from delegating certain kinds of legislative decisions to agencies—such as decisions that would raise a serious constitutional problem.

Consider, in this regard, Kent v. Dulles, 357 U.S. 116 (1958), which involved a statutory provision that granted the Secretary of State the exclusive authority to "grant and issue passports . . . under such rules as the President shall designate and prescribe." Pursuant to this authority, in 1952 the President and the Secretary promulgated regulations that forbade the issuance of passports to members of the Communist Party. Two U.S. citizens who had been denied passports under this regulation argued that denying them passports on the basis of their political views deprived them of their constitutional right to travel (a liberty interest asserted to be protected by the Due Process Clause of the Fifth Amendment). In a 5–4 decision authored by Justice Douglas, the Court invalidated the regulation, but did so on statutory rather than constitutional grounds:

> Since we start with an exercise by an American citizen of an activity included in constitutional protection, we will not readily infer that Congress gave the Secretary of State unbridled discretion to grant or withhold it. . . . [A passport's] crucial function today is control over exit. And, as we have seen, the right of exit is a personal right included within the word "liberty" as used in the Fifth Amendment. If that "liberty" is to be regulated, it must be pursuant to the lawmaking functions of the Congress. And if that power is delegated, the standards must be adequate to pass scrutiny by the accepted tests. Where activities or enjoyment, natural and often necessary to the well-being of an American citizen, such as travel, are involved, we will construe narrowly all delegated powers that curtail or dilute them. We hesitate to find in this broad generalized power an authority to trench so heavily on the rights of the citizen.

> Thus we do not reach the question of constitutionality. We only conclude that [the statutory provisions at issue] do not delegate to the Secretary the kind of authority exercised here. . . .

> To repeat, we deal here with a constitutional right of the citizen, a right which we must assume Congress will be faithful to respect. We would be faced with important constitutional questions were we to hold that Congress by [these statutory provisions] had given the Secretary authority to withhold passports to citizens because of their beliefs or associations. Congress has made no such provision in explicit terms; and absent one, the Secretary may not employ that standard to restrict the citizens' right of free movement.

357 U.S. at 129–30 (internal citations omitted).

Notice that the statute in *Kent*, by its own terms, seemed to confer unqualified discretion on the President to prescribe regulations for issuing passports. But Justice Douglas strained to read that delegation narrowly to avoid the constitutional problem. Indeed, Justice Douglas suggested that whenever "activities or enjoyment, natural and often necessary to the well-being of an American citizen . . . are involved," the Court should "construe narrowly all delegated powers that curtail or dilute them." Does this application of the avoidance canon promote the nondelegation principle by forcing Congress to state explicitly that it wants the Secretary to restrict the right of travel on constitutionally questionable grounds? Or is it more accurate to suggest that the Court displaced an obvious legislative grant of broad discretion in order to promote a vague constitutional value?

It is perhaps also worth noting that while the plurality's approach in *Benzene* is similar to the approach in *Kent*, *Benzene* is different—and more striking—because in *Benzene* the agency's exercise of its delegated authority would not implicate any *other* substantive constitutional limitation. The *only* constitutional problem that the *Benzene* plurality was avoiding was the constitutional concern about the delegation itself.

*3. Contextual Narrowing of Facially Broad Language*—The post-New Deal Court has frequently found an intelligible principle in statutory standards that seem, on their face, to be meaningless or empty. For example, in American Power & Light Co. v. SEC, 329 U.S. 90, 104 (1946), the Court upheld the Public Utility Holding Company Act's proscription of corporate practices that "unduly or unnecessarily complicate the structure" of a public utility or "unfairly or inequitably distribute voting power among [its] security holders," reasoning that such standards, though seemingly meaningless to a lay person, would be intelligible to those "familiar with corporate realities." Similarly, in Federal Radio Comm'n v. Nelson Bros. Bond & Mortgage Co., 289 U.S. 266, 285 (1933), the Court held that the statutory standard "public convenience, interest or necessity," though seemingly broad, supplied an adequate intelligible principle in light of "its context [and] the nature of radio transmission and reception." Do these cases involve different considerations from the application of the canon of avoidance? That is, do cases such as *American Power & Light* and *Nelson Bros.* merely reflect the conventional interpretive principle that seemingly unqualified language, when read in context, will sometimes have a specialized meaning that is narrower than the meaning apparent on the face of the statute? *See, e.g.*, Morissette v. United States, 342 U.S. 246, 263 (1952) (*see also* pp. 113–125, *supra*). If, for example, the corporate bar would have a shared understanding of what criteria go into determining the existence of an "unduly or unnecessarily complicate[d]" corporate structure, that phrase—understood in its technical sense—would presumably have a narrower and more intelligible meaning than it would to a layperson using ordinary language. Does this practice present the same concerns as the application of nondelegation canons described above? Or does it simply reflect the standard technique of reading texts in their (sometimes specialized) contexts?

*4. Requiring Agencies Themselves To Narrow Open–Ended Delegations*—Whitman v. American Trucking Ass'ns, Inc., 531 U.S. 457 (2001) (pp. 410–415, *supra*), as you may recall, involved a nondelegation challenge to the portion of the Clean Air Act (CAA) that instructed the EPA to set air quality standards for various pollutants that would be "requisite to protect the public health" with an "adequate margin of safety." The Supreme Court's *Whitman* opinion represented a fairly conventional application of the nondelegation doctrine, in that the Court yet again affirmed the vitality of the *Hampton* intelligible principle test, while simultaneously upholding a very broad and open-ended standard under that test. The *Whitman* litigation is more notable for the D.C. Circuit's alternative approach to enforcing nondelegation principles—an approach that the Supreme Court (unanimously) rejected.

The D.C. Circuit's *American Trucking* opinion suggested that even if the statutory language itself did not supply an intelligible principle, the agency might remedy the problem by adopting clear, self-constraining regulations that limit its own authority. *See* American Trucking Ass'ns, Inc. v. United States Environmental Protection Agency, 175 F.3d 1027, *modified on rehearing*, 195 F.3d 4 (D.C. Cir. 1999). The D.C. Circuit first concluded that the CAA's standard, as the EPA had interpreted it, failed to supply an intelligible principle to guide the agency's exercise of discretion. The D.C. Circuit did not, however, conclude that the statutory language *inevitably* lacked a sufficiently intelligible principle; rather, the court concluded that the *EPA* had construed the language in a way that made it too open-ended to satisfy *Hampton*. As the court put it:

> EPA appears to have articulated no "intelligible principle" to channel its application of these factors; nor is one apparent from the statute. The nondelegation doctrine requires such a principle. Here it is as though Congress commanded EPA to select "big guys," and EPA announced that it would evaluate candidates based on height and weight, but revealed no cut-off point. The announcement, though sensible in what it does say, is fatally incomplete. The reasonable person responds, "How tall? How heavy?"

175 F.3d at 1034 (internal citation omitted). The fact that the CAA, as previously interpreted by the EPA, did not supply a constitutionally adequate intelligible principle did not, however, mean that the statute was necessarily unconstitutional in the D.C. Circuit's view. Rather, the agency should be given an opportunity to articulate more definite criteria. As Judge Williams' opinion for the court argued:

> Where (as here) statutory language and an existing agency interpretation involve an unconstitutional delegation of power, but an interpretation without the constitutional weakness is or may be available, our response is not to strike down the statute but to give the agency an opportunity to extract a determinate standard on its own. Doing so serves at least two of three basic rationales for the nondelegation doctrine. If the agency develops determinate, binding standards for itself, it is less likely to exercise the delegated authority arbitrarily. And such standards enhance the likelihood that meaningful judicial review will prove feasible. A remand of this sort of course does not serve the third key function of nondelegation doctrine, to "ensure[ ] to the extent consistent with orderly governmental administration that important choices of social policy are made by Congress, the branch of our Government most responsive to the popular will," Industrial Union Dep't, AFL–CIO v. American Petroleum Inst., 448 U.S. 607, 685 (1980) ("*Benzene*") (Rehnquist, J., concurring). The agency will make the fundamental policy choices. But the remand does ensure that the

courts not hold unconstitutional a statute that an agency, with the application of its special expertise, could salvage. . . .

175 F.3d at 1038 (internal citations omitted).

Does that strategy for enforcing the nondelegation doctrine make sense? As Judge Williams argued, this approach would serve at least two of the main purposes of having a nondelegation doctrine: constraining arbitrary agency action and facilitating meaningful judicial review by providing more determinate criteria against which the agency's action could be judged. On the other hand, as Judge Williams admitted, this approach does nothing to further the interest in ensuring that *Congress*, rather than the agency, makes the key policy determinations. But isn't that latter consideration really what the nondelegation doctrine is principally about? As Judge Silberman argued:

> Th[e] purpose [of the nondelegation doctrine] is . . . to ensure that Congress makes the crucial policy choices that are carried into law. The ability to make those policy choices (even if only at a broad level of generality) is what is meant by legislative power. . . . It hardly serves— indeed, it contravenes—that purpose to demand that EPA in effect draft a different, narrower version of the Clean Air Act. Under that view Congress would be able to delegate almost limitless policymaking authority to an agency, so long as the agency provides and consistently applies an "intelligible principle."

195 F.3d at 15 (Silberman, J., dissenting from denial of rehearing en banc).

The Supreme Court did not have to reach the issue, because the Court held that the CAA itself contained a sufficiently intelligible principle to satisfy the *Hampton* test. That said, the Supreme Court in dicta signaled its strong agreement with Judge Silberman's position, reasoning as follows:

> The idea that an agency can cure an unconstitutionally standardless delegation of power by declining to exercise some of that power seems to us internally contradictory. The very choice of which portion of the power to exercise—that is to say, the prescription of the standard that Congress had omitted—would *itself* be an exercise of the forbidden legislative authority.

531 U.S. at 473.

Does the Court's position seem sound to you? If a facially ambiguous or vague statute is susceptible to a narrowing construction that would supply an intelligible principle, why wouldn't it be preferable to ask the agency to determine the best way to narrow the statute, rather than relying on judges to do so? To put this another way, if it was legitimate for Justice Stevens' plurality opinion in *Benzene* to adopt a strained reading of the OSH Act in order to avoid a serious nondelegation concern, why was it not also legitimate for Judge Williams' opinion in *American Trucking* to ask the EPA to see if it could find an acceptable (though perhaps similarly strained) way to read the CAA more narrowly, in order to avoid a similar sort of nondelegation problem? On the other hand, perhaps—as some scholars argued—Judge Williams' approach would do little to advance the core values of the nondelegation doctrine, but would impose substantial costs on agencies by inviting courts to compel agencies to narrow their statutory mandates. *See* Mark Seidenfeld & Jim Rossi, *The False Promise of the "New" Nondelegation Doctrine*, 76 NOTRE DAME L. REV. 1 (2000). What do you think?

**5.  *Prohibiting Delegation of "Naked" Legislative Power*—**If the major difficulty in enforcing a meaningful nondelegation doctrine is the fact that most exercises of executive power involve some degree of policymaking discretion (because the implementation of legislative commands requires decisions regarding how those commands ought to apply in concrete cases, as well as policy decisions regarding enforcement priorities and strategies), then perhaps courts might at least prohibit the exercise of "naked" legislative power, unconnected with any traditionally executive functions, by administrative agencies. Justice Scalia advocated something like this position in his dissenting opinion in Mistretta v. United States, 488 U.S. 361 (1989). *Mistretta* involved a constitutionally grounded nondelegation challenge to the congressional delegation to the U.S. Sentencing Commission, an independent agency, of the power to establish binding guidelines for sentencing offenders convicted of federal crimes. The eight-Justice majority opinion, written by Justice Blackmun, upheld this delegation under a straightforward application of the *Hampton* intelligible principle test. In his solo dissent, Justice Scalia argued that the question whether the Sentencing Reform Act satisfied the intelligible principle test was beside the point:

> Precisely because the scope of delegation is largely uncontrollable by the courts, we must be particularly rigorous in preserving the Constitution's structural restrictions that deter excessive delegation. The major one, it seems to me, is that the power to make law cannot be exercised by anyone other than Congress, except in conjunction with the lawful exercise of executive or judicial power.
>
> The whole theory of *lawful* congressional "delegation" is not that Congress is sometimes too busy or too divided and can therefore assign its responsibility of making law to someone else; but rather that a certain degree of discretion, and thus of lawmaking, *inheres* in most executive or judicial action, and it is up to Congress, by the relative specificity or generality of its statutory commands, to determine—up to a point—how small or how large that degree shall be.... [Thus,] the Executive could be given the power to adopt policies and rules specifying in detail what radio and television licenses will be in the "public interest, convenience or necessity," because that was ancillary to the exercise of its executive powers in granting and policing licenses and making a "fair and equitable allocation" of the electromagnetic spectrum. See Federal Radio Comm'n v. Nelson Brothers Bond & Mortgage Co., 289 U.S. 266, 285 (1933)....
>
> The focus of controversy, in the long line of our so-called excessive delegation cases, has been whether the *degree* of generality contained in the authorization for exercise of executive or judicial powers in a

particular field is so unacceptably high as to *amount* to a delegation of legislative powers. I say "so-called excessive delegation" because although that convenient terminology is often used, what is really at issue is whether there has been *any* delegation of legislative power, which occurs (rarely) when Congress authorizes the exercise of executive or judicial power without adequate standards. Strictly speaking, there is *no* acceptable delegation of legislative power.... In the present case, however, a pure delegation of legislative power is precisely what we have before us. It is irrelevant whether the standards are adequate, because they are not standards related to the exercise of executive or judicial powers; they are, plainly and simply, standards for further legislation.

The lawmaking function of the Sentencing Commission is completely divorced from any responsibility for execution of the law ... because the Commission neither exercises any executive power on its own, nor is subject to the control of the President who does.... The power to make law at issue here, in other words, is not ancillary but quite naked. The situation is no different in principle from what would exist if Congress gave the same power of writing sentencing laws to a congressional agency such as the General Accounting Office, or to members of its staff.

488 U.S. at 416–21 (Scalia, J., dissenting) (emphasis in original) (footnotes omitted). In sum, Justice Scalia concluded, "the Court errs ... not so much because it mistakes the degree of commingling [of executive and legislative power], but because it fails to recognize that this case is not about commingling, but about the creation of a new Branch altogether, a sort of junior-varsity Congress." *Id.* at 427.

Is Justice Scalia's position sound? At a minimum, it requires courts to determine when the exercise of policymaking discretion is merely "ancillary" to the exercise of executive powers. While some degree of policymaking discretion inheres in the application of general rules to specific cases, many statutes that courts have upheld against delegation challenges also give agencies power to make general rules. It is true that most of these agencies *also* exercise what looks like more conventional executive power (investigation and prosecution). But why should this matter? If Congress had assigned the authority to devise sentencing guidelines not to the Sentencing Commission, but to the Department of Justice (DOJ), would that have been acceptable, since the DOJ also performs executive functions (like prosecution)? Or suppose that Congress decided to pass a new statute that would divide the EPA into two separate agencies, one of which would retain the EPA's rulemaking functions (e.g., setting air quality standards), and the other of which would retain the EPA's investigation and enforcement functions. Would the former agency be unconstitutional under Justice Scalia's analysis? To be sure, Justice Scalia does accept that agencies can be "created with no power other than the making of rules," but he cautions that this is legitimate only if such an agency "is subject to the control of the President and the President has executive authority related to the rulemaking," because "[i]n such circumstances, the rulemaking is ultimately ancillary to the President's executive powers." *Id.* at 417 n.2. The Sentencing Commission is different, he says, because it is an *independent* agency, over which the President has only limited control. We will take up issues related to presidential control of agencies, and the special constitutional problems posed by so-called "independent" agencies, in Parts IV and V, *infra*. For now, consider whether the constitutionality of a delegation of pure rulemaking power should turn on the degree of presidential control over the agency's decisions.

Despite these problems with Justice Scalia's approach, isn't his anxiety about the creation of a "junior-varsity Congress" understandable? After all, the intelligible principle test, as the courts have applied it, does not seem to place significant limits on Congress's ability to delegate. If we do not adopt *some* additional constitutional limitation on the scope of permissible delegation, what is to stop Congress from "vot[ing] all power to the President and adjourn[ing]," or (perhaps more realistically), creating all manner of expert commissions "to dispose of thorny, 'no win' political issues"? *Id.* at 415, 422.

\* \* \* \* \*

As the entire course of post-*Schechter* case law demonstrates, the Court has firmly embraced Congress's authority to delegate extensive lawmaking authority to administrative agencies. Congress can, without offending the Constitution, instruct agencies to promulgate binding rules based on criteria as broad as "public interest," "fair and equitable," or "just and reasonable." To be sure, the Court has never overruled *Panama Refining* or *Schechter*, and the Court sometimes strains to read broad legislative grants of administrative power more narrowly, but the bottom line is that most of the details of federal law are devised not by Congress, but by administrative agencies acting pursuant to delegated authority. Whatever the merits of the practice, it has become a part of the fabric of our constitutional order. But the anxiety about delegation—particularly the concerns about administrative arbitrariness and lack of democratic accountability—persist. Much of administrative law, and much of the body of constitutional law that deals specifically with the relationship between agencies and the other branches of government, can be thought of as a response to these concerns. The challenge that runs throughout much of this body of administrative and constitutional law is designing legal rules, procedures, and institutions that will realize the purported benefits of delegation (expertise, efficiency, flexibility, healthy insulation from everyday politics) while avoiding or containing its dangers (arbitrariness, lawlessness, absence of democratic accountability).

## III. CONGRESSIONAL CONTROL OF AGENCIES

As we saw in the previous section, Congress has made it a consistent practice to delegate extensive authority to administrative agencies to fill in the binding policy details of vaguely worded statutes, and the Court has, with only two exceptions, routinely upheld the resulting arrangements. In this part, we consider Congress's natural impulse to try to attach strings to the authority it has delegated—either by retaining a "veto" on agency decisions implementing delegated authority or by securing the right to dismiss the head of the agency exercising that power.

In reviewing these cases, ask yourself the following questions: If a central concern underlying the nondelegation doctrine is legislative accountability for the adoption of binding federal policy, do the arrangements under review make the exercise of agency decisionmaking more or less accountable? If the answer is more accountable, are there specific provisions of the Constitution that nonetheless preclude Congress from adopting the arrangements that give it direct control over agency action? If the Constitution does not speak clearly to the question, what should the Court's default position be? That Congress has broad authority to prescribe the structure of government pursuant to the Necessary and Proper Clause and that the Supreme Court should keep its hands off unless the arrangement is clearly unconstitutional? That doubts should be resolved against legislation that disturbs the background principle of the separation of powers?

## A. The Legislative Veto

---

## Immigration and Naturalization Service v. Chadha

Supreme Court of the United States
462 U.S. 919 (1983)

■ Chief Justice Burger delivered the opinion of the Court.

[Jagdish Chada, a native of Kenya, remained in the United States after the expiration of his nonimmigrant student visa. The INS issued an order to show cause why he should not be deported. Chadha applied to the Attorney General for suspension of deportation under § 244(a)(1) of the Immigration and Nationality Act, 8 U.S.C.§ 1254(a)(1), which permits the Attorney General, in his or her discretion, to suspend deportation.[1] After a

---

**1.** Section 244(a)(1) provides:

"(a) As hereinafter prescribed in this section, the Attorney General may, in his discretion, suspend deportation and adjust the status to that of an alien lawfully admitted for permanent residence, in the case of an alien who applies to the Attorney General for suspension of deportation and—(1) is deportable under any law of the United States except the provisions specified in paragraph (2) of this subsection; has been physically present in the United States for a continuous period of not less than seven years immediately preceding the date of such application, and proves that during all of such period he was and is a person of good moral character; and is a person whose deportation would, in the opinion of the Attorney General, result in extreme hardship to the alien or to his spouse, parent, or child, who is a citizen of the United States or an alien lawfully admitted for permanent residence."

8 U.S.C. § 1254(a).

hearing, the Attorney General granted Chadha's motion for suspension of deportation on the statutorily authorized ground of "extreme hardship." He reported the decision to Congress under § 244(c), which provides in relevant part:

"(2) In the case of an alien specified in paragraph (1) of subsection (a) of this subsection—if during the session of the Congress at which a case is reported, or prior to the close of the session of the Congress next following the session at which a case is reported, either the Senate or the House of Representatives passes a resolution stating in substance that it does not favor the suspension of such deportation, the Attorney General shall thereupon deport such alien or authorize the alien's voluntary departure at his own expense under the order of deportation in the manner provided by law. If, within the time above specified, neither the Senate nor the House of Representatives shall pass such a resolution, the Attorney General shall cancel deportation proceedings."

The House of Representatives passed a timely resolution overturning the Attorney General's decision to suspend Chadha's deportation. The House did so without conducting a public hearing or offering any meaningful statement of reasons for its decision. It did so, moreover, without a recorded vote. On November 8, 1976, Chadha was ordered deported pursuant to the House action. Chadha petitioned for review of the deportation order in the U.S. Court of Appeals for the Ninth Circuit, alleging that the legislative veto procedure was unconstitutional. The Court of Appeals agreed. The case was then taken to the Supreme Court on writ of certiorari.]

### III

### A

We turn now to the question whether action of one House of Congress under § 244(c)(2) violates strictures of the Constitution. We begin, of course, with the presumption that the challenged statute is valid. Its wisdom is not the concern of the courts; if a challenged action does not violate the Constitution, it must be sustained. . . .

By the same token, the fact that a given law or procedure is efficient, convenient, and useful in facilitating functions of government, standing alone, will not save it if it is contrary to the Constitution. Convenience and efficiency are not the primary objectives—or the hallmarks—of democratic government and our inquiry is sharpened rather than blunted by the fact that congressional veto provisions are appearing with increasing frequency in statutes which delegate authority to executive and independent agencies:

"Since 1932, when the first veto provision was enacted into law, 295 congressional veto-type procedures have been inserted in 196 different statutes as follows: from 1932 to 1939, five statutes were affected; from 1940–49, nineteen statutes; between 1950–59, thirty-four statutes; and from 1960–69, forty-nine. From the year 1970 through 1975, at least one hundred sixty-three such provisions were included in eighty-nine laws." Abourezk, The Congressional Veto: A Contemporary Response to Executive Encroachment on Legislative Prerogatives, 52 Ind. L. Rev. 323, 324 (1977)....

Justice White undertakes to make a case for the proposition that the one-House veto is a useful "political invention," and we need not challenge that assertion. We can even concede this utilitarian argument although the long range political wisdom of this "invention" is arguable.... But policy arguments supporting even useful "political inventions" are subject to the demands of the Constitution which defines powers and, with respect to this subject, sets out just how those powers are to be exercised.

Explicit and unambiguous provisions of the Constitution prescribe and define the respective functions of the Congress and of the Executive in the legislative process. Since the precise terms of those familiar provisions are critical to the resolution of this case, we set them out verbatim. Art. I provides:

"All legislative Powers herein granted shall be vested in a Congress of the United States, which shall consist of a Senate *and* a House of Representatives." Art. I, § 1. (Emphasis added).

"Every Bill which shall have passed the House of Representatives *and* the Senate, *shall,* before it becomes a Law, be presented to the President of the United States...." Art. I, § 7, cl. 2. (Emphasis added).

"*Every* Order, Resolution, or Vote to which the Concurrence of the Senate and House of Representatives may be necessary (except on a question of Adjournment) *shall be* presented to the President of the United States; and before the Same shall take Effect, *shall be* approved by him, or being disapproved by him, *shall be* repassed by two thirds of the Senate and House of Representatives, according to the Rules and Limitations prescribed in the Case of a Bill." Art. I, § 7, cl. 3. (Emphasis added).

These provisions of Art. I are integral parts of the constitutional design for the separation of powers. We have recently noted that "[t]he principle of separation of powers was not simply an abstract generalization in the minds of the Framers: it was woven into the documents that they drafted in Philadelphia in the summer of 1787." ... The very structure of the Articles delegating and separating powers under Arts. I, II, and III exemplifies the concept of separation of powers, and we now turn to Art. I.

### B

### *The Presentment Clauses*

The records of the Constitutional Convention reveal that the requirement that all legislation be presented to the President before becoming law was uniformly accepted by the Framers. Presentment to the President and the Presidential veto were considered so imperative that the draftsmen took special pains to assure that these requirements could not be circumvented. During the final debate on Art. I, § 7, cl. 2, James Madison expressed concern that it might easily be evaded by the simple expedient of calling a proposed law a "resolution" or "vote" rather than a "bill." ... As a consequence, Art. I, § 7, cl. 3 ... was added....

The decision to provide the President with a limited and qualified power to nullify proposed legislation by veto was based on the profound conviction of the Framers that the powers conferred on Congress were the powers to be most carefully circumscribed. It is beyond doubt that lawmaking was a power to be shared by both Houses and the President....

The President's role in the lawmaking process also reflects the Framers' careful efforts to check whatever propensity a particular Congress might have to enact oppressive, improvident, or ill-considered measures. The President's veto role in the legislative process was described later during public debate on ratification:

> "It establishes a salutary check upon the legislative body, calculated to guard the community against the effects of faction, precipitancy, or of any impulse unfriendly to the public good which may happen to influence a majority of that body.... The primary inducement to conferring the power in question upon the Executive is to enable him to defend himself; the secondary one is to increase the chances in favor of the community against the passing of bad laws through haste, inadvertence, or design." The Federalist No. 73, [at 458 (A. Hamilton) (H. Lodge ed. 1888)].

The Court also has observed that the Presentment Clauses serve the important purpose of assuring that a "national" perspective is grafted on the legislative process:

> "The President is a representative of the people just as the members of the Senate and of the House are, and it may be, at some times, on some subjects, that the President elected by all the people is rather more representative of them all than are the members of either body of the Legislature whose constituencies are local and not country-wide...." Myers v. United States, [272 U.S. 52, 123 (1926).]

## C

### Bicameralism

The bicameral requirement of Art. I, §§ 1, 7 was of scarcely less concern to the Framers than was the Presidential veto and indeed the two concepts are interdependent. By providing that no law could take effect without the concurrence of the prescribed majority of the Members of both Houses, the Framers reemphasized their belief, already remarked upon in connection with the Presentment Clauses, that legislation should not be enacted unless it has been carefully and fully considered by the Nation's elected officials....

Hamilton argued that a Congress comprised of a single House was antithetical to the very purposes of the Constitution. Were the Nation to adopt a Constitution providing for only one legislative organ, he warned:

"[W]e shall finally accumulate, in a single body, all the most important prerogatives of sovereignty, and thus entail upon our posterity one of the most execrable forms of government that human infatuation ever contrived. Thus we should create in reality that very tyranny which the adversaries of the new Constitution either are, or affect to be, solicitous to avert." The Federalist No. 22, *supra*, at 135.

This view was rooted in a general skepticism regarding the fallibility of human nature later commented on by Joseph Story:

"Public bodies, like private persons, are occasionally under the dominion of strong passions and excitements; impatient, irritable, and impetuous.... If [a legislature] feels no check but its own will, it rarely has the firmness to insist upon holding a question long enough under its own view, to see and mark it in all its bearings and relations on society." 1 J. Story, [Commentaries on the Constitution of the United States 383–384 (1858).]

These observations are consistent with what many of the Framers expressed, none more cogently than Madison in pointing up the need to divide and disperse power in order to protect liberty:

"In republican government, the legislative authority necessarily predominates. The remedy for this inconveniency is to divide the legislature into different branches; and to render them, by different modes of election and different principles of action, as little connected with each other as the nature of their common functions and their common dependence on the society will admit." The Federalist No. 51, *supra*, at 324....

We see therefore that the Framers were acutely conscious that the bicameral requirement and the Presentment Clauses would serve essential constitutional functions. The President's participation in the legislative process was to protect the Executive Branch from Congress and to protect the whole people from improvident laws. The division of the Congress into two distinctive bodies assures that the legislative power would be exercised only after opportunity for full study and debate in separate settings. The President's unilateral veto power, in turn, was limited by the power of two-thirds of both Houses of Congress to overrule a veto thereby precluding final arbitrary action of one person. It emerges clearly that the prescription for legislative action in Art. I, §§ 1, 7 represents the Framers' decision that the legislative power of the Federal Government be exercised in accord with a single, finely wrought and exhaustively considered, procedure.

## IV

The Constitution sought to divide the delegated powers of the new Federal Government into three defined categories, legislative, executive and judicial, to assure, as nearly as possible, that each Branch of government would confine itself to its assigned responsibility. The hydraulic pressure inherent within each of the separate Branches to exceed the outer limits of its power, even to accomplish desirable objectives, must be resisted.

Although not "hermetically" sealed from one another, the powers delegated to the three Branches are functionally identifiable. When any Branch acts, it is presumptively exercising the power the Constitution has delegated to it. See Hampton & Co. v. United States, 276 U.S. 394, 406 (1928). When the Executive acts, he presumptively acts in an executive or administrative capacity as defined in Art. II. And when, as here, one House of Congress purports to act, it is presumptively acting within its assigned sphere. . . .

Examination of the action taken here by one House pursuant to § 244(c)(2) reveals that it was essentially legislative in purpose and effect. In purporting to exercise power defined in Art. I, § 8, cl. 4 to "establish an uniform Rule of Naturalization," the House took action that had the purpose and effect of altering the legal rights, duties and relations of persons, including the Attorney General, Executive Branch officials and Chadha, all outside the Legislative Branch. Section 244(c)(2) purports to authorize one House of Congress to require the Attorney General to deport an individual alien whose deportation otherwise would be cancelled under § 244. The one-House veto operated in this case to overrule the Attorney General and mandate Chadha's deportation; absent the House action, Chadha would remain in the United States. Congress has *acted* and its action has altered Chadha's status.

The legislative character of the one-House veto in these cases is confirmed by the character of the congressional action it supplants. Neither the House of Representatives nor the Senate contends that, absent the veto provision in § 244(c)(2), either of them, or both of them acting together, could effectively require the Attorney General to deport an alien once the Attorney General, in the exercise of legislatively delegated authority,[16] had

---

**16.** Congress protests that affirming the Court of Appeals in these cases will sanction "lawmaking by the Attorney General. . . . Why is the Attorney General exempt from submitting his proposed changes in the law to the full bicameral process?" Brief of the United States House of Representatives 40. To be sure, some administrative agency action—rule making, for example—may resemble "lawmaking." . . . This Court has referred to agency activity as being "quasi-legislative" in character. Humphrey's Executor v. United States, 295 U.S. 602, 628 (1935). Clearly, however, "[i]n the framework of our Constitution, the President's power to see that the laws are faithfully executed refutes the idea that he is to be a lawmaker." Youngstown Sheet & Tube Co. v. Sawyer, 343 U.S. 579, 587 (1952). See Buckley v. Valeo, 424 U.S. 1, 123 (1976). When the Attorney General performs his duties pursuant to § 244, he does not exercise "legislative" power. See Ernst & Ernst v. Hochfelder, 425 U.S. 185, 213–214 (1976). The bicameral process is not necessary as a check on the Executive's administration of the laws because his administrative activity cannot reach beyond the limits of the statute that created it—a statute duly enacted pursuant to Art. I, §§ 1, 7. The constitutionality of the Attorney General's execution of the authority delegated to him by § 244 involves only a question of delegation doctrine. The courts, when a case or controversy arises, can always "ascertain whether the will of Congress has been obeyed," Yakus v. United States, 321 U.S. 414, 425 (1944), and can enforce adherence to statutory standards. See Youngstown Sheet & Tube Co. v. Sawyer, 343 U.S. 579, 585 (1952); Ethyl Corp. v. EPA, 541 F.2d 1, 68 (CADC) (en

determined the alien should remain in the United States. Without the challenged provision in § 244(c)(2), this could have been achieved, if at all, only by legislation requiring deportation. Similarly, a veto by one House of Congress under § 244(c)(2) cannot be justified as an attempt at amending the standards set out in § 244(a)(1), or as a repeal of § 244 as applied to Chadha. Amendment and repeal of statutes, no less than enactment, must conform with Art. I.

The nature of the decision implemented by the one-House veto in this case further manifests its legislative character. After long experience with the clumsy, time-consuming private bill procedure, Congress made a deliberate choice to delegate to the Executive Branch, and specifically to the Attorney General, the authority to allow deportable aliens to remain in this country in certain specified circumstances. It is not disputed that this choice to delegate authority is precisely the kind of decision that can be implemented only in accordance with the procedures set out in Art. I. Disagreement with the Attorney General's decision on Chadha's deportation—that is, Congress' decision to deport Chadha—no less than Congress' original choice to delegate to the Attorney General the authority to make that decision, involves determinations of policy that Congress can implement in only one way; bicameral passage followed by presentment to the President. Congress must abide by its delegation of authority until that delegation is legislatively altered or revoked.

Finally, we see that when the Framers intended to authorize either House of Congress to act alone and outside of its prescribed bicameral legislative role, they narrowly and precisely defined the procedure for such action. There are but four provisions in the Constitution, explicit and unambiguous, by which one House may act alone with the unreviewable force of law, not subject to the President's veto:

(a) The House of Representatives alone was given the power to initiate impeachments. Art. I, § 2, cl. 5;

(b) The Senate alone was given the power to conduct trials following impeachment on charges initiated by the House and to convict following trial. Art. I, § 3, cl. 6;

(c) The Senate alone was given final unreviewable power to approve or to disapprove presidential appointments. Art. II, § 2, cl. 2;

---

banc) (separate statement of Leventhal, J.), cert. denied, 426 U.S. 941 (1976); L. Jaffe, Judicial Control of Administrative Action 320 (1965). It is clear, therefore, that the Attorney General acts in his presumptively Art. II capacity when he administers the Immigration and Nationality Act. Executive action under legislatively delegated authority that might resemble "legislative" action in some respects is not subject to the approval of both Houses of Congress and the President for the reason that the Constitution does not so require. That kind of Executive action is always subject to check by the terms of the legislation that authorized it; and if that authority is exceeded it is open to judicial review as well as the power of Congress to modify or revoke the authority entirely. A one-House veto is clearly legislative in both character and effect and is not so checked; the need for the check provided by Art. I, §§ 1, 7 is therefore clear. Congress' authority to delegate portions of its power to administrative agencies provides no support for the argument that Congress can constitutionally control administration of the laws by way of a Congressional veto.

(d) The Senate alone was given unreviewable power to ratify treaties negotiated by the President. Art. II, § 2, cl. 2.

... Since it is clear that the action by the House under § 244(c)(2) was not within any of the express constitutional exceptions authorizing one House to act alone, and equally clear that it was an exercise of legislative power, that action was subject to the standards prescribed in Article I. The bicameral requirement, the Presentment Clauses, the President's veto, and Congress' power to override a veto were intended to erect enduring checks on each Branch and to protect the people from the improvident exercise of power by mandating certain prescribed steps. To preserve those checks, and maintain the separation of powers, the carefully defined limits on the power of each Branch must not be eroded. To accomplish what has been attempted by one House of Congress in this case requires action in conformity with the express procedures of the Constitution's prescription for legislative action: passage by a majority of both Houses and presentment to the President.

The veto authorized by § 244(c)(2) doubtless has been in many respects a convenient shortcut; the "sharing" with the Executive by Congress of its authority over aliens in this manner is, on its face, an appealing compromise. In purely practical terms, it is obviously easier for action to be taken by one House without submission to the President; but it is crystal clear from the records of the Convention, contemporaneous writings and debates, that the Framers ranked other values higher than efficiency. The records of the Convention and debates in the states preceding ratification underscore the common desire to define and limit the exercise of the newly created federal powers affecting the states and the people. There is unmistakable expression of a determination that legislation by the national Congress be a step-by-step, deliberate and deliberative process.

The choices we discern as having been made in the Constitutional Convention impose burdens on governmental processes that often seem clumsy, inefficient, even unworkable, but those hard choices were consciously made by men who had lived under a form of government that permitted arbitrary governmental acts to go unchecked. There is no support in the Constitution or decisions of this Court for the proposition that the cumbersomeness and delays often encountered in complying with explicit constitutional standards may be avoided, either by the Congress or by the President. See Youngstown Sheet & Tube Co. v. Sawyer, 343 U.S. 579 (1952). With all the obvious flaws of delay, untidiness, and potential for abuse, we have not yet found a better way to preserve freedom than by making the exercise of power subject to the carefully crafted restraints spelled out in the Constitution....

■ JUSTICE POWELL, concurring in the judgment.

The Court's decision, based on the Presentment Clauses, Art. I, § 7, cls. 2 and 3, apparently will invalidate every use of the legislative veto. The breadth of this holding gives one pause. Congress has included the veto in literally hundreds of statutes, dating back to the 1930's. Congress clearly views this procedure as essential to controlling the delegation of power to administrative agencies. One reasonably may disagree with Congress' assessment of the veto's utility, but the respect due its judgment as a coordinate branch of Government cautions that our holding should be no more extensive than necessary to decide these cases. In my view, the case may be decided on a narrower ground. When Congress finds that a particular person does not satisfy the statutory criteria for permanent residence in this country it has assumed a judicial function in violation of the principle of separation of powers. Accordingly, I concur only in the judgment. . . .

## II

. . . Jagdish Rai Chadha, a citizen of Kenya, stayed in this country after his student visa expired. Although he was scheduled to be deported, he requested the Immigration and Naturalization Service to suspend his deportation because he met the statutory criteria for permanent residence in this country. After a hearing, the Service granted Chadha's request and sent—as required by the reservation of the veto right—a report of its action to Congress.

In addition to the report on Chadha, Congress had before it the names of 339 other persons whose deportations also had been suspended by the Service. The House Committee on the Judiciary decided that six of these persons, including Chadha, should not be allowed to remain in this country. Accordingly, it submitted a resolution to the House, which stated simply that "the House of Representatives does not approve the granting of permanent residence in the United States to the aliens hereinafter named." . . .

On its face, the House's action appears clearly adjudicatory.[7] The House did not enact a general rule; rather it made its own determination that six specific persons did not comply with certain statutory criteria. It thus undertook the type of decision that traditionally has been left to other branches. Even if the House did not make a *de novo* determination, but simply reviewed the Immigration and Naturalization Service's findings, it still assumed a function ordinarily entrusted to the federal courts. . . . Where, as here, Congress has exercised a power "that cannot possibly be regarded as merely in aid of the legislative function of Congress," Buckley v. Valeo, 424 U.S. [1, 138 (1976)], the decisions of this Court have held that Congress impermissibly assumed a function that the Constitution entrusted to another branch, see *id.*, at 138–141; cf. Springer v. Philippine Islands, 277 U.S. [189, 202 (1928).]

---

**7.** The Court concludes that Congress' action was legislative in character because each branch "presumptively act[s] within its assigned sphere." The Court's presumption provides a useful starting point, but does not conclude the inquiry. Nor does the fact that the House's action alters an individual's legal status indicate, as the Court reasons, that the action is legislative rather than adjudicative in nature. In determining whether one branch unconstitutionally has assumed a power central to another branch, the traditional characterization of the assumed power as legislative, executive, or judicial may provide some guidance. . . . But reasonable minds may disagree over the character of an act and the more helpful inquiry, in my view, is whether the act in question raises the dangers the Framers sought to avoid.

The impropriety of the House's assumption of this function is confirmed by the fact that its action raises the very danger the Framers sought to avoid—the exercise of unchecked power. In deciding whether Chadha deserves to be deported, Congress is not subject to any internal constraints that prevent it from arbitrarily depriving him of the right to remain in this country. Unlike the judiciary or an administrative agency, Congress is not bound by established substantive rules. Nor is it subject to the procedural safeguards, such as the right to counsel and a hearing before an impartial tribunal, that are present when a court or an agency[10] adjudicates individual rights. The only effective constraint on Congress' power is political, but Congress is most accountable politically when it prescribes rules of general applicability. When it decides rights of specific persons, those rights are subject to "the tyranny of a shifting majority."

. . . In my view, when Congress undertook to apply its rules to Chadha, it exceeded the scope of its constitutionally prescribed authority. I would not reach the broader question whether legislative vetoes are invalid under the Presentment Clauses.

■ Justice White, dissenting.

Today the Court not only invalidates § 244(c)(2) of the Immigration and Nationality Act, but also sounds the death knell for nearly 200 other statutory provisions in which Congress has reserved a "legislative veto." For this reason, the Court's decision is of surpassing importance. . . .

The prominence of the legislative veto mechanism in our contemporary political system and its importance to Congress can hardly be overstated. It has become a central means by which Congress secures the accountability of executive and independent agencies. Without the legislative veto, Congress is faced with a Hobson's choice: either to refrain from delegating the necessary authority, leaving itself with a hopeless task of writing laws with the requisite specificity to cover endless special circumstances across the entire policy landscape, or in the alternative, to abdicate its law-making function to the Executive Branch and independent agencies. To choose the former leaves major national problems unresolved; to opt for the latter risks unaccountable policymaking by those not elected to fill that role. Accordingly, over the past five decades, the legislative veto has been placed in nearly 200 statutes. The device is known in every field of governmental concern: reorganization, budgets, foreign affairs, war powers, and regulation of trade, safety, energy, the environment and the economy. . . .

The history of the legislative veto . . . makes clear that it has not been a sword with which Congress has struck out to aggrandize itself at the expense of the other branches—the concerns of Madison and Hamilton. Rather, the veto has been a means of defense, a reservation of ultimate

---

**10.** We have recognized that independent regulatory agencies and departments of the Executive Branch often exercise authority that is "judicial in nature." Buckley v. Valeo, 424 U.S. 1, 140–141 (1976). This function, however, forms part of the agencies' execution of public law and is subject to the procedural safeguards, including judicial review, provided by the Administrative Procedure Act. . . .

authority necessary if Congress is to fulfill its designated role under Article I as the nation's lawmaker. . . .

. . . The power to exercise a legislative veto is not the power to write new law without bicameral approval or presidential consideration. The veto must be authorized by statute and may only negative what an Executive department or independent agency has proposed. On its face, the legislative veto no more allows one House of Congress to make law than does the presidential veto confer such power upon the President. . . .

The terms of the Presentment Clauses suggest only that bills and their equivalent are subject to the requirements of bicameral passage and presentment to the President. . . . [I]ts purpose was to prevent Congress from circumventing the presentation requirement in the making of new legislation. . . . There is no record that the Convention contemplated, let alone intended, that these Article I requirements would someday be invoked to restrain the scope of congressional authority pursuant to duly-enacted law. . . .

When the Convention did turn its attention to the scope of Congress' lawmaking power, the Framers were expansive. The Necessary and Proper Clause, Art. I, § 8, cl. 18, vests Congress with the power "to make all laws which shall be necessary and proper for carrying into Execution the foregoing Powers [the enumerated powers of § 8] and all other Powers vested by this Constitution in the government of the United States, or in any Department or Officer thereof." It is long settled that Congress may "exercise its best judgment in the selection of measures, to carry into execution the constitutional powers of the government," and "avail itself of experience, to exercise its reason, and to accommodate its legislation to circumstances." McCulloch v. Maryland, 4 Wheat. 316, 415–416, 420 (1819). . . .

If Congress may delegate lawmaking power to independent and executive agencies, it is most difficult to understand Article I as forbidding Congress from also reserving a check on legislative power for itself. Absent the veto, the agencies receiving delegations of legislative or quasi-legislative power may issue regulations having the force of law without bicameral approval and without the President's signature. It is thus not apparent why the reservation of a veto over the exercise of that legislative power must be subject to a more exacting test. In both cases, it is enough that the initial statutory authorizations comply with the Article I requirements.

Nor are there strict limits on the agents that may receive such delegations of legislative authority so that it might be said that the legislature can delegate authority to others but not to itself. While most authority to issue rules and regulations is given to the Executive Branch and the independent regulatory agencies, statutory delegations to private persons have also passed this Court's scrutiny. In Currin v. Wallace, 306 U.S. 1 (1939), the statute provided that restrictions upon the production or marketing of agricultural commodities was to become effective only upon the favorable vote by a prescribed majority of the affected farmers. United States v. Rock Royal Co-operative, 307 U.S. 533, 577 (1939), upheld an act which gave producers of specified commodities the right to veto marketing orders issued by the Secretary of Agriculture. Assuming *Currin* and *Rock Royal Co-operative* remain sound law, the Court's decision today suggests that Congress may place a "veto" power over suspensions of deportation in private hands or in the hands of an independent agency, but is forbidden from reserving such authority for itself. Perhaps this odd result could be justified on other constitutional grounds, such as the separation of powers, but certainly it cannot be defended as consistent with the Court's view of the Article I presentment and bicameralism commands....

[T]he Court concedes that certain administrative agency action, such as rulemaking, "may resemble lawmaking" and recognizes that "[t]his Court has referred to agency activity as being 'quasi-legislative' in character. Humphrey's Executor v. United States, 295 U.S. 602, 628 (1935)." Such rules and adjudications by the agencies meet the Court's own definition of legislative action for they "alter[ ] the legal rights, duties, and relations of persons ... outside the Legislative Branch[ ]" and involve "determinations of policy." Under the Court's analysis, the Executive Branch and the independent agencies may make rules with the effect of law while Congress, in whom the Framers confided the legislative power, Art. I, § 1, may not exercise a veto which precludes such rules from having operative force. If the effective functioning of a complex modern government requires the delegation of vast authority which, by virtue of its breadth, is legislative or "quasi-legislative" in character, I cannot accept that Article I—which is, after all, the source of the nondelegation doctrine—should forbid Congress to qualify that grant with a legislative veto.

The Court also takes no account of perhaps the most relevant consideration: However resolutions of disapproval under § 244(c)(2) are formally characterized, in reality, a departure from the status quo occurs only upon the concurrence of opinion among the House, Senate, and President. Reservations of legislative authority to be exercised by Congress should be upheld if the exercise of such reserved authority is consistent with the distribution of and limits upon legislative power that Article I provides....

The central concern of the presentation and bicameralism requirements of Art. I is that when a departure from the legal status quo is undertaken, it is done with the approval of the President and both Houses of Congress—or, in the event of a presidential veto, a two-thirds majority in both Houses. This interest is fully satisfied by the operation of § 244(c)(2). The President's approval is found in the Attorney General's action in recommending to Congress that the deportation order for a given alien be suspended. The House and the Senate indicate their approval of the Executive's action by not passing a resolution of disapproval within the statutory period. Thus, a change in the legal status quo—the deportability of the alien—is consummated only with the approval of each of the three relevant actors. The disagreement of any one of the three maintains the alien's pre-existing status: the Executive may choose not to recommend suspension; the House and Senate may each veto the recommendation. The effect on the rights and obligations of the affected individuals and upon the legislative system is precisely the same as if a private bill were introduced but failed to receive the necessary approval. "The President and the two Houses enjoy exactly the same say in what the law is to be as would have been true for each without the presence of the one-House veto, and nothing in the law is changed absent the concurrence of the President and a majority in each House." Atkins v. United States, 556 F.2d 1028, 1064 (Ct. Claims, 1977), cert. denied, 434 U.S. 1009 (1978)....

[I]t may be objected that Congress cannot indicate its approval of legislative change by inaction. In the Court of Appeals' view, inaction by Congress "could equally imply endorsement, acquiescence, passivity, indecision or indifference," . . . and the Court appears to echo this concern.... This objection appears more properly directed at the wisdom of the legislative veto than its constitutionality. The Constitution does not and cannot guarantee that legislators will carefully scrutinize legislation and deliberate before acting. In a democracy it is the electorate that holds the legislators accountable for the wisdom of their choices.

. . . [T]he history of the separation-of-powers doctrine is also a history of accommodation and practicality. Apprehensions of an overly powerful branch have not led to undue prophylactic measures that handicap the effective working of the national government as a whole. The Constitution does not contemplate total separation of the three branches of Government. Buckley v. Valeo, 424 U.S. 1, 121 (1976). "[A] hermetic sealing off of the three branches of Government from one another would preclude the establishment of a Nation capable of governing itself effectively." *Ibid*....

I do not suggest that all legislative vetoes are necessarily consistent with separation of powers principles. A legislative check on an inherently executive function, for example, that of initiating prosecutions, poses an entirely different question. But the legislative veto device here—and in many other settings—is far from an instance of legislative tyranny over the Executive. It is a necessary check on the unavoidably expanding power of the agencies, both Executive and independent, as they engage in exercising authority delegated by Congress....

■ [JUSTICE REHNQUIST's dissenting opinion, which JUSTICE WHITE joined, is omitted.]

---

***1.  Delegation and the Legislative Veto***—Was Justice White correct in asserting that the Court's invalidation of the legislative veto is difficult to square with the Court's acceptance of delegation? When Congress authorizes agencies to promulgate legally binding rules pursuant to vague statutory standards, isn't Congress in some sense transferring the kind of legislative power that *Chadha* declares to be nontransferable? As Justice White put it: "If the effective functioning of a complex modern government requires the delegation of vast authority which, by virtue of its breadth, is legislative or 'quasi-legislative' in character, I cannot accept that Article I—which is, after all, the source of the nondelegation doctrine—

should forbid Congress from qualifying that grant with a legislative veto." Quite apart from the apparent formal inconsistency between approving delegations and invalidating the legislative veto (to which we return shortly), doesn't *Chadha*'s invalidation of the legislative veto also disserve the functional goal of political accountability that lies at the heart of the Constitution? In effect, the Court is saying to Congress that it can transfer its lawmaking authority to bureaucrats but cannot condition the bureaucrats' exercise of that authority on the approval of both chambers of Congress. This is the "Hobson's Choice" to which Justice White so strenuously objects.

The Court's answer to Justice White is found in it its oft-cited footnote 16. The Brief of the United States House of Representatives had argued that the Attorney General's decision to suspend deportation pursuant to broad delegated authority under the Immigration and Nationality Act (INA) was an act of lawmaking outside the context of bicameralism and presentment. Hence, said the House, it would be inconsistent for the Court to permit that delegation to stand but to invalidate the legislative veto. The Court responded that while certain agency action, such as rulemaking, "may resemble 'lawmaking,' " the executive is not a lawmaker. Rather, when the Attorney General exercises authority to suspend deportation pursuant to § 244, he or she performs an *executive* function, which does not require bicameralism and presentment because it "is always subject to check by the terms of the legislation that authorized it; and if that authority is exceeded it is open to judicial review as well as the power of Congress to modify or revoke the authority entirely." Notice how the debate between Chief Justice Burger and Justice White tracks the dispute between Justices Scalia and Stevens in *American Trucking Ass'ns v. Whitman* over whether to treat an agency's exercise of delegated authority as executive or legislative power. (*See supra* pp. 410–415.) Indeed, the two disputes are conceptually intertwined. If delegation is upheld because Congress may legitimately transfer legislative power to an executive branch agent (so long as Congress supplies an intelligible principle), then it is hard to see why Congress cannot also do so with "strings attached." In other words, if the executive can permissibly exercise truly *legislative* power without clearing the hurdles of bicameralism and presentment, why shouldn't Congress be able to do so as well? On the other hand, if agencies' exercise of policymaking discretion pursuant to an intelligible statutory principle is really a form of executive power, then there is a much more compelling argument that Congress cannot interfere with the exercise of that power. If what the agency is doing counts as *executive*, then perhaps the constitutional legitimacy of delegation does not undermine the basic idea that the exercise of *legislative* power must clear Article I, § 7's hurdles?

Let us pursue further the question of how to characterize the powers being exercised by the Attorney General and the House that exercises a legislative veto. The Court characterizes the Attorney General's suspension of deportation as an *executive* (rather than legislative) act, but it characterizes the exercise of the legislative veto as a *legislative* act, in part because of a presumption that "[w]hen any Branch acts, it is presumptively exercising the power the Constitution has delegated to it." Is that a sensible presumption to adopt? Is it sensible to classify exactly the same legal act in different ways, depending on the branch that is acting? That may seem odd, but perhaps it is not so unusual. Consider someone who has a monetary claim against the United States, alleging that the government has failed to pay the amount due on a fully performed government contract. The relevant congressional committees could surely hold hearings on the breach of contract claim and, if they found the claim meritorious, recommend legislation to Congress to appropriate money to pay the amount owed. If Congress made such an appropriation, it would be an exercise of legislative power. If, however, Congress delegated to the Secretary of the Treasury the authority to hold hearings on contract claims against the United States and to pay meritorious ones, the decision to pay such a claim would surely qualify as an exercise of executive power. Finally, if Congress created a judicially enforceable right of action against the United States for breach of contract, the adjudication of such a claim in a federal court would qualify as the exercise of judicial power. Even though the net result might be the same in each instance—payment of a contract claim based upon an inquiry into the merits of the claim—the character of the government action would depend on which branch exercised it. Maybe there are good functional reasons for treating the power to alter legal rights and duties as legislative when Congress exercises it but not when the other branches do so. Are you persuaded?

**2.** ***The Separation of Powers and the Legislative Veto***—In invalidating the legislative veto, the *Chadha* Court emphasized that "[t]he principle of separation of powers was not simply an abstract generalization in the minds of the Framers." Instead, the opinion took pains both to tie its decision to specific dictates of Article I, § 7 and to consider the various purposes associated with bicameralism and presentment derived from statements made by the founders. As noted earlier, a deeply rooted canon of interpretation holds that when a legal document such as the Constitution carefully delimits the manner in which a given power is to be exercised, interpreters should presume that the specified manner is exclusive. *See supra* p. 390. In addition, the presidential veto, it was said, would help to control faction and would impose on the legislative process a national perspective. Bicameralism, moreover, would promote caution and deliberation, and would preserve liberty by dispersing power. All of these considerations, the Court reasoned, were inconsistent with allowing Congress to act unicamerally, without presentment to the President.

Is that convincing? In a world in which the default position is broad delegation, couldn't one respond (as Justice White does) that the legislative veto in fact *restores* fidelity to some of the purposes underlying bicameralism and presentment? After all, the legislative veto maintains *congressional* involvement in the exercise of administrative discretion under broadly-worded statutes. If delegation raises a concern about excessive concentration of power in the executive branch of government, and also a concern about impeding democratic accountability for policy decisions, then doesn't the legislative veto at least partially address some of these concerns, thereby advancing rather than undermining the purposes of the federal legislative process? *See, e.g.,* William N. Eskridge, Jr. & John Ferejohn, *The Article I, Section 7 Game,* 80 Geo. L.J. 523, 540–43 (1992).

But maybe the fact that the legislative veto provision purports to reserve some decisionmaking authority to *Congress* is precisely the problem. An influential strand of the separation-of-powers tradition—reflected in the works of important separation-of-powers theorists such as Locke and Blackstone—articulates a norm against *self*-delegation. This norm is thought to promote the rule of law and restrain arbitrary government in two important ways. First, the separation of lawmaking from law exposition makes it harder for lawmakers to write oppressive laws and then spare their supporters from the laws' effects through application. Hence Locke thought it "too great a temptation to human frailty, apt to grasp at power for the same persons, who have the power of making laws, to have also in their hands the power to execute them, whereby they exempt themselves from obedience to the laws they make." John Locke, Second Treatise of Government 76 (C.B. MacPherson ed., 1980) (1690). But if lawmakers cannot control the application of the laws they enact, this fact would impose "a new and near tie upon [legislators], to take care that they make [laws] for the public good." *Id. See also* Einer Elhauge, Statutory Default Rules 100 (2008) (defending *Chadha* on the ground that the legislative veto concentrates too much power in Congress); Jonathan R. Macey, *Separated Powers and Positive Political Theory: The Tug of War Over Administrative Agencies,* 80 Geo. L.J. 671, 695–97 (1992) (arguing that the legislative veto may facilitate Congress's ability to favor influential special-interest groups at the expense of the general public). Second, giving lawmakers control over law implementation would diminish legislators' incentives to pass clear, transparent, and discretion-constraining statutes. In that circumstance, any discretion created by a vague or open-ended law would inure to the benefit of the lawmaker, who would be in a position to control the exercise of that discretion. Hence, as Blackstone wrote, "where the legislative and executive authority are in distinct hands, the former will take care not to entrust the latter with so large a power as may tend to the subversion of its own independence, and therewith of the liberty of the subject." 1 William Blackstone, Commentaries *147. Modern commentators have advanced similar arguments specifically in the context of the legislative veto. *See* Peter L. Strauss & Andrew R. Rutten, *The Game of Politics and Law: A Response to Eskridge and Ferejohn,* 8 J.L. Econ. & Org. 205, 207 (1992) (arguing that devices such as the legislative veto "encourage less precise and less frequent legislation by depriving Congress of motivation to solve its substantial communications problems at the time of enactment"). Is this a persuasive response to Justice White's functional argument for the legislative veto?

More generally, perhaps the decision in *Chadha* signals a retreat from the New Deal critique of the separation of powers, according to which the cumbersome tripartite structure of federal lawmaking is unsuited to the demands of a complex industrial society. *See generally* James M. Landis, The

ADMINISTRATIVE PROCESS (1938); *see also supra* pp. 393–394. The *Chadha* Court seems to have a quite different attitude. Chief Justice Burger thus wrote that the bicameralism and presentment requirements "impose burdens on governmental processes that often seem clumsy, inefficient, even unworkable, but those hard choices were consciously made by men who had lived under a form of government that permitted arbitrary governmental acts to go unchecked." He added that "[w]ith all the obvious flaws of delay, untidiness, and potential for abuse, we have not yet found a better way to preserve freedom than by making the exercise of power subject tô the carefully crafted restraints spelled out in the Constitution." Do these statements signal retrenchment from the New Deal view? Does the Court's continued weak enforcement of the nondelegation doctrine suggest instead that the Court merely decided to draw a line against further expansion of the New Deal philosophy? If *Chadha* represents strong formalism while the nondelegation cases reflect apparent functionalism (*see supra* pp. 376–378), might there be some good reason for the Court to be formalist in some contexts but functionalist in others? Or perhaps the apparent inconsistency between *Chadha* and the nondelegation cases can best be explained by relative judicial competence, in that it is much harder for the courts to police the line between legislative and executive power in the delegation context than in the context of deciding whether a particular institutional mechanism, like the legislative veto, is permissible. *See* Bradford R. Clark, *Federal Lawmaking and the Role of Structure in Constitutional Interpretation*, 96 CAL. L. REV. 699, 718 (2008).

**3. *Rejecting Established Legislative Practice*—**Justice White's dissent emphasized that "over the past five decades, the legislative veto has been placed in nearly 200 statutes" and that "[t]he device is known in every field of governmental concern: reorganization, budgets, foreign affairs, war powers, and regulation of trade, safety, energy, the environment and the economy." As noted earlier, the founders expected the Constitution to contain many ambiguities and for its meaning to become settled over time by practical constructions of the document by the government institutions charged with its implementation (*see supra* pp. 375–376). Should the Court be especially reluctant to invalidate an arrangement that multiple Congresses over many decades have adopted and presumably adjudged to be constitutional? Certainly, the Court has emphasized "the heavy presumption of constitutionality to which a 'carefully considered decision of a coequal and representative branch of our Government' is entitled." United States Dep't of Labor v. Triplett, 494 U.S. 715, 720 (1990) (quoting Walters v. National Ass'n of Radiation Survivors, 473 U.S. 305, 319 (1985)). Should that presumption be even stronger when, as in *Chadha*, the Court's decision would displace a lengthy series of such congressional judgments? Or should the Court be more wary of placing a thumb on the scale of Congress's considered judgments when the governmental arrangement in question results in congressional self-aggrandizement?

**4. *Alternatives to the Legislative Veto*—**After *Chadha*, legislative veto provisions in statutes are formally unenforceable, and a purported "veto" of an agency action by one or both chambers of Congress outside of the Article I, § 7 process has no legal effect. That said, hundreds of statutes with legislative veto provisions are still on the books, and Congress has continued to insert such provisions into statutory language, or sometimes to assert in a committee report that an agency must seek approval from the relevant legislative committees before taking some action that would appear to be within the scope of the agency's delegated authority under the statute. These directives are legally meaningless after *Chadha*, but that does ·not make them practically meaningless. Rather, the other tools that Congress has at its disposal—such as the threat of statutory revision, control over agency budgets, and more informal oversight mechanisms (see pp. 473–476, *infra*)—may lead executive branch agencies to comply with these legally unenforceable veto mechanisms. *See* LOUIS FISHER, CONGRESSIONAL ABDICATION OF WAR AND SPENDING 180–82 (2000); Louis Fisher, *The Legislative Veto: Invalidated, It Survives*, 56 LAW & CONTEMP. PROBS. 273, 288–91 (1993). This point should not be overstated, however. The loss of a legally effective legislative veto does deprive Congress of an important tool to constrain and influence the exercise of administrative discretion.

Might there be alternative institutional mechanisms that would achieve some of the goals of the legislative veto without running afoul of Article I? Some scholars have suggested that Congress delegate to agencies not the power to *adopt* regulations, but only to *propose* regulations to Congress, which would then have the power to enact them pursuant to "fast track" legislative procedures. Congress has not entertained anything that drastic, but it did adopt a more modest piece of legislation—the Congressional Review Act (CRA)—in 1996. Under the CRA, an agency must submit a "major" rule to Congress 60 days before it goes into effect. During that time, if both the House and the Senate pass a disapproval resolution that is signed by the President (or if the President's veto is overridden by a two-thirds majority in each house), the agency rule is "vetoed." Of course, all this means is that Congress can override an agency action by using the Article I, § 7 process to enact new legislation. All the CRA seems to do is to extend the period before a major rule becomes effective from 30 to 60 days, to provide for expedited procedures in the Senate (though not the House) for bringing a disapproval resolution to the floor if the relevant committee fails to act on it, and to provide that a disapproval resolution passed by one chamber must be considered on the floor of the other chamber without referral to committee. *See* Note, *The Mysteries of the Congressional Review Act*, 122 HARV. L. REV. 2162, 2166–68 (2009). Thus the CRA does not appear to be that much of a substitute for the legislative veto, and indeed the CRA has been used only once, in the early days of President George W. Bush's administration to void a workplace ergonomics regulation that the Occupational Safety and Health Administration had promulgated near the very end of the Clinton Administration. For these and other reasons, most observers do not believe that the CRA has had all that much effect.

## B.   CONGRESSIONAL CONTROL OVER LAW EXECUTION

### Bowsher v. Synar

Supreme Court of the United States
478 U.S. 714 (1986)

■ CHIEF JUSTICE BURGER delivered the opinion of the Court.

The question presented by these appeals is whether the assignment by Congress to the Comptroller General of the United States of certain functions under the Balanced Budget and Emergency Deficit Control Act of 1985 violates the doctrine of separation of powers.

I

A

On December 12, 1985, the President signed into law the Balanced Budget and Emergency Deficit Control Act of 1985, Pub.L. 99–177, 99 Stat. 1038, 2 U.S.C. § 901 *et seq.* (1982 ed., Supp. III), popularly known as the "Gramm–Rudman–Hollings Act." The purpose of the Act is to eliminate the federal budget deficit. To that end, the Act sets a "maximum deficit amount" for federal spending for each of fiscal years 1986 through 1991. The size of that maximum deficit amount progressively reduces to zero in fiscal year 1991. If in any fiscal year the federal budget deficit exceeds the maximum deficit amount by more than a specified sum, the Act requires across-the-board cuts in federal spending to reach the targeted deficit level, with half of the cuts made to defense programs and the other half made to nondefense programs. The Act exempts certain priority programs from these cuts. § 255.

These "automatic" reductions are accomplished through a rather complicated procedure, spelled out in § 251, the so-called "reporting provisions" of the Act. Each year, the Directors of the Office of Management and Budget (OMB) and the Congressional Budget Office (CBO) independently estimate the amount of the federal budget deficit for the upcoming fiscal year. If that deficit exceeds the maximum targeted deficit amount for that fiscal year by more than a specified amount, the Directors of OMB and CBO independently calculate, on a program-by-program basis, the budget reductions necessary to ensure that the deficit does not exceed the maximum deficit amount. The Act then requires the Directors to report jointly their deficit estimates and budget reduction calculations to the Comptroller General.

The Comptroller General, after reviewing the Directors' reports, then reports his conclusions to the President. § 251(b). The President in turn must issue a "sequestration" order mandating the spending reductions specified by the Comptroller General. § 252. There follows a period during which Congress may by legislation reduce spending to obviate, in whole or in part, the need for the sequestration order. If such reductions are not enacted, the sequestration order becomes effective and the spending reductions included in that order are made. . . .

[Almost immediately following its passage, various aggrieved persons filed lawsuits challenging the constitutionality of the Gramm–Rudman–

Hollings Act on separation-of-powers grounds. Pursuant to special authority provided by the Act, a three-judge district court in the District of the District of Columbia heard the case on an expedited basis. The court held that the Act violated the separation of powers by giving Congress authority to remove the Comptroller General, who performed executive functions under the Act. The Supreme Court also heard the case on an expedited basis pursuant to the Act.]

## III.

We noted recently that "[t]he Constitution sought to divide the delegated powers of the new Federal Government into three defined categories, Legislative, Executive, and Judicial." INS v. Chadha, 462 U.S. 919, 951 (1983). The declared purpose of separating and dividing the powers of government, of course, was to "diffus[e] power the better to secure liberty." Youngstown Sheet & Tube Co. v. Sawyer, 343 U.S. 579, 635 (1952) (Jackson, J., concurring). Justice Jackson's words echo the famous warning of Montesquieu, quoted by James Madison in The Federalist No. 47, that " 'there can be no liberty where the legislative and executive powers are united in the same person, or body of magistrates'. . . ." The Federalist No. 47, p. 325 (J. Cooke ed. 1961).

Even a cursory examination of the Constitution reveals the influence of Montesquieu's thesis that checks and balances were the foundation of a structure of government that would protect liberty. The Framers provided a vigorous Legislative Branch and a separate and wholly independent Executive Branch, with each branch responsible ultimately to the people. The Framers also provided for a Judicial Branch equally independent with "[t]he judicial Power ... extend[ing] to all Cases, in Law and Equity, arising under this Constitution, and the Laws of the United States." Art. III, § 2.

Other, more subtle, examples of separated powers are evident as well. Unlike parliamentary systems such as that of Great Britain, no person who is an officer of the United States may serve as a Member of the Congress. Art. I, § 6. Moreover, unlike parliamentary systems, the President, under Article II, is responsible not to the Congress but to the people, subject only to impeachment proceedings which are exercised by the two Houses as representatives of the people. Art. II, § 4. And even in the impeachment of a President the presiding officer of the ultimate tribunal is not a member of the Legislative Branch, but the Chief Justice of the United States. Art. I, § 3.

That this system of division and separation of powers produces conflicts, confusion, and discordance at times is inherent, but it was deliberately so structured to assure full, vigorous, and open debate on the great issues affecting the people and to provide avenues for the operation of checks on the exercise of governmental power.

The Constitution does not contemplate an active role for Congress in the supervision of officers charged with the execution of the laws it enacts. The President appoints "Officers of the United States" with the "Advice and Consent of the Senate . . . ." Art. II, § 2. Once the appointment has been made and confirmed, however, the Constitution explicitly provides for removal of Officers of the United States by Congress only upon impeachment by the House of Representatives and conviction by the Senate. An impeachment by the House and trial by the Senate can rest only on "Treason, Bribery or other high Crimes and Misdemeanors." Art. II, § 4. A direct congressional role in the removal of officers charged with the execution of the laws beyond this limited one is inconsistent with separation of powers.

This was made clear in debate in the First Congress in 1789. When Congress considered an amendment to a bill establishing the Department of Foreign Affairs, the debate centered around whether the Congress "should recognize and declare the power of the President under the Constitution to remove the Secretary of Foreign Affairs without the advice and consent of the Senate." [Myers v. United States,] 272 U.S. [52,] 114 [(1926)] . . . . [A] congressional role in the removal process was rejected. This "Decision of 1789" provides "contemporaneous and weighty evidence" of the Constitution's meaning since many of the Members of the First Congress "had taken part in framing that instrument." Marsh v. Chambers, 463 U.S. 783, 790 (1983) . . . .

A decade later, in Humphrey's Executor v. United States, 295 U.S. 602 (1935), relied upon heavily by appellants, a Federal Trade Commissioner who had been removed by the President sought backpay. *Humphrey's Executor* involved an issue not presented either in the *Myers* case or in this case—*i.e.*, the power of Congress to limit the President's powers of removal of a Federal Trade Commissioner.[4] The relevant statute permitted removal "by the President," but only "for inefficiency, neglect of duty, or malfeasance in office." Justice Sutherland, speaking for the Court, upheld the statute, holding that "illimitable power of removal is not possessed by the President [with respect to Federal Trade Commissioners]." *Id.*, at 628–629. The Court distinguished *Myers*, reaffirming its holding that congressional participation in the removal of executive officers is unconstitutional . . . .

In light of these precedents, we conclude that Congress cannot reserve for itself the power of removal of an officer charged with the execution of the laws except by impeachment. To permit the execution of the laws to be vested in an officer answerable only to Congress would, in practical terms, reserve in Congress control over the execution of the laws. As the District

---

4. Appellants therefore are wide of the mark in arguing that an affirmance in this case requires casting doubt on the status of "independent" agencies because no issues involving such agencies are presented here. The statutes establishing independent agencies typically specify either that the agency members are removable by the President for specified causes, see, *e.g.*, 15 U.S.C. § 41 (members of the Federal Trade Commission may be removed by the President "for inefficiency, neglect of duty, or malfeasance in office"), or else do not specify a removal procedure, see, *e.g.*, 2 U.S.C. § 437c (Federal Election Commission). This case involves nothing like these statutes, but rather a statute that provides for direct congressional involvement over the decision to remove the Comptroller General. Appellants have referred us to no independent agency whose members are removable by the Congress for certain causes short of impeachable offenses, as is the Comptroller General . . . .

Court observed: "Once an officer is appointed, it is only the authority that can remove him, and not the authority that appointed him, that he must fear and, in the performance of his functions, obey." 626 F.Supp., at 1401. The structure of the Constitution does not permit Congress to execute the laws; it follows that Congress cannot grant to an officer under its control what it does not possess.

Our decision in INS v. Chadha, 462 U.S. 919 (1983), supports this conclusion.... To permit an officer controlled by Congress to execute the laws would be, in essence, to permit a congressional veto. Congress could simply remove, or threaten to remove, an officer for executing the laws in any fashion found to be unsatisfactory to Congress. This kind of congressional control over the execution of the laws, *Chadha* makes clear, is constitutionally impermissible.

The dangers of congressional usurpation of Executive Branch functions have long been recognized. "[T]he debates of the Constitutional Convention, and the Federalist Papers, are replete with expressions of fear that the Legislative Branch of the National Government will aggrandize itself at the expense of the other two branches." Buckley v. Valeo, 424 U.S. 1, 129 (1976). Indeed, we also have observed only recently that "[t]he hydraulic pressure inherent within each of the separate Branches to exceed the outer limits of its power, even to accomplish desirable objectives, must be resisted." *Chadha*, supra, 462 U.S., at 951. With these principles in mind, we turn to consideration of whether the Comptroller General is controlled by Congress.

## IV

Appellants urge that the Comptroller General performs his duties independently and is not subservient to Congress. We agree with the District Court that this contention does not bear close scrutiny.

The critical factor lies in the provisions of the statute defining the Comptroller General's office relating to removability. Although the Comptroller General is nominated by the President from a list of three individuals recommended by the Speaker of the House of Representatives and the President *pro tempore* of the Senate, see 31 U.S.C. § 703(a)(2), and confirmed by the Senate, he is removable only at the initiative of Congress. He may be removed not only by impeachment but also by joint resolution of Congress "at any time" resting on any one of the following bases:

"(i) permanent disability;

"(ii) inefficiency;

"(iii) neglect of duty;

"(iv) malfeasance; or

"(v) a felony or conduct involving moral turpitude."

31 U.S.C. § 703(e)(1)B.

This provision was included, as one Congressman explained in urging passage of the Act, because Congress "felt that [the Comptroller General] should be brought under the sole control of Congress, so that Congress at any moment when it found he was inefficient and was not carrying on the duties of his office as he should and as the Congress expected, could remove him without the long, tedious process of a trial by impeachment." 61 Cong.Rec. 1081 (1921). . . . The ultimate design was to "give the legislative branch of the Government control of the audit, not through the power of appointment, but through the power of removal." 58 Cong.Rec. 7211 (1919) (Rep. Temple).

JUSTICE WHITE contends: "The statute does not permit anyone to remove the Comptroller at will; removal is permitted only for specified cause, with the existence of cause to be determined by Congress following a hearing. Any removal under the statute would presumably be subject to post-termination judicial review to ensure that a hearing had in fact been held and that the finding of cause for removal was not arbitrary." . . . [T]he dissent's assessment of the statute fails to recognize the breadth of the grounds for removal. The statute permits removal for "inefficiency," "neglect of duty," or "malfeasance." These terms are very broad and, as interpreted by Congress, could sustain removal of a Comptroller General for any number of actual or perceived transgressions of the legislative will. The Constitutional Convention chose to permit impeachment of executive officers only for "Treason, Bribery, or other high Crimes and Misdemeanors." It rejected language that would have permitted impeachment for "maladministration," with Madison arguing that "[s]o vague a term will be equivalent to a tenure during pleasure of the Senate." 2 M. Farrand, Records of the Federal Convention of 1787, p. 550 (1911). . . .

JUSTICE WHITE, however, assures us that "[r]ealistic consideration" of the "practical result of the removal provision" reveals that the Comptroller General is unlikely to be removed by Congress. The separated powers of our Government cannot be permitted to turn on judicial assessment of whether an officer exercising executive power is on good terms with Congress. The Framers recognized that, in the long term, structural protections against abuse of power were critical to preserving liberty. In constitutional terms, the removal powers over the Comptroller General's office dictate that he will be subservient to Congress. . . .

## V

[The Comptroller General's responsibility under the Act is to prepare a report containing detailed estimates of projected federal revenues and expenditures and detailing necessary reductions on a program-by-program basis.] In preparing the report, the Comptroller General is to have "due regard" for the estimates and reductions set forth in a joint report submitted to him by the Director of CBO and the Director of OMB, the President's fiscal and budgetary adviser. However, the Act plainly contemplates that the Comptroller General will exercise his independent judgment and evaluation with respect to those estimates. The Act also provides that the Comptroller General's report "shall explain fully any differences between the contents of such report and the report of the Directors."

§ 251(b)(2).... Interpreting a law enacted by Congress to implement the legislative mandate is the very essence of "execution" of the law. Under § 251, the Comptroller General must exercise judgment concerning facts that affect the application of the Act. He must also interpret the provisions of the Act to determine precisely what budgetary calculations are required. Decisions of that kind are typically made by officers charged with executing a statute.

The executive nature of the Comptroller General's functions under the Act is revealed in § 252(a)(3) which gives the Comptroller General the ultimate authority to determine the budget cuts to be made. Indeed, the Comptroller General commands the President himself to carry out, without the slightest variation (with exceptions not relevant to the constitutional issues presented), the directive of the Comptroller General as to the budget reductions....

■ Justice Stevens, with whom Justice Marshall joins, concurring in the judgment.

... The Gramm–Rudman–Hollings Act assigns to the Comptroller General the duty to make policy decisions that have the force of law. The Comptroller General's report is, in the current statute, the engine that gives life to the ambitious budget reduction process. It is the Comptroller General's report that "provide[s] for the determination of reductions" and that "contain[s] estimates, determinations, and specifications for all of the items contained in the report" submitted by the Office of Management and Budget and the Congressional Budget Office. § 251(b). It is the Comptroller General's report that the President must follow and that will have conclusive effect. § 252. It is, in short, the Comptroller General's report that will have a profound, dramatic, and immediate impact on the Government and on the Nation at large.

Article I of the Constitution specifies the procedures that Congress must follow when it makes policy that binds the Nation: its legislation must be approved by both of its Houses and presented to the President. In holding that an attempt to legislate by means of a "one-House veto" violated the procedural mandate in Article I, we explained:

"We see therefore that the Framers were acutely conscious that the bicameral requirement and the Presentment Clauses would serve essential constitutional functions. The President's participation in the legislative process was to protect the Executive Branch from Congress and to protect the whole people from improvident laws. The division of the Congress into two distinctive bodies assures that the legislative power would be exercised only after opportunity for full study and debate in separate settings. The President's unilateral veto power, in turn, was limited by the power of two-thirds of both Houses of Congress to overrule a veto thereby precluding final arbitrary action of one person.... It emerges clearly that the prescription for legislative action in Art. I, §§ 1, 7, represents the Framers' decision that the legislative power of the Federal Government be exercised in accord with a single, finely wrought and exhaustively considered, procedure." INS v. Chadha, 462 U.S. [919, 951 (1983).]

If Congress were free to delegate its policymaking authority to one of its components, or to one of its agents, it would be able to evade "the carefully crafted restraints spelled out in the Constitution." *Id.,* at 959. That danger—congressional action that evades constitutional restraints—is not present when Congress delegates lawmaking power to the executive or to an independent agency.... [Accordingly,] even though it is well settled that Congress may delegate legislative power to independent agencies or to the Executive, and thereby divest itself of a portion of its lawmaking power, when it elects to exercise such power itself, it may not authorize a lesser representative of the Legislative Branch to act on its behalf. It is for this reason that I believe § 251(b) and § 251(c)(2) of the Act are unconstitutional....

■ JUSTICE WHITE, dissenting.

The Court, acting in the name of separation of powers, takes upon itself to strike down the Gramm–Rudman–Hollings Act, one of the most novel and far-reaching legislative responses to a national crisis since the New Deal. The basis of the Court's action is a solitary provision of another statute that was passed over 60 years ago and has lain dormant since that time. I cannot concur in the Court's action. Like the Court, I will not purport to speak to the wisdom of the policies incorporated in the legislation the Court invalidates; that is a matter for the Congress and the Executive, *both* of which expressed their assent to the statute barely half a year ago. I will, however, address the wisdom of the Court's willingness to interpose its distressingly formalistic view of separation of powers as a bar to the attainment of governmental objectives through the means chosen by the Congress and the President in the legislative process established by the Constitution. Twice in the past four years I have expressed my view that the Court's recent efforts to police the separation of powers have rested on untenable constitutional propositions leading to regrettable results. See Northern Pipeline Construction Co. v. Marathon Pipe Line Co., 458 U.S. 50, 92–118 (1982) (WHITE, J., dissenting); INS v. Chadha, 462 U.S. 919, 967–1003 (1983) (WHITE, J., dissenting). Today's result is even more misguided. As I will explain, the Court's decision rests on a feature of the legislative scheme that is of minimal practical significance and that presents no substantial threat to the basic scheme of separation of powers. In attaching dispositive significance to what should be regarded as a triviality, the Court neglects what has in the past been recognized as a fundamental principle governing consideration of disputes over separation of powers:

> "The actual art of governing under our Constitution does not and cannot conform to judicial definitions of the power of any of its branches based on isolated clauses or even single Articles torn from context. While the Constitution diffuses power the better to secure liberty, it also contemplates that practice will integrate the dispersed powers into a workable government." Youngstown Sheet & Tube Co. v. Sawyer, 343 U.S. 579, 635 (1952) (Jackson, J., concurring).

## I

... Before examining the merits of the Court's argument, I wish to emphasize what it is that the Court quite pointedly and correctly does not hold: namely, that "executive" powers of the sort granted the Comptroller by the Act may only be exercised by officers removable at will by the President. The Court's apparent unwillingness to accept this argument, which has been tendered in this Court by the Solicitor General, is fully consistent with the Court's longstanding recognition that it is within the power of Congress under the "Necessary and Proper" Clause, Art. I, § 8, to vest authority that falls within the Court's definition of executive power in officers who are not subject to removal at will by the President and are therefore not under the President's direct control. See, e.g., Humphrey's Executor v. United States, 295 U.S. 602 (1935); Wiener v. United States, 357 U.S. 349 (1958).[3] In an earlier day, in which simpler notions of the role of government in society prevailed, it was perhaps plausible to insist that all "executive" officers be subject to an unqualified Presidential removal power, see Myers v. United States, 272 U.S. 52 (1926); but with the advent and triumph of the administrative state and the accompanying multiplication of the tasks undertaken by the Federal Government, the Court has been virtually compelled to recognize that Congress may reasonably deem it "necessary and proper" to vest some among the broad new array of governmental functions in officers who are free from the partisanship that may be expected of agents wholly dependent upon the President.

The Court's recognition of the legitimacy of legislation vesting "executive" authority in officers independent of the President does not imply derogation of the President's own constitutional authority—indeed, duty— to "take Care that the Laws be faithfully executed," Art. II, § 3, for any such duty is necessarily limited to a great extent by the content of the laws enacted by the Congress. As Justice Holmes put it: "The duty of the President to see that the laws be executed is a duty that does not go beyond the laws or require him to achieve more than Congress sees fit to leave within his power." *Myers v. United States, supra,* at 177 (dissenting). Justice Holmes perhaps overstated his case, for there are undoubtedly executive functions that, regardless of the enactments of Congress, must be performed by officers subject to removal at will by the President. Whether a particular function falls within this class or within the far larger class

---

**3.** Although the Court in *Humphrey's Executor* characterized the powers of the Federal Trade Commissioner whose tenure was at issue as "quasi-legislative" and "quasi-judicial," it is clear that the FTC's power to enforce and give content to the Federal Trade Commission Act's proscription of "unfair" acts and practices and methods of competition is in fact "executive" in the same sense as is the Comptroller's authority under Gramm–Rudman– Hollings—that is, it involves the implementation (or the interpretation and application) of an Act of Congress. Thus, although the Court in *Humphrey's Executor* found the use of the labels "quasi-legislative" and "quasi-judicial" helpful in "distinguishing" its then-recent decision in Myers v. United States, 272 U.S. 52, (1926), these terms are hardly of any use in limiting the holding of the case; as Justice Jackson pointed out, "[t]he mere retreat to the qualifying 'quasi' is implicit with confession that all recognized classifications have broken down, and 'quasi' is a smooth cover which we draw over our confusion as we might use a counterpane to conceal a disordered bed." FTC v. Ruberoid Co., 343 U.S. 470, 487–488 (1952) (dissenting).

that may be relegated to independent officers "will depend upon the character of the office." *Humphrey's Executor, supra,* at 631. In determining whether a limitation on the President's power to remove an officer performing executive functions constitutes a violation of the constitutional scheme of separation of powers, a court must "focu[s] on the extent to which [such a limitation] prevents the Executive Branch from accomplishing its constitutionally assigned functions." Nixon v. Administrator of General Services, 433 U.S. 425, 443 (1977). "Only where the potential for disruption is present must we then determine whether that impact is justified by an overriding need to promote objectives within the constitutional authority of Congress." Ibid. This inquiry is, to be sure, not one that will beget easy answers; it provides nothing approaching a bright-line rule or set of rules. Such an inquiry, however, is necessitated by the recognition that "formalistic and unbending rules" in the area of separation of powers may "unduly constrict Congress' ability to take needed and innovative action pursuant to its Article I powers." Commodity Futures Trading Comm'n v. Schor, [478 U.S. 833, 851 (1986)].

It is evident (and nothing in the Court's opinion is to the contrary) that the powers exercised by the Comptroller General under the Gramm–Rudman–Hollings Act are not such that vesting them in an officer not subject to removal at will by the President would in itself improperly interfere with Presidential powers. Determining the level of spending by the Federal Government is not by nature a function central either to the exercise of the President's enumerated powers or to his general duty to ensure execution of the laws; rather, appropriating funds is a peculiarly legislative function, and one expressly committed to Congress by Art. I, § 9, which provides that "No Money shall be drawn from the Treasury, but in Consequence of Appropriations made by Law." In enacting Gramm–Rudman–Hollings, Congress has chosen to exercise this legislative power to establish the level of federal spending by providing a detailed set of criteria for reducing expenditures below the level of appropriations in the event that certain conditions are met. Delegating the execution of this legislation—that is, the power to apply the Act's criteria and make the required calculations—to an officer independent of the President's will does not deprive the President of any power that he would otherwise have or that is essential to the performance of the duties of his office. Rather, the result of such a delegation, from the standpoint of the President, is no different from the result of more traditional forms of appropriation: under either system, the level of funds available to the Executive Branch to carry out its duties is not within the President's discretionary control. To be sure, if the budget-cutting mechanism required the responsible officer to exercise a great deal of policymaking discretion, one might argue that having created such broad discretion Congress had some obligation based upon Art. II to vest it in the Chief Executive or his agents. In Gramm–Rudman–Hollings, however, Congress has done no such thing; instead, it has created a precise and articulated set of criteria designed to minimize the degree of policy choice exercised by the officer executing the statute and to ensure that the relative spending priorities established by Congress in the appropriations it passes into law remain unaltered. Given that the exercise of policy choice by the officer executing the statute would be inimical to Congress' goal in enacting "automatic" budget-cutting measures, it is eminently reasonable and proper for Congress to vest the budget-cutting authority in an officer who is to the greatest degree possible nonpartisan and independent of the President and his political agenda and who therefore may be relied upon not to allow his calculations to be colored by political considerations. Such a delegation deprives the President of no authority that is rightfully his.

## II

If, as the Court seems to agree, the assignment of "executive" powers under Gramm–Rudman–Hollings to an officer not removable at will by the President would not in itself represent a violation of the constitutional scheme of separated powers, the question remains whether, as the Court concludes, the fact that the officer to whom Congress has delegated the authority to implement the Act is removable by a joint resolution of Congress should require invalidation of the Act. The Court's decision, as I have stated above, is based on a syllogism: the Act vests the Comptroller with "executive power"; such power may not be exercised by Congress or its agents; the Comptroller is an agent of Congress because he is removable by Congress; therefore the Act is invalid. I have no quarrel with the proposition that the powers exercised by the Comptroller under the Act may be characterized as "executive" in that they involve the interpretation and carrying out of the Act's mandate. I can also accept the general proposition that although Congress has considerable authority in designating the officers who are to execute legislation, the constitutional scheme of separated powers does prevent Congress from reserving an executive role for itself or for its "agents." *Buckley v. Valeo*, 424 U.S., at 120–141, *id.*, at 267–282 (WHITE, J., concurring in part and dissenting in part). I cannot accept, however, that the exercise of authority by an officer removable for cause by a joint resolution of Congress is analogous to the impermissible execution of the law by Congress itself, nor would I hold that the congressional role in the removal process renders the Comptroller an "agent" of the Congress, incapable of receiving "executive" power....

. . . [T]he Court baldly mischaracterizes the removal provision when it suggests that it allows Congress to remove the Comptroller for "executing the laws in any fashion found to be unsatisfactory"; in fact, Congress may remove the Comptroller only for one or more of five specified reasons, which "although not so narrow as to deny Congress any leeway, circumscribe Congress' power to some extent by providing a basis for judicial review of congressional removal." . . . [U]nder the Budget and Accounting Act, Congress may remove the Comptroller only through a joint resolution, which by definition must be passed by both Houses and signed by the President. See United States v. California, 332 U.S. 19, 28 (1947). In other words, a removal of the Comptroller under the statute *satisfies the requirements of bicameralism and presentment laid down in Chadha*.... That such action may represent a more or less successful attempt by Congress to "control" the actions of an officer of the United States surely does not in itself indicate that it is unconstitutional, for no one would dispute that Congress has the power to "control" administration through legislation imposing duties or substantive restraints on executive officers, through legislation increasing or decreasing the funds made available to such officers, or through legislation actually abolishing a particular office. Indeed, *Chadha* expressly recognizes that while congressional meddling with administration of the laws outside of the legislative process is impermissible, congressional control over executive officers exercised through the legislative process is valid. 462 U.S., at 955, n. 19. . . .

That a joint resolution removing the Comptroller General would satisfy the requirements for legitimate legislative action laid down in *Chadha* does not fully answer the separation-of-powers argument, for it is apparent that even the results of the constitutional legislative process may be unconstitutional if those results are in fact destructive of the scheme of separation-of-powers. Nixon v. Administrator of General Services, 433 U.S. 425 (1977). . . . [T]he substantial role played by the President in the process of removal through joint resolution reduces to utter insignificance the possibility that the threat of removal will induce subservience to the Congress. As I have pointed out above, a joint resolution must be presented to the President and is ineffective if it is vetoed by him, unless the veto is overridden by the constitutionally prescribed two-thirds majority of both Houses of Congress. The requirement of Presidential approval obviates the possibility that the Comptroller will perceive himself as so completely at the mercy of Congress that he will function as its tool. If the Comptroller's conduct in office is not so unsatisfactory to the President as to convince the latter that removal is required under the statutory standard, Congress will have no independent power to coerce the Comptroller unless it can muster a two-thirds majority in both Houses—a feat of bipartisanship more difficult than that required to impeach and convict. The incremental *in terrorem* effect of the possibility of congressional removal in the face of a Presidential veto is therefore exceedingly unlikely to have any discernible impact on the extent of congressional influence over the Comptroller. . . .

Realistic consideration of the nature of the Comptroller General's relation to Congress thus reveals that the threat to separation of powers conjured up by the majority is wholly chimerical. The power over removal retained by the Congress is not a power that is exercised outside the legislative process as established by the Constitution, nor does it appear likely that it is a power that adds significantly to the influence Congress may exert over executive officers through other, undoubtedly constitutional exercises of legislative power and through the constitutionally guaranteed impeachment power. . . .

■ [The opinion of JUSTICE BLACKMUN, dissenting, is omitted.]

---

*1. The Nature of the Power Exercised (Redux)*—Central to the Court's opinion were the conclusions (a) that the Comptroller General was a legislative official—an officer of Congress—and (b) that he or she would exercise executive power in implementing the Gramm–Rudman–Hollings

Act. The constitutional situs of the Comptroller General will be discussed below. It is helpful first to consider the nature of the power that the official was being asked to exercise. Under Gramm–Rudman–Hollings, the report prepared by the Comptroller General based on the deficit estimates prepared by the Office of Management and Budget (an executive agency) and the Congressional Budget Office (an arm of Congress) were to *bind* the President to sequester funds as specified by the Comptroller General's report. In other words, unless Congress otherwise met the deficit targets specified in the Act, the Comptroller General had statutory authority to prescribe budget cuts. Because this grant of authority relates to the expenditure of money from the public fisc, it has a distinctively legislative feel to it. As Justice White noted, "appropriating funds is a peculiarly legislative function, and one expressly committed to Congress by Art. I, § 9, which provides that 'No Money shall be drawn from the Treasury, but in Consequence of Appropriations made by Law.'" Yet the Court concluded that the Comptroller General was, in fact, performing an executive function. As Chief Justice Burger wrote for the Court:

> Interpreting a law enacted by Congress to implement the legislative mandate is the very essence of "execution" of the law. Under § 251, the Comptroller General must exercise judgment concerning facts that affect the application of the Act. He must also interpret the provisions of the Act to determine precisely what budgetary calculations are required. Decisions of that kind are typically made by officers charged with executing a statute.

How important is the Court's characterization of that function? How does it relate to the Court's modern justification for upholding delegations as grants of executive rather than legislative power? In a concurring opinion, Justice Stevens took pains to disagree with the characterization that Gramm–Rudman–Hollings gave the executive power to an agent of Congress, arguing instead that the bill authorized *Congress*—through its agent the Comptroller General—to exercise a form legislative power through means short of bicameralism and presentment. Since he reached the same result, why might Justice Stevens have preferred to treat this as a *Chadha* problem? Does Justice Stevens' reliance on the specific requirements of bicameralism and presentment seem more convincing than the Court's assertion in *Bowsher* that congressional control over law execution violates some unspecified premise of the separation-of-powers doctrine? When reading the cases that follow—concerning the President's power of removal—consider whether there may be other, more practical reasons for Justice Stevens' impulse to treat the Comptroller General's budgetary function as legislative and, in *Whitman, see supra* pp. 414–415, to characterize delegations as legislative as well?

**2. *The Status of the Comptroller General*—**The Court treated the Comptroller General as an agent of Congress, thereby setting up the impermissibility of his or her exercising executive powers. The principal basis for the Court's conclusion is that while the President appoints the Comptroller General by and with the advice and consent of the Senate, the organic act creating the Comptroller General vests the removal power in Congress. In particular, the relevant statute provides that Congress may remove the Comptroller General for "(i) permanent disability; (ii) inefficiency; (iii) neglect of duty; (iv) malfeasance; or (v) a felony or conduct involving moral turpitude." 31 U.S.C. § 703(e)(1)B. If the Court's opinion was animated by the premise that the separation of powers does not permit Congress to control the execution of the laws, do the foregoing provisions suggest such capacity for control? The Court read these provisions as broadly authorizing Congress to remove "a Comptroller General for any number of actual or perceived transgressions of the legislative will." Recall the maxim *noscitur a sociis*—which presupposes that words are known by their associates (see pp. 233–249, *supra*). Applying that maxim, the grounds for removal seem to relate to causes that involve the officer's inability or unwillingness to perform his or her statutory functions (i–iii) or that involve some form of wrongdoing (iv–v). Do you read the statute to permit Congress to remove the Comptroller General if Congress collectively disagreed with his or her judgments about the appropriate way to execute Gramm–Rudman–Hollings?

Even if the Court correctly read the grounds for removal to be broad rather than narrow, doesn't Justice White have a powerful point when he argues that Congress has little practical ability to remove a Comptroller General when the President approves of the way he or she is executing the laws? The removal statute—31 U.S.C. § 703(e)(1)B—provides for removal by "joint resolution." A "joint resolution" requires bicameral passage and presentment to the President for his or her signature or veto pursuant to Article I, § 7. As Justice White pointed out in his dissent, for Congress to dismiss a Comptroller General that the President wished to retain, it would have to muster two-thirds of each House to override his or her likely veto of any joint resolution dismissing that officer. Given the difficulty Congress would have in removing the Comptroller General, do any of the functional concerns about self-delegation that may explain *Chadha* have any resonance here? If not, is there anything to explain the Court's opinion other than a very strong formalist conclusion that Congress cannot exercise any direct control over officers charged with executing the law? The Court attempts to ground its conclusion in one specific constitutional provision—Article II, § 4's provision that executive officers may be impeached only for "Treason, Bribery, or other high Crimes and Misdemeanors." And the Court adds that the Philadelphia Convention rejected a proposal "that would have permitted impeachment for 'maladministration.'" Does the Impeachment Clause of Article II, read in light of its drafting history, carry a strong enough negative implication to sustain the Court's opinion?

## C.   Other Forms of Congressional Control

Cases like *Chadha* and *Bowsher* establish important constitutional limits on Congress's ability to exercise *legal* control over the exercise of authority that Congress has delegated. These holdings, while important, should not be read to imply that Congress lacks any means of influencing the exercise of delegated authority other than amending or repealing the organic statute that delegates authority in the first place. Members of Congress have at their disposal a variety of tools with which to influence agency decisionmaking, even though, post-*Chadha*, Congress lacks the legal authority to veto agency decisions. *See generally* Jack M. Beermann, *Congressional Administration*, 43 SAN DIEGO L. REV. 61 (2006). Consider the following forms of congressional influence:

## a. Appropriations

Agencies need resources to operate, and for this and other reasons agencies care a great deal about preserving or increasing the resources at their disposal. *See, e.g.,* THE BUDGET-MAXIMIZING BUREAUCRAT: APPRAISALS AND EVIDENCE (Andre Blais & Stephane Dion, eds., 1991); D. RODERICK KIEWIET & MATTHEW D. MCCUBBINS, THE LOGIC OF DELEGATION: CONGRESSIONAL PARTIES AND THE APPROPRIATIONS PROCESS (1991). These resources are typically appropriated by Congress in its annual budget (though certain agencies are partly funded by the power to impose direct assessments on regulated parties). As Richard Posner has argued, "agencies must go to their capital markets—the legislative appropriations committees—every year." Richard A. Posner, *Theories of Economic Regulation*, 5 BELL J. ECON. & MGMT. SCI. 335, 338 (1974). This "power of the purse" gives Congress (or, perhaps more accurately, the appropriations subcommittees responsible for proposing a given agency's budget) three important sources of influence over administrative agencies.

First, Congress may often attach substantive "riders" to appropriations bills that restrict an agency's authority to make certain decisions—for example, by forbidding the agency from spending money on disfavored activities, or requiring the agency to spend money on favored activities. *See* Beermann, *supra*, at 85–89. Because these riders are included in an appropriations bill that goes through the full Article I, § 7 process, they can be thought of simply as a form of statutory constraint on agencies. But appropriations riders may sometimes be easier to enact than separate substantive statutory amendments because of the nature of the appropriations process.

Second, the congressional power of the purse gives those members of Congress with influence over the agency's budget considerable leverage over the agency, because an agency that antagonizes those members of Congress may see its budget slashed in retaliation, while an agency that pleases those same members of Congress may see its budget expand. *See* Jonathan Bendor, Serge Taylor & Roland van Gaalen, *Politicians, Bureaucrats, and Asymmetric Information*, 31 AM. J. POL. SCI. 796 (1987); Randall L. Calvert, Matthew D. McCubbins & Barry R. Weingast, *A Theory of Political Control and Agency Discretion*, 33 AM. J. POL. SCI. 588 (1989).

Third, Congress can control how aggressively or expansively an agency pursues its delegated tasks by controlling the resources at the agency's disposal. If members of Congress want agencies to enforce their statutory mandates less aggressively, they can cut agency budgets; if they want agencies to do more, they can increase agency budgets. This use of the appropriations power is something of a blunt instrument, as cutting an agency's budget reduces not only the agency's ability to pursue objectives that Congress disfavors, but also those that Congress supports; increasing the agency's budget may lead both to more effective pursuit of certain objectives and to more inefficient or undesirable spending. *See* Michael M. Ting, *The "Power of the Purse" and Its Implications for Bureaucratic Policy–Making*, 106 Pub. Choice 243 (2001). This form of congressional control may raise special concerns about accountability. What should we make of situations in which Congress enacts a substantive statute giving an agency sweeping authority, but then fails to provide anywhere near the resources sufficient for the agency to fulfill Congress's stated objectives? Professor Susan Rose–Ackerman has argued that this drastic mismatch between goals and funding may undermine democratic accountability by allowing Congress to pass "ambitious-sounding laws that it has no intention of funding adequately," knowing that these laws have "little meaning in the absence of the expenditure of government funds." Susan Rose–Ackerman, *Judicial Review and the Power of the Purse*, 12 Int'l Rev. L. & Econ. 191, 192, 201 (1992). Professor Rose–Ackerman concludes from this observation that courts should treat "drastically underfunded" laws as impliedly repealed by Congress. *Id.* at 198–204. The Court has not adopted Professor Rose–Ackerman's proposal—but is it persuasive? Or is a congressional decision to "underfund" an agency (or a specific agency program) a legitimate means of exercising legislative control over agency activity? *See* Matthew C. Stephenson, *Public Regulation of Private Enforcement: The Case for Expanding the Role of Administrative Agencies*, 91 Va. L. Rev. 93, 107 n.40 (2005) (noting the debate over this question).

#### b. Hearings, Investigations, Audits, and Other Forms of Oversight

Congressional oversight committees also have the ability to influence agency behavior through various oversight activities—holding hearings on agency conduct (at which senior agency officials may be called to testify), conducting investigations into agency activities, issuing press releases criticizing agencies, sending sharply worded letters to agency officials, and so forth. These various forms of oversight activity can make life unpleasant for agency officials, especially because of the omnipresent threat that if the agency really antagonizes Congress, Congress may respond by taking more drastic action (like cutting the agency's budget, withholding cooperation on future initiatives, cutting back on the agency's substantive authority, or even eliminating the agency altogether). *See, e.g.,* Einer Elhauge, Statutory Default Rules 80–81. There is quite a bit of evidence that these forms of congressional oversight can indeed have a significant impact on how agencies exercise their policymaking discretion. *See, e.g.,* Joel D. Aberbach, Keeping a Watchful Eye: The Politics of Congressional Oversight (1990); Beermann, *supra*; J.R. DeShazo & Jody Freeman, *The Congressional Competition To Control Delegated Power*, 81 Tex. L. Rev. 1443 (2003). Indeed, the impact of congressional oversight may be even greater than one would infer from looking only to the total quantity of oversight activity, because the *threat* of oversight may be enough to induce sophisticated agency decision-makers to modify their behavior to appease their congressional overseers. *See* Sanford C. Gordon & Catherine Hafer, *Flexing Muscle: Corporate Political Expenditures as Signals to the Bureaucracy*, 99 AM. POL. SCI. REV. 245 (2005); Barry R. Weingast & Mark J. Moran, *Bureaucratic Discretion or Congressional Control? Regulatory Policymaking by the Federal Trade Commission*, 91 J. POL. ECON. 765, 769 (1983).

That said, it is hard to assess the extent or scope of this form of congressional influence over agencies. The correlation between congressional oversight activity and agency policy change does not necessarily tell us whether congressional oversight *caused* the change, or whether some more fundamental factor—such as widespread public dissatisfaction with the agency, or a major policy failure associated with agency action or inaction—was the cause of both the congressional oversight activity and the change in agency policy. And it is difficult to assess the *relative* significance of congressional influence over agencies, compared to, say, the President's influence, or the agency's own policy objectives, or lobbying by interest groups at the agency level. *See* Thomas H. Hammond & Jack H. Knott, *Who Controls the Bureaucracy?: Presidential Power, Congressional Dominance, Legal Constraints, and Bureaucratic Autonomy in a Model of Multi-Institutional Policymaking*, 12 J.L. ECON. & ORG. 119 (1996); Terry M. Moe, *An Assessment of the Positive Theory of "Congressional Dominance"*, 12 LEG. STUD. Q. 475 (1987). Nonetheless, the important point is that Congress (or the relevant oversight committees within Congress) may retain meaningful influence over agency behavior through these informal mechanisms, even if more formal tools like the legislative veto are out of bounds.

## IV. APPOINTMENT AND REMOVAL

Delegation of substantial lawmaking power to administrative agencies, as we have seen, raises serious concerns about democratic accountability and legitimacy. But the fact that agency officials are not directly elected does not necessarily mean that agencies are not subject to control by the political branches, and thus indirectly accountable to the public. One of the most important ways in which the President and Congress may try to influence regulatory policymaking is through the selection of agency officials—particularly the high-level officials who make critical policy decisions. In the American constitutional tradition, the President selects key agency personnel subject to the advice and consent of the Senate. Yet Congress also sometimes seeks to limit or constrain the President's appointment and removal authority in various ways. In this part, we examine constitutional considerations relating to the appointment and removal of agency officials.

In light of the pervasiveness of broad delegations to administrative agencies, the scope of presidential control over agency personnel—and hence agency decisionmaking—carries enormous implications. On the one hand, presidential control of agencies may be thought to increase democratic accountability by virtue of the President's electoral accountability to the people. Indeed, this presidential control over the administration is viewed in some quarters as the key to the democratic legitimacy of the administrative state, as *presidential* accountability for the content of agency regulations substitutes for *congressional* accountability for the content of statutes. *See, e.g.,* Jerry Mashaw, *Prodelegation: Why Administrators Should Make Political Decisions*, 1 J.L. ECON. & ORG. 81 (1985). On the other hand, giving the President sweeping powers over senior agency personnel, with which Congress may not interfere outside of the context of Senate confirmation of presidential nominees, may be thought to dilute checks and balances by shifting the implementation of legislative policy too far away from Congress. Especially in light of cases like *Chadha* and *Bowsher* (*see* Part III, *supra*), which disable Congress from retaining formal control over the exercise of delegated power by executive branch agencies, some believe that allowing Congress to place some limits on the President's control over agency personnel helps prevent excessive concentration of policymaking power in the hands of the President. How should one balance these competing interests? How does the U.S. Constitution balance them?

Although the powers to appoint and to remove agency personnel are obviously related, the Constitution handles the two types of authority quite differently. The Appointments Clause in Article II, § 2 speaks explicitly to the question of appointment as follows:

> [The President] shall nominate, and by and with the Advice and Consent of the Senate, shall appoint Ambassadors, other public Ministers and Consuls, Judges of the supreme Court, and all other Officers of the United States, whose Appointments are not herein otherwise provided for, and which shall be established by Law: but the Congress may by Law vest the Appointment of such inferior Officers, as they think proper, in the President alone, in the Courts of Law, or in the Heads of Departments.

U.S. CONST. art. II, § 2, cl. 2. In contrast, the Constitution does not deal explicitly with the question of removal at all, requiring proponents of inherent presidential removal power to derive that authority by implication from more generally worded provisions of Article II. A host of difficult constitutional questions arise out of the President's appointment and removal powers, particularly with respect to Congress's ability to regulate the President's use of those powers. The constitutional text clearly contemplates a role for at least one chamber of Congress—the Senate—in the appointment of government officials: the Appointments Clause requires senatorial "advice and consent" to confirm presidential nominees. But does the Constitution—and, in particular, the Necessary and Proper Clause, U.S. CONST. art. I, § 8, cl. 18—permit Congress to play any other role in the appointment and removal of executive branch officials?

The materials that follow also illustrate important and longstanding methodological disagreements about constitutional interpretation. Some of the opinions on these appointment and removal questions are quite formalist in their approach; others are more functionalist and pragmatic. Some of the opinions reflect the view that the Court should try to excavate the original understanding of the particular constitutional provision at issue, while others proceed from the premise that the original understanding tells us little if anything about how to approach most of these separation-of-powers questions. As you work through the materials in this section, consider what the styles of reasoning in those cases might tell us about the pluses and minuses of different approaches to constitutional interpretation, as well as the implications for regulatory policymaking.

## A. FOUNDATIONAL CASES ON APPOINTMENT AND REMOVAL

### a. Appointments Clause Exclusivity

## Buckley v. Valeo

Supreme Court of the United States
424 U.S. 1 (1976)

■ PER CURIAM.

These appeals present constitutional challenges to the key provisions of the Federal Election Campaign Act of 1971 (Act), and related provisions of the Internal Revenue Code of 1954, all as amended in 1974.

The Court of Appeals, in sustaining the legislation in large part against various constitutional challenges, viewed it as "by far the most comprehensive reform legislation (ever) passed by Congress concerning the election of the President, Vice–President, and members of Congress." 519 F.2d 821, 831 (1975). The statutes at issue summarized in broad terms, contain the following provisions: (a) individual political contributions are limited to $1,000 to any single candidate per election, with an overall annual limitation of $25,000 by any contributor; independent expenditures by individuals and groups "relative to a clearly identified candidate" are limited to $1,000 a year; campaign spending by candidates for various federal offices and spending for national conventions by political parties are subject to prescribed limits; (b) contributions and expenditures above certain threshold levels must be reported and publicly disclosed; (c) a system for public funding of Presidential campaign activities is established by Subtitle H of the Internal Revenue Code; and (d) a Federal Election Commission is established to administer and enforce the legislation....

### IV.   THE FEDERAL ELECTION COMMISSION

The 1974 amendments to the Act create an eight-member Federal Election Commission (Commission), and vest in it primary and substantial responsibility for administering and enforcing the Act. The question that we address in this portion of the opinion is whether, in view of the manner in which a majority of its members are appointed, the Commission may under the Constitution exercise the powers conferred upon it. We find it unnecessary to parse the complex statutory provisions in order to sketch the full sweep of the Commission's authority. It will suffice for present purposes to describe what appear to be representative examples of its various powers.

Chapter 14 of Title 2 makes the Commission the principal repository of the numerous reports and statements which are required by that Chapter to be filed by those engaging in the regulated political activities. Its duties under § 438(a) with respect to these reports and statements include filing and indexing, making them available for public inspection, preservation, and auditing and field investigations. It is directed to "serve as a national clearinghouse for information in respect to the administration of elections." § 438(b).

Beyond these recordkeeping, disclosure, and investigative functions, however, the Commission is given extensive rulemaking and adjudicative powers.... [T]he Commission is empowered to make such rules "as are necessary to carry out the provisions of this Act." ... The Commission is authorized under § 437f(a) to render advisory opinions with respect to activities possibly violating the Act, ... the effect of which is that "[n]otwithstanding any other provision of law, any person with respect to whom an advisory opinion is rendered ... who acts in good faith in accordance with the provisions and findings [thereof] shall be presumed to be in compliance with the [statutory provision] with respect to which such advisory opinion is rendered." § 437f(b). In the course of administering the provisions for Presidential campaign financing, the Commission may authorize convention expenditures which exceed the statutory limits.

The Commission's enforcement power is both direct and wide ranging. It may institute a civil action for (i) injunctive or other relief against "any acts or practices which constitute or will constitute a violation of this Act," § 437g(a)(5); (ii) declaratory or injunctive relief "as may be appropriate to implement or con[s]true any provisions" of ... Title 26[ ] governing administration of funds for Presidential election campaigns and national party conventions ...; and (iii) "such injunctive relief as is appropriate to implement any provision" of ... Title 26[ ] governing the payment of matching funds for Presidential primary campaigns. If after the Commission's post-disbursement audit of candidates receiving payments under Chapter 95 or 96 it finds an overpayment, it is empowered to seek repayment of all funds due the Secretary of the Treasury.... Finally, as "[a]dditional enforcement authority," [the Act] authorizes the Commission, after notice and opportunity for hearing, to make "a finding that a person ... while a candidate for Federal office, failed to file" a required report of contributions or expenditures. If that finding is made within the applicable limitations period for prosecutions, the candidate is thereby "disqualified from becoming a candidate in any future election for Federal office for a period of time beginning on the date of such finding and ending one year after the expiration of the term of the Federal office for which such person was a candidate."

The body in which this authority is reposed consists of eight members. The Secretary of the Senate and the Clerk of the House of Representatives are ex officio members of the Commission without the right to vote. Two members are appointed by the President pro tempore of the Senate "upon the recommendations of the majority leader of the Senate and the minority leader of the Senate." Two more are to be appointed by the Speaker of the House of Representatives, likewise upon the recommendations of its respective majority and minority leaders. The remaining two members are appointed by the President. Each of the six voting members of the Commission must be confirmed by the majority of both Houses of Congress, and each of the three appointing authorities is forbidden to choose both of their appointees from the same political party....

Appellants urge that since Congress has given the Commission wide-ranging rulemaking and enforcement powers with respect to the substantive provisions of the Act, Congress is precluded under the principle of separation of powers from vesting in itself the authority to appoint those who will exercise such authority. Their argument is based on the language of Art. II, § 2, cl. 2, of the Constitution, which provides in pertinent part as follows:

> "[The President] shall nominate, and by and with the Advice and Consent of the Senate, shall appoint ... all other Officers of the United States, whose Appointments are not herein otherwise provided for, and which shall be established by Law: but the Congress may by Law vest the Appointment of such inferior Officers, as they think proper, in the President alone, in the Courts of Law, or in the Heads of Departments."

... The principle of separation of powers was not simply an abstract generalization in the minds of the Framers: it was woven into the document that they drafted in Philadelphia in the summer of 1787. Article I, § 1, declares: "All legislative Powers herein granted shall be vested in a Congress of the United States." Article II, § 1, vests the executive power "in a President of the United States of America," and Art. III, § 1, declares that "The judicial Power of the United States, shall be vested in one supreme Court, and in such inferior Courts as the Congress may from time to time ordain and establish." The further concern of the Framers of the Constitution with maintenance of the separation of powers is found in the so-called "Ineligibility" and "Incompatibility" Clauses contained in Art. I, § 6:

> "No Senator or Representative shall, during the Time for which he was elected, be appointed to any civil Office under the Authority of the United States, which shall have been created, or the Emoluments whereof shall have been encreased during such time; and no Person holding any Office under the United States, shall be a Member of either House during his Continuance in Office."

... The Appointments Clause could, of course, be read as merely dealing with etiquette or protocol in describing "Officers of the United States," but the drafters had a less frivolous purpose in mind. This conclusion is supported by language from United States v. Germaine, 99 U.S. 508, 509–510 (1879):

"The Constitution for purposes of appointment very clearly divides all its officers into two classes. The primary class requires a nomination by the President and confirmation by the Senate. But foreseeing that when offices became numerous, and sudden removals necessary, this mode might be inconvenient, it was provided that, in regard to officers inferior to those specially mentioned, Congress might by law vest their appointment in the President alone, in the courts of law, or in the heads of departments. *That all persons who can be said to hold an office under the government about to be established under the Constitution were intended to be included within one or the other of these modes of appointment there can be but little doubt.*" ...

We think that the term "Officers of the United States" as used in Art. II, defined to include "all persons who can be said to hold an office under the government" in *United States v. Germaine, supra*, is a term intended to have substantive meaning. We think its fair import is that any appointee exercising significant authority pursuant to the laws of the United States is an "Officer of the United States," and must, therefore, be appointed in the manner prescribed by § 2, cl. 2, of that Article.

If "all persons who can be said to hold an office under the government about to be established under the Constitution were intended to be included within one or the other of these modes of appointment," *United States v. Germaine, supra*, it is difficult to see how the members of the Commission may escape inclusion. If a postmaster first class, Myers v. United States, 272 U.S. 52 (1926), and the clerk of a district court, Ex parte Hennen, 38 U.S. 225 (1839), are inferior officers of the United States within the meaning of the Appointments Clause, as they are, surely the Commissioners before us are at the very least such "inferior Officers" within the meaning of that Clause.[162]

Although two members of the Commission are initially selected by the President, his nominations are subject to confirmation not merely by the Senate, but by the House of Representatives as well. The remaining four voting members of the Commission are appointed by the President pro tempore of the Senate and by the Speaker of the House. While the second part of the Clause authorizes Congress to vest the appointment of the officers described in that part in "the Courts of Law, or in the Heads of Departments," neither the Speaker of the House nor the President *pro tempore* of the Senate comes within this language.

The phrase "Heads of Departments," used as it is in conjunction with the phrase "Courts of Law," suggests that the Departments referred to are themselves in the Executive Branch or at least have some connection with that branch. While the Clause expressly authorizes Congress to vest the

---

**162.** *"Officers of the United States"* does not include all employees of the United States, but there is no claim made that the Commissioners are employees of the United States rather than officers. Employees are lesser functionaries subordinate to officers of the United States, see Auffmordt v. Hedden, 137 U.S. 310, 327 (1890); United States v. Germaine, 99 U.S. 508 (1879), whereas the Commissioners, appointed for a statutory term, are not subject to the control or direction of any other executive, judicial, or legislative authority.

appointment of certain officers in the "Courts of Law," the absence of similar language to include Congress must mean that neither Congress nor its officers were included within the language "Heads of Departments" in this part of cl. 2.

Thus with respect to four of the six voting members of the Commission, neither the President, the head of any department, nor the Judiciary has any voice in their selection. . . .

[The] Commission and amici urge that because of what they conceive to be the extraordinary authority reposed in Congress to regulate elections, this case stands on a different footing than if Congress had exercised its legislative authority in another field. There is, of course, no doubt that Congress has express authority to regulate congressional elections, by virtue of the power conferred in Art. I, § 4. This Court has also held that it has very broad authority to prevent corruption in national Presidential elections. Burroughs v. United States, 290 U.S. 534 (1934). But Congress has plenary authority in all areas in which it has substantive legislative jurisdiction, McCulloch v. Maryland, 17 U.S. 316 (1819), so long as the exercise of that authority does not offend some other constitutional restriction. We see no reason to believe that the authority of Congress over federal election practices is of such a wholly different nature from the other grants of authority to Congress that it may be employed in such a manner as to offend well-established constitutional restrictions stemming from the separation of powers.

The position that because Congress has been given explicit and plenary authority to regulate a field of activity, it must therefore have the power to appoint those who are to administer the regulatory statute is both novel and contrary to the language of the Appointments Clause. Unless their selection is elsewhere provided for, *all* officers of the United States are to be appointed in accordance with the Clause. Principal officers are selected by the President with the advice and consent of the Senate. Inferior officers Congress may allow to be appointed by the President alone, by the heads of departments, or by the Judiciary. No class or type of officer is excluded because of its special functions. The President appoints judicial as well as executive officers. Neither has it been disputed—and apparently it is not now disputed—that the Clause controls the appointment of the members of a typical administrative agency even though its functions, as this Court recognized in Humphrey's Executor v. United States, 295 U.S. 602, 624 (1935), may be "predominantly quasi-judicial and quasi-legislative" rather than executive. . . .

We are also told by appellees and amici that Congress had good reason for not vesting in a Commission composed wholly of Presidential appointees the authority to administer the Act, since the administration of the Act would undoubtedly have a bearing on any incumbent President's campaign for re-election. While one cannot dispute the basis for this sentiment as a practical matter, it would seem that those who sought to challenge incumbent Congressmen might have equally good reason to fear a Commission which was unduly responsive to members of Congress whom they were seeking to unseat. But such fears, however rational, do not by themselves warrant a distortion of the Framers' work.

[The] Commission and amici finally contend . . . that whatever shortcomings the provisions for the appointment of members of the Commission might have under Art. II, Congress had ample authority under the Necessary and Proper Clause of Art. I to effectuate this result. We do not agree. The proper inquiry when considering the Necessary and Proper Clause is not the authority of Congress to create an office or a commission, which is broad indeed, but rather its authority to provide that its own officers may make appointments to such office or commission.

So framed, the claim that Congress may provide for this manner of appointment under the Necessary and Proper Clause of Art. I stands on no better footing than the claim that it may provide for such manner of appointment because of its substantive authority to regulate federal elections. Congress could not, merely because it concluded that such a measure was "necessary and proper" to the discharge of its substantive legislative authority, pass a bill of attainder or *ex post facto* law contrary to the prohibitions contained in § 9 of Art. I. No more may it vest in itself, or in its officers, the authority to appoint officers of the United States when the Appointments Clause by clear implication prohibits it from doing so. . . .

Thus, on the assumption that all of the powers granted in the statute may be exercised by an agency whose members *have been* appointed in accordance with the Appointments Clause, the ultimate question is which, if any, of those powers may be exercised by the present voting Commissioners, none of whom *was* appointed as provided by that Clause. Our previous description of the statutory provisions . . . disclosed that the Commission's powers fall generally into three categories: functions relating to the flow of necessary information—receipt, dissemination, and investigation; functions with respect to the Commission's task of fleshing out the statute rulemaking and advisory opinions; and functions necessary to ensure compliance with the statute and rules—informal procedures, administrative determinations and hearings, and civil suits.

Insofar as the powers confided in the Commission are essentially of an investigative and informative nature, falling in the same general category as those powers which Congress might delegate to one of its own committees, there can be no question that the Commission as presently constituted may exercise them. . . . As this Court stated in [McGrain v. Daugherty, 273 U.S. 135, 175 (1927):]

> "A legislative body cannot legislate wisely or effectively in the absence of information respecting the conditions which the legislation is intended to affect or change; and where the legislative body does not itself possess the requisite information—which not infrequently is true— recourse must be had to others who do possess it. Experience has taught that mere requests for such information often are unavailing, and also that information which is volunteered is not always accurate or complete; so some means of compulsion are essential to obtain what is needed. All this was true before and when the Constitution was

framed and adopted. In that period the power of inquiry, with enforcing process—was regarded and employed as a necessary and appropriate attribute of the power to legislate—indeed, was treated as inhering in it."

But when we go beyond this type of authority to the more substantial powers exercised by the Commission, we reach a different result. The Commission's enforcement power, exemplified by its discretionary power to seek judicial relief, is authority that cannot possibly be regarded as merely in aid of the legislative function of Congress. A lawsuit is the ultimate remedy for a breach of the law, and it is to the President, and not to the Congress, that the Constitution entrusts the responsibility to "take Care that the Laws be faithfully executed." Art. II, § 3.

Congress may undoubtedly under the Necessary and Proper Clause create "offices" in the generic sense and provide such method of appointment to those "offices" as it chooses. But Congress' power under that Clause is inevitably bounded by the express language of Art. II, § 2, cl. 2, and unless the method it provides comports with the latter, the holders of those offices will not be "Officers of the United States." They may, therefore, properly perform duties only in aid of those functions that Congress may carry out by itself, or in an area sufficiently removed from the administration and enforcement of the public law as to permit their being performed by persons not "Officers of the United States."

This Court observed more than a century ago with respect to litigation conducted in the courts of the United States:

"Whether tested, therefore, by the requirements of the Judiciary Act, or by the usage of the government, or by the decisions of this court, it is clear that all such suits, so far as the interests of the United States are concerned, are subject to the direction, and within the control of, the Attorney–General." Confiscation Cases, 74 U.S. 454, 458–459 (1869).

The Court echoed similar sentiments 59 years later in Springer v. Philippine Islands, 277 U.S. [189, 202 (1928)], saying:

"Legislative power, as distinguished from executive power, is the authority to make laws, but not to enforce them or appoint the agents charged with the duty of such enforcement. The latter are executive functions. It is unnecessary to enlarge further upon the general subject, since it has so recently received the full consideration of this court. Myers v. United States, 272 U.S. 52.

We hold that these provisions of the Act, vesting in the Commission primary responsibility for conducting civil litigation in the courts of the United States for vindicating public rights, violate Art. II, § 2, cl. 2, of the Constitution. Such functions may be discharged only by persons who are "Officers of the United States" within the language of that section.

All aspects of the Act are brought within the Commission's broad administrative powers: rulemaking, advisory opinions, and determinations of eligibility for funds and even for federal elective office itself. These functions, exercised free from day-to-day supervision of either Congress or the Executive Branch, are more legislative and judicial in nature than are the Commission's enforcement powers, and are of kinds usually performed by independent regulatory agencies or by some department in the Executive Branch under the direction of an Act of Congress. Congress viewed these broad powers as essential to effective and impartial administration of the entire substantive framework of the Act. Yet each of these functions also represents the performance of a significant governmental duty exercised pursuant to a public law. While the President may not insist that such functions be delegated to an appointee of his removable at will, Humphrey's Executor v. United States, 295 U.S. 602 (1935), none of them operates merely in aid of congressional authority to legislate or is sufficiently removed from the administration and enforcement of public law to allow it to be performed by the present Commission. These administrative functions may therefore be exercised only by persons who are "Officers of the United States." . . .

In summary, we . . . hold that most of the powers conferred by the Act upon the Federal Election Commission can be exercised only by "Officers of the United States," appointed in conformity with Art. II, § 2, cl. 2, of the Constitution, and therefore cannot be exercised by the Commission as presently constituted. . . .

■ [JUSTICE WHITE dissented from the Court's invalidation of FECA on Appointments Clause grounds. His opinion is omitted.]

---

*1. The Appointments Clause versus the Necessary and Proper Clause*—*Buckley* presents in sharp form a perennial conflict between the explicit assignment of executive power to the President under Article II and Congress's explicit authority to define the shape of government pursuant to the Article I Necessary and Proper Clause. *Buckley* held that, at least in the appointments context, the former takes priority over the latter; the Appointments Clause provides the exclusive mechanism for appointing "Officers of the United States," and Congress has no authority, under the Necessary and Proper Clause or anything else, to specify a different method of appointment. The Court reached this conclusion by observing, first, that the Appointments Clause divides officers into two classes—principal "Officers of the United States" and "inferior Officers"—and then carefully specifies a method for appointing officers in each class. From this the Court reasoned that there can be "but little doubt" that "all persons who can be said to hold an office under the government about to be established under the Constitution were intended to be included within one or the other of these modes of appointment." That conclusion seems to derive, at least in part, from an application of the traditional maxim that the specification of a particular method for implementing a newly granted power implicitly excludes all other such methods.

But did the Court dismiss the Necessary and Proper Clause argument too quickly? Consider the following argument in favor of the unusual appointments scheme struck down in *Buckley*: Under Article I, § 4, Congress has broad authority to regulate the time, place, and manner of holding elections for Senators and Representatives, and the Court has recognized broad congressional authority to regulate aspects of presidential elections. In 1789, the founders could never have contemplated the extent to which the American political system would depend on large campaign contributions to fund the organization of political activity. Given the potential for the corruption of our system by factions and the consequent need for the regulation of such contributions, Congress thought it "necessary and proper" to create an administrative agency to implement new legislation regulating campaign contributions. Because of the sensitive nature of the agency's task, all three branches needed to be involved in the appointment of its officials. Hence, the President nominated two Commissioners; the House nominated two; and the Senate nominated two; and all six were subject to the advice and consent of the Senate and the House. Rather than diminishing the checks and balances inherent in the Appointments Clause, this system *enhanced* those checks and balances. Hence, if one treats the Appointments Clause as a floor on the degree of checks and balances, this statute should pass muster.

Is that argument convincing? What if the Appointments Clause was meant not to be a floor on the procedures that were needed, but rather a ceiling *and* a floor? Since the power of appointment had traditionally belonged exclusively to the executive under English common law, perhaps the Appointments Clause was meant to limit that traditional authority only to the extent specified explicitly in the clause. Isn't it sensible to assume that when a provision is as detailed and specific as the Appointments Clause, it should it be understood as a compromise that went so far and no farther? *See* JEREMY WALDRON, LAW AND DISAGREEMENT 125 (1999) (noting that "specific provisions" in an enacted law may reflect the end-product "of compromise and line-item voting"). Might we further argue that in fact the Constitution expressly (though perhaps obliquely) states that the Appointments Clause is exclusive? After all, the first part of the clause makes clear that its advice and consent requirements extend to certain specified officers and then also to "all other Officers of the United States, *whose Appointments are not herein otherwise provided for*" (emphasis added). Since the text that follows it gives Congress authority to "vest the Appointment of such inferior Officers, as they think proper, in the President alone, in the Courts of Law, or in the Heads of Departments," might the italicized phrase suggest that all Officers of the United States who are not "inferior Officers" are subject to advice and consent? On that reading, the word "herein" in "not otherwise herein provided for" internally refers to the Appointments Clause itself. Is that interpretation convincing?

**2. *Officer versus Employee***—Later in this chapter (pp. 539–543, *infra*), we consider the distinction between "principal officers," who must be appointed by the President with the advice and consent of the Senate, and "inferior Officers," whose appointment Congress may vest "in the President alone, in the Courts of Law, or in the Heads of Departments." Because the procedure set forth in the Federal Election Campaign Act did not comply with the clause's default procedure for appointing "Officers of the United States" or the special procedures available for appointing "inferior Officers," the Court did not have to decide whether FEC Commissioners were "inferior officers" or "principal officers." The *Buckley* Court did, however, have to decide whether the Commissioners were some form of "Officer of the United States," whether inferior or not, because the procedures set forth by the Appointments Clause only apply to federal *officers*, not to other federal employees. The Constitution does not specifically define the category of non-officer "employees"; the Court in *Buckley* defined this category by implication, holding that the "fair import" of the Appointments Clause "is that any appointee exercising significant authority pursuant to the laws of the United States is an 'Officer of the United States[.]' " Thus, *Buckley* endorsed a "significant authority" test for distinguishing "officers" from "employees." *See also* Freytag v. Commissioner of Internal Revenue, 501 U.S. 868, 880–82 (1991) (finding Tax Court judges to be "inferior officers" rather than "employees" because they exercise "significant discretion" and are not limited to the performance of "ministerial tasks"); Walter Dellinger, *The Constitutional Separation of Powers Between the President and Congress*, Memorandum for the General Counsels of the Federal Government (May 7, 1996), *reprinted in* 63 LAW & CONTEMP. PROBS. 514, 533–35 (2000) (summarizing case law and concluding from it that "any appointee in federal service who exercises significant authority pursuant to the laws of the United States must be an officer in the constitutional sense," whereas "employees do not wield independent discretion and act only at the direction of officers") (internal quotation marks, citations, and alterations omitted).

### b. The President's Removal Power

---

# Myers v. United States

Supreme Court of the United States
272 U.S. 52 (1926)

■ MR. CHIEF JUSTICE TAFT delivered the opinion of the Court.

This case presents the question whether under the Constitution the President has the exclusive power of removing executive officers of the United States whom he has appointed by and with the advice and consent of the Senate.

Myers, appellant's intestate, was on July 21, 1917, appointed by the President, by and with the advice and consent of the Senate, to be a postmaster of the first class at Portland, Oregon, for a term of four years. On January 20, 1920, Myers' resignation was demanded. He refused the demand. On February 2, 1920, he was removed from office by order of the Postmaster General, acting by direction of the President. February 10th, Myers sent a petition to the President and another to the Senate Committee on Post Offices, asking to be heard, if any charges were filed. He protested to the department against his removal, and continued to do so until the end of his term. He pursued no other occupation and drew compensation for no other service during the interval. On April 21, 1921, he brought this suit in the Court of Claims for his salary from the date of his removal. . . .

By the 6th section of the Act of Congress of July 12, 1876, 19 Stat. 80, 81, c. 179 (Comp. St. § 7190), under which Myers was appointed with the advice and consent of the Senate as a first-class postmaster, it is provided that: "Postmasters of the first, second, and third classes shall be appointed and may be removed by the President by and with the advice and consent of the Senate, and shall hold their offices for four years unless sooner removed or suspended according to law."

The Senate did not consent to the President's removal of Myers during his term. . . . The government maintains that the requirement is invalid, for the reason that under Article II of the Constitution the President's power of removal of executive officers appointed by him with the advice and consent of the Senate is full and complete without consent of the Senate. If this view is sound, the removal of Myers by the President without the Senate's consent was legal. . . .

The question where the power of removal of executive officers appointed by the President by and with the advice and consent of the Senate was vested, was presented early in the first session of the First Congress. There is no express provision respecting removals in the Constitution, except as Section 4 of Article II . . . provides for removal from office by impeachment. The subject was not discussed in the Constitutional Convention. Under the Articles of Confederation, Congress was given the power of appointing certain executive officers of the Confederation, and during the Revolution and while the articles were given effect, Congress exercised the power of removal. . . .

Consideration of the executive power was initiated in the Constitutional Convention by the seventh resolution in the Virginia Plan introduced by Edmund Randolph. 1 Farrand. Records of the Federal Convention, 21. It gave to the executive "all the executive powers of the Congress under the Confederation," which would seem therefore to have intended to include the power of removal which had been exercised by that body as incident to the power of appointment. As modified by the committee of the whole this resolution declared for a national executive of one person to be elected by the legislature, with power to carry into execution the national laws and to appoint to offices in cases not otherwise provided for. It was referred to the committee on detail (1 Farrand, 230), which recommended that the executive power should be vested in a single person to be styled the President of the United States, that he should take care that the laws of the United States be duly and faithfully executed, and that he should commission all the officers of the United States and appoint officers in all cases not otherwise provided by the Constitution (2 Farrand, 185). The committee further recommended that the Senate be given power to make treaties, and to appoint ambassadors and judges of the Supreme Court.

After the great compromises of the convention—the one giving the states equality of representation in the Senate, and the other placing the election of the President, not in Congress, as once voted, but in an electoral college, in which the influence of larger states in the selection would be more nearly in proportion to their population—the smaller states led by Roger Sherman, fearing that under the second compromise the President would constantly be chosen from one of the larger states, secured a change by which the appointment of all officers, which theretofore had been left to the President without restriction, was made subject to the Senate's advice and consent, and the making of treaties and the appointments of ambassadors, public ministers, consuls, and judges of the Supreme Court were transferred to the President, but made subject to the advice and consent of the Senate. This third compromise was affected in a special committee in which Gouverneur Morris of Pennsylvania represented the larger states, and Roger Sherman the smaller states. Although adopted finally without objection by any state in the last days of the convention, members from the larger states, like Wilson and others, criticized this limitation of the President's power of appointment of executive officers and the resulting increase of the power of the Senate. 2 Farrand, 537, 538, 539. . . .

[During the First Congress], [o]n June 16, 1789, the House resolved itself into a committee of the whole on a bill proposed by Mr. Madison for establishing an executive department to be denominated the Department of Foreign Affairs, in which the first clause, after stating the title of the officer and describing his duties, had these words "to be removable from office by the President of the United States." 1 Annals of Congress, 455. After a very full discussion the question was put: Shall the words "to be removable by the President" be struck out? It was determined in the negative-yeas 20, nays 34. 1 Annals of Congress, 576.

On June 22, in the renewal of the discussion: "Mr. Benson moved to amend the bill, by altering the second clause, so as to imply the power of removal to be in the President alone. The clause enacted that there should be a chief clerk, to be appointed by the Secretary of Foreign Affairs, and employed as he thought proper, and who, in case of vacancy, should have the charge and custody of all records, books, and papers appertaining to the department. The amendment proposed that the chief clerk, 'whenever the said principal officer shall be removed from office by the President of the United States, or in any other case of vacancy,' should during such vacancy, have the charge and custody of all records, books, and papers appertaining to the department." 1 Annals of Congress, 578. "Mr. Benson stated that his objection to the clause 'to be removable by the President' arose from an idea that the power of removal by the President hereafter might appear to be exercised by virtue of a legislative grant only, and consequently be subjected to legislative instability, when he was well satisfied in his own mind that it was fixed by a fair legislative construction of the Constitution." 1 Annals of Congress, 579. "Mr. Benson declared, if he succeeded in this amendment, he would move to strike out the words in the first clause, 'to be removable by the President,' which appeared somewhat like a grant. Now, the mode he took would evade that point and establish a legislative construction of the Constitution. He also hoped his amendment would succeed in reconciling both sides of the House to the decision, and quieting the minds of gentlemen." 1 Annals of Congress, 578.

Mr. Madison admitted the objection made by the gentleman near him (Mr. Benson) to the words in the bill. He said: "They certainly may be construed to imply a legislative grant of the power. He wished everything like ambiguity expunged, and the sense of the House explicitly declared, and therefore seconded the motion...." 1 Annals of Congress, 578, 579....

The first amendment was then approved by a vote of 30 to 18. 1 Annals of Congress, 580. Mr. Benson then moved to strike out in the first clause the words "to be removable by the President," in pursuance of the purpose he had already declared, and this second motion of his was carried by a vote of 31 to 19. 1 Annals of Congress, 585.

The bill as amended was ordered to be engrossed, and read the third time the next day, June 24, 1789, and was then passed by a vote of 29 to 22, and the clerk was directed to carry the bill to the Senate and desire their concurrence. 1 Annals of Congress, 591.

[After summarizing the legislative debate and a series of votes, the Court concluded that this history showed that] the exact question which the House voted upon was whether it should recognize and declare the power of the President under the Constitution to remove the Secretary of Foreign Affairs without the advice and consent of the Senate. That was what the vote was taken for.... [T]he vote was, and was intended to be, a legislative declaration that the power to remove officers appointed by the President and the Senate vested in the President alone, and until the Johnson impeachment trial in 1868 its meaning was not doubted, even by those who questioned its soundness.

The discussion was a very full one.... Fourteen out of the 29 who voted for the passage of the bill and 11 of the 22 who voted against the bill took part in the discussion. Of the members of the House, 8 had been in the Constitutional Convention, and of these 6 voted with the majority, and 2, Roger Sherman and Elbridge Gerry, the latter of whom had refused to sign the Constitution, voted in the minority. After the bill as amended had passed the House, it was sent to the Senate, where it was discussed in secret session, without report. The critical vote there was upon the striking out of the clause recognizing and affirming the unrestricted power of the President to remove. The Senate divided by 10 to 10, requiring the deciding vote of the Vice President, John Adams, who voted against striking out, and in favor of the passage of the bill as it had left the House.[ ] Ten of the Senators had been in the Constitutional Convention, and of them 6 voted that the power of removal was in the President alone. The bill, having passed as it came from the House, was signed by President Washington and became a law. Act July 27, 1789, 1 Stat. 28, c. 4.

The bill was discussed in the House at length and with great ability. The report of it in the Annals of Congress is extended. James Madison was then a leader in the House, as he had been in the convention. His arguments in support of the President's constitutional power of removal independently of congressional provision, and without the consent of the Senate, were masterly, and he carried the House....

First. Mr. Madison insisted that Article II by vesting the executive power in the President was intended to grant to him the power of appointment and removal of executive officers except as thereafter expressly provided in that article. He pointed out that one of the chief purposes of the convention was to separate the legislative from the executive functions. He said: "If there is a principle in our Constitution, indeed in any free Constitution more sacred than another, it is that which separates the legislative, executive and judicial powers. If there is any point in which the separation of the legislative and executive powers ought to be maintained with great caution, it is that which relates to officers and offices." 1 Annals of Congress, 581.

Their union under the Confederation had not worked well, as the members of the convention knew. Montesquieu's view that the maintenance of independence, as between the legislative, the executive and the judicial branches, was a security for the people had their full approval. Madison in the Convention, 2 Farrand, Records of the Federal Convention, 56.... Accordingly the Constitution was so framed as to vest in the Congress all legislative powers therein granted, to vest in the President the executive power, and to vest in one Supreme Court and such inferior courts as Congress might establish the judicial power. From this division on principle, the reasonable construction of the Constitution must be that the branches should be kept separate in all cases in which they were not expressly blended, and the Constitution should be expounded to blend them no more than it affirmatively requires. Madison, 1 Annals of Congress, 497....

The debates in the Constitutional Convention indicated an intention to create a strong executive, and after a controversial discussion the executive power of the government was vested in one person and many of his important functions were specified so as to avoid the humiliating weakness of the Congress during the Revolution and under the Articles of Confederation. 1 Farrand, 66–97.

Mr. Madison and his associates in the discussion in the House dwelt at length upon the necessity there was for construing Article II to give the President the sole power of removal in his responsibility for the conduct of the Executive Branch, and enforced this by emphasizing his duty expressly declared in the third section of the article to "take care that the laws be faithfully executed." Madison, 1 Annals of Congress, 496, 497.

The vesting of the executive power in the President was essentially a grant of the power to execute the laws. But the President alone and unaided could not execute the laws. He must execute them by the assistance of subordinates. This view has since been repeatedly affirmed by this Court.... As he is charged specifically to take care that they be faithfully executed, the reasonable implication, even in the absence of express words, was that as part of his executive power he should select those who were to act for him under his direction in the execution of the laws. The further implication must be, in the absence of any express limitation respecting removals, that as his selection of administrative officers is essential to the execution of the laws by him, so must be his power of removing those for whom he cannot continue to be responsible. Fisher Ames, 1 Annals of Congress, 474. It was urged that the natural meaning of the term "executive power" granted the President included the appointment and removal of executive subordinates. If such appointments and removals were not an exercise of the executive power, what were they? They certainly were not the exercise of legislative or judicial power in government as usually understood.

It is quite true that, in state and colonial governments at the time of the Constitutional Convention, power to make appointments and removals had sometimes been lodged in the Legislatures or in the courts, but such a disposition of it was really vesting part of the executive power in another branch of the government. In the British system, the crown, which was the executive, had the power of appointment and removal of executive officers, and it was natural, therefore, for those who framed our Constitution to regard the words "executive power" as including both. Ex parte Grossman, 267 U.S. 87, 110. Unlike the power of conquest of the British crown, considered and rejected as a precedent for us in Fleming v. Page, 9 How. 603, 618, the association of removal with appointment of executive officers is not incompatible with our republican form of government. . . .

Second. The view of Mr. Madison and his associates was that not only did the grant of executive power to the President in the first section of Article II carry with it the power of removal, but the express recognition of the power of appointment in the second section enforced this view on the well-approved principle of constitutional and statutory construction that the power of removal of executive officers was incident to the power of appointment. It was agreed by the opponents of the bill, with only one or two exceptions, that as a constitutional principle the power of appointment carried with it the power of removal. Roger Sherman, 1 Annals of Congress, 491. This principle as a rule of constitutional and statutory construction, then generally conceded, has been recognized ever since. . . . The reason for the principle is that those in charge of and responsible for administering functions of government, who select their executive subordinates, need in meeting their responsibility to have the power to remove those whom they appoint.

Under section 2 of Article II, however, the power of appointment by the executive is restricted in its exercise by the provision that the Senate, a part of the legislative branch of the government, may check the action of the executive by rejecting the officers he selects. Does this make the Senate part of the removing power? And this, after the whole discussion in the House is read attentively, is the real point which was considered and decided in the negative by the vote already given.

The history of the clause by which the Senate was given a check upon the President's power of appointment makes it clear that it was not prompted by any desire to limit removals. As already pointed out, the important purpose of those who brought about the restriction was to lodge in the Senate, where the small states had equal representation with the larger states, power to prevent the President from making too many appointments from the larger states. Roger Sherman and Oliver Ellsworth, delegates from Connecticut, reported to its Governor: "The equal representation of the states in the Senate and the voice of that branch in the appointment to offices will secure the rights of the lesser as well as of the greater states." 3 Farrand, 99. The formidable opposition to the Senate's veto on the President's power of appointment indicated that in construing its effect, it should not be extended beyond its express application to the matter of appointments. This was made apparent by the remarks of Abraham Baldwin, of Georgia, in the debate in the First Congress. He had been a member of the Constitutional Convention. In opposing the construction which would extend the Senate's power to check appointments to removals from office, he said: "I am well authorized to say that the mingling of the powers of the President and Senate was strongly opposed in the convention which had the honor to submit to the consideration of the United States and the different States the present system for the government of the Union.... This objection was not confined to the walls of the convention; it has been subject of newspaper declamation and perhaps justly so. Ought we not, therefore, to be careful not to extend this unchaste connection any further?" 1 Annals of Congress, 557....

It was pointed out in this great debate that the power of removal, though equally essential to the executive power, is different in its nature from that of appointment. Madison, 1 Annals of Congress, 497 et seq.; Clymer, 1 Annals, 489; Sedgwick, 1 Annals, 522; Ames, 1 Annals, 541, 542; Hartley, 1 Annals, 481. A veto by the Senate—a part of the legislative branch of the government—upon removals is a much greater limitation upon the executive branch, and a much more serious blending of the legislative with the executive, than a rejection of a proposed appointment. It is not to be implied. The rejection of a nominee of the President for a particular office does not greatly embarrass him in the conscientious discharge of his high duties in the selection of those who are to aid him, because the President usually has an ample field from which to select for office, according to his preference, competent and capable men. The Senate has full power to reject newly proposed appointees whenever the President shall remove the incumbents. Such a check enables the Senate to prevent the filling of offices with bad or incompetent men, or with those against whom there is tenable objection.

The power to prevent the removal of an officer who has served under the President is different from the authority to consent to or reject his appointment. When a nomination is made, it may be presumed that the Senate is, or may become, as well advised as to the fitness of the nominee as the President, but in the nature of things the defects in ability or intelligence or loyalty in the administration of the laws of one who has served as an officer under the President, are facts as to which the President, or his trusted subordinates, must be better informed than the

Senate, and the power to remove him may therefore be regarded as confined for very sound and practical reasons, to the governmental authority which has administrative control. The power of removal is incident to the power of appointment, not to the power of advising and consenting to appointment, and when the grant of the executive power is enforced by the express mandate to take care that the laws be faithfully executed, it emphasizes the necessity for including within the executive power as conferred the exclusive power of removal. . . .

The constitutional construction that excludes Congress from legislative power to provide for the removal of superior officers finds support in the second section of Article II. By it the appointment of all officers, whether superior or inferior, by the President is declared to be subject to the advice and consent of the Senate. In the absence of any specific provision to the contrary, the power of appointment to executive office carries with it, as a necessary incident, the power of removal. Whether the Senate must concur in the removal is aside from the point we now are considering. That point is that by the specific constitutional provision for appointment of executive officers with its necessary incident of removal, the power of appointment and removal is clearly provided for by the Constitution, and the legislative power of Congress in respect to both is excluded save by the specific exception as to inferior offices in the clause that follows, *viz.*, is "but the Congress may by law vest the appointment of such inferior officers, as they think proper, in the President alone, in the Courts of Law, or in the Heads of Departments." . . .

A reference of the whole power of removal to general legislation by Congress is quite out of keeping with the plan of government devised by the framers of the Constitution. It could never have been intended to leave to Congress unlimited discretion to vary fundamentally the operation of the great independent Executive Branch of government and thus most seriously to weaken it. It would be a delegation by the convention to Congress of the function of defining the primary boundaries of another of the three great divisions of government. The inclusion of removals of executive officers in the executive power vested in the President by Article II according to its usual definition, and the implication of his power of removal of such officers from the provision of section 2 expressly recognizing in him the power of their appointment, are a much more natural and appropriate source of the removing power.

It is reasonable to suppose also that had it been intended to give to Congress power to regulate or control removals in the manner suggested, it would have been included among the specifically enumerated legislative powers in Article I, or in the specified limitations on the executive power in Article II. The difference between the grant of legislative power under Article I to Congress which is limited to powers therein enumerated, and the more general grant of the executive power to the President under Article II is significant. The fact that the executive power is given in general terms strengthened by specific terms where emphasis is appropriate, and limited by direct expressions where limitation is needed, and that no express limit is placed on the power of removal by the executive is a convincing indication that none was intended....

... Mr. Madison and his associates pointed out with great force the unreasonable character of the view that the convention intended, without express provision, to give to Congress or the Senate, in case of political or other differences, the means of thwarting the executive in the exercise of his great powers and in the bearing of his great responsibility by fastening upon him, as subordinate executive officers, men who by their inefficient service under him, by their lack of loyalty to the service, or by their different views of policy might make his taking care that the laws be faithfully executed most difficult or impossible....

Made responsible under the Constitution for the effective enforcement of the law, the President needs as an indispensable aid to meet it the disciplinary influence upon those who act under him of a reserve power of removal. But it is contended that executive officers appointed by the President with the consent of the Senate are bound by the statutory law, and are not his servants to do his will, and that his obligation to care for the faithful execution of the laws does not authorize him to treat them as such. The degree of guidance in the discharge of their duties that the President may exercise over executive officers varies with the character of their service as prescribed in the law under which they act. The highest and most important duties which his subordinates perform are those in which they act for him. In such cases they are exercising not their own but his discretion. This field is a very large one. It is sometimes described as political. Kendall v. United States, 12 Pet 524, 610. Each head of a department is and must be the President's alter ego in the matters of that department where the President is required by law to exercise authority....

But this is not to say that there are not strong reasons why the President should have a like power to remove his appointees charged with other duties than those above described. The ordinary duties of officers prescribed by statute come under the general administrative control of the President by virtue of the general grant to him of the executive power, and he may properly supervise and guide their construction of the statutes under which they act in order to secure that unitary and uniform execution of the laws which Article II of the Constitution evidently contemplated in vesting general executive power in the President alone. Laws are often passed with specific provision for adoption of regulations by a department or bureau head to make the law workable and effective. The ability and judgment manifested by the official thus empowered, as well as his energy and stimulation of his subordinates, are subjects which the President must consider and supervise in his administrative control. Finding such officers to be negligent and inefficient, the President should have the power to remove them. Of course there may be duties so peculiarly and specifically committed to the discretion of a particular officer as to raise a question whether the President may overrule or revise the officer's interpretation of his statutory duty in a particular instance. Then there may be duties of a quasi-judicial character imposed on executive officers and members of executive tribunals whose decisions after hearing affect interests of individuals, the discharge of which the President cannot in a particular case properly influence or control. But even in such a case he may consider the decision after its rendition as a reason for removing the officer, on the ground that the discretion regularly entrusted to that officer by statute has not been on the whole intelligently or wisely exercised. Otherwise he does not discharge his own constitutional duty of seeing that the laws be faithfully executed.

We have devoted much space to this discussion and decision of the question of the presidential power of removal in the First Congress, not because a congressional conclusion on a constitutional issue is conclusive, but first, because of our agreement with the reasons upon which it was avowedly based; second, because this was the decision of the First Congress on a question of primary importance in the organization of the government made within two years after the Constitutional Convention and within a much shorter time after its ratification; and third, because that Congress numbered among its leaders those who had been members of the convention. . . .

[The Court then discussed at length the subsequent constitutional history of presidential removal. The Court noted that the views that prevailed in 1789 continued to be prevalent until the Reconstruction Congress enacted the Tenure in Office Act in 1867, which limited President Andrew Johnson's power to remove executive officers. Subsequently, the Court observed, the removal issue had been regarded as unresolved.]

What, then, are the elements that enter into our decision of this case? We have, first, a construction of the Constitution made by a Congress which was to provide by legislation for the organization of the government in accord with the Constitution which had just then been adopted, and in which there were, as Representatives and Senators, a considerable number of those who had been members of the convention that framed the Constitution and presented it for ratification. It was the Congress that launched the government. It was the Congress that rounded out the Constitution itself by the proposing of the first 10 amendments which had in effect been promised to the people as a consideration for the ratification. It was the Congress in which Mr. Madison, one of the first in the framing of the Constitution, led also in the organization of the government under it. It was a Congress whose constitutional decisions have always been regarded, as they should be regarded, as of the greatest weight in the interpretation of that fundamental instrument. This construction was followed by the legislative department and the executive department continuously for 73 years, and this although the matter, in the heat of political differences between the executive and the Senate in President Jackson's time, was the subject of bitter controversy, as we have seen. This Court has repeatedly laid down the principle that a contemporaneous legislative exposition of the Constitution, when the founders of our government and framers of our

Constitution were actively participating in public affairs, acquiesced in for a long term of years, fixes the construction to be given its provisions. . . .

For the reasons given, we must therefore hold that the provision of the law of 1876 by which the unrestricted power of removal of first-class postmasters is denied to the President is in violation of the Constitution and invalid. . . .

■ Mr. Justice Holmes, dissenting.

My Brothers McReynolds and Brandeis have discussed the question before us with exhaustive research and I say a few words merely to emphasize my agreement with their conclusion.

The arguments drawn from the executive power of the President, and from his duty to appoint officers of the United States (when Congress does not vest the appointment elsewhere), to take care that the laws be faithfully executed, and to commission all officers of the United States, seem to me spider's webs inadequate to control the dominant facts.

We have to deal with an office that owes its existence to Congress and that Congress may abolish tomorrow. Its duration and the pay attached to it while it lasts depend on Congress alone. Congress alone confers on the President the power to appoint to it and at any time may transfer the power to other hands. With such power over its own creation, I have no more trouble in believing that Congress has power to prescribe a term of life for it free from any interference than I have in accepting the undoubted power of Congress to decree its end. I have equally little trouble in accepting its power to prolong the tenure of an incumbent until Congress or the Senate shall have assented to his removal. The duty of the President to see that the laws be executed is a duty that does not go beyond the laws or require him to achieve more than Congress sees fit to leave within his power.

■ Mr. Justice McReynolds, dissenting.

. . . May the President oust at will all postmasters appointed with the Senate's consent for definite terms under an act which inhibits removal without consent of that body? May he approve a statute which creates an inferior office and prescribes restrictions on removal, appoint an incumbent, and then remove without regard to the restrictions? Has he power to appoint to an inferior office for a definite term under an act which prohibits removal except as therein specified, and then arbitrarily dismiss the incumbent and deprive him of the emoluments? I think there is no such power. Certainly it is not given by any plain words of the Constitution; and the argument advanced to establish it seems to me forced and unsubstantial. . . .

The long struggle for . . . legislation designed to insure some security of official tenure ought not to be forgotten. Again and again Congress has enacted statutes prescribing restrictions on removals, and by approving them many Presidents have affirmed its power therein.

The following are some of the officers who have been or may be appointed with consent of the Senate under such restricting statutes:

Members of the Interstate Commerce Commission, Board of General Appraisers, Federal Reserve Board, Federal Trade Commission, Tariff

Commission, Shipping Board, Federal Farm Loan Board, Railroad Labor Board; officers of the Army and Navy; Comptroller General; Postmaster General and his assistants; Postmasters of the first, second, and third classes; judge of the United States Court for China; judges of the Court of Claims, established in 1855, the judges to serve "during good behavior"; judges of territorial (statutory) courts; judges of the Supreme Court and Court of Appeals for the District of Columbia (statutory courts), appointed to serve "during good behavior." . . .

Every one of these officers, we are now told in effect, holds his place subject to the President's pleasure or caprice. . . .

. . . Nothing short of language clear beyond serious disputation should be held to clothe the President with authority wholly beyond congressional control arbitrarily to dismiss every officer whom he appoints except a few judges. There are no such words in the Constitution, and the asserted inference conflicts with the heretofore accepted theory that this government is one of carefully enumerated powers under an intelligible charter. . . .

The Legislature may create post offices and prescribe qualifications, duties, compensation, and term. And it may protect the incumbent in the enjoyment of his term unless in some way restrained therefrom. The real question, therefore, comes to this: Does any constitutional provision definitely limit the otherwise plenary power of Congress over postmasters, when they are appointed by the President with the consent of the Senate? The question is not the much-mooted one whether the Senate is part of the appointing power under the Constitution and therefore must participate in removals. . . .

[Justice McReynolds wrote at length concerning the Court's reading of the history of presidential removal power. As to the decision of 1789, Justice McReynolds concluded that of the 24 Members of the House of Representatives who spoke about the removal of the Secretary of Foreign Affairs, "only nine members said anything which tends to support the present contention, and fifteen emphatically opposed it." In addition, he cited a number of early instances in the Republic's history where Congress limited the removability of federal officers (usually in the Territories).]

If the framers of the Constitution had intended "the executive power," in Article II, Sec. 1, to include all power of an executive nature, they would not have added the carefully defined grants of Sec. 2. They were scholarly men, and it exceeds belief "that the known advocates in the convention for a jealous grant and cautious definition of federal powers should have silently permitted the introduction of words and phrases in a sense rendering fruitless the restrictions and definitions elaborated by them." Why say, the President shall be commander-in-chief; may require opinions in writing of the principal officers in each of the executive departments; shall have power to grant reprieves and pardons; shall give information to Congress concerning the state of the union; shall receive ambassadors; shall take care that the laws be faithfully executed—if all of these things and more had already been vested in him by the general words? The Constitution is exact in statement. . . . That the general words of a grant are limited, when followed by those of special import is an established canon; and an accurate writer would hardly think of emphasizing a general grant by adding special and narrower ones without explanation. . . .

If it be admitted that the Constitution by direct grant vests the President with all executive power, it does not follow that he can proceed in defiance of congressional action. Congress, by clear language, is empowered to make all laws necessary and proper for carrying into execution powers vested in him. Here he was authorized only to appoint an officer of a certain kind, for a certain period, removable only in a certain way. He undertook to proceed under the law so far as agreeable, but repudiated the remainder. I submit that no warrant can be found for such conduct....

... The federal Constitution is an instrument of exact expression. Those who maintain that Art. II, Sec. 1, was intended as a grant of every power of executive nature not specifically qualified or denied, must show that the term "executive power" had some definite and commonly accepted meaning in 1787. This court has declared that it did not include all powers exercised by the King of England; and, considering the history of the period, none can say that it had then (or afterwards) any commonly accepted and practical definition. If any one of the descriptions of "executive power" known in 1787 had been substituted for it, the whole plan would have failed....

■ Mr. Justice Brandeis, dissenting.

... It is ... argued that the clauses in Article II, § 3, of the Constitution, which declare that the President "shall take Care that the Laws be faithfully executed, and shall Commission all the Officers of the United States" imply a grant to the President of the alleged uncontrollable power of removal. I do not find in either clause anything which supports this claim. The provision that the President "shall Commission all the Officers of the United States" clearly bears no such implication. Nor can it be spelled out of the direction that "he shall take Care that the Laws be faithfully executed." There is no express grant to the President of incidental powers resembling those conferred upon Congress by clause 18 of Article I, § 8. A power implied on the ground that it is inherent in the executive, must, according to established principles of constitutional construction, be limited to "the least possible power adequate to the end proposed." ...

To imply a grant to the President of the uncontrollable power of removal from statutory inferior executive offices involves an unnecessary and indefensible limitation upon the constitutional power of Congress to fix the tenure of the inferior statutory offices.... In none of the original 13 states did the chief executive possess such power at the time of the adoption of the federal Constitution. In none of the 48 states has such power been conferred at any time since by a state Constitution,[ ] with a single possible exception....

The practice of Congress to control the exercise of the executive power of removal from inferior offices is evidenced by many statutes which restrict it in many ways besides the removal clause here in question. Each of these restrictive statutes became law with the approval of the President.

The historical data submitted present a legislative practice, established by concurrent affirmative action of Congress and the President, to make consent of the Senate a condition of removal from statutory inferior, civil, executive offices to which the appointment is made for a fixed term by the President with such consent. They show that the practice has existed, without interruption, continuously for the last 58 years; that throughout this period, it has governed a great majority of all such offices; that the legislation applying the removal clause specifically to the office of postmaster was enacted more than half a century ago; and that recently the practice has, with the President's approval, been extended to several newly created offices. The data show further that the insertion of the removal clause in acts creating inferior civil offices with fixed tenures is part of the broader legislative practice, which has prevailed since the formation of our government, to restrict or regulate in many ways both removal from and nomination to such offices. A persistent legislative practice which involves a delimitation of the respective powers of Congress and the President, and which has been so established and maintained, should be deemed tantamount to judicial construction, in the absence of any decision by any court to the contrary....

Nor does the debate [over the decision of 1789] show that the majority of those then in Congress thought that the President had the uncontrollable power of removal. The Senators divided equally in their votes. As to their individual views we lack knowledge; for the debate was secret. In the House only 24 of the 54 members voting took part in the debate. Of the 24, only 6 appear to have held the opinion that the President possessed the uncontrollable power of removal....

The separation of the powers of government did not make each branch completely autonomous. It left each in some measure, dependent upon the others, as it left to each power to exercise, in some respects, functions in their nature executive, legislative and judicial. Obviously the President cannot secure full execution of the laws, if Congress denies to him adequate means of doing so. Full execution may be defeated because Congress declines to create offices indispensable for that purpose. Or because Congress, having created the office, declines to make the indispensable appropriation; or because Congress, having both created the office and made the appropriation, prevents, by restrictions which it imposes, the appointment of officials who in quality and character are indispensable to the efficient execution of the law. If, in any such way, adequate means are denied to the President, the fault will lie with Congress....

Checks and balances were established in order that this should be "a government of laws and not of men." ... The doctrine of the separation of powers was adopted by the convention of 1787, not to promote efficiency but to preclude the exercise of arbitrary power. The purpose was not to avoid friction, but, by means of the inevitable friction incident to the distribution of the governmental powers among three departments, to save the people from autocracy....

***1. Is a Plenary Removal Power Implicit in the President's Executive Power?***—The Constitution contains no provision that expressly addresses the President's power to remove executive officers. Yet *Myers* derived a very strong and sweeping presidential removal power from the Constitution, relying principally on structural inferences from two closely related provisions. First, Chief Justice Taft observed that Article II explicitly vests the "executive Power" in the President. Chief Justice Taft reasoned that "the President alone and unaided could not execute the laws"; rather, the President must rely on subordinates. Thus, officers wielding the executive power are acting as agents of, or surrogates for, the President. The President must therefore have plenary authority to remove such officials in order to wield the executive power effectively. In the same vein, Chief Justice Taft emphasized that Article II, § 3 provides that the President "shall take Care that the Laws be faithfully executed," And he inferred from this constitutional duty that the President must have the "power of removing those for whom he cannot continue to be responsible." These structural inferences from the constitutional text are also connected to a particular vision of what the Constitution, and the office of the President in particular, is meant to accomplish. According to this vision, the concentration of all executive power in the President facilitates democratic accountability (because voters know whom to blame or credit for the conduct of the administration), promotes coherence and energy in the execution of the laws, and ensures an executive branch that is strong enough to provide a counterweight to Congress.

Those structural and pragmatic arguments in favor of plenary presidential removal authority are powerful, but there are some countervailing considerations. With respect to the structural cues from the constitutional text, some constitutional provisions suggest that the President's removal power may be more limited. For example, Article II authorizes the President to "require the Opinion, in writing, of the Principal Officer in each of the executive Departments, relating to the Duties of their respective Offices." U.S. CONST. art. II, § 2, cl. 1. Some commentators have questioned why the founders would bother to insert such a seemingly trivial power if the President had the authority to remove the officers covered by the Opinions Clause. *See, e.g.*, Lawrence Lessig & Cass R. Sunstein, *The President and the Administration*, 94 COLUM. L. REV. 1, 32 (1994). The Necessary and Proper Clause, moreover, looms as a potential source of congressional authority to regulate removal. *See, e.g., id.* at 67; *see also* Peter M. Shane, *Independent Policymaking and Presidential Power: A Constitutional Analysis*, 57 GEO. WASH. L. REV. 596, 611 (1989). Does the Constitution's silence on the removal power imply that this is one of those powers for which Congress may make any law "necessary and proper" for carrying into execution "other Powers vested by [the] Constitution in the Government of the United States," including the executive power vested in the President?

One can, of course, contest these objections by arguing that the structural inferences one can draw from the Article II Vesting Clause and Take Care Clause are strong enough to overcome these countervailing pieces of structural evidence. Another way one might seek to resolve the issue in favor of the *Myers* position is by leaning more heavily on the functionalist claim that a plenary presidential removal power is more consistent with the overall purposes and goals of the constitutional scheme. In their important article on this subject, Professors Lawrence Lessig and Cass Sunstein opt for this latter approach; they argue that although the original understanding of Article II did not encompass illimitable presidential removal power, subsequent developments—including the rise of broad delegations of discretionary lawmaking power to administrative agencies—favor the conclusion that contemporary courts should infer from Article II a plenary presidential removal power. *See* Lessig & Sunstein, *supra*, at 93–106. More specifically, they argue that broad presidential removal power may be necessary to serve the constitutional goals of coordination, accountability, and efficiency in government, as well as checking the influence of factions. *See id.* Others, including some who disagree with Lessig and Sunstein's conclusions regarding the original understanding of the Constitution, agree that plenary presidential removal power is required to serve these fundamental constitutional commitments. *See, e.g.*, Steven G. Calabresi, *Some Normative Arguments for the Unitary Executive*, 48 Ark. L. Rev. 23 (1994).

Consider three possible responses to this line of argument. One is to deny the legitimacy of an interpretive approach that seeks to ground constitutional jurisprudence in a functionalist analysis of what rules would best serve constitutional "commitments" or "values" (defined at a high level of generality) under present circumstances, rather than in a close analysis of how the text and structure would have been understood by those who framed and ratified the document. Second, one might adopt something like Lessig and Sunstein's methodology but conclude that the rise of the modern administrative state makes it *more* dangerous to give the President unconstrained authority to remove agency officials. *See* Abner S. Greene, *Checks and Balances in an Era of Presidential Lawmaking*, 61 U. Chi. L. Rev. 123, 126–28 (1994). On this view, while the founding generation viewed the legislature as the main threat to liberty, and so sought to bolster the President as a counterweight, under modern conditions the ever-growing power of the executive branch—the rise of the so-called "imperial presidency"—means that the President is the greater threat. *See* Arthur M. Schlesinger, Jr., The Imperial Presidency (1973). If so, then allowing Congress to limit presidential removal power may recapture some of the diffusion of power that was intended under the constitutional system of checks and balances. *See* Martin S. Flaherty, *The Most Dangerous Branch*, 105 Yale L.J. 1725 (1996).

Third, while it is usually reasonable to assume that the *President*'s interests are best-served by an unlimited removal power, the President may sometimes view limitations on presidential removal power as *facilitating*, rather than *impeding*, the President's policy objectives. For example, limitations on the President's removal power over an agency's principal officers might influence the amount of discretion that Congress is willing to confer on that agency. If Congress knows that the agency is subject to direct presidential control (because of the President's unlimited removal authority), Congress may be reluctant to delegate substantial authority to that agency; this reluctance to delegate might make both Congress and the President worse off. *See* Nolan McCarty, *The Appointments Dilemma*, 48 Am. J. Pol. Sci. 413 (2004). The President might also find that limitations on *ex post* control of agency officials enable the executive branch to make a credible commitment to certain policies. The classic example here is monetary policy: The President may recognize that optimal monetary policy (under most circumstances) entails a commitment to a "tight money" policy that keeps inflation low, but there may be short-term political pressure to stimulate the economy through an expansionary monetary policy, even if in the long run it will increase inflation and harm the economy's long-term health. A familiar institutional solution to this problem is for the government to delegate substantial authority over monetary policy to an independent central bank. *See* Finn E. Kydland & Edward C. Prescott, *Rules Rather Than Discretion: The Inconsistency of Optimal Plans*, 85 J. Pol. Econ. 473 (1977). The President, moreover, might sometimes benefit politically from the existence of independent commissions, as they may remove certain politically contentious issues from the President's agenda. *See* Michael A. Fitts, *The Paradox of Power in the Modern State: Why a Unitary, Centralized Presidency May Not Exhibit Effective or Legitimate Leadership*, 144 U. Pa. L. Rev. 827, 898–99 (1996).

Do these possibilities undermine the arguments that the President's constitutional responsibility to "take care" that the laws be faithfully executed implies a plenary removal power? Might one reasonably respond that, independent of the President's view as to the desirability of limits on the removal power, the Constitution vests executive power solely in the President in order to ensure that voters know exactly whom to credit or blame for decisions taken by executive branch officials? In addition, if removal restrictions benefit the President, in part, by encouraging Congress to make broader delegations to agencies over which he or she has at least some influence or control, might that outcome itself undermine constitutional values implicit in the nondelegation doctrine? Do such considerations militate in favor of a plenary removal power regardless of whether the President wants that power or not?

**2. *Historical Understandings*—**Many constitutional interpreters would argue that the place to start, when trying to determine whether the President's executive power includes a plenary removal power despite the absence of any express provision on removal in the text, is with the historical understanding of the removal power. The historical debate concerning the removal question is too wide-ranging and elaborate to summarize in full. *See, e.g.,* Steven G. Calabresi & Christopher S. Yoo, The Unitary Executive: Presidential Power from Washington to Bush (2008); Steven G. Calabresi & Saikrishna B. Prakash, *The President's Power to Execute the Laws,* 104 Yale L.J. 541 (1994); Edward S. Corwin, *Tenure of Office and the Removal Power under the Constitution,* 27 Colum. L. Rev. 353 (1927); Martin S. Flaherty, *The Most Dangerous Branch,* 105 Yale L.J. 1725 (1996); Lawrence Lessig & Cass R. Sunstein, *The President and the Administration,* 94 Colum. L. Rev. 1 (1994); Saikrishna Prakash, *New Light on the Decision of 1789,* 91 Cornell L. Rev. 1021 (2006); Peter L. Strauss, *The Place of Agencies in Government: Separation of Powers and the Fourth Branch,* 84 Colum. L. Rev. 573, 596–625 (1984). In this brief note we limit ourselves to introducing some of the more significant pieces of historical evidence that *Myers* employed in interpreting the constitutional structure.

    ***a.  English common law background.*** Chief Justice Taft's opinion relied on the related premises that "[i]n the British system, the crown, which was the executive, had the power of appointment and removal of executive officers, and [that] it was natural, therefore, for those who framed our Constitution to regard the words 'executive power' as including both." This conclusion built on the frequently used canon of interpretation holding that when the Constitution borrows technical concepts familiar to the English system, it is reasonable to assume that the founders—who began life as English subjects—would have understood those concepts in their common law sense. *See, e.g.,* United States v. Williams, 504 U.S. 36, 51 (1992); Ex parte Grossman, 267 U.S. 87, 110 (1925). Yet the U.S. Constitution differs in material respects from English government, and the Supreme Court has made clear in other contexts that the English common law tradition sometimes will not fit with American constitutional assumptions. *See, e.g.,* Clinton v. Jones, 520 U.S. 681, 697 n.24 (1997). In this regard, what does one make of the fact that the Appointments Clause explicitly deviates from the English tradition by conditioning presidential appointments upon the consent of the Senate, rather than leaving the matter to the executive alone? No less prominent a figure than Alexander Hamilton believed that because the power of removal typically ran with the power of appointment at common law, conditioning the appointment power similarly qualified the removal power. *See* The Federalist No. 77, at 458–63 (Alexander Hamilton) (Clinton Rossiter ed., 1961). Chief Justice Taft, in contrast, argued that the contours of the Appointments Clause demonstrate that when the founders wished to deviate from the English practice, they did so expressly; hence, conditioning the traditional executive prerogative of appointment upon advice and consent, if anything, revealed an intention to leave the related executive prerogative of removal unqualified.

    How would one decide between these competing understandings of the constitutional history? If the evidence suggests that the founders generally took the common law prerogatives of the executive as their starting point for understanding executive power, but then modified, divided, and reassigned those prerogatives where appropriate, should the Court presume that the President retained whatever was not modified or reallocated? *See, e.g.,* 1 William Winslow Crosskey, Politics and the Constitution in the

HISTORY OF THE UNITED STATES 428 (1953); Antonin Scalia, *Originalism: The Lesser Evil*, 57 U. CINN. L. REV. 849, 859–60 (1989). *But see* Curtis A. Bradley & Martin S. Flaherty, *Executive Power Essentialism and Foreign Affairs*, 102 MICH. L. REV. 545, 592–626 (2003) (citing statements in the Philadelphia Convention and the ratifying debates that indicate the founders did not want to replicate in the President the broad and ill-defined prerogatives of the crown). Should the Court fall back on the presumption that Congress has the power to establish the government's institutional structure unless its decisions are clearly unconstitutional? In his famous treatment of the question, Professor Edward Corwin suggested that the crown possessed appointment and removal authority at common law "as an outgrowth" of the "much wider prerogative" to create the offices themselves. *See* Corwin, *supra*, at 383. On that assumption, does the Constitution's vesting of power to create federal agencies in *Congress* under the Necessary and Proper Clause suggest a transfer of the authority over appointment or removal as well, as long as there is no express statement to the contrary?

  ***b. Contemporaneous state practice.*** Professor Martin Flaherty has argued that the New York and Massachusetts Constitutions served as important models for the U.S. Constitution, and that neither of those state charters embraced a strong version of gubernatorial control over executive officers. *See* Martin S. Flaherty, *The Most Dangerous Branch*, 105 YALE L.J. 1725, 1768–69, 1776–77 (1996). Indeed, "the clause requiring the President to 'take care that the laws be faithfully executed' was taken almost verbatim from the New York constitution of 1777, which none the less gave the executive of that state very little voice in either appointments or removals." Corwin, *supra*, at 385. Chief Justice Taft acknowledged that state constitutional practice did not favor his position, but he argued that where state or colonial governments vested "power to make appointments and removals . . . in the Legislatures or in the courts," that arrangement "was really vesting part of the executive power in another branch of the government." Is that a satisfying response to the fact that state practice suggested anything but a uniform view of where the power of appointment and removal should lie? How much weight, if any, should someone trying to understand the *federal* constitutional structure place on contemporaneous *state* practice, given the fact that much of the federal structure represented a reaction *against* early state practices? *See* GORDON WOOD, THE CREATION OF THE AMERICAN REPUBLIC, 1776–1787, at 463–67 (1969).

  ***c. Early legislation.*** Much of Chief Justice Taft's opinion turns on the conclusion that in creating the Department of Foreign Affairs, the First Congress determined that the President possesses illimitable removal power over executive officers. In crediting the First Congress's apparent judgment in the so-called "Decision of 1789," Chief Justice Taft wrote in bold terms that "[t]his court has repeatedly laid down the principle that a contemporaneous legislative exposition of the Constitution, when the founders of our government and framers of our Constitution were actively participating in public affairs, acquiesced in for a long term of years, fixes the construction to be given its provisions." *See also* Ex Parte Hennen, 38

U.S. (13 Pet.) 230, 259 (1839). But for Chief Justice Taft to be able to say that Congress resolved the constitutional question of illimitable removal power in the Decision of 1789, he had to be able to find that Congress squarely resolved that precise issue. Critiquing Chief Justice Taft's opinion, Professor Corwin had this to say about the debate leading up to the Decision of 1789:

> Three fairly equal parties eventually disclosed themselves: first, those who believed that the power of removal was the President's alone by the intention of the Constitution; secondly, those who believed, on like grounds, that it belonged to the President acting by and with the advice and consent of the Senate; thirdly, those who held that the Constitution had not settled the question, and that, therefore, it remained for Congress to settle it by virtue of its powers under the "necessary and proper" clause. A fourth group, comprising apparently only two or three members, were of opinion that impeachment was the only constitutional method of removal.

Edward S. Corwin, *Tenure of Office and the Removal Power under the Constitution*, 27 COLUM. L. REV. 352, 361 (1927). According to this line of argument, Representative Benson managed to exploit these internal divisions to produce a result that *appeared* to favor the view that the President's removal power was absolute. *See* John F. Manning, *The Independent Counsel Statute*: *Reading "Good Cause" in Light of Article II*, 83 MINN. L. REV. 1285, 1323–25 (1999). He did this by first making a motion to add language to the bill creating the Foreign Affairs Department that would *imply* the existence of a plenary presidential removal power—in particular, by designating an officer to take custody of the department's records "whenever the principal officer shall be removed from office by the President." He then made a second motion to delete the *express* grant of removal power present in the original bill. Professor David Currie explains the political dynamic as follows:

> For better or worse, the two halves of Benson's proposal were put to the House separately. The members first voted thirty to eighteen [in favor of Benson's first motion]. All those who had spoken in favor of presidential removal voted aye, whether they thought that Article II settled the question or left the matter to Congress. The House then voted thirty-one to nineteen [in favor of Benson's second motion] to drop the phrase "to be removable by the President." The numbers were virtually identical, but it was a different majority. For on this question, the proponents of Article II power prevailed only because they were joined by a substantial number of members who had opposed presidential removal altogether.
>
> The original coalition was patched up again when it came time for the House to pass the amended bill.... Thus it was the considered judgment of the majority in both Houses that the President could remove the Secretary of Foreign Affairs, *but there was no consensus as to whether he got that authority from Congress or from the Constitution itself.*

David P. Currie, The Constitution in Congress: The Federalist Period, 1789–1801, at 40–41 (1997) (emphasis added); *see also* Charles C. Thach, Jr., The Creation of the Presidency 1775–1789, at 154–55 (1969). *But see* Saikrishna Prakash, *New Light on the Decision of 1789*, 91 Cornell L. Rev. 1021, 1047–67 (2006) (arguing that a majority of the House agreed that the Constitution gave the President plenary removal power, and that the faction that voted against Benson's second amendment but for the amended bill did so for unrelated tactical or symbolic reasons).

Recall Chapter One's discussion of Condorcet's Paradox, in which a legislative body choosing among three options (say, A, B, and C) may exhibit apparently incoherent collective preferences (for example, preferring A to B to C to A). (*See* pp. 173–176, *supra*.) Did Representative Benson's two-step motion exploit such a situation? If it did, how much does the outcome tell us about how the First Congress collectively understood the Constitution? Recall, moreover, that however difficult it may be to interpret the meaning of the House vote, the Senate split evenly on the removal question, with no meaningful record explaining why particular Senators voted as they did. More generally, if one believes that the legislative process is opaque, complex, path-dependent, and that its outcomes often turn on agenda control and logrolling, how reliable is it for modern interpreters to treat an Act of Congress, such as the Decision of 1789, as a reasoned and authoritative exposition of the Constitution? *See, e.g.*, Note, *Should the Supreme Court Presume that Congress Acts Constitutionally? The Role of the Canon of Avoidance and Reliance on Early Legislative Practice in Constitutional Interpretation*, 116 Harv. L. Rev. 1798 (2003).

Quite apart from the concerns about how to read the Decision of 1789 itself, does it make sense to focus exclusively on one cabinet department in understanding the way the founders conceived of executive power? Professors Lessig and Sunstein argue that Congress differentiated among various departments of the government:

> Congress established the Departments of Foreign Affairs and War as "executive departments," with little detail, and with secretaries who were obligated to "perform and execute such duties as shall from time to time be enjoined on or intrusted to them by the President of the United States." But the treatment of the Department of the Treasury was wholly different. Unlike with Foreign Affairs and War, the enacting Congress (1) did not denominate Treasury an "executive department," (2) did specify in detail the offices and functions of Treasury, (3) did impose on the Treasurer specific duties, and (4) did shield the Comptroller (an office within Treasury) from presidential direction.

Lessig & Sunstein, *supra*, at 27. Under this view, officials who exercised powers that were at the core of the President's authority (foreign affairs and military) were considered to be the President's agents, while officials whose duties were more closely related to implementing legislative programs might not be. *But see* Prakash, *supra*, at 1064–65 (contesting Lessig and Sunstein's claims and arguing that Congress in fact debated and endorsed the President's inherent constitutional authority to remove the

Treasury Secretary). Should Chief Justice Taft have looked at the evidence from other departments before relying on the Decision of 1789? Does the evidence cited by Professors Lessig and Sunstein refute Chief Justice Taft's position, or merely suggest that the story is more complicated than he lets on?

### c.   The Rise of the Independent Agency

---

## Humphrey's Executor v. United States

Supreme Court of the United States
295 U.S. 602 (1935)

■ Mr. Justice Sutherland delivered the opinion of the Court.

Plaintiff brought suit in the Court of Claims against the United States to recover a sum of money alleged to be due the deceased for salary as a Federal Trade Commissioner from October 8, 1933, when the President undertook to remove him from office, to the time of his death on February 14, 1934.... The material facts which give rise to the questions are as follows:

William E. Humphrey, the decedent, on December 10, 1931, was nominated by President Hoover to [be] ... a member of the Federal Trade Commission, and was confirmed by the United States Senate. He was duly commissioned for a term of seven years, expiring September 25, 1938; and, after taking the required oath of office, entered upon his duties. On July 25, 1933, President Roosevelt addressed a letter to the commissioner asking for his resignation, on the ground "that the aims and purposes of the Administration with respect to the work of the Commission can be carried out most effectively with personnel of my own selection," but disclaiming any reflection upon the commissioner personally or upon his services. The commissioner replied, asking time to consult his friends. After some further correspondence upon the subject, the President on August 31, 1933, wrote the commissioner expressing the hope that the resignation would be forthcoming, and saying: "You will, I know, realize that I do not feel that your mind and my mind go along together on either the policies or the administering of the Federal Trade Commission, and, frankly, I think it is best for the people of this country that I should have a full confidence."

The commissioner declined to resign; and on October 7, 1933, the President wrote him: "Effective as of this date you are hereby removed from the office of Commissioner of the Federal Trade Commission."

Humphrey never acquiesced in this action, but continued thereafter to insist that he was still a member of the commission, entitled to perform its duties and receive the compensation provided by law at the rate of $10,000 per annum. Upon these and other facts ..., the following questions are certified:

"1. Do the provisions of section 1 of the Federal Trade Commission Act, stating that 'any commissioner may be removed by the President for inefficiency, neglect of duty, or malfeasance in office', restrict or limit the power of the President to remove a commissioner except upon one or more of the causes named?

"If the foregoing question is answered in the affirmative, then—

"2. If the power of the President to remove a commissioner is restricted or limited as shown by the foregoing interrogatory and the answer made thereto, is such a restriction or limitation valid under the Constitution of the United States?"

The Federal Trade Commission Act, c. 311, 38 Stat. 717, 718, §§ 1, 2, 15 U.S.C. §§ 41, 42, creates a commission of five members to be appointed by the President by and with the advice and consent of the Senate, and § 1 provides: "Not more than three of the commissioners shall be members of the same political party. The first commissioners appointed shall continue in office for terms of three, four, five, six, and seven years, respectively, from the date of the taking effect of this Act [September 26, 1914], the term of each to be designated by the President, but their successors shall be appointed for terms of seven years, except that any person chosen to fill a vacancy shall be appointed only for the unexpired term of the commissioner whom he shall succeed. The commission shall choose a chairman from its own membership. No commissioner shall engage in any other business, vocation, or employment. Any commissioner may be removed by the President for inefficiency, neglect of duty, or malfeasance in office...."

Section 5 of the act in part provides:

"That unfair methods of competition in commerce are declared unlawful.

"The commission is empowered and directed to prevent persons, partnerships, or corporations, except banks, and common carriers subject to the Acts to regulate commerce, from using unfair methods of competition in commerce."

. . .

Section 6, among other things, gives the commission wide powers of investigation in respect of certain corporations subject to the act, and in respect of other matters, upon which it must report to Congress with recommendations. Many such investigations have been made, and some have served as the basis of congressional legislation.

Section 7 provides that: "In any suit in equity brought by or under the direction of the Attorney General as provided in the antitrust Acts, the court may, upon the conclusion of the testimony therein, if it shall be then of opinion that the complainant is entitled to relief, refer said suit to the commission, as a master in chancery, to ascertain and report an appropriate form of decree therein. The commission shall proceed upon such notice to the parties and under such rules of procedure as the court may prescribe, and upon the coming in of such report such exceptions may be filed and such proceedings had in relation thereto as upon the report of a master in other equity causes, but the court may adopt or reject such report, in whole or in part, and enter such decree as the nature of the case may in its judgment require."

*First.* The question first to be considered is whether, by the provisions of § 1 of the Federal Trade Commission Act already quoted, the President's power is limited to removal for the specific causes enumerated therein. . . .

. . . [T]he language of the act, the legislative reports, and the general purposes of the legislation as reflected by the debates, all combine to demonstrate the congressional intent to create a body of experts who shall gain experience by length of service; a body which shall be independent of executive authority—except in its selection—and free to exercise its judgment without the leave or hindrance of any other official or any department of the government. To the accomplishment of these purposes, it is clear that Congress was of opinion that length and certainty of tenure would vitally contribute. And to hold that, nevertheless, the members of the commission continue in office at the mere will of the President, might be to thwart, in large measure, the very ends which Congress sought to realize by definitely fixing the term of office.

We conclude that the intent of the act is to limit the executive power of removal to the causes enumerated, the existence of none of which is claimed here; and we pass to the second question.

*Second.* To support its contention that the removal provision of § 1, as we have just construed it, is an unconstitutional interference with the executive power of the President, the government's chief reliance is Myers v. United States, 272 U.S. 52. That case has been so recently decided, and the prevailing and dissenting opinions so fully review the general subject of the power of executive removal, that further discussion would add little of value to the wealth of material there collected. These opinions examine at length the historical, legislative, and judicial data bearing upon the question, beginning with what is called "the decision of 1789" in the first Congress and coming down almost to the day when the opinions were delivered. They occupy 243 pages of the volume in which they are printed. Nevertheless, the narrow point actually decided was only that the President had power to remove a postmaster of the first class, without the advice and consent of the Senate as required by act of Congress. In the course of the opinion of the court, expressions occur which tend to sustain the government's contention, but these are beyond the point involved and, therefore, do not come within the rule of stare decisis. In so far as they are out of harmony with the views here set forth, these expressions are disapproved. . . .

The office of a postmaster is so essentially unlike the office now involved that the decision in the *Myers* Case cannot be accepted as controlling our decision here. A postmaster is an executive officer restricted to the performance of executive functions. He is charged with no duty at all related to either the legislative or judicial power. The actual decision in the

*Myers* Case finds support in the theory that such an officer is merely one of the units in the executive department and, hence, inherently subject to the exclusive and illimitable power of removal by the Chief Executive, whose subordinate and aid he is. Putting aside dicta, which may be followed if sufficiently persuasive but which are not controlling, the necessary reach of the decision goes far enough to include all purely executive officers. It goes no farther; much less does it include an officer who occupies no place in the executive department and who exercises no part of the executive power vested by the Constitution in the President.

The Federal Trade Commission is an administrative body created by Congress to carry into effect legislative policies embodied in the statute in accordance with the legislative standard therein prescribed, and to perform other specified duties as a legislative or as a judicial aid. Such a body cannot in any proper sense be characterized as an arm or an eye of the executive. Its duties are performed without executive leave and, in the contemplation of the statute, must be free from executive control. In administering the provisions of the statute in respect of "unfair methods of competition"—that is to say, in filling in and administering the details embodied by that general standard—the commission acts in part quasi-legislatively and in part quasi-judicially. In making investigations and reports thereon for the information of Congress under § 6, in aid of the legislative power, it acts as a legislative agency. Under § 7, which authorizes the commission to act as a master in chancery under rules prescribed by the court, it acts as an agency of the judiciary. To the extent that it exercises any executive function, as distinguished from executive power in the constitutional sense, it does so in the discharge and effectuation of its quasi-legislative or quasi-judicial powers, or as an agency of the legislative or judicial departments of the government.

If Congress is without authority to prescribe causes for removal of members of the trade commission and limit executive power of removal accordingly, that power at once becomes practically all-inclusive in respect of civil officers with the exception of the judiciary provided for by the Constitution. The Solicitor General, at the bar, apparently recognizing this to be true, with commendable candor, agreed that his view in respect of the removability of members of the Federal Trade Commission necessitated a like view in respect of the Interstate Commerce Commission and the Court of Claims. We are thus confronted with the serious question whether not only the members of these quasi-legislative and quasi-judicial bodies, but the judges of the legislative Court of Claims, exercising judicial power ... continue in office only at the pleasure of the President.

We think it plain under the Constitution that illimitable power of removal is not possessed by the President in respect of officers of the character of those just named. The authority of Congress, in creating quasi-legislative or quasi-judicial agencies, to require them to act in discharge of their duties independently of executive control cannot well be doubted; and that authority includes, as an appropriate incident, power to fix the period during which they shall continue, and to forbid their removal except for cause in the meantime. For it is quite evident that one who holds his office only during the pleasure of another, cannot be depended upon to maintain an attitude of independence against the latter's will.

The fundamental necessity of maintaining each of the three general departments of government entirely free from the control or coercive influence, direct or indirect, of either of the others, has often been stressed and is hardly open to serious question. So much is implied in the very fact of the separation of the powers of these departments by the Constitution; and in the rule which recognizes their essential coequality. The sound application of a principle that makes one master in his own house precludes him from imposing his control in the house of another who is master there. . . .

The power of removal here claimed for the President falls within this principle, since its coercive influence threatens the independence of a commission, which is not only wholly disconnected from the executive department, but which, as already fully appears, was created by Congress as a means of carrying into operation legislative and judicial powers, and as an agency of the legislative and judicial departments.

In the light of the question now under consideration, we have re-examined the precedents referred to in the *Myers* Case, and find nothing in them to justify a conclusion contrary to that which we have reached. The so-called "decision of 1789" had relation to a bill proposed by Mr. Madison to establish an executive Department of Foreign Affairs. The bill provided that the principal officer was "to be removable from office by the President of the United States." This clause was changed to read "whenever the principal officer shall be removed from office by the President of the United States," certain things should follow, thereby, in connection with the debates, recognizing and confirming, as the court thought in the Myers Case, the sole power of the President in the matter. We shall not discuss the subject further, . . . except to say that the office under consideration by Congress was not only purely executive, but the officer one who was responsible to the President, and to him alone, in a very definite sense. A reading of the debates shows that the President's illimitable power of removal was not considered in respect of other than executive officers. And it is pertinent to observe that when, at a later time, the tenure of office for the Comptroller of the Treasury was under consideration, Mr. Madison quite evidently thought that, since the duties of that office were not purely of an executive nature but partook of the judiciary quality as well, a different rule in respect of executive removal might well apply. 1 Annals of Congress, cols. 611–612.

In Marbury v. Madison, 1 Cranch, 137, at pages 162, 165–166, it is made clear that Chief Justice Marshall was of opinion that a justice of the peace for the District of Columbia was not removable at the will of the President; and that there was a distinction between such an officer and officers appointed to aid the President in the performance of his constitutional duties. In the latter case, the distinction he saw was that "their acts are his acts" and his will, therefore, controls; and, by way of illustration, he adverted to the act establishing the Department of Foreign Affairs, which was the subject of the "decision of 1789."

The result of what we now have said is this: Whether the power of the President to remove an officer shall prevail over the authority of Congress to condition the power by fixing a definite term and precluding a removal except for cause will depend upon the character of the office; the *Myers* decision, affirming the power of the President alone to make the removal, is confined to purely executive officers; and as to officers of the kind here under consideration, we hold that no removal can be made during the prescribed term for which the officer is appointed, except for one or more of the causes named in the applicable statute.

To the extent that, between the decision in the *Myers* Case, which sustains the unrestrictable power of the President to remove purely executive officers, and our present decision that such power does not extend to an office such as that here involved, there shall remain a field of doubt, we leave such cases as may fall within it for future consideration and determination as they may arise. . . .

---

**1.  *The Holding of* Humphrey's Executor**—*Humphrey's Executor* affirmed a significant restriction on presidential removal a mere nine years after *Myers* had (apparently) held that the President may remove executive officials at will. *Humphrey's Executor* distinguished *Myers* on the ground that the regional postmaster dismissed in *Myers* performed purely executive functions, whereas the FTC performed "quasi-legislative" functions (such as making investigations and issuing reports to Congress) and "quasi-judicial" functions (such as adjudicating individual cases involving alleged transgressions of the statutory prohibition on unfair methods of competition). Another important function of administrative agencies—making substantive regulations pursuant to statutory delegations of rulemaking authority—is also usually characterized as a "quasi-legislative" activity under the *Humphrey's Executor* framework. *See* INS v. Chadha, 462 U.S. 919, 953 n.16 (1983); *id.* at 989 (White, J., dissenting). (In the specific context of the FTC, however, it was—and remains—surprisingly unsettled whether the FTC has the authority to adopt regulations specifying "unfair methods of competition," which may be why the *Humphrey's Executor* Court did not refer explicitly to rulemaking as one of the FTC's "quasi-legislative" powers. *See* EINER ELHAUGE, UNITED STATES ANTITRUST LAW AND ECONOMICS 11–12 n.11 (2008).)

Do these "quasi-legislative" or "quasi-judicial" powers that the Court identifies lie outside the three powers established in the first three articles of the Constitution? If an agency's rulemaking and adjudicative authority is not merely an aspect of its *executive* power, then is it even permissible for this agency, which after all is located in the executive branch, to exercise these powers? (In this regard, it might be worth recalling the conceptual disagreement between those, like Justice Scalia, who rationalize delegation on the grounds that agency policymaking is merely incidental to the executive power, and those, like Justice Stevens, who rationalize delegation by asserting that the legislative power vested in Congress by Article I is delegable to the agencies. *See* pp. 410–415, *supra*.) Perhaps the "quasi-legislative" and "quasi-judicial" categories identified by *Humphrey's Executor* are meant to capture the idea that some agency functions (e.g., regulatory rulemaking and adjudication), while sufficiently close to the executive power that they may legitimately be delegated, are also sufficiently removed from the traditional core of executive power that Congress may insulate agencies exercising these functions from presidential control. Does that seem like an appropriately nuanced approach to questions regarding the nature of the power that agencies exercise? Or is it an unprincipled rationalization for a fundamental departure from the constitutional design? Consider, in this regard, Justice Jackson's oft-cited observation that:

> [a]dministrative agencies have been called quasi-legislative, quasi-executive or quasi-judicial, as the occasion required, in order to validate their functions within the separation-of-powers scheme of the Constitution. The mere retreat to the qualifying "quasi" is implicit with confession that all recognized classifications have broken down, and "quasi" is a smooth cover which we draw over our confusion as we might use a counterpane to conceal a disordered bed.

FTC v. Ruberoid Co., 343 U.S. 470, 487–88 (1952) (Jackson, J., dissenting).

If the distinction between purely executive functions and quasi-legislative or quasi-judicial functions strikes you as difficult to sustain, are there alternative ways one might reconcile the results in *Myers* and *Humphrey's Executor*? Consider the following possibility: The statute at issue in *Myers* not only limited the President's removal power, but gave a chamber of Congress (the Senate) a direct role in removal decisions; by contrast, the statute at issue in *Humphrey's Executor* limited the President's removal power but did not purport to involve Congress directly in individual removal decisions. Thus, while the latter statute does raise a legitimate concern about congressional *encroachment* on presidential prerogatives, it does not raise any concern that Congress sought to *aggrandize* its own power. If aggrandizement is viewed as a more significant threat to the separation of powers than encroachment, perhaps this can explain why the removal restriction in *Humphrey's Executor* was permissible while the restriction in *Myers* was not. Indeed, Professor Jonathan Molot argues that this distinction between aggrandizement and encroachment is critical for understanding the Court's separation-of-powers jurisprudence:

> When Congress merely "encroaches" on the President's power—restricting the President's power without claiming that power for itself—the Court has been willing to acquiesce in new arrangements. Faced with congressional efforts to limit ever-expanding executive power in the New Deal ..., the Court has been flexible in its approach to separation of powers. Despite its strong "unitary executive" language in *Myers*—language that seemed to prohibit any encroachment at all on presidential power—the Court signed off on independent agencies in *Humphrey's Executor*.... But when Congress has sought not only to limit the President's power but to aggrandize its own

power—as it did in *Myers*, *Chadha*, and *Bowsher*—the Court has adhered to the formal separation of powers and invalidated these new arrangements. The Court's decisions thus can be reconciled based on principle, even if each appears to be a product of its political times.

Jonathan T. Molot, *Principled Minimalism: Restriking the Balance between Judicial Minimalism and Neutral Principles*, 90 Va. L. Rev. 1753, 1823–24 (2004) (footnotes omitted). *See also* Lawrence Lessig & Cass Sunstein, *The President and the Administration*, 94 Colum. L. Rev. 114–15 (1994); Peter L. Strauss, *The Place of Agencies in Government: Separation of Powers and the Fourth Branch*, 84 Colum. L. Rev. 573, 614–15 (1984). How well does the distinction between encroachment and aggrandizement reconcile the case law? Is the distinction a sensible one? If the Constitution was designed to ensure that the coordinate branches can check one another's ambitions, does Congress's right to encroach upon the President's authority inherently allow Congress to aggrandize its own power? If the President cannot remove agency heads, for example, doesn't that increase Congress's relative authority over the exercise of whatever power it has delegated to such agencies?

One final wrinkle in the *Humphrey's Executor* holding is worth noting: Mr. Humphrey, and later his estate, pursued only the remedy of back pay. Could the grant of such a remedy *ever* interfere with the President's executive power or duty to "take Care that the Laws be faithfully executed"? Allowing a back pay remedy for wrongful dismissal does not prevent the President from dismissing someone he or she believes is not faithfully executing the laws. Do you think that *Humphrey's Executor* would or should have come out differently if Humphrey had survived and sought reinstatement to his position? *See* Daniel J. Gifford, *The Separation of Powers Doctrine and the Regulatory Agencies after* Bowsher v. Synar, 55 Geo. Wash. L. Rev. 441, 473–74 (1987).

**2. How Much Do "For Cause" Removal Restrictions Constrain the President?**—The Court in *Humphrey's Executor* treated the restriction on the President's removal power at issue—which prohibits the President from removing an FTC Commissioner except in cases of "inefficiency, neglect of duty, or malfeasance in office"—as quite restrictive of the President's removal authority. Is such a reading justified? In the actual case, President Roosevelt made no attempt to argue that he had sufficient cause, within the meaning of the statute, to dismiss Mr. Humphrey. Suppose he had. Imagine, for example, that President Roosevelt had instructed Commissioner Humphrey to vote to dismiss a complaint filed by the FTC that the President regarded as unwarranted by the terms of the governing statute. If Humphrey had refused to comply with such a directive, would that count as "neglect of duty" within the meaning of the statute? *See* Geoffrey P. Miller, *Independent Agencies*, 1986 Sup. Ct. Rev. 41, 87. Would such a reading be necessary to avoid a serious constitutional question under the Take Care Clause? *See* Shurtleff v. United States, 189 U.S. 311, 316 (1903) (holding that the Court would insist upon "explicit language . . . before holding the [removal] power of the President to have been taken away by an act of Congress"); *see also* John F. Manning, *The Independent Counsel Statute: Reading "Good Cause" in Light of Article II*, 83 MINN. L. REV. 1285 (1999). Because the President so infrequently attempts to remove independent agency commissioners, those questions remain largely unresolved.

    ***3.  Independent Agencies and Statutory Limitations on Removal**—Humphrey's Executor* blesses the congressional practice of creating so-called "independent agencies" or "independent regulatory commissions." The defining feature of an independent agency is the organic act's provision for limitations on removability by the President. Why might Congress want to create such independent agencies? What functions might they serve?

    The most traditional justification for creating independent regulatory commissions is the idea—associated strongly with the New Deal—that often the best way to solve pressing social and economic problems is to empower expert decision-makers, insulated from the distorting or corrupting influence of politics, to apply their specialized skills and knowledge to the problem that the political branches have identified. This New Deal faith in technocratic problem-solving was well captured by James Landis, who wrote that "[w]ith the rise of regulation, the need for expertness became dominant; for the art of regulating an industry requires knowledge of the details of its operation, ability to shift requirements as the condition of the industry may dictate, the pursuit of energetic measures upon the appearance of an emergency, and the power through enforcement to realize conclusions as to policy." JAMES M. LANDIS, THE ADMINISTRATIVE PROCESS 23–24 (1938). *See also* Robert L. Rabin, *Federal Regulation in Historical Perspective*, 38 STAN. L. REV. 1189, 1267–68 (1986). As Landis further explained, while executive agencies often responded to "political pressure" or "the varying tempers of changing administrations," independent agencies might achieve "a degree of permanence and consistency" in their formulation and implementation of regulatory policy. LANDIS, *supra*, at 112–13. Thus it is somewhat ironic that, while *Humphrey's Executor* is often thought (with good reason) to reflect a largely conservative Supreme Court's rebuke to President Roosevelt, *see, e.g.*, Neal Devins, *Government Lawyers and the New Deal*, 96 COLUM. L. REV. 237, 245 (1996); Paul Verkuil, *The Status of Independent Agencies after* Bowsher v. Synar, 1986 DUKE L.J. 779, 784, the Court's interpretation of the FTCA ended up fitting comfortably with the New Deal emphasis on agency expertise as a means to achieve effective regulatory policy. Indeed, Landis—though a Roosevelt ally and New Deal supporter—wrote approvingly that *Humphrey's Executor* "underwrites the legislative desire for protection of the administrative from interference as to the disposition of detail, which in so great a measure is the objective sought by the creation of the independent Commission." LANDIS, *supra*, at 115.

    The New Deal optimism about the capacity of independent agencies, staffed by experts and insulated from politics, to solve difficult regulatory policy questions has eroded substantially since the 1930s. This erosion is due primarily to two related changes in mainstream thinking about administrative agency decisionmaking. First, it is now generally accepted that virtually all significant regulatory policy decisions are shot through with value judgments—judgments that are essentially "political" in the sense that they require not just empirical findings and predictions, but also decisions about priorities and ultimate objectives. This is not to say that technical expertise is no longer considered significant. But few today would subscribe to the view that the application of such expertise can or should be politically "neutral." *See* Alfred C. Aman, Jr., *Administrative Law in a Global Era: Progress, Deregulatory Change, and the Rise of the Administrative Presidency*, 73 Cornell L. Rev. 1101, 1218–23 (1988) (noting this "value skepticism" as a reason for the erosion of the "expertise" justification for agency power). The second development that has contributed to the erosion of the "neutral expertise" justification for independent regulatory commissions is an increasing concern that agency bureaucrats, even if insulated from Congress and the President, are not insulated from the kind of special interest politics that many New Dealers viewed as a threat to coherent, just, and efficient regulation. Indeed, in the post-World War II era, the view that regulatory agencies are often "captured" by the interests they are regulating became widespread. *See, e.g.*, Thomas W. Merrill, *Capture Theory and the Courts: 1967–1983*, 72 Chi.-Kent L. Rev. 1039, 1050–52 (1997); Richard B. Stewart, *The Reformation of American Administrative Law*, 88 Harv. L. Rev. 1669, 1684–87 (1975). Advocates of this "capture theory" have typically emphasized that concentrated interest groups, with high stakes and common interests, would have an easier time organizing and lobbying agencies (or their political overseers) for favorable policies; that agencies depend on the regulated community for information and political support; and that agency officials often come from, and frequently seek subsequent employment with, firms that the agency is supposed to regulate. *See, e.g.*, Mancur Olson, The Logic of Collective Action (1965); Jean-Jacques Laffont & Jean Tirole, *The Politics of Government Decision-Making: A Theory of Regulatory Capture*, 106 Q. J. Econ. 1089 (1991); George J. Stigler, *The Theory of Economic Regulation*, 2 Bell J. of Econ. & Mgmt. Sci. 3 (1971). To be sure, many scholars have challenged the strong version of capture theory, and the empirical evidence in support of widespread agency capture is not as robust as some of its proponents assert. *See, e.g.*, Steven P. Croley, Regulation and Public Interests: The Possibility of Good Regulatory Government (2008); James Q. Wilson, *The Politics of Regulation*, *in* The Politics of Regulation 357 (James Q. Wilson ed., 1980); Jessica Leight, *Public Choice: A Critical Reassessment*, in Government and Markets: Toward a New Theory of Regulation 230–38 (Edward J. Balleisen & David A. Moss eds., 2009). That said, few would now defend the view that independent agencies can be as insulated from special interest politics as Landis and other New Dealers seemed to suggest.

To what extent do these developments undermine the traditional justification for insulating independent agencies from presidential control? If regulatory policy decisions are inseparable from political value judgments, does this mean that principles of democratic accountability require greater control of agencies by the President? And if we think that so-called independent agencies are not truly independent, but instead may be particularly susceptible to manipulation by parochial interest groups, might we be better off if the President—who answers to a national constituency—has greater influence over agency policymaking? *See* Cass R. Sunstein, *Paradoxes of the Regulatory State*, 57 U. CHI. L. REV. 407, 428 (1990). On the other hand, while New Dealers like Landis may have overstated the degree to which independent regulatory commissions are repositories of politically neutral expertise, don't they still have a point that sometimes a certain degree of insulation from political oversight is valuable for all of the reasons they suggested? Even if the concerns about a lack of democratic accountability and the potential for special interest manipulation are real, do they outweigh the advantages associated with putting greater decision-making authority in the hands of agency experts?

   *4. The Balance of Power Between the President and Congress—* There is another potential justification for restricting the President's power to remove the leaders of certain administrative agencies that emphasizes not the *insulation* of agencies from politics, but rather the need to maintain an appropriate *balance* between presidential and congressional control over regulatory policy. On this view, so-called "independent" agencies are not so much independent of political control as they are more responsive to congressional influence, relative to that of the President. As Justice Scalia recently asserted in his majority opinion in F.C.C. v. Fox Television Stations, Inc., 129 S.Ct. 1800, 1815 (2009): "The independent agencies are sheltered not from politics but from the President, and . . . their freedom from presidential oversight (and protection) has simply been replaced by increased subservience to congressional direction." *See also* Frank H. Easterbrook, *The State of Madison's Vision of the State: A Public Choice Perspective*, 107 HARV. L. REV. 1328, 1341 (1994). If this is so, does it strengthen or weaken the case for permitting Congress to create independent agencies, over which the President has only restricted removal authority? On the one hand, the democratic legitimacy concern with independent agencies has less bite if the impact of removal restrictions is not so much a shift in decisionmaking authority from the (elected) President to (unelected) administrators, but rather a shift in influence from the (elected) President to the (elected) Congress. On the other hand, shifting influence over regulatory policymaking from the President to Congress might be problematic not only because of the formalist concern that Congress has no business interfering with the execution of the laws, but also because of a more functionalist concern that congressional control will exacerbate problems of special interest capture. Part of this concern arises out of the general observation that factions can influence agencies indirectly through legislators. *See, e.g.*, Einer R. Elhauge, *Does Interest Group Theory Justify More Intrusive Judicial Review?*, 101 YALE L.J. 31, 41–42 (1991); Sanford C. Gordon & Catherine Hafer, *Flexing Muscle: Corporate Political Expenditures as Signals to the Bureaucracy*, 99 AM. POL. SCI. REV. 245 (2005); Richard A. Posner, *Theories of Economic Regulation*, 5 BELL J. ECON. & MGMT. SCI. 335, 338 (1974). The concern is intensified by the fear that congressional influence over agencies is more likely to reflect parochial rather than general interests. As Professor Sunstein argues, the restrictions on the President's power to control independent agencies "leave[ ] agencies vulnerable both to individual members and committees of Congress, which sometimes represent narrow factions and well-organized private groups with significant stakes in the outcome of regulatory decisions." Cass R. Sunstein, *Paradoxes of the Regulatory State*, 57 U. CHI. L. REV. 407, 427 (1990). Judge Easterbrook offers a similar assessment:

> A President may resist claims by factions in the way Madison envisioned: by adding other items to the agenda. But agencies devoted to single industries lack threats; they cannot promise to veto bill X if Congress takes step Y. Because agencies cannot engage in logrolling, committees in Congress gain relative influence. The loser is the President (with a national constituency), and the principal beneficiaries are committee chairmen, who hold, on average, beliefs farther from the national median view of politics. Chairmen are tied to the very local interests that Madison dubbed faction; Presidents are not.

Frank H. Easterbrook, *The State of Madison's Vision of the State: A Public Choice Perspective*, 107 HARV. L. REV. 1328, 1341 (1994) (footnotes omitted); *see also* Jonathan R. Macey, *Separated Powers and Positive Political Theory: The Tug of War Over Administrative Agencies*, 80 GEO. L.J. 671, 697–98 (1992).

But is that critical assessment appropriate? As we have observed elsewhere (*see* pp. 177–178, *supra*), the assertion that committees (and committee chairs) have beliefs that deviate substantially from those of the chamber median is hotly contested, and the evidence is much more equivocal than Sunstein or Easterbrook suggest. Recent scholarship has also challenged the idea that the President is more responsive to a national constituency than is Congress (when considered as a whole); this scholarship suggests that the President is more susceptible to influence by parochial factions, and Congress is more nationalist, than Sunstein, Easterbrook, and other scholars have argued. *See* Jide Nzelibe, *The Fable of the Nationalist President and the Parochial Congress*, 53 UCLA L. REV. 1217 (2006). Does the constitutional legitimacy of independent agencies turn, to any meaningful degree, on the answers to these sorts of empirical questions?

**5. *Partisan Balance Requirements on Multi–Member Commissions*—**The defining feature of an "independent agency," as noted above, is the restriction on the President's power to remove senior agency officials. Many of the most important independent regulatory commissions—including the FTC—also share a number of other common institutional features: Many are led not by single heads but by multi-member boards who serve staggered terms of years, and many of the statutes creating such commissions contain "partisan balance" requirements that mandate that not more than a bare majority of the commissioners (e.g., three out of five) belong to the same political party. *See, e.g.,* 5 U.S.C. § 7104 (Federal Labor Relations Authority); 15 U.S.C. § 41 (FTC); 29 U.S.C. § 661 (Occupational Safety & Health Review Commission). These partisan balance requirements are another means by which Congress seeks to insulate independent agencies from presidential control. It is not clear how effective they are, especially given that the President can usually ensure that a majority of the commissioners are members of the President's party, and that the President also has the power to select the commission chair, who exerts disproportionate influence over the commission's policymaking and administrative functions. *See* Lisa Schultz Bressman, *Procedures as Politics in Administrative Law*, 107 COLUM. L. REV. 1749 (2007); Peter L. Strauss, *The Place of Agencies in Government: Separation of Powers and the Fourth Branch*, 84 COLUM. L. REV. 573, 590–91 (1984). That said, there does seem to be some suggestive empirical evidence that these partisan balance requirements have an effect on agency behavior. *See* DAVID E. LEWIS, PRESIDENTS AND THE POLITICS OF AGENCY DESIGN (2003); Daniel E. Ho, *Congressional Agency Control: The Impact of Statutory Partisan Requirements on Regulation* (unpublished manuscript, 2007).

Although these requirements are widespread and generally accepted, they may raise questions under the Appointments Clause. If the Constitution specifies no role for Congress in the appointment of principal officers other than the Senate's power to grant or withhold its consent on presidential nominations, why is it permissible for Congress to place conditions on whom the President can appoint? There is no Supreme Court case that addresses this question directly, but the D.C. Circuit considered it in *Federal Election Commission v. NRA Political Victory Fund*, 6 F.3d 821 (D.C. Cir. 1993). In that case, a political action committee argued that the partisan balance requirement in the Federal Election Commission Act (FECA), under which no more than three of the six FEC commissioners could be members of the same political party, unconstitutionally interfered with the President's appointment power. The D.C. Circuit rejected the challenge not on the merits, but on the ground that the appellants could not show that the statutory partisan balance requirement was the source of their alleged injury:

> Congressional limitations—even the placement of burdens—on the President's appointment power may raise serious constitutional questions. But it is impossible to determine in this case whether the *statute* actually limited the President's appointment power. Appellants do not argue, nor can we assume, that the President wished to appoint more than three members of one party and was restrained by FECA from doing so. Presidents have often viewed restrictions on their appointment power not to be legally binding. Of course, such legislation may impose political restraints. Particularly with respect to the Commission ... it is hard to imagine that the President would wish to alter that balance, even if the understanding had not been reflected in the statutory language. More important, as appellants recognize, under its Advice and Consent authority the Senate may reject or approve the President's nominees for whatever reason it deems proper. Since all commissioners must be confirmed by the Senate, it would seem that a Senate resolution or even an informal communication to the President would have the same effect as the statute. It is not the law, therefore,

which arguably restrains the President, but his perception of the present Senate's view as it may be assumed to be reflected in the statute.

... We cannot assume ... that the bipartisanship requirement has any effect on the Commission's work, for without the statute the President could have appointed exactly the same members.... It may well be that only if the President appoints and the Senate confirms a fourth same-party member to the Commission could the unconstitutionality of the bipartisanship requirement be regarded as justiciable, when the government raises it as a defense to the charge that the member's participation violates FECA.

6 F.3d at 824–25 (internal citations and footnotes omitted) (emphasis in original).

Do you find that analysis convincing? Does Judge Silberman's opinion in *NRA Political Victory Fund* imply that statutory partisan balance requirements likely *are* unconstitutional insofar as they purport to constrain the President's discretion, but that as a practical matter their legal status is irrelevant because political factors induce presidential compliance? What would or should happen if a President with a sufficient majority in the Senate violated the partisan balance requirement? If such requirements don't have binding legal force, why would Congress write them into statutes? For further discussion of the issue, *see, e.g.*, Note, *Congressional Restrictions on the President's Appointment Power and the Role of Longstanding Practice in Constitutional Interpretation*, 120 HARV. L. REV. 1914 (2007); Adam J. Rappaport, Comment, *The Court of International Trade's Political Party Diversity Requirement: Unconstitutional Under Any Separation of Powers Theory*, 68 U. CHI. L. REV. 1429 (2001).

**6. A Note on Contrasting Styles**—*Myers* was decided almost three years after the case was initially argued, and the opinions were extraordinarily lengthy and detailed (Chief Justice Taft's majority opinion ran 70 pages, and there was also a one-page dissent by Justice Holmes, a 61–page dissent by Justice McReynolds, and a 55–page dissent by Justice Brandeis.) *Myers* exhaustively aired sharply contrasting views on the meaning of the constitutional text and the accompanying historical context. *Humphrey's Executor*, which was decided twenty-six days after argument, relied principally on pragmatic arguments about the importance of independence and expert administrative judgment in the modern administrative state. Quite apart from your agreement or disagreement with the ultimate holding in either case, how do these cases affect your views of the relative merits of formalism and functionalism? Although *Myers* obviously entailed a great deal more effort, does its conclusion appear to you to rest on firmer footing? Does it seem realistic to try to reconstruct how the founding generation would have understood an issue that the constitutional text does not address expressly? Do contemporary concerns about the relative virtues of expertise and accountability provide any prospect of firmer ground for making a constitutional judgment?

## B.   The Modern Approach to Appointment and Removal

In the aftermath of *Humphrey's Executor*, the legal culture came largely to accept the constitutional legitimacy of independent agencies. *See* Geoffrey P. Miller, *Independent Agencies*, 1986 Sup. Ct. Rev. 41, 43. Indeed, in the half century after *Humphrey's Executor*, only the rarest reported case even presented the occasion to consider the legitimacy of statutory restrictions on the President's authority to remove an administrative officer, and those few cases upheld such restrictions as constitutional without exception. *See, e.g.*, Wiener v. United States, 357 U.S. 349 (1958); Morgan v. TVA, 115 F.2d 990 (6th Cir. 1940). Late in the twentieth century, however, lawyers and legal scholars who read the Constitution as mandating a "unitary executive"—including many senior lawyers and officials in the Reagan Administration—began to question the legitimacy of *Humphrey's Executor*. *See* Neal Devins & David E. Lewis, *Not–So Independent Agencies: Party Polarization and the Limits of Institutional Design*, 88 B.U. L. Rev. 459, 480–81 (2008). During this period, the Supreme Court confronted a broadly framed constitutional challenge to the legitimacy of statutory restrictions on the President's removal powers in the *Morrison v. Olson* case.

*Morrison* dealt not with ordinary administrative agencies, but with so-called "independent counsels" who investigate alleged criminal wrongdoing by high government officials. The Ethics in Government Act, which established the independent counsel scheme at issue in *Morrison*, was a response to the post-Watergate perception that the executive branch could not be relied on to conduct an impartial investigation into alleged criminal wrongdoing by officials close to the President or by the President him- or herself. During an investigation of whether President Nixon and others had participated in a cover-up of his campaign's involvement in a break-in at the Democratic National Committee headquarters at the Watergate Hotel during the 1972 presidential election, President Nixon ordered the firing of special prosecutor Archibald Cox, who was investigating the Watergate scandal under a special appointment within the U.S. Department of Justice. *See* John J. Scirica, To Set the Record Straight 166 (1979). In response to this episode, Congress thought it necessary to create an independent counsel scheme that effectively insulated prosecutors investigating high government officials from the President in their appointment and removal. *See* S. Rep. No. 170, 95th Cong., 1st Sess. 2–3 (1977). After the Act had been in effect for some years, targets of an independent counsel investigation challenged its constitutionality. Joined by the U.S. Department of Justice in an *amicus curiae* brief, they asked the Court to reaffirm the idea that Congress may not limit the President's authority to remove a federal officer performing an executive function, and to apply this principle to hold the independent counsel provision unconstitutional. In resolving this claim, the Supreme Court substantially reconceptualized important aspects of both its appointment and removal jurisprudence.

## Morrison v. Olson

Supreme Court of the United States
487 U.S. 654 (1988)

■ Chief Justice Rehnquist delivered the opinion of the Court.

This case presents us with a challenge to the independent counsel provisions of the Ethics in Government Act of 1978, 28 U.S.C. §§ 49, 591 *et seq.* (1982 ed., Supp. V).... Briefly stated, Title VI of the Ethics in Government Act (Title VI or the Act), 28 U.S.C. §§ 591–599 (1982 ed., Supp. V), allows for the appointment of an "independent counsel" to investigate and, if appropriate, prosecute certain high-ranking Government officials for violations of federal criminal laws. The Act requires the Attorney General, upon receipt of information that he determines is "sufficient to constitute grounds to investigate whether any person [covered by the Act] may have violated any Federal criminal law," to conduct a preliminary investigation of the matter. When the Attorney General has completed this investigation, or 90 days has elapsed, he is required to report to a special court (the Special Division) created by the Act "for the purpose of appointing independent counsels." 28 U.S.C. § 49 (1982 ed., Supp. V). If the Attorney General determines that "there are no reasonable grounds to believe that further investigation is warranted," then he must notify the Special Division of this result. In such a case, "the division of the court shall have no power to appoint an independent counsel." § 592(b)(1). If, however, the Attorney General has determined that there are "reasonable grounds to believe that further investigation or prosecution is warranted," then he "shall apply to the division of the court for the appointment of an independent counsel." The Attorney General's application to the court "shall contain sufficient information to assist the [court] in selecting an independent counsel and in defining that independent counsel's prosecutorial jurisdiction." § 592(d). Upon receiving this application, the Special Division "shall appoint an appropriate independent counsel and shall define that independent counsel's prosecutorial jurisdiction." § 593(b).

With respect to all matters within the independent counsel's jurisdiction, the Act grants the counsel "full power and independent authority to exercise all investigative and prosecutorial functions and powers of the Department of Justice, the Attorney General, and any other officer or employee of the Department of Justice." § 594(a). The functions of the independent counsel include conducting grand jury proceedings and other investigations, participating in civil and criminal court proceedings and litigation, and appealing any decision in any case in which the counsel participates in an official capacity. §§ 594(a)(1)–(3). Under § 594(a)(9), the counsel's powers include "initiating and conducting prosecutions in any court of competent jurisdiction, framing and signing indictments, filing informations, and handling all aspects of any case, in the name of the United States." The counsel may appoint employees, § 594(c), may request and obtain assistance from the Department of Justice, § 594(d), and may accept referral of matters from the Attorney General if the matter falls within the counsel's jurisdiction as defined by the Special Division,

§ 594(e). The Act also states that an independent counsel "shall, except where not possible, comply with the written or other established policies of the Department of Justice respecting enforcement of the criminal laws." § 594(f). In addition, whenever a matter has been referred to an independent counsel under the Act, the Attorney General and the Justice Department are required to suspend all investigations and proceedings regarding the matter. § 597(a). An independent counsel has "full authority to dismiss matters within [his or her] prosecutorial jurisdiction without conducting an investigation or at any subsequent time before prosecution, if to do so would be consistent" with Department of Justice policy. § 594(g).

Two statutory provisions govern the length of an independent counsel's tenure in office. The first defines the procedure for removing an independent counsel. Section 596(a)(1) provides:

> "An independent counsel appointed under this Chapter may be removed from office, other than by impeachment and conviction, only by the personal action of the Attorney General and only for good cause, physical disability, mental incapacity, or any other condition that substantially impairs the performance of such independent counsel's duties."

If an independent counsel is removed pursuant to this section, the Attorney General is required to submit a report to both the Special Division and the Judiciary Committees of the Senate and the House "specifying the facts found and the ultimate grounds for such removal." § 596(a)(2). Under the current version of the Act, an independent counsel can obtain judicial review of the Attorney General's action by filing a civil action in the United States District Court for the District of Columbia. Members of the Special Division "may not hear or determine any such civil action or any appeal of a decision in any such civil action." The reviewing court is authorized to grant reinstatement or "other appropriate relief." § 596(a)(3).

The other provision governing the tenure of the independent counsel defines the procedures for "terminating" the counsel's office. Under § 596(b)(1), the office of an independent counsel terminates when he or she notifies the Attorney General that he or she has completed or substantially completed any investigations or prosecutions undertaken pursuant to the Act. In addition, the Special Division, acting either on its own or on the suggestion of the Attorney General, may terminate the office of an independent counsel at any time if it finds that "the investigation of all matters within the prosecutorial jurisdiction of such independent counsel . . . have been completed or so substantially completed that it would be appropriate for the Department of Justice to complete such investigations and prosecutions." § 596(b)(2).

Finally, the Act provides for congressional oversight of the activities of independent counsel. An independent counsel may from time to time send Congress statements or reports on his or her activities. § 595(a)(2). The "appropriate committees of the Congress" are given oversight jurisdiction in regard to the official conduct of an independent counsel, and the counsel is required by the Act to cooperate with Congress in the exercise of this jurisdiction. § 595(a)(1). The counsel is required to inform the House of Representatives of "substantial and credible information which [the counsel] receives ... that may constitute grounds for an impeachment." § 595(c). In addition, the Act gives certain congressional committee members the power to "request in writing that the Attorney General apply for the appointment of an independent counsel." § 592(g)(1). The Attorney General is required to respond to this request within a specified time but is not required to accede to the request. § 592(g)(2).

[The case arose out of the Reagan Administration's assertion of executive privilege in response to two congressional subcommittees' 1982 subpoenas directing the Environmental Protection Agency (EPA) to produce documents relating to the enforcement of the so-called "Superfund Law" by the EPA and the U.S. Department of Justice. After considerable procedural wrangling, the administration in 1983 agreed to give the relevant House subcommittees "limited access to the documents." In the aftermath of this dispute between Congress and the Executive Branch, the House Judiciary Committee investigated the Justice Department's role in the dispute. In connection with this investigation, Theodore B. Olson, then the Assistant Attorney General for the Office of Legal Counsel (OLC), testified before a House subcommittee concerning the handling of the document requests. In 1985, the Judiciary Committee majority published a lengthy report that "suggested that ... Olson had given false and misleading testimony to the Subcommittee on March 10, 1983." Pursuant to the Ethics in Government Act, the Chairman of the Judiciary Committee forwarded the report to the Attorney General "with a request, pursuant to 28 U.S.C. § 592(c), that he seek the appointment of an independent counsel to investigate the allegations against Olson." After a preliminary investigation, the Attorney General requested appointment of an independent counsel to investigate whether Olson had given false testimony to Congress, in violation of federal criminal law, as well as "any other matter related to that allegation." The Special Division of the D.C. Circuit ultimately appointed Alexia Morrison to be the Independent Counsel.]

... [I]n May and June 1987, [the Independent Counsel] caused a grand jury to issue and serve subpoenas ... on [Mr. Olson, who] moved to quash the subpoenas, claiming ... that the independent counsel provisions of the Act were unconstitutional and that appellant accordingly had no authority to proceed....

### III

The Appointments Clause of Article II reads as follows:

"[The President] shall nominate, and by and with the Advice and Consent of the Senate, shall appoint Ambassadors, other public Ministers and Consuls, Judges of the Supreme Court, and all other Officers of the United States, whose Appointments are not herein otherwise provided for, and which shall be established by Law: but the Congress may by Law vest the Appointment of such inferior Officers, as they think proper, in the President alone, in the Courts of Law, or in the Heads of Departments." U.S. Const., Art. II, § 2, cl. 2.

The parties do not dispute that "[t]he Constitution for purposes of appointment ... divides all its officers into two classes." United States v. Germaine, 99 U.S. (9 Otto) 508, 509 (1879). As we stated in Buckley v. Valeo, 424 U.S. 1, 132 (1976): "Principal officers are selected by the President with the advice and consent of the Senate. Inferior officers Congress may allow to be appointed by the President alone, by the heads of departments, or by the Judiciary." The initial question is ... whether appellant is an "inferior" or a "principal" officer. If she is the latter, ... then the Act is in violation of the Appointments Clause.

The line between "inferior" and "principal" officers is one that is far from clear, and the Framers provided little guidance into where it should be drawn.... We need not attempt here to decide exactly where the line falls between the two types of officers, because in our view appellant clearly falls on the "inferior officer" side of that line. Several factors lead to this conclusion.

First, appellant is subject to removal by a higher Executive Branch official. Although appellant may not be "subordinate" to the Attorney General (and the President) insofar as she possesses a degree of independent discretion to exercise the powers delegated to her under the Act, the fact that she can be removed by the Attorney General indicates that she is to some degree "inferior" in rank and authority. Second, appellant is empowered by the Act to perform only certain, limited duties. An independent counsel's role is restricted primarily to investigation and, if appropriate, prosecution for certain federal crimes. Admittedly, the Act delegates to appellant "full power and independent authority to exercise all investigative and prosecutorial functions and powers of the Department of Justice," § 594(a), but this grant of authority does not include any authority to formulate policy for the Government or the Executive Branch, nor does it give appellant any administrative duties outside of those necessary to operate her office. The Act specifically provides that in policy matters appellant is to comply to the extent possible with the policies of the Department. § 594(f).

Third, appellant's office is limited in jurisdiction. Not only is the Act itself restricted in applicability to certain federal officials suspected of certain serious federal crimes, but an independent counsel can only act within the scope of the jurisdiction that has been granted by the Special Division pursuant to a request by the Attorney General. [Fourth,] appellant's office is limited in tenure. There is concededly no time limit on the appointment of a particular counsel. Nonetheless, the office of independent counsel is "temporary" in the sense that an independent counsel is appointed essentially to accomplish a single task, and when that task is over the office is terminated, either by the counsel herself or by action of the Special Division. Unlike other prosecutors, appellant has no ongoing responsibilities that extend beyond the accomplishment of the mission that she was appointed for and authorized by the Special Division to undertake.

In our view, these factors relating to the "ideas of tenure, duration ... and duties" of the independent counsel, [United States v. Germaine, 9 Otto 508, 511 (1878)], are sufficient to establish that appellant is an "inferior" officer in the constitutional sense.

This conclusion is consistent with our few previous decisions that considered the question whether a particular Government official is a "principal" or an "inferior" officer. In United States v. Eaton, 169 U.S. 331 (1898), for example, we approved Department of State regulations that allowed executive officials to appoint a "vice-consul" during the temporary absence of the consul, terming the "vice-consul" a "subordinate officer" notwithstanding the Appointment Clause's specific reference to "Consuls" as principal officers. As we stated: "Because the subordinate officer is charged with the performance of the duty of the superior for a limited time and under special and temporary conditions he is not thereby transformed into the superior and permanent official." *Id.*, at 343. In Ex parte Siebold, 100 U.S. [(10 Otto)] 371 (1880), the Court found that federal "supervisor[s] of elections," who were charged with various duties involving oversight of local congressional elections, [10 Otto] at 379–380, were inferior officers for purposes of the Clause. In Go–Bart Importing Co. v. United States, 282 U.S. 344, 352–353 (1931), we held that "United States commissioners are inferior officers." *Id.*, at 352. These commissioners had various judicial and prosecutorial powers, including the power to arrest and imprison for trial, to issue warrants, and to institute prosecutions under "laws relating to the elective franchise and civil rights." *Id.*, at 353, n. 2. All of this is consistent with our reference in United States v. Nixon, 418 U.S. 683, 694, 696 (1974), to the office of Watergate Special Prosecutor—whose authority was similar to that of appellant, see *id.*, at 694, n. 8—as a "subordinate officer." ...

## V

We now turn to consider whether the Act is invalid under the constitutional principle of separation of powers. ...

## A

... Unlike both [Bowsher v. Synar, 478 U.S. 714 (1986),] and [Myers v. United States, 272 U.S. 52 (1926),] this case does not involve an attempt by Congress itself to gain a role in the removal of executive officials other than its established powers of impeachment and conviction. The Act instead puts the removal power squarely in the hands of the Executive Branch; an independent counsel may be removed from office, "only by the personal action of the Attorney General, and only for good cause." § 596(a)(1). ... In our view, the removal provisions of the Act make this case more analogous to Humphrey's Executor v. United States, 295 U.S. 602 (1935), and Wiener v. United States, 357 U.S. 349(1958), than to *Myers* or *Bowsher*.

In *Humphrey's Executor,* [we held that] the President's power to remove Government officials simply was not "all-inclusive in respect of civil officers with the exception of the judiciary provided for by the Constitution." 295 U.S., at 629. At least in regard to "quasi-legislative" and "quasi-judicial" agencies such as the FTC, "[t]he authority of Congress, in creating [such] agencies, to require them to act in discharge of their duties independently of executive control . . . includes, as an appropriate incident, power to fix the period during which they shall continue in office, and to forbid their removal except for cause in the meantime." *Ibid* . . . .

We undoubtedly did rely on the terms "quasi-legislative" and "quasi-judicial" to distinguish the officials involved in *Humphrey's Executor* . . . from those in *Myers,* but our present considered view is that the determination of whether the Constitution allows Congress to impose a "good cause"-type restriction on the President's power to remove an official cannot be made to turn on whether or not that official is classified as "purely executive." The analysis contained in our removal cases is designed not to define rigid categories of those officials who may or may not be removed at will by the President,[28] but to ensure that Congress does not interfere with the President's exercise of the "executive power" and his constitutionally appointed duty to "take care that the laws be faithfully executed" under Article II. *Myers* was undoubtedly correct in its holding, and in its broader suggestion that there are some "purely executive" officials who must be removable by the President at will if he is to be able to accomplish his constitutional role. See 272 U.S., at 132–134. . . .

At the other end of the spectrum from *Myers,* the characterization of the agencies in *Humphrey's Executor* and *Wiener* as "quasi-legislative" or "quasi-judicial" in large part reflected our judgment that it was not essential to the President's proper execution of his Article II powers that these agencies be headed up by individuals who were removable at will. We do not mean to suggest that an analysis of the functions served by the officials at issue is irrelevant. But the real question is whether the removal restrictions are of such a nature that they impede the President's ability to perform his constitutional duty, and the functions of the officials in question must be analyzed in that light.

---

**28.** The difficulty of defining such categories of "executive" or "quasi-legislative" officials is illustrated by a comparison of our decisions in cases such as *Humphrey's Executor,* Buckley v. Valeo, 424 U.S. 1, 140–141 (1976), and *Bowsher, supra,* 478 U.S., at 732–734. In *Buckley,* we indicated that the functions of the Federal Election Commission are "administrative," and "more legislative and judicial in nature," and are "of kinds usually performed by independent regulatory agencies or by some department in the Executive Branch under the direction of an Act of Congress." 424 U.S., at 140–141. In *Bowsher,* we found that the functions of the Comptroller General were "executive" in nature, in that he was required to "exercise judgment concerning facts that affect the application of the Act," and he must "interpret the provisions of the Act to determine precisely what budgetary calculations are required." 478 U.S., at 733. Compare this with the description of the FTC's powers in *Humphrey's Executor,* which we stated "occupie[d] no place in the executive department": "The [FTC] is an administrative body created by Congress to carry into effect legislative policies embodied in the statute in accordance with the legislative standard therein prescribed, and to perform other specified duties as a legislative or as a judicial aid." 295 U.S., at 628. As Justice White noted in his dissent in *Bowsher,* it is hard to dispute that the powers of the FTC at the time of *Humphrey's Executor* would at the present time be considered "executive," at least to some degree. See 478 U.S., at 761, n. 3.

Considering for the moment the "good cause" removal provision in isolation from the other parts of the Act at issue in this case, we cannot say that the imposition of a "good cause" standard for removal by itself unduly trammels on executive authority. There is no real dispute that the functions performed by the independent counsel are "executive" in the sense that they are law enforcement functions that typically have been undertaken by officials within the Executive Branch. As we noted above, however, the independent counsel is an inferior officer under the Appointments Clause, with limited jurisdiction and tenure and lacking policymaking or significant administrative authority. Although the counsel exercises no small amount of discretion and judgment in deciding how to carry out his or her duties under the Act, we simply do not see how the President's need to control the exercise of that discretion is so central to the functioning of the Executive Branch as to require as a matter of constitutional law that the counsel be terminable at will by the President.

Nor do we think that the "good cause" removal provision at issue here impermissibly burdens the President's power to control or supervise the independent counsel, as an executive official, in the execution of his or her duties under the Act. This is not a case in which the power to remove an executive official has been completely stripped from the President, thus providing no means for the President to ensure the "faithful execution" of the laws. Rather, because the independent counsel may be terminated for "good cause," the Executive, through the Attorney General, retains ample authority to assure that the counsel is competently performing his or her statutory responsibilities in a manner that comports with the provisions of the Act. Although we need not decide in this case exactly what is encompassed within the term "good cause" under the Act, the legislative history of the removal provision also makes clear that the Attorney General may remove an independent counsel for "misconduct." See H.R.Conf.Rep. No. 100–452, p. 37 (1987). Here, as with the provision of the Act conferring the appointment authority of the independent counsel on the special court, the congressional determination to limit the removal power of the Attorney General was essential, in the view of Congress, to establish the necessary independence of the office. We do not think that this limitation as it presently stands sufficiently deprives the President of control over the independent counsel to interfere impermissibly with his constitutional obligation to ensure the faithful execution of the laws.

### B

The final question to be addressed is whether the Act, taken as a whole, violates the principle of separation of powers by unduly interfering with the role of the Executive Branch. . . .

We observe first that this case does not involve an attempt by Congress to increase its own powers at the expense of the Executive Branch. Cf. *Commodity Futures Trading Comm'n v. Schor,* 478 U.S. [833, 856 (1986)]. Unlike some of our previous cases, most recently *Bowsher v. Synar,* this case simply does not pose a "dange[r] of congressional usurpation of

Executive Branch functions." 478 U.S., at 727; see also INS v. Chadha, 462 U.S. 919, 958 (1983). . . .

[Similarly], we do not think that the Act "impermissibly under-mine[s]" the powers of the Executive Branch, *Schor, supra,* 478 U.S., at 856, or "disrupts the proper balance between the coordinate branches [by] prevent[ing] the Executive Branch from accomplishing its constitutionally assigned functions," *Nixon v. Administrator of General Services,* [433 U.S. 425, 443 (1977)]. It is undeniable that the Act reduces the amount of control or supervision that the Attorney General and, through him, the President exercises over the investigation and prosecution of a certain class of alleged criminal activity. The Attorney General is not allowed to appoint the individual of his choice; he does not determine the counsel's jurisdic-tion; and his power to remove a counsel is limited. Nonetheless, the Act does give the Attorney General several means of supervising or controlling the prosecutorial powers that may be wielded by an independent counsel. Most importantly, the Attorney General retains the power to remove the counsel for "good cause," a power that we have already concluded provides the Executive with substantial ability to ensure that the laws are "faithful-ly executed" by an independent counsel. No independent counsel may be appointed without a specific request by the Attorney General, and the Attorney General's decision not to request appointment if he finds "no reasonable grounds to believe that further investigation is warranted" is committed to his unreviewable discretion. The Act thus gives the Executive a degree of control over the power to initiate an investigation by the independent counsel. In addition, the jurisdiction of the independent coun-sel is defined with reference to the facts submitted by the Attorney General, and once a counsel is appointed, the Act requires that the counsel abide by Justice Department policy unless it is not "possible" to do so. Notwithstanding the fact that the counsel is to some degree "independent" and free from executive supervision to a greater extent than other federal prosecutors, in our view these features of the Act give the Executive Branch sufficient control over the independent counsel to ensure that the President is able to perform his constitutionally assigned duties. . . .

Reversed.

■ JUSTICE KENNEDY took no part in the consideration or decision of this case.

■ JUSTICE SCALIA, dissenting.

It is the proud boast of our democracy that we have "a government of laws and not of men." Many Americans are familiar with that phrase; not many know its derivation. It comes from Part the First, Article XXX, of the Massachusetts Constitution of 1780, which reads in full as follows:

> "In the government of this Commonwealth, the legislative depart-ment shall never exercise the executive and judicial powers, or either of them: The executive shall never exercise the legislative and judicial powers, or either of them: The judicial shall never exercise the legisla-tive and executive powers, or either of them: to the end it may be a government of laws and not of men."

The Framers of the Federal Constitution similarly viewed the principle of separation of powers as the absolutely central guarantee of a just Government. In No. 47 of The Federalist, Madison wrote that "[n]o political truth is certainly of greater intrinsic value, or is stamped with the authority of more enlightened patrons of liberty." The Federalist No. 47, p. 301 (C. Rossiter ed. 1961) (hereinafter Federalist). Without a secure structure of separated powers, our Bill of Rights would be worthless, as are the bills of rights of many nations of the world that have adopted, or even improved upon, the mere words of ours. . . .

. . . "[T]he great security," wrote Madison, "against a gradual concentration of the several powers in the same department consists in giving to those who administer each department the necessary constitutional means and personal motives to resist encroachments of the others. The provision for defense must in this, as in all other cases, be made commensurate to the danger of attack." Federalist No. 51, pp. 321–322. Madison continued:

> "But it is not possible to give to each department an equal power of self-defense. In republican government, the legislative authority necessarily predominates. The remedy for this inconveniency is to divide the legislature into different branches; and to render them, by different modes of election and different principles of action, as little connected with each other as the nature of their common functions and their common dependence on the society will admit. . . . As the weight of the legislative authority requires that it should be thus divided, the weakness of the executive may require, on the other hand, that it should be fortified." *Id.*, at 322–323.

The major "fortification" provided, of course, was the veto power. But in addition to providing fortification, the Founders conspicuously and very consciously declined to sap the Executive's strength in the same way they had weakened the Legislature: by dividing the executive power. Proposals to have multiple executives, or a council of advisers with separate authority were rejected. See 1 M. Farrand, Records of the Federal Convention of 1787, pp. 66, 71–74, 88, 91–92 (rev. ed. 1966); 2 *id.*, at 335–337, 533, 537, 542. Thus, while "[a]ll legislative Powers herein granted shall be vested in a Congress of the United States, which shall consist of a Senate *and* House of Representatives," U.S. Const., Art. I, § 1 (emphasis added), "[t]he executive Power shall be vested in *a President of the United States,*" Art. II, § 1, cl. 1 (emphasis added).

That is what this suit is about. Power. The allocation of power among Congress, the President, and the courts in such fashion as to preserve the equilibrium the Constitution sought to establish—so that "a gradual concentration of the several powers in the same department," Federalist No. 51, p. 321 (J. Madison), can effectively be resisted. Frequently an issue of this sort will come before the Court clad, so to speak, in sheep's clothing: the potential of the asserted principle to effect important change in the equilibrium of power is not immediately evident, and must be discerned by a careful and perceptive analysis. But this wolf comes as a wolf. . . .

## II

If to describe this case is not to decide it, the concept of a government of separate and coordinate powers no longer has meaning. The Court devotes most of its attention to such relatively technical details as the Appointments Clause and the removal power, addressing briefly and only at the end of its opinion the separation of powers. As my prologue suggests, I think that has it backwards. Our opinions are full of the recognition that it is the principle of separation of powers, and the inseparable corollary that each department's "defense must . . . be made commensurate to the danger of attack," Federalist No. 51, p. 322 (J. Madison), which gives comprehensible content to the Appointments Clause, and determines the appropriate scope of the removal power. Thus, while I will subsequently discuss why our appointments and removal jurisprudence does not support today's holding, I begin with a consideration of the fountainhead of that jurisprudence, the separation and equilibration of powers. . . .

To repeat, Article II, § 1, cl. 1, of the Constitution provides:

"The executive Power shall be vested in a President of the United States."

As I described at the outset of this opinion, this does not mean *some of* the executive power, but *all of* the executive power. It seems to me, therefore, that the decision of the Court of Appeals invalidating the present statute must be upheld on fundamental separation-of-powers principles if the following two questions are answered affirmatively: (1) Is the conduct of a criminal prosecution (and of an investigation to decide whether to prosecute) the exercise of purely executive power? (2) Does the statute deprive the President of the United States of exclusive control over the exercise of that power? . . .

The Court concedes that "[t]here is no real dispute that the functions performed by the independent counsel are 'executive'," though it qualifies that concession by adding "in the sense that they are law enforcement functions that typically have been undertaken by officials within the Branch." The qualifier adds nothing but atmosphere. In what *other* sense can one identify "the executive Power" that is supposed to be vested in the President . . . *except* by reference to what has always and everywhere—if conducted by government at all—been conducted never by the legislature, never by the courts, and always by the executive. . . .

As for the second question, whether the statute before us deprives the President of exclusive control over that quintessentially executive activity: The Court does not, and could not possibly, assert that it does not. That is indeed the whole object of the statute. Instead, the Court points out that the President, through his Attorney General, has at least *some* control. That concession is alone enough to invalidate the statute, but I cannot refrain from pointing out that the Court greatly exaggerates the extent of that "some" Presidential control. "Most importan[t]" among these controls, the Court asserts, is the Attorney General's "power to remove the counsel for 'good cause.'" This is somewhat like referring to shackles as an effective means of locomotion. As we recognized in Humphrey's Executor v. United States, 295 U.S. 602 (1935)—indeed, what *Humphrey's Executor* was all about—limiting removal power to "good cause" is an impediment to, not an effective grant of, Presidential control. . . .

Moving on to the presumably "less important" controls that the President retains, the Court notes that no independent counsel may be appointed without a specific request from the Attorney General. [But] the condition that renders such a request mandatory (inability to find "no reasonable grounds to believe" that further investigation is warranted) is so insubstantial that the Attorney General's discretion is severely confined. And once the referral is made, it is for the Special Division to determine the scope and duration of the investigation. See 28 U.S.C. § 593(b) (1982 ed., Supp. V). And in any event, the limited power over referral is irrelevant to the question whether, *once appointed,* the independent counsel exercises executive power free from the President's control. Finally, the Court points out that the Act directs the independent counsel to abide by general Justice Department policy, except when not "possible." See 28 U.S.C. § 594(f) (1982 ed., Supp. V). The exception alone shows this to be an empty promise. Even without that, however, one would be hard put to come up with many investigative or prosecutorial "policies" (other than those imposed by the Constitution or by Congress through law) that are absolute. Almost all investigative and prosecutorial decisions—including the ultimate decision whether, after a technical violation of the law has been found, prosecution is warranted—involve the balancing of innumerable legal and practical considerations. . . . To take this away is to remove the core of the prosecutorial function, and not merely "some" Presidential control. . . .

Is it unthinkable that the President should have such exclusive power, even when alleged crimes by him or his close associates are at issue? No more so than that Congress should have the exclusive power of legislation, even when what is at issue is its own exemption from the burdens of certain laws. See Civil Rights Act of 1964, Title VII, 42 U.S.C. § 2000e *et seq.* (prohibiting "employers," not defined to include the United States, from discriminating on the basis of race, color, religion, sex, or national origin). No more so than that this Court should have the exclusive power to pronounce the final decision on justiciable cases and controversies, even those pertaining to the constitutionality of a statute reducing the salaries of the Justices. See United States v. Will, 449 U.S. 200, 211–217 (1980). A system of separate and coordinate powers necessarily involves an acceptance of exclusive power that can theoretically be abused. . . . The checks against any branch's abuse of its exclusive powers are twofold: First, retaliation by one of the other branch's use of *its* exclusive powers: Congress, for example, can impeach the executive who willfully fails to enforce the laws; the executive can decline to prosecute under unconstitutional statutes . . . ; and the courts can dismiss malicious prosecutions. Second, and ultimately, there is the political check that the people will replace those in the political branches . . . who are guilty of abuse. Political pressures produced special prosecutors—for Teapot Dome and for Watergate, for example—long before this statute created the independent counsel. See Act of Feb. 8, 1924, ch. 16, 43 Stat. 5–6. . . .

The Court has . . . replaced the clear constitutional prescription that the executive power belongs to the President with a "balancing test." What are the standards to determine how the balance is to be struck, that is, how much removal of Presidential power is too much? . . . Once we depart from the text of the Constitution, just where short of that do we stop? The most amazing feature of the Court's opinion is that it does not even purport to give an answer. It simply *announces,* with no analysis, that the ability to control the decision whether to investigate and prosecute the President's closest advisers, and indeed the President himself, is not "so central to the functioning of the Executive Branch" as to be constitutionally required to be within the President's control. Apparently that is so because we say it is so. . . . Evidently, the governing standard is to be what might be called the unfettered wisdom of a majority of this Court, revealed to an obedient people on a case-by-case basis. This is not only not the government of laws that the Constitution established; it is not a government of laws at all.

In my view, moreover, even as an ad hoc, standardless judgment the Court's conclusion must be wrong. Before this statute was passed, the President, in taking action disagreeable to the Congress, or an executive officer giving advice to the President or testifying before Congress concerning one of those many matters on which the two branches are from time to time at odds, could be assured that his acts and motives would be adjudged—insofar as the decision whether to conduct a criminal investigation and to prosecute is concerned—in the Executive Branch, that is, in a forum attuned to the interests and the policies of the Presidency. That was one of the natural advantages the Constitution gave to the Presidency, just as it gave Members of Congress (and their staffs) the advantage of not being prosecutable for anything said or done in their legislative capacities. See U.S. Const., Art. I, § 6, cl. 1; Gravel v. United States, 408 U.S. 606 (1972). It is the very object of this legislation to eliminate that assurance of a sympathetic forum. . . . [This statute] deeply wounds the President, by substantially reducing the President's ability to protect himself and his staff. That is the whole object of the law, of course, and I cannot imagine why the Court believes it does not succeed. . . .

### III

. . . Article II, § 2, cl. 2, of the Constitution provides as follows:

"[The President] shall nominate, and by and with the Advice and Consent of the Senate, shall appoint Ambassadors, other public Ministers and Consuls, Judges of the supreme Court, and all other Officers of the United States, whose Appointments are not herein otherwise provided for, and which shall be established by Law: but the Congress may by Law vest the Appointment of such inferior Officers, as they think proper, in the President alone, in the Courts of Law, or in the Heads of Departments."

Because appellant (who all parties and the Court agree is an officer of the United States) was not appointed by the President with the advice and consent of the Senate, but rather by the Special Division of the United States Court of Appeals, her appointment is constitutional only if . . . she is an "inferior" officer within the meaning of the above Clause . . . .

. . . [T]he Court does not attempt to "decide exactly" what establishes the line between principal and "inferior" officers, but is confident that, whatever the line may be, appellant "clearly falls on the 'inferior officer' side" of it. The Court gives three reasons: *First,* she "is subject to removal by a higher Executive Branch official," namely, the Attorney General. *Second,* she is "empowered by the Act to perform only certain, limited duties." *Third,* her office is "limited in jurisdiction" and "limited in tenure."

The first of these lends no support to the view that appellant is an inferior officer. Appellant is removable only for "good cause" or physical or mental incapacity. 28 U.S.C. § 596(a)(1) (1982 ed., Supp. V). By contrast, most (if not all) *principal* officers in the Executive Branch may be removed by the President *at will.* I fail to see how the fact that appellant is more difficult to remove than most principal officers helps to establish that she is an inferior officer. . . . If she were removable at will by the Attorney General, then she would be subordinate to him and thus properly designated as inferior; but the Court essentially admits that she is not subordinate. . . .

The second reason offered by the Court—that appellant performs only certain, limited duties—may be relevant to whether she is an inferior officer, but it mischaracterizes the extent of her powers. As the Court states: "Admittedly, the Act delegates to appellant [the] *'full power and independent authority to exercise all investigative and prosecutorial functions and powers of the Department of Justice.'*" (quoting 28 U.S.C. § 594(a) (1982 ed., Supp. V) (emphasis added)). . . .

The final set of reasons given by the Court for why the independent counsel clearly is an inferior officer emphasizes the limited nature of her jurisdiction and tenure. Taking the latter first, I find nothing unusually limited about the independent counsel's tenure. To the contrary, unlike most high ranking Executive Branch officials, she continues to serve until she (or the Special Division) decides that her work is substantially completed. See §§ 596(b)(1), (b)(2). This particular independent prosecutor has already served more than two years, which is at least as long as many Cabinet officials. As to the scope of her jurisdiction, there can be no doubt that is small (though far from unimportant). But within it she exercises more than the full power of the Attorney General. The Ambassador to Luxembourg is not anything less than a principal officer, simply because Luxembourg is small. And the federal judge who sits in a small district is not for that reason "inferior in rank and authority." If the mere fragmentation of executive responsibilities into small compartments suffices to render the heads of each of those compartments inferior officers, then Congress could deprive the President of the right to appoint his chief law enforcement officer by dividing up the Attorney General's responsibilities among a number of "lesser" functionaries.

More fundamentally, however, it is not clear from the Court's opinion why the factors it discusses—even if applied correctly to the facts of this case—are determinative of the question of inferior officer status.... I think it preferable to look to the text of the Constitution and the division of power that it establishes. These demonstrate, I think, that the independent counsel is not an inferior officer because she is not *subordinate* to any officer in the Executive Branch (indeed, not even to the President). Dictionaries in use at the time of the Constitutional Convention gave the word "inferiour" two meanings which it still bears today: (1) "[l]ower in place, ... station, ... rank of life, ... value or excellency," and (2) "[s]ubordinate." S. Johnson, Dictionary of the English Language (6th ed. 1785). In a document dealing with the structure (the constitution) of a government, one would naturally expect the word to bear the latter meaning—indeed, in such a context it would be unpardonably careless to use the word *unless* a relationship of subordination was intended. If what was meant was merely "lower in station or rank," one would use instead a term such as "lesser officers." At the only other point in the Constitution at which the word "inferior" appears, it plainly connotes a relationship of subordination. Article III vests the judicial power of the United States in "one supreme Court, and in such *inferior* Courts as the Congress may from time to time ordain and establish." U.S. Const., Art. III, § 1 (emphasis added). In Federalist No. 81, Hamilton pauses to describe the "inferior" courts authorized by Article III as inferior in the sense that they are "subordinate" to the Supreme Court....

To be sure, it is not a *sufficient* condition for "inferior" officer status that one be subordinate to a principal officer. Even an officer who is subordinate to a department head can be a principal officer.... But it is surely a *necessary* condition for inferior officer status that the officer be subordinate to another officer.... The independent counsel is not even subordinate to the President....

## IV

... Since our 1935 decision in Humphrey's Executor v. United States, 295 U.S. 602—which was considered by many at the time the product of an activist, anti-New Deal Court bent on reducing the power of President Franklin Roosevelt—it has been established that the line of permissible restriction upon removal of principal officers lies at the point at which the powers exercised by those officers are no longer purely executive.... Today, however, *Humphrey's Executor* is swept into the dustbin of repudiated constitutional principles. "[O]ur present considered view," the Court says, "is that the determination of whether the Constitution allows Congress to impose a 'good cause'-type restriction on the President's power to remove an official cannot be made to turn on whether or not that official is classified as 'purely executive.'" What *Humphrey's Executor* (and presumably *Myers*) really means, we are now told, is not that there are any "rigid categories of those officials who may or may not be removed at will by the President," but simply that Congress cannot "interfere with the President's exercise of the 'executive power' and his constitutionally appointed duty to 'take care that the laws be faithfully executed[.]' "

One can hardly grieve for the shoddy treatment given today to *Humphrey's Executor*, which, after all, accorded the same indignity (with much less justification) to Chief Justice Taft's opinion 10 years earlier in *Myers v. United States*, 272 U.S. 52 (1926)—gutting, in six quick pages devoid of textual or historical precedent for the novel principle it set forth, a carefully researched and reasoned 70–page opinion. It is in fact comforting to witness the reality that he who lives by the *ipse dixit* dies by the *ipse dixit*. But one must grieve for the Constitution. *Humphrey's Executor* at least had the decency formally to observe the constitutional principle that the President had to be the repository of *all* executive power, which, as *Myers* carefully explained, necessarily means that he must be able to discharge those who do not perform executive functions according to his liking.... There are now no lines. If the removal of a prosecutor, the virtual embodiment of the power to "take care that the laws be faithfully executed," can be restricted, what officer's removal cannot? This is an open invitation for Congress to experiment. What about a special Assistant Secretary of State, with responsibility for one very narrow area of foreign policy, who would not only have to be confirmed by the Senate but could also be removed only pursuant to certain carefully designed restrictions? Could this possibly render the President "[un]able to accomplish his constitutional role"? Or a special Assistant Secretary of Defense for Procurement? The possibilities are endless, and the Court does not understand what the separation of powers, what "[a]mbition ... counteract[ing] ambition," Federalist No. 51, p. 322 (Madison), is all about, if it does not expect Congress to try them. As far as I can discern from the Court's opinion, it is now open season upon the President's removal power for all executive officers, with not even the superficially principled restriction of *Humphrey's Executor* as cover. The Court essentially says to the President: "Trust us. We will make sure that you are able to accomplish your constitutional role." I think the Constitution gives the President—and the people—more protection than that.

V

The purpose of the separation and equilibration of powers in general, and of the unitary Executive in particular, was not merely to assure effective government but to preserve individual freedom. Those who hold or have held offices covered by the Ethics in Government Act are entitled to that protection as much as the rest of us, and I conclude my discussion by considering the effect of the Act upon the fairness of the process they receive....

Under our system of government, the primary check against prosecutorial abuse is a political one. The prosecutors who exercise this awesome discretion are selected and can be removed by a President, whom the people have trusted enough to elect. Moreover, when crimes are not investigated and prosecuted fairly, nonselectively, with a reasonable sense of proportion, the President pays the cost in political damage to his administration. . . .

. . . An independent counsel is selected, and the scope of his or her authority prescribed, by a panel of judges. What if they are politically partisan, as judges have been known to be, and select a prosecutor antagonistic to the administration, or even to the particular individual who has been selected for this special treatment? There is no remedy for that, not even a political one. Judges, after all, have life tenure, and appointing a surefire enthusiastic prosecutor could hardly be considered an impeachable offense. So if there is anything wrong with the selection, there is effectively no one to blame. The independent counsel thus selected proceeds to assemble a staff. As I observed earlier, in the nature of things this has to be done by finding lawyers who are willing to lay aside their current careers for an indeterminate amount of time, to take on a job that has no prospect of permanence and little prospect for promotion. One thing is certain, however: it involves investigating and perhaps prosecuting a particular individual. Can one imagine a less equitable manner of fulfilling the executive responsibility to investigate and prosecute? What would be the reaction if, in an area not covered by this statute, the Justice Department posted a public notice inviting applicants to assist in an investigation and possible prosecution of a certain prominent person? Does this not invite what Justice Jackson described as "picking the man and then searching the law books, or putting investigators to work, to pin some offense on him"? . . . It seems to me not conducive to fairness. But even if it were entirely evident that unfairness was in fact the result—the judges hostile to the administration, the independent counsel an old foe of the President, the staff refugees from the recently defeated administration—*there would be no one accountable to the public to whom the blame could be assigned.* . . .

. . . Today's decision on the basic issue of fragmentation of executive power is ungoverned by rule, and hence ungoverned by law. It extends into the very heart of our most significant constitutional function the "totality of the circumstances" mode of analysis that this Court has in recent years become fond of. Taking all things into account, we conclude that the power taken away from the President here is not really *too* much. The next time executive power is assigned to someone other than the President we may conclude, taking all things into account, that it *is* too much. That opinion, like this one, will not be confined by any rule. We will describe, as we have today (though I hope more accurately) the effects of the provision in question, and will authoritatively announce: "The President's need to control the exercise of the [subject officer's] discretion *is* so central to the functioning of the Executive Branch as to require complete control." This is not analysis; it is ad hoc judgment. And it fails to explain why it is not true that—as the text of the Constitution seems to require, as the Founders seemed to expect, and as our past cases have uniformly assumed—all purely executive power must be under the control of the President.

The ad hoc approach to constitutional adjudication has real attraction, even apart from its work-saving potential. It is guaranteed to produce a result, in every case, that will make a majority of the Court happy with the law. The law is, by definition, precisely what the majority thinks, taking all things into account, it *ought* to be. I prefer to rely upon the judgment of the wise men who constructed our system, and of the people who approved it, and of two centuries of history that have shown it to be sound. Like it or not, that judgment says, quite plainly, that "[t]he executive Power shall be vested in a President of the United States."

---

**1. The Appointments Clause**—*Morrison* has given rise to a rich body of scholarship on the question whether and to what extent the President should exercise control over criminal prosecution in general, and criminal prosecution of high government officials in particular. *See, e.g.,* Stephen L. Carter, *The Independent Counsel Mess*, 102 HARV. L. REV. 105 (1988); William B. Gwyn, *The Indeterminacy of the Separation of Powers and the Federal Courts*, 57 GEO. WASH. L. REV. 474, 476 (1989); Harold J. Krent, *Executive Control over Criminal Law Enforcement: Some Lessons from History*, 38 AM. U. L. REV. 275 (1989); Saikrishna Prakash, *The Chief Prosecutor*, 73 GEO. WASH. L. REV. 521 (2005). Given our focus here on the regulatory process, however, we will put this issue to one side and focus instead on *Morrison*'s implications for the competition between Congress and the President for control over administrative agencies.

*Morrison* is significant in part because of how the Court approached the question whether the independent counsel is an "inferior Officer" for Appointments Clause purposes. In reaching the conclusion that the special prosecutor was an inferior officer, rather than a principal officer, *Morrison* adopted a balancing test that took account of four nonexclusive factors. First, because the Attorney General could remove the independent counsel for cause, the independent counsel was "to some degree 'inferior' in rank and degree." Second, the independent counsel only had "certain, limited duties"—namely, investigating and prosecuting crimes, rather than "formulat[ing] policy for the Government or the Executive Branch." Third, the independent counsel had limited jurisdiction; she was restricted by the organic statute to investigating only certain federal officials and then limited further to the particular officials and offenses specified in the order appointing her and defining her jurisdiction. Fourth, the office of the independent counsel was limited in duration in the sense that it expired at the conclusion of the investigation.

How did the Court derive these four factors? If, as the Court suggested, the meaning of the term "inferior Officer" is vague or opaque, then perhaps the Court's test was a commonsensical way to determine whether someone could plausibly be called an "inferior" officer within the federal government hierarchy. *See* Peter M. Shane, *Independent Policymaking and Presidential Power: A Constitutional Analysis*, 57 GEO. WASH. L. REV. 596, 599 (1989) ("[B]ecause an independent counsel is apparently a temporary appointee for the investigation of criminal charges relating to a single individual, such an official surely has the feel of 'inferior-ness.' ") Even on this sympathetic reading of *Morrison*, however, there remain some difficult questions about how this test would apply in cases where the four factors listed by the *Morrison* Court point in different directions. Imagine, for example, that Congress established a Permanent Office of the Independent Counsel to examine all claims of criminal wrongdoing by any of the high government officials covered by the Ethics in Government Act. If that official were removable for "good cause," would he or she be an inferior officer? How much of a problem are these questions of application? Do they indicate, as Justice Scalia suggested, that the *Morrison* approach to distinguishing principal from inferior officers is devoid of content? Or do these questions merely indicate that the precise contours of the distinction have not yet been fully worked out, and can be clarified in subsequent cases?

There are also legitimate questions, raised by Justice Scalia in dissent, about whether the *Morrison* majority correctly applied its own test. For example, *Morrison* asserts that the independent counsel has only "limited duties." But while it is true that the independent counsel did not have government-wide policymaking authority, she did exercise all of the powers of the Attorney General within her area of jurisdiction. And even though that jurisdiction is "limited" in the sense that the independent counsel is only authorized to investigate a narrowly defined set of individuals, that set consists of high-level government officials. Hence the independent counsel's jurisdiction, though "limited," is extremely important. *See* Ken Gormley, *An Original Model of the Independent Counsel Statute*, 97 MICH. L. REV. 601, 641 n.166 (1998); Donald C. Smaltz, *The Independent Counsel: A View from Inside*, 86 GEO. L.J. 2307, 2323–24 (1998). Also, while *Morrison* suggests that the independent counsel's tenure is limited, because a particular independent counsel's office ceases to exist once its investigation has come to a close, it is not clear why that limitation is particularly important in determining whether the independent counsel is a principal or inferior officer. Is this aspect of Justice Scalia's critique persuasive? Did the majority correctly apply its own test?

Justice Scalia's dissent advocates a different, and seemingly much simpler, approach to distinguishing principal officers from inferior officers; in his view, "inferior" in the context of the Appointments Clause means "subordinate," and "subordinate" means subject to the direction and control of another executive branch official (other than the President). Justice Scalia's conclusion that "inferior" in this context means "subordinate" rests on two pieces of evidence: First, a leading late-eighteenth-century dictionary defined "inferiour" as "(1) '[l]ower in place, ... station, ... rank of life, ... value or excellency,' and (2) '[s]ubordinate.' " In Justice Scalia's view, when used in a constitutional provision dealing with the structure of government, "one would naturally expect the word to bear the latter meaning—indeed, in such a context it would be unpardonably careless to use the word *unless* a relationship of subordination was intended." Second, Justice Scalia concluded that the word "inferior" as used in Article III—which vests the judicial power in "one supreme Court, and in such *inferior* Courts as the Congress may from time to time ordain and establish" (emphasis added)—"plainly connotes a relationship of subordination." (In making this latter point, Justice Scalia implicitly applied to the Constitution the interpretive principle that identical terms should be presumed to have the same meaning, which we have previously encountered in the context of *statutory* interpretation (*see* pp. 243–245, *supra*)). Are these two pieces of evidence sufficiently convincing to justify striking down an Act of Congress? Why didn't the Court or the dissent examine how early statutes—or for that matter, how statutes over time—drew the line between inferior and principal officers?

**2. Morrison *Reconsidered?*—**Almost a decade after *Morrison*, the Court issued another major opinion construing the phrase "inferior Officer" in a manner that, some believe, overruled *Morrison*'s four-part balancing without saying so. *See* William K. Kelley, *The Constitutional Dilemma of Litigation Under the Independent Counsel System*, 83 Minn. L. Rev. 1197, 1258 (1999); Nick Bravin, Note, *Is* Morrison v. Olson *Still Good Law? The Court's New Appointments Clause Jurisprudence*, 98 Colum. L. Rev. 1103, 1125–35 (1998). In Edmond v. United States, 520 U.S. 651 (1997), the Court purported to apply the *Morrison* four-part framework for determining whether someone was an inferior officer, but gave dispositive weight to only one of the four factors. At issue was the appointment of the judges of the Coast Guard Court of Criminal Appeals (CGCCA), a military court residing within the executive branch. Under the relevant statute, the Secretary of Transportation appoints CGCCA Judges. This is permissible only if these judges are inferior officers eligible for appointment by "Heads of Departments." U.S. Const. art. II, § 2, cl. 2.

In an opinion by Justice Scalia, the Court held that the CGCCA Judges were, in fact, inferior officers. In so holding, the Court started by finding that these judges failed three of the four prongs of *Morrison*'s test for inferior officers: First, CGCCA Judges do not have "limited tenure," in the sense that *Morrison* used this term, because a CGCCA Judge's office does not expire upon the completion of a discrete task. Second, CGCCA Judges are not "limited in jurisdiction" in the *Morrison* sense, because these Judges are not constrained to adjudicate only cases involving certain individuals' offenses specified in advance. Third, CGCCA Judges could not be said to perform "limited duties," because the court-martial proceedings over which they preside may "result in the most serious sentences," including dismissal, confinement, or even capital punishment, and in these proceedings the CGCCA Judges have substantial power to review findings of fact and to make conclusions of law. Despite all this, Justice Scalia's *Edmond* opinion concluded that the CGCCA Judges were inferior officers because they were subject to supervision by a higher-ranking executive branch official (below the President):

> [W]hether one is an "inferior" officer depends on whether he has a superior. It is not enough that other officers may be identified who formally maintain a higher rank, or possess responsibilities of a greater magnitude. If that were the intention, the Constitution might have used the phrase "lesser officer." Rather, in the context of a Clause

designed to preserve political accountability relative to important Government assignments, we think it evident that "inferior officers" are officers whose work is directed and supervised at some level by others who were appointed by presidential nomination with the advice and consent of the Senate.

The Court held that the CGCCA Judges satisfied this criterion because they were effectively supervised in three respects. First, the Judge Advocate General (JAG)—a senior Coast Guard official who answers to the Secretary of Transportation—"is charged with the responsibility to 'prescribe uniform rules of procedure' for the court, and must 'meet periodically [with other Judge Advocates General] to formulate policies and procedure in regard to review of court-martial cases.' " 10 U.S.C. § 866(f). Second, the JAG possesses authority to "remove a Court of Criminal Appeals judge from his judicial assignment without cause," though he or she may not use that power to affect the outcome of any case. Third, another component of the executive branch, the Court of Appeals for the Armed Forces (CAAF), "reviews every decision of the Courts of Criminal Appeals in which: (a) the sentence extends to death; (b) the Judge Advocate General orders such review; or (c) the court itself grants review upon petition of the accused." 10 U.S.C. § 867(a). Although Justice Scalia acknowledged that the CAAF exercised only narrow review that required it to sustain the CGCCA's judgments "so long as there is some competent evidence in the record to establish each element of the offense beyond a reasonable doubt," he found it significant that CGCCA Judges under this scheme "have no power to render a final decision on behalf of the United States unless permitted to do so by other executive officers." 10 U.S.C. § 867(c).

In a concurring opinion, Justice Souter suggested that the Court's opinion focused too narrowly on the question of supervision and was therefore not true to the *Morrison* test it purported to apply:

> Because the term "inferior officer" implies an official superior, one who has no superior is not an inferior officer. . . . It does not follow, however, that if one is subject to some supervision and control, one is an inferior officer. Having a superior officer is necessary for inferior officer status, but not sufficient to establish it. . . . Accordingly, in *Morrison*, the Court's determination that the independent counsel was "to some degree 'inferior' " to the Attorney General . . . did not end the enquiry. The Court went on to weigh the duties, jurisdiction, and tenure associated with the office . . . before concluding that the independent counsel was an inferior officer. Thus, under *Morrison*, the Solicitor General of the United States, for example, may well be a principal officer, despite his statutory "inferiority" to the Attorney General. . . .

If the supervision test articulated by Justice Scalia for eight members of the Court in *Edmond* supplants the four-part *Morrison* test, is it an improvement? Perhaps *Edmond* supplies a clearer and more easily administrable test than did *Morrison*. Then again, the *Edmond* opinion might indicate that the question whether an officer is "supervised" by another is not as straightforward as it might first appear. In *Edmond*, the Court relied on three factors in concluding that the CGCCA Judges were subject to sufficient supervision: the JAG's prescription of rules of procedure, the JAG's power to remove, and the CAAF's power to review. Were all three necessary? If not, which combination of factors would have sufficed? What if the only supervision had been the CAAF's sharply limited review? If an officer higher in the executive branch had illimitable removal authority, would that alone suffice to establish supervision? If Congress reenacted the independent counsel statute, would the "good cause" removal provision suffice to establish supervision under *Edmond*? (For an argument that it would not, see Kelley, *supra*, at 1258–59.) If it did not, would the fact that the officer had limited duties, jurisdiction, and tenure still be able to sustain the independent counsel's status as an inferior officer? Does anything in the holding of *Edmond* preclude such a result?

*Edmond* might also have a superior claim to furthering the Appointments Clause's purpose "to preserve political accountability relative to important government assignments." But is the *Edmond* "supervision" test obviously superior to the four-part *Morrison* test in preserving this sort of political accountability? Given the complexities of sorting through the various tests, should the Court rely more heavily on common law reasoning in this area—examining whether a disputed officer shares fundamental attributes of officers that Congress and the Court have, in the past, treated as inferior officers? If so, what attributes should the Court look for? Scope and importance of responsibilities? Explicit accountability to superiors? Both?

**3. The Removal Power After Morrison**—*Morrison* is perhaps even more significant for its holding regarding statutory limitations on the President's power to remove agency officials. Strikingly, *Morrison* seems to reject both *Myers*' position that executive officers are subject to the President's illimitable removal power and *Humphrey's Executor*'s position that Congress can restrict the President's removal power only over agency officials that perform quasi-legislative or quasi-judicial functions. The *Morrison* Court apparently viewed the lines drawn by *Humphrey's Executor* as too difficult to sustain, but still wished to preserve a basis for upholding independent agencies as constitutional.

Noting "the difficulty of defining such categories of 'executive' or 'quasi-legislative'" and explaining that "the powers of the FTC at the time of *Humphrey's Executor* would at the present time be considered 'executive' in some degree," the Court made clear that "our present considered view is that the determination of whether the Constitution allows Congress to impose a 'good cause'-type restriction on the President's power to remove an official cannot be made to turn on whether or not that official is classified as 'purely executive.'" *Morrison* thus eliminates the incongruity between *Humphrey's Executor* and the conception of delegated power as law execution that runs from *Chadha* through *Bowsher* to *Whitman*.

If the formal line between executive power, on the one hand, and quasi-legislative or quasi-judicial power, on the other, no longer determines the permissibility of removal restrictions, what does? The Court asserted: "The analysis contained in our removal cases is designed not to define rigid categories of those officials who may or may not be removed at will by the President, but to ensure that Congress does not interfere with the President's exercise of the 'executive power' and his constitutionally appointed duty to 'take care that the laws be faithfully executed' under Article II." In this case, the Court concluded that the "good cause" restriction on removal did not "unduly trammel[ ] on executive authority," even though no one in the case disputed that the prosecutorial functions performed by the independent counsel were executive. The Court observed that "we simply do not see how the President's need to control the exercise of that discretion is so central to the functioning of the Executive Branch as to require as a matter of constitutional law that the counsel be terminable at will by the President."

How can one tell whether a removal restriction "unduly trammels" on the President's executive authority? The Court considered several factors. First, the Court made clear that the *type of function* remains relevant. Even though the quasi-legislative and quasi-judicial categories are no longer dispositive, *Morrison* indicated that an officer's performance of such functions made it less likely that that officer's functions would be deemed central to the functioning of the executive branch, while the President would be more likely to have plenary removal power over officers performing functions related to core aspects of the President's executive authority. Second, the Court considered the *degree of authority* exercised by the independent counsel, noting that she had "limited jurisdiction and tenure and lack[ed] policymaking or significant administrative authority." Third, the removal restriction did not, in the Court's view "impermissibly burden[ ] the President's power to control and supervise the independent counsel." What did the Court mean by that? On one side of the ledger, the Court believed that the "good cause" standard left the President, through the Attorney General, "with ample authority" both "to assure that the independent counsel is competently performing his or her statutory responsibilities in a manner that comports with the provisions of the Act" and to "remove an independent counsel for misconduct." On the other side of the ledger, the limitation on removal "was essential, in the view of Congress, to establish the necessary independence of the office."

Where did the Court get this elaborate test? Is Justice Scalia correct in stating that the Court "replaces [a] clear constitutional prescription [announced in *Myers*] that the executive power belongs to the President with a 'balancing test'"? Justice Scalia argued that the conclusion that the removal limitation does not impermissibly intrude on the President's Article II power "is so [only] because we say it is so." Is that a fair criticism? Or does the Court's standard represent a commonsensical way of determining whether there is more than a *de minimis* intrusion on presidential power, and whether Congress had good reason for such intrusion as there is?

How easy or hard is the *Morrison* test to apply? Consider different positions in the Department of Justice. Presumably it would be unlawful, under *Morrison*, for Congress to establish an Independent Attorney General, even though the Attorney General wields the same type of executive power as the independent counsel. But what if Congress created an Independent Solicitor General? Although the Solicitor General performs the important function of representing the United States in the Supreme Court, he or she also has special obligations of candor and scrupulousness in dealing with the Court. *See* Lincoln Caplan, The Tenth Justice (1987). Could Congress impose a "good cause" restriction on the President's authority to remove the Solicitor General, in order to guard his or her independence from political pressure? What if Congress concluded that all of the U.S. Attorneys—the 93 front-line federal prosecutors throughout the nation who supervise all federal prosecutions within their respective districts—should be removable only for "good cause" as a way to insulate prosecutorial decisionmaking from political influence? *See* James Eisenstein, *The U.S. Attorney Firings of 2006: Main Justice's Centralization Efforts in Historical Context*, 31 Seattle U. L. Rev. 219 (2008) (same); Daniel Richman, *Political Control of Federal Prosecutions: Looking Back and Looking Forward*, 58 Duke L.J. 2087, 2094–2116 (2009) (discussing recent controversy over the firing of eight U.S. attorneys). Or would such a limitation take too big a bite out of the President's authority over the function of prosecution?

Consider other types of officials. Imagine that Congress decided to insulate the General Counsel of the Defense Department from removal in order to assure that he or she was able to give dispassionate advice about the rule of law, perhaps especially during times of emergency. Would that cut too close to the core of the President's power as commander-in-chief? How about, as per Justice Scalia's example, a limitation on the Assistant Secretary of Defense for Procurement? Although that office has responsibilities that relate to national security, might the Court conclude that dealing with defense contractors represents a fairly small piece of the President's authority over national defense and that there are good reasons to give political insulation to someone who administers large government contracts? How about the Tax Legislative Counsel in the Treasury Department, who plays an important role in crafting the regulations that implement tax policy? Does your take on these examples suggest a coherent intuition that guides the application of *Morrison*'s balancing test, or does it seem ad hoc?

Note also that, in addition to the factors outlined above, *Morrison* seems to endorse more generally the importance of distinguishing between congressional *aggrandizement*—Congress's arrogating to itself powers that ought to reside with the President—and congressional *encroachment* on presidential power in the form of restrictions or limitations on the President that do not enhance the role of Congress. (*See* pp. 514–515, *supra*). As the *Morrison* majority explains, "this case does not involve an attempt by Congress to increase its own powers at the expense of the Executive Branch.... Unlike some of our previous cases, most recently *Bowsher v.*

*Synar,* this case simply does not pose a 'dange[r] of congressional usurpation of Executive Branch functions.' " *See also* Eric R. Glitzenstein & Alan B. Morrison, *The Supreme Court's Decision in* Morrison v. Olson*: A Common Sense Application of the Constitution to a Practical Problem,* 38 AM. U. L. REV. 359, 370–74 (1989). How much work do you think that distinction is doing in the opinion? How much work should it do? Does Justice Scalia make a convincing case that the independent counsel statute *does* aggrandize congressional power by taking from the President constitutionally contemplated means of self-defense in the inevitable interbranch competition?

**4. *Political Safeguards and Judicial Enforcement in Separation-of-Powers Cases*—**Morrison provides a useful opportunity to think about a question that often arises in the separation-of-powers context: To what extent are *legal* restrictions necessary to prevent government officials from abusing their power, and to what extent can we rely on *political* checks to restrain abuses of discretion? This issue arises in *Morrison* in two quite different contexts.

First, consider the functional arguments in favor of the independent counsel statute itself. The *Morrison* majority concluded that Congress had a reasonable interest in insulating the independent counsel from presidential control, in light of the fact that the President may be reluctant to permit aggressive investigation of the President's close associates and allies, or perhaps even of the President him- or herself. Justice Scalia disagreed in part because he views the political check as adequate to prevent Presidents from abusing their power to dismiss a special prosecutor investigating allegations of criminal wrongdoing in the executive branch. For example, when President Nixon ordered the dismissal of Special Prosecutor Archibald Cox, who was investigating the Watergate scandal that ultimately led to President Nixon's resignation, the result was a political firestorm that may have hastened Nixon's political demise. *See* Ken Gormley, *An Original Model of the Independent Counsel Statute,* 97 MICH. L. REV. 601, 603 (1998). While the political ramifications of dismissing an independent counsel investigating allegations of high-level wrongdoing might be particularly dramatic, might there be similar political constraints on the use of removal more generally as a means to dictate regulatory policy outcomes?

Second, consider the question whether it is necessary for the judiciary to enforce aggressively a sharp separation between legislative and executive powers, or whether the judiciary should instead be more tolerant of novel arrangements that do not fit comfortably with traditional conceptions of a tripartite separation of powers. Justice Scalia's dissent emphasized that strict enforcement of the Constitution's formal division of powers is necessary because if Congress has the power to do things like create executive officials whom the President cannot remove, Congress will invariably exploit this power to undermine the presidency. The majority's greater comfort with a functionalist approach seems due in part to an implicit belief that political as well as judicial safeguards will prevent Congress from abusing its power. This difference in view has parallels to the debates over whether the "political safeguards of federalism" protect state autonomy effectively enough to obviate the need for aggressive judicial enforcement of the Tenth Amendment and the Commerce Clause. *See* pp. 289–290, *supra*.

Do subsequent developments with respect to the independent counsel statute vindicate one or the other side of these debates? In the period between the late 1980s and the late 1990s, when a large number of independent counsels aggressively investigated both Republican and Democratic administrations, a growing bipartisan consensus began to emerge that the independent counsel statute was not working well and, in particular, that it presented the potential, if not the reality, for the very sorts of abuses to which Justice Scalia's dissent referred. *See* Nick Bravin, Note, *Is Morrison v. Olson Still Good Law? The Court's New Appointments Clause Jurisprudence*, 98 COLUM. L. REV. 1103, 1125–35 (1998). Do these perceived excesses show that Justice Scalia was right—that the Ethics in Government Act's independent counsel provision put a dangerous political weapon in the hands of Congress to harass and weaken the President? Or does the fact that Congress declined to renew the independent counsel statute when it expired in 1999 suggest that the system has a greater capacity for self-correction than Justice Scalia appreciated? *See, e.g.*, James K. Robinson, *After the Independent Counsel Act: Where Do We Go from Here?*, 51 HASTINGS L.J. 733, 740 (2000) (noting that "faced with a near-total lack of interest or enthusiasm for the continuation of this flawed experiment, Congress let the Independent Counsel Act lapse when it expired on June 30, 1999").

**5. *The Meaning of "Good Cause"***—After *Morrison*, it seems likely that the Court will continue to uphold the "good cause"-type removal restrictions that routinely appear in the organic acts creating independent regulatory agencies. In light of that fact, what does *Morrison* tell us, if anything, about the scope of the President's authority to use such removal authority to direct, influence, and coordinate the federal government's regulatory policy? As discussed in connection with *Humphrey's Executor* (pp. 515–516, *supra*), perhaps the President might have "cause," under the typical removal restriction, to dismiss an agency official who refuses to comply with the President's (reasonable) view of the law. Recall that *Bowsher* described a variant of the "inefficiency, neglect of duty, and malfeasance in office" standard as permitting removal for any "actual or perceived transgression of the [principal's] will" (p. 465, *supra*). Does *Morrison* reinforce that idea? Although the Court took pains to state that it lacked any occasion to decide what "good cause" means, it also stated that the "good cause" provision at least permitted the Attorney General to remove an independent counsel who is not "competently performing his or her statutory responsibilities in a manner that comports with the provisions of the Act." Is that reading of "good cause" in keeping with the spirit of the independent counsel statute or the philosophy underlying the creation of independent agencies? Is such a reading necessary to avoid serious constitutional questions?

## V. PRESIDENTIAL CONTROL OF AGENCIES

Although the President is the head of the executive branch, and the policy decisions of the agencies are frequently associated in the public mind with the sitting President's administration, modern Presidents have struggled to oversee the bureaucracy. Even President Franklin Roosevelt, one of the most powerful Presidents in history and the chief architect of the modern administrative state, had trouble controlling his creation. Indeed, in 1937 he established a special commission (known as the Brownlow Committee, after its chair Louis Brownlow) to propose solutions that would address the fact that the President, though having responsibility for the "direction and control of all departments and agencies in the Executive Branch," nevertheless lacked "adequate legal authority or administrative machinery to enable him to exercise it." *Memorandum from Louis Brownlow, President's Committee on Administrative Management, to President Franklin Delano Roosevelt* (Nov. 5, 1936) (A–II–33 Roosevelt Library), *quoted in* PERI E. ARNOLD, MAKING THE MANAGERIAL PRESIDENCY: COMPREHENSIVE REORGANIZATION PLANNING, 1905–1996, at 103 (2nd ed. 1998). Although the Brownlow Committee's report prompted a number of reforms—perhaps most importantly, the creation of the Executive Office of the President (EOP), the relocation of the Bureau of the Budget from the Treasury Department to the newly-created EOP, and the expansion of the White House staff—Presidents continued to struggle to manage the administrative bureaucracy. President Roosevelt's successor, President Harry Truman, once complained, "I thought I was the president, but when it comes to these bureaucrats, I can't do a damn thing," (quoted in RICHARD P. NATHAN, THE ADMINISTRATIVE PRESIDENCY 2 (1983)), and he predicted that his successor, former general Dwight Eisenhower will "sit here and he'll say, 'Do this! Do that!' *And nothing will happen.* Poor Ike—it won't be a bit like the Army." RICHARD E. NEUSTADT, PRESIDENTIAL POWER AND THE MODERN PRESIDENTS 10 (1990) (internal quotation marks omitted) (emphasis in original). President George H.W. Bush nicely summed up the exasperation many modern Presidents have felt regarding the limits on their power over the agencies when he declared, during complicated negotiations concerning the Food and Drug Administration's nutrition labeling regulations, "I'm a little puzzled. I'm being told that I can't just make a decision and have it promptly executed, that the Department can't just salute smartly and go execute whatever decision I make. Why is that?" DAVID KESSLER, A QUESTION OF INTENT: A GREAT AMERICAN BATTLE WITH A DEADLY INDUSTRY 68 (2001).

As we saw in Part IV of this chapter, one of the most important tools at the President's disposal for exerting control over the administrative bureaucracy is the power to appoint and remove agency officials. Indeed, the President's power over personnel may be the single most important form of presidential influence over the administrative state. *See* DAVID E. LEWIS, THE POLITICS OF PRESIDENTIAL APPOINTMENTS: POLITICAL CONTROL AND BUREAUCRATIC PERFORMANCE (2008); David J. Barron, *From Takeover to*

*Merger: Reforming Administrative Law in an Age of Agency Politicization*, 76 GEO. WASH. L. REV. 1095 (2008). Nevertheless, the appointment and removal powers do not give Presidents as much control as they would like. With respect to appointments, Presidents cannot always predict ahead of time which appointees will consistently act to advance the President's priorities. Furthermore, appointments are not always based exclusively on loyalty to the President's regulatory vision: the interest in appointing technically competent administrators, and the interest in rewarding key supporters or constituency groups, may sometimes induce appointment of officials whose regulatory preferences diverge to some degree from those of the appointing President. The requirement of Senate confirmation may also constrain the President's ability to shape administrative policy exclusively through appointments, especially during periods of divided government. True, Senate rejections of presidential nominees are extremely rare (occurring in fewer than 5% of cases, with most "rejections" taking the form of a nominee's withdrawal rather than a rejection in a floor vote). *See* Glen S. Krutz, Richard Fleisher & Jon R. Bond, *From Abe Fortas to Zöe Baird: Why Some Presidential Nominations Fail in the Senate*, 92 AM. POL. SCI. REV. 871 (1998). Yet this does not render the Senate confirmation process insignificant, as the threat of Senate rejection or substantial delay of a presidential nominee may exert a powerful influence over a President's appointments. *See* Nolan McCarty & Rose Razaghian, *Advice and Consent: Senate Responses to Executive Branch Nominations, 1885–1996*, 43 AM. J. POL. SCI. 1122 (1999); David C. Nixon, *Separation of Powers and Appointee Ideology*, 20 J.L. ECON. & ORG. 438 (2004). Empirical research confirms that the Senate has a substantial influence on the policy preferences of presidential appointees, notwithstanding the fact that almost all appointees are confirmed. *See* Nixon, *supra*; Susan K. Snyder & Barry R. Weingast, *The American System of Shared Powers: The President, Congress, and the NLRB*, 16 J.L. ECON. & ORG. 269 (2000). The preferences of agency officials may also shift after they are appointed, as they are influenced by lobbyists in the field they are supposed to regulate (a form of "capture") or by the career civil servants in the agency. *See* Bruce Ackerman, *The New Separation of Powers*, 113 HARV. L. REV. 633, 700–01 (2000); E. Donald Elliott, *TQM-ing OMB: Or Why Regulatory Review Under Executive Order 12,291 Works Poorly and What President Clinton Should Do About It*, 57 LAW & CONTEMP. PROBS 167 (1994). Taken together, these factors mean that the President's power to appoint agency officials does not guarantee that agencies will always share the President's regulatory philosophy and priorities.

The President's removal power goes some way toward addressing this problem, both because the President can replace unsatisfactory officials, and because the threat of removal may keep agency officials in line. Yet the removal power does not solve the President's control problem. For the independent commissions, as we have seen, Congress may impose legal limits on the President's removal authority (*see* pp. 508–513, *supra*). Removal, moreover, is a blunt instrument: firing an agency official is a drastic measure, and the President may feel politically constrained regarding its use. As Professor Robert Percival suggests, when an agency official rejects presidential direction in the face of threatened removal, that action may "serve as an alarm signal to the public that the president may not be acting with fidelity to the law or in the best interest of the country." Robert V. Percival, *Presidential Management of the Administrative State: The Not–So–Unitary Executive*, 51 DUKE L.J. 963, 1004 (2001); *see also* Richard H. Pildes & Cass R. Sunstein, *Reinventing the Regulatory State*, 62 U. CHI. L. REV. 1, 25 (1995) (arguing that the President may incur a large political cost when he or she dismisses an agency head for reasons of policy disagreement). Recall, furthermore, that if the President dismisses an official whose appointment is subject to advice and consent, he or she gives the Senate leverage to make a public issue of the matter that provoked the dismissal and to block or delay the appointment of a replacement.

The limitations on the President's ability to shape regulatory policy exclusively through the appointment and removal of agency officials have prompted recent Presidents to seek other mechanisms for exercising influence over the administration. This section will consider two such mechanisms: centralized review of regulations by the White House's Office of Management and Budget (OMB), and the Presidential issuance of "directives" to agencies. These are not the only other sources of presidential control over agencies. As Professor Peter Strauss points out, even independent agencies frequently "need goods the President can provide: budgetary and legislative support, assistance in dealing with other agencies, legal services, office space, and advice on national policy." Peter L. Strauss, *The Place of Agencies in Government: Separation of Powers and the Fourth Branch*, 84 COLUM. L. REV. 573, 594 (1984). Yet centralized regulatory review and presidential directives are two of the most important and controversial tools that modern Presidents have used to assert greater control over the administrative state, and so we conclude this chapter with a discussion of these devices.

## A. CENTRALIZED REGULATORY REVIEW

As noted above, the Brownlow Committee's report prompted the creation of the Executive Office of the President (EOP) and the transfer of the Bureau of the Budget from Treasury to EOP. While these reforms were intended to give the White House greater control over agencies, their impact on agency regulatory policy was initially quite limited. This began to change in the 1970s. In 1970, President Richard Nixon reorganized the Bureau of the Budget into the Office of Management and Budget (OMB). As part of his reorganization of this office, President Nixon instituted an interagency review process, supervised by OMB, in which proposed agency rules on environmental, public health, or consumer protection topics were circulated to other agencies for comment before the initiating agency could move forward. *See* Harold H. Bruff, *Presidential Management of Agency Rulemaking*, 57 GEO. WASH. L. REV. 533, 546–47 (1989). Presidents Gerald Ford and Jimmy Carter built on this foundation, with President Ford requiring all agencies to submit to OMB an analysis of the inflationary impact of their regulatory proposals, and President Carter requiring agencies to submit for OMB review an analysis of major regulations (including a statement of the problem, an analysis of economic consequences of both the proposed regulation and major alternatives, and the reason for the ultimate choice). *Id.* at 547–48. President Carter also created a Regulatory Analysis Review Group, consisting of representatives of major agencies and OMB, to review certain regulations with a significant economic impact, as well as a Regulatory Council, made up of the heads of major regulatory agencies, to publish an annual calendar that summarized major regulations under development. *Id.* at 548–49. Nonetheless, these various review programs were not actually all that powerful: only a small number of agency rules were reviewed by the White House, and even when they were reviewed, "all parties understood final decisionmaking authority to rest with the initiating agency," Elena Kagan, *Presidential Administration*, 114 HARV. L. REV. 2245, 2276–77 (2001).

President Ronald Reagan dramatically expanded centralized White House review of agency regulations, and set the template for every President since. In his first month in office, President Reagan issued Executive Order 12291, which required all executive branch agencies (but not independent commissions) to submit proposals for "major" regulations (principally regulations expected to have a significant economic impact) to the Office of Information and Regulatory Affairs (OIRA), a newly created division within OMB. These submissions had to include a "regulatory impact analysis" that included a formal cost-benefit analysis (CBA). E.O. 12291 not only required agencies to provide such an analysis, but further instructed agencies that "to the extent permitted by law," they could adopt a regulation only if the CBA showed that the net benefits of that regulation were positive and that the regulatory alternative selected involved "the least net cost to society." Four years later, President Reagan issued Executive Order 12498, which expanded centralized OMB review by establishing a "regulatory planning process," in which executive branch agencies (but, again, not independent commissions) were required each year to submit to OMB a draft regulatory program describing "all significant regulatory actions" that the agency planned to undertake in the coming year. Pursuant to E.O. 12498, OMB would then review the plan for consistency with the President's regulatory philosophy and priorities, and would send comments on the plan back to the agency.

Neither of these executive orders purported to give the President or OMB the power to dictate substantive results to the agencies. In practice, however, the centralized review process established by these two orders gave the White House substantially greater control over agency policy. *See* Kagan, *supra*, at 2278–79. President Reagan's more aggressive form of centralized regulatory review was controversial. Defenders of this system saw it as a way to improve both the quality of regulation (by ensuring that new regulatory initiatives are cost-justified and by ensuring coordination across different regulatory programs) and the democratic pedigree of regulation (by tying agency decisionmaking more closely to the priorities and philosophy of the elected President). Critics saw President Reagan's expansion of centralized OMB review as a deliberate effort to entrench an anti-regulatory bias in agency decisionmaking, both by imposing a substantive CBA standard that focuses excessively on regulatory costs, and by implementing a burdensome review procedure that is itself a deterrent to new regulations. Critics also saw OMB review as undermining rather than enhancing the democratic character of regulatory policy decisions by shifting more of those decisions from the more transparent and participatory agency rulemaking process to the obscure and secretive OMB review process, where industry groups were suspected of having disproportionate access and influence. The tenor of the debate was nicely captured by a 1986 exchange in the *Harvard Law Review* between OMB review proponents Christopher DeMuth and Douglas Ginsburg (the latter of whom served as OIRA Administrator under President Reagan and was later appointed to the D.C. Circuit Court of Appeals) and Alan Morrison, a prominent critic of the OMB review process who at the time was the director of the Public Citizen Litigation Group. Summarizing the advantages of President Reagan's centralized regulatory review process, DeMuth and Ginsburg asserted:

> ... [A] government agency charged with the responsibility of defending the nation or constructing highways or promoting trade will invariably wish to spend "too much" on its goals. An agency succeeds by accomplishing the goals Congress set for it as thoroughly as possible—not by balancing its goals against other, equally worthy goals. ... Without some countervailing restraint, EPA and OSHA would "spend"—through regulations that spend society's resources but do not appear in the federal government's fiscal budget—"too much" on pollution control and workplace safety. ...
>
> Centralized review of proposed regulations under a cost/benefit standard, by an office that has no program responsibilities and is accountable only to the president, is an appropriate response to the failings of regulation. It encourages policy coordination, greater political accountability, and more balanced regulatory decisions. ... OMB review subjects proposed rules to a "hard look" *before* they are issued and ensures that serious policy disagreements between a president's appointees (one with and the other without programmatic responsibilities in the area in question) will be brought to his attention.
>
> ... In any administration, the president is more likely to take a broad view of the nation's economic interest in a given rulemaking controversy than are any of his agency heads—where "broad" denotes the consideration of all the likely benefits and costs of the rule. ...

Christopher C. DeMuth & Douglas H. Ginsburg, *White House Review of Agency Rulemaking*, 99 HARV. L. REV. 1075, 1081–82 (1986).

Mr. Morrison summarized his critique of these claims as follows:

> ... OMB can perform some useful functions in the rulemaking process. Its role in coordinating related proceedings between agencies and in assuring that relevant scientific information, cost data, and alternative approaches are shared between agencies, are entirely prop-

er.... Similarly, it is proper for OMB to insist that agencies take a hard look at the necessity for a rule, provided OMB does so in an evenhanded manner....

In practice, however, neither Executive Order [12291 nor 12498] is being used to further any of these theoretically beneficial ends.... [T]he system of OMB control imposes costly delays that are paid for through the decreased health and safety of the American public. This system also places the ultimate rulemaking decisions in the hands of OMB personnel who are neither competent in the substantive areas of regulation, nor accountable to Congress or the electorate in any meaningful sense. In addition, the entire process operates in an atmosphere of secrecy and insulation from public debate that makes a mockery of the system of open participation [in agency rulemaking]....

The Administration has principally used the system of OMB review created by the Executive Orders to implement a myopic vision of the regulatory process which places the elimination of cost to industry above all other considerations. In doing so, however, the administration has imposed a significant price on the public resulting from the delay it causes in adoption of needed protections....

Alan B. Morrison, *OMB Interference with Agency Rulemaking: The Wrong Way To Write a Regulation*, 99 HARV. L. REV. 1059, 1064–65 (1986).

In part because of the political tenor of the debate over President Reagan's executive orders—with conservatives typically in support and most liberals in opposition—one might have predicted that when President Bill Clinton, a pro-regulatory Democrat, assumed office in 1993, he would scale back or dismantle much of the apparatus of centralized regulatory review. That, however, is not what happened. President Clinton did rescind Executive Orders 12291 and 12498, but he replaced them with his own order on regulatory review, Executive Order 12866. President Clinton's order did alter several features of the Reagan-era executive orders that progressives had found most objectionable: E.O. 12866 made the OMB review process more transparent, relaxed the requirement that agencies could adopt new regulations only if a cost-benefit showed net positive regulatory benefits, and instructed agencies to include non-quantifiable considerations. Nevertheless, E.O. 12866 retained—and in some ways expanded—the two key features of President Reagan's executive orders: centralized OIRA review of proposed major regulations, and the annual regulatory planning process.

E.O. 12866 remains the governing authority for the regulatory review process. (Late in his second term, President George W. Bush issued an executive order that amended E.O. 12866 but retained its basic structure. President Barack Obama rescinded President Bush's order and initiated a review process to consider possible changes to E.O. 12866, but as of March 2010, that review process had not been completed, and E.O. 12866 remains in place.) Because of its importance, the text of E.O. 12866 is presented, with only minor redaction, below:

# Executive Order 12866

Regulatory Planning and Review
September 30, 1993

The American people deserve a regulatory system that works for them, not against them: a regulatory system that protects and improves their health, safety, environment, and well-being and improves the performance of the economy without imposing unacceptable or unreasonable costs on society; regulatory policies that recognize that the private sector and private markets are the best engine for economic growth; regulatory approaches that respect the role of State, local, and tribal governments; and regulations that are effective, consistent, sensible, and understandable. We do not have such a regulatory system today.

With this Executive order, the Federal Government begins a program to reform and make more efficient the regulatory process. The objectives of this Executive order are to enhance planning and coordination with respect to both new and existing regulations; to reaffirm the primacy of Federal agencies in the regulatory decisionmaking process; to restore the integrity and legitimacy of regulatory review and oversight; and to make the process more accessible and open to the public. In pursuing these objectives, the regulatory process shall be conducted so as to meet applicable statutory requirements and with due regard to the discretion that has been entrusted to the Federal agencies. Accordingly, by the authority vested in me as President by the Constitution and the laws of the United States of America, it is hereby ordered as follows:

## Sec. 1.   Statement of Regulatory Philosophy and Principles.

**(a) The Regulatory Philosophy.** Federal agencies should promulgate only such regulations as are required by law, are necessary to interpret the law, or are made necessary by compelling public need, such as material failures of private markets to protect or improve the health and safety of the public, the environment, or the well-being of the American people. In deciding whether and how to regulate, agencies should assess all costs and benefits of available regulatory alternatives, including the alternative of not regulating. Costs and benefits shall be understood to include both quantifiable measures (to the fullest extent that these can be usefully estimated) and qualitative measures of costs and benefits that are difficult to quantify, but nevertheless essential to consider. Further, in choosing among alternative regulatory approaches, agencies should select those approaches that maximize net benefits (including potential economic, environmental, public health and safety, and other advantages; distributive impacts; and equity), unless a statute requires another regulatory approach.

**(b) The Principles of Regulation.** To ensure that the agencies' regulatory programs are consistent with the philosophy set forth above, agencies should adhere to the following principles, to the extent permitted by law and where applicable:

(1) Each agency shall identify the problem that it intends to address (including, where applicable, the failures of private markets or public institutions that warrant new agency action) as well as assess the significance of that problem.

(2) Each agency shall examine whether existing regulations (or other law) have created, or contributed to, the problem that a new regulation is intended to correct and whether those regulations (or other law) should be modified to achieve the intended goal of regulation more effectively.

(3) Each agency shall identify and assess available alternatives to direct regulation, including providing economic incentives to encourage the desired behavior, such as user fees or marketable permits, or providing information upon which choices can be made by the public.

(4) In setting regulatory priorities, each agency shall consider, to the extent reasonable, the degree and nature of the risks posed by various substances or activities within its jurisdiction.

(5) When an agency determines that a regulation is the best available method of achieving the regulatory objective, it shall design its regulations in the most cost-effective manner to achieve the regulatory objective. In doing so, each agency shall consider incentives for innovation, consistency, predictability, the costs of enforcement and compliance (to the government, regulated entities, and the public), flexibility, distributive impacts, and equity.

(6) Each agency shall assess both the costs and the benefits of the intended regulation and, recognizing that some costs and benefits are difficult to quantify, propose or adopt a regulation only upon a reasoned determination that the benefits of the intended regulation justify its costs.

(7) Each agency shall base its decisions on the best reasonably obtainable scientific, technical, economic, and other information concerning the need for, and consequences of, the intended regulation.

(8) Each agency shall identify and assess alternative forms of regulation and shall, to the extent feasible, specify performance objectives, rather than specifying the behavior or manner of compliance that regulated entities must adopt.

(9) Wherever feasible, agencies shall seek views of appropriate State, local, and tribal officials before imposing regulatory requirements that might significantly or uniquely affect those governmental entities. Each agency shall assess the effects of Federal regulations on State, local, and tribal governments, including specifically the availability of resources to carry out those mandates, and seek to minimize those burdens that uniquely or significantly affect such governmental entities, consistent with achieving regulatory objectives. In addition, as appropriate, agencies shall seek to harmonize Federal regulatory actions with related State, local, and tribal regulatory and other governmental functions.

(10) Each agency shall avoid regulations that are inconsistent, incompatible, or duplicative with its other regulations or those of other Federal agencies.

(11) Each agency shall tailor its regulations to impose the least burden on society, including individuals, businesses of differing sizes, and other entities (including small communities and governmental entities), consistent with obtaining the regulatory objectives, taking into account, among other things, and to the extent practicable, the costs of cumulative regulations.

(12) Each agency shall draft its regulations to be simple and easy to understand, with the goal of minimizing the potential for uncertainty and litigation arising from such uncertainty.

**Sec. 2. Organization.** [This section outlined the role of the agencies, OMB, and the Vice President in shaping regulatory policy.]

**Sec. 3. Definitions.** For purposes of this Executive order:

(a) "Advisors" refers to such regulatory policy advisors to the President as the President and Vice President may from time to time consult....

(b) "Agency," unless otherwise indicated, means any authority of the United States that is an "agency" under 44 U.S.C. 3502(1), other than those considered to be independent regulatory agencies, as defined in 44 U.S.C. 3502(10).

(c) "Director" means the Director of OMB.

(d) "Regulation" or "rule" means an agency statement of general applicability and future effect, which the agency intends to have the force and effect of law, that is designed to implement, interpret, or prescribe law or policy or to describe the procedure or practice requirements of an agency. It does not, however, include:

(1) Regulations or rules issued in accordance with the formal rulemaking provisions of 5 U.S.C. 556, 557;

(2) Regulations or rules that pertain to a military or foreign affairs function of the United States, other than procurement regulations and regulations involving the import or export of non-defense articles and services;

(3) Regulations or rules that are limited to agency organization, management, or personnel matters; or

(4) Any other category of regulations exempted by the Administrator of OIRA.

(e) "Regulatory action" means any substantive action by an agency (normally published in the Federal Register) that promulgates or is expected to lead to the promulgation of a final rule or regulation, including notices of inquiry, advance notices of proposed rulemaking, and notices of proposed rulemaking.

(f) "Significant regulatory action" means any regulatory action that is likely to result in a rule that may:

(1) Have an annual effect on the economy of $100 million or more or adversely affect in a material way the economy, a sector of the economy, productivity, competition, jobs, the environment, public health or safety, or State, local, or tribal governments or communities;

(2) Create a serious inconsistency or otherwise interfere with an action taken or planned by another agency;

(3) Materially alter the budgetary impact of entitlements, grants, user fees, or loan programs or the rights and obligations of recipients thereof; or

(4) Raise novel legal or policy issues arising out of legal mandates, the President's priorities, or the principles set forth in this Executive order.

**Sec. 4.  Planning Mechanism.** In order to have an effective regulatory program, to provide for coordination of regulations, to maximize consultation and the resolution of potential conflicts at an early stage, to involve the public and its State, local, and tribal officials in regulatory planning, and to ensure that new or revised regulations promote the President's priorities and the principles set forth in this Executive order, these procedures shall be followed, to the extent permitted by law:

**(a) Agencies' Policy Meeting.** Early in each year's planning cycle, the Vice President shall convene a meeting of the Advisors and the heads of agencies to seek a common understanding of priorities and to coordinate regulatory efforts to be accomplished in the upcoming year.

**(b) Unified Regulatory Agenda.** For purposes of this subsection, the term "agency" or "agencies" shall also include those considered to be independent regulatory agencies, as defined in 44 U.S.C. 3502(10). Each agency shall prepare an agenda of all regulations under development or review, at a time and in a manner specified by the Administrator of OIRA. The description of each regulatory action shall contain, at a minimum, . . . a brief summary of the action, the legal authority for the action [and] any legal deadline for the action. . . .

**(c) The Regulatory Plan.** For purposes of this subsection, the term "agency" or "agencies" shall also include those considered to be independent regulatory agencies, as defined in 44 U.S.C. 3502(10).

(1) As part of the Unified Regulatory Agenda . . . each agency shall prepare a Regulatory Plan (Plan) of the most important significant regulatory actions that the agency reasonably expects to issue in proposed or final form in that fiscal year or thereafter. The Plan shall be approved personally by the agency head. . . .

(2) Each agency shall forward its Plan to OIRA by June 1st of each year.

(3) Within 10 calendar days after OIRA has received an agency's Plan, OIRA shall circulate it to other affected agencies, the Advisors, and the Vice President.

(4) An agency head who believes that a planned regulatory action of another agency may conflict with its own policy or action taken or planned shall promptly notify, in writing, the Administrator of OIRA, who shall forward that communication to the issuing agency, the Advisors, and the Vice President.

(5) If the Administrator of OIRA believes that a planned regulatory action of an agency may be inconsistent with the President's priorities or the principles set forth in this Executive order or may be in conflict with any policy or action taken or planned by another agency, the Administrator of OIRA shall promptly notify, in writing, the affected agencies, the Advisors, and the Vice President.

(6) The Vice President, with the Advisors' assistance, may consult with the heads of agencies with respect to their Plans and, in appropriate instances, request further consideration or inter-agency coordination.

(7) The Plans developed by the issuing agency shall be published annually in the October publication of the Unified Regulatory Agenda. This publication shall be made available to the Congress; State, local, and tribal governments; and the public. Any views on any aspect of any agency Plan, including whether any planned regulatory action might conflict with any other planned or existing regulation, impose any unintended consequences on the public, or confer any unclaimed benefits on the public, should be directed to the issuing agency, with a copy to OIRA.

. . .

**Sec. 5. Existing Regulations.** [This section required each agency to submit to OIRA a program for periodically reviewing the agency's existing regulations "to determine whether any such regulations should be modified or eliminated so as to make the agency's regulatory program more effective in achieving the regulatory objectives, less burdensome, or in greater alignment with the President's priorities and the principles set forth in this Executive order."]

**Sec. 6. Centralized Review of Regulations.** The guidelines set forth below shall apply to all regulatory actions, for both new and existing regulations, by agencies other than those agencies specifically exempted by the Administrator of OIRA:

**(a) Agency Responsibilities.**

. . .

(3) In addition to adhering to its own rules and procedures and to the requirements of the Administrative Procedure Act . . . and other applicable law, each agency shall develop its regulatory actions in a

timely fashion and adhere to the following procedures with respect to a regulatory action:

(A) Each agency shall provide OIRA, at such times and in the manner specified by the Administrator of OIRA, with a list of its planned regulatory actions, indicating those which the agency believes are significant regulatory actions within the meaning of this Executive order. Absent a material change in the development of the planned regulatory action, those not designated as significant will not be subject to review under this section unless, within 10 working days of receipt of the list, the Administrator of OIRA notifies the agency that OIRA has determined that a planned regulation is a significant regulatory action within the meaning of this Executive order. The Administrator of OIRA may waive review of any planned regulatory action designated by the agency as significant, in which case the agency need not further comply with subsection (a)(3)(B) or subsection (a)(3)(C) of this section.

(B) For each matter identified as, or determined by the Administrator of OIRA to be, a significant regulatory action, the issuing agency shall provide to OIRA:

(i) The text of the draft regulatory action, together with a reasonably detailed description of the need for the regulatory action and an explanation of how the regulatory action will meet that need; and

(ii) An assessment of the potential costs and benefits of the regulatory action, including an explanation of the manner in which the regulatory action is consistent with a statutory mandate and, to the extent permitted by law, promotes the President's priorities and avoids undue interference with State, local, and tribal governments in the exercise of their governmental functions.

(C) For those matters identified as, or determined by the Administrator of OIRA to be, a significant regulatory action within the scope of section 3(f)(1), the agency shall also provide to OIRA the following additional information developed as part of the agency's decisionmaking process (unless prohibited by law):

(i) An assessment, including the underlying analysis, of benefits anticipated from the regulatory action (such as, but not limited to, the promotion of the efficient functioning of the economy and private markets, the enhancement of health and safety, the protection of the natural environment, and the elimination or reduction of discrimination or bias) together with, to the extent feasible, a quantification of those benefits;

(ii) An assessment, including the underlying analysis, of costs anticipated from the regulatory action (such as, but not limited to, the direct cost both to the government in administering the regulation and to businesses and others in complying with the regulation, and any adverse effects on the efficient functioning of the economy, private markets (including productivity, employment, and competitiveness), health, safety, and the natural environment), together with, to the extent feasible, a quantification of those costs; and

(iii) An assessment, including the underlying analysis, of costs and benefits of potentially effective and reasonably feasible alternatives to the planned regulation, identified by the agencies or the public (including improving the current regulation and reasonably viable nonregulatory actions), and an explanation why the planned regulatory action is preferable to the identified potential alternatives.

(D) In emergency situations or when an agency is obligated by law to act more quickly than normal review procedures allow, the agency shall notify OIRA as soon as possible and, to the extent practicable, comply with subsections (a)(3)(B) and (C) of this section. . . .

(E) After the regulatory action has been published in the Federal Register or otherwise issued to the public, the agency shall:

(i) Make available to the public the information set forth in subsections (a)(3)(B) and (C);

(ii) Identify for the public, in a complete, clear, and simple manner, the substantive changes between the draft submitted to OIRA for review and the action subsequently announced; and

(iii) Identify for the public those changes in the regulatory action that were made at the suggestion or recommendation of OIRA.

(F) All information provided to the public by the agency shall be in plain, understandable language.

**(b) OIRA Responsibilities.** The Administrator of OIRA shall provide meaningful guidance and oversight so that each agency's regulatory actions are consistent with applicable law, the President's priorities, and the principles set forth in this Executive order and do not conflict with the policies or actions of another agency. OIRA shall, to the extent permitted by law, adhere to the following guidelines:

(1) OIRA may review only actions identified by the agency or by OIRA as significant regulatory actions under subsection (a)(3)(A) of this section.

(2) OIRA shall waive review or notify the agency in writing of the results of its review within the following time periods:

(A) For any notices of inquiry, advance notices of proposed rulemaking, or other preliminary regulatory actions prior to a

Notice of Proposed Rulemaking, within 10 working days after the date of submission of the draft action to OIRA;

(B) For all other regulatory actions, within 90 calendar days after the date of submission of the information set forth in subsections (a)(3)(B) and (C) of this section, unless OIRA has previously reviewed this information and, since that review, there has been no material change in the facts and circumstances upon which the regulatory action is based, in which case, OIRA shall complete its review within 45 days; and

(C) The review process may be extended (1) once by no more than 30 calendar days upon the written approval of the Director and (2) at the request of the agency head.

(3) For each regulatory action that the Administrator of OIRA returns to an agency for further consideration of some or all of its provisions, the Administrator of OIRA shall provide the issuing agency a written explanation for such return, setting forth the pertinent provision of this Executive order on which OIRA is relying. If the agency head disagrees with some or all of the bases for the return, the agency head shall so inform the Administrator of OIRA in writing.

[The next two subsections contained a number of additional provisions to make the review process more transparent and to limit ex parte contracts with OIRA by parties other than federal government employees.]

**Sec. 7. Resolution of Conflicts.** To the extent permitted by law, disagreements or conflicts between or among agency heads or between OMB and any agency that cannot be resolved by the Administrator of OIRA shall be resolved by the President.... Presidential consideration of such disagreements may be initiated only by the Director, by the head of the issuing agency, or by the head of an agency that has a significant interest in the regulatory action at issue. Such review will not be undertaken at the request of other persons, entities, or their agents....

**Sec. 8. Publication.** [This section set limits on agencies' authority to publish regulatory action prior to the completion or waiver of OIRA review.]

**Sec. 9. Agency Authority.** Nothing in this order shall be construed as displacing the agencies' authority or responsibilities, as authorized by law.

**Sec. 10. Judicial Review.** Nothing in this Executive order shall affect any otherwise available judicial review of agency action. This Executive order is intended only to improve the internal management of the Federal Government and does not create any right or benefit, substantive or procedural, enforceable at law or equity by a party against the United States, its agencies or instrumentalities, its officers or employees, or any other person.

**Sec. 11. Revocations.** Executive Orders Nos. 12291 and 12498; all amendments to those Executive orders; all guidelines issued under those orders; and any exemptions from those orders heretofore granted for any category of rule are revoked.

WILLIAM CLINTON

THE WHITE HOUSE,

September 30, 1993.

---

***1. Centralized Regulatory Review and Presidential Oversight of the Administration***—E.O. 12866, like its predecessors E.O. 12291 and 12498, seeks to achieve greater presidential control over the administrative state by subjecting agency regulatory policymaking to greater White House supervision. Indeed, although E.O. 12866 makes the process more transparent, in some ways it asserts presidential authority over the administration even more boldly than did President Reagan's orders, particularly in § 7 of the order, which declares that, "[t]o the extent permitted by law, disagreements or conflicts between or among agency heads or between OMB and any agency that cannot be resolved by the Administrator of OIRA shall be resolved by the President, or by the Vice President acting at the request of the President, with the relevant agency head (and, as appropriate, other interested government officials)." (It is not clear whether this assertion of presidential authority made much practical difference. The formal dispute-resolution provision in § 7 has rarely been formally invoked, and even under President Reagan's orders the President effectively had the final say in resolving conflicts between OMB and the programmatic agencies charged with implementing specific statutory mandates. *See* Elena Kagan, *Presidential Administration*, 114 Harv. L. Rev. 2245, 2289 (2001).) One of the central objectives of OMB regulatory review under both Democratic and Republican administrations has been to increase presidential control over the administration.

The arguments for centralized White House oversight of rulemaking, like the arguments for presidential supervision of the administration more generally, typically advance both "effective government" and "democratic accountability" arguments. The effective-government argument—essentially, that the President has a uniquely holistic perspective on regulatory policy questions which facilitates coordination, coherence, and rational priority-setting—is well summarized by the passage quoted above from Christopher C. DeMuth & Douglas H. Ginsburg, *White House Review of Agency Rulemaking*, 99 Harv. L. Rev. 1075 (1982) (*see* p. 552, *supra*). *See also* Kagan, *supra*, at 2339–46; Lawrence Lessig & Cass R. Sunstein, *The President and the Administration*, 94 Colum. L. Rev. 1 (1994). The democratic-accountability argument is straightforwardly that "[w]e vote for presidents, not secretaries or administrators," and that "White House oversight places accountability precisely where it should be, namely, where the electorate can do something about it." Philip J. Harter, *Executive Oversight of Rulemaking: The President Is No Stranger*, 36 Am. U. L. Rev. 557, 568 (1987); *see also, e.g.*, Peter L. Strauss & Cass R. Sunstein, *The Role of the President and OMB in Informal Rulemaking*, 38 Admin. L. Rev.

181, 190 (1986); Kagan, *supra*, at 2384. Furthermore, some advocates of centralized OMB review argue that this process improves democratic accountability by shifting influence over agency policy away from congressional oversight committees, in favor of greater presidential control. It may at first seem odd to assert that shifting control away from Congress could make regulatory policy more democratically responsive, but proponents of this argument insist that committee oversight is particularly likely to be dominated by special interest groups and unrepresentative committee members, while the President is more likely to take a broader, national view. *See, e.g.,* Jonathan R. Macey, *Separated Powers and Positive Political Theory: The Tug of War Over Administrative Agencies*, 80 Geo. L.J. 671, 697–98 (1992). (As you may recall from Chapter One, there is a lively empirical debate in the political science literature over whether committee members are "preference outliers," or whether they represent the preferences of the parent chamber reasonably well. *See* pp. 176–178, *supra*.) The political accountability argument for centralized regulatory review is sometimes supplemented with the empirical claim that the sitting President is held accountable for the actions of the agencies in any event; it therefore makes sense to give the President more control over those actions. *See* Kagan, *supra*, at 2310–13. *Cf.* David E. Lewis, Presidents and the Politics of Agency Design 24–27 (2003).

Critics have attacked both of the foregoing justifications for centralized regulatory review; the basic objections are summarized succinctly in the passage from Alan Morrison's article quoted above. Alan B Morrison, *OMB Interference with Agency Rulemaking: The Wrong Way to Write a Regulation*, 99 Harv. L. Rev. 1059 (1986) (*see supra* pp. 552–553). With respect to the claim that centralized White House review promotes more efficient and effective regulatory policymaking, the critics generally argue that neither the President nor OMB has the requisite expertise in the substantive policy areas to second-guess the programmatic agencies, yet in practice this is precisely the sort of second-guessing that OMB oversight both allows and encourages. Critics have also charged that centralized OMB review introduces a powerful and undesirable anti-regulatory bias, for two main reasons. First, as we discuss in the next note, critics allege that the specific analytic technique mandated by E.O. 12866—cost-benefit analysis—has an anti-regulatory cast and is usually deployed as a tool for blocking environmental, health, or safety regulations with difficult-to-quantify benefits. Second, critics contend that the *structure* of OMB review, at least as currently practiced, contains an implicit and inherent status quo bias (which in most cases amounts to an anti-regulatory bias), because the delays caused by OMB review entail significant costs and may cause agencies to play it safe by adopting more modest regulations. *See* Nicholas Bagley & Richard L. Revesz, *Centralized Oversight of the Regulatory State*, 106 Colum. L. Rev. 1260, 1270 (2006).

This deterrent effect might be desirable if one believes—as some proponents of centralized OMB review do—that agencies, if left to their own devices, are generally likely to regulate too much due to agency officials' tendency to focus on their own narrow missions, or to capture by special interest groups. *See* DeMuth & Ginsburg, *supra*; John O. McGinnis, *Presidential Review as Constitutional Restoration*, 51 Duke L.J. 901, 932–38 (2001). The claim that agencies have a tendency to overregulate, however, is controversial; Bagley and Revesz, *supra* at 1286, describe this claim as "wholly implausible" in light of modern political science theory, and they are not alone in that assessment. *See, e.g.,* Steven P. Croley, Regulation and Public Interests: The Possibility of Good Regulatory Government 26–52 (2008); Kagan, *supra*, at 2264. Another potential rejoinder to the claim that OIRA review has a deterrent effect on aggressive agency regulation is that however plausible this hypothesis may appear, as an empirical matter OIRA review has *not* substantially chilled agency regulation. Indeed, most of the extant quantitative evidence on the impact of OIRA review (or analogous mechanisms at the state level) has failed to uncover any significant effect of OIRA review on the speed or volume of agency rulemaking activity. *See* Cary Coglianese, *The Rhetoric and Reality of Regulatory Reform*, 25 Yale J. on Reg. 85 (2008); Cornelius M. Kerwin & Scott R. Furlong, *Time and Rulemaking: An Empirical Test of Theory*, 2 J. Pub. Admin. Res. & Theory 113 (1992); Stuart Shapiro, *Speed Bumps and Roadblocks: Procedural Controls and Regulatory Change*, 12 J. Pub. Admin. Res. & Theory 29 (2002); Susan Webb Yackee & Jason Webb Yackee, *Administrative Procedures and Bureaucratic Performance: Is Federal Rulemaking "Ossified"?*, J. Pub. Admin. Res. & Theory (forthcoming). Then again, this evidence does not necessarily refute the claim that OMB review is a substantial deterrent to agency regulation: it is impossible to observe how much agency regulation there would have been if not for OMB review, and measuring the *quantity* of agency rules does not tell us whether, as Bagley and Revesz hypothesize, OMB review substantially distorts the *content* of agency rules, leading to "watered down" regulations.

What about the claim that because OMB review enhances presidential influence over regulatory policymaking, it improves the democratic accountability of the administrative state? As we noted earlier, a prominent objection to President Reagan's executive orders on regulatory review concerned their lack of transparency, which undercut the claim that White House regulatory review promoted democratic values. *See* Morrison, *supra*; Thomas O. McGarity, *Presidential Control of Regulatory Agency Decisionmaking*, 36 Am. U. L. Rev. 443, 456–57 (1987). President Clinton's revisions to the regulatory review process went some way toward addressing this concern, but many critics still maintain that centralized OMB review tends to undermine rather than advance democratic values. One argument along these lines is that, given the constraints on the President's time, centralized OMB review does not really increase the influence of the elected President vis-à-vis unelected bureaucrats, but rather increases the influence of one set of unelected bureaucrats (in OMB) vis-à-vis another set of unelected bureaucrats (in the programmatic agencies). *See, e.g.,* Thomas O. McGarity, *Some Thoughts on "Deossifying" the Rulemaking Process*, 41 Duke L.J. 1385, 1431 (1992); Thomas O. Sargentich, *Normative Tensions in the Theory of Presidential Oversight of Agency Rulemaking*, 7 Admin. L.J. Am. U. 325, 326 (1993); Sidney A. Shapiro, *Political Oversight and the*

*Deterioration of Regulatory Policy*, 46 ADMIN. L. REV. 1, 12–13 (1994). Furthermore, even if one assumes that centralized OMB review increases presidential influence over agency policymaking, some critics take issue with the premise that the President is more likely than Congress or agency bureaucrats to be responsive to a national constituency. Professor Jide Nzelibe has argued that the idea that Congress is "parochial" while the President is "nationalist" is a "fable." Jide Nzelibe, *The Fable of the Nationalist President and the Parochial Congress*, 53 UCLA L. REV. 1217 (2006). Professor Peter Shane similarly argues that if "bureaucratic accountability to elected politicians is to be used as a structural mechanism aimed at achieving direct responsiveness to public opinion, it would probably make more sense to intensify the influence that Congress—especially the House—has over the agencies." Peter M. Shane, *Political Accountability in a System of Checks and Balances: The Case of Presidential Review of Rulemaking*, 48 ARK. L. REV. 161, 200 (1995).

Others have suggested that although agency officials are not directly elected, the administrative rulemaking process (which we discuss in greater detail in Chapter Four, *infra*) may be well-suited to promote democratic values, and White House review might (paradoxically) undermine that sort of democratic accountability. Based on a study of White House oversight of EPA rulemaking, Professors Lisa Bressman and Michael Vandenbergh have thus argued that "White House involvement may not promote much political accountability in a functional sense—that is, with the aim of ensuring that regulatory activity reflects public preferences and resists narrow influences." Lisa Schultz Bressman & Michael P. Vandenbergh, *Inside the Administrative State: A Critical Look at the Practice of Presidential Control*, 105 MICH. L. REV. 47, 83–84 (2006). Professors Bressman and Vandenbergh emphasize, in particular, "that EPA officials are bound by administrative procedures and subject to media attention in a way that White House involvement is not" and that "EPA officials . . . gather more public input and receive more public scrutiny, both of which tend to ensure that they will better assess public preferences and resist parochial pressures." *See id.* For a contrasting view, see Sally Katzen, *A Reality Check on an Empirical Study: Comments on "Inside the Administrative State"*, 105 MICH. L. REV. 1497, 1502–03, 1505 (2007) (arguing that Bressman and Vandenbergh's study actually shows that "EPA is pursuing a parochial interest," while "OIRA is tempering that with the national interest, as it should").

While Professors Bressman and Vandenbergh emphasize that bureaucratic policy may itself be reasonably responsive to public preferences, an alternative argument holds that *even if* the President is more responsive (on average) to voter preferences than are agency bureaucrats, "a moderate degree of bureaucratic insulation alleviates rather than exacerbates the countermajoritarian problems inherent in bureaucratic policymaking." Matthew C. Stephenson, *Optimal Political Control of the Bureaucracy*, 107 MICH. L. REV. 53, 55 (2008). This argument turns on the claim that bureaucratic insulation reduces the variance in agency policy outcomes, as follows:

[A]n elected politician, though responsive to majoritarian preferences, will almost always deviate from the majority in one direction or the other. Republican presidents, for example, are almost always more conservative than a majority of the electorate, while Democratic presidents are typically more liberal. So even if the *average policy position* of presidential administrations tends to track the policy views of the median voter in the electorate, the *average divergence* between the preferences of the median voter and the president is generally greater than zero. Forcing the politically responsive president to share power with a partially insulated, politically unresponsive bureaucracy tends to reduce the variance in policy outcomes, because bureaucratic insulation creates a kind of compensatory inertia that mutes the significance of variation in the president's policy preferences. Up to a point, the benefit to a majority of voters from a reduction in outcome variance outweighs the cost associated with biasing the expected outcome away from the median voter's ideal outcome. A majority of voters therefore prefers a moderate level of bureaucratic insulation from political control.

*Id.* (emphasis in original). Some critics of centralized OMB review build on these and related observations to argue that the best way to achieve democratic accountability is though the involvement of a *plurality* of institutions—accountable in different ways and to somewhat different constituencies—in regulatory policymaking. *See, e.g.,* Cynthia R. Farina, *The Consent of the Governed: Against Simple Rules for a Complex World,* 72 Chi.-Kent L. Rev. 987, 988 (1997) (arguing that proponents of centralized OMB review invoke a ''fabricated'' idea of the ''will of the people'' that is ''artificially bounded in time, homogenized, shorn of ambiguities'' and that it ''obscures complex problems . . . of information, prediction, and risk perception''); Shane, *supra,* at 195 (''[T]he alternative to 'presidentialism' is not really agency policy independence or even 'congressionalism.' The real-world alternative is probably best described as 'political pluralism.' '').

Do you find these responses to the political accountability argument for White House regulatory review convincing? Even if were to accept the idea that *absolute* presidential control of the administration is unnecessary—or perhaps even inimical—to democratic accountability, how would we know if the particular form of regulatory review embodied in E.O. 12866 entrenches a desirable or undesirable level of presidential oversight? Put another way, if we reject the extreme positions that presidential control of agencies should be absolute or non-existent, how can we figure out what degree of presidential control is ''just right''? Is there a way to address this question empirically? Does a complete answer require making contestable normative judgments about the relative importance of competing values? In the absence of decisive normative and empirical arguments, how should we think about the task of designing or reforming OMB regulatory review?

**2.   *Cost–Benefit Analysis*—**Section 1 of E.O. 12866 instructs that agencies should ''assess all costs and benefits of available regulatory alternatives, including the alternative of not regulating,'' and should, to the extent permitted by law, "propose or adopt a regulation only upon a reasoned determination that the benefits of the intended regulation justify its costs." Similarly, Section 4(c) requires that each agency's annual Regulatory Plan include "preliminary estimates of the anticipated costs and benefits" of each planned significant regulatory action as well as alternatives to be considered. Furthermore, under the centralized regulatory review process laid out in Section 6, an agency proposing a significant regulatory action must provide OIRA with an "assessment, including the underlying analysis" of the benefits and costs of the proposed action, quantified to the extent feasible and permitted by law, as well as an analogous assessment of costs and benefits of "potentially effective and reasonably feasible alternatives." This emphasis in E.O. 12866 (as well as its Reagan-era predecessors) on cost-benefit analysis (CBA) has been extraordinarily controversial.

Our main focus in this chapter is on various mechanisms by which the elected branches of government try to control agency decisionmaking. Questions about whether, or to what extent, the President should have the *authority* to influence agencies' decisionmaking process (e.g., by telling agencies what analytic techniques they should use) are conceptually distinct from questions about *how* the President should use such authority (e.g., whether a President who has such authority should specify this or that particular technique). Yet despite this conceptual distinction, debates about OIRA's role in the regulatory process are so bound up with the debate over the appropriate role of CBA in regulatory analysis that it is worth saying a bit about that latter debate. We can do no more here than scratch the surface of the very complex set of economic, philosophical, and political issues involved in the debates over CBA, but we hope that the discussion and excerpted material below will at least give you a flavor of the contemporary debate.

CBA involves much more than the broad notion that the government should adopt a regulation if but only if the benefits exceed the costs. That philosophical position is the starting point for (most) advocates of CBA, but CBA typically involves not just a loose, intuitive balancing of costs and benefits, but rather an attempt to quantify—on a common scale, usually dollars—all relevant benefits and costs so that they can be directly compared. There are myriad ways of performing cost-benefit analyses, and different practitioners approach the problem in different ways. There is also a range of views within the community of CBA proponents and practitioners about whether or how to incorporate difficult-to-quantify values in the analysis; how to account for distributional concerns, including inter-generational distributional issues; and so forth. There is also disagreement among CBA proponents over whether regulatory policy choices should be made *exclusively* on the basis of whether the net benefits are positive or negative, or whether the CBA of a particular regulation is only one *factor* (though perhaps an important one) that ought to be considered; the latter "soft" view of CBA is probably more widespread among CBA proponents now than it was a generation ago. (Note that E.O. 12866 explicitly endorses this softer version to CBA, instructing agencies to consider "qualitative measures of costs and benefits that are difficult to quantify" along with quantifiable measures, and that the net benefits of a regulation must include not only economic considerations, but also "environmental, public health and safety, and other advantages; distributive impacts; and equity," to the extent permitted by statute.)

Despite these and other intramural differences, CBA proponents agree that some effort to quantify and compare costs and benefits is valuable, and sometimes vital, in formulating rational regulatory policy. Professor John Graham, an influential advocate, practitioner, and teacher of CBA who served as the OIRA Administrator under President George W. Bush, has argued that CBA reflects a "science-based approach" to regulation that can help to "establish regulatory priorities based on relative risk, promote wise investments in lifesaving, minimize the unintended risks and undue burdens of regulation, and deploy market-oriented policy instruments that may stimulate innovation while minimizing costs." John D. Graham, *Saving Lives through Administrative Law and Economics*, 157 U. PA. L. REV. 395, 400–01 (2008). Professor Kip Viscusi, another leading scholar and advocate of CBA, has explained the advantages of CBA over alternative, less quantitative approaches, as follows:

> . . . Our current muddled approach makes it difficult to reach wise, well-informed decisions as to the preferred balance of risk and cost. Some risks we ignore; some small ones we regulate stringently. Worse, our overreaction to very small risks impedes the kind of technological progress that has historically brought dramatic improvements in both health and material well-being. In addition, we are likely to misdirect our efforts, for example, by focusing on risks that command attention in the political process, . . . rather than those where the greatest gains in well-being are available. . . .

W. KIP VISCUSI, FATAL TRADEOFFS: PUBLIC AND PRIVATE RESPONSIBILITIES FOR RISK 149 (1992). Professor Cass Sunstein, currently serving as the OIRA Administrator in the Obama Administration, has elaborated on this theme:

> [T]he strongest arguments for cost-benefit balancing are based not only on neoclassical economics, but also on an understanding of human cognition, on democratic considerations, and on an assessment of the real-world record of such balancing. . . . Ordinary people have difficulty in calculating probabilities. . . . [CBA] is a natural corrective here.
>
> . . . People often have intense, highly emotional reactions to particular incidents, and as a result, they can fail to think much about the *probability* that the underlying risks will come to fruition. When people think about the "worst case," they might not consider the fact that there is an infinitesimal chance that the worst case will actually occur. . . . In addition, people have a hard time understanding the systematic consequences of one-shot regulatory interventions. . . . CBA is a way of producing [a] full accounting. Studies show as well that people tend to be "intuitive toxicologists," making a number of errors about toxic substances, such as, for example, how likely it is that those

exposed to a carcinogen will get cancer. Cost-benefit balancing helps to ensure that these errors are not translated into regulatory policy.

With respect to democracy, the case for CBA is strengthened by the fact that interest groups are often able to use these cognitive problems strategically, thus fending off desirable regulation or pressing for regulation when the argument on its behalf is fragile. Here CBA ... can protect democratic processes by exposing an account of consequences to public view....

Cass R. Sunstein, The Cost-Benefit State: The Future of Regulatory Protection 9–10 (2002) (emphasis in original).

Critics of CBA, however, think that this quantification and comparison of benefits and costs (usually on a monetary scale) is deeply misguided, at least with respect to issues related to the protection of health, safety, and the natural environment. Two of the most prominent and vocal critics of CBA in recent years, Frank Ackerman and Lisa Heinzerling, succinctly summarize the essence of the vast critical literature on CBA as follows:

The basic problem with narrow economic analysis of health and environmental protection is that human life, health, and nature cannot be described meaningfully in monetary terms....

There are hard questions to be answered about protection of human health and the environment, and there are many useful insights about these questions from the field of economics. But there is no reason to think that the right answers will emerge from the strange process of assigning dollar values to human life, human health, and nature itself, and then crunching the numbers. Indeed, in pursuing this approach, formal cost-benefit analysis often hurts more than it helps: it muddies rather than clarifies fundamental clashes about values. By proceeding as if its assumptions are scientific and by speaking a language all its own, economic analysis too easily conceals the basic human questions that lie at its heart and excludes the voices of people untrained in the field....

Frank Ackerman & Lisa Heinzerling, Priceless: On Knowing the Price of Everything and the Value of Nothing 9–10 (2004). Critics assert further that CBA not only creates a false impression of precision and scientific objectivity, but that this false veneer of objectivity has made CBA a powerful tool that opponents of health, safety, and environmental regulation can manipulate to undermine such regulation. *See, e.g.,* Ackerman & Heinzerling, *supra*; Thomas O. McGarity, Sidney Shapiro & David Bollier, Sophisticated Sabotage: The Intellectual Games Used to Subvert Responsible Regulation (2004).

If we reject CBA, how *should* we go about making regulatory policy decisions, according to CBA's progressive critics? Professors Ackerman and Heinzerling summarize their proposal as "an attitude rather than an algorithm": "We advocate a more holistic analysis, one that replaces the reductive approach of cost-benefit analysis with a broader and more integrative perspective. We also urge precaution in the face of scientific uncertainty and fairness in the treatment of the current and future generations. Above all, perhaps, we aim to restore a sense of moral urgency to the protection of life, health, and the environment. . . ." ACKERMAN & HEINZERLING, *supra*, at 11.

Not all self-described progressives, however, are hostile to cost-benefit analysis. Professor Richard Revesz and Michael Livermore, for example, have argued that although "cost-benefit analysis, as currently practiced, is indeed biased against regulation, those biases are not inherent to the methodology. . . . [P]rogressive groups should seek to mend, not end, cost-benefit analysis." RICHARD L. REVESZ & MICHAEL A. LIVERMORE, RETAKING RATIONALITY: HOW COST-BENEFIT ANALYSIS CAN BETTER PROTECT THE ENVIRON-MENT AND OUR HEALTH 10 (2008); *see also* Samuel J. Rascoff & Richard L. Revesz, *The Biases of Risk Tradeoff Analysis: Towards Parity in Environmental and Health-and-Safety Regulation*, 69 U. CHI. L. REV. 1763 (2002). According to Revesz and Livermore, the wholesale rejection of cost-benefit analysis is not only wrongheaded as a substantive matter, but has been counterproductive for progressive, pro-regulatory interest groups:

> The roots of the antiregulatory bias within cost-benefit analysis are historical rather than conceptual. . . . Starting in the early 1980s, conservatives used cost-benefit analysis to squelch economic regula-tion. Groups more sympathetic to regulation found themselves on the defensive. Many liberal groups fought back by rejecting the validity of cost-benefit analysis altogether, claiming that technical and moral problems rendered it worthless. These groups essentially boycotted not just cost-benefit analysis, but any debate over how it should be con-ducted.
>
> . . .
>
> By ceding the field, liberals ensured that their belief about cost-benefit analysis became a reality. . . . [As a result, CBA developed] many antiregulatory biases. Those biases, however, reflect the charac-ter of the masters, and not of the tool. Purged of those biases, cost-benefit analysis can be reclaimed as a neutral instrument.

*Id.* at 10–11. Revesz and Livermore further argue that CBA is fully consistent with—indeed, indispensible for—compassionate and effective regulation:

> There is a temptation to rely on gut-level decisionmaking in order to avoid economic analysis, which, to many, is a foreign language on top of seeming cold and unsympathetic. . . . [But b]ecause of the complex nature of governmental decisions, we have no choice but to deploy complex analytic tools in order to make the best choices possi-ble. Failing to use these tools, which amounts to abandoning our duties to one another, is not a legitimate response.

*Id.*; *see also, e.g.*, SUNSTEIN, *supra*; SUSAN ROSE-ACKERMAN, RETHINKING THE PROGRESSIVE AGENDA: THE REFORM OF THE AMERICAN REGULATORY STATE (2002).

The brief excerpts included in this note provide only a superficial introduction to the extraordinarily sophisticated—and politically charged—debate over the virtues and vices of CBA as a regulatory tool. That said, are you instinctively more sympathetic to any of the positions sketched above?

**3. _Application to Independent Commissions_**—As noted earlier, neither of President Reagan's executive orders on centralized regulatory review applied to the independent regulatory commissions (those agencies, usually governed by multi-member boards, for which Congress has limited the President's removal authority); this decision was likely based more on political than legal calculations. _See_ PETER M. SHANE & HAROLD M. BRUFF, THE LAW OF PRESIDENTIAL POWER 358–60 (1988); Elena Kagan, _Presidential Administration_, 114 HARV. L. REV. 2245, 2278 (2001). While E.O. 12866 also excludes independent commissions from OIRA review of proposed major regulations under § 6 of the Order, independent commissions are required to participate in the annual regulatory planning process under § 4 of the Order. Thus President Clinton's order expanded somewhat—though in relatively modest fashion—the assertion of centralized White House control over the independent commissions.

Would it be lawful for the President to require independent commissions not only to participate in the annual regulatory planning process under § 4, but also to submit proposed major rules to OIRA for review in accordance with § 6? The Supreme Court has never expressly confronted these questions. How do you think they ought to be resolved? On one view, neither § 4 nor § 6 would raise constitutional problems when applied to independent commissions, because although these sections require that agencies provide information to the White House and create an institutionalized mechanism for White House feedback and consultation, they do not actually authorize the White House to dictate any policy result. It would seem that the President has the explicit authority to require information under Article II, § 2 of the Constitution (the "Opinions Clause"), which authorizes the President to "require the Opinion, in writing, of the principal Officer in each of the executive Departments, upon any subject relating to the Duties of their respective Offices." _See_ REPORT OF THE HOUSE OF DELEGATES, 1986 A.B.A. SEC., ADMIN. L. (resolution 100, passed Feb. 10, 1986); Kagan, _supra_, at 2324 & n.311; Peter L. Strauss & Cass R. Sunstein, _The Role of the President and OMB in Informal Rulemaking_, 38 ADMIN. L. REV. 181, 200–02, 204 (1986). And consultation and guidance, even if provided by the White House to independent commissions, would not seem to offend any constitutional provision. _See_ Richard H. Pildes & Cass R. Sunstein, _Reinventing the Regulatory State_, 62 U. CHI. L. REV. 1, 32 (1995). Then again, as Professors Pildes and Sunstein acknowledge, "[i]n some situations, guidance and consultation might actually become policy dictation, in which case different legal issues would be raised." _Id._, at 32–33. Such issues might also be raised if the President subjected independent commissions to something analogous to § 1 of E.O. 12866, requiring these commissions, to the extent permitted by statute, to employ particular analytic techniques (such as cost-benefit analysis) or more generally to exercise their discretion so as to advance the President's regulatory philosophy. Would that be constitutional? How would you analyze the issues? Do the separation-of-powers cases discussed earlier in this chapter (pp. 523–547, *supra*) provide any guidance?

One way to deal with the legal issues raised by a more ambitious presidential attempt to bring independent commissions within the ambit of centralized White House regulatory review would be to avoid the constitutional questions by finding in the statutes that create these independent commissions an implicit grant of authority to the President to supervise these agencies, notwithstanding the express statutory limits on the President's removal power. Professors Pildes and Sunstein make an argument along these lines; they claim that in many cases "[i]t might be possible to interpret the relevant statutes as allowing a degree of ... supervisory power to remain in the President," and they argue for a "clear-statement principle ... that allows the President a degree of supervisory power over the commissions." Pildes & Sunstein, *supra*, at 30, 32. But couldn't one respond that Congress chose to insulate these commissions from this very sort of influence by limiting the President's removal power? *See supra* pp. 508–513; *cf.* Kagan, *supra*, at 2327. As a matter of statutory construction, do you think the organic statutes that create independent commissions can or should be read as giving the President the power to supervise those commissions pursuant to something like the regulatory review process laid out in E.O. 12866? As precluding such power?

## B. PRESIDENTIAL DIRECTIVES

The centralized review process established first by President Reagan's Executive Orders 12291 and 12498, and then by President Clinton's Executive Order 12866, is designed principally to review regulatory proposals that originate with the programmatic agencies. So, while this form of centralized review may indeed enhance presidential influence over regulatory policymaking, it does so in a particular way: by stopping, delaying, or suggesting improvements to the agencies' regulatory initiatives. But the White House may also want to influence agencies by prodding agencies to *undertake*, rather than abandon or modify, regulatory policy changes. Thus, while OIRA review of agency proposals gets comparatively more attention, OIRA also sometimes issues "prompt letters," encouraging agencies to take regulatory action to deal with some perceived problem. *See* CASS R. SUNSTEIN, THE COST-BENEFIT STATE: THE FUTURE IF REGULATORY PROTECTION 7–8 (2002); John D Graham, *Saving Lives through Administrative Law and Economics*, 157 U. PA. L. REV. 395, 460–63 (2008).

Separate and apart from OIRA's occasional practice of issuing prompt letters, the *President* sometimes issues directives to specific agencies. While these directives are not invariably pro-regulatory—sometimes they instruct an agency to stop or suspend a rulemaking, or to initiate a deregulatory rulemaking—they often have the effect of encouraging or demanding that the agency take some regulatory action. President Clinton was especially innovative—and aggressive—in using directives to agencies as a tool for shaping administrative policy. Professor Elena Kagan (who served in the

Clinton Administration as a senior advisor and participated in the formulation of President Clinton's policy strategy) explained that such directives "enabled Clinton and his White House staff to instigate, rather than merely check, administrative action," and that they became "Clinton's primary means ... of setting an administrative agenda ... and of ensuring the execution of this program." Elena Kagan, *Presidential Administration*, 114 HARV. L. REV. 2245, 2290 (2001). Furthermore, Professor Kagan asserts, these directives did not merely ratify agency initiatives, but rather emanated from White House staff, with the "final call" coming "from the President ... [or] from his closest policy advisors." *Id.* at 2297–98.

Consider the following example, issued by President Clinton to the Department of the Interior, the Department of Agriculture, and the Environmental Protection Agency in 1999:

---

# Memorandum on Clean Water Protection

May 29, 1999
Public Papers of the Presidents
William J. Clinton—1999 (Volume 1), pp. 857–858

Memorandum for the Secretary of the Interior, the Secretary of Agriculture, the Administrator of the Environmental Protection Agency

Subject: Clean Water Protection

Fifteen months ago, celebrating the 25th anniversary of the Clean Water Act, my Administration set forth a vision for a new generation of clean water protection through our Clean Water Action Plan. The Action Plan strengthens protections for our Nation's waters, addresses the remaining sources of water quality impairment, and provides the tools and resources that States, Tribes, and communities need to control pollution on a coordinated basis throughout their watersheds.

The Action Plan recognizes that despite significant progress, the challenge for all of us in protecting our Nation's waters remains unfinished. The health of our people continues to be threatened by exposure to harmful organisms in our waters; consumption of fish from many of our waters presents a threat to the most vulnerable among us; polluted runoff has for too long eluded remedy using conventional approaches. The Action Plan was coupled with a challenge to the Congress to reauthorize and strengthen the Clean Water Act, but the Congress has yet to act on this challenge.

As we begin the beach-going season, when families are reminded again about the importance of clean water to their recreation, their well-being, and the economy, we remain anxious to work with the Congress on strengthening the Clean Water Act. We must not wait for the Congress, however, before using our available resources and authority to further accelerate the effort to protect America's waters and the health and safety of the American public.

Accordingly, I direct you to take the following additional steps, consistent with the Clean Water Act and the Clean Water Action Plan, to protect public health and clean water.

First, I direct the Park Service and other units of the Department of the Interior to strengthen water-quality protections at all beaches managed by the Department. . . .

Second, I direct the EPA to work with the States to expedite the pace at which they will strengthen their beach and recreational water quality standards, so that the public will be able to enjoy the same strong level of protection at all the Nation's beaches no later than 2003. In accordance with the EPA's Beach Action Plan, the EPA should promulgate standards in cases where a State does not amend its water quality standards to include the EPA-recommended criteria in a timely manner.

Third, I direct the EPA to improve protection of public health at our Nation's beaches by developing, within 1 year, a strong national regulation to prevent the over 40,000 annual sanitary sewer overflows from contaminating our Nation's beaches and jeopardizing the health of our Nation's families. At a minimum, the program must raise the standard for sewage treatment to adequately protect public health and provide full information to communities about these water quality problems and associated health risks.

Fourth, I direct the Department of the Interior and the Department of Agriculture to enhance management of Federal lands to increase protection of waters on or near Federal lands, and to identify waters on or near Federal lands that require special protection. Specifically, a proposal for a unified Federal policy on watershed management, developed under the Clean Water Action Plan, should be circulated first for consultation with States and Indian Tribes, and then published in the Federal Register for public comment no later than July 15, 1999.

Each of these measures should be implemented through a process that provides appropriate opportunities for participation and comment by States, Tribes, and the affected public.

This memorandum is not intended to create any right, benefit, or trust responsibility, substantive or procedural, enforceable at law or equity by a party against the United States, its agencies or instrumentalities, or any other person.

William J. Clinton

---

**1. Does the President Have the Legal Authority To Direct Agency Action?**—Where does the President get the legal authority to issue directives like President Clinton's Clean Water Memorandum? There is relatively little case law that bears on this issue, but some court of appeals decisions are at least suggestive of how one might approach this question. Consider, for example, the D.C. Circuit's decision in Sierra Club v. Costle, 657 F.2d 298 (D.C. Cir. 1981). In that case, environmental groups argued that the EPA had acted improperly by failing to disclose the details of conversations between White House officials (including the President) and EPA officials regarding the development of an EPA pollution control regulation. While the precise legal issue in *Sierra Club* concerned the agency's alleged obligation to *disclose* contacts with the White House, Judge Wald's opinion made some general observations about the relationship between the President and the agencies that may be relevant to the legality of presidential directives:

> The court recognizes the basic need of the President and his White House staff to monitor the consistency of executive agency regulations with Administration policy. He and his White House advisers surely must be briefed fully and frequently about rules in the making, and their contributions to policymaking considered. The executive power under our Constitution, after all, is not shared[;] it rests exclusively with the President. The idea of a "plural executive," or a President with a council of state, was considered and rejected by the Constitutional Convention. Instead the Founders chose to risk the potential for tyranny inherent in placing power in one person, in order to gain the advantages of accountability fixed on a single source. To ensure the President's control and supervision over the Executive Branch, the Constitution and its judicial gloss vests him with the powers of appointment and removal, the power to demand written opinions from executive officers, and the right to invoke executive privilege to protect consultative privacy. In the particular case of EPA, Presidential authority is clear since it has never been considered an "independent agency," but always part of the Executive Branch.

> The authority of the President to control and supervise executive policymaking is derived from the Constitution; the desirability of such control is demonstrable from the practical realities of administrative rulemaking. Regulations such as those involved here demand a careful weighing of cost, environmental, and energy considerations. They also have broad implications for national economic policy. Our form of government simply could not function effectively or rationally if key executive policymakers were isolated from each other and from the Chief Executive. Single mission agencies do not always have the answers to complex regulatory problems. An overworked administrator exposed on a 24–hour basis to a dedicated but zealous staff needs to know the arguments and ideas of policymakers in other agencies as well as in the White House.

>      .   .   .

> . . . [A]ny [EPA] rule issued here with or without White House assistance must have the requisite factual support in the rulemaking record. . . . Of course, it is always possible that undisclosed Presidential prodding may direct an outcome that is factually based on the record, but different from the outcome that would have obtained in the absence of Presidential involvement. In such a case, it would be true that the political process did affect the outcome in a way the courts

could not police. But we do not believe that Congress intended that the courts convert informal rulemaking into a rarified technocratic process, unaffected by political considerations or the presence of Presidential power....

657 F.2d at 405–08.

While *Sierra Club* does not consider directly the lawfulness of presidential directives to agencies, doesn't Judge Wald's reasoning strongly suggest that such directives are at least presumptively legitimate? Her analysis implies that although the President may not direct an agency to take an action that is unsupported by the record (or otherwise unlawful), if the agency has the discretion to take more than one action, the President may influence, perhaps even direct, the agency's choice among permissible alternatives. The D.C. Circuit seemed to take a similar line a few years later in Center for Auto Safety v. Peck, 751 F.2d 1336 (D.C. Cir. 1985), in which the court upheld a National Highway Traffic Safety Administration (NHTSA) decision to relax the performance standard for automobile bumpers. The challengers had alleged that the agency's action was unduly influenced by the President. In support of this allegation, they pointed to a White House press release, issued shortly before the agency finalized its rule, that proposed a relaxation of the bumper standard as a way to assist the auto industry. *Peck*, 751 F.2d at 1368. The D.C. Circuit, in an opinion by then-Judge Scalia, concluded that there was "nothing either extraordinary or unlawful in the fact that a federal agency opens an inquiry into a matter which the President believes should be inquired into. Indeed, we had thought the system was supposed to work that way." *Id.* Judge Scalia's opinion was careful to note, however, that it "would be a different matter if the President directed the agency, in the course of its inquiry, to disregard the statutory criteria controlling its actions." *Id. Peck* would therefore seem to imply that presidential directives, such as President Clinton's Clean Water Memorandum, would pose no legal difficulties so long as they do not direct the agency to disregard statutory criteria or otherwise act in ways that are unlawful. Then again, *Peck* also emphasized that "the [White House] Press Release was the product of the agency's decisions rather than the cause for them." *Id.* As Professor Kagan observes, *supra* pp. 572–573, this was *not* typically true of President Clinton's directives, which prompted—rather than merely announced or took ownership of—agency decisions. Judge Scalia also emphasized the fact that the White House press release at issue in *Peck* did not assert the legal authority to *direct* the agency action; the press release only "demonstrate[d] an expectation ... that the President would be pleased if the agency ended its rulemaking by reducing the existing standard, and disappointed if it left the current rule in effect." *Id.* at 1368–69. The Clean Water Memorandum excerpted above is phrased in more imperative terms. Do these factors put that memo on a different legal footing from the press release in *Peck*? Or is the distinction immaterial, in light of the fact that in neither case did the President direct the agency to disregard statutory or other legal provisions?

Opinions in cases like *Sierra Club* and *Peck* appear to endorse a robust form of presidential control over the administrative state, on the grounds that as long as the President does not direct agencies to act unlawfully, presidential oversight promotes energy, coherence, and political accountability. But what about the fact that Congress may sometimes prefer to lodge decisionmaking authority in an agency that is independent of—or at least somewhat insulated from—presidential authority? Congress often phrases its delegations as delegations of discretionary authority to an *agency official*, rather than the President: Many statutes say something to the effect that the agency should adopt regulations that, *in the judgment of the Administrator* (or Secretary or Commission), will fulfill the statutory goals. Why should the President's judgment prevail if the statute explicitly delegates to the Administrator? And what about the independent commissions, for which Congress has expressly limited the President's removal power? If a statute expressly delegates a discretionary policy judgment to an independent commission, should the President be able direct how the commissioners should make that judgment? Does the President's duty to ensure that "the Laws be faithfully executed" imply that the President has the ultimate say over how agency officials exercise their discretion? Scholars have reached quite different conclusions on these questions. *See, e.g.,* Steven G. Calabresi & Saikrishna B. Prakash, *The President's Power To Execute the Laws*, 104 YALE L.J. 541 (1994) (arguing that the Constitution mandates that the President be able to direct any administrative official regarding the exercise of lawful discretion); Elena Kagan, *Presidential Administration*, 114 HARV. L. REV. 2245 (2001) (arguing that courts should adopt a default interpretive presumption that, unless a statute clearly states otherwise, the President has directive authority over executive branch agencies, but not independent commissions); Kevin M. Stack, *The President's Statutory Powers To Administer the Laws*, 106 COLUM. L. REV. 263 (2006) (arguing that courts should construe statutes as granting the President the legal authority to direct agency decisionmaking only if that authority is expressly granted to the President); Peter L. Strauss, *Overseer, or "The Decider"? The President in Administrative Law*, 75 GEO. WASH. L. REV. 696 (2007) (arguing that the President has the authority to oversee agency decisionmaking processes but not to decide matters delegated to an agency rather than to the President).

**2.   *Does It Matter Whether the President Has the Legal Authority to Direct Agency Action?*—**One might reasonably question how much it matters whether presidential directives, such as President Clinton's Clean Water Memorandum, are *legally* binding on agency officials. After all, as the D.C. Circuit suggested in *Peck*, the President surely has the authority to declare what he or she would *like* the agency to do, and agency officials—particularly those whom the President can remove at will—may have strong incentives to pay close attention to the President's wishes. But this sort of presidential influence does not depend directly on the *legal* status of presidential directives. And agencies that wish to resist presidential directives may be able to do so effectively whether or not these directives are legally "binding" in some formal sense. Professor Kagan summarizes these points as follows:

> ... Agency officials may accede to [the President's] preferences because they feel a sense of personal loyalty and commitment to him; because they desire his assistance in budgetary, legislative, and appointments matters; or in extreme cases because they respect and fear his removal power.... Conversely, even given the assertion of directive authority, a President may face considerable constraints in imposing his will on administrative actors. Their resistance to or mere criticism of a directive may inflict political costs on the President as heavy as any that would result from an exercise of the removal power....

Elena Kagan, *Presidential Administration*, 114 Harv. L. Rev. 2245, 2298 (2001) (footnotes omitted).

Why, then, does the *legal* status of presidential directives matter? At least with regard to independent commissions, perhaps a commissioner's refusal to comply with a presidential directive might constitute "good cause" for removal if, but only if, the President has the lawful authority to direct agency action. Again, though, this prospect is more hypothetical than real, as no President has ever relied on noncompliance with a presidential directive as a reason for firing a commissioner of an independent agency. Perhaps the practical significance of the legal status of presidential directives lies in the way the President's *legal* authority to direct the administration may affect, in subtle psychological ways, the *political* interaction between the President and the agencies. As Professor Kagan has noted, "the explicit and repeated assertion of directive authority probably alters over time what Peter Strauss has called the 'psychology of government'—the understanding of agency and White House officials alike of their respective roles and powers." Kagan, *supra*, at 2299 (citing Peter L. Strauss, *Presidential Rulemaking*, 72 Chi.-Kent L. Rev. 965, 986 (1997)). If, as a result, agencies come to see presidential intervention in regulatory policymaking as "ever more routine," the net result may be "a significant enhancement of presidential power over regulatory matters." *Id.*; *see also* Ronald A. Cass & Peter L. Strauss, *The Presidential Signing Statements Controversy*, 16 William & Mary Bill of Rights J. 11, 19 (2007) (asserting that "an administrator who sees the legal responsibility for particular decisions as *his* own, not the President's, may find it easier to resist presidential 'instructions'"); Kevin M. Stack, *The President's Statutory Powers to Administer the Laws*, 106 Colum. L. Rev. 263, 322 (2006) (arguing that a conception of an agency official's role "that emphasizes the official's independent duty under the law, as opposed to its acting in the stead of the President" is important because, if that conception is "absorbed by executive branch actors, [it] has the potential to contribute to the protection against presidential abuse of the administrative state"). Do such contentions seem sufficiently plausible to justify paying serious attention to the *legality* of presidential directives, as opposed to the desirability of presidential control as a more general matter of policy?

# CHAPTER FOUR

# THE REGULATORY PROCESS

## CONTENTS

## I.  AN OVERVIEW OF THE REGULATORY PROCESS
## A.  ADMINISTRATIVE PROCEDURES AS A RESPONSE TO THE DELEGATION PROBLEM

In Chapter Three, we saw that despite the serious legal and normative concerns about delegating broad discretionary lawmaking powers to administrative agencies, such delegations are now a well-established and entrenched feature of our system of government, and the Supreme Court has showed little inclination to rein in such delegations directly through a more aggressive version of the constitutional non-delegation doctrine. This does not, however, mean that the serious concerns about excessive concentration of power in unelected bureaucrats are no longer relevant. Indeed, much of what we call "administrative law" can be thought of as a response to these concerns. The central problem or tension that runs throughout much of our administrative law is how to reap the perceived benefits of broad delegations—flexible, expert decision-making insulated from the distorting influence of day-to-day partisan politics—while avoiding the perceived danger of arbitrary, abusive government by unelected and unaccountable bureaucrats.

One of the ways in which our system tries to manage this tension is through the use of carefully designed administrative procedures. The materials in this chapter consider the role and function of administrative procedures, focusing primarily on a statute called the Administrative Procedure Act (APA), which establishes default rules for federal agencies to follow when making, interpreting, and applying regulations. Before turning to the APA, though, it's worth taking a moment to think more generally about the purpose of administrative procedures, and in particular about why proceduralization might be (or might not be) an effective response to some of the concerns associated with delegating extensive powers to administrative agencies.

> **a.  *Improving the Quality of Agency Decision–Making*—**Perhaps the most intuitive argument in favor of imposing procedural requirements on agencies is simply that appropriately designed procedures improve the quality of agency decisions. They do this first and foremost by ensuring that the agency properly considers all relevant information, and that affected parties have a sufficient opportunity to state their views, present evidence, and make reasoned arguments to the agency. Administrative procedures may also help guard against the "capture" of agencies by parochial interest groups. The fact that procedural requirements slow the decision-making process down, and may encourage or require consultation and deliberation, might also help prevent hasty or ill-considered action. The right sort of procedures might further improve the quality of agency decisions by ensuring that the right people within the agency have the greatest influence over the final decision. Procedural requirements may also facilitate judicial review of agency action, enabling courts—which

typically lack the requisite subject matter expertise—to evaluate agency action and ensure that the agency has made a reasoned decision that conforms with governing law. In sum, administrative procedures may be an important way to ensure that agency decision-making really does exhibit the virtues invoked to justify delegation in the first place—expertise, dispassionate analysis, deliberation, fairness, and the like—while containing the risks of arbitrary agency action.

It is far from certain, however, that greater proceduralization of administrative decision-making is always (or even usually) beneficial. Even well-designed procedures can impose significant costs on agencies, making the decision-making process slower, more cumbersome, and less flexible, and the costs associated with this so-called "ossification" of agency decision-making may outweigh whatever benefits the additional procedures confer. Indeed, the costs and delay imposed by excessive proceduralization might hand well-organized interest groups an additional tool for resisting changes in regulatory policy that would produce net benefits for the more diffuse general public. Finally, certain forms of proceduralization—in particular, those patterned after the judicial process—may end up disempowering the agency's technical experts (the people who really understand the complex policy questions at stake), and empowering instead the agency's lawyers (who better understand how to navigate the requisite procedures). One of the central difficulties facing institutional designers (including both the legislators who draft procedural requirements and the judges who interpret them) is how to devise procedures that will improve the quality of agency decision-making and guard against administrative arbitrariness without undermining the agency's ability to achieve its mission with overly burdensome, labyrinthine, and counterproductive procedural rules.

***b.   Enhancing Democratic Legitimacy***—Quite apart from the possibility that administrative procedures may help ensure high-quality regulatory policy decisions, procedures are sometimes thought to serve other important functions as well. For instance, although agency officials are not elected, appropriately designed administrative procedures that facilitate broad public participation in agency decision-making may be an attempt to compensate for the absence of direct democratic accountability. Some have even gone so far as to suggest that if the correct sort of administrative procedures are in place, the agency rulemaking process could approximate the civic republican ideal of a "deliberative democracy" even better than the legislative process. *See* Mark Seidenfeld, *A Civic Republican Justification for the Bureaucratic State*, 105 Harv. L. Rev. 1511 (1992); *see also* Cass R. Sunstein, *Interest Groups in American Public Law*, 38 Stan. L. Rev. 29 (1985). While there may be reason to doubt that administrative procedures can ever fully substitute for the functions performed by democratic elections, administrative procedures may be designed to alleviate at least some of the concerns about the public accountability of agency decision-making.

Administrative procedures may also facilitate or inhibit the control of agencies by the elected branches of government. One hypothesis prominent in the political science literature proposes that administrative procedures can facilitate congressional control of agencies because certain procedures—particularly those that disclose information about agency plans early on, slow down the process of finalizing a decision, and provide opportunities for outside input—make it easier for Congress to monitor what agencies are doing and to intervene when necessary. The metaphor sometimes used here is that of "fire alarm" oversight, as contrasted with "police patrol" oversight. "Police patrol" oversight involves congressionally-initiated inquiries into agency behavior. The problem with such oversight is that it is resource intensive and inefficient for Congress, due to the sheer volume of agency activity. In contrast, "fire alarm" oversight entails congressional response to some signal—such as complaints by constituents—that something is wrong. Administrative procedures may facilitate fire-alarm oversight by enabling Congress to receive trouble signals early and to respond quickly. *See* Mathew D. McCubbins & Thomas Schwartz, *Congressional Oversight Overlooked: Police Patrols Versus Fire Alarms*, 28 AM. J. POL. SCI. 165 (1984); Mathew D. McCubbins, Roger G. Noll & Barry R. Weingast, *Administrative Procedures as Instruments of Political Control*, 3 J. L. ECON. & ORG. 243 (1987); Mathew D. McCubbins, Roger G. Noll & Barry R. Weingast, *Structure and Process, Politics and Policy: Administrative Arrangements and the Political Control of Agencies*, 75 VA. L. REV. 431 (1989). If one believes that a significant problem with delegating power to agencies is that there is often a lack of sufficient oversight by Congress, then procedures that facilitate such oversight may be desirable, and we might expect Congress to try to design these sorts of procedures.

While the above hypothesis posits that administrative procedures facilitate political control of the bureaucracy, others have argued that administrative procedures may have the opposite effect, further insulating agencies from control by Congress, the President, or politically influential interest groups. The idea is that some procedures—such as those that require that decisions be based on a public record and formal findings, place limits on *ex parte* contacts with agency officials, and provide for judicial review—make it harder for outside actors, including elected politicians, to influence agencies. While no one thinks that administrative procedures can eliminate external political influence, such procedures may make this sort of outside influence more difficult and costly, thereby empowering the technocrats in the agency at the expense of politicians and politically influential constituency groups.

These two hypotheses may seem contradictory, in that one suggests administrative procedures facilitate political control, while the other suggests that administrative procedures inhibit political control. There is no necessary contradiction, however: *certain* procedural requirements (alone or in combination) may facilitate political control, while *other* procedural requirements may inhibit such control. Furthermore, the procedural scheme might facilitate *certain forms* of political control, while inhibiting other forms of political control. This, in turn, suggests another central tension or problem for institutional designers: crafting the procedural scheme that promotes beneficial forms of political influence, while impeding other, less desirable forms—achieving the right balance between the interest in political accountability and the interest in political independence. As you read the materials that follow, ask yourself how well the designers of modern administrative procedures have struck that balance.

## B.  The Statutory Framework: The Administrative Procedure Act

This chapter focuses on a statute called the Administrative Procedure Act (APA), and in particular on the "notice-and-comment" procedures that the APA establishes for agencies to use when making rules. The APA, enacted in 1946, emerged as a carefully crafted legislative compromise after a lengthy political struggle over the control of executive agencies, a struggle triggered by the dramatic expansion of the federal administrative bureaucracy that began in the early part of the twentieth century and accelerated rapidly in the 1930s during President Franklin Roosevelt's New Deal. Although the APA ultimately passed both houses of Congress unanimously, this unanimity reflected more a grudging compromise than a universal agreement on optimal administrative procedures. *See generally* George B. Shepherd, *Fierce Compromise: The Administrative Procedure Act Emerges from New Deal Politics*, 90 Nw. U. L. Rev. 1557 (1996).

The APA establishes the basic default rules of procedure for federal agencies to use when promulgating and enforcing regulations. Commentators have sometimes characterized the APA as a kind of quasi-constitutional statute. *See* Bruce Ackerman, *The Emergency Constitution*, 113 Yale L.J. 1029, 1077–78 (2004); Peter H. Schuck, Foundations of Administrative Law 49 (1994). This characterization stems from two related characteristics of the APA. First, the APA is a "framework" statute, laying out the basic structure and procedures for a set of important government institutions, and subjecting these institutions to legal and political controls. *See* Ackerman, *supra*; Michael Asimow, *The Influence of the Federal Administrative Procedure Act on California's New Administrative Procedure Act*, 32 Tulsa L.J. 297, 297 (1996). Second, in part because of its role as a framework statute, and in part because of the open-endedness of many of its main provisions, courts have felt relatively free to adapt the APA to changed circumstances through a process of judicial interpretation, elaboration, and refinement that in some ways more closely resembles conventional understandings of constitutional, rather than statutory, interpretation. *See* Thomas W. Merrill, *Capture Theory and the Courts: 1967–1983*, 72 Chi.-Kent L. Rev. 1039, 1039 (1997); Steven P. Croley, *The Administrative Procedure Act and Regulatory Reform: A Reconciliation*, 10 Admin. L. J. Am. U. 35, 49 (1996). Whether or not such an approach represents a sound and legitimate interpretive posture is a controversial question, as you might expect. *See, e.g.*, Lars Noah, *Interpreting Agency Enabling Acts: Misplaced Metaphors in Administrative Law*, 41 Wm. & Mary L. Rev. 1463 (2000).

Before proceeding, it is important to emphasize that although this chapter will focus almost exclusively on the APA, the APA is not the exclusive source of procedural law for federal administrative agencies. The Constitution, other statutory law, and an agency's own regulations may also impose important constraints on an agency's decision-making process. Section 559 of the APA makes this explicit, stating that the APA's provisions "do not limit or repeal additional requirements imposed by statute or otherwise recognized by law." It is also important to emphasize that the APA's procedural rules are default rules that can be overridden by more specific statutory directives. That said, § 559 purports to impose some constraints on derogation from APA procedures by instructing that a "subsequent statute may not be held to supersede or modify [the APA's procedural or judicial review requirements] . . . except to the extent that it does so expressly." This occasionally leads to interesting legal questions about how clear a subsequent statute must be to effect deviation from the APA's requirements. *See, e.g.,* Marcello v. Bonds, 349 U.S. 302 (1955). Thus, while the APA is a vitally important statute, it does not necessarily apply in all cases (though it usually does), and when it does apply, its requirements may not be exhaustive or exclusive (indeed, they usually aren't).

**a. The Forms of Administrative Action under the APA**—The APA defines two major types of agency action: "rules" and "orders." A "rule" is defined by the APA as "an agency statement of general or particular applicability and future effect designed to implement, interpret, or prescribe law or policy or describing the organization, procedure, or practice requirements of an agency." 5 U.S.C. § 551(4). An "agency process for formulating, amending, or repealing a rule" is defined by the APA as a "rulemaking." 5 U.S.C. § 551(5). An "order" is pretty much any authoritative agency action other than a rule—the APA defines "order" as "a final disposition, whether affirmative, negative, injunctive, or declaratory in form, of an agency in a matter other than rule making but including licensing." 5 U.S.C. § 551(6). The APA labels the "agency process for the formulation of an order" an "adjudication." 5 U.S.C. § 551(7). This label is somewhat misleading, however. Although many agency processes for formulating orders involve adversarial procedures that resemble what one might find in a judicial trial, *any* process producing final agency action that is not a rule is an "adjudication" for APA purposes, including many actions (such as licensing) that do not fit the model of an adversarial adjudicative hearing that resembles a trial.

Each of these two categories of agency action—rules and orders—may be "formal" or "informal." As the names imply, formal proceedings involve more elaborate procedures than do informal proceedings. Thus, the APA divides the universe of possible agency action into four major categories— (1) formal rulemaking, (2) informal rulemaking, (3) formal adjudication, and (4) informal adjudication—and specifies different procedural requirements for each.

Formal rulemakings are governed by an elaborate set of procedures laid out in §§ 556 and 557 of the APA. These sections provide for an adversarial hearing at which the proponent of the rule (that is, the agency) carries the burden of proof on contested issues, and must show that the proposed rule is supported by "reliable, probative, and substantial evidence." The presiding officer at the hearing is an official called an Administrative Law Judge (ALJ). ALJs are agency officials, not members of the Article III judiciary, but—in order to foster their independence and impartiality—ALJs have special statutory civil service protections and some degree of insulation from the rest of the agency. Interested parties are entitled to participate in the agency hearing and to present evidence, and are entitled to present oral testimony and conduct cross-examination unless the agency affirmatively concludes that they will not be prejudiced by the absence of such procedures. The agency's final rule must be based on the official record adduced in the formal proceedings, and there are strict prohibitions on *ex parte* contacts with agency decision-makers. There is a process for internal appeals from the ALJ's determination to the agency leadership, and a final disposition of the matter must include formal findings of fact and conclusions of law.

In contrast, informal rulemaking—widely known as notice-and-comment rulemaking—is governed by § 553 of the APA. Section 553 does not require the elaborate public hearing process associated with formal rulemaking. Rather, § 553 rulemaking entails three main procedural requirements. *First*, an agency that proposes to make a rule through this process must give public <u>notice</u> by publishing its "notice of proposed rulemaking" (NPRM) in the *Federal Register* (the official journal of the federal government, published daily by the Government Printing Office). According to the APA, the NPRM must include "(1) a statement of the time, place, and nature of the public rule making proceedings; (2) reference to the legal authority under which the rule is proposed; and (3) either the terms or substance of the proposed rule or a description of the subjects and issues involved." 5 U.S.C. § 553(b). *Second*, the agency must provide the public with an opportunity to <u>comment</u> on the agency's proposal. In particular, the APA states that after the agency publishes its NPRM in the *Federal Register*, the agency "shall give interested persons an opportunity to participate in the rule making through submission of written data, views, or arguments with or without opportunity for oral presentation." 5 U.S.C. § 553(c). *Third*, if the agency decides to finalize a rule, it must publish an <u>explanation</u> of the rule; that is, agencies must "incorporate in the rules adopted a concise general statement of their basis and purpose." *Id*. In contrast with the express terms of the formal rulemaking provisions, however, § 553 contains no requirement that a final rule be based on any record compiled during the proceedings.

Like formal rulemakings, formal adjudications are governed by §§ 556 and 557 of the APA, as well as additional requirements described in § 554. Formal adjudications are what most people immediately associate with "agency adjudications"—trial-like adversarial hearings that typically involve an agency seeking to impose some sort of penalty on a regulated party, or to resolve a dispute between two or more parties under a regulatory scheme administered by the agency. In contrast with formal rulemaking, formal adjudications require an opportunity for oral presentation (except in cases involving claims for money or benefits or applications for initial licenses, where the agency may forgo those procedures if the parties "will not be prejudiced thereby").

There is no section of the APA that specifies particular procedures for *informal* adjudication. Some generic APA provisions, such as § 555 (which governs certain "ancillary matters" related to agency procedure) and § 706 (the general provision on judicial review, discussed in more detail at pp. ___, *infra*) apply to all agency actions, including informal adjudications. Informal adjudications are also subject to procedural restrictions found in other statutes, the agency's own regulations, and the Constitution. But overall, the procedural requirements for informal adjudication are fairly minimal.

In order to figure out which APA procedures apply to a given agency action, one must ask two questions. The first is whether the agency action in question is a rule or an order. If the former, the agency must promulgate it through a rulemaking process. If the latter, the agency must proceed by adjudication. Once one has determined whether the agency proceeding is a rulemaking or an adjudication, one must then determine whether the proceeding must be formal or whether it may be informal. What does the APA—and the judicial doctrine interpreting the APA—tell us about how to answer these two classification questions?

**b. Distinguishing Rulemaking from Adjudication**—Let us consider first how to distinguish administrative "adjudication" from "rulemaking." For purposes of determining which of the four APA procedural frameworks applies, the APA itself contains express definitions of the relevant terms. Recall that the APA essentially defines an adjudication as anything other than a rulemaking, §§ 551(6)–(7), and defines a rule as "an agency statement of general or particular applicability and future effect designed to implement, interpret, or prescribe law or policy," § 551(4). These definitions appear to reject at least one common, intuitive distinction between rulemaking and adjudication: the idea that rules are general, while adjudications deal with particular parties. Rather, the APA states that a rule can have "general *or particular* applicability," § 551(4) (emphasis added). The APA instead emphasizes the idea that rulemaking is future-oriented, whereas adjudication concerns events that happened in the past. That is to say, rulemaking is typically about prescribing new law, or making new policy, while adjudication is typically about applying existing law or policy to some set of facts. In short, rulemaking resembles what legislators do, while adjudication resembles what courts do. The *Attorney General's Manual on the Administrative Procedure Act*—an explanatory monograph prepared by the Department of Justice shortly after the APA's enactment—described the distinction as follows:

> [T]he entire Act is based upon a dichotomy between rule making and adjudication. Examination of the legislative history of the definitions and of the differences in the required procedures for rule making and for adjudication discloses highly practical concepts of rule making and adjudication. Rule making is agency action which regulates the future conduct of either groups of persons or a single person; it is

essentially legislative in nature, not only because it operates in the future but also because it is primarily concerned with policy considerations. The object of the rule making proceeding is the implementation or prescription of law or policy for the future, rather than the evaluation of a respondent's past conduct. Typically, the issues relate not to the evidentiary facts ... but rather to the policy-making conclusions to be drawn from the facts. Conversely, adjudication is concerned with the determination of past and present rights and liabilities. Normally, there is involved a decision as to whether past conduct was unlawful.... Or, it may involve the determination of a person's right to benefits under existing law.... In such proceedings, the issues of fact are often sharply controverted.

U.S. Department of Justice, Attorney General's Manual on the Administrative Procedure Act 14–15 (1947) (internal citation omitted).

This distinction between rulemaking and adjudication is intuitive, but there are some difficulties in its application. For starters, the APA's temporal distinction—the idea that rules are about the future and adjudication is about the past—does not always hold, at least if we take legislation and judicial adjudication as our paradigm cases for each category of action. Adjudicative decisions can be future oriented, in that they may involve declaratory judgments spelling out the future legal consequences of a course of conduct, or may enjoin a party to take, or abstain from, some action in the future. As for the idea that rulemaking (like legislation) is about *making* law, while adjudication (administrative or judicial) is about *applying* law to facts, this distinction is also problematic, in that many adjudicative decisions involve the adjudicator announcing general principles of law or policy that are used to decide the instant case and subsequently applied as precedent in future cases.

Despite these conceptual difficulties, determining whether an agency proceeding is a rulemaking or an adjudication for APA purposes is usually not too difficult, and the issue is rarely litigated. Often the agency's organic statute will make clear which agency actions count as rules (and are therefore governed by the APA's rulemaking procedures) and which count as orders (governed by the APA's provisions on adjudication). And courts virtually always accept the agency's characterization of its own action— there are very few cases in which a court decides that an agency action described by the agency as a rule is really an adjudication, or vice versa. That said, there are important legal questions, some of which we will discuss later in this chapter (pp. 643–674, *infra*) about when an agency is *allowed* to proceed by adjudication rather than rulemaking, or by rulemaking rather than adjudication. But, with very few exceptions, these cases do not turn on careful parsing of the APA's definition of a "rule."

**c. When Must an Agency Use Formal Procedures?**—As we have seen, the procedural requirements for formal and informal rulemaking differ dramatically. For this reason, a great deal—for the agency and for those affected by agency action—turns on the legal criteria for determining when agency regulations must go through the formal rulemaking process laid out in §§ 556–557 of the APA, and when agencies may adopt regulations through the informal notice-and-comment procedures laid out in § 553.

Section 553 of the APA states that rulemaking is governed by formal procedures if the agency rule in question "[is] required by statute to be made on the record after opportunity for an agency hearing." 5 U.S.C. § 553(c). This seems straightforward enough, but it is not always completely clear whether the agency's organic statute imposes the requirements specified in this provision. Some statutes use essentially the precise triggering language that appears in § 553(c), requiring agencies to issue regulations "on the record after opportunity for a hearing." These are easy cases—formal rulemaking is clearly required. Other statutes say nothing of the sort. These are also easy cases—the agency may proceed via informal rulemaking if it so chooses. But some statutes use words that are suggestive of a more formal process, but without the precise language that appears in § 553(c). Other statutes contain an explicit reference only to one of the two features mentioned in § 553(c) (a "hearing" or a decision "on the record"), but not both. What should courts do when confronted with such ambiguous statutes?

The Supreme Court addressed the issue in the following case, *United States v. Florida East Coast Railway Co.* While the principal issue in the case concerns a question of statutory interpretation, the majority opinion and the dissent both appear to be influenced by the Justices' respective views of the costs and benefits of formal administrative procedures. The opinions also reflect quite distinctive attitudes about how to interpret ambiguous terms in the APA and in related organic acts.

---

## United States v. Florida East Coast Railway Company

Supreme Court of the United States
410 U.S. 224 (1973)

■ Mr. Justice Rehnquist delivered the opinion of the Court.

Appellees, two railroad companies, brought this action in the District Court for the Middle District of Florida to set aside the incentive per diem rates established by appellant Interstate Commerce Commission in a rulemaking proceeding.... They challenged the order of the Commission on both substantive and procedural grounds. The District Court sustained appellees' position that the Commission had failed to comply with the applicable provisions of the Administrative Procedure Act, 5 U.S.C. § 551 *et seq.*, and therefore set aside the order without dealing with the railroads' other contentions. The District Court held that the language of § 1(14)(a) of the Interstate Commerce Act, 49 U.S.C. § 1(14)(a), required the Commission in a proceeding such as this to act in accordance with the Administrative Procedure Act, 5 U.S.C. § 556(d)....

[Section 1(14)(a) of the Interstate Commerce Act provides that the Interstate Commerce Commission may establish rates "after hearing" and must "give consideration" to factors affecting the national supply of railroad freight cars.]

## I. Background of Chronic Freight Car Shortages

This case arises from the factual background of a chronic freight-car shortage on the Nation's railroads.... Congressional concern for the problem was manifested in the enactment in 1966 of an amendment to § 1(14)(a) of the Interstate Commerce Act, enlarging the Commission's authority to prescribe per diem charges for the use by one railroad of freight cars owned by another.... The Commission in 1966 commenced an investigation ... "to determine whether information presently available warranted the establishment of an incentive element increase, on an interim basis, to apply pending further study and investigation." ... In October 1967, the Commission rendered a decision discontinuing the earlier proceeding, but announcing a program of further investigation into the general subject.

In December 1967, the Commission initiated the rulemaking procedure giving rise to the order that appellees here challenge. It directed Class I and Class II line-haul railroads to compile and report detailed information with respect to freight-car demand and supply at numerous sample stations for selected days of the week during 12 four-week periods, beginning January 29, 1968.

Some of the affected railroads voiced questions about the proposed study or requested modification in the study procedures outlined by the Commission in its notice of proposed rulemaking. In response to petitions setting forth these carriers' views, the Commission staff held an informal conference in April 1968, at which the objections and proposed modifications were discussed. Twenty railroads, including appellee Seaboard, were represented at this conference, at which the Commission's staff sought to answer questions about reporting methods to accommodate individual circumstances of particular railroads. The conference adjourned on a note that undoubtedly left the impression that hearings would be held at some future date. A detailed report of the conference was sent to all parties to the proceeding before the Commission.

The results of the information thus collected were analyzed and presented to Congress by the Commission during a hearing before the Subcommittee on Surface Transportation of the Senate Committee on Commerce in May 1969. Members of the Subcommittee expressed dissatisfaction with the Commission's slow pace in exercising the authority that had been conferred upon it by the 1966 Amendments to the Interstate Commerce Act. Judge Simpson in his opinion for the District Court said:

"Members of the Senate Subcommittee on Surface Transportation expressed considerable dissatisfaction with the Commission's apparent inability to take effective steps toward eliminating the national shortage of freight cars. Comments were general that the Commission was conducting too many hearings and taking too little action. Senators pressed for more action and less talk, but Commission counsel expressed doubt respecting the Commission's statutory power to act without additional hearings." 322 F. Supp., at 727.

Judge Friendly, describing the same event in Long Island R. Co. v. United States, *supra*, said:

> "To say that the presentation was not received with enthusiasm would be a considerable understatement. Senators voiced displeasure at the Commission's long delay at taking action under the 1966 amendment, engaged in some merriment over what was regarded as an unintelligible discussion of methodology ... and expressed doubt about the need for a hearing.... But the Commission's general counsel insisted that a hearing was needed ... and the Chairman of the Commission agreed...." 318 F.Supp., at 494.

The Commission, now apparently imbued with a new sense of mission, issued in December 1969 an interim report announcing its tentative decision to adopt incentive per diem charges on standard boxcars based on the information compiled by the railroads. The substantive decision reached by the Commission was that so-called "incentive" per diem charges should be paid by any railroad using on its lines a standard boxcar owned by another railroad. Before the enactment of the 1966 amendment to the Interstate Commerce Act, it was generally thought that the Commission's authority to fix per diem payments for freight car use was limited to setting an amount that reflected fair return on investment for the owning railroad, without any regard being had for the desirability of prompt return to the owning line or for the encouragement of additional purchases of freight cars by the railroads as a method of investing capital. The Commission concluded, however, that in view of the 1966 amendment it could impose additional "incentive" per diem charges to spur prompt return of existing cars and to make acquisition of new cars financially attractive to the railroads. It did so by means of a proposed schedule that established such charges on an across-the-board basis for all common carriers by railroads subject to the Interstate Commerce Act. Embodied in the report was a proposed rule adopting the Commission's tentative conclusions and a notice to the railroads to file statements of position within 60 days, couched in the following language:

> "That verified statements of facts, briefs, and statements of position respecting the tentative conclusions reached in the said interim report, the rules and regulations proposed in the appendix to this order, and any other pertinent matter, are hereby invited to be submitted pursuant to the filing schedule set forth below by an interested person whether or not such person is already a party to this proceeding."

.   .   .   .   .   .

"That any party requesting oral hearing shall set forth with specificity the need therefor and the evidence to be adduced." 337 I.C.C. 183, 213.

Both appellee railroads filed statements objecting to the Commission's proposal and requesting an oral hearing, as did numerous other railroads. In April 1970, the Commission, without having held further "hearings," issued a supplemental report making some modifications in the tentative conclusions earlier reached, but overruling in toto the requests of appellees.

The District Court held that in so doing the Commission violated § 556(d) of the Administrative Procedure Act, and it was on this basis that it set aside the order of the Commission.

## II. Applicability of Administrative Procedure Act

In United States v. Allegheny–Ludlum Steel Corp., we held that the language of § 1(14)(a) of the Interstate Commerce Act authorizing the Commission to act "after hearing" was not the equivalent of a requirement that a rule be made "on the record after opportunity for an agency hearing" as the latter term is used in § 553(c) of the Administrative Procedure Act. Since the 1966 amendment to § 1(14)(a), under which the Commission was here proceeding, does not by its terms add to the hearing requirement contained in the earlier language, the same result should obtain here unless that amendment contains language that is tantamount to such a requirement. Appellees contend that such language is found in the provisions of that Act requiring that:

"[T]he Commission shall give consideration to the national level of ownership of such type of freight car and to other factors affecting the adequacy of the national freight car supply, and shall, on the basis of such consideration, determine whether compensation should be computed...."

While this language is undoubtedly a mandate to the Commission to consider the factors there set forth in reaching any conclusion as to imposition of per diem incentive charges, it adds to the hearing requirements of the section neither expressly nor by implication. We know of no reason to think that an administrative agency in reaching a decision cannot accord consideration to factors such as those set forth in the 1966 amendment by means other than a trial-type hearing or the presentation of oral argument by the affected parties. Congress by that amendment specified necessary components of the ultimate decision, but it did not specify the method by which the Commission should acquire information about those components.

Both of the district courts that reviewed this order of the Commission concluded that its proceedings were governed by the stricter requirements of §§ 556 and 557 of the Administrative Procedure Act, rather than by the provisions of § 553 alone.[6] The conclusion of the District Court for the

---

**6.** ... The dissenting opinion of Mr. Justice Douglas relies in part on indications by the Commission that it proposed to apply the more stringent standards of §§ 556 and 557 of the

Middle District of Florida, which we here review, was based on the assumption that the language in § 1(14)(a) of the Interstate Commerce Act requiring rulemaking under that section to be done "after hearing" was the equivalent of a statutory requirement that the rule "be made on the record after opportunity for an agency hearing." Such an assumption is inconsistent with our decision in *Allegheny–Ludlum, supra.*

The District Court for the Eastern District of New York reached the same conclusion by a somewhat different line of reasoning. That court felt that because § 1(14)(a) of the Interstate Commerce Act had required a "hearing," and because that section was originally enacted in 1917, Congress was probably thinking in terms of a "hearing" such as that described in the opinion of this Court in the roughly contemporaneous case of ICC v. Louisville & Nashville R. Co., 227 U.S. 88, 93 (1913). The ingredients of the "hearing" were there said to be that "[a]ll parties must be fully apprised of the evidence submitted or to be considered, and must be given opportunity to cross-examine witnesses, to inspect documents and to offer evidence in explanation or rebuttal." Combining this view of congressional understanding of the term "hearing" with comments by the Chairman of the Commission at the time of the adoption of the 1966 legislation regarding the necessity for "hearings," that court concluded that Congress had, in effect, required that these proceedings be "on the record after opportunity for an agency hearing" within the meaning of § 553(c) of the Administrative Procedure Act.

Insofar as this conclusion is grounded on the belief that the language "after hearing" of § 1(14)(a), without more, would trigger the applicability of § 556 and 557, it, too, is contrary to our decision in *Allegheny–Ludlum, supra.* The District Court observed that it was "rather hard to believe that the last sentence of § 553(c) was directed only to the few legislative spots where the words 'on the record' or their equivalent had found their way into the statute book." 318 F.Supp., at 496. This is, however, the language which Congress used, and since there are statutes on the books that do use these very words, see e.g., the Fulbright Amendment to the Walsh–Healey Act, 41 U.S.C. § 43a, and 21 U.S.C. § 371(e)(3), the regulations provision of the Food and Drug Act, adherence to that language cannot be said to render the provision nugatory or ineffectual. We recognized in *Allegheny–Ludlum* that the actual words "on the record" and "after ... hearing" used in § 553 were not words of art, and that other statutory language having the same meaning could trigger the provisions of §§ 556 and 557 in rulemaking proceedings. But we adhere to our conclusion, expressed in that

---

Administrative Procedure Act to these proceedings. This Act is not legislation that the Interstate Commerce Commission, or any other single agency, has primary responsibility for administering. An agency interpretation involving, at least in part, the provisions of that Act does not carry the weight, in ascertaining the intent of Congress, that an interpretation by an agency "charged with the responsibility" of administering a particular statute does.... Moreover, since any agency is free under the Act to accord litigants appearing before it more procedural rights than the Act requires, the fact that an agency may choose to proceed under §§ 556 and 557 does not carry the necessary implication that the agency felt it was required to do so.

case, that the phrase "after hearing" in § 1(14)(a) of the Interstate Commerce Act does not have such an effect. . . .

### III. "Hearing" Requirement of § 1(14)(a)
### of the Interstate Commerce Act

Inextricably intertwined with the hearing requirement of the Administrative Procedure Act in this case is the meaning to be given to the language "after hearing" in § 1(14)(a) of the Interstate Commerce Act. Appellees, both here and in the court below, contend that the Commission procedure here fell short of that mandated by the "hearing" requirement of § 1(14)(a), even though it may have satisfied § 553 of the Administrative Procedure Act. The Administrative Procedure Act states that none of its provisions "limit or repeal additional requirements imposed by statute or otherwise recognized by law." 5 U.S.C. § 559. Thus, even though the Commission was not required to comply with §§ 556 and 557 of that Act, it was required to accord the "hearing" specified in § 1(14)(a) of the Interstate Commerce Act. Though the District Court did not pass on this contention, it is so closely related to the claim based on the Administrative Procedure Act that we proceed to decide it now.

If we were to agree with the reasoning of the District Court . . . with respect to the type of hearing required by the Interstate Commerce Act, the Commission's action might well violate those requirements, even though it was consistent with the requirements of the Administrative Procedure Act.

The term "hearing" in its legal context undoubtedly has a host of meanings. Its meaning undoubtedly will vary, depending on whether it is used in the context of a rulemaking-type proceeding or in the context of a proceeding devoted to the adjudication of particular disputed facts. It is by no means apparent what the drafters of the Esch Car Service Act of 1917, 40 Stat. 101, which became the first part of § 1(14)(a) of the Interstate Commerce Act, meant by the term [since the legislative history sheds no light on the meaning of the words "after hearing."] . . .

Under these circumstances, confronted with a grant of substantive authority made after the Administrative Procedure Act was enacted, we think that reference to that Act, in which Congress devoted itself exclusively to questions such as the nature and scope of hearings, is a satisfactory basis for determining what is meant by the term "hearing" used in another statute. Turning to that Act, we are convinced that the term "hearing" as used therein does not necessarily embrace either the right to present evidence orally and to cross-examine opposing witnesses, or the right to present oral argument to the agency's decisionmaker.

Section 553 excepts from its requirements rulemaking devoted to "interpretative rules, general statements of policy, or rules of agency organization, procedure, or practice," and rulemaking "when the agency for good cause finds . . . that notice and public procedure thereon are impracticable, unnecessary, or contrary to the public interest." This exception does not apply, however, "when notice or hearing is required by statute"; in those cases, even though interpretative rulemaking be involved, the requirements of § 553 apply. But since these requirements themselves do not mandate any oral presentation, see *Allegheny–Ludlum, supra*, it cannot be doubted that a statute that requires a "hearing" prior to rulemaking may in some circumstances be satisfied by procedures that meet only the standards of § 553. . . .

Appellee railroads cite a number of our previous decisions dealing in some manner with the right to a hearing in an administrative proceeding. Although appellees have asserted no claim of constitutional deprivation in this proceeding, some of the cases they rely upon expressly speak in constitutional terms, while others are less than clear as to whether they depend upon the Due Process Clause of the Fifth and Fourteenth Amendments to the Constitution, or upon generalized principles of administrative law formulated prior to the adoption of the Administrative Procedure Act. . . .

ICC v. Louisville & Nashville R. Co., 227 U.S. 88 (1913), involved what the Court there described as a "quasi-judicial" proceeding of a quite different nature from the one we review here. The provisions of the Interstate Commerce Act, 24 Stat. 379, as amended, and of the Hepburn Act, 34 Stat. 584, in effect at the time that case was decided, left to the railroad carriers the "primary right to make rates," 227 U.S., at 92, but granted to the Commission the authority to set them aside, if after hearing, they were shown to be unreasonable. The proceeding before the Commission in that case had been instituted by the New Orleans Board of Trade complaint that certain class and commodity rates charged by the Louisville & Nashville Railroad from New Orleans to other points were unfair, unreasonable, and discriminatory. 227 U.S., at 90. The type of proceeding there, in which the Commission adjudicated a complaint by a shipper that specified rates set by a carrier were unreasonable, was sufficiently different from the nationwide incentive payments ordered to be made by all railroads in this proceeding so as to make the *Louisville & Nashville* opinion inapplicable in the case presently before us.

The basic distinction between rulemaking and adjudication is illustrated by this Court's treatment of two related cases under the Due Process Clause of the Fourteenth Amendment. In Londoner v. Denver, . . ., 210 U.S. 373 (1908), the Court held that due process had not been accorded a landowner who objected to the amount assessed against his land as its share of the benefit resulting from the paving of a street. Local procedure had accorded him the right to file a written complaint and objection, but not to be heard orally. This Court held that due process of law required that he "have the right to support his allegations by argument, however brief; and, if need be, by proof, however informal." Id., at 386. But in the later case of Bi–Metallic Investment Co. v. State Board of Equalization, 239 U.S. 441 (1915), the Court held that no hearing at all was constitutionally required prior to a decision by state tax officers in Colorado to increase the valuation of all taxable property in Denver by a substantial percentage. The Court distinguished *Londoner* by stating that there a small number of persons "were exceptionally affected, in each case upon individual grounds." Id., at 446.

Later decisions have continued to observe the distinction adverted to in *Bi–Metallic Investment Co., supra*. In Ohio Bell Telephone Co. v. Public Utilities Comm'n, 301 U.S. 292, 304–305 (1937), the Court noted the fact that the administrative proceeding there involved was designed to require the utility to refund previously collected rate charges. The Court held that in such a proceeding the agency could not, consistently with due process, act on the basis of undisclosed evidence that was never made a part of the record before the agency. The case is thus more akin to *Louisville & Nashville R. Co.*, supra, than it is to this case.... While the line dividing them may not always be a bright one, these decisions represent a recognized distinction in administrative law between proceedings for the purpose of promulgating policy-type rules or standards, on the one hand, and proceedings designed to adjudicate disputed facts in particular cases on the other.

Here, the incentive payments proposed by the Commission in its tentative order, and later adopted in its final order, were applicable across the board to all of the common carriers by railroad subject to the Interstate Commerce Act. No effort was made to single out any particular railroad for special consideration based on its own peculiar circumstances. Indeed, one of the objections of appellee Florida East Coast was that it and other terminating carriers should have been treated differently from the generality of the railroads. But the fact that the order may in its effects have been thought more disadvantageous by some railroads than by others does not change its generalized nature. Though the Commission obviously relied on factual inferences as a basis for its order, the source of these factual inferences was apparent to anyone who read the order of December 1969. The factual inferences were used in the formulation of a basically legislative-type judgment, for prospective application only, rather than in adjudicating a particular set of disputed facts....

■ Mr. Justice Powell took no part in the consideration or decision of this case.

■ Mr. Justice Douglas, with whom Mr. Justice Stewart concurs, dissenting.

The present decision makes a sharp break with traditional concepts of procedural due process. The Commission order under attack is tantamount to a rate order. Charges are fixed that nonowning railroads must pay owning railroads for boxcars of the latter that are on the tracks of the former.... I do not believe it is within our traditional concepts of due process to allow an administrative agency to saddle anyone with a new rate, charge, or fee without a full hearing that includes the right to present oral testimony, cross-examine witnesses, and present oral argument. That is required by the Administrative Procedure Act, 5 U.S.C. § 556(d); § 556(a) states that § 556 applies to hearings required by § 553. Section 553(c) provides that § 556 applies "[w]hen rules are required by statute to be made on the record after opportunity for an agency hearing." A hearing under § 1(14) (a) of the Interstate Commerce Act fixing rates, charges, or fees is certainly adjudicatory, not legislative in the customary sense....

The rules in question here established "incentive" per diem charges to spur the prompt return of existing cars and to make the acquisition of new cars financially attractive to the railroads. Unlike those we considered in *Allegheny–Ludlum*, these rules involve the creation of a new financial liability. Although quasi-legislative, they are also adjudicatory in the sense that they determine the measure of the financial responsibility of one road for its use of the rolling stock of another road. The Commission's power to promulgate these rules pursuant to § 1(14)(a) is conditioned on the preliminary finding that the supply of freight cars to which the rules apply is inadequate. Moreover, in fixing incentive compensation once this threshold finding has been made, the Commission "shall give consideration to the national level of ownership of such type of freight car and to other factors affecting the adequacy of the national freight car supply...."

The majority finds ICC v. Louisville & Nashville R. Co., 227 U.S. 88, "sufficiently different" as to make the opinion in that case inapplicable to the case now before us. I would read the case differently, finding a clear mandate that where, as here, ratemaking must be based on evidential facts, § 1(14)(a) requires that full hearing which due process normally entails. There we considered Commission procedures for setting aside as unreasonable, after a hearing, carrier-made rates. The Government maintained that the Commission, invested with legislative ratemaking power, but required by the Commerce Act to obtain necessary information, could act on such information as the Congress might. The Government urged that we presume that the Commission's findings were supported by such information, "even though not formally proved at the hearing." *Id.*, at 93. We rejected the contention, holding that the right to a hearing included "an opportunity to test, explain, or refute.... All parties must be fully apprised of the evidence submitted or to be considered, and must be given opportunity to cross-examine witnesses, to inspect documents, and to offer evidence in explanation or rebuttal." *Ibid.* I would agree with the District Court in *Long Island R. Co.*, supra, that Congress was fully cognizant of our decision in *Louisville & Nashville R. Co.* when it first adopted the hearing requirement of § 1(14)(a) in 1917. And when Congress debated the 1966 amendment that empowered the Commission to adopt incentive per diem rates, it had not lost sight of the importance of hearings. Questioned about the effect that incentive compensation might have on terminating lines, Mr. Staggers, Chairman of the House Committee on Interstate and Foreign Commerce and floor manager of the bill, responded: "I might say to the gentleman that this will not be put into practice until there have been *full hearings* before the Commission and all sides have had an opportunity to argue and present their facts on the question." 112 Cong.Rec. 10443 (emphasis added). Nor should we overlook the Commission's own interpretation of the hearing requirement in § 1(14)(a) as it applies to this case. The Commission's order initiating the rulemaking proceeding notified the parties that it was acting "under authority of Part I of the Interstate Commerce Act (49 U.S.C. § 1 et seq.); more particularly, section 1(14)(a) and the Administrative Procedure Act (5 U.S.C. §§ 553, 556, and 557)." Clearly, the Commission believed that it was required to hold a hearing on the record. This interpretation, not of the Administrative Procedure Act, but of § 1(14)(a) of the Commission's own Act, is "entitled to great weight." United States v. American Trucking Assns., 310 U.S. 534, 549; Norwegian Nitrogen Products Co. v. United States, 288 U.S. 294, 315....

Section 1(14)(a) of the Interstate Commerce Act bestows upon the Commission broad discretionary power to determine incentive rates. These rates may have devastating effects on a particular line. According to the brief of one of the appellees, the amount of incentive compensation paid by debtor lines amounts to millions of dollars each six-month period. Nevertheless, the courts must defer to the Commission as long as its findings are supported by substantial evidence and it has not abused its discretion. "All the more insistent is the need, when power has been bestowed so freely, that the 'inexorable safeguard' ... of a fair and open hearing be maintained in its integrity." Ohio Bell Telephone Co. v. Public Utilities Comm'n of Ohio, 301 U.S. 292, 304.

Accordingly, I would hold that appellees were not afforded the hearing guaranteed by § 1(14)(a) of the Interstate Commerce Act and 5 U.S.C. §§ 553, 556, and 557, and would affirm the decision of the District Court.

---

*1. The Impact of* **Florida East Coast Railway**—The principal consequence of *Florida East Coast Railway* (as well as its predecessor, United States v. Allegheny–Ludlum Steel Corp., 406 U.S. 742 (1972)) was to limit sharply the applicability of the APA's formal rulemaking category. There are some statutes that explicitly use both the "after hearing" and "on the record" language, but such statutes are rare. And, although the *Florida East Coast Railway* opinion insists that "other statutory language having the same meaning could trigger the provisions of §§ 556 and 557," the Supreme Court has never actually found any other language (that is, language that does not state explicitly that a decision must be made both "on the record" and "after [a] hearing") sufficient to trigger the APA's formal rulemaking requirements.

If that was the (predictable) consequence of *Florida East Coast Railway*, why do you suppose the Court decided the case the way it did? After all, while the Court's interpretation of the statute is certainly plausible, it is hardly inevitable. One possibility is that the Court was worried about the overproceduralization of agency rulemaking. You may recall from the introductory note at the beginning of this chapter that one of the concerns about imposing extensive procedural requirements on agencies is that doing so makes it extremely difficult for them to act quickly, or at all. By the 1970s, when the Court decided *Allegheny–Ludlum* and *Florida East Coast Railway*, this concern about overproceduralization had already begun to emerge. One particularly notorious and widely discussed illustration of the alleged defects of the APA's formal rulemaking procedures involved the Food and Drug Administration's proposal, in 1959, to raise the minimum peanut content in products sold as "peanut butter" from 87 percent to 90 percent. This formal rulemaking took over nine years and produced a

7,736–page transcript. *See* Robert W. Hamilton, *Rulemaking on a Record by the Food and Drug Administration*, 50 TEX. L. REV. 1132, 1143–45 (1972).

If the overproceduralization concern indeed influenced the Court's decision in *Florida East Coast Railway*, do you think the Court acted properly in taking that consideration into account? Would or should the case have come out the other way if the prior experience with formal rulemaking had demonstrated that the process was reasonably efficient and yielded significant benefits? If this is essentially a matter of statutory interpretation, should the Court focus on whether Congress (or a reasonable observer) *in 1946* would have concluded that the APA's formal rulemaking procedures would be triggered by language comparable to that in the Interstate Commerce Act? Or should the inquiry focus instead on the broader purposes of the APA, and ask which interpretation of the triggering language would best serve those purposes in light of empirical evidence and contemporary views of administrative performance?

Also, when evaluating the overproceduralization concern in *Florida East Coast Railway*, it is worth considering the case's implications for concerns about *under*proceduralization of agency decision-making. After all, if an agency rulemaking governed by the APA is not subject to the formal rulemaking requirements in §§ 556 and 557, then it is presumably subject only to the informal notice-and-comment procedures in § 553. But § 553's procedural requirements do not appear, at least on their face, terribly demanding. We might conclude that agency rulemaking procedures should not be so onerous that it takes a decade and thousands of transcript pages to enact a relatively modest regulation. But we might also conclude that *some* meaningful procedural constraints are necessary. Does § 553 supply such constraints? Could one reasonably criticize the APA for laying out only two procedural formats for rulemaking, one of which is too stringent and the other of which is not stringent enough?

**2. *Background Understandings about Ratemaking*—**When Congress enacted the APA, the modern administrative state already had a long history. Beginning with the establishment of the ICC in 1887, Congress had created a large number of agencies and, in many cases, the organic acts contained familiar terms (such as "hearing" requirements) that had been the subject of authoritative judicial or administrative interpretations. The *Attorney General's Manual* offered the following description of the "hearing" requirement in ratemaking statutes:

> Statutes authorizing agencies to prescribe future rates (i.e., rules of either general or particular applicability) for public utilities and common carriers typically require that such rates be established only after an opportunity for a hearing before the agency. Such statutes rarely specify in terms that the agency action must be taken on the basis of the "record" developed in the hearing. However, where rates or prices are established by an agency after a hearing required by statute, the agencies themselves and the courts have long assumed that the agency's action must be based upon the evidence adduced at the hearing. Sometimes the requirement of decision on the record is

readily inferred from other statutory provisions defining judicial review. . . .

The Interstate Commerce Commission and the Secretary of Agriculture may, after hearing, prescribe rates for carriers and stockyard agencies, respectively. Both types of rate orders are reviewable under the Urgent Deficiencies Act of 1913 (28 U.S.C. 47). Nothing in [the relevant organic acts] requires in terms that such rate orders be "made on the record", or provides for the filing of a transcript of the administrative record with the reviewing court. . . . However, both of these agencies and the courts have long assumed that such rate orders must be based upon the record made in the hearing; furthermore, it has long been the practice under the Urgent Deficiencies Act to review such orders on the basis of the administrative record, which is submitted to the reviewing court. . . .

With respect to the types of rule making discussed above, the statutes not only specifically require the agencies to hold hearings but also, specifically, or by clear implication, or by established administrative and judicial construction, require such rules to be formulated upon the basis of the evidentiary record made in the hearing.

U.S. Department of Justice, Attorney General's Manual on the Administrative Procedure Act 33–34 (1947). Should the Court in *Florida East Coast Railway* have credited the *Attorney General's Manual* and held that the term "after hearing" in the ICA meant, by implication, "required to be determined on the record after an opportunity for an agency hearing" within the meaning of § 554? Should the Court impute to the Members of Congress who enacted the APA an awareness of the pre-APA administrative practice? *See, e.g.*, Pierce v. Underwood, 487 U.S. 552, 564–65 (1988) (interpreting a provision of the APA in light of the settled pre-APA understanding of that term). How much weight should the Court give to the fact that the *Attorney General's Manual* concluded, on the basis of pre-APA practice and precedent, that ICC ratemaking had to be on the record, thereby triggering the formal rulemaking requirements? The *Attorney General's Manual* was published after the APA's enactment, but the Court has concluded that the manual reflects the contemporaneous understanding of the Department of Justice, which was deeply involved in the drafting and negotiations surrounding the APA's enactment. *See, e.g.*, Chrysler Corp. v. Brown, 441 U.S. 281, 302 n.31 (1979); Vermont Yankee Nuclear Power Corp. v. Natural Res. Def. Council, Inc., 435 U.S. 519, 546 (1978). Is the Court's posture appropriate, given that the Department of Justice's views of the relevant provisions may have differed from other players in the process? Should the weight attached to the *Attorney General's Manual* depend on how persuasive its account of the APA's meaning is on the merits?

**3.  *A General Note on Interpreting the APA*—***Florida East Coast Railway* raises general questions about how to interpret the APA. As noted earlier, the APA is broad framework legislation, and partly for that reason some commentators and judges believe that courts are justified in adopting a more expansive, purposive, and dynamic approach to interpreting the APA than might be appropriate for an "ordinary" statute. Others, however, view this approach as mistaken, both in principle and in practice.

A well-known and widely cited articulation of the view that the APA should be interpreted broadly, in order to advance its fundamental purposes, appears in Justice Jackson's majority opinion in Wong Yang Sung v. McGrath, 339 U.S. 33 (1950). After summarizing the history leading up to the APA's enactment, Justice Jackson declared:

> The [APA] thus represents a long period of study and strife; it settles long-continued and hard-fought contentions, and enacts a formula upon which opposing social and political forces have come to rest. It contains many compromises and generalities and, no doubt, some ambiguities. Experience may reveal defects. But it would be a disservice to our form of government and to the administrative process itself if the courts should fail, so far as the terms of the Act warrant, to give effect to its remedial purposes where the evils it was aimed at appear.

339 U.S. at 40–41. Later in the opinion, Justice Jackson reemphasized this theme, stating, "It is the plain duty of the courts, regardless of their views of the wisdom or policy of the [APA], to construe this remedial legislation to eliminate, so far as its text permits, the practices it condemns." *Id.* at 45.

Isn't there a tension between Justice Jackson's assertion that the APA reflects a difficult compromise—that it "enacts a formula upon which opposing social and political forces have come to rest"—and his assertion that courts should construe the Act as broadly as the text permits in order to effectuate its remedial purposes? If the text of the APA reflects the fact that "opposing social and political forces" were unable to come to a consensus regarding how aggressively the Act should combat the "evils" identified—or indeed regarding whether these features of the administrative process counted as "evils" at all—what is the justification for construing the Act broadly? Wouldn't that effectively give one side of a political struggle a victory that it was unable to secure in the legislative arena?

But perhaps that criticism doesn't give Justice Jackson enough credit. Maybe he is suggesting that although "opposing social and political forces" were able to identify a particular set of problems with a reasonable degree of clarity, they were not able to specify with precision all the details of the procedural scheme necessary to achieve the statute's goals, leaving that "filling-in-the-details" role to the courts. According to this understanding, judges are both authorized and obligated to construe the ambiguous provisions of the APA to effect its overall purposes or policies, regardless of their views of those purposes and policies. Still, though, doesn't this approach to interpretation give a great deal of power to judges? Might we be concerned that in practice judges' views of the policy of the APA will tend to reflect a bit too closely the judges' own views of sound policy, rather than the policy Congress thought it was enacting? Does Justice Jackson's approach have relevance in those instances in which the text of the APA is clear?

Another approach to interpreting the APA emphasizes the need to give its terms the effect they would have been understood to have by legislators in 1946, when the statute was enacted. *See* Director, Office of Workers' Compensation Programs v. Greenwich Collieries, 512 U.S. 267, 275–76 (1994). Despite the breadth of many of the APA's terms, a number of these terms had been used either in organic acts or in a pre-APA judge-made law of administrative procedure. *See, e.g.*, Consolidated Edison Co. of New York v. NLRB, 305 U.S. 197, 217 (1938) (defining the term "substantial evidence" that was later adopted in the APA's judicial review section); Pacific States Box & Basket Co. v. White, 296 U.S. 176, 182 (1935) (setting out the "arbitrary and capricious" standard that Congress later used in the APA). Should courts assume that when Congress used these terms in the APA, Congress intended them as technical terms of art, with a fixed and well-known legal meaning at the time of enactment? On the one hand, treating terms of art as having a fixed meaning credits Congress's apparent choice to adopt a well-known term in the first place—an impulse perhaps reinforced by the APA's goal of providing greater uniformity in administrative procedure. On the other hand, if the interpretation of those open-ended terms had required some judicial creativity prior to the APA, then perhaps courts should not treat their codification as having fixed their meaning for all time.

The basic tensions regarding the proper approach to interpreting the APA were nicely summarized in a commentary written by Judge Stephen Williams. In considering arguments over whether courts should interpret the APA "dynamically," Judge Williams identified three criteria that the "public might reasonably expect from courts in their interpretation of a statute such as the APA":

> [First,] Congress's decision to adopt the APA expressed, presumably, its belief that the courts—and perhaps the citizenry—needed some help. If Congress had fully embraced the judicial answers to the questions posed by administrative proliferation, a statute would not have been necessary. . . . Thus, to state the obvious, one criterion for sound interpretation of the APA must be fidelity to what Congress meant.

> A second criterion is that interpretations should lend themselves to reasonable application across the range of agencies and agency activities governed by the statute. For example, a very demanding view of [the] requirement that an agency make its decisions "available for public inspection," well suited to the Social Security Administration with offices scattered over the country and tens of millions of clients, might be quite unsuitable for the Federal Energy Regulatory Commission. . . .

> Third, there is surely an interest . . . in interpretations that fit current circumstances. Congress's provision that in a formal hearing any "oral or documentary evidence may be received," subject to the agency's power to exclude "irrelevant, immaterial or unduly repetitious evidence," should doubtless be construed in a way that recognizes

the advantages (and hazards) of information on a disk, or at least in a way that allows agencies to adjust to changing technology. Further, in some contexts, later congressional enactments or other exogenous developments might change background assumptions strongly enough to shift the meaning of an APA term.

Stephen F. Williams, *The Era of "Risk–Risk" and the Problem of Keeping the APA Up to Date*, 63 U. CHI. L. REV. 1375, 1385–86 (1996) (footnotes omitted).

Do you agree with Judge Williams' identification of the relevant criteria for evaluating the judicial approach to interpretation under the APA? Given that these criteria may come into conflict, and that there may be room for reasonable disagreement about which interpretations best satisfy each of them, how should courts resolve these tensions? These are very difficult questions to answer in the abstract, but you should keep them in mind as we turn to more specific questions regarding the interpretation of various APA provisions, particularly those related to notice-and-comment rulemaking and to the standard of judicial review.

   **4. Due Process and the Interpretation of Administrative Statutes**—Notice that Justice Rehnquist considered the implications of the Due Process Clause of the Constitution in fleshing out the "hearing" requirement in the Interstate Commerce Act. In particular, he suggested that the type of agency action at issue—which involved the adoption of a forward-looking policy applicable to a broad swath of regulated parties—did not require any type of specialized procedures, such as oral presentation or a decision on the record. In so doing, he invoked a famous pair of cases—Londoner v. Denver, 210 U.S. 373 (1908) and Bi–Metallic Investment Co. v. State Board of Equalization, 239 U.S 441 (1915)—that distinguish rulemaking from adjudication *for constitutional purposes*. Although these cases have no bearing on the appropriate classification of a given procedure as rulemaking or adjudication in the technical sense used by the APA, the constitutional categories are important in determining the minimum procedures required apart from the APA.

   In *Londoner*, the city of Denver assessed a special tax on a small group of property owners without granting them an oral hearing. The Supreme Court held that the failure to provide a hearing constituted a deprivation of property without due process of law, in violation of the Due Process Clause of the Fourteenth Amendment. In *Bi–Metallic*, the state of Colorado issued a general increase in property value assessments, and hence property taxes, throughout the city of Denver. A group of property owners sued, claiming that under *Londoner* they were entitled to a public hearing prior to the tax increase. The Supreme Court rejected the claim, distinguishing *Londoner* on the ground that in the earlier case "[a] relatively small number of persons was concerned, who were exceptionally affected, in each case upon individual grounds," whereas *Bi–Metallic* involved "a general determination dealing only with the principle upon which all assessments in a county had been laid." 239 U.S. at 446. Thus, *Londoner* and *Bi–Metallic* together made clear that agency adjudication (in the constitutional sense) is subject to more stringent hearing requirements than agency rulemaking (in the constitutional sense). As Justice Holmes' opinion for the Court in *Bi–Metallic* explained, "Where a rule of conduct applies to more than a few people, it is impracticable that everyone should have a direct voice in its adoption.... There must be a limit to individual argument in such matters if government is to go on." *Id.* at 445. So, in the due process context, the distinction between rulemaking and adjudication has been—and remains—important. *See, e.g.,* Minnesota State Board for Community Colleges v. Knight, 465 U.S. 271, 283–87 (1984).

*Florida East Coast Railway* made clear that because the APA's definitions of rulemaking and adjudication do not correspond precisely to those in the due process cases, one can be engaged in rulemaking for purposes of determining the applicable APA procedural categories but adjudication for purposes of determining the relevant due process frame of analysis. For example, while ratemaking is defined as a form of rulemaking for APA purposes (*see* 5 U.S.C. § 551(4)), an agency's decision to set rates for *a single* common carrier might place the procedure on the adjudication side of the line for purposes of the Due Process Clause. Thus, in ICC v. Louisville & Nashville Railroad Co., 227 U.S. 88 (1913), the Court treated as "quasi-judicial" for constitutional purposes a ratemaking proceeding that applied to a single railroad. Given the due process implications of that holding, the Court read the word "hearing" as used in the relevant section of the Interstate Commerce Act to mean that "[a]ll parties must be fully apprised of the evidence submitted or to be considered, and must be given opportunity to cross-examine witnesses, to inspect documents, and to offer evidence in explanation or rebuttal." 227 U.S. at 93. In contrast, having found that the relevant procedure for determining incentive payments was rulemaking in the constitutional sense, *Florida East Coast Railway* held that the term "hearing" in a different provision of the Interstate Commerce Act did not require such procedures.

Should the word "hearing" have the same meaning throughout the same statute? *See supra* pp. 243–245. If Congress adopts a vague term like "hearing" on the assumption that the courts will read that term on a context-specific basis in light of due process requirements, does that arrangement introduce undesirable uncertainty into the administrative process? Under present case law, the Court determines precisely what process is due in adjudication by weighing the following three factors:

> First, the private interest that will be affected by the official action; second, the risk of an erroneous deprivation of such interest through the procedures used, and the probable value, if any, of additional or substitute procedural safeguards; and finally, the Government's interest, including the function involved and the fiscal and administrative burdens that the additional or substitute procedural requirement would entail.

Mathews v. Eldridge, 424 U.S. 319, 335 (1976). Does that test supply a firm enough basis for agencies conducting adjudication (in the constitutional sense) to know what procedures they will have to supply?

## II.   NOTICE-AND-COMMENT RULEMAKING

Formal rulemakings governed by APA §§ 556 and 557 are relatively rare, in no small part because of decisions like *Florida East Coast Railway*. For that reason, our focus will be on the procedural requirements for so-called "informal" or "notice-and-comment" rulemaking, which appear in § 553. The three main procedural requirements of § 553 are: (1) notice; (2) opportunity for comment; and (3) a concise statement of basis and purpose accompanying the final rule.

The notice requirement, in § 553(b), provides in relevant part:

General notice of proposed rule making shall be published in the Federal Register, unless persons subject thereto are named and either personally served or otherwise have actual notice thereof in accordance with law. The notice shall include—

(1) a statement of the time, place, and nature of public rule making proceedings;

(2) reference to the legal authority under which the rule is proposed; and

(3) either the terms or substance of the proposed rule or a description of the subjects and issues involved.

5 U.S.C. § 553(b).

The requirements pertaining to the opportunity for public comment and to the statement of basis and purpose appear in the following subsection, § 553(c), the relevant portion of which states:

After notice required by this section, the agency shall give interested persons an opportunity to participate in the rule making through submission of written data, views, or arguments with or without opportunity for oral presentation. After consideration of the relevant matter presented, the agency shall incorporate in the rules adopted a concise general statement of their basis and purpose.

5 U.S.C. § 553(c).

On their face, these requirements seem straightforward and not particularly burdensome. They appear to require simply that the agency announce in advance what it intends to do (at least in broad terms); allow interested parties to submit written comments and relevant material; and provide a brief explanation of the final rule. It turns out, however, that in practice these seemingly simple notice-and-comment requirements, as interpreted by the courts, are much more complex and demanding. The following materials illustrate this, and also provide an opportunity for reflecting on the causes and consequences of the doctrinal developments in this area.

## A. THE PAPER HEARING REQUIREMENT

Section 553 of the APA requires that agencies provide information to the general public at both the beginning and the end of the rulemaking procedure. At the beginning of the process, § 553(b) requires that the agency provide advance notice of "either the terms or substance of the proposed rule or a description of the subjects and issues involved." At the end of the process, if the agency chooses to promulgate a final rule, § 553(c) requires that the agency provide "a concise general statement of [the rule's] basis and purpose." The text of the APA, at least on an initial reading, would seem to suggest that neither the notice provided at the beginning of the process nor the explanatory statement provided at the end has to be particularly detailed or elaborate. After all, § 553(b) requires only a description of the "terms or substance" of the proposed rule, or a "description of the subjects or issues involved." And § 553(c) specifies that the statement explaining a rule's basis and purpose is supposed to be "concise" and "general." But courts have invoked the structure and purpose of the APA to interpret these provisions to require much more than that initial reading might suggest.

The following case, *United States v. Nova Scotia Food Products Corp.*, illustrates this broad purposive reasoning as applied both to the question of what the agency's initial notice of proposed rulemaking must include, and to the question of what the statement of basis and purpose must contain. *Nova Scotia* is a classic example of how courts have read the APA's procedural provisions to impose requirements that are more stringent than their text would seem to suggest—and that, according to some commentators, go well beyond what the APA's drafters envisioned. The case is therefore useful for thinking about the costs and benefits of this purposive approach to interpreting the APA, as well as the costs and benefits of imposing more rigorous notification and explanatory burdens on administrative agencies.

---

# United States v. Nova Scotia Food Products Corp.

U.S. Court of Appeals for the Second Circuit
568 F.2d 240 (2d Cir. 1977)

■ Before WATERMAN and GURFEIN, CIRCUIT JUDGES, and BLUMENFELD, DISTRICT JUDGE.

■ GURFEIN, CIRCUIT JUDGE:

This appeal involving a regulation of the Food and Drug Administration is . . . an appeal from a judgment of the District Court for the Eastern District of New York . . . enjoining the appellants, after a hearing, from processing hot smoked whitefish except in accordance with time-temperature-salinity (T–T–S) regulations contained in 21 C.F.R. Part 122 (1977). . . .

The injunction was sought and granted on the ground that smoked whitefish which has been processed in violation of the T–T–S regulation is "adulterated." Food, Drug and Cosmetics Act ("the Act") §§ 302(a) and 301(k), 21 U.S.C. §§ 332(a), 331(k).

Appellant Nova Scotia receives frozen or iced whitefish in interstate commerce which it processes by brining, smoking and cooking. The fish are then sold as smoked whitefish.

The regulations cited above require that hot-process smoked fish be heated by a controlled heat process that provides a monitoring system positioned in as many strategic locations in the oven as necessary to assure a continuous temperature through each fish of not less than 180° F. for a minimum of 30 minutes for fish which have been brined to contain 3.5% Water phase salt or at 150° F. for a minimum of 30 minutes if the salinity was at 5% Water phase. Since each fish must meet these requirements, it is necessary to heat an entire batch of fish to even higher temperatures so that the lowest temperature for any fish will meet the minimum requirements.

Government inspection of appellants' plant established without question that the minimum T–T–S requirements were not being met. There is no substantial claim that the plant was processing whitefish under "insanitary conditions" in any other material respect. Appellants, on their part, do not defend on the ground that they were in compliance, but rather that the requirements could not be met if a marketable whitefish was to be produced. They defend upon the grounds that the regulation is invalid (1) because it is beyond the authority delegated by the statute; (2) because the FDA improperly relied upon undisclosed evidence in promulgating the regulation and because it is not supported by the administrative record; and (3) because there was no adequate statement setting forth the basis of the regulation. We reject the contention that the regulation is beyond the authority delegated by the statute, but we find serious inadequacies in the procedure followed in the promulgation of the regulation and hold it to be invalid as applied to the appellants herein.

The hazard which the FDA sought to minimize was the outgrowth and toxin formation of Clostridium botulinum Type E spores of the bacteria which sometimes inhabit fish. There had been an occurrence of several cases of botulism traced to consumption of fish from inland waters in 1960 and 1963 which stimulated considerable bacteriological research. These bacteria can be present in the soil and water of various regions. They can invade fish in their natural habitat and can be further disseminated in the course of evisceration and preparation of the fish for cooking. A failure to destroy such spores through an adequate brining, thermal, and refrigeration process was found to be dangerous to public health.

The Commissioner of Food and Drugs ("Commissioner"), employing informal "notice-and-comment" procedures under 21 U.S.C. § 371(a), issued a proposal for the control of C. botulinum bacteria Type E in fish. 34 F.R. 17,176 (Oct. 23, 1969). For his statutory authority to promulgate the regulations, the Commissioner specifically relied only upon § 342(a)(4) of the Act which provides:

"A food shall be deemed to be adulterated—

"(4) if it has been prepared, packed, or held under insanitary conditions whereby it may have become contaminated with filth, or whereby it may have been rendered injurious to health;"

Similar guidelines for smoking fish had been suggested by the FDA several years earlier, and were generally made known to people in the industry. At that stage, however, they were merely guidelines without substantive effect as law. Responding to the Commissioner's invitation in the notice of proposed rulemaking, members of the industry, including appellants ... submitted comments on the proposed regulation.

The Commissioner thereafter issued the final regulations in which he adopted certain suggestions made in the comments, including a suggestion by the National Fisheries Institute, Inc. ("the Institute"), the intervenor herein. The original proposal provided that the fish would have to be cooked to a temperature of 180° F. for at least 30 minutes, if the fish have been brined to contain 3.5% water phase salt, with no alternative. In the final regulation, an alternative suggested by the intervenor "that the parameter of 150° F. for 30 minutes and 5% salt in the water phase be established as an alternate procedure to that stated in the proposed regulation for an interim period until specific parameters can be established" was accepted, but as a permanent part of the regulation rather than for an interim period.

The intervenor suggested that "specific parameters" be established. This referred to particular processing parameters for different species of fish on a "species by species" basis. Such "species by species" determination was proposed not only by the intervenor but also by the Bureau of Commercial Fisheries of the Department of the Interior. That Bureau objected to the general application of the T–T–S requirement proposed by the FDA on the ground that application of the regulation to all species of fish being smoked was not commercially feasible, and that the regulation should therefore specify time-temperature-salinity requirements, as developed by research and study, on a species-by-species basis. The Bureau suggested that "wholesomeness considerations could be more practically and adequately realized by reducing processing temperature and using suitable concentrations of nitrite and salt." The Commissioner took cognizance of the suggestion, but decided, nevertheless, to impose the T–T–S requirement on *all* species of fish (except chub, which were regulated by 21 C.F.R. 172.177 (1977) [dealing with food additives]).

He did acknowledge, however, in his "basis and purpose" statement required by the Administrative Procedure Act ("APA"), 5 U.S.C. § 553(c), that "adequate times, temperatures and salt concentrations have not been demonstrated for each individual species of fish presently smoked". 35 F.R. 17,401 (Nov. 13, 1970). The Commissioner concluded, nevertheless, that "the processing requirements of the proposed regulations are the safest now known to prevent the outgrowth and toxin formation of *C. botulinum* Type E". He determined that "the conditions of current good manufacturing practice for this industry should be established without further delay." *Id.*

The Commissioner did not answer the suggestion by the Bureau of Fisheries that nitrite and salt as additives could safely lower the high temperature otherwise required, a solution which the FDA had accepted in the case of chub. Nor did the Commissioner respond to the claim of Nova Scotia through its trade association, the Association of Smoked Fish Processors, Inc., Technical Center that "[t]he proposed process requirements suggested by the FDA for hot processed smoked fish are neither commercially feasible nor based on sound scientific evidence obtained with the variety of smoked fish products to be included under this regulation."

Nova Scotia, in its own comment, wrote to the Commissioner that "the heating of certain types of fish to high temperatures will completely destroy the product". It suggested, as an alternative, that "specific processing procedures could be established for each species after adequate work and experimention [sic] has been done—but not before." (*Id.*). We have noted above that the response given by the Commissioner was in general terms. He did not specifically aver that the T–T–S requirements as applied to whitefish were, in fact, commercially feasible.

When, after several inspections and warnings, Nova Scotia failed to comply with the regulation, an action by the United States Attorney for injunctive relief was filed on April 7, 1976, six years later, and resulted in the judgment here on appeal. The District Court denied a stay pending appeal, and no application for a stay was made to this court.

## I

[The court considered but ultimately rejected Nova Scotia's claim that the FDA lacked the statutory authority to promulgate the regulation at issue.]

## II

Appellants contend that there is an inadequate administrative record upon which to predicate judicial review, and that the failure to disclose to interested persons the factual material upon which the agency was relying vitiates the element of fairness which is essential to any kind of administrative action. Moreover, they argue that the "concise general statement of . . . basis and purpose" by the Commissioner was inadequate. 5 U.S.C. § 553.

The question of what is an adequate "record" in informal rulemaking has engaged the attention of commentators for several years. The extent of the administrative record required for judicial review of informal rulemaking is largely a function of the scope of judicial review. Even when the standard of review is whether the promulgation of the rule was "arbitrary, capricious, an abuse of discretion, or otherwise not in accordance with law," as specified in 5 U.S.C. § 706(2)(A), judicial review must nevertheless, be based on the "whole record" (*id.*). Adequate review of a determination requires an adequate record, if the review is to be meaningful.... What will constitute an adequate record for meaningful review may vary with the nature of the administrative action to be reviewed.... Review must be based on the whole record even when the judgment is one of policy, except that findings of fact such as would be required in an adjudicatory proceeding or in a formal "on the record" hearing for rulemaking need not be made. [Citizens to Preserve] Overton Park [v. Volpe], 401 U.S. [402,] 416–18 (1971). Though the action was informal, without an evidentiary record, the review must be "thorough, probing, [and] in depth". *Id.*, 401 U.S. at 415....

This raises several questions regarding the informal rulemaking procedure followed here: (1) What record does a reviewing court look to? (2) How much of what the agency relied on should have been disclosed to interested persons? (3) To what extent must the agency respond to criticism that is material?

## A

With respect to the content of the administrative "record," the Supreme Court has told us that in informal rulemaking, "the focal point for judicial review should be the administrative record already in existence, not some new record made initially in the reviewing court." *See* Camp v. Pitts, 411 U.S. 138, 142 (1973).

No contemporaneous record was made or certified.[13] When, during the enforcement action, the basis for the regulation was sought through pretrial discovery, the record was created by searching the files of the FDA and the memories of those who participated in the process of rulemaking. This resulted in what became Exhibit D at the trial of the injunction action. Exhibit D consists of (1) Tab A containing the comments received from outside parties during the administrative "notice-and-comment" proceeding and (2) Tabs B through L consisting of scientific data and the like upon which the Commissioner now says he relied but which were not made known to the interested parties.

Appellants object to the exclusion of evidence in the District Court "aimed directly at showing that the scientific evidence relied upon by the FDA was inaccurate and not based upon a realistic appraisal of the true facts. Appellants attempted to introduce scientific evidence to demonstrate that in fixing the processing parameters FDA relied upon tests in which ground fish were injected with many millions of botulism [sic] spores and then tested for outgrowth at various processing levels whereas the spore levels in nature are far less and outgrowth would have been prevented by far less stringent processing parameters." The District Court properly excluded the evidence.

---

**13.** A practice developed in the early years of the APA of not making a formal contemporaneous record, but rather, when challenged, to put together a historical record of what had been available for agency consideration at the time the regulation was promulgated....

In an enforcement action, we must rely exclusively on the record made before the agency to determine the validity of the regulation. The exception to the exclusivity of that record is that "there may be independent judicial fact-finding when issues that were not before the agency are raised in a proceeding to *enforce* non-adjudicatory agency action." *Overton Park, supra*, 401 U.S. at 415 (1971). (Emphasis added.)

Though this is an enforcement proceeding and the question is close, we think that the "issues" were fairly before the agency and hence that de novo evidence was properly excluded. . . . Our concern is, rather, with the manner in which the agency treated the issues tendered.

### B

The key issues were (1) whether, in the light of the rather scant history of botulism in whitefish, that species should have been considered separately rather than included in a general regulation which failed to distinguish species from species; (2) whether the application of the proposed T–T–S requirements to smoked whitefish made the whitefish commercially unsaleable; and (3) whether the agency recognized that prospect, but nevertheless decided that the public health needs should prevail even if that meant commercial death for the whitefish industry. The procedural issues were whether, in the light of these key questions, the agency procedure was inadequate because (i) it failed to disclose to interested parties the scientific data and the methodology upon which it relied; and (ii) because it failed utterly to address itself to the pertinent question of commercial feasibility.

### 1.

### *The History of Botulism in Whitefish*

The history of botulism occurrence in whitefish, as established in the trial record, which we must assume was available to the FDA in 1970, is as follows. Between 1899 and 1964 there were only eight cases of botulism reported as attributable to hot-smoked whitefish. In all eight instances, vacuum-packed whitefish was involved. All of the eight cases occurred in 1960 and 1963. The industry has abandoned vacuum-packing, and there has not been a single case of botulism associated with commercially prepared whitefish since 1963, though 2,750,000 pounds of whitefish are processed annually. Thus, in the seven-year period from 1964 through 1970, 17.25 million pounds of whitefish have been commercially processed in the United States without a single reported case of botulism. The evidence also disclosed that defendant Nova Scotia has been in business some 56 years, and that there has never been a case of botulism illness from the whitefish processed by it.

### 2.

### *The Scientific Data*

Interested parties were not informed of the scientific data, or at least of a selection of such data deemed important by the agency, so that comments could be addressed to the data. Appellants argue that unless the scientific data relied upon by the agency are spread upon the public records, criticism of the methodology used or the meaning to be inferred from the data is rendered impossible.

We agree with appellants in this case, for although we recognize that an agency may resort to its own expertise outside the record in an informal rulemaking procedure, we do not believe that when the pertinent research material is readily available and the agency has no special expertise on the precise parameters involved, there is any reason to conceal the scientific data relied upon from the interested parties. As Judge Leventhal said in Portland Cement Ass'n v. Ruckelshaus, 486 F.2d 375, 393 (1973): "It is not consonant with the purpose of a rulemaking proceeding to promulgate rules on the basis of inadequate data, or on data that [in] critical degree, *is known only to the agency*." (Emphasis added.) This is not a case where the agency methodology was based on material supplied by the interested parties themselves.... Here all the scientific research was collected by the agency, and none of it was disclosed to interested parties as the material upon which the proposed rule would be fashioned.[15] Nor was an articulate effort made to connect the scientific requirements to available technology that would make commercial survival possible, though the burden of proof was on the agency. This required it to "bear a burden of adducing a reasoned presentation supporting the reliability of its methodology." *International Harvester, supra*, 478 F.2d at 643.

Though a reviewing court will not match submission against counter-submission to decide whether the agency was correct in its conclusion on scientific matters (unless that conclusion is arbitrary), it will consider whether the agency has taken account of all "relevant factors and whether there has been a clear error of judgment." *Overton Park, supra*, 401 U.S. at 415–16.... In this circuit we have said that "it is 'arbitrary or capricious' for an agency not to take into account all relevant factors in making its determination." Hanly v. Mitchell, 460 F.2d 640, 648 (2d Cir.), *cert. denied*, 409 U.S. 990 (1972)....

If the failure to notify interested persons of the scientific research upon which the agency was relying actually prevented the presentation of relevant comment, the agency may be held not to have considered all "the relevant factors." We can think of no sound reasons for secrecy or reluctance to expose to public view (with an exception for trade secrets or national security) the ingredients of the deliberative process.... Indeed, the FDA's own regulations now specifically require that every notice of proposed rulemaking contain "references to all data and information on which the Commissioner relies for the proposal (copies or a full list of which shall be a part of the administrative file on the matter...)." 21 C.F.R. § 10.40(b)(1) (1977). And this is, undoubtedly, the trend....

---

**15.** We recognize the problem posed by Judge Leventhal in *International Harvester*, that a proceeding might never end if such submission required a reply *ad infinitum*. Here the exposure of the scientific research relied on simply would have required a single round of comment addressed thereto.

We think that the scientific data should have been disclosed to focus on the proper interpretation of "insanitary conditions." When the basis for a proposed rule is a scientific decision, the scientific material which is believed to support the rule should be exposed to the view of interested parties for their comment. One cannot ask for comment on a scientific paper without allowing the participants to read the paper. Scientific research is sometimes rejected for diverse inadequacies of methodology; and statistical results are sometimes rebutted because of a lack of adequate gathering technique or of supportable extrapolation. Such is the stuff of scientific debate. To suppress meaningful comment by failure to disclose the basic data relied upon is akin to rejecting comment altogether. For unless there is common ground, the comments are unlikely to be of a quality that might impress a careful agency. The inadequacy of comment in turn leads in the direction of arbitrary decision-making. We do not speak of findings of fact, for such are not technically required in the informal rulemaking procedures. We speak rather of what the agency should make known so as to elicit comments that probe the fundamentals. Informal rulemaking does not lend itself to a rigid pattern. Especially, in the circumstance of our broad reading of statutory authority in support of the agency, we conclude that the failure to disclose to interested persons the scientific data upon which the FDA relied was procedurally erroneous. Moreover, the burden was upon the agency to articulate rationally why the rule should apply to a large and diverse class, with the same T–T–S parameters made applicable to *all* species. . . .

### C

Appellants additionally attack the "concise general statement" required by APA, 5 U.S.C. § 553, as inadequate. We think that, in the circumstances, it was less than adequate. It is not in keeping with the rational process to leave vital questions, raised by comments which are of cogent materiality, completely unanswered. The agencies certainly have a good deal of discretion in expressing the basis of a rule, but the agencies do not have quite the prerogative of obscurantism reserved to legislatures. . . . As was said in Environmental Defense Fund, Inc. v. EPA, 465 F.2d 528, 540–51 (1972): "We cannot discharge our role adequately unless we hold EPA to a high standard of articulation. Kennecott Copper Corp. v. EPA, . . . 462 F.2d 846 (1972)."

The test of adequacy of the "concise general statement" was expressed by Judge McGowan in the following terms:

> "We do not expect the agency to discuss every item of fact or opinion included in the submissions made to it in informal rulemaking. We do expect that, if the judicial review which Congress has thought it important to provide is to be meaningful, the 'concise general statement of . . . basis and purpose' mandated by Section 4 will enable us to see what major issues of policy were ventilated by the informal proceedings and why the agency reacted to them as it did." Automotive Parts & Accessories Ass'n v. Boyd, 407 F.2d 330, 338 (1968). . . .

The Secretary was squarely faced with the question whether it was necessary to formulate a rule with specific parameters that applied to all species of fish, and particularly whether lower temperatures with the addition of nitrite and salt would not be sufficient. Though this alternative was suggested by an agency of the federal government, its suggestion, though acknowledged, was never answered.

Moreover, the comment that to apply the proposed T–T–S requirements to whitefish would destroy the commercial product was neither discussed nor answered. We think that to sanction silence in the face of such vital questions would be to make the statutory requirement of a "concise general statement" less than an adequate safeguard against arbitrary decision-making.

We cannot improve on the statement of the District of Columbia Circuit in Industrial Union Dep't, AFL–CIO v. Hodgson, 499 F.2d 467, 475 (1974).

> "What we are entitled to at all events is a careful identification by the Secretary, when his proposed standards are challenged, of the reasons why he chooses to follow one course rather than another. Where that choice purports to be based on the existence of certain determinable facts, the Secretary must, in form as well as in substance, find those facts from evidence in the record. By the same token, when the Secretary is obliged to make policy judgments where no factual certainties exist or where facts alone do not provide the answer, he should so state and go on to identify the considerations he found to be persuasive."

One may recognize that even commercial infeasibility cannot stand in the way of an overwhelming public interest. Yet the administrative process should disclose, at least, whether the proposed regulation is considered to be commercially feasible, or whether other considerations prevail even if commercial infeasibility is acknowledged. This kind of forthright disclosure and basic statement was lacking in the formulation of the T–T–S standard made applicable to whitefish. It is easy enough for an administrator to ban everything. In the regulation of food processing, the worldwide need for food also must be taken into account in formulating measures taken for the protection of health. In the light of the history of smoked whitefish to which we have referred, we find no articulate balancing here sufficient to make the procedure followed less than arbitrary.

After seven years of relative inaction, the FDA has apparently not reviewed the T–T–S regulations in the light of present scientific knowledge and experience. In the absence of a new statutory directive by Congress regarding control of micro-organisms, which we hope will be worthy of its consideration, we think that the T–T–S standards should be reviewed again by the FDA.

We cannot, on this appeal, remand to the agency to allow further comments by interested parties, addressed to the scientific data now disclosed at the trial below. We hold in this enforcement proceeding, therefore, that the regulation, as it affects non-vacuum-packed hot-smoked whitefish, was promulgated in an arbitrary manner and is invalid. . . .

### 1. Must Agencies Disclose Data and Studies Supporting a Proposed Rule?

—The text of § 553(b) would seem to allow an agency to give general notice that it is considering regulations in some substantive area, without giving much detail about the specific proposal or proposals that the agency is considering. After all, § 553(b) says that, as an *alternative* to giving notice of the terms or substance of a specific proposed rule, the agency may give notice of the "subjects and issues involved." But courts have held that such general notice is insufficient, arguing that the notice requirement must be read in conjunction with the requirement that the agency provide an "opportunity" for comment, along with a sense that the purpose of § 553 would be thwarted if the agency's notice of proposed rulemaking were insufficiently specific about what the agency is considering. *See, e.g.*, Small Refiner Lead Phase–Down Task Force v. EPA, 705 F.2d 506, 549 (D.C. Cir. 1983); Home Box Office, Inc. v. FCC, 567 F.2d 9, 36 (D.C. Cir. 1977).

Of course, the objection to the FDA's notice in *Nova Scotia* was not that it failed to describe in sufficient detail what the agency was planning to do. Rather, the Nova Scotia company—and the Second Circuit—objected to the agency's failure to disclose, in its original notice, the *scientific studies* on which the agency based its proposed rulemaking. Is it more problematic to ask the agency to disclose those studies? Section 553(b)(3)'s detailed notice requirement says nothing about any obligation to disclose the *evidentiary basis* for proposed rules. Furthermore, the preceding subsection, § 553(b)(2), explicitly requires that the agency's notice include "reference to the legal authority under which the rule is proposed." Couldn't one invoke the *expressio unius* principle here to argue that the explicit obligation to disclose the *legal* basis for the proposed rule implies the absence of any obligation to disclose the *factual* basis for the proposed rule?

The *Nova Scotia* court derived the agency's legal obligation to disclose the studies supporting its proposed rule from two sources, which the court viewed as inextricably linked. As in the cases requiring a sufficiently detailed notice of the agency's proposals, *Nova Scotia* first relied on § 553(c)'s requirement that agencies provide interested parties with "an opportunity to participate in the rule making through submission of written data, views, or arguments." The *Nova Scotia* court construed this "opportunity" not merely in the narrow, formal sense that the agency must receive and consider comments, but in the broader, functional sense that outside parties must have a *meaningful* opportunity to comment. A meaningful opportunity to comment, Judge Gurfein reasoned, requires not only that interested parties have a sufficiently clear idea of the rule the agency is considering, but also the evidentiary basis for that proposal, including scientific studies or other data on which the agency relied. Following the D.C. Circuit's influential opinion in Portland Cement Ass'n v. Ruckelshaus, 486 F.2d 375 (D.C. Cir. 1973), the *Nova Scotia* court concluded that "failure to disclose the basic data relied upon" would "suppress meaningful comment"—indeed, such nondisclosure would be "akin to rejecting comment altogether."

*Nova Scotia*'s second ground rested on the general judicial review provision in § 706(2)(A) of the APA. According to this section, a court must invalidate any agency action that is "arbitrary, capricious, an abuse of discretion, or otherwise not in accordance with law." Part IV of this chapter will consider judicial review under this standard in greater depth (pp. 717–790, *infra*). For present purposes, the important thing to understand is that a line of cases—most prominently, Citizens to Preserve Overton Park, Inc. v. Volpe, 401 U.S. 402 (1971)—had held that although reviewing courts should be deferential to agency factual or policy judgments, a court should nonetheless strike down agency action as "arbitrary" if the agency had failed to consider all the "relevant factors" in making its decision. *Id.* at 416. In *Nova Scotia*, Judge Gurfein reasoned that because the agency's failure to disclose the relevant scientific studies "prevented the presentation of relevant comment," the court could not confidently conclude that the agency had "considered all 'the relevant factors,'" and this, in turn, meant the decision was arbitrary under § 706. As the opinion explained, if the studies underlying the proposed rule are not disclosed to interested parties, these parties will not be able to use the comment period effectively to challenge those studies, and the "inadequacy of comment in turn leads in the direction of arbitrary decision-making."

Do you find that interpretation of the APA convincing? Or do you think the *Nova Scotia* decision (and the *Portland Cement* decision on which *Nova Scotia* relied) are guilty of reading requirements into the APA that are simply not there (and perhaps should not be there)? How much of your view on this question turns on your understanding of what the notice-and-comment process is supposed to accomplish? Consider two perspectives. On the one hand, if § 553 notice-and-comment procedures are designed to create a quasi-adversarial process in which interested parties have a fair opportunity to defend their interests and advocate vigorously for their favored positions—and if one views this sort of adversarial process as more likely to generate good public policy—then *Nova Scotia*'s disclosure rule holds considerable appeal. On the other hand, if the § 553 process is mostly about mimicking a legislative-style process in which the agency gathers information from interested parties so that the agency can make the best possible policy decision, then perhaps the *Nova Scotia* court is overreaching. On this latter view, the notice-and-comment process isn't supposed to be an opportunity for interested parties to engage in a "scientific debate" with the agency (or with other parties), but simply an opportunity to submit relevant material to the agency, which alone is responsible for assessing the merits of the evidence before it. Which of these views do you find more compelling?

**2.  *Must Agencies Disclose Publicly Available Material?*—**The disclosure rule announced in *Nova Scotia* would seem most plausible when the agency's proposal is based on unpublished studies to which the agency alone has access. This was the situation in Portland Cement Ass'n v. Ruckelshaus, 486 F.2d 375 (D.C. Cir. 1973), *cert. denied sub nom.* 417 U.S. 921 (1974). In that case, the EPA had based an air pollution regulation on tests that the EPA and its contractors had conducted. The EPA did not reveal the details of these tests until after the close of the comment period. 486 F.2d at 392. But in *Nova Scotia*, the FDA's proposed rule was based on published scientific studies that were generally available. The objection in *Nova Scotia* was therefore not that the agency had relied on studies to which the agency alone had access. Rather, the objection was that the FDA's notice had failed to *identify* the studies on which its rule was based. In that sort of case, is it really accurate to say—as the *Nova Scotia* court did, quoting *Portland Cement*—that the agency promulgated a rule on the basis of data "known only to the agency"? Why should an agency have to identify the specific studies on which it has relied, if those studies are publicly available?

Perhaps the idea is that the notice-and-comment process can only work effectively if the comments are sufficiently focused. Even if the studies the agency views as important are publicly available, it might not be efficient (or fair) to compel interested parties to comb through the extant literature themselves and to try to guess which studies should be the focus of their comments. If the agency has already identified the handful of studies that it views as most important, what justification is there for keeping this information to itself? Is there any reason an agency might do so other than a discreditable desire to sidestep a vigorous methodological debate over the validity of those studies? On the other hand, is it really unreasonable to expect Nova Scotia to identify the studies that provide empirical support for the proposition that the proposed T–T–S regulations will prevent botulism? This is, after all, a relatively narrow issue.

What if an agency's proposed regulation is based not on a handful of studies on the precise regulatory policy question at issue, but rather on the entire body of scientific and technical literature that bears on the topic? Does the agency need to disclose *all* the sources that are relevant to its rulemaking proposal? Does it need to specify, in detail, how each source relates to the agency's proposal? Doesn't that seem overly burdensome? Then again, when the potentially relevant body of published literature is very large, perhaps it is even more important that agencies identify in advance the materials they view as most relevant, so potential commenters know where to focus their attention. What do you think?

In a recent case, Chamber of Commerce v. SEC, 443 F.3d 890 (D.C. Cir. 2006), the D.C. Circuit attempted to summarize the doctrine on when an agency may rely on "publicly available" material without specifically disclosing it in the notice of proposed rulemaking:

> ... In some instances, "publicly available" information, such as "published literature in the fields relevant to the [agency's] proposal," may be so obviously relevant that requiring it be specifically noticed and included in the rulemaking record would advance none of the goals of the APA, *see* Richard J. Pierce, Administrative Law Treatise § 7.3, at

436–38 (2004), such as improving the quality of the information used by the agency, ensuring fairness to affected parties, or enhancing the quality of judicial review. The public availability of such information might fall into an implied exception to the general requirement that extra-record data critical to support a legislative rule be subject to public comment, or, alternatively, go towards negating the petitioner's claims of prejudice when such extra-record information is used to cure deficiencies in the rulemaking record. . . .

. . . However, the mere availability of [extra-record sources] . . . is insufficient to demonstrate that [these materials] are generally considered reliable sources of information that should be treated as the inevitable background source of information. . . . *See* Pierce, Administrative Law Treatise, § 7.3, at 436–38. . . . [The agency in the case before the court failed to establish that this undisclosed material] is so reliable or ubiquitous that the procedural requirements for comment should be relaxed when these materials serve as the critical data on which the [agency] relies [for a critical point]. . . .

443 F.3d at 906 (internal citations omitted). Does this seem like a satisfactory way to approach the problem? Does it supply a sufficiently definite standard for courts to apply?

**3. What About Data or Studies Generated During or After the Comment Period?**—Cases like *Nova Scotia* and *Portland Cement* require agencies to disclose the studies on which their rulemaking proposals are based, so that interested parties have an opportunity to challenge and criticize the data, methods, and implications of those studies. This is a relatively straightforward principle to apply to material that the agency has in its possession at the time it publishes the notice of proposed rulemaking in the *Federal Register*. But often the agency will base its final rule on data or other materials that the agency acquires *after* the publication of this notice—including material supplied by outside parties as part of the public comment process. Is the agency ever obligated to disclose *this* material, and to allow more time for public comment? The Second Circuit did not have to address that issue in *Nova Scotia*, which was "not a case where the agency methodology was based on material supplied by the interested parties themselves." Such cases do arise, however. How should courts resolve them? The Supreme Court has not addressed the issue, and the courts of appeals have not developed an altogether consistent or transparent doctrine on this question, so it is difficult to make confident generalizations about when courts will require disclosure of, and opportunity to comment on, evidentiary material acquired by the agency after the initial notice. That said, a few themes have emerged in the case law.

First, if commenters criticize the studies on which the agency initially relied, and the agency responds by conducting new studies that do not lead to any fundamental changes in the agency's proposal, then the agency usually does not have to provide an opportunity to comment on these new studies as well. For example, in Community Nutrition Institute v. Block, 749 F.2d 50 (D.C. Cir. 1984), consumer groups challenged a Department of

Agriculture regulation concerning labeling requirements for certain meat products. During the comment period, several parties alleged that the studies on which the Department had relied (and which had been disclosed in the notice of proposed rulemaking) were methodologically flawed. In response, the Department conducted additional studies, which it referenced in the explanatory statement accompanying the final rule. The D.C. Circuit, in an opinion by then-Judge Scalia, concluded that the Department had no obligation to provide an opportunity to comment on these new studies, principally because they "did not provide entirely new information," but merely "expanded on and confirmed" the conclusions of the earlier studies. *Id.* at 58. Judge Scalia's opinion found it "impossible to perceive why correction of an asserted deficiency in earlier studies—which correction confirms the accuracy of those studies—should give rise to an additional opportunity to comment." *Id. See also* Kern County Farm Bureau v. Allen, 450 F.3d 1072, 1079–80 (9th Cir. 2006); Idaho Farm Bureau Federation v. Babbitt, 58 F.3d 1392, 1402–03 (9th Cir. 1995); Solite Corp. v. EPA, 952 F.2d 473, 484 (D.C. Cir. 1991).

Second, several courts of appeals have held that an agency may generate additional data using a "methodology disclosed in the rulemaking record," even if the actual data is not made available until after the close of the comment period. *See* Chamber of Commerce v. SEC, 443 F.3d 890, 900 (D.C. Cir. 2006) (citing Air Transp. Ass'n of Am. v. Civil Aeronautics Bd., 732 F.2d 219, 224 (D.C. Cir. 1984)). As the First Circuit explained in BASF Wyandotte Corp. v. Costle, 598 F.2d 637 (1st Cir. 1979), a case involving a challenge to a set of pollution regulations established by the Environmental Protection Agency:

> Certainly nothing is more important than the bottom line numbers which determine whether individual plants are or are not in compliance with the regulations. The data that an agency has used to set proposed limits obviously should be subject to public comment if possible. . . .

> This does not mean, however, that any new numbers gathered after publication of proposed regulations must be submitted for comment. It is perfectly predictable that new data will come in during the comment period, either submitted by the public with comments or collected by the agency in a continuing effort to give the regulations a more accurate foundation. The agency should be encouraged to use such information in its final calculations without thereby risking the requirement of a new comment period. . . .

> . . . [The notice provided in connection with the interim rules] disclosed the method by which EPA calculated the [pollution] limits. This methodology was substantially the same for the [interim] and final regulations. EPA afforded petitioners the chance to make the most meaningful possible contribution to the regulatory process because the petitioners could use the information to collect data at their own plants, analyze it, and submit it to EPA. . . .

... [P]etitioners knew all they needed to know in order to make a meaningful contribution to the regulatory process and a meaningful comment on the regulations proposed. All they did not know was what the actual raw numbers would be. While these numbers were certainly crucial in setting the limits and of obviously great interest to the petitioners, we are not convinced that knowing them would have significantly improved petitioners' opportunity to comment. They would have had a different numerical target for their many complaints about the limits set, but that would not have greatly advanced their ability to make positive contributions to the process by criticizing[, among other things,] ... the analytical and statistical methodology EPA used to turn the raw numbers into effluent limits. In short, in this case, we think it was far more important for EPA to solicit comments on how it intended to collect and use data than on the data itself.

598 F.2d at 644–45 (footnote omitted); *see also* American Coke & Coal Chems. Inst. v. EPA, 452 F.3d 930, 939–41 (D.C. Cir. 2006).

A more difficult situation arises when the new material generated in response to comments adds genuinely new information, rather than merely confirming evidence that the agency had already disclosed or supplying the raw data that the agency processes pursuant to a method that the agency had disclosed in the original notice. Here the case law is much sparser, and it is more difficult to predict how a reviewing court will evaluate the claim of inadequate notice. This uncertainty in the case law is illustrated by a pair of Ninth Circuit cases, Rybachek v. EPA, 904 F.2d 1276 (9th Cir. 1990), and Ober v. EPA, 84 F.3d 304 (9th Cir. 1996). In *Rybachek*, the EPA proposed certain regulations under the Clean Water Act that affected Alaskan mining operations. During the comment period, a number of parties objected to the impact the proposed regulations would have on smaller mines. In response, the EPA solicited additional comments, and also conducted a number of additional analyses. When the EPA finalized its rule, it included over 6,000 pages of additional material that had been generated in response to the critical comments about the impact of the rule on small mines. A group of miners (led by the named plaintiffs, the Rybackeks) argued that the EPA's reliance on this additional material deprived them of their right to comment. The Ninth Circuit disagreed:

The EPA has not violated the Rybacheks' right to meaningful public participation. The additional material was the EPA's response to comments made during a public-comment period. Nothing prohibits the Agency from adding supporting documentation for a final rule in response to public comments. In fact, adherence to the Rybacheks' view might result in the EPA's never being able to issue a final rule capable of standing up to review: every time the Agency responded to public comments, such as those in this rulemaking, it would trigger a new comment period. Thus, either the comment period would continue in a never-ending circle, or, if the EPA chose not to respond to the last set of public comments, any final rule could be struck down for lack of

> support in the record. The Rybacheks' unviolated right was to comment on the proposed regulations, not to comment in a never-ending way on the EPA's responses to their comments.

904 F.2d at 1286 (citations omitted). Does that reasoning seem convincing? What do you make of the *Rybachek* court's broad assertion that "*[n]othing* prohibits the Agency from adding supporting documentation for a final rule in response to public comments" (emphasis added)?

In *Ober*, decided only six years later, the Ninth Circuit suggested some important limits on the apparently sweeping language in *Rybachek*. *Ober* involved the EPA's approval of Arizona's plan for achieving its federally-mandated air quality standards under the Clean Air Act. (The Clean Air Act permits individual states to come up with their own plans for meeting federal air quality standards, but each state plan must be approved by the EPA, and the approval process takes the form of a notice-and-comment rulemaking.) During the comment period on Arizona's proposed implementation plan, several environmental advocacy groups objected to Arizona's failure to include a number of specific pollution control measures. After the close of the comment period, the EPA requested from Arizona additional information as to why it had rejected those measures. Arizona responded by providing the EPA with approximately 300 pages of additional material to show that the control measures at issue were either infeasible or would have no significant benefits, and the EPA cited this additional information when it issued its final rule approving the Arizona plan. The Ninth Circuit held that this deprived petitioners of their right to adequate notice and opportunity to comment:

> The challenged post-comment period justifications did not merely expand on prior information and address alleged deficiencies. Instead, they addressed the submitted Implementation Plan's failure to comply with an essential provision of the Clean Air Act. Therefore, they were relied on and were critical to the EPA's approval of the Implementation Plan. Furthermore, the accuracy of the additional information submitted after the comment period is in question because Petitioners argue that many of the asserted justifications do not in fact support rejection of the control measures. These justifications should have been available for public comment *before* the EPA proposed approval of the Implementation Plan.

84 F.3d at 314 (emphasis in original). The Ninth Circuit distinguished *Rybachek* on the ground that in *Rybachek* the additional materials reflected "the EPA's internal assessment of comments from the public; whereas, here, the new information was solicited by the EPA from an interested party." In addition, the *Ober* court noted that in *Rybachek*, "[t]he additional information was not relied on or critical to the EPA's decision"; rather, the agency merely "decided not to alter the regulation based on the additional information." *Id.* Do you find these distinctions persuasive?

**4. *Limits to the Disclosure Requirement*—***Nova Scotia* suggested some important qualifications to its general requirement that agencies disclose the data or studies on which their proposals are based. First, *Nova*

Scotia *indicated that its general disclosure rule would not apply to trade secrets or sensitive national security information. Second,* Nova Scotia *noted that the FDA did not have any "special expertise on the precise parameters involved." On this latter point, the court's meaning is somewhat opaque, but perhaps the court meant to suggest that when the agency has relied principally on a study, rather than its own experience and analysis, it must disclose the study; the corollary would be that in some cases the agency can rely on its general expertise and experience, without a need to identify and disclose all the data on which the agency's views are based. Does that seem persuasive to you? Is the distinction one that courts can meaningfully enforce? Third,* Nova Scotia*'s emphasis on the idea that disclosure is required to facilitate meaningful comment might imply that a petitioner asserting inadequate disclosure must show not only that the agency failed to disclose important studies, but also that the petitioner could have mounted a plausible attack on the validity or relevance of those studies. Put another way, one might read* Nova Scotia *as implicitly requiring a showing of* actual prejudice, *not the simple fact of non-disclosure. But it is not entirely clear what is required to make this showing. Must the petitioner establish, to the court's satisfaction, that it would have succeeded in changing the agency's mind if it had been given an opportunity to comment? Or must the petitioner show only that its objections to the new study would have been non-frivolous—the sort of thing the agency couldn't completely ignore without rendering its decision arbitrary?*

**5.   *The "Concise General Statement of Basis and Purpose"*—** *Nova Scotia* also found fault with the FDA's statement of basis and purpose accompanying its final T–T–S rule. The opinion indicated, first, that the agency's most important obligation is to say *something* in response to significant comments. Thus, with regard to the Bureau of Fisheries' suggestion that the FDA could have allowed lower temperatures coupled with higher salinity, the *Nova Scotia* court complained that "[t]hough this alternative was suggested by an agency of the federal government, its suggestion, though acknowledged, was never answered." Likewise, the court objected to the fact that the comment regarding the devastating economic impact of the rule on the smoked whitefish industry "was neither discussed nor answered." Summing up its basic objection to the FDA's statement of basis and purpose, the Second Circuit declared: "We think that to sanction silence in the face of such vital questions would be to make the statutory requirement of a 'concise general statement' less than an adequate safeguard against arbitrary decision-making."

The idea that an agency must say *something* in its explanatory statement about "vital questions" sounds reasonable, but it raises at least two difficult issues. First, which questions or issues are so "vital" that they require an explicit response? Second, how much must the agency say in response in order to satisfy its procedural obligation to provide an adequate statement of the rule's basis and purpose?

On the first question, the obvious place to begin is with the comments submitted during the notice-and-comment process. As the D.C. Circuit put it in Rodway v. United States Department of Agriculture, 514 F.2d 809 (D.C. Cir. 1975), "[t]he basis and purpose statement is inextricably intertwined with the receipt of comments" because this statement "is not intended to be an abstract explanation addressed to imaginary complaints," but rather is supposed "to respond in a reasoned manner to the comments received." 514 F.2d at 817. But must the agency respond explicitly to *every* (non-frivolous) comment that outside parties submit? It might be tempting to say yes, on the logic that this ensures adequate engagement with all the issues, but such a requirement would place substantial burdens on agencies. After all, many § 553 rulemakings produce hundreds of pages of comments. *Nova Scotia* tried to strike the right balance by asserting that agencies have an obligation to address comments that raise questions "of cogent materiality." Elsewhere, *Nova Scotia* quoted favorably the D.C. Circuit's opinion in Automotive Parts & Accessories Ass'n v. Boyd, 407 F.2d 330 (1968), which held that although agencies are not expected "to discuss every item of fact or opinion included in the submissions made to it," nonetheless the statement of basis and purpose must "enable [a court] to see what major issues of policy were ventilated by the . . . proceedings and why the agency reacted to them as it did." 407 F.2d at 338. How satisfying or helpful are those linguistic formulations for determining what comments an agency must address explicitly in its explanatory statement? What marks an issue as "major" or "cogent[ly] material[]"? What incentives do you suppose this doctrine creates for agencies? Do cases like *Nova Scotia*, *Rodway*, and *Boyd* in practice compel agencies to respond to every comment received, except for those that are obviously frivolous or repetitive?

The second question—concerning the *content* of the agency's response to comments—is more difficult, and perhaps also more important. It is fairly easy (if time consuming) for agencies to say *something* about every non-frivolous comment, but just saying something is arguably not enough. Consider how the FDA responded to the suggestion that it adopt species-by-species T–T–S requirements in light of the enormous variation across species with respect to botulism risk. The FDA was *not* completely silent in response to this comment, but its answer was terse: The FDA's statement of basis and purpose said only that (1) appropriate species-by-species T–T–S requirements had not (yet) been demonstrated; (2) that its proposed regulations "are the safest now known" for preventing botulism; and (3) that it is important to establish new regulations "without further delay." Is that adequate? There are many circumstances in which it makes sense to adopt an overly broad rule in order to deal with some perceived risk, because the costs and delays of coming up with a more nuanced rule or standard are just not worth it. Reasonable minds might disagree about whether quick adoption of a broad but simple rule was appropriate in this case, but is it fair to say that the FDA had failed to supply an adequate statement of the "basis and purpose" of its decision to adopt an across-the-board rule? On the other hand, if the Second Circuit had found the FDA's explanation sufficient, couldn't an agency (almost) always make some coherent boilerplate statement about how it considered the comments and the alternatives that had been proposed, but decided that on balance its rule was better?

**6.  The "Statement of Basis and Purpose" and Judicial Review for Arbitrariness**—*Nova Scotia*'s interpretation of the "statement of basis and purpose" requirement raises again the question of how the court derives broad procedural requirements from the text of § 553. The legislative history of the APA provides some support for the *Nova Scotia* court's approach. The Senate Report on the APA stated that "[t]he agency must analyze and consider all relevant matter presented [and that the] required statement of the basis and purpose of rules issued should not only relate to the data so presented but with reasonable fullness explain the actual basis and objectives of the rule." S. Rep. No. 752, 79th Cong., 1st Sess. at 15 (1945); *see also* H.R. Rep. No. 1980, 79th Cong., 2d Sess. at 25 (1946). Nonetheless, it is hard to square the elaborate requirements of explanation and response set forth in cases such as *Nova Scotia* with § 553(c)'s requirement that the agency produce a "concise" and "general" statement along with a final rule. The prevailing doctrine, according to which agencies risk reversal if they fail to respond adequately to any non-frivolous, non-repetitive comment means that many of these final statements are neither concise nor general—rather, they are lengthy and detailed, often running dozens, or sometimes hundreds, of pages. What is the legal basis for this apparent transformation of the "statement of basis and purpose" requirement?

The answer, which parallels a theme discussed earlier in the context of the notice requirement (p. 615, *supra*), lies in the connection courts have made between the procedural requirements for informal rulemaking found in § 553 and the APA's general judicial review provision, found in § 706(2)(A), pursuant to which a court must invalidate any agency action that is "arbitrary, capricious, [or] an abuse of discretion." Accordingly, *Nova Scotia* held that requiring an agency's statement of basis and purpose to address important issues raised by the commenters is a necessary "safeguard against arbitrary decision-making." Other courts have been even more explicit in tying the agency's procedural obligation to explain its rule pursuant to § 553(c) to the court's obligation to review agency action for arbitrariness pursuant to § 706(2)(A). The point was made perhaps most succinctly by a 1979 Federal Court of Claims opinion, which explained that "[t]he purpose of requiring a statement of the basis and purpose is to enable courts, which have the duty to exercise review, to be aware of the legal and factual framework underlying the agency's action." American Standard, Inc. v. United States, 602 F.2d 256, 269 (Ct. Cl. 1979); *see also* Trans–Pacific Freight Conference of Japan/Korea v. Federal Maritime Commission, 650 F.2d 1235, 1249 (D.C. Cir. 1980); Amoco Oil Co. v. EPA, 501 F.2d 722, 739 (D.C. Cir. 1974). Thus the question whether the agency has satisfied its procedural obligation under § 553(c) to supply an adequate statement of basis and purpose has merged with the question whether the agency's action is arbitrary or capricious under the general review standard laid out in § 706(2)(A).

We address the "arbitrary and capricious" standard of review in greater depth in Part IV of this chapter, pp. 717–790 *infra*. For now, consider whether it makes sense to link the § 553(c) statement of basis and purpose requirement so closely to the § 706 standard of review. Even if there were no "concise general statement of ... basis and purpose" requirement in § 553(c), would the agency still be obligated to explain its decision adequately, on the logic that failure to do so would render the decision arbitrary? More generally, couldn't one question the assertion that § 553(c)'s requirements must be interpreted in a way that facilitates a particular approach to judicial review under § 706(2)(A)? Perhaps the courts have gotten it all backwards: The fact that the prevailing judicial approach to "arbitrary and capricious" review under § 706 implies a more lengthy and detailed explanatory statement—one that seems to go well beyond the "concise general statement" required by the text of § 553(c)— may be a sign that the courts have misconstrued their obligations under § 706, not that § 553(c) must be read broadly. Then again, perhaps the courts have it basically right, in that § 706(2)(A) helps give content to § 553(c) by making it clear that the sort of explanatory statement required is one that would enable an outsider to assess whether the agency action is arbitrary, while § 553(c) simultaneously shapes the courts' understanding of their obligations under § 706(2)(A) by focusing attention not so much on the *content* of an agency's decision but on the *reasoning* behind it. Is that convincing? We will return to questions of this sort when we consider the material on § 706 review in Part IV.

**7. *The Judicial Expansion of § 553 and the "Ossification" Problem*—**The courts' expansive reading of § 553's procedural requirements has transformed so-called "informal" rulemaking into a much more elaborate and formal process—a " 'paper hearing' that includes extensive and often repeated notice to affected groups of a proposed rule, provision to them of the factual and analytical material supporting it, and detailed responses to any group's adverse comment or alternative proposal." Elena Kagan, *Presidential Administration*, 114 HARV. L. REV. 2245, 2267 (2001). Why has this occurred? And what are the consequences?

With respect to the causes of this judicial transformation of notice-and-comment rulemaking, one straightforward explanation is that judges (and others) are uncomfortable with the idea that agencies can make important policy decisions without adequate procedural safeguards. Recall, again, the fundamental anxiety about broad delegations of power to administrative agencies. Recall further that our legal and political system has traditionally sought to legitimize (or rationalize) such delegations in part by ensuring that agency decisions are subject to procedural controls and judicial review. A narrow reading of § 553's procedural requirements would arguably permit agencies to exercise extraordinarily broad policymaking powers without adequate procedural safeguards (because the notice, comment, and explanatory statement requirements, read narrowly, seem to require so little) and without adequate judicial oversight (because a more robust understanding of these procedures, as we have seen, is believed to facilitate meaningful judicial review). This problem is arguably exacerbated by *Flori-*

*da East Coast Railway* (pp. 588–597, *supra*), which shifted more cases from the heavily proceduralized formal rulemaking category to the less-formal notice-and-comment category. As judges confront the fact that a large number of substantial policy decisions are being made by agencies through the notice-and-comment rulemaking process, they may feel the need to interpret the requirements of that process in ways that constrain and legitimize these exercises of administrative power. Whether they have the legal authority to do so under the APA is another matter. The answer to that legal question depends in part on one's attitude toward statutory interpretation in general, and the interpretation of the APA in particular.

But might this judge-driven expansion of § 553 have adverse practical consequences? Many scholars and judges have asserted that it does. One concern is that judges' procedural rulings are outcome-driven. *See, e.g.,* Richard L. Revesz, *Environmental Regulation, Ideology, and the D.C. Circuit*, 83 Va. L. Rev. 1717 (1997); Emerson H. Tiller, *Controlling Policy by Controlling Process: Judicial Influence on Regulatory Decision Making*, 14 J. L. Econ. & Org. 114 (1998). Another concern is that even if judges act entirely in good faith, the expansive judicial construction of § 553 has led to an overproceduralization of notice-and-comment rulemaking, rendering it too cumbersome, costly, and lawyer-driven, which in turn undermines the benefits associated with this more flexible form of agency rulemaking. Thus many scholars have warned that judge-driven overproceduralization of informal rulemaking has "ossified" the rulemaking process, substantially delaying, or deterring altogether, vital regulatory policy changes. *See* Thomas O. McGarity, *Some Thoughts on "Deossifying" the Rulemaking Process*, 41 Duke L.J. 1385, 1400–01 (1992); Richard J. Pierce, Jr., *Seven Ways To Deossify Agency Rulemaking*, 47 Admin. L. Rev. 59, 65 (1995). Judge Kavanaugh recently summed up the argument as follows:

> ... [Section] 553 of the APA requires only a notice providing a "description of the subjects and issues involved"; time for interested persons to comment; and a "concise general statement" of the rule's "basis and purpose." 5 U.S.C. § 553. Courts have incrementally expanded those APA procedural requirements well beyond what the text provides. And courts simultaneously have grown ... § 706 arbitrary-and-capricious review into a far more demanding test....
>
> Over time, those twin lines of decisions have gradually transformed rulemaking—whether regulatory or deregulatory rulemaking—from the simple and speedy practice contemplated by the APA into a laborious, seemingly never-ending process. The judicially created obstacle course can hinder Executive Branch agencies from rapidly and effectively responding to changing or emerging issues within their authority ... or effectuating policy or philosophical changes in the Executive's approach to the subject matter at hand. The trend has not been good as a jurisprudential matter, and it continues to have significant practical consequences for the operation of the Federal Government and those affected by federal regulation and deregulation.

American Radio Relay League, Inc. v. FCC, 524 F.3d 227, 248 (D.C. Cir. 2008) (Kavanaugh, J., concurring in part, concurring in the judgment in part, and dissenting in part).

Is this pessimistic view in fact correct? The ossification hypothesis, though influential in some quarters, has generated a spirited debate among scholars who have tried to assess both the empirical question of whether judicially-imposed procedural burdens actually do have a substantial impact on the speed or frequency of agency rulemaking, and the more normative question of how to balance the costs of this alleged "ossification" against the countervailing benefits associated with more stringent procedural safeguards. *See, e.g.*, William S. Jordan III, *Ossification Revisited: Does Arbitrary and Capricious Review Significantly Interfere with Agency Ability To Achieve Regulatory Goals Through Informal Rulemaking?*, 94 Nw. U. L. Rev. 393 (2000); Thomas O. McGarity, *The Courts and the Ossification of Rulemaking: A Response to Professor Seidenfeld*, 75 Tex. L. Rev. 525 (1997); Anne Joseph O'Connell, *Political Cycles of Rulemaking: An Empirical Portrait of the Modern Administrative State*, 94 Va. L. Rev. 889 (2008); Richard J. Pierce, Jr., *The Unintended Effects of Judicial Review of Agency Rules: How Federal Courts Have Contributed to the Electricity Crisis of the 1990s*, 43 Admin. L. Rev. 7 (1991); Jim Rossi, *Redeeming Judicial Review: The Hard Look Doctrine and Federal Regulatory Efforts To Restructure the Electric Utility Industry*, 1994 Wis. L. Rev. 763; Mark Seidenfeld, *Demystifying Deossification: Rethinking Recent Proposals To Modify Judicial Review of Notice and Comment Rulemaking*, 75 Tex. L. Rev. 483 (1997); Susan Webb Yackee & Jason Webb Yackee, *Administrative Procedures and Bureaucratic Performance: Is Federal Rulemaking "Ossified"?*, 20 J. Pub. Admin. Res. & Theory, 261 (2010). Given that the ossification concern rests at least in part on contestable empirical assertions about the actual effect of the § 553 process on agency behavior, how should courts (or others) respond to this concern? And given that the concern about ossification also implicates judgments about the relative importance of speed, flexibility, and efficiency on the one hand, versus deliberation, restraint, and stability on the other, how should courts balance those interests in the context of § 553 rulemaking?

## B. When Is a Supplemental Notice Required?

The notice-and-comment rulemaking process seems premised on two simple and appealing ideas. The first is that parties whose interests are affected by a proposed agency rule should have fair notice of the proposal, as well as the opportunity to make timely objections and to suggest modifications. The second is that public participation in the agency rulemaking process enables the agency to draw on input from interested parties to improve the quality of its final rules. Thus, a participatory process of the sort established by § 553 is supposed to advance both the interest in protecting affected parties, and the interest in improving public policy. In many respects, these interests are complementary: It is precisely the affected parties' desire to protect their own interests by participating in the agency process that enhances the agency's decision-making capacity.

The notion that broad public participation in the agency rulemaking process can improve the quality of agency rules presumes that an agency might alter its proposed rule in response to the outside input it receives during the comment period: "The whole rationale of notice and comment rests on the expectation that the final rules will be somewhat different— and improved—from the rules originally proposed by the agency." Trans-Pacific Freight Conference of Japan/Korea v. Federal Maritime Commission, 650 F.2d 1235, 1249 (D.C. Cir. 1980). But suppose that an agency does change its proposed rule in response to comments by interested parties. Might this change deprive *other* potentially interested parties of adequate notice and opportunity for comment? After all, these other parties likely directed their comments at the original proposal rather than the subsequent revision. Sometimes this isn't really a problem, as the range of possible policy choices is known to all parties at the outset of the rulemaking process, and the only question is which among a limited set of known alternatives the agency will adopt. But sometimes commenters will suggest alternatives or modifications to the original proposal that the agency had not previously considered. The agency could always provide public notice of the revised proposal and allow additional time for comment, but doing so might significantly slow down the rulemaking process, impeding the interest in efficiency and flexibility.

To put this problem in sharper doctrinal form: When does the APA obligate an agency to do a second round of notice and comment, due to the fact that it has substantially modified its proposed rule in light of comments received during the first round of notice and comment? The following case, *Chocolate Manufacturers Association v. Block*, addresses this question, and the opinion illustrates the standard doctrinal approach. As you read the case, consider the degree to which the court's holding—and your view—is influenced by a sense of what the § 553 notice-and-comment provisions are supposed to accomplish. What does the *Chocolate Manufacturers* court seem to think is the principal purpose of these provisions? Does the court's approach—both as stated and as applied—strike the right balance between fairness, efficiency, and other relevant values? The case also provides an opportunity to consider the questions raised earlier (pp. 599–602, *supra*) about how courts should approach the task of interpreting the APA. Is *Chocolate Manufacturers* a case where an expansive, purposive approach to interpreting the APA is appropriate? Or could the case be resolved on the basis of § 553's text, without reliance on inferences from the substantive purposes served by the APA's notice-and-comment provisions?

---

# Chocolate Manufacturers Association v. Block

Court of Appeals for the Fourth Circuit
755 F.2d 1098 (4th Cir. 1985)

■ SPROUSE, CIRCUIT JUDGE:

Chocolate Manufacturers Association (CMA) appeals from the decision of the district court denying it relief from a rule promulgated by the Food and Nutrition Service (FNS) of the United States Department of Agriculture (USDA or Department). CMA protests that part of the rule that prohibits the use of chocolate flavored milk in the federally funded Special Supplemental Food Program for Women, Infants and Children (WIC Program). Holding that the Department's proposed rulemaking did not provide adequate notice that the elimination of flavored milk would be considered in the rulemaking procedure, we reverse.

I

... The WIC Program was established by Congress in 1972 to assist pregnant, postpartum, and breastfeeding women, infants and young children from families with inadequate income whose physical and mental health is in danger because of inadequate nutrition or health care. Under the program, the Department designs food packages reflecting the different nutritional needs of women, infants, and children and provides cash grants to state or local agencies, which distribute cash or vouchers to qualifying individuals in accordance with Departmental regulations as to the type and quantity of food.

In 1975 Congress revised and extended the WIC Program through fiscal year 1978 and, for the first time, defined the "supplemental foods" which the program was established to provide. The term

> shall mean those foods containing nutrients known to be lacking in the diets of populations at nutritional risk and, in particular, those foods and food products containing high-quality protein, iron, calcium, vitamin A, and vitamin C.... The contents of the food package shall be made available in such a manner as to provide flexibility, taking into account medical and nutritional objectives and cultural eating patterns....

Pursuant to this statutory definition, the Department promulgated new regulations specifying the contents of WIC Program food packages. These regulations specified that flavored milk was an acceptable substitute for fluid whole milk in the food packages for women and children, but not infants. This regulation formalized the Department's practice of permitting the substitution of flavored milk, a practice observed in the WIC Program since its inception in 1973....

In 1978 Congress, in extending the WIC Program through fiscal year 1982, redefined the term "supplemental foods" to mean

> those foods containing nutrients determined by nutritional research to be lacking in the diets of pregnant, breastfeeding, and postpartum women, infants, and children, as prescribed by the Secretary. State agencies may, with the approval of the Secretary, substitute different foods providing the nutritional equivalent of foods prescribed by the Secretary, to allow for different cultural eating patterns.

... Congress stated further:

The Secretary shall prescribe by regulation supplemental foods to be made available in the program under this section. To the degree possible, the Secretary shall assure that the fat, sugar, and salt content of the prescribed foods is appropriate.

... To comply with this statutory redefinition, the Department moved to redraft its regulations specifying the WIC Program food packages. In doing so it relied upon information collected during an extensive investigative effort which had begun in 1977....

Using this information as well as its own research as a basis, the Department in November 1979 published for comment the proposed rule at issue in this case.... Along with the proposed rule, the Department published a preamble discussing the general purpose of the rule and acknowledging the congressional directive that the Department design food packages containing the requisite nutritional value and appropriate levels of fat, sugar, and salt.... Discussing the issue of sugar at length, it noted, for example, that continued inclusion of high sugar cereals may be "contrary to nutrition education principles and may lead to unsound eating practices." It also noted that high sugar foods are more expensive than foods with lower sugar content, and that allowing them would be "inconsistent with the goal of teaching participants economical food buying patterns."

The rule proposed a maximum sugar content specifically for authorized cereals. The preamble also contained a discussion of the sugar content in juice, but the Department did not propose to reduce the allowable amount of sugar in juice because of technical problems involved in any reduction. Neither the rule nor the preamble discussed sugar in relation to flavoring in milk. Under the proposed rule, the food packages for women and children without special dietary needs included milk that could be "flavored or unflavored."

The notice allowed sixty days for comment and specifically invited comment on the entire scope of the proposed rules: "The public is invited to submit written comments in favor of or in objection to the proposed regulations or to make recommendations for alternatives not considered in the proposed regulations." Over 1,000 comments were received from state and local agencies, congressional offices, interest groups, and WIC Program participants and others. Seventy-eight commenters, mostly local WIC administrators, recommended that the agency delete flavored milk from the list of approved supplemental foods.

In promulgating the final rule, the Department, responding to these public comments, deleted flavored milk from the list, explaining:

In the previous regulations, women and children were allowed to receive flavored or unflavored milk. No change in this provision was proposed by the Department. However, 78 commenters requested the deletion of flavored milk from the food packages since flavored milk has a higher sugar content than unflavored milk. They indicated that providing flavored milk contradicts nutrition education and the Department's proposal to limit sugar in the food packages. Furthermore, flavored milk is more expensive than unflavored milk. The Department agrees with these concerns[....] Therefore, to reinforce nutrition education, for consistency with the Department's philosophy about sugar in the food packages, and to maintain food package costs at economic levels, the Department is deleting flavored milk from the food packages for women and children. Although the deletion of flavored milk was not proposed, the comments and the Department's policy on sugar validate this change.

After the final rule was issued, CMA petitioned the Department to reopen the rulemaking to allow it to comment, maintaining that it had been misled into believing that the deletion of flavored milk would not be considered.... [The Department] declined to reopen the rulemaking procedure.

On this appeal, CMA contends ... that the Department did not provide notice that the disallowance of flavored milk would be considered.... The Department responds ... by arguing that its notice advised the public of its general concern about high sugar content in the proposed food packages and that this should have alerted potentially interested commenters that it would consider eliminating any food with high sugar content. It also argues in effect that the inclusion of flavored milk in the proposed rule carried with it the implication that both inclusion and exclusion would be considered in the rulemaking process....

## II

The requirement of notice and a fair opportunity to be heard is basic to administrative law.... We must decide whether inclusion of flavored milk in the allowable food packages under the proposed rule should have alerted interested persons that the Department might reverse its position and exclude flavored milk if adverse comments recommended its deletion from the program.

Section 4 of the Administrative Procedure Act (APA) requires that the notice in the Federal Register of a proposed rulemaking contain "either the terms or substance of the proposed rule or a description of the subjects and issues involved." 5 U.S.C. § 553(b)(3) (1982). The purpose of the notice-and-comment procedure is both "to allow the agency to benefit from the experience and input of the parties who file comments ... and to see to it that the agency maintains a flexible and open-minded attitude towards its own rules." National Tour Brokers Ass'n v. United States, 591 F.2d 896, 902 (D.C.Cir.1978). The notice-and-comment procedure encourages public participation in the administrative process and educates the agency, thereby helping to ensure informed agency decisionmaking. Spartan Radiocasting Co. v. FCC, 619 F.2d 314, 321 (4th Cir.1980); BASF Wyandotte Corp. v. Costle, 598 F.2d 637, 642 (1st Cir.1979), *cert. denied*, 444 U.S. 1096 (1980).

The Department's published notice here consisted of the proposed rule and a preamble discussing the negative effect of high sugar content in general and specifically in relation to some foods such as cereals and juices, but it did not mention high sugar content in flavored milk. The proposed rule eliminated certain foods with high sugar content but specifically authorized flavored milk as part of the permissible diet. In a discussion characterized by pointed identification of foods with high sugar content, flavored milk was conspicuous by its exclusion. If after comments the agency had adopted without change the proposed rule as its final rule, there could have been no possible objection to the adequacy of notice. The public was fully notified as to what the Department considered to be a healthy and adequate diet for its target group. The final rule, however, dramatically altered the proposed rule, changing for the first time the milk content of the diet by deleting flavored milk. The agency concedes that the elimination of flavored milk by the final rule is a complete reversal from its treatment in the proposed rule, but it explains that the reversal was caused by the comments received from 78 interested parties—primarily professional administrators of the WIC Program.

This presents then not the simple question of whether the notice of a proposed rule adequately informs the public of its intent, but rather the question of how to judge the adequacy of the notice when the proposal it describes is replaced by a final rule which reaches a conclusion exactly opposite to that proposed, on the basis of comments received from parties representing only a single view of a controversy. In reviewing the propriety of such agency action, we are not constrained by the same degree of deference we afford most agency determinations....

There is no question that an agency may promulgate a final rule that differs in some particulars from its proposal. Otherwise the agency "can learn from the comments on its proposals only at the peril of starting a new procedural round of commentary." International Harvester Co. v. Ruckelshaus, 478 F.2d 615, 632 n. 51 (D.C.Cir.1973). An agency, however, does not have carte blanche to establish a rule contrary to its original proposal simply because it receives suggestions to alter it during the comment period. An interested party must have been alerted by the notice to the possibility of the changes eventually adopted from the comments.... Although an agency, in its notice of proposed rulemaking, need not identify precisely every potential regulatory change, the notice must be sufficiently descriptive to provide interested parties with a fair opportunity to comment and to participate in the rulemaking....

... [A]ppellate review of changes in a proposed rule after comments is more specifically controlled by the circumstances of each case than most administrative appeals. Nevertheless, a review of decisions of our sister circuits performing similar tasks is helpful. In BASF Wyandotte Corp. v. Costle, 598 F.2d 637 (1st Cir.1979), *cert. denied*, 444 U.S. 1096 (1980), the court considered an EPA regulation controlling the discharge of pollutants into navigable waters by the pesticide industry. The EPA originally proposed dividing the organic pesticide industry into three subcategories, setting different pollutant standards for each one. The industry, arguing for expansion of the number of subcategories and, therefore, pollutant standards, submitted comments demonstrating that the proposed three subcategories were indistinguishable. The EPA, while agreeing with the comments, chose a different solution: it altered its initial rule by eliminating the subcategories and applying uniform standards throughout the entire organic pesticide industry. The industry complained that the EPA's decision to contract rather than expand the number of subcategories took them entirely by surprise. "The essential inquiry," the court said, "is whether the commentators have had a fair opportunity to present their views on the contents of the final plan." The First Circuit reasoned that even if the initial rule had proposed uniform standards, the content of petitioner's comments would not have been different for they still would have argued, albeit more voluminously and vociferously, for more subcategories. The petitioners, therefore, "had a fair opportunity to present their views."

In South Terminal Corp. v. EPA, 504 F.2d 646 (1st Cir.1974), the court considered an air quality transportation control plan for Boston, Massachusetts, which varied substantially from the proposal described in the notice. The petitioners contended that they had no meaningful notice of the substance of the plan. The *South Terminal* court identified two factors of primary importance in determining whether a substantially revised final rule is promulgated in accordance with the APA: the changes in the original rule must be "in character with the original scheme" and "a logical outgrowth" of the notice and comment already given. In rejecting the petitioners' claim, the court stated: "Although the changes were substantial, they were in character with the original scheme and were additionally foreshadowed in proposals and comments advanced during the rulemaking. [In addition, the parties] had been warned that strategies might be modified in light of their suggestions." 504 F.2d at 658. A proposed rule, therefore, must fairly apprise interested parties of the potential scope and substance of a substantially revised final rule and, under this approach, a substantial change must relate in part to the comments received. . . .

The test devised by the First Circuit for determining adequacy of notice of a change in a proposed rule occurring after comments appears to us to be sound: notice is adequate if the changes in the original plan "are in character with the original scheme," and the final rule is a "logical outgrowth" of the notice and comments already given. Other circuits also have adopted some form of the "logical outgrowth" test. . . .

There can be no doubt that the final rule in the instant case was the "outgrowth" of the original rule proposed by the agency, but the question of whether the change in it was in character with the original scheme and whether it was a *"logical* outgrowth" is not easy to answer. In resolving this difficult issue, we recognize that, although helpful, verbal formulations are not omnipotent talismans, and we agree that in the final analysis each case "must turn on how well the notice that the agency gave serves the policies underlying the notice requirement." Small Refiner Lead Phase–Down Task Force v. EPA, 705 F.2d 506, 547 (D.C.Cir.1983). Under either view, we do not feel that CMA was fairly treated or that the administrative rulemaking process was well served by the drastic alteration of the rule without an opportunity for CMA to be heard.

It is apparent that for many years the Department of Agriculture has permitted the use of chocolate in some form in the food distribution programs that it administers. The only time the Department has proposed to remove chocolate in any form from its programs was in April 1978 when it sought to characterize chocolate as a candy and remove it from the School Lunch Program. That proposal was withdrawn after CMA commented, supporting chocolate as a part of the diet. Chocolate flavored milk has been a permissible part of the WIC Program diet since its inception and there have been no proposals for its removal until the present controversy.

The Department sponsored commendable information-gathering proceedings prior to publishing its proposed rule.... In all of these activities setting out and discussing food packages, including the proposed rule and its preamble, the Department never suggested that flavored milk be removed from the WIC Program.

The published preamble to the proposed rule consisted of twelve pages in the Federal Register discussing in detail factors that would be considered in making the final rule. Two pages were devoted to a general discussion of nutrients ... and the dangers of overconsumption of sugar, fat, and salt. The preamble discussed some foods containing these ingredients and foods posing specific problems. It did not discuss flavored milk.

In the next eight pages of the preamble, the nutrition content of food packages was discussed—under the general headings of "cereal" and "juice" for infants; and "eggs," "milk," "cheese," "peanut butter and mature dried beans and peas," "juice," "additional foods," "cereals," "iron," "sugar," "whole grain cereals," "highly fortified cereals," and "artificial flavors and colors" for women and children. The only reference to milk concerned the correct quantity to be provided to children.... Although there was considerable discussion of the sugar content of juice and cereal, there was none concerning flavored milk. Likewise, there was considerable discussion of artificial flavor and color in cereal but none concerning flavored milk. The only reference to flavored milk was in the two-page discussion of the individual food packages, which noted that the proposed rule would permit the milk to be flavored or unflavored. The proposed rule which followed the preamble expressly noted that flavored or unflavored milk was permitted in the individual food packages for women and children without special dietary needs.

At the time the proposed rulemaking was published, neither CMA nor the public in general could have had any indication from the history of either the WIC Program or any other food distribution programs that flavored milk was not part of the acceptable diet for women and children without special dietary needs. The discussion in the preamble to the proposed rule was very detailed and identified specific foods which the agency was examining for excess sugar. This specificity, together with total silence concerning any suggestion of eliminating flavored milk, strongly indicated that flavored milk was not at issue. The proposed rule positively and unqualifiedly approved the continued use of flavored milk. Under the specific circumstances of this case, it cannot be said that the ultimate changes in the proposed rule were in character with the original scheme or a logical outgrowth of the notice. We can well accept that, in general, an approval of a practice in a proposed rule may properly alert interested parties that the practice may be disapproved in the final rule in the event of adverse comments. The total effect of the history of the use of flavored milk, the preamble discussion, and the proposed rule, however, could have led interested persons only to conclude that a change in flavored milk would not be considered. Although ultimately their comments may well have been futile, CMA and other interested persons at least should have had the opportunity to make them. We believe that there was insufficient notice that the deletion of flavored milk from the WIC Program would be considered if adverse comments were received, and, therefore, that affected parties did not receive a fair opportunity to contribute to the administrative rulemaking process. That process was ill-served by the misleading or inadequate notice concerning the permissibility of chocolate flavored milk in the WIC Program and "does not serve the policy underlying the notice requirement."

The judgment of the district court is therefore reversed, and the case is remanded to the administrative agency with instructions to reopen the comment period and thereby afford interested parties a fair opportunity to comment on the proposed changes in the rule.

---

***1. The "Logical Outgrowth" Test***—The dilemma posed by cases like *Chocolate Manufacturers* is straightforward. On the one hand, a requirement that the agency must start a new notice-and-comment period if it decides to alter its original proposal drags out the rulemaking process. Such a requirement may also make agencies reluctant to modify proposed rules in response to comments, even if those comments suggest sensible revisions or alternatives. Agencies might also respond by making their initial rulemaking proposals vaguer and more general, in order to preserve greater flexibility to alter these proposals after receiving comments. On the other hand, if an agency enacts a final rule that differs substantially from the rule it initially proposed, this may deprive interested parties of a meaningful opportunity to participate in the notice-and-comment process. Furthermore, a doctrine that gives agencies great latitude to adopt final rules that differ substantially from proposed rules, without further notice and comment, might encourage inefficient and wasteful "over-participation" in agency rulemaking proceedings by potentially interested parties, who would have an incentive to submit extensive commentary on anything they could imagine the agency might do, whether or not it appeared in the initial proposal.

Did *Chocolate Manufacturers* handle this dilemma satisfactorily? As you saw, the Fourth Circuit applied something called the "logical outgrowth" test, according to which the agency does not have to initiate a new round of notice and comment if the final rule is the "logical outgrowth" of the proposed rule and is "in character with the original scheme." (While some courts, including the D.C. Circuit, have sometimes framed the inquiry as whether the original notice "sufficiently foreshadowed" the final rule, in practice there appears to be no meaningful difference between the "logical outgrowth" test and the "sufficiently foreshadowed" test. *See* Phillip M. Kannan, *The Logical Outgrowth Doctrine in Rulemaking*, 48 ADMIN. L. REV. 213, 217 (1996).) Is this the right way to frame the issue? Does this doctrinal formulation help resolve the question, or merely restate it? Is there a way to decide whether a final rule is a "logical outgrowth" of a proposed rule that does not depend on whether a new round of notice and comment should be required on some other grounds? *Chocolate Manufacturers* explained that the key question is whether a new round of notice and comment is important to serve the policies underlying the notice requirement—in particular, the principle that "affected parties ... [should] receive a fair opportunity" to participate. Do you agree with the Fourth Circuit's identification and application of the policies underlying the notice requirement?

    **2. *The Specificity of the Agency's Initial Proposal*—**One of the things that got the agency into trouble in *Chocolate Manufacturers* was the fact that the agency's notice of proposed rulemaking had listed, in reasonable detail, the food products the agency was considering removing from the WIC program. Suppose the agency had not done this, but had simply stated its intention to exclude from the WIC program "foods excessively high in fat, salt, or sugar." Might the outcome of the case have been different? If so, wouldn't this give agencies an incentive to be less specific in their initial proposals than they would be otherwise? What if the agency had said simply that it was planning to enact a rule revising the list of approved foods "to improve the nutritional quality of the WIC program"?

    The concern that a demanding version of the logical outgrowth test might give agencies an incentive to be excessively vague in their initial proposals is a serious one, but there are at least two mitigating considerations, one legal and the other practical. The legal consideration is that if the initial notice is too vague, a court might deem it legally inadequate. *See, e.g.*, Small Refiner Lead Phase–Down Task Force v. EPA, 705 F.2d 506, 549 (D.C. Cir. 1983) (stating that for notice to be adequate for purposes of § 553(b), the agency "must describe the range of alternatives being considered with reasonable specificity"); Rodway v. Department of Agriculture, 514 F.2d 809, 814 (D.C. Cir. 1975) (finding that the Department of Agriculture's general notice that it intended "to revise the regulations governing the operation of the Food Stamp Program" was "insufficient to include [the specific regulatory change at issue] by inference").

    A potential problem with this legal argument is that the text of § 553(b) requires that a notice of proposed rulemaking include "*either* the terms or substance of the proposed rule *or* a description of the subjects and issues involved" (emphasis added). Presumably an agency could give notice of the "subjects and issues involved" (e.g., the nutritional content of WIC-approved foods) in open-ended terms without going into great detail about specifics. But *Chocolate Manufacturers* and other cases suggest a possible response: The agency's obligation to be reasonably precise in its initial proposal derives not only from the notice requirement in § 553(b), but also from the agency's obligation under § 553(c) to provide an "opportunity to participate in the rule making through submission of written data, views, or arguments." If the initial notice does not provide a sufficiently clear indication of what the agency is thinking about doing, then potentially interested parties do not have a meaningful "opportunity to participate," even if the notice does describe, in general terms, the "subjects and issues involved." *See, e.g., Small Refiner*, 705 F.2d at 549 (concluding that if the notice does not "describe the range of alternatives being considered with reasonable specificity . . . interested parties will not know what to comment on, and notice will not lead to better-informed agency decisionmaking"); Home Box Office, Inc. v. FCC, 567 F.2d 9, 36 (D.C. Cir. 1977) ("[A]n agency proposing informal rulemaking has an obligation to make its views known to the public in a concrete and focused form so as to make criticism or formulation of alternatives possible."). But couldn't one plausibly respond that if the agency had said merely that it was initiating a rulemaking "to revise the list of WIC program foods to improve nutritional content," and then allowed anyone to submit whatever comments they would like, the agency would have provided both notice of "the subjects and issues involved" and also "an opportunity"—in the formal sense—for interested persons to submit written comments? Why is that not the right way to approach the issue?

In addition to whatever legal constraints there may be on an agency's ability to issue a vague or open-ended rulemaking proposal, practical considerations might deter agencies from adopting such an approach. The rulemaking process may be more efficient—and less costly to the agency—if the initial notice focuses potential commenters' attention on a particular proposal or limited set of proposals, so that the agency does not have to deal with a large number of irrelevant comments. And perhaps the agency has an interest in maintaining good relationships with both the regulated community and the agency's political overseers by striving for a reasonable degree of transparency.

Notwithstanding these legal and pragmatic constraints on excessively vague rulemaking notices, does *Chocolate Manufacturers* give agencies an incentive to draft their initial proposals in ways that will give the agency more wiggle room to alter those proposals after the conclusion of the comment period? If so, is this a good or bad thing?

**3. *Can the Comments of Other Parties Provide Adequate Notice?*—**The *Chocolate Manufacturers* decision was written in a way that suggests the CMA had no way of knowing that the elimination of chocolate milk from the list of WIC-approved foods was even a possibility until the Department announced its final rule. But, as we have noted, the suggestion to eliminate chocolate milk was submitted by a number of local WIC program administrators during the public comment period, and although those comments were not immediately published in the *Federal Register*, they were part of a public rulemaking docket. If these comments came in early enough that the CMA could have seen and responded to them before the close of the comment period, does it make sense to conclude that the CMA had no notice of the possibility that the Department might eliminate chocolate milk from the WIC list? Don't the comments themselves provide adequate notice and an opportunity to respond?

One possible reason to reject the idea that other comments submitted to the Department gave the CMA adequate notice is that there is no guarantee that the CMA ever actually saw these comments. "Commenting parties," the D.C. Circuit has asserted, "cannot be expected to monitor all other comments submitted to an agency." Fertilizer Institute v. EPA, 935 F.2d 1303, 1312 (D.C. Cir. 1991). A doctrine that treats other comments as adequate notice could "turn notice into an elaborate treasure hunt, in which interested parties, assisted by high-priced guides (called 'lawyers'), must search the record for the buried treasure of a possibly relevant comment. Inevitably, many parties will not attempt this costly search and many others will fail in their search." *Small Refiner*, 705 F.2d at 549. Furthermore, "[e]ven if a party knows that a commenter has made some novel proposal to an agency during a rulemaking, the party cannot be expected to respond unless it has some reason to believe the agency will take the proposal seriously. Actual notice, then, depends on awareness that the agency, despite its failure to alert the public, is considering adopting what the commenter has suggested." National Mining Ass'n v. Mine Safety & Health Admin., 116 F.3d 520, 531–32 (D.C. Cir. 1997).

On the other hand, isn't it reasonable to presume that sophisticated parties often have a very good sense of what is going on in an agency rulemaking process, and are usually aware of significant comments made by other interested parties that the agency is likely to take seriously? Considerations of this sort have sometimes led courts to depart from the usual rule that comments submitted by other parties cannot supply adequate notice of an alternative rule that differs substantially from the initial proposal. *See, e.g.*, Natural Res. Def. Council, Inc. v. Thomas, 838 F.2d 1224, 1243 (D.C. Cir. 1988) (noting that while nothing in the EPA's initial notice would have suggested the final form of the EPA's regulation, "the public comments raised the possibility of adopting [the rule the EPA ultimately promulgated]," which alerted industry participants of the "foreseeable risk" that the agency would adopt such a rule and gave them "a clear opportunity to shoot the idea down"). Does such an approach comport with either the letter or the spirit of the "logical outgrowth" test?

**4.  *The Content of Submitted Comments***—In *Chocolate Manufacturers*, the CMA argued that it did not know that the agency was even considering a rule that would affect its members' interests. In other cases, though, the attack on the adequacy of agency notice comes from a party that *did* participate in the rulemaking process by submitting comments. The aggrieved party in such cases typically argues that even though it submitted comments, these comments did not adequately address and critique the alternative the agency ended up adopting, because the agency's notice did not make clear that this was one of the alternatives on the table. In some cases, moreover, an aggrieved party asserts not only that the agency's inadequate notice led the party to fail to comment on certain alternatives, but also that the comments the party submitted would have been different if it had known the other options the agency was considering. (The aggrieved party says, in effect, "The agency only gave notice of $X$, so I commented on $X$, but then the agency adopted $Y$. If the agency had given notice of both $X$ and $Y$ as possibilities, not only would I have commented on both $X$ and $Y$, but *the substance of my comments on X would have been different*.") Such cases, while unusual, are useful for thinking about the purposes that the notice-and-comment process is supposed to serve.

A particularly useful example of this sort of case is BASF Wyandotte Corp. v. Costle, 598 F.2d 637 (1st Cir. 1979), discussed (and distinguished) by *Chocolate Manufacturers*. *BASF Wyandotte* involved EPA regulations governing discharge of pollutants by pesticide manufacturers. In 1976 the EPA adopted interim regulations and simultaneously initiated a notice-and-comment proceeding to produce a set of final regulations. The interim regulations had divided organic pesticides into three categories ("halogenated organic pesticides," "organo-phosphorous pesticides," and "organo-nitrogen pesticides") and adopted somewhat different pollution control restrictions for each. In their comments on the regulations, industry groups argued for a larger number of categories. In support of this argument, industry commenters asserted that the EPA's three categories did not make sense: many pesticides would fit into more than one of these categories, others didn't seem fit into any of them, and many pesticides classified in the same category had dramatically different characteristics.

The EPA accepted these criticisms of its interim regulations but responded in a way that the industry did not expect: The EPA decided to abandon the attempt to define sub-categories of organic pesticides, and chose instead to apply a single pollution control regulation to *all* organic pesticides. The industry viewed this outcome as even worse than the original three-category scheme. The industry challenged the EPA on grounds of inadequate notice, arguing that collapsing the three organic pesticide subcategories and applying a single emissions control standard to all organic pesticide manufacturers was not a "logical outgrowth" of the agency's initial proposal. The First Circuit rejected the argument, and its analysis of the issue is worth quoting at length:

> [Petitioners complain] that EPA failed to comply with the requirements of the Administrative Procedure Act in that the final regulations were so different from the interim final regulations that the interims were not notice of "either the terms or substance of the proposed rule or a description of the subjects and issues involved." 5 U.S.C. § 553(b)(3)....
>
> In this case EPA issued interim final regulations and sought comments on them. Industry representatives, government agencies, and others submitted voluminous comments on many aspects of the

interim regulations. It is clear that EPA gave careful consideration to these comments. . . .

The procedural rules in § 553 were meant to ensure meaningful public participation in agency proceedings, not to be a straitjacket for agencies. An agency's promulgation of proposed rules is not a guarantee that those rules will be changed only in the ways the targets of the rules suggest. . . .

The essential inquiry is whether the commenters have had a fair opportunity to present their views on the contents of the final plan. We must be satisfied, in other words, that given a new opportunity to comment, commenters would not have their first occasion to offer new and different criticisms which the Agency might find convincing. . . . [W]here the Agency adds a new pollution control parameter without giving notice of intention to do so or receiving comments, there must be a remand to allow public comment. The question, however, always requires careful consideration on a case-by-case basis.

The . . . principal change complained of is the Agency's decision to merge the . . . three interim subcategories into a single Organic Pesticide Chemicals Manufacturing subcategory. So far as the record discloses, petitioners were not aware of this change until the final regulations were promulgated and the time for comment had expired. EPA consolidated the former subcategories because it "recognized certain ambiguities were present in its subcategorization based on chemical structure. Many pesticides contain more than one functional group . . . and do not fit the former subcategorization scheme." 43 Fed.Reg. 17777 (1978). Consequently, "and in response to industry comments", EPA undertook further research and found that "the quantities of pollutants in the effluents of those plants with the properly operated model technologies installed were similar regardless of the organic pesticide chemicals manufactured. The Agency . . . therefore concluded that the waste waters of all organic pesticide chemicals can be treated or controlled to the levels documented. . . . Thus, the final regulations do not differentiate among halogenated organic, organo-phosphorus, or organo-nitrogen pesticide chemicals." *Id.*

The industry comments were almost unanimous in condemning the three original subcategories both for being internally inconsistent and insufficiently differentiated from the other categories. Comments presented statistical tests of EPA's data, purporting to show that the subcategories were not distinguishable from each other. Comments also pointed to the inclusion of very different compounds within particular subcategories. The comments made a strong case against use of the interim subcategories, and EPA decided that the criticism was persuasive. It follows that EPA had to decide on an alternative unless it was to abandon regulation of the pesticide industry. Industry's preference was clear. They wanted EPA to expand the number of subcategories. They are now aggrieved because EPA accepted their criticism of the original subcategories but chose a different solution, collapsing rather than expanding them. Petitioners suggest that EPA's response took them entirely by surprise and that EPA had somehow indicated that the only issue for comments would be whether three subcategories were enough or there should be more.

Neither suggestion is grounds for remand. It should be clear to commenters when they criticize a regulatory scheme that if the agency accepts those criticisms, a new scheme will be substituted. The commenters cannot claim they had no notice to propose and discuss alternatives. And in fact they did so, suggesting a number of new approaches based on different ways to subcategorize the industry....

Another repeated call of the industry commenters was that the subcategories should be more equitably treated because the record did not support the significantly different guideline limits assigned to the different subcategories. They should have realized that these criticisms, if accepted, could be resolved, among other ways, by applying the same limits to all organic pesticides. Again, though EPA's solution was not the one for which industry argued, it was suggested by and, in part, a logical outgrowth of industry's comments. They cannot now complain because they misread the regulatory waters, incorrectly anticipated how EPA would react to their criticisms, and, consequently, submitted comments that left some things unsaid.

Not only do we think that petitioners had fair notice that consolidation of subcategories was an issue to comment upon, but we cannot think how their comments would have differed fundamentally if they had known what EPA would do. Though they would have had a different proposition against which to argue, their proposed solutions would, presumably, have been the same for the same reasons. They might have responded in greater volume or more vociferously, but they have not shown us that the content of their criticisms would have been different to the point that they would have stood a better chance of convincing the Agency to use more subcategories. In short, they had a fair opportunity to present their views on how the industry ought to be subcategorized. Their real complaint is that EPA rejected those views.

598 F.2d at 641–44 (footnotes and citation omitted).

Perhaps the most interesting feature of this discussion is the court's characterization of the purpose of the notice requirement. The court explains that the "essential inquiry," when evaluating a claim of inadequate notice, "is whether the commenters have had a fair opportunity to present their views on the contents of the final plan." More specifically, the reviewing court must focus on whether, if given a new opportunity to comment, the aggrieved commenters would "have their first occasion to offer new and different criticisms which the Agency might find convincing." In this case, the First Circuit concluded that even if one were to stipulate that the industry representatives did not foresee that the EPA might eliminate subcategories altogether, this is irrelevant under the above standard because one "cannot think how [the industry representatives'] comments would have differed fundamentally if they had known what EPA would do."

Is that right? If you represented the industry petitioners, aren't there at least two obvious ways in which your comments would have been different had you anticipated that the EPA might seriously consider eliminating subcategories and applying a uniform standard to all organic pesticides? First, the industry might have been much less aggressive in criticizing the tripartite scheme adopted by the interim regulations; indeed, the industry might have emphasized the benefits of that system, rather than focusing on the problems. Second, the industry might have devoted considerably more time and effort to pointing out the serious flaws in a system of uniform treatment for all organic pesticides. Isn't it a bit odd, then, for the court to suggest that it cannot imagine how the industry representatives' comments would have "differed fundamentally" if they had known what the EPA would do?

But perhaps these likely differences in the industry's comments are not relevant to the legal inquiry, given the purposes of the notice requirement. The claim that the industry might not have pointed out the flaws in the EPA's original three subcategories if the industry had foreseen the possibility of a one-category solution is not likely to attract a great deal of sympathy, since the claim boils down to an admission that the industry would have withheld relevant information and analysis from the agency. As for the industry's claim that it would have devoted more of its energies to an attack on a uniform standard (including an unfavorable comparison of such an approach to the admittedly flawed three-category scheme), the *BASF Wyandotte* court noted that although the industry representatives "would have had a different proposition against which to argue, their proposed solutions would, presumably, have been the same for the same reasons." 598 F.2d at 644.

Are those responses satisfactory? Perhaps they are if one conceives of the notice-and-comment process principally as a way for agencies to gather relevant information—though even then the industry may have a plausible claim that it would have advanced significant criticisms of the one-category solution if that option had been fully disclosed. But what if one conceives of the notice-and-comment process not simply as an efficient means for the agency to gather information, but as a quasi-adversarial process that gives potentially affected parties an opportunity to defend their interests in the administrative arena? Do cases like *BASF Wyandotte* require courts to make judgments about the ultimate purposes of APA notice-and-comment procedures?

## III.  Alternatives to Notice-and-Comment Rulemaking

As we have seen, judicial interpretation of the notice-and-comment procedures in § 553 has transformed this process into one that, while nominally "informal," is in fact quite elaborate and time-consuming. As we have further seen, many scholars and judges have hypothesized that this proceduralization—some would say over-proceduralization—has made notice-and-comment rulemaking less attractive to agencies as a means of making policy. This follows from a straightforward economic logic: As the cost of producing rules goes up, the quantity produced tends to go down, all else equal. Of course, this may be a good thing on balance, both because proceduralization may improve the quality of the rules that the agency does enact, and because additional procedural costs may curb an agency's tendency toward overzealousness. (So understood, the proceduralization of agency rulemaking may promote some of the same interests often attributed to bicameralism and presentment in the legislative context. *See* pp. 24–25, *supra*.) That said, greater proceduralization of the notice-and-comment process raises significant concerns.

Perhaps the most straightforward concern is that increasing the procedural costs of notice and comment may defeat the purposes for which Congress delegated rulemaking authority to agencies in the first place—namely, to create a flexible, efficient process for agencies to use in addressing complex social and economic problems. (*See* pp. 379–384, *supra*.) Another concern is that increasing the procedural costs of notice-and-comment rulemaking gives agencies a stronger incentive to find other, less costly ways to pursue their policy objectives. The strongest version of this hypothesis asserts that judicial strengthening of the procedural safeguards of notice-and-comment rulemaking has made things worse overall by channeling agencies into other forms of policymaking that have even fewer safeguards.

Whether or not one finds that strong version of the hypothesis convincing, it is undoubtedly true that agencies sometimes make policy decisions that look a lot like "rules" outside of the APA's rulemaking process. This is not necessarily illegitimate—as we will see, the APA expressly contemplates at least some circumstances in which agencies issue rules (or rule-like directives) without going through the notice-and-comment process laid out in § 553 (or the more formal process laid out in §§ 556 and 557). These exemptions serve important functions. In particular, they allow agencies to respond quickly and flexibly to new situations, and to fill in gaps or ambiguities in existing rules without having to incur the costs and delays of formally amending those rules. Nonetheless, the availability of these lower cost alternatives raises concerns that agencies will be tempted to rely too heavily on them, thereby circumventing the § 553 process. *See, e.g.*, James T. Hamilton & Christopher H. Schroeder, *Strategic Regulators and the Choice of Rulemaking Procedures: The Selection of Formal vs. Informal Rules in Regulating Hazardous Waste*, 57 Law & Contemp. Probs. 111, 120, 127–32, 139–48 (Spring 1994).

How should the law respond to this difficulty? How can courts distinguish between agency pronouncements that must be enacted pursuant to § 553's notice-and-comment process and those that an agency may promulgate in another form? The following materials consider this problem, focusing in particular on three ways that agencies may issue what look like "rules" without going through the rulemaking process. The first of these potential alternatives to rulemaking is administrative adjudication. When, and under what conditions, may agencies announce a new general principle in the context of issuing an order in a specific case? The second alternative to notice-and-comment rulemaking derives from a provision in the APA that expressly exempts from § 553 "general statements of [agency] policy," 5 U.S.C. § 553(b)(A), sometimes known as guidance documents. How do we distinguish an agency *rule* from an agency *policy statement*? Third, the APA also exempts so-called "interpretative rules" from notice-and-comment procedures. *Id.* This exemption implies a distinction between so-called *legislative rules*—which must go through notice and comment—and interpretive rules, which do not. How should courts draw that distinction? As you work through these materials, think about whether the doctrines that the courts have developed on these questions are effective in matching a given type of agency decision to the appropriate procedural vehicle, and the degree to which these doctrines seem well-grounded in the APA.

## A.  ADJUDICATION

Recall that the APA divides the universe of agency action into two basic categories: *rulemaking* and *adjudication*. Our focus in this book is principally on rulemaking, but much important agency activity takes the form of adjudication. Under a variety of statutory schemes, parties must apply to an agency for licenses or permits; the orders granting or denying such permits are issued pursuant to an administrative adjudication. Likewise, many agencies are responsible for allocating government benefits; an agency process for determining whether a particular applicant is eligible for a government benefit is also an adjudication for APA purposes. Furthermore, many agencies are authorized to enforce statutes and regulations by bringing civil enforcement actions that are heard in the first instance by an administrative tribunal and appealed up the administrative hierarchy prior to judicial review by an Article III court.

The usual image of "adjudication" involves the application of existing law to specific facts. But that picture does not fully capture what goes on in administrative adjudications any more than it fully captures what courts do. When courts adjudicate specific cases, they sometimes apply existing law or precedent to new sets of facts, but sometimes in the process of deciding particular cases judges will announce, refine, or elaborate general legal principles that not only resolve the case at hand, but will govern (or at least influence) the resolution of future cases that present similar issues. What is true of courts is also frequently true of agencies: In the process of adjudicating a specific case—deciding whether to grant this license or that benefit, whether to assess penalties against a certain regulated firm, and so forth—agencies sometimes announce what look like general principles, and these principles are often treated by the agency as precedents in future cases. *See, e.g.,* NLRB v. Curtin Matheson Scientific, Inc., 494 U.S. 775, 780–81 (1990); Atchison, T. & S.F. Ry. Co. v. Wichita Bd. of Trade, 412 U.S. 800, 807–08 (1973) (plurality); *see also* David L. Shapiro, *The Choice of*

*Rulemaking or Adjudication in the Development of Administrative Policy,* 78 HARV. L. REV. 921, 926 (1965).

The seminal case on agencies' ability to make new "rules" in the context of administrative adjudications is *SEC v. Chenery,* a pre-APA case. (Although the Supreme Court issued its *Chenery* decision in 1947, after the APA was enacted, the relevant conduct and governing law predated the APA.) *Chenery*'s approach has remained influential, and the analysis in the case now supplies the doctrinal framework under the APA for approaching the question whether, or under what conditions, an agency may announce a new policy decision in an adjudicative order rather than through a rulemaking.

The factual and procedural background of *Chenery* is a bit complicated. The case involved a 1935 statute called the Public Utility Holding Company Act (PUHCA), which mandated a change in the ownership structures of certain public utilities. (The pyramidal ownership structures of these utilities were thought to have contributed to their fragility, and ultimate collapse, in the Great Depression.) The PUHCA allowed existing utilities to submit reorganization plans to the Securities and Exchange Commission (SEC). Following an administrative adjudication, the SEC could issue an order approving, conditionally approving, or disapproving the proposed reorganization plan. The statute required that the SEC approve only those reorganization plans that were "fair and equitable." If the SEC disapproved a reorganization, and if the company was unable to develop an acceptable alternative plan, the SEC could impose its own reorganization plan on the company.

One of the public utility companies affected by the PUHCA was the Federal Water Service Corporation (Federal). Some of Federal's shareholders held "preferred" stock in the company, which meant they were supposed to have priority in receiving dividends, but preferred shares did not have voting power in the election of the corporation's directors. Other shareholders held "common" stock, which had voting power. Christopher Chenery and his associates (the "Chenery group") held a controlling block of the common stock, giving the Chenery group the power to select the directors and management of the corporation. The SEC rejected the first several reorganization plans submitted by Federal on the grounds that they did not sufficiently distribute shareholder voting power; the SEC insisted that any acceptable reorganization plan would have to convert the nonvoting preferred stock into voting common stock, in order to dilute the concentration of ownership.

In response, Federal submitted another reorganization plan that did what the SEC requested: Pursuant to that plan, preferred shares would be converted to common shares. This, however, meant that the Chenery group might no longer control the company. So, while the reorganization plan was pending, the Chenery group bought up enough of the preferred stock to retain control of the company even after the reorganization. The Chenery group was completely transparent about what it was doing, and it paid a market price for the shares that presumably reflected the expectation that these shares would have voting rights in the reorganized company. The SEC, however, again refused to approve the reorganization plan if the converted preferred shares bought up by the Chenery group were given the same voting rights as other converted preferred shares. Instead, the SEC amended the plan (over the Chenery group's objection), such that the Chenery group would have to surrender the preferred stock it had purchased, at cost plus any accumulated dividends. The SEC explained that its decision was based on an existing judge-made rule of equity jurisprudence, according to which fiduciaries of a corporation have a "duty of fair dealing" not to trade in the corporation's securities while a reorganization plan is pending with the SEC.

In SEC v. Chenery Corp., 318 U.S. 80 (1943) ("*Chenery I*"), the Supreme Court, in an opinion by Justice Frankfurter, rejected the SEC's position that any such fiduciary duty had been recognized by the courts. *Id.* at 85–89. In its brief to the Court, the SEC had argued in the alternative that even if there was no existing judge-made equitable principle that would prohibit what the Chenery group had done, the Court should nonetheless uphold the SEC's order on the grounds that approving this reorganization plan would not be "fair and equitable" within the meaning of the PUHCA. The Court refused to consider this argument. Justice Frankfurter's majority opinion acknowledged that "[d]etermination of what is 'fair and equitable' calls for the application of ethical standards to particular sets of facts," and that "[i]n evolving standards of fairness and equity, the Commission is not bound by settled judicial precedents." *Id.* at 89. But, the Court went on, the SEC's order rejecting Federal's proposed reorganization plan had relied *only* on the assertion that existing *judicial* doctrine would have prohibited Chenery's behavior, and the SEC's order therefore had to stand or fall on that rationale:

> Since the Commission professed to decide the case before it according to settled judicial doctrines, its action must be judged by the standards which the Commission itself invoked. And judged by those standards, i.e., those which would be enforced by a court of equity, we must conclude that the Commission was in error in deeming its action controlled by established judicial principles.

*Id.* at 89–90.

*Chenery I* thus established an important principle of administrative law, separate and apart from the issues related to adjudication and rulemaking that are our main focus in this section: A court reviewing an agency action will consider *only* the basis for that action proffered by the agency in the rule or order at issue; agencies may not offer additional *post hoc* justifications during litigation. As *Chenery I* explained:

> Judged ... as a determination based upon judge-made rules of equity, the Commission's order cannot be upheld. Its action must be measured by what the Commission did, not by what it might have done. It is not for us to determine independently what is 'detrimental to the public interest or the interest of investors or consumers' or 'fair and equitable' within the meaning of §§ 7 and 11 of the Public Utility

Holding Company Act of 1935. The Commission's action cannot be upheld merely because findings might have been made and considerations disclosed which would justify its order as an appropriate safeguard for the interests protected by the Act. There must be such a responsible finding. . . . There is no such finding here.

. . . [C]ourts cannot exercise their duty of review unless they are advised of the considerations underlying the action under review. . . . [T]he orderly functioning of the process of review requires that the grounds upon which the administrative agency acted by clearly disclosed and adequately sustained. . . . We are not suggesting that the Commission must justify its exercise of administrative discretion in any particular manner or with artistic refinement. We are not sticking in the bark of words. We merely hold that an administrative order cannot be upheld unless the grounds upon which the agency acted in exercising its powers were those upon which its action can be sustained.

*Id.* at 93–95.

Perhaps unsurprisingly, after its defeat in *Chenery I*, the SEC re-issued essentially the same order that the Supreme Court had vacated. This time, instead of arguing that its order merely applied an existing judge-made equitable principle, the SEC formally adopted the alternative justification the Supreme Court had refused to consider in *Chenery I*: that independent of any pre-existing judge-made principles, a prohibition on fiduciaries trading in their corporation's shares during a reorganization would best effectuate the purposes of the PUHCA. Having announced that general principle, the SEC proceeded to deny Federal's proposed reorganization plan. The Chenery group again challenged the order, and the case again made its way up to the Supreme Court. The Court's decision in this second case (*Chenery II*) addressed the issue of when an agency may announce what looks like a rule in an adjudication rather than a rulemaking.

---

## Securities and Exchange Commission v. Chenery Corporation

Supreme Court of the United States
332 U.S. 194 (1947)

■ MR. JUSTICE MURPHY delivered the opinion of the Court.

This case is here for the second time. In S.E.C. v. Chenery Corporation, 318 U.S. 80, we held that an order of the Securities and Exchange Commission could not be sustained on the grounds upon which that agency acted. We therefore directed that the case be remanded to the Commission for such further proceedings as might be appropriate. On remand, the Commission reexamined the problem, recast its rationale and reached the same result. The issue now is whether the Commission's action is proper in light of the principles established in our prior decision. . . .

The Commission had been dealing with the reorganization of the Federal Water Service Corporation (Federal), a holding company registered under the Public Utility Holding Company Act of 1935, 49 Stat. 803. During the period when successive reorganization plans proposed by the management were before the Commission, the officers, directors and controlling stockholders of Federal purchased a substantial amount of Federal's preferred stock on the over-the-counter market. Under the fourth reorganization plan, this preferred stock was to be converted into common stock of a new corporation; on the basis of the purchases of preferred stock, the management would have received more than 10% of this new common stock. It was frankly admitted that the management's purpose in buying the preferred stock was to protect its interest in the new company. It was also plain that there was no fraud or lack of disclosure in making these purchases.

But the Commission would not approve the fourth plan so long as the preferred stock purchased by the management was to be treated on a parity with the other preferred stock. It felt that the officers and directors of a holding company in process of reorganization under the Act were fiduciaries and were under a duty not to trade in the securities of that company during the reorganization period. And so the plan was amended to provide that the preferred stock acquired by the management, unlike that held by others, was not to be converted into the new common stock; instead, it was to be surrendered at cost plus dividends accumulated since the purchase dates. As amended, the plan was approved by the Commission over the management's objections.

The Court interpreted the Commission's order approving this amended plan as grounded solely upon judicial authority. The Commission appeared to have treated the preferred stock acquired by the management in accordance with what it thought were standards theretofore recognized by courts. If it intended to create new standards growing out of its experience in effectuating the legislative policy, it failed to express itself with sufficient clarity and precision to be so understood. Hence the order was judged by the only standards clearly invoked by the Commission. On that basis, the order could not stand...

The opinion further noted that neither Congress nor the Commission had promulgated any general rule proscribing such action as the purchase of preferred stock by Federal's management....

After the case was remanded to the Commission, ... [t]he Commission denied the application [of Federal's management to amend the reorganization plan to issue common stock in the reorganized company to Federal's management] in an order issued on February 7, 1945. That order was reversed by the Court of Appeals, which felt that our prior decision precluded such action by the Commission.

The latest order of the Commission definitely avoids the fatal error of relying on judicial precedents which do not sustain it. This time, after a thorough reexamination of the problem in light of the purposes and standards of the Holding Company Act, the Commission has concluded that the proposed transaction is inconsistent with the standards of §§ 7 and 11 of the Act. It has drawn heavily upon its accumulated experience in dealing with utility reorganizations. And it has expressed its reasons with a clarity and thoroughness that admit of no doubt as to the underlying basis of its order.

The argument is pressed upon us, however, that the Commission was foreclosed from taking such a step following our prior decision. It is said that, in the absence of findings of conscious wrongdoing on the part of Federal's management, the Commission could not determine by an order in this particular case that it was inconsistent with the statutory standards to permit Federal's management to realize a profit through the reorganization purchases.... Under this view, the Commission would be free only to promulgate a general rule outlawing such profits in future utility reorganizations; but such a rule would have to be prospective in nature and have no retroactive effect upon the instant situation.

We reject this contention, for it grows out of a misapprehension of our prior decision and of the Commission's statutory duties. We held no more and no less than that the Commission's first order was unsupportable for the reasons supplied by that agency. But when the case left this Court, the problem whether Federal's management should be treated equally with other preferred stockholders still lacked a final and complete answer. It was clear that the Commission could not give a negative answer by resort to prior judicial declarations. And it was also clear that the Commission was not bound by settled judicial precedents in a situation of this nature. Still unsettled, however, was the answer the Commission might give were it to bring to bear on the facts the proper administrative and statutory considerations, a function which belongs exclusively to the Commission in the first instance. The administrative process had taken an erroneous rather than a final turn. Hence we carefully refrained from expressing any views as to the propriety of an order rooted in the proper and relevant considerations....

When the case was directed to be remanded to the Commission for such further proceedings as might be appropriate, it was with the thought that the Commission would give full effect to its duties in harmony with the views we had expressed.... After the remand was made, therefore, the Commission was bound to deal with the problem afresh, performing the function delegated to it by Congress. It was again charged with the duty of measuring the proposed treatment of the management's preferred stock holdings by relevant and proper standards. Only in that way could the legislative policies embodied in the Act be effectuated.

The absence of a general rule or regulation governing management trading during reorganization did not affect the Commission's duties in relation to the particular proposal before it. The Commission was asked to grant or deny effectiveness to a proposed amendment to Federal's reorganization plan whereby the management would be accorded parity treatment on its holdings. It could do that only in the form of an order, entered after a due consideration of the particular facts in light of the relevant and proper standards. That was true regardless of whether those standards previously had been spelled out in a general rule or regulation. Indeed, if the Commission rightly felt that the proposed amendment was inconsistent with those standards, an order giving effect to the amendment merely because there was no general rule or regulation covering the matter would be unjustified.

It is true that our prior decision explicitly recognized the possibility that the Commission might have promulgated a general rule dealing with this problem under its statutory rule-making powers, in which case the issue for our consideration would have been entirely different from that which did confront us. But we did not mean to imply thereby that the failure of the Commission to anticipate this problem and to promulgate a general rule withdrew all power from that agency to perform its statutory duty in this case. To hold that the Commission had no alternative in this proceeding but to approve the proposed transaction, while formulating any general rules it might desire for use in future cases of this nature, would be to stultify the administrative process. That we refuse to do.

Since the Commission, unlike a court, does have the ability to make new law prospectively through the exercise of its rule-making powers, it has less reason to rely upon *ad hoc* adjudication to formulate new standards of conduct within the framework of the Holding Company Act. The function of filling in the interstices of the Act should be performed, as much as possible, through this quasi-legislative promulgation of rules to be applied in the future. But any rigid requirement to that effect would make the administrative process inflexible and incapable of dealing with many of the specialized problems which arise. See Report of the Attorney General's Committee on Administrative Procedure in Government Agencies, S. Doc. No. 8, 77th Cong., 1st Sess., p. 29. Not every principle essential to the effective administration of a statute can or should be cast immediately into the mold of a general rule. Some principles must await their own development, while others must be adjusted to meet particular, unforeseeable situations. In performing its important functions in these respects, therefore, an administrative agency must be equipped to act either by general rule or by individual order. To insist upon one form of action to the exclusion of the other is to exalt form over necessity.

In other words, problems may arise in a case which the administrative agency could not reasonably foresee, problems which must be solved despite the absence of a relevant general rule. Or the agency may not have had sufficient experience with a particular problem to warrant rigidifying its tentative judgment into a hard and fast rule. Or the problem may be so specialized and varying in nature as to be impossible of capture within the boundaries of a general rule. In those situations, the agency must retain power to deal with the problems on a case-to-case basis if the administrative process is to be effective. There is thus a very definite place for the case-by-case evolution of statutory standards. And the choice made between proceeding by general rule or by individual, ad hoc litigation is one that lies primarily in the informed discretion of the administrative agency....

Hence we refuse to say that the Commission, which had not previously been confronted with the problem of management trading during reorganization, was forbidden from utilizing this particular proceeding for announcing and applying a new standard of conduct.... That such action might have a retroactive effect was not necessarily fatal to its validity. Every case of first impression has a retroactive effect, whether the new principle is announced by a court or by an administrative agency. But such retroactivity must be balanced against the mischief of producing a result which is contrary to a statutory design or to legal and equitable principles. If that mischief is greater than the ill effect of the retroactive application of a new standard, it is not the type of retroactivity which is condemned by law....

And so in this case, the fact that the Commission's order might retroactively prevent Federal's management from securing the profits and control which were the objects of the preferred stock purchases may well be outweighed by the dangers inherent in such purchases from the statutory standpoint. If that is true, the argument of retroactivity becomes nothing more than a claim that the Commission lacks power to enforce the standards of the Act in this proceeding. Such a claim deserves rejection.

The problem in this case thus resolves itself into a determination of whether the Commission's action in denying effectiveness to the proposed amendment to the Federal reorganization plan can be justified on the basis upon which it clearly rests. As we have noted, the Commission avoided placing its sole reliance on inapplicable judicial precedents. Rather it has derived its conclusions from the particular facts in the case, its general experience in reorganization matters and its informed view of statutory requirements. It is those matters which are the guide for our review.

The Commission concluded that it could not find that the reorganization plan, if amended as proposed, would be "fair and equitable to the persons affected thereby" within the meaning of § 11(e) of the Act, under which the reorganization was taking place. Its view was that the amended plan would involve the issuance of securities on terms "detrimental to the public interest or the interest of investors" contrary to §§ 7(d)(6) and 7(e), and would result in an "unfair or inequitable distribution of voting power" among the Federal security holders within the meaning of § 7(e). It was led to this result "not by proof that the interveners [Federal's management] committed acts of conscious wrongdoing but by the character of the conflicting interests created by the interveners' program of stock purchases carried out while plans for reorganization were under consideration."

The Commission noted that Federal's management controlled a large multi-state utility system and that its influence permeated down to the lowest tier of operating companies. The financial, operational and accounting policies of the parent and its subsidiaries were therefore under the management's strict control. The broad range of business judgments vested in Federal's management multiplied opportunities for affecting the market price of Federal's outstanding securities and made the exercise of judgment on any matter a subject of greatest significance to investors. Added to these normal managerial powers, the Commission pointed out that a holding company management obtains special powers in the course of a voluntary reorganization under § 11(e) of the Holding Company Act. The management represents the stockholders in such a reorganization, initiates the proceeding, draws up and files the plan, and can file amendments thereto at any time. These additional powers may introduce conflicts between the management's normal interests and its responsibilities to the various classes of stockholders which it represents in the reorganization. Moreover, because of its representative status, the management has special opportunities to obtain advance information of the attitude of the Commission.

Drawing upon its experience, the Commission indicated that all these normal and special powers of the holding company management during the course of a § 11(e) reorganization placed in the management's command "a formidable battery of devices that would enable it, if it should choose to use them selfishly, to affect in material degree the ultimate allocation of new securities among the various existing classes, to influence the market for its own gain and to manipulate or obstruct the reorganization required by the mandate of the statute." In that setting, the Commission felt that a management program of stock purchase would give rise to the temptation and the opportunity to shape the reorganization proceeding so as to encourage public selling on the market at low prices. No management could engage in such a program without raising serious questions as to whether its personal interests had not opposed its duties "to exercise disinterested judgment in matters pertaining to subsidiaries' accounting, budgetary and dividend policies, to present publicly an unprejudiced financial picture of the enterprise, and to effectuate a fair and feasible plan expeditiously."

The Commission further felt that its answer should be the same even where proof of intentional wrongdoing on the management's part is lacking. Assuming a conflict of interests, the Commission thought that the absence of actual misconduct is immaterial; injury to the public investors and to the corporation may result just as readily.... Moreover, the Commission was of the view that the delays and the difficulties involved in probing the mental processes and personal integrity of corporate officials do not warrant any distinction on the basis of evil intent, the plain fact being "that an absence of unfairness or detriment in cases of this sort would be practically impossible to establish by proof."

Turning to the facts in this case, the Commission noted the salient fact that the primary object of Federal's management in buying the preferred stock was admittedly to obtain the voting power that was accruing to that stock through the reorganization and to profit from the investment therein.... The Commission admitted that the good faith and personal integrity of this management were not in question; but as to the management's justification of its motives, the Commission concluded that it was merely trying to "deny that they made selfish use of their powers during the period when their conflict of interest, vis-à-vis public investors was in existence owing to their purchase program." Federal's management had thus placed itself in a position where it was "peculiarly susceptible to temptation to conduct the reorganization for personal gain rather than the public good" and where its desire to make advantageous purchases of stock could have an important influence, even though subconsciously, upon many of the decisions to be made in the course of the reorganization. Accordingly, the Commission felt that all of its general considerations of the problem were applicable to this case.

The scope of our review of an administrative order wherein a new principle is announced and applied is no different from that which pertains to ordinary administrative action. The wisdom of the principle adopted is none of our concern.... Our duty is at an end when it becomes evident that the Commission's action is based upon substantial evidence and is consistent with the authority granted by Congress....

We are unable to say in this case that the Commission erred in reaching the result it did. The facts being undisputed, we are free to disturb the Commission's conclusion only if it lacks any rational and statutory foundation. In that connection, the Commission has made a thorough examination of the problem, utilizing statutory standards and its own accumulated experience with reorganization matters. In essence, it has made what we indicated in our prior opinion would be an informed, expert judgment on the problem....

... The "fair and equitable" rule of § 11(e) and the standard of what is "detrimental to the public interest or the interest of investors or consumers" under § 7(d)(6) and § 7(e) were inserted by the framers of the Act in order that the Commission might have broad powers to protect the various interests at stake. The application of those criteria, whether in the form of a particular order or a general regulation, necessarily requires the use of informal discretion by the Commission. The very breadth of the statutory language precludes a reversal of the Commission's judgment save where it has plainly abused its discretion in these matters.... Such an abuse is not present in this case.

The purchase by a holding company management of that company's securities during the course of a reorganization may well be thought to be so fraught with danger as to warrant a denial of the benefits and profits accruing to the management. The possibility that such a stock purchase program will result in detriment to the public investors is not a fanciful one. The influence that program may have upon the important decisions to be made by the management during reorganization is not inconsequential. Since the officers and directors occupy fiduciary positions during this period, their actions are to be held to a higher standard than that imposed upon the general investing public. There is thus a reasonable basis for a value judgment that the benefits and profits accruing to the management from the stock purchases should be prohibited, regardless of the good faith involved. And it is a judgment that can justifiably be reached in terms of fairness and equitableness, to the end that the interests of the public, the investors and the consumers might be protected. But it is a judgment based upon public policy, a judgment which Congress has indicated is of the type for the Commission to make.

The Commission's conclusion here rests squarely in that area where administrative judgments are entitled to the greatest amount of weight by appellate courts. It is the product of administrative experience, appreciation of the complexities of the problem, realization of the statutory policies, and responsible treatment of the uncontested facts. It is the type of judgment which administrative agencies are best equipped to make and which justifies the use of the administrative process.... Whether we agree or disagree with the result reached, it is an allowable judgment which we cannot disturb.

Reversed.

■ Mr. Justice Burton concurs in the result.

■ The Chief Justice and Mr. Justice Douglas took no part in the consideration or decision of these cases.

■ Mr. Justice Jackson, dissenting.

The Court by this present decision sustains the identical administrative order which only recently it held invalid.... As the Court correctly notes, the Commission has only "recast its rationale and reached the same result." There being no change in the order, no additional evidence in the record and no amendment of relevant legislation, it is clear that there has been a shift in attitude between that of the controlling membership of the Court when the case was first here and that of those who have the power of decision on this second review.

I feel constrained to disagree with the reasoning offered to rationalize this shift. It makes judicial review of administrative orders a hopeless formality for the litigant, even where granted to him by Congress. It reduces the judicial process in such cases to a mere feint. While the opinion does not have the adherence of a majority of the full Court, if its pronouncements should become governing principles they would, in practice, put most administrative orders over and above the law.

## I.

The essential facts are few and are not in dispute. This corporation filed with the Securities and Exchange Commission a voluntary plan of reorganization. While the reorganization proceedings were pending sixteen officers and directors bought on the open market about 7½% of the corporation's preferred stock. Both the Commission and the Court admit that these purchases were not forbidden by any law, judicial precedent, regulation or rule of the Commission. Nevertheless, the Commission has ordered these individuals to surrender their shares to the corporation at cost, plus 4% interest, and the Court now approves that order.

It is helpful, before considering whether this order is authorized by law, to reflect on what it is and what it is not. It is not conceivably a discharge of the Commission's duty to determine whether a proposed plan of reorganization would be "fair and equitable." It has nothing to do with the corporate structure, or the classes and amounts of stock, or voting rights or dividend preferences. It does not remotely affect the impersonal financial or legal factors of the plan. It is a personal deprivation denying particular persons the right to continue to own their stock and to exercise its privileges. Other persons who bought at the same time and price in the open market would be allowed to keep and convert their stock. Thus, the order is in no sense an exercise of the function of control over the terms and relations of the corporate securities. . . .

II.

The reversal of the position of this Court is due to a fundamental change in prevailing philosophy. The basic assumption of the earlier opinion as therein stated was, *"But before transactions otherwise legal can be outlawed or denied their usual business consequences, they must fall under the ban of some standards of conduct prescribed by an agency of government authorized to prescribe such standards."* Securities and Exchange Commission v. Chenery Corp., 318 U.S. 80, 92, 93. The basic assumption of the present opinion is stated thus: *"The absence of a general rule or regulation governing management trading during reorganization did not affect the Commission's duties in relation to the particular proposal before it."* This puts in juxtaposition the two conflicting philosophies which produce opposite results in the same case and on the same facts. The difference between the first and the latest decision of the Court is thus simply the difference between holding that administrative orders must have a basis in law and a holding that absence of a legal basis is no ground on which courts may annul them.

As there admittedly is no law or regulation to support this order we peruse the Court's opinion diligently to find on what grounds it is now held that the Court of Appeals . . . was required to stamp this order with its approval. We find but one. That is the principle of judicial deference to administrative experience. . . .

What are we to make of this reiterated deference to "administrative experience" when in another context the Court says, "Hence we refuse to say that the Commission, *which had not previously been confronted with the problem of management trading during reorganization*, was forbidden from utilizing this particular proceeding for announcing and applying *a new standard of conduct."*? (Emphasis supplied.)

The Court's reasoning adds up to this: The Commission must be sustained because of its accumulated experience in solving a problem with which it had never before been confronted!

Of course, thus to uphold the Commission by professing to find that it has enunciated a "new standard of conduct," brings the Court squarely against the invalidity of retroactive law-making. But the Court does not falter. "That such action might have a retroactive effect was not necessarily fatal to its validity." "But such retroactivity must be balanced against the mischief of producing a result which is contrary to a statutory design or to legal and equitable principles." Of course, if what these parties did really was condemned by "statutory design" or "legal and equitable principles," it could be stopped without resort to a new rule and there would be no retroactivity to condone. But if it had been the Court's view that some law already prohibited the purchases, it would hardly have been necessary three sentences earlier to hold that the Commission was not prohibited "from utilizing this particular proceeding for announcing and applying a *new standard of conduct*." (Emphasis supplied.)

I give up. Now I realize fully what Mark Twain meant when he said, "The more you explain it, the more I don't understand it."

### III.

. . . [A]dministrative experience is of weight in judicial review only to this point—it is a persuasive reason for deference to the Commission in the exercise of its discretionary powers under and within the law. It cannot be invoked to support action outside of the law. And what action is, and what is not, within the law must be determined by courts, when authorized to review, no matter how much deference is due to the agency's fact finding. . . .

Even if the Commission had, as the Court says, utilized this case to announce a new legal standard of conduct, there would be hurdles to be cleared, but we need not dwell on them now. Because to promulgate a general rule of law, either by regulation or by case law, is something the Commission expressly declined to do. It did not previously promulgate, and it does not by this order profess to promulgate, any rule or regulation to prohibit such purchases absolutely or under stated conditions. On the other hand, its position is that no such rule or standard would be fair and equitable in all cases.

### IV.

Whether, as matter of policy, corporate managers during reorganization should be prohibited from buying or selling its stock, is not a question for us to decide. But it is for us to decide whether, so long as no law or regulation prohibits them from buying, their purchases may be forfeited, or not, in the discretion of the Commission. If such a power exists in words of the statute or in their implication, it would be possible to point it out and thus end the case. Instead, the Court admits that there was no law prohibiting these purchases when they were made, or at any time thereafter. And, except for this decision, there is none now.

The truth is that in this decision the Court approves the Commission's assertion of power to govern the matter *without* law, power to force surrender of stock so purchased whenever it will, and power also to overlook such acquisitions if it so chooses. The reasons which will lead it to take one course as against the other remain locked in its own breast, and it has not and apparently does not intend to commit them to any rule or regulation. This administrative authoritarianism, this power to decide without law, is what the Court seems to approve in so many words: "The absence of a general rule or regulation governing management trading during reorganization did not affect the Commission's duties. . . ." This seems to me to undervalue and to belittle the place of law, even in the system of administrative justice. It calls to mind Mr. Justice Cardozo's statement that "Law as a guide to conduct is reduced to the level of mere futility if it is unknown and unknowable."[4]

### V.

The Court's averment concerning this order that "It is the type of judgment which administrative agencies are best equipped to make and which justifies the use of the administrative process," is the first instance in which the administrative process is sustained by reliance on that disregard of law which enemies of the process have always alleged to be its principal evil. It is the first encouragement this Court has given to conscious lawlessness as a permissible rule of administrative action. This decision is an ominous one to those who believe that men should be governed by laws that they may ascertain and abide by, and which will guide the action of those in authority as well as of those who are subject to authority.

I have long urged, and still believe, that the administrative process deserves fostering in our system as an expeditious and nontechnical method of *applying law* in specialized fields. I can not agree that it be used, and I think its continued effectiveness is endangered when it is used, as a method of *dispensing with law* in those fields.

■ MR. JUSTICE FRANKFURTER joins in this opinion.

---

*1. The Consistency of* **Chenery II** *with* **Chenery** I—In *Chenery I*, the Supreme Court struck down an SEC order disapproving Federal's proposed reorganization plan and substituting an amended plan. In *Chenery II*, the Supreme Court upheld an order with exactly the same effect. Are these two decisions consistent? In one important sense, they are perfectly consistent. Justice Frankfurter's *Chenery I* opinion was quite clear that it invalidated the SEC's order only because the legal basis that the SEC had offered was flawed. *Chenery I* explicitly left the door open for the kind of alternative justification that the SEC subsequently offered, and that was upheld as legitimate in *Chenery II*. Then again, does it seem significant to you that of the five Justices who participated in both *Chenery I* and *Chenery II* (Justices Frankfurter, Jackson, Black, Murphy, and Reed), not one was in the majority in both cases? (Justice Black, joined by Justices Murphy and Reed, had dissented in *Chenery I*, while Justice Jackson had joined Justice Frankfurter's majority opinion in that case.)

*2. The Legitimacy of Policymaking through Adjudication—Chenery I* had suggested that the SEC could use its rulemaking power to promulgate a new general standard of conduct governing this sort of situation. *Chenery II* reiterated this preference for rulemaking, asserting that "[t]he function of filling in the interstices of the Act should be performed, as much as possible, through this quasi-legislative promulgation of rules to be applied in the future." Yet the Court seemed unwilling to

---

**4.** *The Growth of the Law*, p. 3.

back up that exhortation with any substantial legal obligation. Was it right not to do so? Let us consider some of the reasons the Court offered for its conclusion that the SEC could announce in an adjudication the principle that management may not trade in its own firm's securities during a reorganization.

The Court seemed most concerned with preserving agencies' flexibility to address new, unforeseen problems as they arise. Justice Murphy's majority opinion frets that any "rigid requirement" that the SEC flesh out the details of the Act's meaning *only* through the promulgation of general rules would "stultify the administrative process," rendering it "inflexible and incapable of dealing with many of the specialized problems which arise." The Court further elaborated that sometimes it is simply not feasible for an agency to formulate rules in advance given the great variety of situations the agency may confront. A related but somewhat distinct idea is that a gradual, case-by-case method of developing rules—similar to the traditional common law process—might actually lead to better rules, because "[n]ot every principle essential to the effective administration of a statute can or should be cast immediately into the mold of a general rule. Some principles must await their own development, while others must be adjusted to meet particular, unforeseeable situations." Considerations of this sort may be especially salient in contexts, like securities regulation, where sophisticated parties have the incentive and ability to game the system, finding and exploiting any loopholes in the existing rules.

To Justice Jackson, however, this is a recipe for "administrative authoritarianism." In his view, the majority's *Chenery II* opinion gave agencies license to make up the rules as they go along—governing without law. Justice Jackson's rhetoric was certainly impassioned, but was he right? While Justice Jackson insisted that the SEC had created and applied a new standard of conduct, Justice Murphy's majority opinion asserted that the SEC was merely applying an existing statutory requirement (that reorganization plans be "fair and equitable") to new and unforeseen circumstances. This disagreement may seem trivial or semantic, as both Justice Murphy and Justice Jackson seemed to be in general agreement about what happened: The SEC asserted, correctly, that under the statute it could approve a reorganization plan only if that plan was "fair and equitable," and the SEC further asserted—for the first time in any binding agency statement—that a reorganization plan would not be "fair and equitable" if it allowed corporate insiders to derive benefit from trades in the corporation's securities while the reorganization proposal was pending. But if the SEC's order merely filled in a detail that was already implicit in the existing statutory command, then Justice Jackson's claim that the Commission was acting lawlessly loses much of its force. After all, as we have seen over and over again, no legal command can fully anticipate every circumstance. On the other hand, does Justice Murphy's assertion that the SEC's order was merely an "application of [the statutory] criteria" feel a bit forced given the seemingly loose connection between the general statutory standard ("fair and equitable") and the particular mid-level rule of conduct applied by the SEC (no trading by corporate insiders during a pending reorganization)? And isn't Justice Jackson right that the majority opinion seems somewhat inconsistent on this point, sometimes characterizing the SEC's order as an application of existing statutory standards, but at other points frankly characterizing the SEC order as "announcing and applying a new standard of conduct"? Which is the right way to characterize the SEC's action for purposes of deciding whether the SEC was obligated to promulgate this standard of conduct in a rule before relying on it in an adjudication?

Another way to think about this is to ask how the SEC could have satisfied Justice Jackson's demand that it announce the applicable policy in advance through rulemaking. Presumably, it would not have sufficed for the agency to have adopted a rule stating that "management trading in securities during reorganization must be fair and equitable." What if the agency had adopted a rule that stated that "management cannot trade during reorganizations in ways that create a conflict of interest"? Would that be specific enough to satisfy the "advance rulemaking" requirement that Justice Jackson urged upon the Court? Since any rule would leave some ambiguity, and consequently some discretion for the agency adjudicator, any requirement of advance rulemaking would presumably impel the Court to determine not only whether a rule had been made, but whether the rule articulated the relevant policy with *sufficient* clarity or specificity. Would the inquiry be whether the agency, through rulemaking, sufficiently defined and constrained its own discretion as adjudicator? Would such a requirement be any more manageable than the seemingly analogous intelligible principle test that the Court has found unadministrable in the nondelegation context? *See* John F. Manning, *Nonlegislative Rules*, 72 GEO. WASH. L. REV. 893, 910 (2004).

Furthermore, what of the fact that the sort of case-by-case "lawmaking" that *Chenery II* permits for agencies is characteristic of much judicial decision-making—most obviously in the context of the common law, but also in cases involving statutory and constitutional interpretation? If it is "administrative authoritarianism" for the SEC, in administrative adjudications, to announce and apply more specific rules of conduct in order to implement a general statutory requirement that reorganization plans be "fair and equitable," is it also "judicial authoritarianism" for courts, in individual lawsuits alleging anti-competitive practices to announce and apply more specific rules of conduct in order to implement the general statutory prohibition in the antitrust laws on contracts, combinations, or conspiracies in restraint of trade? *See* William F. Baxter, *Separation of Powers, Prosecutorial Discretion, and the "Common Law" Nature of Antitrust Law*, 60 TEX. L. REV. 661, 662–73 (1982) (asserting that the open-ended antitrust statutes in effect delegate to the courts the power to develop more specific antitrust rules through a common law process). Justice Jackson might reply by noting two critical differences between courts and agencies. First, most agencies, unlike courts, have rulemaking authority in addition to adjudicative authority, and this authority entails an obligation—which courts do not have—to separate more sharply the promulgation of general principles from the application of those principles in particular cases. Second, agencies might be thought to pose a greater threat than do courts to the separation of powers, given their resources and their location in the executive branch; it follows that it is more important to constrain agencies by limiting their flexibility and imposing strict procedural safeguards. Do you find these distinctions compelling?

Finally, is it relevant to this debate that earlier in the twentieth century, both before and after the passage of the APA, adjudication was the policy-making method of choice for many agencies? *See* Richard J. Pierce, Jr., *Rulemaking and the Administrative Procedure Act*, 32 TULSA L.J. 185, 187 (1996); Reuel E. Schiller, *Rulemaking's Promise: Administrative Law and Legal Culture in the 1960s and 1970s*, 53 ADMIN. L. REV. 1139, 1144–47 (2001). Can we draw any inferences from this fact about the intent of the Congress that enacted the APA? Even if so, does this intent matter?

**3. Rulemaking Procedures and the Circumvention Concern—** Might we be concerned that permitting agencies to make policy in adjudicative settings will facilitate circumvention of the procedural safeguards associated with rulemaking? It is often argued that procedural safeguards are necessary to legitimate the exercise of quasi-legislative power by agencies. But formal adjudications are *also* heavily proceduralized—in some ways more so than rulemakings. Given that fact, why might one be concerned that agencies could use formal administrative adjudication to circumvent notice-and-comment rulemaking procedures? From the agency's perspective, wouldn't it be out of the frying pan, into the fire?

Then again, maybe there *are* important differences between rulemaking and adjudicative procedures that make the latter an inadequate substitute for the former, at least when general policy issues are at stake. First, although formal adjudications involve substantial procedural constraints, those constraints are designed to further the interest in assuring the correct application of law to facts; they are arguably not well-suited for ensuring good general policy decisions. *See, e.g.*, Colin S. Diver, *Policymaking Paradigms in Administrative Law*, 95 HARV. L. REV. 393, 401 (1981); Richard A. Posner, *The Rise and Fall of Administrative Law*, 72 CHI.-KENT L. REV. 953, 962 (1997). More specifically, although an agency conducting an adjudication may at times invite the participation of a broad range of interested parties, *see* David L. Shapiro, *The Choice of Rulemaking or Adjudication in the Development of Administrative Policy*, 78 HARV. L. REV. 921, 931 (1965), notice-and-comment rulemaking procedures are generally better designed to elicit input from a broad range of constituencies, and to encourage the agency to view its proposed rule from a more general, holistic perspective. *See, e.g.*, Alan B. Morrison, *The Administrative Procedure Act: A Living and Responsive Law*, 72 VA. L. REV. 253, 255 (1986). Additionally, the general policy considerations at stake may be more transparent to Congress and affected interest groups when they are ventilated in a rulemaking. Adjudication, by contrast, may enable agencies to make general policy decisions under the political radar. *See, e.g.*, KENNETH CULP DAVIS, DISCRETIONARY JUSTICE: A PRELIMINARY INQUIRY 66–67 (1969).

Second, if an agency must conduct a formal adjudication anyway—if it has to rule on a reorganization plan, for example—then it's not really true that the procedural constraints on agencies are the same whether the agency makes a rule in an adjudication or in a rulemaking. If the agency opts for the former, then it does not have to comply with any procedural requirements over and above what it was already using. If rulemaking were obligatory, however, an agency that wanted to create a new rule to apply in a particular case would have to suspend the adjudication and initiate a separate rulemaking process. The majority in *Chenery II* recognized this fact and viewed it as a bad thing: Such a requirement, Justice Murphy warned, would "stultify" the administrative process. But if one believes that extra procedural safeguards are particularly important when agencies exercise quasi-legislative powers to make general rules, then perhaps these additional procedural hurdles are desirable. How should the Court in *Chenery II* have gone about investigating these competing concerns? Did it address them adequately?

**4. *Retroactivity*—**Another concern about this case is the fact that the SEC applied its new rule (or, if you prefer, its newly-announced elaboration of requirements immanent in the PUHCA) to Federal's proposed reorganization plan, even though the Chenery group would have had no way of anticipating that the SEC would impose such a requirement. Indeed, it is likely that Mr. Chenery and his associates were advised by counsel that their activities were perfectly lawful and would pose no obstacle to the approval of the reorganization plan, in light of the fact that—as the Supreme Court subsequently confirmed in *Chenery I*—prevailing understandings of managers' and directors' fiduciary duties did not proscribe the Chenery group's open-market purchases of Federal's preferred stock. *See* Roy A. Schotland, *A Sporting Proposition:* SEC v. Chenery, in ADMINISTRATIVE LAW STORIES 168, 176–77 (Peter L. Strauss ed. 2006). For this reason, the Chenery group argued that application of the SEC's new principle to penalize the Chenery group's prior conduct amounted to an impermissible retroactive application of a new rule.

The Supreme Court, as you saw, rejected this retroactivity claim. Interestingly, the Court did not reject the claim that the SEC's order had retroactive effect, even though the Court might have resisted this conclusion on the ground that the SEC was merely applying a standard immanent in the statute rather than declaring a new rule. The Court instead emphasized that retroactivity was not *per se* unlawful, as "[e]very case of first impression has a retroactive effect, whether the new principle is announced by a court or by an administrative agency." Retroactivity would render an adjudicative order invalid, according to the Court, only when "the ill effect of the retroactive application of a new standard" outweighs "the mischief of producing a result which is contrary to a statutory design or to legal and equitable principles." Subsequent court of appeals cases have elaborated on this balancing inquiry. For example, the D.C. Circuit in Retail, Wholesale & Department Store Union v. NLRB, 466 F.2d 380 (D.C. Cir. 1972) explained that an assessment of the legality of retroactive administrative action under *Chenery* required consideration of five factors:

(1) whether the particular case is one of first impression, (2) whether the new rule represents an abrupt departure from well established practice or merely attempts to fill a void in an unsettled area of law, (3) the extent to which the party against whom the new rule is applied relied on the former rule, (4) the degree of the burden which a retroactive order imposes on a party, and (5) the statutory interest in applying a new rule despite the reliance of a party on the old standard.

466 F.2d at 390. *See also* District Lodge 64, Int'l Ass'n of Machinists and Aerospace Workers v. NLRB, 949 F.2d 441, 447–49 (D.C. Cir. 1991) (reformulating the five-factor test as a three-factor test, but without substantively changing the inquiry); Clark–Cowlitz Joint Operating Agency v. FERC, 826 F.2d 1074, 1081–85 (D.C. Cir. 1987) (en banc) (elaborating and applying these factors). Does this approach—which remains the guiding frame of reference in assessing the legality of retroactive administrative adjudication—seem sound to you? Does it seem workable?

**5. *The Consequences of* Chenery II**—Under *Chenery II*, there are few legal constraints on agencies' ability to announce and apply general principles—principles that look a lot like rules—in orders issued pursuant to administrative adjudications. Perhaps the most significant consequence of *Chenery II* is that certain agencies—most notably the National Labor Relations Board (NLRB)—do virtually all of their policymaking in adjudicative orders rather than rulemakings. *See, e.g.*, Merton C. Bernstein, *The NLRB's Adjudication–Rule Making Dilemma Under the Administrative Procedure Act*, 79 YALE L.J. 571, 574 (1970); Cornelius J. Peck, *The Atrophied Rule–Making Powers of the National Labor Relations Board*, 70 YALE L.J. 729, 729–30 (1961). Other agencies, including the SEC, make policy through a mix of rulemaking and adjudication, and likely rely more on adjudication than they would have had Justice Jackson's views carried the day in *Chenery II*. *See, e.g.*, Donna M. Nagy, *Judicial Reliance on Regulatory Interpretations in SEC No–Action Letters: Current Problems and a Proposed Framework*, 83 CORNELL L. REV. 921, 929–31 & n.34 (1998).

The impact of the *Chenery II* doctrine on agencies' choices between rulemaking and adjudication, while certainly important, should not be exaggerated. While some agencies make most of their important policy decisions through adjudication, most engage in a substantial amount of rulemaking activity. One reason for this is that agencies do not always have a choice: Certain policy decisions are required by statute to take the form of regulations (that is, rules). But even when agencies *do* have a choice between adjudication and rulemaking, they sometimes opt for rulemaking. Why might this be so? Perhaps agencies themselves sometimes conclude that they will be able to make higher-quality decisions if they solicit the sort of broad public input associated with rulemaking. Agencies may also find it easier to frame their policies at the right level of generality if they do not need to rely on an appropriate enforcement action or on a private party to file a complaint on a subject of policymaking interest to the agency. Agencies might also find it more efficient to announce a general rule that clarifies the law ahead of time. There might also be political demand for rulemaking from the relevant congressional oversight committees or the interest groups that routinely work with the agency. How much does your view of the debate between Justices Murphy and Jackson in *Chenery II* turn on your assessment of the degree to which non-legal policy considerations of this sort will press agencies to use rulemaking without the compulsion of law?

\* \* \* \*

Although *Chenery II* accurately captures the state of current doctrine on agencies' freedom to announce general principles in adjudicative proceedings, the Supreme Court and many lower courts have sometimes displayed considerable ambivalence about *Chenery II*'s hands-off approach. Much of this ambivalence may be traceable to the fact, noted above, that some agencies (most prominently, the NLRB) have chosen to rely almost exclusively on adjudications rather than rulemakings to establish agency policy. This ambivalence came to a head in NLRB v. Wyman–Gordon Co., 394 U.S. 759 (1969), a case that involved workplace elections in which employees decide whether they want union representation. The NLRB is responsible for determining when a union representation election must be held, and for certifying the results of such elections. In Excelsior Underwear, Inc., 156 N.L.R.B. 1236 (1966), the NLRB considered a claim by two unions that the NLRB should refuse to certify the results of certain representation elections because the companies involved had refused to provide the unions with lists of the names and addresses of all employees eligible to vote. After a hearing, the NLRB issued an order declaring that, as a general matter, employers are obligated to provide such lists to unions. The order, however, said that the NLRB would only apply this principle prospectively. Thus, the NLRB certified the results of the elections at issue in *Excelsior*, but stated that in the future it would not certify election results if the employer had refused to disclose the names and addresses of all employees eligible to vote. A few months later, the NLRB issued an order mandating a union representation election at the Wyman–Gordon Company. Citing *Excelsior*, this order specifically required Wyman–Gordon to furnish the unions with a list of the names and addresses of employees eligible to vote. Wyman–Gordon refused to comply, arguing that the *Excelsior* "rule" was invalid because it had been issued in an adjudication rather than a rulemaking.

The NLRB ultimately prevailed in the Supreme Court, but the opinions cast doubt on the scope of agencies' authority to announce general principles via adjudication. Justice Fortas, writing for a plurality that included himself, Chief Justice Warren, and Justices Stewart and White, concluded that the *Excelsior* "order" was in fact an invalid rule:

> ... There is no question that, in an adjudicatory hearing, the Board could validly decide the issue whether the employer must furnish a list of employees to the union. But that is not what the Board did in *Excelsior*. The Board did not even apply the rule it made to the parties in the adjudicatory proceeding, the only entities that could

properly be subject to the order in that case. Instead, the Board purported to make a rule: *i.e.*, to exercise its quasi-legislative power.

Adjudicated cases may and do, of course, serve as vehicles for the formulation of agency policies, which are applied and announced therein. They generally provide a guide to action that the agency may be expected to take in future cases. Subject to the qualified role of *stare decisis* in the administrative process, they may serve as precedents. But this is far from saying ... that commands, decisions, or policies announced in adjudication are "rules" in the sense that they must, without more, be obeyed by the affected public.

394 U.S. at 765–66 (plurality opinion) (footnote and citation omitted). The plurality, however, upheld the NLRB's order to the Wyman–Gordon Company, explaining:

Even though the direction to furnish the list was followed by citation to *"Excelsior Underwear Inc.*, 156 NLRB No. 111," it is an order in the present case that [Wyman–Gordon] was required to obey. Absent this direction by the Board, the respondent was under no compulsion to furnish the list because no statute and no validly adopted rule required it to do so.

*Id.* at 766.

Justice Douglas and Justice Harlan, in separate dissents, agreed with the plurality that *Excelsior* was a procedurally invalid rule, but they concluded that the NLRB's order to Wyman–Gordon was premised on the validity of that rule, and so could not be sustained. *Id.* at 779–80 (Douglas, J., dissenting), 780–83 (Harlan, J., dissenting).

Justice Black, joined by Justices Brennan and Marshall, concurred in the result, but took issue with the assertion that the disclosure requirement announced in *Excelsior* was not legally valid and binding. In Justice Black's view, "the *Excelsior* practice was adopted by the Board as a legitimate incident to the adjudication of a specific case before it, and for that reason I would hold that the Board properly followed the procedures applicable to 'adjudication' rather than 'rule making.' " *Id.* at 770 (Black, J., concurring in the result). Justice Black further declared that if *Excelsior* were *not* a valid rule, then he would have invalidated the Board's order to Wyman–Gordon, as that order, in his view, clearly relied on the *Excelsior* rule.

*Wyman–Gordon* illustrates the so-called "doctrinal paradox" of collective judicial decision-making. *See* Lewis A. Kornhauser & Lawrence G. Sager, *The One and the Many: Adjudication in Collegial Courts*, 81 Cal. L. Rev. 1 (1993); Michael I. Meyerson, *The Irrational Supreme Court*, 84 Neb. L. Rev. 895, 957 (2006). In *Wyman–Gordon*, the Board's order would be valid if (a) *Excelsior* announced a valid rule, or (b) the Board's order were valid even without reliance on *Excelsior*. If neither of those conditions is satisfied, then the Board's order in *Wyman–Gordon* is invalid. A 6–3 majority (the four-Justice plurality plus the two dissenters) concluded that the *Excelsior* rule was invalid. A 5–4 majority (the three-Justice concurrence in the result plus the two dissenters) concluded that the Board's order to Wyman–Gordon could not be sustained if the *Excelsior* rule were invalid. So, if the Justices voted issue by issue, the NLRB should have lost. But a 7–2 majority voted to sustain the Board's order. Does this seem problematic? Given that six out of nine justices concluded that *Excelsior* was in fact an invalid rule, does this cast doubt on the vitality of *Chenery II*, despite the fact that the NLRB ultimately prevailed in *Wyman–Gordon?*

On that latter question, both the plurality and the dissents suggested a more skeptical attitude toward the use of administrative adjudication to announce general rules. Consider the following passages from Justice Fortas's plurality opinion and from Justice Douglas's dissent:

> The rule-making provisions of [the Administrative Procedure Act], which the Board would avoid, were designed to assure fairness and mature consideration of rules of general application. They may not be avoided by the process of making rules in the course of adjudicatory proceedings. There is no warrant in law for the Board to replace the statutory scheme with a rule-making procedure of its own invention.

*Id.* at 764 (Fortas, J.) (plurality opinion) (citation omitted).

> The rule-making procedure performs important functions. It gives notice to an entire segment of society of those controls or regimentation that is forthcoming. It gives an opportunity for persons affected to be heard....

> This is a healthy process that helps make a society viable. The multiplication of agencies and their growing power make them more and more remote from the people affected by what they do and make more likely the arbitrary exercise of their powers. Public airing of problems through rule making makes the bureaucracy more responsive to public needs and is an important brake on the growth of absolutism in the regime that now governs all of us....

> ... [W]hen we are lax and allow federal agencies to play fast and loose with rule making, we set a precedent with dangerous repercussions.

*Id.* at 777–78 (Douglas, J., dissenting).

Justice Black's concurrence in the judgment provides a useful contrast, as it succinctly restates the case for preserving the sort of administrative flexibility that *Chenery II* had endorsed:

> ... The line between [rulemaking and adjudication] is not always a clear one and in fact the two functions merge at many points. For example, in exercising its quasi-judicial function an agency must frequently decide controversies on the basis of new doctrines, not theretofore applied to a specific problem, though drawn to be sure from broader principles reflecting the purposes of the statutes involved and from the rules invoked in dealing with related problems. If the agency decision reached under the adjudicatory power becomes a precedent, it guides future conduct in much the same way as though it were a new

rule promulgated under the rule-making power, and both an adjudicatory order and a formal "rule" are alike subject to judicial review....

... Congress had a laudable purpose in prescribing [the APA's rulemaking requirements], and it was evidently contemplated that administrative agencies like the Labor Board would follow them when setting out to announce a new rule of law to govern parties in the future. In this same statute, however, Congress also conferred on the affected administrative agencies the power to proceed by adjudication, and Congress specified a distinct procedure by which this adjudicatory power is to be exercised.... Thus, although it is true that the adjudicatory approach frees an administrative agency from the procedural requirements specified for rule making, the Act permits this to be done whenever the action involved can satisfy the definition of "adjudication" and then imposes separate procedural requirements that must be met in adjudication. Under these circumstances, so long as the matter involved can be dealt with in a way satisfying the definition of either "rule making" or "adjudication" under the Administrative Procedure Act, that Act ... should be read as conferring upon the Board the authority to decide, within its informed discretion, whether to proceed by rule making or adjudication....

In the present case ... [t]he Board did not abstractly decide out of the blue to announce a brand new rule of law to govern labor activities in the future, but rather established the procedure as a direct consequence of the proper exercise of its adjudicatory powers.

*Id.* at 770–73 (Black, J., concurring in the result).

The notion that *Wyman–Gordon* signaled a retreat from *Chenery II* was put to rest a few years later in another labor relations case, *NLRB v. Bell Aerospace Co.* The substantive question in that case was whether buying agents at Bell Aerospace's factories could unionize. The answer to this question turned on whether buyers were "managerial" employees. Traditionally, the NLRB had excluded "managerial employees" from collective bargaining under the National Labor Relations Act (NLRA), reasoning that Congress did not intend managers to come within the Act's protections. The Board had defined managerial employees to include those "so closely related to or aligned with management as to place the employee[s] in a position of potential conflict of interest between [the] employer on the one hand and ... fellow workers on the other" *and* those charged with "formulating, determining and effectuating [the] employer's policies or [exercising] discretion, independent of an employer's established policy, in the performance of [their] duties," Illinois State Journal–Register, Inc. v. NLRB, 412 F.2d 37, 41 (7th Cir. 1969). The Board had also long held that buyers—those who exercise discretion in procuring materials on behalf of management—were managerial employees. Swift & Co., 115 N.L.R.B. 752, 753–54 (1956); American Locomotive Co., 92 N.L.R.B. 115, 116–17 (1950). The Board had made both sets of determinations—about the exclusion of managerial employees from the NLRA and about the status of "buyers" as managerial employees—through adjudication. In the formal adjudication that precipitated the *Bell Aerospace* litigation, the Board had reversed its prior position and held that managerial employees could unionize if their duties did not create a conflict of interest with membership in a labor organization. The Board had also held, in the alternative, that buyers were not managerial employees. The Court of Appeals for the Second Circuit (in an opinion written by the distinguished Judge Henry Friendly) first rejected the Board's principal contention that the Act's protections extend to most managerial employees, reasoning that this contradicted Congress's apparent intent. Turning to the Board's alternative holding that buyers are not managerial employees, the court considered whether the Board could overturn its earlier adjudicative precedents treating buyers as "managerial." The court concluded that the Board was not precluded from doing so but that it could not reverse those decisions through adjudication. In reaching this result, Judge Friendly's opinion cobbled together statements from the plurality and two dissents in *Wyman–Gordon* in an attempt to identify a principled limitation on *Chenery II*. The Supreme Court rejected Judge Friendly's synthesis, reemphasizing *Chenery II*'s recognition of broad agency discretion to choose between rulemaking and adjudication. As you read the cases that follow, ask yourself who has the better of the argument.

## Bell Aerospace Co. v. National Labor Relations Board

U.S. Court of Appeals for the Second Circuit
475 F.2d 485 (2d Cir. 1973)

■ FRIENDLY, CHIEF JUDGE:

. . .

### III.

. . . [W]hile the Board was not precluded from reversing itself on the position that buyers, or some buyers, were not "managerial employees," we hold that, particularly in light of the justified contrary belief the Board had engendered, it could not do this in the manner that was done here. This is an appropriate case in which to give effect to the Supreme Court's observation in the second *Chenery* decision, 332 U.S. 194, 202 (1947), largely disregarded by the Board for a quarter century:

> The function of filling in the interstices of the Act should be performed, as must as possible, through this quasi-legislative promulgation of rules to be applied in the future.

Such a holding is also in line with the considered dicta in NLRB v. Wyman–Gordon Co., 394 U.S. 759 (1969).

Although the precise issues in *Wyman–Gordon* were whether a direction made in a previous decision, Excelsior Underwear Inc., 156 N.L.R.B. 1236 (1966), that was to apply prospectively only, in fact constituted rule-making, . . . expressions by a majority of the Justices point against the procedure the Board followed here. The plurality opinion of Mr.

Justice Fortas, joined by the Chief Justice, Mr. Justice Stewart and Mr. Justice White, emphasized, 394 U.S. at 764:

> The rule-making provisions of that Act, which the Board would avoid, were designed to assure fairness and mature consideration of rules of general application. . . . They may not be avoided by the process of making rules in the course of adjudicatory proceedings.

Mr. Justice Douglas, dissenting from the holding that the Board's violation in *Excelsior* had been cured in *Wyman–Gordon* because the rule adopted in *Excelsior* was being applied as part of a later adjudicative order, said this, 394 U.S. at 777–779 (footnote omitted):

> A rule like the one in *Excelsior* is designed to fit all cases at all times. It is not particularized to special facts. It is a statement of far-reaching policy covering all future representation elections.
>
> It should therefore have been put down for the public hearing prescribed by the Act.
>
> The rule-making procedure performs important functions. It gives notice to an entire segment of society of those controls or regimentation that is forthcoming. It gives an opportunity for persons affected to be heard. . . .
>
> Agencies discover [through rule-making proceedings] that they are not always repositories of ultimate wisdom; they learn from the suggestions of outsiders and often benefit from that advice.
>
> \* \* \* \* \* \*
>
> I would hold the agencies governed by the rule-making procedure strictly to its requirements and not allow them to play fast and loose as the National Labor Relations Board apparently likes to do.

Mr. Justice Harlan, likewise dissenting, after pointing to the Board's decision to apply the *Excelsior* rule only prospectively as implying that it was "such a departure from pre-existing understandings that it would be unfair to impose the rule upon the parties in pending matters," 394 U.S. at 780–781, continued:

> [I]t is precisely in these situations, in which established patterns of conduct are revolutionized, that rule-making procedures perform the vital functions that my Brother Douglas describes so well in a dissenting opinion with which I basically agree.
>
> \* \* \* \* \* \*
>
> Either the rule-making provisions are to be enforced or they are not. Before the Board may be permitted to adopt a rule that so significantly alters pre-existing labor-management understandings, it must be required to conduct a satisfactory rule-making proceeding, so that it will have the benefit of wide-ranging argument before it enacts its proposed solution to an important problem.

Despite all this, *Wyman–Gordon* does not supply a bright line for determining just when the Board, or other agencies, must proceed by rule-making.... Certainly the decision does not proscribe the use of adjudication as a vehicle for the formulation of new agency policies, which "are applied and announced therein" and "generally provide a guide to action that the agency may be expected to take in future cases." 394 U.S. at 765–766 (Fortas, J.). But if the statements ... from the opinions of six Justices in *Wyman–Gordon* are to mean anything, they must be read as demanding rule-making here, and given the Board's long-standing negative attitude, as requiring a court to order it. The Board was prescribing a new policy, not just with respect to 25 buyers in [this case], but in substance, to use Mr. Justice Douglas' phrase, "to fit all cases at all times." 394 U.S. at 777. There must be tens of thousands of manufacturing, wholesale and retail units which employ buyers, and hundreds of thousands of the latter. Yet the Board did not even attempt to inform industry and labor organizations, by means providing some notice ... of its proposed new policy and to invite comment thereon.... Although policy-making by adjudication often cannot be avoided in unfair labor practice cases, since the parties have already acted and the Board must decide one way or the other, there is no such problem in a representation case. Finally, the argument for rule-making is especially strong when the Board is proposing to reverse a long-standing and oft-repeated policy on which industry and labor have relied. To be sure, the change of policy here in question did not expose an employer to new and unexpected liability.... The point rather is that when the Board has so long been committed to a position, it should be particularly sure that it has all available information before adopting another, in a setting where nothing stands in the way of a rule-making proceeding except the Board's congenital disinclination to follow a procedure which, as said in Texaco, Inc. v. FPC, 412 F.2d 740, 744 (3[d] Cir. 1969), "enables the agency promulgating the rule to educate itself before establishing rules and procedures which have a substantial impact on those regulated," despite the Court's pointed admonitions....

---

## National Labor Relations Board v. Bell Aerospace Co.

Supreme Court of the United States
416 U.S. 267 (1974)

■ Mr. Justice Powell delivered the opinion of the Court.

This case presents [the question whether] the [National Labor Relations] Board must proceed by rulemaking rather than by adjudication in determining whether certain buyers are "managerial employees." We answer [this question] in the negative....

### III

The Court of Appeals ... held that, although the Board was not precluded from determining that buyers or some types of buyers were not "managerial employees," it could do so only by invoking its rulemaking procedures. . . . We disagree.

. . . [The] question is whether . . . the Board must invoke its rulemaking procedures if it determines . . . that these buyers are not "managerial employees" under the Act. The Court of Appeals thought that rulemaking was required because *any* Board finding that the company's buyers are not "managerial" would be contrary to its prior decisions and would presumably be in the nature of a general rule designed "to fit all cases at all times."

A similar issue was presented to this Court in its second decision in SEC v. Chenery Corp., 332 U.S. 194 (1947) (*Chenery II*). There, the respondent corporation argued that in an adjudicative proceeding the Commission could not apply a general standard that it had formulated for the first time in that proceeding. Rather, the Commission was required to resort instead to its rulemaking procedures if it desired to promulgate a new standard that would govern future conduct. In rejecting this contention, the Court first noted that the Commission had a statutory duty to decide the issue at hand in light of the proper standards and that this duty remained "regardless of whether those standards previously had been spelled out in a general rule or regulation." *Id.*, at 201. . . .

The Court concluded that "the choice made between proceeding by general rule or by individual, *ad hoc* litigation is one that lies primarily in the informed discretion of the administrative agency." *Id.*, at 203.

And in NLRB v. Wyman–Gordon Co., 394 U.S. 759 (1969), the Court upheld a Board order . . . first promulgated in an earlier adjudicative proceeding. . . . The plurality opinion of Mr. Justice Fortas, joined by THE CHIEF JUSTICE, MR. JUSTICE STEWART, and MR. JUSTICE WHITE, recognized that "[a]djudicated cases may and do . . . serve as vehicles for the formulation of agency policies, which are applied and announced therein," and that such cases "generally provide a guide to action that the agency may be expected to take in future cases." *NLRB v. Wyman–Gordon Co., supra*, at 765–766. The concurring opinion of MR. JUSTICE BLACK, joined by MR. JUSTICE BRENNAN and MR. JUSTICE MARSHALL, also noted that the Board had both adjudicative and rulemaking powers and that the choice between the two was "within its informed discretion." *Id.*, at 772.

The views expressed in *Chenery II* and *Wyman–Gordon* make plain that the Board is not precluded from announcing new principles in an adjudicative proceeding and that the choice between rulemaking and adjudication lies in the first instance within the Board's discretion. Although there may be situations where the Board's reliance on adjudication would amount to an abuse of discretion or a violation of the Act, nothing in the present case would justify such a conclusion. Indeed, there is ample indication that adjudication is especially appropriate in the instant context. As the Court of Appeals noted, "[t]here must be tens of thousands of manufacturing, wholesale and retail units which employ buyers, and hundreds of thousands of the latter." 475 F.2d, at 496. Moreover, duties of buyers vary widely depending on the company or industry. It is doubtful whether any generalized standard could be framed which would have more than marginal utility. The Board thus has reason to proceed with caution, developing its standards in a case-by-case manner with attention to the specific character of the buyers' authority and duties in each company. The Board's judgment that adjudication best serves this purpose is entitled to great weight.

The possible reliance of industry on the Board's past decisions with respect to buyers does not require a different result. It has not been shown that the adverse consequences ensuing from such reliance are so substantial that the Board should be precluded from reconsidering the issue in an adjudicative proceeding. Furthermore, this is not a case in which some new liability is sought to be imposed on individuals for past actions which were taken in good-faith reliance on Board pronouncements. Nor are fines or damages involved here. . . .

It is true, of course, that rulemaking would provide the Board with a forum for soliciting the informed views of those affected in industry and labor before embarking on a new course. But surely the Board has discretion to decide that the adjudicative procedures in this case may also produce the relevant information necessary to mature and fair consideration of the issues. Those most immediately affected, the buyers and the company in the particular case, are accorded a full opportunity to be heard before the Board makes its determination. . . .

■ [JUSTICE WHITE's opinion, joined by JUSTICES BRENNAN, STEWART, and MARSHALL, concurring in part and dissenting in part, is omitted. JUSTICE WHITE concurred in Part III of the majority opinion, excerpted above.]

---

***1. A Retreat from* Wyman–Gordon*?*—**Doesn't there seem to be deep tension between the tenor of the plurality and dissenting opinions in *Wyman–Gordon* and Justice Powell's assertion in *Bell Aerospace* that although "rulemaking would provide the Board with a forum for soliciting the informed views of those affected in industry and labor," the Board "has discretion to decide that the adjudicative procedures in this case may also produce the relevant information necessary to mature and fair consideration of the issues"? What do you make of the fact that Justice Douglas, whose strongly worded dissent in *Wyman–Gordon* insisted on the need to restrict agencies' ability to use adjudicative orders to avoid rulemaking, joined Justice Powell's *Bell Aerospace* opinion without comment? Or that Justice White, who joined Justice Fortas's plurality opinion in *Wyman–Gordon*, likewise concurred in the relevant portion of Justice Powell's *Bell Aerospace* opinion? Does this imply that *Wyman–Gordon* is confined to cases in which an agency announces a new rule in an adjudication that applies *only* prospectively? If so, perhaps *Wyman–Gordon* merely reflects the fact that the APA defines a "rule" to be "an agency statement of general or particular applicability and *future effect*." 5 U.S.C. § 551(4) (emphasis added). Does that imply that the *Excelsior* order would have been binding if the NLRB had applied the disclosure requirement in *Excelsior* itself?

**2.  *Proposed Limits on* Chenery II**—Judge Friendly's *Bell Aerospace* opinion accepted the general *Chenery II* proposition that agencies may sometimes make general policy decisions in adjudicative orders, but tried to cabin that principle by identifying specific factors that might limit agencies' freedom to make rules through the adjudication process. Although the Supreme Court reversed, Judge Friendly's proposed limits are nonetheless worth considering.

*First*, Judge Friendly made much of the fact that the NLRB had changed its position. In prior orders, the NLRB had declared explicitly that buyers similar to those at issue in *Bell Aerospace* were not entitled to the NLRA's collective bargaining protections. In *Chenery II*, by contrast, although the prior judge-made law on fiduciary duties would not have proscribed the Chenery group's stock purchases, the SEC had never taken any formal position on whether a public utility corporation's managers may trade in the corporation's shares while a reorganization proposal is pending.

*Second*, Judge Friendly emphasized the scope of the rule at issue. Citing Justice Douglas's criterion that an agency must make a rule if it wishes to announce a policy that "fits all cases at all times," Judge Friendly pointed out that the NLRB's new ruling affects not only the 25 buyers at Bell Aerospace's factory, but "tens of thousands of manufacturing, wholesale and retail units which employ buyers, and hundreds of thousands of the latter."

*Third*, Judge Friendly suggested a difference between cases in which "policy-making by adjudication . . . cannot be avoided"—because an issue is brought before the agency that the agency must resolve one way or another—and those cases in which the agency has some discretion as to how to proceed. *Chenery II* arguably fell into the first category: the SEC had to decide whether or not to approve the reorganization plan, and if it thought that the proposed plan was not "fair and equitable," it was under an obligation to reject it and to explain why. *Bell Aerospace*, Judge Friendly argued, fell into the second category, presumably because the NLRB could have delayed a decision on whether the buyers could unionize until it had completed a rulemaking on the subject.

Do you find any of these three criteria convincing? Are they judicially manageable? Was the Supreme Court right to reject them?

**3.  *Are There Doctrinal Limits on Making Rules through Adjudication?***—The Supreme Court's *Bell Aerospace* opinion did not completely shut the door on the enforcement of legal limits on an agency's freedom to announce general principles in adjudicative orders. The Court recognized that "there may be situations where the Board's reliance on adjudication would amount to an abuse of discretion" under § 706(2)(A) of the APA. Some courts of appeals have picked up on this language to strike down agency orders that rested on general propositions announced in the orders themselves, rather than in prior rulemakings. *See, e.g.*, First Bancorporation v. Board of Governors of the Federal Reserve System, 728 F.2d 434, 437–38 (10th Cir. 1984); Ford Motor Co. v. FTC, 673 F.2d 1008, 1009–10

(9th Cir. 1981), *cert. denied*, 459 U.S. 999 (1982); Patel v. INS, 638 F.2d 1199, 1204–05 & n.5 (9th Cir. 1980). But such decisions are extremely unusual. *See* M. Elizabeth Magill, *Agency Choice of Policymaking Form*, 71 U. Chi. L. Rev. 1383, 1408 (2004) (observing that the Supreme Court's decisions on this issue are "now clearly read to hold that an agency can proceed by adjudication even in circumstances that might, based on the *Chenery II* discussion, call for the promulgation of a legislative rule"); *see also* E. Donald Elliott, *Re–Inventing Rulemaking*, 41 Duke L.J. 1490, 1492 (1992) (approving this development in the doctrine).

*Bell Aerospace* acknowledged that there may be a retroactivity concern when an agency applies a newly announced policy to the case at hand. But *Bell Aerospace* reaffirmed the *Chenery II* balancing approach to retroactivity, requiring a showing either of substantial adverse reliance on the past agency policy, or the imposition of some penalty (e.g., fines or damages) for past conduct that was consistent with the agency's then-prevailing policy. The combination of this aspect of *Bell Aerospace* with *Wyman–Gordon's* prohibition on purely prospective adjudicative "rules" does place some limits on agencies' ability to make policy via adjudication: If a new agency policy implicates substantial reliance interests or subjects regulated entities to new liability, an agency cannot announce that new policy in an adjudication. The new policy would be impermissibly retroactive under *Bell Aerospace* if it were applied to the parties to the dispute, but if the agency purported to make the new policy purely prospective, it would be an invalid rule under *Wyman–Gordon*. That said, judicial reversals of agency adjudicative orders on grounds of impermissible retroactivity, while certainly not unheard of, are rare.

*4. Limits on the Announcement of New Policy Through Rulemaking*—The Court has also established some limits on the use of rulemaking to impose a new policy retroactively. In Bowen v. Georgetown University Hospitals, 488 U.S. 204 (1988), the Secretary of Health and Human Services had used notice-and-comment rulemaking to correct a cost-limit formula governing the reimbursements hospitals could claim for services rendered to Medicare beneficiaries under the Medicare Act, 42 U.S.C. § 1395 *et seq.* Because a court had declared an earlier formula invalid, the Secretary promulgated a new cost-limit rule in 1984 that applied retroactively to reimbursements for a period commencing in 1981. Although a provision of the Medicare Act gave the Secretary some authority to adopt regulations for "the making of suitable retroactive corrective adjustments" to reimbursements, *id.* § 1395x(v)(1)(A), the Court read that authority narrowly to permit the adoption of procedures for case-by-case adjustments, not the categorical revision of the overall reimbursement formula. In so holding, Justice Kennedy's opinion for the Court articulated a strong interpretive presumption against reading an organic act to permit retroactive rulemaking:

> Retroactivity is not favored in the law. Thus, congressional enactments and administrative rules will not be construed to have retroactive effect unless their language requires this result. . . . By

the same principle, a statutory grant of legislative rulemaking authority will not, as a general matter, be understood to encompass the power to promulgate retroactive rules unless that power is conveyed by Congress in express terms. See Brimstone R. Co. v. United States, 276 U.S. 104, 122 (1928) ("The power to require readjustments for the past is drastic. It ... ought not to be extended so as to permit unreasonably harsh action without very plain words"). Even where some substantial justification for retroactive rulemaking is presented, courts should be reluctant to find such authority absent an express statutory grant.

488 U.S. at 208–09. This passage implements the Court's more general framework of disfavoring retroactive legislation on the ground that such legislation, even when constitutional, contradicts important constitutional values implicit in clauses such as the Due Process Clause, the Takings Clause, and the Ex Post Facto Clause. *See* pp. 336–337, *supra*. But if the Court readily relies on this nonretroactivity value to constrain rulemaking, why do its opinions in *Chenery II* and *Bell Aerospace* seem to give agencies such broad latitude to announce and apply new policies retroactively in adjudication?

One potential explanation is that, since adjudication entails the application of law to fact, there will always be some retroactive policymaking when an agency (or, for that matter, a court) applies an ambiguous text to a novel fact situation. In that respect, recall that the rulemaking process was intended to approximate a legislative process, perhaps suggesting to the Court that the usual presumption of nonretroactive legislation should extend to the rulemaking process as well.

Might there, however, be a more formal explanation for the difference? In a concurring opinion in *Bowen*, Justice Scalia suggested that the true source of the relevant nonretroactivity constraint lies in the APA itself:

> The first part of the APA's definition of "rule" states that a rule
>
>> "means the whole or a part of an agency statement of general or particular applicability *and future effect* designed to implement, interpret, or prescribe law or policy or describing the organization, procedure, or practice requirements of an agency...." 5 U.S.C. § 551(4) (emphasis added).

The only plausible reading of the italicized phrase is that rules have legal consequences only for the future. It could not possibly mean that merely *some* of their legal consequences must be for the future, though they may also have legal consequences for the past, since that description would not enable rules to be distinguished from "orders," see 5 U.S.C. § 551(6), and would thus destroy the entire dichotomy upon which the most significant portions of the APA are based.

488 U.S. at 216 (Scalia, J., concurring). Noting that adjudications can have future as well as past consequences (because adjudications serve as prece-

dents for future cases), Justice Scalia made clear that the very essence of rulemaking was that it prescribed policy solely for the future.

Did Justice Scalia convincingly parse the language of the APA's definitional section? Is his conclusion consistent with the *Wyman–Gordon* plurality's reasons for concluding that a purely prospective adjudication violated the APA? Is it altogether clear what should count as "future effect" for purposes of the APA? The House Report accompanying the APA states that "[t]he phrase 'future effect' does not preclude agencies from considering and, so far as legally authorized, dealing with past transactions in prescribing rules for the future." H.R. REP. No. 1980, 79th Cong., 2d Sess., 49 n.1 (1946). So, for example, the EPA can presumably rely on rulemaking to require sharp reductions in *future* emissions of air pollutants, even if *in the past* a firm built a factory in reliance upon a more relaxed regulatory posture. Similarly, even if one sets up a trust in reliance on an Internal Revenue Service ruling suggesting that streams of income from that type of trust will be taxed a certain way, such reliance does not necessarily preclude the IRS from later adopting a rule that changes its tax treatment of future income from that trust. Justice Scalia suggested that such agency rulemaking would be permissible—*i.e.*, not retroactive in the sense prohibited by the APA—because it does not "alter[] the *past* legal consequences of past actions." *Bowen*, 488 U.S. at 219. Does that distinction seem workable? If a reviewing court did not treat rules as being of purely "future effect," is there any other plausible way to distinguish rulemaking from adjudication under the APA's definitions—especially since rulemaking can be "of general or particular applicability"?

## B.  EXCEPTIONS TO § 553

Although § 551(4) of the APA defines a "rule" as "an agency statement of general or particular applicability and future effect designed to implement, interpret, or prescribe law or policy," not every agency statement meeting this definition must be issued pursuant to the notice-and-comment procedures laid out in § 553 (or the more formal procedures described in §§ 556 and 557). Even putting to one side the fact that, as the previous section discussed, agency adjudicative orders sometimes contain what look like "rules" meeting the above definition, § 553 itself specifies a number of exemptions from notice-and-comment rulemaking requirements.

First, § 553(a) states that notice-and-comment procedures are not required for matters pertaining to "a military or foreign affairs function of the United States," 5 U.S.C. § 553(a)(1), nor for matters "relating to agency management or personnel or to public property, loans, grants, benefits, or contracts," 5 U.S.C. § 553(a)(2). The exemptions for rules covering military, foreign affairs, personnel, and internal management are important, but they are also (mostly) straightforward and rarely litigated. The exemptions in § 553(a)(2) for matters relating to loans, grants, benefits, or contracts are significant in that these exemptions have been held to exclude a variety of rules related to various government benefit programs from the notice-and-comment requirements of § 553, though many of the agencies administering such programs have established their own regulations mandating notice-and-comment rulemaking.

The more significant and controversial exemptions are those contained in § 553(b), which specifies that § 553's notice-and-comment requirements do not apply:

> (A) to interpretative rules, general statements of policy, or rules of agency organization, procedure, or practice; or

> (B) when the agency for good cause finds ... that notice and public procedure thereon are impracticable, unnecessary, or contrary to the public interest.

These exemptions are quite important because they permit agencies to announce rules without going through the increasingly onerous procedural constraints associated with notice-and-comment rulemaking. But their scope is not altogether clear. The APA nowhere defines the key terms, and the Supreme Court has addressed the meaning of these exceptions to notice-and-comment rulemaking only rarely and indirectly. This section will explore how the federal courts of appeals have fleshed out open-ended terms such as "good cause," "interpretative rule," and "general statement of policy."

### a. The "Good Cause" Exemption

The so-called "good cause" exemption in § 553(b)(B) says that an agency need not go through the ordinary notice-and-comment rulemaking process if that process would be "impracticable, unnecessary, or contrary to the public interest." The courts have noted at least three sorts of circumstances that may justify invocation of this exemption.

*First*, compliance with § 553's notice-and-comment requirements may be "unnecessary" if the rule in question is "a routine determination, insignificant in nature and impact, and inconsequential to the industry and to the public." South Carolina ex rel. Patrick v. Block, 558 F.Supp. 1004, 1016 (D. S.C. 1983) (internal citations and quotation marks omitted); *see also* Utility Solid Waste Activities Group v. EPA, 236 F.3d 749, 755 (D.C. Cir. 2001); Texaco, Inc. v. Federal Power Comm'n, 412 F.2d 740, 743 (3d Cir. 1969). The courts, however, construe this exception quite narrowly, limiting it to cases in which there is no controversy whatsoever about the rule.

Some agencies have tried to take maximum possible advantage of this exception through a practice called "direct final rulemaking," in which the agency announces an "interim rule," which it expects to be non-controversial and thus immediately effective pursuant to the § 553(b)(B) exemption, and the agency simultaneously solicits comments on the interim rule as if it were an ordinary notice of proposed rulemaking. If the agency receives no adverse comments, the rule remains in effect. If the agency does receive adverse comments, then the interim rule is withdrawn, but the agency nonetheless completes the rulemaking as it would in the ordinary course of things. Scholars have debated both the desirability and legality of this approach. *See, e.g.,* Michael Asimow, *Interim–Final Rules: Making Haste Slowly,* 51 ADMIN. L. REV. 703 (1999); Michael Kolber, *Rulemaking Without Rules: An Empirical Study of Direct Final Rulemaking,* 72 ALB. L. REV. 79 (2009); Ronald M. Levin, *Direct Final Rulemaking,* 64 GEO. WASH. L. REV. 1 (1995); Ronald M. Levin, *More on Direct Final Rulemaking: Streamlining, Not Corner–Cutting,* 51 ADMIN. L. REV. 757 (1999); Lars Noah, *Doubts About Direct Final Rulemaking,* 51 ADMIN. L. REV. 401 (1999).

*Second,* rulemaking may be deemed "impracticable" if there is some kind of emergency situation that makes the delay associated with the ordinary notice-and-comment process intolerable. For example, in the immediate aftermath of the terrorist attacks in New York and Washington, D.C. on September 11, 2001, the Federal Aviation Administration (FAA) promulgated, without notice and comment, new regulations allowing for speedier revocation of pilot's licenses for pilots deemed to pose a security threat. The D.C. Circuit held this was a valid invocation of the § 553(b)(B) "good cause" exception, in light of the FAA's reasonable determination that delay in promulgating these new regulations could pose a serious security risk. *See* Jifry v. FAA, 370 F.3d 1174, 1179–80 (D.C. Cir. 2004). Courts have consistently required an agency wishing to rely on this exception to demonstrate some sort of emergency situation or substantial harm caused by delay. *See, e.g.,* Hawaii Helicopter Operators Ass'n v. FAA, 51 F.3d 212, 214 (9th Cir. 1995); American Federation of Government Employees, AFL–CIO v. Block, 655 F.2d 1153, 1156–58 (D.C. Cir. 1981).

Agencies that invoke this exception usually declare that the rule in question is "temporary," and simultaneously initiate the regular notice-and-comment rulemaking process, using the emergency rule as the proposed final rule. (This is similar to the direct final rulemaking process described above, but the agency does not automatically withdraw the rule in response to adverse comments.) Many courts have indicated that the interim rule's temporary status is a necessary precondition for upholding the agency's use of the § 553(b)(B) exemption as legitimate. For example, in *Mid–Tex Electric Cooperative, Inc. v. Federal Energy Regulatory Commission,* 822 F.2d 1123 (D.C. Cir. 1987), then-Judge Ruth Bader Ginsburg declared that "a rule's temporally limited scope is among the key considerations in evaluating an agency's 'good cause' claim," and she noted further that an agency claiming such an exemption has an obligation to demonstrate that it is engaging in good faith efforts to complete the regular rulemaking process expeditiously. *Id.* at 1132; *see also Block,* 655 F.2d at 1156–59; Council of the Southern Mountains, Inc. v. Donovan, 653 F.2d 573, 582 (D.C. Cir. 1981).

*Third,* courts have sometimes found that ordinary notice-and-comment procedures would be "contrary to the public interest" because advance notice of the proposed rule would prompt undesirable anticipatory behavior by affected parties. This exception, while rarely invoked, is particularly relevant to price-control regulations. For example, in the early 1970s, the federal government tried to combat inflation by imposing a set of wage and price controls pursuant to a 1970 statute called the Economic Stabilization

Act (ESA). In 1973, a then-existing federal agency called the Cost of Living Council decided to increase the maximum allowable price for a certain class of crude oil without notice or comment. In rejecting the argument that the agency had violated the APA, the Temporary Emergency Court of Appeals (which at the time had exclusive jurisdiction to hear appeals arising from disputes under the ESA) held that notice would have been contrary to the public interest within the meaning of § 553(b)(B) because "the announcement of a price increase at a future date could have resulted in producers withholding crude oil from the market until such time as they could take advantage of the price increase." Nader v. Sawhill, 514 F.2d 1064, 1068 (Em. App. 1975); *see also* DeRieux v. The Five Smiths, Inc., 499 F.2d 1321, 1332 (Em. App. 1974) (holding that an order freezing the prices for season tickets to professional football games could be issued without notice and comment because advance notice of the price freeze would have caused "a massive rush to raise prices and conduct 'actual transactions'—or avoid them—before the freeze deadline[, and] [e]ach price increase would have generated further increases in a growing spiral of inflation.").

### b.  General Statements of Policy

Section 553(b)(A) states that notice-and-comment requirements do not apply to an agency's "general statements of policy." What does this mean? Unfortunately, the APA nowhere defines "general statements of policy," and the committee reports accompanying the APA do not shed further light on the question. *See* Chrysler Corp. v. Brown, 441 U.S. 281, 301–02 & n.31 (1979). As we will see in a moment, it can be quite difficult to delimit the scope of the term with precision. That said, the basic idea, as developed by a large body of (mainly lower court) case law, is fairly straightforward: An agency "policy statement" (sometimes also referred to as a "guidance document") is an agency memorandum, letter, speech, press release, manual, or other official declaration by the agency of its agenda, its policy priorities, or how it plans to exercise its discretionary authority. Such policy statements can be valuable both for the agency and for those potentially affected by agency decisions, because these statements provide advance warning about how the agency is likely to resolve questions that come before it.

Consider, as an example, a variant on the scenario discussed in the *Chenery* litigation (*see* pp. 646–656, *supra*). In the actual case, the SEC declared that the corporation's reorganization plan was not "fair and equitable" within the meaning of the governing statute, because corporate insiders (the Chenery group) had traded in the corporation's securities while the reorganization proposal was pending. The SEC's decision caught the Chenery group by surprise; until the SEC's ruling on the reorganization plan, neither the Chenery group nor anyone else knew that the SEC wouldn't consider a reorganization plan "fair and equitable" under these circumstances. Suppose that well before the corporation had submitted its reorganization plan, the SEC had published an official notice that it would not consider "fair" any reorganization plan that permitted managers to benefit from trades in the corporation's securities while the plan was under consideration. The Chenery group would then have had notice of what the SEC was likely to do in its case, and could have planned accordingly. Mr. Chenery and his associates presumably would have been unhappy, but if they'd known about the SEC's likely disposition of their proposal, at least they would not have been caught off guard.

That hypothetical example, however, suggests one of the difficulties with exempting "general statements of policy" from the ordinary strictures of notice-and-comment rulemaking. While part of the concern in *Chenery* was that the SEC was announcing a new rule that interested parties would not have been able to anticipate, another important concern had to do with agency circumvention of the safeguards built into the notice-and-comment rulemaking process. *See* Steven P. Croley, *Theories of Regulation: Incorporating the Administrative Process*, 98 COLUM. L. REV. 1, 116–17 (1998); Nina A. Mendelson, *Regulatory Beneficiaries and Informal Agency Policymaking*, 92 CORNELL L. REV. 397, 424–33 (2007). An advance statement by the SEC that it would not approve any reorganization plan that allowed insiders to benefit from trades in the corporation's securities has the look and feel of a rule—it announces in advance that certain conduct is not permitted—but if it were considered merely a "policy statement," it would not have to go through notice and comment.

The following D.C. Circuit case, *Pacific Gas & Electric Co. v. Federal Power Commission*, illustrates the difficulties of distinguishing between *rules* (which have to go through notice and comment) and *policy statements* (which do not). The *PG&E* holding also exemplifies the most common doctrinal approach to drawing this difficult distinction.

To understand what's going on in *PG&E*, it's helpful to know a bit about the statutory and regulatory background of natural gas regulation. The 1938 Natural Gas Act (NGA) gave the Federal Power Commission (FPC) (now the Federal Energy Regulatory Commission (FERC)) broad authority to regulate the transmission and sale of natural gas. According to § 7 of the NGA, 15 U.S.C. § 717f, no party may sell or transport natural gas in interstate commerce unless the FPC first issues a "certificate of public convenience and necessity," to which the Commission may attach reasonable terms and conditions. Section 4 of the NGA, 15 U.S.C. § 717c, further requires that natural gas companies charge "just and reasonable rates," § 717c(a), and that the companies file their rate schedules and charges with the Commission, § 717c(c). Most importantly for present purposes, § 4(b) of the Act prohibits any natural gas company from "mak[ing] or grant[ing] any undue preference or advantage to any person or subject[ing] any person to any undue prejudice or disadvantage," and also prohibits "maintain[ing] any unreasonable difference in rates, charges, service, facilities, or in any other respect, either as between localities or as between classes of service." § 717c(b).

Beginning in 1970, parts of the United States faced serious natural gas shortages. When a natural gas company found itself unable to meet all of its customers' demand, it had to decide how to allocate the available gas, since not all customers could get all they had purchased at the regulated rate. Recognizing the problem, the FPC in 1971 issued (without notice and comment) a directive, Order No. 431, that declared "as a statement of general policy that ... pipeline companies shall take all steps necessary for the protection of as reliable and adequate service as ... supplies and capacities will permit...." 45 F.P.C. 570, 571 (1971). More specifically, Order No. 431 instructed each pipeline company under the Commission's jurisdiction to inform the FPC whether it anticipated a shortage, and, if so, to submit a "curtailment plan" indicating which deliveries the company planned to curtail. *Id.* at 572. These plans would have to be approved by the FPC as "just and reasonable" within the meaning of § 717c(a), and could not grant any "undue preference or advantage" to any party, or maintain any "unreasonable difference" in service or facilities for different consumers, within the meaning of § 717c(b).

But there are many different approaches to curtailing service, and it was not immediately obvious which ones the FPC would permit. One possibility would be to reduce all customers' gas deliveries on a *pro rata* basis (that is, if there's a 10% shortfall in total supply, each customer's gas supply could be cut by 10%). Another possibility would be to prioritize certain customers over others based on the end use of the gas (for instance, pipelines could prioritize residential customers over industrial customers, or vice versa). Yet a third option would be to give priority to those customers with whom the gas pipeline had made prior contractual agreements regarding the amount of gas to be delivered, at the expense of those customers whose demand was variable, and who therefore lacked a firm contractual right to a certain quantity of gas. As a result of this uncertainty, the hundreds of curtailment plans the FPC received in response to Order No. 431 used a wide variety of methods for allocating limited natural gas supplies. In response to this inconsistency and uncertainty, the FPC weighed in again in early 1973, offering guidance to natural gas pipelines in the form of the following "statement of policy," entitled Order No. 467:

---

# Federal Power Commission (FPC) Order No. 467

49 F.P.C. 85 (Jan. 8, 1973)

STATEMENT OF POLICY

Before Commissioners: John N. Nassikas, Chairman; Albert B. Brooke, Jr. and Rush Moody, Jr.

This order contains a statement of policy by the Commission on priorities-of-deliveries by jurisdictional pipeline companies during periods of curtailment. The Commission proposes to implement such policy in all matters arising under the Natural Gas Act.

When applied in specific cases, opportunity will be afforded interested parties to challenge or support this policy through factual or legal presentation as may be appropriate in the circumstances presented. It is the

Commission's intention in this statement to focus the attention of all parties concerned with the natural gas industry upon the general policy views of the Commission in advance of the filing of particular applications with the Commission and thereby to permit affected entities the opportunity to evolve a rational energy resource development program considering national energy goals and objectives as they may be stated from time-to-time, and to minimize the complexity and length of administrative proceedings before this Commission.

... [We find] that procedures should be adopted to maximize the high priority usage of natural gas during curtailment periods on a pipeline's system.

*General Discussion*—... [T]he Commission has been called upon to determine the propriety of curtailment procedures to be invoked by jurisdictional pipeline companies during periods of curtailed deliveries. In reaching its decisions, the Commission has reviewed the records in those proceedings and, based upon those reviews, has concluded that the customers' use of the natural gas fall into certain set categories. Accordingly, we believe that those categories are generally applicable industry-wide and can be utilized for establishing priorities-of-delivery during periods of short supply on any jurisdictional pipeline's system. We, of course, recognize that extraordinary circumstances may preclude the strict adherence to the priorities established and, consequently, we will permit those persons who allege that their circumstances require such extraordinary treatment to file petitions for relief under ... our Rules of Practice and Procedure. Barring such circumstances, our review of those curtailment proceedings and our knowledge of the industry convinces us that the priorities-of-delivery set forth below should be applied to all jurisdictional pipeline companies during periods of curtailment.

The curtailment procedures to be followed must have as their basic objective the protection of deliveries for the residential and small volume consumers who cannot be safely curtailed on a daily basis and requiring, as the initial level of curtailment, reduction in deliveries for large volume interruptible sales....

Secondly, we have determined that interruptible sales are for the most part, predicated on end-use considerations; those customers, be they direct sales or indirect sales, who require gas for human needs service or nonsubstitutable industrial service do not contract on an interruptible basis. Interruptible service, at the lower rates charged for such service, envisions interruption. And accordingly, interruptible customers can most reasonably be expected to have alternate fuel facilities already operational. We conclude, therefore, that curtailment should first fall on those who have not historically borne the full-fixed costs of providing gas service, particularly since these customers are best prepared to accept interruptions in service and clearly do not require uninterrupted service for protection of life or property.

Finally, if curtailment reaches beyond the level of interruptible service into firm contract service, we commit ourselves to the proposition that large volume boiler fuel usage is inferior and should be curtailed before other firm service. Aside from the established physical fact that combustion of natural gas for raising steam in boilers and its subsequent conversion into electricity or mechanical energy results in a loss of roughly two-thirds of the heating value of the gas used—which we regard as unacceptably inefficient in time of shortage—we note also that those who use gas as boiler fuel generally can substitute other fuels more readily and at lower overall cost than other gas users; additionally, pollution control is more practical because of the large size of individual installations.... 

In determining our priority-of-service listing, we are cognizant of the economic impacts that will flow from that listing. However, we believe that we have no choice but to impose certain restrictions on the sale of natural gas within the limits of our jurisdiction during this time of supply shortages.... 

*The Commission finds:*

(1) The notice and effective date provisions of 5 U.S.C. 553 do not apply with respect to the policy statement here adopted.

(2) It is appropriate and in the public interest in administering the Natural Gas Act to adopt the policy statement as herein ordered.... 

---

Order No. 467 was issued without notice and comment, which the Commission justified with its assertion that Order No. 467 was a "policy statement." Those natural gas customers disadvantaged by the Order, however, brought a legal challenge alleging that Order No. 467 did not qualify for the "general statements of policy" exception to § 553's notice-and-comment requirements. The D.C. Circuit addressed that challenge in the following opinion, which contains a particularly lucid and influential discussion of the distinction between rules and policy statements:

---

# Pacific Gas & Electric Co. v. Federal Power Commission

U.S. Court of Appeals for the D.C. Circuit
506 F.2d 33 (D.C. Cir. 1974)

■ MacKINNON, CIRCUIT JUDGE:

Petitioners assert that we have jurisdiction ... to review Order No. 467, which the Federal Power Commission issued on January 8, 1973. Order No. 467 is a "Statement of Policy" on "priorities-of-deliveries by jurisdictional pipelines during periods of curtailment" which the Commission indicated it proposes to implement in all matters arising under the [Natural Gas] Act. The petitioning customers of pipeline companies, whose deliveries are subject to curtailment during natural gas shortages, contend that Order No. 467 is procedurally defective for failure to comply with the Administrative Procedure Act....

## I.  BACKGROUND

This country appears to be experiencing a natural gas shortage which necessitates the curtailment of supplies to certain customers during peak demand periods. The problem confronting many pipeline companies is whether to curtail on the basis of existing contractual commitments or on the basis of the most efficient end use of the gas. In some instances the pipeline companies are concerned that withholding gas due under existing contracts may subject them to civil liability.

Recognizing these uncertainties and mindful of the desirability of providing uniform curtailment regulation, the FPC in 1971 issued a Statement of General Policy in the form of Order No. 431 directing jurisdictional pipeline companies which expected periods of shortages to file tariff sheets containing a curtailment plan. Order No. 431 hinted that curtailment priorities should be based on the end use of the gas and stated that curtailment plans approved by the Commission "will control in all respects notwithstanding inconsistent provisions in [prior] sales contracts...." In response to Order No. 431, numerous pipeline companies which had not already done so submitted a variety of curtailment plans for the Commission's approval. As could be expected, the curtailment plans reflected a wide range of views as to the proper priorities for delivery. Some plans were based on end use; others, on contract entitlements. The industry was forced to speculate as to which priorities would later be found to be just and reasonable by the Commission, and the absence of any stated Commission policy hindered effective long range planning by pipelines, distributors and consumers.

Sensing a need for guidance and uniformity in the curtailment area, on January 8, 1973 the Commission promulgated Order No. 467, the order presently under review.... Entitled "Statement of Policy," Order No. 467 was issued without prior notice or opportunity for comment. The statement sets forth the Commission's view of a proper priority schedule and expresses the Commission's policy that the national interest would be best served by assigning curtailment priorities on the basis of end use rather than on the basis of prior contractual commitments. Order No. 467 further states the Commission's intent to follow this priority schedule unless a particular pipeline company demonstrates that a different curtailment plan is more in the public interest....

The Commission immediately received numerous petitions for rehearing, reconsideration, modification or clarification of [Order No. 467].... Most of the petitioners were customers of pipeline companies subject to curtailment, particularly electric generating companies to whom Order No. 467 had assigned a low priority....

Petitioners seek review of Order No. 467 ... [They argue] that Order No. 467 is in effect a substantive rule which the Commission should have promulgated after a rulemaking proceeding under the Administrative Procedure Act (APA)....

## II. STATEMENTS OF POLICY

... [I]t is necessary ... to determine whether Order No. 467 is a substantive rule or merely a general statement of policy....

### A. *General Principles*

The APA requires that before an agency adopts a substantive rule, it must publish a notice of the proposed rule and provide interested persons an opportunity to comment. 5 U.S.C. § 553. The FPC did not utilize this rulemaking procedure in adopting Order No. 467. However, section 553(b)(A) of the APA provides an exception to the general rulemaking requirements:

> Except when notice or hearing is required by statute, this subsection does not apply—
>
> (A) to interpretative rules, *general statements of policy*, or rules of agency organization, procedure, or practice; ....

*Id.* § 553(b)(A) (emphasis added). The Commission maintains that Order No. 467 was exempt from the rulemaking requirements because it is a "general statement of policy" within the meaning of section 553(b)(A).

The APA never defines "general statements of policy" but it does define "rule" to

> [mean] the whole or a part of an agency statement of general or particular applicability and future effect designed to implement, interpret, or prescribe law or policy or describing the organization, procedure, or practice requirements of an agency ....

*Id.* § 551(4). This broad definition obviously could be read literally to encompass virtually any utterance by an agency, including statements of general policy. But the statutory provision of an exception to the rulemaking requirements for "general statements of policy" indicates that Congress did not intend the definition of "rule" to be construed so broadly. Congress recognized that certain administrative pronouncements did not require public participation in their formulation. These types of pronouncements are listed in section 553(b)(A) and include "general statements of policy."[14]

Professor [Kenneth Culp] Davis has described the distinction between substantive rules and general statements of policy as a "fuzzy product." Unfortunately the issues in this case compel us to attempt to define the fuzzy perimeters of a general statement of policy.

An administrative agency has available two methods for formulating policy that will have the force of law. An agency may establish binding policy through rulemaking procedures by which it promulgates substantive

---

14. Section 553(b)(A) also excludes "interpretative rules" from the rulemaking requirements. Interpretative rules are similar in some respects to general statements of policy. An interpretative rule expresses the agency's view of what another rule, regulation or statute means.... The agency's announced interpretation is usually followed until it is overruled by a court, but the scope of judicial review is broad because the interpretation of statutory language does not involve the agency's discretion....

rules, or through adjudications which constitute binding precedents. A general statement of policy is the outcome of neither a rulemaking nor an adjudication; it is neither a rule nor a precedent but is merely an announcement to the public of the policy which the agency hopes to implement in future rulemakings or adjudications. A general statement of policy, like a press release, presages an upcoming rulemaking or announces the course which the agency intends to follow in future adjudications.

As an informational device, the general statement of policy serves several beneficial functions. By providing a formal method by which an agency can express its views, the general statement of policy encourages public dissemination of the agency's policies prior to their actual application in particular situations. Thus the agency's initial views do not remain secret but are disclosed well in advance of their actual application. Additionally, the publication of a general statement of policy facilitates long range planning within the regulated industry and promotes uniformity in areas of national concern.

The critical distinction between a substantive rule and a general statement of policy is the different practical effect that these two types of pronouncements have in subsequent administrative proceedings. A properly adopted substantive rule establishes a standard of conduct which has the force of law. In subsequent administrative proceedings involving a substantive rule, the issues are whether the adjudicated facts conform to the rule and whether the rule should be waived or applied in that particular instance. The underlying policy embodied in the rule is not generally subject to challenge before the agency.

A general statement of policy, on the other hand, does not establish a "binding norm." It is not finally determinative of the issues or rights to which it is addressed. The agency cannot apply or rely upon a general statement of policy as law because a general statement of policy only announces what the agency seeks to establish as policy. A policy statement announces the agency's tentative intentions for the future. When the agency applies the policy in a particular situation, it must be prepared to support the policy just as if the policy statement had never been issued. An agency cannot escape its responsibility to present evidence and reasoning supporting its substantive rules by announcing binding precedent in the form of a general statement of policy.

Often the agency's own characterization of a particular order provides some indication of the nature of the announcement. The agency's express purpose may be to establish a binding rule of law not subject to challenge in particular cases. On the other hand the agency may intend merely to publish a policy guideline that is subject to complete attack before it is finally applied in future cases. When the agency states that in subsequent proceedings it will thoroughly consider not only the policy's applicability to the facts of a given case but also the underlying validity of the policy itself, then the agency intends to treat the order as a general statement of policy.

... The tentative effect of a general statement of policy has ramifications in subsequent judicial review proceedings as well as in administrative proceedings. Because a general statement of policy is adopted without public participation, the scope of review may be broader than the scope of review for a substantive rule. The rulemaking process prescribed by the APA insures a thorough exploration of the relevant issues. The public is notified of the proposed rule and interested parties submit arguments supporting their positions. The rulemaking process culminates in the agency applying its experience and expertise to the issues. A court reviewing a rule that was adopted pursuant to this extensive rulemaking process will defer to the agency's judgment if the rule satisfies the minimal criterion of reasonableness.

But when an agency promulgates a general statement of policy, the agency does not have the benefit of public exploration of the issues. Judicial review may be the first stage at which the policy is subjected to full criticism by interested parties. Consequently a policy judgment expressed as a general statement of policy is entitled to less deference than a decision expressed as a rule or an adjudicative order. Although the agency's expertise and experience cannot be ignored, the reviewing court has some leeway to assess the underlying wisdom of the policy and need not affirm a general statement of policy that merely satisfies the test of reasonableness.

### B. Order No. 467

Applying these general principles to the problem at hand, we conclude that Order No. 467 is a general statement of policy. Order No. 467 is entitled and consistently referred to by the Commission as a general statement of policy. Recognizing the "need for Commission guidance in curtailment planning," the Commission announced in Order No. 467 the curtailment policy which it "proposes to implement," the "plan preferred by the Commission" which "will serve as a guide in other proceedings." Thus, the stated purpose of Order No. 467 was not to provide an inflexible, binding rule but to give advance notice of the general policy with respect to curtailment priorities that the Commission prefers.

Order No. 467 does not establish a curtailment plan for any particular pipeline. The effect of the order is to inform the public of the types of plans which will receive initial and tentative FPC approval, but there is no assurance that any such plan will be finally approved. As the Commission stated:

> When applied in specific cases, opportunity will be afforded interested parties to challenge or support this policy through factual or legal presentation as may be appropriate in the circumstances presented[ . . . . ]

> [Order No. 467 is] not finally determinative of the rights and duties of a given pipeline, its customers or ultimate consumers; it expressly envisions further proceedings[ . . . . ]

> Not only will petitioners have an opportunity to challenge the merits of the proposed plan, they will also have an opportunity to demonstrate that the plan is inappropriate in particular circumstances[ . . . . ]

We recognized that some flexibility is essential as curtailments first occur, in order to ameliorate the economic dislocations which necessarily ensue, and for that reason we made clear in Order No. 467 that the policy therein stated could, and would, be adjusted in appropriate cases where the hearing record so required[. . . .]

Thus it is apparent from Order No. 467 itself that there is no final, inflexible impact upon the petitioners. And since the statement will be applied prospectively, the courts are in a position to police the Commission's application of the policy and to insure that the Commission gives no greater effect to Order No. 467 than the order is entitled to as a general statement of policy.

The FPC of course was under no compulsion to issue Order No. 467. The Commission issued the policy statement because the curtailment plans being submitted reflected sharp differences in philosophy which necessitated Commission guidance in the curtailment area. In the absence of such a policy statement, the Commission could have proceeded on an ad hoc basis and tentatively approved curtailment plans . . . which the Commission found to be just and reasonable. In following such a course the only difference from the present situation would be that the Commission would be acting under a secret policy rather than under the publicized guidelines of Order No. 467. The argument that an agency must follow rulemaking procedures when it elects to formulate policy by a substantive rule has no application in this case. Order No. 467 does not establish a substantive rule. Although the Commission is free to initiate a rulemaking proceeding to establish a binding substantive rule, the Commission apparently intends to establish its curtailment policies by proceeding through individual adjudications. Order No. 467 merely announces the general policy which the Commission hopes to establish in subsequent proceedings.

A comparison of the present case with Columbia Broadcasting System, Inc. v. United States, 316 U.S. 407 (1942), provides a good illustration of the difference between a substantive rule and a general statement of policy. After conducting extensive hearings with public participation, the Federal Communications Commission promulgated regulations purporting to require the Commission to refuse to grant or renew a license to any station which entered into certain types of contracts with a chain broadcasting network. Plaintiff, a chain broadcasting network, sued in district court for injunctive relief against the regulation. Although the FCC maintained that the regulations merely announced a general policy . . . , the Supreme Court concluded that the regulations had the effect of a substantive rule. . . . [25]

A distinguishing feature of the regulations in *Columbia Broadcasting* was their immediate and significant impact upon plaintiff's business. There was evidence that the issuance of the regulations caused the immediate cancellation of or failure to renew plaintiff's contracts. These ''wholesale

---

**25.** . . . The case arose prior to the enactment of the APA, and while the Court's holding was limited to determining the district court's jurisdiction, the treatment of the issues is helpful in understanding the difference between a rule and a general statement of policy under the APA. . . .

cancellations" seriously disorganized plaintiff's organization and impaired plaintiff's very "ability to conduct its business." The effect of Order No. 467 in the present case is not so direct or immediate. Any abrogation of contractual commitments will occur only after individual curtailment plans have been filed and approved by the Commission. In those proceedings all interested parties can appear, present their case and, if aggrieved, obtain judicial review. Assuming the Commission approves curtailment plans that override some contractual obligations, the result will be that during occasional periods of shortage coupled with high demand, deliveries to some customers rather than others might be curtailed. The possibility that petitioners might receive a lower curtailment priority at some future time as the result of a subsequent tariff filing does not compare with the significant and immediate impact of the regulations in *Columbia Broadcasting*.

A further important distinction between *Columbia Broadcasting* and the present case is that the FCC regulations in that case had the "force of law." Unlike Order No. 467, the FCC regulations were the product of a full rulemaking procedure, were "avowedly" adopted in the exercise of rulemaking power, and were "couched in terms of command." There was no assurance that the underlying validity of the regulations could be challenged in subsequent adjudications—the only issue in future proceedings would be whether a particular contract was within the regulations. Indeed, the FCC acknowledged that the regulations afforded a "legal basis" for subsequent administrative action. None of these features are present here. In this case the FPC has consistently viewed Order No. 467 as a general statement of policy and . . . the order does not have the binding force of a substantive rule.

Petitioners contend that Order No. 467 has an immediate and significant practical effect by shifting the burden of proof in curtailment cases from the pipeline companies to their customers because the order "established a presumption that the curtailment rules prescribed are consistent with the Natural Gas Act in any and all situations. . . ." Under section 4 of the Natural Gas Act a pipeline company filing a new curtailment plan has the burden of proving that its plan is reasonable and fair. . . . Petitioners maintain that by stating that tariffs which conform to the proposed plan will be permitted to become effective, Order No. 467 relieves the pipeline companies of their burden of justifying their plans. However, the language of Order No. 467 is as follows:

> Proposed tariff sheets which conform to the policies expressed in [Order No. 467] will be accepted for filing, and permitted to become effective, *subject to the rights of intervenors to hearing and adjudication of any claim of preference, discrimination, unjustness or unreasonableness* of the provisions contained in the proposed tariff sheets, and subject to the further right of anyone adversely affected to seek individualized special relief because of extraordinary circumstances.

49 F.P.C. at 585 (emphasis added). We interpret the italicized proviso to mean that in appropriate cases the Commission will conduct a section 4

proceeding to consider a challenge to the underlying validity of a curtailment plan, even though the plan conforms to Order No. 467. Section 4 renders unlawful curtailment plans which are preferential, discriminatory, unreasonable or unfair and provides for a hearing concerning the lawfulness of newly filed curtailment plans.... We expect the Commission generally to continue processing curtailment plans in section 4 proceedings, in which the pipeline company has the burden of proof, and to refrain from treating Order No. 467 as anything more than a general statement of policy....

---

**1. The "Force of Law" Test**—Substantive rules and policy statements are often difficult to distinguish from one another because both appear to declare, in advance and as a general matter, what sorts of conduct the agency will permit or prohibit when it considers individual cases in subsequent proceedings. Judge MacKinnon's opinion in *PG&E*, however, emphasizes that the "critical distinction" between substantive rules and policy statements is that they have a different *legal* status in these subsequent administrative proceedings. A valid substantive rule has the "force of law," meaning that the only question in the subsequent proceedings is whether the regulated parties conformed their conduct to the rule. The validity of the "underlying policy embodied in the rule" is not subject to challenge at that point. In contrast, a policy statement merely declares in advance how the agency intends to exercise its discretion in the future; the agency cannot rely on the policy statement in subsequent proceedings. As the *PG&E* opinion explains, when "the agency applies the policy [announced in the statement] in a particular situation, it must be prepared to support the policy just as if the policy statement had never been issued." Courts have consistently emphasized this "force of law" distinction as the most important means for differentiating substantive rules (which must go through notice and comment) from policy statements (which need not).

To illustrate, suppose that instead of issuing Order No. 467 as a "general statement of policy," the Commission had promulgated the substance of the Order as a notice-and-comment rule. Then, if a natural gas pipeline had responded to a shortage by proposing a curtailment plan that prioritized industrial consumers over residential customers, the Commission could reject the proposed plan as inconsistent with the rule. As long as the rule was valid, then the Commission would not need to say anything more, because the rule itself established a binding norm with which pipelines must comply. But in the real case, where Order No. 467 merely stated the agency's policy, if the Commission subsequently decided to reject a curtailment plan that gave priority to industrial over residential consumers, the Commission could not rely on the plan's inconsistency with the Order, because the Order itself has no legal effect—it's the equivalent of a press release or a speech by an agency official. Instead, the Commission would have to justify why, *in the individual adjudication at issue*, the proposed curtailment plan was "unjust" or "unreasonable" within the meaning of the Natural Gas Act.

But is this difference more formal than real? Suppose that the Commission had promulgated Order No. 467 as a notice-and-comment rule. If the Commission refused to approve a curtailment plan due to its inconsistency with that rule, why couldn't the pipeline (or other adversely affected party) challenge the Commission's decision on the grounds that the rule on which it was based was arbitrary, capricious, or otherwise not in accordance with law? Isn't the *PG&E* opinion incorrect, or at least seriously incomplete, when it declares that the "underlying policy embodied in the rule is not generally subject to challenge" in a subsequent administrative adjudication? (Recall the as-applied challenge to the rule in *Nova Scotia*, pp. 605–614, *supra*). Likewise, even if Order No. 467 was merely a "policy statement" with no binding "force of law," why couldn't the Commission, in denying approval for a curtailment plan that failed to prioritize residential customers, cite "the reasons given in Order No. 467," or, if the cross-reference would be deemed inadequate, simply cut-and-paste the language from Order No. 467 into the administrative order denying approval of the curtailment plan? After all, in light of decisions like *Chenery II* and *Bell Aerospace* (pp. 646–656, 668–670, *supra*), there would presumably be no problem with the Commission declaring its policy on this question in an adjudicative order. Do these observations undermine the utility of the "force of law" test as a means for distinguishing substantive rules from general statements of policy?

Maybe, but not necessarily. The fact that a substantive rule has the "force of law," while a policy statement does not, can sometimes make an important practical difference. First, and most straightforwardly, sometimes an agency would not have any legal basis to act unless it first promulgates a substantive rule. Second, although it is often possible for an adversely affected party to challenge the substantive validity of an agency rule as a defense to an enforcement action (as in *Nova Scotia*), it is not always possible to do so. For example, if the statute of limitations for a challenge to the rule has run, then adversely affected parties cannot collaterally attack the rule in an enforcement action. Do these points satisfy you that the "force of law" test draws a meaningful distinction between those general agency statements that must go through § 553 notice and comment and those that need not?

**2. *The Scope of Judicial Review*—**As noted above, the D.C. Circuit's opinion in *PG&E* may have overstated the practical significance of the fact that substantive rules have the "force of law," in light of the fact that adversely affected parties often *can* challenge the policy of the underlying substantive rule in subsequent adjudicative proceedings, as well as the fact that agencies can cross-reference or restate the reasoning provided in ostensibly "non-binding" policy statements when issuing binding orders in individual adjudications. Judge MacKinnon's opinion did demonstrate some awareness of this concern. One of his principal responses seemed to be that although an adversely affected party may challenge the policy underlying a substantive rule when seeking judicial review of an adjudicative order, and an agency may invoke the reasoning contained in a policy statement when defending an adjudicative order from a legal challenge, the odds that the agency will actually *prevail* in such disputes may turn on whether the agency promulgated its policy choice as a substantive rule or as a non-binding policy statement.

The reason, *PG&E* explained, is that courts may review administrative policy choices more deferentially if they are embodied in binding rules that go through notice and comment. As Judge MacKinnon put it, "[b]ecause a general statement of policy is adopted without public participation, the scope of review may be broader than the scope of review for a substantive rule. . . . A court reviewing a rule that was adopted pursuant to [the] extensive rulemaking process will defer to the agency's judgment if the rule satisfies the minimal criterion of reasonableness." In contrast, when an agency issues a general statement of policy, "[j]udicial review [of an enforcement action] may be the first stage at which the policy is subjected to full criticism by interested parties. Consequently a policy judgment expressed as a general statement of policy is entitled to less deference than a decision expressed as a rule or an adjudicative order." Thus, although Judge MacKinnon emphasized that a court should be respectful of the agency's expertise and experience, "the reviewing court has some leeway to assess the underlying wisdom of the policy and need not affirm a general statement of policy that merely satisfies the test of reasonableness."

If this is correct, then even if the agency had absolute discretion to designate its general pronouncements as substantive rules or as policy statements, the agency would not necessarily always opt for the latter in order to avoid the strictures of § 553's notice-and-comment procedures, because the agency might prefer to secure more deferential judicial review. In other words, the agency has a choice: It can shoulder the procedural costs of § 553, knowing that its final policy choice will be reviewed more deferentially, or it can dispense with § 553 and accept more aggressive judicial scrutiny. Is that a sensible way to structure the doctrine? What incentives does it create for agencies? Does it suggest that agencies will tend to use notice and comment for those rules that courts are likely to view skeptically, but to eschew notice and comment for rules that courts are expected to view sympathetically? If so, is that effect desirable? *See* Matthew C. Stephenson, *The Strategic Substitution Effect: Textual Plausibility, Procedural Formality, and Judicial Review of Agency Statutory Interpretations*, 120 HARV. L. REV. 528 (2006). We have not yet covered issues related to the standard of review of agency action, but when we turn to those issues we will revisit the question whether the standard of review does, or should, turn on the procedural form of the agency action in question. *See* pp. 935–937, *infra*.

**3. *Limitation on the Agency's Subsequent Discretion*—**Although *PG&E* emphasized the question whether an agency pronouncement has the "force of law," Judge MacKinnon's opinion also noted that Order No. 467 was not "inflexible" or "binding"; instead, the order indicated which sorts of curtailment plans would receive "initial and tentative FPC approval." The opinion stressed the Commission's pledge to consider each proposed plan on a case-by-case basis, and its insistence that Order No. 467 established only general guidelines. Thus, *PG&E* suggested that another important factor in differentiating policy statements from substantive rules is the degree to which an agency statement purports to limit the agency's subsequent discretion.

This consideration is often conflated with the question whether an agency statement has the force of law—both are sometimes characterized as related to whether the agency statement has "binding effect"—but these considerations are distinct. The "force of law" inquiry has to do with the formal legal effect of an agency statement in a subsequent proceeding. The flexibility or inflexibility of the policy announced in that statement has to do with the degree to which the agency anticipates adjusting its specific decisions to the circumstances of individual cases. It is not hard to imagine extremely inflexible policy statements that do not have any binding legal effect. Suppose, for example, that the FPC issued a press release declaring that it planned to exercise its statutory discretion to reject any proposed curtailment plan that failed to prioritize residential consumers. That announcement would not have the force of law—the Commission in subsequent proceedings would have to rely on its statutory authority to reject any individual plan—but the announced policy is extremely inflexible. Likewise, many notice-and-comment regulations that *do* have the force of law allow for discretionary exceptions when justified by the circumstances. These rules may be just as "flexible" as Order No. 467, but they have the force of law.

Once we see that the flexibility of an agency's pronouncement (that is, the degree to which it purports to restrict or limit the action that the agency may take in the future) is distinct from the "force of law" question, we may naturally ask whether, or to what extent, the flexibility of the agency pronouncement should be a factor in distinguishing substantive rules from policy statements for purposes of § 553. Some court of appeals decisions have emphasized this "flexibility" factor. For example, in *Community Nutrition Institute v. Young*, 818 F.2d 943 (D.C. Cir. 1987), the D.C. Circuit considered a challenge to an FDA "policy statement" (styled by the FDA as an "action level") that said the agency would initiate enforcement proceedings against any food producer that sold corn with an aflatoxin content above a specified numerical concentration level, on the grounds that such corn would be "adulterated" within the meaning of the Food, Drugs, and Cosmetics Act. The D.C. Circuit held that this alleged "policy statement" was actually a substantive rule. The court acknowledged that the action level did not have the force of law, noting:

> [I]n a suit to enjoin shipment of allegedly contaminated corn, it appears that FDA would be obliged to prove that the corn is "adulterated," within the meaning of the [Food, Drugs, and Cosmetics] Act, rather than merely prove non-compliance with the action level. The action level thus does not bind food producers in the sense that

producers are automatically subject to enforcement proceedings for violating the action level.

*Id.* at 948 (internal citations omitted). The court nonetheless concluded that the action level's lack of binding legal effect on food producers was "not determinative" because the "FDA has bound itself." *Id.* "[T]his type of cabining of an agency's prosecutorial discretion," the court reasoned, "can in fact rise to the level of a substantive, legislative rule." Id. *See also* United States Telephone Ass'n v. FCC, 28 F.3d 1232, 1234 (D.C. Cir. 1994) (claiming that the distinction between substantive rules and general statements of policy "turns on an agency's intention to bind itself to a particular legal policy position"); Nader v. Civil Aeronautics Bd., 657 F.2d 453, 456 (D.C. Cir. 1981) (finding agency guidelines that "narrowly circumscribe[ ] the Board's discretion" qualify as a substantive rule); Guardian Fed. Sav. & Loan Ass'n v. Federal Sav. & Loan Ins. Corp., 589 F.2d 658, 666–67 (D.C. Cir. 1978) (holding that "[i]f it appears that a so-called policy statement is in purpose or likely effect one that narrowly limits administrative discretion, it will be taken for what it is—a binding rule of substantive law").

Is that correct? Assuming that an agency statement does not have the formal force and effect of law, should it still be classified as a substantive rule if the statement appears to declare an inflexible policy that the agency plans to follow in all future cases, rather than a speculative or tentative general intention, which the agency declares it may not follow in all individual cases? The position has some intuitive appeal, in that the more the agency appears to treat its prior pronouncement as binding on the agency itself, the more that pronouncement looks like a binding substantive rule, whether or not it has a formal legal effect on the conduct of outside parties. This observation gains added force when considered in light of the fact that, as noted above, the formal legal status of an agency statement may not make that much practical difference in many cases.

Then again, if the agency has decided to exercise its discretion in a relatively inflexible manner, and the agency would have the lawful statutory discretion to do so, why shouldn't the agency be able to announce this policy ahead of time? *See* Ronald M. Levin, *Nonlegislative Rules and the Administrative Open Mind*, 41 Duke L.J. 1497, 1499 (1992). Consider, again, the *Chenery II* case, which held that it was perfectly legitimate for the SEC to declare, in an adjudicative order, that it would reject any reorganization plan that permitted corporate insiders to benefit from trades in the corporation's securities while the plan was pending with the SEC. Nowhere did *Chenery II* indicate that the SEC had to frame this principle in tentative or otherwise flexible terms; the agency could simply declare the policy and then follow it in future cases, using its earlier decision as a precedent. Suppose that the SEC had announced its views in an earlier policy statement, which was not phrased in tentative or speculative terms. On the logic of *Community Nutrition Institute* and the other cases cited above, would this statement have been a substantive rule that required compliance with notice-and-comment rulemaking procedures? If not, how do you distinguish the cases? If so, then isn't the end result that the agency would simply abstain from issuing the policy statement, but would none-theless adhere to its inflexible policy? Doesn't that undermine one of the main benefits of general policy statements—that, as the *PG&E* court put it, "[b]y providing a formal method by which an agency can express its views, the general statement of policy encourages public dissemination of the agency's policies prior to their actual application in particular situations . . . [and ensures that] the agency's initial views do not remain secret but are disclosed well in advance of their actual application"?

**4. *The Practical Effect on Regulated Parties*—**We have seen that when courts and commentators assert that the key difference between substantive rules and general policy statements is that the former but not the latter have "binding effect," they could mean one or both of two conceptually distinct things. The first is the idea that substantive rules, but not policy statements, have the force of law as a formal matter. The second is the idea that substantive rules are less flexible than policy statements, in that they announce more definite limits on how the agency will exercise its discretion. There is yet a third sense in which courts and commentators sometimes use the phrase "binding effect" to capture the difference be-tween substantive rules and policy statements: the idea that rules have a more practical binding (or coercive) effect on regulated parties than do policy statements. *PG&E* invoked this idea when distinguishing Order No. 467 from the FCC "policy statement" at issue in Columbia Broadcasting System, Inc. v. United States, 316 U.S. 407 (1942), which the Supreme Court concluded was in fact an invalid substantive rule. In the statement that precipitated the *Columbia Broadcasting* litigation, the FCC had de-clared that it would refuse to grant or renew broadcasting licenses under specified circumstances. This certainly resembles the sort of advance decla-ration contained in Order No. 467. *PG&E* nonetheless concluded that the FCC statement at issue in *Columbia Broadcasting* was distinguishable because of its "immediate and significant impact" on the business of the adversely affected petitioners. "The effect of Order No. 467 in the present case," *PG&E* reasoned, "is not so direct or immediate," and the "possibili-ty that petitioners might receive a lower curtailment priority at some future time . . . does not compare with the significant and immediate impact of the regulations in *Columbia Broadcasting*." In a more recent case, the D.C. Circuit summed up this basic idea as follows: "[I]f [an agency document] leads private parties . . . to believe that [the agency] will declare permits invalid unless they comply with the terms of the document, then the agency's document is for all practical purposes 'binding.' " Appalachian Power Co. v. EPA, 208 F.3d 1015, 1021 (D.C. Cir. 2000).

While an agency statement with the force of law may often exert a greater coercive effect than one without the force of law, statements of the latter variety can still exert a powerful coercive effect, as *Columbia Broad-casting* recognized. If potentially affected parties can anticipate what the agency plans to do, they may alter their conduct so as to comply. An agency statement that is framed in non-discretionary terms (e.g., that the agency "shall"—as opposed to "may"—approve a given proposal, or initiate en-forcement proceedings under specified circumstances) might well have a greater practical coercive effect on affected parties, but such mandatory language is not always necessary for such an effect. As Professor Robert Anthony, a prominent critic of agencies' alleged overuse of the "policy statement" exception to § 553, has argued:

> [D]espite any professed reservation of discretion, a nonlegislative document as a practical matter can quite readily impose binding standards or obligations upon private parties. Their discretion is constrained even if the agency's is not. A test more consistent with the spirit of the APA than one looking to the constraints on an agency's discretion would be one that considered whether the intended or actual constraints on the *private persons' discretion* (that is, upon their freedom of action) amount to binding them in a practical sense. If so, the recitation that discretion is reserved should be of no moment, and the agency's circumvention of legislative rulemaking procedures should be redressed.

Robert A. Anthony, *Interpretive Rules, Policy Statements, Guidances, Manuals, and the Like—Should Federal Agencies Use Them To Bind the Public?*, 41 DUKE L.J. 1311, 1360–61 (1992) (emphasis in original). Indeed, Professor Anthony argues that if courts are more likely to treat an agency pronouncement as a policy statement exempt from § 553 if the agency reserves more discretion to itself, without regard for the practical coercive effect of the statement on the conduct of outside parties, then we get the perverse result that "the agency is rewarded for stating its rules with less precision and authority than might otherwise be required of it ... [even though] as a practical matter it still may be able to apply or threaten to apply the rule in a binding way." *Id.* at 1362; *see also* James T. Hamilton & Christopher H. Schroeder, *Strategic Regulators and the Choice of Rulemaking Procedures: The Selection of Formal vs. Informal Rules in Regulating Hazardous Waste*, 57 LAW & CONTEMP. PROBS. 111, 147 (Spring 1994) (arguing that "the prospect of multiple future interactions between [the regulatory agency and regulated entities] ... may provide the regulators with leverage to secure adherence to rules that have not been formally promulgated [through the notice-and-comment process]").

Do you find that critique persuasive? Should the distinction between substantive rules and general statements of policy turn principally on the degree to which the agency statement exerts a practical coercive effect on regulated parties? How can such an effect be predicted or measured?

* * * * * *

As we have seen, although most courts emphasize that the distinction between substantive rules and general statements of policy turns on whether the policy statement in question has a "binding effect," there are a number of different senses in which an agency's statement may be "binding": (1) It may be legally binding, in that the statement is in and of itself a valid legal norm; (2) it may be practically binding on the agency, in that the statement seems to announce a firm rule that the agency plans to apply inflexibly; and (3) it may be practically binding on regulated parties, who may feel compelled to conform their conduct to the standards announced in the agency statement. These different sorts of "binding effects" often go together, but they need not. The most challenging cases are those in which the agency statement does not have *legally* binding effects, but nonetheless appears to cabin the discretion of the agency and/or to exert a coercive effect on regulated parties. Although cases like *PG&E* emphasize the "force of law" factor as the "critical distinction between a substantive rule and a general statement of policy," other cases focus more on practical consequences. The following case, *Chamber of Commerce v. Department of Labor*, is a case of that type. As you read the case, consider whether the analysis in *Chamber of Commerce* is consistent with *PG&E*. To the extent the cases are inconsistent, which do you think is more persuasive?

---

# Chamber of Commerce of the United States v. United States Department of Labor

U.S. Court of Appeals for the D.C. Circuit
174 F.3d 206 (D.C. Cir. 1999)

■ GINSBURG, CIRCUIT JUDGE:

The Occupational Safety and Health Administration, part of the United States Department of Labor, issued a "Directive" pursuant to which each employer in selected industries will be inspected unless it adopts a comprehensive safety and health program designed to meet standards that in some respects exceed those required by law. The Chamber of Commerce objects to the Directive on the grounds that prior notice and an opportunity to comment were required by the Administrative Procedure Act. . . .

## I.  Background

According to the OSHA, the Directive, which establishes the "OSHA High Injury/Illness Rate Targeting and Cooperative Compliance Program," represents a new, cooperative approach to the problem of worker safety at some 12,500 relatively dangerous workplaces. The Directive first provides that each of these sites will be placed on a so-called "primary inspection list" and subjected to a comprehensive inspection before the end of 1999. (But for the Directive, the OSHA might have searched some of the sites, but it does not claim that it would have searched all of them). The Directive next provides that the agency will remove a workplace from the primary inspection list, and reduce by 70 to 90 percent the probability that it will be inspected, if the employer participates in the agency's "Cooperative Compliance Program."

Participation in the CCP obligates the employer to satisfy eight requirements. An employer must agree, for example, to "[i]dentify and correct hazards" and to "[w]ork toward a significant reduction of injuries and illnesses." Most important is the requirement that the employer implement a "comprehensive safety and health program" (CSHP) that meets the standard established in the OSHA's 1989 Safety and Health Program Management Guidelines.

... Although many aspects of a CSHP are, not surprisingly, directed toward the prevention or correction of violations of the Occupational Safety and Health Act, the Directive makes clear that compliance with the Act is not in itself sufficient for participation in the new CCP: "An effective [CSHP] looks beyond specific requirements of law to address all hazards. It will seek to prevent injuries and illnesses, whether or not compliance is at issue." Further to this point, an acceptable CSHP also obligates the employer to be generally in compliance with applicable "voluntary standards," "industry practices," and even "suppliers' safety recommendations."

## II.  Analysis

The Chamber of Commerce petitions for review of the Directive first on the ground that the agency should have conducted a notice and comment rulemaking proceeding prior to issuing it....

Under the APA, 5 U.S.C. § 553, an agency seeking to promulgate a rule must first provide the public with notice of, and an opportunity to comment upon, a proposed version of it. The OSHA concedes that the Directive is, in APA parlance, a "rule," and therefore that § 553 applies.... The agency takes the position, however, that notice and comment rulemaking was not required because the Directive falls into the exception[] provided in § 553(b)(3)(A) for ... "general statements of policy."...

A general statement of policy "does not establish a binding norm. It is not finally determinative of the issues or rights to which it is addressed. The agency cannot apply or rely upon [such a] policy as law because a general statement of policy only announces what the agency seeks to establish as policy." Pacific Gas & Elec. Co. v. FPC, 506 F.2d 33, 38 (D.C.Cir.1974). The OSHA argues that the Directive meets this definition, raising ... the point that the rule imposes no formal legal obligation upon an employer that chooses not to participate in the CCP.

In this context, the agency's contention has some intuitive appeal: At first glance, one might think that a rule could not be considered a "binding norm" unless it is backed by a threat of legal sanction. Beyond that first glance, however, its appeal is fleeting.

In American Bus Association v. United States, 627 F.2d 525 (1980), we held that the question whether a rule is a policy statement is to be determined by whether it (1) has only a prospective effect, and (2) leaves agency decisionmakers free to exercise their informed discretion in individual cases. Both criteria lead us here to the conclusion that the Directive is a substantive rule rather than a policy statement. First, the Directive provides that every employer that does not participate in the CCP will be searched. The effect of the rule is therefore not to "announce[] the agency's tentative intentions for the future," *Pacific Gas*, 506 F.2d at 38, but to inform employers of a decision already made. See American Bus Ass'n, 627

F.2d at 531 (order indicating that applicants providing certain documents would receive "immediate issuance" of certificate permitting transport of goods to Canada had current, not prospective, effect and therefore was not statement of policy); *cf. Pacific Gas*, 506 F.2d at 40–41 (order intended to inform public of types of plans that will receive "initial and tentative" agency approval is policy statement). Indeed, the OSHA admits in its brief that the inspection plan "leave[s] no room for discretionary choices by inspectors in the field." And the Directive itself suggests that the agency will not remove an employer from the CCP unless the employer fails to abide by the terms of the program. Therefore, although the Directive does not impose a binding norm in the sense that it gives rise to a legally enforceable duty, neither can it be shoehorned into the exception for policy statements. . . .

■ [Judge Silberman's dissent on jurisdictional grounds is omitted.]

### c.  Interpretive Rules

Section 553(b)(A) exempts interpretative rules (also know as interpretive rules) from § 553's notice-and-comment requirements. Interpretive rules and general statements of policy are similar in many respects, and they are often referred to collectively as "non-legislative rules" (as distinct from substantive rules, also known as "legislative rules"). But there are some important differences between them. A policy statement is a preliminary announcement by the agency of how it intends to exercise its discretion in some future case, given a relatively open-ended grant of legal authority. An interpretive rule is a declaration of how the agency interprets an ambiguous statute or regulation. This is often a difficult distinction to draw, especially since an agency's plans for exercising its discretion often depend on how the agency interprets some ambiguous legal provision. But as we shall see, the distinction can be important for both agencies and regulated parties.

The next case, *American Mining Congress v. MSHA*, contains an influential—though sometimes contested—outline of the doctrine for distinguishing interpretive rules from legislative rules. When reading the case, pay particular attention to the similarities and differences between the doctrinal test the court lays out in this context and the doctrinal test (or tests) the courts have applied when distinguishing legislative rules from "general statements of policy" (pp. 677–697, *supra*).

## American Mining Congress v. Mine Safety & Health Administration

U.S. Court of Appeals for the D.C. Circuit
995 F.2d 1106 (D.C. Cir. 1993)

■ Stephen F. Williams, Circuit Judge:

This case presents a single issue: whether Program Policy Letters of the Mine Safety and Health Administration, stating the agency's position that certain x-ray readings qualify as "diagnose[s]" of lung disease within the meaning of agency reporting regulations, are interpretive rules under the Administrative Procedure Act. We hold that they are.

\* \* \* \* \* \*

The Federal Mine Safety and Health Act ... extensively regulates health and safety conditions in the nation's mines and empowers the Secretary of Labor to enforce the statute and relevant regulations. In addition, the Act requires "every operator of a ... mine ... [to] establish and maintain such records, make such reports, and provide such information, as the Secretary ... may reasonably require from time to time to enable him to perform his functions." The Act makes a general grant of authority to the Secretary to issue "such regulations as ... [he] deems appropriate to carry out" any of its provisions.

Pursuant to its statutory authority, the Mine Safety and Health Administration (acting on behalf of the Secretary of Labor) maintains regulations known as "Part 50" regulations, which cover the "Notification, Investigation, Reports and Records of Accidents, Injuries, Illnesses, Employment, and Coal Production in Mines." These were adopted via notice-and-comment rulemaking. Subpart C deals with the "Reporting of Accidents, Injuries, and Illnesses" and requires mine operators to report to the MSHA within ten days "each accident, occupational injury, or occupational illness" that occurs at a mine. Of central importance here, the regulation also says that whenever any of certain occupational illnesses are *"diagnosed,"* the operator must similarly report the diagnosis within ten days. (emphasis added). . . . An operator's failure to report may lead to citation and penalty.

As the statute and formal regulations contain ambiguities, the MSHA from time to time issues Program Policy Letters ("PPLs") intended to coordinate and convey agency policies, guidelines, and interpretations to agency employees and interested members of the public. One subject on which it has done so—apparently in response to inquiries from mine operators about whether certain x-ray results needed to be reported as "diagnos[es]"—has been the meaning of the term diagnosis for purposes of Part 50.

The first of the PPLs at issue here ... stated that any chest x-ray of a miner who had a history of exposure to pneumoconiosis ... would be considered a "diagnosis that the x-rayed miner has silicosis or one of the other pneumoconioses" for the purposes of the Part 50 reporting requirements. . . .

The second letter ... stated the MSHA's position that mere diagnosis of an occupational disease or illness within the meaning of Part 50 did not automatically entitle a miner to benefits for disability or impairment under a workers' compensation scheme. The PPL also said that the MSHA did not intend for an operator's mandatory reporting of an x-ray reading to be equated with an admission of liability for the reported disease.

The final PPL under dispute . . . restated the MSHA's basic view that a chest x-ray . . . constituted a "diagnosis" of silicosis or some other pneumoconiosis. . . .

The MSHA did not follow the notice and comment requirements of 5 U.S.C. § 553 in issuing any of the three PPLs. In defending its omission of notice and comment, the agency relies solely on the interpretive rule exemption of § 553(b)(3)(A). . . .

\* \* \* \* \* \*

The distinction between those agency pronouncements subject to APA notice-and-comment requirements and those that are exempt has been aptly described as "enshrouded in considerable smog," General Motors Corporation v. Ruckelshaus, 742 F.2d 1561, 1565 (D.C.Cir.1984) (en banc) (quoting Noel v. Chapman, 508 F.2d 1023, 1030 (2d Cir.1975)); see also American Hospital Association v. Bowen, 834 F.2d 1037, 1046 (D.C.Cir. 1987) (calling the line between interpretive and legislative rules "fuzzy"); Community Nutrition Institute v. Young, 818 F.2d 943, 946 (D.C.Cir.1987) (quoting authorities describing the present distinction between legislative rules and policy statements as "tenuous," "blurred" and "baffling").

Given the confusion, it makes some sense to go back to the origins of the distinction in the legislative history of the Administrative Procedure Act. Here the key document is the *Attorney General's Manual on the Administrative Procedure Act* (1947), which offers "the following working definitions":

> *Substantive rules*—rules [ . . . ] issued by an agency pursuant to statutory authority and which implement the statute, as, for example, the proxy rules issued by the Securities and Exchange Commission pursuant to section 14 of the Securities Exchange Act of 1934 (15 U.S.C. 78n). Such rules have the force and effect of law.

> *Interpretative rules*—rules or statements issued by an agency to advise the public of the agency's construction of the statutes and rules which it administers. . . .

> *General statements of policy*—statements issued by an agency to advise the public prospectively of the manner in which the agency proposes to exercise a discretionary power.

. . . Our own decisions have often used similar language, inquiring whether the disputed rule has "the force of law". We have said that a rule has such force only if Congress has delegated legislative power to the agency and if the agency intended to exercise that power in promulgating the rule.

On its face, the "intent to exercise" language may seem to lead only to more smog, but in fact there are a substantial number of instances where such "intent" can be found with some confidence. The first and clearest case is where, in the absence of a legislative rule by the agency, the legislative basis for agency enforcement would be inadequate. The example used by the Attorney General's Manual fits exactly—the SEC's proxy authority under § 14 of the Securities Exchange Act of 1934, 15 U.S.C. § 78n. Section 14(b), for example, forbids certain persons, "to give, or to refrain from giving a proxy" "in contravention of such rules and regulations as the Commission may prescribe". The statute itself forbids *nothing* except acts or omissions to be spelled out by the Commission in "rules or regulations". The present case is similar, as to Part 50 itself, in that § 813(h) merely requires an operator to maintain "such records . . . as the Secretary . . . may reasonably require from time to time". Although the Secretary might conceivably create some "require[ments]" ad hoc, clearly some agency creation of a duty is a necessary predicate to any enforcement against an operator for failure to keep records. Analogous cases may exist in which an agency may offer a government benefit only after it formalizes the prerequisites.

Second, an agency seems likely to have intended a rule to be legislative if it has the rule published in the Code of Federal Regulations; 44 U.S.C. § 1510 limits publication in that code to rules "having general applicability and legal effect". See Brock v. Cathedral Bluffs Shale Oil Co., 796 F.2d 533, 539 (D.C.Cir.1986) (Scalia, J.).

Third, " '[i]f a second rule repudiates or is irreconcilable with [a prior legislative rule], the second rule must be an amendment of the first; and, of course, an amendment to a legislative rule must itself be legislative.' " National Family Planning & Reproductive Health Ass'n v. Sullivan, 979 F.2d 227, 235 (D.C.Cir.1992) (quoting Michael Asimow, *Nonlegislative Rulemaking and Regulatory Reform,* 1985 Duke L.J. 381, 396). . . .

There are variations on these themes. For example, in Chamber of Commerce v. OSHA, 636 F.2d 464 (D.C.Cir.1980), the agency had on a prior occasion claimed that a certain statutory term, correctly understood, itself imposed a specific requirement on affected businesses. We found that interpretation substantively invalid, but noted the agency's power to promulgate such a requirement on the basis of more general authority. Leone v. Mobil Oil Corp.,i 523 F.2d 1153 (D.C.Cir.1975). The agency then issued a purported interpretive rule to fill the gap (without notice and comment), and we struck it down as an invalid exercise of the agency's legislative powers.

We reviewed a similar juxtaposition of different agency modes in Fertilizer Institute v. EPA, 935 F.2d 1303, 1308 (D.C.Cir.1991). There a statute created a duty to report any "release" of a "reportable quantity" or "RQ" of certain hazardous materials, specifying the RQs but authorizing the EPA to change them by regulation. In the preamble to a legislative rule exercising its authority to amend the RQs, the EPA also expatiated on the meaning of the statutory term "release"—improperly broadening it, as petitioners claimed and as we ultimately found. But we rejected a claim that the agency's attempted exposition of the term "release" was not an interpretation and therefore required notice and comment.

In United States v. Picciotto, 875 F.2d 345 (D.C.Cir.1989), the Park Service had issued an indisputably legislative rule containing an "open-ended" provision stating that a "permit may contain additional reasonable conditions". Then, in a rule issued without notice and comment, it established some such conditions. We struck down the disputed condition, as it was not an interpretation of the prior regulation but an exercise of the legislative authority reserved by the prior legislative rule.

This focus on whether the agency *needs* to exercise legislative power (to provide a basis for enforcement actions or agency decisions conferring benefits) helps explain some distinctions that may, out of context, appear rather metaphysical. For example, in *Fertilizer Institute* we drew a distinction between instances where an agency merely "declare[s] its understanding of what a statute requires" (interpretive), and ones where an agency "go[es] beyond the text of a statute" (legislative).... The difficulty with the distinction is that almost every rule may seem to do both. But if the dividing line is the necessity for agency legislative action, then a rule supplying that action will be legislative no matter how grounded in the agency's "understanding of what the statute requires", and an interpretation that spells out the scope of an agency's or regulated entity's pre-existing duty (such as EPA's interpretation of "release" in *Fertilizer Institute*), will be interpretive....

Similarly, we have distinguished between cases where a rule is "based on specific statutory provisions" (interpretive), and where one is instead "based on an agency's power to exercise its judgment as to how best to implement a general statutory mandate" (legislative). United Technologies Corp. v. EPA, 821 F.2d 714, 719–20 (D.C.Cir.1987). A statute or legislative rule that actually establishes a duty or a right is likely to be relatively specific (and the agency's refinement will be interpretive), whereas an agency's authority to create rights and duties will typically be relatively broad (and the agency's actual establishment of rights and duties will be legislative). But the legislative or interpretive status of the agency rules turns not in some general sense on the narrowness or breadth of the statutory (or regulatory) term in question, but on the prior existence or non-existence of legal duties and rights.

Of course an agency may for reasons of its own choose explicitly to invoke its general legislating authority—perhaps, for example, out of concern that its proposed action might be invalid as an interpretation of some existing mandate.... In that event, even if a court believed that the agency had been unduly cautious about the legislative background, it would presumably treat the rule as an attempted exercise of legislative power.

In an occasional case we have appeared to stress whether the disputed rule is one with "binding effect"—"binding" in the sense that the rule does not " 'genuinely leave[ ] the agency ... free to exercise discretion.' " State of Alaska v. DOT, 868 F.2d at 445 (quoting Community Nutrition Institute v. Young, 818 F.2d 943, 945–46 (D.C.Cir.1987)). That inquiry arose in a quite different context, that of distinguishing *policy statements,* rather than interpretive rules, from legislative norms. The classic application is Pacific Gas & Electric Co. v. FPC, 506 F.2d 33, 38 (D.C.Cir.1974)....

But while a good rule of thumb is that a norm is less likely to be a general policy statement when it purports (or, even better, has proven) to restrict agency discretion, restricting discretion tells one little about whether a rule is interpretive.... Nor is there much explanatory power in any distinction that looks to the use of mandatory as opposed to permissive language. While an agency's decision to use "will" instead of "may" may be of use when drawing a line between *policy statements* and legislative rules, the endeavor miscarries in the interpretive/legislative rule context. Interpretation is a chameleon that takes its color from its context; therefore, an interpretation will use imperative language—or at least have imperative meaning—if the interpreted term is part of a command; it will use permissive language—or at least have a permissive meaning—if the interpreted term is in a permissive provision.

A non-legislative rule's capacity to have a binding effect is limited in practice by the fact that agency personnel at every level act under the shadow of judicial review. If they believe that courts may fault them for brushing aside the arguments of persons who contest the rule or statement, they are obviously far more likely to entertain those arguments. And, as failure to provide notice-and-comment rulemaking will usually mean that affected parties have had no prior formal opportunity to present their contentions, judicial review for want of reasoned decisionmaking is likely, in effect, to take place in review of specific agency actions implementing the rule. Similarly, where the agency must defend its view [of the statute as reasonable,] agency disregard of significant policy arguments will clearly count against it. As Donald Elliott has said, agency attentiveness to parties' arguments must come sooner or later. "As in the television commercial in which the automobile repairman intones ominously 'pay me now, or pay me later,' the agency has a choice...." E. Donald Elliott, *Reinventing Rulemaking,* 41 Duke L.J. 1490, 1491 (1992). Because the threat of judicial review provides a spur to the agency to pay attention to facts and arguments submitted in derogation of any rule not supported by notice and comment, even as late as the enforcement stage, *any* agency statement not subjected to notice-and-comment rulemaking will be more vulnerable to attack not only in court but also within the agency itself.

Not only does an agency have an incentive to entertain objections to an interpretive rule, but the ability to promulgate such rules, without notice and comment, does not appear more hazardous to affected parties than the likely alternative. Where a statute or legislative rule has created a legal basis for enforcement, an agency can simply let its interpretation evolve ad hoc in the process of enforcement or other applications (e.g., grants). The protection that Congress sought to secure by requiring notice and comment for legislative rules is not advanced by reading the exemption for "interpretive rule" so narrowly as to drive agencies into pure ad hocery—an ad hocery, moreover, that affords less notice, or less convenient notice, to affected parties.

Accordingly, insofar as our cases can be reconciled at all, we think it almost exclusively on the basis of whether the purported interpretive rule has "legal effect", which in turn is best ascertained by asking (1) whether in the absence of the rule there would not be an adequate legislative basis for enforcement action or other agency action to confer benefits or ensure the performance of duties, (2) whether the agency has published the rule in the Code of Federal Regulations, (3) whether the agency has explicitly invoked its general legislative authority, or (4) whether the rule effectively amends a prior legislative rule. If the answer to any of these questions is affirmative, we have a legislative, not an interpretive rule.

Here we conclude that the August 1992 PPL is an interpretive rule. The Part 50 regulations themselves require the reporting of diagnoses of the specified diseases, so there is no legislative gap that required the PPL as a predicate to enforcement action. Nor did the agency purport to act legislatively, either by including the letter in the Code of Federal Regulations, or by invoking its general legislative authority under [the statute]. . . . The remaining possibility therefore is that the August 1992 PPL is a de facto amendment of prior legislative rules, namely the Part 50 regulations.

A rule does not, in this inquiry, become an amendment merely because it supplies crisper and more detailed lines than the authority being interpreted. If that were so, no rule could pass as an interpretation of a legislative rule unless it were confined to parroting the rule or replacing the original vagueness with another. . . .

Although petitioners cite some definitions of "diagnosis" suggesting that with pneumoconiosis and silicosis, a diagnosis requires more than a chest x-ray—specifically, additional diagnostic tools as tissue examination or at least an occupational history. . .—MSHA points to some administrative rules that make x-rays at the level specified here the basis for a finding of pneumoconiosis. . . . A finding of a disease is surely equivalent, in normal terminology, to a diagnosis, and thus the PPLs certainly offer no interpretation that repudiates or is irreconcilable with an existing legislative rule.

We stress that deciding whether an interpretation is an amendment of a legislative rule is different from deciding the substantive validity of that interpretation. An interpretive rule may be sufficiently within the language of a legislative rule to be a genuine interpretation and not an amendment, while at the same time being an incorrect interpretation of the agency's statutory authority. . . . Here, petitioners have made no attack on the PPLs' substantive validity. Nothing that we say upholding the agency's decision to act without notice and comment bars any such substantive claims. . . .

---

*1.  Easy Cases?*—Although distinguishing between legislative and interpretive rules is among the most complex problems in administrative law, Judge Williams' opinion in *AMC* attempted to identify straightforward criteria for doing so in some cases. Perhaps most obviously, if the agency explicitly announces that it is issuing a legislative rule pursuant to a valid statutory grant of authority to enact such rules, then courts will treat the resulting rule as legislative rather than interpretive. (*AMC* also indicated that an agency may implicitly classify a rule as legislative by publishing it in the Code of Federal Regulations (CFR), but a subsequent D.C. Circuit opinion, also written by Judge Williams, backed away from that position. *See* Health Ins. Ass'n of Am. v. Shalala, 23 F.3d 412, 423 (D.C. Cir. 1994) (treating publication in the CFR as no more than "a snippet of evidence of agency intent").)

But what if the agency has not explicitly declared that a rule is legislative rather than interpretive? Indeed, what if the agency insists that the rule is interpretive, and therefore exempt from notice and comment? *AMC* addressed this question by noting several circumstances in which an agency rule is necessarily legislative, even if the agency says otherwise. The first is when, in the absence of the rule, the agency would lack any authority to take subsequent legal action. *AMC* noted the example, drawn from a discussion in the *Attorney General's Manual*, of the provision in the Securities Exchange Act that prohibits any issuer of a security from violating "such rules and regulations as the [Securities and Exchange Commission (SEC)] may prescribe." If the SEC issues no such rules or regulations, then it is not possible to violate this section of the statute, so any rule on which the SEC relies in enforcing this section must be legislative. Also, if the alleged interpretive rule is irreconcilable with a prior legislative rule, then the former rule will be deemed legislative rather than interpretive. While these rules of thumb mitigate the complexity of the inquiry, they do not eliminate the need to adopt more general criteria for distinguishing interpretive rules from legislative rules.

**2. *The Defining Characteristics of Interpretive Rules*—**As with general statements of policy, interpretive rules lack the binding legal force of a legislative rule in the sense that one cannot incur legal liability simply for "violating" an interpretive rule. (Contrast this with the SEC's Rule 10b–5, which prohibits, among other things, insider trading in securities. Because 10b–5 is a legislative rule, a willful violation of that rule itself provides the basis for legal liability.) But the similarities appear to end there. In contrast with the law surrounding general statements of policy, *AMC* suggested that an agency document may qualify as an interpretive rule even if it narrows agency discretion or exerts a coercive effect on regulated parties. *AMC*'s reasoning was straightforward: An interpretive rule is an agency's declaration of what it thinks some statutory or regulatory command *actually means*. Either MSHA thinks that an x-ray is a "diagnosis" within the meaning of its existing regulations, or it does not. If the underlying command is inflexible, the agency's interpretation will also be inflexible. If the underlying statutory or regulatory provision that the agency is interpreting has coercive effects on regulated parties, then an interpretation of that provision will also have coercive effects.

This implies that it may matter a great deal whether an agency's statement can be characterized as an "interpretive rule" rather than as a "general statement of policy"—a question taken up in greater detail below. *See infra* pp. 710–714. Suppose that an agency issues a statement regarding how it intends to implement some statutory provision, and this statement is framed in mandatory, inflexible terms. If the agency tries to characterize its declaration as a "general statement of policy," then even though it may not have any binding legal effect, its inflexibility, definiteness, and likely coercive effect on regulated parties may lead the court to reject this characterization. If, however, the agency can characterize the statement as an interpretive rule, then the fact that the agency's statement is inflexible, mandatory, and coercive may not matter.

How, then, can courts distinguish an interpretive rule from a policy statement or an (invalid) legislative rule? Some D.C. Circuit precedents ask whether an interpretive rule genuinely "interprets" a statute or regulation. Accordingly, the D.C. Circuit suggested that "an interpretive statement simply indicates an agency's reading of a statute or a rule." Orengo Caraballo v. Reich, 11 F.3d 186, 195 (D.C. Cir. 1993). If the rule invokes "specific statutory provisions, and its validity stands or falls on the correctness of the agency's interpretation of those provisions, it is an interpretive rule." United Technologies Corp. v. EPA, 821 F.2d 714, 719–20 (D.C. Cir. 1987). Put another way, the court is looking for "reasoned statutory interpretation, with reference to the language, purpose, and legislative history" of the relevant provision. General Motors Corp. v. Ruckelshaus, 742 F.2d 1561, 1565 (D.C. Cir. 1984) (en banc); *see also United Technologies*, 821 F.2d. at 720 (noting that an agency rule qualified as an interpretive rule because its validity "depend[ed] on whether or not the Agency ha[d] correctly interpreted congressional intent"). Conversely, "if by its action the agency intends to create new law, rights or duties, the rule is properly considered to be a legislative rule." *General Motors*, 742 F.2d at 1565. The D.C. Circuit nicely summarized this line of reasoning in Fertilizer Institute v. EPA, 935 F.2d 1303, 1308 (D.C. Cir. 1991), as follows: "[A]n agency can declare its understanding of what a statute requires without providing notice and comment, but an agency cannot go beyond the text of a statute and exercise its delegated powers without first providing adequate notice and comment."

How manageable is that distinction? Does it ask a question analogous to the question that the Court has found so difficult to administer in the nondelegation context—namely, where one draws the line between lawmaking and law implementation? (*See* pp. 415–416, *supra*.) Especially when the underlying grant of statutory or regulatory authority is framed in relatively open-ended terms, how can we decide whether the agency's more detailed and specific rule qualifies as an "interpretation" of the underlying provision, or whether the agency has instead issued either a legislative rule (specifying new legal rights and obligations) or a general statement of policy (declaring how the agency intends to exercise its policy discretion)? The next case, *Hoctor v. Department of Agriculture*, is a useful illustration of the challenges of distinguishing "interpretation" from other forms of discretionary policymaking. Do you think Judge Posner's analysis in *Hoctor* is consistent with Judge Williams' analysis in *AMC*, or do they approach the problem differently? How would you define "interpretation" for purposes of the § 553(b)(A) interpretive rule exemption?

## Hoctor v. United States Department of Agriculture

U.S. Court of Appeals for the Seventh Circuit
82 F.3d 165 (7th Cir. 1996)

■ POSNER, CHIEF JUDGE.

A rule promulgated by an agency that is subject to the Administrative Procedure Act is invalid unless the agency first issues a public notice of proposed rulemaking, describing the substance of the proposed rule, and gives the public an opportunity to submit written comments; and if after receiving the comments it decides to promulgate the rule it must set forth the basis and purpose of the rule in a public statement. 5 U.S.C. §§ 553(b), (c). These procedural requirements do not apply, however, to "interpretative rules, general statements of policy, or rules of agency organization, procedure, or practice." 5 U.S.C. § 553(b)(A). Distinguishing between a "legislative" rule, to which the notice and comment provisions of the Act apply, and an interpretive rule, to which these provisions do not apply, is often very difficult—and often very important to regulated firms, the public, and the agency. Notice and comment rulemaking is time-consuming, facilitates the marshaling of opposition to a proposed rule, and may result in the creation of a very long record that may in turn provide a basis for a judicial challenge to the rule if the agency decides to promulgate it. There are no formalities attendant upon the promulgation of an interpretive rule, but this is tolerable because such a rule is "only" an interpretation. Every governmental agency that enforces a less than crystalline statute must interpret the statute, and it does the public a favor if it announces the interpretation in advance of enforcement, whether the announcement takes the form of a rule or of a policy statement, which the Administrative Procedure Act assimilates to an interpretive rule. It would be no favor to the public to discourage the announcement of agencies' interpretations by burdening the interpretive process with cumbersome formalities.

The question presented by this appeal from an order of the Department of Agriculture is whether a rule for the secure containment of animals, a rule promulgated by the Department under the Animal Welfare Act, 7 U.S.C. §§ 2131 *et seq.*, without compliance with the notice and comment requirements of the Administrative Procedure Act, is nevertheless valid because it is merely an interpretive rule. Enacted in 1966, the Animal Welfare Act, as its title implies, is primarily designed to assure the humane treatment of animals. The Act requires the licensing of dealers ... and exhibitors, and authorizes the Department to impose sanctions on licensees who violate either the statute itself or the rules promulgated by the Department under the authority of 7 U.S.C. § 2151, which authorizes the Secretary of Agriculture "to promulgate such rules, regulations, and orders as he may deem necessary in order to effectuate the purposes of [the

Act]." The Act provides guidance to the exercise of this rulemaking authority by requiring the Department to formulate standards "to govern the humane handling, care, treatment, and transportation of animals by dealers," and these standards must include minimum requirements "for handling, housing, feeding, watering, sanitation," etc. 7 U.S.C. § 2143(a).

The Department has employed the notice and comment procedure to promulgate a regulation, the validity of which is not questioned, that is entitled "structural strength" and that provides that "the facility [housing the animals] must be constructed of such material and of such strength as appropriate for the animals involved. The indoor and outdoor housing facilities shall be structurally sound and shall be maintained in good repair to protect the animals from injury and to contain the animals."

Enter the petitioner, Patrick Hoctor, who in 1982 began dealing in exotic animals on his farm outside of Terre Haute. In a 25–acre compound he raised a variety of animals including "Big Cats"—a typical inventory included three lions, two tigers, seven ligers (a liger is a cross between a male lion and a female tiger, and is thus to be distinguished from a tigon), six cougars, and two snow leopards. The animals were in pens. . . . The area in which the pens were located was surrounded by a fence ("containment fence"). In addition, Hoctor erected a fence around the entire compound ("perimeter fence"). At the suggestion of a veterinarian employed by the Agriculture Department who was assigned to inspect the facility when Hoctor started his animal dealership in 1982, Hoctor made the perimeter fence six feet high.

The following year the Department issued an internal memorandum addressed to its force of inspectors in which it said that all "dangerous animals," defined as including, among members of the cat family, lions, tigers, and leopards, must be inside a perimeter fence at least eight feet high. This provision is the so-called interpretive rule, interpreting the housing regulation quoted above. . . .

On several occasions beginning in 1990, Hoctor was cited by a Department of Agriculture inspector for . . . failing to have an eight-foot perimeter fence. . . . The parties agree that unless the rule requiring a perimeter fence at least eight feet high is a valid interpretive rule, the sanction for violating it was improper.

We may assume, though we need not decide, that the Department of Agriculture has the statutory authority to require dealers in dangerous animals to enclose their compounds with eight-foot-high fences. . . .

Another issue that we need not resolve . . . is whether the Department might have cited Hoctor for having a perimeter fence that was *in fact*, considering the number and type of his animals, the topography of the compound, the design and structure of the protective enclosures and the containment fence, the proximity of highways or inhabited areas, and the design of the perimeter fence itself, too low to be safe, as distinct from merely being lower than eight feet. . . .

The only ground on which the Department defends sanctioning Hoctor for not having a high enough fence is that requiring an eight-foot-high perimeter fence for dangerous animals is an interpretation of the Department's own structural-strength regulation, and "provided an agency's interpretation of its own regulations does not violate the Constitution or a federal statute, it must be given 'controlling weight unless it is plainly erroneous or inconsistent with the regulation.' " Stinson v. United States, 508 U.S. at 44–46. The "provided" clause does not announce a demanding standard of judicial review, although the absence of any reference in the housing regulation to fences or height must give us pause. The regulation appears only to require that pens and other animal housing be sturdy enough in design and construction, and sufficiently well maintained, to prevent the animals from breaking through the enclosure—not that any enclosure, whether a pen or a perimeter fence, be high enough to prevent the animals from escaping by jumping over the enclosure. . . .

Our doubts about the scope of the regulation that the eight-foot rule is said to be "interpreting" might seem irrelevant, since even if a rule requiring an eight-foot perimeter fence could not be based on the regulation, it could be based on the statute itself, which in requiring the Department to establish minimum standards for the housing of animals presumably authorizes it to promulgate standards for secure containment. But if the eight-foot rule were deemed one of those minimum standards that the Department is required by statute to create, it could not possibly be thought an *interpretive* rule. For what would it be interpreting? When Congress authorizes an agency to create standards, it is delegating legislative authority, rather than itself setting forth a standard which the agency might then particularize through interpretation. Put differently, when a statute does not impose a duty on the persons subject to it but instead authorizes (or requires—it makes no difference) an agency to impose a duty, the formulation of that duty becomes a legislative task entrusted to the agency. Provided that a rule promulgated pursuant to such a delegation is intended to bind, and not merely to be a tentative statement of the agency's view, which would make it just a policy statement, and not a rule at all, the rule would be the clearest possible example of a legislative rule, as to which the notice and comment procedure not followed here is mandatory, as distinct from an interpretive rule; for there would be nothing to interpret. American Mining Congress v. Mine Safety & Health Administration, 995 F.2d 1106, 1109 (D.C.Cir.1993). . . . That is why the Department *must* argue that its eight-foot rule is an interpretation of the structural-strength regulation—itself a standard, and therefore interpretable, in order to avoid reversal.

Even if . . . the eight-foot rule is consistent with, even in some sense authorized by, the structural-strength regulation, it would not necessarily follow that it is an interpretive rule. It is that only if it can be derived from the regulation by a process reasonably described as interpretation. Supposing that the regulation imposes a general duty of secure containment, the question is, then, Can a requirement that the duty be implemented by erecting an eight-foot-high perimeter fence be thought an interpretation of that general duty?

"Interpretation" in the narrow sense is the ascertainment of meaning. It is obvious that eight feet is not part of the meaning of secure containment. But "interpretation" is often used in a much broader sense. A process of "interpretation" has transformed the Constitution into a body of law undreamt of by the framers. . . . But our task in this case is not to plumb the mysteries of legal theory; it is merely to give effect to a distinction that the Administrative Procedure Act makes, and we can do this by referring to the purpose of the distinction. The purpose is to separate the cases in which notice and comment rulemaking is required from the cases in which it is not required. As we noted at the outset, unless a statute or regulation is of crystalline transparency, the agency enforcing it cannot avoid interpreting it, and the agency would be stymied in its enforcement duties if every time it brought a case on a new theory it had to pause for a bout, possibly lasting several years, of notice and comment rulemaking. Besides being unavoidably continuous, statutory interpretation normally proceeds without the aid of elaborate factual inquiries. When it is an executive or administrative agency that is doing the interpreting it brings to the task a greater knowledge of the regulated activity than the judicial or legislative branches have, and this knowledge is to some extent a substitute for formal fact-gathering.

At the other extreme from what might be called normal or routine interpretation is the making of reasonable but arbitrary (not in the "arbitrary or capricious" sense) rules that are consistent with the statute or regulation under which the rules are promulgated but not derived from it, because they represent an arbitrary choice among methods of implementation. A rule that turns on a number is likely to be arbitrary in this sense. There is no way to reason to an eight-foot perimeter-fence rule as opposed to a seven-and-a-half foot fence or a nine-foot fence or a ten-foot fence. None of these candidates for a rule is uniquely appropriate to, and in that sense derivable from, the duty of secure containment. This point becomes even clearer if we note that the eight-foot rule actually has another component—the fence must be at least three feet from any animal's pen. Why three feet? Why not four? Or two?

. . . Legislators have the democratic legitimacy to make choices among value judgments, choices based on hunch or guesswork or even the toss of a coin, and other arbitrary choices. When agencies base rules on arbitrary choices they are legislating, and so these rules are legislative or substantive and require notice and comment rulemaking, a procedure that is analogous to the procedure employed by legislatures in making statutes. The notice of proposed rulemaking corresponds to the bill and the reception of written comments to the hearing on the bill.

The common sense of requiring notice and comment rulemaking for legislative rules is well illustrated by the facts of this case. There is no process of cloistered, appellate-court type reasoning by which the Department of Agriculture could have excogitated the eight-foot rule from the structural-strength regulation. The rule is arbitrary in the sense that it could well be different without significant impairment of any regulatory purpose. But this does not make the rule a matter of indifference to the people subject to it. There are thousands of animal dealers, and some unknown fraction of these face the prospect of having to tear down their existing fences and build new, higher ones at great cost. The concerns of these dealers are legitimate and since, as we are stressing, the rule could well be otherwise, the agency was obliged to listen to them before settling on a final rule and to provide some justification for that rule, though not so tight or logical a justification as a court would be expected to offer for a new judge-made rule. Notice and comment is the procedure by which the persons affected by legislative rules are enabled to communicate their concerns in a comprehensive and systematic fashion to the legislating agency. The Department's lawyer speculated that if the notice and comment route had been followed in this case the Department would have received thousands of comments. The greater the public interest in a rule, the greater reason to allow the public to participate in its formation.

We are not saying that an interpretive rule can never have a numerical component. See, e.g., *American Mining Congress v. Mine Safety & Health Administration, supra,* 995 F.2d at 1108, 1113.... There is merely an empirical relation between interpretation and generality on the one hand, and legislation and specificity on the other. Especially in scientific and other technical areas, where quantitative criteria are common, a rule that translates a general norm into a number may be justifiable as interpretation. The mine safety agency in the *American Mining* case could refer to established medical criteria, expressed in terms of numerical evaluations of x-rays, for diagnosing black-lung disease. Even in a nontechnical area the use of a number as a rule of thumb to guide the application of a general norm will often be legitimately interpretive. Had the Department of Agriculture said in the internal memorandum that it could not imagine a case in which a perimeter fence for dangerous animals that was lower than eight feet would provide secure containment, and would therefore presume, subject to rebuttal, that a lower fence was insecure, it would have been on stronger ground. For it would have been tying the rule to the animating standard, that of secure containment, rather than making it stand free of the standard, self-contained, unbending, arbitrary. To switch metaphors, the "flatter" a rule is, the harder it is to conceive of it as merely spelling out what is in some sense latent in a statute or regulation, and the eight-foot rule in its present form is as flat as they come. At argument the Department's lawyer tried to loosen up the rule, implying that the Department might have bent it if Hoctor proposed to dig a moat or to electrify his six-foot fence. But an agency's lawyer is not authorized to amend its rules in order to make them more palatable to the reviewing court....

---

**1.  A Workable Test for "Interpretive" Rules?**—It is important to emphasize that *Hoctor* was *not* a case in which the Department of Agriculture would lack a legal basis for bringing an enforcement action against Mr.

Hoctor in the absence of the alleged interpretive rule. Even if the Department had never announced that it thought an eight-foot fence was required, it could have brought an enforcement action against Mr. Hoctor on the grounds that his facility, in light of its shorter perimeter fence, was not "constructed . . . of such strength as appropriate for the animals involved" within the meaning of the Department's existing (and validly-promulgated) "structural-strength" regulation. Indeed, the Department could not and did not rely on the alleged interpretive rule as the legal basis for its enforcement action. Rather, the Department alleged a violation of the structural-strength regulation itself, and declared that it was interpreting that regulation to require an eight-foot fence. Mr. Hoctor (and ultimately Judge Posner) argued that the eight-foot-fence requirement could not fairly be characterized as an interpretation of the existing structural-strength regulation. Why not? If MSHA can interpret the term "diagnosis" as including an x-ray, why can't the Department of Agriculture interpret the phrase "constructed of . . . such strength as appropriate for the animals involved" as including facilities with eight-foot perimeter fences, but excluding facilities with shorter fences?

Judge Posner's *Hoctor* opinion took an unabashedly purposivist approach to construing the APA's exemption for interpretive rules. He noted that "interpretation" is ordinarily used in the narrow sense of "ascertainment of meaning," and in that ordinary usage it would be difficult—perhaps impossible—to see the eight-foot-fence requirement as a reasonable "ascertainment" of the semantic meaning of the phrase "constructed . . . of such strength as appropriate." Judge Posner also noted, however, that in legal discourse the term "interpretation" is sometimes used in a much broader sense to describe the process of fleshing out or giving more precise content to open-ended legal terms. The appropriate understanding of "interpretation" for purposes of delineating the scope of the § 553(b)(A) exemption, in Judge Posner's view, depends on the purpose of that exemption in the APA—"to separate the cases in which notice and comment rulemaking is required from the cases in which it is not required." The purpose of notice-and-comment rulemaking, Judge Posner continued, is to ensure that "the persons affected by legislative rules are enabled to communicate their concerns in a comprehensive and systematic fashion to the legislating agency," a process analogous to "the reception of written comments to the hearing on [a proposed] bill" in the legislative process, which ensures the "democratic legitimacy" of "choices among value judgments, choices based on hunch or guesswork or even the toss of a coin, and other arbitrary choices." On the other hand, the purpose of exempting interpretive rules from this notice-and-comment process is to accommodate the inevitable ambiguity of legal commands and the utility of permitting agencies to provide advance notice of how they interpret those commands. As *Hoctor* put it, "Every governmental agency that enforces a less than crystalline statute must interpret the statute, and it does the public a favor if it announces the interpretation in advance of enforcement. . . . It would be no favor to the public to discourage the announcement of agencies' interpretations by burdening the interpretive process with cumbersome formalities."

Judge Posner suggested that understanding these purposes helps courts distinguish interpretive rules from legislative rules and general statements of policy. From this starting point, *Hoctor* emphasized that the height requirements in the Department of Agriculture rule were "arbitrary," not in the sense of being unreasonable but rather in the sense of relying on bright-line numerical rules instead of flexible standards. Judge Posner's logic is that legislatures can—and often must—make decisions that are "arbitrary" in the sense of defining a category or picking a cut-off rule. This action is legislative in nature because it is general, and does not take into account the particular facts and circumstances of individual cases. Judge Posner reasoned that in light of the purpose of the APA's procedural requirements, these sorts of arbitrary decisions must go through notice and comment.

While Judge Posner's analysis is compelling in many respects, it is also problematic. First, the opinion's emphasis on the "flatness" of the Department of Agriculture's rule—its generality and inflexibility—recalls the distinction drawn in the "general statements of policy" context between agency statements that preserve the agency's discretion in future cases and those that do not. Perhaps Judge Posner meant to suggest that a similar consideration may help distinguish interpretive rules from legislative rules: the more an agency statement is framed in presumptive rather than absolute terms, the more likely it is to be interpretive rather than legislative. But why should that be? Recall Judge Williams' comment in *AMC* that the degree to which a rule restricts agency discretion is not useful in distinguishing legislative and interpretive rules, because the degree to which the *interpretation* is mandatory or inflexible depends on the degree to which the underlying *statute or regulation* is mandatory or inflexible. Moreover, isn't there some tension between the *Hoctor* analysis and the holding in *AMC* (which *Hoctor* cited approvingly) that the MSHA policy letter in that case was an interpretive rule? We can imagine a continuum of medical evidence that might tend to show black lung disease, ranging from superficial symptoms (respiratory irritation, coughing), to an x-ray, to analysis of tissue samples. MSHA "arbitrarily" (in the sense used by Judge Posner in *Hoctor*) selected the x-ray as the point at which a miner would be considered "diagnosed" with black lung disease. MSHA, that is, picked a bright-line rule that was not dictated by the language of the governing statute or regulation, even though that bright-line rule would doubtless be both over-and under-inclusive in relation to the statutory or regulatory purpose. Why isn't that just as "arbitrary" as selecting eight feet rather than seven or nine feet when deciding whether a perimeter fence is "constructed of . . . such strength as appropriate" for containing big cats? Furthermore, the MSHA interpretive rule at issue in *AMC* seems just as "flat" as the Department of Agriculture rule at issue in *Hoctor*: the MSHA rule declared that an x-ray will *always* count as a diagnosis for purposes of the regulatory reporting requirement, not that it will *presumptively* count as a diagnosis. Why, then, is the MSHA policy letter a valid interpretive rule, while the Department of Agriculture memorandum is an invalid legislative rule?

Perhaps the key to understanding the distinction—if there is one—lies not in the specificity, flexibility, or arbitrariness of the alleged interpretive rule, but rather in the generality or specificity of the underlying statute or regulation that the agency is allegedly interpreting. In *AMC*, the reporting requirement was already fairly specific. The question whether an x-ray alone could count as a "diagnosis" can perhaps be characterized as an interstitial or subsidiary question that arose in the process of implementing a reasonably detailed set of regulatory requirements. Indeed, Judge Posner's opinion in *Hoctor* suggested that in *AMC*, "established medical criteria" may have determined or at least guided the determination of how many x-rays were needed to diagnose black-lung disease—thereby identifying "diagnosis" as a term of art in this context. The structural-strength regulation at issue in *Hoctor*, by contrast, was itself quite open-ended, requiring only that the facilities be "appropriate" "to protect the animals from injury and to contain the animals." Perhaps, then, Judge Posner was right that there is "an empirical relation between interpretation and generality on the one hand, and legislation and specificity on the other," but he erred in focusing on the generality or specificity of the *interpretation*, as opposed to the generality or specificity of the *language being interpreted*. Cf. Jacob E. Gersen, *Legislative Rules Revisited*, 74 U. CHI. L. REV. 1705, 1715–16 (2007) (suggesting that the "empirical relation" hypothesized by Judge Posner may in fact be the reverse, with legislative rules tending to be more general and interpretive rules more specific). This way of approaching the problem may be attractive in that it fits with Judge Posner's account of the purposes of notice-and-comment and of the § 553 exemption: Where some pre-existing statute or regulation already spells out legal rights and obligations in some detail, an agency should be able to fill in gaps and resolve ambiguities without invoking the cumbersome notice-and-comment process, but when the underlying statutory or regulatory command is so open-ended that the most significant policy choices are being made in the process of "interpretation," then notice-and-comment rulemaking ought to be required.

This approach, however, presents two difficulties. First, how can courts figure out when an underlying command is too vague or open-ended to allow the agency to "interpret" it by issuing much more detailed and specific commands? Barring the existence of a well-settled medical convention, reasonable people can disagree about the amount and kind of evidence necessary to "diagnose" black lung disease, just as they can disagree about the "appropriate" height of a perimeter fence for a facility housing big cats. By what metric can or should courts treat the implementation of one such regulation as interpretation and the other as new legislative policy? Second, remember that under *Chenery* and *Bell Aerospace* the Department of Agriculture could have validly announced and applied its eight-foot fence interpretation of the enclosure regulation in an enforcement action against Mr. Hoctor adjudicated before the agency. If we assume that the underlying regulation would supply an adequate legal basis for the enforcement action, why should we *ever* require the agency to go through notice and comment before announcing that interpretation? Why wouldn't it be better to permit the agency to announce the interpretation informally, if the alternative is for the agency to announce it for the first time in an enforcement order?

  **2.   *Implications for Judicial Review of the Agency's Interpretation*—**As was true with respect to general statements of policy, one way courts can reconcile themselves to the difficulty of distinguishing interpretive rules from legislative rules is to emphasize that judicial review of the reasonableness of an agency's interpretation serves as a check on the agency's ability or incentive to circumvent notice-and-comment rulemaking. Judge Williams' *AMC* opinion contained a nice summary of this point, noting that because "failure to provide notice-and-comment rulemaking will usually mean that affected parties have had no prior formal opportunity to present their contentions, judicial review for want of reasoned decisionmaking is likely ... to take place in review of specific agency actions implementing the rule." For this reason, Judge Williams suggested, affected parties *will* have an opportunity to present their objections to the rule, and the agency will be compelled to offer a reasoned response. In Judge Williams' view, the agency cannot escape its obligation to defend the reasonableness of its position and to respond to adverse comments.

  Is that persuasive? If it is, does it suggest that Judge Posner was too quick in *Hoctor* to reject the Department's claim that its memorandum was simply an interpretive rule? Judge Posner asserted that notice and comment should have been required, given that many affected parties would have legitimate concerns about the agency's interpretation of its structural-strength rule. Since these concerns "are legitimate and since ... the rule could well be otherwise, the agency was obliged to listen to [these interested parties] before settling on a final rule and to provide some justification for that rule.... Notice and comment is the procedure by which the persons affected by legislative rules are enabled to communicate their concerns in a comprehensive and systematic fashion to the legislating agency." But if Judge Williams is right that "the threat of judicial review provides a spur to the agency to pay attention to facts and arguments submitted in derogation of any rule not supported by notice and comment, even as late as the enforcement stage," then is the sort of public comment that Judge Posner emphasized really necessary? Think about it this way: Suppose there really are good arguments as to why an adequate perimeter fence need only be six feet high, and that if the Department had proposed its fence-height regulation as a notice-and-comment rule, Mr. Hoctor and others would have been able to submit comments to that effect. If these arguments would have been sufficient to convince a court that the eight-foot requirement was unreasonable (in the language of the APA, that it was "arbitrary [and] capricious"), then the rule would have been struck down. But Mr. Hoctor could raise those very same arguments as a defense in the enforcement proceeding against him, and if the agency's eight-foot-fence rule really is unreasonable, Mr. Hoctor should win. Because of this, the agency has a strong incentive to consider in advance the most salient objections to its proposed interpretation. *See, e.g.,* E. Donald Elliott, *Re-*

*Inventing Rulemaking*, 41 Duke L.J. 1490, 1491 (1992); John F. Manning, *Nonlegislative Rules*, 72 Geo. Wash. L. Rev. 893, 932–33 & n.99 (2004). By contrast, if the agency's rule is reasonable, then it should be upheld whether it is challenged at the rulemaking stage or at the enforcement stage. This line of argument suggests that courts perhaps could do without *any* formal test for distinguishing interpretative rules from legislative rules.

Then again, doesn't this argument presuppose that judicial review at the enforcement stage is an adequate substitute for notice and comment? That would seem to prove too much. By that logic, there is little point in having notice-and-comment procedures in the first place. But the notice-and-comment requirements are rooted in important goals of promoting accurate, informed, and reasoned agency decisions. Perhaps Mr. Hoctor might not be able to establish in an enforcement action that an eight-foot-fence rule is so unreasonable as to be unlawful. But if he and others like him had been given a chance to comment ahead of time in a rulemaking proceeding, they might have been able to persuade the agency to adopt a six-foot-fence rule instead.

Perhaps there is another way to interpret Judge Williams' emphasis on judicial review, one that echoes an argument that Judge MacKinnon emphasized in *PG&E* (*see* pp. 681–688, *supra*): Maybe the idea is that the standard of judicial review is different—and more rigorous—for interpretive rules. This approach implies that while there are some interpretations that are sufficiently reasonable that they would be upheld even if they were promulgated as interpretive rules, and some interpretations that are so unreasonable that the court would reject them even if they were enacted as notice-and-comment legislative rules, there is a set of interpretations that courts would uphold as reasonable if they were issued pursuant to § 553 proceedings, but would reject as unreasonable if they were announced as interpretive rules. Does it seem realistic to suppose that courts would adjust the standard of review in this way? Should they do so?

**3. *Agencies' Interpretation of Their Own Regulations*—**One important fact about *AMC* and *Hoctor* is that the alleged "interpretive rule" in both cases purported to interpret an ambiguous provision in the agency's *own regulations*. The formal doctrine on differentiating interpretive from legislative rules does not usually distinguish between cases in which an agency purports to interpret a statute and cases in which an agency purports to interpret its own regulations. Should it? If so, how?

There is a lively scholarly debate, which sometimes spills over into judicial opinions, about the appropriate standard of review to apply to an agency's interpretation of its own regulations. The standard doctrinal position, announced in several Supreme Court cases, is that an agency's interpretation of its regulations should be upheld so long as the interpretation is reasonable—a standard that is very similar to the one courts apply when reviewing an agency's interpretation of an ambiguous statutory provision. *See, e.g.*, Auer v. Robbins, 519 U.S. 452, 461 (1997); Thomas Jefferson University v. Shalala, 512 U.S. 504, 512 (1994); Bowles v. Seminole Rock & Sand Co., 325 U.S. 410, 414 (1945). (For more on the standard of review the courts apply when reviewing agency statutory interpretations, see Chapter Five, *infra*.) Some scholars, however, have argued that courts should be less deferential to an agency's interpretation of its own regulations than to an agency's interpretation of statutes, on the grounds that the agency can determine the precision or vagueness of its regulations. A doctrine that requires deference to an agency's interpretation of its own rules, on this view, gives an agency an incentive to "promulgate mush"—vague, open-ended regulations that the agency will give substantive content by issuing "interpretive rules" without notice and comment. *See, e.g.*, Robert A. Anthony, *The Supreme Court and the APA: Sometimes They Just Don't Get It*, 10 ADMIN. L.J. AM. U. 1, 11–12 (1996); John F. Manning, *Constitutional Structure and Judicial Deference to Agency Interpretations of Agency Rules*, 96 COLUM. L. REV. 612, 654–80 (1996). Others, however, have argued that this concern is both overstated and outweighed by the interests in preserving agencies' flexibility and their ability to announce their interpretive views in advance. *See, e.g.*, Scott H. Angstreich, *Shoring Up* Chevron: *A Defense of* Seminole Rock *Deference to Agency Regulatory Interpretations*, 34 U.C. DAVIS L. REV. 49 (2000); Peter L. Strauss, *Publication Rules in the Rulemaking Spectrum: Assuring Proper Respect for an Essential Element*, 53 ADMIN. L. REV. 803, 838–42 (2001).

Does this debate have any bearing on when, or under what conditions, a reviewing court should characterize a subsequent rule as "legislative" rather than "interpretive"? Consider the following argument: Agencies do not have any (direct) control over the specificity or generality of the statutory provisions they administer, so agencies should be given greater latitude in announcing *statutory* interpretations without going through notice and comment. On the other hand, because an agency has considerable control over whether its own rules are framed in specific or general terms, courts should be more skeptical when an agency invokes the interpretive rule exemption to give more definite content to a vague or open-ended agency regulation. The advantage of this approach is that it would give agencies an incentive to make their own regulations more specific and detailed. On the other hand, if the open-ended regulation would still supply an adequate legal basis for subsequent enforcement actions or other adjudicative proceedings, and if the agency would remain free (in light of *Chenery II*) to announce and apply its more detailed interpretations in that context, then narrowing the scope of the interpretive rule exemption for an agency's interpretation of its own regulations might lead the agency to continue to promulgate vague rules, but to flesh them out in adjudications rather than giving advance warning in published interpretive rules.

The basic problem here is that restricting an agency's ability to invoke the interpretive rule exemption when the agency interprets its own (open-textured) regulations may have two different effects on the agency's behavior: It might lead the agency to make its legislative rules more precise and detailed (which in most cases is a desirable result), or it might lead the agency to do more of its interpretation in the context of adjudication rather than giving advance notice through interpretive rules (which is usually undesirable). Or both of these effects might occur simultaneously: the agency might be somewhat more precise in its initial legislative rules, but also more likely to develop and announce its interpretations on an ad hoc basis in individual adjudicative orders. How can we assess which effect is more likely? In the absence of hard evidence on this issue, what should courts do?

---

## IV.  JUDICIAL REVIEW OF AGENCY RULES
## A.  THE "ARBITRARY AND CAPRICIOUS" STANDARD: COMPETING APPROACHES

As we have seen, one way that our legal system deals with the concern about the delegation of broad policymaking authority to administrative agencies is to impose procedural requirements on agency decision-making. In doing so, the system relies on the judiciary to enforce these procedural requirements. This responsibility gives the judiciary an important role in shaping the regulatory process, as the courts must interpret the scope, content, and applicability of the various procedural requirements of the APA and other statutes.

The judiciary's role in constraining and shaping agency decision-making, however, goes well beyond its role in enforcing statutory procedural requirements. Two other forms of judicial oversight are also critically important (and the subject of considerable conflict and controversy). First, challengers often allege that an agency has acted in a way that is inconsistent with the terms of the underlying statute. In such cases, courts must interpret the statute and decide whether the agency acted lawfully. This sort of judicial review, which focuses on the interpretation of substantive statutory provisions, will be the principal subject of Chapter Five. Second, the APA empowers courts to engage in a more general review of agency decisions to ensure that those decisions are not "arbitrary" or "capricious." A court may strike down an agency action, even if the agency complied with all procedural requirements and acted within the scope of its statutory discretion, if the court decides that the agency's decision was so unreasonable as to be arbitrary. *See* Gary Lawson, *Outcome, Procedure, and Process: Agency Duties of Explanation for Legal Conclusions*, 48 RUTGERS L. REV. 313, 318–19 (1996). It is this sort of review that will occupy our attention for the remainder of this chapter.

Chapter Seven of the APA (5 U.S.C. §§ 701 *et seq.*) contains the default provisions for judicial review of agency action. (They are only default provisions because sometimes the organic acts themselves alter or supplement the APA's standards). Sections 701–705 deal with the availability, timing, and form of judicial review, as well as certain issues related to forms of judicial relief. We do not cover these issues in detail, leaving them instead to advanced courses in administrative law. Our focus here is on § 706, the "Scope of Review" provision. This provision is sufficiently important that we set it out in full:

## Administrative Procedure Act

5 U.S.C. § 706–Scope of Review

To the extent necessary to decision and when presented, the reviewing court shall decide all relevant questions of law, interpret constitutional and statutory provisions, and determine the meaning or applicability of the terms of an agency action. The reviewing court shall—

(1) compel agency action unlawfully withheld or unreasonably delayed; and

(2) hold unlawful and set aside agency action, findings, and conclusions found to be—

(A) arbitrary, capricious, an abuse of discretion, or otherwise not in accordance with law;

(B) contrary to constitutional right, power, privilege, or immunity;

(C) in excess of statutory jurisdiction, authority, or limitations, or short of statutory right;

(D) without observance of procedure required by law;

(E) unsupported by substantial evidence in a case subject to sections 556 and 557 of this title or otherwise reviewed on the record of an agency hearing provided by statute; or

(F) unwarranted by the facts to the extent that the facts are subject to a trial de novo by the reviewing court.

In making the foregoing determinations, the court shall review the whole record or those parts of it cited by a party, and due account shall be taken of the rule of prejudicial error.

Section 706 contains a number of different provisions for judicial review of agency action. Many of these are (at least apparently) straightforward. Section 706(1) announces that courts can order agencies to take action, though in practice such orders are relatively uncommon. Sections 706(2)(B), (C), and (D) make clear that courts can strike down agency action that is unconstitutional, contrary to statutory law, or procedurally defective. Section 706(2)(F) is a rarely invoked provision that applies to cases in which, during judicial proceedings to enforce administrative action, the court concludes that the fact-finding procedures the agency used in its prior administrative adjudication were inadequate. Section 706(2)(E) requires that in *formal* agency proceedings (that is, proceedings governed by §§ 556 and 557), all agency conclusions must be supported by "substantial evidence." This provision is particularly important for judicial review of formal agency adjudications, which are relatively common, but it is less relevant to rulemaking, given that very few rulemakings are required to be formal (*see* pp. 597–598, *supra*). The most important of the APA's standard-of-review provisions, for our purposes, is § 706(2)(A), which instructs a reviewing court to hold unlawful and set aside any agency action that is "arbitrary, capricious, [or] an abuse of discretion[.]" This standard, often referred to as the "arbitrary and capricious" standard, is critically important, as it empowers courts to invalidate an agency action as "arbitrary" even when there is no specific statutory or constitutional provision forbidding that action. But what, exactly, does the § 706(2)(A) "arbitrary and capricious" standard mean? How rigorous should judicial review under this standard be? What factors should such review emphasize?

These questions are difficult because of a basic, and by now familiar, tension or ambivalence about the appropriate role of courts in overseeing the regulatory process. On the one hand, Congress's delegation of substantial lawmaking authority to administrative agencies raises serious concerns about unchecked bureaucratic power, and judicial review is seen as a vital check on the dangers of administrative arbitrariness. As the distinguished administrative law scholar Louis Jaffe once put it: "The availability of judicial review is a necessary condition, psychologically if not logically, of a system of administrative power which purports to be legitimate, or legally valid." LOUIS L. JAFFE, JUDICIAL CONTROL OF ADMINISTRATIVE ACTION 320 (1965); *see also* Nina A. Mendelson, *Regulatory Beneficiaries and Informal Agency Policymaking*, 92 CORNELL L. REV. 397, 419 (2007). On the other hand, courts typically lack the subject-matter expertise that agencies are thought to possess, and judges are even less democratically accountable than agency bureaucrats. We might therefore worry about excessive judicial interference with the content of regulatory policy. In light of these conflicting interests, what role should judges have in assessing whether an agency action is "arbitrary and capricious"?

For the first two decades after the APA was enacted, the answer to that question seemed to be "very little." In the pre-APA case Pacific States Box & Basket Co. v. White, 296 U.S. 176 (1935), the Supreme Court indicated that judicial review for "arbitrary or capricious" agency action is extraordinarily deferential, with essentially no independent judicial scrutiny into the evidence proffered in support of an agency's decision. Under the *Pacific States Box & Basket* standard, as long as "any state of facts reasonably can be conceived that would sustain [the agency action], there is a presumption of the existence of that state of facts, and [the party challenging the agency action] must carry the burden of showing . . . that the action is arbitrary." *Id.* at 185; *see generally* Reuel E. Schiller, *The Era of Deference: Courts, Expertise, and the Emergence of New Deal Administrative Law*, 106 MICH. L. REV. 399 (2007) (discussing judicial review of agency action before and immediately after the New Deal). After the APA was enacted in 1946, most lower courts continued to apply something like the *Pacific States Box & Basket* standard (though without necessarily citing the case explicitly) to cases governed by the § 706(2)(A) standard of review, and the Supreme Court barely revisited the issue. (That said, during the same time period, both the Supreme Court and the lower courts established a more rigorous, though still deferential, standard of review under the "substantial evidence" provision in § 706(2)(E), which governs formal proceedings.)

In the late 1960s, partly in response to growing concerns about the "capture" of administrative agencies by special interests, some courts of appeals began to adopt a more aggressive approach to judicial review of agency action for "arbitrariness" or "abuse of discretion." *See, e.g.*, Thomas W. Merrill, *Capture Theory and the Courts: 1967–1983*, 72 CHI. KENT L. REV. 1039, 1050–52 (1997). This more aggressive approach to judicial review also emerged—perhaps not coincidentally—around the same time as did increased public demand that agencies, which since the passage of the APA had relied principally on adjudication, engage in more rulemaking. *See* Richard J. Pierce, Jr., *Rulemaking and the Administrative Procedure Act*, 32 TULSA L.J. 185, 187–89 (1996); Reuel E. Schiller, *Rulemaking's Promise: Administrative Law and Legal Culture in the 1960s and 1970s*, 53 ADMIN. L. REV. 1139, 1145–51 (2001). While courts in this period continued to emphasize that judicial review of agency action should be deferential, many judges nonetheless suggested that such review should go beyond the minimal inquiry associated with cases like *Pacific States Box & Basket*.

One of the leading judicial proponents of a more robust form of judicial review was Judge Harold Leventhal of the D.C. Circuit. In a series of opinions in the late 1960s, Judge Leventhal advocated an approach to judicial review that he and others dubbed "hard look" review. The idea was that although a reviewing court should be deferential to the agency's factual findings and policy judgments, the court was nonetheless obligated to make sure the agency had carefully considered all relevant aspects of the problem—that is, had taken a "hard look" at the issues—and had exercised its discretion in a reasonable manner. Judge Leventhal cogently summarized this vision in Greater Boston Television Corp. v. FCC, 444 F.2d 841 (D.C. Cir. 1970). The relevant section of this influential opinion is worth quoting at length:

> Its supervisory function calls on the court to intervene not merely in case of procedural inadequacies, or bypassing of the mandate in the legislative charter, but more broadly if the court becomes aware, especially from a combination of danger signals, that the agency has not really taken a "hard look" at the salient problems, and has not genuinely engaged in reasoned decision-making. If the agency has not shirked this fundamental task, however, the court exercises restraint and affirms the agency's action even though the court would on its own account have made different findings or adopted different standards.... If satisfied that the agency has taken a hard look at the issues with the use of reasons and standards, the court will uphold its findings, though of less than ideal clarity, if the agency's path may reasonably be discerned, though of course the court must not be left to guess as to the agency's findings or reasons.

> The process thus combines judicial supervision with a salutary principle of judicial restraint, an awareness that agencies and courts together constitute a "partnership" in furtherance of the public inter-

est, and are "collaborative instrumentalities of justice." The court is in a real sense part of the total administrative process, and not a hostile stranger to the office of first instance. This collaborative spirit does not undercut, it rather underlines the court's rigorous insistence on the need for conjunction of articulated standards and reflective findings, in furtherance of evenhanded application of law, rather than impermissible whim, improper influence, or misplaced zeal. Reasoned decision promotes results in the public interest by requiring the agency to focus on the values served by its decision, and hence releasing the clutch of unconscious preference and irrelevant prejudice. It furthers the broad public interest of enabling the public to repose confidence in the process as well as the judgments of its decision-makers.

> ... [T]he applicable doctrine that has evolved with the enormous growth and significance of administrative determination in the past forty or fifty years has insisted on reasoned decision-making....

*Id.* at 851–852 (internal footnotes and citations omitted). Note the contrast between the standard of review articulated in *Pacific States Box & Basket*, which calls on courts to uphold administrative action as non-arbitrary so long as "any state of facts reasonably can be conceived" that would support the action (regardless of whether or not the agency had explicitly found and articulated such facts), and the doctrine that Judge Leventhal claims has "evolved" since the enactment of the APA, which insists on "reasoned decision-making" by the agency.

Around the same time (the late 1960s and early 1970s), other scholars and judges, most notably D.C. Circuit Judge David Bazelon, had begun to emphasize the importance of judicial scrutiny into whether an agency had employed *procedures* that were conducive to "reasoned decision-making." As Judge Bazelon explained in Environmental Defense Fund, Inc. v. Ruckelshaus, 439 F.2d 584 (D.C. Cir. 1971):

> To protect [interests in life, health, and liberty] from administrative arbitrariness, it is necessary, but not sufficient, to insist on strict judicial scrutiny of administrative action. For judicial review alone can correct only the most egregious abuses. Judicial review must operate to ensure that the administrative process itself will confine and control the exercise of discretion. Courts should require administrative officers to articulate the standards and principles that govern their discretionary decisions in as much detail as possible.... When administrators provide a framework for principled decision-making, the result will be to diminish the importance of judicial review by enhancing the integrity of the administrative process, and to improve the quality of judicial review in those cases where judicial review is sought.

*Id.* at 598.

The Supreme Court weighed in, and started to give shape to what has emerged as the dominant modern framework for § 706(2)(A) "arbitrary and capricious" review, in Citizens to Preserve Overton Park, Inc. v. Volpe, 401 U.S. 402 (1971). *Overton Park* involved the Secretary of Transportation's decision to approve federal funds for a highway project in Memphis, Tennessee that ran through a public park. Local citizens' and environmental groups challenged the decision. Under the statute, the Department could approve federal highway funds for projects on public parklands only if the Secretary of Transportation determined that there was "no feasible and prudent alternative" to the use of these lands and that the proposed highway project "includes all possible planning to minimize harm" to the park. In approving the funding for the Overton Park project, the Secretary had made such a determination, but the public interest groups asserted that the Secretary's conclusions were arbitrary and capricious within the meaning of § 706(2)(A).

In evaluating this challenge, Justice Marshall's opinion for the Court laid out some general principles for § 706(2)(A) review. To make a finding that an agency action is "arbitrary, capricious, [or] an abuse of discretion," according to *Overton Park*, the reviewing court "must consider whether the decision was based on a consideration of the relevant factors and whether there has been a clear error of judgment." 401 U.S. at 416. The Court went on to caution that "[a]lthough this inquiry into the facts is to be searching and careful, the ultimate standard of review is a narrow one. The court is not empowered to substitute its judgment for that of the agency." *Id.* The Court decided that the case had to be remanded to the district court to make a new determination as to whether the Secretary's action was valid under this standard. The Secretary lost on remand, and ultimately rescinded his decision to approve federal funding for the highway.

The language quoted above is important and widely cited, but its meaning is not entirely certain. Notice that Justice Marshall emphasized two things that a reviewing court should consider under the § 706(2)(A) standard: first, whether the agency based its decision on "a consideration of the relevant factors"—which sounds like an inquiry into whether the agency's reasoning process was sound and drew upon the guiding statutory criteria, rather than an evaluation of the reasonableness of the decision itself; and second, whether the agency had made "a clear error of judgment"—which sounds like a more substantive standard. Inquiry into the rationality of the *decision process* and evaluation of the rationality of the *decision* are of course not mutually exclusive. But what is their relative significance? Is § 706(2)(A) more about process rationality or substance rationality? *Overton Park* also seemed to struggle with the tension noted earlier between the desire for meaningful judicial review as a check on agency action and the fear of aggressive judicial review's potential adverse effects. The opinion thus states that § 706(2)(A) requires review that is both "searching and careful" but also "narrow." As a result, proponents of very different visions of judicial review of agency action could—and did— find support for their views in *Overton Park*, and the case, while important, did not put an end to the ongoing debates about the best way to interpret the § 706(2)(A) standard.

That debate was particularly sophisticated—and particularly heated— among the judges on the D.C. Circuit. Judge Leventhal, quite naturally, viewed *Overton Park* as a vindication of the "hard look" review he had advocated in cases like *Greater Boston Television Corp.* Other judges on the

D.C. Circuit, including Judge Bazelon, had different notions about how courts should approach their responsibilities under § 706(2)(A), and they also found support (or at least absence of rejection) in *Overton Park*. Throughout the 1970s, these judges engaged in a spirited argument about this topic. The following case, *Ethyl Corp. v. EPA*, is one of the leading D.C. Circuit cases of that period. The four principal opinions in *Ethyl Corp.* lay out contrasting visions of judicial review of agency action. As you read these opinions, pay close attention to the differences (sometimes subtle, sometimes not) between different judges' understandings of what is required (or permitted) of reviewing courts applying the § 706(2)(A) standard. Consider also the different visions of the appropriate relationship between courts and agencies that underlie these contrasting viewpoints.

---

# Ethyl Corp. v. Environmental Protection Agency

U.S. Court of Appeals for the D.C. Circuit
541 F.2d 1 (D.C. Cir. 1976) (en banc)

■ J. Skelly Wright, Circuit Judge:

... It is only recently that we have begun to appreciate the danger posed by unregulated modification of the world around us, and have created watchdog agencies whose task it is to warn us, and protect us, when technological "advances" present dangers unappreciated or unrevealed by their supporters. Such agencies, unequipped with crystal balls and unable to read the future, are nonetheless charged with evaluating the effects of unprecedented environmental modifications.... Necessarily, they must deal with predictions and uncertainty, with developing evidence, with conflicting evidence, and, sometimes, with little or no evidence at all. Today we address the scope of the power delegated one such watchdog, the Environmental Protection Agency (EPA). We must determine the certainty required by the Clean Air Act before EPA may act to protect the health of our populace from the lead particulate emissions of automobiles.

... [T]he Clean Air Act [CAA] authorizes the Administrator of EPA to regulate gasoline additives whose emission products "will endanger the public health or welfare ...." Acting pursuant to that power, the Administrator, after notice and comment, determined that the automotive emissions caused by leaded gasoline present "a significant risk of harm" to the public health. Accordingly, he promulgated regulations that reduce ... the lead content of leaded gasoline. We must decide whether the Administrator properly interpreted the meaning of [the CAA] ... and, if so, whether the evidence adduced at the rule-making proceeding supports his final determination. Finding in favor of the Administrator on both grounds, and on all other grounds raised by petitioners, we affirm his determination.

## I.  THE FACTS, THE STATUTE, THE PROCEEDINGS, AND THE REGULATIONS

... Today, approximately 90 percent of motor gasoline manufactured in the United States contains lead additives.... [S]cientists have questioned whether the addition of lead to gasoline, and its consequent diffusion into the atmosphere from the automobile emission, poses a danger to the public health.... Despite ... reasons for concern, hard proof of any danger caused by lead automotive emissions has been hard to come by. Part of the reason for this lies in the multiple sources of human exposure to lead.

... In the Clean Air Act Amendments of 1970, ... Congress ... gave the newly-created EPA authority to control or prohibit the sale or manufacture of any fuel additive whose emission products "will endanger the public health or welfare ...." ...

Given this mandate, EPA published on January 31, 1971 advance notice of proposed rule-making. The Administrator announced he was considering possible controls on lead additives in gasolines....

On January 10, 1973 the Administrator ... [proposed] the health-based regulations now at issue.... The Agency concluded ... that it was virtually impossible to identify the precise amount of airborne lead that will endanger public health. Instead, the control strategy would concentrate on evaluating the cumulative effect of airborne lead on total human lead exposure and the significance of that contribution.... The Agency again invited public comment....

On October 28, 1973, ... this court ordered EPA to reach within 30 days a final decision on whether lead additives should be regulated for health reasons. EPA published its final health document ... on November 28, 1973.... This document ... extensively details and reviews the state of knowledge of the health effects of airborne lead.... The same day, ... EPA promulgated its final regulations, accompanied by a thorough discussion of its health conclusions, the impact of the regulations, and the alternative courses of action considered and rejected....

Petitioners ... appealed the promulgation of low-lead regulations to this court.... The appeal was heard by a division of the court... On December 20, 1974, the division, one judge dissenting, ordered the regulations set aside.... Because of the importance of the issues presented, we granted EPA's petition for rehearing *en banc* on March 17, 1975, vacating the judgment and opinions of the division and setting the case for reargument....

The regulations are challenged by petitioners on a variety of grounds.... Their primary claims ... are that the Administrator misinterpreted the statutory standard of "will endanger" and that his application of that standard is without support in the evidence and arbitrary and capricious....

### III.  THE EVIDENCE

A. *The Standard of Review*

In promulgating the low-lead regulations ... EPA engaged in informal rule-making. As such, ... its procedures are conducted pursuant to ... 5

U.S.C. § 553 and must be reviewed under 5 U.S.C. § 706(2) (A)–(D). Our review of the evidence is governed by [§ 702(2)(A)], which requires us to strike "agency action, findings, and conclusions" that we find to be "arbitrary, capricious, an abuse of discretion, or otherwise not in accordance with law . . . ." 5 U.S.C. § 706(2)(A). This standard of review is a highly deferential one. It presumes agency action to be valid. Citizens to Preserve Overton Park v. Volpe, 401 U.S. 402, 415 (1971); Pacific States Box & Basket Co. v. White, 296 U.S. 176, 185–186 (1935). . . . Moreover, it forbids the court's substituting its judgment for that of the agency, *Citizens to Preserve Overton Park v. Volpe, supra*, 401 U.S. at 416, and requires affirmance if a rational basis exists for the agency's decision.[73] Bowman Transportation, Inc. v. Arkansas–Best Freight System, Inc., 419 U.S. 281, 290 (1974). . . .

This is not to say, however, that we must rubber-stamp the agency decision as correct. To do so would render the appellate process a superfluous (although time-consuming) ritual. Rather, the reviewing court must assure itself that the agency decision was "based on a consideration of the relevant factors . . . ."[74] Moreover, it must engage in a "substantial inqui-

---

[73]. Of course, that basis must be expressed by the agency itself and not supplied by the court. SEC v. Chenery Corp., 332 U.S. 194, 196 (1947). Nonetheless, a decision of "less than ideal clarity" will be upheld if the agency's rationale "may reasonably be discerned." Bowman Transportation, Inc. v. Arkansas–Best Freight System, Inc., 419 U.S. 281, 286 (1974). See also Colorado Interstate Gas Co. v. FPC, 324 U.S. 581, 595 (1945).

[74]. *Overton Park* also requires the reviewing court to consider "whether there has been a clear error of judgment." . . . While as used, carefully bracketed by traditional statements of the restraint of "arbitrary and capricious" review, the phrase works no change in the law, the Court's choice of language is troublesome. The phrase sounds much like the "clearly erroneous" standard used to review the factual findings of a trial court sitting without a jury. . . . Unlike an agency determination or a jury verdict, such findings may be fairly readily reversed. . . . Indeed, under "clearly erroneous" review a court may substitute its judgment for that of the trial court and upset findings that are not unreasonable. . . .

Since *Overton Park* expressly forbade such intrusive review, . . . it plainly did not intend to use the "clear error of judgment" phrase to replace *sub silentio* "arbitrary and capricious" review with "clearly erroneous" review. Nonetheless, more than linguistic echoes of "clearly erroneous" review accompany the Court's turn of phrase. To the extent the cases relied upon by the Court support consideration of "clear errors of judgment," they all involve review of trial courts', and not agencies', abuses of discretion. . . . On the other hand, the Court also cited a case in which Judge Friendly recognized that an agency's abuse of discretion, unlike a court's, is reviewed under the "arbitrary and capricious" standard . . . and that review in such cases should be much more deferential than under the "clearly erroneous" standard. . . .

All of this makes the Court's intent in *Overton Park* somewhat difficult to plumb and its standard even more uncertain of application. We do not think the Court's use of the "clear error of judgment" phrase was an attempt vastly to revamp traditional "arbitrary and capricious" review. . . . Nonetheless, we fear its use of this phrase so familiar to judges in another, and significantly more intrusive, context may unintentionally prompt judicial distortion of the "arbitrary and capricious" standard. . . .

Post–*Overton Park* decisions, as well as the internal evidence in *Overton Park* itself . . . have made clear that the Court does not intend the "clear error of judgment" phrase to sanction review more intrusive than traditional "arbitrary and capricious" review; rather, the Court has reaffirmed that the reviewing court must defer if the agency has a rational basis for its decision. . . . Thus it is important that courts not think themselves licensed to embark upon

ry" into the facts, one that is "searching and careful." Citizens to Preserve Overton Park v. Volpe, 401 U.S. at 415, 416. This is particularly true in highly technical cases such as this one.

A court does not depart from its proper function when it undertakes a study of the record, hopefully perceptive, even as to the evidence on technical and specialized matters, for this enables the court to penetrate to the underlying decisions of the agency, to satisfy itself that the agency has exercised a reasoned discretion, with reasons that do not deviate from or ignore the ascertainable legislative intent. . . .

There is no inconsistency between the deferential standard of review and the requirement that the reviewing court involve itself in even the most complex evidentiary matters; rather, the two indicia of arbitrary and capricious review stand in careful balance. The close scrutiny of the evidence is intended to educate the court. It must understand enough about the problem confronting the agency to comprehend the meaning of the evidence relied upon and the evidence discarded; the questions addressed by the agency and those bypassed; the choices open to the agency and those made. The more technical the case, the more intensive must be the court's effort to understand the evidence, for without an appropriate understanding of the case before it the court cannot properly perform its appellate function. But that function must be performed with conscientious awareness of its limited nature. The enforced education into the intricacies of the problem before the agency is not designed to enable the court to become a superagency that can supplant the agency's expert decision-maker. To the contrary, the court must give due deference to the agency's ability to rely on its own developed expertise. . . . The immersion in the evidence is designed solely to enable the court to determine whether the agency decision was rational and based on consideration of the relevant factors. . . . It is settled that we must affirm decisions with which we disagree so long as this test is met. . . .

Thus, after our careful study of the record, we must take a step back from the agency decision. We must look at the decision not as the chemist, biologist or statistician that we are qualified neither by training nor experience to be, but as a reviewing court exercising our narrowly defined duty of holding agencies to certain minimal standards of rationality. . . . We must affirm unless the agency decision is arbitrary or capricious. . . .

B.  *Overview of the Evidence*

Petitioners vigorously attack both the sufficiency and the validity of the many scientific studies relied upon by the Administrator, while advancing for consideration various studies allegedly supportive of their position.

---

wide-ranging searches for "clear errors of judgment." Such searches can only distort the established appellate role in reviewing informal agency action. Rather, we think *Overton Park*'s troublesome phrase is best read as no more than an affirmation of the traditional standard of review. Accordingly, in the context of "arbitrary and capricious" review, we shall reverse for a "clear error of judgment" only if the error is so clear as to deprive the agency's decision of a rational basis.

The record in this case is massive—over 10,000 pages. Not surprisingly, evidence may be isolated that supports virtually any inference one might care to draw. Thus we might well have sustained a determination by the Administrator not to regulate lead additives on health grounds. That does not mean, however, that we cannot sustain his determination to so regulate. [W]e need not decide whether his decision is supported by the preponderance of the evidence, nor, for that matter, whether it is supported by substantial evidence.[79] To the contrary, we must sustain if it has a rational basis in the evidence... [W]e have no difficulty in terming [the Administrator's] decision rational.

. . . Contrary to the apparent suggestion of some of the petitioners, we need not seek a single dispositive study that fully supports the Administrator's determination. Science does not work that way; nor, for that matter, does adjudicatory fact-finding. Rather, the Administrator's decision may be fully supportable if it is based, as it is, on the inconclusive but suggestive results of numerous studies. By its nature, scientific evidence is cumulative: the more supporting, albeit inconclusive, evidence available, the more likely the accuracy of the conclusion.... Thus, after considering the inferences that can be drawn from the studies supporting the Administrator, and those opposing him, we must decide whether the cumulative effect of all this evidence, and not the effect of any single bit of it, presents a rational basis for the low-lead regulations.

While we have studied the record with great care, we do not discuss it all here; to do so would make this already lengthy opinion completely unwieldy. Instead, we shall briefly review the bases for the Administrator's conclusions that petitioners have singled out for special attack.....

[The court's lengthy discussion of the record and explanation for its conclusion that the EPA's decision was not arbitrary or capricious is omitted.]

## V. CONCLUSION

The complex scientific questions presented by this rule-making proceeding were "resolved in the crucible of debate through the clash of informed but opposing scientific and technological viewpoints." International Harvester Co. v. Ruckelshaus, 478 F.2d 615, 652 (1973) (concurring opinion of Chief Judge Bazelon).... [A]lmost three years after the debate was joined, the EPA promulgated its regulations accompanied by a 10,000–word opinion, thoroughly and comprehensively analyzing the various scien-

---

**79.** Review for substantial evidence is mandated only for agency adjudications and formal rule-making proceedings. 5 U.S.C. § 706(2)(E). Since "arbitrary and capricious" review does not involve determining whether the agency decision is supported by substantial evidence, it is considered the more lenient form of review. Nonetheless, some have noted that in reviewing the evidence relied upon in agency proceedings, the two standards often seem to merge.... The primary difference between the two in such cases would seem to be that "substantial evidence" review is limited to evidence developed in formal hearings, while "arbitrary and capricious" review of an agency engaged in informal rule-making is not so limited, but rather may consider the agency's developed expertise and any evidence referenced by the agency or otherwise placed in the record....

tific studies and giving its reasons why it resolved the scientific debate it had provoked in favor of protecting the public from the danger of lead emissions. A ... [d]ocument, extensively detailing and reviewing the current state of scientific knowledge of the health effects of airborne lead, also accompanied the regulations and the reasons for their issuance.

Because of the importance of the issues raised, we have accorded this case the most careful and exhaustive consideration. We find that in this rule-making proceeding the EPA['s] ... reasons as stated in its opinion provide a rational basis for its action....

■ BAZELON, CHIEF JUDGE, with whom McGOWAN, CIRCUIT JUDGE, joins (concurring):

I concur in Judge Wright's opinion for the court, and wish only to further elucidate certain matters.

I agree with the court's construction of the statute that the Administrator is called upon to make "essentially legislative policy judgments" in assessing risks to public health. But I cannot agree that this automatically relieves the Administrator's decision from the "procedural ... rigor proper for questions of fact." Quite the contrary, this case strengthens my view that[4]

> ... in cases of great technological complexity, the best way for courts to guard against unreasonable or erroneous administrative decisions is not for the judges themselves to scrutinize the technical merits of each decision. Rather, it is to establish a decision-making process that assures a reasoned decision that can be held up to the scrutiny of the scientific community and the public.

This record provides vivid demonstration of the dangers implicit in the contrary view, ably espoused by Judge Leventhal, which would have judges "steeping" themselves "in technical matters to determine whether the agency 'has exercised a reasoned discretion' ".[5] It is one thing for judges to scrutinize FCC judgments concerning diversification of media ownership to determine if they are rational. But I doubt judges contribute much to improving the quality of the difficult decisions which must be made in highly technical areas when they take it upon themselves to decide, as did the panel in this case, that "in assessing the scientific and medical data the Administrator made clear errors of judgment." The process making a de novo evaluation of the scientific evidence inevitably invites judges of

---

4. International Harvester Co. v. Ruckelshaus, 478 F.2d 615, 652 (1973) (Bazelon, C. J., concurring).

5. ... The *Greater Boston TV* case, from which Judge Leventhal draws this language, involved FCC non-renewal of a license in part because it was held by parties controlling a major newspaper in the area. As indicated in the text, such issues are much more amenable to judicial comprehension than the scientific judgments in a case such as the present. While acknowledging that the general rules of administrative law might be modified, rather than imported wholesale, into scientific and technical areas, Judge Leventhal apparently concludes that encouraging judges to parse the evidence themselves is necessary if courts are to remain "fully vigilant to exercise rather than abdicate their supervisory role" in areas such as environmental law which touch fundamental interests in life and health....

opposing views to make plausible-sounding, but simplistic, judgments of the relative weight to be afforded various pieces of technical data.[7]

It is true that, where ... a panel has reached the result of invalidating agency action by undue involvement in the uncertainties of the typical informal rulemaking record, the court *en banc* will be tempted to justify its affirmation of the agency by confronting the panel on its own terms. But this is a temptation which, if not resisted, will not only impose severe strains upon the energies and resources of the court but also compound the error of the panel in making legislative policy determinations alien to its true function. We would be wiser to heed the admonition of the Supreme Court that: "[e]xperience teaches ... that the affording of procedural safeguards, which by their nature serve to illuminate the underlying facts, in itself often operates to prevent erroneous decisions on the merits from occurring."[8]

Because substantive review of mathematical and scientific evidence by technically illiterate judges is dangerously unreliable, I continue to believe we will do more to improve administrative decision-making by concentrating our efforts on strengthening administrative procedures:[9]

> When administrators provide a framework for principled decision-making, the result will be to diminish the importance of judicial review by enhancing the integrity of the administrative process, and to improve the quality of judicial review in those cases where judicial review is sought.

It does not follow that courts may never properly find that an administrative decision in a scientific area is irrational. But I do believe that in highly technical areas, where our understanding of the import of the evidence is attenuated, our readiness to review evidentiary support for decisions must be correspondingly restrained.

As I read the court's opinion, it severely limits judicial weighing of the evidence by construing the Administrator's decision to be a matter of "legislative policy," and consequently not subject to review with the

---

**7.** For example, Judge Wright states little weight is to be given the absence of studies documenting actual harm from lead in auto emissions with the observation ... that "... lead exposure from the ambient air is pervasive, so that valid control groups cannot be found against which the effects of lead on our population can be measured." ...

Similarly, Judge Wilkey, in his original panel opinion, discounts the value of a particular study with the observation: "Realistically, it is impossible to say that any definite scientific or medical conclusion can be drawn from the observation of one or two subjects." ...

I do not know whether or not these observations are valid, although it was my impression that techniques had been devised which minimized these problems in certain cases. Be that as it may, these overt examples of homespun scientific aphorisms indicate that on more subtle, and less visible, matters of scientific judgment we judges are well beyond our institutional competency.

**8.** Silver v. New York Stock Exchange, 373 U.S. 341 (1963).

**9.** Environmental Defense Fund, Inc. v. Ruckelshaus, 439 F.2d 584, 598 (1971) (Bazelon, C. J.).

"substantive rigor proper for questions of fact."[10] Since this result would bar the panel's close analysis of the evidence, it satisfies my concerns.

\* \* \* \* \* \*

An additional matter which emerges from this record deserves comment: namely, the failure of the record to clearly disclose the procedural steps followed by EPA. As a result, an onerous, time-consuming burden was cast upon the court to reconstruct these steps by inference and surmise. It is not enough for an agency to prepare a record compiling all the evidence it relied upon for its action; it must also organize and digest it, so that a reviewing court is not forced to scour the four corners of the record to find that evidence for itself. These principles apply with no less force to judicial review of agency procedures. In informal rule-making, the record should clearly disclose when each piece of new information is received and when and how it was made available for comment. If information is received too late for comment, the agency must at least clearly indicate how the substance of its consideration would be affected.

It is regrettable that EPA did not give the same care to clearly setting forth procedural matters for the record as it gave to substantive matters. It may well be that this court's 30–day order interfered with the opportunity to do so. Based on that possibility, and the court's own reconstruction of the procedural record . . . , I am persuaded that the petitioner's rights were not prejudiced. Ordinarily, however, I think a record which so burdens judicial review would require a remand for clarification.

■ Statement of Circuit Judge Leventhal:

I concur without reservation in the excellent opinion for the court.

I write an additional word only because of observations in the concurring opinion authored by Chief Judge Bazelon. I would not have thought they required airing today, since they in no way relate, so far as I can see, to the court's en banc opinion. But since they have been floated I propose to bring them to earth, though I can here present only the highlights of analysis.

What does and should a reviewing court do when it considers a challenge to technical administrative decision-making? In my view, the panel opinion in this case overstepped the bounds of proper judicial supervision in its willingness to substitute its own scientific judgments for that of the EPA. In an effort to refute that approach convincingly the panel dissent may have over-reacted and responded too much in kind. In a kind of sur-rebuttal against such overzealousness, Judge Bazelon has also over-reacted. His opinion if I read it right advocates engaging in no substantive review at all, whenever the substantive issues at stake involve technical matters that the judges involved consider beyond their individual technical competence.

If he is not saying that, if he agrees there must be some substantive review, then I am at a loss to discern its significance. Certainly it does not help those seeking enlightenment to recognize when the difference in degree of substantive review becomes a difference in kind.

---

**10.** . . . This construction of the proper scope of review makes unnecessary Judge Wright's exhaustive analysis of the scientific evidence, which is evidently undertaken to answer those who believe we must judge the technical data for ourselves.

Taking the opinion in its fair implication, as a signal to judges to abstain from any substantive review, it is my view that while giving up is the easier course, it is not legitimately open to us at present. In the case of legislative enactments, the sole responsibility of the courts is constitutional due process review. In the case of agency decision-making the courts have an additional responsibility set by Congress. Congress has been willing to delegate its legislative powers broadly and courts have upheld such delegation because there is court review to assure that the agency exercises the delegated power within statutory limits, and that it fleshes out objectives within those limits by an administration that is not irrational or discriminatory. Nor is that envisioned judicial role ephemeral, as *Overton Park*[2] makes clear.

Our present system of review assumes judges will acquire whatever technical knowledge is necessary as background for decision of the legal questions. It may be that some judges are not initially equipped for this role, just as they may not be technically equipped initially to decide issues of obviousness and infringement in patent cases. If technical difficulties loom large, Congress may push to establish specialized courts. Thus far, it has proceeded on the assumption that we can both have the important values secured by generalist judges and rely on them to acquire whatever technical background is necessary.

The aim of the judges is not to exercise expertise or decide technical questions, but simply to gain sufficient background orientation. Our obligation is not to be jettisoned because our initial technical understanding may be meagre. . . . When called upon to make de novo decisions, individual judges have had to acquire the learning pertinent to complex technical questions in such fields as economics, science, technology and psychology. Our role is not as demanding when we are engaged in review of agency decisions, where we exercise restraint, and affirm even if we would have decided otherwise so long as the agency's decisionmaking is not irrational or discriminatory.

The substantive review of administrative action is modest, but it cannot be carried out in a vacuum of understanding. Better no judicial review at all than a charade that gives the imprimatur without the substance of judicial confirmation that the agency is not acting unreasonably. Once the presumption of regularity in agency action is challenged with a factual submission, and even to determine whether such a challenge has been made, the agency's record and reasoning has to be looked at. If there is some factual support for the challenge, there must be either evidence or judicial notice available explicating the agency's result, or a remand to supply the gap.

Mistakes may mar the exercise of any judicial function. While in this case the panel made such a mistake, it did not stem from judicial incom-

---

**2.** [*Overton Park*] requires the reviewing court to scrutinize the facts and consider whether the agency decision was "based on a consideration of the relevant factors" in the context of nonformalized, discretionary executive decisionmaking. A fortiori, at least that rigor of review should apply to more formal decisionmaking processes like informal rulemaking.

petence to deal with technical issues, but from confusion about the proper stance for substantive review of agency action in an area where the state of current knowledge does not generate customary definitiveness and certainty. . . .

On issues of substantive review, on conformance to statutory standards and requirements of rationality, the judges must act with restraint. Restraint, yes, abdication, no.

■ [JUDGE MACKINNON's separate dissent is omitted.]

■ WILKEY, CIRCUIT JUDGE, with whom joined TAMM and ROBB, CIRCUIT JUDGES (dissenting):

. . .

## III.   SCOPE OF REVIEW

EPA in promulgating these regulations followed the informal rulemaking procedure outlined in the Administrative Procedure Act, 5 U.S.C. § 553. . . . [O]ur scope of review of these regulations is limited to a determination of whether "agency action, findings . . . [or] conclusions . . . [are] arbitrary, capricious, an abuse of discretion, or otherwise not in accordance with law. . . ." or "in excess of statutory jurisdiction, authority, or limitations, or short of statutory right," or "without observance of procedure required by law."

It is well recognized that in reviewing the record we are not to substitute our judgment for that of the Administrator. Thus, we are required to affirm agency determinations with which we disagree. However, we are also under an obligation not to act as a rubber stamp of agency rulemaking action. As a result, in reviewing agency rulemaking under § 553, we are obligated to engage in a "substantial inquiry," and "inquiry into the facts is to be searching and careful. . . ."[132] As the Supreme Court has indicated, we "must 'consider whether the decision [. . .] was based on a consideration of the relevant factors and whether there has been *a clear error of judgment.*'"[133]

Certainly a determination made in the absence of any evidence in the record to support it would lead a reviewing court to conclude that a "clear error of judgment" had occurred. However, a reviewing court could reach a similar conclusion in the presence of some evidence supporting the agency determination. Since a court must review "the entire record," it may well be that the evidence detracting from the agency's conclusion is so overwhelming or so persuasive, or the agency's approach so one-sided, or the decision-making process so flawed, that a reviewing court must conclude that the agency erred in the exercise of its rulemaking power. Or, if there is an essential point or element missing in the logical progression toward the conclusion that the agency reaches, then the agency's action likewise may

---

**132.**   Citizens to Preserve Overton Park, Inc. v. Volpe, 401 U.S. 402, 415, 416 (1971).

**133.**   *Id.* (emphasis added). This statement of the scope of review was reaffirmed very recently by a unanimous Supreme Court in Bowman Transp., Inc. v. Arkansas–Best Freight Sys., Inc., 419 U.S. 281, 284–86 (1974). . . .

be arbitrary or capricious, because it is not supported by a logical thought process.

. . . [T]he thought process by which an agency reaches its conclusion on informal rulemaking resembles a chain. If there is a link missing, then the agency, to reach the conclusion that it did, was required to take an arbitrary jump in its logic to reach that conclusion. . . . [I]f no such scientifically proved chain exists, the Administrator's decision can only be arbitrary and capricious. . . .

In the case at hand, it seems obvious that the Administrator made "clear error[s] of judgment." This conclusion is based upon a "searching and careful" inquiry into the facts underlying the determination that airborne lead will endanger the public health. At several points in the Administrator's reasoning we have found little or no evidence to support his conclusions, and at several points we have noted clear errors of a substantial nature in the Administrator's analytical and evaluative methodology and EPA's decision-making process. Several vital links in the chain are unsupported; for the Administrator to leap to the conclusion he did can only be termed arbitrary and capricious. We submit that "a clear error of judgment" has occurred,[139] as our concluding analysis of the evidence and methodology demonstrates.

## IV. THE EVIDENCE

### A. *This Court's Task*

It is of crucial importance to recognize that this court's task on review of agency rulemaking is twofold. One of these tasks is universally acknowledged. We must explore the evidentiary record to determine whether the statements and conclusions of facts have an adequate basis in the underlying evidence. However, an equally important role is our review of agency analysis in order to determine whether it is principled and reasonable. Properly understood, our role is not to review directly the evidence, but to review the agency's treatment and analysis of the evidence. Of course, in so doing we will defer to the agency's expertise and experience in the subject matter of the decision.

In our view, the court's treatment of the evidence neglects this second, equally important function of a reviewing court. . . . Just as agency counsel cannot supply a post hoc rationalization for agency determinations, neither can a reviewing court.[140] . . .

---

**139.** We find our colleagues do not differ materially with us on the standard for review. . . . We believe [ ] that the error of the Administrator was so clear as to deprive the agency's decision of a rational basis. . . .

**140.** In a footnote the court does pay lip service to this well-settled principle of judicial restraint: "Of course, [the rational] basis must be expressed by the agency itself *and not supplied by the court.* SEC v. Chenery Corp., 332 U.S. 194, 196 (1947)." Court's opinion at n.73 (emphasis added). *Accord, Environmental Defense Fund v. EPA,* where Judge Leventhal speaks for this court,

*1. How Rigorously Should Courts Evaluate Agency Reasoning?*—Judge Wright's majority opinion and Judge Wilkey's dissent appear, at least on the surface, to articulate similar standards of review. Judge Wright described the § 706(2)(A) standard as a "highly deferential one" that "presumes agency action to be valid ... [,] forbids the court's substituting its judgment for that of the agency ... [,] and requires affirmance if a rational basis exists for the agency's decision...." At the same time, Judge Wright emphasized that the court should not "rubber-stamp" agency decisions, but should instead "assure itself that the agency decision was based on a consideration of the relevant factors" after a searching and careful inquiry. Using almost identical language, Judge Wilkey's dissent declared that the court should "not substitute [its] judgment for that of the Administrator" and must often "affirm agency determinations with which [the court] disagree[s]," but also that the court is "under an obligation not to act as a rubber stamp" and must therefore engage in a searching and careful inquiry.

Yet despite these similarities, Judge Wright and Judge Wilkey appeared to approach the task of reviewing agency action in quite different ways. The major differences seem to be how willing they are to infer agency reasoning that is not stated expressly, and to allow the agency to make explicit or implicit assumptions that are not supported by direct evidence. In the key passage of Judge Wilkey's dissent, he characterized the agency's decision process as a "chain" of reasoning that must connect the evidence before the agency to the agency's ultimate policy conclusion. Each step in this reasoning process—every piece of evidence, intermediate logical or factual inference, value judgment, and the like—is a link in this chain. Thus, Judge Wilkey explained, "[i]f there is a link missing, then the agency, to reach the conclusion that it did, was required to take an *arbitrary* jump in its logic to reach that conclusion" (emphasis added). Furthermore, even if the reviewing court can imagine sensible arguments or inferences the agency *might* have made to reach its conclusion, the court is forbidden to consider these points if the agency did not include them in the rulemaking record. The reason is grounded in the *Chenery I* principle (pp. 645–646 *supra*) that neither agency counsel, nor a reviewing court, can supply a post hoc rationalization for an agency decision. The only appropriate remedy in such cases is to remand the decision to the agency.

Judge Wright approached the issue differently. Rather than seeing the agency's reasoning process as a "chain," Judge Wright viewed the process

---

> The interests at stake here are too important to permit the decision to be sustained on the basis of speculative inference as to what the Administrator's findings and conclusions *might* have been regarding benefits. Sound principle sustains the practice of vesting choice of policy with the Administrator. Its corollary is that the *specific decision must be explained, not merely explainable*, in terms of the ingredients announced by the Administrator as comprising the Agency's policies and standards.

465 F.2d 528, 539 (1972) (emphasis added). Here, too, the interests at stake are too important to permit EPA's decision to be sustained on the basis of speculative inference as to why the Administrator *might have* embraced certain studies and rejected others....

more holistically, explaining that an agency's decision "may be fully supportable if it is based ... on the inconclusive but suggestive results of numerous studies." For Judge Wright, the question whether the agency acted "arbitrarily" turned not on whether it is possible to identify steps in the decision-making process where the agency failed to supply an explicit rationale for some contestable factual or logical inference, or failed to explain in detail why it credited the results of certain studies over the results of other studies, but rather on whether the agency's decision had a "rational basis" in the evidence, given the "cumulative effect" of all the evidence available. Thus, for Judge Wilkey an agency decision is "arbitrary" if it relies on unstated or unsupported inferences, while for Judge Wright a decision is "arbitrary" if no reasonable person, confronted with the evidence before the agency, could reach the conclusion that the agency did. Which of these approaches is the better one?

The Supreme Court has sent mixed signals on just how demanding reviewing courts must be. *Chenery I*, of course, insisted that an agency's action can be upheld only on the basis of the justification proffered by the agency in promulgating the rule or order; neither a reviewing court nor agency lawyers can supply a post hoc rationale for the agency's decision. That said, only a couple years before *Chenery I*, the Supreme Court decided a case called Colorado Interstate Gas Co. v. Federal Power Commission, 324 U.S. 581 (1945), in which parties challenging a set of Federal Power Commission orders argued that the Commission's findings, as stated in the orders, were "inadequate" and that the cases therefore "should be remanded to the Commission so that appropriate findings may be made." *Id.* at 595. Although the Supreme Court agreed that "[t]he findings of the Commission ... leave much to be desired since they are quite summary," the Court nonetheless concluded that "the path which [the Commission] followed can be discerned." *Id.* Because the Commission's findings were not "so vague and obscure as to make ... judicial review ... a perfunctory process," the Court refused to remand the case to the agency. *Id.*

*Chenery I* and *Colorado Interstate Gas* are not inconsistent, but taken together they illustrate a basic tension that was also manifest in the dispute between Judges Wright and Wilkey in *Ethyl Corp.* We want agencies to explain their decisions clearly, but at the same time we don't want to subject agencies to unreasonable burdens or to expose agencies to judicial remand every time some clever and aggressive lawyer can identify a logical or evidentiary gap. This tension was nicely summed up in Bowman Transportation, Inc. v. Arkansas–Best Freight Systems, Inc., 419 U.S. 281 (1974), decided only six months before the en banc oral argument in *Ethyl Corp. Bowman* summarized the doctrine on the agency's obligation to adequately explain its decision by stating: "While we may not supply a reasoned basis for the agency's action that the agency itself has not given, SEC v. Chenery Corp., 332 U.S. 194, 196 (1947), we will uphold a decision of less than ideal clarity if the agency's path may reasonably be discerned. Colorado Interstate Gas Co. v. FPC, 324 U.S. 581, 595 (1945)." 419 U.S. at 285–86. This sentence from *Bowman* is oft-quoted, both in cases where courts remand agency action in light of the agency's failure to provide a sufficiently well-reasoned explanation, and in cases where courts uphold agency action despite arguments that the agency's explanation was incomplete or inadequate. Opinions in the former category tend to emphasize the first clause in the quoted sentence (and the citation of *Chenery I*), while opinions in the latter category tend to emphasize the second clause (and the citation to *Colorado Interstate Gas*). How would you resolve this tension? How much detail should an agency have to supply in order for a reviewing court to conclude that "the agency's path may reasonably be discerned"?

It's also worth restating here the connection between the question of how much detail an agency must supply such that its decision is not "arbitrary" within the meaning of § 706(2)(A) and the questions concerning the adequacy of the agency's "statement of [the final rule's] basis and purpose" as required by § 553(c). As you may recall if you have covered the *Nova Scotia* case (pp. 605–614, *supra*), courts have drawn an explicit connection between the requirement that agencies supply an adequate statement of a rule's basis and purpose with the requirement that an agency demonstrate that its final rule was the product of a reasoned decision-making process. Thus, while *Nova Scotia* framed the relevant inquiry as whether the agency had complied with a procedural requirement of § 553(c), and *Ethyl Corp.* framed the inquiry in terms of whether the agency's action was arbitrary within the meaning of § 706(2)(A), the ultimate question in both cases was essentially identical: Did the agency statement accompanying the final rule adequately explain and justify the agency's policy choice, in light of the available evidence?

**2. Should Review Focus on Substance or Procedure?**—The difference in how Judges Wright and Wilkey interpreted the § 706(2)(A) standard of review, though important, is subtle. The difference in how Judges Bazelon and Leventhal viewed the court's role under this standard is much more dramatic. As noted in the materials introducing this section, Judge Leventhal was one of the driving forces behind the development of what he called "hard look" review—an approach that, while deferential, entails close judicial scrutiny of the agency's decision-making process to ensure that the agency has carefully considered the relevant factors and reasonably explained the choices it had made. Judge Bazelon was more skeptical of judges' capacity to engage in searching review of the agency's reasoning, but he was also committed to a significant role for courts in overseeing agency decisions. As a result, Judge Bazelon began to champion an approach to § 706(2)(A) review that focused on whether the agency had employed appropriate decision-making *procedures*. Judge Bazelon's concurrence in *Ethyl Corp.* is probably the clearest and most emphatic statement of his alternative conception of § 706(2)(A) review, while Judge Leventhal's opinion presented a succinct and forceful rebuttal. As we will see, the Supreme Court weighed in a few years later in *Vermont Yankee v. NRDC* (pp. 740–748, *infra*), which decisively rejected Judge Bazelon's approach. Yet the Bazelon–Leventhal debate is of more than historical interest, as their arguments touch on important—and still unsettled—questions about the appropriate role of courts in overseeing agency action. *See* Ronald J.

Krotoszynski, Jr., *"History Belongs to the Winners": The Bazelon–Leventhal Debate and the Continuing Relevance of the Process/Substance Dichotomy in Judicial Review of Agency Action*, 58 ADMIN. L. REV. 995 (2006).

Judge Bazelon's concurrence made two separate points that, while related, are logically distinct. He argued, first, that judges should not attempt to evaluate an agency's reasoning process on the merits by delving into the rulemaking record and scrutinizing the agency's substantive explanation for its choices. Second, he argued that judges should concentrate their efforts on "strengthening administrative procedures," focusing on whether the agency had "establish[ed] a decision-making process that assures a reasoned decision." Acceptance of the first point does not necessarily entail acceptance of the second point. Indeed, under the old *Pacific States Box & Basket* standard, judges neither engaged in careful scrutiny of the agency's reasoning nor insisted on more stringent procedures; instead, courts applied a kind of minimal rational basis review to the agency's final policy choice. Likewise, one could accept Judge Bazelon's call for judicial insistence on more rigorous procedures as a *supplement* to a searching inquiry into the substance of the agency's reasoning. That said, the two points are related insofar as substantive and procedural review might be seen as (partial) substitutes.

Let us consider first Judge Bazelon's critique of the sort of hard look review advocated by Judge Leventhal. Judge Bazelon's main criticism was straightforward: Generalist judges, in his view, are simply not competent to evaluate complex scientific and technical issues; substantive review of such issues "by technically illiterate judges," according to Judge Bazelon, "is dangerously unreliable." The danger derives from the fact that judges—especially those that have invested substantial time in studying the administrative record—are likely to overestimate their understanding of the complex issues involved, and therefore will tend "to make plausible-sounding, but simplistic, judgments of the relative weight to be afforded various pieces of technical data," relying on "homespun scientific aphorisms" rather than a real understanding of the evidence. This danger is compounded by the fact that judges may have strong policy preferences that may color their interpretation of technical data and analysis that they don't really understand.

Judge Leventhal's response was equally straightforward, and nicely summed up by the closing words of his opinion: "Restraint, yes, abdication, no." Judge Leventhal did not deny that generalist judges lack the time and expertise to develop an understanding of the administrative record comparable to that of the responsible agency officials. He also agreed that in some cases reviewing judges may lose sight of their proper role and inappropriately second-guess agency technical judgments. Indeed, he thought that was what the judges on the original panel had done in *Ethyl Corp.* But he believed Judge Bazelon had overreacted to this legitimate concern by calling for the abolition of any form of substantive judicial review of agency decision-making. Judge Leventhal made two major arguments here. The first argument engaged Judge Bazelon's institutional competence argument on its own terms; the second emphasized the illegitimacy of abandoning substantive hard look review in light of congressional intent. Let us consider each in turn, and assess whether these arguments, considered separately or together, convincingly refute Judge Bazelon's critique of hard look review.

Judge Leventhal's first point was that judges, though not experts, can learn enough about the issues to engage in deferential but meaningful review to ensure that the agency has considered the relevant factors and not made a clear error of judgment. Judges, that is, can "acquire whatever technical knowledge is necessary as background for decision of the legal questions." Judge Leventhal pointed out that in numerous other contexts (such as patent cases) "individual judges have had to acquire the learning pertinent to complex technical questions in such fields as economics, science, technology and psychology." As long as judges properly understand their limited role—which is to ensure that "the agency's decisionmaking is not irrational or discriminatory"—they should be able to acquire enough expertise to engage in meaningful review.

Is that convincing? Are administrative review cases comparable to other cases involving technical issues—like patent, antitrust, or complex mass torts—with respect to the challenges they pose to judges' technical competence? What about Judge Bazelon's suggestion that even though the sort of informed but deferential review that Judge Leventhal advocates might be possible in theory, judges *in practice* will overestimate their technical competence, and hence overstep their appropriate institutional role? How would you go about evaluating the competing claims? Should the approach to judicial review depend on whether the question is highly technical (as Judge Bazelon seems to suggest)?

Judge Leventhal's second argument was that whatever the merits of Judge Bazelon's pragmatic concerns, Congress intended courts to engage in something like hard look review. Instead of relying on the text of § 706(2)(A) in making this argument, Judge Leventhal emphasized that Congress delegated extensive powers to agencies on the assumption that meaningful (i.e., substantive) judicial review would ensure that agencies did not exercise that delegated power in ways that were "irrational or discriminatory." He added that because Congress had generally not created specialized courts to review technical agency decisions, it stood to reason that Congress made a considered judgment that the advantages of substantive review by generalist courts outweigh the disadvantages.

As a matter of statutory interpretation, is Judge Leventhal's argument persuasive? Judge Bazelon did not address the point directly. How do you think he might respond? Start with the text of § 706(2)(A), which empowers courts to set aside agency action that is "arbitrary, capricious[, or] an abuse of discretion." Does that text favor Judge Leventhal's conception of hard look review over Judge Bazelon's alternative, procedure-focused review? Notice that a *separate* provision of the same statutory section, § 706(2)(D), obligates a court to set aside agency action that is "without observance of procedure required by law." Does this imply that

§ 706(2)(A)'s "arbitrary and capricious" standard mandates some form of meaningful judicial review *beyond* procedural review? On the other hand, if Congress enacted the § 706(2)(A) "arbitrary and capricious" standard against a background legal understanding that equated that term with the minimal rational basis review prescribed by *Pacific States Box & Basket*, might that suggest that Judge Leventhal had, if anything, inverted congressional expectations about how judges would conduct review of delegated agency policymaking?

One interesting fact about Judge Leventhal's response to Judge Bazelon is that it defended hard look review but did little to address Judge Bazelon's proposed alternative of focusing on the adequacy of the agency's decision-making *procedures* (as opposed to the adequacy of the agency's reasoning). There are, however, difficult and important questions regarding the degree to which courts may demand that agencies employ more rigorous decision-making procedures—questions that are distinct from those concerning the appropriate scope of judicial review of the substantive reasonableness of an agency's decision-making. The next section, on the *Vermont Yankee* case, engages these questions.

## B. JUDICIAL REGULATION OF ADMINISTRATIVE PROCEDURES

In a series of cases decided in the 1970s, Judge Bazelon argued that judicial review of agency rules should focus on the adequacy of agency procedures, rather than the soundness of the agency's reasoning. *See* O'Donnell v. Shaffer, 491 F.2d 59, 62 (D.C. Cir. 1974); International Harvester Co. v. Ruckelshaus, 478 F.2d 615, 650–52 (D.C. Cir. 1973) (Bazelon, C.J., concurring in the result); Environmental Defense Fund, Inc. v. Ruckelshaus, 439 F.2d 584, 597–98 (D.C. Cir. 1971); *see also* David L. Bazelon, *Coping with Technology Through the Legal Process*, 62 CORNELL L. REV. 817 (1977). Other judges sometimes adopted a similar approach. *See, e.g.*, Mobil Oil Corp. v. Federal Power Comm'n, 483 F.2d 1238, 1251–54 (D.C. Cir. 1973); Appalachian Power Co. v. EPA, 477 F.2d 495, 500–03 (4th Cir. 1973). Others resisted Judge Bazelon's approach. Sometimes, as in Judge Leventhal's *Ethyl Corp.* opinion (pp. 730–732, *supra*), that resistance focused on the impermissibility of abandoning all judicial inquiry into the validity of the agency's reasoning process. *See* Harold Leventhal, *Environmental Decisionmaking and the Role of the Courts*, 122 U. PA. L. REV. 509, 532–41 (1974). An equally important line of criticism questioned the legitimacy of judicial imposition of procedural requirements beyond those explicitly required by the Constitution, the APA, other statutes, or the agency's own regulations. *See* J. Skelly Wright, *The Courts and the Rulemaking Process: The Limits of Judicial Review*, 59 CORNELL L. REV. 375 (1974). (For more on the debate in the D.C. Circuit over this issue, see generally Ronald J. Krotoszynski, Jr., *"History Belongs to the Winners": The Bazelon–Leventhal Debate and the Continuing Relevance of the Process/Substance Dichotomy in Judicial Review of Agency Action*, 58 ADMIN. L. REV. 995 (2006); Reuel E. Schiller, *Rulemaking's Promise: Administrative Law and Legal Culture in the 1960s and 1970s*, 53 ADMIN. L. REV. 1139 (2001); Matthew Warren, *Active Judging: Judicial Philosophy and the*

*Development of the Hard Look Doctrine in the D.C. Circuit*, 90 GEO. L.J. 2599 (2002).)

This schism was eventually addressed, apparently conclusively, by the Supreme Court in *Vermont Yankee Nuclear Power Corp. v. Natural Resources Defense Council*. In *Vermont Yankee*, the Supreme Court reviewed two D.C. Circuit opinions authored by Judge Bazelon, both of which had invalidated decisions to license nuclear power plants. These decisions had relied principally on the conclusion that the procedures the responsible agency had used to make the rule on which the licensing decisions were based were inadequate, even though the agency had complied with the express procedural requirements of the APA's notice-and-comment rulemaking provisions. Natural Res. Def. Council, Inc. v. Nuclear Regulatory Comm'n, 547 F.2d 633, 643–46, 653–54 (D.C. Cir. 1976); Aeschliman v. Nuclear Regulatory Comm'n, 547 F.2d 622, 632 (D.C. Cir. 1976). Judge Bazelon's opinion in *NRDC v. NRC* acknowledged that courts ordinarily should not "prescribe the procedural format which an agency must use," and further asserted that courts "are no more expert at fashioning administrative procedures than they are in the substantive areas of responsibility which are left to agency discretion." 547 F.2d at 644. But notwithstanding these disclaimers, Judge Bazelon concluded that while it would usually be improper for a reviewing court to mandate that an agency use particular procedures, the court nonetheless must "decide whether the procedures provided by the agency were sufficient to ventilate the issues." *Id.* at 643. In other words, to ensure that the agency's decision was not arbitrary and capricious, the court needed to "scrutinize the record as a whole to insure that genuine opportunities [for the parties] to participate in a meaningful way were provided." *Id.* at 644. Judge Bazelon then concluded that the rulemaking procedures used by the agency were inadequate.

The Supreme Court's review of these decisions presented the Court with an opportunity to decide whether Judge Bazelon's procedurally oriented approach to judicial review of agency action was permissible. The Supreme Court concluded unanimously that it was not. As you read *Vermont Yankee*, consider whether its rejection of Judge Bazelon's approach is well-justified. What might Judge Bazelon have said in response to the arguments in then-Justice Rehnquist's opinion for the Court? What do you think the world of judicial review of agency action would look like today if the Supreme Court had validated, rather than rejected, Judge Bazelon's approach?

## Vermont Yankee Nuclear Power Corp. v. Natural Resources Defense Council, Inc.

Supreme Court of the United States
435 U.S. 519 (1978)

■ MR. JUSTICE REHNQUIST delivered the opinion of the Court.

In 1946, Congress enacted the Administrative Procedure Act, which as we have noted elsewhere was not only "a new, basic and comprehensive regulation of procedures in many agencies," Wong Yang Sung v. McGrath, 339 U.S. 33 (1950), but was also a legislative enactment which settled "long-continued and hard-fought contentions, and enacts a formula upon which opposing social and political forces have come to rest." *Id.*, at 40. Section 4 of the Act, 5 U.S.C. § 553 (1976 ed.), dealing with rulemaking, requires in subsection (b) that "notice of proposed rule making shall be published in the Federal Register ...," describes the contents of that notice, and goes on to require in subsection (c) that after the notice the agency "shall give interested persons an opportunity to participate in the rule making through submission of written data, views, or arguments with or without opportunity for oral presentation. After consideration of the relevant matter presented, the agency shall incorporate in the rules adopted a concise general statement of their basis and purpose." Interpreting this provision of the Act in United States v. Allegheny–Ludlum Steel Corp., 406 U.S. 742 (1972), and United States v. Florida East Coast R. Co., 410 U.S. 224 (1973), we held that generally speaking this section of the Act established the maximum procedural requirements which Congress was willing to have the courts impose upon agencies in conducting rulemaking procedures. Agencies are free to grant additional procedural rights in the exercise of their discretion, but reviewing courts are generally not free to impose them if the agencies have not chosen to grant them. This is not to say necessarily that there are no circumstances which would ever justify a court in overturning agency action because of a failure to employ procedures beyond those required by the statute. But such circumstances, if they exist, are extremely rare.

Even apart from the Administrative Procedure Act this Court has for more than four decades emphasized that the formulation of procedures was basically to be left within the discretion of the agencies to which Congress had confided the responsibility for substantive judgments. In FCC v. Schreiber, 381 U.S. 279, 290 (1965), the Court explicated this principle, describing it as "an outgrowth of the congressional determination that administrative agencies and administrators will be familiar with the industries which they regulate and will be in a better position than federal courts or Congress itself to design procedural rules adapted to the peculiarities of the industry and the tasks of the agency involved." ...

It is in the light of this background of statutory and decisional law that we granted certiorari to review two judgments of the Court of Appeals for the District of Columbia Circuit because of our concern that they had seriously misread or misapplied this statutory and decisional law cautioning reviewing courts against engrafting their own notions of proper procedures upon agencies entrusted with substantive functions by Congress.... We conclude that the Court of Appeals has done just that in these cases, and we therefore remand them to it for further proceedings....

## I

### A

Under the Atomic Energy Act of 1954, 68 Stat. 919, as amended, 42 U.S.C. § 2011 *et seq.*, the Atomic Energy Commission was given broad regulatory authority over the development of nuclear energy. Under the terms of the Act, a utility seeking to construct and operate a nuclear power plant must obtain a separate permit or license at both the construction and the operation stage of the project. In order to obtain the construction permit, the utility must file a preliminary safety analysis report, an environmental report, and certain information regarding the antitrust implications of the proposed project. This application then undergoes exhaustive review by the Commission's staff and by the Advisory Committee on Reactor Safeguards (ACRS), a group of distinguished experts in the field of atomic energy. Both groups submit to the Commission their own evaluations, which then become part of the record of the utility's application. The Commission staff also undertakes the review required by the National Environmental Policy Act of 1969 (NEPA), 83 Stat. 852, 42 U.S.C. § 4321 *et seq.*, and prepares a draft environmental impact statement, which, after being circulated for comment, is revised and becomes a final environmental impact statement. Thereupon a three-member Atomic Safety and Licensing Board conducts a public adjudicatory hearing ... and reaches a decision which can be appealed to the Atomic Safety and Licensing Appeal Board, and currently, in the Commission's discretion, to the Commission itself. The final agency decision may be appealed to the courts of appeals....

These cases arise from two separate decisions of the Court of Appeals for the District of Columbia Circuit. In the first, the court remanded a decision of the Commission to grant a license to petitioner Vermont Yankee Nuclear Power Corp. to operate a nuclear power plant. Natural Resources Defense Council v. NRC, 547 F.2d 633 (1976). In the second, the court remanded a decision of that same agency to grant a permit to petitioner Consumers Power Co. to construct two pressurized water nuclear reactors to generate electricity and steam. Aeschliman v. NRC, 547 F.2d 622.

### B

In December 1967, after the mandatory adjudicatory hearing and necessary review, the Commission granted petitioner Vermont Yankee a permit to build a nuclear power plant in Vernon, Vt. Thereafter, Vermont Yankee applied for an operating license. Respondent Natural Resources Defense Council (NRDC) objected to the granting of a license, however, and therefore a hearing on the application commenced on August 10, 1971. Excluded from consideration at the hearings, over NRDC's objection, was the issue of the environmental effects of operations to reprocess fuel or dispose of wastes resulting from the reprocessing operations.[6] This ruling was affirmed by the Appeal Board in June 1972.

---

   **6.** The nuclear fission which takes place in light-water nuclear reactors apparently converts its principal fuel, uranium, into plutonium, which is itself highly radioactive but can be used as reactor fuel if separated from the remaining uranium and radioactive waste products. Fuel reprocessing refers to the process necessary to recapture usable plutonium. Waste disposal, at the present stage of technological development, refers to the storage of the very long lived and highly radioactive waste products until they detoxify sufficiently that they

In November 1972, however, the Commission, making specific reference to the Appeal Board's decision with respect to the Vermont Yankee license, instituted rulemaking proceedings "that would specifically deal with the question of consideration of environmental effects associated with the uranium fuel cycle in the individual cost-benefit analyses for light water cooled nuclear power reactors." The notice of proposed rulemaking offered two alternatives, both predicated on a report prepared by the Commission's staff entitled Environmental Survey of the Nuclear Fuel Cycle. The first would have required no quantitative evaluation of the environmental hazards of fuel reprocessing or disposal because the Environmental Survey had found them to be slight. The second would have specified numerical values for the environmental impact of this part of the fuel cycle, which values would then be incorporated into a table, along with the other relevant factors, to determine the overall cost-benefit balance for each operating license.

Much of the controversy in this case revolves around the procedures used in the rulemaking hearing which commenced in February 1973. In a supplemental notice of hearing the Commission indicated that while discovery or cross-examination would not be utilized, the Environmental Survey would be available to the public before the hearing along with the extensive background documents cited therein. All participants would be given a reasonable opportunity to present their position and could be represented by counsel if they so desired. Written and, time permitting, oral statements would be received and incorporated into the record. All persons giving oral statements would be subject to questioning by the Commission. At the conclusion of the hearing, a transcript would be made available to the public and the record would remain open for 30 days to allow the filing of supplemental written statements. More than 40 individuals and organizations representing a wide variety of interests submitted written comments. On January 17, 1973, the Licensing Board held a planning session to schedule the appearance of witnesses and to discuss methods for compiling a record. The hearing was held on February 1 and 2, with participation by a number of groups, including the Commission's staff, the United States Environmental Protection Agency, a manufacturer of reactor equipment, a trade association from the nuclear industry, a group of electric utility companies, and a group called Consolidated National Intervenors which represented 79 groups and individuals including respondent NRDC.

After the hearing, the Commission's staff filed a supplemental document for the purpose of clarifying and revising the Environmental Survey. Then the Licensing Board forwarded its report to the Commission without rendering any decision. The Licensing Board identified as the principal procedural question the propriety of declining to use full formal adjudicatory procedures. The major substantive issue was the technical adequacy of the Environmental Survey.

---

no longer present an environmental hazard. There are presently no physical or chemical steps which render this waste less toxic, other than simply the passage of time.

In April 1974, the Commission issued a rule which adopted the second of the two proposed alternatives described above. The Commission also approved the procedures used at the hearing,[7] and indicated that the record, including the Environmental Survey, provided an "adequate data base for the regulation adopted." . . .

Respondents appealed from both the Commission's adoption of the rule and its decision to grant Vermont Yankee's license to the Court of Appeals for the District of Columbia Circuit. . . .

### D

With respect to the challenge of Vermont Yankee's license, the court . . . examined the rulemaking proceedings and, despite the fact that it appeared that the agency employed all the procedures required by 5 U.S.C. § 553 (1976 ed.) and more, the court determined the proceedings to be inadequate and overturned the rule. Accordingly, the Commission's determination with respect to Vermont Yankee's license was also remanded for further proceedings. . . .

### II

. . .

### B

. . . [B]efore determining whether the Court of Appeals reached a permissible result, we must determine exactly what result it did reach, and in this case that is no mean feat. Vermont Yankee argues that the court invalidated the rule because of the inadequacy of the procedures employed in the proceedings. Respondents, on the other hand, labeling petitioner's view of the decision a "straw man," argue to this Court that the court merely held that the record was inadequate to enable the reviewing court to determine whether the agency had fulfilled its statutory obligation. But we unfortunately have not found the parties' characterization of the opinion to be entirely reliable. . . .

After a thorough examination of the opinion itself, we conclude that while the matter is not entirely free from doubt, the majority of the Court of Appeals struck down the rule because of the perceived inadequacies of the procedures employed in the rulemaking proceedings. The court first determined the intervenors' primary argument to be "that the decision to preclude 'discovery or cross-examination' denied them a meaningful oppor-

---

**7.** The Commission stated:

"In our view, the procedures adopted provide a more than adequate basis for formulation of the rule we adopted. All parties were fully heard. Nothing offered was excluded. The record does not indicate that any evidentiary material would have been received under different procedures. Nor did the proponent of the strict 'adjudicatory' approach make an offer of proof—or even remotely suggest—what substantive matters it would develop under different procedures. In addition, we note that 11 documents including the Survey were available to the parties several weeks before the hearing, and the Regulatory staff, though not requested to do so, made available various drafts and handwritten notes. Under all of the circumstances, we conclude that adjudicatory type procedures were not warranted here."

tunity to participate in the proceedings as guaranteed by due process." 547 F.2d, at 643. The court then went on to frame the issue for decision thus:

> "Thus, we are called upon to decide whether the procedures provided by the agency were sufficient to ventilate the issues." 547 F.2d, at 643.

The court conceded that absent extraordinary circumstances it is improper for a reviewing court to prescribe the procedural format an agency must follow, but it likewise clearly thought it entirely appropriate to "scrutinize the record as a whole to insure that genuine opportunities to participate in a meaningful way were provided...." 547 F.2d, at 644. The court also refrained from actually ordering the agency to follow any specific procedures, but there is little doubt in our minds that the ineluctable mandate of the court's decision is that the procedures afforded during the hearings were inadequate. This conclusion is particularly buttressed by the fact that after the court examined the record, particularly the testimony of Dr. Pittman, and declared it insufficient, the court proceeded to discuss at some length the necessity for further procedural devices or a more "sensitive" application of those devices employed during the proceedings. The exploration of the record and the statement regarding its insufficiency might initially lead one to conclude that the court was only examining the sufficiency of the evidence, but the remaining portions of the opinion dispel any doubt that this was certainly not the sole or even the principal basis of the decision. Accordingly, we feel compelled to address the opinion on its own terms, and we conclude that it was wrong.

In prior opinions we have intimated that even in a rulemaking proceeding when an agency is making a " 'quasi-judicial' " determination by which a very small number of persons are " 'exceptionally affected, in each case upon individual grounds,' " in some circumstances additional procedures may be required in order to afford the aggrieved individuals due process.[16] United States v. Florida East Coast R. Co., 410 U.S., at 242–245, quoting from Bi–Metallic Investment Co. v. State Board of Equalization, 239 U.S. 441, 446 (1915). It might also be true, although we do not think the issue is presented in this case and accordingly do not decide it, that a totally unjustified departure from well-settled agency procedures of long standing might require judicial correction.

But this much is absolutely clear. Absent constitutional constraints or extremely compelling circumstances the "administrative agencies 'should be free to fashion their own rules of procedure and to pursue methods of inquiry capable of permitting them to discharge their multitudinous duties.' " FCC v. Schreiber, 381 U.S., at 290, quoting from FCC v. Pottsville Broadcasting Co., 309 U.S., at 143. Indeed, our cases could hardly be more explicit in this regard....

---

**16.** Respondent NRDC does not now argue that additional procedural devices were required under the Constitution. Since this was clearly a rulemaking proceeding in its purest form, we see nothing to support such a view....

We have continually repeated this theme through the years, most recently in FPC v. Transcontinental Gas Pipe Line Corp., 423 U.S. 326 (1976), decided just two Terms ago. In that case, in determining the proper scope of judicial review of agency action under the Natural Gas Act, we held that while a court may have occasion to remand an agency decision because of the inadequacy of the record, the agency should normally be allowed to "exercise its administrative discretion in deciding how, in light of internal organization considerations, it may best proceed to develop the needed evidence and how its prior decision should be modified in light of such evidence as develops." *Id.*, at 333. We went on to emphasize:

> "At least in the absence of substantial justification for doing otherwise, a reviewing court may not, after determining that additional evidence is requisite for adequate review, proceed by dictating to the agency the methods, procedures, and time dimension of the needed inquiry and ordering the results to be reported to the court without opportunity for further consideration on the basis of the new evidence by the agency. Such a procedure clearly runs the risk of 'propel[ling] the court into the domain which Congress has set aside exclusively for the administrative agency.' SEC v. Chenery Corp., 332 U.S. 194, 196 (1947)." *Ibid.*

Respondent NRDC argues that [§ 553] of the Administrative Procedure Act ... merely establishes lower procedural bounds and that a court may routinely require more than the minimum when an agency's proposed rule addresses complex or technical factual issues or "Issues of Great Public Import." We have, however, previously shown that our decisions reject this view....

There are compelling reasons for construing [§ 553] in this manner. In the first place, if courts continually review agency proceedings to determine whether the agency employed procedures which were, in the court's opinion, perfectly tailored to reach what the court perceives to be the "best" or "correct" result, judicial review would be totally unpredictable. And the agencies, operating under this vague injunction to employ the "best" procedures and facing the threat of reversal if they did not, would undoubtedly adopt full adjudicatory procedures in every instance. Not only would this totally disrupt the statutory scheme, through which Congress enacted "a formula upon which opposing social and political forces have come to rest," Wong Yang Sung v. McGrath, 339 U.S., at 40, but all the inherent advantages of informal rulemaking would be totally lost.

Secondly, it is obvious that the court in these cases reviewed the agency's choice of procedures on the basis of the record actually produced at the hearing, and not on the basis of the information available to the agency when it made the decision to structure the proceedings in a certain way. This sort of Monday morning quarterbacking not only encourages but almost compels the agency to conduct all rulemaking proceedings with the full panoply of procedural devices normally associated only with adjudicatory hearings.

Finally, and perhaps most importantly, this sort of review fundamentally misconceives the nature of the standard for judicial review of an agency rule. The court below uncritically assumed that additional procedures will automatically result in a more adequate record because it will give interested parties more of an opportunity to participate in and contribute to the proceedings. But informal rulemaking need not be based solely on the transcript of a hearing held before an agency. Indeed, the agency need not even hold a formal hearing. See 5 U.S.C. § 553(c) (1976 ed.). Thus, the adequacy of the "record" in this type of proceeding is not correlated directly to the type of procedural devices employed, but rather turns on whether the agency has followed the statutory mandate of the Administrative Procedure Act or other relevant statutes. If the agency is compelled to support the rule which it ultimately adopts with the type of record produced only after a full adjudicatory hearing, it simply will have no choice but to conduct a full adjudicatory hearing prior to promulgating every rule. In sum, this sort of unwarranted judicial examination of perceived procedural shortcomings of a rulemaking proceeding can do nothing but seriously interfere with that process prescribed by Congress.

. . . In short, nothing in the APA, . . . the circumstances of this case, the nature of the issues being considered, past agency practice, or the statutory mandate under which the Commission operates permitted the court to review and overturn the rulemaking proceeding on the basis of the procedural devices employed (or not employed) by the Commission so long as the Commission employed at least the statutory *minima*, a matter about which there is no doubt in this case.

There remains, of course, the question of whether the challenged rule finds sufficient justification in the administrative proceedings that it should be upheld by the reviewing court. Judge Tamm, concurring in the result reached by the majority of the Court of Appeals, thought that it did not. There are also intimations in the majority opinion which suggest that the judges who joined it likewise may have thought the administrative proceedings an insufficient basis upon which to predicate the rule in question. We accordingly remand so that the Court of Appeals may review the rule as the Administrative Procedure Act provides. We have made it abundantly clear before that when there is a contemporaneous explanation of the agency decision, the validity of that action must "stand or fall on the propriety of that finding, judged, of course, by the appropriate standard of review. If that finding is not sustainable on the administrative record made, then the Comptroller's decision must be vacated and the matter remanded to him for further consideration." Camp v. Pitts, 411 U.S. 138, 143 (1973). See also SEC v. Chenery Corp., 318 U.S. 80 (1943). The court should engage in this kind of review and not stray beyond the judicial province to explore the procedural format or to impose upon the agency its own notion of which procedures are "best" or most likely to further some vague, undefined public good.

## III

. . . Nuclear energy may some day be a cheap, safe source of power or it may not. But Congress has made a choice to at least try nuclear energy, establishing a reasonable review process in which courts are to play only a limited role. The fundamental policy questions appropriately resolved in Congress and in the state legislatures are *not* subject to reexamination in the federal courts under the guise of judicial review of agency action. Time may prove wrong the decision to develop nuclear energy, but it is Congress or the States within their appropriate agencies which must eventually make that judgment. In the meantime courts should perform their appointed function.... Administrative decisions should be set aside in this context, as in every other, only for substantial procedural or substantive reasons as mandated by statute, not simply because the court is unhappy with the result reached....

*Reversed and remanded.*

■ MR. JUSTICE BLACKMUN and MR. JUSTICE POWELL took no part in the consideration or decision of these cases.

---

*1. The Legal Basis for Judicial Imposition of Procedural Requirements*—Assume for the moment that the D.C. Circuit opinions under review in *Vermont Yankee* did indeed require the NRC to use administrative procedures other than those mandated by the Constitution, the APA, other statutes, or the agency's own regulations. From what legal source might judges derive the authority to impose such constraints? One possibility is that the courts might develop these procedural requirements as part of a federal common law of administrative procedure. Indeed, prior to the enactment of the APA, much of the federal law on judicial review of administrative action was this type of judge-made common law, and in the first several decades after the APA's enactment, federal judges continued to exercise what they viewed as their legitimate authority to fashion administrative common law. Thus Professor Kenneth Culp Davis, in the 1978 edition of his administrative law treatise (published 32 years after the APA was enacted), declared that "nine-tenths of administrative law is judge-made law, and the other tenth is statutory." 1 KENNETH CULP DAVIS, ADMINISTRATIVE LAW TREATISE § 2:18, at 140 (2d. ed. 1978); *see also* John F. Duffy, *Administrative Common Law in Judicial Review*, 77 TEX. L. REV. 113, 121–52 (1998).

On at least some plausible readings of the APA, this is entirely permissible: One might read § 706(2)(D), which allows a court to set aside agency action that is "without observance of procedure required *by law*" (emphasis added) as including procedure required by *judge-made administrative common law*, as well as by statutory, constitutional, or regulatory law. In addition, § 559 states that the APA "do[es] not limit or repeal additional requirements imposed by statute *or otherwise recognized by law*" (emphasis added). The last phrase clearly indicates that the APA does not displace non-statutory procedural law. While that category could be understood as referring to agency-created regulatory law, it could also be read as preserving the administrative common law that was pervasive at the time of the APA's enactment. Then again, given that one of the main purposes of the APA was to provide for more uniform administrative procedures, is it plausible that Congress meant to maintain the courts' role in fashioning a common law of administrative procedure? The legislative history of the APA gives conflicting signals. *Compare* Duffy, *supra*, at 186 (contending that the "text, structure, and legislative history of the APA strongly support the conclusion that an agency's choice of procedure is reviewable only for violations of law; otherwise, the matter lies within the unreviewable discretion of the agency"), *with* Kenneth Culp Davis, *Administrative Common Law and the* Vermont Yankee *Opinion*, 1980 Utah L. Rev. 3, 11 (claiming that "[t]he legislative history of the APA ... fully supports the conclusion that the APA imposed only minimum requirements and did not impose any maximum limit on procedural protections that ... courts might require").

*Vermont Yankee* is usually read as the Supreme Court's decisive rejection of the idea that there is any longer a federal common law of administrative procedure after the enactment of the APA. *See, e.g.*, Davis, *supra*; Antonin Scalia, Vermont Yankee: *The APA, the D.C. Circuit, and the Supreme Court*, 1978 Sup. Ct. Rev. 345, 390–91; *cf.* Jack M. Beermann & Gary Lawson, *Reprocessing* Vermont Yankee, 75 Geo. Wash. L. Rev. 856, 871–74 (2007) (suggesting that courts have read *Vermont Yankee* too narrowly and urging a broader reading that does in fact reject federal common lawmaking in this area). *But see* Duffy, *supra*, at 182–87 (arguing that *Vermont Yankee* is better understood as a statutory decision that did not reject the possibility of a federal administrative common law). For this reason, *Vermont Yankee* is sometimes characterized as an administrative law version of Erie Railroad Co. v. Tompkins, 304 U.S. 64, 78 (1938), which famously held that "[t]here is no federal general common law." *See* Cass R. Sunstein, *Is the Clean Air Act Unconstitutional?*, 98 Mich. L. Rev. 303, 341–42 (1999); Adrian Vermeule, *Our Schmittian Administrative Law*, 122 Harv. L. Rev. 1095, 1146 (2009). Do you think the Court was right to reject the idea of a common law of administrative procedure?

Even if *Vermont Yankee* is read as a sweeping rejection of a federal common law of administrative procedure, there may be other legal bases for the proposition that courts can set aside an agency rule due to procedural inadequacies, even if the agency has complied with all the specific requirements of § 553. One possibility might be to ground this judicial authority in § 706(2)(A), which, as we have seen, empowers courts to set aside agency action that is "arbitrary, capricious[, or] an abuse of discretion." There are at least two possible legal arguments as to why the agency's failure to use additional procedures could, under certain circumstances, render the agency's action arbitrary and capricious. *First*, the agency's decision not to use additional procedures may *itself* be an arbitrary and capricious decision. *See* Stephen F. Williams, *Hybrid Rulemaking under the Administrative Procedure Act: A Legal and Empirical Analysis*, 42 U. Chi. L. Rev. 401, 411–12 & n.33 (1975). *But see* John F. Duffy, *Administrative Common Law in Judicial Review*, 77 Tex. L. Rev. 113, 184–86 (1998) (arguing that an agency's procedural decisions would not be "agency actions" reviewable under § 706(2)(A)). *Second*, one might argue that a final agency rule is arbitrary and capricious if the rule was not issued pursuant to a decision-making process adequate to ensure a thorough consideration of the issues and adequate attention to alternative viewpoints. On this view, the administrative procedures used in a given case are the best available proxy that judges can use to evaluate whether the agency acted arbitrarily and capriciously. Is that legal theory adequate to support judicial imposition of additional administrative procedures? Is there any meaningful difference between these approaches—which turn on an expansive conception of how courts may legitimately implement § 706(2)(A)—and the common law approach to administrative procedure?

**2. Vermont Yankee *and the Over–Proceduralization Concern***—Justice Rehnquist's *Vermont Yankee* opinion listed three pragmatic reasons for rejecting the idea that courts can demand rulemaking procedures beyond those laid out in § 553 or in other statutory or constitutional law. All three reasons appear to be variants on the concern that if courts can impose additional procedural requirements on agencies, the consequence will be the over-proceduralization of informal rulemaking. The basic empirical claim is that "if courts continually review agency proceedings to determine whether the agency employed procedures which were, in the court's opinion, perfectly tailored to reach what the court perceives to be the 'best' or 'correct' result," rational agencies "would undoubtedly adopt full adjudicatory procedures in every instance," rather than risk judicial reversal. The reasons for this, *Vermont Yankee* explained, are: (1) that agencies cannot predict what procedures courts would deem appropriate; (2) that courts engaged in after-the-fact review are likely to engage in "Monday morning quarterbacking," finding fault with agency procedures on the basis of the record produced by those proceedings rather than the information the agency had at the time it designed those proceedings; and (3) that courts will typically assume that additional procedures—especially those that give interested parties more of an opportunity to participate—will always produce a better record for review. Because of this anticipated judicial behavior, agencies are likely to respond defensively by adopting "the full panoply of procedural devices normally associated only with adjudicatory hearings," which nullifies the main advantages of informal, notice-and-comment rulemaking.

Do you find Justice Rehnquist's argument persuasive? Isn't there at least a tinge of hyperbole in his claims? After all, lower federal courts had been occasionally remanding agency decisions for procedural inadequacy since at least the late 1960s and possibly earlier, yet agencies continued throughout the 1970s to promulgate rules using the § 553 notice-and-comment process, without the "full panoply" of formal procedures associated with §§ 556 and 557. Indeed, the fact that such judicial decisions were relatively rare (when compared to the overall number of agency decisions subject to judicial review) may suggest that Justice Rehnquist exaggerated the degree to which courts would find fault with an agency's procedural choices.

That said, doesn't it seem reasonable to suppose that if *Vermont Yankee* had come out the other way—if it had validated Judge Bazelon's procedurally oriented form of judicial review—agencies would be more likely to adopt additional procedural safeguards than they would otherwise? Justice Rehnquist suggested that this would be an undesirable outcome. On the other side, though, Judge Bazelon's position rests on an express concern about *under*-proceduralization; in his view, the additional proceduralization that his approach might induce is desirable—indeed, it is precisely the point. How can a court resolve this disagreement? Is it possible for courts to figure out the optimal set of administrative procedures for any given agency action? To answer these questions, wouldn't we also need to have some sense of the magnitude of the incentive effect created by different doctrinal approaches on agencies' choice of procedures? How could we figure that out?

Finally, what of *Vermont Yankee*'s claim that Judge Bazelon's approach would make judicial review "totally unpredictable"? Is that right? Even though common law adjudication—or adjudication under open-textured statutory or constitutional provisions—is often unpredictable at first, it can gradually take a more definite shape as precedents accumulate and courts develop doctrinal tests and frameworks to distinguish between different situations. Does this possibility mitigate *Vermont Yankee*'s concern that unpredictable doctrine will induce over-proceduralization? Or would a doctrine that permitted judges to demand additional procedures inevitably lead to ad hoc, case-by-case decisions, given the enormous variation in the subjects of agency rulemaking and the fact that so much turns on the reviewing court's sense of the "importance" of the underlying policy issue and the specific factual disputes at issue in each case?

**3.  *Procedural Review and Judicial Overreaching*—**A subtext of the *Vermont Yankee* opinion is the Supreme Court's apparent irritation that, in the Court's view, the D.C. Circuit judges allowed their skepticism about nuclear power to influence their ostensibly procedural ruling. This comes across most clearly in the concluding paragraph of Justice Rehnquist's opinion, which reminded the D.C. Circuit that "[t]he fundamental policy questions appropriately resolved in Congress . . . are *not* subject to reexamination in the federal courts under the guise of judicial review of agency action. . . . Administrative decisions should be set aside . . . only for substantial procedural or substantive reasons as mandated by statute, not simply because the court is unhappy with the result reached." Whether or not the Supreme Court's criticism is fair in this particular case, the Court's admonition that judges should not allow their policy preferences to influence their decisions regarding the lawfulness of agency action raises a more general question about which approach to judicial review is more likely to constrain such "judicial activism."

A defender of Judge Bazelon's approach might argue that judicial decisions are less likely to be distorted by judges' policy views when judges focus on the adequacy of agency procedures, rather than trying to evaluate whether the agency had engaged in "reasoned decision-making" as a substantive matter. Although Judge Bazelon's proceduralist approach requires some assessment of the *importance* of the underlying policy issue, as well as some attention to the types of issues on which there were serious factual disputes that needed airing, it does not require judges to decide whether the agency resolved these disputes correctly (or "reasonably"). On this view, while no doctrinal formulation can eliminate completely the risk of inappropriate policy considerations infecting judges' decisions, a focus on procedural adequacy may be less susceptible to that risk than a focus on the agency's reasoning process.

A critic of Judge Bazelon's proceduralist approach might maintain, to the contrary, that his approach actually magnifies the risk that judges' policy preferences will impermissibly influence their rulings. On this view, it is (almost) always possible—with the benefit of hindsight—to declare that the agency should have adopted more or different procedures than it did. Hence, even in cases where the reviewing court cannot find anything unreasonable about the agency's decision-making, a court could always find the agency's procedures wanting in some way. Thus a court hostile to the agency's policy decision might find itself compelled to uphold the agency action as reasonable under Judge Leventhal's preferred form of "hard look" review, while a court using Judge Bazelon's proceduralist approach could vacate and remand.

Which view is more convincing? Let us assume that most judges act in good faith—they do not *consciously* try to impose their policy preferences on administrative agencies—but they may be *subconsciously* influenced by those preferences when evaluating agency action. If we want to constrain that tendency, which doctrinal approach is preferable? Does forcing judges to consider only the adequacy of administrative procedures, without a substantive assessment of the merits of agency's reasoning, focus judges on more politically neutral questions of procedural adequacy? Or is this apparent neutrality an illusion, as procedural review actually makes it easier, not harder, for judges to strike down agency actions they dislike, without the disciplining effect of having to identify any specific substantive fault in the agency's analysis?

**4. Vermont Yankee *and the Paper Hearing Requirements*—** *Vermont Yankee* held that courts may not impose procedural requirements that go beyond those mandated by statute, the Constitution, or the agency's own regulations. How does that holding square with the line of judicial opinions that have interpreted the § 553 notice-and-comment procedures to require much more than their plain text would suggest? As discussed earlier, courts have, among other things, interpreted § 553 (in conjunction with § 706(2)(A)), to require agencies to give notice of their proposed rules in reasonably specific terms (pp. 635–636, *supra*); to disclose the evidence on which the proposal is based (pp. 614–621, *supra*); to provide a new round of notice and comment if the agency significantly changes its proposed rule in response to comments (pp. 634–635, *supra*); and to provide, in the statement of basis and purpose accompanying a final rule, detailed responses to all significant comments, as well as an explanation for why the agency chose its final rule over other possible alternatives (pp. 621–626, *supra*).

As a formal matter, these opinions are all consistent with *Vermont Yankee* because they all purport to derive those requirements from the APA. But is that formal distinction practically meaningful? If one takes the *Vermont Yankee* concern about over-proceduralization of notice-and-comment rulemaking seriously, doesn't this imply that courts should also take a more restrained approach to interpreting § 553's procedural requirements? Alternatively, if one believes that a more open-ended, purposive approach to interpreting § 553 performs valuable functions—particularly in light of the APA's status as a quasi-constitutional framework statute—then doesn't this undermine *Vermont Yankee*'s uncompromising rejection of judicial initiative in fashioning procedural requirements that are not explicitly grounded in the statutory text?

This tension between *Vermont Yankee*'s rejection of a federal common law of administrative procedure, on the one hand, and a creative, purposive, quasi-common law approach to interpreting the APA's requirements, on the other, is nowhere more evident than in the context of judicial review for "arbitrariness" under § 706(2)(A). Recall that in *Citizens to Preserve Overton Park, Inc. v. Volpe* (pp. 721–722, *supra*), the Supreme Court, applying the § 706(2)(A) standard, vacated the agency's decision and remanded for further proceedings in light of the fact that the agency had failed to generate an adequate contemporaneous record of its decision-making process. As Professor Richard Stewart argued in a critical commentary on *Vermont Yankee* shortly after the case was decided:

> . . . *Vermont Yankee* is self-contradictory. The decision explicitly recognizes that courts should review notice and comment rulemaking on the basis of an evidentiary "record" in order to determine whether there is an adequate analytical and factual basis for the agency's decision, and that APA notice and comment procedures may sometimes fail to produce an adequate record, necessitating judicial remand for creation of an improved record. This requirement of review in informal rulemaking on the basis of a record is consonant with . . . *Citizens to Preserve Overton Park, Inc. v. Volpe* . . . which . . . empower[s] reviewing courts to require that administrators engaged in informal adjudication prepare a record as the basis for judicial review.

> This requirement of an evidentiary "record" plainly goes beyond the APA, which provides for administrative creation of such a record only in cases of formal adjudication and rulemaking; the APA fails to require such a record in either notice and comment rulemaking or informal adjudication. The Supreme Court's recognition of a "record" requirement in such informal proceedings accordingly represents the very sort of procedural innovation which *Vermont Yankee* purports to condemn. Moreover, in authorizing courts to remand an administrative record as inadequate even though the agency has complied fully with APA notice and comment procedures, *Vermont Yankee* in effect authorizes judges to conclude that APA procedures are insufficient and must be supplemented.

Richard B. Stewart, Vermont Yankee *and the Evolution of Administrative Procedure*, 91 HARV. L. REV. 1805, 1816–17 (1978) (internal footnotes omitted).

The courts, however, have rejected the claim that *Vermont Yankee* is inconsistent with *Overton Park*. In explaining how these cases can be reconciled, Judge Douglas Ginsburg's opinion for the D.C. Circuit in Occidental Petroleum Corp. v. SEC, 873 F.2d 325 (D.C. Cir. 1989), drew a helpful analogy to the distinction between "performance standards" (regulations framed in terms of ultimate goals that must be achieved) and "design standards" (regulations that specify exactly how a product must be constructed), as follows:

> Nothing in the general principles of *Vermont Yankee* is inconsistent ... with the standards for judicial review set forth in *Overton Park*. Section 706, as interpreted in the latter case, establishes a performance standard for informal action by an agency: in order to allow for meaningful judicial review, the agency must produce an administrative record that delineates the path by which it reached its decision. If the record does not meet the *Overton Park* standard, the district court may insist that the agency produce, by whatever means the agency chooses, a record that does meet the required level of performance. The general principles of *Vermont Yankee*, on the other hand, would simply forbid the reviewing court from imposing upon the agency specific procedural steps that must be followed in order to create a reviewable record, *i.e.*, a design standard.

873 F.2d at 338.

Shortly afterwards, the Supreme Court endorsed a similar distinction in Pension Benefit Guaranty Corp. v. LTV Corp., 496 U.S. 633 (1990). The details of the underlying substantive dispute in the case are complicated and not particularly pertinent. As relevant here, the Pension Benefit Guaranty Corporation (PBGC), a federal agency responsible for overseeing a government insurance program that protects private employee pension plans, issued an order, following an informal adjudication, that adversely affected the interests of the LTV Corporation. As you may recall, the APA provides little in the way of specific procedural requirements for informal adjudications. LTV argued that the PBGC's order was arbitrary and capricious within the meaning of § 706(2)(A) because the PBGC's decision-making process lacked adequate safeguards. The Court of Appeals for the Second Circuit agreed, holding that because "PBGC neither apprised LTV of the material on which it was to base its decision, gave LTV an adequate opportunity to offer contrary evidence, proceeded in accordance with ascertainable standards ..., nor provided a statement showing its reasoning in applying those standards," the PBGC's decision was "arbitrary and capricious." Pension Ben. Guar. Corp. v. LTV Corp., 875 F.2d 1008, 1021 (2d Cir. 1989). The PBGC argued that the Second Circuit's reasoning contravened *Vermont Yankee*, because the Second Circuit had effectively mandated that the PBGC use additional administrative procedures that were not required by the APA. LTV countered that *Overton Park* held that a court may (indeed, must) reverse and remand an agency decision as arbitrary if the agency has not provided an adequate explanation for its decision that permits meaningful judicial review. LTV insisted that the procedural requirements articulated by the Second Circuit were necessary to produce an agency record that satisfies the *Overton Park* standard. Justice Blackmun's opinion for the Court in *PBGC v. LTV Corp.* sided with the agency, and explained the relationship between *Vermont Yankee* and *Overton Park* as follows:

> ... [A]lthough one initially might feel that there is some tension between *Vermont Yankee* and *Overton Park,* the two cases are not necessarily inconsistent. *Vermont Yankee* stands for the general proposition that courts are not free to impose upon agencies specific procedural requirements that have no basis in the APA. At most, *Overton Park* suggests that § 706(2)(A), which directs a court to ensure that an agency action is not arbitrary and capricious or otherwise contrary to law, imposes a general "procedural" requirement of sorts by mandating that an agency take whatever steps it needs to provide an explanation that will enable the court to evaluate the agency's rationale at the time of decision.
>
> Here, unlike in *Overton Park,* the Court of Appeals did not suggest that the administrative record was inadequate to enable the court to fulfill its duties under § 706. Rather, to support its ruling, the court focused on "fundamental fairness" to LTV.... With the possible exception of the absence of "ascertainable standards"—by which we are not exactly sure what the Court of Appeals meant—the procedural inadequacies cited by the court all relate to LTV's role in the PBGC's decisionmaking process. But the court did not point to any provision in [the organic statute] or the APA which gives LTV the procedural rights the court identified. Thus, the court's holding runs afoul of *Vermont Yankee* and finds no support in *Overton Park.*

496 U.S. at 654–55 (internal citations omitted).

Is this distinction satisfactory? A proponent of Judge Bazelon's approach might respond that even if the distinction between "performance standards" and "design standards" is conceptually meaningful, it is bad legal policy to insist on a performance standard rather than a design standard in this context, principally because judges are more expert in evaluating procedures than in assessing the adequacy of the technical record compiled. Even for someone sympathetic to Justice Rehnquist's arguments in *Vermont Yankee,* the distinction between the sort of review that *Overton Park* requires and the sort of review that *Vermont Yankee* prohibits might appear elusive. In the aftermath of *Vermont Yankee,* reviewing courts that are dissatisfied with agency procedures can frame their adverse rulings not in terms of procedural inadequacies per se, but rather as more general objections to the quality of the agency's record. Without overtly mandating particular procedures, the latter form of review may still invite excessive judicial intervention, after-the-fact second-guessing, and unpredictability—thereby creating strong incentives for agencies to adopt cumbersome additional procedures. Scholars who have this latter concern have been waiting and advocating—so far in vain—for a *"Vermont Yankee II"* that would end rigorous hard look review of agency policy decisions, at least in the rulemaking context. *See, e.g.*, Paul R. Verkuil, *Judicial Review of Informal Rulemaking: Waiting for* Vermont Yankee II, 55 TUL. L. REV. 418 (1981); *see also, e.g.*, Jack M. Beermann & Gary Lawson, *Reprocessing* Vermont Yankee, 75 GEO. WASH. L. REV. 856 (2007) (noting the inconsistency between *Vermont Yankee* and some of the expansive interpretations of § 553 that are still on the books); Stephen Breyer, Vermont Yankee *and the Courts' Role in the Nuclear Energy Controversy*, 91 HARV. L. REV. 1833 (1978) (same); Richard J. Pierce, Jr., *Waiting for* Vermont Yankee II, 57 ADMIN. L. REV. 669 (2005) (same). On the other hand, a "performance standard" would not necessarily have to result in overproceduralization—at least not if reviewing courts could maintain the discipline to limit themselves to a deferential inquiry into whether the agency considered the relevant factors. Might your assessment, then, depend on the way reviewing courts apply the hard look doctrine and allied doctrines governing rulemaking?

## C.   MODERN "HARD LOOK" REVIEW

As we have seen, there is a significant tension between *Vermont Yankee* and *Overton Park*, notwithstanding the formal doctrinal consistency of their holdings. In the immediate aftermath of *Vermont Yankee*, many commentators thought (and some hoped) that *Vermont Yankee* was a harbinger of a narrower, more deferential form of judicial review that would sharply limit (if not expressly repudiate) the more robust form of hard look review that *Overton Park* seemed to permit. In our next case, however, the Supreme Court reaffirmed—and even expanded on—*Overton Park*'s endorsement of "hard look" review. As you read *State Farm*, consider whether it reinforces or alleviates concerns about a reviewing court's capacity to conduct such review without second-guessing the agency on the merits.

---

## Motor Vehicle Manufacturers Association v. State Farm Mutual Automobile Insurance Co.

Supreme Court of the United States
463 U.S. 29 (1983)

■ JUSTICE WHITE delivered the opinion of the Court.

The development of the automobile gave Americans unprecedented freedom to travel, but exacted a high price for enhanced mobility. Since 1929, motor vehicles have been the leading cause of accidental deaths and injuries in the United States. In 1982, 46,300 Americans died in motor vehicle accidents and hundreds of thousands more were maimed and injured. While a consensus exists that the current loss of life on our highways is unacceptably high, improving safety does not admit to easy solution. In 1966, Congress decided that at least part of the answer lies in improving the design and safety features of the vehicle itself. But much of the technology for building safer cars was undeveloped or untested. Before changes in automobile design could be mandated, the effectiveness of these changes had to be studied, their costs examined, and public acceptance considered. This task called for considerable expertise and Congress responded by enacting the National Traffic and Motor Vehicle Safety Act of 1966, (Act), 15 U.S.C. §§ 1381 *et seq.* (1976 and Supp. IV 1980). The Act, created for the purpose of "reduc[ing] traffic accidents and deaths and injuries to persons resulting from traffic accidents," 15 U.S.C. § 1381, directs the Secretary of Transportation or his delegate to issue motor vehicle safety standards that "shall be practicable, shall meet the need for motor vehicle safety, and shall be stated in objective terms." 15 U.S.C. § 1392(a). In issuing these standards, the Secretary is directed to consider "relevant available motor vehicle safety data," whether the proposed standard "is reasonable, practicable and appropriate" for the particular type of motor vehicle, and the "extent to which such standards will contribute to carrying out the purposes" of the Act. 15 U.S.C. § 1392(f)(1), (3), (4).[3]

The Act also authorizes judicial review under the provisions of the Administrative Procedure Act (APA), 5 U.S.C. § 706 (1976), of all "orders establishing, amending, or revoking a Federal motor vehicle safety standard," 15 U.S.C. § 1392(b). Under this authority, we review today whether NHTSA acted arbitrarily and capriciously in revoking the requirement in Motor Vehicle Safety Standard 208 that new motor vehicles produced after September 1982 be equipped with passive restraints to protect the safety of the occupants of the vehicle in the event of a collision. Briefly summarized, we hold that the agency failed to present an adequate basis and explanation for rescinding the passive restraint requirement and that the agency must either consider the matter further or adhere to or amend Standard 208 along lines which its analysis supports.

## I

The regulation whose rescission is at issue bears a complex and convoluted history. Over the course of approximately 60 rulemaking notices, the requirement has been imposed, amended, rescinded, reimposed, and now rescinded again.

As originally issued by the Department of Transportation in 1967, Standard 208 simply required the installation of seatbelts in all automobiles. It soon became apparent that the level of seatbelt use was too low to reduce traffic injuries to an acceptable level. The Department therefore began consideration of "passive occupant restraint systems"—devices that

---

3. The Secretary's general authority to promulgate safety standards under the Act has been delegated to the Administrator of the National Highway Traffic Safety Administration (NHTSA). 49 CFR § 1.50(a) (1982). This opinion will use the terms NHTSA and agency interchangeably when referring to the National Highway Traffic Safety Administration, the Department of Transportation, and the Secretary of Transportation.

do not depend for their effectiveness upon any action taken by the occupant except that necessary to operate the vehicle. Two types of automatic crash protection emerged: automatic seatbelts and airbags. The automatic seatbelt is a traditional safety belt, which when fastened to the interior of the door remains attached without impeding entry or exit from the vehicle, and deploys automatically without any action on the part of the passenger. The airbag is an inflatable device concealed in the dashboard and steering column. It automatically inflates when a sensor indicates that deceleration forces from an accident have exceeded a preset minimum, then rapidly deflates to dissipate those forces. The life-saving potential of these devices was immediately recognized, and in 1977, after substantial on-the-road experience with both devices, it was estimated by NHTSA that passive restraints could prevent approximately 12,000 deaths and over 100,000 serious injuries annually.

In 1969, the Department formally proposed a standard requiring the installation of passive restraints, thereby commencing a lengthy series of proceedings. In 1970, the agency revised Standard 208 to include passive protection requirements, and in 1972, the agency amended the standard to require full passive protection for all front seat occupants of vehicles manufactured after August 15, 1975. In the interim, vehicles built between August 1973 and August 1975 were to carry either passive restraints or lap and shoulder belts coupled with an "ignition interlock" that would prevent starting the vehicle if the belts were not connected.[4] On review, the agency's decision to require passive restraints was found to be supported by "substantial evidence" and upheld. Chrysler Corp. v. Dep't of Transportation, 472 F.2d 659 (CA6 1972).

In preparing for the upcoming model year, most car makers chose the "ignition interlock" option, a decision which was highly unpopular, and led Congress to amend the Act to prohibit a motor vehicle safety standard from requiring or permitting compliance by means of an ignition interlock or a continuous buzzer designed to indicate that safety belts were not in use. . . .

The effective date for mandatory passive restraint systems was extended for a year until August 31, 1976. But in June 1976, Secretary of Transportation William Coleman initiated a new rulemaking on the issue. After hearing testimony and reviewing written comments, Coleman extended the optional alternatives indefinitely and suspended the passive restraint requirement. Although he found passive restraints technologically and economically feasible, the Secretary based his decision on the expectation that there would be widespread public resistance to the new systems. He instead proposed a demonstration project involving up to 500,000 cars

---

**4.** Early in the process, it was assumed that passive occupant protection meant the installation of inflatable airbag restraint systems. In 1971, however, the agency observed that "[s]ome belt-based concepts have been advanced that appear to be capable of meeting the complete passive protection options," leading it to add a new section to the proposed standard "[t]o deal expressly with passive belts." 36 Fed.Reg. 12,859.

installed with passive restraints, in order to smooth the way for public acceptance of mandatory passive restraints at a later date.

Coleman's successor as Secretary of Transportation disagreed. Within months of assuming office, Secretary Brock Adams decided that the demonstration project was unnecessary. He issued a new mandatory passive restraint regulation, known as Modified Standard 208. The Modified Standard mandated the phasing in of passive restraints beginning with large cars in model year 1982 and extending to all cars by model year 1984. The two principal systems that would satisfy the Standard were airbags and passive belts; the choice of which system to install was left to the manufacturers. In Pacific Legal Foundation v. Dep't of Transportation, 593 F.2d 1338 (CADC), cert. denied, 444 U.S. 830 (1979), the Court of Appeals upheld Modified Standard 208 as a rational, nonarbitrary regulation consistent with the agency's mandate under the Act. . . .

Over the next several years, the automobile industry geared up to comply with Modified Standard 208. As late as July, 1980, NHTSA reported:

> "On the road experience in thousands of vehicles equipped with airbags and automatic safety belts has confirmed agency estimates of the life-saving and injury-preventing benefits of such systems. When all cars are equipped with automatic crash protection systems, each year an estimated 9,000 more lives will be saved and tens of thousands of serious injuries will be prevented." NHTSA, Automobile Occupant Crash Protection, Progress Report No. 3, p. 4.

In February 1981, however, Secretary of Transportation Andrew Lewis reopened the rulemaking due to changed economic circumstances and, in particular, the difficulties of the automobile industry. Two months later, the agency ordered a one-year delay in the application of the standard to large cars, extending the deadline to September 1982, and at the same time, proposed the possible rescission of the entire standard. After receiving written comments and holding public hearings, NHTSA issued a final rule (Notice 25) that rescinded the passive restraint requirement contained in Modified Standard 208.

## II

In a statement explaining the rescission, NHTSA maintained that it was no longer able to find, as it had in 1977, that the automatic restraint requirement would produce significant safety benefits. This judgment reflected not a change of opinion on the effectiveness of the technology, but a change in plans by the automobile industry. In 1977, the agency had assumed that airbags would be installed in 60% of all new cars and automatic seatbelts in 40%. By 1981 it became apparent that automobile manufacturers planned to install the automatic seatbelts in approximately 99% of the new cars. For this reason, the life-saving potential of airbags would not be realized. Moreover, it now appeared that the overwhelming majority of passive belts planned to be installed by manufacturers could be detached easily and left that way permanently. Passive belts, once detached, then required "the same type of affirmative action that is the stumbling block to obtaining high usage levels of manual belts." 46 Fed.Reg., at 53421. For this reason, the agency concluded that there was no longer a basis for reliably predicting that the standard would lead to any significant increased usage of restraints at all.

In view of the possibly minimal safety benefits, the automatic restraint requirement no longer was reasonable or practicable in the agency's view. The requirement would require approximately $1 billion to implement and the agency did not believe it would be reasonable to impose such substantial costs on manufacturers and consumers without more adequate assurance that sufficient safety benefits would accrue. In addition, NHTSA concluded that automatic restraints might have an adverse effect on the public's attitude toward safety. Given the high expense and limited benefits of detachable belts, NHTSA feared that many consumers would regard the standard as an instance of ineffective regulation, adversely affecting the public's view of safety regulation and, in particular, "poisoning popular sentiment toward efforts to improve occupant restraint systems in the future." 46 Fed.Reg., at 53424.

State Farm Mutual Automobile Insurance Co. and the National Association of Independent Insurers filed petitions for review of NHTSA's rescission of the passive restraint standard. The United States Court of Appeals for the District of Columbia Circuit held that the agency's rescission of the passive restraint requirement was arbitrary and capricious ... for three reasons. First, the court found insufficient as a basis for rescission NHTSA's conclusion that it could not reliably predict an increase in belt usage under the Standard. The court held that there was insufficient evidence in the record to sustain NHTSA's position on this issue, and that, "only a well-justified refusal to seek more evidence could render rescission non-arbitrary." 680 F.2d, at 232. Second, a majority of the panel concluded that NHTSA inadequately considered the possibility of requiring manufacturers to install nondetachable rather than detachable passive belts. Third, the majority found that the agency acted arbitrarily and capriciously by failing to give any consideration whatever to requiring compliance with Modified Standard 208 by the installation of airbags.

... [W]e granted certiorari....

### III

... Both the Motor Vehicle Safety Act and the 1974 Amendments concerning occupant crash protection standards indicate that motor vehicle safety standards are to be promulgated under the informal rulemaking procedures of § 553 of the Administrative Procedure Act. 5 U.S.C. § 553 (1976). The agency's action in promulgating such standards therefore may be set aside if found to be "arbitrary, capricious, an abuse of discretion, or otherwise not in accordance with law." 5 U.S.C. § 706(2)(A). Citizens to Preserve Overton Park v. Volpe, 401 U.S. 402 (1971); Bowman Transportation, Inc. v. Arkansas–Best Freight System, Inc., 419 U.S. 281 (1974). We believe that the rescission or modification of an occupant protection standard is subject to the same test. Section 103(b) of the Motor Vehicle Safety Act, 15 U.S.C. § 1392(b), states that the procedural and judicial review provisions of the Administrative Procedure Act "shall apply to all orders establishing, amending, or revoking a Federal motor vehicle safety standard," and suggests no difference in the scope of judicial review depending upon the nature of the agency's action.

Petitioner Motor Vehicle Manufacturers Association (MVMA) disagrees, contending that the rescission of an agency rule should be judged by the same standard a court would use to judge an agency's refusal to promulgate a rule in the first place—a standard Petitioner believes considerably narrower than the traditional arbitrary and capricious test and "close to the borderline of nonreviewability." We reject this view. The Motor Vehicle Safety Act expressly equates orders "revoking" and "establishing" safety standards; neither that Act nor the APA suggests that revocations are to be treated as refusals to promulgate standards. Petitioner's view would render meaningless Congress' authorization for judicial review of orders revoking safety rules. Moreover, the revocation of an extant regulation is substantially different than a failure to act. Revocation constitutes a reversal of the agency's former views as to the proper course. A "settled course of behavior embodies the agency's informed judgment that, by pursuing that course, it will carry out the policies committed to it by Congress. There is, then, at least a presumption that those policies will be carried out best if the settled rule is adhered to." Atchison, T. & S.F.R. Co. v. Wichita Bd. of Trade, 412 U.S. 800, 807–808 (1973). Accordingly, an agency changing its course by rescinding a rule is obligated to supply a reasoned analysis for the change beyond that which may be required when an agency does not act in the first instance.

In so holding, we fully recognize that "regulatory agencies do not establish rules of conduct to last forever," American Trucking Assoc., Inc. v. Atchison, T. & S.F.R. Co., 387 U.S. 397, 416 (1967), and that an agency must be given ample latitude to "adapt their rules and policies to the demands of changing circumstances." Permian Basin Area Rate Cases, 390 U.S. 747, 784 (1968). But the forces of change do not always or necessarily point in the direction of deregulation. In the abstract, there is no more reason to presume that changing circumstances require the rescission of prior action, instead of a revision in or even the extension of current regulation. If Congress established a presumption from which judicial review should start, that presumption—contrary to petitioners' views—is not *against* safety regulation, but *against* changes in current policy that are not justified by the rulemaking record. While the removal of a regulation may not entail the monetary expenditures and other costs of enacting a new standard, and accordingly, it may be easier for an agency to justify a deregulatory action, the direction in which an agency chooses to move does not alter the standard of judicial review established by law.

The Department of Transportation accepts the applicability of the "arbitrary and capricious" standard. It argues that under this standard, a reviewing court may not set aside an agency rule that is rational, based on consideration of the relevant factors and within the scope of the authority delegated to the agency by the statute. We do not disagree with this formulation.[9] The scope of review under the "arbitrary and capricious" standard is narrow and a court is not to substitute its judgment for that of the agency. Nevertheless, the agency must examine the relevant data and articulate a satisfactory explanation for its action including a "rational connection between the facts found and the choice made." Burlington Truck Lines v. United States, 371 U.S. 156, 168 (1962). In reviewing that explanation, we must "consider whether the decision was based on a consideration of the relevant factors and whether there has been a clear error of judgment." *Bowman Transp. Inc. v. Arkansas–Best Freight System, supra,* 419 U.S., at 285; *Citizens to Preserve Overton Park v. Volpe, supra,* 401 U.S., at 416. Normally, an agency rule would be arbitrary and capricious if the agency has relied on factors which Congress has not intended it to consider, entirely failed to consider an important aspect of the problem, offered an explanation for its decision that runs counter to the evidence before the agency, or is so implausible that it could not be ascribed to a difference in view or the product of agency expertise. The reviewing court should not attempt itself to make up for such deficiencies: "We may not supply a reasoned basis for the agency's action that the agency itself has not given." SEC v. Chenery Corp., 332 U.S. 194, 196 (1947). We will, however, "uphold a decision of less than ideal clarity if the agency's path may reasonably be discerned." *Bowman Transp. Inc. v. Arkansas–Best Freight System, supra,* 419 U.S., at 286. . . .

### V

The ultimate question before us is whether NHTSA's rescission of the passive restraint requirement of Standard 208 was arbitrary and capricious. We conclude, as did the Court of Appeals, that it was. . . . We deal separately with the rescission as it applies to airbags and as it applies to seatbelts.

### A

The first and most obvious reason for finding the rescission arbitrary and capricious is that NHTSA apparently gave no consideration whatever to modifying the Standard to require that airbag technology be utilized. Standard 208 sought to achieve automatic crash protection by requiring automobile manufacturers to install either of two passive restraint devices: airbags or automatic seatbelts. There was no suggestion in the long rulemaking process that led to Standard 208 that if only one of these options were feasible, no passive restraint standard should be promulgated. Indeed, the agency's original proposed standard contemplated the installation of inflatable restraints in all cars. Automatic belts were added as a

---

**9.** The Department of Transportation suggests that the arbitrary-and-capricious standard requires no more than the minimum rationality a statute must bear in order to withstand analysis under the Due Process Clause. We do not view as equivalent the presumption of constitutionality afforded legislation drafted by Congress and the presumption of regularity afforded an agency in fulfilling its statutory mandate.

means of complying with the standard because they were believed to be as effective as airbags in achieving the goal of occupant crash protection. At that time, the passive belt approved by the agency could not be detached. Only later, at a manufacturer's behest, did the agency approve of the detachability feature—and only after assurances that the feature would not compromise the safety benefits of the restraint. Although it was then foreseen that 60% of the new cars would contain airbags and 40% would have automatic seatbelts, the ratio between the two was not significant as long as the passive belt would also assure greater passenger safety.

The agency has now determined that the detachable automatic belts will not attain anticipated safety benefits because so many individuals will detach the mechanism. Even if this conclusion were acceptable in its entirety, standing alone it would not justify any more than an amendment of Standard 208 to disallow compliance by means of the one technology which will not provide effective passenger protection. It does not cast doubt on the need for a passive restraint standard or upon the efficacy of airbag technology. In its most recent rule-making, the agency again acknowledged the life-saving potential of the airbag:

> "The agency has no basis at this time for changing its earlier conclusions in 1976 and 1977 that basic airbag technology is sound and has been sufficiently demonstrated to be effective in those vehicles in current use. . . ." NHTSA Final Regulatory Impact Analysis (RIA) at XI–4 (Oct. 1981).

Given the effectiveness ascribed to airbag technology by the agency, the mandate of the Safety Act to achieve traffic safety would suggest that the logical response to the faults of detachable seatbelts would be to require the installation of airbags. At the very least this alternative way of achieving the objectives of the Act should have been addressed and adequate reasons given for its abandonment. But the agency not only did not require compliance through airbags, it did not even consider the possibility in its 1981 rulemaking. Not one sentence of its rulemaking statement discusses the airbags-only option. Because, as the Court of Appeals stated, "NHTSA's . . . analysis of airbags was nonexistent," 680 F.2d, at 236, what we said in Burlington Truck Lines v. United States, 371 U.S., at 167, is apropos here:

> "There are no findings and no analysis here to justify the choice made, no indication of the basis on which the [agency] exercised its expert discretion. We are not prepared to and the Administrative Procedure Act will not permit us to accept such . . . practice. . . . Expert discretion is the lifeblood of the administrative process, but 'unless we make the requirements for administrative action strict and demanding, *expertise,* the strength of modern government, can become a monster which rules with no practical limits on its discretion.' New York v. United States, 342 U.S. 882, 884 (dissenting opinion)." (footnote omitted).

We have frequently reiterated that an agency must cogently explain why it has exercised its discretion in a given manner, . . . and we reaffirm this principle again today.

The automobile industry has opted for the passive belt over the airbag, but surely it is not enough that the regulated industry has eschewed a given safety device. For nearly a decade, the automobile industry waged the regulatory equivalent of war against the airbag and lost—the inflatable restraint was proven sufficiently effective. Now the automobile industry has decided to employ a seatbelt system which will not meet the safety objectives of Standard 208. This hardly constitutes cause to revoke the standard itself. Indeed, the Motor Vehicle Safety Act was necessary because the industry was not sufficiently responsive to safety concerns. The Act intended that safety standards not depend on current technology and could be "technology-forcing" in the sense of inducing the development of superior safety design. See Chrysler Corp. v. Dept. of Transp., 472 F.2d, at 672–673. If, under the statute, the agency should not defer to the industry's failure to develop safer cars, which it surely should not do, *a fortiori* it may not revoke a safety standard which can be satisfied by current technology simply because the industry has opted for an ineffective seatbelt design.

Although the agency did not address the mandatory airbags option and the Court of Appeals noted that "airbags seem to have none of the problems that NHTSA identified in passive seatbelts," petitioners recite a number of difficulties that they believe would be posed by a mandatory airbag standard. These range from questions concerning the installation of airbags in small cars to that of adverse public reaction. But these are not the agency's reasons for rejecting a mandatory airbag standard. Not having discussed the possibility, the agency submitted no reasons at all. The short—and sufficient—answer to petitioners' submission is that the courts may not accept appellate counsel's *post hoc* rationalizations for agency action. *Burlington Truck Lines v. United States, supra,* 371 U.S., at 168. It is well-established that an agency's action must be upheld, if at all, on the basis articulated by the agency itself. *Ibid.; SEC v. Chenery,* 332 U.S. 194, 196 (1947); American Textile Manufacturers Inst. v. Donovan, 452 U.S. 490, 539 (1981).[15]

Petitioners also invoke our decision in Vermont Yankee Nuclear Power Corp. v. NRDC, 435 U.S. 519 (1978), as though it were a talisman under which any agency decision is by definition unimpeachable. Specifically, it is submitted that to require an agency to consider an airbags-only alternative is, in essence, to dictate to the agency the procedures it is to follow. Petitioners both misread *Vermont Yankee* and misconstrue the nature of the remand that is in order. In *Vermont Yankee,* we held that a court may not impose additional procedural requirements upon an agency. We do not

---

**15.** The Department of Transportation expresses concern that adoption of an airbags-only requirement would have required a new notice of proposed rulemaking. Even if this were so, and we need not decide the question, it would not constitute sufficient cause to rescind the passive restraint requirement. The Department also asserts that it was reasonable to withdraw the requirement as written to avoid forcing manufacturers to spend resources to comply with an ineffective safety initiative. We think that it would have been permissible for the agency to temporarily suspend the passive restraint requirement or to delay its implementation date while an airbags mandate was studied. But, as we explain in text, that option had to be considered before the passive restraint requirement could be revoked.

require today any specific procedures which NHTSA must follow. Nor do we broadly require an agency to consider all policy alternatives in reaching decision. It is true that a rulemaking "cannot be found wanting simply because the agency failed to include every alternative device and thought conceivable by the mind of man ... regardless of how uncommon or unknown that alternative may have been...." 435 U.S., at 551. But the airbag is more than a policy alternative to the passive restraint standard; it is a technological alternative within the ambit of the existing standard. We hold only that given the judgment made in 1977 that airbags are an effective and cost-beneficial life-saving technology, the mandatory passive-restraint rule may not be abandoned without any consideration whatsoever of an airbags-only requirement.

## B

Although the issue is closer, we also find that the agency was too quick to dismiss the safety benefits of automatic seatbelts. NHTSA's critical finding was that, in light of the industry's plans to install readily detachable passive belts, it could not reliably predict "even a 5 percentage point increase as the minimum level of expected usage increase." 46 Fed.Reg., at 53,423. The Court of Appeals rejected this finding because there is "not one iota" of evidence that Modified Standard 208 will fail to increase nationwide seatbelt use by at least 13 percentage points, the level of increased usage necessary for the standard to justify its cost. Given the lack of probative evidence, the court held that "only a well-justified refusal to seek more evidence could render rescission non-arbitrary." 680 F.2d, at 232.

Petitioners object to this conclusion. In their view, "substantial uncertainty" that a regulation will accomplish its intended purpose is sufficient reason, without more, to rescind a regulation. We agree with petitioners that just as an agency reasonably may decline to issue a safety standard if it is uncertain about its efficacy, an agency may also revoke a standard on the basis of serious uncertainties if supported by the record and reasonably explained. Rescission of the passive restraint requirement would not be arbitrary and capricious simply because there was no evidence in direct support of the agency's conclusion. It is not infrequent that the available data does not settle a regulatory issue and the agency must then exercise its judgment in moving from the facts and probabilities on the record to a policy conclusion. Recognizing that policymaking in a complex society must account for uncertainty, however, does not imply that it is sufficient for an agency to merely recite the terms "substantial uncertainty" as a justification for its actions. The agency must explain the evidence which is available, and must offer a "rational connection between the facts found and the choice made." *Burlington Truck Lines, Inc. v. United States, supra,* 371 U.S., at 168. Generally, one aspect of that explanation would be a justification for rescinding the regulation before engaging in a search for further evidence.

In these cases, the agency's explanation for rescission of the passive restraint requirement is *not* sufficient to enable us to conclude that the rescission was the product of reasoned decisionmaking. To reach this conclusion, we do not upset the agency's view of the facts, but we do appreciate the limitations of this record in supporting the agency's decision. We start with the accepted ground that if used, seatbelts unquestionably would save many thousands of lives and would prevent tens of thousands of crippling injuries. Unlike recent regulatory decisions we have reviewed, Industrial Union Department v. American Petroleum Institute, 448 U.S. 607 (1980); American Textile Manufacturers Inst., Inc. v. Donovan, 452 U.S. 490 (1981), the safety benefits of wearing seatbelts are not in doubt and it is not challenged that were those benefits to accrue, the monetary costs of implementing the standard would be easily justified. We move next to the fact that there is no direct evidence in support of the agency's finding that detachable automatic belts cannot be predicted to yield a substantial increase in usage. The empirical evidence on the record, consisting of surveys of drivers of automobiles equipped with passive belts, reveals more than a doubling of the usage rate experienced with manual belts.[16] Much of the agency's rulemaking statement—and much of the controversy in this case—centers on the conclusions that should be drawn from these studies. The agency maintained that the doubling of seatbelt usage in these studies could not be extrapolated to an across-the-board mandatory standard because the passive seatbelts were guarded by ignition interlocks and purchasers of the tested cars are somewhat atypical. Respondents insist these studies demonstrate that Modified Standard 208 will substantially increase seatbelt usage. We believe that it is within the agency's discretion to pass upon the generalizability of these field studies. This is precisely the type of issue which rests within the expertise of NHTSA, and upon which a reviewing court must be most hesitant to intrude.

But accepting the agency's view of the field tests on passive restraints indicates only that there is no reliable real-world experience that usage rates will substantially increase. To be sure, NHTSA opines that "it cannot reliably predict even a 5 percentage point increase as the minimum level of increased usage." Notice 25, 46 Fed.Reg., at 53423. But this and other statements that passive belts will not yield substantial increases in seatbelt usage apparently take no account of the critical difference between detachable automatic belts and current manual belts. A detached passive belt does require an affirmative act to reconnect it, but—unlike a manual seat belt— the passive belt, once reattached, will continue to function automatically unless again disconnected. Thus, inertia—a factor which the agency's own studies have found significant in explaining the current low usage rates for seatbelts[18]—works in *favor* of, not *against*, use of the protective device.

---

**16.** Between 1975 and 1980, Volkswagen sold approximately 350,000 Rabbits equipped with detachable passive seatbelts that were guarded by an ignition interlock. General Motors sold 8,000 1978 and 1979 Chevettes with a similar system, but eliminated the ignition interlock on the 13,000 Chevettes sold in 1980. NHTSA found that belt usage in the Rabbits averaged 34% for manual belts and 84% for passive belts. For the 1978–1979 Chevettes, NHTSA calculated 34% usage for manual belts and 72% for passive belts. On 1980 Chevettes, the agency found these figures to be 31% for manual belts and 70% for passive belts.

**18.** NHTSA commissioned a number of surveys of public attitudes in an effort to better understand why people were not using manual belts and to determine how they would react to

Since 20 to 50% of motorists currently wear seatbelts on some occasions, there would seem to be grounds to believe that seatbelt use by occasional users will be substantially increased by the detachable passive belts. Whether this is in fact the case is a matter for the agency to decide, but it must bring its expertise to bear on the question.

The agency is correct to look at the costs as well as the benefits of Standard 208. The agency's conclusion that the incremental costs of the requirements were no longer reasonable was predicated on its prediction that the safety benefits of the regulation might be minimal. Specifically, the agency's fears that the public may resent paying more for the automatic belt systems is expressly dependent on the assumption that detachable automatic belts will not produce more than "negligible safety benefits." 46 Fed.Reg., at 53,424. When the agency reexamines its findings as to the likely increase in seatbelt usage, it must also reconsider its judgment of the reasonableness of the monetary and other costs associated with the Standard. In reaching its judgment, NHTSA should bear in mind that Congress intended safety to be the preeminent factor under the Motor Vehicle Safety Act. . . .

The agency also failed to articulate a basis for not requiring nondetachable belts under Standard 208. It is argued that the concern of the agency with the easy detachability of the currently favored design would be readily solved by a continuous passive belt, which allows the occupant to "spool out" the belt and create the necessary slack for easy extrication from the vehicle. The agency did not separately consider the continuous belt option, but treated it together with the ignition interlock device in a category it titled "option of use-compelling features." 46 Fed.Reg., at 53,424. The agency was concerned that use-compelling devices would "complicate extrication of [a]n occupant from his or her car." *Ibid.* "To require that passive belts contain use-compelling features," the agency observed, "could be counterproductive [given] . . . widespread, latent and irrational fear in many members of the public that they could be trapped by the seat belt after a crash." *Ibid.* In addition, based on the experience with the ignition interlock, the agency feared that use-compelling features might trigger adverse public reaction.

By failing to analyze the continuous seatbelts option in its own right, the agency has failed to offer the rational connection between facts and judgment required to pass muster under the arbitrary and capricious standard. We agree with the Court of Appeals that NHTSA did not suggest that the emergency release mechanisms used in nondetachable belts are any less effective for emergency egress than the buckle release system used in detachable belts. In 1978, when General Motors obtained the agency's

---

passive restraints. The surveys reveal that while 20% to 40% of the public is opposed to wearing manual belts, the larger proportion of the population does not wear belts because they forgot or found manual belts inconvenient or bothersome. In another survey, 38% of the surveyed group responded that they would welcome automatic belts, and 25% would "tolerate" them. NHTSA did not comment upon these attitude surveys in its explanation accompanying the rescission of the passive restraint requirement.

approval to install a continuous passive belt, it assured the agency that nondetachable belts with spool releases were as safe as detachable belts with buckle releases.... While the agency is entitled to change its view on the acceptability of continuous passive belts, it is obligated to explain its reasons for doing so.

The agency also failed to offer any explanation why a continuous passive belt would engender the same adverse public reaction as the ignition interlock, and, as the Court of Appeals concluded, "every indication in the record points the other way." 680 F.2d, at 234. We see no basis for equating the two devices: the continuous belt, unlike the ignition interlock, does not interfere with the operation of the vehicle. More importantly, it is the agency's responsibility, not this Court's, to explain its decision.

## VI

"An agency's view of what is in the public interest may change, either with or without a change in circumstances. But an agency changing its course must supply a reasoned analysis...." Greater Boston Television Corp. v. FCC, 444 F.2d 841, 852 [(CADC 1970)], cert. denied, 403 U.S. 923 (1971). We ... conclude that the agency has failed to supply the requisite "reasoned analysis" in this case....

■ JUSTICE REHNQUIST, with whom THE CHIEF JUSTICE, JUSTICE POWELL, and JUSTICE O'CONNOR join, concurring in part and dissenting in part.

I join parts I, II, III, IV, and V–A of the Court's opinion. In particular, I agree that, since the airbag and continuous spool automatic seatbelt were explicitly approved in the Standard the agency was rescinding, the agency should explain why it declined to leave those requirements intact. In this case, the agency gave no explanation at all. Of course, if the agency can provide a rational explanation, it may adhere to its decision to rescind the entire Standard.

I do not believe, however, that NHTSA's view of detachable automatic seatbelts was arbitrary and capricious. The agency adequately explained its decision to rescind the Standard insofar as it was satisfied by detachable belts.

The statute that requires the Secretary of Transportation to issue motor vehicle safety standards also requires that "[e]ach such ... standard shall be practicable [and] shall meet the need for motor vehicle safety." 15 U.S.C. § 1392(a). The Court rejects the agency's explanation for its conclusion that there is substantial uncertainty whether requiring installation of detachable automatic belts would substantially increase seatbelt usage. The agency chose not to rely on a study showing a substantial increase in seatbelt usage in cars equipped with automatic seatbelts *and* an ignition interlock to prevent the car from being operated when the belts were not in place *and* which were voluntarily purchased with this equipment by consumers. It is reasonable for the agency to decide that this study does not support any conclusion concerning the effect of automatic seatbelts that are installed in all cars whether the consumer wants them or not and are not linked to an ignition interlock system.

The Court rejects this explanation because "there would seem to be grounds to believe that seatbelt use by occasional users will be substantially increased by the detachable passive belts," and the agency did not adequately explain its rejection of these grounds. It seems to me that the agency's explanation, while by no means a model, is adequate. The agency acknowledged that there would probably be some increase in belt usage, but concluded that the increase would be small and not worth the cost of mandatory detachable automatic belts. The agency's obligation is to articulate a "rational connection between the facts found and the choice made." I believe it has met this standard.

The agency explicitly stated that it will increase its educational efforts in an attempt to promote public understanding, acceptance, and use of passenger restraint systems. 46 Fed. Reg. 53425 (1981). It also stated that it will "initiate efforts with automobile manufacturers to ensure that the public will have [automatic crash protection] technology available. If this does not succeed, the agency will consider regulatory action to assure that the last decade's enormous advances in crash protection technology will not be lost." *Id.*, at 53426.

The agency's changed view of the standard seems to be related to the election of a new President of a different political party. It is readily apparent that the responsible members of one administration may consider public resistance and uncertainties to be more important than do their counterparts in a previous administration. A change in administration brought about by the people casting their votes is a perfectly reasonable basis for an executive agency's reappraisal of the costs and benefits of its programs and regulations. As long as the agency remains within the bounds established by Congress, it is entitled to assess administrative records and evaluate priorities in light of the philosophy of the administration.

---

*1. The Hard Look Standard*—*State Farm* is important primarily for its reaffirmation and elaboration of the "hard look" approach advocated by Judge Leventhal in cases like *Greater Boston Television Corp.* (pp. 720–721, *supra*) and endorsed by the Supreme Court in *Overton Park*. (It is perhaps worth noting that in Judge Leventhal's original formulation, the term "hard look" referred to the agency's obligation to take a "hard look" at the relevant factors, but over time the phrase has come to connote the court's "hard look" at the agency's reasoning. *See* National Lime Ass'n v. EPA, 627 F.2d 416, 451 n.126 (D.C. Cir. 1980).) *State Farm* and *Overton Park* remain the leading cases on the hard look standard. In the most important passage in *State Farm*, the Court held that although "[t]he scope of review under the 'arbitrary and capricious' standard is narrow and a court is not to substitute its judgment for that of the agency," the agency must nevertheless "examine the relevant data and articulate a satisfactory explanation for its action including a rational connection between the facts found and the choice made," and the reviewing court must "consider whether the decision was based on a consideration of the relevant factors and whether there has been a clear error of judgment" (internal citations and quotation marks omitted). *State Farm* then identified three situations in which an agency rule would likely be arbitrary and capricious within the meaning of § 706(2)(A). Let us consider each of these three forms of arbitrary and capricious action (though in a different order than the *State Farm* opinion lists them):

### (a) Agency action is arbitrary and capricious if the agency has "entirely failed to consider an important aspect of the problem."

A court may invalidate agency action as "arbitrary and capricious" if the agency has failed to address some significant criticism of, or proposed alternative to, the agency's final policy choice. In *State Farm*, for example, NHTSA apparently failed to consider (or at least said nothing about) the possibility of adopting a passive restraints rule that would require airbags and/or continuously spooling automatic seatbelts. In many ways, *State Farm* (or at least this portion of *State Farm*) presented an easy case: The alternative was so obvious, and the agency's failure to say anything about it was so glaring, that the Court had no difficulty ruling unanimously that the agency acted arbitrarily in failing to address it. Yet the idea that a reviewing court can set aside an agency action if the agency has "entirely failed to consider an important aspect of the problem" raises at least two potentially difficult classification problems. First, what counts as an "*important* aspect of the problem" that the agency must consider? Second, under what conditions has an agency "*entirely* failed to consider" an important aspect of the problem?

The first question arises because there are generally a great number of potential objections and alternatives to a proposed agency rule, and it would therefore be extraordinarily burdensome to require an agency to address *every* conceivable "aspect of the problem." Pragmatically, courts and agencies need to be able to figure out which objections and alternatives are sufficiently "important" to merit explicit consideration and discussion by the agency. *See* Portland Cement Ass'n v. Ruckelshaus, 486 F.2d 375, 394 (D.C. Cir. 1973), *cert. denied sub nom.* 417 U.S. 921 (1974) (stating that, although an agency must take a "hard look" at potentially important matters raised by public comments on a proposed rule, those "comments must be significant enough to step over a threshold requirement of materiality before any lack of agency response or consideration becomes of concern"); *cf. Vermont Yankee*, 435 U.S. at 551–54 (observing, in a different but related doctrinal context, that an agency's discussion of alternatives "cannot be found wanting simply because the agency failed to include every alternative device and thought conceivable to the mind of man," *id.* at 551). As a rule of thumb, then, agencies are usually safe if they focus only on public comments that make significant objections or propose sufficiently concrete and reasonable alternatives to the proposed rule. *State Farm* also made clear, however, that some alternatives—including those the agency itself had previously proposed or considered—may be sufficiently obvious that the agency is obligated to say something about them.

But how much does the agency have to say? This second question doesn't come up if the agency said literally nothing about some significant objection or alternative. In such cases the reviewing court can assert without hesitation that the agency has "entirely failed" to address an important issue. The harder cases are those in which the agency has said *something*—it has acknowledged the existence of the objection or alternative—but what the agency has said is so cursory that it is not clear that the agency gave the matter any *genuine* consideration. For example, suppose that in its statement explaining the rescission of the passive restraints rule, NHTSA had said something like, "We recognize that our conclusion that detachable automatic belts are not cost-justified might imply that we should mandate either airbags or continuously spooling belts. We have decided, however, that such a regulation would impose excessive burdens on the auto industry." Or suppose NHTSA had said, "Giving automakers a range of compliance options was an important feature of our original passive restraints rule. Having determined that one of those options is undesirable, we have concluded that it is more appropriate to revisit the issue from scratch, rather than limiting automakers' choices to the other passive restraints contemplated by the original rule, in order to achieve an appropriate balance between safety and cost." If the agency had made such statements, then one could not say, as a literal matter, that the agency had entirely failed to consider the alternative of requiring airbags or spooling seatbelts. Is that enough? If it is *not* enough, just how much does the agency have to say in order to demonstrate that it has adequately considered a proposed alternative? If it *is* enough, then isn't it quite easy for the agency to meet this standard, even if it never does engage in a genuine assessment of the proposed alternatives? *See* Natural Res. Def. Council, Inc. v. Nuclear Regulatory Comm'n, 547 F.2d 633, 646 (D.C. Cir. 1976) ("Boilerplate generalities brushing aside detailed criticism on the basis of agency 'judgment' or 'expertise' avail nothing; what is required is a reasoned response, in which the agency points to particulars in the record which, when coupled with its reservoir of expertise, support its resolution of the controversy."), *rev'd on other grounds*, *Vermont Yankee*, *supra*.

### (b) Agency action is arbitrary and capricious "if the agency has relied on factors which Congress has not intended it to consider."

While statutes sometimes authorize an agency to enact regulations that are "reasonable" or "in the public interest," or that satisfy some similarly general standard, many statutes implicitly or explicitly supply factors that the agency is supposed to consider, or is forbidden to consider, when making its judgment. Such statutory provisions may affect how courts review agency action under § 706(2)(A), in that an otherwise reasonable agency explanation may be unreasonable if it neglects the factors Congress has identified as important and/or relies on considerations that Congress has indicated ought not to be considered.

An example of a case in which an agency rule was invalidated as arbitrary because the agency had "relied on factors which Congress has not intended it to consider" is Independent U.S. Tanker Owners Committee v. Dole, 809 F.2d 847 (D.C. Cir. 1987), *cert. denied* 484 U.S. 819. In *Dole*, the D.C. Circuit struck down as arbitrary and capricious a rule promulgated by the Department of Transportation that would have allowed federally subsidized merchant ships greater access to domestic shipping markets. Judge Bork's opinion for the court emphasized that the governing statute, the Merchant Marine Act, identified a set of very specific goals that the Department was supposed to further in promulgating regulations under that Act. In particular, these regulations were supposed to help foster and maintain a domestic merchant marine fleet that is "sufficient to carry its domestic water-borne commerce and a substantial portion of the water-borne export and import foreign commerce," "capable of serving as a naval and military auxiliary," "owned and operated under the United States flag by citizens of the United States," "composed of the best-equipped, safest, and most suitable types of vessels, constructed in the United States and manned with a trained and efficient citizen personnel," and "supplemented by efficient facilities for shipbuilding and ship repair." 809 F.2d at 852. The attention given to these factors by the Department's statement of basis and purpose, Judge Bork complained, was "cursory at best." *Id.* Instead, the Department "cho[se] to rely on other policies in defending the rule," such as the assertion that the rule would promote "economic efficiency, use of underemployed resources, increased competition, and deregulation." *Id.* at 853 (internal quotation marks omitted). Importantly, the D.C. Circuit did *not* hold that such considerations were irrational in the abstract, or that the Department's explanation was unreasonable as a general policy matter. Instead, *Dole* held that the Department had acted arbitrarily and capriciously because it had failed to justify its rule in terms of the *particular objectives* specified by Congress in the Merchant Marine Act:

> [The Department's] policy [of promoting efficient competition] may well be defensible, yet it is not among the objectives specified in the Act....
>
> In exercising her decisionmaking authority, the Secretary [of Transportation] is certainly free to consider factors that are not mentioned explicitly in the governing statute, yet she is not free to substitute new goals in place of the statutory objectives without explaining how these actions are consistent with her authority under the statute. Her failure to link these non-statutory criteria with Congress' stated objectives in the Act thus makes it impossible for us to uphold the Secretary's decision.... Her reliance on these non-statutory criteria is consistently a key point in her justifications for adopting this rule. In order to defend this action as "reasoned decision-making," the Secretary must spell out in more detail how her decision to adopt this rule and reject alternative measures by relying on policies of competition and deregulation can be squared with the statutory objectives that Congress specified as the primary guidelines for administrative action in this area.

*Id.* at 853–54.

Another, more recent example is the Supreme Court's decision in Massachusetts v. Environmental Protection Agency, 549 U.S. 497 (2007), which invalidated the EPA's decision not to regulate emissions of greenhouse gasses from motor vehicles under the Clean Air Act. After first rejecting the EPA's argument that it lacked statutory authority to regulate these emissions, Justice Stevens' opinion for the Court turned to the EPA's alternative argument that, even if it had such authority, the EPA had reasonably chosen not to regulate greenhouse gasses in light of the EPA's conclusions

> that a number of voluntary executive branch programs already provide an effective response to the threat of global warming, that regulating greenhouse gases might impair the President's ability to negotiate with key developing nations to reduce emissions, and that curtailing motor-vehicle emissions would reflect an inefficient, piecemeal approach to address the climate change issue.

*Id.* at 533 (internal citations and quotation marks omitted). In rejecting this argument, the Supreme Court did not say that consideration of such factors would be unreasonable as a general matter. Rather, the Court held that the Clean Air Act requires the EPA to regulate greenhouse gas emissions if the EPA makes a judgment that these emissions pose a threat to public health or welfare within the meaning of the statute. The EPA's "reasons for action or inaction," the Court explained, "must conform to the authorizing statute." *Id.* The "laundry list of reasons" the EPA had advanced for not regulating greenhouse gas emissions from motor vehicles, however, "ha[d] nothing to do with whether greenhouse gas emissions contribute to climate change," which the Supreme Court held was the only consideration the statute permits. *Id.*

**(c) Agency action is arbitrary and capricious if the agency has "offered an explanation for its decision that runs counter to the evidence before the agency, or is so implausible that it could not be ascribed to a difference in view or the product of agency expertise."**

As we have seen, an agency action may be arbitrary and capricious if the agency has either failed to consider some alternative or objection, or has tried to justify its decision in terms of considerations that differ from those that Congress specified in the governing statute. What if the agency has addressed an issue in the proper terms, but its explanation seems substantively implausible in light of the evidence in the record? How much authority should a reviewing court have to assert that an agency's action is "arbitrary and capricious" on the grounds that no reasonable interpretation of the available evidence could support the agency's ultimate decision? *State Farm* is careful to reaffirm the standard position that a reviewing court "is not to substitute its judgment for that of the agency." Yet *State Farm* also holds open the possibility that a court might strike down an agency action as substantively irrational, a position that echoes the assertion in *Overton Park* that a court may set aside an agency action as arbitrary if the agency has made "a clear error of judgment."

Along these lines, *State Farm* held (by a 5–4 vote) that NHTSA had acted irrationally in concluding that a passive restraint rule that included a detachable passive seat belt option would not be worthwhile. On that point, Justice White's majority opinion insisted that while the Court would accept "the agency's view of the facts," the Court nonetheless could not ignore "the limitations of this record in supporting the agency's decision." Justice White emphasized that although there was no reliable quantitative empirical evidence based on actual experience with detachable passive belts, the existing evidence that many drivers use seatbelts occasionally, coupled with the fact that inertia favors use rather than non-use of passive belts, strongly suggests that passive belts would increase seatbelt usage. Yet NHTSA had not addressed that consideration. Although the Court was careful to emphasize that the factual question whether requiring detachable passive belts would in fact increase seatbelt usage was "a matter for the agency to decide," the Court nevertheless held that the agency "must bring its expertise to bear on the question." In other words, the Court indicated that the existing evidence that requiring passive belts *would* increase usage was sufficiently strong that the agency could not reasonably reach a contrary conclusion without either more specific evidence or a convincing refutation of the claim that inertia favors substantial increases in belt usage. Do you find this convincing? Did NHTSA's conclusion that its existing passive restraints rule would not save enough lives to justify the costs "run[] counter to the evidence before the agency," or was the court impermissibly "substitute[ing] its judgment for that of the agency"?

A closely related issue, also raised by this portion of the *State Farm* decision, is when (if ever) a court may conclude that an agency has acted arbitrarily and capriciously by enacting a rule without first trying to gather additional evidence on some uncertain factual question. After all, NHTSA did not conclude that requiring detachable passive belts would *not* sufficiently increase usage; the agency instead concluded only that there was "substantial uncertainty" on that question in light of the methodological flaws in the existing studies. In holding that NHTSA had acted arbitrarily, the D.C. Circuit had held that even if one were to accept NHTSA's conclusion that the existing evidence was inconclusive, "then only a well justified *refusal to seek more evidence* could render rescission non-arbitrary." State Farm Mut. Auto. Ins. Co. v. Department of Transp., 680 F.2d 206, 232 (D.C. Cir. 1982) (emphasis added), *vacated and remanded, State Farm, supra.* For example, the D.C. Circuit suggested, the agency "could have conducted surveys or experimented with detachable belt prototypes." *Id.* The agency's failure to do so, in the D.C. Circuit's view, rendered its decision arbitrary.

Is this analysis correct? Administrative agencies, like other policymakers, often have to make decisions under extreme uncertainty. Sometimes it is literally impossible for agencies to acquire better information about relevant facts; more often, gathering additional information is possible but costly, consuming time and resources that the agency might prefer to allocate to other tasks. In deciding what proportion of its scarce resources to devote to gathering information on any particular empirical question, rational agency decision-makers need to compare the expected value of additional information (particularly with respect to improving the quality of the agency's decision) with the expected cost of gathering and analyzing this information. *See, e.g.*, Matthew C. Stephenson, *Bureaucratic Decision Costs and Endogenous Agency Expertise*, 23 J. L. ECON. & ORG. 469 (2007); Matthew C. Stephenson, *Evidentiary Standards and Information Acquisition in Public Law*, 10 AMER. L. & ECON. REV. 351 (2008). When, if ever, does an agency's decision not to seek additional information, and to instead make what seems like the best decision in light of the existing evidence, render the policy decision arbitrary and capricious? Should courts have a substantial role in assessing the rationality of an agency's decision not to gather evidence, as opposed to assessing whether the agency has acted reasonably in light of the evidence before it?

**2. *The Costs and Benefits of Hard Look Review***—The principal justification for deferential but meaningful review of the agency's reasoning under the "hard look" standard, as we have seen, is that judicial review is necessary to constrain administrative arbitrariness and to ensure that agency decisions are based on legitimate rather than illegitimate consider-ations. As William Pederson, former General Counsel at the Environmental Protection Agency, put it in his commentary on some of the early "hard look" cases coming out of the D.C. Circuit:

> The effect of such detailed factual review by the courts on the portion of the agency subject to it is entirely beneficial. It is a great tonic to a program to discover that even if a regulation can be slipped or wrestled through various layers of internal or external review without significant change, the final and most prestigious reviewing forum of all—a circuit court of appeals—will inquire into the minute details of methodology, data sufficiency and test procedure and will send the regulations back if these are lacking. The effect of such judicial opinions within the agency reaches beyond those who were concerned with the specific regulations reviewed. They serve as a precedent for future rule-writers and give those who care about well-documented and well-reasoned decisionmaking a lever with which to move those who do not.

William F. Pedersen, Jr., *Formal Records and Informal Rulemaking*, 85 YALE L.J. 38, 59–60 (1975).

Other scholars have extended this basic line of argument to suggest that the shadow of judicial review, and the incentive it creates for thorough and careful agency consideration of all significant aspects of a regulatory proposal, improves the agency decision-making process by: (1) ensuring broader participation by a more diverse group of agency staff members in developing regulations, *see, e.g.*, Mark Seidenfeld, *Demystifying Deossifica-tion: Rethinking Recent Proposals To Modify Judicial Review of Notice and Comment Rulemaking*, 75 TEX. L. REV. 483, 506–10 (1997); (2) reducing various cognitive biases, such as overconfidence and "tunnel vision," that may afflict agency decision-makers, *see, e.g.*, Jeffrey J. Rachlinski & Cyn-thia R. Farina, *Cognitive Psychology and Optimal Government Design*, 87

Cornell L. Rev. 549, 559–61 588–89, 596–97 (2002); (3) mitigating the ability of parochial special interest groups to exert undue influence over regulatory policy, *see, e.g.*, Sidney A. Shapiro & Richard E. Levy, *Heightened Scrutiny of the Fourth Branch: Separation of Powers and the Requirement of Adequate Reasons for Agency Decisions*, 1987 Duke L.J. 387, 412–13; and (4) facilitating meaningful citizen participation in agency decision-making, both by giving agencies a greater incentive to take public comments seriously, *see, e.g.*, Jim Rossi, *Redeeming Judicial Review: The Hard Look Doctrine and Federal Regulatory Efforts To Restructure the Electric Utility Industry*, 1994 Wis. L. Rev. 763, 819–20, and by forcing agencies to present their analyses and conclusions in a form that courts and the general public can understand well enough to assess their reasonableness, *see, e.g.*, Patricia M. Wald, *Judicial Review in the Time of Cholera*, 49 Admin. L. Rev. 659, 665–66 (1997).

Critics, however, echo the concern Judge Bazelon stressed in his *Ethyl Corp.* opinion (pp. 728–730, *supra*): Because judges do not have the necessary technical background to evaluate the evidence or arguments proffered by the agency in most of the complex regulatory matters that come before the courts, hard look review of the sort endorsed in *State Farm* is unlikely to significantly improve agency decision-making. Professor Martin Shapiro puts the point bluntly: "Courts cannot take a hard look at materials they cannot understand nor be partners to technocrats in a realm in which only technocrats speak the language." Martin Shapiro, *Administrative Discretion: The Next Stage*, 92 Yale L.J. 1487, 1507 (1983); *see also* Thomas O. McGarity, *Some Thoughts on "Deossifying" the Rulemaking Process*, 41 Duke L.J. 1385, 1452 (1992); Richard J. Pierce, Jr., *Seven Ways To Deossify Agency Rulemaking*, 47 Admin. L. Rev. 59, 69–70 (1995). This alleged judicial incompetence, according to critics, means that *State Farm*-style hard look review is likely to have a number of adverse effects.

First, and most straightforwardly, generalist judges are likely to misunderstand the issues involved and to make mistakes, thus leading to bad decisions on the merits. Despite the fact that *State Farm* and other cases emphasize that hard look review should be narrow and deferential, critics assert that in practice judges will be overly likely to strike down agency action. *See, e.g.*, Frank B. Cross, *Pragmatic Pathologies of Judicial Review of Administrative Rulemaking*, 78 N.C. L. Rev. 1013, 1054–55 (2000); Thomas O. McGarity, *The Courts and the Ossification of Rulemaking: A Response to Professor Seidenfeld*, 75 Tex. L. Rev. 525, 547–49 (1997). Relatedly, judges may not have a good sense of which issues are really significant—they may display instead an "instinct for the capillary," treating trivial omissions as important defects. *See* Richard J. Pierce, Jr., *Unruly Judicial Review of Rulemaking*, Nat. Resources & Env't, Fall 1990, at 23, 24–25; *cf.* Jerry L. Mashaw, Bureaucratic Justice: Managing Social Security Disability Claims 19 (1983). These problems may be especially acute when judges review agency regulations, as opposed to case-specific remedial orders. This could have the perverse effect of incentivizing agencies to make policy through case-by-case adjudications. *See* Jerry L. Mashaw & David L. Harfst, The Struggle for Auto Safety 147–71 (1990).

Second, hard look review might lead judges—perhaps subconsciously—to improperly "substitute their judgment for that of the agency" by finding ostensible failures to adequately address important issues in those cases where the judges disagree with the agency's policy choice on substantive or ideological grounds. As Professor William Rodgers observed, "the suspicion has arisen, certainly among practitioners who can say such things, that the grand synthesizing principle that tells us whether the court will dig deeply or bow cursorily depends exclusively on whether the judge agrees with the result of the administrative decision." William H. Rodgers, Jr., *Judicial Review of Risk Assessments: The Role of Decision Theory in Unscrambling the Benzene Decision*, 11 ENVTL. L. 301, 302 (1981); *see also* Richard J. Pierce, Jr., *Legislative Reform of Judicial Review of Agency Actions*, 44 DUKE L.J. 1110, 1110–11, 1120 (1995); McGarity, *supra*, at 539, 549. Quantitative empirical studies have found evidence broadly consistent with the hypothesis that judges' political ideologies are indeed correlated with their decisions in hard look review cases. *See, e.g.*, Thomas J. Miles & Cass R. Sunstein, *The Real World of Arbitrariness Review*, 75 U. CHI. L. REV. 761 (2008).

Third, while proponents of hard look review argue that requiring agencies to demonstrate "reasoned decision-making" will lead to higher-quality regulatory policy for the reasons sketched above, critics contend that judicial review will not have that effect because the "reasons" offered in official agency statements bear little connection to the actual process of agency decision-making. These formal reasons are, according to critics, usually concocted after the fact, often with substantial input from agency lawyers who don't know much about the substantive issues involved. According to Professor Martin Shapiro:

> [I]nstead of telling the truth, agencies can lie; this is mostly what they do these days. They can dress each of their guestimates about the facts ... in enormous, multilayered costumes of technocratic rationality. They can weave shrouds of data and analysis designed to proclaim the scientific rationality of every choice they have made.

MARTIN SHAPIRO, WHO GUARDS THE GUARDIANS? JUDICIAL CONTROL OF ADMINISTRATION 151–52 (1988). Hard look review, on this account, has exactly the opposite effect as that suggested by many of its proponents: It obscures rather than clarifies the true basis for administrative decisions. Furthermore, instead of empowering a broader set of agency experts to shape bureaucratic policy, hard look review may instead lead agencies to "hire more lawyers and give them more of a role in producing decisions that will withstand court scrutiny," thus reducing rather than enhancing the expert nature of administrative decisions. *Id.* at 154; *see also* R. SHEP MELNICK, REGULATION AND THE COURTS: THE CASE OF THE CLEAN AIR ACT 302–03 (1983) (asserting that hard look judicial review of Clean Air Act rules "greatly enhanced the bureaucratic position of politically naïve and technically ignorant attorneys within the [Environmental Protection Agency]"); Thomas O. McGarity, *The Role of Government Attorneys in Regulatory Agency Rulemaking*, 61 LAW & CONTEMP. PROBS. 19, 26 (Winter 1998) (arguing that "[t]he evolution of the 'hard look' doctrine of judicial review ... demanded that agency lawyers perform the ... controversial function of ensuring that the rule at least appear to be rational").

Fourth, critics contend that although the elaborate records that agencies must generate to survive hard look review do not reflect or improve the agency's actual decision-making process, producing these records is nonetheless very costly for agencies. Professor McGarity remarks that "assimilating the record and drafting the preambles to proposed and final rules" requires a "Herculean effort" and "may well be the most time-consuming aspect of informal rulemaking." Thomas O. McGarity, *Some Thoughts on "Deossifying" the Rulemaking Process*, 41 DUKE L.J. 1385, 1401 (1992); *see also* Richard J. Pierce, Jr., *Unruly Judicial Review of Rulemaking*, NAT. RESOURCES & ENV'T, Fall 1990, at 23, 49–50; Richard J. Pierce, Jr., *Judicial Review of Agency Actions in a Period of Diminishing Agency Resources*, 49 ADMIN. L. REV. 61, 71 (1997). This problem, critics say, is exacerbated by the fact that opponents of proposed agency rules can "hire consultants and lawyers to pick apart the agencies' preambles and background documents and launch blunderbuss attacks on every detail of the legal and technical bases for the agencies' rules[, and] ... agencies cannot afford to allow any of the multifaceted attacks to go unanswered for fear the courts will remand...." McGarity, *supra*, at 1400; *see also* Richard Stewart, *Administrative Law in the Twenty–First Century*, 78 N.Y.U. L. REV. 437, 442, 447 (2003). Critics further assert that the unpredictability of hard look review tends to make agencies more reluctant to initiate rulemaking, because they are unsure of what exactly they need to do to insulate their rules from judicial reversal, and any gap in an agency's reasoning may lead to judicial invalidation. *See, e.g.*, Richard J. Pierce, Jr., *Seven Ways To Deossify Agency Rulemaking*, 47 ADMIN. L. REV. 59, 65 (1995). The net result, according to these critics, is the "ossification" of agency rulemaking—a concern also raised in the closely analogous (perhaps functionally identical) context of judicial interpretation of the APA's procedural requirements (*see* pp. 624–626, *supra*). Thus, even if hard look review has positive effects when considered in the context of any individual rule, the net effect might still be negative. As Professor Frank Cross argues, "improved quality [of enacted rules] is an insufficient justification for [hard look] judicial review if quantity suffers unduly.... A marginal increase in regulation quality (from explicitly proving the obvious) could cause a substantial decrease in quantity; the net result, therefore, may be an overall decrease in the quality of regulation." Frank B. Cross, *Pragmatic Pathologies of Judicial Review of Administrative Rulemaking*, 78 N.C. L. REV. 1013, 1044 (2000).

Defenders of hard look review believe these criticisms are inapposite or exaggerated. Following Judge Leventhal's argument in *Ethyl Corp.* (pp. 730–732, *supra*), proponents of hard look review insist that generalist judges can acquire the background information they need to conduct deferential but meaningful assessment of agencies' reasoning process. According to Judge Patricia Wald, one of Judge Leventhal's colleagues on the D.C. Circuit:

> It is ... important to remember that the nature of the judicial review process is not necessarily geared to finally settling disputed scientific or technological facts. Rather, the appellate court's job is only to decide if the agency's choices between varying scientific or technological theories or proofs are reasonable ones....
>
> Of course, to conduct a "hard look" into the substance of agency decision making, a judge needs command of the subject matter involved, no matter how complex, technical, or uninviting it is. In a way, the reviewing court performs a function like the jury in common law; it gets a sense of the case based on all the evidence that is placed before it, whether or not it understands in detail every piece of that evidence. [The judges'] role is to make sure that agency "expertise" does not disguise agency refusal to deal with agonizing questions or with cogent opposition to its intended direction....
>
> Given all this, it seems to me that courts and the country are better off relying upon Article III judges who, despite occasional bumblings or mistakes, are engaged in the everyday business of accommodating ... [the] problems of a regulated industrial society to democratic constitutional principles.

Patricia M. Wald, *Judicial Review of Complex Administrative Agency Decisions*, 462 ANNALS AM. ACAD. POL. & SOC. SCI. 72, 76–77 (1982); *see also* Thomas O. Sargentich, *The Critique of Active Judicial Review of Administrative Agencies: A Reevaluation*, 49 ADMIN. L. REV. 599, 634 (1997); Mark Seidenfeld, *Demystifying Deossification: Rethinking Recent Proposals To Modify Judicial Review of Notice and Comment Rulemaking*, 75 TEX. L. REV. 483, 521 (1997).

Defenders of hard look review also dispute the empirical claim that hard look review in fact substantially increases rulemaking costs. *See, e.g.*, Patricia M. Wald, *Judicial Review in the Time of Cholera*, 49 ADMIN. L. REV. 659, 666 (1997). In support of this view, some hard look proponents note that despite the alleged ossification of agency rulemaking, agencies continue to make a substantial number of new rules, these rules are rarely reversed by courts, and even when such a reversal does occur it usually does not derail or significantly delay an agency's ability to achieve its regulatory goals. *See* Cary Coglianese, *Empirical Analysis and Administrative Law*, 2002 U. ILL. L. REV. 1111, 1125–31; William S. Jordan, III, *Ossification Revisited: Does Arbitrary and Capricious Review Significantly Interfere with Agency Ability To Achieve Regulatory Goals Through Informal Rulemaking?*, 94 NW. U. L. REV. 393 (2000); Anne Joseph O'Connell, *Political Cycles of Rulemaking: An Empirical Portrait of the Modern Administrative State*, 94 VA. L. REV. 889 (2008); Susan Webb Yackee & Jason Webb Yackee, *Administrative Procedures and Bureaucratic Performance: Is Federal Rulemaking "Ossified"?*, 20 J. PUB. ADMIN. RES. & THEORY 261 (2010). Of course, the fact that agencies promulgate a large number of rules and usually prevail in court does not necessarily refute the ossification hypothesis. We do not know what would have happened in the counterfactual world in which courts adopted a more deferential approach.

Nonetheless, defenders of hard look review emphasize that proponents of the ossification thesis have failed to supply systematic (as opposed to anecdotal) empirical evidence for their position, and the limited quantitative evidence that does exist, though not dispositive, tends to cut the other way.

Furthermore, some proponents of hard look review suggest that raising agencies' costs of promulgating new rules can actually be a good thing, at least under some conditions. If hard look review makes piecemeal agency rulemaking slower and less reliable, interested parties may have a greater incentive to form coalitions to seek comprehensive *legislative* reform. *See* Jim Rossi, *Redeeming Judicial Review: The Hard Look Doctrine and Federal Regulatory Efforts To Restructure the Electric Utility Industry*, 1994 WIS. L. REV. 763, 807–11. In other words, it is possible that raising the costs of rulemaking will lead to more desirable forms of legislative policymaking, even if there is less overall rulemaking. Others suggest that hard look review may counteract agency tendencies toward overregulation: "[B]y requiring agencies to show that the benefits of regulation justify its costs, or that a significant problem is involved," hard look review may operate as "a means of promoting private ordering." Cass R. Sunstein, *In Defense of the Hard Look: Judicial Activism and Administrative Law*, 7 HARV. J. L. & PUB. POL'Y 51, 53 (1984); *cf.* Richard H. Fallon, Jr., *The Core of an Uneasy Case for Judicial Review*, 121 HARV. L. REV. 1693, 1704–09 (2008) (arguing that institutional devices that make the legislative process more cumbersome help to guard against the tendency to overlegislate); James R. Rogers & Georg Vanberg, *Resurrecting* Lochner: *A Defense of Unprincipled Judicial Activism*, 23 J. L. ECON. & ORG. 442 (2007) (same). Another argument, along somewhat similar lines, is that the costs to agencies of providing courts with satisfactory explanations may force agencies to give priority to those rules that are truly important over those that are less so. The agency's willingness to bear these additional costs may provide useful information to the reviewing court about the net benefits of the proposed rule:

> Because the production of a high-quality explanation is costly to the agency—consuming time, money, and staff that could have been devoted to other things—the quality of the agency's defense of its regulatory decision provides a signal of the benefits the agency expects to receive if the court upholds the regulation. The quality of the agency's regulation therefore provides valuable information to the court even if the court cannot understand or verify any of the agency's substantive analysis. . . .
>
> . . . [O]ssification, understood as the deterrence of rulemaking in cases where the agency views the judicially-imposed explanation costs as greater than the rule's expected net benefits, may be precisely what hard look review is supposed to accomplish. Courts cannot assess regulatory benefits directly, so they establish a type of review under which it is too expensive for agencies to enact regulations that have low positive value to the agency and negative expected value to the

courts. Ossification, on this view, need not be the result of an individual or collective failure of judicial rationality or foresight. Instead, ossification may be the pejorative name assigned to the effective screening out by judges of regulations that are of sufficiently low value that they would be considered irrational, and therefore unlawful, by a fully informed reviewing court.

Matthew C. Stephenson, *A Costly Signaling Theory of "Hard Look" Judicial Review*, 58 ADMIN. L. REV. 753, 766, 776 (2006).

The debate over the merits of hard look review has been going on for at least four decades, perhaps longer. As we have seen, this debate involves both uncertain empirical questions—such as the impact of hard look review on agency behavior and performance—and difficult normative questions involving the appropriate trade-offs between the values of rationality, transparency, speed, flexibility, expertise, and accountability. Based on the materials we have covered, what approach do you think courts should take when reviewing agency action under the "arbitrary and capricious" standard of § 706(2)(A) or analogous review provisions?

**3. *Hard Look Review and Congressional Intent*—**Whatever the pragmatic arguments for and against hard look review, is this approach consistent with the APA? If you read *Ethyl Corp.* (pp. 723–733, *supra*), you may recall Judge Leventhal's argument that because Congress intended this searching form of judicial review under § 706(2)(A), courts are not free to abstain from such review even if they have doubts about its efficacy. But is that correct? After all, at the time the APA was enacted, courts applying an "arbitrariness" standard of review to agency decisions typically applied the very deferential test associated with cases like *Pacific States Box & Basket* (*see* p. 719, *supra*). Furthermore, many scholars have concluded that the APA was a political compromise that gave conservatives a more proceduralized agency adjudication process, but preserved for New Dealers a less formal, more legislative-style process for rulemaking. *See, e.g.*, Lisa Schultz Bressman, *Procedures as Politics in Administrative Law*, 107 COLUM. L. REV. 1749, 1756 (2007); Martin Shapiro, *APA: Past, Present, and Future*, 72 VA. L. REV. 447, 453 (1986). If these propositions are true, then hard look review may differ from the arbitrary and capricious test that Congress thought it was enacting in 1946. On the other hand, some have argued that hard look review has been implicitly endorsed by all three branches of government over a long period of time (with Congress on several occasions rejecting proposals to alter the review standard by amending § 706), and that this consensus ought to be respected. *See* Peter L. Strauss, *The Rulemaking Continuum*, 41 DUKE L.J. 1463, 1471–72 (1992); Cass R. Sunstein, *In Defense of the Hard Look: Judicial Activism and Administrative Law*, 7 HARV. J. L. & PUB. POL'Y 51, 56 (1984); Patricia M. Wald, *Judicial Review in the Time of Cholera*, 49 ADMIN. L. REV. 659, 663 (1997). Do either of these positions strike you as sufficiently persuasive to resolve the controversy over hard look review without reference to the pragmatic arguments outlined above?

*4. Judicial Review of an Agency's Rescission of an Existing Rule*—While *State Farm* announced and applied a general approach to judicial review under the § 706(2)(A) "arbitrary and capricious" standard, the Motor Vehicle Manufacturers Association had argued that that standard, even if appropriate when reviewing an agency's decision to *adopt* a new regulation, was inappropriate in cases involving an agency's *rescission* of an existing (but in this case not yet effective) regulation. To understand the Motor Vehicle Manufacturers Association's argument, it is important to have a bit of background on how courts typically review an agency's decision *not* to adopt a new rule.

An agency's decision not to initiate a rulemaking proceeding is judicially reviewable under § 706 of the APA. First, § 706(1) requires a reviewing court to "compel agency action unlawfully withheld." Applying this standard, courts sometimes compel an agency to initiate rulemaking proceedings when a statute unambiguously requires the agency to do so, or when the agency's reasons for refusing to initiate a rulemaking are expressly precluded by statute. *See, e.g.*, Massachusetts v. EPA, 549 U.S. 497, 528–32 (2007); Atlantic States Legal Found. v. EPA, 114 F.3d 1032 (10th Cir. 1997). Second, and more relevant to our discussion here, § 706(2)(A) instructs reviewing courts to set aside arbitrary and capricious "agency action," and § 551(13) explicitly defines "agency action" as including "failure to act." Thus, a reviewing court can, in principle, hold that an agency's decision not to initiate a rulemaking proceeding is arbitrary and capricious. *See, e.g.*, Massachusetts v. EPA, 549 U.S. 497, 533–34 (2007); *cf.* American Lung Ass'n v. EPA, 134 F.3d 388, 392–93 (D.C. Cir. 1998) (applying an analogous standard under the organic statute). (In contrast, an agency's decision not to bring an *enforcement action* against a particular party under existing laws or regulations is presumptively unreviewable. *See* Heckler v. Chaney, 470 U.S. 821 (1985).)

That said, most courts have held that judicial review of an agency's decision not to initiate rulemaking proceedings is more deferential than review of an agency's decision to adopt a new rule. As the D.C. Circuit explained in WWHT, Inc. v. Federal Communications Commission, 656 F.2d 807 (D.C. Cir. 1981), "the parameters of the 'arbitrary and capricious' standard of review will vary with the context of the case," and in the context of an agency decision not to initiate rulemaking, the scope of review is especially narrow. *Id.* at 817. Under this "extremely limited, highly deferential" version of "arbitrary and capricious" review, a court will "overturn an agency's decision not to initiate a rulemaking only for compelling cause, such as plain error of law or a fundamental change in the factual premises previously considered by the agency." National Customs Brokers & Forwarders Ass'n of America, Inc. v. United States, 883 F.2d 93, 96–97 (D.C. Cir. 1989); *see also* American Horse Protection Ass'n, Inc. v. Lyng, 812 F.2d 1, 4–5 (D.C. Cir. 1987) ("Review under the 'arbitrary and capricious' tag line . . . encompasses a range of levels of deference to the agency, and . . . an agency's refusal to institute rulemaking proceedings is at the high end of the range") (internal citations omitted). *But see* Professional Pilots Fed'n v. FAA, 118 F.3d 758, 764 (D.C. Cir. 1997). Indeed, courts have occasionally asserted (with only slight exaggeration) that although an agency's refusal to initiate rulemaking is technically reviewable, such a refusal "is evaluated with a deference so broad as to make the process akin to non-reviewability." Cellnet Communication, Inc. v. FCC, 965 F.2d 1106, 1111 (D.C. Cir. 1992). As for an agency decision to *terminate* a rulemaking proceeding that has already started, the standard of review is somewhat less deferential than that applied to a decision not to initiate rulemaking in the first place, but more deferential than the standard for review of an enacted rule. *See* Williams Natural Gas Co. v. Federal Energy Regulatory Comm'n, 872 F.2d 438, 443–44 (D.C. Cir. 1989); Natural Res. Def. Council, Inc. v. SEC, 606 F.2d 1031, 1045–46 (D.C. Cir. 1979).

The D.C. Circuit explained the basic rationale for applying a more deferential version of "arbitrary and capricious" review to decisions not to initiate rulemaking proceedings in its 1979 *NRDC v. SEC* decision, *supra*:

> Requiring an agency to defend in court its decision not to adopt proposed rules will divert scarce institutional resources into an area that the agency in its expert judgment has already determined is not even worth the effort already expended. The danger of throwing good money after bad, moreover, also exists in a more subtle form because the very prospect of litigation may cause the agency to give a proposal more elaborate consideration than it might actually merit....

> ... An agency's discretionary decision *not* to regulate a given activity is inevitably based, in large measure, on factors not inherently susceptible to judicial resolution—e.g., internal management considerations as to budget and personnel; evaluations of its own competence; weighing of competing policies within a broad statutory framework.... Further, even if an agency considers a particular problem worthy of regulation, it may determine for reasons lying within its special expertise that the time for action has not yet arrived.... The area may be one of such rapid technological development that regulations would be outdated by the time they could become effective, or the scientific state of the art may be such that sufficient data are not yet available on which to premise adequate regulations.... The circumstances in the regulated industry may be evolving in a way that could vitiate the need for regulation, ... or the agency may still be developing the expertise necessary for effective regulation....

> Moreover, added to the problems already inherent in reviewing the record support for informal rulemaking decisions is the additional concern that, in the context of an agency's non-adoption of a rule, the record and reasons statement will be of little use to a reviewing court unless they are narrowly focused on the particular rule advocated by plaintiff or petitioner. There are an infinite number of rules that an agency could adopt in its discretion; unless the agency has carefully focused its considerations, judicial review will have an undesirably abstract and hypothetical quality.

606 F.2d at 1045–47; *see also* Eric Biber, *Two Sides of the Same Coin: Judicial Review of Administrative Agency Action and Inaction*, 26 VA.

ENVTL. L. J. 461 (2008) (explaining deference to agency inaction as reflecting reluctance to interfere with agency resource allocation decisions).

The essence of the Motor Vehicle Manufacturers' argument in *State Farm* was that a decision to *rescind* a regulation should be treated as the equivalent—for judicial review purposes—of a decision not to enact the regulation in the first place. The Supreme Court (unanimously) disagreed. Part of the Court's conclusion was based on a specific provision in the National Motor Vehicle Safety Act that provided for judicial review of agency decisions to "revoke" a safety standard. But the Court's rationale for rejecting the Motor Vehicle Manufacturers' argument was much broader, and has since been applied in cases where there was no specific statutory provision covering judicial review of "revocations." The Court's more general argument was that Congress established a presumption not against *regulation*, but against *policy change*. Thus, the Court's sliding-scale approach to judicial review under § 706(2)(A) creates a *status quo bias*, rather than an *anti-regulatory bias*.

Is that sensible? The Court did not offer much in the way of explanation for its position. In rejecting the idea that courts should vary the standard of review so as to favor deregulation, the Court asserted that "there is no more reason to presume that changing circumstances require the rescission of prior action, instead of a revision in or even the extension of current regulation." And the Court's argument for subjecting changes in the status quo to a more rigorous standard of review was its assertion, quoting the plurality opinion in Atchison, Topeka & Santa Fe Railway Co. v. Wichita Board of Trade, 412 U.S. 800, 807–08 (1973), that a "settled course of behavior embodies the agency's informed judgment that, by pursuing that course, it will carry out the policies committed to it by Congress. There is, then, at least a presumption that those policies will be carried out best if the settled rule is adhered to."

Is this convincing? Do the arguments advanced by the D.C. Circuit in *NRDC v. SEC* for reviewing decisions not to initiate rulemakings more deferentially support the Motor Vehicle Manufacturers' position, or the Supreme Court's? Some of the considerations raised by the D.C. Circuit in *NRDC*—such as the resource cost of developing the new rule, and the absence of a well-developed record focused on a specific proposal—would seem inapplicable in cases where the agency proposes rescission of a rule that has already been enacted. Then again, other considerations raised in *NRDC* seem more consonant with the Motor Vehicle Manufacturers' position. The *NRDC* court, after all, noted that "even if an agency considers a particular problem worthy of regulation, it may determine for reasons lying within its special expertise that the time for action has not yet arrived," and further suggested that "[t]he area may be one of such rapid technological development that regulations would be outdated by the time they could become effective, or . . .[, or] [t]he circumstances in the regulated industry may be evolving in a way that could vitiate the need for regulation. . . ." If these are valid reasons to review more deferentially an agency's decision *not to enact* a new regulation, wouldn't they also counsel more deferential judicial review of an agency's decision *to rescind* a regulation—especially one that has not yet gone into effect? Or was the Supreme Court correct that although these and other considerations may make it "easier for an agency to justify a deregulatory action, the direction in which an agency chooses to move does not alter the standard of judicial review established by law"? *See generally* Merrick B. Garland, *Deregulation and Judicial Review*, 98 Harv. L. Rev. 505, 513–25 (1985).

   **5.  *Hard Look Review of Changes in Agency Policy*—***State Farm* decisively rejected the argument that an agency's decision to rescind a regulation should be reviewed more deferentially than a decision to enact a regulation. Some judges and commentators would go beyond *State Farm* to hold an agency to an even more *rigorous* standard of review when the agency rescinds or reverses a pre-existing policy, especially a longstanding policy. *See, e.g.*, Office of Communication of United Church of Christ v. FCC, 707 F.2d 1413, 1425 (D.C. Cir. 1983); NAACP v. FCC, 682 F.2d 993, 998 (D.C. Cir. 1982). The Supreme Court, however, recently rejected that view in Federal Communications Commission v. Fox Television Stations, Inc., 129 S.Ct. 1800 (2009). In his opinion for the Court in *Fox Television*, Justice Scalia declared:

> We find no basis in the Administrative Procedure Act or in our opinions for a requirement that all agency change be subjected to more searching review.... [O]ur opinion in *State Farm* neither held nor implied that every agency action representing a policy change must be justified by reasons more substantial than those required to adopt a policy in the first instance. That case, which involved the rescission of a prior regulation, said only that such action requires "a reasoned analysis for the change beyond that which may be required when an agency *does not act* in the first instance." (emphasis added). Treating failures to act and rescissions of prior action differently for purposes of the standard of review makes good sense, and has basis in the text of the statute, which likewise treats the two separately. It instructs a reviewing court to "compel agency action unlawfully withheld or unreasonably delayed," 5 U.S.C. § 706(1), and to "hold unlawful and set aside agency action, findings, and conclusions found to be [among other things] ... arbitrary [or] capricious," § 706(2)(A). The statute makes no distinction, however, between initial agency action and subsequent agency action undoing or revising that action.

> To be sure, the requirement that an agency provide reasoned explanation for its action would ordinarily demand that it display awareness that it *is* changing position.... And of course the agency must show that there are good reasons for the new policy. But it need not demonstrate to a court's satisfaction that the reasons for the new policy are *better* than the reasons for the old one; it suffices that the new policy is permissible under the statute, that there are good reasons for it, and that the agency *believes* it to be better, which the conscious change of course adequately indicates. This means that the agency need not always provide a more detailed justification than what would

suffice for a new policy created on a blank slate. Sometimes it must—
when, for example, its new policy rests upon factual findings that
contradict those which underlay its prior policy; or when its prior
policy has engendered serious reliance interests that must be taken
into account. It would be arbitrary or capricious to ignore such matters. In such cases it is not that further justification is demanded by
the mere fact of policy change; but that a reasoned explanation is
needed for disregarding facts and circumstances that underlay or were
engendered by the prior policy.

129 S.Ct. at 1810–11 (internal citations and footnote omitted) (emphasis in
original).

Several other Justices weighed in with different perspectives on whether an agency's change of a previous policy requires a heightened form of
review under the "arbitrary and capricious" standard. Justice Stevens
argued in dissent that "[t]here should be a strong presumption that the
FCC's initial views, reflecting the informed judgment of independent commissioners with expertise in the regulated area, also reflect the views of the
Congress that delegated the Commission authority to flesh out details not
fully defined in the enacting statute." *Id.* at 1826 (Stevens, J., dissenting).
This consideration, coupled with a preference for "stability over administra-
trative whim," counsels in favor of placing on an agency a heightened
burden to explain why "its prior policy is no longer sound before allowing it
to change course." *Id.* Justice Breyer, in a separate dissent joined by
Justices Stevens, Souter, and Ginsburg, had a somewhat different take on
this issue. Justice Breyer argued:

To explain a change requires more than setting forth reasons why
the new policy is a good one. It also requires the agency to answer the
question, "Why did you change?" And a rational answer to this
question typically requires a more complete explanation than would
prove satisfactory were change itself not at issue. An (imaginary)
administrator explaining why he chose a policy that requires driving on
the right-side, rather than the left-side, of the road might say, "Well,
one side seemed as good as the other, so I flipped a coin." But even
assuming the rationality of that explanation for an *initial* choice, that
explanation is not at all rational if offered to explain why the administrator *changed* driving practice, from right-side to left-side, 25 years
later. . . .

I recognize that *sometimes* the ultimate explanation for a change
may have to be, "We now weigh the relevant considerations differently." But at other times, an agency can and should say more. Where, for
example, the agency rested its previous policy on particular factual
findings; or where an agency rested its prior policy on its view of the
governing law or where an agency rested its previous policy on, say, a
special need to coordinate with another agency, one would normally
expect the agency to focus upon those earlier views of fact, of law, or of
policy and explain why they are no longer controlling. Regardless, to
say that the agency here must answer the question "why change" is

... to recognize the obvious fact that *change* is sometimes (not always) a relevant background feature that sometimes (not always) requires focus (upon prior justifications) and explanation lest the adoption of the new policy (in that circumstance) be "arbitrary, capricious, an abuse of discretion."

*Id.* at 1830–32 (Breyer, J., dissenting) (internal citations omitted) (emphasis in original). Justice Breyer, however, was careful to insist that he was *not* calling for a "heightened" standard of judicial review for agency decisions to reverse previous policies; rather, he argued that "the law requires application of the *same standard* of review to different circumstances, namely circumstances characterized by the fact that *change* is at issue." *Id.* at 1831 (emphasis in original).

Which of these approaches do you find most attractive? How different are they? Do formal differences, or differences in application, mask underlying agreement on the basic principle? Or perhaps the opposite is true— perhaps agreement on the formal characteristics of review (e.g., that there is no "heightened standard," but agencies may be obligated to explain rejection of earlier factual findings) is illusory, masking a genuine disagreement over the proper standard of review. What do you think?

**6.  *The Role of Politics in Administrative Decision–Making*—** One of the most interesting—and oft-quoted—passages in *State Farm* is the last paragraph of Justice Rehnquist's partial dissent. While Justice White's majority opinion faulted NHTSA for failing to supply either empirical evidence or logical arguments to support the claim that passive belts would not increase seatbelt usage as much as NHTSA had previously estimated, Justice Rehnquist did not think the agency had really based its change in position on a new assessment of the *facts* about likely belt usage rates. Rather, the agency had decided to resolve the uncertainty differently in light of newly-elected President Reagan's different regulatory philosophy, which was more skeptical of the benefits of government regulation and more confident in the ability of private markets to promote public welfare. Justice Rehnquist thus wrote: "A change in administration brought about by the people casting their votes is a perfectly reasonable basis for an executive agency's reappraisal of the costs and benefits of its programs and regulations. As long as the agency remains within the bounds established by Congress, it is entitled to assess administrative records and evaluate priorities in light of the philosophy of the administration."

To put Justice Rehnquist's point in a slightly different way, in a case like *State Farm*, no one really knows how many lives NHTSA's original passive restraints rule will save. In light of this uncertainty, it would be reasonable to adopt the rule—erring on the side of safety, even though the rule might end up imposing significant costs for no meaningful safety gains. It would also, however, be reasonable to forgo the rule—erring on the side of reducing regulatory costs, even though this might be a mistake if the safety benefits of the rule would have been substantial. Reasonable people can disagree on the best course of action when confronted with this sort of uncertainty. These differences in regulatory philosophy need not derive from any difference in empirical assessment of the available evidence. If the agency's change in position is due to a change in regulatory philosophy—especially when that change is the result of a democratic election in which regulatory philosophy was a major issue in the campaign—the courts should not reject that change as "arbitrary" simply because the agency has not provided a technocratic explanation for its new position.

Is that argument convincing? Does it matter that NHTSA itself did not explain its decision as the result of a change in regulatory philosophy, but rather defended its changed position as a rational, technocratic, allegedly neutral response to the uncertainties of the existing data? Consider Judge Stephen Williams diagnosis of how the agency erred in *State Farm*:

> [NHTSA] appeared to adopt a substantive standard tilting strongly toward regulation, under which it would require a proposed safety device if it offered any significant benefits (at least if they were not overwhelmed by costs). It then found that passive restraints did not measure up even to this criterion. Given those agency choices, the vulnerable point of the decision was its science, and there the challengers attacked.... Had the agency invoked an authority to rely on standard cost-benefit analysis, presumably the Court would have asked whether the statute permitted such a view and (if so) whether the agency had arrived at it without being arbitrary or capricious....
>
> ... [A]n agency's order must have adequate underpinnings in fact, law, and policy.... An agency's caution in one domain may require it to extend itself in another, just as a stretch—going to the edge—in one may enable it to occupy safe territory in another. A broad law-policy judgment by the agency in *State Farm* might have sustained its rejection of passive restraints despite the frailties of its science, but it chose a narrower view of its mandate and thus needed "stronger" science.... Every agency order hangs on a kind of chain, and the challengers naturally go for what they perceive as the weakest link; the court must decide if it is strong enough.

Stephen F. Williams, *The Roots of Deference*, 100 Yale L.J. 1103, 1107–08 (1991) (footnote omitted). Does that strike you as a compelling response to Justice Rehnquist's dissent? Perhaps the Court was right to invalidate the agency's decision to rescind the passive restraints rule given that the agency had chosen to explain its decision as reflecting a revised assessment of the empirical evidence, but the Court should have upheld the agency (at least on this point) if the agency had forthrightly declared that it no longer viewed requiring detachable automatic seatbelts as worthwhile, due to a change in the agency's regulatory priorities. *See* Kathryn A. Watts, *Proposing a Place for Politics in Arbitrary and Capricious Review*, 119 Yale L.J. 2, 8, 40–41 (2009) (arguing that courts should explicitly declare that " 'valid' reasons under arbitrary and capricious review ... include certain political influences from the President, other executive officials, and members of Congress, so long as the political influences are openly and transparently disclosed," and that such an express judicial recognition of the legitimacy of these considerations would eliminate agencies' temptation to fudge their science in order to reach favored political outcomes). Does that seem to be the right approach? Why do you suppose the agency chose *not* to explain its policy change in those terms?

Justice Rehnquist's dissent also implicates a more general set of issues regarding the appropriate bases for administrative policymaking. As you may recall from Chapter Three (p. 382, *supra*), delegation to administrative agencies is considered problematic in part because it threatens to undermine democratic accountability. One response to that concern is to emphasize that agency officials, though not themselves elected, are part of the executive branch under the control of the President, who of course *is* elected. *See, e.g.*, Jerry L. Mashaw, *Prodelegation: Why Administrators Should Make Political Decisions*, 1 J. L. Econ. & Org. 81, 95–99 (1985); Elena Kagan, *Presidential Administration*, 114 Harv. L. Rev. 2245, 2332–39 (2001). Insofar as we view presidential control of the administration as important in reconciling the felt need for administrative governance with our commitment to democratic accountability, Justice Rehnquist's argument has considerable force: Courts, on this view, should not stand as obstacles to the President's ability to align administrative policy choices with the President's regulatory philosophy. *See* Richard Pierce, *Democratizing the Administrative State*, 48 Wm. & Mary L. Rev. 559, 582 (2006); Watts, *supra*, at 42–45.

On the other hand, one of the most important arguments in favor of permitting broad delegations to agencies, as we also discussed in Chapter Three (p. 381, *supra*), is the desire for technocratic decision-making that is at least partially *insulated* from day-to-day partisan politics. Those who are sympathetic to this argument are often skeptical of assertions of a broad presidential prerogative to direct the administration, viewing such presidential control as a threat to agency autonomy. *See, e.g.*, Lisa Schultz Bressman, *Beyond Accountability: Arbitrariness and Legitimacy in the Administrative State*, 78 N.Y.U. L. Rev. 461 (2003); Cynthia R. Farina, *The Consent of the Governed: Against Simple Rules for a Complex World*, 72 Chi.-Kent L. Rev. 987 (1997); Matthew C. Stephenson, *Optimal Political Control of the Bureaucracy*, 107 Mich. L. Rev. 53 (2008). On this view, Justice Rehnquist's argument is problematic: If one of Congress's chief purposes in creating and empowering NHTSA was to ensure that automobile safety regulations were made by experts using the best available science, then it may not be enough for the agency to reverse its position simply because the President has a different "regulatory philosophy." Finally, recall that one of the central conceptual elements behind the Court's approval of delegations is the notion that an agency is not exercising legislative power, but rather implementing an "intelligible principle" set down by Congress. *See supra* pp. 391–392. If an agency could alter policy because of a new President's political preferences—without regard to whether the change could be defended by application of the guiding statutory criteria to relevant facts and policy considerations—might that possibility cast doubt on the very legitimacy of the delegation?

Should the analysis be any different if the agency in question is an independent commission rather than an executive branch agency? Justice Breyer's dissenting opinion in FCC v. Fox Television Stations, Inc., 129 S.Ct. 1800 (2009), argued explicitly that there should be such a difference:

> ... [A]pplicable law ... grants those in charge of independent administrative agencies broad authority to determine relevant policy. But it does not permit them to make policy choices for purely political reasons nor to rest them primarily upon unexplained policy preferences. Federal Communications Commissioners have fixed terms of office; they are not directly responsible to the voters; and they enjoy an independence expressly designed to insulate them, to a degree, from the exercise of political oversight. That insulation helps to secure important governmental objectives, such as the constitutionally related objective of maintaining broadcast regulation that does not bend too readily before the political winds. But that agency's comparative freedom from ballot-box control makes it all the more important that courts review its decisionmaking to assure compliance with applicable provisions of the law—including law requiring that major policy decisions be based upon articulable reasons.

*Id.* at 1829–30 (Breyer, J., dissenting) (internal citations and quotation marks omitted).

Justice Scalia's majority opinion in *Fox Television*, however, rejected this view:

> [Justice Breyer] claims that the FCC's status as an "independent" agency sheltered from political oversight requires courts to be "all the more" vigilant in ensuring "that major policy decisions be based upon articulable reasons." Not so. The independent agencies are sheltered not from politics but from the President, and it has often been observed that their freedom from presidential oversight (and protection) has simply been replaced by increased subservience to congressional direction....
>
> Regardless, it is assuredly not "applicable law" that rulemaking by independent regulatory agencies is subject to heightened scrutiny. The Administrative Procedure Act, which provides judicial review, makes no distinction between independent and other agencies, neither in its definition of agency, 5 U.S.C. § 701(b)(1), nor in the standards for reviewing agency action, § 706.... There is no reason to magnify the separation-of-powers dilemma posed by the Headless Fourth Branch by letting Article III judges—like jackals stealing the lion's kill—expropriate some of the power that Congress has wrested from the unitary Executive.

*Id.* at 1815–17 (majority opinion) (internal citations omitted).

Which view do you find more persuasive?

# CHAPTER FIVE

# STATUTORY INTERPRETATION IN THE ADMINISTRATIVE STATE

## CONTENTS

## I.  Judicial Review of Agency Statutory Interpretation

The last section of Chapter Four (pp. 717–790, *supra*) focused on judicial review of agency action under the "arbitrary and capricious" standard laid out in § 706 of the APA. In this chapter, we focus on how courts review an agency's interpretation of the statute the agency is charged with administering. This issue is important because many crucial agency policy decisions rest on potentially contestable interpretations of the governing legislation. When, or under what conditions, should a reviewing court accept an agency's interpretation of the relevant statutory language even if the court would reach a different conclusion if deciding the question on its own? When, or under what conditions, should the reviewing court determine the meaning of the statute for itself, using tools and techniques like those covered in Chapters One and Two, without deference to the agency's contrary interpretation? These are difficult questions. On one hand, we typically think of the judiciary, rather than the executive, as having the authority to "say what the law is," Marbury v. Madison, 5 U.S. (1 Cranch) 137, 177 (1803), and judicial review is thought to be an important means for ensuring that agencies comply with congressional directives. On the other hand, many issues of statutory interpretation are linked, perhaps inextricably, with questions of fact and policy—questions that may be best resolved by expert agencies under the supervision of the elected branches of government, rather than by unelected generalist judges. This chapter deals with how courts have struggled to address this fundamental tension.

## A.  Early Cases

The most important Supreme Court case on judicial review of agency statutory interpretations is Chevron, U.S.A. v. Natural Resources Defense Council, 467 U.S. 837 (1984), which we will take up in Part C (pp. 814–835, *infra*). It is helpful, however, to begin with the pre–*Chevron* doctrine. The following case, *NLRB v. Hearst Publications*, was the leading case on judicial review of agency statutory interpretation prior to *Chevron*. Pay particular attention to the way *Hearst* attempted to distinguish those questions of statutory interpretation that courts ought to resolve de novo (that is, without deference to the agency's views) from those interpretive questions that courts ought to answer by deferring to the reasonable interpretation of the responsible administrative agency.

## National Labor Relations Board v. Hearst Publications

Supreme Court of the United States
322 U.S. 111 (1944)

■ Mr. Justice Rutledge delivered the opinion of the Court.

These cases arise from the refusal of respondents, publishers of four Los Angeles daily newspapers, to bargain collectively with a union representing newsboys who distribute their papers on the streets of that city. Respondents' contention that they were not required to bargain because the newsboys are not their "employees" within the meaning of that term in the National Labor Relations Act, 29 U.S.C. § 152,[1] presents the important question which we granted certiorari to resolve.

The proceedings before the National Labor Relations Board were begun with the filing of four petitions for investigation and certification by Los Angeles Newsboys Local Industrial Union No. 75. Hearings were held in a consolidated proceeding after which the Board made findings of fact and concluded that the regular full-time newsboys selling each paper were employees within the Act and that questions . . . concerning the representation of employees had arisen. It designated appropriate units and ordered elections. At these the union was selected as their representative by majorities of the eligible newsboys. After the union was appropriately certified, the respondents refused to bargain with it. Thereupon proceedings under Section 10, 29 U.S.C. § 160, were instituted, a hearing was held and respondents were found to have violated Section 8(1) and (5) of the Act, 29 U.S.C. § 158(1), (5). They were ordered to cease and desist from such violations and to bargain collectively with the union upon request.

Upon respondents' petitions for review and the Board's petitions for enforcement, the Circuit Court of Appeals, one judge dissenting, set aside the Board's orders. Rejecting the Board's analysis, the court independently examined the question whether the newsboys are employees within the Act, decided that the statute imports common-law standards to determine that question, and held the newsboys are not employees. . . .

The newsboys work under varying terms and conditions. They may be "bootjackers," selling to the general public at places other than established corners, or they may sell at fixed "spots." They may sell only casually or part-time, or full-time; and they may be employed regularly and continuously or only temporarily. The units which the Board determined to be appropriate are composed of those who sell full-time at established spots. Those vendors, misnamed boys, are generally mature men, dependent upon the proceeds of their sales for their sustenance, and frequently supporters of families. Working thus as news vendors on a regular basis often for a number of years, they form a stable group with relatively little turnover, in contrast to schoolboys and others who sell as bootjackers, temporary and casual distributors. . . .

---

1. Section 2(3) of the Act provides that "The term 'employee' shall include any employee, and shall not be limited to the employees of a particular employer, unless the Act explicitly states otherwise, and shall include any individual whose work has ceased as a consequence of, or in connection with, any current labor dispute or because of any unfair labor practice, and who has not obtained any other regular and substantially equivalent employment, but shall not include any individual employed as an agricultural laborer, or in the domestic service of any family or person at his home, or any individual employed by his parent or spouse."

The newsboys' compensation consists in the difference between the prices at which they sell the papers and the prices they pay for them. [Both of these prices are fixed by the publishers.] . . . In practice the newsboys receive their papers on credit. They pay for those sold either sometime during or after the close of their selling day, returning for credit all unsold papers. Lost or otherwise unreturned papers, however, must be paid for as though sold. Not only is the "profit" per paper thus effectively fixed by the publisher, but substantial control of the newsboys' total "take home" can be effected through the ability to designate their sales areas and the power to determine the number of papers allocated to each. . . .

. . . [R]espondents . . . urge that on the entire record the [newsboys] cannot be considered their employees. They base this conclusion on the argument that by common-law standards the extent of their control and direction of the newsboys' working activities creates no more than an "independent contractor" relationship and that common-law standards determine the "employee" relationship under the Act. . . .

## I.

The principal question is whether the newsboys are "employees." Because Congress did not explicitly define the term, respondents say its meaning must be determined by reference to common-law standards. In their view "common-law standards" are those the courts have applied in distinguishing between "employees" and "independent contractors" when working out various problems unrelated to the [National Labor Relations Act's] purposes and provisions.

The argument assumes that there is some simple, uniform and easily applicable test which the courts have used, in dealing with such problems, to determine whether persons doing work for others fall in one class or the other. Unfortunately this is not true. . . . Few problems in the law have given greater variety of application and conflict in results than the cases arising in the borderland between what is clearly an employer-employee relationship and what is clearly one of independent entrepreneurial dealing. This is true within the limited field of determining vicarious liability in tort. It becomes more so when the field is expanded to include all of the possible applications of the distinction.

It is hardly necessary to stress particular instances of these variations or to emphasize that they have arisen principally, first, in the struggle of the courts to work out common-law liabilities where the legislature has given no guides for judgment, more recently also under statutes which have posed the same problem for solution in the light of the enactment's particular terms and purposes. It is enough to point out that, with reference to an identical problem, results may be contrary over a very considerable region of doubt in applying the distinction, depending upon the state or jurisdiction where the determination is made; and that within a single jurisdiction a person who, for instance, is held to be an "independent contractor" for the purpose of imposing vicarious liability in tort may be an "employee" for the purposes of particular legislation, such as unemployment compensation.... In short, the assumed simplicity and uniformity, resulting from application of "common-law standards," does not exist.

Mere reference to these possible variations as characterizing the application of the [National Labor Relations Act] in the treatment of persons identically situated in the facts surrounding their employment and in the influences tending to disrupt it, would be enough to require pause before accepting a thesis which would introduce them into its administration. This would be true, even if the statute itself had indicated less clearly than it does the intent they should not apply.

Two possible consequences could follow. One would be to refer the decision of who are employees to local state law. The alternative would be to make it turn on a sort of pervading general essence distilled from state law. Congress obviously did not intend the former result. It would introduce variations into the statute's operation as wide as the differences the forty-eight states and other local jurisdictions make in applying the distinction for wholly different purposes....

Both the terms and the purposes of the statute, as well as the legislative history, show that Congress had in mind no such patchwork plan for securing freedom of employees' organization and of collective bargaining. The [National Labor Relations Act] is federal legislation, administered by a national agency, intended to solve a national problem on a national scale.... It is an Act, therefore, in reference to which it is not only proper, but necessary for us to assume, "in the absence of a plain indication to the contrary, that Congress ... is not making the application of the federal act dependent on state law." Jerome v. United States, 318 U.S. 101, 104.... Consequently, so far as the meaning of "employee" in this statute is concerned, "the federal law must prevail no matter what name is given to the interest or right by state law." Morgan v. Commissioner, 309 U.S. 78, 81....

## II.

Whether, given the intended national uniformity, the term "employee" includes such workers as these newsboys must be answered primarily from the history, terms and purposes of the legislation. The word "is not treated by Congress as a word of art having a definite meaning...." Rather "it takes color from its surroundings ... [in] the statute where it appears," United States v. American Trucking Associations, Inc., 310 U.S. 534, 545, and derives meaning from the context of that statute, which "must be read in the light of the mischief to be corrected and the end to be attained." South Chicago Coal & Dock Co. v. Bassett, 309 U.S. 251, 259....

It will not do, for deciding this question as one of uniform national application, to import wholesale the traditional common-law conceptions or some distilled essence of their local variations as exclusively controlling limitations upon the scope of the statute's effectiveness. To do this would be merely to select some of the local, hairline variations for nation-wide application and thus to reject others for coverage under the Act. That result hardly would be consistent with the statute's broad terms and purposes. . . .

The mischief at which the Act is aimed and the remedies it offers are not confined exclusively to "employees" within the traditional legal distinctions separating them from "independent contractors." Myriad forms of service relationship, with infinite and subtle variations in the terms of employment, blanket the nation's economy. Some are within this Act, others beyond its coverage. Large numbers will fall clearly on one side or on the other, by whatever test may be applied. But intermediate there will be many, the incidents of whose employment partake in part of the one group, in part of the other, in varying proportions of weight. And consequently the legal pendulum, for purposes of applying the statute, may swing one way or the other, depending upon the weight of this balance and its relation to the special purpose at hand.

Unless the common-law tests are to be imported and made exclusively controlling, without regard to the statute's purposes, it cannot be irrelevant that the particular workers in these cases are subject, as a matter of economic fact, to the evils the statute was designed to eradicate and that the remedies it affords are appropriate for preventing them or curing their harmful effects in the special situation. Interruption of commerce through strikes and unrest may stem as well from labor disputes between some who, for other purposes, are technically "independent contractors" and their employers as from disputes between persons who, for those purposes, are "employees" and their employers. . . . Inequality of bargaining power in controversies over wages, hours and working conditions may as well characterize the status of the one group as of the other. The former, when acting alone, may be as "helpless in dealing with an employer," as "dependent . . . on his daily wage" and as "unable to leave the employ and to resist arbitrary and unfair treatment" as the latter. For each, "union . . . [may be] essential to give . . . opportunity to deal on equality with their employer." And for each, collective bargaining may be appropriate and effective for the "friendly adjustment of industrial disputes arising out of differences as to wages, hours, or other working conditions." [29 U.S.C. § 151]. In short, when the particular situation of employment combines these characteristics, so that the economic facts of the relation make it more nearly one of employment than of independent business enterprise with respect to the ends sought to be accomplished by the legislation, those characteristics may outweigh technical legal classification for purposes unrelated to the statute's objectives and bring the relation within its protections.

To eliminate the causes of labor disputes and industrial strife, Congress thought it necessary to create a balance of forces in certain types of economic relationships. These do not embrace simply employment associations in which controversies could be limited to disputes over proper "physical conduct in the performance of the service."[27] On the contrary,

---

**27.** Control of "physical conduct in the performance of the service" is the traditional test of the "employee relationship" at common law. Cf., e.g., Restatement of the Law of Agency § 220(1).

Congress recognized those economic relationships cannot be fitted neatly into the containers designated "employee" and "employer" which an earlier law had shaped for different purposes. Its Reports on the bill disclose clearly the understanding that "employers and employees not in proximate relationship may be drawn into common controversies by economic forces," and that the very disputes sought to be avoided might involve "employees [who] are at times brought into an economic relationship with employers who are not their employers." In this light, the broad language of the Act's definitions, which in terms reject conventional limitations on such conceptions as "employee," "employer," and "labor dispute," leaves no doubt that its applicability is to be determined broadly, in doubtful situations, by underlying economic facts rather than technically and exclusively by previously established legal classifications. . . .

Hence "technical concepts pertinent to an employer's legal responsibility to third persons for the acts of his servants" have been rejected in various applications of this Act both here . . . and in other federal courts. . . . There is no good reason for invoking them to restrict the scope of the term "employee" sought to be done in this case. That term, like other provisions, must be understood with reference to the purpose of the Act and the facts involved in the economic relationship. . . .

It is not necessary in this case to make a completely definitive limitation around the term "employee." That task has been assigned primarily to the agency created by Congress to administer the Act. Determination of "where all the conditions of the relation require protection" involves inquiries for the Board charged with this duty. Everyday experience in the administration of the statute gives it familiarity with the circumstances and backgrounds of employment relationships in various industries, with the abilities and needs of the workers for self-organization and collective action, and with the adaptability of collective bargaining for the peaceful settlement of their disputes with their employers. The experience thus acquired must be brought frequently to bear on the question who is an employee under the Act. Resolving that question, like determining whether unfair labor practices have been committed, "belongs to the usual administrative routine" of the Board. Gray v. Powell, 314 U.S. 402, 411. . . .

In making that body's determinations as to the facts in these matters conclusive, if supported by evidence, Congress entrusted to it primarily the decision whether the evidence establishes the material facts. Hence in reviewing the Board's ultimate conclusions, it is not the court's function to substitute its own inferences of fact for the Board's, when the latter have support in the record. . . . Undoubtedly questions of statutory interpretation, especially when arising in the first instance in judicial proceedings, are for the courts to resolve, giving appropriate weight to the judgment of those whose special duty is to administer the questioned statute. . . . But where the question is one of specific application of a broad statutory term in a proceeding in which the agency administering the statute must determine it initially, the reviewing court's function is limited. Like the commissioner's determination under the Longshoremen's & Harbor Workers' Act, that a man is not a "member of a crew" (South Chicago Coal & Dock Co. v. Bassett, 309 U.S. 251) or that he was injured "in the course of his employment" (Parker v. Motor Boat Sales, Inc., 314 U.S. 244) and the Federal Communications Commission's determination that one company is under the "control" of another (Rochester Telephone Corp. v. United States, 307 U.S. 125), the Board's determination that specified persons are "employees" under this Act is to be accepted if it has "warrant in the record" and a reasonable basis in law.

In this case the Board found that the designated newsboys work continuously and regularly, rely upon their earnings for the support of themselves and their families, and have their total wages influenced in large measure by the publishers who dictate their buying and selling prices, fix their markets and control their supply of papers. Their hours of work and their efforts on the job are supervised and to some extent prescribed by the publishers or their agents. Much of their sales equipment and advertising materials is furnished by the publishers with the intention that it be used for the publisher's benefit. Stating that "the primary consideration in the determination of the applicability of the statutory definition is whether effectuation of the declared policy and purposes of the Act comprehend securing to the individual the rights guaranteed and protection afforded by the Act," the Board concluded that the newsboys are employees. The record sustains the Board's findings and there is ample basis in the law for its conclusion. . . .

■ [Justice Reed's separate concurrence is omitted.]

■ Mr. Justice Roberts.

. . . I think it plain that newsboys are not "employees" of the respondents within the meaning and intent of the National Labor Relations Act. When Congress, in § 2(3), [29 U.S.C. § 152(3)], said: "The term 'employee' shall include any employee, . . ." it stated as clearly as language could do it that the provisions of the Act were to extend to those who, as a result of decades of tradition which had become part of the common understanding of our people, bear the named relationship. Clearly also Congress did not delegate to the National Labor Relations Board the function of defining the relationship of employment so as to promote what the Board understood to be the underlying purpose of the statute. The question who is an employee, so as to make the statute applicable to him, is a question of the meaning of the Act and, therefore, is a judicial and not an administrative question. . . .

---

1. *"Pure" Questions of Law vs. "Mixed" Questions of Law and Fact*—The key to understanding the doctrinal importance of *Hearst* is to observe that although the ultimate legal question is whether these "newsboys"—who were, in fact, more likely adult newsvendors—were "employees" within the meaning of the National Labor Relations Act (NLRA), Justice Rutledge's opinion carefully divided this question into two distinct sub-questions. The first is whether the term "employee" as used in the relevant sections of the NLRA incorporated the pre-existing common law

definition of "employee" (as distinct from "independent contractor") that would have been applied, for example, in a tort suit. (It is usually the case that firms are liable for torts committed by their employees, but not for torts committed by independent contractors.) If the answer to this question is "Yes," then the NLRA does not cover the newsvendors, because they would likely count as "independent contractors" under the common law. If the answer to this first question is "No"—that is, if the NLRA did *not* incorporate the common law definition of "employee"—one must proceed to the second question: Do these newsvendors count as "employees" within the meaning of that term *as used in the NLRA*?

On the first question—whether the NLRA incorporated the common law definition of "employee"—the Court concluded that the answer was no. The Court reached this conclusion by applying many of the tools of statutory interpretation that are covered in Chapters One and Two, including consideration of the context in which the word "employee" is used, the purpose of the NLRA, and the legislative history. In this section of the opinion, the Court said virtually nothing about the NLRB's construction of the Act, despite the fact that the NLRB also concluded that the Act did not incorporate the common law definition of "employee." Although the Court ultimately agreed with the NLRB on this point, the Court apparently reached this result after its own independent analysis of the legal issues.

On the second question—whether the term "employee" in the NLRA specifically encompasses the newsvendors at issue—the Court's approach was markedly different. Once the Court concluded that "employee" in the NLRA did *not* have the same meaning that it has at common law, one might think the next logical step would be to decide exactly what the word "employee" *does* mean in the NLRA. But the Court expressly eschewed any attempt at a precise definition. Why is this? The Court explained that the duty to determine whether a *particular* group of individuals should be treated as "employees" under the NLRA "has been assigned primarily to the agency created by Congress to administer the Act [i.e., the NLRB]," rather than to the judiciary. The Court elaborated that "where the question is one of specific application of a broad statutory term in a proceeding in which the agency administering the statute must determine it initially, the reviewing court's function is limited.... The Board's determination that specified persons are 'employees' under this Act is to be accepted if it has 'warrant in the record' and a reasonable basis in law."

Thus in *Hearst*, the degree to which the Court defers to the agency's judgment on a question of statutory construction appears to turn on the degree to which the resolution of that interpretive question (that is, the "question of law") is bound up with the resolution of contested "questions of fact" (for example, the details of the publisher-newsvendor relationship, the parties' relative bargaining power, and more generally whether extending NLRA coverage to newsvendors would facilitate the peaceful settlement of labor disputes). While a court may have to resolve for itself so-called "pure" questions of law—such as whether the NLRA incorporated the common law definition of employee—on "mixed questions of law and fact"—such as whether application of the NLRA to newsvendors would advance or undermine the goals of the Act—courts should defer to the agency's conclusion, so long as that conclusion has both sufficient evidentiary support in the record and a *"reasonable basis in law"* (emphasis added).

How well does *Hearst's* doctrinal distinction—de novo review for pure questions of law, deferential review for mixed questions of law and fact—resolve the tension between the interest in judicial resolution of legal questions and the interest in administrative resolution of factual and policy questions? Was the Court suggesting that Congress delegated the authority to interpret mixed questions to the NLRB? That the NLRB has greater expertise and merits deference for pragmatic reasons?

   **2.  *The Separability of Legal and Factual Questions*—**The *Hearst* approach to judicial review of agency statutory interpretations turns on the ability of courts to distinguish "pure" questions of law from "mixed" questions of law and fact. The Court's emphasis on this distinction drew divergent reactions from important administrative law scholars in the period during which *Hearst* supplied the governing standard of review. Professor Louis Jaffe argued that courts could appropriately differentiate conclusions of law from findings of fact through what some have termed the "analytical approach":

> A *finding of fact is the assertion that a phenomenon has happened or is or will be happening independent of or anterior to any assertion as to its legal effect.* It can, for example, be made by a person who is ignorant of the applicable law. Thus, a statute may provide compensation for injuries arising out of and during the course of employment. It has been found that an employee while at work has been intentionally hit on the head by a fellow employee. This is a finding of fact. It owes nothing to the compensation statute. If, however, it is asserted that the injury arose out of the employment and is therefore compensable, the assertion is something more than a finding of fact; it is, in our view, a conclusion of law. The assertion cannot be derived by one who is ignorant of the applicable statutes. It is, unless it is a purely arbitrary exercise of power, an assertion that the purpose of the statute will be served by awarding compensation.

LOUIS L. JAFFE, JUDICIAL CONTROL OF ADMINISTRATIVE ACTION 548 (1965).

   In contrast, Professor Kenneth Culp Davis, another leading administrative law scholar, advanced what he called the "practical approach," which holds that courts should—and, in practice, do—differentiate questions of "law" from those of "fact" based on policy considerations relating to the appropriate allocation of power between courts and agencies. *See* 4 KENNETH CULP DAVIS, ADMINISTRATIVE LAW TREATISE § 30.01 *et seq.* (1958). In his view, because any finding of fact is inevitably measured against some legal baseline, the "conceptual" line between questions of law and questions of fact is too thin to do meaningful work. "Every determination which refines the meaning of a legal concept," he wrote, "is to that extent analytically a determination of law, even though the facts to which the concept is applied are unique and may never occur again." *Id.* § 30.02, at 195. Accordingly, Professor Davis believed that "[i]n the context of juridical review of administrative action the term 'question of fact' means an administrative question on which a reviewing court should not substitute judgment and the term 'question of law' means a question on which the reviewing court may properly substitute judgment." *Id.* § 30.02, at 193. Who has the better of the argument? Do you agree with Professor Davis that it is impossible to distinguish legal and factual questions independently of, and prior to, deciding whether the question is one where judicial deference is appropriate?

Consider an alternative objection to the *Hearst* framework, which Justice Roberts' dissent nicely summarized: it *is* possible to distinguish legal and factual questions, and for that reason, even in cases that present so-called "mixed questions," the court should have sole responsibility to resolve the *legal aspects* of those questions. So, even if we conclude that the word "employee" in the NLRA has whatever meaning would best advance the purposes of that Act, it is up to the Court, not the NLRB, to decide what those "purposes" are, using the best available evidence of congressional intent. Isn't Justice Roberts correct that the Court could defer to the Board's *factual* conclusions—for example, what and how the newsvendors are paid, the degree to which they are subject to the direction and control of the publishing companies, and so forth—while still deciding for itself, on the basis of those factual conclusions, whether extending NLRA coverage to newsvendors is consistent with the overall structure and purposes of the Act? Then again, the resolution of some mixed questions, such as whether collective bargaining by the newsvendors will lead to more or less labor strife—would seem to turn almost entirely on the resolution of the factual questions. If so, perhaps *Hearst* is correct to defer to the agency's judgment, rather than trying to disentangle the issues of fact and law. What do you think?

**3. *Hearst's Compatibility with the APA's Judicial Review Provisions*—***Hearst* was a pre–APA case, but the APA went into effect only two years later. The section of the APA dealing with judicial review of agency action, § 706, states: "To the extent necessary to decision and when presented, the reviewing court *shall decide all relevant questions of law [and] interpret constitutional and statutory provisions...*" (emphasis added). Furthermore, § 706(2)(C) requires reviewing courts to set aside any agency action that is "in excess of statutory jurisdiction, authority, or limitations, or short of statutory right." That sounds an awful lot like a de novo standard of review for statutory interpretation issues, doesn't it? *Hearst's* use of a de novo standard of review for pure questions of law would seem entirely consistent with the above-quoted language from § 706. But what about *Hearst's* instruction that, for mixed questions of law and fact, a court should accept the agency's views as long as they are reasonable? Can we reconcile that aspect of *Hearst* with the APA?

On one view, *Hearst* is compatible with the APA's judicial review provisions because in a mixed law-fact case the factual and legal questions cannot be disentangled, and the correct resolution of the legal question depends on a prior resolution of the factual questions. For those factual questions, the APA itself adopts a deferential standard for judicial review, imposing only the general requirement that the agency's findings not be "arbitrary [or] capricious," § 706(2)(A), or, in cases decided in a formal hearing process, the requirement that the agency's findings be supported "by substantial evidence," § 706(2)(E). A contrary view, however, echoes Justice Roberts' dissent by maintaining that although the court should defer to the agency's *factual* findings, under the APA the reviewing court must decide for itself whether those facts would support the agency's legal conclusion. Does the resolution of concerns about *Hearst's* consistency with the APA depend on whether Professor Jaffe was correct that there is a discernible conceptual line between questions of law and questions of fact?

For better or worse, the enactment of the APA did not seem to have any noticeable impact on how courts reviewed agency interpretations of statutes. Indeed, courts discussing the relevant standard of review after the enactment of the APA would often cite only to prior case law (including pre–APA decisions like *Hearst*) without bothering even to mention § 706. Perhaps this is because courts thought that the *Hearst* framework was so clearly compatible with the APA that there was no need to address the issue.

\* \* \* \*

*Hearst* was enormously influential. That said, it became clear almost immediately after *Hearst* was decided that the sharp categorical distinction between pure and mixed questions was difficult to sustain and to apply consistently. The following case, *Packard Motor Car Co. v. NLRB*, decided only three years after *Hearst*, illustrates this point. As you read the case, pay particular attention to whether the *Packard* Court treats the interpretive question at issue—which, as in *Hearst*, involved whether certain individuals are "employees" under the NLRA—as a pure question of law or as a mixed question of law and fact, and how this classification affects the degree to which the Court defers to the NLRB's resolution of this question.

## Packard Motor Car Co. v. National Labor Relations Board

Supreme Court of the United States
330 U.S. 485 (1947)

■ MR. JUSTICE JACKSON delivered the opinion of the Court.

The question presented by this case is whether foremen are entitled as a class to the rights of self-organization, collective bargaining, and other concerted activities as assured to employees generally by the National Labor Relations Act. [29 U.S.C.A. § 151 *et seq.*] The case grows out of conditions of the automotive industry, and so far as they are important to the legal issues here the facts are simple.

The Packard Motor Car Company employs about 32,000 rank-and-file workmen. Since 1937 they have been represented by the United Automobile Workers of America affiliated with the Congress of Industrial Organizations. These employees are supervised by approximately 1,100 employees of foremen rank. . . .

The function of these foremen in general is typical of the duties of foremen in mass production industry generally. Foremen carry the responsibility for maintaining quantity and quality of production, subject, of course, to the overall control and supervision of the management. . . .

The foremen as a group are highly paid and, unlike the workmen, are paid for justifiable absence and for holidays, are not docked in pay when tardy, receive longer paid vacations, and are given severance pay upon release by the Company.

These foremen determined to organize as a unit of the Foremen's Association of America, an unaffiliated organization which represents supervisory employees exclusively. Following the usual procedure, after the Board had decided that "all general foremen, foremen, assistant foremen, and special assignment men employed by the Company at its plants in Detroit, Michigan, constitute a unit appropriate for the purposes of collective bargaining within the meaning of section 9(b) of the Act," the Foremen's Association was certified as the bargaining representative. The Company asserted that foremen were not "employees" entitled to the advantages of the Labor Act, and refused to bargain with the union. After hearing on charge of unfair labor practice, the Board issued the usual cease and desist order. The Company resisted and challenged validity of the order. The judgment of the court below decreed its enforcement, and we granted certiorari.

The issue of law as to the power of the National Labor Relations Board under the National Labor Relations Act is simple and our only function is to determine whether the order of the Board is authorized by the statute.

The privileges and benefits of the Act are conferred upon employees, and § 2(3) of the Act, so far as relevant, provides "The term 'employee' shall include any employee. . . ." 49 Stat. 450. The point that these foremen are employees both in the most technical sense at common law as well as in common acceptance of the term, is too obvious to be labored. The Company, however, turns to the Act's definition of employer, which it contends reads foremen out of the employee class and into the class of employers. Section 2(2) reads: "The term 'employer' includes any person acting in the interest of an employer, directly or indirectly. . . ." 49 Stat. 450. The context of the Act, we think, leaves no room for a construction of this section to deny the organizational privilege to employees because they act in the interest of an employer. Every employee, from the very fact of employment in the master's business, is required to act in his interest. . . .

The purpose of § 2(2) seems obviously to render employers responsible in labor practices for acts of any persons performed in their interests. It is an adaptation of the ancient maxim of the common law, *respondeat superior*, by which a principal is made liable for the tortious acts of his agent and the master for the wrongful acts of his servants.... [Congress] provided that in administering this act the employer ... should be not merely the individual or corporation which was the employing entity, but also others, whether employee or not, who are "acting in the interest of an employer."

Even those who act for the employer in some matters, including the service of standing between management and manual labor, still have interests of their own as employees. Though the foreman is the faithful representative of the employer in maintaining a production schedule, his interest properly may be adverse to that of the employer when it comes to fixing his own wages, hours, seniority rights or working conditions. He does not lose his right to serve himself in these respects because he serves his master in others. And we see no basis in this Act whatever for holding that foremen are forbidden the protection of the Act when they take collective action to protect their collective interests.

The company's argument is really addressed to the undesirability of permitting foremen to organize.... But the effect of the National Labor Relations Act is otherwise, and it is for Congress, not for us, to create exceptions or qualifications at odds with its plain terms....

... Our power of review also is circumscribed by the provision that findings of the Board as to the facts, if supported by evidence, shall be conclusive. § 10(e), 49 Stat. 454. So we have power only to determine whether there is substantial evidence to support the Board, or its order oversteps the law....

There is clearly substantial evidence in support of the determination that foremen are an appropriate [collective bargaining unit].... Hence the order insofar as it depends on facts is beyond our power of review. The issue as to what unit is appropriate for bargaining is one for which no absolute rule of law is laid down by statute, and none should be by decision. It involves of necessity a large measure of informed discretion and the decision of the Board, if not final, is rarely to be disturbed. While we do not say that a determination of a unit of representation cannot be so unreasonable and arbitrary as to exceed the Board's power, we are clear that the decision in question does not do so. That settled, our power is at an end.

We are invited to make a lengthy examination of views expressed in Congress while this and later legislation was pending to show that exclusion of foremen was intended. There is, however, no ambiguity in this Act to be clarified by resort to legislative history, either of the Act itself or of subsequent legislative proposals which failed to become law.

Counsel also would persuade us to make a contrary interpretation by citing a long record of inaction, vacillation and division of the National Labor Relations Board in applying this Act to foremen. If we were obliged to depend upon administrative interpretation for light in finding the meaning of the statute, the inconsistency of the Board's decisions would leave us in the dark.[3] But there are difficult questions of policy involved in these cases which, together with changes in Board membership, account for the contradictory views that characterize their history in the Board.... We are not at liberty to be governed by those policy considerations in deciding the naked question of law whether the Board is now, in this case, acting within the terms of the statute.

It is also urged upon us most seriously that unionization of foremen is from many points bad industrial policy, that it puts the union foreman in the position of serving two masters, divides his loyalty and makes generally for bad relations between management and labor. However we might appraise the force of these arguments as a policy matter, we are not authorized to base decision of a question of law upon them. They concern the wisdom of the legislation; they cannot alter the meaning of otherwise plain provisions....

■ [JUSTICE DOUGLAS's dissent, joined by CHIEF JUSTICE VINSON and JUSTICE BURTON, and joined in part by JUSTICE FRANKFURTER, is omitted.]

---

*1.  The Tension between* **Hearst** *and* **Packard**—*Packard* is, in many respects, quite similar to *Hearst*, as both cases involve the scope of the term "employee" in the NLRA. In *Packard*, the automaker argued that its foremen were not "employees" within the meaning of the NLRA because, as supervisors, they act in the interests of the employer. The first question the NLRB (and, subsequently, the Court) had to resolve was whether this claim was correct. If so, the case would be over. If, however, foremen are "employees" within the meaning of the NLRA's collective bargaining provisions, the next question is whether this group of foremen can organize into an independent union and bargain collectively with the automaker. The *Packard* Court was quite clear that this second question is a mixed question of law and fact, and that the Court would uphold the Board's judgment so long as it was not "arbitrary" or "unreasonable." So far, everything in *Packard* appears consistent with *Hearst*.

But what about the first question, whether foremen count as "employees" within the meaning of the NLRA? On this question, the Court noted that the Board itself had been inconsistent, and that the Board's changing positions reflected the Board's changing views on "difficult questions of policy." The *Packard* Court, however, declared that it was "not at liberty to be governed by those policy considerations in deciding the *naked question of law* whether the Board is now, in this case, acting within the terms of the statute" (emphasis added). If the question whether the general term "employee" encompassed newsvendors was a mixed question of law and

---

**3.** The Board had held that supervisory employees may organize in an independent union ...; and in an affiliated union.... Then it held that there was no unit appropriate to the organization of supervisory employees.... In this case, ... the Board re-embraced its earlier conclusions with the same progressive boldness it had shown in the [earlier decisions]. In none of this series of cases did the Board hold that supervisors were not employees....

fact in *Hearst*, why was the question whether the general term "employee" covers foremen a "naked" question of law in *Packard*?

**2. *Possible Distinctions Between* Hearst *and* Packard**—If it seems implausible that the question whether foremen are "employees" is a pure question of law, while the question whether newsvendors are "employees" is a mixed question of law and fact, then perhaps we might look to other factors to explain *Hearst* and *Packard*'s different approaches to judicial review of the NLRB's decisions.

One possible distinction might be the NLRB's inconsistency in the treatment of foremen under the NLRA's collective bargaining provisions. In its initial rulings, issued in 1942, the Board had decided that foremen could unionize. In 1943, however, the Board issued a spate of orders that concluded, first, that the NLRA was ambiguous as to whether supervisory employees like foremen counted as employees, and second, that supervisory employees ought not to be allowed to unionize. Only three years later, in 1946, the Board again reversed itself. On the face of the opinion, *Packard* seemed unconcerned with the Board's inconsistency, but perhaps the Court was more troubled by this factor than it let on. Indeed, maybe this inconsistency was part of the reason that the Court decided to resolve this interpretive issue without deference to the Board. Should reviewing courts be less deferential when an agency's position, even on a mixed law-fact question, has been inconsistent?

One might also distinguish *Packard* and *Hearst* by noting that the social and economic significance of the question in *Packard* was arguably much greater. Allowing factory foremen to unionize would have enormous consequences, far more significant than those associated with unionization of newsvendors. Perhaps the Court concluded—implicitly or subconsciously—that it was more important to decide such an important issue on the basis of the Court's best reading of the statute, in order to be as faithful as possible to the intent or understanding of the enacting Congress. Should reviewing courts be less deferential to agency interpretations on questions of greater legal, social, or economic significance? Would a rational legislator more likely prefer agencies or courts to decide such questions?

\* \* \* \*

*Packard* suggested the possibility of some limitations on *Hearst* deference, and further suggested other factors that courts might consider when deciding how much deference is due an agency's interpretation even on a mixed law-fact question. A much more explicit and important limitation on the scope of *Hearst* deference appeared in another case, *Skidmore v. Swift & Co.*, decided only a few months after *Hearst*. When you read *Skidmore*, pay particular attention both to the reasons why the Court does not apply *Hearst* deference to what looks like a mixed law-fact question, and also to the alternative standard of review that *Skidmore* indicates is appropriate.

# Skidmore v. Swift & Co.

Supreme Court of the United States
323 U.S. 134 (1944)

■ Mr. Justice Jackson delivered the opinion of the Court.

Seven employees of the Swift and Company packing plant at Fort Worth, Texas, brought an action under the Fair Labor Standards Act, [29 U.S.C.A. § 201 *et seq.*], to recover overtime, liquidated damages, and attorneys' fees, totaling approximately $77,000. The District Court rendered judgment denying this claim wholly, and the Circuit Court of Appeals for the Fifth Circuit affirmed.

It is not denied that the daytime employment of these persons was working time within the Act. Two were engaged in general fire hall duties and maintenance of fire-fighting equipment of the Swift plant. The others operated elevators or acted as relief men in fire duties. They worked from 7:00 a.m. to 3:30 p.m., with a half-hour lunch period, five days a week. They were paid weekly salaries.

Under their oral agreement of employment, however, petitioners undertook to stay in the fire hall on the Company premises, or within hailing distance, three and a half to four nights a week. This involved no task except to answer alarms, either because of fire or because the sprinkler was set off for some other reason. No fires occurred during the period in issue, the alarms were rare, and the time required for their answer rarely exceeded an hour. For each alarm answered the employees were paid in addition to their fixed compensation an agreed amount, fifty cents at first, and later sixty-four cents. The Company provided a brick fire hall equipped with steam heat and air-conditioned rooms. It provided sleeping quarters, a pool table, a domino table, and a radio. The men used their time in sleep or amusement as they saw fit, except that they were required to stay in or close by the fire hall and be ready to respond to alarms. It is stipulated that "they agreed to remain in the fire hall and stay in it or within hailing distance, subject to call, in event of fire or other casualty, but were not required to perform any specific tasks during these periods of time, except in answering alarms." The trial court found the evidentiary facts as stipulated; it made no findings of fact as such as to whether under the arrangement of the parties and the circumstances of this case . . . the fire hall duty or any part thereof constituted working time. It said, however, as a "conclusion of law" that "the time plaintiffs spent in the fire hall subject to call to answer fire alarms does not constitute hours worked, for which overtime compensation is due them under the Fair Labor Standards Act, as interpreted by the Administrator and the Courts," and in its opinion observed, "of course we know pursuing such pleasurable occupations or performing such personal chores does not constitute work." The Circuit Court of Appeals affirmed.

. . . [W]e hold that no principle of law found either in the statute or in Court decisions precludes waiting time from also being working time. We have not attempted to, and we cannot, lay down a legal formula to resolve cases so varied in their facts as are the many situations in which employment involves waiting time. Whether in a concrete case such time falls within or without the Act is a question of fact to be resolved by appropriate findings of the trial court.... This involves scrutiny and construction of the agreements between the particular parties, appraisal of their practical construction of the working agreement by conduct, consideration of the nature of the service, and its relation to the waiting time, and all of the surrounding circumstances. Facts may show that the employee was engaged to wait, or they may show that he waited to be engaged. His compensation may cover both waiting and task, or only performance of the task itself. Living quarters may in some situations be furnished as a facility of the task and in another as a part of its compensation. The law does not impose an arrangement upon the parties. It imposes upon the courts the task of finding what the arrangement was.

We do not minimize the difficulty of such an inquiry where the arrangements of the parties have not contemplated the problem posed by the statute. But it does not differ in nature or in the standards to guide judgment from that which frequently confronts courts where they must find retrospectively the effect of contracts as to matters which the parties failed to anticipate or explicitly to provide for.

Congress did not utilize the services of an administrative agency to find facts and to determine in the first instance whether particular cases fall within or without the Act. Instead, it put this responsibility on the courts.... But it did create the office of Administrator, impose upon him a variety of duties, endow him with powers to inform himself of conditions in industries and employments subject to the Act, and put on him the duties of bringing injunction actions to restrain violations. Pursuit of his duties has accumulated a considerable experience in the problems of ascertaining working time in employments involving periods of inactivity and a knowledge of the customs prevailing in reference to their solution. From these he is obliged to reach conclusions as to conduct without the law, so that he should seek injunctions to stop it, and that within the law, so that he has no call to interfere. He has set forth his views of the application of the Act under different circumstances in an interpretative bulletin and in informal rulings. They provide a practical guide to employers and employees as to how the office representing the public interest in its enforcement will seek to apply it. Wage and Hour Division, Interpretative Bulletin No. 13.

The Administrator thinks the problems presented by inactive duty require a flexible solution, rather than the all-in or all-out rules respectively urged by the parties in this case, and his Bulletin endeavors to suggest standards and examples to guide in particular situations. In some occupations, it says, periods of inactivity are not properly counted as working time even though the employee is subject to call. Examples are an operator of a small telephone exchange where the switchboard is in her home and she ordinarily gets several hours of uninterrupted sleep each night; or a pumper of a stripper well or watchman of a lumber camp during the off season, who may be on duty twenty-four hours a day but ordinarily "has a normal night's sleep, has ample time in which to eat his meals, and has a certain amount of time for relaxation and entirely private pursuits." Exclusion of all such hours the Administrator thinks may be justified. In general, the answer depends "upon the degree to which the employee is free to engage in personal activities during periods of idleness when he is subject to call and the number of consecutive hours that the employee is subject to call without being required to perform active work." "Hours worked are not limited to the time spent in active labor but include time given by the employee to the employer. . . ."

The facts of this case do not fall within any of the specific examples given, but the conclusion of the Administrator, as expressed in the brief amicus curiae, is that the general tests which he has suggested point to the exclusion of sleeping and eating time of these employees from the work-week and the inclusion of all other on-call time: although the employees were required to remain on the premises during the entire time, the evidence shows that they were very rarely interrupted in their normal sleeping and eating time, and these are pursuits of a purely private nature which would presumably occupy the employees' time whether they were on duty or not and which apparently could be pursued adequately and comfortably in the required circumstances; the rest of the time is different because there is nothing in the record to suggest that, even though pleasurably spent, it was spent in the ways the men would have chosen had they been free to do so.

There is no statutory provision as to what, if any, deference courts should pay to the Administrator's conclusions. And, while we have given them notice, we have had no occasion to try to prescribe their influence. The rulings of this Administrator are not reached as a result of hearing adversary proceedings in which he finds facts from evidence and reaches conclusions of law from findings of fact. They are not, of course, conclusive, even in the cases with which they directly deal, much less in those to which they apply only by analogy. They do not constitute an interpretation of the Act or a standard for judging factual situations which binds a district court's processes, as an authoritative pronouncement of a higher court might do. But the Administrator's policies are made in pursuance of official duty, based upon more specialized experience and broader investigations and information than is likely to come to a judge in a particular case. They do determine the policy which will guide applications for enforcement by injunction on behalf of the Government. Good administration of the Act and good judicial administration alike require that the standards of public enforcement and those for determining private rights shall be at variance only where justified by very good reasons. The fact that the Administrator's policies and standards are not reached by trial in adversary form does not mean that they are not entitled to respect. This Court has long given considerable and in some cases decisive weight to Treasury Decisions and to interpretative regulations of the Treasury and of other bodies that were not of adversary origin.

We consider that the rulings, interpretations and opinions of the Administrator under this Act, while not controlling upon the courts by reason of their authority, do constitute a body of experience and informed judgment to which courts and litigants may properly resort for guidance. The weight of such a judgment in a particular case will depend upon the thoroughness evident in its consideration, the validity of its reasoning, its consistency with earlier and later pronouncements, and all those factors which give it power to persuade, if lacking power to control.

. . . Each case must stand on its own facts. But in this case, although the District Court referred to the Administrator's Bulletin, its evaluation and inquiry were apparently restricted by its notion that waiting time may not be work, an understanding of the law which we hold to be erroneous. Accordingly, the judgment is reversed and the cause remanded for further proceedings consistent herewith.

---

**1.  *The Distinction between* Hearst *and* Skidmore**—As in *Hearst* and *Packard*, the *Skidmore* Court treated the ultimate interpretative question as entailing both a pure question of law (Can waiting time *ever* count as working time under the FLSA?) and, if the answer to that question is "Yes," a logically subsequent mixed law-fact question (Does *this particular* waiting time count as working time under the FLSA, in light of the employees' obligations and constraints during this time, the alternate uses of their time, and so forth?). On the pure question of law, the trial court and appellate court concluded that waiting time could never qualify as working time under the FLSA. While the Supreme Court reversed on that point, it did so after de novo review of the legal question, without any deference to the agency. So far, so good: This seems exactly like the approach we saw in *Hearst*.

But what about the mixed question of law and fact? *Skidmore* could hardly have been clearer that these firefighters' entitlement to overtime pay presented a quintessential mixed fact-law question: "We . . . cannot lay down a legal formula to resolve cases so varied in their facts as are the many situations in which employment involves waiting time. Whether in a concrete case such time falls within or without the Act is a question of fact. . . ." In *Hearst*, the Court treated the views of the responsible administrative agency (there, the NLRB) as very important—indeed, practically determinative—on a mixed question of this sort. In *Skidmore*, the Court's approach seemed quite different: The Court did not say that the agency's view on the mixed question ought to be adopted so long as that view is reasonable.

The key distinctions between *Hearst* and *Skidmore* seem to be, first, the difference in the nature of the agencies' responsibilities under the relevant statutes, and second, the legal status of their interpretive statements. The NLRA had empowered the NLRB to adjudicate disputes relating to unionization and collective bargaining, and in *Hearst* the NLRA had announced its views on how the NLRA applied to newsvendors in a binding order following a formal public hearing. In contrast, under the FLSA, the

Wages and Hours Administrator (a Labor Department official) has a variety of duties relating to the administration and enforcement of the FLSA, but the Administrator does not have the authority to conduct hearings and issue formal administrative orders finding violations of the Act's terms. Thus the Administrator did not and could not announce his views on the meaning of the FLSA in a binding administrative order, but rather did so in a non-binding interpretive bulletin and in an amicus brief. Justice Jackson's opinion suggested that these differences in the statutory authority of the agencies, the legal force of their interpretive pronouncements, and the formality of the process leading up to the interpretive decision together explain why strong *Hearst*-style deference is inappropriate in a case like *Skidmore*. Does that approach make sense? Why should judicial deference to the agency's view on a mixed fact-law question turn on the legal form in which the agency makes its view known?

**2. The Nature of Skidmore "Respect"**—Although *Skidmore* did not apply the deferential *Hearst* standard, the opinion *did not* say that a reviewing court should simply ignore the agency's opinion. Rather, in light of the agency's "specialized expertise" and "experience," the reviewing court should give the agency's interpretive opinions "respect." What is the difference between *Hearst*-style deference and *Skidmore*-style respect? Most straightforwardly, it would seem that *Hearst* is a more deferential standard than *Skidmore*: It is at least conceptually possible to imagine a court concluding that an agency interpretation is likely wrong (even giving the agency's view its due respect), but that the interpretation is nonetheless reasonable. Presumably in such a case a reviewing court should uphold the interpretation under *Hearst* but reject it under *Skidmore*.

Another possible difference is that *Hearst* seemed to endorse a categorical rule of deference to any reasonable agency resolution of a mixed question, while *Skidmore* endorsed more of a "sliding scale" approach. Indeed, in perhaps the most important and frequently-quoted passage from *Skidmore*, Justice Jackson explained that the weight a reviewing court should give to an agency's interpretation in a case governed by the *Skidmore* standard depends "upon the thoroughness evident in [the agency's] consideration, the validity of its reasoning, its consistency with earlier and later pronouncements, and all those factors which give it power to persuade, if lacking power to control." That sounds eminently reasonable. But if that's what *Skidmore* means—that non-binding agency interpretive opinions should influence courts to the extent that those opinions are thorough, well-reasoned, and persuasive—then does *Skidmore* "respect" have any special significance? Shouldn't a court take seriously *any* opinion on a legal question—whether in an agency bulletin, a litigant brief, a law review article, or anything else—that is thorough, well-reasoned, and persuasive? Does *Skidmore* "respect" amount to anything more than the truism that courts should uphold an agency's view if the court is persuaded that the agency's view is correct?

Some take this position, but others argue that *Skidmore* clearly indicates that courts should treat an *agency's* opinion on an interpretive question—even if informal and non-binding—as entitled to more respect than an ordinary litigant's brief. *See* Kristin E. Hickman & Matthew D. Krueger, *In Search of the Modern* Skidmore *Standard*, 107 Colum. L. Rev. 1235, 1251–59 (2007) (surveying competing understandings of *Skidmore*). The idea seems to be that although the *degree* of judicial respect for an agency's opinion depends on the thoroughness and persuasiveness of the agency's argument, the court should also be mindful of the special position and expertise of the agency. One might draw an analogy between the agency and a uniquely well-qualified expert witness, or perhaps one might think of *Skidmore* respect as similar to how the courts of appeals treat "persuasive" authority from other circuits: non-binding, and not to be followed if poorly reasoned or otherwise unpersuasive, but more significant than a litigant's brief by virtue of peer circuits' special status.

## B.  Evolution of the Doctrine, 1944–1984

The 1944 Supreme Court decisions in *Hearst* and *Skidmore*, taken together, appeared to establish the following framework for deciding how much weight to put on an administrative agency's interpretation of a statutory provision: *First*, for pure questions of law, the reviewing court should resolve the issue de novo, without any special deference to the agency's views. *Second*, for mixed questions of law and fact, if the agency announces its view in an authoritative, legally binding rule or order following some kind of formal process, then the reviewing court should defer to the agency, upholding its determination so long as it is reasonable. *Third*, if an agency announces its view of a mixed fact-law question in an informal and non-binding statement (e.g., an opinion letter, guidance document, interpretive rule, or litigation brief), then the court is not obligated to defer to the agency's interpretation, but at the same time the court should treat the agency's view with special respect in light of the agency's unique expertise and experience (though the degree of respect depends on the thoroughness and persuasiveness of the agency's reasoning). This doctrinal framework is not exactly simple—among other things, it requires a conceptually tricky distinction between pure and mixed questions (*see* pp. 800–801, *supra*), and in those cases where *Skidmore* supplies the governing standard the court must consider a variety of contextual factors. While not simple, however, the doctrinal framework at least purported to supply a reasonably discernible formula.

Almost immediately, however, the categorical distinctions implied by the above framework began to erode. We have already seen one early example: *Packard*, while arguably consistent with *Hearst* and *Skidmore* as a formal matter, indicated a possible concern with factors that did not fit comfortably into the scheme just described. In the four decades following *Hearst* and *Skidmore*, the doctrine developed into a more standard-like multi-factor approach, rather than a more rule-like categorical approach. During this period, the factors that courts would consider when deciding how much weight to give to an agency's interpretive views included some of the factors we have already seen in cases like *Hearst*, *Packard*, and *Skidmore*. For example, in keeping with *Skidmore*, courts called for greater deference to agencies that had broad policymaking or adjudicative power, and to agency interpretations issued in legislative rules or binding orders rather than interpretive rules or guidance documents. *See, e.g.,* Batterton v. Francis, 432 U.S. 416, 424–426 & nn.8–9 (1977); Pittston Stevedoring Corp. v. Dellaventura, 544 F.2d 35, 49–50 (2d Cir. 1976), *aff'd sub nom*, Northeast Marine Terminal Co. v. Caputo, 432 U.S. 249 (1977). Also, while the sharp distinction between pure and mixed questions became less significant in the years following *Hearst*, the Supreme Court continued to emphasize that a court need not defer to an agency's interpretation if the court could discern the "plain meaning" of the relevant statutory text using the standard tools of statutory construction. *See, e.g.,* NLRB v. Amax Coal Co., 453 U.S. 322, 329–330 (1981); FEC v. Democratic Senatorial Campaign Committee, 454 U.S. 27, 32 (1981). In addition, recall that both *Packard* and *Skidmore* suggested that the consistency of an agency's interpretation might bear on the appropriate level of deference. Later cases picked up on this consideration, suggesting that an agency's interpretation might be entitled to more deference if the agency's view has been longstanding and consistent. *See, e.g.,* Udall v. Tallman, 380 U.S. 1, 16 (1965); NLRB v. Bell Aerospace, 416 U.S. 267, 275, 289 (1974); Haig v. Agee, 453 U.S. 280, 293 (1981).

Courts looked to other factors as well. For instance, they sometimes emphasized that because agency technical expertise was one of the main justifications for judicial deference, courts should be more deferential on interpretive questions involving complex technical subject matter, *see, e.g.,* E.I. du Pont de Nemours & Co. v. Train, 430 U.S. 112, 134–35 & n.25 (1977); Aluminum Company of America v. Central Lincoln Peoples' Utility District, 467 U.S. 380, 390 (1984), or empirical predictions about the practical consequences of different interpretive choices, *see, e.g.,* NLRB v. Seven–Up Bottling Co., 344 U.S. 344, 348 (1953). Also, courts sometimes looked to indirect evidence that an agency's interpretation was consistent with congressional intent, such as whether the agency's interpretation was adopted contemporaneously with the statute's passage, *see, e.g.,* Norwegian Nitrogen Products Co. v. United States, 288 U.S. 294, 315 (1933); SEC v. Sloan, 436 U.S. 103, 126 (1978) (Brennan, J., concurring), or whether Congress implicitly acquiesced in the agency's interpretation by failing to modify the statute in response, *see, e.g.,* Zemel v. Rusk, 381 U.S. 1, 11 (1965); Red Lion Broadcasting Co. v. FCC, 395 U.S. 367, 381 (1969); NLRB v. Hendricks County Rural Electric Corp., 454 U.S. 170, 177 (1981). Occasionally courts also considered the legal or practical importance of the interpretive question as another factor bearing on the deference due to the agency's interpretation, although it was not entirely clear how this factor should or did affect the standard of review. *See* Stephen Breyer, *Judicial Review of Questions of Law and Policy,* 38 ADMIN. L. REV. 363, 370 (1986) (surveying the case law during this period and finding that courts were less deferential if the legal question was especially important, on the logic that "Congress is more likely to have focused upon, and answered, major questions, while leaving interstitial matters to answer themselves in the course of the statute's daily administration").

This multi-factor approach arguably captured the tenor of its time. Justice Breyer observed that courts applying this framework "looked to the practical features of the particular circumstance to decide whether it 'makes sense,' in terms of the need for fair and efficient administration of a statute in light of its substantive purpose, to imply a congressional intent that courts defer to the agency's interpretation." Breyer, *supra*, at 370. In other words, in light of the surrounding circumstances, judges were "to imagine what a hypothetically 'reasonable' legislator would have wanted (given the statute's objective) as an interpretive method." *Id.* That approach reflects the interpretive assumptions of the Legal Process school that supplied the prevalent interpretive methodology during much of the post–World War II period. *See* HENRY M. HART, JR. & ALBERT M. SACKS, THE LEGAL PROCESS (William N. Eskridge, Jr. & Philip P. Frickey eds., 1994) (1958). As discussed in Chapter One (*see* p. 45, *supra*), the Legal Process framework directed statutory interpreters to "assume unless the contrary unmistakably appears, that the legislature was made up of reasonable persons pursuing reasonable goals reasonably." *Id.* at 1378.

An important general objection to the Legal Process approach, however, is that it risks excessive unpredictability and judicial subjectivity. *Cf.* Philip P. Frickey, *From the Big Sleep to the Big Heat: The Revival of Theory in Statutory Interpretation*, 77 MINN. L. REV. 241, 251 (1992) (noting the possibility that "if I ask what 'reasonable people pursuing reasonable purposes reasonably' would have wanted in a given context, am I not likely to assume that those reasonable people are similar to the reasonable person I know best—myself—and, thus, would want what I think is the right answer?"). Many commentators thought that this concern was borne out in the specific context of judicial review of agency interpretations of law throughout the post–*Hearst* period. Leading scholarly commentators have characterized the pre–*Chevron* doctrine on this standard-of-review question as puzzling, ad hoc, incoherent, and unpredictable. *See* Thomas W. Merrill, *Judicial Deference to Executive Precedent*, 101 YALE L.J. 969, 974–75 (1992); Cass R. Sunstein, *Law and Administration after* Chevron, 90 COLUM. L. REV. 2071, 2082 (1990). Perhaps in response to this set of concerns—or perhaps inadvertently—in 1984 the Supreme Court dramatically altered the doctrinal framework in its *Chevron v. NRDC* decision. That decision, its consequences, and questions about its application will be our focus for the remainder of this chapter.

## C. THE MODERN APPROACH: *CHEVRON V. NRDC*

*Chevron v. NRDC* is one of the most important cases in administrative law. As you read the case, observe the ways in which the *Chevron* framework differs (as well as the ways in which it does *not* differ) from the multi-factor analysis described in the previous section. Also think about the respective roles of courts and agencies in determining statutory meaning under the *Chevron* framework. When must the reviewing court strike down an agency interpretation of a statute, and when must the court uphold an agency interpretation that differs from the interpretation the court would favor? Finally, pay close attention to the *Chevron* opinion's *justifications* (both theoretical and pragmatic) for its preferred approach.

---

# Chevron, U.S.A., Inc., v. Natural Resources Defense Council, Inc.

Supreme Court of the United States
467 U.S. 837 (1984)

■ JUSTICE STEVENS delivered the opinion of the Court.

In the Clean Air Act Amendments of 1977, Congress enacted certain requirements applicable to States that had not achieved the national air quality standards established by the Environmental Protection Agency (EPA) pursuant to earlier legislation. The amended Clean Air Act required these "nonattainment" States to establish a permit program regulating "new or modified major stationary sources" of air pollution. Generally, a permit may not be issued for a new or modified major stationary source unless several stringent conditions are met. The EPA regulation promulgated to implement this permit requirement allows a State to adopt a plantwide definition of the term "stationary source."[2] Under this definition, an existing plant that contains several pollution-emitting devices may install or modify one piece of equipment without meeting the permit conditions if the alteration will not increase the total emissions from the plant. The question presented by these cases is whether EPA's decision to allow States to treat all of the pollution-emitting devices within the same industrial grouping as though they were encased within a single "bubble" is based on a reasonable construction of the statutory term "stationary source."

I

The EPA regulations containing the plantwide definition of the term stationary source were promulgated on October 14, 1981. Respondents filed a timely petition for review in the United States Court of Appeals for the District of Columbia Circuit....

The Court of Appeals set aside the regulations.

The court observed that the relevant part of the amended Clean Air Act "does not explicitly define what Congress envisioned as a 'stationary source,['] to which the permit program ... should apply," and further

---

**2.** [The EPA defined "stationary source" as follows:]

"(i) 'Stationary source' means any building, structure, facility, or installation which emits or may emit any air pollutant subject to regulation under the Act.

"(ii) 'Building, structure, facility, or installation' means all of the pollutant-emitting activities which belong to the same industrial grouping, are located on one or more contiguous or adjacent properties, and are under the control of the same person (or persons under common control) except the activities of any vessel." 40 CFR §§ 51.18(j)(1)(i) and (ii) (1983).

stated that the precise issue was not "squarely addressed in the legislative history." 685 F.2d, at 723. In light of its conclusion that the legislative history bearing on the question was "at best contradictory," it reasoned that "the purposes of the nonattainment program should guide our decision here." 685 F.2d, at 726, n. 39.... [T]he court stated that the bubble concept ... was "inappropriate" in programs enacted to improve air quality. 685 F.2d, at 726. Since the purpose of the permit program—its "raison d'être," in the court's view—was to improve air quality, the court held that the bubble concept was inapplicable in these cases.... It therefore set aside the regulations embodying the bubble concept as contrary to law....

The basic legal error of the Court of Appeals was to adopt a static judicial definition of the term "stationary source" when it had decided that Congress itself had not commanded that definition....

## II.

When a court reviews an agency's construction of the statute which it administers, it is confronted with two questions. First, always, is the question whether Congress has directly spoken to the precise question at issue. If the intent of Congress is clear, that is the end of the matter; for the court, as well as the agency, must give effect to the unambiguously expressed intent of Congress.[9] If, however, the court determines Congress has not directly addressed the precise question at issue, the court does not simply impose its own construction on the statute, as would be necessary in the absence of an administrative interpretation. Rather, if the statute is silent or ambiguous with respect to the specific issue, the question for the court is whether the agency's answer is based on a permissible construction of the statute.[11]

"The power of an administrative agency to administer a congressionally created ... program necessarily requires the formulation of policy and the making of rules to fill any gap left, implicitly or explicitly, by Congress." Morton v. Ruiz, 415 U.S. 199, 231 (1974). If Congress has explicitly left a gap for the agency to fill, there is an express delegation of authority to the agency to elucidate a specific provision of the statute by regulation. Such legislative regulations are given controlling weight unless they are arbitrary, capricious, or manifestly contrary to the statute. Sometimes the legislative delegation to an agency on a particular question is implicit rather than explicit. In such a case, a court may not substitute its own construction of a statutory provision for a reasonable interpretation made by the administrator of an agency.

---

**9.** The judiciary is the final authority on issues of statutory construction and must reject administrative constructions which are contrary to clear congressional intent.... If a court, employing traditional tools of statutory construction, ascertains that Congress had an intention on the precise question at issue, that intention is the law and must be given effect.

**11.** The court need not conclude that the agency construction was the only one it permissibly could have adopted to uphold the construction, or even the reading the court would have reached if the question initially had arisen in a judicial proceeding.

We have long recognized that considerable weight should be accorded to an executive department's construction of a statutory scheme it is entrusted to administer, and the principle of deference to administrative interpretations

> "has been consistently followed by this Court whenever decision as to the meaning or reach of a statute has involved reconciling conflicting policies, and a full understanding of the force of the statutory policy in the given situation has depended upon more than ordinary knowledge respecting the matters subjected to agency regulations.... If this choice represents a reasonable accommodation of conflicting policies that were committed to the agency's care by the statute, we should not disturb it unless it appears from the statute or its legislative history that the accommodation is not one that Congress would have sanctioned."

United States v. Shimer, 367 U.S. 374, 382, 383 (1961).

In light of these well-settled principles it is clear that the Court of Appeals misconceived the nature of its role in reviewing the regulations at issue. Once it determined, after its own examination of the legislation, that Congress did not actually have an intent regarding the applicability of the bubble concept to the permit program, the question before it was not whether in its view the concept is "inappropriate" in the general context of a program designed to improve air quality, but whether the Administrator's view that it is appropriate in the context of this particular program is a reasonable one. Based on the examination of the legislation and its history which follows, we agree with the Court of Appeals that Congress did not have a specific intention on the applicability of the bubble concept in these cases, and conclude that the EPA's use of that concept here is a reasonable policy choice for the agency to make....

V

The legislative history of the portion of the 1977 Amendments dealing with nonattainment areas does not contain any specific comment on the "bubble concept" or the question whether a plantwide definition of a stationary source is permissible under the permit program. It does, however, plainly disclose that in the permit program Congress sought to accommodate the conflict between the economic interest in permitting capital improvements to continue and the environmental interest in improving air quality. Indeed, the House Committee Report identified the economic interest as one of the "two main purposes" of this section of the bill. It stated:

> "Section 117 of the bill, adopted during full committee markup establishes a new section 127 of the Clean Air Act. The section has two main purposes: (1) to allow reasonable economic growth to continue in an area while making reasonable further progress to assure attainment of the standards by a fixed date; and (2) to allow States greater flexibility for the former purpose than EPA's present interpretative regulations afford.

"The new provision allows States with nonattainment areas to pursue one of two options. First, the State may proceed under EPA's present 'tradeoff' or 'offset' ruling. The Administrator is authorized, moreover, to modify or amend that ruling in accordance with the intent and purposes of this section.

"The State's second option would be to revise its implementation plan in accordance with this new provision."

H.R.Rep. No. 95–294, p. 211 (1977).

The portion of the Senate Committee Report dealing with nonattainment areas states generally that it was intended to "supersede the EPA administrative approach," and that expansion should be permitted if a State could "demonstrate that these facilities can be accommodated within its overall plan to provide for attainment of air quality standards." S.Rep. No. 95–127, p. 55 (1977). The Senate Report notes the value of "case-by-case review of each new or modified major source of pollution that seeks to locate in a region exceeding an ambient standard," explaining that such a review "requires matching reductions from existing sources against emissions expected from the new source in order to assure that introduction of the new source will not prevent attainment of the applicable standard by the statutory deadline." *Ibid.* This description of a case-by-case approach to plant additions, which emphasizes the net consequences of the construction or modification of a new source, as well as its impact on the overall achievement of the national standards, was not, however, addressed to the precise issue raised by these cases. . . .

## VI

[Prior to 1981, the EPA had implemented a "point source" approach to determining whether something was a "stationary source." That is to say, each smokestack was considered a "stationary source," meaning that the addition of any new equipment to a plant would trigger the Act's strict requirements, even if the plant's overall emissions were reduced by the retirement of older, dirtier equipment.] In 1981 a new administration took office and initiated a "Government-wide reexamination of regulatory burdens and complexities." 46 Fed.Reg. 16281. In the context of that review, the EPA reevaluated the various arguments that had been advanced in connection with the proper definition of the term "source" and concluded that the term should be [defined in terms of a plantwide or "bubble" concept in nonattainment areas.]

In explaining its conclusion, the EPA first noted that the definitional issue was not squarely addressed in either the statute or its legislative history and therefore that the issue involved an agency "judgment as how to best carry out the Act." *Ibid.* It then set forth several reasons for concluding that the plantwide definition was more appropriate. It pointed out that the dual definition "can act as a disincentive to new investment and modernization by discouraging modifications to existing facilities" and "can actually retard progress in air pollution control by discouraging replacement of older, dirtier processes or pieces of equipment with new, cleaner ones." . . . [T]he agency [also] explained that additional require-ments that remained in place would accomplish the fundamental purposes of achieving attainment [of the national ambient air quality standards] as expeditiously as possible. These conclusions were set forth in a proposed rulemaking in August 1981 that was formally promulgated in October. . . .

## VII

. . .

### Statutory Language

. . . We are not persuaded that parsing of general terms in the text of the statute will reveal an actual intent of Congress. We know full well that this language is not dispositive; the terms are overlapping and the language is not precisely directed to the question of the applicability of a given term in the context of a larger operation. . . .

### Legislative History

In addition, respondents argue that the legislative history and policies of the Act foreclose the plantwide definition, and that the EPA's interpreta-tion is not entitled to deference because it represents a sharp break with prior interpretations of the Act.

Based on our examination of the legislative history, we agree with the Court of Appeals that it is unilluminating. The general remarks pointed to by respondents "were obviously not made with this narrow issue in mind and they cannot be said to demonstrate a Congressional desire. . . ." Jewell Ridge Coal Corp. v. Mine Workers, 325 U.S. 161, 168–169 (1945). . . . We find that the legislative history as a whole is silent on the precise issue before us. It is, however, consistent with the view that the EPA should have broad discretion in implementing the policies of the 1977 Amend-ments.

More importantly, that history plainly identifies the policy concerns that motivated the enactment; the plantwide definition is fully consistent with one of those concerns—the allowance of reasonable economic growth—and, whether or not we believe it most effectively implements the other, we must recognize that the EPA has advanced a reasonable explana-tion for its conclusion that the regulations serve the environmental objec-tives as well. Indeed, its reasoning is supported by the public record developed in the rulemaking process,[36] as well as by certain private stud-ies.[37]

---

**36.** See, for example, the statement of the New York State Department of Environmen-tal Conservation, pointing out that denying a source owner flexibility in selecting options made it "simpler and cheaper to operate old, more polluting sources than to trade up. . . ."

**37.** "Economists have proposed that economic incentives be substituted for the cumber-some administrative-legal framework. The objective is to make the profit and cost incentives that work so well in the marketplace work for pollution control. . . . [The 'bubble' or 'netting' concept] is a first attempt in this direction. By giving a plant manager flexibility to find the places and processes within a plant that control emissions most cheaply, pollution control can

Our review of the EPA's varying interpretations of the word "source"—both before and after the 1977 Amendments—convinces us that the agency primarily responsible for administering this important legislation has consistently interpreted it flexibly—not in a sterile textual vacuum, but in the context of implementing policy decisions in a technical and complex arena. The fact that the agency has from time to time changed its interpretation of the term "source" does not, as respondents argue, lead us to conclude that no deference should be accorded the agency's interpretation of the statute. An initial agency interpretation is not instantly carved in stone. On the contrary, the agency, to engage in informed rulemaking, must consider varying interpretations and the wisdom of its policy on a continuing basis. Moreover, the fact that the agency has adopted different definitions in different contexts adds force to the argument that the definition itself is flexible, particularly since Congress has never indicated any disapproval of a flexible reading of the statute. . . .

*Policy*

The arguments over policy that are advanced in the parties' briefs create the impression that respondents are now waging in a judicial forum a specific policy battle which they ultimately lost in the agency and in the 32 jurisdictions opting for the "bubble concept," but one which was never waged in the Congress. Such policy arguments are more properly addressed to legislators or administrators, not to judges.

In these cases, the Administrator's interpretation represents a reasonable accommodation of manifestly competing interests and is entitled to deference: the regulatory scheme is technical and complex, the agency considered the matter in a detailed and reasoned fashion, and the decision involves reconciling conflicting policies. Congress intended to accommodate both interests, but did not do so itself on the level of specificity presented by these cases. Perhaps that body consciously desired the Administrator to strike the balance at this level, thinking that those with great expertise and charged with responsibility for administering the provision would be in a better position to do so; perhaps it simply did not consider the question at this level; and perhaps Congress was unable to forge a coalition on either side of the question, and those on each side decided to take their chances with the scheme devised by the agency. For judicial purposes, it matters not which of these things occurred.

Judges are not experts in the field, and are not part of either political branch of the Government. Courts must, in some cases, reconcile competing political interests, but not on the basis of the judges' personal policy preferences. In contrast, an agency to which Congress has delegated policy-making responsibilities may, within the limits of that delegation, properly rely upon the incumbent administration's views of wise policy to inform its judgments. While agencies are not directly accountable to the people, the Chief Executive is, and it is entirely appropriate for this political branch of

---

be achieved more quickly and cheaply." L. Lave & G. Omenn, Cleaning Air: Reforming the Clean Air Act 28 (1981) (footnote omitted).

the Government to make such policy choices—resolving the competing interests which Congress itself either inadvertently did not resolve, or intentionally left to be resolved by the agency charged with the administration of the statute in light of everyday realities.

When a challenge to an agency construction of a statutory provision, fairly conceptualized, really centers on the wisdom of the agency's policy, rather than whether it is a reasonable choice within a gap left open by Congress, the challenge must fail. In such a case, federal judges—who have no constituency—have a duty to respect legitimate policy choices made by those who do. The responsibilities for assessing the wisdom of such policy choices and resolving the struggle between competing views of the public interest are not judicial ones: "Our Constitution vests such responsibilities in the political branches." TVA v. Hill, 437 U.S. 153, 195 (1978).

We hold that the EPA's definition of the term "source" is a permissible construction of the statute which seeks to accommodate progress in reducing air pollution with economic growth. . . .

■ JUSTICE MARSHALL and JUSTICE REHNQUIST took no part in the consideration or decision of these cases.

■ JUSTICE O'CONNOR took no part in the decision of these cases.

---

***1. The Structure of the* Chevron *Doctrine***—*Chevron* established a two-step test for courts to apply when deciding whether or not to uphold an agency's interpretation of a statute. At *Chevron* Step One, the reviewing court must ask "whether Congress has directly spoken to the precise question at issue." In making this determination, the reviewing court is supposed to "employ[] the traditional tools of statutory construction." If the reviewing court concludes that Congress had a clear intent on the precise question, then the court must give effect to that intent, regardless of the agency's position. If, however, the reviewing court concludes that the statute is "silent or ambiguous with respect to the specific issue," then the reviewing court should proceed to *Chevron* Step Two. At Step Two, the reviewing court should uphold the agency's resolution of the statutory ambiguity so long as the agency has adopted "a permissible construction of the statute"—that is, so long as the agency's interpretation is "reasonable."

How does *Chevron* differ from the pre–*Chevron* doctrine on judicial review of agency interpretations of law? Most obviously, *Chevron* appeared to jettison (without comment) the multi-factor inquiry that had developed in the preceding decades in favor of an apparently clear categorical approach. For example, pre–*Chevron* courts often placed considerable emphasis on whether the agency's interpretation was longstanding and consistent, whether it was issued contemporaneously with the enactment of the statute, and whether Congress had acquiesced in the agency's interpretation (*see* pp. ___, *supra*). Not only did *Chevron* not make reference to any of these considerations, it seemed to reject at least some of them: The EPA interpretation of "stationary source" at issue in *Chevron* was of recent vintage, was issued several years after the statute was enacted, and conflicted with the agency's own earlier interpretation of the same provision. Yet *Chevron* treated this as irrelevant, noting that "an initial agency interpretation is not instantly carved in stone." Also, while *Chevron* emphasized the importance of agency expertise, the doctrinal structure of *Chevron* appears to make the level of deference independent of any case-specific judgment of the agency's expertise or the technical complexity of the issue.

Although *Chevron*'s two-step framework has been enormously influential in structuring how courts frame questions involving judicial review of agency statutory interpretations, the precise relationship between the two steps is not entirely clear. Indeed, some have argued that the two-step structure is redundant and misleading. *See* Clark Byse, *Judicial Review of Administrative Interpretation of Statutes: An Analysis of* Chevron's *Step Two*, 2 Admin. L. Rev. 255, 256 n.10 (1988); Matthew C. Stephenson & Adrian Vermeule, Chevron *Has Only One Step*, 95 Va. L. Rev. 597 (2009). *But see* Kenneth A. Bamberger & Peter Strauss, Chevron's *Two Steps*, 95 Va. L. Rev. 611 (2009). After all, if Congress has expressed a clear intention on the "precise question at issue," then wouldn't it always be the case that a contrary agency interpretation would not be "a permissible construction of the statute"? Isn't Step One, then, merely a special case of Step Two? While most Supreme Court and lower court opinions continue to employ the two-step framework, many do not, without much apparent loss of content or affect on outcomes. *See* Orin Kerr, *Shedding Light on* Chevron: *An Empirical Study of the* Chevron *Doctrine in the U.S. Courts of Appeals*, 15 Yale J. on Reg. 1, 30–31 (1998).

Partly because of this apparent redundancy, some courts and scholars have interpreted *Chevron* Step One as a requirement that the agency's interpretation be permissible as a matter of statutory construction, while *Chevron* Step Two imposes an analytically distinct requirement that the agency's interpretive decision be the product of a reasoned decisionmaking process. That is, *Chevron* Step Two is sometimes viewed as roughly analogous to *State Farm*-style review under the arbitrary and capricious standard of APA § 706(2)(A): the agency must adequately explain its choice, responding to reasonable objections and proposed alternatives (*see* pp. 769–775, *supra*). *See, e.g.*, Gary Lawson, *Outcome, Procedure, and Process: Agency Duties of Explanation for Legal Conclusions*, 48 Rutgers L. Rev. 313, 314–16 (1996); Ronald M. Levin, *The Anatomy of* Chevron: *Step Two Reconsidered*, 72 Chi.-Kent L. Rev. 1253 (1997); Mark Seidenfeld, *A Syncopated* Chevron: *Emphasizing Reasoned Decisionmaking in Reviewing Agency Interpretations of Statutes*, 73 Tex. L. Rev. 83 (1994). This understanding eliminates the redundancy between *Chevron* Steps One and Two, but at the cost of creating an apparent redundancy between *Chevron* Step Two and *State Farm*. *See* Stephenson & Vermeule, *supra*.

Despite these conceptual questions about the relationship between Steps One and Two, the overall thrust of *Chevron* is fairly clear: If the responsible administrative agency has reasonably resolved a statutory ambiguity, the reviewing court should accept the agency's resolution, even if the court would have resolved the question differently. If the agency's interpretation is not reasonable—if, for example, it contravenes the clear text of the statute—then the reviewing court should reject it. This seems to be quite a deferential standard, though as we will see a great deal depends on the degree to which courts are willing to discern sufficiently clear statutory meaning to preclude deference to the agency.

Another notable feature of the *Chevron* doctrine is that although agencies must demonstrate (either under *Chevron* Step Two or *State Farm*) that their statutory interpretations were the product of reasoned decision-making, *Chevron* does not require that agencies demonstrate that they used a valid *interpretive method*. *See* Bernard W. Bell, *Using Statutory Interpretation to Improve the Legislative Process: Can It Be Done in the Post–Chevron Era?*, 13 J.L. & POL. 105 (1997) (noting and criticizing this aspect of *Chevron*). To illustrate, consider a hypothetical variant of *Chevron* in which the EPA explained its adoption of the bubble concept as follows: "Although the most natural semantic reading of the statutory text would seem to require that each point source of pollution count as a 'source' under the Act, our reading of the legislative history indicates that the bubble concept is closer to Congress's true intent." Now imagine that the judges reviewing the agency's decision are strict textualists who reject any reference to legislative history, but who also believe (unlike the agency) that the bubble concept is consistent with the statute's semantic meaning. Under *Chevron*, the agency would almost certainly win, because the court views the agency's interpretation (the bubble concept) as reasonable, even though the court disagrees with the agency's interpretive methodology. But why should this be so? In an ordinary *State Farm* case, if the agency has supplied an unacceptable explanation for an otherwise reasonable policy choice, the reviewing court will vacate and remand. Why should the same standard not apply to an agency that has adopted a reasonable interpretation of a statute on the basis of an interpretive method that the court considers flawed?

Then again, perhaps the problem with the agency's reasoning in the above example is not that the agency used a flawed *method* for ascertaining congressional intent, but that the agency was trying to ascertain congressional intent in the first place. After all, as we discuss in greater detail below (pp. 824–825, *infra*), one of the leading justifications for *Chevron* deference is the idea that Congress has not expressed any intent, and that the agency resolving the "interpretive" issue is in fact making a policy choice. Indeed, if it were otherwise—if the agency were basing its decision on an inquiry into legislative intent, rather than a judgment about what policy would be best—then why does it make sense to defer to the agency, rather than allowing the courts to exercise their independent judgment? *See* EINER ELHAUGE, STATUTORY DEFAULT RULES 97–99 (2008) (arguing that "courts defer to agencies because the policy views of agencies are more in tune with prevailing political preferences, not because agencies are better at legal interpretation than courts," and that it follows from this that courts should not defer to agency interpretations that are based on arguments about legislative intent rather than policy judgments). *But see* ADRIAN VERMEULE, JUDGING UNDER UNCERTAINTY 209–10 (2006) (arguing that agencies may be better at determining legislative intent than judges due to agencies' greater political responsiveness); Peter L. Strauss, *When the Judge Is Not the Primary Official With Responsibility To Read: Agency Interpretation and the Problem of Legislative History*, 66 CHI.-KENT L. REV. 321, 334, 346–52 (1990) (arguing that an agency is a "particularly capable reader" of its statutes, and especially well-positioned to ascertain the intent of the enacting legislature).

**2. *Normative Evaluation of* Chevron**—A prominent objection to the *Chevron* framework is that it entails judicial abdication of the responsibility to interpret the law, a responsibility famously asserted by Chief Justice John Marshall's opinion in *Marbury v. Madison*, 5 U.S. (1 Cranch) 137, 177 (1803) ("It is emphatically the province and duty of the Judicial Department to say what the law is."). Because *Chevron* instructs reviewing courts to accept an executive branch agent's interpretation of a congressional statute, *Chevron* has been characterized as the "counter-*Marbury* [] for the administrative state." Cass R. Sunstein, *Law and Administration after* Chevron, 90 COLUM. L. REV. 2071, 2075 (1990). What are we to make of this objection? There are really two questions here. First, there is a purely normative question about whether the *Chevron* rule is desirable. Is it a good idea for courts to adopt such a deferential posture, even if this effectively transfers much of the authority to interpret congressional statutes from the federal courts to the agencies? The second question—which we address in the next note (pp. 827–831, *infra*)—is whether *Chevron* deference is legally permissible, whether or not it is normatively attractive.

There is a voluminous scholarly literature debating the normative desirability of *Chevron*. Here, we scratch the surface of this enormously complex debate by considering a few of the most influential arguments for and against the *Chevron* doctrine. The most well-known arguments in favor of *Chevron* appear in the opinion itself. These arguments start from the premise that when a statute is silent or ambiguous on some interpretive question, the law has "run out," and the resolution of the ambiguity is essentially a policy choice. The question thus becomes whether the agency or the court should make that choice. *See, e.g.*, Lawrence Lessig, *Understanding Changed Readings: Fidelity and Theory*, 47 STAN. L. REV. 395, 436–37 (1995); Laurence H. Silberman, Chevron—*The Intersection of Law & Policy*, 58 GEO. WASH. L. REV. 821, 823 (1990). *Chevron* emphasized two reasons why the choice should reside with the agency. The first is the now familiar argument that agencies have superior expertise. Of course, as noted above, *Chevron* does not condition deference on a showing that the resolution of the interpretive issue requires, or that the agency actually possesses, any sort of specialized expertise. Nonetheless, if we opt for an easy-to-administer categorical approach, we might prefer a general presumption that agency interpretations merit deference because agencies usually have more relevant expertise than do courts. *See* Cass R. Sunstein, *Is Tobacco a Drug? Administrative Agencies as Common Law Courts*, 47 DUKE L.J. 1013, 1058 (1998). On the other hand, might the resolution of statutory ambiguities also require a different kind of specialized expertise—an expertise in techniques of legal interpretation—that courts typically have and agencies typically lack?

In addition to the expertise argument, *Chevron* advanced a second, perhaps more striking explanation for why courts should defer to reasonable agency constructions of ambiguous statutes: democratic accountability. This argument also starts from the premise that when the statute does not resolve a policy question decisively, the resolution of statutory ambiguity inevitably entails the exercise of policymaking discretion. In the absence of a clear congressional choice, the question thus becomes whether this policy decision should be made by the agency or by the court. As *Chevron* explained, agencies compare favorably to courts on the democratic accountability dimension: "Judges . . . are not part of either political branch of the Government. . . . While agencies are not directly accountable to the people, the Chief Executive is, and it is entirely appropriate for this political branch of the Government to make such policy choices. . . ." Note that this justification for *Chevron* might be grounded not only in pragmatic considerations, but in an underlying *constitutional* commitment to democratic decision-making (*see* pp. 829–830, *infra*).

A third common justification for *Chevron* deference, which is not explicit in the opinion itself, is that *Chevron* promotes coordination in the interpretation of federal law. The enormous volume of interpretive questions that agencies must address, and the limited number of cases that the Supreme Court is able to review, means that under a regime of de novo review, many interpretive questions will be decided by the courts of appeals. But these courts of appeals may reach different conclusions regarding the meaning of the same federal statute, and, again, resource constraints may make it difficult for the Supreme Court to impose uniformity. *Chevron* promotes greater uniformity because different courts of appeals are more likely to defer to the agency's construction. *See, e.g.,* Peter L. Strauss, *One Hundred Fifty Cases per Year: Some Implications of the Supreme Court's Limited Resources for Judicial Review of Agency Action*, 87 Colum. L. Rev. 1093 (1987). Furthermore, in the administrative context interpretive issues arising under the same statute or set of related statutes are particularly likely to be interdependent, such that it makes sense to have a single interpreter resolve these issues. *Chevron* deference enhances federal agencies' ability to implement legal interpretations that are consistent across the country and compatible with one another. *See* Matthew C. Stephenson, *Legislative Allocation of Delegated Power: Uncertainty, Risk, and the Choice Between Agencies and Courts*, 119 Harv. L. Rev. 1035 (2006) (making this point, but also arguing that deference is more likely to reduce consistency over time).

If expertise, accountability, and coordination are the main normative justifications for *Chevron* deference, what are the main objections? Perhaps the most prominent criticism of *Chevron* is that it concentrates too much power—both lawmaking and law-interpreting power—in the executive branch. This concentration of power may be objectionable on both pragmatic and constitutional grounds. A staple of separation-of-powers theory—going back at least to Montesquieu, running through the *Federalist Papers*, and formalized in the tripartite structure of the U.S. Constitution—is the notion that the separation of law-interpreting and law-enforcing power is an important safeguard against arbitrary and abusive government. As we saw in Chapter Three, the modern administrative state fits uncomfortably with this traditional notion of separation of powers (*see* pp. ___, *supra*). *Chevron*'s critics charge that by transferring even more law-interpreting authority from independent courts to executive branch agencies, *Chevron* further erodes important checks and balances. Simply put, for those who are concerned about excessive concentration of power in agency bureaucrats, and who believe that strict judicial oversight is a necessary precondition for the legitimacy of substantial delegation to agencies, *Chevron* is cause for serious concern. *See, e.g.,* Cynthia R. Farina, *Statutory Interpretation and the Balance of Power in the Administrative State*, 89 COLUM. L. REV. 452 (1989).

Furthermore, *Chevron* might undermine democratic accountability in subtle ways. Although *Chevron* may increase political accountability in a *particular* case by giving policymaking authority to agencies rather than courts, *Chevron* may diminish political accountability over the long run by making delegation more attractive to Congress. On this theory, Congress may often prefer to draft ambiguous statutes and leave the resolution of the resultant ambiguities to agencies because Congress (or powerful subgroups within Congress, such as oversight and appropriations committees) can influence how agencies interpret these statutory ambiguities. *See* Kathleen Bawn, *Choosing Strategies To Control the Bureaucracy: Statutory Constraints, Oversight, and the Committee System*, 13 J.L. ECON. & ORG. 101 (1997); J.R. DeShazo & Jody Freeman, *The Congressional Competition To Control Delegated Power*, 81 TEX. L. REV. 1443 (2003); *see also* pp. 473–476, *supra*. If courts rather than agencies assumed principal interpretive authority, members of Congress might find the strategy of adopting deliberately vague or ambiguous statutes less appealing, because they would be less sure of their ability to influence *judicial* resolution of these ambiguities. In other words, a less deferential standard might induce Congress to write clearer statutes. *Cf.* John F. Manning, *Constitutional Structure and Judicial Deference to Agency Interpretations of Agency Rules*, 96 COLUM. L. REV. 612 (1996). It is not certain, however, whether this argument's empirical premises are actually correct, as Congress may often distrust agencies, especially during periods of divided government. *See, e.g.,* Michael Herz, *Judicial Textualism Meets Congressional Micromanagement: A Potential Collision in Clean Air Act Interpretation*, 16 HARV. ENVTL. L. REV. 175, 179 (1992); [*c.f.*] Sidney A. Shapiro & Robert L. Glicksman, *Congress, the Supreme Court, and the Quiet Revolution in Administrative Law*, 1988 DUKE L.J. 819, 836–45. Furthermore, even if we accept the empirical claim that a less deferential standard would lead to an increase in the clarity of congressional statutes, we still have a trade-off: Unless we endorse the unrealistic claim that a non-deferential regime would *eliminate* statutory ambiguities, then a non-deferential regime would still involve many cases in which statutory ambiguities were resolved by less accountable courts rather than by more accountable agencies. Is that accountability cost greater or less than the accountability benefit of inducing greater statutory clarity?

**3.** *Legal Justifications for* **Chevron**—Whatever the pros and cons of *Chevron*'s deferential approach from a policy perspective, the question remains: On what basis can one *legally* justify this approach, given the background assumptions of *Marbury* (that the judiciary has the responsibility to "say what the law is") and the express directions contained in the APA (according to which reviewing courts have the duty to "interpret . . . statutory provisions")? *Chevron* itself, and subsequent cases and commentary, have grounded *Chevron* deference in a presumption (perhaps a legal fiction) about congressional intent. It is essential to understand the theoretical and doctrinal moves the Court makes here:

First, *Chevron* pointed out that settled constitutional law allows Congress to delegate to an agency the authority to make discretionary policy decisions, so long as Congress satisfies the weak requirement of supplying a sufficiently intelligible principle. (*See* pp. 410–417, *supra*). Congress may therefore adopt statutes that do not define the public's rights and duties directly, but instead instruct an administrative agency to specify those rights and responsibilities within the broad parameters set by the statute. *See, e.g.,* Richard J. Pierce, Jr., *The Role of the Judiciary in Implementing an Agency Theory of Government*, 64 N.Y.U. L. REV. 1239, 1244–47 (1989); Edward L. Rubin, *Law and Legislation in the Administrative State*, 89 COLUM. L. REV. 369, 380–85 (1989). In the context of such statutes, a court fulfills its responsibility to "say what the law is" (for purposes of *Marbury*) or to "interpret . . . statutory provisions" (for purposes of the APA) by ascertaining whether the agency has stayed within the bounds of its delegated authority. *See* Henry P. Monaghan, Marbury *and the Administrative State*, 83 COLUM. L. REV. 1, 6, 27 (1983); *see also, e.g.,* Ronald M. Levin, *Identifying Questions of Law in Administrative Law*, 74 GEO. L.J. 1, 21 (1985). Imagine, for example, that the 1977 Clean Air Act Amendments had said explicitly: "These regulatory requirements shall apply to any 'new or modified stationary source of pollution,' as defined by the EPA, and the EPA may in its discretion determine by rule whether a 'stationary source' shall be defined as an individual point source or as a collection of point sources that are all part of the same facility." Given the express delegation to the agency in this hypothetical example, the legal question for a reviewing court would not be to determine the meaning of "stationary source," but rather to determine whether the agency permissibly exercised its discretion within the boundaries set by the statute. In this example, moreover, there would be little doubt that the EPA has the authority to adopt either the pre–1981 definition of "stationary source" (any individual point source) or the post–1981 "bubble concept." As long as the agency complied with all applicable procedures and can show that its choice between these two options was not arbitrary, the court should uphold whatever choice the agency makes.

That much is uncontroversial. *Chevron's* critical move was to equate statutory silence or ambiguity with the sort of explicit delegation described above. After first noting that some statutes contain "an express delegation of authority [by Congress] to the agency to elucidate a specific provision of the statute by regulation," *Chevron* explained that "the legislative delegation to an agency on a particular question is [sometimes] implicit rather than explicit." In other words, the actual Clean Air Act, which simply uses the term "stationary source" without specifying either the point source definition or the bubble definition, is analytically and legally equivalent to the hypothetical statute described above, in which Congress explicitly delegated the choice between these two possible definitions to the agency. According to *Chevron*, because implicit and explicit delegations are equivalent, reviewing courts should be as deferential in the former case as they are in the latter. By equating statutory ambiguity with permissible delegation, *Chevron* supplies a ready answer to the charge that the decision is inconsistent with *Marbury* or the APA: Not so, because the reviewing court's obligation to "say what the law is" and to "interpret ... statutory provisions" in a delegation case is satisfied by determining that the agency acted within the scope of the authority delegated to it by Congress. *See* Thomas W. Merrill & Kristin E. Hickman, Chevron's *Domain*, 89 Geo. L.J. 833, 870–72 (2001).

But *why* should courts presume that when Congress has enacted a statute that is silent or ambiguous on some point, Congress meant to delegate the resolution of that ambiguity to the agency? That conclusion is by no means inevitable. One could just as easily adopt the presumption that when Congress left an ambiguity in a statute, it meant for the *court* to decide the issue in just the same way the court would decide any ordinary question of statutory construction. Furthermore, there is rarely any direct evidence of congressional intent regarding the allocation of interpretive authority. If *Chevron* is not grounded in an *empirical* proposition about likely subjective legislative intent, derived from the language or legislative history of either the APA or the organic statutes, on what ground might it be justified?

One possibility is that *Chevron* is grounded in the same sorts of considerations that were used to support the pre–*Chevron* approach: An imputation of legislative intent based on pragmatic arguments in favor of deference (expertise, accountability, and coherence), coupled with the classic Legal Process assumption that legislators are reasonable people pursuing reasonable goals reasonably. (*See* p. 45, *supra*). On that view, *Chevron* presumes that Congress intended courts to treat statutory ambiguities as equivalent to express delegations because it would be a *good idea* for courts to adopt this approach—an idea the courts then impute to the presumptively sensible legislators who enacted the ambiguous statutory text. In other words, this account of *Chevron* presumes that a reasonable Member of Congress would intend courts to treat statutory ambiguities as equivalent to express delegations in light of the agency's comparative advantage in expertise and accountability.

Putting aside general concerns about the legitimacy and utility of the Legal Process method (*see* pp. 61–65, *supra*), can *Chevron* be defended as an appropriate application of that method? Might even a proponent of the Legal Process approach be concerned by the degree to which *Chevron* apparently altered a doctrinal framework that had been in place for 40 years? *See, e.g.*, Stephen Breyer, *Judicial Review of Questions of Law and Policy*, 38 ADMIN. L. REV. 363, 370–71 (1986); Louis L. Jaffe, *Judicial Review: Question of Law*, 69 HARV. L. REV. 239, 273 (1955). As the Court has observed in another context, it is "not only appropriate but also realistic to presume that Congress was thoroughly familiar with . . . unusually important precedents" establishing rules of construction, and that Congress "expect[s] its enactment[s] to be interpreted in conformity with them." Cannon v. University of Chicago, 441 U.S. 677, 699 (1979). Does this consideration make it difficult to defend *Chevron* even as a policy-based imputation of congressional intent? On the other hand, as noted earlier (*see* p. 814, *supra*), many have characterized the pre–*Chevron* framework as confused and internally inconsistent. *See* Pittston Stevedoring Corp. v. Dellaventura, 544 F.2d 35, 49 (2d Cir. 1976) (Friendly, J.) (stating that "it is time to recognize . . . that there are two lines of Supreme Court decisions on [the standard of review for agency statutory interpretations] which are analytically in conflict"), *aff'd sub nom.* Northeast Marine Terminal Co. v. Caputo, 432 U.S. 249 (1977). If that is indeed the case, then maybe the argument that Congress legislated against the background of a well-established doctrinal framework loses much of its force.

Furthermore, it might well be that, as a descriptive empirical matter, Congress had no intent one way or the other regarding how courts should review agency interpretations of statutory ambiguities, or this intent might have been inconsistent or incoherent. If that is the case, perhaps it would be possible—and more honest—for the Court to defend *Chevron* simply as a policy-based legal fiction grounded in pragmatic considerations regarding the optimal allocation of interpretive authority rather than any real inquiry into actual legislative intent. *See, e.g.*, David J. Barron & Elena Kagan, *Chevron's Nondelegation Doctrine*, 2001 SUP. CT. REV. 201, 203; Stephen Breyer, *Judicial Review of Questions of Law and Policy*, 38 ADMIN L. REV. 363, 370 (1986); Eric A. Posner & Cass R. Sunstein, *Chevronizing Foreign Relations Law*, 116 YALE L.J. 1170, 1220 (2007); Matthew C. Stephenson, *Public Regulation of Private Enforcement*, 91 VA. L. REV. 93, 149 (2005). But what might be the source of judicial authority to adopt such a policy-based fiction about congressional intent? Could the Court, with equal justification, adopt a pragmatic fiction that instead seeks to promote cost-effective regulation, to limit interest group influence on the regulatory process, to promote individual liberty, or to advance any other goal the Court thought desirable on pragmatic grounds?

For those who do not believe that *Chevron* can be justified either as a matter of actual or imputed legislative intent, and who question the legitimacy of grounding *Chevron* in pragmatic policy concerns, might *Chevron* nonetheless be justified as a constitutionally inspired clear statement rule? (*See* pp. 288–337, *supra*). On this account, *Chevron* is analogous to other constitutionally inspired substantive canons. For example, the various federalism canons assert that courts should presume that Congress wants to preserve the usual balance between state and federal authority, and so courts should not construe statutes to upset that balance (say, by imposing federal requirements on core aspects of state sovereignty or by preempting state law) unless the statute clearly directs such a result (pp. 288–327, *supra*). In much the same way, *Chevron* may rest on the premise that because our constitutional system's commitment to democracy favors policymaking by relatively accountable agencies rather than relatively unaccountable courts, ambiguity in an organic act is presumed to reflect a delegation of primary decisionmaking authority to the agency unless the act *unmistakably* precludes such deference. *See, e.g.,* John F. Manning, *Constitutional Structure and Judicial Deference to Agency Interpretations of Agency Rules*, 96 COLUM. L. REV. 612, 626, 634 (1996); Richard L. Pierce, *Reconciling* Chevron *and Stare Decisis*, 85 GEO. L.J. 2225, 2229–33 (1997). Is that defense of *Chevron* convincing? Recall that many scholars are generally skeptical of the legitimacy of constitutionally inspired clear statement rules. (*See* pp. 299–300, *supra.*) In addition, many of the major objections to *Chevron* are *also* grounded in constitutional values—in particular, the constitutional commitment to separation of powers and checks and balances. *See* Cynthia R. Farina, *Statutory Interpretation and the Balance of Power in the Administrative State*, 89 COLUM. L. REV. 452, 511–26 (1989). If constitutional values, broadly conceived, point in different directions, how should the Court determine their priority?

The forgoing rationales all imply that Congress has the authority to overturn *Chevron*, either with respect to an individual statute or generically. Although Congress rarely does anything like this, the possibility is not entirely hypothetical. Even before *Chevron*, there were some attempts to amend the APA in order to compel courts to review questions of statutory interpretation de novo. The most well-known of these was the "Bumpers Amendment," a legislative proposal repeatedly introduced by Senator Dale Bumpers in the late 1970s and early 1980s. The Bumpers Amendment would have amended the APA to require reviewing courts to decide, without deference to the agency's views, whether a proposed agency action was within the agency's statutory authority. The Bumpers Amendment never became law, but it came close several times, and in one instance it failed only because Congress was unable to reach consensus on the larger regulatory reform bill to which the Bumpers Amendment was attached. *See* Ronald M. Levin, *Identifying Questions of Law in Administrative Law*, 74 GEO. L.J. 1, 2–9 & n.10 (1985); Ronald M. Levin, *Review of "Jurisdictional" Issues Under the Bumpers Amendment*, 1983 DUKE L.J. 355, 358–66. Also, Congress has occasionally (though extremely rarely) included specific language about the appropriate standard of judicial review in individual statutes in order to alter the *Chevron* default rule. For example, the 1999 Financial Modernization Act (also known as the Gramm–Leach–Bliley Act) instructed that when there is a dispute between the federal Office of the Comptroller of the Currency (OCC) and a State insurance commission about whether a particular financial product should count as part of the business of "banking" (regulated by the OCC, not the States) or as a form of "insurance" (regulated by the states, not the federal government), the federal courts shall resolve this legal question "without unequal deference" to the federal agency. 15 U.S.C. § 6714(e). That language—sometimes called the "jump ball" provision—is usually construed as withdrawing *Chevron* deference from the OCC's views on the application of the terms "banking" and "insurance" to particular financial products. *See* Baron & Kagan, *supra*, at 216 n.58; Lissa L. Broome & Jerry W. Markham, *Banking and Insurance: Before and After the Gramm–Leach–Bliley Act*, 25 J. Corp. L. 723, 764 (2000). (As we will see later, there is some question whether the OCC's views on this issue would receive *Chevron* deference even without the jump ball provision, because this interpretive issue implicates questions involving federal preemption of State law. *See* pp. 910–916, *infra*.)

Such examples of express congressional alteration of the *Chevron* default are, however, relatively rare. Does that rarity suggest implicit congressional acquiescence in the *Chevron* standard? *See* Elizabeth Garrett, *Legislating* Chevron, 101 Mich. L. Rev. 2637 (2003) (exploring this and similar questions).

**4. Chevron's *Practical Impact*—**While many judges and scholars are fascinated by the doctrinal and theoretical puzzles associated with *Chevron*, more practically minded people—agency officials, parties affected by agency action, and the lawyers who represent them—may be more interested in the actual impact of *Chevron* on the behavior of the federal judges who review agency action. The most basic question in this regard is whether *Chevron* actually increased the overall level of judicial deference to agency interpretations of statutes (as is widely believed), or whether *Chevron*'s impact on the degree of judicial deference was, at best, marginal and fleeting. In addition to this question about the impact of *Chevron* on the overall *level* of deference, we might also ask about the *distribution* of deference: Are agency interpretations in certain types of cases more (or less) likely to get deference after *Chevron* than before? We might also want to know whether *Chevron* has substantially narrowed the impact of judicial policy preferences on rulings in agency statutory interpretation cases. Let us consider each of these questions in turn.

With respect to *Chevron*'s impact on the overall level of judicial deference to agency statutory interpretations, it is important to keep in mind that the pre–*Chevron* regime was *not* a regime of de novo judicial review (notwithstanding the text of the APA). As we have seen (pp. 812–814, *supra*), prior to *Chevron* reviewing courts took into account a variety of factors, but in the end they often deferred to agency interpretations, especially on complex questions involving significant factual or policy considerations. *Chevron* did modify the doctrine in several important respects, but did these changes lead to an overall increase in judicial deference to agency interpretations? This is a difficult question to answer empirically. One cannot look simply at the frequency with which courts uphold agency interpretations pre- and post-*Chevron*, because agencies (if they have good lawyers) will adjust their behavior depending on how deferential they expect a reviewing court to be. If the agency's level of interpretive aggressiveness were fixed, then increasing judicial deference would increase agency win rates. Likewise, if the level of judicial deference were fixed, increasing agency interpretive aggressiveness would decrease agency win rates. The problem is that increasing judicial deference is likely to increase agencies' interpretive aggressiveness, which means an increase in deference might not show up in the form of higher overall agency win rates. One could try to assess directly the aggressiveness of agency interpretations—how much they stretch the statutory text—but that approach is likely to be extremely difficult and perhaps hopelessly subjective.

There are a couple of things one might do to get around this problem. First, agency win rates in the years immediately following *Chevron* might be more informative as to the doctrine's effect on judicial behavior, if we assume (reasonably) that it takes time for agencies to recognize that they are operating in a new, more favorable environment and to adjust their interpretive strategies accordingly. Here, the quantitative evidence supports the claim that *Chevron* led to at least a short-term boost in agency win rates. *See* Mark J. Richards, Joseph L. Smith & Herbert M. Kritzer, *Does* Chevron *Matter?*, 28 L. & POLICY 444 (2006); Peter H. Schuck & E. Donald Elliott, *To the* Chevron *Station: An Empirical Study of Federal Administrative Law*, 1990 DUKE L.J. 984. Of course, this evidence by itself cannot distinguish between (a) the hypothesis that *Chevron's* effect on win rates was temporary because agencies strategically adapted to this new higher level of deference; and (b) the hypothesis that *Chevron's* effect on judicial behavior was only temporary, and quickly dissipated a few years after the decision. One way we might try to figure out which account is more accurate is to look to the subjective reports of agency officials (including General Counsels and other senior agency officials) to see whether *Chevron* led agencies to behave differently. Here, at least one former official—E. Donald Elliott, who served as EPA General Counsel from 1989 to 1991—has asserted that *Chevron* had precisely this effect. *See* E. Donald Elliott, Chevron *Matters: How the* Chevron *Doctrine Redefined the Roles of Congress, Courts and Agencies in Environmental Law*, 16 VILL. ENVTL L.J. 1 (2005). Taken together, this and other evidence seems to support the claim that *Chevron* increased the overall level of judicial deference to agency statutory interpretations, though the magnitude of the effect is difficult to assess.

What about the more nuanced question whether *Chevron* had a more pronounced effect on the level of deference in *particular categories* of cases? Here, the empirical evidence is even sparser, but it does suggest that *Chevron's* impact was more pronounced in some areas than in others. For example, one factor that pre–*Chevron* cases sometimes deemed important was the consistency of the agency's interpretation. As a doctrinal matter, *Chevron* and its progeny have sent mixed signals as to whether interpretive inconsistency matters under *Chevron*. That said, a survey of post–*Chevron* court of appeals opinions found that interpretive inconsistency hardly ever leads courts to reject agency interpretations. *See* David M. Gossett, Chevron, *Take Two: Deference to Revised Agencies' Interpretation of Statutes*, 64

U. Chi. L. Rev. 681, 695–96 (1997). While there is no direct comparison to a similar sample of pre–*Chevron* cases, this finding is broadly suggestive that *Chevron* did indeed render agency inconsistency less relevant than it had been. Additionally, pre–*Chevron* case law indicated that the procedural form of the agency action might affect the level of judicial deference. While there is some question about the scope of *Chevron*'s applicability to informal opinion letters and guidance documents (*see* pp. 935–937, *infra*), the Supreme Court has clearly held that *Chevron* applies to formal adjudications in exactly the same way it applies to rulemakings. *See, e.g.*, INS v. Aguirre–Aguirre, 526 U.S. 415, 424–425 (1999). And, one study of pre- and post–*Chevron* cases found that the impact of *Chevron* on agency win rates was substantially greater for agency adjudications than for rulemakings. *See* Richards, Smith, & Kritzer, *supra*, at 456. This suggests that *Chevron* altered not just the level of deference overall, but had a particularly strong impact on certain categories of cases.

What about the third question, regarding the degree to which *Chevron* "de-politicized" judicial review of agency statutory interpretations by transferring the resolution of interpretive questions from the courts to the agencies? Here, the most recent empirical evidence generally supports the conclusion that a judge's political or jurisprudential views—usually measured using the party of the appointing President as a crude proxy—has a significant effect on rulings in *Chevron* cases: Conservative judges are more likely to uphold agency interpretations issued under Republican administrations, and more likely to reject agency interpretations issued under Democratic administrations; liberal judges display the opposite tendencies, though the magnitude of the difference (indeed, whether it exists at all) remains the subject of debate. *See* Frank B. Cross & Emerson H. Tiller, *Judicial Partisanship and Obedience to Legal Doctrine: Whistleblowing on the Federal Courts of Appeals*, 107 Yale L.J. 2155, 2163 (1998); Jason J. Czarnezki, *An Empirical Investigation of Judicial Decisionmaking, Statutory Interpretation, and the* Chevron *Doctrine in Environmental Law*, 79 U. Colo. L. Rev. 767 (2008); Thomas J. Miles & Cass R. Sunstein, *Do Judges Make Regulatory Policy? An Empirical Investigation of* Chevron, 73 U. Chi. L. Rev. 823 (2006); Joseph L. Smith, *Presidents, Justices, and Deference to Administrative Action*, 23 J.L. Econ. & Org. 346 (2007). *But see* Oren S. Kerr, *Shedding Light on* Chevron: *An Empirical Study of the* Chevron *Doctrine in the U.S. Courts of Appeals*, 15 Yale J. on Reg. 1, 35–37 (finding no statistically significant differences between Republican and Democratic appointees in *Chevron* cases); Richard L. Revesz, *Congressional Influence on Judicial Behavior? An Empirical Examination of Challenges to Agency Action in the D.C. Circuit*, 76 N.Y.U. L. Rev. 1100, 1104–15 (2001) (finding differences between the votes of Republican and Democratic appointees on procedural issues, but not in *Chevron* cases). An interesting subtlety about these findings is that, at the court of appeals level, the composition of the judicial panel seems to matter a great deal: A panel with two Republican appointees and one Democratic appointee may be somewhat more likely to vote in a "conservative" fashion in a *Chevron* case than a panel with one Republican and two Democrats, but the effect is slight. Panels with three Republicans, however, seem *much* more conservative than mixed panels, while panels with three Democrats seem much more liberal. *See* Cross & Tiller, *supra*; Miles & Sunstein, *supra*.

Should we infer from this that *Chevron* has not fulfilled its implicit promise to shift the authority to resolve statutory ambiguities from courts to agencies? The evidence lends itself to such an interpretation, but at least two important caveats are in order. The first concerns the baseline: *Chevron* may not have eliminated the impact of judicial ideology in this class of cases, but perhaps it reduced the impact of ideology relative to what we would have seen had *Chevron* not been decided. We have very little empirical evidence that addresses that question satisfactorily, but the evidence that does exist tends to support the view that *Chevron* at least dampened the impact of judges' political ideology on their votes, even if it did not eliminate it. *See* Richards, Smith & Kritzer, *supra*, at 462. Second, the set of litigated and decided cases is not a random sample of all agency statutory interpretations. Rather, these are the cases in which some aggrieved party viewed challenging an agency action on statutory grounds as worthwhile. Moreover, the cases that end up in the Supreme Court consist of a subset of those disputes—those that at least four Justices thought were worth a spot on the Court's docket. Thus, reported cases are likely to include a disproportionate number of hard cases, where judges' policy views are most likely to make a difference.

Moreover, even if one views the impact of judicial ideology on the outcome of *Chevron* cases as troubling, it is not obvious what one could or should do about this. After all, even if we conclude that these partisan effects are both real and normatively problematic (both of which are contested claims), we cannot tell whether the problem is too *little* deference to agencies from ideologically hostile judges, or too *much* deference to agencies from ideologically sympathetic judges. Is the problem that *Chevron* makes it too easy for a judge who dislikes the agency's choice on policy grounds to find that the statute "unambiguously" precludes the agency's decision? Or is the problem that *Chevron* makes it too easy for a judge who sympathizes with the agency's policy to uphold the agency's interpretation in the name of "deference," despite strong evidence that the agency's interpretation is inconsistent with the governing statute? *See* Cass R. Sunstein & Thomas J. Miles, *Depoliticizing Administrative Law*, 58 Duke L.J. 2193, 2215–16, 2224–25 (2009). These questions, in turn, implicate a larger set of issues about the appropriate relationship between *Chevron* and other tools and techniques of statutory construction. We take up those issues in Parts II and III of this chapter, *infra*.

**5.   Chevron *and the Hard Look Doctrine*—**Recall that in *Motor Vehicle Manufacturers Ass'n v. State Farm Mutual Automobile Insurance Co.*, 463 U.S. 29 (1983) (*see* pp. 756–769 *supra*), the Court embraced the hard look doctrine for judicial review of agency policy determinations. In particular, the Court reasoned that "an agency rule would be arbitrary and capricious if the agency has relied on factors which Congress has not intended it to consider, entirely failed to consider an important aspect of the problem, offered an explanation for its decision that runs counter to the evidence before the agency, or is so implausible that it could not be ascribed to a difference in view or the product of agency expertise." *Id.* at 43. *Chevron* was decided one year after *State Farm*. But as compared with the Court's extensive analysis of the agency's reasoning in *State Farm*, the *Chevron* Court's review of the EPA's reasoning was relatively terse:

> ... [The legislative] history plainly identifies the policy concerns that motivated the enactment; the plantwide definition is fully consistent with one of those concerns—the allowance of reasonable economic growth—and, whether or not we believe it most effectively implements the other, we must recognize that the EPA has advanced a reasonable explanation for its conclusion that the regulations serve the environmental objectives as well. Indeed, its reasoning is supported by the public record developed in the rulemaking process, as well as by certain private studies.

Does this analysis represent a misapplication or dilution of hard-look review? Or can it be explained in terms of the different nature of the inquiry in each case? In *State Farm*, the Court was reviewing a technical decision that rested, in part, on a factual prediction concerning the likely increase in seatbelt use if automakers were required to install detachable automatic seatbelts. In contrast, the agency decision in *Chevron* sought to justify striking a balance between interests in economic growth and environmental protection. In that context, might the burden of explanation— even under a hard-look approach—be easier to satisfy?

Assuming that *Chevron* is consistent with *State Farm*, do the two cases create an anomalous pattern of judicial review? Consider then-Judge Breyer's observations about the contrast between the two approaches to judicial review embodied by these two seminal cases:

> [T]he present law of judicial review of administrative decisionmaking, the heart of administrative law, contains an important anomaly. The law 1) requires courts to defer to agency judgments about *matters of law*, but 2) it also suggests that courts conduct independent, "in-depth" reviews of agency judgments about *matters of policy*. Is this not the exact opposite of a rational system? Would one not expect courts to conduct a stricter review of matters of law, where courts are more expert, but more lenient review of matters of policy, where agencies are more expert?

Stephen Breyer, *Judicial Review of Questions of Law and Policy*, 38 Admin. L. Rev. 363, 397 (1986). How might a defender of these two decisions respond to Justice Breyer's critique?

## II. *Chevron* and Textual Interpretation

*Chevron* instructs judges reviewing an agency construction of a statute to ask whether the statute clearly precludes the agency's interpretation, and if the answer is no, to ask whether the agency's interpretation is reasonable. Much of the action under the *Chevron* standard then, occurs at the point when the reviewing court decides whether the relevant statutory language is in fact ambiguous—that is, whether or not "Congress has directly spoken to the precise question at issue."

How is a court supposed to decide whether the statute's meaning is sufficiently clear that the agency's interpretation is impermissible? Footnote 9 of the *Chevron* opinion offers some guidance, asserting that reviewing courts should employ the "traditional tools of statutory construction" in order to decide whether "Congress had an intention on the precise question at issue." These "traditional tools" of statutory construction presumably include the familiar techniques covered in Chapters One and Two: textual analysis, inferences from statutory structure and context, inferences from statutory purpose, legislative history, and semantic and substantive canons of construction. Not all judges accept the legitimacy of all of these interpretive tools, of course, but the gist of footnote 9 seems to be that courts should use all legitimate techniques of statutory construction at the first step of *Chevron*, and defer to the agency only if the application of those techniques fails to yield a clear answer to the interpretive question.

But this raises a difficulty: Won't the application of the "traditional tools of statutory construction" *always* (or almost always) provide an answer to the question of what a particular statutory phrase means? After all, in an ordinary statutory interpretation case, with no agency involved, the court would proceed by applying whatever tools it thought appropriate to arrive at the best understanding of the statute—an understanding that the court would then ascribe to Congress. *Chevron* cannot mean that the reviewing court may defer to the agency only when the traditional tools of statutory construction provide *no answer whatsoever* to the interpretive question; that reading of footnote 9 would render *Chevron* practically meaningless. *Chevron* instead must mean that a reviewing court should defer to the agency if the application of the traditional tools of statutory construction fails to supply a *sufficiently clear* answer to the interpretive question. But how are courts supposed to determine whether the answer supplied by the traditional tools of construction is sufficiently clear to preclude a contrary agency interpretation? Are there some "traditional tools of statutory construction" that, notwithstanding footnote 9, are per se inapplicable in a *Chevron* case? Can courts distinguish between an *answer* to an interpretive question, and a *clear answer* to that question?

This Part will consider these questions in the context of a series of cases in which the *Chevron* doctrine interacts with—and arguably conflicts with—one or more of the tools of statutory construction that we covered in Chapters One and Two.

## A.   *Chevron*, Textual Analysis, and Structural Inference

The starting point in almost all statutory interpretation cases is the text of the statute. Sometimes textual analysis focuses on the "plain meaning" of statutory language to an ordinary speaker of English. Often, textual analysis will go beyond the particular statutory language at issue, inferring meaning from the context in which that language is used and how it fits into the overall statutory scheme. Sometimes, contextual or other evidence implies that a statutory phrase is a "term of art" with a specialized meaning that is narrower, broader, or simply different from the term's ordinary-language meaning (*see* pp. 111–140, *supra*). And sometimes courts invoke so-called semantic canons of construction as an aid to parsing statutory texts, on the logic that these canons are reasonable generalizations about how we ordinarily use and understand language (*see* pp. 222–266, *supra*). To what extent, or under what conditions, do these tools of textual analysis provide sufficiently clear evidence of statutory meaning to preclude a contrary agency interpretation? At what point should courts acknowledge that the text of the statute is sufficiently ambiguous that the agency interpretation should prevail?

The following case, *MCI v. AT & T*, highlights both the importance of the statutory text as a constraint on agency discretion and the difficulties involved in deciding when the text is "clear." The majority and dissenting opinions in *MCI* also highlight the underlying normative tension between the interest in giving administrative agencies sufficient latitude to pursue their policy agendas without excessive judicial interference, and the interest in judicial enforcement of the constraints that Congress meant to impose on the agencies. As you read the case, pay attention to the different approaches that the majority and the dissent take toward the analysis of the statutory language. Also, observe the ways Justice Scalia's majority opinion, though focused principally on the dictionary definition of the critical statutory term, also makes use of structural and contextual inferences to bolster this interpretation. Justice Stevens' dissent deploys structural and contextual arguments as well, but reaches a much different conclusion. Which arguments do you find more compelling? Do you find either view sufficiently compelling to overcome the *Chevron* presumption that the agency's interpretation should prevail?

# MCI Telecommunications Corp. v. American Telephone and Telegraph Co.

Supreme Court of the United States
512 U.S. 218 (1994)

■ Justice Scalia delivered the opinion of the Court.

Section 203(a) of Title 47 of the United States Code requires communications common carriers to file tariffs with the Federal Communications Commission, and § 203(b) authorizes the Commission to "modify" any requirement of § 203. These cases present the question whether the Commission's decision to make tariff filing optional for all nondominant long-distance carriers is a valid exercise of its modification authority.

I

Like most cases involving the role of the American Telephone and Telegraph Company (AT & T) in our national telecommunication system, these have a long history. An understanding of the cases requires a brief review of the Commission's efforts to regulate and then deregulate the telecommunications industry. When Congress created the Commission in 1934, AT & T, through its vertically integrated Bell system, held a virtual monopoly over the Nation's telephone service. The Communications Act of 1934 authorized the Commission to regulate the rates charged for communication services to ensure that they were reasonable and nondiscriminatory. The requirements of § 203 that common carriers file their rates with the Commission and charge only the filed rate were the centerpiece of the Act's regulatory scheme.

In the 1970's, technological advances reduced the entry costs for competitors of AT & T in the market for long-distance telephone service. The Commission, recognizing the feasibility of greater competition, passed regulations to facilitate competitive entry. By 1979, competition in the provision of long-distance service was well established, and some urged that the continuation of extensive tariff filing requirements served only to impose unnecessary costs on new entrants and to facilitate collusive pricing. The Commission held hearings on the matter, following which it issued a series of rules that have produced this litigation.

[The Court then described a long and complex procedural history that resulted in the FCC's decision to adopt a rule that relieved "nondominant [long-distance] carriers" (that is, carriers other than AT & T) of the obligation to file tariffs under § 203(a) of the Act. The Commission did so pursuant to authority under § 203(b) to "modify any requirement made by or under the authority of this section."]

II

Section 203 of the Communications Act contains both the filed rate provisions of the Act and the Commission's disputed modification authority. It provides in relevant part:

"(a) Filing; public display.

"Every common carrier, except connecting carriers, shall, within such reasonable time as the Commission shall designate, file with the Commission and print and keep open for public inspection schedules showing all charges ..., whether such charges are joint or separate, and showing the classifications, practices, and regulations affecting such charges. . . .

"(b) Changes in schedule; discretion of Commission to modify requirements.

"(1) No change shall be made in the charges, classifications, regulations, or practices which have been so filed and published except after one hundred and twenty days notice to the Commission and to the public, which shall be published in such form and contain such information as the Commission may by regulations prescribe.

"(2) The Commission may, in its discretion and for good cause shown, modify any requirement made by or under the authority of this section either in particular instances or by general order applicable to special circumstances or conditions except that the Commission may not require the notice period specified in paragraph (1) to be more than one hundred and twenty days.

"(c) Overcharges and rebates.

"No carrier, unless otherwise provided by or under authority of this chapter, shall engage or participate in such communication unless schedules have been filed and published in accordance with the provisions of this chapter and with the regulations made thereunder; and no carrier shall (1) charge, demand, collect, or receive a greater or less or different compensation for such communication ... than the charges specified in the schedule then in effect, or (2) refund or remit by any means or device any portion of the charges so specified, or (3) extend to any person any privileges or facilities in such communication, or employ or enforce any classifications, regulations, or practices affecting such charges, except as specified in such schedule." 47 U.S.C. § 203 (1988 ed. and Supp. IV).

The dispute between the parties turns on the meaning of the phrase "modify any requirement" in § 203(b)(2). Petitioners argue that it gives the Commission authority to make even basic and fundamental changes in the scheme created by that section. We disagree. The word "modify"—like a number of other English words employing the root "mod-" (deriving from the Latin word for "measure"), such as "moderate," "modulate," "modest," and "modicum"—has a connotation of increment or limitation. Virtually every dictionary we are aware of says that "to modify" means to change moderately or in minor fashion. See, *e.g.,* Random House Dictionary of the English Language 1236 (2d ed. 1987) ("to change somewhat the form or qualities of; alter partially; amend"); Webster's Third New International Dictionary 1452 (1981) ("to make minor changes in the form or structure of: alter without transforming"); 9 Oxford English Dictionary 952 (2d ed. 1989) ("[t]o make partial changes in; to change (an object) in respect of some of its qualities; to alter or vary without radical transformation"); Black's Law Dictionary 1004 (6th ed. 1990) ("[t]o alter; to change in incidental or subordinate features; enlarge; extend; amend; limit; reduce").

In support of their position, petitioners cite dictionary definitions contained in, or derived from, a single source, Webster's Third New International Dictionary 1452 (1981) (Webster's Third), which includes among the meanings of "modify," "to make a basic or important change in."[2] Petitioners contend that this establishes sufficient ambiguity to enti-

---

**2.** Petitioners also cite Webster's Ninth New Collegiate Dictionary 763 (1991), which includes among its definitions of "modify," "to make basic or fundamental changes in often to give a new orientation to or to serve a new end." They might also have cited the eighth

tle the Commission to deference in its acceptance of the broader meaning, which in turn requires approval of its permissive detariffing policy. *See Chevron U.S.A. Inc. v. Natural Resources Defense Council, Inc.,* 467 U.S. 837, 843 (1984). In short, they contend that the courts must defer to the agency's choice among available dictionary definitions, citing *National Railroad Passenger Corporation v. Boston & Maine Corp.,* 503 U.S. 407, 418 (1992).

But *Boston & Maine* does not stand for that proposition.... [T]he opinion did not rely exclusively upon dictionary definitions, but also upon contextual indications—which in the present cases, as we shall see, contradict petitioners' position. Moreover, when the *Boston & Maine* opinion spoke of "alternative dictionary definitions," it did not refer to what we have here: one dictionary whose suggested meaning contradicts virtually all others. It referred to alternative definitions *within the dictionary cited* (Webster's Third, as it happens), which was not represented to be the *only* dictionary giving those alternatives. To the contrary, the Court said "these alternative interpretations are as old as the jurisprudence of this Court," *id.,* at 419, citing *McCulloch v. Maryland,* 4 Wheat. 316 (1819). See also Webster's New International Dictionary 2117 (2d ed. 1934); 2 New Shorter Oxford English Dictionary 2557 (1993) (giving both alternatives).

Most cases of verbal ambiguity in statutes involve ... a selection between accepted alternative meanings shown as such by many dictionaries. One can envision (though a court case does not immediately come to mind) having to choose between accepted alternative meanings, one of which is so newly accepted that it has only been recorded by a single lexicographer. (Some dictionary must have been the very first to record the widespread use of "projection," for example, to mean "forecast.") But what petitioners demand that we accept as creating an ambiguity here is a rarity even rarer than that: a meaning set forth in a single dictionary (and, as we say, its progeny) which not only *supplements* the meaning contained in all other dictionaries, but *contradicts* one of the meanings contained in virtually all other dictionaries. Indeed, contradicts one of the alternative meanings contained in the out-of-step dictionary itself—for as we have observed, Webster's Third itself defines "modify" to connote *both* (specifically) major change *and* (specifically) minor change. It is hard to see how that can be. When the word "modify" has come to mean *both* "to change in some respects" *and* "to change fundamentally" it will in fact mean *neither* of those things. It will simply mean "to change," and some adverb will have to be called into service to indicate the great or small degree of the change.

---

version of Webster's New Collegiate Dictionary 739 (1973), which contains that same definition; and Webster's Seventh New Collegiate Dictionary 544 (1963), which contains the same definition as Webster's Third New International Dictionary quoted in text. The Webster's New Collegiate Dictionaries, published by G. & C. Merriam Company of Springfield, Massachusetts, are essentially abridgments of that company's Webster's New International Dictionaries, and recite that they are based upon those lengthier works. The last New Collegiate to be based upon Webster's Second New International, rather than Webster's Third, does not include "basic or fundamental change" among the accepted meanings of "modify." See Webster's New Collegiate Dictionary 541 (6th ed. 1949).

If that is what the peculiar Webster's Third definition means to suggest has happened—and what petitioners suggest by appealing to Webster's Third—we simply disagree. "Modify," in our view, connotes moderate change. It might be good English to say that the French Revolution "modified" the status of the French nobility—but only because there is a figure of speech called understatement and a literary device known as sarcasm. And it might be unsurprising to discover a 1972 White House press release saying that "the Administration is modifying its position with regard to prosecution of the war in Vietnam"—but only because press agents tend to impart what is nowadays called "spin." Such intentional distortions, or simply careless or ignorant misuse, must have formed the basis for the usage that Webster's Third, and Webster's Third alone, reported.[3] It is perhaps gilding the lily to add this: In 1934, when the Communications Act became law—the most relevant time for determining a statutory term's meaning . . .—Webster's Third was not yet even contemplated. To our knowledge *all* English dictionaries provided the narrow definition of "modify". . . . We have not the slightest doubt that is the meaning the statute intended.

Beyond the word itself, a further indication that the § 203(b)(2) authority to "modify" does not contemplate fundamental changes is the sole exception to that authority which the section provides. One of the requirements of § 203 is that changes to filed tariffs can be made only after 120 days' notice to the Commission and the public. § 203(b)(1). The *only* exception to the Commission's § 203(b)(2) modification authority is as follows: "except that the Commission may not require the notice period specified in paragraph (1) to be more than one hundred and twenty days." Is it conceivable that the statute is indifferent to the Commission's power to eliminate the tariff-filing requirement entirely for all except one firm in the long-distance sector, and yet strains out the gnat of extending the waiting period for tariff revision beyond 120 days? We think not. The exception is not as ridiculous as a Lilliputian in London only because it is to be found in Lilliput: in the small-scale world of "modifications," it is a big deal.

Since an agency's interpretation of a statute is not entitled to deference when it goes beyond the meaning that the statute can bear, see, *e.g.,* . . . *Chevron,* 467 U.S., at 842–843, the Commission's permissive detariffing policy can be justified only if it makes a less than radical or fundamental change in the Act's tariff-filing requirement. The Commission's attempt to establish that no more than that is involved greatly understates the extent to which its policy deviates from the filing requirement, and greatly undervalues the importance of the filing requirement itself.

To consider the latter point first: For the body of a law, as for the body of a person, whether a change is minor or major depends to some extent upon the importance of the item changed to the whole. Loss of an entire

**3.** That is not an unlikely hypothesis. Upon its long-awaited appearance in 1961, Webster's Third was widely criticized for its portrayal of common error as proper usage. . . . An example is its approval (without qualification) of the use of "infer" to mean "imply". . . .

toenail is insignificant; loss of an entire arm tragic. The tariff-filing requirement is, to pursue this analogy, the heart of the common-carrier section of the Communications Act. In the context of the Interstate Commerce Act, which served as its model, . . . this Court has repeatedly stressed that rate filing was Congress's chosen means of preventing unreasonableness and discrimination in charges: "[T]here is not only a relation, but an indissoluble unity between the provision for the establishment and maintenance of rates until corrected in accordance with the statute and the prohibitions against preferences and discrimination." *Texas & Pacific R. Co. v. Abilene Cotton Oil Co.,* 204 U.S. 426, 440 (1907). . . . "The duty to file rates with the Commission, [the analog to § 203(a)], and the obligation to charge only those rates, [the analog to § 203(c)], have always been considered essential to preventing price discrimination and stabilizing rates." *Maislin Industries, U.S., Inc. v. Primary Steel, Inc.,* 497 U.S. 116, 126 (1990) . . . . As the *Maislin* Court concluded, compliance with these provisions "is 'utterly central' to the administration of the Act." 497 U.S., at 132, quoting *Regular Common Carrier Conference v. United States,* 793 F.2d 376, 379 (CADC 1986).

Much of the rest of the Communications Act subchapter applicable to Common Carriers . . . and the Act's Procedural and Administrative Provisions . . . are premised upon the tariff-filing requirement of § 203. For example, § 415 defines "overcharges" (which customers are entitled to recover) by reference to the filed rate. See § 415(g). The provisions allowing customers and competitors to challenge rates as unreasonable or as discriminatory . . . would not be susceptible of effective enforcement if rates were not publicly filed. *See Maislin, supra,* 497 U.S., at 132. Rate filings are, in fact, the essential characteristic of a rate-regulated industry. It is highly unlikely that Congress would leave the determination of whether an industry will be entirely, or even substantially, rate-regulated to agency discretion—and even more unlikely that it would achieve that through such a subtle device as permission to "modify" rate-filing requirements.

Bearing in mind, then, the enormous importance to the statutory scheme of the tariff-filing provision, we turn to whether what has occurred here can be considered a mere "modification." The Commission stresses that its detariffing policy applies only to nondominant carriers, so that the rates charged to over half of all consumers in the long-distance market are on file with the Commission. It is not clear to us that the proportion of customers affected, rather than the proportion of carriers affected, is the proper measure of the extent of the exemption (of course *all* carriers in the long-distance market are exempted, except AT & T). But even assuming it is, we think an elimination of the crucial provision of the statute for 40% of a major sector of the industry is much too extensive to be considered a "modification." What we have here, in reality, is a fundamental revision of the statute, changing it from a scheme of rate regulation in long-distance common-carrier communications to a scheme of rate regulation only where effective competition does not exist. That may be a good idea, but it was not the idea Congress enacted into law in 1934. . . .

Finally, petitioners earnestly urge that their interpretation of § 203(b) furthers the Communications Act's broad purpose of promoting efficient telephone service. They claim that although the filing requirement prevented price discrimination and unfair practices while AT & T maintained a monopoly over long-distance service, it frustrates those same goals now that there is greater competition in that market. Specifically, they contend that filing costs raise artificial barriers to entry and that the publication of rates facilitates parallel pricing and stifles price competition. We have considerable sympathy with these arguments (though we doubt it makes sense, if one is concerned about the use of filed tariffs to communicate pricing information, to require filing by the dominant carrier, the firm most likely to be a price leader).... But our estimations, and the Commission's estimations, of desirable policy cannot alter the meaning of the federal Communications Act of 1934. For better or worse, the Act establishes a rate-regulation, filed-tariff system for common-carrier communications, and the Commission's desire "to 'increase competition' cannot provide [it] authority to alter the well-established statutory filed rate requirements," *Maislin,* 497 U.S., at 135. As we observed in the context of a dispute over the filed-rate doctrine more than 80 years ago, "such considerations address themselves to Congress, not to the courts," *Armour Packing,* 209 U.S., at 82.

We do not mean to suggest that the tariff-filing requirement is so inviolate that the Commission's existing modification authority does not reach it at all. Certainly the Commission can modify the form, contents, and location of required filings, and can defer filing or perhaps even waive it altogether in limited circumstances. But what we have here goes well beyond that. It is effectively the introduction of a whole new regime of regulation (or of free-market competition), which may well be a better regime but is not the one that Congress established....

■ Justice O'Connor took no part in the consideration or decision of these cases.

■ Justice Stevens, with whom Justice Blackmun and Justice Souter join, dissenting.

The communications industry has an unusually dynamic character. In 1934, Congress authorized the Federal Communications Commission (FCC or Commission) to regulate "a field of enterprise the dominant characteristic of which was the rapid pace of its unfolding." *National Broadcasting Co. v. United States,* 319 U.S. 190, 219 (1943). The Communications Act of 1934 (Act) gives the FCC unusually broad discretion to meet new and unanticipated problems in order to fulfill its sweeping mandate "to make available, so far as possible, to all the people of the United States, a rapid, efficient, Nation-wide and world-wide wire and radio communication service with adequate facilities at reasonable charges." 47 U.S.C. § 151. This Court's consistent interpretation of the Act has afforded the Commission ample leeway to interpret and apply its statutory powers and responsibilities.... The Court today abandons that approach in favor of a rigid literalism that deprives the FCC of the flexibility Congress meant it to have in order to implement the core policies of the Act in rapidly changing conditions.

I

At the time the Act was passed, the telephone industry was dominated by the American Telephone & Telegraph Company (AT & T) and its affiliates. Title II of the Act, which establishes the framework for FCC regulation of common carriers by wire, was clearly a response to that dominance. . . .

The wire communications provisions of the Act address problems distinctly associated with monopoly. Section 201 requires telephone carriers to "furnish . . . communication service upon reasonable request therefor," and mandates that their "charges, practices, classifications, and regulations" be "just and reasonable." 47 U.S.C. § 201. Section 202 forbids carriers to "make any unjust or unreasonable discrimination in charges, practices, classifications, regulations, facilities, or services . . . or give any undue or unreasonable preference or advantage to any particular person, class of persons, or locality." 47 U.S.C. § 202(a). The Commission, upon complaint or its own motion, may hold hearings upon, and declare the lawfulness of, proposed rate increases, § 204, and may prescribe just and reasonable charges upon a finding that a carrier's actual or proposed charges are illegal, § 205. Persons damaged by a carrier's violation of the statute have a right to damages, §§ 206–207, and any person may file with the Commission a complaint of violation of the Act, § 208.

Section 203 . . . requires that common carriers other than connecting carriers "file with the Commission and print and keep open for public inspection schedules showing all charges for itself and its connecting carriers." 47 U.S.C. § 203(a). A telephone carrier must allow a 120–day period of lead time before a tariff goes into effect, and, "unless otherwise provided by or under authority of this Chapter," may not provide communication services except according to a filed schedule, §§ 203(c), (d). The tariff-filing section of the Act, however, contains a provision [§ 203(b)] that states:

> "(2) The Commission may, in its discretion and for good cause shown, modify any requirement made by or under the authority of this section either in particular instances or by general order applicable to special circumstances or conditions except that the Commission may not require the notice period specified in paragraph (1) to be more than one hundred and twenty days." 47 U.S.C. § 203(b)(2) (1988 ed., Supp. IV).

Congress doubtless viewed the filed rate provisions as an important mechanism to guard against abusive practices by wire communications monopolies. But it is quite wrong to suggest that the mere process of filing rate schedules—rather than the substantive duty of reasonably priced and nondiscriminatory service—is "the heart of the common-carrier section of the Communications Act."

## II

In response to new conditions in the communications industry, including stirrings of competition in the long-distance telephone market, the FCC ... began reexamining its regulatory scheme. The Commission tentatively concluded that costly tariff-filing requirements were unnecessary and actually counterproductive as applied to nondominant carriers, *i.e.,* those whose lack of market power leaves them unable to extract supra-competitive or discriminatory rates from customers.... Relaxing the regulatory burdens upon new entrants would foster competition into the telecommunications markets; at the same time, the forces of competition would ensure that firms without monopoly power would comply with the Act's prohibitions on "unreasonable rates" and price discrimination....

In the instant [case], the FCC adhered to its policy of excusing nondominant providers of long-distance telephone service from the § 203 filing requirement, and codified that longstanding forbearance policy. ... [T]he Commission found principal statutory authority for detariffing in the "modify any requirement" language of § 203(b)(2)....

## III

Although the majority observes that further relaxation of tariff-filing requirements might more effectively enhance competition, it does not take issue with the Commission's conclusions that mandatory filing of tariff schedules serves no useful purpose and is actually counterproductive in the case of carriers who lack market power....

In my view, each of the Commission's detariffing orders was squarely within its power to "modify any requirement" of § 203. Section 203(b)(2) plainly confers at least some discretion to modify the general rule that carriers file tariffs, for it speaks of "*any* requirement."[2] Section 203(c) of the Act, ignored by the Court, squarely supports the FCC's position; it prohibits carriers from providing service without a tariff "*unless otherwise provided by or under authority of this Act.*" Section 203(b)(2) is plainly one provision that "otherwise provides," and thereby authorizes, service without a filed schedule. The FCC's authority to modify § 203's requirements in "particular instances" or by "general order applicable to special circumstances or conditions" emphasizes the expansive character of the Commission's authority: modifications may be narrow or broad, depending upon the Commission's appraisal of current conditions. From the vantage of a Congress seeking to regulate an almost completely monopolized industry, the advent of competition is surely a "special circumstance or condition" that might legitimately call for different regulatory treatment.

The only statutory exception to the Commission's modification authority provides that it may not extend the 120–day notice period set out in § 203(b)(1). See § 203(b)(2). The Act thus imposes a specific limit on the Commission's authority to *stiffen* that regulatory imposition on carriers,

---

**2.** Section 203(b)(2) must do more than merely allow the Commission to dictate the form and contents of tariff filings, for § 203(b)(1) separately grants it that authority.

but does not confine the Commission's authority to *relax* it. It was no stretch for the FCC to draw from this single, unidirectional statutory limitation on its modification authority the inference that its authority is otherwise unlimited. . . .

According to the Court, the term "modify," as explicated in all but the most unreliable dictionaries, rules out the Commission's claimed authority to relieve nondominant carriers of the basic obligation to file tariffs. Dictionaries can be useful aids in statutory interpretation, but they are no substitute for close analysis of what words mean as used in a particular statutory context. . . . Even if the sole possible meaning of "modify" were to make "minor" changes,[3] further elaboration is needed to show why the detariffing policy should fail. The Commission came to its present policy through a series of rulings that gradually relaxed the filing requirements for nondominant carriers. Whether the current policy should count as a cataclysmic or merely an incremental departure from the § 203(a) baseline depends on whether one focuses on particular carriers' obligations to file (in which case the Commission's policy arguably works a major shift) or on the statutory policies behind the tariff-filing requirement (which remain satisfied because market constraints on nondominant carriers obviate the need for rate filing). When § 203 is viewed as part of a statute whose aim is to constrain monopoly power, the Commission's decision to exempt non-dominant carriers is a rational and "measured" adjustment to novel circumstances—one that remains faithful to the core purpose of the tariff-filing section. See Black's Law Dictionary 1198 (3d ed. 1933) (defining "modification" as "A change; an alteration which introduces new elements into the details, or cancels some of them, but leaves *the general purpose and effect of the subject-matter* intact").

The Court seizes upon a particular sense of the word "modify" at the expense of another, long-established meaning that fully supports the Commission's position. That word is first defined in Webster's Collegiate Dictionary 628 (4th ed. 1934) as meaning "to limit or reduce in extent or degree."[5] The Commission's permissive detariffing policy fits comfortably within this common understanding of the term. The FCC has in effect adopted a general rule stating that "if you are dominant you must file, but if you are nondominant you need not." The Commission's partial detariff-

---

**3.** As petitioner MCI points out, the revolutionary consent decree providing for the breakup of the Bell System was, per AT & T's own proposal, entitled "Modification of Final Judgment." *See United States v. American Telephone & Telegraph Co.,* 552 F.Supp. 131 (D.C.1982), aff'd, 460 U.S. 1001 (1983).

**5.** See also 9 Oxford English Dictionary 952 (2d ed. 1989) ("2. To alter in the direction of moderation or lenity; to make less severe, rigorous, or decided; to qualify, tone down. . . ."); Random House Dictionary of the English Language 1236 (2d ed. 1987) ("5. to reduce or lessen in degree or extent; moderate; soften; *to modify one's demands*"); Webster's Third New International Dictionary 1452 (1981) ("1: to make more temperate and less extreme: lessen the severity of; . . . 'traffic rules were *modified* to let him pass' "); Webster's New Collegiate Dictionary 739 (1973) ("1. to make less extreme; MODERATE"); Webster's Seventh New Collegiate Dictionary 544 (1963) (same); Webster's Seventh New International Dictionary 1577 (2d ed. 1934) ("2. To reduce in extent or degree; to moderate; qualify; lower; as, to *modify* heat, pain, punishment"). . . .

ing policy—which excuses nondominant carriers from filing *on condition that* they remain nondominant—is simply a relaxation of a costly regulatory requirement that recent developments had rendered pointless and counterproductive in a certain class of cases.

A modification pursuant to § 203(b)(1), like any other order issued under the Act, must of course be consistent with the purposes of the statute. On this point, the Court asserts that the Act's prohibition against unreasonable and discriminatory rates "would not be susceptible of effective enforcement if rates were not publicly filed." That determination, of course, is for the Commission to make in the first instance. But the Commission has repeatedly explained that (1) a carrier that lacks market power is entirely unlikely to charge unreasonable or discriminatory rates, (2) the statutory bans on unreasonable charges and price discrimination apply with full force regardless of whether carriers have to file tariffs, (3) any suspected violations by nondominant carriers can be addressed on the Commission's own motion or on a damages complaint filed pursuant to § 206, and (4) the FCC can reimpose a tariff requirement should violations occur.... The Court does not adequately respond to the FCC's explanations....

The filed tariff provisions of the Communications Act are not ends in themselves, but are merely one of several procedural *means* for the Commission to ensure that carriers do not charge unreasonable or discriminatory rates.... The Commission has reasonably concluded that this particular means of enforcing the statute's substantive mandates will prove counterproductive in the case of nondominant long-distance carriers. Even if the 1934 Congress did not define the scope of the Commission's modification authority with perfect scholarly precision, this is surely a paradigm case for judicial deference to the agency's interpretation, particularly in a statutory regime so obviously meant to maximize administrative flexibility.[7] Whatever the best reading of § 203(b)(2), the Commission's reading cannot in my view be termed unreasonable. It is informed (as ours is not) by a practical understanding of the role (or lack thereof) that filed tariffs play in the modern regulatory climate and in the telecommunications industry. Since 1979, the FCC has sought to adapt measures originally designed to control monopoly power to new market conditions. It has carefully and consistently explained that mandatory tariff-filing rules frustrate the core statutory interest in rate reasonableness. The Commission's use of the "discretion" expressly conferred by § 203(b)(2) reflects "a reasonable accommodation of manifestly competing interests and is entitled to deference: the regulatory

---

7. The majority considers it unlikely that Congress would have conferred power on the Commission to exempt carriers from the supposedly pivotal rate-filing obligation. But surely such a delegation is not out of place in a statute that also empowers the FCC, for example, to decide what the "public convenience, interest, or necessity" requires, see, *e.g.,* 47 U.S.C. § 303, and to "prescribe such rules and regulations as may be necessary in the public interest," § 201(b); see also § 154(i). The Court's rigid reading of § 203(b)(2) is out of step with our prior recognition that the 1934 Act was meant to be a "supple instrument for the exercise of discretion by the expert body which Congress has charged to carry out its legislative policy." *FCC v. Pottsville Broadcasting Co.,* 309 U.S. 134, 138 (1940).

scheme is technical and complex, the agency considered the matter in a detailed and reasoned fashion, and the decision involves reconciling conflicting policies." *Chevron U.S.A. Inc. v. Natural Resources Defense Council, Inc.*, 467 U.S. 837, 865 (1984) (footnotes omitted). The FCC has permissibly interpreted its § 203(b)(2) authority in service of the goals Congress set forth in the Act. We should sustain its eminently sound, experience-tested, and uncommonly well-explained judgment.

I respectfully dissent.

---

1. ***Textualism and* Chevron *Deference*—**The decision in *MCI v. AT & T* raises questions about the relationship between "textualism" as an interpretive philosophy and the *Chevron* doctrine. Some scholars have hypothesized, in light of *MCI* and cases like it, that textualist judges are less likely to defer to agency interpretations under *Chevron*, because textualists are more likely to discern a "clear" statutory meaning. *See, e.g.,* Thomas W. Merrill, *Textualism and the Future of the* Chevron *Doctrine*, 72 Wash. U. L.Q. 351, 366 (1994); Richard J. Pierce, Jr., *The Supreme Court's New Hypertextualism: An Invitation to Cacophony and Incoherence in the Administrative State*, 95 Colum. L. Rev. 749, 752 (1995); Peter L. Strauss, *On Resegregating the Worlds of Statute and Common Law*, 1994 Sup. Ct. Rev. 429, 498. Justice Scalia in particular has provided some evidence in support of this hypothesis, both through his voting patterns and in his public statements and writings. With regard to voting behavior, although Justice Scalia is a strong supporter and vigorous defender of the *Chevron* doctrine, he actually has one of the lowest overall rates of deference to agencies in the *Chevron* cases that come before the Supreme Court. *See* Thomas J. Miles & Cass R. Sunstein, *Do Judges Make Regulatory Policy? An Empirical Investigation of* Chevron, 73 U. Chi. L. Rev. 823 (2006). One plausible explanation for this seeming contradiction is that although Justice Scalia strongly supports deferring to the responsible agency *when a statute is ambiguous*, his preferred textualist mode of interpretation is more likely to yield unambiguous answers to questions of statutory meaning. Justice Scalia has explicitly advanced this argument, explaining:

> One who finds *more* often (as I do) that the meaning of a statute is apparent from its text and from its relationship with other laws, thereby finds *less* often that the triggering requirement for *Chevron* deference exists. It is thus relatively rare that *Chevron* will require me to accept an interpretation which, though reasonable, I would not personally adopt.

Antonin Scalia, *Judicial Deference to Administrative Interpretations of Law*, 1989 Duke L.J. 511, 521 (emphasis in original). Justice Scalia further hypothesized that judges who consider a broader range of interpretive sources, such as legislative history, are more likely to find "agency-liberating ambiguity." *Ibid*. Justice Breyer, who advocates a more contextual, pragmatic, multi-factor approach to statutory interpretation, provides a broadly corroborative counterpoint to Justice Scalia in this regard. Although Justice Breyer has expressed skepticism about a broad reading of

*Chevron* and argued for limits on the scope of judicial deference to agency interpretations, *see* Stephen Breyer, *Our Democratic Constitution*, 77 N.Y.U. L. REV. 245, 266–67 (2002), in practice he defers to agency interpretations at a higher rate than most of the other justices. *See* Miles & Sunstein, *supra*.

While Justices Breyer and Scalia's examples are consistent with the hypothesis that textualism correlates inversely with the propensity to defer under *Chevron*, it is far from clear that this hypothesis is well-grounded in principle or generally true in practice. With respect to principle, Justice Scalia and others have asserted that looking beyond the text of a statute to factors like legislative history will tend to expand rather than contract the range of "reasonable" interpretations. But is that necessarily true? Isn't it easy to imagine a case where the text is susceptible to several reasonable interpretations, but some other factor, such as the legislative history, clearly points to one of those interpretations as the correct one? (For an example of a case that arguably falls in this category, see *Exxon–Mobil v. Allapattah Services*, pp. 185–189, *supra*.) Moreover, if legislative history is less "costly" to produce or acquire than statutory text, one would expect it to contain more policy detail than the text itself. As Professor Jerry Mashaw has argued:

> [T]he exclusion of legislative history is more likely to increase the flexibility of statutes than to render them static or rigid. After all, inquiry is directed necessarily away from pre-statutory history and toward later text including administrative decisions, judicial decisions, and later statutes. Suppressing the working documents . . . of codes or constitutions is a common technique for ensuring that texts have a long, useful life . . . . By eliminating legislative history as a less costly method of pre-interpreting a statute—of settling the details of meaning in advance—textualism may in fact decrease the specificity of the overall legislative work-product, enhancing the adaptability and flexibility of the public law.

Jerry L. Mashaw, *Textualism, Constitutionalism, and the Interpretation of Federal Statutes*, 32 WM. & MARY L. REV. 827, 836 (1991). Furthermore, if courts look to legislative history *only if the text is ambiguous* (*see supra* pp. 190–191), doesn't that suggest that legislative history will tend to reduce rather than expand the scope for *Chevron* deference?

Of course, even if this is possible in theory, one would need to know something about the *relative frequencies* with which consideration of extra-textual interpretive tools expand rather than contract the range of permissible constructions. The contrasting examples of Justice Scalia and Justice Breyer might suggest that in practice textualists defer less often, under *Chevron*, than do purposivists. But the Supreme Court decides only a very small number of administrative law cases, and Justices Scalia and Breyer, while undoubtedly influential, are not necessarily representative of all textualists or purposivists, respectively. There is little systematic empirical evidence on the question whether textualist judges are less likely to defer to agency constructions under *Chevron* as a general matter. One notable study, by Professor Orin Kerr, explored this issue by analyzing court of appeals opinions in *Chevron* cases decided over a two-year period (1995–1996). *See* Orin S. Kerr, *Shedding Light on* Chevron: *An Empirical Study of the* Chevron *Doctrine in the U.S. Courts of Appeals*, 15 YALE J. ON REG. 1 (1998). Professor Kerr used the party of the appointing President as a proxy for "textualism," on the assumption that during the relevant time period, judges appointed by Presidents Reagan and Bush were more likely to espouse a textualist approach. *Id.* at 23–29, 54–56. Professor Kerr found no correlation between judges' partisan affiliation and the rate at which they upheld agency interpretations, *id.* at 40–43, though the crudeness of the proxy for textualism means that the significance of this non-finding may not tell us very much. (Note also that Professor Kerr's findings are potentially in some tension with those of Professors Miles and Sunstein. *See* p. 833 *supra*).

**2.   *What Constitutes "Ambiguity"?***—The dispute between Justices Scalia and Stevens in *MCI* raises a more basic question about *Chevron*. All language has *some* ambiguity, at least at the margins. Accordingly, *Chevron* raises questions about how strenuously reviewing courts should try to resolve such ambiguity through an application of the various tools of statutory construction. Should courts defer only after an exhaustive judicial effort to resolve a surface ambiguity has left lingering doubt? Or should a court defer whenever the resolution of a surface ambiguity would require close, intricate analysis of the sort observed in both the majority and dissenting opinions in *MCI*? As discussed in the previous note, Justice Scalia believes that a judge applying the traditional tools of statutory construction can usually ascertain a clear signal about statutory meaning. *See* Antonin Scalia, *Judicial Deference to Administrative Interpretations of Law*, 1989 DUKE L.J. 511, 521. His former D.C. Circuit colleague Judge Laurence Silberman expressed a different view:

> [M]ore often than not we, as a court, cannot resolve a case at the first step of *Chevron*. . . . Finding a specific congressional intent is particularly unlikely if the agency is applying statutory language that calls for an administrative judgment, such as what is "feasible" or "probable." But often there is also ambiguity when statutes are extensively detailed, because the more Congress writes the more difficulty it seems to have making legislation clear. That should not be all that surprising when one thinks about it: the more detailed the instructions drafted in an effort to anticipate every twist and turn that a regulation will undergo, the more likely it is—given the difficulty in predicting human behavior—that a draftsman will create ambiguity. . . .
>
> Still, even assuming one is scrupulously honest in reading a statute thoroughly and looking carefully at its linguistic structure, legitimate ambiguities, which give room for differing good-faith interpretations, more often than not appear in our cases. If a case is resolved at the first step of *Chevron*, one must assume a situation where either a petitioner has brought a particularly weak case to the

court of appeals, or the agency is sailing directly against a focused legislative wind. Neither eventuality occurs very often. Litigation is expensive for private parties and agencies are rarely so cavalier in interpreting their statutes.

Laurence H. Silberman, Chevron—*The Intersection of Law & Policy*, 58 GEO. WASH. L. REV. 821, 825–26 (1990).

Is this difference of opinion a matter for empirical study, or does it boil down to a difference in attitude about *Chevron*? Professor Thomas Merrill believes that when judges exhaustively seek the meaning of a statutory term using dictionaries, canons of construction, and other verbal cues, they undermine the values of the *Chevron* doctrine: democratic accountability, expert decisionmaking, statutory flexibility, and nationwide legal uniformity. *See* Thomas W. Merrill, *Textualism and the Future of the* Chevron *Doctrine*, 72 WASH. U. L.Q. 351, 376 (1994). Professor Adrian Vermeule, moreover, finds it doubtful that a reviewing court's exhaustive use of traditional tools of statutory interpretation will produce a more accurate account of legislative intent or purpose than the agency's own interpretation would, given that "specialized agencies are closer to the statute, its legislative history, and its original purposes and compromises than are generalist judges" and that agencies are "typically far more familiar with the congressional process and its heterogeneous outputs." ADRIAN VERMEULE, JUDGING UNDER UNCERTAINTY 209–10 (2006). If one accepts such views, then the parsing of dictionaries, the close structural reading, and the aggressive purposive analysis found in *both* the majority and dissent in *MCI* might seem at odds with the spirit of *Chevron*. On this view, the Court should have observed simply that it is not obvious whether elimination of the filed rate doctrine for nondominant carriers "modifies" the statutory requirements, leaving that question to the agency.

On the other hand, might such an approach risk ignoring important indicia of statutory meaning? Presumably courts couldn't ignore entirely basic rules of grammar or the conventional meaning of terms. As Judge Posner has observed, "[a]ll sorts of linguistic and cultural tools must be brought to bear on even the simplest text to get meaning out of it." Richard A. Posner, *Legal Formalism, Legal Realism, and the Interpretation of Statutes and the Constitution*, 37 CASE W. RES. L. REV. 179, 187 (1986). If that's true, isn't it important for courts to make some serious use of this wide range of tools in order to ascertain whether the statute has a clear meaning before allowing the agency to do what it wants? Wouldn't failure to do so shift too much power from Congress to the agencies? *Cf.* William N. Eskridge, Jr. & John Ferejohn, *Making the Deal Stick: Enforcing the Original Constitutional Structure of Lawmaking in the Modern Regulatory State*, 8 J.L. ECON. & ORG. 165 (1992) (arguing that an expansive version of *Chevron* undermines the original constitutional design by shifting power from Congress to the executive). Or would a more aggressive approach in fact shift power from the agencies to the *courts*, as Professors Merrill and Vermeule suggest?

### 3.  The Role of Structural, Contextual, and Purposive Argument in Chevron Analysis—*MCI v. AT & T* is most striking for its "war of dictionaries," but both Justice Scalia and Justice Stevens buttressed their arguments with inferences from statutory context, structure, and purpose. While a number of such arguments appear in the opinions, perhaps the most interesting is Justice Scalia's suggestion that one reason for rejecting the FCC's interpretation of "modify" is the fact that such an interpretation would allow the FCC to eliminate entirely the tariff-filing requirement—an "essential characteristic" of the overall statutory scheme—for some or all regulated entities. "It is highly unlikely," Justice Scalia asserted, "that Congress would leave the determination of whether an industry will be entirely, or even substantially, rate-regulated to agency discretion—and even more unlikely that it would achieve that through such a subtle device as permission to 'modify' rate-filing requirements." What do you make of this argument? Is Justice Scalia's inference about Congress's likely intent strong enough to find the statute unambiguous for *Chevron* purposes, even if there were a reasonable dictionary definition of "modify" that was consistent with the FCC's interpretation?

Justice Stevens did not contest the notion that the analysis of the statutory language in a *Chevron* case should take into account what Congress was trying to achieve, and how the agency's interpretation affects the other provisions of the statute. But Justice Stevens disputed the claim that the filed-rate requirement was really so central to the overall scheme, arguing that "[t]he filed tariff provisions of the Communications Act are not ends in themselves, but are merely one of several procedural *means* for the Commission to ensure that carriers do not charge unreasonable or discriminatory rates" (emphasis in original). Justice Stevens also argued that while Congress may not have anticipated this *particular* exercise of the modification authority, certainly Congress meant for the FCC to interpret the 1934 Communications Act flexibly, so as to advance its underlying purposes. "[T]his," insisted Justice Stevens, "is surely a paradigm case for judicial deference to the agency's interpretation, particularly in a statutory regime so obviously meant to maximize administrative flexibility."

Is it consistent with *Chevron* to assert that courts should reject (or at least should be more willing to reject) an agency interpretation that would alter the overall regulatory scheme in some fundamental way that the enacting Congress is unlikely to have anticipated? Perhaps Justice Scalia's argument, properly understood, is that where the agency's interpretation entails a substantially broader delegation of power to the agency, or implicates a particularly fundamental legal question, ordinary *Chevron* deference should not apply, or should be limited in some way. If so, perhaps *MCI* resembles earlier cases in which reviewing courts read statutes narrowly in order to avoid a concern about an excessively broad delegation of power to the agency, including *Kent v. Dulles* (pp. 436–437, *supra*) and *Benzene* (pp. 418–433, *supra*). *MCI* does not endorse that view explicitly, but some have read the case as one of several suggesting a background "nondelegation canon" that can limit *Chevron* deference in some situations. *See, e.g.,* John F. Manning, *Nonlegislative Rules*, 72 GEO. WASH. L.

REV. 893, 928 & n.180 (2004); Cass R. Sunstein, Chevron *Step Zero*, 92 VA. L. REV. 187, 244–47 (2006) (discussing but ultimately rejecting this interpretation of *MCI*). We will return to this issue in the notes following the *FDA v. Brown & Williamson* case (pp. 867–881, *infra*).

## B. CHEVRON, SEMANTIC CANONS AND TERMS OF ART

Cases like *MCI v. AT & T* raise the difficult question of when a statute's text is sufficiently clear that a contrary agency interpretation is impermissible, even under the deferential *Chevron* standard. As we saw, the analysis in *MCI* focused on two important techniques for discerning textual meaning: consideration of the "plain" or "ordinary" meaning of statutory terms (often with the aid of dictionaries), and inferences from statutory structure and context. There are other important techniques of textual interpretation, however, and applications of these techniques in *Chevron* cases also raise vexing questions about when the "traditional tools of statutory construction" generate a sufficiently clear statutory meaning that an agency's contrary interpretation must give way.

First, while courts usually presume that statutes use words in their "ordinary" sense, this presumption can be overcome when there is sufficient evidence that a statutory phrase is a "term of art" with a specialized meaning. (*See* pp. 111–140, *supra*.) It is therefore possible that an agency might interpret a statutory term in a way that is inconsistent with the term's ordinary meaning, but nonetheless defend its interpretation on the ground that the word or phrase could reasonably be viewed as a term of art with the specialized meaning the agency ascribes to it. Likewise, there might be cases in which the agency's construction of a statutory phrase is consistent with a standard dictionary definition of that phrase, but the court concludes—on the basis of context, history, or other evidence—that Congress was using the phrase as a term of art with a narrower, more specialized meaning. In either case, the agency is likely to argue that if there is ambiguity as to whether a particular term has a general or specialized meaning, the court should defer to agency's view under *Chevron*. When should the agency prevail in such an argument?

Second, courts frequently invoke a variety of so-called semantic canons of construction as guides to textual meaning. These canons, covered in Chapter Two, include the presumptions that statutory terms have a consistent meaning throughout the statute (*see* pp. 243–245, *supra*); that each statutory term is meaningful (i.e., that redundancy is disfavored) (*see* pp. 247–249, *supra*); that the explicit inclusion of certain things implies the exclusion of other things (*expressio unius*) (*see* pp. 224–232, *supra*); that statutory terms, especially those in a list, draw meaning from surrounding words (*noscitur a sociis*) (*see* pp. 245–247, *supra*); and that general catch-all terms at the end of a list are to be construed as including only items of the same general type as those specifically listed (*ejusdem generis*) (*see* pp. 249–266, *supra*). How do these canons apply in a *Chevron* case? Does the application of these canons enable courts to discern "clear" statutory meaning (in which case they might take precedence over *Chevron* deference)? Or are these canons merely ways for courts to construct statutory meaning when the text is not clear (in which case an agency's contrary interpretation would presumably take precedence under *Chevron*)?

The following case, *Babbitt v. Sweet Home Chapter of Communities for a Great Oregon*, is a useful starting point for thinking about these questions. In addition, the opinions in *Sweet Home* make use of a number of other interpretive techniques, including contextual and structural arguments similar to those we saw in *MCI v. AT & T*, as well as inferences from legislative history, which we will address in more detail in the note at pp. 885–888, *infra*.

## Babbitt v. Sweet Home Chapter of Communities for a Great Oregon

Supreme Court of the United States
515 U.S. 687 (1995)

■ JUSTICE STEVENS delivered the opinion of the Court.

The Endangered Species Act of 1973 (ESA or Act) contains a variety of protections designed to save from extinction species that the Secretary of the Interior designates as endangered or threatened. Section 9 of the Act makes it unlawful for any person to "take" any endangered or threatened species. The Secretary has promulgated a regulation that defines the statute's prohibition on takings to include "significant habitat modification or degradation where it actually kills or injures wildlife." This case presents the question whether the Secretary exceeded his authority under the Act by promulgating that regulation.

I

Section 9(a)(1) of the Act provides the following protection for endangered species:

"Except as provided in sections 1535(g)(2) and 1539 of this title, with respect to any endangered species of fish or wildlife listed pursuant to section 1533 of this title it is unlawful for any person subject to the jurisdiction of the United States to—

. . . . .

"(B) take any such species within the United States or the territorial sea of the United States." 16 U.S.C. § 1538(a)(1).

Section 3(19) of the Act defines the statutory term "take":

"The term 'take' means to harass, harm, pursue, hunt, shoot, wound, kill, trap, capture, or collect, or to attempt to engage in any such conduct." 16 U.S.C. § 1532(19).

The Act does not further define the terms it uses to define "take." The Interior Department regulations that implement the statute, however, define the statutory term "harm":

> "*Harm* in the definition of 'take' in the Act means an act which actually kills or injures wildlife. Such act may include significant habitat modification or degradation where it actually kills or injures wildlife by significantly impairing essential behavioral patterns, including breeding, feeding, or sheltering."

This regulation has been in place since 1975.

A limitation on the § 9 "take" prohibition appears in § 10(a)(1)(B) of the Act. . . . That section authorizes the Secretary to grant a permit for any taking otherwise prohibited . . . "if such taking is incidental to, and not the purpose of, the carrying out of an otherwise lawful activity." 16 U.S.C. § 1539(a)(1)(B).

. . . Respondents in this action are small landowners, logging companies, and families dependent on the forest products industries in the Pacific Northwest and in the Southeast, and organizations that represent their interests. They brought this declaratory judgment action against petitioners, the Secretary of the Interior and the Director of the Fish and Wildlife Service, in the United States District Court for the District of Columbia to challenge the statutory validity of the Secretary's regulation defining "harm," particularly the inclusion of habitat modification and degradation in the definition. . . .

II

Because this case was decided on motions for summary judgment, we may appropriately make certain factual assumptions in order to frame the legal issue. First, we assume respondents have no desire to harm either the red-cockaded woodpecker or the spotted owl; they merely wish to continue logging activities that would be entirely proper if not prohibited by the ESA. On the other hand, we must assume, *arguendo*, that those activities will have the effect, even though unintended, of detrimentally changing the natural habitat of both listed species and that, as a consequence, members of those species will be killed or injured. . . .

The text of the Act provides three reasons for concluding that the Secretary's interpretation is reasonable. First, an ordinary understanding of the word "harm" supports it. The dictionary definition of the verb form of "harm" is "to cause hurt or damage to: injure." Webster's Third New International Dictionary 1034 (1966). In the context of the ESA, that definition naturally encompasses habitat modification that results in actual injury or death to members of an endangered or threatened species.

Respondents argue that the Secretary should have limited the purview of "harm" to direct applications of force against protected species, but the dictionary definition does not include the word "directly" or suggest in any way that only direct or willful action that leads to injury constitutes "harm."[10] Moreover, unless the statutory term "harm" encompasses indirect as well as direct injuries, the word has no meaning that does not duplicate the meaning of other words that § 3 uses to define "take." A reluctance to treat statutory terms as surplusage supports the reasonableness of the Secretary's interpretation.[11]

Second, the broad purpose of the ESA supports the Secretary's decision to extend protection against activities that cause the precise harms Congress enacted the statute to avoid. . . .

Respondents . . . ask us to invalidate the Secretary's understanding of "harm" in every circumstance, even when an actor knows that an activity, such as draining a pond, would actually result in the extinction of a listed species by destroying its habitat. Given Congress' clear expression of the ESA's broad purpose to protect endangered and threatened wildlife, the Secretary's definition of "harm" is reasonable.[13]

Third, the fact that Congress in 1982 authorized the Secretary to issue permits for takings that § 9(a)(1)(B) would otherwise prohibit, "if such taking is incidental to, and not the purpose of, the carrying out of an otherwise lawful activity," strongly suggests that Congress understood

---

**10.** Respondents and the dissent emphasize what they portray as the "established meaning" of "take" in the sense of a "wildlife take," a meaning respondents argue extends only to "the effort to exercise dominion over some creature, and the concrete effect of [sic] that creature." This limitation ill serves the statutory text, which forbids not taking "some creature" but "tak[ing] any [endangered] species"—a formidable task for even the most rapacious feudal lord. More importantly, Congress explicitly defined the operative term "take" in the ESA, no matter how much the dissent wishes otherwise, thereby obviating the need for us to probe its meaning as we must probe the meaning of the undefined subsidiary term "harm." Finally, Congress' definition of "take" includes several words—most obviously "harass," "pursue," and "wound," in addition to "harm" itself—that fit respondents' and the dissent's definition of "take" no better than does "significant habitat modification or degradation."

**11.** In contrast, if the statutory term "harm" encompasses such indirect means of killing and injuring wildlife as habitat modification, the other terms listed in § 3—"harass," "pursue," "hunt," "shoot," "wound," "kill," "trap," "capture," and "collect"—generally retain independent meanings. Most of those terms refer to deliberate actions more frequently than does "harm," and they therefore do not duplicate the sense of indirect causation that "harm" adds to the statute. In addition, most of the other words in the definition describe either actions from which habitat modification does not usually result (e.g., "pursue," "harass") or effects to which activities that modify habitat do not usually lead (e.g., "trap," "collect"). To the extent the Secretary's definition of "harm" may have applications that overlap with other words in the definition, that overlap reflects the broad purpose of the Act.

**13.** The dissent incorrectly asserts that the Secretary's regulation (1) "dispenses with the foreseeability of harm" and (2) "fail[s] to require injury to particular animals," . . . . As to the first assertion, the regulation merely implements the statute, and it is therefore subject to the statute's "knowingly violates" language, and ordinary requirements of proximate causation and foreseeability. Nothing in the regulation purports to weaken those requirements. To the contrary, the word "actually" in the regulation should be construed to limit the liability about which the dissent appears most concerned, liability under the statute's "otherwise violates" provision. The Secretary did not need to include "actually" to connote "but for" causation, which the other words in the definition obviously require. As to the dissent's second assertion, every term in the regulation's definition of "harm" is subservient to the phrase "an act which actually kills or injures wildlife."

§ 9(a)(1)(B) to prohibit indirect as well as deliberate takings .... No one could seriously request an "incidental" take permit to avert § 9 liability for direct, deliberate action against a member of an endangered or threatened species, but respondents would read "harm" so narrowly that the permit procedure would have little more than that absurd purpose. "When Congress acts to amend a statute, we presume it intends its amendment to have real and substantial effect." Stone v. INS, 514 U.S. 386, 397 (1995)....

The Court of Appeals [erred] in asserting that "harm" must refer to a direct application of force because the words around it do.[15] First, the court's premise was flawed. Several of the words that accompany "harm" in the § 3 definition of "take," especially "harass," "pursue," "wound," and "kill," refer to actions or effects that do not require direct applications of force. Second, to the extent the court read a requirement of intent or purpose into the words used to define "take," it ignored § 11's express provision that a "knowin[g]" action is enough to violate the Act. Third, the court employed *noscitur a sociis* to give "harm" essentially the same function as other words in the definition, thereby denying it independent meaning. The canon, to the contrary, counsels that a word "gathers meaning from the words around it." Jarecki v. G.D. Searle & Co., 367 U.S. 303, 307 (1961). The statutory context of "harm" suggests that Congress meant that term to serve a particular function in the ESA, consistent with, but distinct from, the functions of the other verbs used to define "take." The Secretary's interpretation of "harm" to include indirectly injuring endangered animals through habitat modification permissibly interprets "harm" to have "a character of its own not to be submerged by its association." Russell Motor Car Co. v. United States, 261 U.S. 514, 519 (1923)....

We need not decide whether the statutory definition of "take" compels the Secretary's interpretation of "harm," because our conclusions that Congress did not unambiguously manifest its intent to adopt respondents' view and that the Secretary's interpretation is reasonable suffice to decide this case. See generally Chevron U.S.A. Inc. v. Natural Resources Defense Council, Inc., 467 U.S. 837 (1984). The latitude the ESA gives the Secretary in enforcing the statute, together with the degree of regulatory expertise necessary to its enforcement, establishes that we owe some degree of deference to the Secretary's reasonable interpretation.

---

**15.** The dissent ... tries to impose on § 9 a limitation of liability to "affirmative conduct intentionally directed against a particular animal or animals." Under the dissent's interpretation of the Act, a developer could drain a pond, knowing that the act would extinguish an endangered species of turtles, without even proposing a conservation plan or applying for a permit under § 10(a)(1)(B); unless the developer was motivated by a desire "to get at a turtle," no statutory taking could occur. Because such conduct would not constitute a taking at common law, the dissent would shield it from § 9 liability, even though the words "kill" and "harm" in the statutory definition could apply to such deliberate conduct. We cannot accept that limitation. In any event, our reasons for rejecting the Court of Appeals' interpretation apply as well to the dissent's novel construction.

## III

Our conclusion that the Secretary's definition of "harm" rests on a permissible construction of the ESA gains further support from the legislative history of the statute. The Committee Reports accompanying the bills that became the ESA do not specifically discuss the meaning of "harm," but they make clear that Congress intended "take" to apply broadly to cover indirect as well as purposeful actions. . . .

Two endangered species bills, S. 1592 and S. 1983, were introduced in the Senate and referred to the Commerce Committee. Neither bill included the word "harm" in its definition of "take," although the definitions otherwise closely resembled the one that appeared in the bill as ultimately enacted. Senator Tunney, the floor manager of the bill in the Senate, subsequently introduced a floor amendment that added "harm" to the definition, noting that this and accompanying amendments would "help to achieve the purposes of the bill." Respondents argue that the lack of debate about the amendment that added "harm" counsels in favor of a narrow interpretation. We disagree. An obviously broad word that the Senate went out of its way to add to an important statutory definition is precisely the sort of provision that deserves a respectful reading.

The definition of "take" that originally appeared in S. 1983 differed from the definition as ultimately enacted in one other significant respect: It included "the destruction, modification, or curtailment of [the] habitat or range" of fish and wildlife. Respondents make much of the fact that the Commerce Committee removed this phrase from the "take" definition before S. 1983 went to the floor. We do not find that fact especially significant. The legislative materials contain no indication why the habitat protection provision was deleted. That provision differed greatly from the regulation at issue today. Most notably, the habitat protection provision in S. 1983 would have applied far more broadly than the regulation does because it made adverse habitat modification a categorical violation of the "take" prohibition, unbounded by the regulation's limitation to habitat modifications that actually kill or injure wildlife . . . . We do not believe the Senate's unelaborated disavowal of the provision in S. 1983 undermines the reasonableness of the more moderate habitat protection in the Secretary's "harm" regulation.

The history of the 1982 amendment that gave the Secretary authority to grant permits for "incidental" takings provides further support for his reading of the Act. The House Report expressly states that "[b]y use of the word 'incidental' the Committee intends to cover situations in which it is known that a taking will occur if the other activity is engaged in but such taking is incidental to, and not the purpose of, the activity." This reference to the foreseeability of incidental takings undermines respondents' argument that the 1982 amendment covered only accidental killings of endangered and threatened animals that might occur in the course of hunting or trapping other animals. . . . Thus, Congress in 1982 focused squarely on the aspect of the "harm" regulation at issue in this litigation. Congress' implementation of a permit program is consistent with the Secretary's interpretation of the term "harm."

## IV

... The proper interpretation of a term such as "harm" involves a complex policy choice. When Congress has entrusted the Secretary with broad discretion, we are especially reluctant to substitute our views of wise policy for his. See *Chevron*, 467 U.S., at 865–66. In this case, that reluctance accords with our conclusion, based on the text, structure, and legislative history of the ESA, that the Secretary reasonably construed the intent of Congress when he defined "harm" to include "significant habitat modification or degradation that actually kills or injures wildlife."

In the elaboration and enforcement of the ESA, the Secretary and all persons who must comply with the law will confront difficult questions of proximity and degree; for, as all recognize, the Act encompasses a vast range of economic and social enterprises and endeavors. These questions must be addressed in the usual course of the law, through case-by-case resolution and adjudication....

■ Justice O'Connor, concurring.

My agreement with the Court is founded on two understandings. First, the challenged regulation is limited to significant habitat modification that causes actual, as opposed to hypothetical or speculative, death or injury to identifiable protected animals. Second, ... the regulation's application is limited by ordinary principles of proximate causation, which introduce notions of foreseeability....

... I do not find it as easy as Justice Scalia does to dismiss the notion that significant impairment of breeding injures living creatures.... To "injure" is, among other things, "to impair." Webster's Ninth New Collegiate Dictionary 623 (1983). One need not subscribe to theories of "psychic harm," to recognize that to make it impossible for an animal to reproduce is to impair its most essential physical functions and to render that animal, and its genetic material, biologically obsolete....

In any event, even if impairing an animal's ability to breed were not, *in and of itself*, an injury to that animal, interference with breeding can cause an animal to suffer other, perhaps more obvious, kinds of injury. The regulation has clear application, for example, to significant habitat modification that kills or physically injures animals which, because they are in a vulnerable breeding state, do not or cannot flee or defend themselves, or to environmental pollutants that cause an animal to suffer physical complications during gestation....

■ Justice Scalia, with whom The Chief Justice and Justice Thomas join, dissenting.

I think it unmistakably clear that the legislation at issue here (1) forbade the hunting and killing of endangered animals, and (2) provided federal lands and federal funds for the acquisition of private lands, to preserve the habitat of endangered animals. The Court's holding that the hunting and killing prohibition incidentally preserves habitat on private lands imposes unfairness to the point of financial ruin—not just upon the rich, but upon the simplest farmer who finds his land conscripted to national zoological use. I respectfully dissent.

I

... In my view petitioners must lose—the regulation must fall—even under the test of Chevron U.S.A. Inc. v. Natural Resources Defense Council, Inc., 467 U.S. 837, 843 (1984), so I shall assume that the Court is correct to apply *Chevron*.

The regulation has three features which ... do not comport with the statute. First, it interprets the statute to prohibit habitat modification that is no more than the cause-in-fact of death or injury to wildlife. *Any* "significant habitat modification" that in fact produces that result by "impairing essential behavioral patterns" is made unlawful, regardless of whether that result is intended or even foreseeable, and no matter how long the chain of causality between modification and injury....

Second, the regulation does not require an "act": The Secretary's officially stated position is that an *omission* will do....

The third and most important unlawful feature of the regulation is that it encompasses injury inflicted, not only upon individual animals, but upon populations of the protected species. "Injury" in the regulation includes "significantly impairing essential behavioral patterns, including *breeding*." Impairment of breeding does not "injure" living creatures; it prevents them from propagating, thus "injuring" a population of animals which would otherwise have maintained or increased its numbers....

*None* of these three features of the regulation can be found in the statutory provisions supposed to authorize it. The term "harm" in § 1532(19) has no legal force of its own ... for the only *operative* term in the statute is to "take." If "take" were not elsewhere defined in the Act, none could dispute what it means, for the term is as old as the law itself. To "take," when applied to wild animals, means to reduce those animals, by killing or capturing, to human control.... This is just the sense in which "take" is used elsewhere in federal legislation and treaty.... And that meaning fits neatly with the rest of § 1538(a)(1), which makes it unlawful not only to take protected species, but also to import or export them; to possess, sell, deliver, carry, transport, or ship any taken species; and to transport, sell, or offer to sell them in interstate or foreign commerce. The taking prohibition, in other words, is only part of the regulatory plan of § 1538(a)(1), which covers all the stages of the process by which protected wildlife is reduced to man's dominion and made the object of profit. It is obvious that "take" in this sense—a term of art deeply embedded in the statutory and common law concerning wildlife—describes a class of acts (not omissions) done directly and intentionally (not indirectly and by accident) to particular animals (not populations of animals).

The Act's definition of "take" does expand the word slightly (and not unusually), so as to make clear that it includes not just a completed taking, but the process of taking, and all of the acts that are customarily identified with or accompany that process ("to harass, harm, pursue, hunt, shoot, wound, kill, trap, capture, or collect"); and so as to include attempts. The tempting fallacy—which the Court commits with abandon—is to assume that *once defined*, "take" loses any significance, and it is only the definition that matters. The Court treats the statute as though Congress had directly enacted the § 1532(19) definition as a self-executing prohibition, and had not enacted § 1538(a)(1)(B) at all. But § 1538(a)(1)(B) *is* there, and if the terms contained in the definitional section are susceptible of two readings, one of which comports with the standard meaning of "take" as used in application to wildlife, and one of which does not, an agency regulation that adopts the latter reading is necessarily unreasonable, for it reads the defined term "take"—the only operative term—out of the statute altogether.[2]

That is what has occurred here. The verb "harm" has a range of meaning: "to cause injury" at its broadest, "to do hurt or damage" in a narrower and more direct sense.... In fact the more directed sense of "harm" is a somewhat more common and preferred usage.... To define "harm" as an act or omission that, however remotely, "actually kills or injures" a population of wildlife through habitat modification is to choose a meaning that makes nonsense of the word that "harm" defines—requiring us to accept that a farmer who tills his field and causes erosion that makes silt run into a nearby river which depletes oxygen and thereby "impairs [the] breeding" of protected fish has "taken" or "attempted to take" the fish. It should take the strongest evidence to make us believe that Congress has defined a term in a manner repugnant to its ordinary and traditional sense.

Here the evidence shows the opposite. "Harm" is merely one of 10 prohibitory words in § 1532(19), and the other 9 fit the ordinary meaning of "take" perfectly. To "harass, pursue, hunt, shoot, wound, kill, trap, capture, or collect" are all affirmative acts ... which are directed immediately and intentionally against a particular animal—not acts or omissions that indirectly and accidentally cause injury to a population of animals. The Court points out that several of the words ("harass," "pursue," "wound," and "kill") "refer to actions or effects that do not require direct *applications of force*." (emphasis added). That is true enough, but force is not the point. Even "taking" activities in the narrowest sense, activities traditionally engaged in by hunters and trappers, do not all consist of direct applications of force; pursuit and harassment are part of the business of

---

**2.** The Court suggests halfheartedly that "take" cannot refer to the taking of particular animals, because § 1538(a)(1)(B) prohibits "tak[ing] any [endangered] *species*." The suggestion is halfhearted because that reading obviously contradicts the statutory intent. It would mean no violation in the intentional shooting of a single bald eagle—or, for that matter, the intentional shooting of 1,000 bald eagles out of the extant 1,001. The phrasing of § 1538(a)(1)(B), as the Court recognizes elsewhere, is shorthand for "take any [*member of* an endangered] species."

"taking" the prey even before it has been touched. What the nine other words in § 1532(19) have in common—and share with the narrower meaning of "harm" described above, but not with the Secretary's ruthless dilation of the word—is the sense of affirmative conduct intentionally directed against a particular animal or animals.

... [Under the principle of statutory construction,] *noscitur a sociis*, ... [t]he fact that "several items in a list share an attribute counsels in favor of interpreting the other items as possessing that attribute as well," Beecham v. United States, 511 U.S. 368, 371 (1994). The Court contends that the canon cannot be applied to deprive a word of all its "independent meaning," .... That proposition is questionable to begin with, especially as applied to long lawyers' listings such as this. If it were true, we ought to give the word "trap" in the definition its rare meaning of "to clothe" (whence "trappings")—since otherwise it adds nothing to the word "capture." In any event, the Court's contention that "harm" in the narrow sense adds nothing to the other words underestimates the ingenuity of our own species in a way that Congress did not. To feed an animal poison, to spray it with mace, to chop down the very tree in which it is nesting, or even to destroy its entire habitat in order to take it (as by draining a pond to get at a turtle), might neither wound nor kill, but would directly and intentionally harm.

... The Court says that "[to] read a requirement of intent or purpose into the words used to define 'take' ... ignore[s] [§ 1540's] express provision that a 'knowin[g]' action is enough to violate the Act." This presumably means that because the reading of § 1532(19) advanced here ascribes an element of purposeful injury to the prohibited acts, it makes superfluous (or inexplicable) the more severe penalties provided for a "knowing" violation. That conclusion does not follow, for it is quite possible to take protected wildlife purposefully without doing so knowingly. A requirement that a violation be "knowing" means that the defendant must "know the facts that make his conduct illegal," Staples v. United States, 511 U.S. 600, 606 (1994). The hunter who shoots an elk in the mistaken belief that it is a mule deer has not knowingly violated § 1538(a)(1)(B)—not because he does not know that elk are legally protected ..., but because he does not know what sort of animal he is shooting. The hunter has nonetheless committed a purposeful taking of protected wildlife, and would therefore be subject to the (lower) strict-liability penalties for the violation....

## II

The Court makes four other arguments. First, "the broad purpose of the [Act] supports the Secretary's decision to extend protection against activities that cause the precise harms Congress enacted the statute to avoid." I thought we had renounced the vice of "simplistically ... assum[ing] that *whatever* furthers the statute's primary objective must be the law." Rodriguez v. United States, 480 U.S. 522, 526 (1987) (per curiam) (emphasis in original). Deduction from the "broad purpose" of a statute begs the question if it is used to decide by what *means* (and hence to what *length*) Congress pursued that purpose; to get the right answer to that question there is no substitute for the hard job (or, in this case, the quite simple one) of reading the whole text. . . .

Second, the Court maintains that the legislative history of the 1973 Act supports the Secretary's definition. Even if legislative history were a legitimate and reliable tool of interpretation (which I shall assume in order to rebut the Court's claim); and even if it could appropriately be resorted to when the enacted text is as clear as this; here it shows quite the opposite of what the Court says. . . .

Much of the Court's discussion of legislative history is devoted to two items: first, the Senate floor manager's introduction of an amendment that added the word "harm" to the definition of "take," with the observation that . . . it would " 'help to achieve the purposes of the bill' "; second, the relevant Committee's removal from the definition of a provision stating that "take" includes " 'the destruction, modification or curtailment of [the] habitat or range' " of fish and wildlife. The Court inflates the first and belittles the second, even though the second is on its face far more pertinent. But this elaborate inference from various pre-enactment actions and inactions is quite unnecessary, since we have *direct* evidence of what those who brought the legislation to the floor thought it meant. . . .

Both the Senate and House floor managers of the bill explained it in terms which leave no doubt that the problem of habitat destruction on private lands was to be solved principally by the land acquisition program of § 1534, while § 1538 solved a different problem altogether—the problem of takings. . . .

Habitat modification and takings, in other words, were viewed as different problems, addressed by different provisions of the Act. The Court really has no explanation for these statements . . . . [T]hey display the clear understanding (1) that habitat modification is separate from "taking," and (2) that habitat destruction on private lands is to be remedied by public acquisition, and not by making particular unlucky landowners incur "excessive cost to themselves." . . . .

. . . [T]he Court seeks support from a provision that was added to the Act in 1982, the year after the Secretary promulgated the current regulation. The provision states:

"[T]he Secretary may permit, under such terms and conditions as he shall prescribe—

. . . . .

"any taking otherwise prohibited by section 1538(a)(1)(B) . . . if such taking is incidental to, and not the purpose of, the carrying out of an otherwise lawful activity." 16 U.S.C. § 1539(a)(1)(B).

. . . The Court claims . . . that the provision "strongly suggests that Congress understood [§ 1538(a)(1)(B)] to prohibit indirect as well as deliberate takings." That would be a valid inference if habitat modification were the only substantial "otherwise lawful activity" that might incidentally and nonpurposefully cause a prohibited "taking." Of course it is not. This provision applies to the many otherwise lawful takings that incidentally take a protected species—as when fishing for unprotected salmon also takes an endangered species of salmon .... Congress has referred to such "incidental takings" in other statutes as well.... The Court shows that it misunderstands the question when it says that "[n]o one could seriously request an 'incidental' take permit to avert ... liability for direct, deliberate action *against a member of an endangered or threatened species.*" (emphasis added). That is not an *incidental* take at all.

This is enough to show ... that the 1982 permit provision does not support the regulation. I must acknowledge that the Senate Committee Report on this provision, and the House Conference Committee Report, clearly contemplate that it will enable the Secretary to permit environmental modification. But the text of the amendment cannot possibly bear that asserted meaning, when placed within the context of an Act that must be interpreted (as we have seen) not to prohibit private environmental modification. The neutral language of the amendment cannot possibly alter that interpretation, nor can its legislative history be summoned forth to contradict, rather than clarify, what is in its totality an unambiguous statutory text.... There is little fear, of course, that giving no effect to the relevant portions of the Committee Reports will frustrate the real-life expectations of a majority of the Members of Congress. If they read and relied on such tedious detail on such an obscure point ... the Republic would be in grave peril....

## III

In response to the points made in this dissent, the Court's opinion stresses two points, neither of which is supported by the regulation, and so cannot validly be used to uphold it. First, the Court and the concurrence suggest that the regulation should be read to contain a requirement of proximate causation or foreseeability, principally *because the statute does....* I quite agree that the statute contains such a limitation, because the verbs of purpose in § 1538(a)(1)(B) denote action directed at animals. But the Court has rejected that reading. The critical premise on which it has upheld the regulation is that, despite the weight of the other words in § 1538(a)(1)(B), "the statutory term 'harm' encompasses indirect as well as direct injuries,"…. Consequently, unless there is some strange category of causation that is indirect and yet also proximate, the Court has already rejected its own basis for finding a proximate-cause limitation in the regulation....

The regulation says (it is worth repeating) that "harm" means (1) an act that (2) actually kills or injures wildlife. If that does not dispense with a proximate-cause requirement, I do not know what language would. And changing the regulation by judicial invention, even to achieve compliance with the statute, is not permissible. Perhaps the agency itself would prefer to achieve compliance in some other fashion. We defer to reasonable agency interpretations of ambiguous statutes precisely in order that agencies, rather than courts, may exercise policymaking discretion in the interstices of statutes. See *Chevron*, 467 U.S., at 843–845....

The second point the Court stresses in its response seems to me a belated mending of its holding. It apparently concedes that the statute requires injury *to particular animals* rather than merely to populations of animals.... The Court then rejects my contention that the regulation ignores this requirement, since, it says, "every term in the regulation's definition of 'harm' is subservient to the phrase 'an act which actually kills or injures wildlife.' " As I have pointed out, this reading is incompatible with the regulation's specification of impairment of "breeding" as one of the *modes* of "kill[ing] or injur[ing] wildlife."[5]

But since the Court is reading the regulation and the statute incorrectly in other respects, it may as well introduce this novelty as well—law à la carte. As I understand the regulation that the Court has created and held consistent with the statute that it has also created, habitat modification can constitute a "taking," but only if it results in the killing or harming of *individual animals*, and only if that consequence is the direct result of the modification. This means that the destruction of privately owned habitat that is essential, not for the feeding or nesting, but for the *breeding*, of butterflies, would not violate the Act, since it would not harm or kill any living butterfly. I, too, think it would not violate the Act—not for the utterly unsupported reason that habitat modifications fall outside the regulation if they happen not to kill or injure a living animal, but for the textual reason that only action directed at living animals constitutes a "take." ...

---

**1. *How Much Work Is* Chevron *Doing in* Sweet Home?**—Justice Stevens' majority opinion in *Sweet Home* emphasized repeatedly that the question in the case was not whether the Interior Department's interpreta-

---

**5.** Justice O'CONNOR supposes that an "impairment of breeding" intrinsically injures an animal because "to make it impossible for an animal to reproduce is to impair its most essential physical functions and to render that animal, and its genetic material, biologically obsolete." (concurring opinion). This imaginative construction does achieve the result of extending "impairment of breeding" to individual animals; but only at the expense of also expanding "injury" to include elements beyond physical harm to individual animals. For surely the only harm to the individual animal from impairment of that "essential function" is not the failure of issue (which harms only the issue), but the *psychic harm* of perceiving that it will leave this world with no issue (assuming, of course, that the animal in question, perhaps an endangered species of slug, is capable of such painful sentiments). If it includes *that* psychic harm, then why not the psychic harm of not being able to frolic about—so that the draining of a pond used for an endangered animal's recreation, but in no way essential to its survival, would be prohibited by the Act? That the concurrence is driven to such a dubious redoubt is an argument for, not against, the proposition that "injury" in the regulation includes injury to populations of animals. Even more so with the concurrence's alternative explanation: that "impairment of breeding" refers to nothing more than concrete injuries inflicted by the habitat modification on the animal who does the breeding, such as "physical complications [suffered] during gestation," ... Quite obviously, if "impairment of breeding" meant such physical harm to an individual animal, it would not have had to be mentioned....

tion of "take" was *correct*, but whether it was sufficiently *reasonable* to merit deference under *Chevron*. From your reading of the opinion, does it seem that the holding depends on this deferential standard of review? Put another way, if a de novo standard of review applied in this case, do you think Justice Stevens would still uphold the Department's interpretation as the best reading of § 9 of the Endangered Species Act? Alternatively, suppose that the agency had adopted the dissent's interpretation of "take." Would (or should) the Court have upheld that definition as reasonable, or would the evidence the Court identified to support its holding—the concerns about avoiding statutory surplusage, the inferences from statutory structure, the dictionary definition of "harm," the legislative history— impel a holding that the interpretation of "take" favored by Justice Scalia's dissent would be unreasonable under *Chevron* even if the agency had endorsed it?

**2. *The Relationship between Operative Provisions and Statutory Definitions*—**The dissent's emphasis on the traditional meaning of "take," and the majority's response, raises an interesting question about the relationship between operative statutory terms and the statutory definitions of those terms. Justice Scalia's argument here has two components: (1) "take," in this context, is a term of art with a traditional meaning restricted to killing or capturing animals; and (2) the words that appear in the statutory definition of "take"—including the word "harm"— should be read in a way that is consistent with the essential elements of the traditional meaning of "take," rather than in a way that substantially expands the meaning of that term. Justice Stevens' majority opinion did not seem to take issue with the first point. Rather, the majority emphasized that "Congress explicitly defined the operative term 'take' in the ESA," which in turn meant that that the Court did not need "to probe its meaning as [the court had to] probe the meaning of the undefined subsidiary term 'harm.' "

Justice Scalia's position thus seems to be that the operative term in the statute is most important; the definitional terms, while also important, can and should be limited by the nature of the operative term they define. Justice Stevens' position, by contrast, seems to be that once an operative statutory term is specifically defined in the statute itself, that statutory definition alone determines the operative term's meaning, and any additional limitations or connotations contained in the operative term itself do not matter. Which of those positions would you favor in an ordinary statutory interpretation case? Should *Chevron* make a difference here? If one could plausibly read the broad definitional section in light of the narrower common law meaning of "take," or could read the operative term "take" as broadened by the statutory definition, is that the sort of statutory ambiguity the agency should resolve under *Chevron*? If not, why not?

**3. *Chevron and Semantic Canons*—**What about the dueling semantic canons? The dissent (and the D.C. Circuit opinion under review) emphasized the *noscitur a sociis* canon: Because the other words in the definition of "take" connote direct and intentional applications of physical force, and because the word "harm" sometimes has a similar narrow meaning, application of the *noscitur* canon implies that "harm" should be given this narrower construction in the context of the ESA's definition of "take." The majority, on the other hand, emphasized the presumption against statutory surplusage: According to the majority, the narrower reading of "harm" favored by the dissent would render that term redundant with the other terms in the statutory definition.

The notes following *Gustafson v. Alloyd* (pp. 248–249, *supra*), suggested that the tension between the *noscitur* canon and the presumption against statutory redundancy may be one of the best illustrations of Karl Llewellyn's claim that for every canon there is a counter-canon that leads to the opposite conclusion. Does the debate between the majority and the dissent in *Sweet Home* bear that out? Does the "dueling canon" phenomenon imply that the courts should give the canons little weight under the *Chevron* framework? Or are these canons, if applied appropriately and with sensitivity to the overall context, still a legitimate and valuable source of insight into whether Congress had a specific intention on the precise question at issue?

## C. Structure, Context, and History in *Chevron* Analysis

In most cases in which a court rejects an agency's statutory interpretation under the *Chevron* framework, the court emphasizes the inconsistency of the agency's interpretation with the *clear semantic meaning* of the statutory text; courts in such cases typically invoke arguments from structure, context, purpose, or history to buttress or augment the textual claim. But in certain cases, courts have rejected agency statutory interpretations as contrary to the clear intent of Congress *solely* on the basis of inferences from structure, purpose, and history, without any real argument that the semantic meaning of the statutory term itself is inconsistent with the agency's interpretation. The following case, *FDA v. Brown & Williamson Tobacco Corp.*, is a case of that sort. As you read the case, pay close attention to the reasons the Court gives for its conclusion that the Food, Drugs, and Cosmetics Act clearly prohibits the FDA from asserting jurisdiction over tobacco products. What do these reasons suggest to you about the scope and limits of *Chevron* deference?

---

## Food and Drug Administration v. Brown & Williamson Tobacco Corp.

Supreme Court of the United States
529 U.S. 120 (2000)

■ Justice O'Connor delivered the opinion of the Court.

This case involves one of the most troubling public health problems facing our Nation today: the thousands of premature deaths that occur each year because of tobacco use. In 1996, the Food and Drug Administration (FDA) ... asserted jurisdiction to regulate tobacco products.... The FDA concluded that nicotine is a "drug" within the meaning of the Food, Drug, and Cosmetic Act (FDCA or Act) .... Pursuant to this authority, it promulgated regulations intended to reduce tobacco consumption among children and adolescents....

... [A]lthough agencies are generally entitled to deference in the interpretation of statutes that they administer, a reviewing "court, as well as the agency, must give effect to the unambiguously expressed intent of Congress." *Chevron U.S.A. Inc. v. Natural Resources Defense Council, Inc.,* 467 U.S. 837, 842–843 (1984). In this case, we believe that Congress has clearly precluded the FDA from asserting jurisdiction to regulate tobacco products. Such authority is inconsistent with the intent that Congress has expressed in the FDCA's overall regulatory scheme and in the tobacco-specific legislation that it has enacted subsequent to the FDCA. In light of this clear intent, the FDA's assertion of jurisdiction is impermissible.

I

The FDCA grants the FDA ... the authority to regulate ... "drugs" ... [and] defines "drug" to include "articles (other than food) intended to affect the structure or any function of the body." 21 U.S.C. § 321(g)(1)(C)....

[After notice and comment,] the FDA issued a final rule entitled "Regulations Restricting the Sale and Distribution of Cigarettes and Smokeless Tobacco to Protect Children and Adolescents." The FDA determined that nicotine is a "drug" ... [,] and therefore it had jurisdiction under the FDCA to regulate tobacco products as customarily marketed— that is, without manufacturer claims of therapeutic benefit. First, the FDA found that tobacco products " 'affect the structure or any function of the body' " because nicotine "has significant pharmacological effects." ... Second, the FDA determined that these effects were "intended" under the FDCA because they "are so widely known and foreseeable that [they] may be deemed to have been intended by the manufacturers," ...; consumers use tobacco products "predominantly or nearly exclusively" to obtain these effects ...; and the statements, research, and actions of manufacturers revealed that they "have 'designed' cigarettes to provide pharmacologically active doses of nicotine to consumers,"....

Having resolved the jurisdictional question, the FDA next explained the policy justifications for its regulations, detailing the deleterious health effects associated with tobacco use....

Based on these findings, the FDA promulgated regulations concerning tobacco products' promotion, labeling, and accessibility to children and adolescents. The access regulations prohibit the sale of cigarettes or smokeless tobacco to persons younger than 18; require retailers to verify through photo identification the age of all purchasers younger than 27; prohibit the sale of cigarettes in quantities smaller than 20; prohibit the distribution of free samples; and prohibit sales through self-service displays and vending machines except in adult-only locations. The promotion regulations require that any print advertising appear in a black-and-white, text-only format unless the publication in which it appears is read almost exclusively by adults; prohibit outdoor advertising within 1,000 feet of any public playground or school; prohibit the distribution of any promotional items, such as T-shirts or hats, bearing the manufacturer's brand name; and prohibit a manufacturer from sponsoring any athletic, musical, artistic, or other social or cultural event using its brand name. The labeling regulation requires that the statement, "A Nicotine–Delivery Device for Persons 18 or Older," appear on all tobacco product packages....

## II

... Because this case involves an administrative agency's construction of a statute that it administers, our analysis is governed by *Chevron U.S.A. Inc. v. Natural Resources Defense Council, Inc.,* 467 U.S. 837 (1984). Under *Chevron,* a reviewing court must first ask "whether Congress has directly spoken to the precise question at issue." ... If Congress has done so, the inquiry is at an end.... But if Congress has not specifically addressed the question, a reviewing court must respect the agency's construction of the statute so long as it is permissible....

In determining whether Congress has specifically addressed the question at issue, a reviewing court should not confine itself to examining a particular statutory provision in isolation. The meaning—or ambiguity—of certain words or phrases may only become evident when placed in context.... Similarly, the meaning of one statute may be affected by other Acts, particularly where Congress has spoken subsequently and more specifically to the topic at hand.... In addition, we must be guided to a degree by common sense as to the manner in which Congress is likely to delegate a policy decision of such economic and political magnitude to an administrative agency. Cf. *MCI Telecommunications Corp. v. American Telephone & Telegraph Co.,* 512 U.S. 218, 231 (1994)....

### A

Viewing the FDCA as a whole, it is evident that one of the Act's core objectives is to ensure that any product regulated by the FDA is "safe" and "effective" for its intended use.... For instance, 21 U.S.C. § 393(b)(2) ... defines the FDA's "[m]ission" to include "protect[ing] the public health by ensuring that ... drugs are safe and effective" and that "there is reasonable assurance of the safety and effectiveness of devices intended for human use." The FDCA requires premarket approval of any new drug, with some limited exceptions, and states that the FDA "shall issue an order refusing to approve the application" of a new drug if it is not safe and effective for its intended purpose. §§ 355(d)(1)–(2), (4)–(5). If the FDA discovers ... that a drug is unsafe or ineffective, it "shall, after due notice and opportunity for hearing to the applicant, withdraw approval" of the drug. 21 U.S.C. §§ 355(e)(1)–(3)....

In its rulemaking proceeding, the FDA quite exhaustively documented that "tobacco products are unsafe," "dangerous," and "cause great pain and suffering from illness." . . . .

These findings logically imply that, if tobacco [is a "drug"] under the FDCA, the FDA would be required to remove [tobacco products] from the market. . . . Contrary to the dissent's contention, the Act admits no remedial discretion. . . .

Congress, however, has foreclosed the removal of tobacco products from the market. A provision of the United States Code currently in force states that "[t]he marketing of tobacco constitutes one of the greatest basic industries of the United States with ramifying activities which directly affect interstate and foreign commerce at every point, and stable conditions therein are necessary to the general welfare." 7 U.S.C. § 1311(a). More importantly, Congress has directly addressed the problem of tobacco and health through legislation on six occasions since 1965. See Federal Cigarette Labeling and Advertising Act (FCLAA), Pub.L. 89–92, 79 Stat. 282; Public Health Cigarette Smoking Act of 1969, Pub.L. 91–222, 84 Stat. 87; Alcohol and Drug Abuse Amendments of 1983, Pub.L. 98–24, 97 Stat. 175; Comprehensive Smoking Education Act, Pub.L. 98–474, 98 Stat. 2200; Comprehensive Smokeless Tobacco Health Education Act of 1986, Pub.L. 99–252, 100 Stat. 30; Alcohol, Drug Abuse, and Mental Health Administration Reorganization Act, Pub.L. 102–321, § 202, 106 Stat. 394. When Congress enacted these statutes, the adverse health consequences of tobacco use were well known. . . . Nonetheless, Congress stopped well short of ordering a ban. Instead, it has generally regulated the labeling and advertisement of tobacco products, expressly providing that it is the policy of Congress that "commerce and the national economy may be . . . protected to the maximum extent consistent with" consumers "be[ing] adequately informed about any adverse health effects." 15 U.S.C. § 1331. Congress' decisions to regulate labeling and advertising and to adopt the express policy of protecting "commerce and the national economy . . . to the maximum extent" reveal its intent that tobacco products remain on the market. Indeed, the collective premise of these statutes is that cigarettes and smokeless tobacco will continue to be sold in the United States. A ban of tobacco products by the FDA would therefore plainly contradict congressional policy.

The FDA apparently recognized this dilemma and concluded, somewhat ironically, that tobacco products are actually "safe" within the meaning of the FDCA. In promulgating its regulations, the agency conceded that "tobacco products are unsafe, as that term is conventionally understood." . . . Nonetheless, the FDA reasoned that, in determining whether a device is safe under the Act, it must consider "not only the risks presented by a product but also any of the countervailing effects of use of that product, including the consequences of not permitting the product to be marketed." . . . Applying this standard, the FDA found that, because of the high level of addiction among tobacco users, a ban would likely be "dangerous." . . . In particular, current tobacco users could suffer from extreme withdrawal, the health care system and available pharmaceuticals might not be able to meet the treatment demands of those suffering from withdrawal, and a black market offering cigarettes even more dangerous than those currently sold legally would likely develop....

It may well be, as the FDA asserts, that "these factors must be considered when developing a regulatory scheme that achieves the best public health result for these products." ... But the FDA's judgment that leaving tobacco products on the market "is more effective in achieving public health goals than a ban," ... is no substitute for the specific safety determinations required by the [FDCA]. Several provisions in the Act require the FDA to determine that the *product itself* is safe as used by consumers.... In contrast, the FDA's conception of safety would allow the agency ... to compare the aggregate health effects of alternative administrative actions. This is a qualitatively different inquiry. Thus, although the FDA has concluded that a ban would be "dangerous," it has *not* concluded that tobacco products are "safe" as that term is used throughout the Act....

... Consequently, the analogy made by the FDA and the dissent to highly toxic drugs used in the treatment of various cancers is unpersuasive.... Although "dangerous" in some sense, these drugs are safe within the meaning of the Act because, for certain patients, the therapeutic benefits outweigh the risk of harm.... The same is not true for tobacco products....

The dissent contends that our conclusion means that "the FDCA requires the FDA to ban outright 'dangerous' drugs or devices," ... and that this is a "perverse" reading of the statute.... This misunderstands our holding. The FDA, consistent with the FDCA, may clearly regulate many "dangerous" products without banning them.... What the FDA may not do is conclude that a drug or device cannot be used safely for any therapeutic purpose and yet, at the same time, allow that product to remain on the market....

Considering the FDCA as a whole, it is clear that Congress intended to exclude tobacco products from the FDA's jurisdiction. A fundamental precept of the FDCA is that any product regulated by the FDA—but not banned—must be safe for its intended use.... [T]he FDA has concluded that, although tobacco products might be effective in delivering certain pharmacological effects, they are "unsafe" and "dangerous" when used for these purposes. Consequently, if tobacco products were within the FDA's jurisdiction, the Act would require the FDA to remove them from the market entirely. But a ban would contradict Congress' clear intent as expressed in its more recent, tobacco-specific legislation. The inescapable conclusion is that there is no room for tobacco products within the FDCA's regulatory scheme. If they cannot be used safely for any therapeutic purpose, and yet they cannot be banned, they simply do not fit.

### B

In determining whether Congress has spoken directly to the FDA's authority to regulate tobacco, we must also consider in greater detail the tobacco-specific legislation that Congress has enacted over the past 35 years. At the time a statute is enacted, it may have a range of plausible meanings. Over time, however, subsequent acts can shape or focus those meanings. The "classic judicial task of reconciling many laws enacted over time, and getting them to 'make sense' in combination, necessarily assumes that the implications of a statute may be altered by the implications of a later statute." United States v. Fausto, 484 U.S. [439, 453 (1988)]. This is particularly so where the scope of the earlier statute is broad but the subsequent statutes more specifically address the topic at hand. As we recognized recently in *United States v. Estate of Romani,* "a specific policy embodied in a later federal statute should control our construction of the [earlier] statute, even though it ha[s] not been expressly amended." 523 U.S. [517, 530–531 (1998)].

Congress has enacted six separate pieces of legislation since 1965 addressing the problem of tobacco use and human health. Those statutes, among other things, require that health warnings appear on all packaging and in all print and outdoor advertisements . . . ; prohibit the advertisement of tobacco products through "any medium of electronic communication" subject to regulation by the Federal Communications Commission (FCC) . . . ; require the Secretary of HHS to report every three years to Congress on research findings concerning "the addictive property of tobacco," . . . ; and make States' receipt of certain federal block grants contingent on their making it unlawful "for any manufacturer, retailer, or distributor of tobacco products to sell or distribute any such product to any individual under the age of 18," . . . .

In adopting each statute, Congress has acted against the backdrop of the FDA's consistent and repeated statements that it lacked authority under the FDCA to regulate tobacco absent claims of therapeutic benefit by the manufacturer. In fact, on several occasions over this period, and after the health consequences of tobacco use and nicotine's pharmacological effects had become well known, Congress considered and rejected bills that would have granted the FDA such jurisdiction. Under these circumstances, it is evident that Congress' tobacco-specific statutes have effectively ratified the FDA's long-held position that it lacks jurisdiction under the FDCA to regulate tobacco products. Congress has created a distinct regulatory scheme to address the problem of tobacco and health, and that scheme, as presently constructed, precludes any role for the FDA.

[In 1964, for example,] Congress convened hearings to consider legislation addressing "the tobacco problem." During those deliberations, FDA representatives testified before Congress that the agency lacked jurisdiction under the FDCA to regulate tobacco products. . . .

[Before ultimately enacting its first major piece of tobacco legislation, the Federal Cigarette Labeling and Advertising Act (FCLAA),] Congress considered and rejected several proposals to give the FDA the authority to regulate tobacco. In April 1963, Representative Udall introduced a bill "[t]o amend the Federal Food, Drug, and Cosmetic Act so as to make that Act applicable to smoking products." H.R. 5973, 88th Cong., 1st Sess., 1. Two months later, Senator Moss introduced an identical bill in the Senate. S. 1682, 88th Cong., 1st Sess. (1963). . . . In December 1963, Representative Rhodes introduced another bill that would have amended the FDCA "by striking out 'food, drug, device, or cosmetic,' each place where it appears therein and inserting in lieu thereof 'food, drug, device, cosmetic, or smoking product.' " H.R. 9512, 88th Cong., 1st Sess., § 3 (1963). And in January 1965, five months before passage of the FCLAA, Representative Udall again introduced a bill to amend the FDCA "to make that Act applicable to smoking products." H.R. 2248, 89th Cong., 1st Sess., 1. None of these proposals became law.

Congress ultimately decided in 1965 to subject tobacco products to the less extensive regulatory scheme of the FCLAA, which created a "comprehensive Federal program to deal with cigarette labeling and advertising with respect to any relationship between smoking and health." Pub.L. 89–92, § 2, 79 Stat. 282. The FCLAA rejected any regulation of advertising, but it required the warning, "Caution: Cigarette Smoking May Be Hazardous to Your Health," to appear on all cigarette packages. Id., § 4, 79 Stat. 283. . . .

Subsequent tobacco-specific legislation followed a similar pattern. . . . [The Court then went on to describe various other statutory enactments addressing the regulation of tobacco. The Court emphasized that in the deliberations that formed the background of each such statute, the FDA consistently took the position that it lacked jurisdiction to regulate tobacco.]

. . . The FDA's disavowal of jurisdiction was consistent with the position that it had taken since the agency's inception. As the FDA concedes, it never asserted authority to regulate tobacco products as customarily marketed until it promulgated the regulations at issue here. . . .

The FDA's position was also consistent with Congress' specific intent when it enacted the FDCA. . . . [A]s the FDA admits, there is no evidence in the text of the FDCA or its legislative history that Congress in 1938 even considered the applicability of the Act to tobacco products. Given the economic and political significance of the tobacco industry at the time, it is extremely unlikely that Congress could have intended to place tobacco within the ambit of the FDCA absent any discussion of the matter. Of course, whether the Congress that enacted the FDCA specifically intended the Act to cover tobacco products is not determinative. . . . Nonetheless, this intent is certainly relevant to understanding the basis for the FDA's representations to Congress and the background against which Congress enacted subsequent tobacco-specific legislation. . . .

Taken together, these actions by Congress over the past 35 years preclude an interpretation of the FDCA that grants the FDA jurisdiction to regulate tobacco products. We do not rely on Congress' failure to act—its consideration and rejection of bills that would have given the FDA this authority—in reaching this conclusion. Indeed, this is not a case of simple inaction by Congress that purportedly represents its acquiescence in an agency's position. To the contrary, Congress has enacted several statutes addressing the particular subject of tobacco and health, creating a distinct regulatory scheme for cigarettes and smokeless tobacco. In doing so, Congress has been aware of tobacco's health hazards and its pharmacological effects. It has also enacted this legislation against the background of the FDA repeatedly and consistently asserting that it lacks jurisdiction under the FDCA to regulate tobacco products as customarily marketed. Further, Congress has persistently acted to preclude a meaningful role for *any* administrative agency in making policy on the subject of tobacco and health. . . .

Under these circumstances, it is clear that Congress' tobacco-specific legislation has effectively ratified the FDA's previous position that it lacks jurisdiction to regulate tobacco. . . . Congress has affirmatively acted to address the issue of tobacco and health, relying on the representations of the FDA that it had no authority to regulate tobacco. It has created a distinct scheme to regulate the sale of tobacco products, focused on labeling and advertising, and premised on the belief that the FDA lacks such jurisdiction under the FDCA. As a result, Congress' tobacco-specific statutes preclude the FDA from regulating tobacco products as customarily marketed.

Although the dissent takes issue with our discussion of the FDA's change in position, . . . our conclusion does not rely on the fact that the FDA's assertion of jurisdiction represents a sharp break with its prior interpretation of the FDCA. Certainly, an agency's initial interpretation of a statute that it is charged with administering is not "carved in stone." *Chevron*, 467 U.S., at 863. . . . The consistency of the FDA's prior position is significant in this case for a different reason: It provides important context to Congress' enactment of its tobacco-specific legislation. When the FDA repeatedly informed Congress that the FDCA does not grant it the authority to regulate tobacco products, its statements were consistent with the agency's unwavering position since its inception, and with the position that its predecessor agency had first taken in 1914. Although not crucial, the consistency of the FDA's prior position bolsters the conclusion that when Congress created a distinct regulatory scheme addressing the subject of tobacco and health, it understood that the FDA is without jurisdiction to regulate tobacco products and ratified that position.

The dissent also argues that the proper inference to be drawn from Congress' tobacco-specific legislation is "critically ambivalent." . . . We disagree. In that series of statutes, Congress crafted a specific legislative response to the problem of tobacco and health, and it did so with the understanding, based on repeated assertions by the FDA, that the agency has no authority under the FDCA to regulate tobacco products. . . . And in addressing the subject, Congress consistently evidenced its intent to preclude any federal agency from exercising significant policymaking authority in the area. Under these circumstances, we believe the appropriate inference—that Congress intended to ratify the FDA's prior position that it lacks jurisdiction—is unmistakable.

## C

Finally, our inquiry into whether Congress has directly spoken to the precise question at issue is shaped, at least in some measure, by the nature of the question presented. Deference under *Chevron* to an agency's construction of a statute that it administers is premised on the theory that a statute's ambiguity constitutes an implicit delegation from Congress to the agency to fill in the statutory gaps. See *Chevron, supra,* at 844. In extraordinary cases, however, there may be reason to hesitate before concluding that Congress has intended such an implicit delegation. . . .

This is hardly an ordinary case. Contrary to its representations to Congress since 1914, the FDA has now asserted jurisdiction to regulate an industry constituting a significant portion of the American economy. In fact, the FDA contends that, were it to determine that tobacco products provide no "reasonable assurance of safety," it would have the authority to ban cigarettes and smokeless tobacco entirely. Owing to its unique place in American history and society, tobacco has its own unique political history. Congress, for better or for worse, has created a distinct regulatory scheme for tobacco products, squarely rejected proposals to give the FDA jurisdiction over tobacco, and repeatedly acted to preclude any agency from exercising significant policymaking authority in the area. Given this history and the breadth of the authority that the FDA has asserted, we are obliged to defer not to the agency's expansive construction of the statute, but to Congress' consistent judgment to deny the FDA this power.

Our decision in *MCI Telecommunications Corp. v. American Telephone & Telegraph Co.,* 512 U.S. 218 (1994), is instructive. That case involved the proper construction of the term "modify" in § 203(b) of the Communications Act of 1934. The FCC contended that, because the Act gave it the discretion to "modify any requirement" imposed under the statute, it therefore possessed the authority to render voluntary the otherwise mandatory requirement that long distance carriers file their rates. *Id.* at 225. We rejected the FCC's construction, finding "not the slightest doubt" that Congress had directly spoken to the question. *Id.* at 228. In reasoning even more apt here, we concluded that "[i]t is highly unlikely that Congress would leave the determination of whether an industry will be entirely, or even substantially, rate-regulated to agency discretion—and even more unlikely that it would achieve that through such a subtle device as permission to 'modify' rate-filing requirements." *Id.,* at 231.

As in *MCI,* we are confident that Congress could not have intended to delegate a decision of such economic and political significance to an agency in so cryptic a fashion. . . .

\* \* \*

[N]o matter how "important, conspicuous, and controversial" the issue, and regardless of how likely the public is to hold the Executive Branch politically accountable, . . . an administrative agency's power to regulate in the public interest must always be grounded in a valid grant of authority from Congress. . . . Reading the FDCA as a whole, as well as in conjunction with Congress' subsequent tobacco-specific legislation, it is plain that Congress has not given the FDA the authority that it seeks to exercise here. . . .

■ JUSTICE BREYER, with whom JUSTICE STEVENS, JUSTICE SOUTER, and JUSTICE GINSBURG join, dissenting.

The Food and Drug Administration (FDA) has the authority to regulate "articles (other than food) intended to affect the structure or any function of the body. . . ." Federal Food, Drug, and Cosmetic Act (FDCA), 21 U.S.C. § 321(g)(1)(C). Unlike the majority, I believe that tobacco products fit within this statutory language.

In its own interpretation, the majority nowhere denies the following two salient points. First, tobacco products (including cigarettes) fall within the scope of this statutory definition, read literally. . . .

Second, the statute's basic purpose—the protection of public health—supports the inclusion of cigarettes within its scope. . . .

Despite the FDCA's literal language and general purpose . . . the majority nonetheless reads the statute as *excluding* tobacco products for two basic reasons:

(1) the FDCA does not "fit" the case of tobacco because the statute requires the FDA to prohibit dangerous drugs or devices (like cigarettes) outright, and the agency concedes that simply banning the sale of cigarettes is not a proper remedy . . . ; and

(2) Congress has enacted other statutes, which, when viewed in light of the FDA's long history of denying tobacco-related jurisdiction and considered together with Congress' failure explicitly to grant the agency tobacco-specific authority, demonstrate that Congress did not intend for the FDA to exercise jurisdiction over tobacco. . . .

In my view, neither of these propositions is valid. Rather, the FDCA does not significantly limit the FDA's remedial alternatives. . . . And the later statutes do not tell the FDA it cannot exercise jurisdiction, but simply leave FDA jurisdictional law where Congress found it. . . .

## I

. . . [T]he literal language of the [FDCA's] definition [of "drug"] and the FDCA's general purpose both strongly support a projurisdiction reading of the statute. . . .

That Congress would grant the FDA such broad jurisdictional authority should surprise no one. In 1938, the President and much of Congress believed that federal administrative agencies needed broad authority and would exercise that authority wisely—a view embodied in much Second New Deal legislation. . . .

Nor is it surprising that such a statutory delegation of power could lead after many years to an assertion of jurisdiction that the 1938 legislators might not have expected. Such a possibility is inherent in the very nature of a broad delegation. . . .

I shall not pursue these general matters further, for neither the companies nor the majority denies that the FDCA's literal language, its general purpose, and its particular legislative history favor the FDA's present jurisdictional view. Rather, they have made several specific arguments in support of one basic contention: Even if the statutory delegation is broad, it is not broad *enough* to include tobacco. I now turn to each of those arguments.

### II

. . .

### C

The majority . . . reaches the "inescapable conclusion" that the language and structure of the FDCA as a whole "simply do not fit" the kind of public health problem that tobacco creates. . . . That is because, in the majority's view, the FDCA requires the FDA to ban outright "dangerous" drugs or devices (such as cigarettes); yet, the FDA concedes that an immediate and total cigarette-sale ban is inappropriate. . . .

This argument is curious because it leads with similarly "inescapable" force to precisely the opposite conclusion, namely, that the FDA *does* have jurisdiction but that it must ban cigarettes. More importantly, the argument fails to take into account the fact that a statute interpreted as requiring the FDA to pick a more dangerous over a less dangerous remedy would be a perverse statute, *causing,* rather than preventing, unnecessary harm whenever a total ban is likely the more dangerous response. And one can at least imagine such circumstances.

Suppose, for example, that a commonly used, mildly addictive sleeping pill (or, say, a kind of popular contact lens) . . . turned out to pose serious health risks for certain consumers. Suppose further that many of those addicted consumers would ignore an immediate total ban, turning to a potentially more dangerous black-market substitute, while a less draconian remedy (say, adequate notice) would wean them gradually away to a safer product. Would the FDCA still *force* the FDA to impose the more dangerous remedy? For the following reasons, I think not.

. . . [The dissent argued that the relevant provisions of the statute are framed in a way that gives the FDA discretion to consider the overall safety of various regulatory alternatives, including the comparative safety effects of imposing restrictions upon the sale and distribution of a product, rather than banning it outright.] For example, where the FDA cannot "otherwise" obtain "reasonable assurance" of a device's "safety and effectiveness," the agency may restrict by regulation a product's "sale, distribution, or use" upon "*such . . . conditions as the Secretary may prescribe.*" § 360j(e)(1) (emphasis added). . . .

. . . [S]urely the agency can determine that a substance is comparatively "safe" . . . whenever it would be *less* dangerous to make the product available (subject to regulatory requirements) than suddenly to withdraw it from the market. Any other interpretation risks substantial harm of the sort that my sleeping pill example illustrates .... And nothing in the statute prevents the agency from adopting a view of "safety" that would avoid such harm. Indeed, the FDA already seems to have taken this position when permitting distribution of toxic drugs, such as poisons used for chemotherapy, that are dangerous for the user but are not deemed "dangerous to health" in the relevant sense....

. . . [D]espite the majority's assertions to the contrary, the statute does not distinguish among the kinds of health effects that the agency may take into account when assessing safety. The Court insists that the statute only permits the agency to take into account the health risks and benefits of the *"product itself"* as used by individual consumers . . . and, thus, that the FDA is prohibited from considering that a ban on smoking would lead many smokers to suffer severe withdrawal symptoms or to buy possibly stronger, more dangerous, black market cigarettes—considerations that the majority calls "the aggregate health effects of alternative administrative actions." . . .

[But] one cannot distinguish in this context between a "specific" health risk incurred by an individual and an "aggregate" risk to a group. *All* relevant risk is, at bottom, risk to an individual; *all* relevant risk attaches to "the product itself"; and *all* relevant risk is "aggregate" in the sense that the agency aggregates health effects in order to determine risk to the individual consumer .... A "specific" risk to an individual consumer and "aggregate" risks are two sides of the same coin; each calls attention to the same set of facts. While there may be a theoretical distinction between the risk of the product itself and the risk related to the presence or absence of an intervening voluntary act (*e.g.,* the search for a replacement on the black market), the majority does not rely upon any such distinction, and the FDA's history of regulating "replacement" drugs such as methadone [(used for treating heroin addiction)] shows that it has long taken likely actual alternative consumer behavior into account.

I concede that, as a matter of logic, one could consider the FDA's "safety" evaluation to be different from its choice of remedies. But to read the statute to forbid the agency from taking account of the realities of consumer behavior either in assessing safety or in choosing a remedy could increase the risks of harm .... Why would Congress insist that the FDA ignore such realities, even if the consequent harm would occur only unusually, say, where the FDA evaluates a product (a sleeping pill; a cigarette; a contact lens) that is already on the market, potentially habit forming, or popular? I can find no satisfactory answer to this question. And that, I imagine, is why the statute itself says nothing about any of the distinctions that the Court has tried to draw....

. . . [T]he view the Court advances undermines the FDCA's overall health-protecting purpose . . . [T]he majority maintains that the FDA "may clearly regulate many 'dangerous' products without banning them." . . . But it then adds that the FDA *must* ban . . . a drug or device that "cannot be used safely for any therapeutic purpose." . . . [T]his linchpin of the majority's conclusion remains unexplained. *Why* must a widely used but unsafe device be withdrawn from the market when that particular remedy threatens the health of many and is thus more dangerous than another regulatory response? It is, indeed, a perverse interpretation that reads the FDCA to require the ban of a device that has no "safe" therapeutic purpose where a ban is the most dangerous remedial alternative.

. . . [W]here linguistically permissible, we should interpret the FDCA in light of Congress' overall desire to protect health. That purpose requires a flexible interpretation that both permits the FDA to take into account the realities of human behavior and allows it, in appropriate cases, to choose from its arsenal of statutory remedies. A statute so interpreted easily "fit[s]" this, and other, drug- and device-related health problems.

### III

In the majority's view, laws enacted since 1965 require us to deny jurisdiction, whatever the FDCA might mean in their absence. But why? Do those laws contain language barring FDA jurisdiction? The majority must concede that they do not. Do they contain provisions that are inconsistent with the FDA's exercise of jurisdiction? With one exception, the majority points to no such provision. Do they somehow repeal the principles of law . . . that otherwise would lead to the conclusion that the FDA has jurisdiction in this area? The companies themselves deny making any such claim. Perhaps the later laws "shape" and "focus" what the 1938 Congress meant a generation earlier. But this Court has warned against using the views of a later Congress to construe a statute enacted many years before. . . . And, while the majority suggests that the subsequent history "control[s] our construction" of the FDCA, this Court expressly has held that such subsequent views are not "controlling." Haynes v. United States, 390 U.S. 85, 87–88, n. 4 (1968). . . .

Regardless, the later statutes do not support the majority's conclusion. That is because, whatever individual Members of Congress after 1964 may have assumed about the FDA's jurisdiction, the laws they enacted did not embody any such "no jurisdiction" assumption. And one cannot automatically *infer* an antijurisdiction intent . . . for the later statutes are . . . consistent with quite a different congressional desire, namely, the intent to proceed without interfering with whatever authority the FDA otherwise may have possessed. . . . [T]he subsequent legislative history is critically ambivalent, for it can be read *either* as (a) "ratif[ying]" a no-jurisdiction assumption, *or* as (b) leaving the jurisdictional question just where Congress found it. . . .

Consider, for example, Congress' failure to provide the FDA with express authority to regulate tobacco. . . . In fact, Congress *both* failed to grant express authority to the FDA when the FDA denied it had jurisdiction over tobacco *and* failed to take that authority expressly away when the agency later asserted jurisdiction. . . . Consequently, the defeat of various different proposed jurisdictional changes proves nothing. This history shows only that Congress could not muster the votes necessary either to grant or to deny the FDA the relevant authority. . . .

## IV

I now turn to the ... FDA's former denials of its tobacco-related authority.

Until the early 1990's, the FDA expressly maintained that the 1938 statute did not give it the power that it now seeks to assert. It then changed its mind. The majority agrees with me that the FDA's change of positions does not make a significant legal difference .... Nevertheless, it labels those denials "important context" for drawing an inference about Congress' intent. In my view, the FDA's change of policy, like the subsequent statutes themselves, does nothing to advance the majority's position.

When it denied jurisdiction to regulate cigarettes, the FDA consistently stated *why* that was so. In 1963, for example, FDA administrators wrote that cigarettes did not satisfy the relevant FDCA definitions—in particular, the "intent" requirement—because cigarette makers did not sell their product with accompanying "therapeutic claims." ... And subsequent FDA Commissioners made roughly the same assertion....

What changed? For one thing, the FDA obtained evidence sufficient to prove [that the tobacco products were "intended" to affect the structure or function of the body] despite the absence of specific [claims about such effects by the tobacco companies]. This evidence, which first became available in the early 1990's, permitted the agency to demonstrate that the tobacco companies *knew* nicotine achieved appetite-suppressing, mood-stabilizing, and habituating effects through chemical (not psychological) means, even at a time when the companies were publicly denying such knowledge.

Moreover, scientific evidence of adverse health effects mounted, until, in the late 1980's, a consensus on the seriousness of the matter became firm. That is not to say that concern about smoking's adverse health effects is a new phenomenon.... [T]he health conclusions [regarding smoking] were the subject of controversy, diminishing somewhat over time, until recently—and only recently—has it become clear that there is a wide consensus about the health problem....

Finally, administration policy changed. Earlier administrations may have hesitated to assert jurisdiction for the reasons prior Commissioners expressed.... Commissioners of the current administration simply took a different regulatory attitude.

Nothing in the law prevents the FDA from changing its policy for such reasons. By the mid–1990's, the evidence needed to prove objective intent ... had been found. The emerging scientific consensus about tobacco's adverse, chemically induced, health effects may have convinced the agency that it should spend its resources on this important regulatory effort. As for the change of administrations, I agree with then-Justice Rehnquist's statement in a different case, where he wrote:

> "The agency's changed view ... seems to be related to the election of a new President of a different political party. It is readily apparent that the responsible members of one administration may consider public

resistance and uncertainties to be more important than do their counterparts in a previous administration. A change in administration brought about by the people casting their votes is a perfectly reasonable basis for an executive agency's reappraisal of the costs and benefits of its programs and regulations. As long as the agency remains within the bounds established by Congress, it is entitled to assess administrative records and evaluate priorities in light of the philosophy of the administration." *Motor Vehicle Mfrs. Assn. of United States, Inc. v. State Farm Mut. Automobile Ins. Co.,* 463 U.S. 29, 59 (1983) (concurring in part and dissenting in part).

V

... [O]ne might claim that courts ... should assume in close cases that a decision with "enormous social consequences," ... should be made by democratically elected Members of Congress rather than by unelected agency administrators .... If there is such a background canon of interpretation, however, I do not believe it controls the outcome here.

Insofar as the decision to regulate tobacco reflects the policy of an administration, it is a decision for which that administration, and those politically elected officials who support it, must (and will) take responsibility. And the very importance of the decision taken here, as well as its attendant publicity, means that the public is likely to be aware of it and to hold those officials politically accountable. Presidents, just like Members of Congress, are elected by the public. Indeed, the President and Vice President are the *only* public officials whom the entire Nation elects. I do not believe that an administrative agency decision of this magnitude—one that is important, conspicuous, and controversial—can escape the kind of public scrutiny that is essential in any democracy. And such a review will take place whether it is the Congress or the Executive Branch that makes the relevant decision....

---

***1. Can a Statute Be "Clear" Even if the Language Is Not?***— *Brown & Williamson* raises interesting questions about the outer limits of a court's ability to declare that Congress has "clearly spoken" to the precise question at issue. After all, although the majority concluded that Congress had indeed "directly spoken to the issue here and precluded the FDA's jurisdiction to regulate tobacco products," the opinion did not seriously dispute that the statutory definitions of "drug" and "drug delivery device," read literally, would include nicotine, cigarettes, and other tobacco products. Indeed, it is hard to see how one could make such an argument persuasively (though the tobacco companies tried) in light of the fact that the statutory definition of "drug" includes "articles (other than food) intended to affect the structure or any function of the body." Once one factors in the modern evidence revealing the physical and psychopharmacological effects of tobacco and the further evidence showing that the tobacco companies were aware of these effects when they sold their products, one might have thought that the statutory definition clearly *includes* tobacco and tobacco products. Yet the majority not only rejected that reading, but concluded that it was so clearly inconsistent with the statute that *Chevron* deference was inappropriate.

The majority opinion laid the groundwork for this striking conclusion by emphasizing that, "[i]n determining whether Congress has specifically addressed the question at issue, a reviewing court should not confine itself to examining a particular statutory provision in isolation. The meaning—or ambiguity—of certain words or phrases may only become evident when placed in context." What "context" did the Court have in mind? As you saw, the Court emphasized two things: (1) inferences from statutory structure, including the implications of the agency's interpretation for the operation of other statutory provisions; and (2) the history, not so much of this particular statutory provision, but of past agency and congressional action (or inaction) in this area of tobacco regulation more generally. Let us consider each in turn.

    *a.  Arguments from Statutory Structure*—Consider first the Court's inferences from statutory structure. The argument here is intricate (or convoluted, depending on your point of view). The nub of the Court's structural argument was that if the FDA had jurisdiction over tobacco *at all*—if nicotine counts as a "drug" under the Act—then *other provisions* of the Act would compel the FDA to ban tobacco outright, rather than to adopt more limited advertising and marketing restrictions. But, the Court continued, Congress could not possibly have intended an outright tobacco ban, as a series of subsequent legislative enactments makes clear. So, the conclusion necessarily follows that tobacco and tobacco products do not fall within the Act's scope at all.

Justice Breyer's principal attack on this structural argument focused on the Court's intermediate claim that if the Act covers tobacco, the FDA would have no choice but to ban it because tobacco is not "safe and effective" for any use. Justice Breyer (and presumably the FDA) had a different understanding of what it means for a drug to be "safe" than did the *Brown & Williamson* majority. Which of these interpretations do you find more persuasive? Is the question whether tobacco is sufficiently "safe" to be marketed *itself* a question of statutory interpretation? After all, the dispute between the majority and the dissent on this point turns on whether the statutorily required "safety" assessment can take into account only the physiological impact of the product on the user (the majority's view), or whether this safety assessment can take into account the adverse behavioral effects of a ban (the dissent's view). Does the statute clearly favor one or the other of these interpretations? If not, then should the Court have deferred to the interpretation preferred by the FDA? Why or why not?

    *b.  Arguments from Context and History*—Relying on the legislative history surrounding tobacco-related statutes enacted after the FDCA, Justice O'Connor concluded that Congress effectively ratified the FDA's longstanding position that it lacked jurisdiction over tobacco. Justice O'Connor's main arguments were: (1) in congressional hearings relating to proposed tobacco statutes, the FDA repeatedly disclaimed any authority to regulate tobacco products under the FDCA; (2) Congress, partly in reliance on these disclaimers, enacted a series of separate statutes that were meant to address concerns about the health hazards of tobacco products, but stopped well short of the aggressive regulations the FDA adopted in 1996; and (3) Congress on several occasions considered and rejected bills that would have given the FDA the authority that the FDA claimed in 1996 to have under the FDCA. According to Justice O'Connor's majority opinion, these arguments, especially when taken together, indicate that Congress clearly understood the FDCA as not giving the FDA jurisdiction over tobacco, and that Congress subsequently approved and reaffirmed that result.

It is important to recognize that Justice O'Connor's argument here was *not* that agencies cannot alter their prior statutory interpretations, or that they get less deference when they do so. Rather, she asserted that the FDA's consistent disavowals of jurisdiction provide "important context" for Congress's subsequent enactment of tobacco-specific legislation, which can thus be interpreted as "ratif[ying]" the FDA's position that it lacked jurisdiction to regulate tobacco. This "implicit congressional ratification" argument is striking in part because the *Brown & Williamson* majority included the Court's two strictest textualists (Justices Scalia and Thomas), and the other three Justices in this majority (Chief Justice Rehnquist and Justices O'Connor and Kennedy) have in other contexts expressed skepticism about, and called for greater caution in using, legislative history. Does it seem odd that these Justices would place so much emphasis on representations that the FDA made at committee hearings about *other legislation*, decades after the enactment of the FDCA, in determining the meaning of the FDCA? Such legislative history would have been considered dubious even under the more traditional post–New Deal standard. Then again, doesn't Justice O'Connor have a point that this long, consistent history shows a clear, stable consensus that the FDA lacked jurisdiction under the FDCA to regulate tobacco?

Justice Breyer interpreted the FDA's denials of jurisdiction, and Congress's apparent acquiescence in those denials, quite differently. In his view, when Congress "accepted" the FDA's claim that it lacked jurisdiction over tobacco, Congress was not necessarily embracing the view that the FDCA *clearly precluded* the FDA from exercising such jurisdiction. Rather, Congress might have viewed the statute as ambiguous on this point, such that the FDA had discretion under the statute to decide whether to regulate tobacco. Accordingly, Congress might reasonably have enacted the post–FDCA tobacco legislation in response to the fact that the FDA *at the time* believed—and intended to act on the belief—that it lacked jurisdiction over tobacco.

With respect to the majority's separate point that Congress declined to pass proposed legislation giving the FDCA explicit authority over tobacco, Justice Breyer emphasized that congressional inaction generally has little probative value, not only because the intent of the enacting Congress may differ from that of subsequent Congresses, but also because there are many reasons Congress might fail to act. In support of that latter point, Justice Breyer noted that a bill was introduced after the rulemaking at issue that would have stripped the FDA of jurisdiction over tobacco, but that bill *also* failed to pass. The essence of Justice Breyer's argument is that the FDCA consistently gave the FDA the *option* to regulate tobacco, and that Congress consistently acquiesced in this understanding of the statute.

Perhaps *Brown & Williamson*'s reliance on these other congressional statutes might be defended on different grounds. Instead of treating these other tobacco-specific enactments as an implicit congressional ratification of the FDA's position that it lacked jurisdiction, the Court might have invoked the "commonplace [principle] of statutory construction that the specific governs the general." Morales v. Trans World Airlines, Inc., 504 U.S. 374, 384 (1992); *see also* Clifford F. MacEvoy Co. v. United States, 322 U.S. 102, 107 (1944) (asserting that "[h]owever inclusive may be the language of a statute, . . . specific terms prevail over the general in the same or another statute which otherwise might be controlling") (internal citations and quotation marks omitted). The rationale for this principle is that when Congress addresses a topic with specificity, it may be striking a compromise that could be upset if a court or agency were to invoke general authority from another statute to reach the same subject matter. Might one conclude that even if the FDA *did* have general authority to regulate tobacco under the FDCA when enacted, Congress's enactment of *specific* legislation touching on some of the same topics (e.g., tobacco labeling and advertising) displaced this general authority? Couldn't Justice Breyer respond that these other statutes merely set a minimum level of regulation rather than a minimum *and* a maximum? For example, the fact that the Public Health Cigarette Smoking Act banned certain types of cigarette advertising does not necessarily mean that Congress affirmatively decided to *permit* all other forms of such advertising. The Court has famously observed that a legislature often can and does approach problems "one step at a time, addressing itself to the phase of the problem that seems most acute to the legislative mind." Williamson v. Lee Optical, Inc., 348 U.S. 483, 489 (1955). If the Court had no reliable way to know whether Congress meant merely to handle particular phases of the problem or instead to adopt a comprehensive and exclusive regulatory scheme, should the Court rely on the existence of that other legislation to narrow the broad authority that Congress conferred upon the FDA in 1938?

**2. Chevron *and "Major" or "Extraordinary" Questions***—Perhaps *Brown & Williamson*'s reliance on otherwise questionable sorts of legislative history was driven by a deeper concern about whether Congress would have delegated to the FDA the authority to regulate tobacco. Indeed, the majority suggested that *Chevron* deference is less appropriate in an "extraordinary" case, where the legal question is so significant that it is simply implausible that Congress would have implicitly delegated the resolution of that question to an agency. As support for this proposition, the Court cited to *MCI*'s conclusion that "Congress could not have intended to delegate a decision of such economic and political significance to an agency in so cryptic a fashion." So, we again have the suggestion that the Court, motivated in part by anxiety about delegation, might reverse the ordinary *Chevron* presumption when the question of statutory construction is somehow "extraordinary." *See also* Barnhart v. Walton, 535 U.S. 212, 222 (2002) (finding that *Chevron* deference was appropriate in part because of the "interstitial" nature of the issue involved); National Cable & Telecommunications Ass'n v. Brand X Internet Services, 545 U.S. 967, 1004 (2005) (Breyer, J., concurring) (suggesting that *Chevron* deference might be inappropriate when "an unusually basic legal question is at issue"); Negusie v. Holder, 129 S.Ct. 1159, 1172 (2009) (Stevens, J., concurring in part and dissenting in part) (arguing that courts should "distinguish . . . between central legal issues and interstitial questions" when deciding whether *Chevron* deference applies).

Whether there is a "major questions" exception to *Chevron* remains unresolved. (For recent discussions of this issue, see Einer Elhauge, Statutory Default Rules 103–04 (2008); Jody Freeman & Adrian Vermeule, Massachusetts v. EPA: *From Politics to Expertise*, 2007 Sup. Ct. Rev. 51, 71–78; Abigail R. Moncrieff, *Reincarnating the "Major Questions" Exception to* Chevron *Deference as a Doctrine of Noninterference (or Why* Massachusetts v. EPA *Got It Wrong)*, 60 Admin. L. Rev. 593 (2008); Cass R. Sunstein, Chevron *Step Zero*, 92 Va. L. Rev. 187 (2006).) Should there be such an exception? One obvious problem is the difficulty of articulating a judicially manageable standard for determining when a subject is too important to presume that Congress implicity delegated authority to regulate it. Even putting this difficulty aside, it is not clear whether the case for *Chevron* is weaker in cases raising exceptionally important issues. Consider Justice Breyer's suggestion that the extraordinarily high political salience of the issue in *Brown & Williamson* strengthened rather than weakened the case for *Chevron* deference, because the administration—and the President— had taken responsibility, and would be held accountable, for the agency's decision. The majority, by contrast, thought that the political accountability of the executive branch was not enough, because for important decisions like this, *Congress* must make an authoritative decision. Which of these views do you find more persuasive?

Finally, although *Brown & Williamson* relied on *MCI*, are those cases distinguishable? The interpretive question at issue in *MCI* arguably had enormous significance for the operation of the statutory scheme, but probably had relatively little public salience. In contrast, the interpretive question in *Brown & Williamson* had enormous political salience but limited implications for the functioning of the statutory scheme as a whole. Does that matter? Does it make sense to distinguish different sorts of "major questions" along these lines, and if so, where (if anywhere) is the case for *Chevron* deference stronger and where is it weaker?

## D. *Chevron* and Legislative History

As you know from Chapter One (pp. 140–201, *supra*), legislative history is one of the most controversial tools of statutory construction.

Many textualists argue that legislative history lacks both legitimacy and probative value. (*See* pp. 169–178, *supra*.) Proponents of the use of legislative history, in contrast, argue that it may provide useful insights into the understandings expressed by key members of the enacting coalition, that legislators expect interpreters to read statutes in light of such material, and that allowing judges to consult legislative history, while imperfect, may be superior to leaving judges to resolve ambiguities without the benefit of these sources. (*See* pp. 169–178, *supra*.) In recent years the Supreme Court has for the most part steered a middle course: While the Court has not abandoned legislative history, it has emphasized that legislative history materials must be analyzed with caution and may generally be consulted only when the text of the statute is ambiguous. *See, e.g.,* Lamie v. United States Trustee, 540 U.S. 526, 533–36 (2004); Green v. Bock Laundry Machine Co., 490 U.S. 504, 511 (1989).

Whatever one's baseline about legislative history, should a reviewing court be more or less inclined to consult it in a *Chevron* case? Suppose that a statute is textually ambiguous—the language could reasonably be construed to mean $X$ or $Y$. Suppose further that the responsible administrative agency has interpreted the statute to mean $X$, but some strong evidence in the legislative history (say, an explicit statement in one or more of the committee reports) indicates that the statute means $Y$. What should a reviewing court do? If we assume that legislative history qualifies as one of the "traditional tools" of statutory construction, then perhaps the court should not defer to the agency's contrary interpretation. On the other hand, one might take the position that courts may consult legislative history in a non-*Chevron* context only as a last resort to resolve an otherwise intractable statutory ambiguity. In a *Chevron* case, by contrast, the court has an alternative—and superior—way to resolve the ambiguity: It can defer to the agency. What we have, in essence, is a choice between two hierarchies of interpretive rules. One says, "First, look to the text. If the text is ambiguous, look to the legislative history. If the legislative history does not clearly resolve the question, defer to the agency's view (if there is one)." The other says, "First, look to the text. If the text is ambiguous, defer to the agency. Look to the legislative history only if there is no agency interpretation." Which of these is preferable?

As a matter of doctrine, the courts have not been entirely clear about how to resolve the above dilemma. *Chevron* itself examined the legislative history of the Clean Air Act Amendments in trying to determine whether Congress had spoken to the precise question at issue, and other Supreme Court cases have suggested that courts can look to a statute's history when deciding whether the agency's interpretation is reasonable. *See, e.g.,* Babbitt v. Sweet Home Chapter of Communities for a Great Oregon, 515 U.S. 687, 704–08 (1995) (pp. 854–865, *supra*); Wisconsin Public Intervenor v. Mortier, 501 U.S. 597, 609–14 (1991). In other cases, however, the Court has suggested that *only* the statute's text and structure are relevant for the first step of the *Chevron* inquiry, which implies that legislative history cannot be used to override an agency's otherwise reasonable interpretation. *See, e.g.,* National Railroad Passenger Corp. v. Boston & Maine Corp., 503

U.S. 407, 417–18 (1992) ("If the agency interpretation is not in conflict with the plain language of the statute, deference is due.").

Perhaps because of these conflicting signals from the Supreme Court, different court of appeals decisions have come out different ways on this issue, creating apparent conflicts between (and sometimes within) the circuits. For example, the Third Circuit held in *United States v. Geiser* that "legislative history should not be considered at *Chevron* step one," and that courts should look only to the "plain and literal language of the statute" to determine whether Congress has expressed its unambiguous intent. 527 F.3d 288, 294 (3d Cir. 2008) (internal citations and quotation marks omitted). In contrast, the Second Circuit concluded that if the statutory language is ambiguous, the court should look to evidence in the "legislative history . . . to see if these interpretive clues permit [the court] to identify Congress's clear intent"; the court should defer to the agency only if the legislative history does not resolve the issue. Cohen v. JP Morgan Chase & Co., 498 F.3d 111, 116 (2d Cir. 2007) (internal citations and quotation marks omitted). Some other court of appeals cases have acknowledged the uncertainty surrounding this issue without conclusively taking a position one way or the other. *See, e.g.,* American Rivers v. Federal Energy Regulatory Commission, 201 F.3d 1186, 1196 n. 16 (9th Cir. 1999); Perez–Olivio v. Chavez, 394 F.3d 45, 50 n.2 (1st Cir. 2005). A few opinions have suggested that although legislative history is irrelevant at *Chevron* Step One (the "precise question" inquiry), it should be considered at *Chevron* Step Two (the "reasonableness" inquiry). *See, e.g.,* Bankers Life and Casualty Co. v. United States, 142 F.3d 973, 983 (7th Cir. 1998); Coke v. Long Island Care at Home, Ltd., 376 F.3d 118, 128 (2d Cir. 2004), *rev'd* 546 U.S. 1147 (2006). It is not clear, though, whether that distinction makes any substantive difference. *Cf.* Matthew C. Stephenson & Adrian Vermeule, Chevron *Has Only One Step*, 95 VA. L. REV. 597 (2009).

In a recent empirical study, Professor William Eskridge and Lauren Baer attempted to move beyond these anecdotal examples to determine whether, as a general rule, the Supreme Court treats legislative history as relevant in *Chevron* cases. After analyzing all Supreme Court cases involving a *Chevron* question between 1984 and 2005, Eskridge and Baer found that in "62.3% of the cases that apply the *Chevron* test, the Court provides at least some reference to legislative history," and in "44.7% of the *Chevron* cases, there is either a genuine positive reliance on legislative history, or it is a determining factor in the Court's reasoning process." William N. Eskridge, Jr. & Lauren Baer, *The Continuum of Deference: Supreme Court Treatment of Agency Statutory Interpretations from* Chevron *to* Hamdan, 96 GEO. L.J. 1083, 1136 (2008). From this, they conclude that the Supreme Court treats legislative history as a routine part of the *Chevron* analysis. *See id.* While Eskridge and Baer clearly demonstrate that the Court has invoked legislative history in a significant number of *Chevron* cases, do their findings necessarily refute the idea that the Court has been ambivalent, ambiguous, or simply inconsistent on the proper role of legislative history in *Chevron* cases? For example, by Eskridge and Baer's own account, in over half of the *Chevron* cases they study, the Court either made no reference to legislative history or rejected it as irrelevant, or at least as not controlling. Furthermore, a significant percentage of the 44.7% of cases that positively rely on legislative history invoked it merely to confirm the meaning suggested by the statute's text and structure. Thus, while Eskridge and Baer have no doubt shown that many *Chevron* cases treat legislative history as relevant, do we need additional information to determine whether, under present law, legislative history can *foreclose* an agency's reasonable interpretation of an otherwise ambiguous text?

## III. *CHEVRON* AND SUBSTANTIVE CANONS OF CONSTRUCTION

*Chevron*, as we have seen, can be considered a kind of substantive canon of interpretation, similar in structure and justification to the substantive canons considered in Chapter Two (pp. 266–337, *supra*). But what happens when the *Chevron* canon conflicts with some other substantive canon? It is not hard to imagine how this might occur. Indeed, the basic problem is structurally similar to the possibility of conflict between *Chevron* and legislative history (*see* pp. 885–888, *supra*). Suppose that a statute administered by some agency is textually ambiguous—it could mean *X* or *Y*—and the agency adopts interpretation *X*. Interpretation *X*, however, raises a serious constitutional question, or encroaches on traditional state authority, whereas interpretation *Y* would not. What should courts do in this situation?

One of the reasons this sort of conflict is so hard to resolve is that *Chevron* and the other substantive canons with which it may clash are sometimes justified by assertions about congressional intent. Courts at times present these assertions as descriptive claims about what Congress (usually) wants. Yet there is often good reason to think that these assertions are actually legal fictions meant to rationalize judicial policy judgments, to promote constitutionally inspired values, or to encourage Congress to deliberate more carefully about certain issues. In order to resolve conflicts between these presumptions about congressional intent, we need to determine which presumption has priority, either generally or with respect to a particular case. The cases in this section focus on potential conflicts between the *Chevron* principle and three of the substantive canons that were discussed in depth in Chapter Two: (1) the constitutional avoidance canon (pp. 268–288, *supra*); (2) the clear statement rule for federal interference with traditional state functions (pp. 289–306, *supra*); and (3) the presumption against preemption (pp. 306–327, *supra*). This focus, however, should not obscure the fact that *Chevron* often comes into conflict with other substantive canons, including the rule that federal conditions on grants to states should be construed narrowly, *see, e.g.*, Virginia Department of Education v. Riley, 106 F.3d 559 (4th Cir. 1997) (en banc) (per curiam); the rule of lenity, *see, e.g.*, Dolfi v. Pontesso, 156 F.3d 696 (6th Cir. 1998); the presumption against retroactivity, *see, e.g.*, INS v. St. Cyr, 533 U.S. 289 (2001); and many other such canons. *See generally* Kenneth A. Bamberger, *Normative Canons in the Review of Administrative*

*Policymaking*, 118 Yale L.J. 64 (2008); Curtis A. Bradley, Chevron *Deference and Foreign Affairs*, 86 Va. L. Rev. 649 (2000); David Freeman Engstrom, *Drawing Lines Between* Chevron *and* Pennhurst: *A Functional Analysis of the Spending Power, Federalism, and the Administrative State*, 82 Tex. L. Rev. 1197 (2004); Elliot Greenfield, *A Lenity Exception to* Chevron *Deference*, 58 Baylor L. Rev. 1 (2006); William V. Luneburg, *Retroactivity and Administrative Rulemaking*, 1991 Duke L.J. 106.

## A. Constitutional Avoidance

What happens when an agency's otherwise reasonable interpretation of a statute raises a serious constitutional issue? The Supreme Court addressed this question in the following case. Can you discern the Court's reasons for resolving the tension between *Chevron* and the avoidance canon the way it did?

---

# Edward J. DeBartolo Corp. v. Florida Gulf Coast Building and Construction Trades Council

Supreme Court of the United States
485 U.S. 568 (1988)

■ Justice White delivered the opinion of the Court.

[The respondent labor union was involved in a wage dispute with a construction company that had been retained by the H.J. Wilson Company to construct a department store in a shopping mall owned by the petitioner Edward J. DeBartolo Corp. (DeBartolo). The union peacefully distributed handbills in the mall, asking mall customers not to shop at any mall stores until DeBartolo publicly promised that all construction at the mall would be done "using contractors who pay their employees fair wages and fringe benefits." DeBartolo, which had no contractual right to influence the selection of contractors by its tenants, filed a complaint with the National Labor Relations Board (Board), charging the union with unfair labor practices under § 8(b)(4) of the National Labor Relations Act (NLRA).]

[After some preliminary proceedings not relevant here, the Board concluded that the union's handbilling activities violated § 8(b)(4)(ii)(B), which makes it an unfair labor practice for a labor organization "to threaten, coerce, or restrain any person engaged in commerce" if the object is to induce that person to cease doing business with any other person, unless the activity in question is a primary strike or primary picketing. The Board, relying on its prior cases, concluded that handbilling urging a consumer boycott constituted "coercion" within the meaning of § 8(b)(4)(ii)(B), and that the object of this coercion was to pressure mall tenants to cease doing business with DeBartolo in order to force DeBartolo not to do business with the construction company. The Board noted the First Amendment objections to this interpretation of § 8(b)(4)(ii)(B), but concluded that the statute's literal language and the applicable case law required the finding of a violation. The Board also stated that, as a congressionally-created administrative agency, it would presume the constitutionality of the statutes it administers. The court of appeals for the Eleventh Circuit denied enforcement of the Board's order. The Court of Appeals, noting the serious constitutional difficulties with the Board's interpretation of § 8(b)(4)(ii)(B), construed the statutory phrase "threaten, coerce, or restrain" to cover secondary picketing and strikes but not consumer publicity.]

The Board, the agency entrusted by Congress with the authority to administer the NLRA, has the "special function of applying the general provisions of the Act to the complexities of industrial life." NLRB v. Erie Resistor Corp., 373 U.S. 221, 236 (1963).... Here, the Board has construed § 8(b)(4) of the Act to cover handbilling at a mall entrance urging potential customers not to trade with any retailers in the mall, in order to exert pressure on the proprietor of the mall to influence a particular mall tenant not to do business with a nonunion construction contractor. That statutory interpretation by the Board would normally be entitled to deference unless that construction were clearly contrary to the intent of Congress. Chevron U.S.A. Inc. v. Natural Resources Defense Council, Inc., 467 U.S. 837, 842–843, and n. 9 (1984).

Another rule of statutory construction, however, is pertinent here: where an otherwise acceptable construction of a statute would raise serious constitutional problems, the Court will construe the statute to avoid such problems unless such construction is plainly contrary to the intent of Congress.... This cardinal principle has its roots in Chief Justice Marshall's opinion for the Court in Murray v. The Charming Betsy, 2 Cranch 64, 118 (1804), and has for so long been applied by this Court that it is beyond debate.... As was stated in Hooper v. California, 155 U.S. 648, 657 (1895), "[t]he elementary rule is that every reasonable construction must be resorted to, in order to save a statute from unconstitutionality." This approach not only reflects the prudential concern that constitutional issues not be needlessly confronted, but also recognizes that Congress, like this Court, is bound by and swears an oath to uphold the Constitution. The courts will therefore not lightly assume that Congress intended to infringe constitutionally protected liberties or usurp power constitutionally forbidden it....

[T]he Board's construction of the statute, as applied in this case, poses serious questions of the validity of § 8(b)(4) under the First Amendment. The handbills involved here truthfully revealed the existence of a labor dispute and urged potential customers of the mall to follow a wholly legal course of action, namely, not to patronize the retailers doing business in the mall. The handbilling was peaceful. No picketing or patrolling was involved. On its face, this was expressive activity arguing that substandard wages should be opposed by abstaining from shopping in a mall where such wages were paid. Had the union simply been leafletting the public generally, including those entering every shopping mall in town, pursuant to an annual educational effort against substandard pay, there is little doubt that legislative proscription of such leaflets would pose a substantial issue of validity under the First Amendment. The same may well be true in this case, although here the handbills called attention to a specific situation in the mall allegedly involving the payment of unacceptably low wages by a construction contractor. . . .

The Board was urged to construe the statute in light of the asserted constitutional considerations, but thought that it was constrained by its own prior authority and cases in the Courts of Appeals, as well as by the express language of the Act, to hold that § 8(b)(4) must be construed to forbid the handbilling involved here. Even if this construction of the Act were thought to be a permissible one, we are quite sure that in light of the traditional rule [of construing statutes to avoid serious constitutional concerns], we must independently inquire whether there is another interpretation, not raising these serious constitutional concerns, that may fairly be ascribed to § 8(b)(4)(ii)(B). . . .

We follow this course here and conclude, as did the Court of Appeals, that the section is open to a construction that obviates deciding whether a congressional prohibition of handbilling on the facts of this case would violate the First Amendment.

The case turns on whether handbilling such as involved here must be held to "threaten, coerce, or restrain any person" to cease doing business with another, within the meaning of § 8(b)(4)(ii)(B). . . . Those words, we have said, are "nonspecific, indeed vague," and should be interpreted with "caution" and not given a "broad sweep," *Drivers, supra*, 362 U.S., at 290. . . . [It is unnecessary] to construe such language to reach the handbills involved in this case. There is no suggestion that the leaflets had any coercive effect on customers of the mall. There was no violence, picketing, or patrolling and only an attempt to persuade customers not to shop in the mall.

[The Court went on to reject the Board's conclusion that any attempt to influence a secondary employer to cease doing business with the employer involved in a labor dispute is "coercion" within the meaning of § 8(b)(4)(ii)(B). The Court distinguished the cases on which the Board relied and cited other cases to support the Court's view. The Court also rejected the argument that a proviso to § 8(b)(4) made clear that § 8(b)(4) covers handbilling urging a consumer boycott of a neutral employer. The Court then examined the legislative history of § 8(b)(4)(ii)(B) and found no "clear indication" that Congress intended this section to "proscribe peaceful handbilling, unaccompanied by picketing, urging a consumer boycott of a neutral employer."]

In our view, interpreting § 8(b)(4) as not reaching the handbilling involved in this case is not foreclosed either by the language of the section or its legislative history. That construction makes unnecessary passing on the serious constitutional questions that would be raised by the Board's understanding of the statute. . . .

*Affirmed.*

■ JUSTICE O'CONNOR and JUSTICE SCALIA concur in the judgment.

■ JUSTICE KENNEDY took no part in the consideration or decision of this case.

***Did*** DeBartolo ***Get the Order of Priority Right?***—*DeBartolo* seems to say quite clearly that the constitutional avoidance canon takes precedence over *Chevron*. Did you find the Court's reasoning compelling? Observe that the Court emphasized two of the substantive justifications for the avoidance canon: the "prudential concern that constitutional issues not be needlessly confronted" and the principle that courts should not "lightly assume that Congress intended to infringe constitutionally protected liberties or usurp power constitutionally forbidden it." Do these considerations apply in the same way when an agency has affirmatively decided to push constitutional limits in a way the statute's text does not clearly preclude?

In addition to the standard arguments in favor of the avoidance canon, one might justify prioritizing the avoidance canon over *Chevron* as a way to narrow congressional delegations of lawmaking power to agencies, at least in certain domains. In that sense, *DeBartolo* is consistent with *Kent v. Dulles* (pp. 436–437, *supra*), which construed the scope of the power Congress delegated to the agency narrowly—and perhaps artificially—as not including the power to act in ways that raised serious constitutional questions. In an important article, Professor Cass Sunstein argued that prioritizing the avoidance canon and other "nondelegation" canons over *Chevron* (which is itself a kind of pro-delegation canon) has two related benefits. *See* Cass R. Sunstein, *Nondelegation Canons*, 67 U. CHI. L. REV. 315 (2000). First, where a policy choice potentially intrudes upon the Constitution or threatens recognized constitutional values, giving priority to the substantive canon ensures that "Congress must make that choice explicitly and take the political heat for deciding to do so." *Id.* at 332. Second, giving these nondelegation canons precedence over *Chevron* offers a more judicially administrable way of promoting the purposes of the practically defunct constitutional nondelegation doctrine, because reviewing courts applying such canons "do not ask the hard-to-manage question whether the legislature has exceeded the permissible level of discretion, but pose instead the far more manageable question whether the agency has been given the discretion to decide something that (under the appropriate canon) only legislatures may decide." *Id.* at 338.

Is Professor Sunstein's argument convincing? In addition to the now-familiar objections to the modern version of the avoidance canon and other constitutionally inspired substantive canons (*see* pp. 287–288, 299–300, *supra*), is it obvious that these so-called nondelegation canons present less of a judicial administrability problem than the constitutional nondelegation doctrine? Since all statutes present some degree of ambiguity on the margins, with what *degree* of clarity must Congress speak in order to satisfy the requirements of a nondelegation canon? *See* David Driesen, *Loose Canons: Statutory Construction and the New Nondelegation Doctrine*, 64 U. PITT. L. REV. 1, 23–33 (2002); John F. Manning, *Lessons from a Nondelegation Canon*, 83 NOTRE DAME L. REV. 1541, 1555–56 (2008). Also, even if privileging these nondelegation canons over *Chevron* may advance one set of constitutionally inspired values, might doing so undermine a *different* constitutional value: respect for the prerogative of executive branch agencies to implement the law? After all, "all executive ... Officers" swear an oath to the Constitution, U.S. CONST. art. VI, cl. 3, and Article II enjoins the President to "take Care that the Laws be faithfully executed," U.S. CONST. art. II, § 3. If an executive official (or the President) has determined, implicitly or explicitly, that a given interpretation is constitutionally permissible, and decided to force the issue by explicitly adopting that interpretation as the basis for authoritative agency action, then could a court's use of the avoidance canon in such circumstances intrude on the President's Article II responsibilities? As Professor William Kelley has argued, when the Court rejects an agency's interpretation on avoidance grounds, the court has, in effect, disregarded the agency's "view of how the law should be executed, not because any statute or the Constitution affirmatively ruled out the Executive's preferred course, but only because the Court deemed it desirable not to decide a constitutional question." William K. Kelley, *Avoiding Constitutional Questions as a Three–Branch Problem*, 86 CORNELL L. REV. 831, 872 (2001). Furthermore, some have argued that the executive branch may have superior knowledge about the underlying purposes of legislation, giving it greater insight into when avoidance of a constitutional issue would be appropriate. *See* Trevor W. Morrison, *Constitutional Avoidance in the Executive Branch*, 106 COLUM. L. REV. 1189, 1240–41 (2006). Why do you think *DeBartolo* implicitly rejected those views? Was it right to do so?

\* \* \* \*

Putting the normative issues to one side, it might seem that *DeBartolo* at least resolved the doctrinal question clearly: When an otherwise reasonable agency interpretation would raise a serious constitutional question, the court should reject the agency's interpretation in favor of a reasonable alternative construction that does not raise the question. In practice, though, *DeBartolo* achieved less doctrinal settlement of this issue than one might have thought, in part because of the malleability of the constitutional avoidance canon itself. This fact is nicely illustrated by the following case, *Rust v. Sullivan*, decided only a few years after *DeBartolo*.

# Rust v. Sullivan

Supreme Court of the United States
500 U.S. 173 (1991)

■ CHIEF JUSTICE REHNQUIST delivered the opinion of the Court.

These cases concern a facial challenge to Department of Health and Human Services (HHS) regulations which limit the ability of Title X fund recipients to engage in abortion-related activities....

I

A

In 1970, Congress enacted Title X of the Public Health Service Act (Act), 84 Stat. 1506, as amended, 42 U.S.C. §§ 300 to 300a–6, which provides federal funding for family-planning services. The Act authorizes the Secretary to "make grants to and enter into contracts with public or nonprofit private entities to assist in the establishment and operation of voluntary family planning projects which shall offer a broad range of acceptable and effective family planning methods and services." § 300(a). Grants and contracts under Title X must "be made in accordance with such regulations as the Secretary may promulgate." § 300a–4(a). Section 1008 of the Act, however, provides that "[n]one of the funds appropriated under this subchapter shall be used in programs where abortion is a method of family planning." 42 U.S.C. § 300a–6. . . .

In 1988, the Secretary promulgated new regulations designed to provide " 'clear and operational guidance' to grantees about how to preserve the distinction between Title X programs and abortion as a method of family planning." 53 Fed.Reg. 2923–2924 (1988). The regulations clarify, through the definition of the term "family planning," that Congress intended Title X funds "to be used only to support *preventive* family planning services." H.R.Conf.Rep. No. 91–1667, p. 8 (emphasis added). Accordingly, Title X services are limited to "preconceptional counseling, education, and general reproductive health care," and expressly exclude "pregnancy care (including obstetric or prenatal care)." 42 CFR § 59.2 (1989). The regulations "focus the emphasis of the Title X program on its traditional mission: The provision of preventive family planning services specifically designed to enable individuals to determine the number and spacing of their children, while clarifying that pregnant women must be referred to appropriate prenatal care services." 53 Fed.Reg. 2925 (1988).

The regulations attach three principal conditions on the grant of federal funds for Title X projects. First, the regulations specify that a "Title X project may not provide counseling concerning the use of abortion as a method of family planning or provide referral for abortion as a method of family planning." 42 CFR § 59.8(a)(1) (1989). . . . The Title X project is expressly prohibited from referring a pregnant woman to an abortion provider, even upon specific request. . . .

Second, the regulations broadly prohibit a Title X project from engaging in activities that "encourage, promote or advocate abortion as a method of family planning." § 59.10(a). Forbidden activities include lobbying for legislation that would increase the availability of abortion as a method of family planning, developing or disseminating materials advocating abortion as a method of family planning, providing speakers to promote abortion as a method of family planning, using legal action to make abortion available in any way as a method of family planning, and paying dues to any group that advocates abortion as a method of family planning as a substantial part of its activities.

Third, the regulations require that Title X projects be organized so that they are "physically and financially separate" from prohibited abortion activities. § 59.9. . . .

B

Petitioners are Title X grantees and doctors who supervise Title X funds suing on behalf of themselves and their patients. Respondent is the Secretary of HHS. After the regulations had been promulgated, but before they had been applied, petitioners filed two separate actions, later consolidated, challenging the facial validity of the regulations and seeking declaratory and injunctive relief to prevent implementation of the regulations. Petitioners challenged the regulations on the grounds that they were not authorized by Title X and that they violate the First and Fifth Amendment rights of Title X clients and the First Amendment rights of Title X health providers. . . .

Applying this Court's decision in *Chevron U.S.A. Inc. v. Natural Resources Defense Council, Inc.*, 467 U.S. 837, 842–843 (1984), the Court of Appeals [for the Second Circuit] determined that the regulations were a permissible construction of the statute that legitimately effectuated congressional intent. The court rejected as "highly strained," petitioners' contention that the plain language of § 1008 forbids Title X projects only from performing abortions. . . .

Turning to petitioners' constitutional challenges to the regulations, the Court of Appeals rejected petitioners' Fifth Amendment challenge. It held that the regulations do not impermissibly burden a woman's right to an abortion because the "government may validly choose to favor childbirth over abortion and to implement that choice by funding medical services relating to childbirth but not those relating to abortion." . . .

The court likewise found that the "Secretary's implementation of Congress's decision not to fund abortion counseling, referral or advocacy also does not, under applicable Supreme Court precedent, constitute a facial violation of the First Amendment rights of health care providers or of women." The court explained that under *Regan v. Taxation with Representation of Wash.*, 461 U.S. 540 (1983), the Government has no obligation to subsidize even the exercise of fundamental rights, including "speech rights." The court also held that the regulations do not violate the First Amendment by "condition[ing] receipt of a benefit on the relinquishment of constitutional rights" because Title X grantees and their employees "remain free to say whatever they wish about abortion outside the Title X project." Finally, the court rejected petitioners' contention that the regulations "facially discriminate on the basis of the viewpoint of the speech involved."

II

. . . We turn first to petitioners' contention that the regulations exceed the Secretary's authority under Title X. . . . We then address petitioner's claim that the regulations must be struck down because they raise a substantial constitutional question.

## A

We need not dwell on the plain language of the statute because ... the language is ambiguous. The language of § 1008—that "[n]one of the funds appropriated under this subchapter shall be used in programs where abortion is a method of family planning"—does not speak directly to the issues of counseling, referral, advocacy, or program integrity. If a statute is "silent or ambiguous with respect to the specific issue, the question for the court is whether the agency's answer is based on a permissible construction of the statute." *Chevron,* 467 U.S., at 842–843....

The broad language of Title X plainly allows the Secretary's construction of the statute. By its own terms, § 1008 prohibits the use of Title X funds "in programs where abortion is a method of family planning." Title X does not define the term "method of family planning," nor does it enumerate what types of medical and counseling services are entitled to Title X funding. Based on the broad directives provided by Congress in Title X in general and § 1008 in particular, we are unable to say that the Secretary's construction of the prohibition in § 1008 to require a ban on counseling, referral, and advocacy within the Title X project is impermissible....

## B

... Petitioners also contend that the regulations must be invalidated because they raise serious questions of constitutional law. They rely on *Edward J. DeBartolo Corp. v. Florida Gulf Coast Building & Construction Trades Council,* 485 U.S. 568 (1988), and *NLRB v. Catholic Bishop of Chicago,* 440 U.S. 490 (1979), which hold that "an Act of Congress ought not be construed to violate the Constitution if any other possible construction remains available." *Id.,* at 500. Under this canon of statutory construction, " '[t]he elementary rule is that every reasonable construction must be resorted to, in order to *save a statute* from unconstitutionality.' " *DeBartolo Corp., supra,* 485 U.S., at 575 (emphasis added), quoting *Hooper v. California,* 155 U.S. 648, 657 (1895).

The principle enunciated in *Hooper v. California, supra,* and subsequent cases, is a categorical one: "as between two possible interpretations of a statute, by one of which it would be unconstitutional and by the other valid, our plain duty is to adopt that which will save the Act." *Blodgett v. Holden,* 275 U.S. 142, 148 (1927) (opinion of Holmes, J.). This principle is based at least in part on the fact that a decision to declare an Act of Congress unconstitutional "is the gravest and most delicate duty that this Court is called on to perform." *Ibid.* Following *Hooper, supra,* cases such as *United States ex rel. Attorney General v. Delaware & Hudson Co.,* 213 U.S. 366, 408 (1909), and *United States v. Jin Fuey Moy,* 241 U.S. 394, 401 (1916), developed the corollary doctrine that "[a] statute must be construed, if fairly possible, so as to avoid not only the conclusion that it is unconstitutional but also grave doubts upon that score." This canon is followed out of respect for Congress, which we assume legislates in the light of constitutional limitations. *FTC v. American Tobacco Co.,* 264 U.S. 298, 305–307 (1924). It is qualified by the proposition that "avoidance of a difficulty will not be pressed to the point of disingenuous evasion." *George Moore Ice Cream Co. v. Rose,* 289 U.S. 373, 379 (1933).

Here Congress forbade the use of appropriated funds in programs where abortion is a method of family planning. It authorized the Secretary to promulgate regulations implementing this provision. The extensive litigation regarding governmental restrictions on abortion since our decision in *Roe v. Wade,* 410 U.S. 113 (1973), suggests that it was likely that any set of regulations promulgated by the Secretary—other than the ones in force prior to 1988 and found by him to be relatively toothless and ineffectual— would be challenged on constitutional grounds. While we do not think that the constitutional arguments made by petitioners in these cases are without some force, in Part III, *infra*, we hold that they do not carry the day. Applying the canon of construction under discussion as best we can, we hold that the regulations promulgated by the Secretary do not raise the sort of "grave and doubtful constitutional questions," *Delaware & Hudson Co., supra,* 213 U.S., at 408, that would lead us to assume Congress did not intend to authorize their issuance. Therefore, we need not invalidate the regulations in order to save the statute from unconstitutionality.

[In Parts III and IV of its opinion, the Court considered and rejected petitioners' constitutional objections to the Department's regulations.]

■ JUSTICE BLACKMUN, with whom JUSTICE MARSHALL joins, with whom JUSTICE STEVENS joins as to Parts II and III, and with whom JUSTICE O'CONNOR joins as to Part I, dissenting.

Casting aside established principles of statutory construction and administrative jurisprudence, the majority in these cases today unnecessarily passes upon important questions of constitutional law.... I conclude that the Secretary's regulation of referral, advocacy, and counseling activities exceeds his statutory authority, and, also, that the regulations violate the First and Fifth Amendments of our Constitution. Accordingly, I dissent....

## I

The majority does not dispute that "[f]ederal statutes are to be so construed as to avoid serious doubt of their constitutionality." *Machinists v. Street,* 367 U.S. 740, 749 (1961) .... Nor does the majority deny that this principle is fully applicable to cases such as the instant ones, in which a plausible but constitutionally suspect statutory interpretation is embodied in an administrative regulation. See *Edward J. DeBartolo Corp. v. Florida Gulf Coast Building & Construction Trades Council,* 485 U.S. 568, 575 (1988); *NLRB v. Catholic Bishop of Chicago,* 440 U.S. 490 (1979); *Kent v. Dulles,* 357 U.S. 116, 129–130 (1958). Rather, in its zeal to address the constitutional issues, the majority sidesteps this established canon of construction with the feeble excuse that the challenged regulations "do not raise the sort of 'grave and doubtful constitutional questions,' ... that would lead us to assume Congress did not intend to authorize their issuance." *Ante,* quoting *United States ex rel. Attorney General v. Delaware & Hudson Co.,* 213 U.S. 366, 408 (1909).

This facile response to the intractable problem the Court addresses today is disingenuous at best. Whether or not one believes that these regulations are valid, it avoids reality to contend that they do not give rise to serious constitutional questions. The canon is applicable to these cases not because "it was likely that [the regulations] . . . would be challenged on constitutional grounds," *ante,* but because the question squarely presented by the regulations—the extent to which the Government may attach an otherwise unconstitutional condition to the receipt of a public benefit— implicates a troubled area of our jurisprudence in which a court ought not entangle itself unnecessarily. . . .

. . . [T]he regulations impose viewpoint-based restrictions upon protected speech and are aimed at a woman's decision whether to continue or terminate her pregnancy. In both respects, they implicate core constitutional values. This verity is evidenced by the fact that two of the three Courts of Appeals that have entertained challenges to the regulations have invalidated them on constitutional grounds. See *Massachusetts v. Secretary of Health and Human Services,* 899 F.2d 53 (CA1 1990); *Planned Parenthood Federation of America v. Sullivan,* 913 F.2d 1492 (CA10 1990).

. . . That a bare majority of this Court today reaches a different result does not change the fact that the constitutional questions raised by the regulations are both grave and doubtful. . . .

. . . [O]ur duty to avoid passing unnecessarily upon important constitutional questions is strongest where, as here, the language of the statute is decidedly ambiguous. It is both logical and eminently prudent to assume that when Congress intends to press the limits of constitutionality in its enactments, it will express that intent in explicit and unambiguous terms. See Sunstein, Law and Administration After *Chevron,* 90 Colum. L. Rev. 2071, 2113 (1990) ("It is thus implausible that, after *Chevron,* agency interpretations of ambiguous statutes will prevail even if the consequence of those interpretations is to produce invalidity or to raise serious constitutional doubts").

Because I conclude that a plainly constitutional construction of § 1008 "is not only 'fairly possible' but entirely reasonable," *Machinists,* 367 U.S., at 750, I would reverse the judgment of the Court of Appeals on this ground without deciding the constitutionality of the Secretary's regulations. . . .

[Parts II and III of Justice Blackmun's dissent argued that the regulations did indeed violate the First and Fifth Amendments of the Constitution.]

■ [JUSTICE STEVENS' separate dissent is omitted.]

■ JUSTICE O'CONNOR, dissenting.

"[W]here an otherwise acceptable construction of a statute would raise serious constitutional problems, the Court will construe the statute to avoid such problems unless such construction is plainly contrary to the intent of Congress." *Edward J. DeBartolo Corp. v. Florida Gulf Coast Building & Construction Trades Council*, 485 U.S. 568, 575 (1988). Justice BLACKMUN has explained well why this longstanding canon of statutory construction applies in these cases, and I join Part I of his dissent. Part II demonstrates why the challenged regulations, which constitute the Secretary's interpretation of § 1008 of the Public Health Service Act, 84 Stat. 1508, 42 U.S.C. § 300a–6, "raise serious constitutional problems": the regulations place content-based restrictions on the speech of Title X fund recipients, restrictions directed precisely at speech concerning one of "the most divisive and contentious issues that our Nation has faced in recent years." *Ante*.

One may well conclude, as Justice BLACKMUN does in Part II, that the regulations are unconstitutional for this reason. I do not join Part II of the dissent, however, for the same reason that I do not join Part III, in which Justice BLACKMUN concludes that the regulations are unconstitutional under the Fifth Amendment. The canon of construction that Justice BLACKMUN correctly applies here is grounded in large part upon our time-honored practice of not reaching constitutional questions unnecessarily. See *DeBartolo, supra*, at 575. "It is a fundamental rule of judicial restraint ... that this Court will not reach constitutional questions in advance of the necessity of deciding them." *Three Affiliated Tribes of Fort Berthold Reservation v. Wold Engineering, P.C.*, 467 U.S. 138, 157 (1984)....

This Court acts at the limits of its power when it invalidates a law on constitutional grounds. In recognition of our place in the constitutional scheme, we must act with "great gravity and delicacy" when telling a coordinate branch that its actions are absolutely prohibited absent constitutional amendment .... In these cases, we need only tell the Secretary that his regulations are not a reasonable interpretation of the statute; we need not tell Congress that it cannot pass such legislation. If we rule solely on statutory grounds, Congress retains the power to force the constitutional question by legislating more explicitly. It may instead choose to do nothing. That decision should be left to Congress; we should not tell Congress what it cannot do before it has chosen to do it. It is enough in this litigation to conclude that neither the language nor the history of § 1008 compels the Secretary's interpretation, and that the interpretation raises serious First Amendment concerns. On this basis alone, I would reverse the judgment of the Court of Appeals and invalidate the challenged regulations.

***Distinguishing* Rust *from* DeBartolo**—*Rust* seems to involve a doctrinal question similar to the one we saw in *DeBartolo*: The agency's interpretation of the statute is reasonable as a matter of text and structure, but it arguably raises a difficult constitutional question. Yet while *DeBartolo* resolved this conflict by rejecting the agency's interpretation in favor of one that would not raise the constitutional issue, *Rust* upheld the agency's interpretation as reasonable under *Chevron*, and then proceeded to consider (and reject) the constitutional objections on the merits. Chief Justice

Rehnquist's majority opinion insisted, however, that *Rust* is consistent with *DeBartolo*. Let us consider his reasons.

First, *Rust* asserted that a central purpose of the avoidance canon is to allow courts to steer clear of constitutional issues entirely—an idea that is perhaps reminiscent of *DeBartolo*'s warning that the federal judiciary should not "needlessly confront" constitutional questions. But, *Rust* continued, Title X requires the agency to adopt *some* restrictions on federal funding for abortion, and because as a practical matter *any* federal restriction pertaining to abortion is likely to be challenged on constitutional grounds, avoiding the constitutional issue is simply impossible in a case like this. Is that convincing? Is the Court correct that no regulatory interpretation of Title X could avoid the need for the courts to resolve the regulation's constitutionality? Did the dissenters succeed in offering such an interpretation?

Second, and perhaps of more general importance, *Rust* insisted that although the constitutional objections to the agency regulation were not "without some force," they were simply not serious enough to trigger application of the constitutional avoidance canon. *See, e.g.* Whitaker v. Thompson, 353 F.3d 947, 952 (D.C. Cir. 2004) (emphasizing the seriousness of the constitutional problem as the key distinction between *DeBartolo* and *Rust*); Williams v. Babbitt, 115 F.3d 657, 661–63 (9th Cir. 1997) (same). At the level of principle, *Rust* is surely right that the mere presence of a constitutional question is not sufficient to trigger the avoidance canon. But how serious does the question have to be to trigger the canon? Should it have mattered that three of the dissenters thought that the agency regulation was actually unconstitutional, and that all four dissenters believed that the constitutional questions in *Rust* easily passed the conventional threshold for avoidance?

Another question to consider is whether there should be a heightened threshold for applying the avoidance canon in *Chevron* cases. That is, whatever the threshold of seriousness in a non-*Chevron* case, should the application of the avoidance canon require a higher bar in *Chevron* cases? Consider the following rationale: In a non-*Chevron* case, the Court is merely choosing among plausible alternative interpretations of a statute that it is reading in the first instance, while in a *Chevron* case, applying the canon of avoidance requires the Court to disturb the executive's judgment as to the meaning of both the statute and the Constitution. (*See* pp. 892–893, *supra*.) The Supreme Court has never explicitly endorsed a heightened threshold for avoidance in a *Chevron* case. Should it?

## B. Federalism

### a. Traditional State Functions

Recall from Chapter Two that in addition to the avoidance canon, the Supreme Court has fashioned a number of other substantive canons—often in the form of "clear statement rules"—to safeguard what are sometimes described as "constitutional values." This approach is especially prominent in the interpretation of statutes that implicate the relationship between the federal government and the state governments. So, for example, the Court will not read a federal statute to intrude into core aspects of state sovereignty, or to displace traditional state authority, unless the statute clearly mandates such a result (*see* pp. 289–305, *supra*). Courts sometimes characterized these substantive presumptions as applications of the constitutional avoidance canon, but in many cases courts apply these pro-federalism canons to disfavor exercises of federal power that would not raise any serious doubt about their *actual* constitutionality, at least not under prevailing doctrine. These canons thus appear to be derived from a more general, perhaps constitutionally inspired, commitment to federalism, rather than concerns about violation of any particular constitutional provision.

Just as *Chevron* may come into conflict with the constitutional avoidance canon, so too may it come into conflict with these other pro-federalism clear statement rules. The next case, *Solid Waste Agency of Northern Cook County (SWANCC) v. U.S. Army Corps of Engineers*, may illustrate such a situation—though as you will see, the majority opinion frames its argument in terms of the constitutional avoidance canon. Consider whether the opinion does in fact endorse the proposition that pro-federalism canons take precedence over *Chevron*, and if so whether you think this is correct.

---

## Solid Waste Agency of Northern Cook County v. United States Army Corps of Engineers

Supreme Court of the United States
531 U.S. 159 (2001)

■ CHIEF JUSTICE REHNQUIST delivered the opinion of the Court.

Section 404(a) of the Clean Water Act (CWA or Act), 33 U.S.C. § 1344(a), regulates the discharge of dredged or fill material into "navigable waters." The United States Army Corps of Engineers (Corps) has interpreted § 404(a) to confer federal authority over an abandoned sand and gravel pit in northern Illinois which provides habitat for migratory birds. We are asked to decide whether the provisions of § 404(a) may be fairly extended to these waters, and, if so, whether Congress could exercise such authority consistent with the Commerce Clause, U.S. Const., Art. I, § 8, cl. 3. We answer the first question in the negative and therefore do not reach the second.

Petitioner, the Solid Waste Agency of Northern Cook County (SWANCC), is a consortium of 23 suburban Chicago cities and villages that united in an effort to locate and develop a disposal site for baled nonhazardous solid waste. The Chicago Gravel Company informed the municipalities of the availability of a 533–acre parcel, bestriding the Illinois counties Cook and Kane, which had been the site of a sand and gravel pit mining operation for three decades up until about 1960. Long since abandoned, the old mining site eventually gave way to a successional stage forest, with its remnant excavation trenches evolving into a scattering of permanent and seasonal ponds of varying size ... and depth....

The municipalities decided to purchase the site for disposal of their baled nonhazardous solid waste....

Section 404(a) grants the Corps authority to issue permits "for the discharge of dredged or fill material into the navigable waters at specified disposal sites." The term "navigable waters" is defined under the Act as "the waters of the United States, including the territorial seas." § 1362(7). The Corps has issued regulations defining the term "waters of the United States" to include

> "waters such as intrastate lakes, rivers, streams (including intermittent streams), mudflats, sandflats, wetlands, sloughs, prairie potholes, wet meadows, playa lakes, or natural ponds, the use, degradation or destruction of which could affect interstate or foreign commerce...." 33 CFR § 328.3(a)(3) (1999).

In 1986, in an attempt to "clarify" the reach of its jurisdiction, the Corps stated that § 404(a) extends to intrastate waters:

> "a. Which are or would be used as habitat by birds protected by Migratory Bird Treaties; or
>
> "b. Which are or would be used as habitat by other migratory birds which cross state lines; or
>
> "c. Which are or would be used as habitat for endangered species; or
>
> "d. Used to irrigate crops sold in interstate commerce." 51 Fed.Reg. 41217.

This last promulgation has been dubbed the "Migratory Bird Rule."

> ... [A]fter the Illinois Nature Preserves Commission informed the Corps that a number of migratory bird species had been observed at the site, the Corps ... asserted jurisdiction over the balefill site pursuant to subpart (b) of the "Migratory Bird Rule." ...

Congress passed the CWA for the stated purpose of "restor[ing] and maintain[ing] the chemical, physical, and biological integrity of the Nation's waters." 33 U.S.C. § 1251(a). In so doing, Congress chose to "recognize, preserve, and protect the primary responsibilities and rights of States to prevent, reduce, and eliminate pollution, to plan the development and use (including restoration, preservation, and enhancement) of land and water resources, and to consult with the Administrator in the exercise of his authority under this chapter." § 1251(b). Relevant here, § 404(a) authorizes respondents to regulate the discharge of fill material into "navigable waters," 33 U.S.C. § 1344(a), which the statute defines as "the waters of the United States, including the territorial seas," § 1362(7). Respondents have interpreted these words to cover the abandoned gravel pit at issue here because it is used as habitat for migratory birds. We conclude that the "Migratory Bird Rule" is not fairly supported by the CWA.

This is not the first time we have been called upon to evaluate the meaning of § 404(a). In United States v. Riverside Bayview Homes, Inc., 474 U.S. 121 (1985), we held that the Corps had § 404(a) jurisdiction over wetlands that actually abutted on a navigable waterway. In so doing, we noted that the term "navigable" is of "limited import" and that Congress evidenced its intent to "regulate at least some waters that would not be deemed 'navigable' under the classical understanding of that term." *Id.*, at 133. But our holding was based in large measure upon Congress' unequivocal acquiescence to, and approval of, the Corps' regulations interpreting the CWA to cover wetlands adjacent to navigable waters. We found that Congress' concern for the protection of water quality and aquatic ecosystems indicated its intent to regulate wetlands "inseparably bound up with the 'waters' of the United States." *Id.*, at 134.

It was the significant nexus between the wetlands and "navigable waters" that informed our reading of the CWA in *Riverside Bayview Homes*. Indeed, we did not "express any opinion" on the "question of the authority of the Corps to regulate discharges of fill material into wetlands that are not adjacent to bodies of open water...." Id., at 131–132, n. 8. In order to rule for respondents here, we would have to hold that the jurisdiction of the Corps extends to ponds that are not adjacent to open water. But we conclude that the text of the statute will not allow this....

... We thus decline respondents' invitation to take what they see as the next ineluctable step after *Riverside Bayview Homes*: holding that isolated ponds, some only seasonal, wholly located within two Illinois counties, fall under § 404(a)'s definition of "navigable waters" because they serve as habitat for migratory birds. As counsel for respondents conceded at oral argument, such a ruling would assume that "the use of the word navigable in the statute ... does not have any independent significance." We cannot agree that Congress' separate definitional use of the phrase "waters of the United States" constitutes a basis for reading the term "navigable waters" out of the statute. We said in *Riverside Bayview Homes* that the word "navigable" in the statute was of "limited import" 474 U.S., at 133, and went on to hold that § 404(a) extended to nonnavigable wetlands adjacent to open waters. But it is one thing to give a word limited effect and quite another to give it no effect whatever. The term "navigable" has at least the import of showing us what Congress had in mind as its authority for enacting the CWA: its traditional jurisdiction over waters that were or had been navigable in fact or which could reasonably be so made.

Respondents ... contend that, at the very least, it must be said that Congress did not address the precise question of § 404(a)'s scope with regard to nonnavigable, isolated, intrastate waters, and that, therefore, we should give deference to the "Migratory Bird Rule." See, *e.g.*, Chevron U.S.A. Inc. v. Natural Resources Defense Council, Inc., 467 U.S. 837 (1984). We find § 404(a) to be clear, but even were we to agree with respondents, we would not extend Chevron deference here.

Where an administrative interpretation of a statute invokes the outer limits of Congress' power, we expect a clear indication that Congress intended that result. See Edward J. DeBartolo Corp. v. Florida Gulf Coast Building & Constr. Trades Council, 485 U.S. 568, 575 (1988). This requirement stems from our prudential desire not to needlessly reach constitutional issues and our assumption that Congress does not casually authorize administrative agencies to interpret a statute to push the limit of congressional authority. This concern is heightened where the administrative interpretation alters the federal-state framework by permitting federal encroachment upon a traditional state power ... See United States v. Bass, 404 U.S. 336, 349 (1971) ("[U]nless Congress conveys its purpose clearly, it will not be deemed to have significantly changed the federal-state balance"). Thus, "where an otherwise acceptable construction of a statute would raise serious constitutional problems, the Court will construe the statute to avoid such problems unless such construction is plainly contrary to the intent of Congress." *DeBartolo, supra*, at 575.

Twice in the past six years we have reaffirmed the proposition that the grant of authority to Congress under the Commerce Clause, though broad, is not unlimited. See United States v. Morrison, 529 U.S. 598 (2000); United States v. Lopez, 514 U.S. 549 (1995). Respondents argue that the "Migratory Bird Rule" falls within Congress' power to regulate intrastate activities that "substantially affect" interstate commerce. They note that the protection of migratory birds is a "national interest of very nearly the first magnitude," Missouri v. Holland, 252 U.S. 416, 435 (1920), and that ... millions of people spend over a billion dollars annually on recreational pursuits relating to migratory birds. These arguments raise significant constitutional questions. For example, we would have to evaluate the precise object or activity that, in the aggregate, substantially affects interstate commerce. This is not clear, for although the Corps has claimed jurisdiction over petitioner's land because it contains water areas used as habitat by migratory birds, respondents now ... focus upon the fact that the regulated activity is petitioner's municipal landfill, which is "plainly of a commercial nature." But this is a far cry, indeed, from the "navigable waters" and "waters of the United States" to which the statute by its terms extends.

These are significant constitutional questions raised by respondents' application of their regulations, and yet we find nothing approaching a clear statement from Congress that it intended § 404(a) to reach an abandoned sand and gravel pit such as we have here. Permitting respondents to claim federal jurisdiction over ponds and mudflats falling within the "Migratory Bird Rule" would result in a significant impingement of the States' traditional and primary power over land and water use .... Rather than expressing a desire to readjust the federal-state balance in this manner, Congress chose to "recognize, preserve, and protect the primary responsibilities and rights of States ... to plan the development and use ... of land and water resources...." 33 U.S.C. § 1251(b). We thus read the statute as written to avoid the significant constitutional and federalism questions raised by respondents' interpretation, and therefore reject the request for administrative deference. . . .

■ JUSTICE STEVENS, with whom JUSTICE SOUTER, JUSTICE GINSBURG, and JUSTICE BREYER join, dissenting.

. . . It is fair to characterize the Clean Water Act as "watershed" legislation. The statute endorsed fundamental changes in both the purpose and the scope of federal regulation of the Nation's waters. In § 13 of the Rivers and Harbors Appropriation Act of 1899 (RHA), 33 U.S.C. § 407, Congress had assigned to the Army Corps of Engineers (Corps) the mission of regulating discharges into certain waters in order to protect their use as highways for the transportation of interstate and foreign commerce; the scope of the Corps' jurisdiction under the RHA accordingly extended only to waters that were "navigable." In the CWA, however, Congress broadened the Corps' mission to include the purpose of protecting the quality of our Nation's waters for esthetic, health, recreational, and environmental uses. The scope of its jurisdiction was therefore redefined to encompass all of "the waters of the United States, including the territorial seas." § 1362(7). That definition requires neither actual nor potential navigability.

The Court has previously held that the Corps' broadened jurisdiction under the CWA properly included an 80–acre parcel of low-lying marshy land that was not itself navigable, directly adjacent to navigable water, or even hydrologically connected to navigable water, but which was part of a larger area, characterized by poor drainage, that ultimately abutted a navigable creek. United States v. Riverside Bayview Homes, Inc., 474 U.S. 121 (1985). . . . [O]nce Congress crossed the legal watershed that separates navigable streams of commerce from marshes and inland lakes, there is no principled reason for limiting the statute's protection to those waters or wetlands that happen to lie near a navigable stream.

In its decision today, the Court draws a new jurisdictional line, one that invalidates the 1986 migratory bird regulation as well as the Corps' assertion of jurisdiction over all waters except for actually navigable waters, their tributaries, and wetlands adjacent to each. . . .

[S]imple common sense cuts against the particular definition of the Corps' jurisdiction favored by the majority.

## I

. . . Section 404 of the CWA resembles § 13 of the RHA, but, unlike the earlier statute, the primary purpose of which is the maintenance of navigability, § 404 was principally intended as a pollution control measure. . . .

Because of the statute's ambitious and comprehensive goals, it was, of course, necessary to expand its jurisdictional scope. Thus, although Congress opted to carry over the traditional jurisdictional term "navigable waters" from the RHA and prior versions of the FWPCA, it broadened the *definition* of that term to encompass all "waters of the United States." § 1362(7). . . . The Conference Report explained that the definition in

§ 502(7) was intended to "be given the broadest possible constitutional interpretation." S. Conf. Rep. No. 92–1236, p. 144 (1972), reprinted in 1 Leg. Hist. 327. . . .

. . . Why should Congress intend that its assertion of federal jurisdiction be given the "broadest possible constitutional interpretation" if it did not intend to reach beyond the very heartland of its commerce power? The activities regulated by the CWA have nothing to do with Congress' "commerce power over navigation." Indeed, the goals of the 1972 statute have nothing to do with *navigation* at all. . . .

### III

Although it might have appeared problematic on a "linguistic" level for the Corps to classify "lands" as "waters" in *Riverside Bayview*, 474 U.S., at 131–132, we squarely held that the agency's construction of the statute that it was charged with enforcing was entitled to deference under Chevron U.S.A. Inc. v. Natural Resources Defense Council, Inc., 467 U.S. 837 (1984). Today, however, the majority refuses to extend such deference to the same agency's construction of the same statute. This refusal is unfaithful to both *Riverside Bayview* and *Chevron*. For it is the majority's reading, not the agency's, that does violence to the scheme Congress chose to put into place.

Contrary to the Court's suggestion, the Corps' interpretation of the statute does not "encroac[h]" upon "traditional state power" over land use. . . . The CWA is not a land-use code; it is a paradigm of environmental regulation. Such regulation is an accepted exercise of federal power.

. . . [T]he federalism concerns to which the majority adverts are misplaced. The Corps' interpretation of the statute as extending beyond navigable waters, tributaries of navigable waters, and wetlands adjacent to each is manifestly reasonable and therefore entitled to deference.

### IV

Because I am convinced that the Court's miserly construction of the statute is incorrect, I shall comment briefly on petitioner's argument that Congress is without power to prohibit it from filling any part of the 31 acres of ponds on its property in Cook County, Illinois. The Corps' exercise of its § 404 permitting power over "isolated" waters that serve as habitat for migratory birds falls well within the boundaries set by this Court's Commerce Clause jurisprudence.

In United States v. Lopez, 514 U.S. 549, 558–559 (1995), this Court identified "three broad categories of activity that Congress may regulate under its commerce power": (1) channels of interstate commerce; (2) instrumentalities of interstate commerce, or persons and things in interstate commerce; and (3) activities that "substantially affect" interstate commerce. The migratory bird rule at issue here is properly analyzed under the third category. In order to constitute a proper exercise of Congress' power over intrastate activities that "substantially affect" interstate commerce, it is not necessary that each individual instance of the activity substantially affect commerce; it is enough that, taken in the aggregate, the *class of activities* in question has such an effect. . . .

The activity being regulated in this case (and by the Corps' § 404 regulations in general) is the discharge of fill material into water. The Corps did not assert jurisdiction over petitioner's land simply because the waters were "used as habitat by migratory birds." It asserted jurisdiction because petitioner planned to *discharge fill* into waters "used as habitat by migratory birds." . . . There can be no doubt that, unlike the class of activities Congress was attempting to regulate in United States v. Morrison, 529 U.S. 598, 613 (2000) ("[g]ender-motivated crimes"), and Lopez, 514 U.S., at 561 (possession of guns near school property), the discharge of fill material into the Nation's waters is almost always undertaken for economic reasons. . . .

Moreover, no one disputes that the discharge of fill into "isolated" waters that serve as migratory bird habitat will, in the aggregate, adversely affect migratory bird populations. . . .

In addition to the intrinsic value of migratory birds, . . . it is undisputed that literally millions of people regularly participate in birdwatching and hunting and that those activities generate a host of commercial activities of great value. The causal connection between the filling of wetlands and the decline of commercial activities associated with migratory birds is not "attenuated," *Morrison*, 529 U.S., at 612; it is direct and concrete. . . .

Finally, the migratory bird rule does not blur the "distinction between what is truly national and what is truly local." *Morrison*, 529 U.S., at 617–618. Justice Holmes cogently observed in Missouri v. Holland that the protection of migratory birds is a textbook example of a national problem. . . . Identifying the Corps' jurisdiction by reference to waters that serve as habitat for birds that migrate over state lines also satisfies this Court's expressed desire for some "jurisdictional element" that limits federal activity to its proper scope. Morrison, 529 U.S., at 612.

The power to regulate commerce among the several States necessarily and properly includes the power to preserve the natural resources that generate such commerce. . . . Migratory birds, and the waters on which they rely, are such resources. Moreover, the protection of migratory birds is a well-established federal responsibility. . . .

---

**1. Should Federalism Canons Limit Chevron's Scope?**—Chief Justice Rehnquist's majority opinion invoked the constitutional avoidance canon, noting that the Migratory Bird Rule raised serious questions about the outer limit of Congress's power under the Commerce Clause. In so doing, Chief Justice Rehnquist asserted the priority of the avoidance canon over *Chevron*, citing *DeBartolo*. On that understanding, *SWANCC*'s discussion of the limits on *Chevron* deference did not break significant new doctrinal ground. That understanding of *SWANCC*, however, is complicated by Justice Stevens' assertion, in dissent, that under prevailing constitutional doctrine the Corps' interpretation of the statute did not raise any serious constitutional questions. But there is another way to interpret the majority's analysis in *SWANCC*: Even if a statute that authorized the Migratory Bird Rule would not raise sufficiently serious constitutional doubts to trigger *DeBartolo*, *SWANCC* might be read more broadly as declaring that an ambiguous statute should not be interpreted to authorize agency regulations that "alter[] the federal-state framework by permitting federal encroachment upon a traditional state power." Recall, after all, that there are a number of cases, such as *Gregory v. Ashcroft* (*see* pp. 291–296, *supra*), in which the Court has applied a substantive canon of construction to protect traditional state prerogatives from federal encroachment, even when there was no serious constitutional doubt sufficient to trigger the conventional version of the avoidance canon. *SWANCC* might be—and sometimes has been—read as standing for the proposition that *Chevron* deference yields to *Gregory*-style federalism canons, such that agencies can only encroach on traditional state authority if the statute clearly authorizes them to do so. On the other hand, *SWANCC* is also sometimes read more narrowly as an application of *DeBartolo*—that is, as a case in which the Court rejected an agency interpretation that raised a serious constitutional doubt.

A recent illustration of the conflicting understandings of *SWANCC* can be found in the Ninth Circuit opinions in *Oregon v. Ashcroft*, 368 F.3d 1118 (9th Cir. 2004), *aff'd* 546 U.S. 243 (2006). After the state of Oregon enacted a law that permitted physician-assisted suicide under certain conditions, then-Attorney General John Ashcroft issued a statement (the "Ashcroft Directive") that declared that prescribing a controlled substance to assist in suicide would violate the federal Controlled Substances Act (CSA). Oregon argued that the Ashcroft Directive was inconsistent with the CSA; the United States argued, among other things, that the language of the CSA was at least ambiguous, and that the Ashcroft Directive should be upheld under *Chevron*. In rejecting the federal government's interpretation of the CSA, the Ninth Circuit majority relied in large measure on a broad reading of *SWANCC*. Under that reading, the majority held (1) that federal regulations that interfere with traditional state functions, like the substantive regulation of medical practice, must be clearly authorized by the federal statute, and (2) that this principle takes precedence over *Chevron*. As Judge Tallman argued:

> Unless Congress' authorization is "unmistakably clear," the Attorney General may not exercise control over an area of law traditionally reserved for state authority, such as regulation of medical care. [*Gregory v. Ashcroft*, 501 U.S. 452,] 460–61 [(1991)] (quoting *Atascadero State Hosp.* [*v. Scanlon*], 473 U.S. [234, 242 (1985)]); *see also Solid Waste Agency of N. Cook County v. U.S. Army Corps of Eng'rs*, 531 U.S. 159, 173 (2001). . . .

> The Ashcroft Directive is invalid because Congress has provided no indication—much less an "unmistakably clear" indication—that it intended to authorize the Attorney General to regulate the practice of physician assisted suicide. By attempting to regulate physician assisted suicide, the Ashcroft Directive invokes the outer limits of Congress'

power by encroaching on state authority to regulate medical practice. Because Congress has not clearly authorized such an intrusion, the Ashcroft Directive violates the clear statement rule. *See Solid Waste Agency*, 531 U.S. at 172–73. . . .

*Id.* at 1125 (some internal citations omitted). By contrast, Judge Wallace's dissent read *SWANCC* more narrowly as holding that "federalism concerns" take precedence over *Chevron* "[o]nly if the [agency's] proposed interpretation would likely render the statute unconstitutional." *Id.* at 1141 (Wallace, J., dissenting).

Thus while the Ninth Circuit majority read *SWANCC* broadly as holding that significant federalism concerns could trigger a clear statement requirement—one that takes priority over *Chevron*—even in the absence of a serious constitutional doubt, Judge Wallace's dissent read *SWANCC* narrowly as entailing merely an application of the standard constitutional avoidance canon and the holding in *DeBartolo*. Interestingly, although the Supreme Court affirmed the Ninth Circuit, Justice Kennedy's majority opinion rejected the U.S. government's arguments for *Chevron* deference principally on other grounds, and found resort to the federalism clear statement rules articulated in cases like *SWANCC* and *Gregory* "unnecessary." Gonzales v. Oregon, 546 U.S. 243, 274 (2006). Thus the question whether pro-federalism clear statement rules take precedence over *Chevron* even in cases that do not involve a serious constitutional doubt remains somewhat unsettled.

What should the doctrine be on this point? If we assume that these pro-federalism canons are appropriate in non-*Chevron* cases, should the fact that a responsible executive branch agency has endorsed the interpretation that encroaches on traditional state power mean that the pro-federalism canon gives way? Or are these federalism canons "traditional tools" of statutory construction that can clairify a statute such that deference to the agency is inappropriate? How would you argue for one or the other view?

**2. *The Relationship between Operative Provisions and Definitional Provisions*—**Although the focus of this section is on the interaction of *Chevron* with substantive canons of construction, it's worth noting that the debate in *SWANCC* about the significance of the term "navigable" is reminiscent of the debate in *Sweet Home* about the significance of the term "take." (*See* p. 866, *supra*.) In *SWANCC*, the relevant operative section of the Clean Water Act gives the Army Corps of Engineers jurisdiction to regulate discharge of dredge or fill materials into "navigable waters," and the Act defines "navigable waters" as including all "waters of the United States"—a phrase that has been interpreted to include all waters under the federal government's jurisdiction. What, then, is the significance of the word "navigable" in the operative section of the Act? On one view, it is irrelevant, because "navigable waters" is a defined term, and the definition alone determines the term's scope. On another view, "navigable" must have some independent significance; even if the statutory definition of "navigable waters" broadens the usual understanding of that term somewhat, it can't render the word "navigable" entirely superfluous. This is quite similar to the question in *Sweet Home* about whether the traditional meaning of the operative term "take" should matter, or whether its meaning is determined solely by the statutory definition.

In *SWANCC*, as in *Sweet Home*, this statutory interpretation question is complicated by *Chevron*. Even if the *best* reading of the Clean Water Act would preserve some independent meaning for "navigable," might we still conclude that there is a statutory ambiguity, and that the court should uphold as permissible the agency's view that the expansive language in the definitions section takes precedence? Or would an agency interpretation that renders a term in the operative provision of the statute meaningless be unreasonable, even under *Chevron*?

### b. Preemption

One of the most difficult problems involving the interaction of *Chevron* with other substantive canons of construction concerns the presumption against preemption (*see* pp. 306–327, *supra*). Many federal regulations may have the effect of preempting state law. These regulations are sometimes clearly authorized by statute, but in other cases the statute is ambiguous as to whether it authorizes the preemptive regulations in question. In such cases, should courts apply *Chevron* and defer to the agency's interpretation, or does the presumption against preemption trump *Chevron*? In situations in which the statute contains an express preemption clause, should courts defer to the responsible agency's interpretation of the scope of this clause? What about cases where a state law arguably stands as an obstacle to achieving the objectives of a federal regulatory program? Should courts defer to the responsible federal agency's view on whether a given state law presents such an obstacle, or is *Chevron* inapplicable in such cases?

As was true with the conflict between *Chevron* and other substantive canons, the conflict between *Chevron* and the presumption against preemption is essentially a conflict between substantive commitments. The proper way to reconcile the underlying commitments has generated a range of scholarly views. Some commentators have suggested that courts should forgo *Chevron* deference to agency decisions regarding preemption of state law, principally on the grounds that refusing *Chevron* deference in this context would channel the decision to preempt state law into the legislative process, where the bicameralism and presentment requirements serve to protect the interests of the states. *See, e.g.*, Bradford R. Clark, *Process–Based Preemption*, in PREEMPTION CHOICE: THE THEORY, LAW, AND REALITY OF FEDERALISM'S CORE QUESTION 192 (William W. Buzbee ed., 2008); Cass R. Sunstein, *Nondelegation Canons*, 67 U. CHI. L. REV. 315, 331 (2000); Ernest A. Young, *Executive Preemption*, 102 NW. U. L. REV. 869, 870–71 (2008). Others have questioned this conclusion, arguing that the administrative process may protect state interests at least as effectively as the legislative process. *See* Nina Mendelson, Chevron *and Preemption*, 102 MICH. L. REV. 737, 759–79 (2004). Furthermore, insofar as *Chevron* deference is grounded in considerations of comparative institutional competence, might agencies be more equipped than courts to determine the degree to which state law interferes with the purposes or objectives of a federal regulatory scheme? If so, perhaps *Chevron* ought to take priority over the presumption against preemption. *See* Thomas W. Merrill, *Preemption and Institutional Choice*, 102 Nw. U. L. Rev. 727 (2008). Others have suggested that courts should apply the intermediate standard set forth in *Skidmore v. Swift & Co.* (*see* pp. 807–810, *supra*) to any agency's view of a statute's preemptive scope. *See, e.g.,* Catherine M. Sharkey, *Products Liability Preemption: An Institutional Approach*, 76 Geo. Wash. L. Rev. 449, 491–98 (2008).

The Supreme Court has offered surprisingly little guidance on this issue. The following case, *Smiley v. Citibank*, touched on one aspect of the issue, but pointedly left many important questions unresolved.

---

# Smiley v. Citibank (South Dakota), N.A.

Supreme Court of the United States
517 U.S. 735 (1996)

■ Justice Scalia delivered the opinion of the Court.

Section 30 of the National Bank Act of 1864, 12 U.S.C. § 85, provides that a national bank may charge its loan customers "interest at the rate allowed by the laws of the State ... where the bank is located." In Marquette Nat. Bank of Minneapolis v. First of Omaha Service Corp., 439 U.S. 299 (1978), we held that this provision authorizes a national bank to charge out-of-state credit-card customers an interest rate allowed by the bank's home State, even when that rate is higher than what is permitted by the States in which the cardholders reside. The question in this case is whether § 85 also authorizes a national bank to charge late-payment fees that are lawful in the bank's home State but prohibited in the States where the cardholders reside—in other words, whether the statutory term "interest" encompasses late-payment fees.

### I

Petitioner, a resident of California, held two credit cards ... issued by respondent, a national bank located in Sioux Falls, South Dakota.... Petitioner was charged late fees on both cards.

These late fees are permitted by South Dakota law. Petitioner, however, is of the view that exacting such "unconscionable" late charges from California residents violates California law....

### II

... [I]t would be difficult indeed to contend that the word "interest" in the National Bank Act is unambiguous with regard to the point at issue here. It is our practice to defer to the reasonable judgments of agencies with regard to the meaning of ambiguous terms in statutes that they are charged with administering. See Chevron U.S.A. Inc. v. Natural Resources Defense Council, Inc., 467 U.S. 837, 842–845 (1984). As we observed only last Term, that practice extends to the judgments of the Comptroller of the Currency with regard to the meaning of the banking laws. . . .

On March 3, 1995, which was after the California Superior Court's dismissal of petitioner's complaint, the Comptroller of the Currency noticed for public comment a proposed regulation dealing with the subject before us, and on February 9, 1996, which was after the California Supreme Court's decision, he adopted the following provision:

> "The term 'interest' as used in 12 U.S.C. § 85 includes any payment compensating a creditor or prospective creditor for an extension of credit, making available of a line of credit, or any default or breach by a borrower of a condition upon which credit was extended. It includes, among other things, the following fees connected with credit extension or availability: numerical periodic rates, late fees, not sufficient funds (NSF) fees, overlimit fees, annual fees, cash advance fees, and membership fees. It does not ordinarily include appraisal fees, premiums and commissions attributable to insurance guaranteeing repayment of any extension of credit, finders' fees, fees for document preparation or notarization, or fees incurred to obtain credit reports." 61 Fed.Reg. 4869 (to be codified in 12 CFR § 7.4001(a)).

Petitioner proposes several reasons why the ordinary rule of deference should not apply to this regulation. First, petitioner points to the fact that this regulation was issued more than 100 years after the enactment of § 85, and seemingly as a result of this and similar litigation in which the Comptroller has participated as *amicus curiae* on the side of the banks. The 100–year delay makes no difference. . . . We accord deference to agencies under *Chevron,* not because of a presumption that they drafted the provisions in question, or were present at the hearings, or spoke to the principal sponsors; but rather because of a presumption that Congress, when it left ambiguity in a statute meant for implementation by an agency, understood that the ambiguity would be resolved, first and foremost, by the agency, and desired the agency (rather than the courts) to possess whatever degree of discretion the ambiguity allows. Nor does it matter that the regulation was prompted by litigation, including this very suit. . . . [W]e have before us here a full-dress regulation, issued by the Comptroller himself and adopted pursuant to the notice-and-comment procedures of the Administrative Procedure Act designed to assure due deliberation. That it was litigation which disclosed the need for the regulation is irrelevant.

Second, petitioner contends that the Comptroller's regulation is not deserving of our deference because "there is no rational basis for distinguishing the various charges [it] has denominated interest . . . from those charges it has denominated 'non-interest.' " We disagree. . . . [I]t seems to us perfectly possible to draw a line, as the regulation does, between (1) "payment compensating a creditor or prospective creditor for an extension of credit, making available of a line of credit, or any default or breach by a borrower of a condition upon which credit was extended," and (2) all other payments. . . . In its logic, at least, the line is not "arbitrary [or] capricious," and thereby disentitled to deference under *Chevron*. . . .

In addition to offering these reasons why 12 CFR § 7.4001(a) in particular is not entitled to deference, petitioner contends that *no* Comptroller interpretation of § 85 is entitled to deference, because § 85 is a provision that pre-empts state law. She argues that the "presumption against . . . pre-emption" announced in Cipollone v. Liggett Group, Inc., 505 U.S. 504, 518 (1992), in effect trumps *Chevron,* and requires a court to make its own interpretation of § 85 that will avoid (to the extent possible) pre-emption of state law. This argument confuses the question of the substantive (as opposed to pre-emptive) *meaning* of a statute with the question of *whether* a statute is pre-emptive. We may assume (without deciding) that the latter question must always be decided *de novo* by the courts. That is *not* the question at issue here; there is no doubt that § 85 pre-empts state law. . . . What *is* at issue here is simply the meaning of a provision that does not (like the provision in *Cipollone*) deal with pre-emption, and hence does not bring into play the considerations petitioner raises. . . .

### III

Since we have concluded that the Comptroller's regulation deserves deference, the question before us is not whether it represents the best interpretation of the statute, but whether it represents a reasonable one. The answer is obviously yes. . . .

---

*1.  **The Decision To Preempt Versus the Scope of Preemption***— The most important feature of *Smiley* (as relevant to the applicability of *Chevron* deference to preemption questions) is the distinction Justice Scalia drew between (1) cases involving an agency's view on the *meaning* of a statutory provision (which may have preemptive consequences), and (2) cases involving an agency's view on *whether* a provision of a federal statute preempts state law. According to Justice Scalia, *Smiley* falls into the first category, not the second. There is no dispute that the National Bank Act preempts any state regulation of "interest" charges by out-of-state banks; the only question is what counts as "interest." A broad construction of "interest" would have the effect of preempting more state law than would a narrow construction, but *Smiley* treated the presumption against preemption as irrelevant to the question whether the agency should get *Chevron* deference on its interpretation of this term. The Court's logic was apparently that if the presumption against preemption displaced *Chevron* in this sort of case, agencies would be under a presumptive obligation to interpret their statutory mandates as narrowly as possible, since any affirmative agency regulation could conflict with a contrary state law. Thus *Smiley* concluded that the presumption against preemption does not apply to the first category of cases, but expressly declined to say anything about whether the presumption against preemption would take precedence over *Chevron* in the second category of cases, where the question is whether a federal statute preempts state law at all. How convincing is *Smiley*'s categorical distinction between these types of cases?

It is perhaps worth noting that Justice Scalia's distinction between the question *whether* a statute preempts state law and the question of *how much* state law a statutory preemption provision covers is similar to the distinction that he drew in his dissenting opinion in *Cipollone v. Liggett Group* (pp. 311–320, *supra*), in which he argued that the presumption against preemption applies to the question *whether* a statute (impliedly) preempts state law, but not to the question of how broadly or narrowly a court ought to read substantive terms in an express preemption clause. In *Cipollone*, a majority of the Court seemed to reject the relevance of that distinction, yet in *Smiley* a unanimous Court endorsed a similar distinction in addressing the question whether *Chevron* applied to an agency's interpretation of a substantive term in an express preemption clause. What do you make of this?

**2.  The Unsettled State of the Doctrine**—*Smiley*, as noted above, expressly declined to address whether an agency would be entitled to *Chevron* deference when it determined whether a particular class of state laws was impliedly preempted (on obstacle or field preemption grounds) by a federal statute. The Supreme Court has yet to resolve this issue clearly. Furthermore, the Court has not consistently adhered to *Smiley*'s assertion that the presumption against preemption yields to *Chevron* on all questions concerning the substantive meaning of the terms in a statutory preemption clause. Consider, in this regard, Medtronic v. Lohr, 518 U.S. 470 (1996), which was decided only two weeks after *Smiley*. *Medtronic* involved a state law claim brought against a medical device manufacturer for an allegedly defective pacemaker. The defendant argued that the claim was preempted by the federal Medical Device Amendments (MDA), which bar states from maintaining any "requirement" related to a medical device that is "different from, or in addition to, any requirement under" the federal statute. 21 U.S.C. § 360(k). In resolving the case in favor of the plaintiffs, Justice Stevens' opinion for the Court (joined by Justices Kennedy, Souter, Ginsburg, and Breyer) emphasized the traditional presumption against preemption:

> . . . [B]ecause the States are independent sovereigns in our federal system, we have long presumed that Congress does not cavalierly preempt state-law causes of action. In all pre-emption cases, and particularly in those in which Congress has "legislated . . . in a field which the States have traditionally occupied," Rice v. Santa Fe Elevator Corp., 331 U.S. 218, 230 (1947), we "start with the assumption that the historic police powers of the States were not to be superseded by the Federal Act unless that was the clear and manifest purpose of Congress." *Ibid.* . . . That approach is consistent with both federalism concerns and the historic primacy of state regulation of matters of health and safety.

517 U.S. at 485.

Notably, Justice Stevens' opinion also asserted that its conclusion of non-preemption was "substantially informed" by regulations promulgated by the Food and Drug Administration (FDA), according to which suits of this kind were not preempted by the federal MDA. As the *Medtronic* opinion explained:

> Because the FDA is the federal agency to which Congress has delegated its authority to implement the provisions of the Act, the agency is uniquely qualified to determine whether a particular form of state law "stands as an obstacle to the accomplishment and execution of the full purposes and objectives of Congress," Hines v. Davidowitz, 312 U.S. 52, 67 (1941), and, therefore, whether it should be pre-empted.... The ambiguity in the statute—and the congressional grant of authority to the agency on the matter contained within it—provide a "sound basis," (O'Connor, J., concurring in part and dissenting in part), for giving substantial weight to the agency's view of the statute. See Chevron U.S.A. Inc. v. Natural Resources Defense Council, Inc., 467 U.S. 837 (1984)....

517 U.S. at 495–96; *see also id.* at 505–06 (Breyer, J., concurring in part and concurring in the judgment).

Thus *Medtronic* ultimately did little to resolve the order of priority between *Chevron* deference and the presumption against preemption, because *Medtronic* happened to be a (somewhat unusual) case in which *both* the presumption against preemption *and* deference to the federal agency's regulations supported a conclusion of non-preemption; there was thus no conflict between these interpretive canons. What would or should have happened if these canons pointed in opposite directions—as when a federal agency responsible for administering a federal statute concludes that this statute *does* preempt certain state laws?

The Supreme Court has repeatedly avoided answering this question, usually by concluding that the federal statute in question is not ambiguous. For example, in Watters v. Wachovia Bank, 550 U.S. 1 (2007), the Supreme Court considered whether the federal National Bank Act (NBA) preempted certain state banking laws. The Office of the Comptroller of the Currency (OCC), the federal agency with the authority to regulate banks under the NBA, had issued a regulation that declared, in effect, that a variety of state banking laws were preempted by the NBA. The Sixth Circuit applied the *Chevron* framework to resolve this question and concluded both that Congress had not spoken precisely on the issue and that the OCC's interpretation was reasonable. Wachovia Bank v. Watters, 431 F.3d 556 (6th Cir. 2005); *see also* Wells Fargo Bank, N.A. v. Boutris, 419 F.3d 949 (9th Cir. 2005); Wachovia Bank, N.A. v. Burke, 414 F.3d 305 (2d Cir. 2005). Although the Supreme Court affirmed, Justice Ginsburg's majority opinion did not rely on *Chevron* deference, but rather held that the NBA clearly authorized the preemptive regulations at issue. Because the federal statute was clear, Justice Ginsburg asserted, "the level of deference owed to [the OCC's] regulation is an academic question"—one that the Court chose not to answer. *Watters*, 550 U.S. at 20–21.

Interestingly, Justice Stevens' dissent in *Watters* (joined by Chief Justice Roberts and Justice Scalia), addressed this issue more directly. Perhaps surprisingly, given some of the language in his majority opinion in

*Medtronic*, Justice Stevens' dissent argued that *Chevron* should *not* apply to an agency's decision to preempt state law:

> [E]xpert agency opinions as to which state laws conflict with a federal statute may be entitled to "some weight," especially when "the subject matter is technical" and "the relevant history and background are complex and extensive." Geier v. American Honda Motor Co., 529 U.S. 861, 883 (2000). But "[u]nlike Congress, administrative agencies are clearly not designed to represent the interests of States, yet with relative ease they can promulgate comprehensive and detailed regulations that have broad preemption ramifications for state law." *Id.*, at 908 (STEVENS, J., dissenting). For that reason, when an agency purports to decide the scope of federal preemption, a healthy respect for state sovereignty calls for something less than *Chevron* deference.

*Watters*, 550 U.S. at 41 (Stevens, J., dissenting) (footnotes omitted).

The Supreme Court's failure to address and resolve questions about *Chevron*'s relative priority vis-à-vis the presumption against preemption has led to divergent approaches in the courts of appeals. *Compare, e.g.,* Brannan v. United Student Aid Funds, Inc., 94 F.3d 1260, 1264 (9th Cir. 1996) (granting *Chevron* deference to an agency's conclusion that a state law is impliedly preempted by the federal statute, on the grounds that the agency " 'is uniquely qualified to determine whether [a state law stands as an obstacle to the accomplishment of Congress's objectives], and therefore, whether it should be preempted' ") (quoting Medtronic v. Lohr, 518 U.S. 470, 496 (1996)), *with* Commonwealth of Massachusetts v. United States Department of Transportation, 93 F.3d 890, 894 (D.C. Cir. 1996) (concluding that an agency's determination that a state law would stand as an obstacle to the achievement of the purposes of a federal law could not be upheld under *Chevron* "in light of the strong presumption against federal preemption"). What is your view on the proper resolution of this doctrinal problem?

## IV.   THE LIMITS OF *CHEVRON*'S DOMAIN

*Chevron*, as we have seen, establishes a presumption of judicial deference to agency statutory interpretations, and this presumption is based on an assertion, or legal fiction, regarding congressional intent. But is this presumption always reasonable? In the previous section, we saw that courts sometimes refuse to give *Chevron* deference to an agency's construction of an otherwise ambiguous statute because the agency's interpretation would implicate some other substantive canon of statutory construction, such as the constitutional avoidance canon or the presumption against preemption. Those cases, however, are still at least ostensibly governed by the *Chevron* framework; when the agency loses, it is because the reviewing court has concluded that the statute is not, in fact, ambiguous once one has applied the appropriate tools of statutory construction.

Are there also some agency statutory interpretations that should not get *Chevron* deference on the grounds it is implausible (or undesirable) to presume Congress meant to delegate the resolution of that particular statutory ambiguity to an agency? Perhaps before courts apply the *Chevron* framework, they first need to ask a preliminary question (or set of questions) about whether *Chevron* applies at all to the agency interpretation at issue. This preliminary inquiry is sometimes characterized as the question of "*Chevron*'s domain" or as a kind of "*Chevron* Step Zero." *See* Thomas W. Merrill & Kristin E. Hickman, Chevron*'s Domain*, 89 Geo. L.J. 833 (2001); Cass R. Sunstein, Chevron *Step Zero*, 92 Va. L. Rev. 187 (2006).

Among the most important and controversial questions regarding possible limits to *Chevron*'s domain is whether the legal effect and/or procedural formality of the agency's interpretive statement are relevant to whether that interpretation is entitled to *Chevron* deference. So far, this chapter has discussed cases in which the reviewing court applied the *Chevron* framework to agency interpretations announced in notice-and-comment rules, or in orders following a formal administrative adjudication. But what about agency interpretations that are announced as interpretive rules that do not go through notice and comment? What about interpretations issued in *informal* adjudications, which are subject to minimal procedural requirements? Should *Chevron* apply to these sorts of interpretations as well?

For the first 15 years after the *Chevron* decision, the Supreme Court did not address these questions directly. During this period, circuit courts sometimes applied *Chevron* to these less formal interpretive statements, but sometimes they declined to do so on the grounds that these informal pronouncements lacked the "force of law." *See* John F. Manning, *Nonlegislative Rules*, 72 Geo. Wash. L. Rev. 893, 937 & n.215 (2004). The Supreme Court finally weighed in on this issue with two important decisions issued in consecutive terms: Christensen v. Harris County, 529 U.S. 576 (2000), and United States v. Mead Corp., 533 U.S. 218 (2001).

*Christensen* involved a dispute over the proper interpretation of the Fair Labor Standards Act (FLSA). Simplifying somewhat, the FLSA allows state and local governments to compensate employees for overtime work by giving these employees additional "comp time," which entitles them to take time off from work at full pay. If employees don't use their accumulated comp time, though, the employer can be required to pay cash compensation. A local sheriff's department in Harris County, Texas was worried that many of its employees were accruing so much unused comp time that if these employees sought cash compensation, it would place a serious fiscal strain on the county treasury. The county therefore decided to adopt a rule requiring its employees to schedule time off in order to use up some of their accumulated comp time. Before Harris County adopted its new policy, it asked the Administrator of the Labor Department's Wages and Hours Division (the federal agency that oversees enforcement of the FLSA) whether this policy would be acceptable. The Administrator's reply letter stated that unless there was a prior contractual agreement permitting this sort of thing, the FLSA prohibited an employer from compelling an employee to use accumulated comp time. Harris County nonetheless went ahead and adopted its new policy. Several employees sued, alleging that this policy was inconsistent with the FLSA.

The Supreme Court, in an opinion by Justice Thomas, found the interpretation urged by the employees and the Labor Department "unpersuasive." The Court acknowledged, however, that the statute was not entirely clear. Given that concession, the Court had to confront the employees' claim that *Chevron* required the Court to defer to the Administrator's interpretation. In rejecting this argument, Justice Thomas wrote:

> [W]e confront an interpretation contained in an opinion letter, not one arrived at after, for example, a formal adjudication or notice-and-comment rulemaking. Interpretations such as those in opinion letters—like interpretations contained in policy statements, agency manuals, and enforcement guidelines, all of which lack the force of law—do not warrant *Chevron*-style deference... Instead, interpretations contained in formats such as opinion letters are "entitled to respect" under our decision in Skidmore v. Swift & Co., 323 U.S. 134, 140 (1944), but only to the extent that those interpretations have the 'power to persuade,' *ibid.*

529 U.S. at 587.

Justice Scalia concurred in the judgment, but he disagreed with the passage quoted above. In Justice Scalia's view, *Chevron* supplied the correct standard of review, and he concurred in the judgment only because he thought that the Administrator's interpretation of the FLSA was unreasonable. Justice Scalia described *Skidmore* as an "anachronism" that had been displaced by *Chevron*, and he emphasized that on numerous occasions the Court had accorded *Chevron* deference to agency positions contained in opinion letters and informal adjudications. *Id.* at 589–91 (Scalia, J., concurring in part and concurring in the judgment). Justice Breyer (who, along with Justices Stevens and Ginsburg, dissented on the merits) argued, to the contrary, that *Skidmore* deference would apply where "*Chevron*-type deference is inapplicable—*e.g.,* where one has doubt that Congress actually intended to delegate interpretive authority to the agency...." *Id.* at 596–97 (Breyer, J., dissenting). To this, Justice Scalia replied that *Chevron* would only be "inapplicable" if the statute were unambiguous (or if there were no authoritative agency interpretation), in which case *Skidmore* would also be inapplicable. Doubts about whether Congress actually intended to delegate interpretive authority to the agency, according to Justice Scalia, are properly considered when the reviewing court is deciding *whether* the statute is ambiguous, but "once ambiguity is established the consequences of *Chevron* attach." *Id.* at 589 n.*(Scalia, J., concurring in part and concurring in the judgment).

*Christensen* was a kind of dress rehearsal for the more significant decision in *United States v. Mead Corp.* the following Term. As you read the opinions in *Mead*, consider the degree to which it is consistent with

*Chevron* at the level of theory, and what the practical consequences of the decision might be.

---

# United States v. Mead Corp.

Supreme Court of the United States
533 U.S. 218 (2001)

■ JUSTICE SOUTER delivered the opinion of the Court.

The question is whether a tariff classification ruling by the United States Customs Service deserves judicial deference. The Federal Circuit rejected Customs's invocation of Chevron U.S.A. Inc. v. Natural Resources Defense Council, Inc., 467 U.S. 837 (1984), in support of such a ruling, to which it gave no deference. We agree that a tariff classification has no claim to judicial deference under *Chevron,* there being no indication that Congress intended such a ruling to carry the force of law, but we hold that under Skidmore v. Swift & Co., 323 U.S. 134 (1944), the ruling is eligible to claim respect according to its persuasiveness.

I

A

Imports are taxed under the Harmonized Tariff Schedule of the United States (HTSUS), 19 U.S.C. § 1202. Title 19 U.S.C. § 1500(b) provides that Customs "shall, under rules and regulations prescribed by the Secretary [of the Treasury,] ... fix the final classification and rate of duty applicable to ... merchandise" under the HTSUS. Section 1502(a) provides that

> "[t]he Secretary of the Treasury shall establish and promulgate such rules and regulations not inconsistent with the law (including regulations establishing procedures for the issuance of binding rulings prior to the entry of the merchandise concerned), and may disseminate such information as may be necessary to secure a just, impartial, and uniform appraisement of imported merchandise and the classification and assessment of duties thereon at the various ports of entry."[1]

... The Secretary provides for tariff rulings before the entry of goods by regulations authorizing "ruling letters" setting tariff classifications for particular imports. 19 CFR § 177.8 (2000). A ruling letter

> "represents the official position of the Customs Service with respect to the particular transaction or issue described therein and is binding on all Customs Service personnel in accordance with the provisions of this section until modified or revoked. In the absence of a change of practice or other modification or revocation which affects the principle of the ruling set forth in the ruling letter, that principle may be cited

---

**1.**  The statutory term "ruling" is defined by regulation as "a written statement ... that interprets and applies the provisions of the Customs and related laws to a specific set of facts." 19 CFR § 177.1(d)(1) (2000).

as authority in the disposition of transactions involving the same circumstances." § 177.9(a).

After the transaction that gives it birth, a ruling letter is to "be applied only with respect to transactions involving articles identical to the sample submitted with the ruling request or to articles whose description is identical to the description set forth in the ruling letter." § 177.9(b)(2). As a general matter, such a letter is "subject to modification or revocation without notice to any person, except the person to whom the letter was addressed," § 177.9(c), and the regulations consequently provide that "no other person should rely on the ruling letter or assume that the principles of that ruling will be applied in connection with any transaction other than the one described in the letter," *ibid.* Since ruling letters respond to transactions of the moment, they are not subject to notice and comment before being issued, may be published but need only be made "available for public inspection," 19 U.S.C. § 1625(a), and, at the time this action arose, could be modified without notice and comment under most circumstances, 19 CFR § 177.10(c) (2000). A broader notice-and-comment requirement for modification of prior rulings was added by statute in 1993, . . . and took effect after this case arose.

Any of the 46 port-of-entry Customs offices may issue ruling letters, and so may the Customs Headquarters Office, in providing "[a]dvice or guidance as to the interpretation or proper application of the Customs and related laws with respect to a specific Customs transaction [which] may be requested by Customs Service field offices . . . at any time, whether the transaction is prospective, current, or completed," 19 CFR § 177.11(a) (2000). Most ruling letters contain little or no reasoning, but simply describe goods and state the appropriate category and tariff. A few letters, like the Headquarters ruling at issue here, set out a rationale in some detail.

### B

Respondent, the Mead Corporation, imports "day planners," three-ring binders with pages having room for notes of daily schedules and phone numbers and addresses, together with a calendar and suchlike. The tariff schedule on point falls under the HTSUS heading for "[r]egisters, account books, notebooks, order books, receipt books, letter pads, memorandum pads, diaries and similar articles," HTSUS subheading 4820.10, which comprises two subcategories. Items in the first, "[d]iaries, notebooks and address books, bound; memorandum pads, letter pads and similar articles," were subject to a tariff of 4.0% at the time in controversy. . . . Objects in the second, covering "[o]ther" items, were free of duty. . . .

Between 1989 and 1993, Customs repeatedly treated day planners under the "other" HTSUS subheading. In January 1993, however, Customs changed its position, and issued a Headquarters ruling letter classifying Mead's day planners as "Diaries . . ., bound" subject to tariff under subheading 4820.10.20. That letter was short on explanation, but after Mead's protest, Customs Headquarters issued a new letter, carefully reasoned but never published, reaching the same conclusion. This letter considered two definitions of "diary" from the Oxford English Dictionary, the first covering a daily journal of the past day's events, the second a book including " 'printed dates for daily memoranda and jottings; also ... calendars....' " Customs concluded that "diary" was not confined to the first, in part because the broader definition reflects commercial usage and hence the "commercial identity of these items in the marketplace." As for the definition of "bound," Customs concluded that HTSUS was not referring to "bookbinding," but to a less exact sort of fastening described in the Harmonized Commodity Description and Coding System Explanatory Notes to Heading 4820, which spoke of binding by " 'reinforcements or fittings of metal, plastics, etc.' "

Customs rejected Mead's further protest of the second Headquarters ruling letter, and Mead filed suit in the Court of International Trade (CIT). The CIT granted the Government's motion for summary judgment, adopting Customs's reasoning without saying anything about deference.

... [Mead then took the case to the U.S. Court of Appeals for the Federal Circuit, which] reversed the CIT and held that Customs classification rulings should not get *Chevron* deference.... Rulings are not preceded by notice and comment as under the Administrative Procedure Act (APA), 5 U.S.C. § 553, they "do not carry the force of law and are not, like regulations, intended to clarify the rights and obligations of importers beyond the specific case under review." The appeals court thought classification rulings had a weaker *Chevron* claim even than Internal Revenue Service interpretive rulings, to which that court gives no deference; unlike rulings by the IRS, Customs rulings issue from many locations and need not be published....

We granted certiorari in order to consider the limits of *Chevron* deference owed to administrative practice in applying a statute. We hold that administrative implementation of a particular statutory provision qualifies for *Chevron* deference when it appears that Congress delegated authority to the agency generally to make rules carrying the force of law, and that the agency interpretation claiming deference was promulgated in the exercise of that authority. Delegation of such authority may be shown in a variety of ways, as by an agency's power to engage in adjudication or notice-and-comment rulemaking, or by some other indication of a comparable congressional intent. The Customs ruling at issue here fails to qualify, although the possibility that it deserves some deference under *Skidmore* leads us to vacate and remand.

## II

### A

When Congress has "explicitly left a gap for an agency to fill, there is an express delegation of authority to the agency to elucidate a specific provision of the statute by regulation," *Chevron*, 467 U.S., at 843–844, and any ensuing regulation is binding in the courts unless procedurally defective, arbitrary or capricious in substance, or manifestly contrary to the statute. See *id.,* at 844.... But whether or not they enjoy any express delegation of authority on a particular question, agencies charged with applying a statute necessarily make all sorts of interpretive choices, and while not all of those choices bind judges to follow them, they certainly may influence courts facing questions the agencies have already answered. "[T]he well-reasoned views of the agencies implementing a statute 'constitute a body of experience and informed judgment to which courts and litigants may properly resort for guidance,' " *Bragdon v. Abbott,* 524 U.S. 624, 642 (1998) (quoting *Skidmore,* 323 U.S., at 139–140), and "[w]e have long recognized that considerable weight should be accorded to an executive department's construction of a statutory scheme it is entrusted to administer...." *Chevron, supra,* at 844 (footnote omitted).... The fair measure of deference to an agency administering its own statute has been understood to vary with circumstances, and courts have looked to the degree of the agency's care, its consistency, formality, and relative expertness, and to the persuasiveness of the agency's position, see *Skidmore, supra,* at 139–140. The approach has produced a spectrum of judicial responses, from great respect at one end ... to near indifference at the other.... Justice Jackson summed things up in *Skidmore v. Swift & Co.:*

> "The weight [accorded to an administrative] judgment in a particular case will depend upon the thoroughness evident in its consideration, the validity of its reasoning, its consistency with earlier and later pronouncements, and all those factors which give it power to persuade, if lacking power to control." 323 U.S., at 140.

Since 1984, we have identified a category of interpretive choices distinguished by an additional reason for judicial deference. This Court in *Chevron* recognized that Congress not only engages in express delegation of specific interpretive authority, but that "[s]ometimes the legislative delegation to an agency on a particular question is implicit." 467 U.S., at 844. Congress, that is, may not have expressly delegated authority or responsibility to implement a particular provision or fill a particular gap. Yet it can still be apparent from the agency's generally conferred authority and other statutory circumstances that Congress would expect the agency to be able to speak with the force of law when it addresses ambiguity in the statute or fills a space in the enacted law, even one about which "Congress did not actually have an intent" as to a particular result. *Id.,* at 845. When circumstances implying such an expectation exist, a reviewing court has no business rejecting an agency's exercise of its generally conferred authority to resolve a particular statutory ambiguity simply because the agency's chosen resolution seems unwise, see *id.,* at 845–846, but is obliged to accept the agency's position if Congress has not previously spoken to the point at issue and the agency's interpretation is reasonable, see *id.,* at 842–845....

We have recognized a very good indicator of delegation meriting *Chevron* treatment in express congressional authorizations to engage in the process of rulemaking or adjudication that produces regulations or rulings for which deference is claimed. See, *e.g., EEOC v. Arabian American Oil Co.,* 499 U.S. 244, 257 (1991) (no *Chevron* deference to agency guideline where congressional delegation did not include the power to " 'promulgate rules or regulations' " (quoting General Elec. Co. v. Gilbert, 429 U.S. 125, 141 (1976))); see also Christensen v. Harris County, 529 U.S. 576, 596–597 (2000) (BREYER, J., dissenting) (where it is in doubt that Congress actually intended to delegate particular interpretive authority to an agency, *Chevron* is "inapplicable"). It is fair to assume generally that Congress contemplates administrative action with the effect of law when it provides for a relatively formal administrative procedure tending to foster the fairness and deliberation that should underlie a pronouncement of such force.[11] . . . Thus, the overwhelming number of our cases applying *Chevron* deference have reviewed the fruits of notice-and-comment rulemaking or formal adjudication. That said, and as significant as notice-and-comment is in pointing to *Chevron* authority, the want of that procedure here does not decide the case, for we have sometimes found reasons for *Chevron* deference even when no such administrative formality was required and none was afforded, see, *e.g., NationsBank of N.C., N.A. v. Variable Annuity Life Ins. Co.,* 513 U.S. 251, 256–257, 263. The fact that the tariff classification here was not a product of such formal process does not alone, therefore, bar the application of *Chevron*.

There are, nonetheless, ample reasons to deny *Chevron* deference here. The authorization for classification rulings, and Customs's practice in making them, present a case far removed not only from notice-and-comment process, but from any other circumstances reasonably suggesting that Congress ever thought of classification rulings as deserving the deference claimed for them here.

### B

No matter which angle we choose for viewing the Customs ruling letter in this case, it fails to qualify under *Chevron*. On the face of the statute, to begin with, the terms of the congressional delegation give no indication that Congress meant to delegate authority to Customs to issue classification rulings with the force of law. We are not, of course, here making any global statement about Customs's authority, for it is true that the general rulemaking power conferred on Customs, see 19 U.S.C. § 1624, authorizes some regulation with the force of law. . . . It is true as well that Congress had classification rulings in mind when it explicitly authorized, in a parenthetical, the issuance of "regulations establishing procedures for the issuance of binding rulings prior to the entry of the merchandise concerned," 19 U.S.C. § 1502(a). The reference to binding classifications does not, however, bespeak the legislative type of activity that would naturally bind more than the parties to the ruling, once the goods classified are admitted into this country. And though the statute's direction to dissemi-

---

11. See Merrill & Hickman, *Chevron*'s Domain, 89 Geo. L.J. 833, 872 (2001) ("[I]f *Chevron* rests on a presumption about congressional intent, then *Chevron* should apply only where Congress would want *Chevron* to apply. In delineating the types of delegations of agency authority that trigger *Chevron* deference, it is therefore important to determine whether a plausible case can be made that Congress would want such a delegation to mean that agencies enjoy primary interpretational authority").

nate "information" necessary to "secure" uniformity, *ibid.*, seems to assume that a ruling may be precedent in later transactions, precedential value alone does not add up to *Chevron* entitlement; interpretive rules may sometimes function as precedents ... and they enjoy no *Chevron* status as a class. In any event, any precedential claim of a classification ruling is counterbalanced by the provision for independent review of Customs classifications by the CIT, see 28 U.S.C. §§ 2638–2640....

It is difficult, in fact, to see in the agency practice itself any indication that Customs ever set out with a lawmaking pretense in mind when it undertook to make classifications like these. Customs does not generally engage in notice-and-comment practice when issuing them, and their treatment by the agency makes it clear that a letter's binding character as a ruling stops short of third parties; Customs has regarded a classification as conclusive only as between itself and the importer to whom it was issued, 19 CFR § 177.9(c) (2000), and even then only until Customs has given advance notice of intended change, §§ 177.9(a), (c). Other importers are in fact warned against assuming any right of detrimental reliance. § 177.9(c).

Indeed, to claim that classifications have legal force is to ignore the reality that 46 different Customs offices issue 10,000 to 15,000 of them each year.... Any suggestion that rulings intended to have the force of law are being churned out at a rate of 10,000 a year at an agency's 46 scattered offices is simply self-refuting. Although the circumstances are less startling here, with a Headquarters letter in issue, none of the relevant statutes recognizes this category of rulings as separate or different from others; there is thus no indication that a more potent delegation might have been understood as going to Headquarters even when Headquarters provides developed reasoning, as it did in this instance....

In sum, classification rulings are best treated like "interpretations contained in policy statements, agency manuals, and enforcement guidelines." *Christensen,* 529 U.S., at 587. They are beyond the *Chevron* pale.

C

To agree with the Court of Appeals that Customs ruling letters do not fall within *Chevron* is not, however, to place them outside the pale of any deference whatever. *Chevron* did nothing to eliminate *Skidmore*'s holding that an agency's interpretation may merit some deference whatever its form, given the "specialized experience and broader investigations and information" available to the agency, 323 U.S., at 139, and given the value of uniformity in its administrative and judicial understandings of what a national law requires, *id.*, at 140....

There is room at least to raise a *Skidmore* claim here, where the regulatory scheme is highly detailed, and Customs can bring the benefit of specialized experience to bear on the subtle questions in this case: whether the daily planner with room for brief daily entries falls under "diaries," when diaries are grouped with "notebooks and address books, bound; memorandum pads, letter pads and similar articles," HTSUS subheading

4820.10.20; and whether a planner with a ring binding should qualify as "bound," when a binding may be typified by a book, but also may have "reinforcements or fittings of metal, plastics, etc.," Harmonized Commodity Description and Coding System Explanatory Notes to Heading 4820, p. 687 (cited in Customs Headquarters letter). A classification ruling in this situation may therefore at least seek a respect proportional to its "power to persuade," *Skidmore, supra,* at 140; see also *Christensen,* 529 U.S., at 587; *id.,* at 595 (Stevens, J., dissenting); *id.,* at 596–597 (Breyer, J., dissenting). Such a ruling may surely claim the merit of its writer's thoroughness, logic, and expertness, its fit with prior interpretations, and any other sources of weight.

## D

Underlying the position we take here, like the position expressed by Justice Scalia in dissent, is a choice about the best way to deal with an inescapable feature of the body of congressional legislation authorizing administrative action. That feature is the great variety of ways in which the laws invest the Government's administrative arms with discretion, and with procedures for exercising it, in giving meaning to Acts of Congress. Implementation of a statute may occur in formal adjudication or the choice to defend against judicial challenge; it may occur in a central board or office or in dozens of enforcement agencies dotted across the country; its institutional lawmaking may be confined to the resolution of minute detail or extend to legislative rulemaking on matters intentionally left by Congress to be worked out at the agency level.

Although we all accept the position that the Judiciary should defer to at least some of this multifarious administrative action, we have to decide how to take account of the great range of its variety. If the primary objective is to simplify the judicial process of giving or withholding deference, then the diversity of statutes authorizing discretionary administrative action must be declared irrelevant or minimized. If, on the other hand, it is simply implausible that Congress intended such a broad range of statutory authority to produce only two varieties of administrative action, demanding either *Chevron* deference or none at all, then the breadth of the spectrum of possible agency action must be taken into account. Justice Scalia's first priority over the years has been to limit and simplify. The Court's choice has been to tailor deference to variety. This acceptance of the range of statutory variation has led the Court to recognize more than one variety of judicial deference, just as the Court has recognized a variety of indicators that Congress would expect *Chevron* deference.

Our respective choices are repeated today. Justice Scalia would pose the question of deference as an either-or choice. On his view that *Chevron* rendered *Skidmore* anachronistic, when courts owe any deference it is *Chevron* deference that they owe. Whether courts do owe deference in a given case turns, for him, on whether the agency action (if reasonable) is "authoritative[.]" The character of the authoritative derives, in turn, not from breadth of delegation or the agency's procedure in implementing it, but is defined as the "official" position of an agency, and may ultimately be a function of administrative persistence alone.

The Court, on the other hand, said nothing in *Chevron* to eliminate *Skidmore*'s recognition of various justifications for deference depending on statutory circumstances and agency action; *Chevron* was simply a case recognizing that even without express authority to fill a specific statutory gap, circumstances pointing to implicit congressional delegation present a particularly insistent call for deference. Indeed, in holding here that *Chevron* left *Skidmore* intact and applicable where statutory circumstances indicate no intent to delegate general authority to make rules with force of law, or where such authority was not invoked, we hold nothing more than we said last Term in response to the particular statutory circumstances in *Christensen,* to which Justice SCALIA then took exception, see 529 U.S., at 589, just as he does again today.

We think, in sum, that Justice SCALIA's efforts to simplify ultimately run afoul of Congress's indications that different statutes present different reasons for considering respect for the exercise of administrative authority or deference to it. Without being at odds with congressional intent much of the time, we believe that judicial responses to administrative action must continue to differentiate between *Chevron* and *Skidmore,* and that continued recognition of *Skidmore* is necessary for just the reasons Justice Jackson gave when that case was decided.[19]

\* \* \*

Since the *Skidmore* assessment called for here ought to be made in the first instance by the Court of Appeals for the Federal Circuit or the CIT, we go no further than to vacate the judgment and remand the case for further proceedings consistent with this opinion.

*It is so ordered.*

■ JUSTICE SCALIA, dissenting.

---

**19.** Surely Justice Jackson's practical criteria, along with *Chevron*'s concern with congressional understanding, provide more reliable guideposts than conclusory references to the "authoritative" or "official." Even if those terms provided a true criterion, there would have to be something wrong with a standard that accorded the status of substantive law to every one of 10,000 "official" customs classifications rulings turned out each year from over 46 offices placed around the country at the Nation's entryways. Justice SCALIA tries to avoid that result by limiting what is "authoritative" or "official" to a pronouncement that expresses the "judgment of central agency management, approved at the highest levels," as distinct from the pronouncements of "underlings[.]" But that analysis would not entitle a Headquarters ruling to *Chevron* deference; the "highest level" at Customs is ... the Commissioner of Customs with the approval of the Secretary of the Treasury. The Commissioner did not issue the Headquarters ruling. What Justice SCALIA has in mind here is that because the Secretary approved the Government's position in its brief to this Court, *Chevron* deference is due. But if that is so, *Chevron* deference was not called for until sometime after the litigation began, when central management at the highest level decided to defend the ruling, and the deference is not to the classification ruling as such but to the brief. This explains why the Court has not accepted Justice SCALIA's position.

Today's opinion makes an avulsive change in judicial review of federal administrative action. Whereas previously a reasonable agency application of an ambiguous statutory provision had to be sustained so long as it represented the agency's authoritative interpretation, henceforth such an application can be set aside unless "it appears that Congress delegated authority to the agency generally to make rules carrying the force of law," as by giving an agency "power to engage in adjudication or notice-and-comment rulemaking, or . . . some other [procedure] indicati[ng] comparable congressional intent," and "the agency interpretation claiming deference was promulgated in the exercise of that authority."[1] What was previously a general presumption of authority in agencies to resolve ambiguity in the statutes they have been authorized to enforce has been changed to a presumption of no such authority, which must be overcome by affirmative legislative intent to the contrary. And whereas previously, when agency authority to resolve ambiguity did not exist the court was free to give the statute what it considered the best interpretation, henceforth the court must supposedly give the agency view some indeterminate amount of so-called *Skidmore* deference. *Skidmore v. Swift & Co.*, 323 U.S. 134 (1944). We will be sorting out the consequences of the *Mead* doctrine, which has today replaced the *Chevron* doctrine, *Chevron U.S.A. Inc. v. Natural Resources Defense Council, Inc.*, 467 U.S. 837 (1984), for years to come. I would adhere to our established jurisprudence, defer to the reasonable interpretation the Customs Service has given to the statute it is charged with enforcing, and reverse the judgment of the Court of Appeals.

## I

Only five years ago, the Court described the *Chevron* doctrine as follows: "We accord deference to agencies under *Chevron* . . . because of a presumption that Congress, when it left ambiguity in a statute meant for implementation by an agency, understood that the ambiguity would be resolved, first and foremost, by the agency, and desired the agency (rather than the courts) to possess whatever degree of discretion the ambiguity allows," Smiley v. Citibank (South Dakota), N. A., 517 U.S. 735, 740–741 (1996) (citing *Chevron, supra,* at 843–844). Today the Court collapses this doctrine, announcing instead a presumption that agency discretion does not exist unless the statute, expressly or impliedly, says so. While the Court disclaims any hard-and-fast rule for determining the existence of discretion-conferring intent, it asserts that "a very good indicator [is] express congressional authorizations to engage in the process of rulemaking or adjudication that produces regulations or rulings for which deference is claimed[.]" Only when agencies act through "adjudication[,] notice-and-comment rulemaking, or . . . some other [procedure] indicati[ng] comparable congressional intent [whatever that means]" is *Chevron* deference applicable—because these "relatively formal administrative procedure[s] [designed] to foster . . . fairness and deliberation" bespeak (according to

---

1. It is not entirely clear whether the formulation newly minted by the Court today extends to both formal and informal adjudication, or simply the former.

the Court) congressional willingness to have the agency, rather than the courts, resolve statutory ambiguities. Once it is determined that *Chevron* deference is not in order, the uncertainty is not at an end—and indeed is just beginning. Litigants cannot then assume that the statutory question is one for the courts to determine, according to traditional interpretive principles and by their own judicial lights. No, the Court now resurrects, in full force, the pre–*Chevron* doctrine of *Skidmore* deference ... whereby "[t]he fair measure of deference to an agency administering its own statute ... var[ies] with circumstances," including "the degree of the agency's care, its consistency, formality, and relative expertness, and ... the persuasiveness of the agency's position[.]" The Court has largely replaced *Chevron,* in other words, with that test most beloved by a court unwilling to be held to rules (and most feared by litigants who want to know what to expect): th'ol' "totality of the circumstances" test.

The Court's new doctrine is neither sound in principle nor sustainable in practice.

A

As to principle: The doctrine of *Chevron*—that all *authoritative* agency interpretations of statutes they are charged with administering deserve deference—was rooted in a legal presumption of congressional intent, important to the division of powers between the Second and Third Branches. When, *Chevron* said, Congress leaves an ambiguity in a statute that is to be administered by an executive agency, it is presumed that Congress meant to give the agency discretion, within the limits of reasonable interpretation, as to how the ambiguity is to be resolved. By committing enforcement of the statute to an agency rather than the courts, Congress committed its initial and primary interpretation to that branch as well.

There is some question whether *Chevron* was faithful to the text of the Administrative Procedure Act (APA), which it did not even bother to cite.[2] But it was in accord with the origins of federal-court judicial review. Judicial control of federal executive officers was principally exercised through the prerogative writ of mandamus.... That writ generally would not issue unless the executive officer was acting plainly beyond the scope of his authority.... Statutory ambiguities, in other words, were left to reasonable resolution by the Executive.

---

**2.** Title 5 U.S.C. § 706 provides that, in reviewing agency action, the court shall "decide all relevant questions of law"—which would seem to mean that all statutory ambiguities are to be resolved judicially.... It could be argued, however, that the legal presumption identified by *Chevron* left as the only "questio[n] of law" whether the agency's interpretation had gone beyond the scope of discretion that the statutory ambiguity conferred. Today's opinion, of course, is no more observant of the APA's text than *Chevron* was—and indeed is even more difficult to reconcile with it. Since the opinion relies upon actual congressional intent to suspend § 706, rather than upon a legal presumption against which § 706 was presumably enacted, it runs head-on into the provision of the APA which specifies that the Act's requirements (including the requirement that judges shall "decide all relevant questions of law") cannot be amended except expressly. See § 559.

The basis in principle for today's new doctrine can be described as follows: The background rule is that ambiguity in legislative instructions to agencies is to be resolved not by the agencies but by the judges. Specific congressional intent to depart from this rule must be found—and while there is no single touchstone for such intent it can generally be found when Congress has authorized the agency to act through (what the Court says is) relatively formal procedures such as informal rulemaking and formal (and informal?) adjudication, and when the agency in fact employs such procedures. The Court's background rule is contradicted by the origins of judicial review of administrative action. But in addition, the Court's principal criterion of congressional intent to supplant its background rule seems to me quite implausible. There is no necessary connection between the formality of procedure and the power of the entity administering the procedure to resolve authoritatively questions of law. The most formal of the procedures the Court refers to—formal adjudication—is modeled after the process used in trial courts, which of course are not generally accorded deference on questions of law. The purpose of such a procedure is to produce a closed record for determination and review of the facts—which implies nothing about the power of the agency subjected to the procedure to resolve authoritatively questions of law.

As for informal rulemaking: While formal adjudication procedures are *prescribed* (either by statute or by the Constitution) . . . informal rulemaking is more typically *authorized* but not required. Agencies with such authority are free to give guidance through rulemaking, but they may proceed to administer their statute case-by-case, "making law" as they implement their program (not necessarily through formal adjudication). See NLRB v. Bell Aerospace Co., 416 U.S. 267, 290–295 (1974); SEC v. Chenery Corp., 332 U.S. 194, 202–203 (1947). Is it likely—or indeed even plausible—that Congress meant, when such an agency chooses rulemaking, to accord the administrators of that agency, *and their successors,* the flexibility of interpreting the ambiguous statute now one way, and later another; but, when such an agency chooses case-by-case administration, to eliminate all future agency discretion by having that same ambiguity resolved authoritatively (and forever) by the courts? Surely that makes no sense. It is also the case that certain significant categories of rules—those involving grant and benefit programs, for example—are exempt from the requirements of informal rulemaking. See 5 U.S.C. § 553(a)(2). Under the Court's novel theory, when an agency takes advantage of that exemption its rules will be deprived of *Chevron* deference, *i.e.,* authoritative effect. Was this either the plausible intent of the APA rulemaking exemption, or the plausible intent of the Congress that established the grant or benefit program? . . .

B

As for the practical effects of the new rule:

1

The principal effect will be protracted confusion. As noted above, the one test for *Chevron* deference that the Court enunciates is wonderfully imprecise: whether "Congress delegated authority to the agency generally to make rules carrying the force of law, . . . as by . . . adjudication[,] notice-and-comment rulemaking, or . . . some other [procedure] indicati[ng] comparable congressional intent." But even this description does not do justice to the utter flabbiness of the Court's criterion, since, in order to maintain the fiction that the new test is really just the old one, applied consistently throughout our case law, the Court must make a virtually open-ended exception to its already imprecise guidance: In the present case, it tells us, the absence of notice-and-comment rulemaking (and "[who knows?] [of] some other [procedure] indicati[ng] comparable congressional intent") is not enough to decide the question of *Chevron* deference, "for we have sometimes found reasons for *Chevron* deference even when no such administrative formality was required and none was afforded." The opinion then goes on to consider a grab bag of other factors—including the factor that used to be the sole criterion for *Chevron* deference: whether the interpretation represented the *authoritative* position of the agency. It is hard to know what the lower courts are to make of today's guidance.

### 2

Another practical effect of today's opinion will be an artificially induced increase in informal rulemaking. Buy stock in the [Government Printing Office]. Since informal rulemaking and formal adjudication are the only more-or-less safe harbors from the storm that the Court has unleashed; and since formal adjudication is not an option but must be mandated by statute or constitutional command; informal rulemaking—which the Court was once careful to make voluntary unless required by statute, see *Bell Aerospace*, *supra*, and *Chenery*, *supra*—will now become a virtual necessity. As I have described, the Court's safe harbor requires not merely that the agency have been given rulemaking authority, but also that the agency have *employed* rulemaking as the means of resolving the statutory ambiguity. (It is hard to understand why that should be so. Surely the mere *conferral* of rulemaking authority demonstrates—if one accepts the Court's logic—a congressional intent to allow the agency to resolve ambiguities. And given that intent, what difference does it make that the agency chooses instead to use another perfectly permissible means for that purpose?) Moreover, the majority's approach will have a perverse effect on the rules that do emerge, given the principle (which the Court leaves untouched today) that judges must defer to reasonable agency interpretations of their own regulations. . . . Agencies will now have high incentive to rush out barebones, ambiguous rules construing statutory ambiguities, which they can then in turn further clarify through informal rulings entitled to judicial respect.

### 3

Worst of all, the majority's approach will lead to the ossification of large portions of our statutory law. Where *Chevron* applies, statutory ambiguities remain ambiguities subject to the agency's ongoing clarification. They create a space, so to speak, for the exercise of continuing agency discretion. As *Chevron* itself held, the Environmental Protection Agency can interpret "stationary source" to mean a single smokestack, can later replace that interpretation with the "bubble concept" embracing an entire plant, and if that proves undesirable can return again to the original interpretation. 467 U.S., at 853–859, 865–866. For the indeterminately large number of statutes taken out of *Chevron* by today's decision, however, ambiguity (and hence flexibility) will cease with the first judicial resolution. *Skidmore* deference gives the agency's current position some vague and uncertain amount of respect, but it does not, like *Chevron, leave* the matter within the control of the Executive Branch for the future. Once the court has spoken, it becomes *unlawful* for the agency to take a contradictory position; the statute now *says* what the court has prescribed.... It will be bad enough when this ossification occurs as a result of judicial determination (under today's new principles) that there is no affirmative indication of congressional intent to "delegate"; but it will be positively bizarre when it occurs simply because of an agency's failure to act by rulemaking (rather than informal adjudication) before the issue is presented to the courts.

One might respond that such ossification would not result if the agency were simply to readopt its interpretation, after a court reviewing it under *Skidmore* had rejected it, by repromulgating it through one of the *Chevron*-eligible procedural formats approved by the Court today. Approving this procedure would be a landmark abdication of judicial power. It is worlds apart from *Chevron* proper, where the court does not *purport* to give the statute a judicial interpretation—except in identifying the scope of the statutory ambiguity, as to which the court's judgment is final and irreversible. (Under *Chevron* proper, when the agency's authoritative interpretation comes within the scope of that ambiguity—and the court therefore approves it—the agency will not be "overruling" the court's decision when it later decides that a different interpretation (still within the scope of the ambiguity) is preferable.) By contrast, under this view, the reviewing court will not be holding the agency's authoritative interpretation within the scope of the ambiguity; but will be holding that the agency has not used the "delegation-conferring" procedures, and that the court must therefore *interpret the statute on its own*—but subject to reversal if and when the agency uses the proper procedures....

I know of no case, in the entire history of the federal courts, in which we have allowed a judicial interpretation of a statute to be set aside by an agency—or have allowed a lower court to render an interpretation of a statute subject to correction by an agency....

### 4

And finally, the majority's approach compounds the confusion it creates by breathing new life into the anachronism of *Skidmore,* which sets forth a sliding scale of deference owed an agency's interpretation of a statute that is dependent "upon the thoroughness evident in [the agency's] consideration, the validity of its reasoning, its consistency with earlier and later pronouncements, and all those factors which give it power to persuade, if lacking power to control"; in this way, the appropriate measure of deference will be accorded the "body of experience and informed judgment" that such interpretations often embody, 323 U.S., at 140. Justice Jackson's eloquence notwithstanding, the rule of *Skidmore* deference is an empty truism and a trifling statement of the obvious: A judge should take into account the well-considered views of expert observers.

It was possible to live with the indeterminacy of *Skidmore* deference in earlier times. But in an era when federal statutory law administered by federal agencies is pervasive, and when the ambiguities (intended or unintended) that those statutes contain are innumerable, totality-of-the-circumstances *Skidmore* deference is a recipe for uncertainty, unpredictability, and endless litigation. To condemn a vast body of agency action to that regime (all except rulemaking, formal (and informal?) adjudication, and whatever else might now and then be included within today's intentionally vague formulation of affirmative congressional intent to "delegate") is irresponsible. . . .

II

. . . It is, to be sure, impossible to demonstrate that any of our cases contradicts the rule of decision that the Court prescribes, because the Court prescribes none. More precisely, it at one and the same time (1) renders meaningless its newly announced requirement that there be an affirmative congressional intent to have ambiguities resolved by the administering agency, and (2) ensures that no prior decision can possibly be cited which contradicts that requirement, by simply announcing that all prior decisions according *Chevron* deference exemplify the multifarious ways in which that congressional intent can be manifested: "[A]s significant as notice-and-comment is in pointing to *Chevron* authority, the want of that procedure here does not decide the case, for we have sometimes found reasons for *Chevron* deference even when no such administrative formality was required and none was afforded[.]"[4]

The principles central to today's opinion have no antecedent in our jurisprudence. *Chevron,* the case that the opinion purportedly explicates, made no mention of the "relatively formal administrative procedure[s]" that the Court today finds the best indication of an affirmative intent by Congress to have ambiguities resolved by the administering agency. Which is not so remarkable, since *Chevron* made no mention of any *need* to find such an affirmative intent; it said that in the event of statutory ambiguity agency authority to clarify was to be *presumed* . . . .

. . . [M]any cases flatly contradict the theory of *Chevron* set forth in today's opinion, and *with one exception* not a single case can be found with language that supports the theory. That exception, a very recent one, [is]

---

**4.** As a sole, teasing example of those "sometimes" the Court cites NationsBank of N. C., N.A. v. Variable Annuity Life Ins. Co., 513 U.S. 251 (1995). . . . The many other cases that contradict the Court's new rule will presumably be explained, like *NationsBank,* as other "modes" of displaying affirmative congressional intent. . . .

... Christensen v. Harris County, 529 U.S. 576 (2000), [in which] the Court said the following:

> "[W]e confront an interpretation contained in an opinion letter, not one arrived at after, for example, a formal adjudication or notice-and-comment rulemaking. Interpretations such as those in opinion letters—like interpretations contained in policy statements, agency manuals, and enforcement guidelines, all of which lack the force of law—do not warrant *Chevron*-style deference." *Id.,* at 587.

This statement was dictum, unnecessary to the Court's holding. Since the Court went on to find that the Secretary of Labor's position "ma[de] little sense" given the text and structure of the statute, *id.,* at 585–586, *Chevron* deference could not have been accorded *no matter what* the conditions for its application. See 529 U.S., at 591 (SCALIA, J., concurring in part and concurring in judgment)....

## III

To decide the present case, I would adhere to the original formulation of *Chevron....* *Chevron* sets forth an across-the-board presumption, which operates as a background rule of law against which Congress legislates: Ambiguity means Congress intended agency discretion. Any resolution of the ambiguity by the administering agency that is authoritative—that represents the official position of the agency—must be accepted by the courts if it is reasonable....

There is no doubt that the Customs Service's interpretation represents the authoritative view of the agency. Although the actual ruling letter was signed by only the Director of the Commercial Rulings Branch of Customs Headquarters' Office of Regulations and Rulings, the Solicitor General of the United States has filed a brief, cosigned by the General Counsel of the Department of the Treasury, that represents the position set forth in the ruling letter to be the official position of the Customs Service.... No one contends that it is merely a *"post hoc* rationalizatio[n]" or an "agency litigating positio[n] wholly unsupported by regulations, rulings, or administrative practice," Bowen v. Georgetown Univ. Hospital, 488 U.S. 204, 212 (1988).[6]

---

6.  The Court's parting shot, that "there would have to be something wrong with a standard that accorded the status of substantive law to every one of 10,000 'official' customs classifications rulings turned out each year from over 46 offices placed around the country at the Nation's entryways," misses the mark. I do not disagree. The "authoritativeness" of an agency interpretation does not turn upon whether it has been enunciated by someone who is actually employed by the agency. It must represent the judgment of central agency management, approved at the highest levels. I would find that condition to have been satisfied when, a ruling having been attacked in court, the general counsel of the agency has determined that it should be defended. If one thinks that that does not impart sufficient authoritativeness, then surely the line has been crossed when, as here, the General Counsel of the agency and the Solicitor General of the United States have assured this Court that the position represents the agency's authoritative view. (Contrary to the Court's suggestion, there would be nothing bizarre about the fact that this latter approach would entitle the ruling to deference here, though it would not have been entitled to deference in the lower courts. Affirmation of the

There is also no doubt that the Customs Service's interpretation is a reasonable one, whether or not judges would consider it the best. I will not belabor this point, since the Court evidently agrees: An interpretation that was unreasonable would not merit the remand that the Court decrees for consideration of *Skidmore* deference. . . .

For the reasons stated, I respectfully dissent from the Court's judgment. . . . I dissent even more vigorously from the reasoning that produces the Court's judgment, and that makes today's decision one of the most significant opinions ever rendered by the Court dealing with the judicial review of administrative action. Its consequences will be enormous, and almost uniformly bad.

---

*1. The Theory of* **Mead**—Justice Souter's majority opinion characterized *Mead* simply as an extension of *Chevron*, while Justice Scalia's dissent characterized *Mead* as an "avulsive change" that had (unwisely) displaced *Chevron*. What accounts for this difference? Both Justice Souter and Justice Scalia characterize *Chevron* itself as grounded in a presumption about congressional intent. The principal difference between them seems to be that for Justice Souter, this presumption applies only when "the agency's generally conferred authority and other statutory circumstances" make it apparent that "Congress would expect the agency to be able to speak with the force of law when it addresses ambiguity in the statute or fills a space in the enacted law," whereas Justice Scalia sees *Chevron* as establishing an across-the-board presumption that ambiguities in agency-administered statutes are legally equivalent to a congressional delegation of authority to the agency.

Both Justice Scalia and Justice Souter appear to be making competing claims about congressional intent. Yet Justice Scalia has asserted that the *Chevron* presumption is not a "100% accurate estimation of . . . congressional intent," but rather is better understood to rest upon "fictional, presumed intent." Antonin Scalia, *Judicial Deference to Administrative Interpretations of Law*, 1989 DUKE L.J. 511, 517. If so, perhaps his objection is not that the majority's approach is less faithful to some genuine congressional preference, but rather that *Chevron*'s categorical approach to (presumptive) congressional intent is preferable to *Mead*'s case-by-case approach. If that's right, the dispute between Justice Souter and Justice Scalia may be another manifestation of the longstanding debate over the relative merits of rules and standards, with Justice Scalia extolling the virtues of *Chevron* as a *rule* and Justice Souter (and the other Justices in the *Mead* majority) insisting that this issue calls for a more flexible *standard* that would "tailor deference to variety." *Compare* Scalia, *supra*, at 516–517 (arguing that the pre–*Chevron* multi-factor regime was a "font of uncertainty and litigation" that *Chevron* had properly replaced with a

---

official agency position before this court—if that is thought necessary—is no different from the agency's issuing a new rule after the Court of Appeals determination. It establishes a new legal basis for the decision, which this Court must take into account (or remand for that purpose), even though the Court of Appeals could not. . . .

clear "background rule of law against which Congress can legislate"), *with* Stephen Breyer, *Judicial Review of Questions of Law and Policy*, 38 ADMIN. L. REV. 363 (1986) (arguing that it does not make sense to presume that Congress would prefer to have a uniform judicial review doctrine for the wide variety of agency actions) *and* Clark Byse, *Judicial Review of Administrative Interpretation of Statutes: An Analysis of* Chevron's *Step Two*, 2 ADMIN. L.J. 255, 260–61 (1988) (same). Justices Breyer and Scalia have continued this rules versus standards debate in a number of post-*Mead* cases. *Compare* Barnhart v. Walton, 535 U.S. 212, 222 (2002) (Breyer, J.) (deferring to an agency's interpretation of a statutory term in light of "the interstitial nature of the legal question, the related expertise of the Agency, the importance of the question to administration of the statute, the complexity of that administration, and the careful consideration the Agency has given the question over a long period of time"), *with id.* at 227 (Scalia, J., concurring in part and concurring in the judgment) (arguing that because the agency's "regulations emerged from notice-and-comment rule-making[, they] merit deference [and n]o more need be said"); *compare also* National Cable & Telecom. Ass'n v. Brand X Internet Svcs., 545 U.S. 967, 1004 (2005) (Breyer, J., concurring) (asserting that under *Mead* "the existence of a formal rulemaking proceeding is neither a necessary nor a sufficient condition for according *Chevron* deference to an agency's interpretation of a statute), *with id.* at 1014–15 (Scalia, J., dissenting) (arguing that insofar as *Mead* managed to set forth *any* comprehensible rule, it is that some degree of formal process "[is] required—or [is] at least the only safe harbor" for an agency that wants to ensure *Chevron* deference for its interpretation).

Can we resolve this rules-standards dispute based on a judgment as to which approach displays greater fidelity to congressional intent? If not, should we be influenced by policy considerations, such as which approach gives greater power to judges or agencies, or creates more predictability, or is more sensitive to context, or is more likely to track prevailing political preferences? *See* EINER ELHAUGE, STATUTORY DEFAULT RULES 90–96 (2008); Thomas W. Merrill, *The* Mead *Doctrine: Rules and Standards, Meta–Rules and Meta–Standards*, 54 ADMIN. L. REV. 807 (2002). Does it matter, in this regard, whether the basis for *Chevron* deference is an assumption or prediction about *real* congressional intent, or rather a legal fiction designed to further certain underlying values? (*See* pp. 828–830, *supra*.)

**2. Mead's *Emphasis on Procedural Formality*—**If *Mead* calls upon courts to make case-specific determinations as to whether Congress would have wanted *Chevron* deference in the case at hand, then courts need some guidance regarding what sorts of evidence tend to indicate that Congress did (or did not) intend to delegate interpretive authority to the agency. Following *Christensen*, the *Mead* Court declared that "a very good indicator of delegation meriting *Chevron* treatment [is] express congressional authorization[] to engage in the process of rulemaking or adjudication that produces regulations or rulings for which deference is claimed." So, *Chevron* will presumably apply in cases involving notice-and-comment rulemaking or formal adjudication. *See, e.g.*, Yellow Transp., Inc. v. Michigan, 537 U.S. 36, 45 (2002). But, as *Mead* also made clear, procedural formality is not a *necessary* condition for *Chevron* deference. *See, e.g.,* Edelman v. Lynchburg Coll., 535 U.S. 106, 114 (2002). It is somewhat less clear from *Mead* whether this sort of procedural formality is a *sufficient* condition for *Chevron* deference. Justice Breyer has suggested that it is not, although it is not clear how many other Justices agree with him on this. *See* National Cable & Telecom Ass'n v. Brand X Internet Svcs., 545 U.S. 967, 1004–05 (2005) (Breyer, J., concurring).

Justice Scalia's principal objection to *Mead*, as we have seen, was that it abandoned a rule-like conception of *Chevron* deference in favor of a more standard-like case-by-case analysis. Justice Scalia also objected to *Mead*'s emphasis on formal procedures as indicative of congressional intent. Indeed, he described the idea that procedural formality is a good indicator that *Chevron* ought to apply as "quite implausible," because there "is no necessary connection between the formality of procedure and the power of the entity administering the procedure to resolve authoritatively questions of law." Is Justice Scalia right about this? Could one imagine a reasonable legislator concluding that agencies should only have the authority to make decisions that bind with the force of law if they do so through procedures that provide assurances of either broad public participation (notice-and-comment rulemaking) or trial-type guarantees of procedural fairness (formal adjudication)? Even if there is no necessary *theoretical* connection between procedural formality and the authoritativeness of an agency's interpretation, might procedural formality nevertheless be a good *proxy* for congressional intent to delegate to the agency? *See* Thomas W. Merrill, *The* Mead *Doctrine: Rules and Standards, Meta–Rules and Meta–Standards*, 54 Admin. L. Rev. 807, 814–15 (2002). Would establishing this doctrinal connection have good or bad *practical* effects? If it would have good effects, could it be defended on the same grounds as *Chevron* itself: as a useful legal fiction about congressional intent that furthers substantive policy interests?

Could one also argue that something like *Mead* is necessary to prevent agencies from exploiting the "interpretive rule" exception to § 553 notice-and-comment procedures? Recall from Chapter Four (pp. 704–706, *supra*) that one of the key distinctions between interpretive rules and legislative rules is that the former lack the "force and effect of law." If courts were to give *Chevron* deference to agency statutory constructions contained in interpretive rules, on the logic that Congress had implicitly delegated these policy choices to the agency, wouldn't that be equivalent to treating interpretive rules as if they *did* have the "force of law"? *See* John F. Manning, *Nonlegislative Rules*, 72 Geo. Wash. L. Rev. 893, 940 (2004). Furthermore, one of the reasons that courts often give agencies great latitude in invoking the interpretive rule exception to notice-and-comment rulemaking is the expectation of more aggressive judicial review of agency interpretations issued in such contexts—the "pay me now or pay me later" idea that the agency can avoid procedural formality only at the cost of subjecting its decision to more rigorous judicial scrutiny on the merits. (*See* pp. 714–715, *supra*.) Does this imply that *Mead* (or at least *Christensen*) must be the right way to approach judicial review of the interpretations contained in such documents? How might Justice Scalia respond?

**3. *"Force of Law"* in the Mead *Analysis*—**Although *Mead*, like *Christensen*, emphasized that *Chevron* applies only to agency interpretations that have the "force of law," the agency interpretations at issue in *Mead* and *Christensen* are quite different from one another with respect to their legal force and effect. The opinion letter in *Christensen* was an interpretive rule that had no legal effect. The agency might initiate an enforcement proceeding against a party that took action contrary to the interpretation stated in the opinion letter, but in such a case, the agency's legal argument would necessarily be that the defendant violated the *statute*, not the opinion letter. In contrast, the Customs Ruling Letter at issue in *Mead* had legal force and effect with respect to the Mead Corporation. The Customs Service went to great lengths to limit the legal consequences of its Ruling Letters, stating that each such Letter applies only to the particular transaction in which the Letter was issued, and has limited precedential effect. Nonetheless, these Ruling Letters are legally binding orders with respect to the parties whom they address. Could one therefore argue that *Christensen* is right but *Mead* is wrong? Should an agency get *Chevron* deference as long as its interpretation has independent legal effect, even if it is issued with minimal procedural formality? Or is the degree of procedural formality more significant than whether the interpretation has formal legal force?

*Mead*, then, did not seem to be using the phrase "force of law" in the traditional, formal sense. Rather, the opinion instructed reviewing courts to consult a range of factors to determine whether Congress intended the agency's statutory constructions to be authoritative. Does *Mead* adequately justify its multi-factor approach to determining the force of law question? Are there other factors one might look to when making this determination? *See* Thomas W. Merrill & Kathryn Tongue Watts, *Agency Rules with the Force of Law: The Original Convention*, 116 HARV. L. REV. 467 (2002) (arguing that the pre–APA convention held that agency rules bind with the force of law when the organic act provides sanctions for such rules); Russell L. Weaver, *The Emperor Has No Clothes:* Christensen, Mead, *and Dual Deference Standards*, 54 ADMIN. L. REV. 173, 175 (2002) (arguing that *Mead*'s "force of law" test is inherently flawed because "Congress never explicitly states that agency interpretations should be 'given the force of law' if articulated in particular formats, and it rarely gives implicit indications of its intent").

**4. *When Is an Agency Interpretation "Authoritative"?*—**Note the striking disagreement between the *Mead* majority opinion and Justice Scalia's dissent regarding what it takes for an agency decision to be "authoritative." For the majority, an agency interpretation is "authoritative," in the sense of being entitled to *Chevron* deference, if there are enough salient indicators that congress intended to delegate interpretive authority in this particular context. Procedural formality is the most important indicator of such intent, but *Mead* also emphasized that "46 different Customs offices issue 10,000 to 15,000 of [these Ruling Letters] each year" and that "[a]ny suggestion that rulings intended to have the force of law are being churned out at a rate of 10,000 a year at an agency's 46 scattered offices is simply self-refuting." Justice Scalia agreed that an interpretation issued by a low-level agency official might not be entitled to *Chevron* deference, but in his view once the agency's leadership has endorsed that interpretation, and the United States Department of Justice has defended that view in court, the interpretation becomes the authoritative position of the agency and is therefore worthy of *Chevron* deference.

Doesn't Justice Scalia have a point that the majority's argument about the large number of Ruling Letters issued by low-level officials loses much of its force once the head of the Customs Service, the Secretary of the Treasury, and the Solicitor General of the United States all endorse and defend the interpretation contained in such a letter? On the other hand, isn't there a tension between Justice Scalia's criterion for "authoritativeness" and the *Chenery I* principle that courts should not consider post hoc litigating positions when evaluating agency action (*see* pp. 845–846, *supra*)? Should it matter whether the agency's leadership endorsed the subordinate official's construction of the statute before litigation commenced? Perhaps the agency should get *Chevron* deference in those cases, but not in cases where the agency leadership only takes a position during litigation? For a proposal along these lines, see David J. Barron & Elena Kagan, Chevron's *Nondelegation Doctrine*, 2001 Sup. Ct. Rev. 201.

**5. The Practical Effects of** Mead—Let us now consider Justice Scalia's three criticisms of *Mead*'s practical consequences.

**a. Unpredictability**—Justice Scalia claimed that *Mead* would lead to confusion and protracted litigation in light of both the uncertainty of the criteria for applying *Chevron* deference and the open-endedness of the *Skidmore* standard that would now apply when *Chevron* does not. Some commentators have concluded that Justice Scalia's concerns proved well-founded, at least in the immediate aftermath of the decision. *See* Lisa Schultz Bressman, *How* Mead *Has Muddled Judicial Review of Agency Action*, 58 Vand. L. Rev. 1443 (2005); Kristin E. Hickman & Matthew D. Krueger, *In Search of the Modern* Skidmore *Standard*, 107 Colum. L. Rev. 1235 (2007); Adrian Vermeule, Mead *in the Trenches*, 71 Geo. Wash. L. Rev. 347 (2003). Then again, perhaps that confusion will be short-lived: After all, new doctrines often engender some degree of short-term uncertainty as the courts work out their details. Or perhaps, as Justice Souter argued, some degree of uncertainty is a price worth paying for a more flexible, nuanced approach to judicial review of agency statutory interpretations. Is this just another instance of the conflict between rule-based and standard-based approaches? If so, how should we figure out which is more appropriate in this context? Is our preference as between these approaches based on anything more well-grounded than intuition? Could it be?

**b. Increase in notice-and-comment rulemaking**—Justice Scalia's second practical objection to *Mead* was that it would result in "an artificially induced increase in informal rulemaking," as agencies try to ensure that their interpretations will receive *Chevron* deference by issuing them in notice-and-comment rules rather than in interpretive rules or informal orders. Do you agree with Justice Scalia that this effect is likely? Recall that when an agency conducts an adjudication and issues a final order on a policy matter covered by an interpretive rule, the agency order must independently defend the merits of its interpretation and its policy position, rather than simply invoking the interpretive rule (which lacks the force of law). (*See* pp. 688–689, 704–705, *supra*.) When an agency does so, its interpretation may be eligible for *Chevron* deference under *Mead*, at least if the adjudication is formal. This effect may diminish the differential impact of *Mead* on the availability of deference. *See* John F. Manning, *Nonlegislative Rules*, 72 GEO. WASH. L. REV. 893, 940–41 (2004).

Furthermore, even if *Mead* were to cause agencies to do more notice-and-comment rulemaking, is that necessarily a bad thing? After all, as we saw in Chapter Four (pp. 642, 659–660, 693–694, 714–715, *supra*), many judges and commentators have expressed concerns about agencies' doing too *little* notice-and-comment rulemaking, avoiding the strictures of § 553 by, for example, taking too much advantage of the exception for interpretive rules. If this is indeed a problem, mightn't the alleged vice identified by Justice Scalia actually be a virtue? Then again, perhaps Justice Scalia has a point: If agencies start investing substantial resources in notice-and-comment rulemakings when such elaborate procedures are not necessary, agencies might divert resources from other, more pressing tasks.

Justice Scalia also expressed concern that, in order to guarantee themselves *Chevron* deference, agencies would "rush out barebones, ambiguous rules," which the agencies would then construe. (Justice Scalia's argument here invokes another judicial doctrine, which we do not cover in depth, under which courts generally defer to an agency's construction of the agency's own regulation. (*See* pp. 715–717, *supra*, for a brief discussion.)) Without going into this topic in too much detail, perhaps one might respond to Justice Scalia's concern by limiting judicial deference to administrative interpretations of overly ambiguous notice-and-comment rules. *See, e.g.*, Paralyzed Veterans of America v. D.C. Arena L.P., 117 F.3d 579, 584 (D.C. Cir. 1997) ("A substantive regulation must have sufficient content and definitiveness as to be a meaningful exercise in agency lawmaking. It is certainly not open to an agency to promulgate mush and then give it concrete form only through subsequent less formal 'interpretations.' "). Might such an approach, however, run into the same sort of line-drawing problems that trouble the Court's efforts to enforce the nondelegation doctrine? That is, might it require the Court to ask at what point an agency rule is so ambiguous that any resulting interpretation cannot meaningfully be attributed to the rulemaking process—an inquiry that may not be susceptible to judicially manageable standards?

**c.  *Ossification through premature judicial construction***—Justice Scalia argued that, because a court may need to resolve an interpretive dispute before the agency has had time to issue a *Chevron*-worthy construction, after *Mead* a greater number of interpretive issues would be resolved conclusively by courts rather than agencies. This, Justice Scalia asserted, is bad for all the reasons that *Chevron* deference is good. Note, however, that Justice Scalia's argument presumes that once a court interprets a statute, the agency cannot issue a different interpretation, even if the agency's interpretation would be considered reasonable under *Chevron*. Four years after *Mead*, the Supreme Court, in an opinion by Justice Thomas, rejected that view: The Court instead held that a judicial construction of a statute administered by an agency is merely provisional; as long as the underlying statutory term is ambiguous, the courts should uphold an agency's alternative interpretation notwithstanding the prior judicial construction. *See* National Cable & Telecom Ass'n v. Brand X Internet Svcs., 545 U.S. 967 (2005); *see also* Kenneth A. Bamberger, *Provisional Precedent: Protecting Flexibility in Administrative Policymaking*, 77 N.Y.U. L. Rev. 1272 (2002). This did not satisfy Justice Scalia, who viewed *Brand X* as "continu[ing] the administrative law improvisation project [the Court] began ... in [*Mead*]" by "inventing yet another breathtaking novelty: judicial decisions subject to reversal by executive officers," an outcome Justice Scalia described as both "bizarre" and "probably unconstitutional." *Brand X*, 545 U.S. at 1016–17 (Scalia, J., dissenting). The *Brand X* majority, however, insisted that it was not holding that an agency could "overrule" a judicial construction. Rather, because "*Chevron* teaches that a court's opinion as to the best reading of an ambiguous statute an agency is charged with administering is not authoritative, the agency's decision to construe that statute differently from a court does not say that the court's holding was legally wrong." *Id.* at 983 (majority opinion). Explaining this point further, *Brand X* insisted that the judicial precedent "has not been 'reversed' by the agency, any more than a federal court's interpretation of a State's law can be said to have been 'reversed' by a state court that adopts a conflicting (yet authoritative) interpretation of state law." *Id.* at 983–84. Which of these positions seems more compelling to you? Does *Brand X* solve the ossification problem Justice Scalia had warned about in *Mead*? Or does it do so only by creating much more serious problems?

# APPENDIX A: UNITED STATES CONSTITUTION

### ARTICLE I

### SECTION 1

All legislative Powers herein granted shall be vested in a Congress of the United States, which shall consist of a Senate and House of Representatives.

### SECTION 2

[1]  The House of Representatives shall be composed of Members chosen every second Year by the People of the several States, and the Electors in each State shall have the Qualifications requisite for Electors of the most numerous Branch of the State Legislature.

[2]  No Person shall be a Representative who shall not have attained to the Age of twenty five Years, and been seven Years a Citizen of the United States, and who shall not, when elected, be an Inhabitant of that State in which he shall be chosen.

[3]  Representatives and direct Taxes shall be apportioned among the several States which may be included within this Union, according to their respective Numbers, which shall be determined by adding to the whole Number of free Persons, including those bound to Service for a Term of Years, and excluding Indians not taxed, three fifths of all other Persons. The actual Enumeration shall be made within three Years after the first Meeting of the Congress of the United States, and within every subsequent Term of ten Years, in such Manner as they shall by Law direct. The Number of Representatives shall not exceed one for every thirty Thousand, but each State shall have at Least one Representative; and until such enumeration shall be made, the State of New Hampshire shall be entitled to chuse three, Massachusetts eight, Rhode–Island and Providence Plantations one, Connecticut five, New–York six, New Jersey four, Pennsylvania eight, Delaware one, Maryland six, Virginia ten, North Carolina five, South Carolina five, and Georgia three.

[4]  When vacancies happen in the Representation from any State, the Executive Authority thereof shall issue Writs of Election to fill such Vacancies.

[5]  The House of Representatives shall chuse their Speaker and other Officers; and shall have the sole Power of Impeachment.

### SECTION 3

[1]  The Senate of the United States shall be composed of two Senators from each State, chosen by the Legislature thereof, for six Years; and each Senator shall have one Vote.

[2]   Immediately after they shall be assembled in Consequence of the first Election, they shall be divided as equally as may be into three Classes. The Seats of the Senators of the first Class shall be vacated at the Expiration of the second Year, of the second Class at the Expiration of the fourth Year, and of the third Class at the Expiration of the sixth Year, so that one third may be chosen every second Year; and if Vacancies happen by Resignation, or otherwise, during the Recess of the Legislature of any State, the Executive thereof may make temporary Appointments until the next Meeting of the Legislature, which shall then fill such Vacancies.

[3]   No Person shall be a Senator who shall not have attained to the Age of thirty Years, and been nine Years a Citizen of the United States, and who shall not, when elected, be an Inhabitant of that State for which he shall be chosen.

[4]   The Vice President of the United States shall be President of the Senate, but shall have no Vote, unless they be equally divided.

[5]   The Senate shall chuse their other Officers, and also a President pro tempore, in the Absence of the Vice President, or when he shall exercise the Office of President of the United States.

[6]   The Senate shall have the sole Power to try all Impeachments. When sitting for that Purpose, they shall be on Oath or Affirmation. When the President of the United States is tried, the Chief Justice shall preside: And no Person shall be convicted without the Concurrence of two thirds of the Members present.

[7]   Judgment in Cases of Impeachment shall not extend further than to removal from Office, and disqualification to hold and enjoy any Office of honor, Trust or Profit under the United States: but the Party convicted shall nevertheless be liable and subject to Indictment, Trial, Judgment and Punishment, according to Law.

### SECTION 4

[1]   The Times, Places and Manner of holding Elections for Senators and Representatives, shall be prescribed in each State by the Legislature thereof; but the Congress may at any time by Law make or alter such Regulations, except as to the Places of chusing Senators.

[2]   The Congress shall assemble at least once in every Year, and such Meeting shall be on the first Monday in December, unless they shall by Law appoint a different Day.

### SECTION 5

[1]   Each House shall be the Judge of the Elections, Returns and Qualifications of its own Members, and a Majority of each shall constitute a Quorum to do Business; but a smaller Number may adjourn from day to day, and may be authorized to compel the Attendance of absent Members, in such Manner, and under such Penalties as each House may provide.

[2]   Each House may determine the Rules of its Proceedings, punish its Members for disorderly Behaviour, and, with the Concurrence of two thirds, expel a Member

[3]   Each House shall keep a Journal of its Proceedings, and from time to time publish the same, excepting such Parts as may in their Judgment require Secrecy; and the Yeas and Nays of the Members of either House on any question shall, at the Desire of one fifth of those Present, be entered on the Journal.

[4]   Neither House, during the Session of Congress, shall, without the consent of the other, adjourn for more than three days, nor to any other Place than that in which the two Houses shall be sitting.

## SECTION 6

[1]   The Senators and Representatives shall receive a Compensation for their Services, to be ascertained by Law, and paid out of the Treasury of the United States. They shall in all Cases, except Treason, Felony and Breach of the Peace, be privileged from Arrest during their Attendance at the Session of their respective Houses, and in going to and returning from the same; and for any Speech or Debate in either House, they shall not be questioned in any other Place.

[2]   No Senator or Representative shall, during the Time for which he was elected, be appointed to any civil Office under the Authority of the United States, which shall have been created, or the Emoluments whereof shall have been encreased during such time; and no Person holding any Office under the United States, shall be a Member of either House during his Continuance in Office.

## SECTION 7

[1]   All Bills for raising Revenue shall originate in the House of Representatives; but the Senate may propose or concur with Amendments as on other Bills.

[2]   Every Bill which shall have passed the House of Representatives and the Senate, shall, before it become a Law, be presented to the President of the United States: If he approve he shall sign it, but if not he shall return it, with his Objections to that House in which it shall have originated, who shall enter the Objections at large on their Journal, and proceed to reconsider it. If after such Reconsideration two thirds of that House shall agree to pass the Bill, it shall be sent, together with the Objections, to the other House, by which it shall likewise be reconsidered, and if approved by two thirds of that House, it shall become a Law. But in all such Cases the Votes of both Houses shall be determined by yeas and Nays, and the Names of the Persons voting for and against the Bill shall be entered on the Journal of each House respectively. If any Bill shall not be returned by the President within ten days (Sundays excepted) after it shall have been presented to him, the Same shall be a Law, in like Manner as if he had signed it, unless the Congress by their Adjournment prevent its Return in which Case it shall not be a Law.

[3]  Every Order, Resolution, or Vote to which the Concurrence of the Senate and House of Representatives may be necessary (except on a question of Adjournment) shall be presented to the President of the United States; and before the Same shall take Effect, shall be approved by him, or being disapproved by him, shall be repassed by two thirds of the Senate and House of Representatives, according to the Rules and Limitations prescribed in the Case of a Bill.

## SECTION 8

[1]  The Congress shall have Power To lay and collect Taxes, Duties, Imposts and Excises, to pay the Debts and provide for the common Defence and general Welfare of the United States; but all Duties, Imposts and Excises shall be uniform throughout the United States;

[2]  To borrow Money on the credit of the United States;

[3]  To regulate Commerce with foreign Nations, and among the several States, and with the Indian Tribes;

[4]  To establish an uniform Rule of Naturalization, and uniform Laws on the subject of Bankruptcies throughout the United States;

[5]  To coin Money, regulate the Value thereof, and of foreign Coin, and fix the Standard of Weights and Measures;

[6]  To provide for the Punishment of counterfeiting the Securities and current Coin of the United States;

[7]  To establish Post Offices and post Roads;

[8]  To promote the Progress of Science and useful Arts, by securing for limited Times to Authors and Inventors the exclusive Right to their respective Writings and Discoveries;

[9]  To constitute Tribunals inferior to the supreme Court;

[10]  To define and punish Piracies and Felonies committed on the high Seas, and Offences against the Law of Nations;

[11]  To declare War, grant Letters of Marque and Reprisal, and make Rules concerning Captures on Land and Water;

[12]  To raise and support Armies, but no Appropriation of Money to that Use shall be for a longer Term than two Years;

[13]  To provide and maintain a Navy;

[14]  To make Rules for the Government and Regulation of the land and naval Forces;

[15]  To provide for calling forth the Militia to execute the Laws of the Union, suppress Insurrections and repel Invasions;

[16]  To provide for organizing, arming, and disciplining, the Militia, and for governing such Part of them as may be employed in the Service of the United States, reserving to the States respectively, the Appointment of the Officers, and the Authority of training the Militia according to the discipline prescribed by Congress;

[17]  To exercise exclusive Legislation in all Cases whatsoever, over such District (not exceeding ten Miles square) as may, by Cession of particular States, and the Acceptance of Congress, become the Seat of the Government of the United States, and to exercise like Authority over all Places purchased by the Consent of the Legislature of the State in which the Same shall be, for the Erection of Forts, Magazines, Arsenals, dock-Yards, and other needful Buildings;—And

[18]  To make all Laws which shall be necessary and proper for carrying into Execution the foregoing Powers, and all other Powers vested by this Constitution in the Government of the United States, or in any Department or Officer thereof.

### Section 9

[1]  The Migration or Importation of such Persons as any of the States now existing shall think proper to admit, shall not be prohibited by the Congress prior to the Year one thousand eight hundred and eight, but a Tax or duty may be imposed on such Importation, not exceeding ten dollars for each Person.

[2]  The Privilege of the Writ of Habeas Corpus shall not be suspended, unless when in Cases of Rebellion or Invasion the public Safety may require it.

[3]  No Bill of Attainder or ex post facto Law shall be passed.

[4]  No Capitation, or other direct, Tax shall be laid, unless in Proportion to the Census or Enumeration herein before directed to be taken.

[5]  No Tax or Duty shall be laid on Articles exported from any State.

[6]  No Preference shall be given by any Regulation of Commerce or Revenue to the Ports of one State over those of another: nor shall Vessels bound to, or from, one State, be obliged to enter, clear, or pay Duties in another.

[7]  No Money shall be drawn from the Treasury, but in Consequence of Appropriations made by Law; and a regular Statement and Account of the Receipts and Expenditures of all public Money shall be published from time to time.

[8]  No Title of Nobility shall be granted by the United States: And no Person holding any Office of Profit or Trust under them, shall, without the Consent of the Congress, accept of any present, Emolument, Office, or Title, of any kind whatever, from any King, Prince, or foreign State.

### Section 10

[1]  No State shall enter into any Treaty, Alliance, or Confederation; grant Letters of Marque and Reprisal; coin Money; emit Bills of Credit; make any Thing but gold and silver Coin a Tender in Payment of Debts; pass any Bill of Attainder, ex post facto Law, or Law impairing the Obligation of Contracts, or grant any Title of Nobility.

[2]   No State shall, without the Consent of the Congress, lay any Imposts or Duties on Imports or Exports, except what may be absolutely necessary for executing it's inspection Laws: and the net Produce of all Duties and Imposts, laid by any State on Imports or Exports, shall be for the Use of the Treasury of the United States; and all such Laws shall be subject to the Revision and Controul of the Congress.

[3]   No State shall, without the Consent of Congress, lay any Duty of Tonnage, keep Troops, or Ships of War in time of Peace, enter into any Agreement or Compact with another State, or with a foreign Power, or engage in War, unless actually invaded, or in such imminent Danger as will not admit of delay.

## ARTICLE II

### SECTION 1

[1]   The executive Power shall be vested in a President of the United States of America. He shall hold his Office during the Term of four Years, and, together with the Vice President, chosen for the same Term, be elected as follows

[2]   Each State shall appoint, in such Manner as the Legislature thereof may direct, a Number of Electors, equal to the whole Number of Senators and Representatives to which the State may be entitled in the Congress: but no Senator or Representative, or Person holding an Office of Trust or Profit under the United States, shall be appointed an Elector.

[3]   The Electors shall meet in their respective States, and vote by Ballot for two Persons, of whom one at least shall not be an Inhabitant of the same State with themselves. And they shall make a List of all the Persons voted for, and of the Number of Votes for each; which List they shall sign and certify, and transmit sealed to the Seat of the Government of the United States, directed to the President of the Senate. The President of the Senate shall, in the Presence of the Senate and House of Representatives, open all the Certificates, and the Votes shall then be counted. The Person having the greatest Number of Votes shall be the President, if such Number be a Majority of the whole Number of Electors appointed; and if there be more than one who have such Majority, and have an equal Number of Votes, then the House of Representatives shall immediately chuse by Ballot one of them for President; and if no Person have a Majority, then from the five highest on the List the said House shall in like Manner chuse the President. But in chusing the President, the Votes shall be taken by States, the Representation from each State having one Vote; A quorum for this Purpose shall consist of a Member or Members from two thirds of the States, and a Majority of all the States shall be necessary to a Choice. In every Case, after the Choice of the President, the Person having the greatest Number of Votes of the Electors shall be the Vice President. But if there should remain two or more who have equal Votes, the Senate shall chuse from them by Ballot the Vice President.

[4]   The Congress may determine the Time of chusing the Electors, and the Day on which they shall give their Votes; which Day shall be the same throughout the United States.

[5]   No Person except a natural born Citizen, or a Citizen of the United States, at the time of the Adoption of this Constitution, shall be eligible to the Office of President; neither shall any Person be eligible to that Office who shall not have attained to the Age of thirty five Years, and been fourteen Years a Resident within the United States.

[6]   In Case of the Removal of the President from Office, or of his Death, Resignation, or Inability to discharge the Powers and Duties of the said Office, the Same shall devolve on the Vice President, and the Congress may by Law provide for the Case of Removal, Death, Resignation or Inability, both of the President and Vice President, declaring what Officer shall then act as President, and such Officer shall act accordingly, until the Disability be removed, or a President shall be elected.

[7]   The President shall, at stated Times, receive for his Services, a Compensation, which shall neither be increased nor diminished during the Period for which he shall have been elected, and he shall not receive within that Period any other Emolument from the United States, or any of them.

[8]   Before he enter on the Execution of his Office, he shall take the following Oath or Affirmation:—"I do solemnly swear (or affirm) that I will faithfully execute the Office of President of the United States, and will to the best of my Ability, preserve, protect and defend the Constitution of the United States."

## SECTION 2

[1]   The president shall be Commander in Chief of the Army and Navy of the United States, and of the Militia of the several States, when called into the actual Service of the United States; he may require the Opinion, in writing, of the principal Officer in each of the executive Departments, upon any Subject relating to the Duties of their respective Offices, and he shall have Power to grant Reprieves and Pardons for Offences against the United States, except in Cases of Impeachment.

[2]   He shall have Power, by and with the Advice and Consent of the Senate, to make Treaties, provided two thirds of the Senators present concur; and he shall nominate, and by and with the Advice and Consent of the Senate, shall appoint Ambassadors, other public Ministers and Consuls, Judges of the supreme Court, and all other Officers of the United States, whose Appointments are not herein otherwise provided for, and which shall be established by Law: but the Congress may by Law vest the Appointment of such inferior Officers, as they think proper, in the President alone, in the Courts of Law, or in the Heads of Departments.

[3]   The President shall have Power to fill up all Vacancies that may happen during the Recess of the Senate, by granting Commissions which shall expire at the End of their next Session.

### SECTION 3

He shall from time to time give to the Congress Information of the State of the Union, and recommend to their Consideration such Measures as he shall judge necessary and expedient; he may, on extraordinary Occasions, convene both Houses, or either of them, and in Case of Disagreement between them, with Respect to the Time of Adjournment, he may adjourn them to such Time as he shall think proper; he shall receive Ambassadors and other public Ministers; he shall take Care that the Laws be faithfully executed, and shall Commission all the Officers of the United States.

### SECTION 4

The President, Vice President and all civil Officers of the United States, shall be removed from Office on Impeachment for, and Conviction of, Treason, Bribery, or other high Crimes and Misdemeanors.

## ARTICLE III

### SECTION 1

The judicial Power of the United States, shall be vested in one supreme Court, and in such inferior Courts as the Congress may from time to time ordain and establish. The Judges, both of the supreme and inferior Courts, shall hold their Offices during good Behaviour, and shall, at stated Times, receive for their Services, a Compensation, which shall not be diminished during their Continuance in Office.

### SECTION 2

[1]   The judicial Power shall extend to all Cases, in Law and Equity, arising under this Constitution, the Laws of the United States, and Treaties made, or which shall be made, under their Authority;—to all Cases affecting Ambassadors, other public Ministers and Consuls;—to all Cases of admiralty and maritime Jurisdiction;—to Controversies to which the United States shall be a Party;—to Controversies between two or more States;—between a State and Citizens of another State;—between Citizens of different States,—between Citizens of the same State claiming Lands under Grants of different States, and between a State, or the Citizens thereof, and foreign States, Citizens or Subjects.

[2]   In all cases affecting Ambassadors, other public Ministers and Consuls, and those in which a State shall be Party, the supreme Court shall have original Jurisdiction. In all the other Cases before mentioned, the supreme Court shall have appellate Jurisdiction, both as to Law and Fact, with such Exceptions, and under such Regulations as the Congress shall make.

[3]   The Trial of all Crimes, except in Cases of Impeachment, shall be by Jury; and such Trial shall be held in the State where the said Crimes shall have been committed; but when not committed within any State, the

Trial shall be at such Place or Places as the Congress may by Law have directed.

## SECTION 3

[1] Treason against the United States, shall consist only in levying War against them, or in adhering to their Enemies, giving them Aid and Comfort. No Person shall be convicted of Treason unless on the Testimony of two Witnesses to the same overt Act, or on Confession in open Court.

[2] The Congress shall have Power to declare the Punishment of Treason, but no Attainder of Treason shall work Corruption of Blood, or Forfeiture except during the Life of the Person attainted.

## ARTICLE IV

### SECTION 1

Full Faith and Credit shall be given in each State to the public Acts, Records, and judicial Proceedings of every other State. And the Congress may by general Laws prescribe the Manner in which such Acts, Records and Proceedings shall be proved, and the Effect thereof.

### SECTION 2

[1] The Citizens of each State shall be entitled to all Privileges and Immunities of Citizens in the several States.

[2] A person charged in any State with Treason, Felony, or other Crime, who shall flee from Justice, and be found in another State, shall on Demand of the executive Authority of the State from which he fled, be delivered up, to be removed to the State having Jurisdiction of the Crime.

[3] No Person held to Service or Labour in one State, under the Laws thereof, escaping into another, shall, in Consequence of any Law or Regulation therein, be discharged from such Service or Labour, but shall be delivered up on Claim of the Party to whom such Service or Labour may be due.

### SECTION 3

[1] New States may be admitted by the Congress into this Union; but no new State shall be formed or erected within the Jurisdiction of any other State; nor any State be formed by the Junction of two or more States, or Parts of States, without the Consent of the Legislatures of the States concerned as well as of the Congress.

[2] The Congress shall have Power to dispose of and make all needful Rules and Regulations respecting the Territory or other Property belonging to the United States; and nothing in this Constitution shall be so construed as to Prejudice any Claims of the United States, or of any particular State.

### SECTION 4

The United States shall guarantee to every State in this Union a Republican Form of Government, and shall protect each of them against

Invasion; and on Application of the Legislature, or of the Executive (when the Legislature cannot be convened) against domestic Violence.

## ARTICLE V

The Congress, whenever two thirds of both Houses shall deem it necessary, shall propose Amendments to this Constitution, or on the Application of the Legislatures of two thirds of the several States, shall call a Convention for proposing Amendments, which, in either Case, shall be valid to all Intents and Purposes, as Part of this Constitution, when ratified by the Legislatures of three fourths of the several States, or by Conventions in three fourths thereof, as the one or the other Mode of Ratification may be proposed by the Congress; Provided that no Amendment which may be made prior to the Year One thousand eight hundred and eight shall in any Manner affect the first and fourth Clauses in the Ninth Section of the first Article; and that no State, without its Consent, shall be deprived of its equal Suffrage in the Senate.

## ARTICLE VI

[1]  All Debts contracted and Engagements entered into, before the Adoption of this Constitution, shall be as valid against the United States under this Constitution, as under the Confederation.

[2]  This Constitution, and the Laws of the United States which shall be made in Pursuance thereof; and all Treaties made, or which shall be made, under the Authority of the United States, shall be the supreme Law of the Land; and the Judges in every State shall be bound thereby, any Thing in the Constitution or Laws of any State to the Contrary notwithstanding.

[3]  The Senators and Representatives before mentioned, and the Members of the several State Legislatures, and all executive and judicial Officers, both of the United States and of the several States, shall be bound by Oath or Affirmation, to support this Constitution; but no religious Test shall ever be required as a Qualification to any Office or public Trust under the United States.

## ARTICLE VII

The Ratification of the Conventions of nine States, shall be sufficient for the Establishment of this Constitution between the States so ratifying the Same.

## AMENDMENT I (1791)

Congress shall make no law respecting an establishment of religion, or prohibiting the free exercise thereof; or abridging the freedom of speech, or of the press; or the right of the people peaceably to assemble, and to petition the Government for a redress of grievances.

## AMENDMENT II (1791)

A well regulated Militia, being necessary to the security of a free State, the right of the people to keep and bear Arms, shall not be infringed.

### AMENDMENT III (1791)

No Soldier shall, in time of peace be quartered in any house, without the consent of the Owner, nor in time of war, but in a manner to be prescribed by law.

### AMENDMENT IV (1791)

The right of the people to be secure in their persons, houses, papers, and effects, against unreasonable searches and seizures, shall not be violated, and no Warrants shall issue, but upon probable cause, supported by Oath or affirmation, and particularly describing the place to be searched, and the persons or things to be seized.

### AMENDMENT V (1791)

No person shall be held to answer for a capital, or otherwise infamous crime, unless on a presentment or indictment of a Grand Jury, except in cases arising in the land or naval forces, or in the Militia, when in actual service in time of War or public danger; nor shall any person be subject for the same offence to be twice put in jeopardy of life or limb; nor shall be compelled in any criminal case to be a witness against himself, nor be deprived of life, liberty, or property, without due process of law; nor shall private property be taken for public use, without just compensation.

### AMENDMENT VI (1791)

In all criminal prosecutions, the accused shall enjoy the right to a speedy and public trial, by an impartial jury of the State and district wherein the crime shall have been committed, which district shall have been previously ascertained by law, and to be informed of the nature and cause of the accusation; to be confronted with the witnesses against him; to have compulsory process for obtaining witnesses in his favor, and to have the Assistance of Counsel for his defence.

### AMENDMENT VII (1791)

In Suits at common law, where the value in controversy shall exceed twenty dollars, the right of trial by jury shall be preserved, and no fact tried by a jury, shall be otherwise reexamined in any Court of the United States, than according to the rules of the common law.

### AMENDMENT VIII (1791)

Excessive bail shall not be required, nor excessive fines imposed, nor cruel and unusual punishments inflicted.

### AMENDMENT IX (1791)

The enumeration in the Constitution, of certain rights, shall not be construed to deny or disparage others retained by the people.

### AMENDMENT X (1791)

The powers not delegated to the United States by the Constitution, nor prohibited by it to the States, are reserved to the States respectively, or to the people.

**AMENDMENT XI (1798)**

The Judicial power of the United States shall not be construed to extend to any suit in law or equity, commenced or prosecuted against one of the United States by Citizens of another State, or by Citizens or Subjects of any Foreign State.

**AMENDMENT XII (1804)**

The Electors shall meet in their respective states and vote by ballot for President and Vice–President, one of whom, at least, shall not be an inhabitant of the same state with themselves; they shall name in their ballots the person voted for as President, and in distinct ballots the person voted for as Vice–President, and they shall make distinct lists of all persons voted for as President, and of all persons voted for as Vice–President, and of the number of votes for each, which lists they shall sign and certify, and transmit sealed to the seat of the government of the United States, directed to the President of the Senate;—the President of the Senate shall, in the presence of the Senate and House of Representatives, open all the certificates and the votes shall then be counted;—The person having the greatest number of votes for President, shall be the President, if such number be a majority of the whole number of Electors appointed; and if no person have such majority, then from the persons having the highest numbers not exceeding three on the list of those voted for as President, the House of Representatives shall choose immediately, by ballot, the President. But in choosing the President, the votes shall be taken by states, the representation from each state having one vote; a quorum for this purpose shall consist of a member or members from two-thirds of the states, and a majority of all the states shall be necessary to a choice. And if the House of Representatives shall not choose a President whenever the right of choice shall devolve upon them, before the fourth day of March next following, then the Vice–President shall act as President, as in the case of the death or other constitutional disability of the President.—The person having the greatest number of votes as Vice–President, shall be the Vice–President, if such number be a majority of the whole number of Electors appointed, and if no person have a majority, then from the two highest numbers on the list, the Senate shall choose the Vice–President; a quorum for the purpose shall consist of two-thirds of the whole number of Senators, and a majority of the whole number shall be necessary to a choice. But no person constitutionally ineligible to the office of President shall be eligible to that of Vice–President of the United States.

**AMENDMENT XIII (1865)**

SECTION 1

Neither slavery nor involuntary servitude, except as a punishment for crime whereof the party shall have been duly convicted, shall exist within the United States, or any place subject to their jurisdiction.

## Section 2

Congress shall have power to enforce this article by appropriate legislation.

## Amendment XIV (1868)

### Section 1

All persons born or naturalized in the United States, and subject to the jurisdiction thereof, are citizens of the United States and of the State wherein they reside. No State shall make or enforce any law which shall abridge the privileges or immunities of citizens of the United States; nor shall any State deprive any person of life, liberty, or property, without due process of law; nor deny to any person within its jurisdiction the equal protection of the laws.

### Section 2

Representatives shall be apportioned among the several States according to their respective numbers, counting the whole number of persons in each State, excluding Indians not taxed. But when the right to vote at any election for the choice of electors for President and Vice President of the United States, Representatives in Congress, the Executive and Judicial officers of a State, or the members of the Legislature thereof, is denied to any of the male inhabitants of such State, being twenty-one years of age, and citizens of the United States, or in any way abridged, except for participation in rebellion, or other crime, the basis of representation therein shall be reduced in the proportion which the number of such male citizens shall bear to the whole number of male citizens twenty-one years of age in such State.

### Section 3

No person shall be a Senator or Representative in Congress, or elector of President and Vice President, or hold any office, civil or military, under the United States, or under any State, who, having previously taken an oath, as a member of Congress, or as an officer of the United States, or as a member of any State legislature, or as an executive or judicial officer of any State, to support the Constitution of the United States, shall have engaged in insurrection or rebellion against the same, or given aid or comfort to the enemies thereof. But Congress may by a vote of two-thirds of each House, remove such disability.

### Section 4

The validity of the public debt of the United States, authorized by law, including debts incurred for payment of pensions and bounties for services in suppressing insurrection or rebellion, shall not be questioned. But neither the United States nor any State shall assume or pay any debt or obligation incurred in aid of insurrection or rebellion against the United States, or any claim for the loss or emancipation of any slave; but all such debts, obligations and claims shall be held illegal and void.

SECTION 5

The Congress shall have power to enforce, by appropriate legislation, the provisions of this article.

## AMENDMENT **XV** (1870)

SECTION 1

The right of citizens of the United States to vote shall not be denied or abridged by the United States or by any State on account of race, color, or previous condition of servitude.

SECTION 2

The Congress shall have power to enforce this article by appropriate legislation.

## AMENDMENT **XVI** (1913)

The Congress shall have power to lay and collect taxes on incomes, from whatever source derived, without apportionment among the several States, and without regard to any census or enumeration.

## AMENDMENT **XVII** (1913)

The Senate of the United States shall be composed of two Senators from each State, elected by the people thereof, for six years; and each Senator shall have one vote. The electors in each State shall have the qualifications requisite for electors of the most numerous branch of the State legislatures.

When vacancies happen in the representation of any State in the Senate, the executive authority of such State shall issue writs of election to fill such vacancies: *Provided*, That the legislature of any State may empower the executive thereof to make temporary appointments until the people fill the vacancies by election as the legislature may direct.

This amendment shall not be so construed as to affect the election or term of any Senator chosen before it becomes valid as part of the Constitution.

## AMENDMENT **XVIII** (1919)

SECTION 1

After one year from the ratification of this article the manufacture, sale, or transportation of intoxicating liquors within, the importation thereof into, or the exportation thereof from the United States and all territory subject to the jurisdiction thereof for beverage purposes is hereby prohibited.

SECTION 2

The Congress and the several States shall have concurrent power to enforce this article by appropriate legislation.

### SECTION 3

This article shall be inoperative unless it shall have been ratified as an amendment to the Constitution by the legislatures of the several States, as provided in the Constitution, within seven years from the date of the submission hereof to the States by the Congress.

## AMENDMENT **XIX** (1920)

The right of citizens of the United States to vote shall not be denied or abridged by the United States or by any State on account of sex.

Congress shall have power to enforce this article by appropriate legislation.

## AMENDMENT **XX** (1933)

### SECTION 1

The terms of the President and the Vice President shall end at noon on the 20th day of January, and the terms of Senators and Representatives at noon on the 3d day of January, of the years in which such terms would have ended if this article had not been ratified; and the terms of their successors shall then begin.

### SECTION 2

The Congress shall assemble at least once in every year, and such meeting shall begin at noon on the 3d day of January, unless they shall by law appoint a different day.

### SECTION 3

If, at the time fixed for the beginning of the term of the President, the President elect shall have died, the Vice President elect shall become President. If a President shall not have been chosen before the time fixed for the beginning of his term, or if the President elect shall have failed to qualify, then the Vice President elect shall act as President until a President shall have qualified; and the Congress may by law provide for the case wherein neither a President elect nor a Vice President elect shall have qualified, declaring who shall then act as President, or the manner in which one who is to act shall be selected, and such person shall act accordingly until a President or Vice President shall have qualified.

### SECTION 4

The Congress may by law provide for the case of the death of any of the persons from whom the House of Representatives may choose a President whenever the right of choice shall have devolved upon them, and for the case of the death of any of the persons from whom the Senate may choose a Vice President whenever the right of choice shall have devolved upon them.

## SECTION 5

Sections 1 and 2 shall take effect on the 15th day of October following the ratification of this article.

## SECTION 6

This article shall be inoperative unless it shall have been ratified as an amendment to the Constitution by the legislatures of three-fourths of the several States within seven years from the date of its submission.

## AMENDMENT **XXI** (1933)

### SECTION 1

The eighteenth article of amendment to the Constitution of the United States is hereby repealed.

### SECTION 2

The transportation or importation into any State, Territory, or Possession of the United States for delivery or use therein of intoxicating liquors, in violation of the laws thereof, is hereby prohibited.

### SECTION 3

This article shall be inoperative unless it shall have been ratified as an amendment to the Constitution by conventions in the several States, as provided in the Constitution, within seven years from the date of the submission hereof to the States by the Congress.

## AMENDMENT **XXII** (1951)

### SECTION 1

No person shall be elected to the office of the President more than twice, and no person who has held the office of President, or acted as President, for more than two years of a term to which some other person was elected President shall be elected to the office of the President more than once. But this Article shall not apply to any person holding the office of President when this Article was proposed by the Congress, and shall not prevent any person who may be holding the office of President, or acting as President, during the term within which this Article becomes operative from holding the office of President or acting as President during the remainder of such term.

### SECTION 2

This article shall be inoperative unless it shall have been ratified as an amendment to the Constitution by the legislatures of three-fourths of the several States within seven years from the date of its submission to the States by the Congress.

### AMENDMENT **XXIII** (1961)

#### SECTION 1

The Disctrict constituting the seat of Government shall appoint in such manner as Congress may direct:

A number of electors of President and Vice President equal to the whole number of Senators and Representatives in Congress to which the District would be entitled if it were a State, but in no event more than the least populous State; they shall be in addition to those appointed by the States, but they shall be considered, for the purposes of the election of President and Vice President, to be electors appointed by a State; and they shall meet in the District and perform such duties as provided by the twelfth article of amendment.

#### SECTION 2

The Congress shall have power to enforce this article by appropriate legislation.

### AMENDMENT **XXIV** (1964)

#### SECTION 1

The right of citizens of the United States to vote in any primary or other election for President or Vice President, for electors for President or Vice President, or for Senator or Representative in Congress, shall not be denied or abridged by the United States or any State by reason of failure to pay any poll tax or other tax.

#### SECTION 2

The Congress shall have power to enforce this article by appropriate legislation.

### AMENDMENT **XXV** (1967)

#### SECTION 1

In case of the removal of the President from office or of his death or resignation, the Vice President shall become President.

#### SECTION 2

Whenever there is a vacancy in the office of the Vice President, the President shall nominate a Vice President who shall take office upon confirmation by a majority vote of both Houses of Congress.

#### SECTION 3

Whenever the President transmits to the President pro tempore of the Senate and the Speaker of the House of Representatives his written declaration that he is unable to discharge the powers and duties of his office, and until he transmits to them a written declaration to the contrary, such powers and duties shall be discharged by the Vice President as Acting President.

#### SECTION 4

Whenever the Vice President and a majority of either the principal officers of the executive departments or of such other body as Congress may by law provide, transmit to the President pro tempore of the Senate and the Speaker of the House of Representatives their written declaration that the President is unable to discharge the powers and duties of his office, the Vice President shall immediately assume the powers and duties of the office as Acting President.

Thereafter, when the President transmits to the President pro tempore of the Senate and the Speaker of the House of Representatives his written declaration that no inability exists, he shall resume the powers and duties of his office unless the Vice President and a majority of either the principal officers of the executive department or of such other body as Congress may by law provide, transmit within four days to the President pro tempore of the Senate and the Speaker of the House of Representatives their written declaration that the President is unable to discharge the powers and duties of his office. Thereupon Congress shall decide the issue, assembling within forty-eight hours for that purpose if not in session. If the Congress, within twenty-one days after receipt of the latter written declaration, or, if Congress is not in session, within twenty-one days after Congress is required to assemble, determines by two-thirds vote of both Houses that the President is unable to discharge the powers and duties of his office, the Vice President shall continue to discharge the same as Acting President; otherwise, the President shall resume the powers and duties of his office.

## AMENDMENT **XXVI** (1971)

### SECTION 1

The right of citizens of the United States, who are eighteen years of age or older, to vote shall not be denied or abridged by the United States or by any State on account of age.

### SECTION 2

The Congress shall have power to enforce this article by appropriate legislation.

## AMENDMENT **XXVII** (1992)

No law, varying the compensation for the services of the Senators and Representatives, shall take effect, until an election of Representatives shall have intervened.

# Appendix B: Selected Provisions of the Administrative Procedure Act (as amended)

## 5 U.S.C. § 551. Definitions

For the purpose of this subchapter—

(1) "agency" means each authority of the Government of the United States, whether or not it is within or subject to review by another agency, but does not include—

(A) the Congress;

(B) the courts of the United States;

(C) the governments of the territories or possessions of the United States;

(D) the government of the District of Columbia;

or except as to the requirements of section 552 of this title—

(E) agencies composed of representatives of the parties or of representatives of organizations of the parties to the disputes determined by them;

(F) courts martial and military commissions;

(G) military authority exercised in the field in time of war or in occupied territory; or

(H) functions conferred by sections 1738, 1739, 1743, and 1744 of title 12; chapter 2 of title 41; subchapter II of chapter 471 of title 49; or sections 1884, 1891–1902, and former section 1641(b)(2), of title 50, appendix;

(2) "person" includes an individual, partnership, corporation, association, or public or private organization other than an agency;

(3) "party" includes a person or agency named or admitted as a party, or properly seeking and entitled as of right to be admitted as a party, in an agency proceeding, and a person or agency admitted by an agency as a party for limited purposes;

(4) "rule" means the whole or a part of an agency statement of general or particular applicability and future effect designed to implement, interpret, or prescribe law or policy or describing the organization, procedure, or practice requirements of an agency and includes the approval or prescription for the future of rates, wages, corporate or financial structures or reorganizations thereof, prices, facilities, appliances, services or allowances

therefor or of valuations, costs, or accounting, or practices bearing on any of the foregoing;

(5) "rule making" means agency process for formulating, amending, or repealing a rule;

(6) "order" means the whole or a part of a final disposition, whether affirmative, negative, injunctive, or declaratory in form, of an agency in a matter other than rule making but including licensing;

(7) "adjudication" means agency process for the formulation of an order;

(8) "license" includes the whole or a part of an agency permit, certificate, approval, registration, charter, membership, statutory exemption or other form of permission;

(9) "licensing" includes agency process respecting the grant, renewal, denial, revocation, suspension, annulment, withdrawal, limitation, amendment, modification, or conditioning of a license;

(10) "sanction" includes the whole or a part of an agency—

(A) prohibition, requirement, limitation, or other condition affecting the freedom of a person;

(B) withholding of relief;

(C) imposition of penalty or fine;

(D) destruction, taking, seizure, or withholding of property;

(E) assessment of damages, reimbursement, restitution, compensation, costs, charges, or fees;

(F) requirement, revocation, or suspension of a license; or

(G) taking other compulsory or restrictive action;

(11) "relief" includes the whole or a part of an agency—

(A) grant of money, assistance, license, authority, exemption, exception, privilege, or remedy;

(B) recognition of a claim, right, immunity, privilege, exemption, or exception; or

(C) taking of other action on the application or petition of, and beneficial to, a person;

(12) "agency proceeding" means an agency process as defined by paragraphs (5), (7), and (9) of this section;

(13) "agency action" includes the whole or a part of an agency rule, order, license, sanction, relief, or the equivalent or denial thereof, or failure to act; and

(14) "ex parte communication" means an oral or written communication not on the public record with respect to which reasonable prior notice to all parties is not given, but it shall not include requests for status reports on any matter or proceeding covered by this subchapter.

### 5 U.S.C. § 552. Public information; agency rules, opinions, orders, records, and proceedings.

(a) Each agency shall make available to the public information as follows:

(1) Each agency shall separately state and currently publish in the Federal Register for the guidance of the public—

(A) descriptions of its central and field organization and the established places at which, the employees (and in the case of a uniformed service, the members) from whom, and the methods whereby, the public may obtain information, make submittals or requests, or obtain decisions;

(B) statements of the general course and method by which its functions are channeled and determined, including the nature and requirements of all formal and informal procedures available;

(C) rules of procedure, descriptions of forms available or the places at which forms may be obtained, and instructions as to the scope and contents of all papers, reports, or examinations;

(D) substantive rules of general applicability adopted as authorized by law, and statements of general policy or interpretations of general applicability formulated and adopted by the agency; and

(E) each amendment, revision, or repeal of the foregoing.

Except to the extent that a person has actual and timely notice of the terms thereof, a person may not in any manner be required to resort to, or be adversely affected by, a matter required to be published in the Federal Register and not so published. For the purpose of this paragraph, matter reasonably available to the class of persons affected thereby is deemed published in the Federal Register when incorporated by reference therein with the approval of the Director of the Federal Register.

(2) Each agency, in accordance with published rules, shall make available for public inspection and copying—

(A) final opinions, including concurring and dissenting opinions, as well as orders, made in the adjudication of cases;

(B) those statements of policy and interpretations which have been adopted by the agency and are not published in the Federal Register;

(C) administrative staff manuals and instructions to staff that affect a member of the public;

(D) copies of all records, regardless of form or format, which have been released to any person under paragraph (3) and which, because of the nature of their subject matter, the agency determines have become or are likely to become the subject of subsequent requests for substantially the same records; and

(E) a general index of the records referred to under subparagraph (D);

unless the materials are promptly published and copies offered for sale. For records created on or after November 1, 1996, within one year after such date, each agency shall make such records available, including by computer telecommunications or, if computer telecommunications means have not been established by the agency, by other electronic means. To the extent required to prevent a clearly unwarranted invasion of personal privacy, an agency may delete identifying details when it makes available or publishes an opinion, statement of policy, interpretation, staff manual, instruction, or copies of records referred to in subparagraph (D). However, in each case the justification for the deletion shall be explained fully in writing, and the extent of such deletion shall be indicated on the portion of the record which is made available or published, unless including that indication would harm an interest protected by the exemption in subsection (b) under which the deletion is made. If technically feasible, the extent of the deletion shall be indicated at the place in the record where the deletion was made. Each agency shall also maintain and make available for public inspection and copying current indexes providing identifying information for the public as to any matter issued, adopted, or promulgated after July 4, 1967, and required by this paragraph to be made available or published. Each agency shall promptly publish, quarterly or more frequently, and distribute (by sale or otherwise) copies of each index or supplements thereto unless it determines by order published in the Federal Register that the publication would be unnecessary and impracticable, in which case the agency shall nonetheless provide copies of such index on request at a cost not to exceed the direct cost of duplication. Each agency shall make the index referred to in subparagraph (E) available by computer telecommunications by December 31, 1999. A final order, opinion, statement of policy, interpretation, or staff manual or instruction that affects a member of the public may be relied on, used, or cited as precedent by an agency against a party other than an agency only if—

> (i) it has been indexed and either made available or published as provided by this paragraph; or

> (ii) the party has actual and timely notice of the terms thereof.

(3)(A) Except with respect to the records made available under paragraphs (1) and (2) of this subsection, and except as provided in subparagraph (E), each agency, upon any request for records which (i) reasonably describes such records and (ii) is made in accordance with published rules stating the time, place, fees (if any), and procedures to be followed, shall make the records promptly available to any person.

(B) In making any record available to a person under this paragraph, an agency shall provide the record in any form or format requested by the person if the record is readily reproducible by the agency in that form or format. Each agency shall make reasonable efforts to maintain its records in forms or formats that are reproducible for purposes of this section.

(C) In responding under this paragraph to a request for records, an agency shall make reasonable efforts to search for the records in electronic form or format, except when such efforts would significantly interfere with the operation of the agency's automated information system.

(D) For purposes of this paragraph, the term "search" means to review, manually or by automated means, agency records for the purpose of locating those records which are responsive to a request.

(E) An agency, or part of an agency, that is an element of the intelligence community (as that term is defined in section 3(4) of the National Security Act of 1947 (50 U.S.C. 401a(4))) shall not make any record available under this paragraph to—

(i) any government entity, other than a State, territory, commonwealth, or district of the United States, or any subdivision thereof; or

(ii) a representative of a government entity described in clause (i).

(4)(A)(i) In order to carry out the provisions of this section, each agency shall promulgate regulations, pursuant to notice and receipt of public comment, specifying the schedule of fees applicable to the processing of requests under this section and establishing procedures and guidelines for determining when such fees should be waived or reduced. Such schedule shall conform to the guidelines which shall be promulgated, pursuant to notice and receipt of public comment, by the Director of the Office of Management and Budget and which shall provide for a uniform schedule of fees for all agencies.

(ii) Such agency regulations shall provide that—

(I) fees shall be limited to reasonable standard charges for document search, duplication, and review, when records are requested for commercial use;

(II) fees shall be limited to reasonable standard charges for document duplication when records are not sought for commercial use and the request is made by an educational or noncommercial scientific institution, whose purpose is scholarly or scientific research; or a representative of the news media; and

(III) for any request not described in (I) or (II), fees shall be limited to reasonable standard charges for document search and duplication.

In this clause, the term "a representative of the news media" means any person or entity that gathers information of potential interest to a segment of the public, uses its editorial skills to turn the raw materials into a distinct work, and distributes that work to an audience. In this clause, the term "news" means information that is about current events or that would be of current interest to the public. Examples of news-media entities are television or radio stations broadcasting to the public at large and publishers of periodicals (but only if such entities qualify as disseminators of "news") who make their products available for purchase by or subscription by or free distribution to the general public. These examples are not all-inclusive. Moreover, as methods of news delivery evolve (for example, the adoption of the electronic dissemination of news-papers through telecommunications services), such alternative media shall be considered to be news-media entities. A free-lance journalist shall be regarded as working for a news-media entity if the journalist can demonstrate a solid basis for expecting publication through that entity, whether or not the journalist is actually employed by the entity. A publication contract would present a solid basis for such an expectation; the Government may also consider the past publication record of the requester in making such a determination.

(iii) Documents shall be furnished without any charge or at a charge reduced below the fees established under clause (ii) if disclosure of the information is in the public interest because it is likely to contribute significantly to public understanding of the operations or activities of the government and is not primarily in the commercial interest of the requester.

(iv) Fee schedules shall provide for the recovery of only the direct costs of search, duplication, or review. Review costs shall include only the direct costs incurred during the initial examination of a document for the purposes of determining whether the documents must be disclosed under this section and for the purposes of withholding any portions exempt from disclosure under this section. Review costs may not include any costs incurred in resolving issues of law or policy that may be raised in the course of processing a request under this section. No fee may be charged by any agency under this section—

(I) if the costs of routine collection and processing of the fee are likely to equal or exceed the amount of the fee; or

(II) for any request described in clause (ii)(II) or (III) of this subparagraph for the first two hours of search time or for the first one hundred pages of duplication.

(v) No agency may require advance payment of any fee unless the requester has previously failed to pay fees in a timely fashion, or the agency has determined that the fee will exceed $250.

(vi) Nothing in this subparagraph shall supersede fees chargeable under a statute specifically providing for setting the level of fees for particular types of records.

(vii) In any action by a requester regarding the waiver of fees under this section, the court shall determine the matter de novo: *Provided*, That the court's review of the matter shall be limited to the record before the agency.

(viii) An agency shall not assess search fees (or in the case of a requester described under clause (ii)(II), duplication fees) under this subparagraph if the agency fails to comply with any time limit under paragraph (6), if no unusual or exceptional circumstances (as those terms are defined for purposes of paragraphs (6)(B) and (C), respectively) apply to the processing of the request.

(B) On complaint, the district court of the United States in the district in which the complainant resides, or has his principal place of business, or in which the agency records are situated, or in the District of Columbia, has jurisdiction to enjoin the agency from withholding agency records and to order the production of any agency records improperly withheld from the complainant. In such a case the court shall determine the matter de novo, and may examine the contents of such agency records in camera to determine whether such records or any part thereof shall be withheld under any of the exemptions set forth in subsection (b) of this section, and the burden is on the agency to sustain its action. In addition to any other matters to which a court accords substantial weight, a court shall accord substantial weight to an affidavit of an agency concerning the agency's determination as to technical feasibility under paragraph (2)(C) and subsection (b) and reproducibility under paragraph (3)(B).

(C) Notwithstanding any other provision of law, the defendant shall serve an answer or otherwise plead to any complaint made under this subsection within thirty days after service upon the defendant of the pleading in which such complaint is made, unless the court otherwise directs for good cause shown.

[(D) Repealed. Pub. L. 98–620, title IV, § 402(2), Nov. 8, 1984, 98 Stat. 3357]

(E)(i) The court may assess against the United States reasonable attorney fees and other litigation costs reasonably incurred in any case under this section in which the complainant has substantially prevailed.

(ii) For purposes of this subparagraph, a complainant has substantially prevailed if the complainant has obtained relief through either—

(I) a judicial order, or an enforceable written agreement or consent decree; or

(II) a voluntary or unilateral change in position by the agency, if the complainant's claim is not insubstantial.

(F)(i) Whenever the court orders the production of any agency records improperly withheld from the complainant and assesses against the United States reasonable attorney fees and other litigation costs, and the court additionally issues a written finding that the circumstances surrounding the withholding raise questions whether agency personnel acted arbitrarily or capriciously with respect to the withholding, the Special Counsel shall promptly initiate a proceeding to determine whether disciplinary action is warranted against the officer or employee who was primarily responsible for the withholding. The Special Counsel, after investigation and consideration of the evidence submitted, shall submit his findings and recommendations to the administrative authority of the agency concerned and shall send copies of the findings and recommendations to the officer or employee or his representative. The administrative authority shall take the corrective action that the Special Counsel recommends.

(ii) The Attorney General shall—

(I) notify the Special Counsel of each civil action described under the first sentence of clause (i); and

(II) annually submit a report to Congress on the number of such civil actions in the preceding year.

(iii) The Special Counsel shall annually submit a report to Congress on the actions taken by the Special Counsel under clause (i).

(G) In the event of noncompliance with the order of the court, the district court may punish for contempt the responsible employee, and in the case of a uniformed service, the responsible member.

(5) Each agency having more than one member shall maintain and make available for public inspection a record of the final votes of each member in every agency proceeding.

(6)(A) Each agency, upon any request for records made under paragraph (1), (2), or (3) of this subsection, shall—

(i) determine within 20 days (excepting Saturdays, Sundays, and legal public holidays) after the receipt of any such request whether to comply with such request and shall immediately notify the person making such request of such determination and the reasons therefor, and of the right of such person to appeal to the head of the agency any adverse determination; and

(ii) make a determination with respect to any appeal within twenty days (excepting Saturdays, Sundays, and legal public holidays) after the receipt of such appeal. If on appeal the denial of the request for records is in whole or in part upheld, the agency shall notify the person making such request of the provisions for judicial review of that determination under paragraph (4) of this subsection.

    The 20–day period under clause (i) shall commence on the date on which the request is first received by the appropriate component of the agency, but in any event not later than ten days after the request is first received by any component of the agency that is designated in the agency's regulations under this section to receive requests under this section. The 20–day period shall not be tolled by the agency except—

    (I) that the agency may make one request to the requester for information and toll the 20–day period while it is awaiting such information that it has reasonably requested from the requester under this section; or

    (II) if necessary to clarify with the requester issues regarding fee assessment. In either case, the agency's receipt of the requester's response to the agency's request for information or clarification ends the tolling period.

(B)(i) In unusual circumstances as specified in this subparagraph, the time limits prescribed in either clause (i) or clause (ii) of subparagraph (A) may be extended by written notice to the person making such request setting forth the unusual circumstances for such extension and the date on which a determination is expected to be dispatched. No such notice shall specify a date that would result in an extension for more than ten working days, except as provided in clause (ii) of this subparagraph.

    (ii) With respect to a request for which a written notice under clause (i) extends the time limits prescribed under clause (i) of subparagraph (A), the agency shall notify the person making the request if the request cannot be processed within the time limit specified in that clause and shall provide the person an opportunity to limit the scope of the request so that it may be processed within that time limit or an opportunity to arrange with the agency an alternative time frame for processing the request or a modified request. To aid the requester, each agency shall make available its FOIA Public Liaison, who shall assist in the resolution of any disputes between the requester and the agency. Refusal by the person to reasonably modify the request or arrange such an alternative time frame shall be considered as a factor in determining whether exceptional circumstances exist for purposes of subparagraph (C).

    (iii) As used in this subparagraph, "unusual circumstances" means, but only to the extent reasonably necessary to the proper processing of the particular requests—

(I) the need to search for and collect the requested records from field facilities or other establishments that are separate from the office processing the request;

(II) the need to search for, collect, and appropriately examine a voluminous amount of separate and distinct records which are demanded in a single request; or

(III) the need for consultation, which shall be conducted with all practicable speed, with another agency having a substantial interest in the determination of the request or among two or more components of the agency having substantial subject-matter interest therein.

(iv) Each agency may promulgate regulations, pursuant to notice and receipt of public comment, providing for the aggregation of certain requests by the same requestor, or by a group of requestors acting in concert, if the agency reasonably believes that such requests actually constitute a single request, which would otherwise satisfy the unusual circumstances specified in this subparagraph, and the requests involve clearly related matters. Multiple requests involving unrelated matters shall not be aggregated.

(C)(i) Any person making a request to any agency for records under paragraph (1), (2), or (3) of this subsection shall be deemed to have exhausted his administrative remedies with respect to such request if the agency fails to comply with the applicable time limit provisions of this paragraph. If the Government can show exceptional circumstances exist and that the agency is exercising due diligence in responding to the request, the court may retain jurisdiction and allow the agency additional time to complete its review of the records. Upon any determination by an agency to comply with a request for records, the records shall be made promptly available to such person making such request. Any notification of denial of any request for records under this subsection shall set forth the names and titles or positions of each person responsible for the denial of such request.

(ii) For purposes of this subparagraph, the term "exceptional circumstances" does not include a delay that results from a predictable agency workload of requests under this section, unless the agency demonstrates reasonable progress in reducing its backlog of pending requests.

(iii) Refusal by a person to reasonably modify the scope of a request or arrange an alternative time frame for processing a request (or a modified request) under clause (ii) after being given an opportunity to do so by the agency to whom the person made the request shall be considered as a factor in determining whether exceptional circumstances exist for purposes of this subparagraph.

(D)(i) Each agency may promulgate regulations, pursuant to notice and receipt of public comment, providing for multitrack processing of requests for records based on the amount of work or time (or both) involved in processing requests.

(ii) Regulations under this subparagraph may provide a person making a request that does not qualify for the fastest multitrack processing an opportunity to limit the scope of the request in order to qualify for faster processing.

(iii) This subparagraph shall not be considered to affect the requirement under subparagraph (C) to exercise due diligence.

(E)(i) Each agency shall promulgate regulations, pursuant to notice and receipt of public comment, providing for expedited processing of requests for records—

(I) in cases in which the person requesting the records demonstrates a compelling need; and

(II) in other cases determined by the agency.

(ii) Notwithstanding clause (i), regulations under this subparagraph must ensure—

(I) that a determination of whether to provide expedited processing shall be made, and notice of the determination shall be provided to the person making the request, within 10 days after the date of the request; and

(II) expeditious consideration of administrative appeals of such determinations of whether to provide expedited processing.

(iii) An agency shall process as soon as practicable any request for records to which the agency has granted expedited processing under this subparagraph. Agency action to deny or affirm denial of a request for expedited processing pursuant to this subparagraph, and failure by an agency to respond in a timely manner to such a request shall be subject to judicial review under paragraph (4), except that the judicial review shall be based on the record before the agency at the time of the determination.

(iv) A district court of the United States shall not have jurisdiction to review an agency denial of expedited processing of a request for records after the agency has provided a complete response to the request.

(v) For purposes of this subparagraph, the term "compelling need" means—

(I) that a failure to obtain requested records on an expedited basis under this paragraph could reasonably be expected to pose an imminent threat to the life or physical safety of an individual; or

(II) with respect to a request made by a person primarily engaged in disseminating information, urgency to inform the public concerning actual or alleged Federal Government activity.

(vi) A demonstration of a compelling need by a person making a request for expedited processing shall be made by a statement certified by such person to be true and correct to the best of such person's knowledge and belief.

(F) In denying a request for records, in whole or in part, an agency shall make a reasonable effort to estimate the volume of any requested matter the provision of which is denied, and shall provide any such estimate to the person making the request, unless providing such estimate would harm an interest protected by the exemption in subsection (b) pursuant to which the denial is made.

(7) Each agency shall—

(A) establish a system to assign an individualized tracking number for each request received that will take longer than ten days to process and provide to each person making a request the tracking number assigned to the request; and

(B) establish a telephone line or Internet service that provides information about the status of a request to the person making the request using the assigned tracking number, including—

(i) the date on which the agency originally received the request; and

(ii) an estimated date on which the agency will complete action on the request.

(b) This section does not apply to matters that are—

(1)(A) specifically authorized under criteria established by an Executive order to be kept secret in the interest of national defense or foreign policy and (B) are in fact properly classified pursuant to such Executive order;

(2) related solely to the internal personnel rules and practices of an agency;

(3) specifically exempted from disclosure by statute (other than section 552b of this title), if that statute—

(A)(i) requires that the matters be withheld from the public in such a manner as to leave no discretion on the issue; or

(ii) establishes particular criteria for withholding or refers to particular types of matters to be withheld; and

(B) if enacted after the date of enactment of the OPEN FOIA Act of 2009, specifically cites to this paragraph.

(4) trade secrets and commercial or financial information obtained from a person and privileged or confidential;

(5) inter-agency or intra-agency memorandums or letters which would not be available by law to a party other than an agency in litigation with the agency;

(6) personnel and medical files and similar files the disclosure of which would constitute a clearly unwarranted invasion of personal privacy;

(7) records or information compiled for law enforcement purposes, but only to the extent that the production of such law enforcement records or information (A) could reasonably be expected to interfere with enforcement proceedings, (B) would deprive a person of a right to a fair trial or an impartial adjudication, (C) could reasonably be expected to constitute an unwarranted invasion of personal privacy, (D) could reasonably be expected to disclose the identity of a confidential source, including a State, local, or foreign agency or authority or any private institution which furnished information on a confidential basis, and, in the case of a record or information compiled by criminal law enforcement authority in the course of a criminal investigation or by an agency conducting a lawful national security intelligence investigation, information furnished by a confidential source, (E) would disclose techniques and procedures for law enforcement investigations or prosecutions, or would disclose guidelines for law enforcement investigations or prosecutions if such disclosure could reasonably be expected to risk circumvention of the law, or (F) could reasonably be expected to endanger the life or physical safety of any individual;

(8) contained in or related to examination, operating, or condition reports prepared by, on behalf of, or for the use of an agency responsible for the regulation or supervision of financial institutions; or

(9) geological and geophysical information and data, including maps, concerning wells.

Any reasonably segregable portion of a record shall be provided to any person requesting such record after deletion of the portions which are exempt under this subsection. The amount of information deleted, and the exemption under which the deletion is made, shall be indicated on the released portion of the record, unless including that indication would harm an interest protected by the exemption in this subsection under which the deletion is made. If technically feasible, the amount of the information deleted, and the exemption under which the deletion is made, shall be indicated at the place in the record where such deletion is made.

(c)(1) Whenever a request is made which involves access to records described in subsection (b)(7)(A) and—

(A) the investigation or proceeding involves a possible violation of criminal law; and

(B) there is reason to believe that (i) the subject of the investigation or proceeding is not aware of its pendency, and (ii) disclosure of the existence of the records could reasonably be expected to interfere with enforcement proceedings,

the agency may, during only such time as that circumstance continues, treat the records as not subject to the requirements of this section.

(2) Whenever informant records maintained by a criminal law enforcement agency under an informant's name or personal identifier are requested by a third party according to the informant's name or personal identifier, the agency may treat the records as not subject to the requirements of this section unless the informant's status as an informant has been officially confirmed.

(3) Whenever a request is made which involves access to records maintained by the Federal Bureau of Investigation pertaining to foreign intelligence or counterintelligence, or international terrorism, and the existence of the records is classified information as provided in subsection (b)(1), the Bureau may, as long as the existence of the records remains classified information, treat the records as not subject to the requirements of this section.

(d) This section does not authorize withholding of information or limit the availability of records to the public, except as specifically stated in this section. This section is not authority to withhold information from Congress.

(e)(1) On or before February 1 of each year, each agency shall submit to the Attorney General of the United States a report which shall cover the preceding fiscal year and which shall include—

(A) the number of determinations made by the agency not to comply with requests for records made to such agency under subsection (a) and the reasons for each such determination;

(B)(i) the number of appeals made by persons under subsection (a)(6), the result of such appeals, and the reason for the action upon each appeal that results in a denial of information; and

(ii) a complete list of all statutes that the agency relies upon to authorize the agency to withhold information under subsection (b)(3), the number of occasions on which each statute was relied upon, a description of whether a court has upheld the decision of the agency to withhold information under each such statute, and a concise description of the scope of any information withheld;

(C) the number of requests for records pending before the agency as of September 30 of the preceding year, and the median and average number of days that such requests had been pending before the agency as of that date;

(D) the number of requests for records received by the agency and the number of requests which the agency processed;

(E) the median number of days taken by the agency to process different types of requests, based on the date on which the requests were received by the agency;

(F) the average number of days for the agency to respond to a request beginning on the date on which the request was received by the agency, the median number of days for the agency to respond to such requests, and the range in number of days for the agency to respond to such requests;

(G) based on the number of business days that have elapsed since each request was originally received by the agency—

(i) the number of requests for records to which the agency has responded with a determination within a period up to and including 20 days, and in 20–day increments up to and including 200 days;

(ii) the number of requests for records to which the agency has responded with a determination within a period greater than 200 days and less than 301 days;

(iii) the number of requests for records to which the agency has responded with a determination within a period greater than 300 days and less than 401 days; and

(iv) the number of requests for records to which the agency has responded with a determination within a period greater than 400 days;

(H) the average number of days for the agency to provide the granted information beginning on the date on which the request was originally filed, the median number of days for the agency to provide the granted information, and the range in number of days for the agency to provide the granted information;

(I) the median and average number of days for the agency to respond to administrative appeals based on the date on which the appeals originally were received by the agency, the highest number of business days taken by the agency to respond to an administrative appeal, and the lowest number of business days taken by the agency to respond to an administrative appeal;

(J) data on the 10 active requests with the earliest filing dates pending at each agency, including the amount of time that has elapsed since each request was originally received by the agency;

(K) data on the 10 active administrative appeals with the earliest filing dates pending before the agency as of September 30 of the preceding year, including the number of business days that have elapsed since the requests were originally received by the agency;

(L) the number of expedited review requests that are granted and denied, the average and median number of days for adjudicating expedited review requests, and the number adjudicated within the required 10 days;

(M) the number of fee waiver requests that are granted and denied, and the average and median number of days for adjudicating fee waiver determinations;

(N) the total amount of fees collected by the agency for processing requests; and

(O) the number of full-time staff of the agency devoted to processing requests for records under this section, and the total amount expended by the agency for processing such requests.

(2) Information in each report submitted under paragraph (1) shall be expressed in terms of each principal component of the agency and for the agency overall.

(3) Each agency shall make each such report available to the public including by computer telecommunications, or if computer telecommunications means have not been established by the agency, by other electronic means. In addition, each agency shall make the raw statistical data used in its reports available electronically to the public upon request.

(4) The Attorney General of the United States shall make each report which has been made available by electronic means available at a single electronic access point. The Attorney General of the United States shall notify the Chairman and ranking minority member of the Committee on Government Reform and Oversight of the House of Representatives and the Chairman and ranking minority member of the Committees on Governmental Affairs and the Judiciary of the Senate, no later than April 1 of the year in which each such report is issued, that such reports are available by electronic means.

(5) The Attorney General of the United States, in consultation with the Director of the Office of Management and Budget, shall develop reporting and performance guidelines in connection with reports required by this subsection by October 1, 1997, and may establish additional requirements for such reports as the Attorney General determines may be useful.

(6) The Attorney General of the United States shall submit an annual report on or before April 1 of each calendar year which shall include for the prior calendar year a listing of the number of cases arising under this section, the exemption involved in each case, the disposition of such case, and the cost, fees, and penalties assessed under subparagraphs (E), (F), and (G) of subsection (a)(4). Such report shall also include a description of the efforts undertaken by the Department of Justice to encourage agency compliance with this section.

(f) For purposes of this section, the term—

(1) "agency" as defined in section 551(1) of this title includes any executive department, military department, Government corporation, Government controlled corporation, or other establishment in the

executive branch of the Government (including the Executive Office of the President), or any independent regulatory agency; and

(2) "record" and any other term used in this section in reference to information includes—

(A) any information that would be an agency record subject to the requirements of this section when maintained by an agency in any format, including an electronic format; and

(B) any information described under subparagraph (A) that is maintained for an agency by an entity under Government contract, for the purposes of records management.

(g) The head of each agency shall prepare and make publicly available upon request, reference material or a guide for requesting records or information from the agency, subject to the exemptions in subsection (b), including—

(1) an index of all major information systems of the agency;

(2) a description of major information and record locator systems maintained by the agency; and

(3) a handbook for obtaining various types and categories of public information from the agency pursuant to chapter 35 of title 44, and under this section.

(h)(1) There is established the Office of Government Information Services within the National Archives and Records Administration.

(2) The Office of Government Information Services shall—

(A) review policies and procedures of administrative agencies under this section;

(B) review compliance with this section by administrative agencies; and

(C) recommend policy changes to Congress and the President to improve the administration of this section.

(3) The Office of Government Information Services shall offer mediation services to resolve disputes between persons making requests under this section and administrative agencies as a non-exclusive alternative to litigation and, at the discretion of the Office, may issue advisory opinions if mediation has not resolved the dispute.

(i) The Government Accountability Office shall conduct audits of administrative agencies on the implementation of this section and issue reports detailing the results of such audits.

(j) Each agency shall designate a Chief FOIA Officer who shall be a senior official of such agency (at the Assistant Secretary or equivalent level).

(k) The Chief FOIA Officer of each agency shall, subject to the authority of the head of the agency—

(1) have agency-wide responsibility for efficient and appropriate compliance with this section;

(2) monitor implementation of this section throughout the agency and keep the head of the agency, the chief legal officer of the agency, and the Attorney General appropriately informed of the agency's performance in implementing this section;

(3) recommend to the head of the agency such adjustments to agency practices, policies, personnel, and funding as may be necessary to improve its implementation of this section;

(4) review and report to the Attorney General, through the head of the agency, at such times and in such formats as the Attorney General may direct, on the agency's performance in implementing this section;

(5) facilitate public understanding of the purposes of the statutory exemptions of this section by including concise descriptions of the exemptions in both the agency's handbook issued under subsection (g), and the agency's annual report on this section, and by providing an overview, where appropriate, of certain general categories of agency records to which those exemptions apply; and

(6) designate one or more FOIA Public Liaisons.

(*l*) FOIA Public Liaisons shall report to the agency Chief FOIA Officer and shall serve as supervisory officials to whom a requester under this section can raise concerns about the service the requester has received from the FOIA Requester Center, following an initial response from the FOIA Requester Center Staff. FOIA Public Liaisons shall be responsible for assisting in reducing delays, increasing transparency and understanding of the status of requests, and assisting in the resolution of disputes.

## 5 U.S.C. § 553. RULE MAKING

(a) This section applies, according to the provisions thereof, except to the extent that there is involved—

(1) a military or foreign affairs function of the United States; or

(2) a matter relating to agency management or personnel or to public property, loans, grants, benefits, or contracts.

(b) General notice of proposed rule making shall be published in the Federal Register, unless persons subject thereto are named and either personally served or otherwise have actual notice thereof in accordance with law. The notice shall include—

(1) a statement of the time, place, and nature of public rule making proceedings;

(2) reference to the legal authority under which the rule is proposed; and

(3) either the terms or substance of the proposed rule or a description of the subjects and issues involved.

Except when notice or hearing is required by statute, this subsection does not apply—

(A) to interpretative rules, general statements of policy, or rules of agency organization, procedure, or practice; or

(B) when the agency for good cause finds (and incorporates the finding and a brief statement of reasons therefor in the rules issued) that notice and public procedure thereon are impracticable, unnecessary, or contrary to the public interest.

(c) After notice required by this section, the agency shall give interested persons an opportunity to participate in the rule making through submission of written data, views, or arguments with or without opportunity for oral presentation. After consideration of the relevant matter presented, the agency shall incorporate in the rules adopted a concise general statement of their basis and purpose. When rules are required by statute to be made on the record after opportunity for an agency hearing, sections 556 and 557 of this title apply instead of this subsection.

(d) The required publication or service of a substantive rule shall be made not less than 30 days before its effective date, except—

(1) a substantive rule which grants or recognizes an exemption or relieves a restriction;

(2) interpretative rules and statements of policy; or

(3) as otherwise provided by the agency for good cause found and published with the rule.

(e) Each agency shall give an interested person the right to petition for the issuance, amendment, or repeal of a rule.

## 5 U.S.C. § 554. ADJUDICATIONS

(a) This section applies, according to the provisions thereof, in every case of adjudication required by statute to be determined on the record after opportunity for an agency hearing, except to the extent that there is involved—

(1) a matter subject to a subsequent trial of the law and the facts de novo in a court;

(2) the selection or tenure of an employee, except a[n] administrative law judge appointed under section 3105 of this title;

(3) proceedings in which decisions rest solely on inspections, tests, or elections;

(4) the conduct of military or foreign affairs functions;

(5) cases in which an agency is acting as an agent for a court; or

(6) the certification of worker representatives.

(b) Persons entitled to notice of an agency hearing shall be timely informed of—

(1) the time, place, and nature of the hearing;

(2) the legal authority and jurisdiction under which the hearing is to be held; and

(3) the matters of fact and law asserted.

When private persons are the moving parties, other parties to the proceeding shall give prompt notice of issues controverted in fact or law; and in other instances agencies may by rule require responsive pleading. In fixing the time and place for hearings, due regard shall be had for the convenience and necessity of the parties or their representatives.

(c) The agency shall give all interested parties opportunity for—

(1) the submission and consideration of facts, arguments, offers of settlement, or proposals of adjustment when time, the nature of the proceeding, and the public interest permit; and

(2) to the extent that the parties are unable so to determine a controversy by consent, hearing and decision on notice and in accordance with sections 556 and 557 of this title.

(d) The employee who presides at the reception of evidence pursuant to section 556 of this title shall make the recommended decision or initial decision required by section 557 of this title, unless he becomes unavailable to the agency. Except to the extent required for the disposition of ex parte matters as authorized by law, such an employee may not—

(1) consult a person or party on a fact in issue, unless on notice and opportunity for all parties to participate; or

(2) be responsible to or subject to the supervision or direction of an employee or agent engaged in the performance of investigative or prosecuting functions for an agency.

An employee or agent engaged in the performance of investigative or prosecuting functions for an agency in a case may not, in that or a factually related case, participate or advise in the decision, recommended decision, or agency review pursuant to section 557 of this title, except as witness or counsel in public proceedings. This subsection does not apply—

(A) in determining applications for initial licenses;

(B) to proceedings involving the validity or application of rates, facilities, or practices of public utilities or carriers; or

(C) to the agency or a member or members of the body comprising the agency.

(e) The agency, with like effect as in the case of other orders, and in its sound discretion, may issue a declaratory order to terminate a controversy or remove uncertainty.

### 5 U.S.C. § 555. ANCILLARY MATTERS

(a) This section applies, according to the provisions thereof, except as otherwise provided by this subchapter.

(b) A person compelled to appear in person before an agency or representative thereof is entitled to be accompanied, represented, and advised by counsel or, if permitted by the agency, by other qualified representative. A party is entitled to appear in person or by or with counsel or other duly qualified representative in an agency proceeding. So far as the orderly conduct of public business permits, an interested person may appear before an agency or its responsible employees for the presentation, adjustment, or determination of an issue, request, or controversy in a proceeding, whether interlocutory, summary, or otherwise, or in connection with an agency function. With due regard for the convenience and necessity of the parties or their representatives and within a reasonable time, each agency shall proceed to conclude a matter presented to it. This subsection does not grant or deny a person who is not a lawyer the right to appear for or represent others before an agency or in an agency proceeding.

(c) Process, requirement of a report, inspection, or other investigative act or demand may not be issued, made, or enforced except as authorized by law. A person compelled to submit data or evidence is entitled to retain or, on payment of lawfully prescribed costs, procure a copy or transcript thereof, except that in a nonpublic investigatory proceeding the witness may for good cause be limited to inspection of the official transcript of his testimony.

(d) Agency subpenas authorized by law shall be issued to a party on request and, when required by rules of procedure, on a statement or showing of general relevance and reasonable scope of the evidence sought. On contest, the court shall sustain the subpena or similar process or demand to the extent that it is found to be in accordance with law. In a proceeding for enforcement, the court shall issue an order requiring the appearance of the witness or the production of the evidence or data within a reasonable time under penalty of punishment for contempt in case of contumacious failure to comply.

(e) Prompt notice shall be given of the denial in whole or in part of a written application, petition, or other request of an interested person made in connection with any agency proceeding. Except in affirming a prior denial or when the denial is self-explanatory, the notice shall be accompanied by a brief statement of the grounds for denial.

### 5 U.S.C. § 556. HEARINGS; PRESIDING EMPLOYEES; POWERS AND DUTIES; BURDEN OF PROOF; EVIDENCE; RECORD AS BASIS OF DECISION

(a) This section applies, according to the provisions thereof, to hearings required by section 553 or 554 of this title to be conducted in accordance with this section.

(b) There shall preside at the taking of evidence—

    (1) the agency;

    (2) one or more members of the body which comprises the agency; or

    (3) one or more administrative law judges appointed under section 3105 of this title.

This subchapter does not supersede the conduct of specified classes of proceedings, in whole or in part, by or before boards or other employees specially provided for by or designated under statute. The functions of presiding employees and of employees participating in decisions in accordance with section 557 of this title shall be conducted in an impartial manner. A presiding or participating employee may at any time disqualify himself. On the filing in good faith of a timely and sufficient affidavit of personal bias or other disqualification of a presiding or participating employee, the agency shall determine the matter as a part of the record and decision in the case.

(c) Subject to published rules of the agency and within its powers, employees presiding at hearings may—

    (1) administer oaths and affirmations;

    (2) issue subpenas authorized by law;

    (3) rule on offers of proof and receive relevant evidence;

    (4) take depositions or have depositions taken when the ends of justice would be served;

    (5) regulate the course of the hearing;

    (6) hold conferences for the settlement or simplification of the issues by consent of the parties or by the use of alternative means of dispute resolution as provided in subchapter IV of this chapter;

    (7) inform the parties as to the availability of one or more alternative means of dispute resolution, and encourage use of such methods;

    (8) require the attendance at any conference held pursuant to paragraph (6) of at least one representative of each party who has authority to negotiate concerning resolution of issues in controversy;

    (9) dispose of procedural requests or similar matters;

    (10) make or recommend decisions in accordance with section 557 of this title; and

    (11) take other action authorized by agency rule consistent with this subchapter.

(d) Except as otherwise provided by statute, the proponent of a rule or order has the burden of proof. Any oral or documentary evidence may be received, but the agency as a matter of policy shall provide for the exclusion of irrelevant, immaterial, or unduly repetitious evidence. A sanction may not be imposed or rule or order issued except on consideration of the whole record or those parts thereof cited by a party and supported by and in accordance with the reliable, probative, and substantial evidence. The agency may, to the extent consistent with the interests of justice and the policy of the underlying statutes administered by the agency, consider a violation of section 557(d) of this title sufficient grounds for a decision adverse to a party who has knowingly committed such violation or knowingly caused such violation to occur. A party is entitled to present his case or defense by oral or documentary evidence, to submit rebuttal evidence, and to conduct such cross-examination as may be required for a full and true disclosure of the facts. In rule making or determining claims for money or benefits or applications for initial licenses an agency may, when a party will not be prejudiced thereby, adopt procedures for the submission of all or part of the evidence in written form.

(e) The transcript of testimony and exhibits, together with all papers and requests filed in the proceeding, constitutes the exclusive record for decision in accordance with section 557 of this title and, on payment of lawfully prescribed costs, shall be made available to the parties. When an agency decision rests on official notice of a material fact not appearing in the evidence in the record, a party is entitled, on timely request, to an opportunity to show the contrary.

### 5 U.S.C. § 557. Initial decisions; conclusiveness; review by agency; submissions by parties; contents of decisions; record

(a) This section applies, according to the provisions thereof, when a hearing is required to be conducted in accordance with section 556 of this title.

(b) When the agency did not preside at the reception of the evidence, the presiding employee or, in cases not subject to section 554(d) of this title, an employee qualified to preside at hearings pursuant to section 556 of this title, shall initially decide the case unless the agency requires, either in specific cases or by general rule, the entire record to be certified to it for decision. When the presiding employee makes an initial decision, that decision then becomes the decision of the agency without further proceedings unless there is an appeal to, or review on motion of, the agency within time provided by rule. On appeal from or review of the initial decision, the agency has all the powers which it would have in making the initial decision except as it may limit the issues on notice or by rule. When the agency makes the decision without having presided at the reception of the evidence, the presiding employee or an employee qualified to preside at hearings pursuant to section 556 of this title shall first recommend a decision, except that in rule making or determining applications for initial licenses—

  (1) instead thereof the agency may issue a tentative decision or one of its responsible employees may recommend a decision; or

  (2) this procedure may be omitted in a case in which the agency finds on the record that due and timely execution of its functions imperatively and unavoidably so requires.

(c) Before a recommended, initial, or tentative decision, or a decision on agency review of the decision of subordinate employees, the parties are entitled to a reasonable opportunity to submit for the consideration of the employees participating in the decisions—

  (1) proposed findings and conclusions; or

  (2) exceptions to the decisions or recommended decisions of subordinate employees or to tentative agency decisions; and

  (3) supporting reasons for the exceptions or proposed findings or conclusions.

The record shall show the ruling on each finding, conclusion, or exception presented. All decisions, including initial, recommended, and tentative decisions, are a part of the record and shall include a statement of—

> (A) findings and conclusions, and the reasons or basis therefor, on all the material issues of fact, law, or discretion presented on the record; and

> (B) the appropriate rule, order, sanction, relief, or denial thereof.

(d)(1) In any agency proceeding which is subject to subsection (a) of this section, except to the extent required for the disposition of ex parte matters as authorized by law—

> (A) no interested person outside the agency shall make or knowingly cause to be made to any member of the body comprising the agency, administrative law judge, or other employee who is or may reasonably be expected to be involved in the decisional process of the proceeding, an ex parte communication relevant to the merits of the proceeding;

> (B) no member of the body comprising the agency, administrative law judge, or other employee who is or may reasonably be expected to be involved in the decisional process of the proceeding, shall make or knowingly cause to be made to any interested person outside the agency an ex parte communication relevant to the merits of the proceeding;

> (C) a member of the body comprising the agency, administrative law judge, or other employee who is or may reasonably be expected to be involved in the decisional process of such proceeding who receives, or who makes or knowingly causes to be made, a communication prohibited by this subsection shall place on the public record of the proceeding:

>> (i) all such written communications;

>> (ii) memoranda stating the substance of all such oral communications; and

>> (iii) all written responses, and memoranda stating the substance of all oral responses, to the materials described in clauses (i) and (ii) of this subparagraph;

> (D) upon receipt of a communication knowingly made or knowingly caused to be made by a party in violation of this subsection, the agency, administrative law judge, or other employee presiding at the hearing may, to the extent consistent with the interests of justice and the policy of the underlying statutes, require the party to show cause why his claim or interest in the proceeding should not be dismissed, denied, disregarded, or otherwise adversely affected on account of such violation; and

> (E) the prohibitions of this subsection shall apply beginning at such time as the agency may designate, but in no case shall they begin to apply later than the time at which a proceeding is noticed

for hearing unless the person responsible for the communication has knowledge that it will be noticed, in which case the prohibitions shall apply beginning at the time of his acquisition of such knowledge.

(2) This subsection does not constitute authority to withhold information from Congress.

### 5 U.S.C. § 558. IMPOSITION OF SANCTIONS; DETERMINATION OF APPLICATIONS FOR LICENSES; SUSPENSION, REVOCATION, AND EXPIRATION OF LICENSES.

(a) This section applies, according to the provisions thereof, to the exercise of a power or authority.

(b) A sanction may not be imposed or a substantive rule or order issued except within jurisdiction delegated to the agency and as authorized by law.

(c) When application is made for a license required by law, the agency, with due regard for the rights and privileges of all the interested parties or adversely affected persons and within a reasonable time, shall set and complete proceedings required to be conducted in accordance with sections 556 and 557 of this title or other proceedings required by law and shall make its decision. Except in cases of willfulness or those in which public health, interest, or safety requires otherwise, the withdrawal, suspension, revocation, or annulment of a license is lawful only if, before the institution of agency proceedings therefor, the licensee has been given—

(1) notice by the agency in writing of the facts or conduct which may warrant the action; and

(2) opportunity to demonstrate or achieve compliance with all lawful requirements.

When the licensee has made timely and sufficient application for a renewal or a new license in accordance with agency rules, a license with reference to an activity of a continuing nature does not expire until the application has been finally determined by the agency.

### 5 U.S.C. § 559. EFFECT ON OTHER LAWS; EFFECT OF SUBSEQUENT STATUTE

This subchapter, chapter 7, and sections 1305, 3105, 3344, 4301(2)(E), 5372, and 7521 of this title, and the provisions of section 5335(a)(B) of this title that relate to administrative law judges, do not limit or repeal additional requirements imposed by statute or otherwise recognized by law. Except as otherwise required by law, requirements or privileges relating to evidence or procedure apply equally to agencies and persons. Each agency is granted the authority necessary to comply with the requirements of this subchapter through the issuance of rules or otherwise. Subsequent statute may not be held to supersede or modify this subchapter, chapter 7, sections 1305, 3105, 3344, 4301(2)(E), 5372, or 7521 of this title, or the provisions of section 5335(a)(B) of this title that relate to administrative law judges, except to the extent that it does so expressly.

## 5 U.S.C. § 701. APPLICATION; DEFINITIONS

(a) This chapter applies, according to the provisions thereof, except to the extent that—

    (1) statutes preclude judicial review; or

    (2) agency action is committed to agency discretion by law.

(b) For the purpose of this chapter—

    (1) "agency" means each authority of the Government of the United States, whether or not it is within or subject to review by another agency, but does not include—

        (A) the Congress;

        (B) the courts of the United States;

        (C) the governments of the territories or possessions of the United States;

        (D) the government of the District of Columbia;

        (E) agencies composed of representatives of the parties or of representatives of organizations of the parties to the disputes determined by them;

        (F) courts martial and military commissions;

        (G) military authority exercised in the field in time of war or in occupied territory; or

        (H) functions conferred by sections 1738, 1739, 1743, and 1744 of title 12; chapter 2 of title 41; subchapter II of chapter 471 of title 49; or sections 1884, 1891–1902, and former section 1641(b)(2), of title 50, appendix; and

    (2) "person", "rule", "order", "license", "sanction", "relief", and "agency action" have the meanings given them by section 551 of this title.

## 5 U.S.C. § 702. RIGHT OF REVIEW

A person suffering legal wrong because of agency action, or adversely affected or aggrieved by agency action within the meaning of a relevant statute, is entitled to judicial review thereof. An action in a court of the United States seeking relief other than money damages and stating a claim that an agency or an officer or employee thereof acted or failed to act in an official capacity or under color of legal authority shall not be dismissed nor relief therein be denied on the ground that it is against the United States or that the United States is an indispensable party. The United States may be named as a defendant in any such action, and a judgment or decree may be entered against the United States: *Provided*, That any mandatory or injunctive decree shall specify the Federal officer or officers (by name or by title), and their successors in office, personally responsible for compliance. Nothing herein (1) affects other limitations on judicial review or the power or duty of the court to dismiss any action or deny relief on any other appropriate legal or equitable ground; or (2) confers authority to grant relief if any other statute that grants consent to suit expressly or impliedly forbids the relief which is sought.

## 5 U.S.C. § 703. FORM AND VENUE OF PROCEEDING

The form of proceeding for judicial review is the special statutory review proceeding relevant to the subject matter in a court specified by statute or, in the absence or inadequacy thereof, any applicable form of legal action, including actions for declaratory judgments or writs of prohibitory or mandatory injunction or habeas corpus, in a court of competent jurisdiction. If no special statutory review proceeding is applicable, the action for judicial review may be brought against the United States, the agency by its official title, or the appropriate officer. Except to the extent that prior, adequate, and exclusive opportunity for judicial review is provided by law, agency action is subject to judicial review in civil or criminal proceedings for judicial enforcement.

## 5 U.S.C. § 704. ACTIONS REVIEWABLE

Agency action made reviewable by statute and final agency action for which there is no other adequate remedy in a court are subject to judicial review. A preliminary, procedural, or intermediate agency action or ruling not directly reviewable is subject to review on the review of the final agency action. Except as otherwise expressly required by statute, agency action otherwise final is final for the purposes of this section whether or not there has been presented or determined an application for a declaratory order, for any form of reconsideration, or, unless the agency otherwise requires by rule and provides that the action meanwhile is inoperative, for an appeal to superior agency authority.

## 5 U.S.C. § 705. RELIEF PENDING REVIEW

When an agency finds that justice so requires, it may postpone the effective date of action taken by it, pending judicial review. On such conditions as may be required and to the extent necessary to prevent irreparable injury, the reviewing court, including the court to which a case may be taken on appeal from or on application for certiorari or other writ to a reviewing court, may issue all necessary and appropriate process to postpone the effective date of an agency action or to preserve status or rights pending conclusion of the review proceedings.

## 5 U.S.C. § 706. SCOPE OF REVIEW

To the extent necessary to decision and when presented, the reviewing court shall decide all relevant questions of law, interpret constitutional and statutory provisions, and determine the meaning or applicability of the terms of an agency action. The reviewing court shall—

(1) compel agency action unlawfully withheld or unreasonably delayed; and

(2) hold unlawful and set aside agency action, findings, and conclusions found to be—

>   (A) arbitrary, capricious, an abuse of discretion, or otherwise not in accordance with law;

>   (B) contrary to constitutional right, power, privilege, or immunity;

>   (C) in excess of statutory jurisdiction, authority, or limitations, or short of statutory right;

>   (D) without observance of procedure required by law;

>   (E) unsupported by substantial evidence in a case subject to sections 556 and 557 of this title or otherwise reviewed on the record of an agency hearing provided by statute; or

>   (F) unwarranted by the facts to the extent that the facts are subject to trial de novo by the reviewing court.

In making the foregoing determinations, the court shall review the whole record or those parts of it cited by a party, and due account shall be taken of the rule of prejudicial error.

## 5 U.S.C. § 3105. Appointment of administrative law judges

Each agency shall appoint as many administrative law judges as are necessary for proceedings required to be conducted in accordance with sections 556 and 557 of this title. Administrative law judges shall be assigned to cases in rotation so far as practicable, and may not perform duties inconsistent with their duties and responsibilities as administrative law judges.

## 5 U.S.C. § 7521. Actions against administrative law judges

(a) An action may be taken against an administrative law judge appointed under section 3105 of this title by the agency in which the administrative law judge is employed only for good cause established and determined by the Merit Systems Protection Board on the record after opportunity for hearing before the Board.

(b) The actions covered by this section are—

>   (1) a removal;

>   (2) a suspension;

>   (3) a reduction in grade;

>   (4) a reduction in pay; and

>   (5) a furlough of 30 days or less;

but do not include—

>   (A) a suspension or removal under section 7532 of this title;

>   (B) a reduction-in-force action under section 3502 of this title; or

>   (C) any action initiated under section 1215 of this title.

# INDEX

References are to Pages.

**987**

†